OUT OF MANY

A History of the American People

Brief Fourth Edition

John Mack Faragher
YALE UNIVERSITY

Mari Jo Buhle
BROWN UNIVERSITY

Daniel Czitrom
MOUNT HOLYOKE COLLEGE

Susan H. Armitage
WASHINGTON STATE UNIVERSITY

PEARSON
Prentice
Hall

Upper Saddle River, New Jersey 07458

Library of Congress Cataloging-in-Publication Data
Out of many : a history of the American people / John Mack Faragher . . . [et al.].-- Brief
4e, combined.
    p. cm.
  Includes bibliographical references and index.
  ISBN 0-13-182430-9 (alk. paper)
   1. United States--History.   I. Faragher, John Mack
E178.1 .O935 2003b
973--dc21   2002030811

Editorial Director: Charlyce Jones Owen
Senior Acquisitions Editor: Charles Cavaliere
Editor-in-Chief, Development: Rochelle Diogenes
Development Editor: Carolyn Smith
Production Liaison: Joanne Hakim
Production Editor: Fran Daniele, Preparé Inc.
Creative Director: Leslie Osher
Art Director: Anne Bonanno Nieglos
Marketing Manager: Heather Shelstad
Interior Designer: C2K, Inc.
Cover Designer: Laura Gardner
Scanning: Central Scanning Services

Cover Image Specialist: Karen Sanatar
AVP, Director of Production and Manufacturing: Barbara Kittle
Manufacturing Manager: Nick Sklitsis
Manufacturing Buyer: Sherry Lewis
Director, Image Resource Center: Melinda Reo
Line Art Manager: Guy Ruggiero
Artist: Mirella Signoretto
Photo Permissions Coordinator: Carolyn Gauntt
Editorial Assistant: Adrienne Paul
Text Permissions: The Permissions Group
Cartographers: Alice and William Thiede/CARTO-GRAPHICS;
    Mirella Signoretto

Cover Art: George Benjamin Luks, American,1867-1933.
    "Hester Street" 1905.
    Oil on canvas. 66.3 x 91.8 (26 1/8 x 36 1/8).
    Brooklyn Museum of Art, Dick S. Ramsay Fund. 40.339

Credits and acknowledgments for materials borrowed from
other sources and reproduced, with permission, in this textbook
appear on page C-1.

This book was set in 11/12 Weiss by Preparé Inc.
and was printed and bound by RR Donnelley & Sons Company.
The cover was printed by Phoenix Color Corp.

 © 2004, 2001, 1999, 1995 by Pearson Education, Inc.
Upper Saddle River, New Jersey 07458

Printed in the United States of America
10 9 8 7 6 5 4 3

ISBN 0-13-182430-9

TO OUR STUDENTS,	
OUR SISTERS,	
AND OUR BROTHERS	

Pearson Education International Ltd., *London*
Pearson Education Australia, PTY. Limited, *Sydney*
Pearson Education *Singapore*, Pte. Ltd.
Pearson Education North Asia Ltd., *Hong Kong*
Pearson Education Canada, Ltd., *Toronto*
Pearson Educación de *Mexico*, S.A. de C.V.
Pearson Education-Japan, *Tokyo*
Pearson Education Malaysia, Pte. Ltd.
Pearson Education, Upper Saddle River, New Jersey

BRIEF CONTENTS

CONTENTS

6 From Empire to Independence, 1750–1776 93

Community & Memory: The Invention of the Liberty Bell 114

7 The Creation of the United States, 1776–1786 116

13 Coming to Terms with the New Age, 1820s–1850s 234

14 The Territorial Expansion of the United States, 1830s–1850s 252

Community & Memory: Representing Chicago's History 386

---

20 Commonwealth and Empire, 1870–1900 388

21 Urban America and the Progressive Era, 1900–1917 407

Community & Memory: Battle for the Lower East Side 425

---

27 America at Midcentury, 1952–1963 527

28 The Civil Rights Movement, 1945–1966 544

**Community & Memory:
Flying the "Stars and Bars"   566**

29 War Abroad, War at Home, 1965–1974 568

30 The Conservative Ascendancy, 1974–1987 598

31 Toward a Transnational America, since 1988 625

**Community & Memory:
The World Trade Center and Ways
of Remembering   647**

MAPS

CHARTS, GRAPHS, AND TABLES

PREFACE

Out of Many: A History of the American People, brief fourth edition, offers a distinctive and timely approach to American history, highlighting the experiences of diverse communities of Americans in the unfolding story of our country. The stories of these communities offer a way of examining the complex historical forces shaping people's lives at various moments in our past. The debates and conflicts surrounding the most momentous issues in our national life—independence, emerging democracy, slavery, westward settlement, imperial expansion, economic depression, war, technological change—were largely worked out in the context of local communities. Through communities we focus on the persistent tensions between everyday life and those larger decisions and events that continually reshape the circumstances of local life. Each chapter opens with a description of a representative community. Some of these portraits feature American communities struggling with one another: African slaves and English masters on the rice plantations of colonial Georgia, or Tejanos and Americans during the Texas war of independence. Other chapters feature portraits of communities facing social change: the feminists of Seneca Falls, New York, in 1848, or the African Americans of Montgomery, Alabama, in 1955. As the story unfolds we find communities growing to include ever larger groups of Americans: the soldiers from every colony who forged the Continental Army into a patriotic national force at Valley Forge during the American Revolution, or the moviegoers who aspired to a collective dream of material prosperity and upward mobility during the 1920s.

We prepared this brief edition to serve the needs of one-semester courses, teachers who assign supplemental readings, or anyone interested in a more condensed narrative of American history. While this volume is about two-thirds the length of the full-length version, it retains the distinct point of view that makes it unique among all college-level American history texts. The community focus remains fully in place as the integrating perspective that allows us to combine political, social, and cultural history.

Out of Many is also the only American history text with a truly continental perspective. With community vignettes from New England to the South, the Midwest to the far West, we encourage students to appreciate the great expanse of our nation. For example, a vignette of seventeenth-century Sante Fé, New Mexico, illustrates the founding of the first European settlements in the New World. We present territorial expansion into the American West from the viewpoint of the Mandan villagers of the upper Missouri River of North Dakota. We introduce the policies of the Reconstruction era through the experience of African Americans in Hale County, Alabama. A continental perspective drives home to students that American history has never been the preserve of any particular region.

In these ways *Out of Many* breaks new ground, but without compromising its coverage of the traditional turning points that we believe are critically important to an understanding of the American past. Among these watershed events are the Revolution and the struggle over the Constitution, the Civil War and Reconstruction, and the Great Depression and World War II. In *Out of Many*, however, we seek to integrate the narrative of national history with the story of the nation's many diverse communities. The Revolutionary and Constitutional period tested the ability of local communities to forge a new unity, and success depended on their ability to build a nation without compromising local identity. The Civil War and Reconstruction formed a second great test of the balance between the national ideas of the Revolution and the power of local and sectional communities. The Depression and the New Deal demonstrated the importance of local communities and the growing power of national institutions during the greatest economic challenge in our history. *Out of Many* also looks back in a new and comprehensive way—from the vantage point of the beginning of a new century and the end of the cold war—at the salient events of the last fifty years and their impact on American communities. The community focus of *Out of Many* weaves the stories of the people and the nation into a single compelling narrative.

Out of Many, brief fourth edition, includes expanded coverage of our diverse heritage. Our country is appropriately known as "a nation of immigrants," and the history of immigration to America, from the seventeenth to the twenty-first centuries, is fully integrated into the text. There is sustained and close attention to our place in the world, with special emphasis on our relations with the nations of the Western Hemisphere, especially our near neighbors, Canada and Mexico. In a completely new final chapter we consider the promises and the risks of American diversity in the new century. The statistical data has been completely updated with the results of the 2000 census. We have also incorporated new scholarship on the South, popular culture, science and technology, and the Cold War.

The brief fourth edition also includes an important new feature, Community & Memory, in which we examine the way American communities have attempted to commemorate and memorialize the past. Communities sometimes come to blows over different ways of looking at history. Arguments over the meaning of the past are not confined to the classroom.

SPECIAL FEATURES

With each edition of *Out of Many* we have sought to strengthen its unique integration of the best of traditional American history with its innovative community-based focus and strong continental perspective. A wealth of special features and pedagogical aids reinforces our narrative and helps students grasp key issues.

- **Community and Diversity.** *Out of Many,* brief fourth edition, opens with an introduction, titled "Community and Diversity," that acquaints students with the major themes of the book, providing them with a framework for understanding American history.

- **Community & Memory.** New to the brief fourth edition, this special illustrated feature, located at the end of Chapters 1, 4, 6, 9, 14, 19, 21, 25, 28, and 31, examines the ways in which American communities have attempted to commemorate the past and the conflicts that arise when the meaning of the past divides the members of a community. Discussion questions and annotated links to relevant Websites for each Community & Memory feature are found on the *Companion Website™* for *Out of Many.*

- **Maps.** *Out of Many,* brief fourth edition contains many maps that include topographical detail to help students appreciate the impact of geography on history. Several maps have been redrawn to better reflect a hemispheric perspective.

- **Overview tables.** Overview tables provide students with a summary of complex issues.

- **Graphs, charts, and tables.** Every chapter includes one or more graphs, charts, or tables that help students understand important events and trends.

- **Photos and Illustrations.** The abundant illustrations in *Out of Many,* 30 percent of them new to the fourth edition, include many that have never before been used in an American history text. None of the images is anachronistic—each one

dates from the historical period under discussion. Extensive captions treat the images as visual primary source documents from the American past, describing their source and explaining their significance.

- **Chapter-opening outlines and key topics lists.** These pedagogical aids provide students with a succinct preview of the material covered in each chapter.

- **Chronologies.** A chronology at the end of each chapter helps students build a framework of key events.

- **Review Questions.** Review questions helps students review, reinforce, and retain the material in each chapter and encourage them to relate the material to broader issues in American history.

- **Recommended Reading and Additional Bibliography.** The works in the short, annotated Recommended Reading list at the end of each chapter have been selected with the interested introductory student in mind. The extensive Additional Bibliography provides a comprehensive overview of current scholarship on the subject of the chapter.

- **On the Web.** New to the brief fourth edition, a section at the end of each chapter lists useful Web resources related to the topics discussed, along with helpful comments describing the material on each site. In addition, these sections include up to two interactive maps directly tied to the ones in each chapter.

CLASSROOM ASSISTANCE PACKAGE

Out of Many, brief fourth edition, brings our dynamic past alive for students with a text and accompanying print and multimedia classroom assistance package that combines sound scholarship, engaging narrative, and a rich array of cutting-edge pedagogical tools.

PRINT SUPPLEMENTS

Instructor's Resource Manual

A true time-saver in developing and preparing lecture presentations, the *Instructor's Resource Manual* contains chapter outlines, detailed chapter overviews, lecture topics, discussion questions, readings, and information about audio-visual resources.

Test Item File

The *Test Item File* offers a menu of more than 1,500 multiple-choice, identification, matching, true-false, and essay test questions and 10–15 questions per chapter on the maps found in each chapter. The guide includes a collection of blank maps that can be photocopied and used for map testing purposes or for other class exercises.

Prentice Hall Custom Test

This commercial-quality computerized test management program, available for Windows and Macintosh environments, allows instructors to select items from the *Test Item File* and design their own exams.

Transparency Pack

This collection of more than 160 full-color transparency acetates provides instructors with all the maps, charts, and graphs in the text for use in the classroom.

Practice Tests, Volumes I and II

Each chapter in the *Practice Tests* includes a chapter commentary and outline, identification terms, multiple-choice questions, short essay questions, and map questions. *Practice Tests* are free when packaged with *Out of Many*.

Documents Set, Volumes I and II

In revising the documents set for the fourth edition, the authors have selected and carefully edited more than 300 documents that relate directly to the themes and content of the text and organized them into five general categories: community, social history, government, culture, and politics. Each document is approximately two pages long and includes a brief introduction and study questions intended to encourage students to analyze the document critically and relate it to the content of the text. The *Documents Set* is available at a substantial discount when packaged with *Out of Many*.

Retrieving the American Past, 2003 Edition

Written and developed by leading historians and educators, this reader is an on-demand history database that offers 300 primary source documents (eight new to the 2003 edition) on key topics in American History, such as: Women on the Frontier, The Salem Witchcraft Scare, The Age of Industrial Violence, and Native American Societies, 1870–1995. Each module includes an introduction, several primary documents and secondary sources, follow-up questions, and recommendations for further reading. By deciding which modules to include and the order in which they will appear, instructors can compile a custom reader to fit their needs. Contact your local Prentice Hall representative for more information about this exciting custom publishing option.

Many Lives, Many Stories: Biographies in American History

New to the brief fourth edition, this two-volume collection of sixty-two biographies in American history was written specifically to match the chapter sequence and themes of *Out of Many*.

Introductions, prereading questions, suggested readings, and a special prologue about the role of biography in the study of American history enrich this important new supplement. Available free when packaged with *Out of Many*. Annotated links to relevant Websites for each biography can be found on the *Companion Website* for *Out of Many*.

Understanding and Answering Essay Questions

Prepared by Mary L. Kelley, San Antonio College

This brief guide suggests helpful study techniques as well as specific analytical tools for understanding different types of essay questions and provides precise guidelines for preparing well-crafted essay answers. The guide is available free to students when packaged with *Out of Many*.

Reading Critically About History

Prepared by Rose Wassman and Lee Rinsky, both of DeAnza College.

This brief guide provides students with helpful strategies for reading a history textbook. It is available free when packaged with *Out of Many*.

eThemes of the Times

eThemes of the Times is a digital newspaper supplement prepared jointly by Prentice Hall and the premier news publication, *The New York Times*. Issued twice a year, it contains up to 30 recent articles pertinent to American history, accessible via the *Companion Website*™ for *Out of Many*. Contact your local Prentice Hall representative for details.

Prentice Hall and Penguin Bundle Program

Prentice Hall and Penguin are pleased to provide adopters of *Out of Many* with an opportunity to receive significant discounts when orders for *Out of Many* are bundled together with Penguin titles in American history. Please contact your local Prentice Hall representative for details.

MULTIMEDIA SUPPLEMENTS

Out of Many Companion Website™

Address: http://www.prenhall.com/brieffaragher

With the *Out of Many* Companion Website™ students can take full advantage of the Web and use it in tandem with the text to enrich their study of American history. The Companion Website™ ties the text to related material available on the Internet. Its many instructional features include learning objectives and study questions organized by the primary subtopics of each chapter, map labeling exercises, annotated links, document questions, and Community & Memory resources.

Mapping American History CD-ROM

This innovative electronic supplement takes advantage of the interactive capabilities of multimedia technology to enrich students' understanding of the geographic dimensions of history with animated maps, timelines, and related on-screen activities tied directly to key issues in each chapter of *Out of Many*. Each new copy of *Out of Many* is packaged with a *Mapping American History* CD-Rom.

Exploring America CD-ROM

The new *Exploring America* CD-Rom features thirty-one activities that drill down to explore the impact of key episodes and developments in United States history. Each activity combines primary sources, illustrations, graphs, audio clips, and interactive maps to provide opportunities to further explore the key themes of *Out of Many*. Available free when packaged with *Out of Many*.

Instructor CD-ROM for *Out of Many*

This new multimedia ancillary section contains a Power Point™ presentation directly linked to the text, as well as maps and graphs from *Out of Many*, lecture outlines, and other instructional materials.

Prentice Hall Guide to Evaluating Online Resources

This brief guide introduces students to the origin and innovations behind the Internet and provides clear strategies for navigating the Web to find historical materials. This 93-page supplementary book is free to students when packaged with *Out of Many*.

 **Research Navigator—Reliable, Relevant, and Resourceful!**

Prentice Hall's new **Research Navigator**™ helps your students make the most of their research time. From finding the right articles and journals, to citing sources, drafting and writing effective papers, and completing research assignments, **Research Navigator**™ simplifies and streamlines the entire process. Here's how:

Complete with extensive help on the research process and three exclusive databases full of relevant and reliable source material including EBSCO's **ContentSelect** Academic Journal Database, *The New York Times* Search by Subject Archive, and *Best of the Web* Link Library, **Research Navigator**™ is the one-stop research solution for your students.

Research Navigator™ is FREE when packaged with *Out of Many*. Contact your local sales representative for more details or take a tour on the web at http://www.researchnavigator.com.

Course Management Systems

As the leader in course-management solutions for teachers and students of history, Prentice Hall provides a variety of online tools. Contact your local Prentice Hall representative for details or visit www.prenhall.com.

ACKNOWLEDGMENTS

In the years it has taken to bring *Out of Many* from idea to reality and to improve it in successive editions, we have often been reminded that although writing history sometimes feels like isolated work, it actually involves a collective effort. We want to thank the dozens of people whose efforts have made the publication of this book possible.

At Prentice Hall, Charles Cavaliere, senior acquisitions editor, gave us his full support and oversaw the entire publication process. Susanna Lesan, senior development editor, edited the first and fourth editions of the book; without her efforts this book would never have been published. Fran Daniele, production editor, oversaw the entire complicated production process in an exemplary fashion. Linda Sykes, our photo researcher, expertly tracked down the many pertinent new images that appear in this edition.

Among our many other friends at Prentice Hall we also want to thank Yolanda de Rooy, president; Charlyce Jones-Owen, editorial director; Rochelle Diogenes, editor-in-chief for development; Heather Shelstad, marketing manager; Leslie Osher, creative design director; Anne Nieglos, art director; Joanne Hakim, production liaison; Stephen Hopkins, copy editor; and Adrienne Paul, editorial assistant.

Although we share joint responsibility for the entire book, the chapters were individually authored: John Mack Faragher wrote chapters 1–8; Susan Armitage wrote chapters 9–16; Mari Jo Buhle wrote chapters 18–20, 25–26, 29; and Daniel Czitrom wrote chapters

17, 21–24, 27–28. (For this edition Buhle and Czitrom co-authored Chapters 30–31.)

Historians around the country greatly assisted us by reading and commenting on our chapters for this and previous editions. We want to thank each of them for the commitment of their valuable time.

Donald Abbe, Texas Tech University, TX
Kathryn Abbott, Western Kentucky University, KY
Richard H. Abbott, Eastern Michigan University, MI
Guy Alchon, University of Delaware, DE
Don Barlow, Prestonburg Community College, KY
William Barney, University of North Carolina, NC
Alwyn Barr, Texas Tech University, TX
Debra Barth, San Jose City College, CA
Peter V. Bergstrom, Illinois State University, IL
William C. Billingsley, South Plains College, TX
Kevin Boyle, University of Massachusetts, MA
Peter H. Buckingham, Linfield College, OR
Bill Cecil-Fronsman, Washburn University
  of Topeka, KS
Victor W. Chen, Chabot College, CA
Jonathan M. Chu, University of Massachusetts, MA
P. Scott Corbett, Oxnard College, CA
Matther Coulter, Collin County Community
  College, TX
Virginia Crane, University of Wisconsin,
  Oshkosh, WI
Jim Cullen, Harvard University, MA
Thomas J. Curran, St. John's University, NY
Richard V. Damms, Ohio State University, OH
Elizabeth Dunn, Baylor University, TX
Emmett G. Essin, Eastern Tennessee State
  University, TN
Mark F. Fernandez, Loyola University, IL
Leon Fink, University of North Carolina, Chapel
  Hill, NC
Michael James Foret, University of Wisconsin,
  Stevens Point, WI
Joshua B. Freeman, Columbia University, NY
Glenda E. Gilmore, Yale University, CT
Don C. Glenn, Diablo Valley College, CA
Lawrence Glickman, University of South Carolina, SC
Kenneth Goings, Florida Atlantic University, FL
Mark Goldman, Tallahassee Community College, FL
Gregory L. Goodwin, Bakersfield College, CA
Gretchen Green, University of Missouri,
  Kansas City, MO
Emily Greenwald, University of Nebraska
  at Lincoln, NE
Mark W. T. Harvey, North Dakota State
  University, ND
Sally Hadden, Florida State University, FL
James A. Hijiya, University of Massachusetts at
  Dartmouth, MA

Jon Hunner, New Mexico State University, NM
Albert Hurtado, University of Oklahoma, OK
Raymond M. Hyser, James Madison University, VA
John Inscoe, University of Georgia, GA
Lesley Ann Kawaguchi, Santa Monica College, CA
John C. Kesler, Lakeland Community College, OH
Peter N. Kirstein, Saint Xavier University, IL
Frank Lambert, Purdue University, IN
Susan Rimby Leighow, Millersville University, PA
Janice M. Leone, Middle Tennessee University, TN
Glenn Linden, Southern Methodist University,
  Dallas, TX
George Lipsitz, University of California,
  San Diego, CA
Judy Barrett Litoff, Bryant College, RI
Jesus Luna, California State University, CA
Larry Madaras, Howard Community College, MD
Lynn Mapes, Grand Valley State University, MI
John F. Marszalek, Mississippi State University, MS
Scott C. Martin, Bowling Green State University, OH
Robert L. Matheny, Eastern New Mexico
  University, NM
Thomas Matijasic, Prestonburg Community
  College, KY
M. Delores McBroome, Humboldt State
  University, CA
Gerald McFarland, University of Massachusetts,
  Amherst, MA
Sam McSeveney, Vanderbilt University, TN
Warren Metcalf, Arizona State University, AZ
M. Catherine Miller, Texas State University, TX
Norman H. Murdoch, University of Cincinnati, OH
Gregory H. Nobles, Georgia Institute
  of Technology, GA
Ellen Nore, Southern Illinois University,
  Edwardsville, IL
Dale Odom, University of Texas at Denton, TX
Sean O'Neill, Grand Valley State University, MI
Edward Opper, Greenville Technical College,
  Greenville, SC
William A. Paquette, Tidewater Community
  College, VA
Charles K. Piehl, Mankato State University, MN
Carolyn Garrett Pool, University of Central
  Oklahoma, OK
Christie Farnham Pope, Iowa State University, IA
Susan Porter-Benson, University of Missouri, MO
Russell Posner, City College of San Francisco, CA
John Powell, Penn State University, Erie, PA
Sarah Purcell, Central Michigan University, MI
Joseph P. Reidy, Howard University, DC
Marilyn D. Rhinehart, North Harris College, TX
Leo P. Ribuffo, George Washington University, DC
Judy Ridner, California State University at
  Northridge, CA

Neal Salisbury, Smith College, MA
Roberto Salmon, University of Texas-Pan American, TX
Steven Schuster, Brookhaven Community College, TX
Megan Seahold, University of Texas, Austin, TX
Nigel Sellars, University of Oklahoma, Norman, OK
John David Smith, North Carolina State University, NC
Patrick Smith, Broward Community College, FL
Mark W. Summers, University of Kentucky, KY
John D. Tanner, Jr., Palomar College, CA
Robert R. Tomes, St. John's University, NY
Michael Miller Topp, University of Texas at El Paso, TX
John Trickel, Richland Community College, IL
Steve Tripp, Grand Valley State University, MI
Fred R. Van Hartesveldt, Fort Valley State University, GA
Philip H. Vaughan, Rose State College, OK
Robert C. Vitz, Northern Kentucky University, KY
Elliot West, University of Arkansas, AR

F. Michael Williams, Brevard Community College, FL
Charles Regan Wilson, University of Mississippi, MS
Harold Wilson, Old Dominion University, VA
Andrew Workman, Mills College, CA
William Woodward, Seattle Pacific University, WA
Loretta E. Zimmerman, University of Florida, FL

Each of us depended on a great deal of support and assistance with the research and writing that went into this book. We want to thank: Nan Boyd, Krista Comer, Jennifer Cote, Crista DeLuzio, Keith Edgerton, Carol Frost, Jesse Hoffnung Garskof, Pailin Gather, Jane Gerhard, Todd Gernes, Mark Krasovic, Melani McAlister, Cristiane Mitchell, J. C. Mutchler, Keith Peterson, Alan Pinkham, Tricia Rose, Gina Rourke, Jessica Shubow, and Maura Young.

Our families and close friends have been supportive and ever so patient over the many years we have devoted to this project. But we want especially to thank Paul Buhle, Meryl Fingrutd, Bob Greene, and Michele Hoffnung.

ABOUT THE AUTHORS

Chris Freitag

JOHN MACK FARAGHER

John Mack Faragher is Arthur Unobskey Professor of American History and Director of the Howard R. Lamar Center for the Study of Frontiers and Borders at Yale University. Born in Arizona and raised in southern California, he received his B.A. at the University of California, Riverside, and his Ph.D. at Yale University. He is the author of *Women and Men on the Overland Trail* (1979), which won the Frederick Jackson Turner Award of the Organization of American Historians, *Sugar Creek: Life on the Illinois Prairie* (1986), *Daniel Boone: The Life and Legend of an American Pioneer* (1992), and (with Robert V. Hine) *The American West: A New Interpretive History* (2000).

MARI JO BUHLE

Mari Jo Buhle is William R. Kenan Jr. University Professor and Professor of American Civilization and History at Brown University, specializing in American women's history. She received her B.A. from the University of Illinois, Urbana–Champaign, and her Ph.D. from the University of Wisconsin, Madison. She is the author of *Women and American Socialism, 1870–1920* (1981) and *Feminism and Its Discontents: A Century of Struggle with Psychoanalysis* (1998). She is also coeditor of *Encyclopedia of the American Left*, second edition (1998). Professor Buhle held a fellowship (1991–1996) from the John D. and Catherine T. MacArthur Foundation.

DANIEL CZITROM

Daniel Czitrom is Professor of History at Mount Holyoke College. Born and raised in New York City, he received his B.A. from the State University of New York at Binghamton and his M.A. and Ph.D. from the University of Wisconsin, Madison. He is the author of *Media and the American Mind: From Morse to McLuhan* (1982), which won the First Books Award of the American Historical Association and has been translated into Spanish and Chinese. He has served as a historical consultant and a featured on-camera commentator for several documentary film projects, including two recent PBS series, *New York: A Documentary Film* and *American Photography: A Century of Images*.

SUSAN H. ARMITAGE

Susan H. Armitage is Claudius O. and Mary R. Johnson Distinguished Professor of History at Washington State University. She earned her Ph.D. from the London School of Economics and Political Science. Among her many publications on western women's history are three coedited books, *The Women's West* (1987), *So Much To Be Done: Women on the Mining and Ranching Frontier* (1991), and *Writing the Range: Race, Class, and Culture in the Women's West* (1997). She currently serves as an editor of a series of books on women and American history for the University of Illinois Press. She is the editor of *Frontiers: A Journal of Women's Studies*.

One of the most characteristic features of our country has always been its astounding variety. The American people include the descendants of native Indians, colonial Europeans, Africans, and migrants from virtually every country and continent. Indeed, as we enter a new century the United States is absorbing a flood of immigrants from Latin America and Asia that rivals the great tide of people from eastern and southern Europe one hundred years ago. What's more, our country is one of the world's most spacious, incorporating more than 3.6 million square miles of territory. The struggle to meld a single nation out of our many far-flung communities is what much of American history is all about. That is the story told in this book.

Every human society is made up of communities. A community is a set of relationships linking men, women, and their families to a coherent social whole that is more than the sum of its parts. In a community people develop the capacity for unified action. In a community people learn, often through trial and error, how to transform and adapt to their environment. The sentiment that binds the members of a community together is the mother of group identity and ethnic pride. In the making of history, communities are far more important than even the greatest of leaders, for the community is the institution most capable of passing a distinctive historical tradition to future generations.

Communities bind people together in multiple ways. They can be as small as local neighborhoods, in which people maintain face-to-face relations, or as large as the nation itself. This book examines American history from the perspective of community life—an ever-widening frame that has included larger and larger groups of Americans.

Networks of kinship and friendship, and connections across generations and among families, establish the bonds essential to community life. Shared feelings about values and history establish the basis for common identity. In communities, people find the power to act collectively in their own interest. But American communities frequently took shape as a result of serious conflicts among groups, and within communities there has often been significant fighting among competing groups or classes. Thus the term *community*, as we use it here, includes tension and discord as well as harmony and agreement.

For years there have been persistent laments about the "loss of community" in modern America. But community has not disappeared—it is continually being reinvented. Until the late eighteenth century, community was defined primarily by space and local geography. But in the nineteenth century communities began to be reshaped by new and powerful historical forces such as the marketplace, industrialization, the corporation, mass immigration, mass media, and the growth of the nation-state. In the twentieth century,

Americans have struggled to balance commitments to several communities simultaneously. These were defined not simply by local spatial arrangements, but by categories as varied as racial and ethnic groups, occupations, political affiliations, and consumer preferences.

The "American Communities" vignettes that open each chapter reflect this shift. Most of the vignettes in the pre–Civil War chapters focus on geographically defined communities, such as the ancient Indian city at Cahokia, or the experiment in industrial urban planning in early nineteenth-century Lowell, Massachusetts. In the post–Civil War chapters different and more modern kinds of communities make their appearance. In the 1920s, movies and radio offered a new kind of community—a community of identification with dreams of freedom, material success, upward mobility, youth and beauty. In the 1950s, rock 'n' roll music helped germinate a new national community of teenagers, with profound effects on the culture of the entire country in the second half of the twentieth century. In the late 1970s, fear of nuclear accidents like the one at Three Mile Island brought concerned citizens together in communities around the country and produced a national movement opposing nuclear power.

The title for our book was suggested by the Latin phrase selected by John Adams, Benjamin Franklin, and Thomas Jefferson for the Great Seal of the United States: *E Pluribus Unum*—"Out of Many Comes Unity." These men understood that unity could not be imposed by a powerful central authority but had to develop out of mutual respect among Americans of different backgrounds. The revolutionary leadership expressed the hope that such respect could grow on the basis of a remarkable proposition: "We hold these truths to be self-evident, that all men are created equal; that they are endowed by their Creator with certain unalienable rights; that among these are life, liberty, and the pursuit of happiness." The national government of the United States would preserve local and state authority but would guarantee individual rights. The nation would be strengthened by guarantees of difference.

"Out of Many"—that is the promise of America, and the premise of this book. The underlying dialectic of American history, we believe, is that as a people we need to locate our national unity in the celebration of the differences that exist among us; these differences can be our strength, as long as we affirm the promise of the Declaration. Protecting the "right to be different," in other words, is absolutely fundamental to the continued existence of democracy, and that right is best protected by the existence of strong and vital communities. We are bound together as a nation by the ideal of local and cultural differences protected by our common commitment to the values of our Revolution.

Today those values are endangered by terrorists using the tactics of mass terror. In the wake of the September 11,

2001, attack on the United States, and with the continuing threat of biological, chemical, or even nuclear assaults, Americans can not afford to lose faith in our historic vision. The United States is a multicultural and transnational society. The thousands of victims buried in the smoking ruins of the World Trade Center included people from dozens of different ethnic and national groups. We must fight to protect and defend the promise of our diverse nation

Our history shows that the promise of American unity has always been problematic. Centrifugal forces have been powerful in the American past, and at times the country has seemed about to fracture into its component parts. Our transformation from a collection of groups and regions into a nation has been marked by painful and often violent struggles. Our past is filled with conflicts between Indians and colonists, masters and slaves, Patriots and Loyalists, Northerners and Southerners, Easterners and Westerners, capitalists and workers, and sometimes the government and the people. War can bring out our best, but it can also bring out our worst. During World War II thousands of Japanese American citizens were deprived of their rights and locked up in isolated detention centers simply because of their ethnic background. Americans often appear to be little more than a contentious collection of peoples with conflicting interests, divided by region and background, race and class.

Our most influential leaders have also sometimes suffered a crisis of faith in the American project of "liberty and justice for all." Thomas Jefferson not only believed in the inferiority of African Americans, but he feared that immigrants from outside the Anglo-American tradition might "warp and bias" the development of the nation "and render it a heterogeneous, incoherent, distracted mass." We have not always lived up to the American promise, and there is a dark side to our history. It took the bloodiest war in American history to secure the human rights of African Americans, and the struggle for full equality for all our citizens has yet to be won. During the great influx of immigrants in the early twentieth century, fears much like Jefferson's led to movements to Americanize the foreign born by forcing them, in the words of one leader, "to give up the languages, customs, and methods of life which they have brought with them across the ocean, and adopt instead the language, habits, and customs of this country, and the general standards and ways of American living." Similar thinking motivated Congress at various times to bar the immigration of Africans, Asians, and other ethnic groups and people of color into the country, and to force assimilation on American Indians by denying them the freedom to practice their religion or even to speak their own language. Such calls for restrictive unity still resound in our own day.

But other Americans have argued for a more fulsome version of Americanization. "What is the American, this new man?" asked the French immigrant Michel Crévecoeur in 1782. "A strange mixture of blood which you will find in no other country." In America, he wrote, "individuals of all nations are melted into a new race of men." A century later Crévecoeur was echoed by historian Frederick Jackson Turner, who believed that "in the crucible of the frontier, the immigrants were Americanized, liberated, and fused into a mixed race, English in neither nationality nor characteristics. The process has gone on from the early days to our own."

The process by which diverse communities have come to share a set of common American values is one of the most fundamental aspects of our history. It did not occur, however, because of compulsory Americanization programs, but because of free public education, popular participation in democratic politics, and the impact of popular culture. Contemporary America does have a common culture: We share a commitment to freedom of thought and expression, we join in the aspirations to own our own homes and send our children to college, we laugh at the same television programs.

To a degree that too few Americans appreciate, this common culture resulted from a complicated process of mutual discovery that took place when different ethnic and regional groups encountered one another. Consider just one small and unique aspect of our culture: the barbecue. Americans have been barbecuing since before the beginning of written history. Early settlers adopted this technique of cooking from the Indians—the word itself comes from a native term for a framework of sticks over a fire on which meat was slowly cooked. Colonists typically barbecued pork, fed on Indian corn. African slaves lent their own touch by introducing the use of hot sauces. The ritual that is a part of nearly every American family's Fourth of July silently celebrates the heritage of diversity that went into making our common culture.

The American educator John Dewey recognized this diversity early in the last century. "The genuine American, the typical American, is himself a hyphenated character," he declared, "international and interracial in his make-up." The point about our "hyphenated character," Dewey believed, "is to see to it that the hyphen connects instead of separates." We, the authors of *Out of Many*, share Dewey's perspective on American history. "Creation comes from the impact of diversity," wrote the American philosopher Horace Kallen. We also endorse Kallen's vision of the American promise: "A democracy of nationalities, cooperating voluntarily and autonomously through common institutions, . . . a multiplicity in a unity, an orchestration of mankind." And now, let the music begin.

ONE

A CONTINENT OF VILLAGES

▶ TO 1500

AMERICAN COMMUNITIES

Cahokia: Thirteenth-Century Life on the Mississippi

AS THE SUN ROSE OVER THE RICH FLOODPLAIN, THE PEOPLE OF THE riverbank city set about their daily tasks. Some went to shops where they manufactured tools, crafted pottery, worked metal, or fashioned ornamental jewelry—goods destined to be exchanged in the far corners of the continent. Others left their densely populated neighborhoods for the outlying countryside, where in the summer heat they worked the seemingly endless fields that fed the city. From almost any point people could see the great temple that rose from the center of their city—the temple where priests in splendid costumes acted out public rituals of death and renewal.

This thirteenth-century city was not in preindustrial Europe but in North America. Its residents lived and worked on the banks of the Mississippi River, across from present-day St. Louis, at a place archaeologists have named Cahokia. In the mid-1200s, Cahokia was an urban cluster of perhaps 30,000 people. Its farm fields were abundant with corn, beans, and pumpkins. The temple, a huge earthwork pyramid, covered fifteen acres at its base and rose as high as a ten-story building. On top were the sacred residences of chiefs and priests, who dressed in elaborate headdresses made from the plumage of American birds.

By the fourteenth century, Cahokia had been abandoned, but its great central temple mound and dozens of smaller ones in the surrounding area, as well as hundreds more throughout the Mississippi Valley, remained to puzzle the European immigrants who resettled the valley in the eighteenth and nineteenth centuries. Treasure seekers plundered the mounds, most of which were eventually dynamited and plowed under for farmland. Only a few were saved, inside parks and estates. Cahokia's central mound survived because in the nineteenth century its summit became the site of a monastery, now long gone.

The Europeans who first explored and excavated these mounds were convinced that they were the ruins of a vanished civilization, but could not believe they were the work of Indians. The first comprehensive study of Cahokia, published in 1848 under the sponsorship of the Smithsonian Institution, noted that "the mound-builders were an agricultural people, considerably advanced in arts, manners, habits, and religion." But because "Indians were hunters averse to labor, and not known to have constructed any works approaching [the] skillfulness of design or [the] magnitude" of Cahokia, surely those wonders were constructed by a "lost race."

The Smithsonian scientists were wrong. Historians now know that the ancestors of contemporary Native Americans constructed massive earthworks in the Mississippi Valley. The vast urban complex of Cahokia flourished from the tenth to the fourteenth century, and at its height stretched six miles along the Mississippi River. Its residents were not nomadic hunters but farmers, members of an agricultural society—which archaeologists call the Mississippian—with highly productive techniques of cultivation. Hundreds of acres of crops fed the people of Cahokia, the most populated urban community north of the complex civilization of the Aztecs in Mexico. Mississippian farmers constructed ingenious raised plots of land on which they heaped compost in wide ridges for improved drainage and protection against unseasonable frosts. To their square houses of wood and mud they attached pens in which they kept flocks of domesticated turkeys and, perhaps, small herds of young deer, which they slaughtered for meat and hides. Cahokia was at the center of a long-distance trading system that linked it to other Indian communities over a vast area. Copper came from Lake Superior, mica from the southern Appalachians, conch shells from the Atlantic coast, and Cahokia's specialized artisans were renowned for the manufacture of high-quality flint hoes, exported throughout the Mississippi Valley.

The archaeological evidence suggests that Cahokia was a city-state supported by tribute and taxation. Like the awe-inspiring public works of early urban societies in other parts of the world—the pyramids of ancient Egypt, the acropolis of Athens—the great temple mound of Cahokia was intended to reflect the city's wealth and power. The mounds and other colossal public works at Cahokia were the monuments of a society ruled by an elite. From their residences atop the mound, priests and governors looked down upon their subjects.

The 1848 Smithsonian report on Cahokia reflected the stereotypical American view that all Indian people lived in hunting bands. But the history of North America before European colonization demonstrates that the native inhabitants of the continent lived in strong, vibrant communities that ranged from small hunting bands to large agricultural cities like Cahokia and splendid imperial capitals like those of the Aztecs of Mexico or the Mayans of Central America. North America before colonization was, as one historian phrases it, "a continent of villages," a land with thousands of local communities. Over many centuries the Indian peoples of North America developed a variety of community types, each with its own system of family and social organization, each integrated with its natural surroundings. The wonders of Cahokia are but one aspect of the little-understood history of the Indians of the Americas. ■

Cahokia

KEY TOPICS

- The peopling of the Americas by migrants from Asia

- The adaptation of native cultures to the regions of North America

- The increase in complexity of many native societies following the development of farming

- The nature of Indian cultures in the three major regions of European invasion and settlement

SETTLING THE CONTINENT

"Why do you call us Indians?" a Massachusetts native complained to Puritan missionary John Eliot in 1646. Christopher Columbus, who mistook the Taino people of the Caribbean for the people of the East Indies, called them *Indios*. By the middle of the sixteenth century this Spanish word had passed into English as "Indians," and was commonly used to refer to all the native peoples of the Americas. Today anthropologists often use the term "Amerindians," and many people prefer "Native Americans." But most indigenous Americans call themselves "Indian people."

Who Are the Indian People?

At the time of their first contacts with Europeans at the beginning of the sixteenth century, the native inhabitants of the Western Hemisphere represented over 2,000 cultures, spoke hundreds of different languages, and made their livings in scores of fundamentally different environments. Just as the term "European" includes the English, French, and Spanish, so "Indian" covers an enormous diversity among the peoples of the Americas.

No single physical type characterized all the native peoples of the Americas. Although most had straight, black hair and dark, almond-shaped eyes, their skin color ranged from mahogany to light brown and few fit the "redskin" descriptions used by North American colonists of the eighteenth and nineteenth centuries. Indeed, it was only when Europeans had compared Indian peoples with natives of other continents, such as Africans, that they seemed similar enough to be classified as a group.

Once Europeans realized that the Americas were in fact a "New World," rather than part of the Asian continent, a debate began over how people might have moved there from Europe and Asia, where the Judeo-Christian Bible indicated God had created the first man and woman. Writers proposed elaborate theories of transoceanic migrations. Common to all these theories was a belief that the Americas had been populated for a few thousand years at most, and that native societies were the degenerate offspring of a far superior Old World culture. A number of Spanish scholars thought more deeply about the question of Indian origins. In 1590, Joseph de Acosta reasoned that because Old World animals were present in the Americas, they must have crossed by a land bridge that could have been used by humans as well.

Migration from Asia

Acosta was the first to propose the Asian migration hypothesis that is today supported by most of the scientific evidence. The first "hard" data linking American Indians with Asians appeared in the 1980s with the finding that Indians and northeast Asians share a common and distinctive pattern in the arrangement of the teeth. But perhaps the most compelling support for the hypothesis comes from genetic research. Studies comparing the DNA variation of populations around the world consistently demonstrate the close genetic relationship of the two populations, and recently geneticists studying a virus sequestered in the kidneys of all humans found that the strain of virus carried by Navajos and Japanese is nearly identical, while that carried by Europeans and Africans is quite different.

The migration could have begun over a land bridge connecting the continents. During the last Ice Age (the Wisconsinan Glaciation, from 70,000 to 10,000 years ago, the final act in the geologic epoch known as the Pleistocene), huge glaciers locked up massive volumes of water, and sea levels were as much as 300 feet lower than today. Asia and North America were joined by a huge subcontinent of ice-free, treeless grassland, 750 miles wide from north to south.

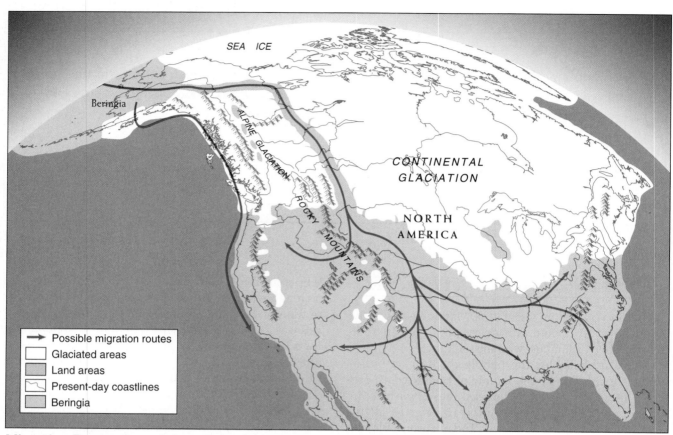

Migration Routes from Asia to America   During the Ice Age, Asia and North America were joined where the Bering Straits are today, forming a migration route for hunting peoples. Either by boat along the coast, or through a narrow corridor between the huge northern glaciers, these migrants began making their way to the heartland of the continent as much as 30,000 years ago.

Geologists have named this area Beringia, from the Bering Straits. Summers there were warm, winters were cold, dry, and almost snow-free. This was a perfect environment for large mammals—mammoth and mastodon, bison, horse, reindeer, camel, and saiga (a goatlike antelope). Small bands of Stone Age hunter-gatherers were attracted by these animal populations. Accompanied by a husky-like species of dog, hunting bands gradually moved as far east as the Yukon River basin of northern Canada, where field excavations have uncovered the fossilized jawbones of several dogs and bone tools estimated to be about 27,000 years old.

Other evidence suggests that the migration from Asia began about 30,000 years ago—around the same time that Japan and Scandinavia were being settled. This evidence is based on blood type. The vast majority of modern Native Americans have type O blood and a few have type A, but almost none have type B. Because modern Asian populations include all three blood types, however, the migrations must have begun before the evolution of type B, which geneticists believe occurred about 30,000 years ago. The study of

the evolution of language offers another kind of evidence. Linguists argue that it would require at least 35,000 years to develop, from a single common base, the nearly 500 distinct languages of the Americas.

By 25,000 years ago human communities were established in western Beringia, which is present-day Alaska. But access to the south was blocked by a huge glacial sheet covering much of what is today Canada. How did the hunters get over those 2,000 miles of deep ice? The argument is that the climate began to warm with the passing of the Ice Age, and about 13,000 B.C.E. (before the Common Era, which began 2,000 years ago) glacial melting created an ice-free corridor—the original "Pan-American Highway"—along the eastern front range of the Rocky Mountains. Soon hunters of big game had reached the Great Plains.

In the past several years, however, new archaeological finds along the Pacific coast of North and South America have thrown this theory into question. Newly excavated early human sites in Washington state, California, and Peru have been radiocarbon dated to be 11,000 to 12,000 years old. The most spectacular find, at Monte Verde in southern Chile, produced striking evidence of tool making, house building, rock painting, and human footprints conservatively dated at 12,500 years ago, long before the highway had been cleared of ice. Many archaeologists now believe that migrants moved south in boats along a coastal route rather than over land—an ancient "Pacific Coast Highway." These people were probably gatherers and fishers rather than hunters of big game.

There were two later migrations into North America. About 5000 B.C.E. the Athapascan or Na-Dene people began to settle the forests in the northwestern area of the continent. Although they eventually adopted a technology similar to that of neighboring peoples, the Na-Dene maintained a separate cultural and linguistic identity. Eventually Athapascan speakers, the ancestors of the Navajos and Apaches, migrated across the Great Plains to the Southwest. The final migration began about 3000 B.C.E., after Beringia had been submerged, when a maritime hunting people crossed the Bering Straits in small boats. The Inuits (also known as the Eskimos) colonized the polar coasts of the Arctic, the Yupiks the coast of southwestern Alaska, and the Aleuts the Aleutian Islands (which are named for them).

While scientists debate the timing and mapping of these migrations, many Indian people hold to their oral traditions that say they have always lived in North America. Every culture has its origin stories, offering explanations of the customs and beliefs of the group. Yet a number of anthropologists argue that these origin stories may shed light on ancient history. The Haida people of the Northwest Pacific coast tell of a time, long ago, when the islands were much larger; but then the oceans rose, they say, and "flood tide woman" forced them to move to higher ground. Could these stories preserve a memory of the changes at the end of the Ice Age? It is notable that many Indian traditions include a long journey from a distant place of origin to a new homeland.

Clovis: The First American Technology

The earliest tools found at North American archaeological sites, crude stone or bone choppers and scrapers, are similar to artifacts from the same period found in Europe or Asia. About 10,000 B.C.E., however, ancient Americans developed a much more sophisticated style of tool making, named after the site of its first discovery near Clovis, New Mexico. The Clovis tradition was a powerful new and sophisticated technology, unlike anything found in the Old World. In the years since the initial discovery, archaeologists have unearthed Clovis artifacts at sites ranging from Montana to Mexico, Nova Scotia to Arizona, all of them dating back to within 1,000 or 2,000 years of one another, suggesting that the Clovis technology spread quickly throughout the continent.

These Clovis points are typical of thousands that archaeologists have found at sites all over the continent, dating from a period about 12,000 years ago. When inserted in a spear shaft, these three- to six-inch fluted points made effective weapons for hunting mammoth and other big game. The ancient craftsmen who made these points often took advantage of the unique qualities of the stone they were working to enhance their aesthetic beauty.

SOURCE: ©Warren Morgan/CORBIS.

The evidence suggests that Clovis bands were mobile communities of foragers numbering perhaps thirty to fifty individuals from several interrelated families. They returned to the same hunting camps year after year, migrating seasonally within territories of several hundred square miles. Near Delbert, Nova Scotia, archaeologists discovered the floors of ten tents arranged in a semicircle, their doors opening south to avoid the prevailing northerly winds. Both this camp and others found throughout the continent overlooked watering places that would attract game. Clovis blades have been excavated amid the remains of mammoth, camel, horse, giant armadillo, and sloth.

NEW WAYS OF LIVING ON THE LAND

About 13,000 B.C.E., a global warming trend began to alter the North American climate. As the giant continental glaciers began to melt, the northern latitudes were colonized by plants, animals, and humans. Meltwater created the lake and river systems of today and raised the level of the surrounding seas, flooding Beringia as well as vast stretches of the Atlantic and Gulf coasts and creating fertile tidal pools and offshore fishing banks. These huge transformations produced new patterns of wind, rainfall, and temperature, reshaping the ecology of the entire continent and gradually producing the distinct North American regions of today. The great integrating force of a single continental climate faded, and with its passing the continental Clovis culture fragmented into many different regional patterns.

Hunting Traditions

One of the most important effects of this massive climatic shift was the stress it placed on the big game animals best suited to an Ice Age environment. The archaeological record shows the extinction of thirty-two classes of large New World animals, including not only the mammoth and mastodon but also the horse and camel, both of which evolved in America and then migrated to Asia across Beringia. Lowered reproduction and survival rates of large animals may have forced hunting bands to intensify their efforts, leading to what some archaeologists have called the "Pleistocene Overkill."

As the other large-mammal populations declined, hunters on the Great Plains concentrated on the herds of American bison, or buffalo. To hunt these animals people needed a weapon they could throw quickly with great accuracy and speed at fast-moving targets over distances of as much as a hundred yards. In archaeological sites dating from about 8000 B.C.E., a new style of tool is found mingled with animal remains. This technology, named "Folsom" after the site of the first major excavation in New Mexico, was a refinement of the Clovis tradition, featuring more delicate but deadlier spear points. Hunters probably hurled the lances to which these points were attached with wooden spear-throwers, with far greater speed than they could achieve with their arms alone. By 7000 B.C.E., Folsom evolved into a tradition that archaeologists call "Plano"; the points are found with grinding tools for vegetable foods, demonstrating the development of a varied diet on the Great Plains.

These archaeological finds suggest the growing complexity of early Indian communities. Hunters frequently stampeded herds of bison into canyon traps or over cliffs. At one such kill site in southeastern Colorado, dated at about 6500 B.C.E., archaeologists uncovered the remains of nearly 200 bison that had been slaughtered and then systematically butchered on a single occasion. Such tasks required a sophisticated division of labor among dozens of men and women and the cooperation of a number of communities. Taking food in such great quantities also suggests a knowledge of basic preservation techniques. These people must have been among the first to make jerky (dried strips of meat) and pemmican (a mixture of dried meat, animal fat, and berries that can keep into the winter when stored in hide containers).

Desert Culture

The retreat of the glaciers led to new ways of finding food in other regions: hunting in the arctic, foraging in the arid deserts, fishing along the coasts, hunting and gathering in the forests. These developments took place roughly 10,000 to 2,500 years ago, during what archaeologists call the Archaic period (corresponding to the late phases of the Stone Age in Eurasia and Africa).

In the Great Basin of present-day Utah and Nevada the warming trend associated with the end of the Ice Age created a desert where once there had been enormous inland seas. Here Indian people developed Desert culture, a way of life based on the pursuit of small game and the intensified foraging of plant foods. Small communities or bands of desert foragers migrated seasonally within a small range. They collected seeds, fiber, and prickly pear from the yucca one season, then moved to highland mesas or plateaus to gather grass seed, acorns, juniper berries, and piñon nuts, and next to mountain streams to spear and net fish.

Archaeologists today find the artifacts of desert foragers in the caves and rock shelters in which they lived. In addition to stone tools, there are objects of wood, hide, and fiber, wonderfully preserved for thousands of years in the dry climate. Desert culture persisted into the nineteenth century among modern Shoshone and Ute communities.

Descriptions of the culture of the modern Shoshones suggest that their emphasis on sharing and gift giving, their condemnation of hoarding, and their limitations on the accumulation of material goods, fostered by a nomadic lifestyle, prevented individuals or families from acquiring excessive wealth and forged a strong sense of community among these people of the desert. Desert communities were characterized by a kind of social equality in which decisions were made by consensus among the adults and leadership tended to be informal, based on achievement and reputation. Men of one band generally married women from another, and wives came to live with the people of their husband's families, creating important linkages between groups that contributed to the sense of shared ethnic identity.

The innovative practices of the Desert culture gradually spread from the Great Basin to the Great Plains and the Southwest, where foraging for plant foods began to supplement hunting. Archaeologists estimate that about 6,000 years ago, Indians carried Desert culture to Cali-

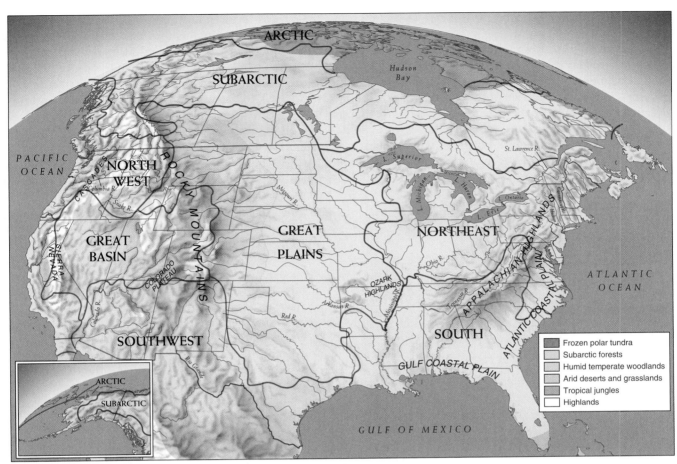

Climatological and Culture Regions of North America   Occupying more than a third of the continent, the United States is alone among the world's nations in encompassing all five general classes of global climate: tropical jungles, arid deserts and grasslands, temperate woodlands, subarctic forests, and frozen polar tundra. All peoples must adjust their diet, shelter, and other material aspects of their lives to the physical conditions of the world around them. By considering the ways in which Indian peoples developed distinct cultures adapted to their environments, anthropologists developed the concept of "culture areas." They divide the continent into nine fundamental regions that have greatly influenced the history of North America over the past 10,000 years. Just as regions shaped the lifeways and history of Indian peoples, after the coming of the Europeans they nurtured the development of regional American cultures.

fornia, where, in the natural abundance of the valleys and coasts, they developed an economy capable of supporting some of the densest populations and the first permanently settled communities in North America. Another dynamic center in the West developed along the Northwest Pacific coast, where Indian communities developed a way of life based on the use of abundant fish and sea mammals. Here, densely populated, permanently settled communities were also possible.

Forest Efficiency

There were similar trends east of the Mississippi. Before European settlers destroyed countless acres of woodland in the eighteenth and nineteenth centuries, the whole of eastern North America was a vast forest.

During the Archaic period, forest communities achieved a comfortable and secure life based on their sophisticated knowledge of the rich and diverse available resources, a principle that archaeologists call "forest efficiency." Indian communities of the forest hunted small game and gathered seeds, nuts, roots, and other wild plant foods. They also developed the practice of burning the woodlands and prairies to stimulate the growth of berries, fruits, and edible roots. These burns created meadows and edge environments that provided harvestable food and attracted grazing animals, which were hunted for their meat and hides. Another important resource was the abundant fish of the rivers.

Archaeological sites in the East suggest that during the late Archaic period community populations grew and settlements became increasingly permanent, providing convincing evidence of the viability of forest efficiency. The artifacts these people buried with their dead—axes, fishhooks, and animal bones with males, nut-cracking stones, beads, and pestles with females—reflect the different roles of men and women in their society.

THE DEVELOPMENT OF FARMING

The use of a wide variety of food sources during the Archaic period eventually led many Indian people to develop and adopt the practice of farming. The dynamic center of this development in North America was in the highlands of Mexico, from which the new technology spread north and east.

Mexico

At the end of the Stone Age ("Stone Age" is generic for all the world, while "Archaic" is specific to the New World and is the equivalent of "mesolithic" for Europe), people in four different parts of the world developed farming systems, each based on a different crop: rice in Southeast Asia, wheat in West Asia, maize (or Indian corn) in Mexico, and potatoes in the Andean highlands of South America. In Mexico a great variety of other crops—most importantly beans and squash, but also tomatoes, peppers, avocados, cocoa (chocolate), and vanilla—supplemented maize. Today, maize and potatoes, the two American crops, contribute more to the world's food supply than do wheat and rice. These "miracle crops" fueled the expansion of European human and livestock populations in the three centuries after 1650.

Archaeological evidence suggests that plant cultivation in the highlands of central Mexico began about 5,000 years ago. Ancient Mexicans developed crops that responded well to human care and produced larger quantities of food in a limited space than did plants growing in the wild. Maize was particularly productive; over time it was adapted to a wide range of American climates, and farming spread throughout the temperate regions of North America, those characterized by relatively mild climates.

As farming became increasingly important, it radically reshaped social life. Where a foraging society might require 100 square miles to support 100 people, a farming society required only one square mile. Population growth and the need for people to remain near

their fields throughout the year led to the appearance of villages and permanent architecture and eventually to the emergence of large, densely settled communities like Cahokia. Autumn harvests had to be stored during winter months, and the storage and distribution of food had to be managed. The division of labor increased with the appearance of specialists like toolmakers, crafts workers, administrators, priests, and rulers as well as farmers and food processors.

By 1000 B.C.E. urban communities governed by permanent bureaucracies had begun to form in Mesoamerica, the region stretching from central Mexico to Central America. By the beginning of the first millennium C.E. (Common Era), highly productive farming was supporting complex urban civilizations in the Valley of Mexico (the location of present-day Mexico City), the Yucatan Peninsula, and other parts of Mesoamerica. Like many of the ancient civilizations of Asia and the Mediterranean, these Mesoamerican civilizations were characterized by the concentration of wealth and power in the hands of an elite class of priests and rulers, the construction of impressive temples and other public structures, and the development of systems of mathematics and astronomy and several forms of hieroglyphic writing. These civilizations also engaged in warfare between states and held terrifying public rituals of human sacrifice.

The great city of Teotihuacan in the Valley of Mexico, which emerged about 100 B.C.E., had a population of as many as 200,000 at the height of its power around C.E. 500. Teotihuacan's elite class of religious and political leaders controlled an elaborate state-sponsored trading system that stretched from present-day Arizona to Central America and may have included coastal shipping connections with the civilizations of Peru. The city had a highly specialized division of labor. Artisans manufactured tools and produced textiles, stoneware, pottery, and obsidian blades. The bureaucratic elite collected taxes and tribute. Farmers worked the fields, and armies of workers constructed such monumental edifices as the Pyramids of the Sun and Moon, which still dominate the site's ruins.

Teotihuacan began to decline in the sixth century, and by the eighth century it was mostly abandoned. A new empire, that of the Toltecs, dominated central Mexico from the tenth to the twelfth century. By the fourteenth century a people known as the Aztecs, migrants from the north, had settled in the Valley of Mexico and begun a dramatic expansion into a formidable imperial power (see Chapter 2).

The Mayan peoples of the Yucatan peninsula developed a group of competing city-states that flourished from about 300 B.C.E. until C.E. 900. Their achievements included advanced writing and calendar systems and a sophisticated knowledge of mathematics.

The Resisted Revolution

Historians once described the development of farming as a revolution. They believed that agricultural communities offered such obvious advantages that their neighbors must have rushed to adopt this way of life. Societies that remained without a farming tradition must simply have been too "primitive" to achieve this breakthrough; vulnerability to fickle nature was the penalty for their ignorance.

But there is very little evidence to support this notion of a "revolution" occurring during a short, critical period. The adoption of farming was a gradual process, one that required hundreds, even thousands of years. Moreover, ignorance of cultivation was never the reason that cultures failed to take up farming, for all hunter-gatherer peoples understand a great deal about plant reproduction. The Menominee Indians of the northern forests of Wisconsin, for example, when gathering wild rice, purposely allowed some of it to fall back into the water to ensure a crop for the next season, and Paiutes of the Great Basin systematically irrigated stands of their favorite wild food sources.

As this new farming technology became available, cultures in different regions assessed its advantages and limitations. In California and the Pacific Northwest, acorn gathering or salmon fishing made the cultivation of food crops seem a waste of time. In the Great Basin, several peoples attempted to farm but without success. Before the invention of modern irrigation systems, which require sophisticated engineering, only the Archaic Desert culture could prevail in this harsh environment. In the neighboring Southwest, however, farming resolved certain ecological dilemmas and transformed the way of life. Like the development of more sophisticated traditions of tool manufacture, farming represented another stage in economic intensifications (like the advance in tool making represented by Clovis technology) that kept populations and available resources in balance. It seems that where the climate favored it, people tended to adopt farming as a way of increasing the production of food, thus continuing the Archaic tradition of squeezing as much productivity as they could from their environment. In a few areas, however, farming truly did result in a revolutionary transformation, creating urban civilizations like the one in central Mexico or at Cahokia, on the banks of the Mississippi.

Increasing Social Complexity

Farming created the basis for much greater social complexity within Indian communities. There were significantly more elaborate systems of kinship. Greater population density prompted families to group themselves into clans. Often different clans became responsible for different social, political, or ritual functions. Clans became an important mechanism for binding together the people of several communities into a tribe. Tribes, based on ethnic, linguistic, and territorial unity, were led by leaders or chiefs from honored clans, who were often advised by councils of elders. These councils sometimes arbitrated disputes between individuals or families, but most crimes—theft, adultery, rape, murder—were avenged by the aggrieved kinship group itself. In all likelihood, the city of Cahokia was governed by such a system.

The primary function of chiefs was the supervision of the economy, the collection and storage of the harvest, and the distribution of food to the clans. Differences in wealth, though small by the standards of modern societies, might develop between the families of a farming tribe. These inequalities were kept in check by redistribution according to principles of sharing similar to those operating in foraging communities. Nowhere in North America did Indian cultures develop a concept of the private ownership of land or other resources, which were usually considered the common resource of the people and were worked collectively.

Indian communities practiced a rather strict division of labor according to gender, which in its details varied tremendously from culture to culture. Among foraging peoples, hunting was generally assigned to men, and the gathering of food and the maintenance of home-base camps were the responsibility of women. This pattern probably originated during the Archaic period. But the development of farming called these patterns into question. In Mexico, where communities became almost totally dependent on crops, both men and women worked in the fields. Where hunting remained important, the older division of labor remained, with women responsible for fieldwork.

In most North American Indian farming communities, women and men belonged to separate social groupings, each with its own rituals and lore. Membership in these societies was one of the most important elements of a person's identity. Marriage ties, on the other hand, were relatively weak, and in most Indian communities divorce was usually simple. The couple separated without a great deal of ceremony, the children almost always remaining with the mother. All Indian women controlled their own bodies, were free to determine the timing of reproduction, and were free to use secret herbs to prevent pregnancy, induce abortion, or ease the pains of childbirth.

Farming communities were far more complex than foraging communities, but they were also less stable. Growing populations demanded increasingly large surpluses of food, and this need often led to social conflict and warfare. Moreover, farming systems were especially vulnerable to changes in climate, such as drought, as well as to crises of their own making, such as soil depletion or erosion.

Farmers of the Southwest

Farming communities began to emerge in the arid Southwest during the first millennium B.C.E. Among the first to develop a settled farming way of life were the Mogollon people, who lived from around 250 B.C.E. to C.E. 1450 along what is today the southern Arizona–New Mexico border. Living along mountain ridges and near streams in permanent villages of ingenious pit houses well suited to the region's temperature extremes, these people used digging sticks to cultivate maize, beans, and squash. Some of the Mogollon pit structures may have been what Southwestern peoples today call *kivas*, which are used for community religious rituals.

From about C.E. 300 to 1500 the people of the Hohokam ("those who are gone," in the language of the modern tribes of the area) culture flourished in the region along the floodplain of the Salt and Gila rivers in southern Arizona. The Hohokams, who lived in agricultural villages, built and maintained the first irrigation system in America north of Mexico, channeling river water many miles to desert fields of maize, beans, squash, tobacco, and cotton. They made jewelry from shells and developed a process for etching shells with animal designs. They shared many traits with Mesoamerican civilization to the south, including platform mounds for religious ceremonies and large courts for ball playing.

The Anasazis

The best-known farming culture of the Southwest is that of the Anasazis, which developed around the first century C.E. several hundred miles to the north of the Hohokam communities in the Four Corners area, where today Arizona, New Mexico, Utah, and Colorado meet on the great plateau of the Colorado River. Around 750, possibly in response to population pressure and an increasingly dry climate, the Anasazis began a shift from pit-house villages to densely populated, multistoried apartment complexes that the Spanish invaders called *pueblos*. These clustered around central complexes with circular underground *kivas*. The Anasazis grew high-yield varieties of maize in terraced fields irrigated by canals flowing from mountain catchment basins. To supplement this vegetable diet, they hunted animals for their meat, using the bow and arrow that first appeared in the region about C.E. 500.

Anasazi culture extended over an area larger than California. The sites of more than 25,000 Anasazi communities are known in New Mexico alone. Only a few

have been excavated, so there is much that archaeologists do not yet understand. The most prominent of the Anasazi centers was Pueblo Bonito in Chaco Canyon. Completed in the twelfth century, this complex of 650 interconnected rooms is a monument to the golden age of the Anasazis.

The Anasazis faced a major crisis in the thirteenth century. The arid climate became even dryer, and growing Anasazi populations had to redouble their efforts to improve food production, building increasingly complex irrigation canals, dams, and terraced fields. A devastating drought from 1276 to 1293 (precisely dated with the aid of tree-ring analysis) resulted in repeated crop failures and eventual famine. This was accompanied by the arrival of Athapascan migrants who for a thousand years or more had been moving south from subarctic regions. These people were the immediate ancestors of the Navajos and the Apaches, and judging by their descendants, they must have been fierce fighters. By the fourteenth and fifteenth centuries, the Athapascans were raiding Anasazi farming communities, taking food, goods, and possibly slaves. (Indeed, the name *Anasazi* means "the place where they fought us" in Athapascan.) Gradually the Anasazis abandoned the Four Corners area altogether. Their movements have not yet been fully traced, but most seem to have resettled in communities along the Rio Grande, joining with local residents to form the Pueblo people of modern times.

Farmers of the Eastern Woodlands

Archaeologists date the beginning of the farming culture of eastern North America, known as Woodland culture, from the first appearances of pottery in the region about 3,000 years ago. The Woodland culture was based on a sophisticated way of life that combined gathering and hunting with the cultivation of a few crops. Sunflowers provided seeds and cooking oil. The presence of pipes in archaeological digs indicates that these farmers grew tobacco, which had spread north from the Caribbean, where it was first domesticated.

Woodland people began cultivating maize during the first millennium C.E., but even before had begun to adopt an increasingly settled existence and a more complex social organization. Between 1700 and 700 B.C.E., the people of the Poverty Point culture in the lower Mississippi Valley erected a remarkable site consisting of a series of concentric semicircular earthen mounds, covering an area about a mile square. The people of the Adena culture occupied the Ohio River basin from present-day Indiana to Pennsylvania from before 1000 B.C.E. to about C.E. 250. They lived in permanent or semipermanent villages and built large burial mounds.

Between about 200 B.C.E. and fifth century C.E., the Hopewell people settled in the Mississippi-Ohio Valley. Hopewell communities were devoted to mortuary cults, in which the dead were honored through ceremony, display, and the construction of enormous and elaborate burial mounds. Hopewell chiefs mobilized an elaborate trade network that acquired obsidian from the Rocky Mountains, copper from the Great Lakes, mica from the Appalachians, and shells from the Gulf coast. Hopewell artisans converted these materials into goods that played an important role in Hopewell trade and were buried with their dead in Hopewell graves.

Mississippian Society

The Hopewell culture collapsed in the fifth century, perhaps as a result of shifting climate patterns. Local communities continued to practice their late Archaic subsistence strategies, but abandoned the expensive cultural displays demanded by the Hopewell mortuary cult. Following the collapse of Hopewell, however, several important innovations were introduced in the East. The bow and arrow, developed on the Great Plains, appeared east of the Mississippi about the seventh century, greatly increasing the efficiency of hunting. Also between 450 and 800, maize farming spread widely in the East. Indian farmers had developed a new variety of maize called Northern Flint, with large cobs and plentiful kernels that matured in a short enough time to make it suitable for cultivation in temperate northern latitudes. A shift from digging sticks to flint hoes also took place about this time, further increasing the productive potential of maize farming.

It was on the basis of these innovations that the powerful new Mississippian culture arose in the seventh or eighth century. The Mississippians were master maize farmers who lived in permanent villages along the floodplain of the Mississippi River. Cahokia, the most important of these, was the urban heart of Mississippian America. Cahokia's dense urban center with its monumental temple, its residential neighborhoods, and its surrounding farmlands were mirrored in many other regional centers, each with thousands of residents. There were cities on the Arkansas River near Spiro, Oklahoma; on the Black Warrior River at Moundville, Al-abama; at Hiawassee Island on the Tennessee River; and along the Etowah and Okmulgee rivers in Georgia. The Great Serpent Mound, the largest effigy earthwork in the world, was constructed by Mississippian peoples in southern Ohio.

These centers, linked by the vast river transportation system of the Mississippi and its many tributaries, became the earliest city-states north of Mexico, hierarchical chiefdoms that extended political control over the farmers of the surrounding countryside. With continued population growth, these cities engaged in vigorous and probably violent competition for the limited space along the rivers. It may have been the need for more orderly ways of allocating territories that stimulated the evolution of political hierarchies. The tasks of preventing local conflict, storing large food surpluses, and redistributing foodstuffs from farmers to artisans and elites required a leadership class with the power to command. Mound building and the use of tribute labor in the construction of other public works testified to the power of chiefs, who lived in sumptuous quarters atop the mounds.

Mississippian culture reached its height between the eleventh and thirteenth centuries C.E., the same period in which the Anasazis constructed their desert cities. Both groups adapted to their own environment the technology that was spreading northward from Mexico. Both developed impressive artistic traditions, and their feats of engineering reflect the beginnings of science and technology. They were complex societies

The Great Serpent Mound in southern Ohio, the shape of an uncoiling snake more than 1,300 feet long, is the largest effigy earthwork in the world. Monumental public works like these suggest the high degree of social organization of the Mississippian people.

SOURCE: George Gerster/Comstock Images.

characterized by urbanism, social stratification, craft specialization, and regional trade—except for the absence of a writing system, all the traits of European civilization.

The Politics of Warfare and Violence

Warfare among Indian peoples certainly predated the colonial era. Organized violence was probably rare among hunting bands, who seldom could manage more than a small raid against an enemy. Certain hunting peoples, though, such as the southward-moving Athapascans, must have engaged in systematic raiding of settled farming communities. Warfare was also common among farming confederacies fighting to gain additional lands for cultivation. The first Europeans to arrive in the southeastern part of the continent described highly organized combat among large tribal armies. The bow and arrow was a deadly weapon of war, and the practice of scalping seems to have originated among warring tribes, who believed one could capture a warrior's spirit by taking his scalp lock.

The archaeological remains of Cahokia reveal that during the thirteenth and fourteenth centuries the residents surrounded the central sections of their city with a heavy log stockade. There must have been a great deal of violent warfare with other nearby communities. Also during this period, numerous towns were formed throughout the river valleys of the Mississippi, each based on the domination of farming countrysides by metropolitan centers. Eventually conditions in the upper Mississippi Valley deteriorated so badly that Cahokia and many other sites were abandoned altogether, and as the cities collapsed, people relocated in smaller, decentralized communities. Among the peoples of the South, however, Mississippian patterns continued into the period of colonization.

CULTURAL REGIONS OF NORTH AMERICA ON THE EVE OF COLONIZATION

An appreciation of the ways human cultures adapted to geography and climate is fundamental to an understanding of American history, for just as regions shaped the development of Indian cultures in the centuries before the arrival of Europeans, so they continued to influence the character of American life in the centuries thereafter.

In order to understand the impact of regions on Indian cultures, anthropologists divide North America into several distinct "culture areas" within which groups shared a significant number of cultural traits:

Arctic, Subarctic, Great Basin, Great Plains, California, Northwest, Plateau, Southwest, South, and Northeast.

The Population of Indian America

In determining the precolonial population of the Americas, historical demographers consider a number of factors—the population densities that different technological and economic systems could support, the archaeological evidence, the very earliest European accounts, and the estimated impact of epidemic diseases. (For a discussion of epidemics among Indian peoples, see Chapter 2.) Although estimates vary, there is general agreement among historians that in the fifteenth century the population of America north of Mexico was between 7 and 10 million. Perhaps as many as 25 million people lived in the complex societies of Mesoamerica. Thus, at the time of their first contact with European explorers and settlers, the peoples of the Western Hemisphere numbered 60 to 70 million, about the same as Europe's population at the time.

The largest populations of the continent were in the Southwest, South, and Northeast. Since it was in these culture areas that European explorers, conquerors, and colonists first concentrated their efforts, they deserve more detailed examination.

The Southwest

The single overwhelming fact of life in the Southwest is aridity. Summer rains average only ten to twenty inches annually, and on much of the dry desert cultivation is impossible. A number of rivers, however, flow out of the pine-covered mountain plateaus. Flowing south to the Gulf of Mexico or the Gulf of California, these narrow bands of green winding through parched browns and reds have made possible irrigation farming along their courses.

On the eve of European colonization, Indian farmers had been cultivating their Southwest fields for nearly 3,000 years. In the floodplain of the Gila and Salt rivers lived the Pimas and Tohono O'Odhams, descendants of the ancient Hohokams. Working small irrigated fields along the Colorado River, even on the floor of the Grand Canyon, were the Yuman peoples. In their oasis communities, desert farmers cultivated corn, beans, squash, sunflowers, and cotton, which they traded throughout the Southwest. Often described as individualists, desert farmers lived in dispersed settlements that the Spanish called *rancherias*, their dwellings separated by as much as a mile. That way, say the Pimas, people avoid getting on each other's nerves. Rancherias were governed by councils of adult men whose decisions required unanimous consent, although a headman was chosen to manage the irrigation works.

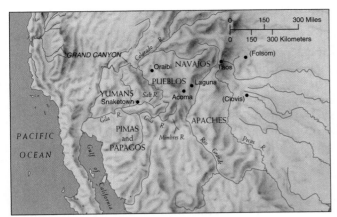

Southwestern Indian Groups on the Eve of Colonization   The Southwest was populated by desert farmers like the Pimas, Tohono O'Odhams, Yumans, and Pueblos, as well as by nomadic hunters and raiders like the Apaches.

Southern Indian Groups on the Eve of Colonization   On the eve of colonization the Indian societies of the South shared many traits of the complex Mississippian farming culture.

East of the Grand Canyon lived the Pueblo peoples, named by the Spanish for their unique dwellings of stacked, interconnected apartments. Although speaking several languages, the Pueblos had a great deal in common, most notably their commitment to communal village life. A strict communal code of behavior that regulated personal conduct was enforced by a maze of matrilineal clans and secret religious societies; unique combinations of these clans and societies formed the governing systems of different Pueblo villages. Seasonal public ceremonies in the village squares included singing and chanting, dancing, colorful impersonations of the ancestral spirits called *kachinas*, and the comic antics of clowns who mocked in slapstick style those who did not conform to the communal ideal (pretending to drink urine or eat dirt, for example, in front of the home of a person who kept an unclean house).

The Pueblos inhabit the oldest continuously occupied towns in the United States. The village of Oraibi, Arizona, dates from the twelfth century, when the Hopis ("peaceful ones") founded it in the isolated central mesas of the Colorado Plateau. Using dry-farming methods and drought-resistant plants, these western Pueblo Indians produced rich harvests of corn and squash amid shifting sand dunes. On a mesa top about fifty miles southwest of present-day Albuquerque, New Mexico, Anasazi immigrants from Mesa Verde built Acoma, the "sky city," in the late thirteenth century. The Pueblo people established approximately seventy other villages during the next 200 years; fifty of these were still in existence in the seventeenth century when the Spanish founded Santa Fé, and two dozen survive today, including the large Indian towns of Laguna, Isleta, Santo Domingo, Jémez, San Felipe, and Taos.

The Athapascans, more recent immigrants, also lived in the arid deserts and mountains. They hunted and foraged, traded meat and medicinal herbs with farmers, and often raided and plundered these same villages and rancherias. Gradually, some of the Athapascan people adopted the farming and handicraft skills of their Pueblo neighbors; they became known as the Navajos. Others, more heavily influenced by the hunting and gathering traditions of the Great Basin and Great Plains, remained nomadic and became known as the Apaches.

The South

The South enjoys a mild, moist climate with short winters and long summers, ideal for farming. From the Atlantic and Gulf coasts, a broad fertile plain extends inland to the Piedmont, a plateau separating the coastal plains from the Appalachian Mountain. The upper courses of the waterways originating in the Appalachian highlands offered ample rich bottom land for farming. The extensive forests, mostly of yellow pine, offered abundant animal resources. In the sixteenth century, large populations of Indian peoples farmed this rich land, fishing or hunting local fauna to supplement their diets. They lived in communities ranging from villages of twenty or so dwellings to large towns of a thousand or more inhabitants.

Mississippian cultural patterns continued among many of the peoples of the South. Along the waterways many farming towns were organized into chiefdoms. Because most of these groups were decimated by disease in the first years of colonization, they are poorly documented. We know most about the Natchez, farmers of the rich floodplains of the lower Mississippi

Delta, who survived into the eighteenth century before being destroyed in a war with the French. Overseeing the Natchez was a ruler known as the Great Sun, who lived in royal splendor on a ceremonial mound in the capital. Natchez was a class society. Noble families ruled the majority, whom they called the "stinkards." Persistent territorial conflict with other confederacies elevated warriors to an honored status among the Natchez. Public torture and human sacrifice of enemies were common.

These chiefdoms were rather unstable. Under the pressure of climate change, population growth, and warfare many were weakened and others collapsed. As a result thousands of people left behind the grand mounds and earthworks to migrate to the woodlands and hill country where they took up hunting and foraging, returning to the tried and true methods of forest efficiency. They formed communities and ethnic confederacies that were less centralized and more egalitarian than the Mississippian chiefdoms and would prove considerably more resilient to conquest.

Among the most prominent of these new ethnic groups were a people in present-day Mississippi and Alabama who came to be known as the Choctaws. Another group in western Tennessee became known as the Chickasaws, and another people in Georgia were known as the Creeks. On the mountain plateaus lived the Cherokees, the single largest confederacy, which included more than sixty towns. For these groups farming was somewhat less important, hunting somewhat more so. There were no ruling classes or kings, and leaders included women as well as men. Most peoples reckoned their descent matrilineally (back through generations of mothers), and after marriage husbands left the homes of their mothers to reside with the families of their wives. Women controlled household and village life and were influential in the matrilineal clans that linked communities together. Councils of elderly men governed the confederacies but were joined by clan matrons for annual meetings at the central council house.

The peoples of the South celebrated a common round of agricultural festivals that brought clans together from surrounding communities. At the harvest festival, for example, people thoroughly cleaned their homes and villages. They fasted and purified themselves by consuming the "black drink," which induced visions. They extinguished the old fires and lit new ones, then celebrated the new crop of sweet corn with dancing and other festivities. During the days that followed, villages, clans, and groups of men and women competed against one another in the ancient stick-and-ball game that the French named lacrosse; in the evenings men and women played chunkey, a gambling game.

The Northeast

The Northeast, the colder sector of the eastern woodlands, has a varied geography of coastal plains and mountain highlands, great rivers, lakes, and valleys. After C.E. 500, cultivation became the main support of the Indian economy in those places where the growing season was long enough to bring a crop of corn to maturity. In such areas of the Northeast, along the coasts and in the river valleys, Indian populations were large and dense.

The Iroquois of present-day Ontario and upstate New York have lived in the region for at least 4,500 years. They were among the first northeastern peoples to adopt cultivation. Iroquois women produced crops of corn, beans, squash, and sunflowers sufficient to support up to fifty longhouses, each occupied by a large matrilineal extended family. Some of those houses were truly long; archaeologists have excavated the foundations of some that extended 400 feet and would have housed dozens of families. Typically, these villages were surrounded by substantial wooden walls or palisades, clear evidence of intergroup conflict and warfare.

Population growth and the resulting intensification of farming in Iroquoia stimulated the development of chiefdoms there as elsewhere. By the fifteenth century several centers of population, each in a separate watershed, had coalesced from east to west across upstate New York. These were the five Iroquois chiefdoms or nations: the Mohawks, Oneidas, Onondagas, Cayugas, and Senecas. Iroquois oral histories collected during the nineteenth century recall this as a period of

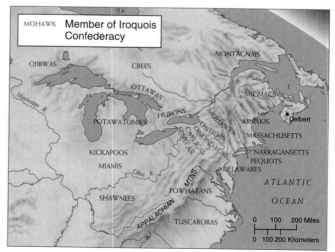

Northeastern Indian Groups on the Eve of Colonization   The Indians of the Northeast were mostly village peoples. In the fifteenth century five Iroquois groups—the Mohawks, Oneidas, Onondagas, Cayugas, and Senecas—joined together to form the Iroquois Five Nation Confederacy.

CHRONOLOGY

30,000–15,000 B.C.E.	First humans in the Americas	**250** B.C.E.	Beginning of Mogollon culture in the Southwest
13,000 B.C.E.	Global warming trend begins	**200** B.C.E.–C.E. **400**	Hopewell culture flourishes
10,000 B.C.E.	Clovis technology	**650**	Bow and arrow, flint hoes, and Northern Flint corn in the Northeast
9000 B.C.E.	Extinction of big-game animals	**775–1150**	Hohokam site of Snaketown reaches its greatest extent
8000 B.C.E.	Beginning of the Archaic period	**1000**	Tobacco in use throughout North America
7000 B.C.E.	First cultivation of plants in the Mexican highlands	**1150**	Founding of Hopi village of Oraibi, oldest continuously occupied town in the United States
5000 B.C.E.	Athapascan migrations to America begin		
4000 B.C.E.	First settled communities along the Pacific coast	**1200**	High point of Mississippian and Anasazi cultures
3000 B.C.E.	Inupiat and Aleut migrations begin	**1276**	Severe drought begins in the Southwest
1500–1000 B.C.E.	Maize and other Mexican crops introduced into the Southwest	**1300**	Arrival of Athapascans in the Southwest
1000 B.C.E.	Beginning of Adena culture First urban communities in Mexico	**1451**	Founding of Iroquois Confederacy

persistent violence, possibly the consequence of conflicts over territory.

Historians believe that the Iroquois founded a confederacy to control this violence. The confederacy outlawed warfare among the member nations and established regulated forms of gift exchange and payment to replace revenge. Iroquois oral history refers to the founder of the confederacy, Chief Deganawida the Lawgiver, as "blocking out the sun" as a demonstration of his powers, suggesting that these events might have taken place during a full solar eclipse, such as the one in the Northeast in 1451. Deganawida's message was proclaimed by his supporter, Hiawatha, a great orator, who convinced all the five Iroquois nations to join in confederacy. As a model of their government, the confederacy used the metaphor of the longhouse; each nation, it was said, occupied a separate hearth but acknowledged a common mother. The confederacy suppressed violence among its members, but did not hesitate to encourage war against neighboring Iroquoian speakers, such as the Hurons or the Eries, who constructed defensive confederacies of their own at about the same time.

The other major language group of the Northeast was Algonquian, whose speakers belonged to at least fifty distinct cultures. The Algonquian peoples north of the Great Lakes and in northern New England were hunters and foragers, organized into bands with loose ethnic affiliations. Several of these peoples, including the Micmacs, Crees, Montagnais, and Ojibwas (also known as the Chippewas), were the first to become involved in the fur trade with European newcomers. Among the Algonquians of the Atlantic coast from present-day Massachusetts south to Virginia, as well as among those in the Ohio Valley, farming led to the development of settlements as densely populated as those of the Iroquois.

In contrast to the Iroquois, most Algonquian peoples were patrilineal. In general, they lived in less extensive dwellings and in smaller villages, often without palisade fortifications. Although Algonquian communities were relatively autonomous, they began to form confederacies during the fifteenth and sixteenth centuries. Among these groupings were those of the Massachusetts, Narragansetts, and Pequots of New England; the Delawares and the peoples of Powhatan's confederacy on the mid-Atlantic coast; and the Shawnees, Miamis, Kickapoos, and Potawatomis of the Ohio Valley.

CONCLUSION

Over the thousands of years that elapsed between the settlement of North America and the invasion of Europeans at the end of the fifteenth century, Indian peoples developed hundreds of distinctive cultures that were fine-tuned to the geographic and climatic possibilities and limitations of their homelands. In the northern forests, they hunted game and perfected the art of processing furs and hides. Along the coasts and rivers they harvested the abundant runs of fish and learned to navigate the waters with sleek and graceful boats. In the arid Southwest, they mastered irrigation farming and made the deserts bloom, while in the humid Southeast, they mastered the large-scale production of crops that could sustain large cities with sophisticated political systems. North America was not a "virgin" continent, as so many of the Europeans believed. Indians had transformed the natural world, making it over into a human landscape.

"Columbus did not discover a new world," wrote historian J. H. Perry. "He established contact between two worlds, both already old." North America had a rich history, one that Europeans did not understand and later generations of Americans have too frequently ignored. The European colonists who came to settle encountered thousands of Indian communities with deep roots and vibrant traditions. In the confrontation that followed, Indian communities viewed the colonists as invaders and called upon their traditions and their gods to help them defend their homelands.

REVIEW QUESTIONS

1. List the evidence for the hypothesis that the Americas were settled by migrants from Asia.
2. Discuss the impact of environmental change and human hunting on the big-game populations of North America.
3. Review the principal regions of the North American continent and the human adaptations that made social life possible in each of them.
4. Define the concept of "forest efficiency." How does it help to illuminate the major development of the Archaic period?
5. Why did the development of farming lead to increasing social complexity? Discuss the reasons why organized political activity began in farming societies.
6. What were the hunting and agrarian traditions? In what ways did the religious beliefs of Indian peoples reflect their environmental adaptations?
7. What factors led to the organization of the Iroquois Confederacy?

RECOMMENDED READING

Tom D. Dillehay, *The Settling of the Americas: A New Prehistory* (2000). A summary of the most recent archaeological findings, suggesting a much earlier migration to the Americas. For the newest discoveries, see the recent issues and websites of *National Geographic* and *Scientific American.*

Roger C. Echo-Hawk and Walter R. Echo-Hawk, *Battlefields and Burial Grounds: The Indian Struggle to Protect Ancestral Graves in the United States* (1994). A passionate discussion by a Pawnee lawyer and historian of the double standard that allows Indian graves to be ransacked while white graves are held sacred.

Thomas E. Emerson, *Cahokia and the Archaeology of Power* (1997). The fascinating story of North America's first metropolis.

Patricia Galloway, *Choctaw Genesis, 1500–1700* (1995). A path-breaking work that uses both archaeological and written evidence to tie together the precolonial and colonial periods of a tribal people of the South.

Alvin M. Josephy Jr., ed., *America in 1492* (1992). Important essays by leading scholars of the North American Indian experience. Includes beautiful illustrations and maps as well as an excellent bibliography.

Alice B. Kehoe, *North American Indians: A Comprehensive Account* (1992). The best general anthropological survey of the history and culture of the Indians of North America. Organized by culture areas, it covers all the peoples of the continent.

Stephen Plog, *Ancient Peoples of the American Southwest* (1998). Covers the shift to agriculture with a focus on both the costs and the benefits. An accessible text with wonderful photographs.

Robert Silverberg, *Mound Builders of Ancient America: The Archaeology of a Myth* (1968). A history of opinion and theory about the mound builders.

William C. Sturtevant, general ed., *Handbook of North American Indians*, 20 vols. proposed (1978–). The most comprehensive collection of the best current scholarship. The completed series will include a volume for each of the culture regions of North America; volumes on origins, Indian–white relations, languages, and art; a biographical dictionary; and a general index.

David Hurst Thomas, *Skull Wars: Kennewick Man, Archaeology, and the Battle for Native American Identity* (2000). A readable account of the controversy over Kennewick Man and the changing ideas about ancient North American history. When scholars, bureaucrats, and Indians go to court over these issues, he argues, everyone loses.

Russell Thornton, *American Indian Holocaust and Survival: A Population History since 1492* (1987). The best introduction to the historical demography of North America. Provides a judicious review of all the evidence in a field of considerable controversy.

ON THE WEB

http://medicine.wustl.edu/~mckinney/cahokia/cahokia.html

Website for the Cahokia Mounds State Historical site (Illinois), it contains information concerning past and present archeological investigations, cultural information about Cahokia, two extensive bibliographies of literature about the Cahokia site, and links to interesting sites about Cahokia and other early Native American cultures.

http://www.its.uidaho.edu/arch499/nonwest/mayan/

Site contains good general information and photos on Mayan architecture, history, society, and culture. This site is maintained by the University of Idaho Architectural Department and possesses links to other websites containing the history and cultur of the Mayan people. Contains good bibliography of works on Mayan archeology, architecture, and general history.

http://www.beloit.edu/~museum/logan/southwest/index.htm

Site maintained by the Logan Museum of Anthropology at Beloit College in Beloit, Wisconsin. Contains comprehensive information about the Anasazi, Mogollon, Membres, Hohokam, and other ancient peoples of the American Southwest. Site also contains a rich and large collection of photos of pottery artifacts along with complete descriptions. Site focuses on material culture but contains extensive information on other aspects of the history of the peoples discussed.

http://www.nmnh.si.edu/naa/

The site containing the National Anthropological Archives, Human Studies Film Archives (Smithsonian Institute) is a rich collection of photos, drawings, and information about Native Americans from Alaska to the Great Plains to Central America and South America. In particular a student should visit online exhibits for a wealth of information. Also visit the Department of Anthropology of the National Museum of Natural History (Smithsonian) at **http://www.nmnh.si.edu/anthro/anthrove.html** for an even richer collection of materials on Native American cultures.

http://www.prenhall.com/faragherbrief/map1.1

Explore the impact of the environment on Indian trade networks. How does the environment influence the relationship between trade and culture?

http://www.prenhall.com/faragherbrief/map1.2

Examine the population densities of various North American regions on the eve of European contact. Why were some regions more populated than others?

► The Battle over Burials

There are thousands of ancient Indian burial mounds in the Midwest and South, dozens of them at Cahokia, maintained as a historical site by the state of Illinois. The people of the Adena, Hopewell, and Mississippian cultures built these mounds as memorials to commemorate their ancestors.

How should Americans manage the care of those mounds today? Should they be excavated for scientific study, exploited as tourist attractions, or treated as sacred sites? In 1990 such a dispute between American Indian activists and local residents wracked the small town of Lewiston, Illinois, about a hundred miles from Cahokia. Often communities come to blows over different ways of looking at history. Arguments over the meaning of the past are not confined to the classroom.

The controversy focused on the Dickson Mounds Museum, built on the site of several impressive mounds constructed by Mississippians around 1000 B.C.E. The museum's central attraction was an exhibit featuring the exposed graves of 237 individuals in one of the mounds. First opened in 1927 by Don Dickson, a local farmer who owned the land on which the mounds were located, the private exhibit attracted thousands of spectators. In the 1940s the state bought the site, constructed a large structure over the excavations, and installed a light and sound system. By the 1980s more than 80,000 visitors were coming each year to see the exposed graves.

As the site became more widely known it also became more controversial. Many Indians found the exhibit disrespectful and activists mounted strong pressure on the state to have the bodies reburied. How would Lewiston residents feel if their own cemeteries were excavated and exposed to public view? "It is my inherited responsibility to see the dead who were buried are responsibly reburied," said one Indian woman. Local residents, however, argued that reburial would deprive them of a valuable part of their heritage. For as long as people could remember, the town had boasted the "World's Greatest Display" of prehistoric Indian skeletons. The protesters were outsiders and didn't have the community's best interests at heart. The exhibit displayed artifacts that local residents had discovered through hard work and persistence. It was "not a desecration but celebration of those who lived on and worked the land," in the words of one local politican. "Those Indians lived and died in our area, they're a part of our history," declared the town's mayor. The two groups interpreted the same site very differently. For one it was a buried treasure, an inheritance that had become a vital part of the life of the community. For the other it was a memorial to a great and departed culture.

While state officials worried over what to do, Indian activists took matters into their own hands. In April 1991 a group of several dozen protestors entered the museum, and using smuggled-in tools, began covering the graves with dirt before being stopped by museum guards. The protest got national attention. "What we did today was call the attention of this country's leaders to the last open burial exhibit in the country," said Charlene Teters, a member of the Spokane Nation and a graduate student at the University of Illinois. "The exhibit is a desecration of these ancients and should be closed."

The Lewistown dispute was part of a contentious national debate over the appropriate ways to memorialize the Indian past. Hundreds of museums around the country held extensive collections of Indian remains and sacred objects. There were, for example, thousands of Indian skulls at the Smithsonian Institution, many of them collected from nineteenth-century battle sites. "It wasn't enough that unarmed Cheyenne people were mowed down by the cavalry at the infamous Sand Creek massacre," wrote Suzan Shown Harjo, executive director of the National Congress of American Indians, "many were decapitated and their heads shipped to Washington." In 1989, after a long review of the question, the Smithsonian agreed to return the human remains in their collections to Indian tribes for reburial. The next year Congress passed the Native American Graves Protection and Repatriation Act (NAGPRA), which gave Indian communities the right to reclaim human remains and sacred objects to which they could establish historical linkage.

Despite fears that the law would result in the wholesale loss of valuable museum collections, for the most part curators, government officials, and Indians have found ways to work together. The return of Mis-

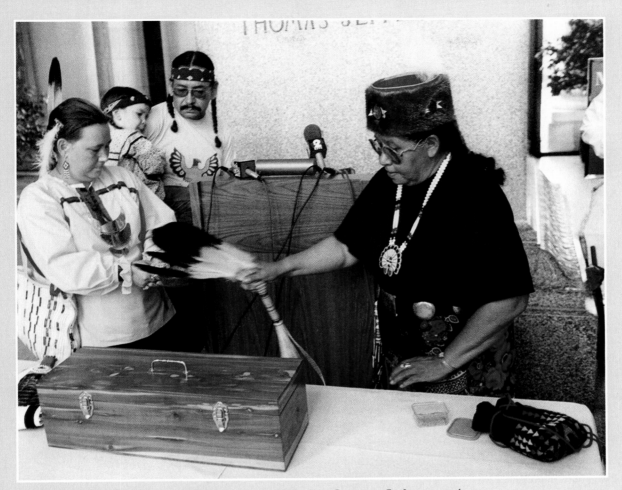

Lynn Kussman and Evelyn Voelker of the American Indian Center in St. Louis conduct a purification ceremony for Indian remains returned by the Missouri Historical Society. Although press reports have often focused on conflicts over remains, for the most part curators, government officials, and Indians have found ways to work together.

SOURCE: Gary Bohn/Saint Louis Post-Dispatch.

sissippian remains by the Missouri Historical Society in St. Louis, across the Mississippi from Cahokia, helped to build a relationship of trust with regional Indian leaders. When the Society acquired a painted rawhide Comanche shield, tribal elders advised curators on how to properly handle it, enabling it to be displayed in a manner that Indians feel honors the spirit of the warrior who carried it.

At Lewistown the state of Illinois arranged a compromise designed to satisfy both Indian activists and local residents. The display was closed and the bones reburied, but the museum got a $4 million renovation. The new Dickson Mounds Museum, which reopened in 1994, is designed to be a site of memory for both Indians and local residents. Instead of gawking at skeletons, visitors watched multimedia presentations on local Indian history prepared in cooperation with Indian scholars and elders. There are also exhibits that interpret the history of the museum itself, with a special display honoring Don Dickson.

This flexible approach works in what cultural critic James E. Young calls the best tradition of memorials— suggesting to people different *ways* to remember, not precisely *what* to remember. Some local residents are still bitter about lost business. But others disagree. "In the past we had a display of bones," one said. "Now we have a museum. Our views and ideas of what is going on have changed." ▪

TWO

WHEN WORLDS COLLIDE

▶ 1 4 9 2 – 1 5 9 0

CHAPTER OUTLINE

AMERICAN COMMUNITIES

The English and the Algonquians at Roanoke

IT WAS LATE AUGUST 1590 WHEN ENGLISH SHIPS SAILED THROUGH Hatteras Inlet into Pamlico Sound, off the coast of present-day North Carolina, and made their way north through rough seas to Roanoke Island, where Governor John White had left the first English community in North America three years before. Anxiously, White went ashore in search of the 115 colonists—mostly single men, but also twenty families, including his own daughter, son-in-law, and granddaughter Virginia Dare, the first English baby born in America. Finding the houses "taken down" and possessions "spoiled and scattered about," White suddenly noticed some writing on a tree trunk: "in fair capital letters was graven CROATOAN." Because this was the name of a friendly Indian village fifty miles south and because White found no sign of a cross, which he had instructed the colonists to leave if they were in trouble, he felt sure that his people awaited him at Croatoan, and he returned to his ship, anxious to speed to their rescue.

The Roanoke settlement had been sponsored by Walter Raleigh, a wealthy adventurer who sought profit and prestige by organizing an English colony to compete with the Spanish, when his men returned from a reconnoitering expedition to the area in 1584, they reported that the coastal region was densely populated by a "very handsome and goodly people." At an island the Indians called Roanoke, the English had been "entertained with all love and kindness" by a chief named Wingina. The leader of several surrounding villages, Wingina welcomed the English as potential allies in his struggle to extend his authority over still others. So when Raleigh's adventurers asked the chief's permission to establish a settlement on the island, he readily granted it, even sending two of his men back to England to assist in preparations for the enterprise. Manteo and Wanchese, the Indian emissaries, worked with Thomas Harriot, an Oxford scholar, and John White, an artist. The four men learned one another's language, and there seems to have been a good deal of mutual respect among them.

But when an all-male force of Englishmen returned in 1585 to establish the colony of Virginia (christened in honor of England's virgin queen, Elizabeth I), the two Indian emissaries offered Chief Wingina conflicting reports. Although Manteo, from the village of Croatoan, argued that their technology would make the English powerful allies, Wanchese described the disturbing inequalities of English society and warned of potential brutality. Wanchese was right to suspect English intentions, for Raleigh's plans were based not on respect for the Indians but on the expectation of exploiting them. He warned of their treachery. Indeed, Raleigh had directed the mission's commander to "proceed with extremity" should the Indians prove difficult and "bring them all in subjection to civility," meaning that they should be made serfs to English colonial masters. Raleigh anticipated that his colony would return profits through the lucrative trade in furs, a flourishing plantation agriculture, or gold and silver mines. In any case, the Indians would supply the labor.

The English colony was incapable of supporting itself. After building a rough fort on the island, the colonists turned to Wingina for supplies. With the harvest in the storage pits, with fish running in the streams and fat game in the woods, Wingina did the hospitable thing. But as fall turned to winter and the stores declined, constant English demands threatened the Indians' resources. Wingina's people were also stunned by the new diseases that came with the intruders. "The people began to die very fast, and many in [a] short space," Harriot wrote. The "disease was so strange that they neither knew what it was, nor how to cure it." In the spring Wingina and his people ran out of patience. But before the Indians could act, the English caught wind of the rising hostility, and in May 1586 they surprised the villagers, killing several of the leading men and beheading Wingina. With the plan of using Indian labor now clearly impossible, the colonists returned to England.

John White and Thomas Harriot, who had spent their time exploring the physical and human world of the coast and recording their findings in notes and sketches, were appalled by this turn of events. Back in England, Harriot insisted to Raleigh that the attack on the villagers came "upon causes that on our part might easily enough have been borne" and argued that "through discreet dealing" the Indians might "honor, obey, fear and love us." White proposed a new plan for a colony of real settlers, who might live in harmony with the Indians. Harriot and White clearly considered English civilization superior to Indian society, but their vision of colonization was considerably different from that of the plunderers.

In 1587, Raleigh arranged for John White to return to America as governor of a new civilian colony.

The party was supposed to land on Chesapeake Bay, but their captain dumped them instead at Roanoke so he could get on with the profitable activity of plundering the Spanish. Thus, the colonists found themselves amid natives who were alienated by the bad treatment of the previous expedition. Within a month one of White's colonists had been shot full of arrows by attackers under the leadership of Wanchese, who after Wingina's death became the most millitant opponent of the English among the Roanoke Indians. White retaliated with a counterattack that increased the hostility of the Indians. The colonists begged White to return home in their only seaworthy ship and to press Raleigh for support. Reluctantly, White set sail but arrived just as a war began between England and Spain. Three anxious years passed before White was able to return to Roanoke, only to find the settlement destroyed and the colonists gone.

As White and his crew set their sights for Croatoan that August morning in 1590, a great storm blew up. White and the ship's captain agreed that they would have to leave the sound for deeper waters. It proved White's last glimpse of America. Tossed home on a stormy sea, he never returned. The English settlers of Roanoke became known as the Lost Colony, their disappearance and ultimate fate one of the enduring mysteries of colonial history.

The Roanoke experience is a reminder of the underlying assumptions of New World colonization. The English, writes the historian and geographer Carl Sauer, had "naked imperial objectives." It also suggests the wasted opportunity of the Indians' initial welcome. But in an unexpected way, the Roanoke story also emphasizes the importance of community. There is evidence that the lost colonists lived out the rest of their lives with the Algonquians. In 1609 the English at Jamestown learned from local Indians that "some of our nation planted by Sir Walter Raleigh [are] yet alive," and many years later an English surveyor at Croatoan Island was greeted by natives who told him that "several of their Ancestors were white People," that "the English were forced to cohabit with them for Relief and Conversation, and that in the process of Time, they conformed themselves to the Manners of their Indian Relations." It may be that Virginia Dare and the other children married into Indian families, creating the first mixed community of English and Indians in North America. ■

Cahokia

KEY TOPICS

- The European background of American colonization

- Creation of the Spanish New World empire and its first extensions to North America

- The large-scale intercontinental exchange of peoples, crops, animals, and diseases

- The French role in the beginnings of the North American fur trade

- England's first overseas colonies in Ireland and America

THE EXPANSION OF EUROPE

Roanoke and other European colonial settlements of the sixteenth century came in the wake of Christopher Columbus's voyage of 1492. There may have been many unrecorded contacts between the peoples of America and the Old World before Columbus. Archaeological excavations at L'Anse aux Meadows on the fogbound Newfoundland coast provide evidence for a Norse landing in North America in the tenth or eleventh century. Norse sagas recounted the exploits of their pioneer heroes, yet they were forgotten within a century. But the contact with the Americas established by Columbus had earthshaking consequences. Within a generation of his voyage, continental exchanges of peoples, crops, animals, and germs had reshaped the Atlantic world. The key to understanding these remarkable events is the transformation of Europe during the several centuries preceding the world of Columbus.

European Communities

Western Europe was an agricultural society, the majority of its people peasant farmers. Farming and livestock raising had been practiced in Europe for thousands of years, but great advances in farming technology took place during the late Middle Ages. Water mills, iron plows, improved devices for harnessing ox and horse power, and systems of crop rotation greatly increased productivity. Over several centuries farmers more than doubled the quantity of European land in cultivation.

Most Europeans were village people, living in family households. Men performed the basic field work; women were responsible for child care, livestock, and food preparation. In the European pattern, daughters usually left the home and village of their families to live among their husband's people. Women were furnished with dowries but generally excluded from inheritance. Divorce was almost unknown.

Europe was a world of social contrasts. Europe was characterized by a social system historians have called "feudalism." The land was divided into hundreds of small territories, each ruled by a family of lords who claimed a disproportionate share of wealth and power. Feudal lords commanded labor service from peasants and tribute in the form of crops. They were the main beneficiaries of medieval economic expansion, accumulating great estates and building castles.

Most Europeans were Christians, united under the authority of the Roman Catholic Church, whose complex organization spanned thousands of local communities with a hierarchy that extended from parish priests all the way to the pope in Rome. At the core of Christian belief was a set of communal values: love of God the father, loving treatment of neighbors, and the fellowship of all believers. Yet the Catholic Church insisted on its dogmas and actively persecuted heretics, nonbelievers, and believers in older "pagan" religions, who were branded "witches." The church legitimized the power relationships of Europe and counseled the poor and downtrodden to place their hopes in heavenly rewards.

Europe was also home to numerous communities of Jews, who had fled from their homeland in Palestine after a series of unsuccessful revolts against Roman rule in the first century C.E. Both church and civic authorities subjected the Jews to discriminatory treatment. Restricted to ghettos and forbidden from owning land, many Jews turned adversity to advantage, becoming merchants who specialized in long-distance trade. But Jewish success only seemed to stimulate Christian hostility. Thus, in the thirteenth and fourteenth centuries the Jews were forced out of England, France, and Spain.

For the great majority of Europeans, living conditions were harsh. Most rural people survived on bread and porridge, supplemented with seasonal vegetables and an occasional piece of meat or fish. Infectious dis-

The Merchant Class and the New Monarchies

Strengthened by the technological breakthroughs of the late Middle Ages, the European economy proved it had a great capacity for recovery. During the fourteenth century disease and famine did not reappear in the same calamatious pattern, and there was an expansion of commerce, especially trade in basic goods, such as cereals and timber, minerals and salt, wine, fish, and wool. Commercial expansion stimulated the growth of markets and towns.

During this revival the monarchs of Western Europe emerged as the new centers of power, building legitimacy by promising internal order as they unified their realms. In the fifteenth century they began the construction of royal bureaucracies and standing armies and navies. In many cases, these new monarchs found support among the rising merchant class, which in return sought lucrative royal contracts and trading monopolies. The alliance between commercial interests and the new states was an important development that prepared the way for European expansion.

The Renaissance

The heart of this dynamic European commercialism lay in the city-states of Italy. During the late Middle Ages, the cities of Venice, Genoa, and Pisa launched armed commercial fleets that seized control of trade in the Mediterranean. Their merchants became the principal outfitters of the Crusades, a series of great military expeditions promoted by the Catholic Church to recover Palestine from the Muslims. The conquest of the Holy Land by Crusaders at the end of the eleventh century delivered the silk and spice trades of Asia into the hands of the Italian merchants. Asian civilization also supplied a number of technical innovations that further propelled European economic growth, including the compass, gunpowder, and the art of printing with movable type—"the three greatest inventions known to man," according to English philosopher Francis Bacon.

Contact with Muslim civilization provided Western scholars with access to important ancient Greek and Roman texts that had been lost to them during the Middle Ages but preserved in the great Muslim libraries. The revival of interest in classical antiquity sparked the period of intellectual and artistic flowering in Europe during the fourteenth, fifteenth, and sixteenth centuries known as the Renaissance. The revolution in publishing (made possible by the perfection of the printing press and movable type), the beginning of regular postal service, and the growth of universities helped spread this revival throughout the elite circles of Europe.

A French peasant labors in the field before a spectacular castle in a page taken from the illuminated manuscript *Tres Riches Heures*, made in the fifteenth century for the duc de Berry. In 1580 the essayist Montaigne talked with several American Indians at the French court who "noticed among us some men gorged to the full with things of every sort while their other halves were beggars at their doors, emaciated with hunger and poverty" and "found it strange that these poverty-stricken halves should suffer such injustice, and that they did not take the others by the throat or set fire to their houses."

SOURCE: Art Resource, Musee Conde, Chantilly/Giraudon, Art Resource, NY.

eases abounded; perhaps a third of all children died before their fifth birthday, and only half the population reached adulthood. Famines periodically ravaged the countryside. A widespread epidemic of bubonic plague, known as the "Black Death," swept in from Asia and wiped out a third of Europe's population between 1347 and 1353. Disease led to famine and violence, as groups fought for shares of a shrinking economy.

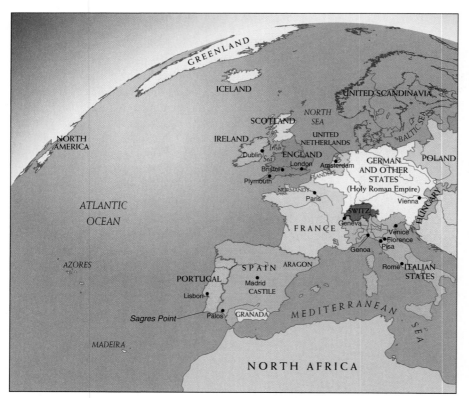

Western Europe in the Fifteenth Century   By the middle of the century, the monarchs of western Europe had unified their realms and begun to build royal bureaucracies and standing armies and navies. These states, all with extensive Atlantic coastlines, sponsored the voyages that inaugurated the era of European colonization.

The Renaissance celebrated human possibility. This human-centered perspective was evident in many endeavors. The Gothic style of medieval cathedrals, whose soaring forms were intended to take human thoughts heavenward, gradually gave way to the use of measured classical styles, thought to encourage rational reflection. In painting and sculpture there was a new focus on the human body. Artists modeled muscles with light and shadow to produce heroic images of men and women. These were aspects of a movement that became known as "humanism," a revolt against religious authority in which the secular took precedence over the purely religious. This Renaissance outlook was a critical component of the spirit that motivated the exploration of the Americas.

Portuguese Explorations

Portugal, a narrow land along the western coast of the Iberian Peninsula with a long tradition of seafaring, became the first of the new Renaissance kingdoms to explore distant lands. Lisbon, the principal port on the sea route between the Mediterranean and northwestern Europe, was a bustling cosmopolitan city with large enclaves of Italian merchants. By 1385 local mer-

chants had grown powerful enough to place their own favorite, João I, on the throne, and he had ambitious plans to establish a Portugese trading empire.

A central figure in this development was the son of the king, Prince Henry, known to later generations as "the Navigator." In the spirit of Renaissance learning, Henry established an academy of eminent geographers, instrument makers, shipbuilders, and seamen at his institute on the southwestern tip of Portugal at Sagres Point. By the mid-fifteenth century, as a result of their efforts, all educated Europeans knew the world was a spherical globe. The idea that fifteenth-century Europeans believed the world to be "flat" is one of the many myths about Columbus's voyage. Studying the seafaring traditions of Asia and the Muslim world, the men of Sagres Point incorporated them into the design of a new ship called the caravel, faster and better handling than any ship previously known in Europe.

Using caravels, the Portuguese explored the Atlantic coast of northwestern Africa for direct access to the lucrative gold and slave trades of that continent. By the time of Prince Henry's death in 1460, they had colonized the Atlantic islands of the Azores and the Madeiras and founded bases along the western African "Gold Coast." In 1488 Portuguese captain Bartholomew Días rounded the southern tip of Africa, and ten years later Vasco da Gama, with the aid of Arab pilots, reached India. The Portuguese eventually erected strategic trading forts along the coasts of Africa, India, and China, the first and longest-lasting outposts of European world colonization, and gained control of much of the Asian spice trade. Most important for the history of the Americas, the Portugese established the Atlantic slave trade. (For a full discussion of slavery, see Chapter 4.)

Columbus Reaches the Americas

In 1476, Christopher Columbus, a young Genoan sailor, joined his brother in Lisbon, where he became a seafaring merchant for Italian traders. Gradually he developed the simple idea of opening a new route to the Indies by sailing west across the Atlantic Ocean, known at that time as the "Western Sea." Such a venture would require royal backing, but when he approached the various monarchs of Europe with his idea, their advisers laughed at his geographic ignorance, pointing out that his calculation of the distance to Asia was much too short. They were right, Columbus was wrong. But it turned out to be an error of monumental good fortune.

Columbus finally sold the plan to the monarchs of Castile and Aragon, Isabel and Ferdinand. These two had just completed the *Reconquista*, a centuries-long struggle between Catholics and Muslims that finally ended Muslim rule in Spain. Through these many generations of warfare, the Spanish had developed a military tradition that thrived on conquest and plunder. The Catholic monarchs of Spain were eager for new lands to conquer, and observing the successful Portuguese push to the south along the west coast of Africa, they became interested in opening lucrative trade routes of their own to the Indies. Columbus called his undertaking "the Enterprise of the Indies," suggesting his commercial intentions. But his mission was more than commercial. His expedition included men and supplies for founding a settlement, for one of his prime goals was to "occupy" the islands he found, establishing title for Spain by the right of occupancy. Like the adventurers who later established the first English colony at Roanoke, Columbus's objectives were starkly imperial.

Columbus's ships left the port of Palos, Spain, in August 1492, pushed west across the Atlantic by the prevailing trade winds. By October, flocks of birds and bits of driftwood announced the ships' approach to land. The first men to sight land were Luis Torres and Rodrigo de Triana. It turned out to be a small, flat island somewhere in the Bahamas, now thought by many to be Samana Cay. But Columbus believed he was in the Indies, somewhere near the Asian mainland.

He explored the northern island coasts of Cuba and Hispaniola before heading home, fortuitously catching the westerly winds that blow from the American coast toward Europe north of the tropics. One of Columbus's most important contributions was the discovery of the clockwise circulation of the Atlantic winds and currents that would carry thousands of European ships back and forth to the Americas.

Leading Columbus's triumphal procession to the royal court were half a dozen kidnapped Taino Indians from the Bahamas, dressed in bright feathers with ornaments of gold. The natives, Columbus noted, were "of a very acute intelligence," but had "no iron or steel weapons." A conflict between the Tainos and several armed Spaniards had ended quickly with the deaths of two natives. "Should your majesties command it," Columbus announced to Ferdinand and Isabel, "all the inhabitants could be made slaves." Moreover, he reported that "there are many spices and great mines of gold and of other metals." In fact, none of the spices familiar to Europeans grew in the Caribbean and there were only small quantities of precious metal in the riverbeds of the islands. But the sight of the little gold ornaments worn by the Indians infected Columbus with gold fever. He left a small force behind in a rough fort on Hispaniola—the first European foothold in the Americas.

The monarchs, enthusiastic about Columbus's report, financed a convoy of seventeen ships and 1,500

This ship, thought to be similar to Columbus's *Niña*, is a caravel, a type of vessel developed by the naval experts at Henry the Navigator's institute at Sagres Point in Portugal. To the traditional square-rigged Mediterranean ship, they added the "lateen" sail of the Arabs, which permitted much greater maneuverability. Other Asian improvements, such as the stern-post rudder and multiple masting, allowed caravels to travel farther and faster than any earlier ships and made possible the invasion of America.

SOURCE: From *Illustrated History of Ships & Boats* by Lionel Casson, © 1964 by Lionel Casson. Used by permission of Doubleday, a division of Random House, Inc.

men that left in late 1493 to begin the colonization of the islands. Like the later English colonists at Roanoke, Columbus expected that Indians would provide the labor. But at Hispaniola Columbus found his fort in ruins and his men killed by Indians who, like the Algonquians at Roanoke, had lost patience with continuing European demands. The Spanish destroyed the nearby native villages, enslaving the Tainos and demanding tribute in gold. Columbus sent boatloads of slaves back to Spain, but most soon sickened and died, and the supply of gold quickly ran out.

Columbus made two additional trips to the Caribbean, both characterized by the same violent raiding for slaves and obsessive searching for gold. He died in Spain in 1506, still convinced that he had opened the way to the Indies. This belief persisted among many Europeans well into the sixteenth century. But others had already begun to see the discoveries from a different perspective. Amerigo Vespucci of Florence, who voyaged to the Caribbean in 1499, was the first to describe Columbus's Indies as *Mundus Novus,* a "New World." When European geographers finally named this continent in the sixteenth century, they honored Vespucci's insight by calling it America.

THE SPANISH IN THE AMERICAS

A century after Columbus's death, before the English had planted a single successful New World colony of their own, the Spanish had created a huge and wealthy empire in the Americas. In theory, all law and policy for the empire came from Spain; in practice, the isolation of the settlements led to a good deal of local autonomy. The Spanish created a caste system, in which a small minority of settlers and their offspring controlled the lives and labor of millions of Indian and African workers. But it was also a society in which colonists, Indians, and Africans mixed to form a new people.

The Invasion of America

The first stages of the Spanish invasion of America included frightful violence. Armies marched across the Caribbean islands, plundering villages, slaughtering men, and capturing women. Columbus and his successors established an institution known as the *encomienda,* in which Indians were compelled to labor in the service of Spanish lords. The relationship was supposed to be reciprocal, with lords protecting Indians in exchange for service, but in practice it amounted to slavery.

Faced with labor shortages, slavers raided the Bahamas and soon had entirely depopulated them. The depletion of gold on Hispaniola led to the invasion of the islands of Puerto Rico and Jamaica in 1508, then Cuba in 1511. Meanwhile, rumors of wealthy societies to the west led to scores of probing expeditions. The Spanish invasion of Central America began in 1511, and two years later Vasco Núñez de Balboa crossed the Isthmus of Panama to the Pacific Ocean. In 1517 Spaniards landed on the coast of Mexico, and within a year they made contact with the Aztec empire.

The Aztecs had migrated to the highland valley of Mexico from the deserts of the American Southwest in the thirteenth century, in the wake of the collapse of the Toltec empire (see Chapter 1). The warlike Aztecs settled a marshy lake district and built the city of Tenochtitlán. By the early fifteenth century they dominated the peoples of the highlands, in the process building a powerful state. By 1519, the population of the Aztec capital numbered approximately 300,000, five times the size of the largest city in Spain.

Hernán Cortés, a veteran of the conquest of Cuba, landed on the Mexican coast with armed troops in 1519. Within two years he overthrew the Aztec empire, a spectacular military accomplishment that has no parallel in the annals of conquest. Cortés skillfully exploited the resentment of the many native peoples who lived under Aztec domination, forging Spanish–Indian alliances that became a model for the subsequent European colonization of the Americas. Here, as at Roanoke and dozens of other sites of European invasion, colonists found Indians eager for allies to support them in their conflicts with their neighbors. Still, the Aztecs were militarily powerful, successfully drove the Spaniards from Tenochtitlán, and put up a bitter and prolonged defense of their besieged capital. But in the meantime the Aztecs suffered a devastating smallpox epidemic that killed thousands and undermined their ability to resist. In the aftermath of conquest, the Spanish unmercifully plundered Aztec society, providing the Catholic monarchs with wealth beyond their wildest imagining.

The Destruction of the Indies

The Indian peoples of the Americas resisted Spanish conquest, but most proved a poor match for mounted warriors with steel swords and man-eating dogs. The record of the conquest, however, includes many brave Indian leaders and thousands of martyrs. The Carib people (from whom the Caribbean takes its name) successfully defended the outermost islands until the end of the sixteenth century, and in the arid lands of northern Mexico the nomadic tribes known collectively as the Chichimecs proved equally difficult to subdue.

The Cruelties used by the Spaniards on the Indians, from a 1699 English edition of *The Destruction of the Indies* by Bartolomé de las Casas. These scenes were copied from a series of engravings produced by Theodore de Bry that accompanied an earlier edition.

SOURCE: British Library.

Some Europeans protested the horrors of the conquest. Principal among them was Bartolomé de las Casas, a Spanish Catholic priest who had participated in the plunder of Cuba in 1511, but who several years later suffered a crisis of conscience and began to denounce the Spanish conquerors. The Christian mission in the New World was to convert the Indians to Christianity, he argued, and "the means to effect this end are not to rob, to scandalize, to capture or destroy them, or to lay waste their lands." Long before the world recognized the concept of universal human rights, las Casas was proclaiming that "the entire human race is one," which earned him a reputation as one of the towering moral figures in the early history of the Americas.

In his brilliant history of the conquest, *The Destruction of the Indies* (1552), las Casas blamed the Spanish for cruelties that resulted in millions of Indian deaths—in effect, genocide. Translated into several languages and widely circulated throughout Europe, las Casas's book was used by other European powers to condemn Spain, thereby covering up their own dismal colonial records—creating a "Black Legend" of Spanish colonization. Although later scholars disputed las Casas's estimates of huge population losses, recent demographic studies suggest that the native people of Hispaniola numbered in the hundreds of thousands when Columbus arrived, and fifty years later they had been reduced to a few hundred. In Mexico, the 1519 population of 25 million plummeted to only a million a century later.

Las Casas was incorrect, however, in attributing most of these losses to warfare. To be sure, thousands of lives were lost in battle, but these deaths accounted for but a small proportion of the overall population decline. Thousands more starved because their economies were destroyed or their food stores taken by conquering armies. Even more important, native birthrates fell drastically after the conquest. Indian women were so "worn out with work," one Spaniard wrote, that they avoided conception, induced abortion, and even "killed their children with their own hands so that they shall not have to endure the same hardships."

Epidemic diseases—influenza, plague, smallpox, measles, typhus—were the primary cause of the drastic reduction of native populations. Indian peoples lacked the antibodies necessary to protect them from European germs and viruses. Smallpox first came from Spain in 1518, exploding in an epidemic so virulent that, in the words of an early Spanish historian, "it left Hispaniola, Puerto Rico, Jamaica, and Cuba desolated of Indians." The epidemic crossed into Mexico in 1520, destroying the Aztecs, then spread along the existing Indian trade network, in 1524 strategically weakening the Inca empire eight years before it was conquered by Spanish conquistador Francisco Pizarro. Spanish chroniclers wrote that this single epidemic killed half the native Americans it touched. Disease was the secret weapon of the Spanish, and it helps explain their extraordinary success in the conquest.

Warfare, famine, lower birthrates, and epidemic disease knocked the population of Indian America into a downward spiral that did not swing upward until the beginning of the twentieth century. By that time the native population had fallen by 90 percent. It was the greatest demographic disaster in world history. The outstanding difference between the European colonial experience in the Americas and Africa or Asia was this radical reduction in the native population.

It is possible that the New World sent one disease, venereal syphilis, back across the Atlantic. The first recorded epidemic of syphilis in Europe took place in Spain in 1493, and many historians think it may have been carried home by the sailors on Columbus's ships. By 1495 the disease was spreading rapidly among Europe's armies, and by the sixteenth century it had found its way to Asia and Africa.

Intercontinental Exchange

The passage of diseases between the Old and New Worlds was one part of the large-scale continental exchange that marks the beginning of the modern era of world history. The most obvious exchange was the vast influx into Europe of the precious metals plundered from the Aztec and Incan empires of the New World. Most of the golden booty was melted down, destroying forever thousands of priceless Indian artifacts. Silver from mines the Spanish discovered and operated in Mexico and Peru tripled the amount of silver coin circulating in Europe between 1500 and 1550, then tripled it again before 1600. The result was runaway inflation, which stimulated commerce and raised profits but lowered the standard of living for most people.

But of even greater long-term importance were the New World crops brought to Europe. Maize (Indian corn) from Mexico, the staff of life for most North Americans, became a staple crop in Mediterranean countries, the dominant feed for livestock elsewhere in Europe, and the primary provision for the slave ships of Africa. Over the next few centuries, potatoes from Peru provided the margin between famine and subsistence for the peasant peoples of northern Europe and Ireland.

Although the Spanish failed to locate valuable spices such as black pepper or cloves in the New World, new tropical crops more than compensated. Tobacco was first introduced to Europe about 1550 as an antidote against disease, but was soon in wide use as a stimulant. American vanilla and chocolate both became highly valued. American cotton proved superior to Asian varieties for the production of cheap textiles.

Each of these native plants, along with tropical transplants from the Old World to the New—sugar, rice, and coffee were among the most important—supplied the basis for important new industries and markets that altered the course of world history.

Columbus introduced domesticated animals into Hispaniola and Cuba, and livestock were later transported to Mexico. The movement of Spanish settlement into northern Mexico was greatly aided by an advancing wave of livestock, for grazing animals seriously disrupted native fields and forests. Horses, used by Spanish stockmen to tend their cattle, also spread northward. In the seventeenth century they reached the Great Plains of North America, where they eventually transformed the lives of the nomadic hunting Indians (see Chapter 5).

The First Europeans in North America

Ponce de León, governor of Puerto Rico, was the first conquistador to attempt to extend the Spanish conquest to North America. In 1513 he landed on the southern Atlantic coast, which he named in honor of the Easter season—*pascua florida*. Warriors from the powerful Indian chiefdoms there beat back Ponce de León's attempts to take slaves and finally succeeded in killing him in 1521. Seven years later another Spanish attempt to colonize Florida, under the command of Pánfilo de Narváez, also ended in disaster. Most of Narváez's men were lost in a shipwreck, but a small group of them survived, living and wandering for several years among the Indian peoples of the Gulf coast and the Southwest until they were finally rescued in 1536 by Spanish slave hunters in northern Mexico. One of these castaways, Alvar Núñez Cabeza de Vaca, published an account of his adventures in which he told of a North American empire known as Cíbola, with golden cities "larger than the city of Mexico."

Cabeza de Vaca's report inspired two Spanish expeditions. The first attempt to penetrate the mystery of North America was mounted by Hernán de Soto, a veteran of the conquest of Peru. After landing in Florida in 1539 with a Cuban army of over 700 men, he pushed hundreds of miles through the heavily populated South, commandeering food and slaves from the Mississippian Indian towns in his path. But de Soto failed to locate another Aztec empire. In present-day Alabama, thousands of warriors besieged his army, and a few months later the ancestors of the modern Chickasaws chewed the Spaniards apart. His army depleted by half, de Soto desperately drove his men westward, crossing the Mississippi and marching deep into present-day Arkansas before returning to the banks of the great river, where he died in 1542. The native peoples of the

South had successfully turned back Spanish invasion. But de Soto also introduced epidemic diseases that drastically depopulated and undermined the Mississippian chiefdoms of the South.

In the year of the de Soto expedition, 1539, Spanish officials in Mexico launched a second attempt to conquer North America, this one aimed at the Southwest. Francisco Vásquez de Coronado led 300 mounted men and infantry and 800 Indian porters north along well-marked Indian trading paths, passing through the settlements of Piman Indians near the present border of the United States and Mexico and finally reaching the Pueblo villages along the Rio Grande. The initial resistance of the Pueblo people was quickly quashed. But Coronado was deeply disappointed by these towns "of stone and mud, rudely fashioned," and sent out expeditions in all directions in search of the legendary golden cities of Cíbola. He led his army as far north as the Great Plains, where they observed great herds of "shaggy cows" (buffalo) and made contact with nomadic hunting peoples but returned without gold. For the next fifty years Spain lost all interest in the Southwest.

The Spanish New World Empire

By the late sixteenth century the Spanish had control of a powerful empire in the Americas. A century after Columbus, some 200,000 European immigrants, most of them Spaniards, had settled in the Americas. Another 125,000 Africans had been forcibly resettled as slaves on the Spanish plantations of the Caribbean, as well as on the Portuguese plantations of Brazil. (The Portuguese colonized Brazil under the terms of the Treaty of Tordesillas, a 1494 agreement dividing the Americas between Spain and Portugal. See Chapter 4.) Most of the Spanish settlers lived in the more than 200 urban communities founded during the conquest, including cities such as Santo Domingo in Hispaniola; Havana in Cuba; Mexico City, built atop the ruins of Tenochtitlán; and Quito and Lima in the conquered empire of the Incas.

Spanish women came to America as early as Columbus's second expedition, but over the course of the sixteenth century they made up only about 10 percent of the immigrants. Thus, from the beginning male colonists married or cohabited with Indian or African women. The result was the growth of large mixed-ancestry groups known respectively as *mestizos* and *mulattoes*. The Spanish established a frontier of inclusion, their communities characterized by a great deal of marriage and sexual mixing between male colonists and native women. Hundreds of thousands of Indians died, but Indian genes were passed on to generations of mixed ancestry people, who became the majority population in the mainland Spanish American empire.

Populated by Indians, Africans, Spanish colonists, and their mixed offspring, the New World colonies of Spain made up one of the largest empires in the history of the world. The empire operated, in theory, as a highly centralized and bureaucratic system. But the Council of the Indies, composed of advisers of the Spanish king who made all the laws and regulations for the empire, was located in Spain. Thus, what looked in the abstract like a centrally administered empire tolerated a great deal of local decision making.

NORTHERN EXPLORATIONS AND ENCOUNTERS

When the Spanish empire was at the height of its power in the sixteenth century, the merchants and monarchs of other European seafaring states looked across the Atlantic for opportunities of their own. France was first to sponsor expeditions to the New World in the early sixteenth century. At first the French attempted to plant settlements on the coasts of Brazil and Florida, but Spanish opposition ultimately persuaded them to concentrate on the North Atlantic. England did not develop its own plans to colonize North America until the second half of the sixteenth century.

Fish and Furs

Long before France and England made attempts to found colonies, however, European fishermen were exploring the coastal North American waters of the North Atlantic. The Grand Banks, off the coast of Newfoundland, had abundant cod. It is possible that European fishermen were working those waters before Columbus's voyages. Certainly by 1500 hundreds of ships and thousands of sailors were sailing annually to the Grand Banks.

The first official voyages of exploration in the North Atlantic used the talents of experienced European sailors and fishermen. With a crew from Bristol, England, Genovese captain John Cabot reached Labrador in 1497, but the English did little to follow up on his voyage. In 1524, Tuscan captain Giovanni da Verrazano, sailing for the French, explored the North American coast from Cape Fear (North Carolina) to the Penobscot River (Maine). Encouraged by his report, the French king commissioned experienced

In his sketch of this "Capitaine" of the Illinois nation (drawn about 1700), the French artist Charles Becard de Granville carefully noted the tattooing of the warrior's face and body, his distinctive costume and feather headdress, his spear and tobacco pipe.

SOURCE: Louis Nicolas, *Capitaine de La Nation*, from the "Codex Canadienses". From the collection of Gilcrease Museum, Tulsa, Oklahoma.

captain Jacques Cartier to locate a "Northwest Passage" to the Indies. Although in his voyages of 1534, 1535, and 1541 Cartier failed to find a Northwest Passage, he reconnoitered the St. Lawrence River, which led deep into the continental interior to the Great Lakes, with easy access to the Ohio and Mississippi rivers, giving France an incomparable geographic edge over other colonial powers. Cartier's attempts to plant settlements on the St. Lawrence failed, but he established France's imperial claim to the lands of Canada.

The French and other northern Europeans thus discovered the Indian people of the northern woodlands, and the Indians in turn discovered them. The contacts between Europeans and natives here took a different form than in the tropics, based on commerce rather than conquest. The Indians immediately appre-

ciated the usefulness of textiles, glass, copper, and ironware. For his part, Cartier was interested in the fur coats of the Indians. Europeans, like Indians, used furs for winter clothing. But the growing population of the late Middle Ages had so depleted the wild game of Europe that the price of furs had risen beyond the reach of most people. The North American fur trade, thus, filled an important demand and produced high profits.

Beginning in the sixteenth century, the fur trade would continue to play an important role in the Atlantic economy for three centuries. By no means were Indians simply the victims of European traders. They had a sharp eye for quality, and cutthroat competition among traders provided them with the opportunity to hold out for what they considered good prices. But the fur trade was essentially an unequal exchange, with furs selling in Europe for ten or twenty times what Indians received for them. The trade also had negative consequences. European epidemic disease followed in the wake of the traders, and violent warfare broke out between tribes over access to hunting grounds. Moreover, as European manufactured goods, such as metal knives, kettles, and firearms, became essential to their way of life, Indians became dependent upon European suppliers. Ultimately, the fur trade was stacked in favor of Europeans.

By 1600, over a thousand European ships were trading for furs each year along the northern coast. The village of Tadoussac on the St. Lawrence, where a wide bay offered Europeans safe anchorage, became the customary place for several weeks of trading each summer, a forerunner of the western fur-trade rendezvous of the nineteenth century. Early in the seventeenth century the French would move to monopolize the trade there by planting colonies along the coast and on the St. Lawrence.

The Protestant Reformation and the First French Colonies

The first French colonies in North America, however, were planted farther south by a group of religious dissenters known as the Huguenots. The Protestant Reformation—the religious revolt against the Roman Catholic Church—had begun in 1517 when German priest Martin Luther publicized his differences with Rome. Luther declared that eternal salvation was a gift from God and not related to works or service to the Catholic Church. His protests—Protestantism—fit into a climate of widespread dissatisfaction with the power and prosperity of the Catholic Church. Luther attracted followers all over northwestern Europe, including France, where they were persecuted by Catholic authorities. Converted to Luther's teachings in 1533, Frenchman John Calvin fled to Switzerland, where he developed a radical theology. His doctrine of predestination declared that God had chosen a small number of men and women for "election," or salvation, while condemning the vast majority to eternal damnation. Calvinists were instructed to cultivate the virtues of thrift, industry, sobriety, and personal responsibility, which Calvin argued were signs of election and essential to the Christian life.

Calvin's followers in France—the Huguenots—were concentrated among merchants and the middle class but also included a portion of the nobility opposed to the central authority of the Catholic monarch. In 1560 the French monarchy defeated the attempt of a group of Huguenot nobles to seize power, which inaugurated nearly forty years of violent religious struggle. In an attempt to establish a religious refuge in the New World, Huguenot leaders were behind the first French attempts to establish colonies in North America. In 1562, Jean Ribault and 150 Protestants from Normandy landed on Parris Island, near present-day Beaufort, South Carolina, and began the construction of a fort and crude mud huts. Ribault soon returned to France for supplies, where he was caught up in the religious wars. The colonists nearly starved and were finally forced to resort to cannibalism before being rescued by a passing British ship. In 1564, Ribault established another Huguenot colony, Fort Caroline on the St. Johns River of Florida, south of present-day Jacksonville.

The Spanish were alarmed by these moves. They had shown no interest in colonizing Florida but worried about protecting their ships, riding home to Spain loaded with gold and silver on the offshore Gulf Stream. Not only was Fort Caroline manned by Frenchmen but also by Protestants—deadly enemies of the Catholic monarchs of Spain. "We are compelled to pass in front of their port," wrote one official, "and with the greatest ease they can sally out with their armadas to seek us." In 1565 the Spanish crown sent Don Pedro Menéndez de Avilés, captain general of the Indies, to crush the Huguenots. After establishing a settlement south of the French at a place called St. Augustine, he marched his men overland through the swamps to surprise the Huguenots from the rear. "I put Jean Ribault and all the rest of them to the knife," Menéndez wrote triumphantly to the king, "judging it to be necessary to the service of the Lord Our God and of Your Majesty." The Spanish built a fort and established a garrison at St. Augustine, which thus became the oldest continuously occupied European city in North America.

Sixteenth-Century England

The English movement across the Atlantic, like the French, was tied to social change at home. Perhaps most important were changes in the economy. As the prices of goods rose steeply—the result of New World inflation—English landlords, their rents fixed by custom, sought ways to increase their incomes. Seeking profits in the woolen trade, many converted the common pasturage used by tenants into grazing land for sheep, dislocating large numbers of farmers. Between 1500 and 1650 a third of all the common lands in England were "enclosed" in this way. Deprived of their livelihoods, thousands of families left their traditional rural homes and sought employment in English cities, crowding the roads with homeless people.

Sixteenth-century England also became deeply involved in the struggles of the Reformation. At first, King Henry VIII of England (reigned 1509–47) supported the Catholic Church and opposed the Protestants. But there was great public resentment in England over the vast properties owned by the Church and the loss of revenue to Rome. When the pope refused to grant Henry an annulment of his marriage to Catherine of Aragon, daughter of Ferdinand and Isabel of Spain, the king exploited this popular mood. Taking up the cause of reform in 1534, he declared himself head of a separate Church of England. He later took over the English estates of the Catholic Church—about a quarter of the country's land—and used their revenues to begin constructing a powerful English state system, including a standing army and navy. Working through Parliament, Henry carefully enlisted the support of the merchants and landed gentry for his program, parceling out a measure of royal prosperity in the form of titles, offices, lands, and commercial favors. By 1547, when Henry died, he had forged a solid alliance with the wealthy merchant class.

Henry was succeeded by his young and sickly son Edward VI, who soon died. Next in succession was Edward's half-sister Mary, who attempted to reverse her father's Reformation from the top by martyring hundreds of English Protestants, gaining herself the title of "Bloody Mary." But upon her death in 1558, her half-sister Elizabeth I (reigned 1558–1603) came to the throne. Elizabeth sought to end the religious turmoil by tolerating a variety of views within the English church. The Spanish monarch, head of the most powerful empire in the world, declared himself the defender of the Catholic faith and vowed to overthrow her.

Fearing Spanish subversion on the neighboring Catholic island of Ireland, Elizabeth urged enterprising supporters such as Walter Raleigh and his half-brother Humphrey Gilbert to subdue the Irish Catholics and settle homeless English families on their land. During the 1560s, Raleigh, Humphrey, and many other commanders invaded the island and viciously attacked the

Irish, forcing them to retreat beyond a frontier line of English settlement along the coast. So ferociously did the Irish resist the conquest that an image of the "wild Irish" became fixed in the English mind. Gilbert retaliated with even greater brutality, decapitating captured Irish men and women and using their heads as paving stones, "so that none should come into his tent for any cause but commonly he must pass through a lane of heads." Such barbarism did not prevent the English from considering the Irish an inferior race, and the notion that civilized people could not mix with such "savages" was an assumption English colonists would carry with them to the Americas.

Early English Efforts in the Americas

England's first ventures in the New World were made against the backdrop of its conflict with Spain. In 1562 John Hawkins violated Spanish regulations by transporting a load of African slaves to the Caribbean, bringing back valuable tropical goods. Thus, the English began their participation in the slave trade. (For a full discussion see Chapter 4.) The Spanish attacked Hawkins on another of his voyages in 1567, an event English privateers such as Francis Drake used as an excuse for launching a series of devastating and lucrative raids against Spanish New World ports and fleets. The voyages of these English "Sea Dogs" greatly enriched their investors, including Elizabeth herself. The English, thus, began their American adventures by slaving and plundering.

A consensus soon developed among Elizabeth's closest advisers that the time had come to enter the competition for America. In a state paper written for the queen, Richard Hakluyt summarized the advantages that would come from colonies: they could provide bases from which to raid the Spanish in the Caribbean, outposts for an Indian market for English goods, and plantations for growing tropical products, freeing the nation from a reliance on the long-distance trade with Asia. Moreover, by populating them with the "multitudes of loiterers and idle vagabonds" of England, colonies offered a solution to the problem of social dislocation and homelessness. He urged Elizabeth to establish such colonies "upon the mouths of the great navigable rivers" from Florida to the St. Lawrence.

Although Elizabeth declined to commit the state to Hakluyt's plan, she authorized and invested in several private attempts at exploration and colonization. In the late 1570s, Martin Frobisher conducted three voyages of exploration in the North Atlantic. Fresh from the Irish wars, Raleigh and Gilbert planned the first true colonizing ventures. In 1583 Gilbert sailed

with a flotilla of ships from Plymouth and landed at St. John's Bay, Newfoundland. He encountered fishermen from several other nations but nevertheless claimed the territory for his queen. But Gilbert's ship was lost on the return voyage.

Following his brother's death, Raleigh decided to establish a colony southward, in the more hospitable climate of the mid-Atlantic coast. Although the Roanoke enterprise of 1584–87 seemed far more promising than Gilbert's, it too eventually failed (as described in the opening of the chapter). The greatest legacy of the expedition was the work of Thomas Harriot and John White, who mapped the area, surveyed its commercial potential, and studied the Indian residents. Harriot's *A Briefe and True Report of the Newfound Land of Virginia* (1588), illustrated by engravings of White's watercolors, provided the single most accurate description of North American Indians at the moment of their contact with Europeans.

King Philip II of Spain was outraged at the English incursions into territory reserved by the pope for Catholics. He had authorized the destruction of the French colony in Florida, and now he committed himself to smashing England. In 1588 he sent a fleet of 130 ships carrying 30,000 men to invade the British Isles. Countered by captains such as Drake and Hawkins, who commanded smaller and more maneuverable ships, and frustrated by an ill-timed storm that the English chose to interpret as an act of divine intervention, the Spanish Armada foundered. The Spanish monopoly of the New World had been broken in the English Channel.

CONCLUSION

The Spanish opened the era of European colonization in the Americas with Columbus's voyage in 1492. The consequences for the Indian peoples of the Americas were disastrous. The Spanish succeeded in constructing the world's most powerful empire on the backs of Indian and African labor. Inspired by the Spanish success, the French and the English attempted to colonize the coast of North America. By the end of the sixteenth century, however, they had not succeeded in establishing any lasting colonial communities. Instead, a very different kind of colonial encounter, based on commerce rather than conquest, was taking place in northeastern North America. In the next century the French would turn this development to their advantage. Along the mid-Atlantic coast in Virginia, however, the English would put their Irish experience to use, pioneering an altogether new kind of American colonialism.

CHRONOLOGY

1000	Norse settlement at L'Anse aux Meadows
1347–53	Black Death in Europe
1381	English Peasants' Revolt
1488	Bartolomeu Días sails around the African continent
1492	Christopher Columbus first arrives in the Caribbean
1494	Treaty of Tordesillas
1497	John Cabot explores Newfoundland
1500	High point of the Renaissance
1508	Spanish invade Puerto Rico
1513	Juan Ponce de León lands in Florida
1514	Bartolomé de las Casas begins preaching against the conquest
1516	Smallpox introduced to the New World
1517	Martin Luther breaks with the Roman Catholic Church
1519	Hernán Cortés lands in Mexico
1534	Jacques Cartier first explores the St. Lawrence River
1539–40	Hernán de Soto and Francisco Vásquez de Coronado expeditions
1550	Tobacco introduced to Europe
1552	Bartolomé de las Casas's *Destruction of the Indies* published
1558	Elizabeth I of England begins her reign
1562	Huguenot colony planted along the mid-Atlantic coast
1565	St. Augustine founded
1572	St. Bartholomew's Day Massacre in France
1583	Humphrey Gilbert attempts to plant a colony in Newfoundland
1584–87	Walter Raleigh's colony on Roanoke Island
1588	English defeat the Spanish Armada
1590	John White returns to find Roanoke colony abandoned

REVIEW QUESTIONS

1. Discuss the roles played by the rising merchant class, the new monarchies, Renaissance humanism, and the Reformation in the development of European colonialism.
2. Define a "frontier of inclusion." In what ways does this description apply to the Spanish empire in the Americas?
3. Make a list of the major exchanges that took place between the Old World and the New World in the centuries following the European invasion of America. Discuss some of the effects these exchanges had on the course of modern history.
4. In what ways did colonial contact in the Northeast differ from contacts in the Caribbean and Mexico?
5. In what ways might the English experience in Ireland have shaped expectations about American colonization?

RECOMMENDED READING

David Noble Cook, *Born to Die: Disease and New World Conquest, 1492–1650* (1998). A synthetic history of the impact of disease, including Indian and European views.

Cyclone Covey, trans. and ed., *Cabeza de Vaca's Adventures in the Unknown Interior of America* (1983). The captivity narrative that lured the Spanish into North America. An eye-opening story of the peoples and places of the preconquest Southwest.

Alfred W. Crosby Jr., *The Columbian Exchange: Biological and Cultural Consequences of 1492* (1972). Pathbreaking account of the intersection of the biospheres of the Old and New Worlds.

Richard Flint, *Great Cruelties Have Been Reported: The 1544 Investigation of the Coronado Expedition* (2001). Testimony regarding the treatment of Indians and subsequent human rights debates in Spain.

Charles Gibson, *Spain in America* (1966). Still the best introductory history of Spain's American empire.

Lewis Hanke, *The Spanish Struggle for Justice in the Conquest of America* (1949; reprint, 1965). The classic account of las Casas's attempts to rectify the wrongs committed by the Spanish against the Indians.

Charles M. Hudson, *Knights of Spain, Warriors of the Sun: Hernando de Soto and the South's Ancient Chiefdoms* (1997). A very readable history of the de Soto expedition, told from the viewpoint of the Indians.

Miguel Leon-Portilla, *The Broken Spears: The Aztec Account of the Conquest of Mexico* (1962; expanded ed., 1992). The history of the Spanish conquest as told by the Aztecs, drawn from manuscripts dating as early as 1528, only seven years after the fall of Tenochtitlán.

Samuel Eliot Morison, *The European Discovery of America: The Northern Voyages*, A.D. 500–1600 (1971) and *The Southern Voyages*, A.D. 1492–1616 (1974). The most detailed treatment of all the important European explorations of the Americas.

David Beers Quinn, *Set Fair for Roanoke: Voyages and Colonies, 1584–1606* (1985). The story of Roanoke—the Indian village, the English settlement, and the Lost Colony.

Kirkpatrick Sale, *The Conquest of Paradise: Christopher Columbus and the Columbian Legacy* (1990). A harsh view of Columbus, but important information on the world of the Caribbean and the disastrous effects of the encounter with Europeans.

Carl Ortwin Sauer, *Sixteenth Century North America: The Land and the People as Seen by the Europeans* (1971). An excellent source for the explorations of the continent, providing abundant descriptions of the Indians.

Hugh Thomas, *Conquest: Montezuma, Cortés, and the Fall of Old Mexico* (1993). A fascinating account, written by a master of historical style, that incorporates the Aztec view as well as the words of the conquerors.

Gustavo Verdesio, *Forgotten Conquests: Rereading New World History from the Margins* (2001). An argument that the old master historical narrative represents only one of many possible histories, and a suggestion for finding the colonial subjects who did not produce documents.

ON THE WEB

http://americanart.si.edu/

The Smithsonian American Art Museum contains hundreds of digitized paintings of every conceivable variety and kind. Most interesting are those of George Catlin of which 617 are catalogued with most displayed in digitized form. Most paintings deal with individuals, tribal life, and tribal activities of early nineteenth century Native Americans. To access these painting engage the Smithsonian search engine, use its "Search for artists represented in our collection" hot button, and then enter "Catlin, George" in the appropriate name blocks.

http://www.joslyn.org/

The Joslyn Art Museum in Omaha, Nebraska, possesses a respectable collection of Native American drawings/artifacts and paintings/watercolors of Native Americans in the early nineteenth century from the Western Plains and Missouri Basin region. Access both the Western American Collection (paintings/watercolors) and the Native American Collection (artifacts/drawings) for detailed cultural, social, and historical information about each museum acquisition. In particular, access Karl Bodmer's watercolor of Mató-T&oacutepe (Four Bears), Mandan Chief, 1834.

http://www.xmission.com/~drudy/mtman/gif/bodmer/index.html

This location contains fifteen paintings by Karl Bodmer from *Travels in the Interior of North America*, an atlas prepared for Maximilian, Prince of Wied, covering Bodmer's travels on the western frontier. The quality of these reproductions of Bodmer's work is excellent.

http://www.umt.edu/history/NAHUATL/florent.txt

This site is an extensive dictionary of Nahauatl (Aztec) words with definitions. It is based on the Florentine Codex.

http://www.prenhall.com/faragherbrief/map2.1

Check your knowledge of European political geography in the fifteenth century. Why were some European states better positioned for colonizing than others?

http://www.prenhall.com/faragherbrief/map2.2

Analyze the environmental factors that influenced French, Spanish, and English explorations. What were the reasons behind the different experiences of each of these countries?

THREE

PLANTING COLONIES IN NORTH AMERICA

▶ 1588–1701

CHAPTER OUTLINE

AMERICAN COMMUNITIES

Communities Struggle with Diversity in Seventeenth-Century Santa Fé

I T WAS A HOT AUGUST DAY IN 1680 WHEN THE FRANTIC MESSENGERS rode into the small mission outpost of El Paso with the news that the Pueblo Indians to the north had risen in revolt. The corpses of more than 400 colonists lay bleeding in the dust. Two thousand Spanish survivors huddled inside the Palace of Governors in Santa Fé, surrounded by 3,000 angry warriors. The Pueblo leaders had sent two crosses into the palace—white for surrender, red for death. Which would the Spaniards choose?

Spanish colonists had been in New Mexico for nearly a century. Franciscan priests came first, followed by a military expedition from Mexico in search of precious metals. In 1609, high in the picturesque foothills of the Sangre de Cristo Mountains, the colonial authorities founded La Villa Real de la Santa Fé de San Francisco—"the royal town of the holy faith of St. Francis"—soon known simply as Santa Fé. Colonization efforts included the conversion of the Pueblo Indians to Christianity, making them subjects of the king of Spain, and forcing them to work for the colonial elite who lived in the town.

In the face of overwhelming Spanish power, the Pueblos adopted a flexible attitude. Twenty thousand of them converted to Christianity, but most of these thought of the new religion as simply an appendage to their complex culture. The Christian God was but a minor addition to their numerous deities; church holidays were included in their own religious calendar and celebrated with native dances and rituals.

Most anthropologists agree that the Pueblos were a spirited people. Many of their public dances included erotic displays and sometimes ended in spectacles of mock public intercourse, symbolizing the powerful force that brought the separate worlds of men and women together, and also created community. The celibacy of the Franciscan priests not only astounded the Pueblos but horrified them, for it marked the priests as only half-persons. The Pueblos also found the Franciscan practice of subjecting themselves to prolonged fasts and tortures, such as self-flagellation, inexplicable. "You Christians are crazy," one Pueblo chief told a priest. "You go through the streets in groups, flagellating yourselves, and it is not well that the people of this pueblo should be encouraged to commit such madness."

The missionaries, outraged by what they considered Pueblo sacrileges, invaded underground kivas, destroyed sacred Indian artifacts, publicly humiliated holy men, and compelled whole villages to perform penance by working in irrigation ditches and fields. Such violations of the deepest traditions of Pueblo community life eventually led to the revolt of 1680. In New Mexico, several years before, the Spanish governor had executed three Pueblo religious leaders and publicly whipped dozens more for secretly practicing their religion. One of those leaders, Popé of San Juan Pueblo, vowed to overthrow the regime. During the next several years he carefully organized a conspiracy among more than twenty Indian towns.

Popé's job was not difficult, for there were plenty of local grievances. The Hopis of northern Arizona, for example, still tell of a missionary who capped his ever-escalating demands on them with the order that all the young women of the village be brought to live with him. When the revolt began, the Hopis surrounded the missionary's house. "I have come to kill you," the chief announced. "You can't kill me," the priest cried from behind his locked door. "I will come [back] to life and wipe out your whole tribe." But the chief shouted back, "my gods have more power than you have." He and his men broke down the door, hung the missionary from the beams, and lit a fire beneath his feet.

When the Indians demanded the surrender of the Spanish inside Santa Fé's Palace of Governors, the besieged colonists sent back the red cross, signaling defiance. But after a siege lasting five days, the Pueblos agreed to allow most of them to flee south to El Paso, "the poor women and children on foot and unshod," in the words of one Spaniard's account, and "of such a hue that they looked like dead people." The Indians then ransacked the missions and churches, desecrating the holy furnishings with human excrement and leaving the mutilated bodies of priests lying on their altars. They transformed the governor's chapel into a traditional kiva, his palace into a communal dwelling. On the elegant inlaid stone floors where the governor had held court, Pueblo women now ground their corn.

Santa Fé became the capital of a Pueblo confederacy led by Popé. He forced Christian Indians to the river to scrub away the taint of baptism. Then he ordered the destruction of everything Spanish. But this the Pueblos could not do. The colonists had introduced horses and sheep, fruit trees and wheat, new tools and new crafts, all of which the Indians found useful. Moreover, the Pueblos sorely missed the support of the Spanish in their struggle against their traditional enemies, the nomadic Navajos and Apaches. Equipped with stolen horses and weapons, these nomadic peoples had become considerably more dangerous, and their raids on the unprotected Pueblo villages became much more destructive after the colonists fled. With chaos mounting, Popé was deposed in 1690, and many of the Indians found themselves thinking the unthinkable: if only the Spanish would come back!

Come back they did, beginning in 1692, and after six years of fighting they succeeded in reestablishing Spanish authority. But both sides had learned a lesson, and over the next generation the colonists and the Indians reached an implicit understanding. Pueblos dutifully observed Catholicism in the missionary chapels, while missionaries tolerated the practice of traditional religion in the Indians' underground kivas. Royal officials guaranteed the inviolability of Indian lands, and Pueblos pledged loyalty to the Spanish monarch. Pueblos turned out for service on colonial lands, and colonists abandoned the system of forced labor. Together the Spanish and the Pueblos held off the nomadic tribes for the next 150 years. Colonist and Indian communities remained autonomous, but they learned to live with one another. ■

Santa Fé

KEY TOPICS

- A comparison of the European colonies established in North America in the seventeenth century

- The English and Algonquian colonial encounter in the Chesapeake

- The role of religious dissent in the planting of the New England colonies

- The restoration of the Stuart monarchy and the creation of new proprietary colonies

- Indian warfare and internal conflict at the end of the seventeenth century

---

SPAIN AND ITS COMPETITORS IN NORTH AMERICA

At the beginning of the seventeenth century the Spanish controlled the only colonial outposts on the mainland, a series of forts along the Florida coast to protect the Gulf Stream sea lanes used by the convoys carrying wealth from their New World colonies to Spain. During the first two decades of the new century, however, the Spanish, French, Dutch, and English were all drawn into planting far more substantial colonies in North America.

In New Spain and New France there was a good deal of cultural and sexual mixing between colonists and natives. These areas became frontiers of inclusion, where native peoples were part of colonial society. The Dutch at first followed the French model when they established their colony on the Hudson River. But soon they changed course, fearing the great success of the English, who from the beginning adopted a different model of colonization, in which settlers and Indians lived in separate societies. The "frontiers of exclusion" in Virginia, New England, and New Netherlands offered a dramatic contrast to the situation in New Spain and New France.

New Mexico in the Seventeenth Century   By the end of the seventeenth century, New Mexico contained 3,000 colonial settlers in several towns, surrounded by an estimated 50,000 Pueblo Indians living in some fifty farming villages. The isolation and sense of danger among the Hispanic settlers are evident in their name for the road linking the colony with New Spain, *Jornada del Muerto,* "the Road of Death."

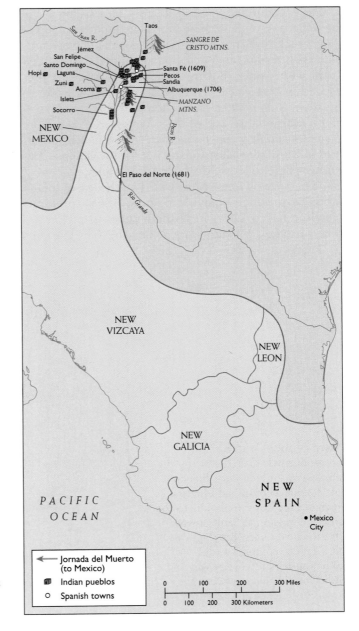

New Mexico

After the 1539 expedition of Francisco Vásquez de Coronado failed to turn up vast Indian empires to conquer in the northern Mexican deserts, the Spanish interest in the Southwest faded. The densely settled farming communities of the Pueblos did offer a harvest of converts for Christianity, however, and by the 1580s Franciscan missionaries were at work in the Southwest. Soon rumors drifted back to Mexico City of rich mines along the Rio Grande, raising the hopes of Spanish officials that they might find another Aztec empire. In 1598, Juan de Oñate, the son of a wealthy mining family of New Spain, financed a colonizing expedition made up of Indian and mestizo soldiers with the purpose of mining both gold and souls.

Moving north into the upper Rio Grande Valley, Oñate encountered varying degrees of resistance. He lay siege at Acoma, set high atop a great outcropping of desert rock. Indian warriors killed dozens of Spaniards with their arrows, and women and children bombarded them with stones. But in the end, the attackers succeeded in climbing the rock walls and laying waste to the town, killing 800 men, women, and children. All surviving warriors had one of their feet severed, and more than 500 people were enslaved. In 1606 Spanish authorities in Mexico recalled Oñate, not for his violence, but for his failure to locate the fabled gold mines.

The Spanish empire was based on the use of Indian labor to produce valuable commodities—precious metals, tobacco, or sugar. Without mines to exploit, interest in New Mexico waned. But the Church con-vinced the Spanish monarchy to subsidize New Mexico as a special missionary colony. In 1609, a new governor founded the capital of Santa Fé, and from this base the Franciscan missionaries penetrated all the surrounding Indian villages. The Pueblos who most resisted Christianity—the Acomas, the Zunis, and the isolated Hopis—retained their old customs, including their way of tracing kinship through the maternal line. But many other communities were dramatically affected by contact with Spanish culture and adopted the Spanish pattern of reckoning descent through both the father and mother's ancestors.

The colonial economy of New Mexico, based on small-scale agriculture and sheep raising, was never very prosperous. Indians labored for both colonists and priests. Population growth was almost entirely the result of marriages between colonial men and Indian women. By the late seventeenth century this northernmost outpost of the far-flung Spanish empire in America contained some 3,000 mestizos (of mixed Indian and European ancestry) in a few towns along the Rio Grande, surrounded by an estimated 50,000 Pueblos in some fifty villages. New Mexico was a "frontier of inclusion."

New France

In the early seventeenth century the French devised a strategy to monopolize the northern fur trade. In 1605 Samuel de Champlain, acting as the agent of a royal monopoly, helped establish the outpost of Port Royal on the Bay of Fundy. It proved impossible, however, to control the coastal trade from that loca-

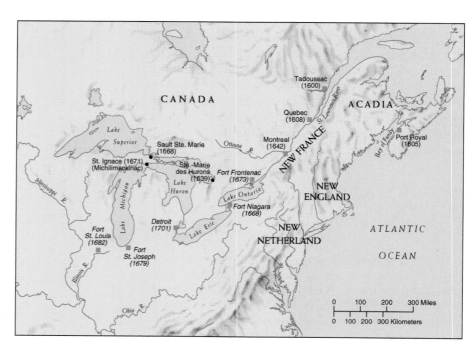

New France in the Seventeenth Century By the late seventeenth century, French settlements were spread from the town of Port Royal in Acadia to the post and mission at Sault Ste. Marie on the Great Lakes. But the heart of New France comprised the communities stretching along the St. Lawrence River between the towns of Quebec and Montreal.

tion. In 1608 he founded the settlement of Quebec on the St. Lawrence River at a site where he could intercept the traffic in furs to the Atlantic. He forged an alliance with the Huron Indians, who controlled access to the rich fur grounds of the Great Lakes, and in 1609 and 1610 joined them in making war on their traditional enemies, the Five Nation Iroquois Confederacy. Champlain sent agents and traders to live among native peoples, where they learned native languages and customs, and directed the flow of furs to Quebec.

The St. Lawrence was like a great roadway leading directly into the heart of the continent, and it provided the French with enormous geographic and political advantage. But the river froze during the winter, isolating the colonists, and the short growing season limited agricultural productivity in the region. Many Frenchmen went to Canada and Acadia as *engagés* ("hired men") in the fur trade or the fishery, as craftsmen or as farmers, but nine out of ten of them returned to France. Huguenot dissenters would have been willing colonists, but French authorities refused to let them emigrate, declaring that New France would be an exclusively Catholic colony. It was the most serious mistake France made, for by closing Canada to Huguenot refugees they destroyed their only hope for mass emigration. As a result the population of Acadia on the Bay of Fundy and Canada on the St. Lawrence grew slowly in the seventeenth century, reaching a total of only about 15,000 by 1700. Quebec City, the administrative capital, was small by Spanish colonial standards, and Montreal, founded in 1642 as a missionary and trading center, remained little more than a frontier outpost. Small clusters of riverbank farmers known as *habitants* lived on the lands of *seigneurs*, or landlords. By using Indian farming techniques, habitants were able to produce subsistence crops, and eventually they developed a modest export economy.

The communities of Canada looked west toward the continental interior rather than toward the Atlantic. It was typical for the sons of habitants to take to the woods in their youth, working as independent traders or as *coureurs de bois*, paid agents of the fur companies. Most eventually returned to take up farming, but others remained in Indian villages, where they married Indian women and raised families. Such French traders were living on the Great Lakes as early as the 1620s, and from the late 1660s to the 1680s the French established outposts at each of the strategic points on the lakes. By the 1670s, French fur traders and missionaries were exploring the reaches of the upper Mississippi River. In 1681–82, fur-trade commandant Robert Sieur de La Salle navigated the mighty river to its mouth on the Gulf of Mexico and claimed its entire watershed for France.

New Netherland

The United Provinces of the Netherlands, commonly known as Holland, was only a fraction of the size of France, but it was the center of Europe's economic transformation in the sixteenth century. On land reclaimed from the sea by an elaborate system of dikes, Dutch farmers used new methods of crop rotation and deep tilling that dramatically increased their yields, producing large surpluses that supported the growth of the world's most urban and commercial nation. After a century of rule by the Hapsburgs, the prosperous Dutch rose up against their Spanish masters and in 1581 suceeded in establishing their political independence. Amsterdam became the site of the world's first stock exchange and investment banks. Dutch investors built the largest commercial fleet in Europe and captured the lucrative Baltic and North Sea trade in fish, lumber, iron, and grain. It was said that the North Sea was Holland's "America."

Soon the Dutch were establishing trading outposts in America itself. Early in the seventeenth century the United Netherlands organized two great monopolies, the Dutch East India Company and the Dutch West India Company, combining naval military might and commercial strength in campaigns to seize the maritime trade of Asia and the Atlantic. Backed by powerfully armed men-of-war ships, during the first half of the seventeenth century Dutch traders built a series of trading posts in China, Indonesia, India, Africa, Brazil, the Caribbean, and North America, and Holland became the greatest commercial power in the world. The Dutch first appeared in North America in 1609 with the explorations of Henry Hudson, and within a few years they had founded settlements on the Hudson River at Fort Orange (today's Albany) and at New Amsterdam, on Manhattan Island, at the river's mouth. Seeking to match French success, they negotiated a commercial alliance with the Iroquois Confederacy to obtain furs. Access to superior Dutch products, including metal tools and firearms, greatly increased the power of the Iroquois, who embarked on a series of military expeditions against their neighbors, known as the Beaver Wars, which made them the strategic middlemen of the Dutch. In the late 1640s, the Iroquois attacked and dispersed the Hurons, who had long controlled the flow of furs from the Great Lakes to their allies the French. The Dutch also succeeded in overwhelming a small colony of Swedes on the lower Delaware River, incorporating that region into their sphere of influence in the 1640s.

ENGLAND IN THE CHESAPEAKE

England first attempted to plant colonies in North America during the 1580s, in Newfoundland and at Roanoke Island in present-day North Carolina (see Chapter 2). Both attempts were failures. England's war with Spain (1588 to 1604) suspended further efforts, but thereafter the English once again turned to the Americas.

Jamestown and the Powhatan Confederacy

Early in his reign, King James I (reigned 1603–25) issued royal charters for the colonization of the mid-Atlantic region, known as Virginia, to English joint-stock com-

This illustration is a detail of John Smith's map of Virginia. It includes the names of many Indian villages, suggesting how densely settled the Indian population was on the coast of Chesapeake Bay. For the inset of Powhatan and his court in the upper left, the engraver borrowed images from John White's drawings of the Indians of the Roanoke area.

SOURCE: Princeton University Library. Manuscripts Division. Department of Rare Books and Special Collections. Princeton University Library.

panies, which raised capital by selling shares. In 1607, a London group of investors known as the Virginia Company sent ships to Chesapeake Bay, where a hundred men built a fort they named Jamestown in honor of the king. It was destined to become the first permanent English settlement in North America.

The Chesapeake was already home to an estimated 24,000 Algonquian people. The English colonists were immediately confronted by Powhatan, the powerful *werowance* (leader) of a confederacy of Algonquian tribes. Powhatan had mixed feelings about the English. The Spanish had already attempted to plant a base nearby, bringing conflict and disease to the region. But he looked forward to valuable trade with the English, as well as their support for his struggle to extend his confederacy over outlying tribes.

The English saw themselves as conquistadors, and like the first Roanoke colonists, they proved unable to support themselves. Hating the idea of physical labor, they survived the first year only with Powhatan's material assistance. Jamestown grew so dependent on Algonquian stores that Smith and his men plundered food from surrounding tribes. In retaliation, Powhatan decided to starve the colonists out. He now realized that the English had come "not for trade, but to invade my people and possess my country." During the terrible winter of 1609–10 hundreds of colonists starved and a number resorted to cannibalism. Of the 500 colonists at Jamestown in the fall, only sixty remained alive by the spring.

Determined to prevail, the Virginia Company sent out a large additional force of men, women, and livestock, committing themselves to a protracted war against the Indians. The grim fighting persisted until 1613, when the English captured Powhatan's favorite daughter, teenaged Pocahontas. Worn down by war and disease, and eager to see his child again, Powhatan accepted a treaty of peace in 1614. Pocahontas adopted English ways and married John Rolfe, one of the leading settlers. But she fell sick and died on a visit to England in 1617. Crushed by the news, Powhatan abdicated in favor of his brother Opechancanough before dying of despair.

Tobacco, Expansion, and Warfare

Tobacco provided the Virginia colonists with the "merchantable commodity" for which Thomas Harriot, the scientist who accompanied the Roanoke expedition, had searched (see Chapter 2). Tobacco had been introduced to the English by Francis Drake in the 1580s, and by the 1610s the smoking craze created strong demand for the product. Pocahontas's husband John Rolfe developed a mild hybrid variety with considerable appeal, and soon the first commercial shipments of cured Virginia leaf reached England. Tobacco provided the Virginia Company with the first returns on its investment. Its cultivation quickly exhausted the soil, however, creating pressures for further expansion into Indian territory.

The settlers pressed the Indians for additional lands. Outraged, Opechancanough prepared the Chesapeake Algonquians for a final assault. He encouraged a cultural revival under the guidance of the shaman Nemattanew, who instructed his followers to reject the English and their ways but to learn the use of firearms. This was the first of many Indian resistance movements led jointly by strong political and religious figures. The uprising, which began on Good Friday, March 22, 1622, completely surprised the English. Nearly a third of the settlers, 347 people, were killed. Yet the colony managed to hang on. The attack stretched into a ten-year war of attrition in which both sides committed horrors.

The Indians finally sued for peace in 1632, but in the meantime the war had bankrupted the Virginia Company. In 1624 the king converted Virginia into a royal colony with civil authorities appointed by the crown, although the colony's House of Burgesses, created in 1619, continued to include representatives of Virginia's boroughs. Although disease, famine, and warfare took a heavy toll, continual emigration from England allowed the colonial population to double every five years from 1625 to 1640, by which time it numbered approximately 10,000. Meanwhile, decimated by violence and disease, the Algonquians shrank to about the same number.

Numerical strength soon shifted in favor of the English. In 1644 Opechancanough organized a final desperate revolt in which more than 500 colonists were killed. But the next year the Virginians crushed the Algonquians, capturing and executing their leader. A formal treaty granted the Indians a number of small reserved territories. By 1670 the Indian population had fallen to just 2,000, overwhelmed by the 40,000 English colonists.

Indentured Servants

At least three-quarters of the English migrants to the Chesapeake came as indentured servants. In exchange for the cost of their transportation to the New World, men and women contracted to labor for a master for a fixed term. Most indentured servants were young, unskilled males, who served for two to seven years; but some were skilled craftsmen, women, or even children (the latter were expected to serve a master until they reached the age of twenty-one).

African slaves were first introduced to the Chesapeake in 1619, but slaves were more expensive than servants, and as late as 1680 they made up less than 7 percent of the Chesapeake population. In the harddriving economy of the Chesapeake, however, masters treated servants as cruelly as they treated slaves. After arriving, bound laborers were inspected by planters who poked muscles, peered into open mouths, and pinched women. Approximately two out of five servants died during indenture. Those who survived were eligible for "freedom dues"—clothing, tools, a gun, or a spinning wheel, help getting started on their own—and many former servants headed west in the hope of cutting a farm from the wilderness. But most former servants who were able to raise the price of passage returned home to England.

Community Life in the Chesapeake

Because most emigrants were men, whether free or indentured, free unmarried women often married as soon as they arrived in the Chesapeake. Moreover, in the disease-ridden environment of the early Chesapeake, English men seemed to suffer a higher rate of mortality than women, and widows remarried quickly, sometimes within days. Their scarcity provided women with certain advantages. Shrewd widows bargained for a remarriage agreement that gave them a larger share of the estate than those set by common law upon the death of their husband. So notable was the concentration of wealth in the hands of these widows that one historian has suggested that early Virginia was a "matriarchy." But because of high mortality rates, family size was smaller and kinship bonds—one of the most important components of community—were weaker than in England.

Visitors from England often remarked on the crude conditions of community life. Prosperous planters, investing everything in tobacco production, lived in rough wooden dwellings. On the western edge of the settlements, freed servants lived with their families in shacks, huts, or even caves. Colonists spread across the countryside in search of new tobacco lands, creating dispersed settlements and few towns. Before 1650 there were few community institutions such as schools and churches. Meanwhile, the Spanish in the Caribbean and Mexico were building communities that would grow into great cities with permanent institutions.

In contrast to the colonists of New France, who were developing a distinctive American identity because of their commercial connections with Native Americans, the population of the Chesapeake maintained close emotional ties to England. Colonial politics were shaped less by local developments than by a continuing relationship with the mother country.

THE NEW ENGLAND COLONIES

Both in climate and in geography, the northern coast of North America was far different from the Chesapeake. "Merchantable commodities" such as tobacco could not be produced there, and thus it was far less favored for investment and settlement. Instead, the region became a haven for Protestant dissenters from England, who gave the colonies of the north a distinctive character.

The Social and Political Values of Puritanism

Most English men and women continued to practice a Christianity little different from traditional Catholicism. But the English followers of John Calvin, known as Puritans because they wished to purify and reform the English church from within, grew increasingly influential during the last years of Elizabeth's reign at the end of the sixteenth century. The Calvinist emphasis on enterprise meant that Puritanism appealed to merchants, entrepreneurs, and commercial farmers, those most responsible for the rapid economic and social transformation of England. But the Puritans were also the most vocal critics of the disruptive effects of that change, condemning the decline of the traditional rural community and the growing number of "idle and masterlessmen" produced by the enclosure of common lands. They argued for reviving communities by placing reformed Christian congregations at their core to monitor the behavior of individuals. By the early seventeenth century Puritans controlled many congregations and had become an influential force at the universities in Oxford and Cambridge, training centers for the future political and religious leaders of England. (For a review of the Protestant Reformation and the enclosure movement in England, see Chapter 2.)

King James I, who assumed the throne after Elizabeth's death, abandoned her policy of religious tolerance. His persecution of the Puritans, however, merely stiffened their resolve and turned them toward open political opposition. An increasingly vocal Puritan minority in Parliament criticized King Charles I (reigned 1625–49), James's son and successor, for supporting "High Church" (of England) policies—which emphasized the authority of the church and its traditional forms of worship—as well as for marrying a Roman Catholic princess. In 1629, determined to rule without these troublesome opponents, Charles dismissed Parliament and launched a campaign of repression against the Puritans. This political turmoil provided the context for the migration of thousands of English Protestants to New England.

Early Contacts in New England

The northern Atlantic coast seemed an unlikely spot for English colonies, for the region was dominated by French and Dutch traders. In 1613, desperate to keep their colonial options open, the English had dispatched a fleet from Jamestown that destroyed the French post on the Bay of Fundy and harassed the Dutch on the Hudson. The following year Captain John Smith of Virginia explored the northern coastline and christened the region "New England." The land was "so planted with Gardens and Corne fields," he wrote, that "I would rather live here than any where." But Smith's plans for a New England colony were aborted when he was captured by the French.

Then a twist of fate transformed English fortunes. From 1616 to 1618 an epidemic ravaged the native peoples of the northern Atlantic coast. Modern estimates confirm the testimony of a surviving Indian that his people were "melted down by this disease, whereof nine-tenths of them have died." The native population of New England as a whole dropped from an estimated 120,000 to less than 70,000. So crippled were the surviving coastal societies that they could not provide effective resistance to the planting of English colonies.

Plymouth Colony and the Mayflower Compact

The first English colony in New England was founded by a group of religious dissenters known to later generations as the Pilgrims. They were called Separatists because rather than reform the English church from within they believed it to be so corrupt that they had to establish their own independent congregations. One group moved to Holland in 1609, but fearful that tolerant Dutch society was seducing their children, they decided on emigration to North America. Backed by the Virginia Company of London and led by tradesman William Bradford, 102 people sailed from Plymouth, England, on the *Mayflower* in September 1620.

The little group, mostly families but including a substantial number of single men hired by the investors, arrived in Massachusetts Bay at the site of the former Indian village of Patuxet, which the English then named Plymouth. Soon the hired men began to grumble about Pilgrim authority, and to reassure them Bradford drafted an agreement by which the male members of the expedition did "covenant and combine [themselves] together into a civil body politic." The Mayflower Compact was the first document of self-government in North America.

Weakened by scurvy and malnutrition, nearly half the Pilgrims perished over the first winter. Like the earlier settlers of Roanoke and Jamestown, however, they were rescued by Indians. Massasoit, the sachem (leader) of the Pokanokets (also known as the Wampanoags), offered the newcomers food and advice in return for an alliance against his enemies, the Narragansets. It was the familiar pattern of Indians attempting to incorporate European colonists into their world.

The Pilgrims succeeded during the first two or three decades in establishing the self-sufficient community they desired. So strong was their communal agreement that the annual meeting of property-owning men reelected William Bradford to thirty consecutive terms as governor. By midcentury, however, the Plymouth population had dispersed into eleven separate communities, and the growth of diverse local interests had begun to disrupt this Separatist retreat.

The Massachusetts Bay Colony

In England, the political climate of the late 1620s convinced a number of influential Puritans that the only way to protect their congregations was by emigration. In 1629 a royal charter was granted to a group of wealthy Puritans who called their enterprise the Massachusetts Bay Company, and an advance force of 200 settlers left for the fishing settlement of Naumkeag on Massachusetts Bay, which they renamed Salem. They hoped to establish what John Winthrop, their leader and first governor, called "a city on a hill," a New England model of reform for old England. The Puritan emigration became known as the Great Migration, a phrase that would be repeated many times in American history. Between 1629 and 1643 some 20,000 people relocated to Massachusetts. They built the town of Boston in 1630 and within five years ringed it with towns as far as thirty miles inland.

Indians and Puritans

The Algonquian Indians of southern New England found the English very different from the French and Dutch traders who had preceded them. The principal concern of the English was not commerce, although the fur trade remained an important part of their economy, but the acquisition of Indian land for their growing settlements.

Ravaged by disease, the Pokanokets' northern neighbors, the Massachusetts, were ill-prepared for the Puritan landings that took place after 1629. The English believed they had the right to take what they thought of as "unused" lands—lands not being used, that is, in the "English way"—and depopulated Massachusetts villages became prime targets for expansion. As one colonist wrote, "Their land is spacious and void, and there are few and [they] do but run over the grass, as do also the foxes and wild beasts." The Indians did not consider that land could be privately owned, but understood it as a community resource. Conflicts between settlers over title, however, made it necessary to obtain

original deeds from Indians, and the English used a variety of tactics to pressure them into signing "quitclaims," or documents in which the signers relinquished all claim to specified properties.

By the late 1630s the most powerful tribes in the vicinity of the Puritans were the Narragansets of present-day Rhode Island and their traditional enemies the Pequots, principal trading partners of the Dutch. The Pequots lived on Long Island Sound near the mouth of the Connecticut River, where they controlled the production of wampum, woven belts of sea shells used as a medium of exchange in the Indian trade. In 1637 the Narragansets, in alliance with the English, who were looking for an excuse to smash the Dutch, went to war against the Pequots. Narraganset warriors and English troops attacked the main Pequot village, killing most of its slumbering residents, including women and children. Unaccustomed to such tactics, the shocked Narragansets cried out to the English: "It is too furious, it slays too many."

The New England Merchants

In England, the conflict between King Charles I and the Puritans in Parliament broke into armed conflict in 1642. Several years of violent confrontation led to the execution of the king in 1649 and the proclamation of an English Commonwealth, headed by the Puritan leader Oliver Cromwell. Because the Puritans were on the victorious side in the English Civil War, they no longer had the same incentive to migrate to New England. A number of settlers even returned to England.

New England's economy had depended on the sale of supplies and land to arriving immigrants, but as the Great Migration ended the importance of this "newcomer market" declined. Lacking a single exportable commodity, New England traders developed a diversified trade with a variety of commodities, including oak barrel staves, pine ship's masts, salted cod fish, and farm products. By the 1660s the New England merchants had a commercial fleet that was the envy of other colonies: 300 trading and fishing vessels that voyaged throughout the Atlantic—to the fishing grounds of the North Atlantic, to the sugar-producing colonies of the West Indies, to the wine-producing islands of the Atlantic, and to Africa and England.

Community and Family in Massachusetts

The Puritans stressed the importance of well-ordered communities. The Massachusetts General Court, the governing body of the colony, granted townships to a group of proprietors, the leaders of a congregation wishing to settle new lands. These men then distributed fields, pasture, and woodlands in quantities proportional to the social status of the recipient, with wealthy families receiving more than others. The Puritans believed that social hierarchy was ordained by God and made for well-ordered communities. Settlers typically clustered their dwellings in a central village, near the meetinghouse that served as both church and civic center. Some towns, particularly those along the coast such as Boston, soon became centers of shipping. These clustered settlements and strong, vital communities made seventeenth-century New England quite different from Chesapeake society.

The ideal Puritan family was also well ordered. Parents often participated in the choice of mates for their offspring, and children typically married in the order of their births, younger siblings waiting until arrangements had been made for their elders. But well-disciplined children also needed education. Another source of New England's strength was the impressive system the Puritans built to educate their young. In 1647 Massachusetts required that towns with 50 families or more support a public school; those with 100 families were to establish a grammar school that taught Latin, knowledge of which was required for admission to Harvard College, founded in 1636. The colony of Connecticut enacted similar requirements. Literacy was higher in New England than elsewhere in North

America, and even in most of Europe. But because girls were excluded from grammar schools, far fewer New England women than men could read and write. By 1639 the first printing press in the English colonies was in operation in Boston, and the following year it brought out the first American English publication, *The Bay Psalm Book.*

Dissent and New Communities

The Puritans emigrated in order to practice their variety of Christianity, but they had little tolerance for other religious points of view. Religious disagreement among the colonists soon provoked the founding of new colonies. Thomas Hooker, minister of the congregation at Cambridge, disagreed with the policy of restricting suffrage to male church members. In 1636 he led his followers west to the Connecticut River, where they founded the town of Hartford near the site of the trading post abandoned by the Dutch after epidemic disease had destroyed nearby Indian communities in 1634.

Another dissenter was the minister Roger Williams, who came to New England in 1631 to take up duties for the congregation in Salem. Williams believed in religious tolerance and the separation of church and state (discussed in Chapter 5). He also preached that the colonists had no absolute right to Indian land but must bargain for it in good faith. These were dangerous ideas, and Williams was banished from the colony in 1636. With a group of his followers, he emigrated to the Narraganset country, where he purchased land from the Indians and founded the town of Providence.

In 1644 Roger Williams received a royal charter creating the colony of Rhode Island, named for the principal island in Narraganset Bay, as a protection for these dissenting communities. A new royal charter of 1663 guaranteed self-government and complete religious liberty.

THE RESTORATION COLONIES

The Puritan Commonwealth established in England after the execution of King Charles attempted to provide a measure of central control over the colonies with the passage in 1651 of an Act of Trade and Navigation, which was intended to keep Dutch ships out of England's overseas possessions. But the regime was preoccupied with English domestic affairs and left the colonies largely to their own devices. Cromwell ruled as Lord Protector of the Commonwealth, but the new order failed to survive his death in 1658. While wishing to reserve for itself certain significant powers of state, Parliament was desperate for political stability after nearly two decades of civil war. In 1660 it restored the

The Mason Children, by an unknown Boston artist, c. 1670. These Puritan children—David, Joanna, and Abigail Mason—are dressed in finery, an indication of the wealth and prominence of their family. The cane in young David's hand indicates his position as the male heir, while the rose held by Abigail is a symbol of childhood innocence.

SOURCE: Attributed to the Freake-Gibbs Painter, American, active Boston, MA, c. 1670. *The Mason Children: David, Joanna, and Abigail,* c.a. 1670. Oil on canvas, 39 x 421⁄2 in. The Fine Arts Museum of San Francisco, Gift of Mr. and Mrs. John D. Rockefeller 3rd, 1979,7.3.

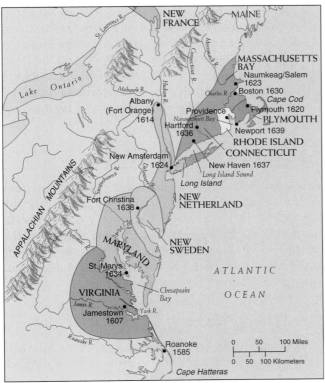

European Colonies of the Atlantic Coast, 1607–39   Virginia on Chesapeake Bay was the first English colony in North America, but by the mid-seventeenth century Virginia was joined by settlements of Scandinavians on the Delaware River, and Dutch on the Hudson River, as well as English religious dissenters in New England. The territories indicated here reflect the vague boundaries of the early colonies.

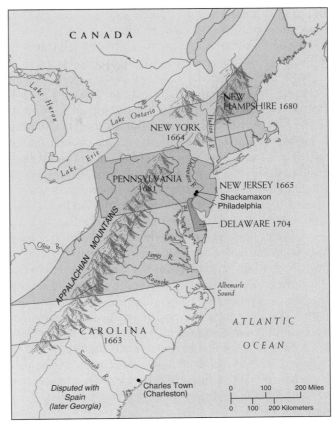

The Restoration Colonies   After the restoration of the Stuart monarchy in 1660, King Charles II of England created the new proprietary colonies of Carolina, New York, Pennsylvania, and New Jersey. New Hampshire was set off as a royal colony in 1680, and in 1704 the lower counties of Pennsylvania became the colony of Delaware.

Stuart monarchy, placing Charles II, son of the former king, on the throne. One of Charles's most important acts was the establishment of several new proprietary colonies, known as the Restoration Colonies.

Early Carolina

In 1663 the king issued his first charters, calling for the establishment of a new colony called Carolina, which stretched from Virginia south to Spanish Florida. Virginians had already begun moving into the northern parts of this territory, and in 1664 the Carolina proprietors appointed a governor for the settlements in the area of Albermarle Sound and created a popularly elected assembly. By 1675 North Carolina, as it became known, was home to 5,000 small farmers and large tobacco planters.

Settlement farther south began in 1670 with the founding of coastal Charles Town (Charleston today). Most South Carolina settlers came from Barbados, a Caribbean colony the English had founded in 1627,

which had grown rich from the production of sugar. By the 1670s the island had become overpopulated with English settlers and Africans. The latter, imported as slaves to work the plantations, made up a majority of the population. Hundreds of Barbadians, both masters and their slaves, relocated to South Carolina, lending a distinctly West Indian character to the colony.

From New Netherland to New York

King Charles II also coveted the lucrative Dutch colony of New Netherland. In response to the growth of New England's population and its merchant economy, in the 1640s the Dutch West India Company began to sponsor the emigration of European settlers to its colony in the Hudson River valley, seeking to convert New Netherland from a specialized fur-trade economy to a diversified supply center for the West Indies. The result was rising conflict with local Indian communities, pressed by the Dutch to cede their lands for agriculture. The British Navigation Act of 1651 was in part a response to what the English viewed as the Dutch threat to the English trade monopoly they sought to establish along the Atlantic coast. England's attempt to control Dutch shipping led to an inconclusive naval war with Holland from 1652 to 1654, and a decade later the two powers clashed again along the West African coast. Finally, in 1664, an English fleet sailed into Manhattan harbor and forced the surrender of New Amsterdam without firing a shot, inagurating a second full-fledged Anglo-Dutch war, which ended with an inconclusive peace in 1667. A third and final conflict from 1672 to 1674 resulted in the bankruptcy of the Dutch West India Company and marked the ascension of the English to dominance in the Atlantic. Holland remained supreme in the Baltic and the East Indies.

Charles II granted the newly acquired Dutch colony to his brother James, the Duke of York, renaming it New York in his honor. Otherwise the English government did little to disturb the existing order, preferring simply to reap the benefits of acquiring this profitable and dynamic colony. Ethnically and linguistically diversified, accommodating a wide range of religious sects, New York boasted the most heterogeneous society in North America. In 1665, the communities of the Delaware Valley were split off as the proprietary colony of New Jersey, although it continued to be governed by New York until the 1680s.

The Founding of Pennsylvania

In 1676 proprietary rights to the western portion of New Jersey were sold to a group of English Quakers that included William Penn, who intended to make the area a religious haven for members of the Society of Friends, or Quakers. A dissenting sect, the Quakers were committed to religious toleration and pacifism. Penn himself had been imprisoned four times for publicly expressing these views. But he was the son of the wealthy and influential English admiral Sir William Penn, a close adviser to the king. In 1681, to settle a large debt owed to Sir William, King Charles granted the younger Penn a huge territory west of the Delaware River. The next year Penn supervised the laying out of his capital of Philadelphia on the Delaware.

Penn wanted this colony to be a "holy experiment." In his first Frame of Government, drafted in 1682, he included guarantees of religious freedom, civil liberties, and elected representation. He also attempted to deal fairly with the Algonquian Indians, not permitting colonization until settlement rights were negotiated and lands purchased. In 1682 and 1683, he made an agreement with the sachem Tammany of the Delaware tribe. Although Pennsylvania's relations with the Indians later soured, during Penn's lifetime his reputation for fair dealing led a number of Indian groups to resettle in the Quaker colony.

During the first decade of Pennsylvania's settlement, over 10,000 colonists arrived from England, and agricultural communities were soon spreading from the Delaware into the fertile interior valleys. In 1704 Penn approved the creation of a separate government for the area formerly controlled by the Scandinavians and Dutch. This area became the colony of Delaware.

CONFLICT AND WAR

Pennsylvania's ability to maintain peaceful relations with the Indians proved the great exception, for the last quarter of the seventeenth century was a time of great violence throughout the colonial regions of the continent. Much of this warfare was between colonists and Indians, but intertribal warfare and intercolonial rivalry greatly contributed to the violence.

King Philip's War

During the nearly forty years of peace that followed the Pequot War of 1637, the Algonquian and English peoples of New England lived in close, if tense, contact. Several Puritan ministers, including John Eliot and Thomas Mayhew, began to preach to the Indians, and several hundred Algonquian converts eventually relocated in Christian Indian communities called "praying towns." Outside the colonial boundaries, however, there remained a number of independent Indian tribes, including the Pokanokets and the Narragansets of Rhode Island and the Abenakis of northern New England. The extraordinary expansion of the Puritan population, and their hunger for land, created pressures for further expansion into those territories.

In 1671 the colonial authorities at Plymouth forced the Pokanokets to concede authority over their home territory. This humiliation convinced the sachem Metacomet (called King Philip by the English), son of Massasoit, that his people must break their half-century alliance with Plymouth and take up armed resistance. Meanwhile, the Puritan colonies prepared for a war of conquest.

In the spring of 1675 Plymouth magistrates arrested and executed three Pokanoket men for the murder of a Christian Indian. Fearing that the moment of confrontation had arrived, Metacomet appealed to the Narragansets for a defensive alliance. The United Colonies (the New England colonies led by Massachusetts Bay) and New York, hoping for territorial gain, took this as the moment to send armed forces into Narraganset country, attacking and burning a number of villages. What became known as King Philip's War soon engulfed all of New England.

At first things went well for the Indians. They forced the abandonment of English settlements on the Connecticut River and torched several towns less than twenty miles from Boston. By the beginning of 1676, however, their campaign was collapsing. A combined colonial army invaded Narraganset country, burning villages, killing women and children, and defeating a large Indian force in a battle known as the Great Swamp Fight. In western New England, Metacomet appealed to the Iroquois for supplies and support, but instead they attacked and defeated his forces. Metacomet retreated back to his homeland, where the colonists annihilated his army in August 1676.

In their attack on Metacomet's army, the Iroquois were motivated by interests of their own. Continuing the role they had played in the Dutch trading system, they now cast themselves in the role of powerful intermediaries between other tribes and the English. By attacking Metacomet they demonstrated where they stood. In a series of negotiations conducted at Albany in 1677, the Iroquois Confederacy and the colony of New York created an alliance known as the Covenant Chain, which sought to establish Iroquois dominance over all other tribes and thus put New York in an economically and politically dominant position among the other colonies.

At the end of King Philip's War, some 4,000 Algonquians and 2,000 English colonists were dead, and dozens of native and colonial towns lay in ruins. Fearing attack from Indians close at hand, colonists destroyed most of the Christian Indian praying towns, killing many of the residents.

Bacon's Rebellion

At the same time as King Philip's War, another English-Indian confrontation took place in the Chesapeake. In the 1670s the Susquehannock people of the upper Potomac River came into conflict with the tobacco planters expanding northward from Virginia. Violent raids in 1675, led by wealthy backcountry settler Nathaniel Bacon, included the indiscriminate murder of Indians. The efforts of Virginia governor William Berkeley to suppress these unauthorized military expe-

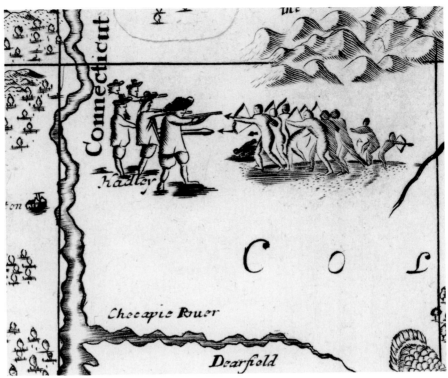

Indians and New Englanders skirmish during King Philip's War in a detail from John Seller's "A Mapp of New England," published immediately after the war in 1675.

SOURCE: Courtesy of the John Carter Brown Library at Brown University.

ditions so infuriated Bacon and his followers—many of them former indentured servants—that in the spring of 1676 they turned their fury against the colonial capital of Jamestown itself. Berkeley fled across the Chesapeake while Bacon pillaged and burned the capital. Soon thereafter Bacon died of dysentery, a common fate of the day, and his rebellion collapsed.

This brief but violent clash marked an important change of direction for Virginia. Bacon had issued a manifesto demanding not only the death or removal of all Indians from the colony but also an end to the rule of aristocratic "grandees" and "parasites." The rebellion thus signaled a developing conflict between frontier districts such as Bacon's and the more established coastal region where the "Indian problem" had long since been settled. In 1677, in a replay of Virginia events known as Culpeper's Rebellion, backcountry men in the Albermarle region of North Carolina suceeded in overthrowing the established government, before being suppressed by English authorities. In the aftermath of these rebellions, colonial authorities in Virginia and North Carolina began to favor armed expansion into Indian territory, hoping to gain the support of backcountry men by enlarging the stock of available colonial land.

OVERVIEW

CONFLICT AND WAR

The Beaver Wars	1640s–80s	The Iroquois extend their authority as middlemen in the Dutch and English trade system by attacking neighbors as far west as Illinois
King Philip's War	1675–76	The Indian peoples of southern New England and the Puritan colonies fight for control of land
Bacon's Rebellion	1675–76	Backcountry settlers attack Indians, and colonial authorities try to suppress these attacks
Wars in the South	1670s–1720s	British colonists in the Carolinas incite Creeks, Cherokees, and other Indian tribes to attack and enslave the mission Indians of Spanish Florida
King William's War	1689–97	The first of a series of colonial struggles between England and France, these conflicts occur principally on the frontiers of northern New England and New York

Wars in the South

There was also massive violence in South Carolina during the 1670s, as colonists there began the operation of a large-scale Indian slave trade. Charleston merchants encouraged Yamasees, Creeks, Cherokees, and Chickasaws to wage war on Indian tribes allied to rival colonial powers: the mission Indians of Spanish Florida, the Choctaw allies of the French, and the Tuscaroras, trading partners of the Virginians. The mission Indians of Florida were hit so hard that by 1710 more than 12,000 of them had been captured and sold, thousands of others had been killed or dispersed, and the Spanish mission system, in operation for more than a century, lay in ruins.

King William's War

The year 1689 marked the beginning of nearly seventy-five years of armed conflict between English and French forces for control of the North American interior. The Iroquois-English Covenant Chain challenged New France's fur-trade empire, and in response the French pressed farther west in search of commercial opportunities. In the far north, the English countered French dominance with the establishment of Hudson's Bay Company, a royal fur-trade monopoly that sought to exploit the watershed of the great northern bay.

Hostilities began with English-Iroquois attacks on Montreal and violence between rival French and English traders on Hudson's Bay. These skirmishes were part of a larger conflict between England and France called the War of the League of Augsburg in Europe. In the North American colonies the conflict was known as King William's War. In 1690, the French and their Algonquian allies counterattacked, burning frontier settlements in New York, New Hampshire, and Maine, and pressing their attacks against the towns of the Iroquois. The same year, a Massachusetts fleet captured and briefly held the strategic French harbor at Port Royal, on the Bay of Fundy in Acadia, but a combined English and colonial force failed in its attempt to conquer the French settlements along the St. Lawrence. This inconclusive war was ended by the Treaty of Ryswick of 1697, which established an equally inconclusive peace. War between England and France resumed only five years later.

The persistent violence of the last quarter of the seventeenth century greatly concerned English authorities, who began to fear the loss of their North American possessions either from outside attack or from internal disorder. To shore up central control, in 1701 the English Board of Trade recommended making all charter and proprietary governments into royal colonies. After a brief period under royal rule, William Penn regained private control of his domain, but Pennsylvania was the only remaining proprietary colony. Among the royal charter colonies, only Rhode Island and Connecticut retained their original governments.

CHRONOLOGY

1598	Juan de Oñate leads Spanish into New Mexico		1660	Stuart monarchy restored, Charles II becomes king
1607	English found Jamestown		1675	King Philip's War
1608	French found Quebec		1676	Bacon's Rebellion
1609	Spanish found Santa Fé		1680	Pueblo Revolt
1620	Pilgrim emigration		1681–82	Robert Sieur de La Salle explores the Mississippi
1622	Indian uprising in Virginia		1689	King William's War
1625	Jesuit missionaries arrive in New France		1698	Spanish reconquest of the Pueblos completed
1629	Puritans begin settlement of Massachusetts Bay		1701	English impose royal governments on all colonies but Massachusetts, Connecticut, and Pennsylvania
1637	Pequot War			
1649	Charles I executed			

CONCLUSION

At the beginning of the seventeenth century the European presence north of Mexico was extremely limited: Spanish bases in Florida, a few Franciscan missionaries among the Pueblos, and fishermen along the North Atlantic coast. By 1700 the human landscape of the Southwest, the South, and the Northeast had been transformed. More than a quarter million migrants from the Old World had moved into these regions, the vast majority to the British colonies. Indian societies had been disrupted, depopulated, and in some cases destroyed. The Spanish and French colonies were characterized by the inclusion of Indians in the social and economic life of the community. But along the Atlantic coast, the English and eventually the Dutch established communities of exclusion, with resulting implications for the future of relations between colonists and Indians that were ominous.

During the long civil war at home the English colonies had been left to run their own affairs. But with the Restoration in 1660 and the establishment of the constitutional monarchy in 1689, the English state began to supervise its troublesome colonists more closely, beginning a long struggle over the limits of self-government. The violence and warfare of the last decades of the century suggested that conflict would continue to play a significant role in the future of colonial America.

REVIEW QUESTIONS

1. Using examples drawn from this chapter, discuss the differences between colonizing "frontiers of inclusion" and "exclusion."
2. What factors turned England's Chesapeake colony of Virginia from stark failure to brilliant success?
3. Discuss the role of religious dissent in the founding of the first New England colonies and in stimulating the creation of others.
4. Compare and contrast William Penn's policy with respect to Indian tribes with the policies of other English settlers, in the Chesapeake and New England, and with the policies of the Spanish, the French, and the Dutch.
5. What were the principal causes of colonial violence and warfare of the late seventeenth century?

RECOMMENDED READING

James Axtell, *The European and the Indian: Essays in the Ethnohistory of Colonial America* (1981). A readable introduction to the dynamics of mutual discovery between natives and colonizers.

Leslie Choquette, *Frenchmen into Peasants: Modernity and Tradition in the Peopling of French Canada* (1997). A history of French immigrants to Canada and Acadia, based on a comprehensive database of hundreds of individuals. The most detailed study of French mobility to date.

Frederic W. Gleach, *Powhatan's World and Colonial Virginia: A Conflict of Cultures* (1997). Reconstructing the worldview of the Chesapeake Algonquians as they attempted to maintain control of their homeland.

Harold Adams Innis, *The Fur Trade in Canada: An Introduction to Canadian Economic History* (1999). A new edition of a classic that remains the definitive history of the fur trade.

Andrew L. Knaut, *The Pueblo Revolt of 1680* (1995). The most complete and sophisticated account of the revolt.

Edmund S. Morgan, *American Slavery, American Freedom* (1975). A classic interpretation of early Virginia. Morgan argues that early American ideas of freedom for some were based on the reality of slavery for others.

Diana Newton, *Papists, Protestants, and Puritans, 1559-1714* (1998). The best survey of religious change during the Protestant Reformation, with a focus on the turmoil in England.

Neal Salisbury, *Manitou and Providence: Indians, Europeans, and the Making of New England* (1982). One of the best examples of the new ethnohistory of Indians; a provocative intercultural approach to the history of the Northeast.

Susan Sleeper-Smith, *Native Women and French Men: Rethinking Cultural Encounter in the Western Great Lakes* (2001). A study of Indian women who married French traders and became cultural brokers and creators of a middle ground.

David J. Weber, *The Spanish Frontier in North America* (1992). A powerful overview that includes the history of New Mexico and Florida.

ON THE WEB

http://www.iath.virginia.edu/vcdh/jamestown/

The University of Virginia has created Virtual Jamestown as a site for students and teachers to explore that early colony and examine original maps, documents, court records, letters, and other historical artifacts. The site is constantly growing but currently the page on Jamestown laws concerning slavery, indentured servants, and religion is very large and interesting. Some pages are under construction and limited in resources, but the maps page is well developed, the newspaper page contains interesting accounts of runaway slaves, and the firsthand accounts and letters page is fairly extensive.

http://www.plimoth.org/Museum/museum.htm

Plimoth Plantation, Inc., a private, nonprofit living history museum, operates this website as a living-history virtual tour of Plymouth Plantation. The web page on the Wampanoag tribe who met the Plymouth settlers is particularly interesting and fact-filled. Other sites are equally rewarding. In using this site, remember that even based on good archeological evidence, it is a living history recreation.

http://www.yale.edu/lawweb/avalon/states/statech.htm

The Avalon Project at the Yale Law School contains documents for the pre-eighteenth century, eighteenth century, nineteenth century, and twentieth century. This page contains the colonial charters for all thirteen colonies plus Maine and Vermont. Where multiple charters were issued, these appear. This web page also contains the 1776 constitutions instituted by the recently independent states at the request of the Continental Congress.

http://www.prenhall.com/faragherbrief/map3.1

Check your knowledge of European colonization of the Atlantic coast. By the middle of the seventeenth century, how many European nations had established colonies on the Atlantic coast?

http://www.prenhall.com/faragherbrief/map3.2

Examine the processes underlying the founding of the Restoration Colonies. How has the political landscape changed since 1639?

FOUR
SLAVERY AND EMPIRE

▶ 1441–1770

AMERICAN COMMUNITIES

African Slaves Build Their Own Community in Coastal Georgia

AFRICANS LABORED IN THE STEAMY HEAT OF THE COASTAL GEORGIA rice fields, the breeches of the men rolled up over their knees, the sack skirts of the women gathered and tied about their hips, leaving them, in the words of one shocked observer, "two thirds naked." Standing on the banks of canals that channeled water to the fields, African slave drivers, whips at the ready, supervised the work. Upriver, groups cut away cypress and gum trees and cleared the swampland's jungle maze of undergrowth; others constructed levees, preparing to bring more land under cultivation. An English overseer or plantation master could be seen here and there, but overwhelmingly it was a country populated by Africans.

These plantations were southern extensions of the South Carolina rice belt. Although slavery had been prohibited by Georgia's original charter of 1732, the restriction was lifted when Georgia became a royal colony two decades later. By 1770, 15,000 African Americans (80 percent of the region's population) lived on several hundred coastal rice plantations owned by a small elite of white people.

Rice was one of the most valuable commodities produced in mainland North America, surpassed in value only by tobacco and wheat. The growth of rice production in the lower South was matched by an enormous expansion in the Atlantic slave trade, and during the eighteenth century rice planters engaged in what one historian calls a "veritable orgy" of slave trading. Although the number of North American black people who were "country born" (native to America and, thus, born into slavery) grew steadily over the century, before the American Revolution the majority of black people on the rice plantations were what were known as "saltwater" Africans. These people had endured the shock of enslavement. Ripped from their homeland communities in West Africa by slave raiders, they were brutally marched to coastal forts. There, they were imprisoned, subjected to humiliating inspections of their bodies, and branded on the buttocks like animals. Packed into the stinking holds of ships, they were forced into a nightmarish passage across the Atlantic Ocean. When finally unloaded on a strange continent, they were sold at dockside auctions, then once again marched overland to their destinations on New World plantations. On the rice plantations of isolated coastal Georgia, enslaved Africans suffered from overwork and numerous physical ailments, the results of poor diet, minimal and inappropriate clothing, and inadequate housing. Mortality rates were exceptionally high, especially for infants. Colonial laws permitted masters to discipline and punish slaves indiscriminately. They were whipped, confined in irons, castrated, or sold away, with little regard for their relations with family or friends.

Africans struggled to make a place for themselves in this inhospitable world. They had little power, but bargained with their masters to win acceptance of the familiar work routines of West Africa. Thus, low-country plantations operated according to the task system: once slaves finished their specific jobs, they could use their remaining time to hunt, fish, or cultivate family gardens. Masters often complained that "tasking" did not produce the same level of profit as the gang labor system of the sugar plantations, but African rice hands refused to work any other way. "Although it is not fixed by law," one planter wrote in 1767, the tasking system was "so well settled by long usage," that any master who tried to increase the workload was faced with "such discontent amongst his slaves as to make them of but little use to him."

Still, many slaves ran away, like slaves everywhere in the Americas. Readers of Savannah newspapers were urged to look out for fugitives: Statira, a woman of the "Gold Coast Country" with tribal markings on her temples, or "a negro fellow named Mingo, about 40 years old, and his wife Quante, a sensible wench about 20 with her child, a boy about 3 years old, all this country born." Some fled in groups, heading for the Creek Indian settlements in northern Florida, or toward St. Augustine, where the Spanish, in an attempt to undermine the English colonies of the Lower South, promised them safe haven. Some struck out violently at their masters: a group of nine Africans from a Savannah plantation killed their master and stole a boat, planning to head upriver, but were apprehended as they lay in wait to murder their hated overseers.

So slaves resisted. But like slaves throughout the New World, the majority of Africans and African Americans of the Georgia coast remained and built communities of

their own within the heartless world of slavery. Plantation slaves married, raised children, and over time constructed kinship networks. They passed on African names and traditions and created new ones. These links between individuals and families formed the basis for reestablished communities. Slave communities combined elements of African languages and English to form dialects that allowed newly arrived people from many different African ethnic groups as well as American-born slaves to communicate with one another. Neither individuals nor families alone can make a language; that is something only a community can do. Common African heritage and common slave status were the foundations of the African American community.

African Americans reworked traditional African dance, song, and story to fit New World circumstances, just as they reestablished traditional arts, such as woodworking, iron making, and weaving. Through their culture, the slaves shared a powerful awareness of their common oppression. They told or sang dialect tales of mistreatment, as in this song of Quow, the punished slave:

> *Was matter Buddy Quow?*
> *I ble Obesha bang you . . . .*
> *Dah Backrow Man go wrong you, Buddy Quow,*
> *Dah Backrow Man go wrong you, Buddy Quow.*
>
> *[What's the matter Brother Quow?*
> *I believe the overseer's beat you . . . .*
> *The white man's wronged you, Brother Quow,*
> *The white man's wronged you, Brother Quow.]*

Just as European settlers planted colonial communities, so Africans, who made up the largest ethnic group to come to North America during the colonial era, constructed distinctive communities of their own. The history of African Americans includes the story of the Atlantic slave trade, the plunder of Africa, and the profits of empire. But it is also a story of achievement under the most difficult circumstances, and of the making of families, kin networks, and communities. They "labor together and converse almost wholly among themselves," a minister wrote of low-country slaves. "They are, as 'twere, a nation within a nation." ■

Georgia
Sea
Islands

KEY TOPICS

- The development of the slavery system
- The history of the slave trade and the Middle Passage
- Community development among African Americans in the eighteenth century

- The connections between the institution of slavery and the imperial system of the eighteenth century
- The early history of racism in America

THE BEGINNINGS OF AFRICAN SLAVERY

Household slaves had long been a part of the world of Mediterranean Europe. Many Europeans were disturbed, however, by the moral implications of enslaving Christians, and in the early fifteenth century the pope excommunicated a number of merchants engaged in selling such captives. Africans and Muslims, however, were sufficiently different in religion to quiet those concerns.

One of the goals of Portuguese expansion in the fifteenth century was access to the lucrative West African trade in gold, wrought iron, ivory, tortoiseshell, textiles, and slaves that had previously been dominated by the Moors of northern Africa. The first African slaves to arrive in Lisbon were kidnapped by a Portuguese captain in 1441. But European traders found it more efficient to leave the capture of men and women for slavery to Africans, who were willing to exchange the captured slaves for European commodities. By the mid-fifteenth century, the Portuguese were shipping a thousand or more slaves per year from Africa.

Sugar and Slavery

Sugar and slaves had gone together since Italian merchants of the fourteenth century had imported the first cane sugar from the Middle East and set up the first modern sugar plantations on the islands of the Mediterranean. Thus, the use of Africans as slaves came to the Americas along with the spread of sugar production. One of the first products Columbus introduced to the New World was sugar cane. Sugar plantations were soon operating on the island of Hispaniola. At first the Spanish tried to use the native Indian people as a slave labor force, but because disease and warfare had so reduced the indigenous population, colonists soon turned to African slaves who were already working in

Spain. Meanwhile, the Portuguese, aided by Dutch financiers, created a center of sugar production in northeast Brazil that became a model of the efficient and brutal exploitation of African labor. By 1600, some 25,000 enslaved Africans labored on the plantations of Hispaniola and Brazil.

The Dutch, using their experience in Brazil, became responsible for the next extension of slavery in the Americas. In 1630 they seized Brazil and for over twenty years they controlled this lucrative colony. Skilled at finance and commerce, they greatly expanded the European market for sugar, converting it from a luxury item for the rich to a staple for European workers. It was the Dutch who introduced sugar cultivation in the tropics. As a result, Barbados became the most valuable of England's colonies. Once the profitability of sugar had been demonstrated, the English sought to expand their Caribbean holdings by seizing the island of Jamaica from the Spanish in 1655 and making it over in the image of Barbados. Jamaica became the crown jewel of Britain's eighteenth-century empire.

The French repeated the process. They first developed sugar plantations on the small island of Martinique, then seized the eastern half of Hispaniola from the Spanish and created a sugar colony called St. Domingue (present-day Haiti). Caribbean sugar and slaves had become the centerpiece of the European colonial system.

West Africans

The men and women whose labor made these tropical colonies so profitable came from the long-established societies and local communities of West Africa. In the sixteenth century more than a hundred different peoples lived along the coast of West Africa, from Cape Verde south to Angola. In the north were the Wolofs, Mandingos, Hausas, Ashantis, and Yorubas; to the south the Ibos, Sekes, Bakongos, and Mbundus.

In all these societies the most important institution was the local community, which was organized by kinship. Decisions about production, storage, and distribution of goods were generally made by clan leaders and village chiefs; local courts arbitrated disputes. Men often took a second or third wife. This marriage system, known as polygyny, produced very large composite families with complex internal relationships.

West African societies were based on sophisticated farming systems many thousands of years old. Africans practiced shifting cultivation: they cleared land by burning, used hoes or digging sticks to cultivate fields, and after several years moved on to other plots while the cleared land lay fallow. Men worked at clearing the land, women at cultivation and the sale of surpluses in the lively West African markets. The West African familiarity with regular agricultural labor was important in the history of slavery, because it proved to be practically impossible to convert large numbers of foraging or nomadic peoples into efficient plantation workers.

Farming sustained large populations and thriving networks of commerce, and in some areas kingdoms and states developed. Along the upper Niger River, where the grassland gradually turns to desert, towns such as Timbuktu developed into trading centers. There were a number of lesser states and kingdoms along the coast, and it was with these that the Portuguese first bargained for Africans who could be sold as slaves.

Varieties of household slavery were common in West African societies, although slaves there were often treated more as members of the family than as mere possessions. The West African familiarity with "unfree" labor made it possible for African and European traders to begin the trade in human merchandise.

THE AFRICAN SLAVE TRADE

The movement of Africans across the Atlantic to the Americas was the largest forced migration in world history. The Atlantic slave trade, which began with the Portuguese in the fifteenth century and did not end in the United States until 1807 (and continued elsewhere in the Americas until the 1870s), is a brutal chapter in the making of America.

The Demography of the Slave Trade

Scholars today estimate that slave ships transported 10 to 11 million Africans to the Americas during the four-century history of the trade. Seventy-six percent arrived from 1701 to 1810—the peak period of colonial demand for labor, when tens of thousands of people were shipped from Africa each year. Of this vast multi-

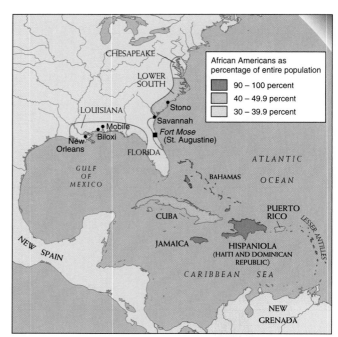

Slave Colonies of the Seventeenth and Eighteenth Centuries   By the eighteenth century the system of slavery had created societies with large African populations throughout the Caribbean and along the southern coast of North America.

tude, about half were delivered to Dutch, French, or British sugar plantations in the Caribbean, a third to Portuguese Brazil, and 10 percent to Spanish America. A much smaller proportion—about one in twenty, or an estimated 600,000 men, women, and children—were transported to the British colonies of North America. With the exception of the 1750s, when the British colonies were engulfed by the Seven Years' War, the slave trade continued to rise in importance in the decades before the Revolution.

Among the Africans brought to the Americas, men generally outnumbered women two to one. Because most Africans were destined for fieldwork, this ratio probably reflected the preferences of plantation owners. The majority of captured and transported Africans were young people, between the ages of fifteen and thirty. Nearly every ethnic group in West Africa was represented among them.

Slavers of All Nations

All the nations of Western Europe participated in the slave trade. Dutch slavers began challenging Portuguese control of the trade at the end of the sixteenth century, and Holland became the most prominent slave-trading nation during the sugar boom of the seventeenth century. The English also entered the trade in the sixteenth century.

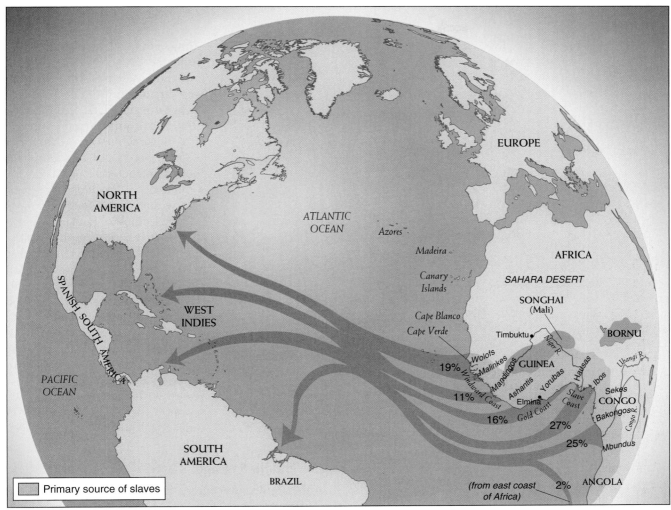

The African Slave Trade   The enslaved men, women, and children transported to the Americas came from West Africa, the majority from the lower Niger River (called the Slave Coast) and the region of the Congo and Angola.

Although the Portugese established a colony in Angola, for the most part the European presence in Africa was confined to coastal outposts. By the early eighteenth century, more than two dozen trading forts dotted the 220 miles of the Gold Coast alone. As the slave trade peaked in the middle of the eighteenth century, however, the forts of trading companies gave way to independent European and American traders who set up operations with the cooperation of local headmen or chiefs. This informal manner of trading offered opportunities for small operators, such as the New England slavers who entered the trade in the early eighteenth century. Many great New England fortunes were built from profits in the slave trade.

The Shock of Enslavement

The slave trade was a collaboration between European or American and African traders. Dependent on the favor of local rulers, many colonial slave traders lived permanently in coastal forts and married African women, reinforcing their commercial ties with family relations. In many areas a mixed-ancestry group became prominent in the coastal slave trade. Continuing the practice of the Portuguese, the grim business of slave raiding was left to the Africans themselves. Slaves were not at all reticent about condemning the participation of their fellow Africans. "I must own to the shame of my own countrymen," wrote Ottobah Cugoano, who was sold into slavery in the mid-eighteenth century, "that I was first kidnapped and betrayed by those of my own complexion."

Most Africans were enslaved through warfare. Sometimes large armies launched massive attacks, burning whole towns and taking hundreds of prisoners. More common were smaller raids in which a group of armed men attacked at nightfall, seized everyone

A slave coffle in an eighteenth-century print. As the demand for slaves increased, raids extended deeper and deeper into the African interior. Tied together with forked logs or bark rope, men, women, and children were marched hundreds of miles toward the coast, where their African captors traded them to Europeans.

SOURCE: North Wind Picture Archives.

the possibility of collective resistance, traders split up families and ethnic groups. Captains carefully inspected each man and woman, and those selected for transport were branded on the back or buttocks with the mark of the buyer. Olaudah Equiano remembered that "those white men with horrible looks, red faces, and long hair, looked and acted . . . in so savage a manner; . . . I had never seen among any people such instances of brutal cruelty." Equiano's narrative, written during the 1780s, after he had secured his freedom, is one of the few that provide an African account of enslavement. He and his fellow captives became convinced that they "had got into a world of bad spirits" and were about to be eaten by cannibals. A French trader wrote that many prisoners were "positively prepossessed with the opinion that we transport them into our country in order to kill and eat them."

within reach, then escaped with their captives. Kidnapping, called "panyaring" in the jargon of the slave trade, was also common.

As the demand for slaves increased in the eighteenth century with the expansion of the plantation system in the Americas, these raids extended deeper and deeper into the African interior. The march to the coast was filled with terrors. One account describes a two-month trip in which many captives died of hunger, thirst, or exhaustion, several attempted suicide, and the whole party was forced to hide to avoid being seized by a rival band of raiders. The captives finally arrived on the coast, where they were sold to an American vessel bound for South Carolina.

Enslavement was an unparalleled shock. Venture Smith, an African born in Guinea in 1729, was eight years old when he was captured. After many years in North American slavery, he still vividly recalled the attack on his village, the torture and murder of his father, and the long march of his people to the coast. "The shocking scene is to this day fresh in my mind," he wrote, "and I have often been overcome while thinking on it."

On the coast, European traders and African raiders assembled their captives. Prisoners waited in dark dungeons or in open pens called "barracoons." To lessen

The Middle Passage

In the eighteenth century, English sailors christened the voyage of slave ships as the "Middle Passage," the middle part of a trading triangle from England to Africa to America and back to England. From coastal forts and barracoons, crews rowed small groups of slaves out to the waiting ships and packed them into shelves below deck only six feet long by two and a half feet high. "Rammed like herring in a barrel," wrote one observer, slaves were "chained to each other hand and foot, and stowed so close, that they were not allowed above a foot and a half for each in breadth." People were forced to sleep "spoon fashion," and the tossing of the ship knocked them about so violently that the skin over their elbows sometimes was worn to the bone from scraping on the planks. "It was more than a week after I left the ship before I could straighten my limbs," one former slave later remembered. One ship designed to carry 450 slaves regularly crossed the Atlantic tightly packed with more than 600.

Their holds filled with human cargo, the ships headed toward Cape Verde to catch the trade winds blowing toward America. A favorable voyage from Senegambia to Barbados might be accomplished in as little as three weeks, but a ship from Guinea or Angola becalmed in the doldrums or driven back by storms might take as much as three months.

The voyage was marked by a daily routine. In the morning the crew opened the hatch and brought the captives on deck, attaching their leg irons to a great chain running the length of the bulwarks. After a breakfast of beans came a ritual known as "dancing the slave." While an African thumped an upturned kettle or plucked a banjo, the crew commanded men and women to jump up and down in a bizarre session of exercise. A day spent chained on deck was concluded by a second bland meal and then the stowing away. During the night, according to one seaman, there issued from below "a howling melancholy noise, expressive of extreme anguish." Down in the hold, the groans of the dying, the shrieks of women and children, and the suffocating heat and stench were, in the words of Olaudah Equiano, "a scene of horror almost inconceivable."

Among the worst of the horrors was the absence of adequate sanitation. There were "necessary tubs" set below deck, but Africans, "endeavoring to get to them, tumble over their companions," as one eighteenth-century ship's surgeon wrote. "And as the necessities of nature are not to be resisted, they ease themselves as they lie." Efficient captains ordered crews to scrape and swab the holds daily, but so sickening was the task that on many ships it was rarely performed and Africans were left to wallow in their urine and feces. When first taken below deck, the boy Equiano remembered, "I received such a salutation in my nostrils as I had never experienced in my life," and "became so sick and low that I was not able to eat." Atlantic sailors said you could "smell a slaver five miles down wind." Many captives sickened and died in these conditions. Many others contracted dysentery, known as the "flux." Frequent shipboard epidemics of smallpox, measles, and yellow fever added to the misery. The dying continued even as the ships anchored at their destinations. Historians estimate that during the Middle Passage of the eighteenth century one in every six Africans perished.

The unwilling voyagers offered plenty of resistance. As long as ships were still within sight of the African coast, hope remained alive and the danger of revolt was great. One historian has found references to fifty-five slave revolts on British and American ships from 1699 to 1845. Once on the open sea, however, the captives' resistance took more desperate form. The sight of the disappearing coast of Africa "left me abandoned to despair," wrote Equiano. "I now saw myself deprived of all chance of returning to my native country, or even the least glimpse of hope of gaining the shore." He witnessed several Africans jump overboard and drown, "and I believe many more would very soon have done the same if they had not been prevented by the ship's crew." Captains took the precaution of spreading netting along the sides of their ships. "Could I have got over the nettings," Equiano declared, "I would have jumped over the side."

Arrival in the New World

As the ship approached its destination the crew prepared the human cargo for market. All but the most rebellious were freed from their chains and allowed to wash themselves and move about the deck. Captains did what they could to get their Africans into presentable condition. To impress buyers, slavers might parade Africans off the ship to the tune of an accordion or the beat of a drum. But the toll of the Middle Passage was difficult to disguise. One observer described a disembarking group as "walking skeletons covered over with a piece of tanned leather."

Some cargoes were destined for a single wealthy planter, or consigned to a merchant who sold the captives in return for a commission; in other cases the captain himself was responsible. Buyers painstakingly examined the Africans, who once again suffered the indignity of probing eyes and poking fingers. This caused "much dread and trembling among us," wrote Equiano, and "bitter cries." In ports such as Charleston, sales were generally made by auction, or by a cruel method known as the scramble—fixed prices set in advance, the Africans driven into a corral, and on cue the buyers rushing among them, grabbing their pick. The noise, clamor, and eagerness of the buyers, Equiano remembered, renewed all the terrible apprehensions of the Africans. "In this manner, without scruple, are relations and friends separated, most of them never to see each other again." Bought by a Virginian, Equiano was taken to an isolated tobacco plantation where he found himself unable to communicate with any of his fellow slaves, who came from other ethnic groups.

Political and Economic Effects on Africa

Africa began the sixteenth century with genuine independence. But as surely as Europe and America grew stronger as a result of the trade and the labor of slaves, so Africa grew weaker by their loss. In the short term, slave-trading kingdoms on the coast increased their power at the expense of interior states. But these coastal states found that the slave trade was a viper that could easily strike back at them. "Merchants daily seize our own subjects, sons of the land and sons of our noblemen, they grab them and cause them to be sold," King Dom Affonso of the Kongo wrote to the Portuguese monarch in the sixteenth century. "And so great, Sir, is their corruption and licentiousness that our country is being utterly depopulated."

More serious still, however, than the loss of millions of men and women over the centuries was the long-term stagnation of the West African economy. Labor was drawn away from farming and other productive activities, and imported consumer goods such as textiles and metal wares stifled local manufacturing. African traders were expert at driving a hard bargain for slaves, but even when they appeared to get the best of the exchange, the ultimate advantage lay with the Europeans, who received wealth-producing workers in return for mere consumer goods.

For every man or woman taken captive, at least another died in the chronic slave raiding. Many of the new West African states became little more than machines for supplying captives to European traders, and a "gun-slave cycle" pushed neighboring kingdoms into a destructive arms race. The resulting political and cultural demoralization prepared the way for the European conquest of Africa in the nineteenth century.

THE DEVELOPMENT OF NORTH AMERICAN SLAVE SOCIETIES

New World slavery was nearly two centuries old before it became an important system of labor in North America. There were slaves in each of the British colonies during the seventeenth century, but in 1700 slaves accounted for only 11 percent of the colonial population. During the eighteenth century slavery greatly expanded, and by 1770 Africans and African Americans in British North America numbered 460,000, or more than 20 percent of the colonial population.

Slavery Comes to North America

The first Africans in Virginia arrived in 1619. But because slaves generally cost twice as much as indentured servants, yet had the same appallingly short life expectancy, they offered planters little economic benefit. Consequently, over the next several decades planters in the Chesapeake region employed far more indentured servants than slaves. Until the 1670s the Chesapeake was what historians term a *society with slaves*, a society in which slavery was one form of labor among several.

In the last quarter of the seventeenth century, however, a number of developments encouraged the transformation of the Chesapeake from a society with slaves into a *slave society*, a society in which slavery was the dominant form of labor. In the aftermath of Bacon's Rebellion, planters consolidated their control of the Virginia colony. Because people were living longer, possibly the result of being better fed and more resistant to disease, more servants were surviving their indentures, and such a population could be troublesome. But these improvements in living conditions also affected Africans, increasing their rates of survival and allowing planters to amortize the pur-

chase price of slaves over a considerably longer span. Also contributing to the transition was the development of better opportunities for European immigrants in colonies such as Pennsylvania, and the beginning of direct shipments of slaves from West Africa to the North American mainland by the English Royal African Company. Thus, the workforce of indentured servants was replaced by a workforce of slaves.

As the proportions of slaves in the colonial population rose, colonists wrote slavery into law, a process best observed in the case of Virginia. In 1662 colonial officials declared that children inherited the status of their slave mothers; five years later they added that baptism as a Christian could no longer alter conditions of servitude. Two important avenues to freedom were thus closed. The colony then placed life-threatening violence in the hands of masters, declaring in 1669 that the death of a slave during punishment "shall not be accounted felony." Such regulations accumulated piecemeal until 1705, when Virginia gathered them into a comprehensive slave code that became a model for other colonies.

Thus, the institution of slavery was strengthened just as the Atlantic slave trade reached flood tide in the eighteenth century. During that century's first decade, more Africans were imported into North America than the total number for the previous century. The English colonies were primed for an unprecedented growth of plantation slavery.

The Tobacco Colonies

During the eighteenth century the European demand for tobacco increased more than tenfold, and it was supplied largely by increased production in the Chesapeake. Tobacco was far and away the single most important commodity produced in eighteenth-century North America, accounting for more than a quarter of the value of all colonial exports.

The expansion of tobacco production could not have taken place without a corresponding growth in the size of the slave labor force. Unlike sugar, tobacco did not require large plantations and could be produced successfully on small farms. But it was a crop that demanded a great deal of hand labor and close attention. As tobacco farming grew, slaveholding became widespread. By 1770 more than a quarter million slaves labored in the colonies of the Upper South (Maryland, Virginia, and North Carolina), and because of the exploding market for tobacco, their numbers were expanding at about double the rate of the general population.

Shipments from Africa accounted for part of the growth of the slave population. In the Caribbean and Brazil, where profits from sugar were high, many sugar planters chose to work their slaves to death, replenishing them with a constant stream of new arrivals, mostly men, from Africa. In Virginia, however, lower rates of profit caused tobacco planters to pay more attention to the health of their labor force, establishing work routines that were not quite so deadly. Moreover, food supplies were more plentiful in North America, which made the Chesapeake populations of Africans more resistant to disease. By the 1730s the slave population of the Chesapeake had become the first in the Western Hemisphere to achieve self-sustained population growth. By the 1750s, about 80 percent of Chesapeake slaves were "country-born."

An Overseer Doing His Duty, a watercolor sketch made by Benjamin Henry Latrobe during a trip to Virginia in 1798. The majority of masters in the tobacco region owned only one or two slaves and worked with them in the fields. In his portrayal of this overseer, relaxing as he supervises his workers, Latrobe clearly expressed his disgust for slavery.

SOURCE: Benjamin Harry Latrobe, *An Overseer Doing His Duty*. Watercolor on paper. Collection of the Maryland Historical Society, Baltimore.

The Lower South

The Chesapeake did not become a slave society until almost a century after its founding. But in South Carolina settlement and slavery went hand in hand, and the colony was a slave society from the beginning. The most valuable part of the early Carolina economy was the Indian slave trade. Practicing a strategy of divide and conquer, using Indian tribes to fight one another, Carolinians enslaved tens of thousands of Indians before the 1730s, shipping many to slave markets in the Caribbean, employing others raising cattle or felling timber.

By 1715, however, planter preference had turned toward African rather than Indian slaves. Rice production was rapidly becoming the most dynamic sector of the South Carolina economy, and with their experience in agriculture West Africans made much better rice workers than Indians. Another important crop was added in the 1740s, when a young South Carolina woman named Elizabeth Lucas Pinckney successfully adapted West Indian indigo to the low-country climate. The indigo plant, native to India, produced a deep blue dye important in textile manufacture. Rice grew in the lowlands, but indigo could be cultivated on high ground, and with different seasonal growing patterns, planters were able to harmonize their production. Rice and indigo were two of the most valuable commodities exported from the mainland colonies of North America.

The boom in these two crops depended on the growth of African slavery. Before the international slave trade to the United States was ended in 1808, at least 100,000 had arrived in South Carolina. It is estimated that one of every five ancestors of today's African Americans passed through Charleston on the way to the rice fields.

By the 1740s, many of the arriving Africans were being taken to Georgia, a colony created by an act of the English Parliament in 1732. Its leader, James Edward Oglethorpe, hoped to establish a buffer against Spanish invasion from Florida and make it a haven for poor British farmers who could then sell their products in the markets of South Carolina. Under Oglethorpe's influence, Parliament agreed to prohibit slavery in Georgia. Soon, however, Georgia's coastal regions were being colonized by South Carolina planters with their slaves. In 1752, Oglethorpe and Georgia's trustees abandoned their experiment, and the colony was opened to slavery under royal authority. The Georgia coast had already become an extension of the Carolina low-country slave system.

By 1770 there were nearly 90,000 African Americans in the Lower South, about 80 percent of the coastal population of South Carolina and Georgia. In the words of one eighteenth-century observer, "Carolina looks more like a negro country than like a country settled by white people." The African American communities of the Lower South achieved self-sustained growth in the middle of the eighteenth century, a generation later than those in the Chesapeake.

Slavery in the Spanish Colonies

Slavery was basic to the Spanish colonial labor system, yet doubts about the enslavement of Africans were raised by both church and crown. The papacy denounced slavery many times as a violation of Christian principles. But the institution of slavery remained intact, and later in the eighteenth century, when sugar production expanded in Cuba, the slave system there was as brutal as any in the history of the Americas.

The character of slavery varied with local conditions. One of the most benign forms operated in Florida. In 1699 the Spanish declared Florida a refuge for escaped slaves from the British colonies, offering free land to fugitives who would help defend their colony. Over the next half-century, refugee Indians and fugitive Africans established many communities in the countryside surrounding St. Augustine.

In New Mexico, the Spanish depended on Indian slavery. In the sixteenth century the colonial governor sent Indian slaves to the mines of Mexico. The enslavement of Indians was one of the causes of the Pueblo Revolt (see Chapter 3). During the eighteenth century, the Spanish were much more cautious in their treatment of the Pueblos, who were officially considered Catholics. But they captured and enslaved "infidel Indians" such as the Apaches or nomads from the Great Plains, using them as house servants and fieldworkers.

French Louisiana

Slavery was also important in Louisiana, the colony founded by the French in the lower Mississippi Valley in the early eighteenth century. The French Company of the Indies imported some 6,000 African slaves, and planters invested in tobacco and indigo plantations on the Mississippi River in the country of the Natchez Indians. But in 1629, the Natchez and the slaves together rose in an armed uprising, the Natchez Rebellion, that took the lives of more than 200 French settlers, 10 percent of the population. Although colonial authorities were able to put down the rebellion, the Louisiana French pulled back from a total commitment to slavery.

After the Natchez Rebellion, Louisiana's economy grew more diversified. Several thousand French colonists established farms and plantations on the Gulf Coast and in a narrow strip of settlement along the Mississippi River. African slaves amounted to no more than a third of the colonial population of 10,000. It was not until the end of the eighteenth century that the colony of Louisiana became an important North American slave society.

Slavery in the North

Although none of the northern colonies could be characterized as a slave society, slavery was an important form of labor in many areas. Over the course of the eighteenth century it grew increasingly significant in the commercial farming regions of southeast Pennsylvania, central New Jersey, and Long Island, where slaves made up about 10 percent of the rural residents. In the vicinity of Newport, Rhode Island, the proportion of slaves in the population reached nearly 25 percent. Elsewhere in the New England countryside slavery was relatively uncommon.

It was widespread in all the port cities, however, including Boston. Slave ownership was nearly universal among the wealthy and ordinary among craftsmen and professionals. By 1750 slaves and small free black populations made up 15 to 20 percent of the residents of Boston, New York City, and Philadelphia.

The Quakers of Pennsylvania and New Jersey, many of whom kept slaves, were the first colonists to voice antislavery sentiment. In *Considerations on the Keeping of Negroes* (1754), John Woolman urged his readers to imagine themselves in the place of the African people. Suppose, he wrote,

> that our ancestors and we had been exposed to constant servitude in the more servile and inferior employments of life; that we had been destitute of the help of reading and good company; that amongst ourselves we had had few wise and pious instructors; that the religious amongst our superiors seldom took notice of us; that while others in ease had plentifully heaped up the fruit of our labour, we had received barely enough to relieve nature, and being wholly at the command of others had generally been treated as a contemptible, ignorant part of mankind. Should we, in that case, be less abject than they now are?

In 1758 the Philadelphia Friends Meeting voted to condemn slavery and urged masters to voluntarily free their slaves. It was not until the Revolution, however, that antislavery attitudes became more widespread in the colonies.

AFRICAN TO AFRICAN AMERICAN

The majority of Africans transported to North America arrived during the eighteenth century. They were met by a rapidly growing population of country-born slaves, or "creoles" (from the French *créole* and Spanish *criollo*, meaning "born" or "raised"), a term first used by slaves in Brazil to distinguish their children, born in the New

World, from newly arrived Africans. The perspective of creoles was shaped by their having grown up under slavery, and that perspective helped them to determine which elements of African culture they would incorporate into the emerging culture of the African American community. That community was formed out of the relationship between creoles and Africans, and between slaves and their European masters.

The Daily Life of Slaves

Because slaves formed the overwhelming majority of the labor force that made the plantation colonies so profitable, it is fair to say that Africans built the South. As an agricultural people, Africans, both women and men, were accustomed to the routines of rural labor, and this was put to use on the plantations. Most Africans were field hands, and even domestic servants labored in the fields when necessary.

Masters provided their workers with rude clothing, sufficient in the summer but nearly always inadequate in the winter. Increasingly the plantations were supplied by cheap goods from the new industrial looms of England. Stiff shoes were a necessity in the cold months, but they so cramped the feet that everyone looked forward to shedding them in the spring and going barefoot all summer and fall. Hand-me-down clothes from the master's family offered slaves an opportunity to brighten their costumes, and many of them dressed in a variety of styles and colors. Similarly, they relieved the monotony of their rations of corn and pork with vegetables from their small gardens, game and fish from field and stream, and wild plant foods from the forests.

On small plantations and farms, which were typical in the tobacco country of the Chesapeake, Africans might work side by side with their owners and, depending on the character of the master, might enjoy a standard of living not too different from those of other family members. The work was more demanding and living conditions less sustaining on the great rice and indigo plantations of the Lower South, where slaves usually lived separately from the master in their own quarters. But large plantations, with large numbers of slaves, created the concentration of population necessary for the emergence of African American communities and African American culture.

Families and Communities

The family was the most important institution for the development of African American community and culture, but slave codes did not provide for legal slave marriages, for that would have contradicted the master's freedom to dispose of his property as he saw fit.

"The endearing ties of husband and wife are strangers to us," declared the Massachusetts slaves who petitioned for their freedom in 1774, "for we are no longer man and wife than our masters or mistresses think proper." Despite the barriers, however, during the eighteenth century slaves in both the Chesapeake and the Lower South created the families that were essential for the development of African American culture.

On large plantations throughout the southern colonies, travelers found Africans living in family households. In the Lower South, where there were greater concentrations of slaves on the great rice plantations, husbands and wives often lived together in the slave quarters, and this was clearly the ideal. On the smaller plantations of the Upper South, men often married women from neighboring farms, and with the permission of both owners visited their families in the evenings or on Sundays.

Emotional ties to particular places, connections between the generations, and relations of kinship and friendship linking neighboring plantations and farms were the foundation stones of African American community life. Kinship was especially important. African American parents encouraged their children to use family terms in addressing unrelated persons: "auntie" or "uncle" became a respectful way of addressing older men and women, "brother" and "sister" affectionate terms for agemates. Fictive kinship may have been one of the first devices enslaved Africans used to humanize the world of slavery. During the Middle Passage, it was common for children to call their elders "aunt" and "uncle," for adults to address all children as "son" or "daughter."

African American Culture

The eighteenth century was the formative period in the development of the African American community, for it was then that the high birthrate and the growing numbers of country-born provided the necessary stability for the evolution of culture. During this period, men and women from dozens of African ethnic groups molded themselves into a new people. Distinctive patterns in music and dance, religion, and oral tradition illustrate the resilience of the human spirit under bondage as well as the successful struggle of African Americans to create a spiritually sustaining culture of their own.

Eighteenth-century masters were reluctant to allow their slaves to become Christians, fearing that baptism would open the way to claims of freedom or give Africans dangerous notions of universal brotherhood and equality with masters. One frustrated missionary was told by a planter that a slave was "ten times worse when a Christian than in his state of paganism." The majority of black southerners before the American

This eighteenth-century painting by an anonymous artist depicts a celebration in the slave quarters on a South Carolina plantation. One planter's description of a slave dance seems to fit this scene: the men leading the women in "a slow shuffling gait, edging along by some unseen exertion of the feet, from one side to the other— sometimes courtesying down and remaining in that posture while the edging motion from one side to the other continued." The woman, he wrote, "always carried a handkerchief held at arm's length, which was waved in a graceful motion to and fro as she moved."

SOURCE: Abby Aldrich Rockefeller Folk Art Museum, Williamsburg, VA.

the Ibos, as "a nation of dancers, musicians, and poets." Thomas Jefferson, raised on a Virginia plantation, wrote that blacks "are more generally gifted than the whites, with accurate ears for tune and time." Many Africans were accomplished players of stringed instruments and drums, and their style featured improvisation and rhythmic complexity, elements that would become prominent in African American music. In America, slaves recreated African instruments, as in the case of the banjo, and mastered the art of the European violin and guitar. Fearing that slaves might communicate by code, authorities often outlawed drums. But using bones, spoons, or sticks, or simply "patting juba" (slapping their thighs), slaves produced elaborate multi-rhythmic patterns.

One of the most important developments of the eighteenth century was the invention of an African American language. An English traveler during the 1770s complained he could not understand Virginia slaves, who spoke "a mixed dialect between the Guinea and English." But such a language made it possible for country-born and "saltwater" Africans to communicate. The two most important dialects were Gullah and Geechee, named after two of the African peoples most prominent in the Carolina and Georgia low country, the Golas and Gizzis of the Windward Coast. These creole languages were a transitional phenomenon, gradually giving way to distinctive forms of black English, although in certain isolated areas, such as the sea islands of the Carolinas and Georgia, they persisted into the twentieth century.

Revolution practiced some form of African religion. Large numbers of African Americans were not converted to Christianity until the Great Awakening, which swept across the South after the 1760s (see Chapter 5).

One of the most crucial areas of religious practice concerned the rituals of death and burial. In their separate graveyards, African Americans often decorated graves with shells and pottery, an old African custom. African Americans generally believed that the spirits of their dead would return to Africa. The burial ceremony was often held at night to keep it secret from masters, who objected to the continuation of African traditions. The deceased was laid out, and around the body men and women would move counterclockwise in a slow dance step while singing ancestral songs. The pace gradually increased, finally reaching a frenzied but joyful conclusion. As slaves from different backgrounds joined together in the circle, they were beginning the process of cultural unification.

Music and dance may have formed the foundation of African American culture, coming even before a common language. Many eighteenth-century observers commented on the musical and rhythmic gifts of Africans. Olaudah Equiano remembered his people,

The Africanization of the South

The African American community often looked to recently arrived Africans for religious leadership and medical magic. Throughout the South, many whites had as much faith in slave conjurers and herb doctors as the slaves themselves did, and slaves won fame for their healing powers. This was one of many ways in which white and black Southerners came to share a common culture. Acculturation was by no means a one-way street; English men and women in the South were also being Africanized.

Slaves worked in the kitchens of their masters, and thus introduced an African style of cooking into colonial diets already transformed by the addition of Indian crops. African American culinary arts are responsible for such southern culinary specialties perennials as barbecue, fried chicken, black-eyed peas, and collard greens. And the liberal African use of red pepper, sesame seeds, and other sharp flavors established the southern preference for highly spiced foods. In Louisiana a combination of African, French, and Indian elements produced a distinguished American regional cuisine, exemplified by gumbos (soups) and jambalayas (stews).

Mutual acculturation is also evident in many aspects of material culture. Southern basket weaving used Indian techniques and African designs. Wood-carving often featured African motifs. African architectural designs featuring high, peaked roofs (to drain off the heat) and broad, shady porches gradually became part of a distinctive southern style. The West African iron-working tradition was evident throughout the South, especially in the ornamentation of the homes of Charleston and New Orleans.

Even more important were less tangible aspects of culture. Slave mothers nursed white children as well as their own. As one English observer wrote, "each child has its [black] Momma, whose gestures and accent it will necessarily copy, for children, we all know, are imitative beings." In this way many Africanisms passed into the English language of the South: goober (peanut), yam, banjo, okay, tote, buddy. Some linguists have argued that the southern "drawl," evident among both black and white speakers, derived from the incorporation of African intonations of words and syllables.

Violence and Resistance

Slavery was a system based on the use of force and violence. Fear underlay the daily life of both masters and slaves. Owners could be humane, but slaves had no guarantees of benevolent treatment, and the kindest master could turn cruel. Even the most cultured plantation owners of the eighteenth century thought nothing about floggings of fifty or seventy-five lashes. "Der prayer was answered," sang the Africans of South Carolina, "wid de song of a whip." Although the typical planter punished slaves with extra work, public humiliation, or solitary confinement, the threat of the lash was omnipresent. There were sadistic masters who stabbed, burned, maimed, mutilated, raped, or castrated their slaves.

Yet African Americans demonstrated a resisting spirit. In their day-to-day existence they often refused to cooperate: they malingered, they mistreated tools and animals, they destroyed the master's property. Flight was also an option, and judging from the advertisements placed by masters in colonial newspapers, even the most trusted Africans ran away.

Runaways sometimes collected together in communities called "maroons," from the Spanish *cimarron*, meaning "wild and untamed." The African communities in Spanish Florida were often called maroons. Indeed, as a whole these mixed African and Creek Indian peoples in Florida called themselves Seminoles, a name deriving from their pronunciation of cimarron. Maroons were also found in the backcountry of the Lower South, and although they were less common in the Upper South, a number of fugitive communities existed in the Great Dismal Swamp between Virginia and North Carolina. In the 1730s, a group of escaped Africans built a community of grass houses and set up a tribal government there, but they were soon dispersed by the authorities.

The most direct form of resistance was revolt. The first notable slave uprising of the colonial era occurred in New York City in 1712. Taking an oath of secrecy, twenty-three Africans vowed revenge for what they called the "hard usage" of their masters. They armed themselves with guns, swords, daggers, and hatchets, killed nine colonists, and burned several buildings before being surrounded by the militia. Six of the conspirators committed suicide rather than surrender. Those captured were hanged, burned at the stake, or broken on the wheel. In 1741 New York authorities uncovered what they thought was another conspiracy. Thirteen black leaders were burned alive, eighteen hanged, and eighty sold and shipped off to the West Indies. A family of colonists and a Catholic priest, accused of providing weapons, were also executed.

There were also isolated but violent uprisings in the Lower South, where slaves were a majority of the population, in 1704, 1720, and 1730. In 1738 a series of violent revolts broke out throughout South Carolina and Georgia. Then in 1739, the largest slave rebellion of the colonial period took place when a group of twenty recently arrived Angolans sacked the armory in Stono, South Carolina. They armed themselves and began a march toward Florida and freedom. Beating drums to attract other slaves to their cause, they grew to nearly one hundred. They plundered a number of planters' homes along the way and killed some thirty colonists. Pausing in a field to celebrate their victory with dance and song, they were overtaken by the militia and destroyed in a pitched battle. That same year there was an uprising in Georgia. Another took place in South Carolina the following year. Attributing these revolts to the influence of newly arrived Africans, colonial officials shut off the slave trade through Charleston for the next ten years.

Wherever masters held slaves, fears of uprisings persisted. But compared with such slave colonies as

Jamaica, Guiana, or Brazil, there were few slave revolts in North America. The conditions favoring revolt— large African majorities, brutal exploitation with correspondingly low survival rates, little acculturation, and geographic isolation—prevailed only in some areas of the Lower South. Indeed, the very success of African Americans in British North America at establishing families, communities, and a culture of their own inevitably made them less likely to take the risks that rebellions required.

SLAVERY AND THE ECONOMICS OF EMPIRE

Slavery contributed enormously to the economic growth and development of Europe during the colonial era, and it was an important factor in Great Britain, just before the Industrial Revolution of the eighteenth century. Slavery was the most dynamic force in the Atlantic economy during that century, creating the conditions for industrialization. But because slave-owning colonists single-mindedly committed their resources to the expansion and extension of the plantation system, they derived very little benefit from the economic diversification that characterized industrialization.

Slavery the Mainspring

The slave colonies—the sugar islands of the West Indies and the colonies of the South—accounted for 95 percent of exports from the Americas to Great Britain from 1714 to 1773. Although approximately half of all Great Britain's American colonists lived in New England and the mid-Atlantic, the colonies in those regions contributed less than 5 percent of total exports during this period. Moreover, there was the prime economic importance of the slave trade itself, which one economist of the day described as the "foundation" of the British economy, "the mainspring of the machine which sets every wheel in motion." The labor of African slaves was largely responsible for the economic success of the British Empire in the Americas.

Slavery greatly contributed to the economic development of Great Britain in three principal ways. First, slavery provided an enormous stimulus to the growth of manufacturing by creating a huge colonial market for exports. Second, slavery generated enormous profits that became a source of investment in the economy. Economic historians estimate that annual profits during the eighteenth century averaged 15 percent of invested capital in the slave trade, 10 percent in plantation agriculture.

The profits of the slave trade and slave production contributed greatly to the accumulation of capital. This capital funded the first modern banks and insurance companies, and eventually found its way into a wide range of economic activities. Merchant capitalists were prominent investors in the expansion of the merchant marine, the improvement of harbors, the construction of canals.

The multiplier effects of these activities are best seen in the growth of English ports such as Liverpool and Bristol. There the African and American trades provided employment for ships' crews, dockmen, construction workers, traders, shopkeepers, lawyers, clerks, factory workers, and officials of all ranks down to the humblest employees of the custom house. It was said of Bristol that "there is not a brick in the city but what is cemented with the blood of a slave."

Third, and finally, slavery contributed to the economic development of Great Britain by supplying

Triangular Trade across the Atlantic The pattern of commerce among Europe, Africa, and the Americas became known as the "Triangular Trade." Sailors called the voyage of slave ships from Africa to America the "Middle Passage" because it formed the crucial middle section of this trading triangle.

OVERVIEW

THE COLONIAL WARS

King William's War	1689–97	France and England battle on the northern frontiers of New England and New York.
Queen Anne's War	1702–13	England fights France and Spain in the Caribbean and on the northern frontier of New France. Part of the European conflict known as the War of the Spanish Succession.
War of Jenkins's Ear	1739–43	Great Britain versus Spain in the Caribbean and Georgia. Part of the European conflict known as the War of the Austrian Succession.
King George's War	1744–48	Great Britain and France fight in Acadia and Nova Scotia; the second American round of the War of the Austrian Succession.
French and Indian War	1754–63	Last of the great colonial wars pitting Great Britain against France and Spain. Known in Europe as the Seven Years War.

the raw cotton essential to the Industrial Revolution. In 1787 slave plantations in the Caribbean supplied 69 percent of the raw cotton for British mills. The insatiable demand for cotton led to the development of the cotton gin and the rise of cotton plantations in the United States (see Chapter 11).

The Politics of Mercantilism

When imperial officials argued that colonies existed solely for the benefit of the mother country, they had in mind principally the great wealth produced by slavery. To ensure that this wealth benefited their states, European imperial powers created a system of regulations that became known as "mercantilism." The essence of mercantilist policy was the political control of the economy by the state. First advanced in France in the seventeenth century under the empire of Louis XIV, in the eighteenth century mercantilist politics were most successfully applied by Great Britain. The monarchy and Parliament established a uniform national monetary system, regulated wages, encouraged agriculture and manufacturing, and erected tariff barriers to protect themselves from foreign competition. England also sought to organize and control colonial trade to the maximum advantage of its own shippers, merchants, manufacturers, and bureaucrats.

The mercantilists viewed the economy as a "zero-sum" game, in which total economic gains were equal to total losses. Profits were thought to result from successful speculation, crafty dealing, or simple plunder—all forms of stealing wealth. The institution of slavery confirmed the theory, for slavery was nothing more than a highly developed system by which some people stole

the labor of others. The essence of the competition between states, the mercantilists argued, was the struggle to acquire and hoard the fixed amount of wealth that existed in the world. The nation that accumulated the largest treasure of gold and silver specie would be the most powerful.

Wars for Empire

The mercantilist era was, thus, a period of intense and violent competition among European states. Wars usually arose out of Old World issues, spilling over into the New World, but they also originated in conflicts over the colonies themselves.

Colonial wars in the southern region had everything to do with slavery. The first fighting of the eighteenth century took place during Queen Anne's War (known in Europe as the War of the Spanish Succession), a conflict that pitted Great Britain and its allies against France and Spain. In 1702 troops from South Carolina invaded Florida, plundering and burning St. Augustine in an attempt to destroy the refuge for fugitive slaves there. A combined French and Spanish fleet took revenge in 1706 by bombarding Charleston. The British finally prevailed, and in 1713, as part of the Peace of Utrecht, Spain ceded to the English the exclusive lucrative right to supply slaves to its American colonies.

The entrance of British slavers into Spanish ports also provided an opportunity for illicit trade, and sporadic fighting between the two empires broke out over this issue a number of times during the next two decades.

In the northern region, the principal focus of this imperial struggle was control of the Indian trade. In

1704, during Queen Anne's War, the French and their Algonquian Indian allies raided New England frontier towns, such as Deerfield, Massachusetts, dragging men, women, and children into captivity in Canada. In turn, the English mounted a series of expeditions against the strategic French fortress of Port Royal in Acadia, which they captured in 1710. At the war's conclusion in 1713, France was forced to cede Acadia, Newfoundland, and Hudson's Bay to Great Britain in exchange for guarantees of security for the French-speaking residents of those provinces. Nearly thirty years of peace followed, but from 1744 to 1748 England again battled France in King George's War (known in Europe as the War of the Austrian Succession). The French attacked the British in Nova Scotia. Indian and Canadian raids again devastated the border towns of New England and New York, and hundreds of British subjects were killed or captured.

British Colonial Regulation

Mercantilists used means other than war to win the wealth of the world. The British monarchy, for example, chartered the East India Company, the Hudson's Bay Company, and the Royal African Company as trading monopolies in their respective regions.

English manufacturers complained that merchant-dominated trading monopolies too frequently carried foreign (particularly Dutch) products to colonial markets, ignoring English domestic industry. Reacting to these charges, between 1651 and 1696 Parliament passed the Navigation Acts, which created the legal and institutional structure of Britain's eighteenth-century colonial system. The acts defined the colonies as both suppliers of raw materials and as markets for English manufactured goods. Merchants from other nations were expressly forbidden to trade in the colonies, and all trade had to be conducted in ships built in England or the British colonies themselves.

The regulations specified a list of colonial products that could be shipped only to England. These included the products of the southern slave colonies (sugar, molasses, rum, tobacco, rice, and indigo), those of the northern Indian trade (furs and skins), and those essential for supplying the shipping industry (pine masts, tar, pitch, resin, and turpentine). The bulk of these products were not destined for English consumption; at great profit they were reexported elsewhere.

England also placed limitations on colonial enterprises that might compete with those at home. A series of enactments—including the Wool Act of 1699, the Hat Act of 1732, and the Iron Act of 1750—forbade the manufacture of those products. Moreover, colonial assemblies were forbidden to impose tariffs on English imports as a way to protect colonial industries. Banking was disallowed, local coinage prohibited, and the export of coin from England forbidden. Badly in need of a circulating monetary medium, Massachusetts illegally minted copper coin, and several colonies issued paper currency, forcing Parliament to explicitly legislate against the practice. The colonists depended mostly on "commodity money" (furs, skins, or hogsheads of tobacco) and the circulation of foreign currency. Official rates of exchange between commodity money, colonial paper, foreign currency, and English pounds allowed this chaotic system to operate without too much difficulty.

As the trade in colonial products increased, the British came to agree that it made little sense to tamper with such a prosperous system. Prime Minister Robert Walpole pursued a policy later characterized as one of "salutory neglect." Any colonial rules and regulations deemed contrary to good business practice were simply ignored and not enforced. Between 1700 and 1760 the quantity of goods exported from the colonies to the mother country rose 165 percent, while imports from Britain to North America increased by more than 400 percent. In part because of the lax enforcement, but mostly because the system operated to the profit of colonial merchants, colonists complained very little about the operation of the mercantilist system before the 1760s.

The Colonial Economy

Despite the seemingly harsh mercantilist regulations, the economic system operated to the benefit of planters, merchants, and white colonists in general. Southern slave owners made healthy profits on the sale of their commodities. They enjoyed a protected market in which competing goods from outside the empire were heavily taxed. Planters found themselves with steadily increasing purchasing power. Pennsylvania, New York, and New England, and increasingly the Chesapeake as well, produced grain, flour, meat, and dairy products. None of these were included in the list of enumerated goods and, thus, they could be sold freely abroad. They found their most ready market in the British West Indies and the Lower South, where food production was slighted in favor of sugar and rice. Most of this trade was carried in New England ships. Indeed, the New England shipbuilding industry was greatly stimulated by the allowance under the Navigation Acts for ships built and manned in the colonies. So many ships were built for English buyers that by midcentury nearly a third of all British tonnage was American made.

The greatest benefits for the port cities of the North came from their commercial relationship to the slave colonies. New England merchants had become important players in the slave trade by the early eighteenth century, and soon thereafter they began to make inroads into the export trade of the West Indian colonies. It was in the Caribbean that northern merchants most blatantly ignored mercantilist regulations. In violation of Spanish, French, and Dutch regulations prohibiting foreign trade, New Englanders traded foodstuffs for sugar in foreign colonies. They illegally sent the sugar to New England. By 1750 more than sixty distilleries in Massachusetts Bay were exporting more than 2 million gallons of rum, most of it produced from sugar obtained illegally. Because the restrictive rules and regulations enacted by Britain for its colonies were not enforced, such growth and prosperity among the merchants and manufacturers of the port cities of the North prospered.

By the mid-eighteenth century, the Chesapeake and Lower South regions were major exporters of tobacco, rice, and indigo, and the middle colonies major exporters of grain to Europe. The carrying trade in the products of slave labor made it possible for the northern and middle colonies to earn the income necessary to purchase British imports despite the lack of valuable products from their own regions. Gradually, the commercial economies of the Northeast and the South were becoming integrated. From the 1730s to the 1770s, for example, while the volume of trade between Great Britain and Charleston doubled, the trade between Charleston and northern ports grew sevenfold. The same relationship was developing between the Chesapeake and the North. Merchants in Boston, Newport, New York, and Philadelphia increasingly provided southern planters not only with shipping services but also with credit and insurance. Like London, Liverpool, and Bristol—though on a smaller scale—the port cities of the North became pivots in the expanding trade network linking slave plantations with Atlantic markets. This trade provided northern merchants with the capital that financed commercial growth and development in their cities and the surrounding countryside. Slavery thus contributed to the growth of a score of northern port cities, forming an indirect but essential part of their economies.

SLAVERY AND FREEDOM

The prosperity of the eighteenth-century plantation economy thus improved the living conditions for the residents of northern cities as well as for a large segment of the population of the South, providing them with the opportunity for a kind of freedom unknown in the previous century. The price of prosperity and freedom was the oppression and exploitation of millions of Africans and African Americans. Freedom for white men based on the slavery of African Americans is the most important contradiction of American history.

The Social Structure of the Slave Colonies

At the summit of southern colonial society stood a small elite of wealthy planters, in contrast with the mass of slave men and women who formed the working population. Slavery had produced a society in which property was concentrated in the hands of a wealthy few. The richest 10 percent of colonists owned more than half the cultivated land and over 60 percent of the wealth. Although there was no colonial aristocracy—no nobility or royal appointments—the landed elite of the slave colonies came very close to constituting one.

The typical wealthy Virginia planter lived in a Tidewater county; owned several thousand acres of prime farmland and more than a hundred slaves; resided in a luxurious plantation mansion, built perhaps in the fashionable Georgian style; and had an estate valued at more than £10,000. Elected to the House of Burgesses and forming the group from which the magistrates and counselors of the colony were chosen, these "first families of Virginia"—the Carters, Harrisons, Lees, Fitzhughs, Washingtons, Randolphs, and others—were a self-perpetuating governing class.

A similar elite ruled the Lower South, although wealthy landowners spent little time on their plantations. They lived instead in fashionable Charleston, where they made up a close-knit group who controlled the colonial government. "They live in as high a style here, I believe, as any part of the world," a visitor wrote.

A considerable distance separated this slave-owning elite from typical southern landowners. About half the adult white males were small planters and farmers. But while the gap between rich and middling colonists grew larger during the eighteenth century, the prosperity of the plantation economy created generally favorable conditions for landowning class as a whole. Slave ownership, for example, became widespread among this group during the eighteenth century. In Virginia at midcentury, 45 percent of heads of household held one to four slaves and even poorer farmers kept one or two.

Despite the prosperity that accompanied slavery in the eighteenth century, however, a substantial portion of colonists owned no land or slaves at all. Some rented land or worked as tenant farmers, some hired out as overseers or farm workers, and still others were indentured servants. Throughout the plantation region, landless men constituted about 40 percent of the population. A New England visitor found a "much greater disparity between the rich and poor in Virginia" than at home.

White Skin Privilege

But all the white colonists of eighteenth-century North America shared the privileged status of their skin color. As slavery became increasingly important, however, Virginia officials took considerable care to create legal

CHRONOLOGY

1441	African slaves first brought to Portugal
1518	Spain grants official license to Portuguese slavers
1535	Africans constitute a majority on Hispaniola
1619	First Africans brought to Virginia
1655	English seize Jamaica
1662	Virginia law makes slavery hereditary
1670	South Carolina founded
1672	Royal African Company organized
1691	Virginia prohibits interracial sexual contact
1698	Britain opens the slave trade to all its merchants
1699	Spanish declare Florida a refuge for escaped slaves
1702	South Carolinians burn St. Augustine
1705	Virginia Slave Code established
1706	French and Spanish navies bombard Charleston

1710	English capture Port Royal in Acadia
1712	Slave uprising in New York City
1713	Peace of Utrecht
1721–48	Robert Walpole leads British cabinet
1729	Natchez Rebellion in French Louisiana
1733	Molasses Act
1739	Stono Rebellion in South Carolina
1739–43	War of Jenkins's Ear
1740–48	King George's War
1741	Africans executed in New York for conspiracy
1752	Georgia officially opened to slavery
1770s	Peak period of the English colonies' slave trade
1808	Importation of slaves into the United States ends

distinctions between the status of colonists and that of Africans. Beginning in 1670, free Africans were prohibited from owning Christian servants. Ten years later, another law declared that any African, free or slave, who struck a Christian would receive thirty lashes on his bare back. One of the most important measures was designed to suppress intimate interracial contacts between white servants and enslaved Africans. A 1691 act "for prevention of that abominable mixture and spurious issue which hereafter may encrease in this dominion" established severe penalties for interracial sexual relationships.

Such penalties were rarely applied to masters, who frequently forced themselves on African women. But some slave women may have willingly established intimate relations with masters to better their condition or the opportunities for their children. After the death of his wife, Thomas Jefferson's father-in-law took a slave woman as his concubine. They had six children. After Jefferson's wife died, it was rumored that he established a sexual relationship with Sally Hemings, the youngest of those children, and his late wife's half-sister. Recent scientific tests have confirmed that Jefferson was likely the father of Sally's children, who enjoyed a privileged position in the household and were freed in Jefferson's will.

Relationships between white masters or indentured servants and African slaves produced a rather large group of mulattoes. Because by law children inherited the bondage or free status of their mothers, the majority of those of mixed ancestry were slaves; a minority, the children of European women and African men, were free. According to a Maryland census of 1755, more than 60 percent of mulattoes were slaves. But Maryland mulattoes also made up three-quarters of a small free African American population. This group, numbering about 4,000 in the 1770s, was denied the right to vote, to hold office, or to testify in court— all on the basis of racial background. Denied the status of citizenship enjoyed by even the poorest white men, free blacks were an outcast group who raised the status of white colonials by contrast.

Racism set up a wall of contempt between colonists and African Americans. Despite their close association, said Thomas Jefferson, the two peoples were divided by "deep rooted prejudices entertained by the whites" and "ten thousand recollections, by the blacks, of the injuries they have sustained." Perhaps he knew of these feelings from his long relationship with Sally Hemings. "I tremble for my country when I reflect that God is just," Jefferson concluded in a deservedly famous passage, and remember "that his justice cannot sleep forever."

CONCLUSION

During the eighteenth century nearly half a million Africans were kidnapped from their homes, marched to the African coast, and packed into ships for up to three months before arriving in British North America. They provided the labor that made colonialism pay. Southern planters, northern merchants, and especially British traders and capitalists benefited greatly from the commerce in slave-produced crops, and that prosperity filtered down to affect many of the colonists of British North America. Slavery was fundamental to the operation of the British empire in North America. Mercantilism was a system designed to channel colonial wealth produced by slaves to the nation-state, but as long as profits were high, the British tended to wink at colonists' violations of mercantilist regulations.

Although African Americans received little in return, their labor helped build the greatest accumulation of capital that Europe had ever seen. But despite enormous hardship and suffering, African Americans survived by forming new communities in the colonies, rebuilding families, restructuring language, and reforming culture. African American culture added important components of African knowledge and experience to colonial agriculture, art, music, and cuisine. The African Americans of the English colonies lived better lives than the slaves worked to death on Caribbean sugar plantations, but lives of misery compared with the men they were forced to serve. As the slaves sang on the Georgia coast, "Dah Backrow Man go wrong you, Buddy Quow."

REVIEW QUESTIONS

1. Trace the development of the system of slavery, and discuss the way it became entrenched in the Americas.
2. Describe the effects of the slave trade both on enslaved Africans and on the economic and political life of Africa.
3. Describe the process of acculturation involved in becoming an African American. In what ways did slaves "Africanize" the South?
4. Explain the connection between the institution of slavery and the building of a commercial empire.
5. In what ways did colonial policy encourage the growth of racism?

RECOMMENDED READING

Ira Berlin, *Many Thousands Gone: The First Two Centuries of Slavery in North America* (1998). A history of colonial slavery with attention to the differences between the regions of the Chesapeake, the Lower South, Louisiana, and the North. Emphasizes the distinction between slave societies and societies with slaves.

Michael Craton, *Sinews of Empire: A Short History of British Slavery* (1974). An introduction to the British mercantilist system that emphasizes the importance of slavery. Includes a comparison of the mainland colonies with the Caribbean.

Philip D. Curtin, *The African Slave Trade: A Census* (1969). The pioneer work in the quantitative history of the slave trade. All subsequent histories of the slave trade are indebted to Curtin.

Winthrop D. Jordan, *White over Black: American Attitudes Toward the Negro, 1550–1812* (1968). Remains the best and most comprehensive history of racial attitudes. A searching examination of British and American literature, folklore, and history.

Herbert S. Klein, *The Atlantic Slave Trade* (1999). A new and important synthesis of the most recent studies of the slave trade, covering the social and cultural effects of the trade, especially for Africans.

Peter Kolchin, *American Slavery, 1619–1877* (1993). This survey features comparisons with slavery in Brazil and the Caribbean and serfdom in Russia. Includes a comprehensive bibliographic essay.

Philip D. Morgan, *Slave Counterpoint: Black Culture in the Eighteenth-Century Chesapeake and Low-Country* (1998). A comprehensive and detailed examination of cultural forms and ways of life in the two regions that leaves hardly a stone unturned.

Walter Rodney, *How Europe Underdeveloped Africa* (1974). This highly influential book traces the relationship between Europe and Africa from the fifteenth to the twentieth century, and demonstrates how Europe's industrialization became Africa's impoverishment.

Mechal Sobel, *The World They Made Together: Black and White Values in Eighteenth-Century Virginia* (1987). Demonstrates the ways in which both Africans and Europeans shaped the formation of American values, perceptions, and identities.

Ian K. Steele, *Warpaths: Invasions of North America* (1994). A new synthesis of the colonial wars from the sixteenth to the eighteenth century that places Indians as well as empires at the center of the action.

ON THE WEB

http://www.csmonitor.com/durable/1999/06/17/ fp16s1-csm.shtml

In 1991 a government building project in Lower Manhattan unearthed a colonial African American cemetery used from 1712 until 1790 for perhaps as many as 10,000 to 20,000 burials. A short but informative *Christian Science Monitor* article (Thursday, June 17, 1999) about this project appears at the site.

http://www.csmonitor.com/durable/1997/10/29/ feat/feat.1.html

This site is a *Christian Science Monitor* article entitled: "Chronicling Black Lives in Colonial New England" (Wednesday October 29, 1999) by Lee Lawrence. This article contains good general information about African Americans in slavery in colonial New England. After reading the article, scroll down to the link entitled: New Hampshire's black history to connect to **http://www.seacoastnh.com/blackhistory/** and read the article "First Blacks of Portsmouth." Added benefits within this site are links to multiple black heritage pages on African American history from the colonial era to the twentieth century.

http://vi.uh.edu/pages/mintz/primary.htm

This is a site of original narratives and documents relating to the history of slavery in the eighteenth and nineteenth centuries maintained by members of the history department of the University of Houston. Pay particular attention to the colonial era narratives by slaves themselves as well as the descriptions given by European observers.

http://www.uwec.edu/Academic/Geography/ Ivogeler/w111/slaves.htm

This site contains a map of the Atlantic slave trade indicating destination and numbers of slaves transported to the Western Hemisphere from 1601 to 1870.

http://www.prenhall.com/faragherbrief/map4.1

Through a series of animated maps, analyze the role of geography and economics in the African slave trade. How and why were the people of Africa enslaved and brought America?

http://www.prenhall.com/faragherbrief/map4.2

In this activity, examine the dynamics that fueled the "Triangular Trade." How were Europe, Africa, and America linked together by commerce?

The Living History of Slavery

The 1,268 acres of freshwater marsh at the Howfyl-Broadfield Plantation State Historic Site, located on the Altamaha River delta of the Georgia sea coast, is maintained by a private trust as a nature center. But historically it was a large rice plantation, its ditches, dikes, and fields arduously cleared, constructed, and cultivated by large numbers of enslaved Africans and African Americans. The plantation supported five generations of owners until the last descendant willed the property to the state of Georgia in the early 1970s. There is a plantation house with period furnishings, and along several miles of trails visitors can observe the relict fields, now gradually returning to salt marsh. This place was once a prime example of the slave society of the Lower South, but until recently slavery wasn't much mentioned at Howfyl-Broadfield Plantation. Huge live oaks festooned with Spanish moss provided a romantic backdrop for the annual "old-fashioned Christmas" observance of the Glynn County Garden Club. Candles lit the way to the plantation house, decorated with greenery and bows, where guests were greeted by actors portraying Scarlet O'Hara and Robert E. Lee. Around back they were served wassail, heated in a 150-year-old black kettle. Howfyl-Broadfield is one of hundreds of historic slave plantations where slavery was a repressed memory, while people memorialized the "moonlight and magnolias" version of Old South history.

But those days are now behind us. During the past quarter-century there has been a growing interest in the history of slavery, in part prompted by the confirmation through DNA testing of Thomas Jefferson's relationship with Sally Hemmings (see discussion in this chapter). Hollywood told a version of that story in *Jefferson in Paris*, and attempted to seriously dramatize slavery itself in the films *Beloved*, *Amistad*, and *Glory*. The United States Congress entered the action, mandating that the National Park Service address the history of slavery at its Civil War sites. President Bill Clinton went to Africa and issued a statement of regret over the historic role of the United States in the slave trade. What accounts for this national attention? Accord-

A runaway slave hides from the slave patrol, a reenactment at Carter's Grove plantation. Many visitors are caught up in these dramas, some offering to help slaves escape, others turning on the owners. Slavery is the most painful topic in American history.

SOURCE: Colonial Williamsburg Foundation, Williamsburg, VA.

ing to distinguished historian of slavery Ira Berlin, behind the interest in slavery is the crisis of race in America. In a society in which blacks and whites hardly talk to each other, slavery is a way to discuss race, a way of addressing some of the deepest hurts that Americans feel.

Incorporating slavery into the interpretation of historic slave plantations has proved controversial. The issue arouses deep anger and bitterness for many African Americans, embarrassment and shame for many white people. According to Rex Ellis, a director of interpretation at Colonial Williamsburg, the historical park where

Interior of a slave cabin at Carter's Grove plantation, Colonial Williamsburg. The incorporation of slavery into the interpretive "living history" programs of colonial plantations is an important part of struggling with the nation's history of race and racism.

SOURCE: Colonial Williamsburg Foundation, Williamsburg, VA.

he works "was never a place for blacks to come to." Although he grew up in the area, neither his African American family nor any of his neighbors would visit. "That place points to slavery," his father would say, "and that's something we don't want to talk about." But in the mid-1980s Colonial Williamsburg made the decision it was something that had to be talked about, and in 1989 the institution opened a reconstruction of the slave quarters at nearby Carter's Grove plantation, staffed by interpreters portraying slaves and masters. For the first time African Americans began to come. Many visitors — white as well as black — found themselves caught up in the reenactments. Some offered to help the slaves escape, while others turned on the slave owners and had to be physically restrained. On the other hand, some of the African American actors reported feeling that they were being treated like slaves, not only by visitors but by those playing roles as masters.

Slavery remains the most painful topic in American history. For years "there was an unwritten rule not to be controversial," says Dwight T. Pitcaithley, chief historian for the National Park Service, but "it didn't make for good history." Pitcaithley oversees the program to include the history of slavery at the nation's Civil War battlefield sites. The idea is to make slavery as vivid in the public imagination as the bloody war it precipi-

tated. Some parts of the slave past, however, may be too sensitive for the medium of living history. When the interpretive staff at Colonial Williamsburg staged a slave auction, civil rights groups picketed and sang "We Shall Overcome." At another living history program in Georgia, middle school students who witnessed a re-enactment of a slave auction were asked to imagine what it would feel like to be a slave. "There I was on the auction block," one African American student wrote. "I had to take off my clothes in front of all those white people. I forgot to be proud and I was ashamed."

So far the movement to incorporate slavery into the interpretation at historic sites has not changed things very much at Howfyl-Broadfield Plantation. An archaeological investigation of the site in the mid-1990s did reveal traces of the old slave quarters out back, not far from the Christmas wassail kettle. Archaeologist Kay Wood would like to do more excavation and create an interpretive exhibit featuring the history of slavery on the rice coast of Georgia, but funds are short. "There really hasn't been a lot done on rice plantations in Georgia," she told a reporter. "This is where history begins on this coast. This is where Georgia begins." But meanwhile the old-fashioned Christmas celebrations continue, perpetuating a different memory of the rice coast, a memory in which slaves are invisible. ■

FIVE

THE CULTURES OF COLONIAL NORTH AMERICA

▶ 1 7 0 0 – 1 7 8 0

AMERICAN COMMUNITIES

From Deerfield to Kahnawake: Crossing Cultural Boundaries

TWO HOURS BEFORE DAYLIGHT ON FEBRUARY 29, 1704, Reverend John Williams and his wife, Eunice, of Deerfield, Massachusetts, awoke to "horrid shouting and yelling" and the crash of axes and hatchets breaking open the doors and windows of their house. Leaping out of bed they knew immediately that the town was under attack by Indians and their French allies; this frontier settlement on the northwestern fringe of New England had already been attacked six times in the perennial fighting with New France. Never before, however, had the enemy penetrated the town's stockade. Suddenly the door burst open and "with painted faces and hideous exclamations" Indians began pushing inside. "I reached up my hands for my pistol," Williams remembered, "cocked it, and put it to the breast of the first Indian that came up." It misfired, and as the couple stood trembling in their nightclothes, they were bound and dragged into the central hall with their seven children. In horror they were forced to watch the invaders club and kill their resisting six-year-old son, their screaming newborn infant daughter, and their black nursemaid. The family was hustled out into the frigid dawn and, with more than a hundred other captives, marched north through snow and ice toward Canada, leaving the frightful sight of the burning town behind.

This raid was one of the most infamous events in a long series of attacks and counterattacks between English and French colonists. At Deerfield, one hundred and forty residents of the town managed to hold off the invasion and survive, but fifty others died in the attack. Among the captives, twenty-one were murdered along the way, in most cases because they were too weak to travel; those murdered included Mrs. Williams, who had not yet recovered from a difficult childbirth just six weeks before. The governor of Massachusetts ordered a day of fasting and prayed that "the Designs of the barbarous Salvages against us be defeated; our exposed Plantations preserved; and the poor Christian Captives in their hands returned." Authorities raised the bounty on Indian scalps from £10 to £100 and organized bloody raids of their own on the French and Indian settlements to the north.

Most of the Deerfield captives were delivered to the French authorities in Montreal. Within two years, fifty-nine of them had been ransomed and returned home to Deerfield, the Reverend Williams and four of his surviving children among them. Williams soon published an account of his captivity, *The Redeemed Captive Returning to Zion.* In colonial America, with its many peoples and cultures, readers were fascinated by the problems and dilemmas of crossing the frontiers between colonial and Indian societies, as well as the borders between the English, French, and Spanish empires. What was life like for you, people wanted to know, on the other side of the frontier? How were you changed by your experience? Did you remain loyal to your community? Can you still be trusted?

Questions of this sort were vitally important to the colonists, for over the years hundreds of Europeans who had been captured by Indians had chosen to remain with their captors rather than return home. Among the Deerfield captives, thirty-one—including ten-year-old Eunice Williams, her mother's namesake—remained in Canada. Eunice and many of the other Deerfield captives lived at Kahnawake, a community of Catholic Indians near Montreal. Like Deerfield, Kahnawake was a farming town of fifty or sixty homes clustered around a central church and surrounded by a stockade to protect it from enemy raiders. The differences between the two communities, however, were more striking than the similarities.

Founded in the seventeenth century by Jesuit missionaries as a refuge for Iroquois converts, Kahnawake not only became home to a great variety of Native American Catholics but also welcomed people of mixed Indian and European ancestry. The "great mixture of the blood of whites with that of aborigines is observable in the persons of the inhabitants," wrote one visitor, struck by the appearance of people who seemed to be Indians in all respects except their blue eyes. Such mixing was also evident in the community's culture, the exotic combination of European and Indian clothing, the use of both Indian and French names, and the special ways the community bent Catholic ritual to fit traditional Iroquois practices. Community members crossed boundaries in other ways, too: many residents were smugglers who engaged in the illegal trade of furs and other Indian products across

the frontier into New York. According to the frustrated authorities in Montreal, Kahnawake operated as "a sort of republic," insisting on its freedom and independence.

As the historian John Demos writes, Kahnawake was "a unique experiment in bicultural living." Its residents were skilled at offering sympathetic sanctuary to traumatized captive children, and by the time Eunice Williams's father and siblings were ransomed, she told the man who had come to fetch her that she was "unwilling to return." Soon she converted to Catholicism. Over the years the father sent several emissaries to retrieve her, but all she would say were two words of Iroquois: *jaghte oghte,* meaning "maybe not." She refused to acknowledge her English name, having taken another: *A'ongonte,* which in Iroquois means "she has been planted as a person." In 1713, at the age of sixteen, she married a Kahnawake Mohawk. Father and daughter would meet only once more, the following year, when he went to Kahnawake a final time to beg her to return. But she would "not so much as give me one pleasant look," Williams wrote mournfully. "She is yet obstinately resolved to live and dye here."

And that is what happened. A'ongonte and her husband remained good Catholics, raising a family and working as traders. John Williams died in 1729, surrounded by his children and grandchildren but longing for his "unredeemed" daughter. It was not until 1739 that A'ongonte found the courage to bring her family south for a visit, for she feared being held in New England against her will. Her brother Stephen wrote in his diary that at long last "we had ye joyfull, Sorrowfull meeting of our poor Sister that we had been Sepratd from fer above 36 years." After that A'ongonte visited only rarely because of the continuing warfare. "We have a great desire of going down to see you," she wrote to her brother through an interpreter near the end of their lives in the 1770s, "but do not know when an oppertunity may offer. . . . I pray the Lord that he may give us grace so to Live in this as to be prepared for a happy meeting in the world to Come." And, perhaps as a sign of reconciliation, she signed the letter, "Loving Sister until death, Eunice Williams." ■

Deerfield

NORTH AMERICAN REGIONS

American colonial history too often is written as if only the British colonists along the Atlantic coast really mattered. But as the experience of the Deerfield community and the Williams family suggests, this is a mistake eighteenth-century colonists could not afford to make. In the first place, Indian America was a critically important part of the eighteenth-century world. From the fringes of colonial societies into the native heart of the continent, from the eastern foothills of the Appalachians to the western flank of the Sierra Nevada in California, hundreds of Indian cultures—despite being deeply affected by the spread of colonial culture—remained firmly in control of their homelands. And in addition to the British provinces stretching along the Atlantic coast, there were Hispanic colonists who defended the northern borderlands of the Spanish Caribbean and Mexican empire in isolated communities from Florida to California, and French communities that occupied the valley of the St. Lawrence River and scattered down the Mississippi Valley from the Great Lakes to the Gulf of Mexico. There were impressive similarities among these colonial societies, representing a continuation in the New World of traditional Old World beliefs, customs, and institutions, as well as a general pattern of European adaptation to American conditions.

Indian America

As the native peoples of the Atlantic coastal plain lost their lands to colonists through battles or treaties and moved into or beyond the Appalachian Mountains, they became active in the fur trade. Indians demonstrated a remarkable capacity for change and adaptation. They began participating in a commercial economy, using metal tools, building their homes of logs as frontier settlers did, but in the process they also became dependent on firearms, metal tools, and other manufactured goods they had no capacity to produce themselves. Yet, until the American Revolution, they continued to assert a proud independence and gained considerable skill at playing colonial powers off against one another.

In general, the French had significantly better relations with native peoples than the English, but inevitably as they pursued their expansionist plans they came into conflict with Indian groups, and when opposed they could be just as cruel and violent as any other European power. In the early eighteenth century the Fox Indians blocked French passage between the Great Lakes and the upper Mississippi, attempting to make themselves into middlemen in the fur trade. Sporadic fighting continued until the French defeated the tribe in 1716. But Fox warriors rose again in 1726, and it took massive violence before the French were able to force the tribe into signing a treaty in 1738. On the lower Mississippi, the Natchez and Chickasaw tribes opposed the arrival of the French, engaging them in a series of bloody conflicts during the 1720s, which concluded only when the French decimated the Natchez in 1731.

The preeminent concern of the Indians of the eastern half of the continent was the tremendous growth of colonial population in the British Atlantic coastal colonies, especially the movement of settlers westward. In the 1730s and 1740s Pennsylvania perpetrated a series of fraudulent seizures of western lands from the Delawares. Particularly in the light of Pennsylvania's previous history of fair dealing with Indian peoples, these acts were another disturbing sign of things to come. Thus, Indian alliances with the French resulted not from any great affection but from their great fear of British expansion.

Meanwhile, a long-term population decline continued among the Indian peoples of North America.

Indian America continued to take a terrific beating from epidemics of European disease. There was no systematic census of North American Indians before the nineteenth century, but historians estimate that from a high of 7 to 10 million Native Americans north of Mexico in 1500, the population had probably fallen to around a million by 1800. Thus, during the eighteenth century colonial population overtook and began to overwhelm the native population of the continent. Population loss did not affect all Indian tribes equally, however. Native peoples with a century or more of colonial contact and interaction had lost 50 percent or more of their numbers, but most Indian societies in the interior had yet to be struck by the horrible epidemics.

Colonization introduced other less distressing changes in Indian cultures. By the early eighteenth century, Indians on the southern fringe of the Great Plains were using horses stolen from the Spanish in New Mexico. Horses enabled Indian hunters to exploit the buffalo herds much more efficiently, and on the base of this more productive economy a number of groups built a distinctive and elaborate nomadic culture. Great numbers of Indian peoples moved onto the plains during the eighteenth century, pulled by this new way of life, pushed by colonial invasions and disruptions radiating southwest from Canada and north from the Spanish borderlands. The invention of nomadic Plains Indian culture was another of the dramatic cultural innovations of the eighteenth century. The mounted Plains Indian, so often used as a symbol of native America, was actually a product of the colonial era.

The Spanish Borderlands

Mexico City, the administrative capital of New Spain, was the most sophisticated urban area in the Western Hemisphere, the site of one of the world's great universities, with broad avenues and spectacular architecture. New Spain's northern borderland provinces of Florida, Texas, New Mexico, and California, however, were far removed from this sophistication. Officials of the viceroyalty of New Spain, who oversaw these colonies, thought of them as buffer zones, protecting New Spain from the expanding colonial empires of Spain's New World rivals.

In Florida, the oldest of European colonies in North America, fierce fighting among the Spanish, the British, and the Indians had by the early eighteenth century reduced the colonial presence to little more than the forts of St. Augustine on the Atlantic and Pensacola on the Gulf of Mexico, each surrounded by small colonized territories populated with the families of Spanish troops. In their weakened condition, the Spanish had

no choice but to establish cooperative relations with the Creek and Seminole Indians who dominated the region, as well as the hundreds of African American runaways who considered St. Augustine a refuge from the cruel slave regimes in Georgia and Carolina. Like the community of Kahnawake, eighteenth-century Florida included a growing mestizo population and a considerable number of free African Americans and Hispanicized Indians from the old missions.

Nearly 2,000 miles to the west, New Mexico was similarly isolated from the mainstream of New Spain. At midcentury New Mexico included some 20,000 Pueblo Indians (their numbers greatly reduced by disease since their first contact with Europeans) and perhaps 10,000 mestizo colonists. The prosperity of these colonists, who supported themselves with subsistence agriculture, was severely limited by a restrictive colonial economic policy that forced them to exchange their wool, pottery, buffalo hides, and buckskin for imported goods at unfavorable rates. Unlike the colonial population of Florida, however, the settlements of New Mexicans were gradually expanding, following the valleys and streams that led east and north from the original colonial outposts scattered along the upper Rio Grande.

The Spanish also founded new northern outposts during the eighteenth century. Concerned about French colonization of the Mississippi Valley, they established a number of military posts or *presidios* on the fringes of the colony of Louisiana and in 1716 began the construction of a string of Franciscan missions among the Indian peoples of Texas. By 1750 the settlement of San Antonio had become the center of a developing frontier province. The Spanish also established new colonial outposts west of New Mexico, in what is today southern Arizona. In the 1690s, Jesuit missionaries, led by Father Eusebio Kino, founded missions among the desert Indians of the lower Colorado River and Gila River valleys. Mission San Xavier del Bac near Tucson is acclaimed the most striking example of Spanish colonial architecture in the United States. Cattle ranching, introduced by the Jesuits, and farming spread along the lower Rio Grande Valley; in fact, ranching continued to define the region's economy for the next 200 years.

Midcentury also found the Spanish considering new settlements along the California coast. Juan Cabrillo, an associate of Hernán Cortés, had first explored the coastal waters in 1542 and was the first European to sail into the fine harbor at San Diego. In 1603 explorer Sebastián Vizcaíno had come upon Monterey Bay. The Spanish did little to follow up on these finds, but in 1769, acting on rumors of Russian expansion along the northern Pacific coast (for a discussion of Russian America, see Chapter 9), officials in Mexico City ordered Gaspar de Portolá, governor

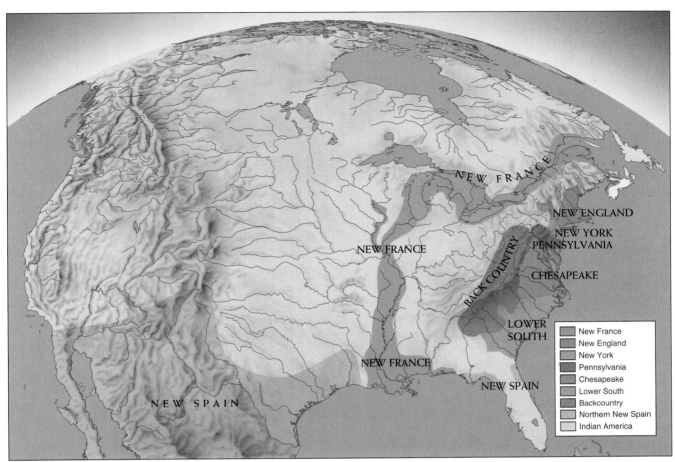

Regions in Eighteenth-Century North America By the middle of the eighteenth century, European colonists had established a number of distinctive colonial regions in North America. The northern periphery of New Spain, the oldest and most prosperous European colony, stretched from Baja California to eastern Texas, then jumped to the settlements on the northern end of the Florida peninsula; cattle ranching was the dominant way of life in this thinly populated region. New France was like a great crescent, extending from the plantation communities along the Mississippi near New Orleans to the French colonial communities along the St. Lawrence; in between were isolated settlements and forts, connected only by the extensive French trading network.

of what is now Baja California, to establish a Spanish presence in the north. With him were Franciscan missionaries led by Junípero Serra, president of the missions in Baja. At the harbor of San Diego, Portolá and Serra founded the first mission and pueblo complex in present-day California. Portolá then proceeded overland, becoming the first European to explore the interior valleys and mountains, and in 1770 he and Serra established their headquarters at Monterey Bay on the central coast. Two years later Juan Bautista de Anza established an overland route across the blistering deserts connecting Arizona and California, and in 1776 he led a colonizing expedition that founded the pueblo of San Francisco. Over the next fifty years the number of California settlements grew to include twenty-one missions and a half-dozen presidios and pueblos, including the town

of Los Angeles. Founded in 1781 by a group of mestizo settlers from Sinaloa, Mexico, by the end of the century Los Angeles, with a population of only 300, was California's largest town.

Region	Population
New France	70,000
New England	400,000
New York	100,000
Pennsylvania	230,000
Chesapeake	390,000
Lower South	100,000
Backcountry	100,000
Northern New Spain	20,000
Indian America	1,500,000

For the Spanish, conquest demanded conversion to Catholicism, which, according to theory, would lead Indians toward "civilization." Like the efforts of the Jesuits at Kahnawake and elsewhere in New France, the Spanish experiment in cultural transformation was designed to make Indians into Catholics and loyal Spanish subjects by educating them and putting them to work raising cattle and crops. The most extensive mission project took place in California, where under the direction of priests thousands of Indian laborers produced a flourishing local economy based on irrigated farming as well as horse, cattle, and sheep ranching. Indian people also constructed the adobe and stone churches, built on Spanish and Moorish patterns, whose ruins symbolize California's colonial society.

To keep the system functioning, the Franciscan missionaries resorted to cruel and sometimes violent means of controlling their Indian subjects: shackles, solitary confinement, and whipping posts. Indians resisted from the very beginning, but the arms and organization of Spanish soldiers were usually sufficient to suppress the uprisings. Another form of protest was flight: whole villages sometimes fled.

Overwork, inadequate nutrition, overcrowding, poor sanitation, and epidemic disease contributed to death rates that exceeded birthrates. During the period of the mission system the native population of California fell by at least 25 percent.

The French Crescent

In France, as in Spain, church and state were closely interwoven. During the seventeenth century the French prime ministers, Cardinal Richelieu and Cardinal Mazarin, laid out a fundamentally Catholic imperial policy, and under their guidance colonists constructed a second Catholic empire in North America. In 1674 church and state collaborated in establishing the bishopric of Quebec, which founded local seminaries, oversaw the appointment and review of priests, and laid the foundation of the resolutely Catholic culture of New France. Meanwhile, Jesuit missionaries continued to carry Catholicism deep into the continent.

The number of French colonists rose from fewer than 15,000 in 1700 to more than 70,000 at midcentury. During the eighteenth century the French used their trade network and alliances with the Indians to establish a great crescent of colonies, military posts, and settlements that extended from the mouth of the St. Lawrence River southwest through the Great Lakes, then down the Mississippi River to the Gulf of Mexico. Although the maritime colony of Acadia was ceded to the British in 1713 (see Chapter 4), the French an-

chored the crescent on the northeast by founding the fortress of Louisbourg on Ile Royale (Cape Breton Island), which soon became the most important French port in the North Atlantic. The colony of Louisiana formed the other end of the crescent at the mouth of the Mississippi. Over this vast territory the French laid a thin colonial veneer, the beginning of what they planned as a great continental empire that would limit the Protestant British to a narrow strip of Atlantic coastline.

At the heart of the French empire in North America were the farming communities of the colony of Canada along the banks of the St. Lawrence, including the towns of Montreal and Quebec. There were also farming communities in the Illinois country, which shipped wheat down the Mississippi to supply the booming sugar plantations of Louisiana. By the mid-eighteenth century, those plantations, extending along the river from Natchez and Baton Rouge to New Orleans, had become the most profitable French enterprise in North America.

The persistence of French colonial long lots in the pattern of modern landholding is clear in this enhanced satellite photograph of the Mississippi River near New Orleans. Long lots, the characteristic form of property holding in New France, were designed to offer as many settlers as possible a share of good bottomland as well as a frontage on the waterways, which served as the basic transportation network.

SOURCE: EROS Data Center, U.S. Geological Survey.

One of the most distinctive French stamps on the North American landscape were the "long lots" stretching back from the rivers that provided each settler family a share of good bottomland to farm as well as frontage on the waterways, the "interstate highway system" of the French Crescent. Long lots were laid out along the lower Mississippi River in Louisiana and at sites on the upper Mississippi such as Kaskaskia and Prairie du Chien, as well as at the strategic passages of the Great Lakes, the communities of Mackinac, Sault Ste. Marie, and Detroit. In 1750, Detroit was a stockaded town with a military garrison, a small administrative center, several stores, a Catholic church, and 100 households of *métis* (French for mestizo) families. French and métis farmers worked the land along the Detroit River, not far from communities inhabited by more than 6,000 Ottawa, Potawatomi, and Huron Indians.

Communities of this sort that combined both French and Indian elements were in the tradition of the inclusive frontier. Detroit looked like "an old French village," said one observer, except that its houses were "mostly covered with bark," in Indian style. Detroit had much of the character of the mixed community of Kahnawake on the St. Lawrence.

Family and kinship in these interior communities were also cast in the Indian pattern. Households often consisted of several related families, but wives limited their births, having on average only two or three children. There were arranged marriages and occasional polygamy, but women had easy access to divorce and enjoyed property rights. Yet the people focused their activities on commerce and identified themselves overwhelmingly as Catholic.

New England

Just as New Spain and New France had their official church, so did the people of New England: local communities in all the New England colonies but Rhode Island were governed by Puritan congregations. Under the plan established in Massachusetts, the local church of a community was free to run its own affairs under the guidance of the General Court (the governor and the representatives selected by the towns). The Puritan colonies allotted each congregation a tract of communal land. Church members divided this land among themselves on the basis of status and seniority, laying out central villages such as Deerfield and building churches (called meetinghouses) that were maintained through taxation. Adult male church members constituted the freemen of the town, and thus there was very little distinction between religious and secular authority. At the town meeting the freemen chose their minister, voted on his salary and support, and elected local men to offices ranging from town clerk to fence viewer.

The Puritan tradition was a curious mix of freedom and repression. Although local communities had considerable autonomy, they were tightly bound by the restrictions of the Puritan faith and the General Court. Contrary to widespread beliefs, the Puritans did not come to America to create a society where religion could be freely practiced. Rather, they sought to establish their own version of the "right and perfect way," which placed severe restraints on individuals. Not only did the Puritans exile dissidents such as Roger Williams and Anne Hutchinson who threatened the religious orthodoxy of Massachusetts (see Chapter 3), but they also banned Anglicans and Baptists and exiled, jailed, whipped, and even executed members of the Society of Friends, who came repeatedly among them to preach the tenets of the Quaker faith.

One of the first formal arguments for religious toleration was made by New Englander Roger Williams, leader of dissenting Rhode Island. "Forced worship," he wrote, "stinks in God's nostrils." After the religious excesses of the English civil war, this argument began to have an appeal. In 1661, King Charles II ordered a stop to religious persecution in Massachusetts. The Toleration Act, passed by Parliament in 1689, was at first resisted by the Puritans. Under pressure from English authorities, however, Massachusetts and Connecticut reluctantly allowed other Protestant denominations to begin practicing their religions openly in 1700, although Congregationalism (as the Puritan Church had become known because the congregations governed themselves) continued to be supported officially through taxation. By the 1730s there were Anglican, Baptist, and Presbyterian congregations in many New England towns.

As towns grew too large for the available land, groups of residents left together, "hiving off" to form new churches and towns elsewhere. The region was knit together by an intricate network of roads and rivers. Seventy-five years after the Indians of southern New England suffered their final defeat in King Philip's War (see Chapter 3), Puritan farm communities had taken up most of the available land of Massachusetts, Connecticut, and Rhode Island, leaving only a few communities of Pequots, Narragansets, and Wampanoags on restricted reservations. Northern Algonquians and Catholic Iroquois allied with the French in Quebec, however, maintained a defensive barrier that prevented New Englanders from expanding northward into Maine, New Hampshire, and the region later called Vermont. Deerfield represented the far northern limit of safe settlement. By midcentury, then, as the result of growing population, New England was reaching the limit of its land supply.

The Middle Colonies

The colony of New York had one of the most ethnically diverse populations on the continent, in striking contrast to the ethnically homogeneous neighboring New England colonies of Connecticut and Massachusetts. At midcentury, society along the lower Hudson River, including the counties in northern New Jersey, was a veritable mosaic of ethnic communities: the Dutch of Flatbush, the Huguenots of New Rochelle, the Flemish of Bergen County, and the Scots of Perth Amboy were but a few. African Americans, both slave and free, made up more than 15 percent of the lower Hudson population. Congregations of Puritans, Baptists, Quakers, and Catholics worshiped without legal hindrance. New York City was also home to the first Jewish community in the country, established in 1654. Several hundred Jewish families attended services in North America's first synagogue, built in 1730. There was a great deal of intermingling (as there was at places such as Kahnawake), but these different communities would long retain their ethnic and religious distinctions, which made New York something of a cultural "salad bowl" rather than a "melting pot."

New York City grew by leaps and bounds in the eighteenth century, but because the elite who had inherited the rich lands and great manors along the upper Hudson chose to rent to tenants rather than to sell, this region was much less attractive to immigrants. By contrast, Pennsylvania was what one German immigrant called "heaven for farmers." The colony's Quaker proprietors were willing to sell land to anyone who could pay the modest prices. Thus, as the region around New York City filled up, immigrants by the thousands made the decision to land at Philadelphia, Pennsylvania's growing port on the Delaware River. During the eighteenth century the population of this region and an extended area that encompassed portions of New Jersey, Delaware, and Maryland grew more dramatically than any other in North America. Boasting some of the best farmland in North America, the region was soon exporting abundant produce through Philadelphia.

The Quakers who had founded Pennsylvania quickly became a minority, but, unlike the Puritans, they were generally comfortable with religious and ethnic pluralism. Many of the founders of the Society of Friends had been imprisoned for their beliefs in pre-Restoration England, and they were determined to prevent a repetition of this injustice in their own province. Indeed, the Quakers were opposed to all signs of rank, and among American Friends, women preached equally with men.

These Quaker attitudes were well suited to the ethnically and religiously diverse population of Pennsylvania. Although the Society of Friends remained the affiliation of the governing elite, it never became an established church. Most German immigrants were Lutherans or Calvinists, most North Britons were Presbyterians, and there were plenty of Anglicans and Baptists as well.

The institutions of government were another pillar of community organization. Colonial officials appointed justices of the peace from among the leading local men, and these justices provided judicial authority for the countryside. Property-owning farmers chose their own local officials. Country communities were tied together by kinship bonds and by bartering and trading among neighbors. The substantial stone houses and great barns of the Pennsylvania countryside testified to the social stability and prosperity of this system. The communities of the middle colonies, however, were more loosely bound than those of New England. Rates of mobility were considerably higher, with about half the population moving in any given decade. Because land was sold in individual lots rather than in communal parcels, farmers tended to disperse themselves at will over the open countryside. Villages gradually developed at crossroads and ferries but with little forethought or planning. It was Pennsylvania, which emphasized individual settlement, that provided the basic model for American expansion.

The Backcountry

By 1750 Pennsylvania's exploding population had pushed beyond the first range of the Appalachian highlands. Settlers occupied the northern reaches of the Great Valley, which extended southwest from Pennsylvania into Virginia. Although they hoped to become commercial farmers, these settlers began more modestly, planting Indian corn and raising hogs, hunting in the woods for meat and furs, and building log cabins. This strategy had originated with the settlers of the New Sweden colony on the lower Delaware River.

The movement into the Pennsylvania and Virginia backcountry that began during the 1720s was the first of the great pioneer treks that would take Americans into the continental interior. Many, perhaps most, of these pioneers held no legal title to the lands they occupied; they simply hacked out and defended their squatters' claims from Indian tribes and all other comers. Many of these settlers came from the northern borders of England and Ireland, where there was considerable clan and ethnic violence, so they adapted well to the violence of the backcountry. To the Delawares and Shawnees, who had been pushed into the interior, or the Cherokees, who occupied the Appalachian highlands to the south, these pioneers presented a new and deadly threat. Rising fears and resentments over this expanding population triggered much eighteenth-century warfare.

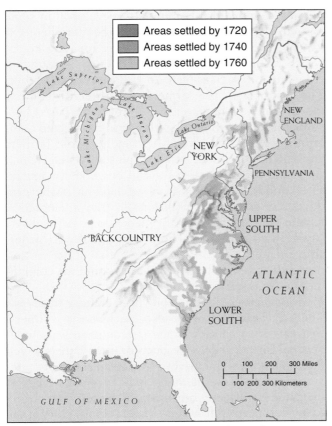

Spread of Settlement: Movement into the Backcountry, 1720–1760   The spread of settlement from 1720 to 1760 shows the movement of population into the backcountry during the midcentury.

One of the distinctive characteristics of the backcountry was the settlers' disdain for rank. But the myth of frontier equality was simply that. Most pioneers owned little or no land, whereas "big men" held great tracts and dominated local communities with their bombastic style of personal leadership. Here the men were warriors, the women workers.

The South

The Chesapeake and the Lower South were triracial societies, with intermingled communities of white colonists and black slaves, along with substantial Indian communities living on the fringes of colonial settlement. Much of the population growth of the region resulted from the forced migration of enslaved Africans, who by 1750 made up 40 percent of the population. Colonial settlement had filled not only the Tidewater area of the southern Atlantic coast but a good deal of the Piedmont as well. Specializing in rice, tobacco, and other commercial crops, these colonies were overwhelmingly rural. Farms and plantations were dispersed across the countryside, and villages or towns were few.

English authorities made the Church of England the state religion in the Chesapeake colonies. Residents paid taxes to support the Church and were required to attend services. No other churches were allowed into Virginia and Maryland (despite being founded by Catholics) and dissenters were excluded or exiled. Before the 1750s, the Toleration Act was little enforced in the South; at the same time, the Anglican establishment was internally weak. It maintained neither a colonial bishop nor local institutions for training clergy.

Along the rice coast, the dominant institution of social life was the large plantation. Transforming the tangle of woods and swamps along the region's rivers into an ordered pattern of dams, dikes, and flooded fields required a heavy capital investment. Consequently, only men of means could undertake rice cultivation. By midcentury, established rice plantations typically were dominated by a large main house, generally located on a spot of high ground overlooking the fields. Nearby, but a world apart, were the slave quarters, rough wooden cabins lining two sides of a muddy pathway near the outbuildings and barns.

Because tobacco, unlike rice, could be grown profitably in small plots, the Chesapeake included a greater variety of farmers and a correspondingly diverse landscape. Tobacco quickly drained the soil of its nutrients, and plantings had to be shifted to fresh ground every few years. Former tobacco land could be planted with corn for several years but then required twenty years or more of rest before reuse. The landscape was, thus, a patchwork of fields, many in various stages of ragged second growth. The poorest farmers lived in wooden cabins little better than the shacks of the slaves. More prosperous farm families lived with two or three slaves in houses that nevertheless were considerably smaller than the substantial homes of New England.

In the Lower South, where the plantations were little worlds unto themselves, there was little community life outside the plantation. But by midcentury the Chesapeake had given rise to well-developed neighborhoods based on kinship networks and economic connections. Encouraging the developing sense of community more than any other institution was the county court, which held both executive and judicial power. On court day, white people of all ranks held a great gathering that included public business, horse racing, and perhaps a barbecue. The gentleman justices of the county, appointed by the governor, included the heads of the leading planter families. These men in turn selected the grand jury, composed of substantial freeholders. One of the most significant bonding forces in this free white population was a growing sense of racial solidarity in response to the increasing proportion of African slaves dispersed throughout the neighborhoods.

Traditional Culture in the New World

In each of these North American colonial societies the family and kinship, the church, and the local community were the most significant factors in everyday life. Throughout the continent, colonists tended to live much as they had in their European homelands at the time their colonies were settled. Thus, the residents of New Mexico, Quebec, and New England continued to be attached to the religious passions of the seventeenth century long after their mother countries had put those religious controversies aside in favor of imperial geopolitics. Nostalgia for Europe helped to fix a conservative colonial attitude toward culture.

These were oral cultures, depending on the transmission of information by the spoken word rather than through print, on the passage of traditions through storytelling, song, music, and crafts. North American colonial folk cultures, traditional and suspicious of change, preserved an essentially medieval worldview. The rhythms of life were regulated by the hours of sunlight and the seasons of the year. People rose with the sun and went to bed soon after it went down. The demands of the season determined their working routines. They farmed with simple tools and were subject to the whims of nature, for drought, flood, or pestilence might quickly sweep away their efforts. Experience told them that the natural world imposed limitations within which men and women had to learn to live. Even patterns of reproduction conformed to nature's cycle: in nearly every European colonial community of North America the number of births peaked in late winter, then fell to a low point during the summer. For African Americans, by contrast, births peaked in early summer. Historians have not yet accounted for this intriguing pattern or provided an explanation for the differences between white and black families, but apparently there was some "inner" seasonal clock tied to old European and African patterns. Human sexual activity itself seemed to fluctuate with the rural working demands created by the seasons.

These were also communal cultures. In Quebec, villagers worked side by side to repair the roads; in New Mexico they collectively maintained the irrigation canals; and in New England they gathered in town meetings to decide the dates when common fields were to be plowed, sowed, and harvested. Houses offered little privacy, with families often sleeping together in the same chamber, sitting together on benches rather than in chairs, and taking their supper from a common bowl or trencher.

Throughout North America, most colonists continued the traditional European occupation of working the land. Plantation agriculture was designed to be a commercial system, in which crops were commodities for sale. Commercial farming also developed in some particularly fertile areas, notably southeastern Pennsylvania, which became known as the breadbasket of North America, as well as in the country surrounding colonial cities such as New York, Boston, and Quebec. The majority of the farmers of eighteenth-century North America, however, grew crops and raised livestock for their own needs or for local barter, and communities were largely self-sufficient. Most farmers attempted to produce small surpluses as well, which they sold to pay their taxes and buy some manufactured goods. But rather than specializing in the production of one or two crops for sale, they attempted to remain as independent of the market as possible, diversifying their activities. The primary goal was ownership of land and the assurance that children and descendants would be able to settle within the community on lands nearby.

Rural households often practiced crafts or trades as a sideline. Farm men were also blacksmiths, coopers, weavers, or carpenters. Some farm women were independent traders in dairy products or eggs. Others served the community as midwives and medicinal experts.

In colonial cities, artisans and craftsmen worked at their trades full time, organizing themselves according to the European craft system. In the colonial cities of the Atlantic coast, carpenters, ironmakers, blacksmiths, shipwrights, and scores of other tradesmen had their own self-governing associations. Young men who wished to pursue a trade served several years as apprentices, working in exchange for learning the skills and secrets of the craft. After completing their apprenticeships they sought employment in a shop. Their search often required them to migrate to some other area, thus becoming "journeymen." As in farming, the ultimate goal was independence.

With the exception of midwifery, there were few opportunities for women outside the household. By law, husbands held managerial rights over family property, but widows received support in the form of a one-third lifetime interest, known as "dower," in a deceased husband's real estate (the rest of the estate being divided among the heirs). And in certain occupations, such as printing (which had a tradition of employing women), widows succeeded their husbands in business.

The Frontier Heritage

The colonial societies of eighteenth-century North America also shared perspectives unique to their common frontier heritage. European colonists came from Old World societies in which land was scarce and monopolized by property-owning elites. They settled in a continent where, for the most part, land was abundant and cheap. This was probably the most important distinction between North America and Europe. American historians once tied the existence of this "free land" directly to the development of democracy. But the colonial experience encouraged assumptions that were anything but democratic.

One of the most important of those colonial assumptions was the popular acceptance of forced labor. A woman of eighteenth-century South Carolina once offered advice on how to achieve a good living. "Get a few slaves," she declared, and "beat them well to make them work hard." There was a labor shortage throughout all the colonies. In a land where free men and women could work for themselves on their own plot of ground, there was little incentive to work for wages. Thus, the use of forced labor was one of the few ways a landowner could secure an agricultural workforce. In the Spanish borderlands, captured Apache children were made lifetime servants, and an Indian slave trade flourished through the eighteenth century. In Quebec one could see African American slaves from the French Caribbean working side-by-side with enslaved Indians captured by other tribes in the West and sold to French traders. In Philadelphia, according to Benjamin Franklin, wages for free workers were so high that most of the unskilled labor was "performed chiefly by indentured servants." All the colonists came from European cultures that believed in social hierarchy and subordination, and involuntary servitude was easily incorporated into their worldview.

At least half the immigrants to eighteenth-century British America arrived as indentured servants. This system allowed poor immigrants to arrange passage across the Atlantic in exchange for four or five years of service in America. Usually indentured servants were single men, often skilled artisans. Sometimes families without means emigrated as "redemptioners." Under this system, they arranged with the ship's owner to pay their passage upon arrival in North America. If no one in the colonies stepped forth to pay, they sold themselves into service for the payment. Family members were sometimes separated. In addition, during the eighteenth century the British sent over, mostly to the Chesapeake, some 50,000 convicts sentenced to seven or fourteen years at hard labor. One historian, accounting for the cost of passage and upkeep, estimates that indentured servants earned their masters, on average, about fifty pounds sterling over their terms of service, the equivalent of something like four or five thousand dollars in today's values. But at the conclusion of their terms of service, eighteenth-century servants enjoyed more opportunity than their seventeenth-century counterparts, probably because of the rise in overall prosperity in the British colonies. Over the course of the century the chance of former servants achieving

positions of moderate comfort rose from one in five in 1700 to better than fifty-fifty by 1750. The majority of redemptioners, for example, appear to have become small farmers.

The expectation of property ownership was a second important assumption that flowed from the frontier heritage and abundance of land in colonial America. This expectation led to rising popular demands in all regions that more and more land be taken from the Indian inhabitants and opened to white settlement. Some colonists justified such wars of dispossession by arguing, as Puritans did, that Indians deserved to lose their lands because they had failed to use their lands to the utmost capacity. Others simply maintained that Indians should be dispossessed because they were "savages." But whatever their specific justifications, the majority of colonists, whether British, Spanish, or French, accepted the violence and brutality directed against Indian tribes as an essential aspect of colonial life. This attitude was as true of inclusive as exclusive societies—with the difference that in the former, native peoples were incorporated into colonial society, while in the latter, tribes were pushed from the frontier. Thus did the Puritan minister Cotton Mather praise Hannah Dustin, a New England woman who escaped her captors during King William's War by killing and scalping nine sleeping Indians, including two women and six children. With this as the prevailing attitude, one can understand why Eunice Williams was hesitant to return to Deerfield after she had married an Indian.

DIVERGING SOCIAL AND POLITICAL PATTERNS

Despite these important similarities among the colonial regions of North America, in the eighteenth century the experience of the British colonies began to diverge sharply from that of the French and Spanish. Immigration, economic growth, and provincial political struggles all pushed British colonists in a radically new direction.

Population Growth and Immigration

All the colonial regions of North America experienced unprecedented growth in the eighteenth century. "Our people must at least be doubled every twenty years," wrote Benjamin Franklin in a remarkable 1751 essay on population, and he was nearly right. In 1700 there were 290,000 colonists north of Mexico; fifty years later they had grown to approximately 1.3 million, an average annual growth rate of about 3 percent. Typical preindustrial societies grow at rates of less than 1 percent per year, approximately the pace of Europe's expansion in the eighteenth century.

High fertility played an important role in this extra-ordinary growth. It was common for women in the British colonies to bear seven or more children during their childbearing years, and colonial women in the French villages along the St. Lawrence or the towns of New Mexico were equally fertile. In addition, mortality rates were low: in most colonial areas there were fewer than 30 deaths for every 1,000 persons, a death rate 15 or 20 percent lower than rates in Europe. Moreover, levels of infant mortality were low. Blessed with fertile lands and the effectiveness of Indian agricultural techniques, North America had no famines. For the colonists, North America was a remarkably healthy environment.

Yet, although all North American colonial societies had high fertility rates, the British colonies grew far more rapidly than did those of other nations. The difference is explained by immigration. The Spanish, fearful of depleting their population at home, severely limited the migration of their own subjects to their colonies, and absolutely forbade the immigration of foreigners. The French, dedicated to keeping their North American colonies exclusively Catholic, ignored the desire of Protestant Huguenots to emigrate. Instead they sent thousands of Catholic *engagés* to Canada, but most returned, discouraged by the climate and the lack of commercial opportunity. The English, however, sent an estimated 400,000 of their own countrymen to populate their North American colonies during the seventeenth and eighteenth centuries. Moreover, the British were the only colonial power to encourage the immigration of foreign nationals.

Social Class

Although traditional working roles were transferred to North America, attempts to transplant the European class system by creating land monopolies were far less successful. In New France the landowning seigneurs claimed privileges similar to those enjoyed by their aristocratic counterparts at home; the Spanish system of encomienda and the great manors created by the Dutch and continued by the English along the Hudson River also represented attempts to bring the essence of European feudalism to North America. But in most areas, because settlers had free access to land, these monopolies proved difficult or impossible to maintain. There was a system of economic rank and an unequal distribution of wealth, prestige, and power. North American society was not aristocratic, but neither was it without social hierarchy.

In New Spain the official criterion for status was racial purity. *Españoles* (Spaniards) or *gente de razon* (literally, "people of reason") occupied the top rung of the social ladder, with mestizos, mulattoes, and others on descending levels. African slaves and Indians were at the bottom. In the isolated northern borderlands, however, these distinctions tended to disappear, with *castas* (persons of mixed background) enjoying considerably more opportunity. Mestizos who acquired land might suddenly be reclassified as españoles. The landlords of New France and the Spanish borderlands may have lacked the means to accumulate real wealth, but they lived lives of elegance compared to the hard toil of the people who owed them labor service or rent.

Despite their lack of titles, the wealthy planters and merchants in the British colonies lived far more extravagantly than the seigneurs of New France or the dons of the Spanish borderlands. What separated the culture of class in the British colonies from that of New France or New Mexico was not so much the material conditions of life as the prevailing attitude toward social rank. In the Catholic cultures, the upper class attempted to obscure its origins, claiming descent from European nobility. But in British North America people celebrated social mobility. The class system was remarkably open, and the entrance of newly successful planters, commercial farmers, and merchants into the upper ranks was not only possible but common, although by midcentury most upper-class families had inherited, not earned, their wealth.

To be sure, there was a large lower class in the British colonies. Slaves, bound servants, and poor laboring families made up at least 40 percent of the population. For them, the standard of living did not rise above bare subsistence. Most lived from hand to mouth, often suffering through seasons of severe privation. A small proportion of poor whites could expect their condition to improve during their lifetimes, but slaves were a permanently servile population. Enslaved African Americans stood apart from the gains in the standard of living enjoyed by immigrants from Europe. Their lives had been degraded beyond measure from the conditions prevailing in their native lands.

The feature of the class system most often commented on by eighteenth-century observers was not the character or composition of the lower ranks but rather the size and strength of the middle class, a rank entirely absent in the colonies of France and Spain. As one Pennsylvanian wrote at midcentury, "The people of this province are generally of the middling sort." More than half the population of the British colonies, and nearly 70 percent of all white settlers, might be so classified. Most were families of landowning farmers of small to moderate means, but the group also included artisans, craftsmen, and small shopkeepers.

Households solidly in the center of this broad ranking owned land or other property worth approximately £500 and earned the equivalent of about £100 per year. They enjoyed a standard of living higher than that of the great majority of people in England and Europe. The low mortality of British Americans was important testimony to generally better living conditions. Touring the British Isles at midcentury, Benjamin Franklin was shocked at the squalid conditions of farmers and workers.

Economic Growth and Increasing Inequality

One of the most important differences among North American colonial regions in the eighteenth century was the economic stagnation in New France and New Spain compared with the impressive economic growth of the British colonies. Weighed down by royal bureaucracies and overbearing regulations, neither the French Crescent nor New Spain evidenced much prosperity. In British North America, however, per capita production grew at an annual rate of 0.5 percent. Granted, this was considerably less than the average annual growth rate of 1.5 percent that prevailed during the era of industrialization, from the early nineteenth through the mid-twentieth century. But as economic growth steadily increased the size of the economic pie, most middle- and upper-class British Americans began to enjoy improved living conditions, better than those of any people in Europe. Improving standards of living and open access to land encouraged British colonists to see theirs as a society where hard work and savings could translate into prosperity, thus producing an upward spiral of economic growth.

At the same time, this growth produced increasing social inequality. In the commercial cities, for example, prosperity was accompanied by a concentration of assets in the hands of wealthy families. In Boston and Philadelphia at the beginning of the century, the wealthiest 10 percent of households owned about half of the taxable property; by about midcentury this small group owned 65 percent or more. In the commercial farming region of Chester County in southeastern Pennsylvania, the holdings of the wealthiest 10 percent of households increased more modestly, from 24 to 30 percent of taxable property during the first half of the century. But at the same time the share of taxable property owned by the poorest third fell from 17 to 6 percent. The general standard of living may have been rising, but the rich were getting richer and the poor poorer. The greatest concentrations of wealth occurred in the cities and in regions dominated by commercial farming, whether slave or free, while the greatest economic equality continued to be found in areas of self-sufficient farming such as the backcountry.

Another eighteenth-century trend worked against the hope of social mobility in the countryside. As pop-

ulation grew and as generations succeeded one another in older settlements, all the available land in the towns was taken up. Under the pressure of increased demand, land prices rose almost beyond the reach of families of modest means. As a family's land was divided among the heirs of the second and third generations, parcels became ever smaller and, thus, more intensively farmed. Eventually the soil was exhausted.

By the eighteenth century, many farm communities did not have sufficient land to provide those of the emerging generation with farms of their own. There were notable increases in the number of landless poor in the towns of New England as well as the disturbing appearance of the "strolling poor," homeless people who traveled from town to town looking for work or a handout. Destitute families crowded into Boston, which by midcentury was spending more than £5,000 annually on relief for the poor, who were required to wear a large red P on their clothing. In other regions, land shortages in the older settlements almost inevitably prompted people to leave in search of cheap or free land.

In New England, young men unable to obtain land in hometowns often moved to the towns and cities of the seaboard, for New England enjoyed a strong seafaring tradition. Fishing and shipping had first become important during the late seventeenth century, as merchants struggled to find a successful method of earning foreign exchange. The expanding slave market in the South opened new opportunities, prompting the growth of thriving coastal ports such as New Haven, Newport, Salem, and Boston. By midcentury New England had become the most urban of all North America's regions. Boston, the largest city in the British colonies, was the metropolis of a region that included not only New England but also the maritime settlements of Nova Scotia and Newfoundland, where New England merchants dominated commerce and recruited seamen for their fishing and shipping fleets.

Contrasts in Colonial Politics

The administration of the Spanish and French colonies was highly centralized. French Canada was ruled by a superior council including the royal governor (in charge of military affairs), the intendant (responsible for civil administration), and the bishop of Quebec. New Spain was governed by the Council of the Indies, which sat in Spain, and direct executive authority over all political affairs was exercised by the viceroy in Mexico City. Although local communities had informal independence, the highly bureaucratized and centralized governments of the French Crescent and the Spanish borderlands left little room for the development of vigorous traditions of self-government.

The situation in the British colonies was quite different. During the early eighteenth century the British government of Prime Minister Robert Walpole assumed that a decentralized administration would best accomplish the nation's economic goals. Contented colonies, Walpole argued, would present far fewer problems. Each of the colonies was administered by royally appointed governors, its taxes and finances set by constituent assemblies. Those who owned property could vote for representatives to the assembly. Because many people—mostly white males—owned property, the proportion of adult white men able to vote was 50 percent or higher in all the British colonies. Proportionally, the electorate of the British colonies was the largest in the world.

That did not mean, however, that the British colonies were democratic. The basic principle of order in eighteenth-century British culture was the ideal of deference to natural hierarchies. The well-ordered family, in which children were to be strictly governed by their parents, and wives by their husbands, was the common metaphor for civil order. Members of subordinate groups, such as women, the non-English, African American slaves, servants, and Indians—who in some colonies constituted nine of every ten adults in the population—could not vote or hold public office. Moreover, for the most part the men who did vote chose wealthy landowners, planters, or merchants to serve as their leaders. Thus, provincial assemblies were controlled by colonial elites.

To educated British colonists, the word "democracy" implied rule by the mob, the normal order of things turned upside-down. Over the century there was, however, an important trend toward stronger institutions of representative government. By midcentury most colonial assemblies in British North America had achieved considerable power over provincial affairs and shared authority with governors and other imperial officials. They collected local revenues and allocated funds for government programs, asserted the right to audit the accounts of public officers, and in some cases even acquired the power to approve the appointment of provincial officials. Because the assemblies controlled the finances of government—the "purse strings"—most royal governors were unable to resist this trend.

The royal governors who were most successful at realizing their agendas were those who became adept at playing one provincial faction off against another. All this conflict had the important effect of schooling the colonial elite in the art of politics. It was not democratic politics, but schooling in the ways of patronage, coalition-building, and behind-the-scenes intrigue that would have important implications for the development of American institutions.

THE CULTURAL TRANSFORMATION OF BRITISH NORTH AMERICA

Despite broad similarities, the colonial regions of North America developed along divergent lines during the eighteenth century. The British colonies were marked by increasing ethnic diversity, economic growth, social tensions, and conflictual politics that proved to be training for self-government. In the middle decades of the eighteenth century, significant cultural transformation began to take place. New ideas and writings associated with the Enlightenment made their way across the Atlantic on the same ships that transported European immigrants and European goods. In New Spain and New France, by contrast, colonial officials worked diligently to suppress these challenging new ideas and writings. The Catholic Church effectively banned the works of hundreds of authors. In Mexico, officials of the Inquisition conducted house-to-house searches in pursuit of prohibited texts that they feared had been smuggled into the country.

The Enlightenment Challenge

Drawing from the discoveries of Galileo, Copernicus, and the seventeenth-century scientists René Descartes and Sir Isaac Newton, Enlightenment thinkers in Britain and on the Continent argued that the universe was governed by natural laws that people could understand and apply to their own advantage. John Locke, for example, articulated a philosophy of reason in proposing that the state existed to provide for the happiness and security of individuals, who were endowed with inalienable rights to life, liberty, and property. Enlightenment writers emphasized rationality, harmony, and order, themes that stood in stark contrast to folk culture's traditional emphasis on the unfathomable mysteries of God and nature and the inevitability of human failure and disorder.

Enlightenment thinking undoubtedly appealed most to those whose ordered lives had improved their lot. The colonial elite had good reason to believe in progress. They sent their sons to college, where the texts of the new thinkers were promoted. Harvard, established in 1636, remained the only institution of higher education in British America until 1693, when Anglicans established the College of William and Mary at Williamsburg, soon to become the new capital of Virginia. Puritans in Connecticut, believing that Harvard was too liberal, founded Yale College in 1701. The curricula of these colleges, modeled on those of Oxford and Cambridge in England, were designed to train ministers, but gradually each institu-

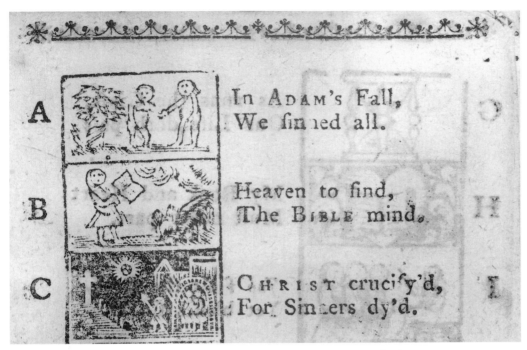

The first page of the *New England Primer* (1689), published in Boston, which in its various editions sold more than 5 million copies. In addition to the letters of the alphabet, illustrated by crude but charming woodcuts and couplets, the book contained simple moral texts based on Biblical history and wisdom.

SOURCE: Courtesy American Antiquarian Society.

tion introduced courses and professors influenced by the Enlightenment.

A mixture of traditional and Enlightenment views characterized the colonial colleges, as it did the thought of men like Cotton Mather. A conservative defender of the old order, Mather wrote a book supporting the existence of witches. On the other hand, he was also a member of the Royal Society, an early supporter of inoculation against smallpox, and a defender of the Copernican sun-centered model of the universe.

About half the adult men and a quarter of the adult women of the British colonies could read, a literacy rate that was comparable to those of England and Scandinavia. In striking contrast, in the French and Spanish colonies reading was a skill confined to a tiny minority of upper-class men. In New England, where the Puritans were committed to Bible reading and developed a system of public education, literacy rates were 85 percent among men and approximately 50 percent among women—the highest in the entire Atlantic world. But the tastes of ordinary readers ran to traditional rather than Enlightenment fare. Not surprisingly, the best-selling book of the colonial era was the Bible. In second place was that unique American literary form, the captivity narrative, (including the

Reverend John Williams's *The Redeemed Captive Returning to Zion*, cited in the beginning of this chapter), most with a lot less religion and a great deal more gore.

Another popular literary form was the almanac, a combination calendar, astrological guide, and sourcebook of medical advice and farming tips reflecting the concerns of traditional folk culture. The best remembered is *Poor Richard's Almanac* (1732–57), published by Philadelphia newspaper publisher Benjamin Franklin, although it was preceded and outlived by a great many others. What was so innovative about Franklin's almanac, and what made it so important, was the manner in which the author used this traditional literary form to promote the new Enlightenment emphasis on useful and practical knowledge. Posing as the simple bumpkin Poor Richard, the highly sophisticated Franklin was one of the first Americans to bring Enlightenment thought to ordinary folk.

The growth of the economy in the British colonies and the development of a colonial upper class stimulated the emergence of a more cosmopolitan Anglican culture, particularly in the cities of the Atlantic coast. A rising demand for drama, poetry, essays, novels, and history was met by urban booksellers who imported British publications.

A Decline in Religious Devotion

At the same time that these new ideas were flourishing, religion seemed in decline. South of New England, the Anglican Church was weak, its ministers uninspiring, and many families remained "unchurched." A historian of religion has estimated that only one adult in fifteen was a member of a congregation. Although this figure may understate the impact of religion on community life, it helps keep things in perspective.

The Puritan churches of New England also suffered declining membership and falling attendance at services, and many ministers began to warn of Puritanism's "declension," pointing to the "dangerous" trend toward the "evil of toleration." By the second decade of the eighteenth century only one in five New Englanders belonged to an established congregation. When Puritanism had been a sect, membership in the church was voluntary and leaders could demand that followers testify to their religious conversion. But when Puritanism became an established church, attendance was expected of all townspeople, and conflicts inevitably arose over the requirement of a conversion experience. An agreement of 1662, known as the Half-Way Covenant, offered a practical solution: members' children who had not experienced conversion themselves could join as "half-way" members, restricted only from participation in communion. Thus, the Puritans chose to manage rather than to resolve the conflicts involved in becoming an established religion. Tensions also developed between congregational autonomy and the central control that traditionally accompanied the establishment of a state church. In 1708 the churches of Connecticut agreed to the Saybrook Platform, which enacted a system of governance by councils of ministers and elders rather than by congregations. This reform also had the effect of weakening the passion and commitment of church members.

In addition, an increasing number of Congregationalists began to question the strict Calvinist theology of predestination—the belief that God had predetermined the few men and women who would be saved in the Second Coming. In the eighteenth century many Puritans turned to the much more comforting idea that God had given people the freedom to choose salvation by developing their faith and by doing good works. This belief, known as Arminianism, was in harmony with the Enlightenment view that men and women were not helpless pawns but rational beings who could actively shape their own destinies. Also implicit in these new views was an image of God as a loving rather than a punishing father. Arminianism became a force at Harvard in the early eighteenth century, and soon a new generation of Arminian ministers began to assume leadership in New England's churches. These liberal ideas appealed to groups experiencing economic and social improvement, especially commercial farmers, merchants, and the comfortable middle class with its rising expectations. But among ordinary people, especially those in the countryside where traditional patterns lingered, there was a good deal of opposition to these unorthodox new ideas.

The Great Awakening

The first stirrings of a movement challenging this rationalist approach to religion occurred during the 1730s, most notably in the movement sparked by Reverend Jonathan Edwards in the community of Northampton, in western Massachusetts. As the leaders of the community increasingly devoted their energies to the pursuit of wealth, the enthusiasm seemed to go out of religion. The congregation adopted rules allowing church membership without evidence of a conversion experience and adopted a seating plan for the church that placed wealthy families in the prominent pews, front and center. But the same economic forces that made the "River Gods"—as the wealthy landowners of the Connecticut Valley were known—also impoverished others. Young people from the community's poorer families grew disaffected as they were forced to postpone marriage because of the scarcity and expense of the land needed to set up a farm household. Increasingly they refused to attend church meetings, instead gathering together at night for "frolics" that only seemed to increase their discontent.

Reverend Edwards made this group of young people his special concern. Believing that they needed to "have their hearts touched," he preached to them in a style that appealed to their emotions. For the first time in a generation, the meetinghouse shook with the fire and passion of Puritan religion. "Before the sermon was done," one Northampton parishioner remembered about one notable occasion, "there was a great moaning and crying through the whole house—What shall I do to be saved?—Oh I am going to Hell!—Oh what shall I do for Christ?" Religious fervor swept through the community, and church membership began to grow. There was more to this than the power of one preacher, for similar revivals were soon breaking out in other New England communities, as well as among German pietists and Scots–Irish Presbyterians in Pennsylvania. Complaining of "spiritual coldness," people abandoned ministers whose sermons read like rational dissertations for those whose preaching was more emotional.

These local revivals became an intercolonial phenomenon thanks to the preaching of George Whitefield, an evangelical Anglican minister from England, who in 1738 made the first of several tours of the colonies. By all accounts, his preaching had a powerful effect. Even Benjamin Franklin, a religious skeptic, wrote of the "extraordinary influence of [Whitefield's] oratory" after attending an outdoor service in Philadelphia where 30,000 people crowded the streets to hear him. Whitefield began as Edwards did, chastising his listeners as "half animals and half devils," but he left them with the hope that God would be responsive to their desire for salvation. Whitefield avoided sectarian differences. "God help us to forget party names and become Christians in deed and truth," he declared.

Historians of religion consider this widespread colonial revival of religion, which later generations called the Great Awakening, to be an American version of the second phase of the Protestant Reformation (see Chapter 2). Religious leaders condemned the laxity, decadence, and officalism of established Protestantism and reinvigorated it with calls for piety and purity. People undergoing the economic and social stresses of the age, unsure about their ability to find land, marry, and participate in the promise of a growing economy, found relief in religious enthusiasm.

In Pennsylvania, two important leaders were William Tennent and his son Gilbert. An Irish-born Presbyterian, the elder Tennent was an evangelical preacher who established a school in Pennsylvania to train like-minded men for the ministry. His lampooned "Log College," as it was called, ultimately evolved into the College of New Jersey—later Princeton University—founded in 1746. In the early 1740s, disturbed by what he called the "presumptuous security" of the colonial church, Tennent toured with Whitefield and delivered the famous sermon "The Dangers of an Unconverted Ministry," in which he called upon Protestants to examine the religious convictions of their own ministers.

Among Presbyterians, open conflict broke out between the revivalists and the old guard, and in some regions the church hierarchy divided into separate organizations. In New England, similar factions, known as the New Lights and the Old Lights, accused each other of heresy. The New Lights railed against Arminianism as a rationalist heresy and called for a revival of Calvinism. The Old Lights condemned emotional enthusiasm as part of the heresy of believing in a personal and direct relationship with God outside the order of the church. Itinerant preachers appeared in the countryside, stirring up trouble. Many congregations split into feuding factions, and ministers found themselves challenged by their newly awakened parishioners. Never had there been such turmoil in New England churches.

Although some historians have raised questions about how cohesive these revivals were, they were so widespread and were typical of so many communities that they might be seen as one of the first national events in American history. They began somewhat later in the South, developing first in the mid-1740s among Scots–Irish Presbyterians, then achieved full impact with the organizational work of Methodists and particularly Baptists in the 1760s and early 1770s. These revivals not only affected white Southerners but also introduced many slaves to Christianity for the first time. Local awakenings were often a phenomenon shared by both whites and blacks. The Baptist churches of the South in the era of the American Revolution included members of both races and featured spontaneous preaching by slaves as well as masters. In the nineteenth century white and black Christians would go their separate ways, but the joint experience of the eighteenth-century Awakening shaped the religious cultures of both groups.

Many other "unchurched" colonists were brought back to Protestantism by eighteenth-century revivalism. But a careful examination of statistics suggests that the proportion of church members in the general population probably did not increase during the middle decades of the century. While the number of churches more than doubled from 1740 to 1780, the colonial population grew even faster, increasing threefold. The greatest impact was on families already associated with the churches. Before the Awakening, attendance at church had been mostly an adult affair, but throughout the colonies the revival of religion had its deepest effects on young people, who flocked to church in greater numbers than ever before. For years the number of people experiencing conversion had been steadily falling, but now full membership surged. Church membership previously had been concentrated among women, leading Cotton Mather, for one, to speculate that perhaps women were indeed more godly. But men were particularly affected by the revival of religion, and their attendance and membership rose.

The Politics of Revivalism

Revivalism appealed most of all to groups who felt bypassed by the economic and cultural development of the British colonies during the first half of the eighteenth century. The New Lights tended to draw their greatest strength from small farmers and less prosperous craftsmen. Many members of the upper class and the comfortable "middling sort" viewed the excesses of revivalism as indications of anarchy, and they became even more committed to rational religion.

Some historians have argued for important political implications of revivalism. In Connecticut, for example, Old Lights politicized the religious dispute by passing a series of laws in the General Assembly designed to suppress revivalism. In one town, separatists

CHRONOLOGY

1636	Harvard College founded
1644	Roger Williams's *Bloudy Tenent of Persecution*
1662	Half-Way Covenant in New England
1674	Bishopric of Quebec established
1680s	William Penn begins recruiting settlers from the European Continent
1682	Mary Rowlandson's *Sovereignty and Goodness of God*
1689	Toleration Act passed by Parliament
1690s	Beginnings of Jesuit missions in Arizona
1693	College of William and Mary founded
1700s	Plains Indians begin adoption of the horse
1701	Yale College founded Iroquois sign treaty of neutrality with France
1704	Deerfield raid
1708	Saybrook Platform in Connecticut
1716	Spanish begin construction of Texas missions
1730s	French decimate the Natchez and defeat the Fox Indians
1732	Franklin begins publishing *Poor Richard's Almanac*
1738	George Whitefield first tours the colonies
1740s	Great Awakening gets under way in the Northeast
1740	Parliament passes a naturalization law for the colonies
1746	College of New Jersey (Princeton) founded
1760s	Great Awakening achieves full impact in the South
1769	Spanish colonization of California begins
1775	Indian revolt at San Diego
1776	San Francisco founded
1781	Los Angeles founded

refused to pay taxes that supported the established church and were jailed. New Light judges were thrown off the bench, and others were denied their elected seats in the assembly. The arrogance of these actions was met with popular outrage: by the 1760s the Connecticut New Lights had organized themselves politically and, in what amounted to a political rebellion, succeeded in turning the Old Lights out of office. These New Light politicians would provide the leadership for the American Revolution in Connecticut.

Such direct connections between religion and politics were rare. There can be little doubt, however, that for many people revivalism offered the first opportunity to participate actively in public debate and public action that affected the direction of their lives. Choices about religious styles, ministers, and doctrine were thrown open for public discourse, and ordinary people began to believe that their opinions actually counted for something. Underlying the debate over

these issues were insecurities about warfare, economic growth, and the development of colonial society. Revivalism empowered ordinary people to question their leaders, an experience that would prove critical in the political struggles to come.

CONCLUSION

By the middle of the eighteenth century a number of distinct colonial regions had emerged in North America, all of them with rising populations who demanded that more land be seized from the Indians. Some colonies attempted to ensure homogeneity, whereas others embraced diversity. Within the British colonies, New England in particular seemed bound to the past, whereas the Middle Colonies and the backcountry pointed the way toward pluralism and expansion. These developments placed them in direct competition with the expansionist plans of the French and at odds with Indian peoples committed to the defense of their homelands.

The economic development of the British colonies introduced new social and cultural tensions that led to the Great Awakening, a massive revival of religion that was the first transcolonial event in American history.

Thousands of people experienced a renewal of religious passions, but rather than resuscitating old traditions, the Awakening pointed people toward a more active role in their own political futures. These transformations added to the differences between the British colonies, on the one hand, and New Spain and the French Crescent, on the other.

REVIEW QUESTIONS

1. What were the principal colonial regions of North America? Discuss their similarities and their differences. Contrast the development of their political systems.
2. Why did the Spanish and the French close their colonies to immigration? Why did the British open theirs? How do you explain the ethnic homogeneity of New England and the ethnic pluralism of New York and Pennsylvania?
3. What were the principal trends in the history of Indian America in the eighteenth century?
4. Discuss the development of class differences in the Spanish, French, and British colonies in the eighteenth century.
5. Discuss the effects of the Great Awakening on the subsequent history of the British colonies.

RECOMMENDED READING

Jon Butler, *Becoming America: The Revolution Before 1776* (2000). A history that emphasizes the diversity, economic prosperity, participatory politics, and religious pluralism of the eighteenth-century British colonies.

Edward Countryman, *Americans: A Collision of Histories* (1996). An important new synthesis that includes the many peoples and cultures of North America.

John Demos, *The Unredeemed Captive: A Family Story from Early America* (1994). A moving history of the Deerfield captives, focusing on the experience of Eunice Williams, the unredeemed captive.

W. J. Eccles, *The Canadian Frontier, 1534–1760* (1983). An introduction to the history of French America by a leading scholar on colonial Canada.

David Hackett Fischer, *Albion's Seed: Four British Folkways in America* (1990). An engaging history with fascinating details on the regions of New England, Pennsylvania, Virginia, and the backcountry.

Jack P. Greene, *Pursuits of Happiness: The Social Development of Early Modern British Colonies and the Formation of American Culture* (1986). A distillation of a tremendous amount of historical material on community life in British North America.

Frank Lambert, *Inventing the "Great Awakening"* (1999). Argues that the revivialists themselves created the idea of the Great Awakening to further their evangelical work.

Jackson Turner Main, *The Social Structure of Revolutionary America* (1965). A detailed treatment of colonial social structure, with statistics, tables, and enlightening interpretations.

D. W. Meinig, *The Shaping of America: Atlantic America, 1492–1800* (1986). A geographer's overview of the historical development of the North American continent in the era of European colonialism. Provides a survey of the British and French colonies.

Lucy Eldersveld Murphy, *A Gathering of Rivers: Indians, Métis, and Mining in the Western Great Lakes, 1737–1832* (2000). Demonstrates the success of Indian communities in adapting to colonialism through the diversification of their economies, intermarriage, and constructing multiethnic communities.

David J. Weber, *The Spanish Frontier in North America* (1992). A magnificent treatment of the entire Spanish borderlands, from Florida to California. Includes important chapters on colonial government and social life.

Marianne S. Wokeck, *Trade in Strangers: The Beginning of Mass Migration to North America* (1999). The first important study of immigration in the eighteenth century, arguing that these migrations served as models for European mass migration in the next century.

ON THE WEB

http://lcweb.loc.gov/exhibits/religion/rel02.html

This web page is a Library of Congress exhibit on religion in eighteenth-century America with links to additional pages on the impact of religion on the American Revolution, the Congress of the Confederation period, state governments, the New Republic, and the federal government. Beside strong factual explanations, this site contains many primary source documents and graphics to support your research.

The following sites are posted by the National Humanities Center. Each essay is a good, general introduction to the topic listed. Some contain connections to web sites with further information.

http://www.nhc.rtp.nc.us:8080/tserve/eighteen/ ekeyinfo/grawaken.htm

"History of the Great Awakening" by Christine Leigh Heyrman, Department of History at the University of Delaware.

http://www.nhc.rtp.nc.us:8080/tserve/eighteen/ ekeyinfo/midcol.htm

"The Middle Colonies as the Birthplace of American Religious Pluralism" by Patricia Bonomi, Professor Emeritus of History at New York University.

http://www.nhc.rtp.nc.us:8080/tserve/eighteen/ ekeyinfo/chureng.htm

"The Church of England in Early America" by Christine Leigh Heyrman, Department of History at the University of Delaware.

http://www.nhc.rtp.nc.us:8080/tserve/eighteen/ ekeyinfo/erelwom.htm

"Religion, Women, and the Family in Early America" by Christine Leigh Heyrman, Department of History at the University of Delaware.

http://www.prenhall.com/faragherbrief/map5.1

Through a series of interactive maps, look at the spread of English settlement in the eighteenth century. How did the movement into the backcountry affect the relations among colonists, Indians, and English authorities?

AMERICAN COMMUNITIES

The First Continental Congress Shapes a National Political Community

BRITAIN'S NORTH AMERICAN COLONIES HAD ENJOYED CONSIDERABLE prosperity during the late seventeenth and early eighteenth centuries. Beginning with the Stamp Act in 1765, however, the British government began to apply pressure, largely in the form of taxes and new trade restrictions, that drew increasing resistance from the colonies. In convening the First Continental Congress in September 1774, the colonies made clear their displeasure with the government's actions. Fifty-six elected delegates from twelve of the colonies met at Philadelphia to draft a common response to what they called the Intolerable Acts—the closing of the port of Boston, the suspension of Massachusetts government, and several other measures of British repression—that were the latest attempt to force the colonies to accept the power of Parliament to make laws binding them "in all cases whatsoever." This was the first meeting of the colonies since the Stamp Act Congress of 1765 (discussed later in this chapter). If the colonies now failed to act together, they would be "attacked and destroyed by piecemeal," declared Arthur Lee of Virginia. "Every part will in its turn feel the vengeance which it would not unite to repel." Abigail Adams, the politically astute wife of John Adams of Massachusetts, agreed. "You have before you," she wrote to her husband, "the greatest national concerns that ever came before any people."

The opening minutes of the first session on September 5 did not bode well. One delegate moved that they begin with prayer; another responded that they were "so divided in religious sentiments, some Episcopalians, some Quakers, some Anabaptists, some Presbyterians and some Congregationalists, so that we could not join in the same act of worship." Were the delegates to be stymied from the very beginning by things that separated rather than united them? John Adams's cousin, fellow Massachusetts delegate Samuel Adams, jumped to his feet. He was no bigot, he said, "and could hear a prayer from any gentleman of piety and virtue who was at the same time a friend to his country." The delegates finally agreed to ask a local clergyman, a supporter of the American cause, to officiate. The minister took for his text the Thirty-fifth Psalm: "Plead my cause, O Lord, with them that strive with me; fight against them that fight against me." John Adams was delighted. The minister "prayed with such fervor, such Ardor, such Earnestness and

Pathos, and in Language so elegant and sublime," he wrote home, that "it has had an excellent Effect upon every Body here."

This incident highlighted the most important task confronting the Continental Congress: they had to develop trust in one another, for what they were doing was considered treason by the British authorities. They had to find a way to support the common cause without compromising their local identities. At first it was as if the delegates were "ambassadors from a dozen belligerent powers of Europe," wrote John Adams. The delegates represented different colonies, whose traditions and histories were as different as those of separate countries. Moreover, these lawyers, merchants, and planters, who were leaders in their respective colonies, were strangers to one another. Their political opinions ranged from loyalty to the British crown and empire to a belief in the necessity of violent revolution. "Every man," Adams wrote, "is a great man, an orator, a critic, a statesman, and therefore every man, upon every question, must show his oratory, his criticism, and his political abilities." As a result, he continued, "business is drawn and spun out to an immeasurable length. I believe that if it was moved and seconded that we should come to a resolution that three and two make five, we should be entertained with logic and rhetorick, law, history, politicks and mathematics concerning the subject for two whole days."

During seven weeks of deliberations, the men of the Continental Congress succeeded in forging an agreement on the principles and policies they would have to follow in addressing the most serious crisis in the history of Britain's North American colonies. Equally important, the delegates found ways to work together and harmonize their interests. They immediately resolved that each colony would have one vote, thereby committing themselves to preserving provincial autonomy. They sent their most vexing problems to committees, whose members could sound each other out on the issues without speaking for the public record, and they added to their daily routine a round of dinners, parties, and late-night drinking. The greatest single accomplishment of the Continental Congress was the creation of a community of leadership for the united colonies. "It has taken us much time to get acquainted," John Adams wrote to Abigail, but he left Philadelphia thinking of his fellow representatives as "a collection of the greatest men upon this continent."

The First Continental Congress, thus, took the first steps toward the creation of a national political community. The bonds of community can be local, regional, national, or international. In a town or village the feeling of association comes from daily, face-to-face contact, but for larger groups these feelings must be created, or "imagined," as the historian Benedict Anderson puts it. The delegates took some of the first steps in this direction. In their final declaration they pledged to "firmly agree and associate, under the sacred ties of virtue, honor and love of our "country." They urged their fellow Americans to "encourage frugality, economy, and industry, and promote agriculture, arts and the manufactures of this country," to "discountenance and discourage every species of extravagance and dissipation, especially all horse-racing, and all kinds of gaming, cock fighting, exhibitions of shows, plays, and other expensive diversions and entertainments." In other words, they called upon the common religious and cultural traditions of British Americans. They asked their countrymen to remember "the poorer sort" among them during the coming economic troubles. And in demanding that their fellow Americans "break off all dealings" and treat with contempt anyone violating the compact, the delegates were declaring who was "inside" and who was "outside" their community. Drawing boundaries is the essential first act in the construction of a new community.

Patrick Henry of Virginia, one of the delegates already committed to independence, was exuberant when the First Continental Congress adjourned in late October. "The distinctions between Virginians, Pennsylvanians, New Yorkers, and New Englanders, are no more. I am not a Virginian, but an American," he declared. Henry voiced an important truth. Great Britain had forced the colonists to recognize that they shared a community of interest distinct from that of the mother country. Theirs was a first attempt to overcome local diversity and difference in pursuit of a common national goal. In the months and years to come the strength of local community would sometimes threaten to pull them apart, and the "imagined community" of America would be sorely tested as the colonies cautiously moved toward independence. ■

Philadelphia

KEY TOPICS

- The final struggle among Great Britain, France, and American Indian tribes for control of eastern North America

- American nationalism in the aftermath of the French and Indian War

- Great Britain's changing policy toward its North American colonies

- The political assumptions of American republicanism

- The colonies' efforts to achieve unity in their confrontation with Great Britain

---

THE SEVEN YEARS' WAR IN AMERICA

The first attempt at cooperation among the leaders of the British colonies occurred in 1754, when representatives from New England, New York, Pennsylvania, and Maryland met to consider a joint approach to the French and Indian challenge. Even as the delegates met, fighting between French Canadians and Virginians began on the Ohio River, the first shots in a great global war for empire, known in Europe as the Seven Years' War, that pitted Britain (allied with Prussia) against the combined might of France, Austria, and Spain. In North America this would be the final and most destructive armed conflict between the British and the French before the French Revolution. Ultimately it decided the future of the vast region between the Appalachian Mountains and the Mississippi River and lay the ground for the conflict between the British and the colonists that led to the American Revolution.

The Albany Conference of 1754

The 1754 meeting, which included an official delegation from the Iroquois Confederacy, took place in the New York town of Albany on the Hudson River, convened by the British Board of Trade. British officials wanted the colonies to consider a collective response to the continuing conflict with New France and the Indians of the interior. High on the agenda was the negotiation of a settlement with the leaders of the Iroquois Confederacy, who had grown impatient with colonial land grabbing. Because the powerful Iroquois Confederacy, with its Covenant Chain of alliances with other Indian tribes, occupied such a strategic location between New France and the British colonies, the British could ill afford Iroquois discontent. But the

official Iroquois delegation walked out of the conference, refusing all offers to join a British alliance.

The Albany Conference did adopt Benjamin Franklin's Plan of Union, which proposed that Indian affairs, western settlement, and other items of mutual interest be placed under the authority of a grand council made up of representatives elected by the colonial assemblies and led by a royally appointed president. But the colonial assemblies rejected the Albany Plan of Union.

Colonial Aims and Indian Interests

The absence of cooperation among the colonies in North America would prove to be one of the greatest weaknesses of the British Empire, because the ensuing war would be fought at a number of widespread locations and required the coordination of command. There were three principal flash points of conflict in North America. The first was along the northern Atlantic coast. In 1713 France had ceded to Britain its colony of Acadia (which the British renamed Nova Scotia), but France then built the fortress of Louisburg, from which it guarded its fishing grounds and the St. Lawrence approach to New France. The French subsequently reinforced Louisburg to such an extent that it became known as the Gibraltar of the New World.

A second zone of conflict was the border region between New France and New York, from Niagara Falls to Lake Champlain, where Canadians and New Yorkers were in furious competition for the Indian trade. Unable to compete effectively against superior English goods, the French resorted to armed might, constructing fortifications on Lake George and reinforcing their base at Niagara. In this zone the strategic advantage was held by the Iroquois Confederacy.

It was the Ohio country—the trans-Appalachian region along the Ohio River—that became the primary

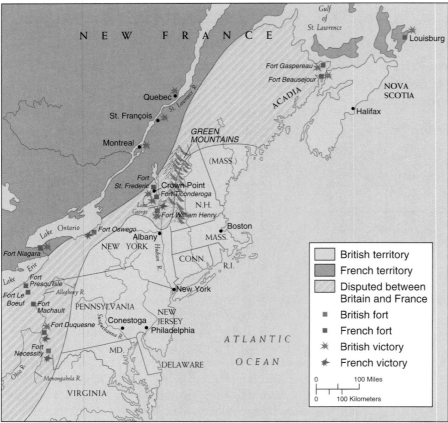

The War for Empire in North America, 1754–1763   The Seven Years' War in America (also known as the French and Indian War) was fought in three principal areas: Nova Scotia and what was then Acadia, the frontier between New France and New York, and the upper Ohio River—gateway to the Old Northwest.

British king decided to directly challenge the French claim to the upper Ohio Valley. He conferred an enormous grant of land on the Ohio Company, organized by Virginia and London capitalists, and the company made plans to build a fort at the Forks of the Ohio River.

The impending conflict did not involve only the competing colonial powers, however, for the Indian peoples of the interior had interests of their own. In addition to its native inhabitants, the Ohio country had become a refuge for Indian peoples who had fled the Northeast—Delawares, Shawnees, Hurons, and Iroquois among them. Most of the Ohio Indians opposed the British and were anxious to preserve the Appalachians as a barrier to westward expansion. They were also disturbed by the French movement into their country. The French outposts, however, unlike those of the British, did not become centers of expanding agricultural settlements.

The Iroquois Confederacy as a whole sought to play off one European power against the other, to its own advantage. In the South the Creeks carved out a similar role for themselves among the British, the French in Louisiana, and the Spanish in Florida. The Cherokees and Choctaws attempted, less successfully, to do the same. It was in the interests of these Indian tribes, in other words, to perpetuate the existing colonial stalemate. Their position would be greatly undermined by an overwhelming victory for either side.

Frontier Warfare

At the Albany Congress the delegates received news that Colonel George Washington, a young militia officer sent by the governor of Virginia to expel the French from the region granted to the Ohio Company, had been forced to surrender his troops to a French force near the headwaters of the Monongahela River. The Canadians now commanded the interior country from their base at Fort Duquesne.

Taking up the challenge, the British government dispatched two Irish regiments under General Edward Braddock across the Atlantic in 1755 to attack and destroy Fort Duquesne. Meanwhile, colonial militias (the

focus of British and French attention. This rich land was a prime target of British backcountry settlers and frontier land speculators. The French worried that their isolated settlements would be overrun by the expanding British population and that the loss of the Ohio River would threaten their entire Mississippi trading empire. To reinforce their claims, in 1749 the French sent a heavily armed force down the Ohio River to ward off the British, and in 1752, supported by their northern Indian allies, they expelled a large number of British traders from the region. To prevent the British from returning to the west, they began the next year to construct a series of forts running south from Lake Erie to the junction of the Allegheny and Monongahela rivers, the site known as the Forks of the Ohio River.

The French "have stripped us of more than nine parts in ten of North America," one British official cried, "and left us only a skirt of coast along the Atlantic shore." In preparation for a general war, the British established the port of Halifax in Nova Scotia as a counter to Louisburg. In northern New York, they strengthened existing forts and constructed new ones. Finally, the equivalent of today's National Guard) commanded by colonial officers were to strike at the New York frontier and the North Atlantic coast. An army of New England militiamen succeeded in capturing two important French forts on the border of Nova Scotia, but the other two prongs of the campaign were failures. The offensive in New York was repulsed. And in the worst defeat of a British army during the eighteenth century, Braddock's force was destroyed by a smaller number of French and Indians on the upper Ohio, and Braddock himself was killed.

Braddock's defeat was followed by the outbreak of full-scale warfare between Britain and France in 1756. Known as the Seven Years' War in Europe, in North America it came to be called the French and Indian War. The fighting of 1756 and 1757 was a near catastrophe for Great Britain. Canadians captured the British forts in northern New York. Indians pounded backcountry settlements, killed thousands of settlers, and raided deep into the coastal colonies, throwing British colonists into panic. The absence of colonial cooperation greatly hampered the British attempt to mount a counterattack. When British commanders tried to exert direct control over provincial troops, in order to coordinate their strategy, they succeeded only in angering local authorities.

The Conquest of Canada

In the darkest days of 1757, William Pitt, an enthusiastic advocate of British expansion, became prime minister of Great Britain. "I know that I can save this country," Pitt declared, "and that no one else can." Deciding that the global war could be won in North America, he subsidized the Prussians to fight the war in Europe and reserved his own forces and resources for naval and colonial operations. Pitt committed the British to the conquest of Canada and the elimination of all French competition in North America. Such a goal could be achieved only with a tremendous outpouring of men and money. By promising that the war would be fought "at His Majesty's expense," Pitt was able to buy colonial cooperation. A massive infusion of British currency and credit greatly stimulated the North American economy. Pitt dispatched over 20,000 regular British troops across the Atlantic. Combining them with colonial forces, he massed over 50,000 armed men against Canada.

The British attracted Indian support for their plans by "redressing the grievances complained of by the Indians, with respect to the lands which have been fraudulently taken from them," in the words of a British official. In 1758 officials promised the Iroquois Confederacy and the Ohio Indians that the crown would "agree upon clear and fixed boundaries between our set-

tlements and their hunting grounds, so that each party may know their own and be a mutual protection to each other of their respective possessions."

Thus did Pitt succeed in reversing the course of the war. Regular and provincial forces captured Louisburg in July 1758, setting the stage for the penetration of the St. Lawrence Valley. A month later a force of New Englanders captured the strategic French fort of Oswego on Lake Ontario, thereby preventing the Canadians from resupplying their western posts. Encouraged by British promises, many Indian tribes abandoned the French alliance. The French were forced to give up Fort Duquesne, and a large British force soon took control of this French fort at the Forks of the Ohio, renaming the post Fort Pitt (Pittsburgh today) in honor of the prime minister. "Blessed be God," wrote a Boston editor. "The long looked for day is arrived that has now fixed us on the banks of the Ohio." The last of the French forts on the New York frontier fell in 1759. In the South, regular and provincial British troops invaded the homeland of the Cherokees and crushed them.

British forces now converged on Quebec, the heart of French Canada. In the summer of 1759 British troops, responding to General James Wolfe's order to "burn and lay waste the country," plundered farms and shelled the city of Quebec. Finally, in an epic battle fought on the Plains of Abraham before the city walls, more than 2,000 British, French, American, and Canadian men lost their lives, including both Wolfe and the French commander, the Marquis de Montcalm. The British army prevailed, and Quebec fell. Finally, the conquest of Montreal in 1760 marked the destruction of the French empire in America.

In the final two years of the war the British swept French ships from the seas, invaded Havana and conquered Cuba, took possession of several other important Spanish and French colonies in the Caribbean, achieved dominance in India, and even captured the Spanish Philippines. In the Treaty of Paris, signed in 1763, France lost all its possessions on the North American mainland. It ceded its claims east of the Mississippi to Great Britain, with the exception of New Orleans. That town, along with the other French trans-Mississippi claims, passed to Spain. For its part, in exchange for the return of all its Caribbean and Pacific colonies, Spain ceded Florida to Britain. The imperial rivalry in eastern North America that had begun in the sixteenth century now came to an end with complete victory for the British Empire.

The Struggle for the West

Both the French and the British had long used gift-giving as a way of gaining favor with Indians. The Spanish officials who replaced the French in Louisiana made an effort to continue the old policy. But the British military governor of the western region, General Jeffery Amherst, in one of his first official actions, banned presents to Indian chiefs and tribes, demanding that they learn to live without "charity." Not only were Indians angered by Amherst's reversal of custom, but they were also frustrated by his refusal to supply them with the ammunition they required for hunting. Many were left starving.

In this climate, hundreds of Ohio Indians became disciples of an Indian visionary named Neolin ("The Enlightened One" in Algonquian), known to the English as the Delaware Prophet. The core of Neolin's teaching was that Indians had been corrupted by European ways and needed to purify themselves by returning to their traditions and preparing for a holy war.

In May 1763, the Indian confederacy simultaneously attacked all the British forts in the West. Although they sacked and burned eight British posts, the Indians failed to take the key forts of Niagara, Detroit, and Pitt. The Indians fought on for another year, but most of the Indians sued for peace, fearing the destruction of their villages. The British came to terms because they knew they could not overwhelm the Indian peoples. The war thus ended in stalemate.

Even before the uprising, the British had been at work on a policy they hoped would help to resolve frontier tensions. In the Royal Proclamation of 1763, the British government set aside the region west of the crest of the Appalachian Mountains as "Indian Country," and required the specific authorization of the crown for any purchase of these protected Indian lands.

Colonists had expected that the removal of the French threat would allow them to move unencumbered into the West, regardless of the wishes of the Indian inhabitants. They could not understand why the British would award territory to Indian enemies who had slaughtered more than 4,000 settlers during the previous war. In fact, the British proved unable and ultimately unwilling to prevent the westward migration that was to be a dynamic part of the colonization of British North America. Within a few years of the war, New Englanders by the thousands were moving into the northern Green Mountain district, known as Vermont. In the middle colonies, New York settlers pushed ever closer to the homeland of the Iroquois, while others settled within the protective radius of Fort Pitt in western Pennsylvania. Hunters, stock herders, and farmers crossed over the first range of the

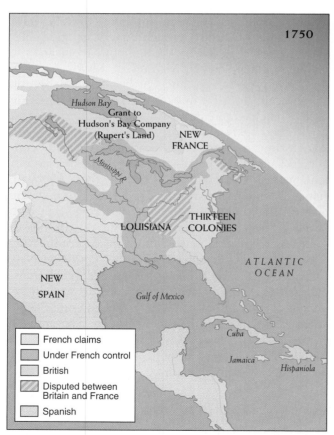

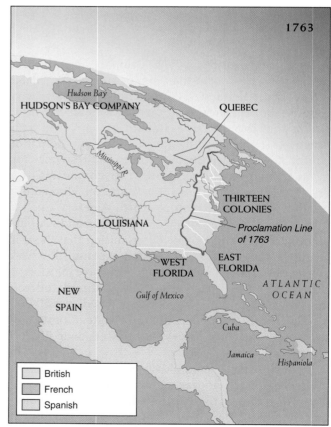

European Claims in North America, 1750 and 1763   As a result of the British victory in the Seven Years' War, the map of colonial claims in North America was fundamentally transformed.

Appalachians in Virginia and North Carolina, planting pioneer communities in what are now West Virginia and eastern Tennessee.

Moreover, the press of population growth and economic development turned the attention of investors and land speculators to the area west of the Appalachians. In response to demands by settlers and speculators, British authorities were soon pressing the Iroquois and Cherokees for cessions of land in Indian Country. No longer able to play off rival colonial powers, Indians were reduced to a choice between compliance and resistance. Weakened by the recent war, they chose to sign away lands.

The individual colonies were even more aggressive. Locked in a dispute with Pennsylvania about jurisdiction in the Ohio country, in 1773 Virginia governor John Murray, Earl of Dunmore, sent a force to occupy Fort Pitt. In 1774, in an attempt to gain legitimacy for his dispute with Pennsylvania, Dunmore provoked a frontier war with the Shawnees. After defeating them, he forced their cession of the upper Ohio River Valley to Virginia.

THE IMPERIAL CRISIS IN BRITISH NORTH AMERICA

No colonial power of the mid-eighteenth century could match Britain in projecting imperial power over the face of the globe. During the years following its victory in the Seven Years' War, Britain turned confidently to the reorganization of its North American empire. This new colonial policy plunged British authorities into a new and ultimately more threatening conflict with the colonists, who had begun to develop a sense of a separate identity.

The Emergence of American Nationalism

Despite the anger of frontier settlers over the Proclamation of 1763, the conclusion of the Seven Years' War had left most colonists proud of their place in the British empire. But during the war many had begun to note important contrasts between themselves and the mother country. The soldiers of the British army, for example, shocked Americans with their profane, lewd, and violent behavior. But the colonists were equally shocked by the swift and terrible punishment that aristocratic officers used to keep these soldiers in line. Those who had witnessed such savage punishments found it easy to believe in the threat of Britain enslaving American colonists.

Colonial forces, by contrast, were composed of volunteer companies. Officers tempered their administration of punishment, knowing they had to maintain the

enthusiasm of their troops. Discipline thus fell considerably below the standards to which British officers were accustomed. "Riff-raff," one British general said of the colonials, "the lowest dregs of the people, both officers and men." For their part, many colonial officers believed that the British ignored the important role the Americans had played in the Seven Years' War. During that war many colonists began to see themselves as distinct from the British.

The Seven Years' War also strengthened a sense of identity among the colonies. Farmers who never before had ventured outside the communities of their birth fought in distant regions with men like themselves from other colonies. Such experiences reinforced a developing nationalist perspective. From 1735 to 1775, while trade with Britain doubled, commerce among the colonies increased by a factor of four. People and ideas moved along with goods. The first stage lines linking seaboard cities began operation in the 1750s. Spurred by Postmaster Benjamin Franklin, many colonies built or improved post roads for transporting the mails.

The Press, Politics, and Republicanism

The pages of the colonial press reveal the political assumptions held by informed colonists. For decades governors had struggled with colonial assemblies over their respective powers. As commentary on the meaning of these struggles, colonial editors often reprinted the writings of the radical Whigs of eighteenth-century England, pamphleteers such as John Trenchard and Thomas Gordon, political theorists such as John Locke, and essayists such as Alexander Pope and Jonathan Swift. They warned of the growing threat to liberty posed by the unchecked exercise of power. In their more emotional writings they argued that a conspiracy existed among the powerful—kings, aristocrats, and Catholics—to quash liberty and institute tyranny. Outside the mainstream of British political opinion, these ideas came to define the political consensus in the British colonies, a point of view called "republicanism."

The Sugar and Stamp Acts

The emerging sense of American political identity was soon tested by British measures designed to raise revenues in the colonies. To quell Indian uprisings and stifle discontent among the French and Spanish populations of Quebec and Florida, 10,000 British troops remained stationed in North America at the conclusion of the Seven Years' War. The cost of maintaining this force added to the enormous debt Britain had run up during the fighting and created a desperate need for additional revenues. In 1764, the Chancellor of the Exchequer, George Grenville, deciding to obtain the needed revenue from America, pushed through Parliament a measure known as the Sugar Act.

The Sugar Act placed a duty on sugar imported into the colonies and revitalized the customs service, introducing stricter registration procedures for ships and adding more officers. In fact, the duty was significantly less than the one that had been on the books and ignored for years, but the difference was that the British now intended to enforce it. In anticipation of American resistance, the legislation increased the jurisdiction of the vice-admiralty court at Halifax, where customs cases were heard. These courts were hated because there was no presumption of innocence and the accused had no right to a jury trial. These new regulations promised not only to squeeze the incomes of American merchants but also to cut off their lucrative smuggling operations. Moreover, colonial taxes, which had been raised during the war, remained at an all-time high. In many cities, merchants as well as artisans protested loudly. Boston was especially vocal: in response to the sugar tax, the town meeting proposed a boycott of certain English imports. This movement for nonimportation soon spread to other port towns.

James Otis, Jr., a Massachusetts lawyer fond of grand oratory, was one of the first Americans to strike a number of themes that would become familiar over the next fifteen years. A man's "right to his life, his liberty, his property" was "written on the heart, and revealed to him by his maker," he argued in language echoing the rhetoric of the Great Awakening. It was "inherent, inalienable, and indefeasible by any laws, pacts, contracts, covenants, or stipulations which man could devise." He declared that "an act against the Constitution is void." There could be "no taxation without representation."

But it was only fair, Grenville argued in return, that the colonists help pay the costs of the empire, and what better way to do so than by a tax? Taxes in the colonies were much lower than taxes at home. In early 1765, unswayed by American protests, he followed the Sugar Act with a second and considerably more sweeping revenue measure, the Stamp Act. This tax required the purchase of specially embossed paper for all newspapers, legal documents, licenses, insurance policies, ship's papers, and even dice and playing cards.

The Stamp Act Crisis

During the summer and autumn of 1765 the American reaction to the Stamp Act created a crisis of unprecedented proportions. The stamp tax had to be paid in hard money, and it came during a period of economic stagnation. Many colonists complained of being "miserably burdened and oppressed with taxes."

Of more importance for the longer term, however, were the constitutional implications. Although colonial male property owners elected their own assemblies, they could not vote in British elections. But the British argued that Americans were subject to the acts of Parliament because of virtual representation. That is, members of Parliament were thought to represent not just their districts, but all citizens of the empire. As one British writer put it, the colonists were "represented in Parliament in the same manner as those inhabitants of Britain are who have not voices in elections." But in an influential pamphlet of 1765, *Considerations on the Propriety of Imposing Taxes*, Maryland lawyer Daniel Dulany rejected this theory. Because Americans were members of a separate political community, he insisted, Parliament could impose no tax on them. Instead, he argued for "actual representation," emphasizing the direct relationship that must exist between the people and their political representatives.

It was just such constitutional issues that were emphasized in the Virginia Stamp Act Resolutions, pushed through the Virginia assembly by the passionate young lawyer Patrick Henry in May 1765. Although the Virginia House of Burgesses rejected the most radical of Henry's resolutions, they were all reprinted throughout the colonies. By the end of 1765 the assemblies of eight other colonies had approved similar measures denouncing the Stamp Act and proclaiming their support of "no taxation without representation."

In Massachusetts the leaders of the opposition to the Stamp Act came from a group of upper- and middle-class men who had long opposed the conservative leaders of the colony. These men had worked years to establish a political alliance with Boston craftsmen and workers who met at taverns, in volunteer fire companies, or at social clubs. One of these clubs, known as the Loyall Nine, included a member named Samuel Adams, an associate and friend of James Otis, who had made his career in local politics. Using his contacts with professionals, craftsmen, and laboring men, Adams helped put together an anti-British alliance that spanned Boston's social classes. In August 1765 Adams and the Loyall Nine were instrumental in organizing a protest of Boston workingmen against the Stamp Act.

Whereas Boston's elite had prospered during the eighteenth century, the conditions for workers and the poor had worsened. Unemployment, inflation, and high taxes had greatly increased the level of poverty during the depression that followed the Seven Years' War, and many were resentful. A large Boston crowd assembled on August 14, 1765, in the shade of an old elm tree and strung up effigies of several British officials, including Boston's stamp distributor, Andrew Oliver. The restless crowd then vandalized Oliver's office and home. At the order of Oliver's brother-in-law, Lieutenant Governor Thomas Hutchinson, leader of the Massachusetts conservatives, the town sheriff tried to break up the crowd, but he was pelted with paving stones and bricks. Soon thereafter, Oliver resigned his commission. The unified action of Boston's social groups had had its intended effect.

Twelve days later, however, a similar crowd gathered at the aristocratic home of Hutchinson himself. As the family fled through the back door, the crowd smashed through the front with axes. Inside they demolished furniture, chopped down the interior walls, consumed the contents of the wine cellar, and looted everything of value, leaving the house a mere shell. As these events demonstrated, it was not always possible to keep popular protests within bounds. During the fall and winter, urban crowds in commercial towns from Halifax in the North to Savannah in the South forced the resignation of many British tax officials.

In many colonial cities and towns, groups of merchants, lawyers, and craftsmen sought to moderate the resistance movement by seizing control of it. Calling themselves the Sons of Liberty, these groups encouraged moderate forms of protest. They circulated petitions, published pamphlets, and encouraged crowd actions only as a last resort; always they emphasized limited political goals. There were few repetitions of mob attacks, but by the end of 1765 almost all the stamp distributors had resigned or fled, making it impossible for Britain to enforce the Stamp Act.

Repeal of the Stamp Act

In the fall of 1765, British merchants, worried about the effects of the growing nonimportation movement among the colonists, began petitioning Parliament to repeal the Stamp Act. However, it was not until March 1766 that a bill for repeal passed the House of Commons. This news was greeted with celebrations throughout the American colonies, and the nonimportation associations were disbanded. Overlooked in the mood of optimism was Parliament's assertion in this Declaratory Act of its full authority to make laws binding the colonies "in all cases whatsoever." The notion of absolute parliamentary supremacy over colonial matters was basic to the British theory of empire. Even Pitt, friend of America that he was, asserted "the authority of this kingdom over the colonies to be sovereign and supreme, in every circumstance of government and legislation whatsoever." The Declaratory Act signaled that the conflict had not been resolved but merely postponed.

Samuel Adams, a second cousin of John Adams, was a leader of the Boston radicals and an organizer of the Sons of Liberty. The artist of this portrait, John Singleton Copley, was known for setting his subjects in the midst of everyday objects; here he portrays Adams in a middle-class suit with the charter guaranteeing the liberties of Boston's freemen.

SOURCE: John Singleton Copley (1738–1815), *Samuel Adams*, c.a. 1772. Oil on canvas, 49 1/2 × 39 1/2 in. (125.7 cm x 100.3 cm). Deposited by the City of Boston, 30.76c. Courtesy, Museum of Fine Arts, Boston. Reproduced with permission. © 2000 Museum of Fine Art.

"SAVE YOUR MONEY AND SAVE YOUR COUNTRY"

Colonial resistance to the Stamp Act was stronger in urban than in rural communities, stronger among merchants, craftsmen, and planters than among farmers and frontiersmen. When Parliament next moved to impose its will, as it had promised to do in the Declaratory Act, imposing new duties on imported goods, the American opposition again adopted the tactic of nonimportation. But this time resistance spread from the cities and towns into the countryside. As the editor of the *Boston Gazette* phrased the issue, "Save your money and you save your country." It became the slogan of the movement.

The Townshend Revenue Acts

During the 1760s there was a rapid turnover of government leaders that made it difficult for Britain to form a consistent and even-handed policy toward the colonies.

In 1767, after several failed governments, King George III asked William Pitt to again become prime minister. Pitt enjoyed enormous goodwill in America, and a government under his leadership stood a good chance of reclaiming colonial credibility. But, suffering from a prolonged illness, he was soon forced to retire, and his place as head of the cabinet was assumed by Charles Townshend, Chancellor of the Exchequer.

One of the first problems facing the new government was the national debt. At home there were massive unemployment, riots over high prices, and tax protests. The large landowners forced a bill through Parliament slashing their taxes by 25 percent. The government feared continued opposition at home far more than opposition in America. So as part of his plan to close the budget gap, Townshend proposed a new revenue measure for the colonies that placed import duties on commodities such as lead, glass, paint, paper, and tea. By means of these new Revenue Acts, enacted in 1767, Townshend hoped to redress colonial grievances against internal taxes such as those imposed by the Stamp Act. For most colonists, however, it proved to be a distinction without a difference.

The most influential response to these Revenue Acts came in a series of articles by John Dickinson, *Letters from a Farmer in Pennsylvania*, that were reprinted in nearly every colonial newspaper. Dickinson was a wealthy Philadelphia lawyer, but in this work he posed as a humble farmer. Parliament had the right to regulate trade through the use of duties, he conceded. It could place prohibitive tariffs, for example, on foreign products. But it had no constitutional authority to tax goods in order to raise revenues in America. As the preface to the Revenue Acts made clear, the income they produced would be used to pay the salaries of royal officials in America. Thus, Dickinson pointed out, since colonial assemblies were no longer paying their salaries, colonial administrators would not be subject to the financial oversight of elected representatives.

Other Americans warned that this was part of the British conspiracy to suppress American liberties. Their fears were reinforced by Townshend's stringent enforcement of the Revenue Acts. He created a new and strengthened Board of Commissioners of the Customs and established a series of vice-admiralty courts at Boston, Philadelphia, and Charleston to prosecute violators of the duties—the first time these hated institutions had appeared in the most important American port cities. To demonstrate his power, he also suspended New York's assembly. That body had refused to vote public funds to support the British troops garrisoned in the colony. Until the citizens of New York relented, Townshend declared, they would no longer be represented.

In response to these measures, some men argued for violent resistance. But it was Dickinson's essays that

had the greatest effect on the public debate, not only because of their convincing arguments but also because of their mild and reasonable tone. "Let us behave like dutiful children," Dickinson urged, "who have received unmerited blows from a beloved parent." As yet, no sentiment for independence existed in America.

Nonimportation: An Early Political Boycott

Associations of nonimportation and nonconsumption, revived in October 1767 when the Boston town meeting drew up a long list of British products to boycott, became the main weapon of the resistance movement. Over the next few months other port cities, including Providence, Newport, and New York, set up nonimportation associations of their own. Artisans took to the streets in towns and cities throughout the colonies to force merchants to stop importing British goods. The associations published the names of uncooperative importers and retailers. These people then became the object of protesters, who sometimes resorted to violence. Coercion was very much a part of the movement.

Adopting the language of Protestant ethics, nonimportation associations pledged to curtail luxuries and stimulate local industry. These aims had great appeal in small towns and rural districts, which previously had been uninvolved in the anti-British struggle. In 1768 and 1769 colonial newspapers paid a great deal of attention to women's support for the boycott. Groups of women, some calling themselves Daughters of Liberty, organized spinning and weaving bees to produce homespun for local consumption. The actual work performed at these bees was less important than the symbolic message. "The industry and frugality of American ladies," wrote the editor of the *Boston Evening Post*, "are contributing to bring about the political salvation of a whole continent." Other women renounced silks and satins and pledged to stop serving tea to their husbands.

Nonimportation was greatly strengthened in May 1769 when the Virginia House of Burgesses enacted the first provincial legislation banning the importation of goods enumerated in the Townshend Acts, and slaves and luxury commodities as well. Over the next few months all the colonies but New Hampshire enacted similar associations. Because of these efforts, the value of colonial imports from Britain declined by 41 percent.

The Massachusetts Circular Letter

Boston and Massachusetts were at the center of the agitation over the Townshend Revenue Acts. In February 1768, the Massachusetts House of Representatives approved a letter, drawn up by Samuel Adams, addressed to the speakers of the other provincial assemblies. Designed largely as a propaganda device and having little practical significance, the letter denounced the Townshend Revenue Acts, attacked the British plan to make royal officials independent of colonial assemblies, and urged the colonies to find a way to "harmonize with each other." Massachusetts governor Francis Bernard condemned the document for stirring up rebellion and dissolved the legislature. In Britain, Lord Hillsborough, secretary of state for the colonies, ordered each royal governor in America to likewise dissolve his colony's assembly if it should endorse the letter. Before this demand reached America, the assemblies of New Hampshire, New Jersey, and Connecticut had commended Massachusetts. Virginia, moreover, had issued a circular letter encouraging a "hearty union" among the colonies and urging common action against the British measures that "have an immediate tendency to enslave us."

Throughout this crisis there were rumors and threats of mob rule in Boston. Because customs agents enforced the law against smugglers and honest traders alike, they enraged merchants, seamen, and dockworkers. In June 1768, a crowd assaulted customs officials who had seized John Hancock's sloop *Liberty* for nonpayment of duties. So frightened were the officials that they fled the city. Hancock, reportedly the wealthiest merchant in the colonies and a vocal opponent of the British measures, had become a principal target of the customs officers. In September the Boston town meeting called on the people to arm themselves, and in the absence of an elected assembly it invited all the other towns to send delegates to a provincial convention. There were threats of armed resistance, but little support for it in the convention, which broke up in chaos. Nevertheless the British, fearing insurrection, occupied Boston with infantry and artillery regiments on October 1, 1768. With this action, they sacrificed a great deal of goodwill and respect and added greatly to the growing tensions.

The Politics of Revolt and the Boston Massacre

The British troops stationed in the colonies were the object of scorn and hostility over the next two years. There were regular conflicts between soldiers and radicals in New York City, often focusing on the Sons of Liberty. These men would erect "liberty poles" festooned with banners and flags proclaiming their cause, and the British troops would promptly destroy them. When the New York assembly finally bowed to Townshend in December 1769 and voted an appropriation to support the troops, the New York City Sons of Liberty organized a demonstration and erected a large liberty pole. The soldiers chopped it down, sawed it into pieces, and left the wood on the steps of a tavern frequented by the Sons. This led to a riot in which British troops used their bayonets against several thousand New Yorkers armed with cutlasses and clubs. Several men were wounded.

Confrontations also took place in Boston. Sam Adams played up reports and rumors of soldiers harassing women, picking fights, or simply taunting residents with versions of "Yankee Doodle." Soldiers were often hauled into Boston's courts, and local judges adopted a completely unfriendly attitude toward these members of the occupying army.

On the evening of March 5, 1770, a crowd gathered at the Customs House and began taunting a guard, calling him a "damned rascally scoundrel lobster" and worse. A captain and seven soldiers went to his rescue, only to be pelted with snowballs and stones. Suddenly, without orders, the frightened soldiers began to fire. Five of the crowd fell dead, and six more were wounded, two of these dying later. The soldiers escaped to their barracks, but a mob numbering in the hundreds rampaged through the streets demanding vengeance. Fearing for the safety of his men and the security of the state, Thomas Hutchinson, now governor of Massachusetts, ordered British troops out of Boston. The Boston Massacre became infamous throughout the colonies, in part because of the circulation of an inflammatory print produced by the Boston engraver Paul Revere, which depicted the British as firing on a crowd of unresisting civilians. But for many colonists, the incident was a disturbing reminder of the extent to which relations with the mother country had deteriorated. During the next two years, many people found themselves pulling back from the brink. "There seems," one Bostonian wrote, "to be a pause in politics."

The growth of American resistance was slowed as well by the news that Parliament had repealed most of the Townshend Revenue Acts on March 5, 1770—the same day as the Boston Massacre. In the climate of apprehension and confusion, there were few celebrations of the repeal, and the nonimportation associations almost immediately collapsed. Over the next three years, the value of British imports rose by 80 percent. The parliamentary retreat on the question of duties, like the earlier repeal of the Stamp Act, was accompanied by a face-saving measure—retention of the tax on tea "as a mark of the supremacy of Parliament," in the words of Frederick Lord North, the new prime minister.

FROM RESISTANCE TO REBELLION

There was a lull in the American controversy during the early 1770s, but the situation turned violent in 1773, when Parliament again infuriated the Americans. This time it was an ill-advised Tea Act, and it propelled the colonists onto a swift track from resistance to outright rebellion.

Intercolonial Cooperation

In June 1772, Governor Hutchinson inaugurated another controversy by announcing that henceforth his salary and those of other royally appointed Massachusetts officials would be paid by the crown. In effect, this made the executive and judiciary branches of the colony's government independent of elected representatives. In October, the Boston town meeting appointed a Committee of Correspondence to communicate with other towns regarding this challenge. The next month the meeting issued what became known as the Boston Pamphlet, a series of declarations written by Samuel Adams and other radicals, concluding that British encroachments on colonial rights pointed to a plot to enslave Americans.

In March 1773, the Virginia House of Burgesses appointed a standing committee for correspondence

In Paul Revere's version of the Boston Massacre, issued three weeks after the incident, the British fire an organized volley into a defenseless crowd. Revere's print—which he plagiarized from another Boston engraver—may have been inaccurate, but it was enormously effective propaganda. It hung in so many Patriot homes that the judge hearing the murder trial of these British soldiers warned the jury not to be swayed by "the prints exhibited in our houses."

SOURCE: The Library of Congress.

among the colonies "to obtain the most early and authentic intelligence" of British actions affecting America, "and to keep up and maintain a correspondence and communication with our sister colonies." The Virginia committee, including Patrick Henry, Richard Henry Lee, and young Thomas Jefferson, served as a model, and within a year all the colonies except Pennsylvania, where conservatives controlled the legislature, had created committees of their own. These committees became the principal channel for sharing information, shaping public opinion, and building cooperation among the colonies before the Continental Congress of 1774.

The information most damaging to British influence came from the radicals in Boston. In June 1773, the Boston committee circulated a set of confidential letters from Governor Hutchinson to the ministry in Britain, obtained in London by Benjamin Franklin from friends within the British government. Because Franklin had pledged to keep the letters to himself, he became the center of a scandal in London and was dismissed from his position as postmaster general. But the British cause in the colonies suffered much more than Franklin's reputation. The letters revealed Hutchinson's call for "an abridgement of what are called English liberties" in the colonies. "I wish to see some further restraint of liberty," he had written, "rather than the connection with the parent state should be broken." This statement seemed to be the "smoking gun" of the conspiracy theory, and it created a torrent of anger against the British and their officials in the colonies.

The Boston Tea Party

It was in this context that the colonists received the news that Parliament had passed a Tea Act. Colonists were major consumers of tea, but because of the tax on it that remained from the Townshend duties, the market for colonial tea had collapsed, bringing the East India Company to the brink of bankruptcy. This company was the sole agent of British power in India, and Parliament could not allow it to fail. The British, therefore, devised a scheme in which they offered tea to Americans at prices that would tempt the most patriotic tea drinker. The radicals argued that this was merely a device to make palatable the payment of unconstitutional taxes—further evidence of the British effort to corrupt the colonists.

In October a mass meeting in Philadelphia denounced anyone importing the tea as "an enemy of his country." The town meeting in Boston passed resolutions patterned on those of Philadelphia, but the tea agents there, including two of Governor Hutchinson's sons, resisted the call to refuse the shipments.

The first of the tea ships arrived in Boston Harbor late in November. Mass meetings in Old South Church, which included many country people drawn to the scene of the crisis, resolved to keep the tea from being unloaded. Governor Hutchinson was equally firm in refusing to allow the ship to leave the harbor. Five thousand people on December 16, 1773, crowded into the church to hear the captain of the tea ship report to Samuel Adams that he could not move his ship. "This meeting can do nothing more to save the country," Adams declared. This was the signal for a disciplined group of fifty or sixty men, including farmers, artisans, merchants, professionals, and apprentices, to march to the wharf disguised as Indians. There they boarded the ship and dumped into the harbor 45 tons of tea, valued at £18,000, all the while cheered on by Boston's citizens. "Boston Harbor's a tea-pot tonight," the crowd chanted.

Boston's was the first tea party. Other incidents of property destruction soon followed. When the Sons of Liberty learned that a cargo of tea had landed secretly in New York, they dressed themselves as Indians and dumped the tea chests into the harbor. At Annapolis a ship loaded with tea was destroyed by fire, and arson also consumed a shipment stored at a warehouse in New Jersey. But it was the action in Boston at which the British railed. The government became convinced that something had to be done about the rebellious colony of Massachusetts.

The Intolerable Acts

During the spring of 1774 an angry Parliament passed a series of acts—called the Coercive Acts, but known by Americans as the Intolerable Acts—that were calculated to punish Massachusetts and strengthen the British hand. The Boston Port Bill prohibited the loading or unloading of ships in any part of Boston Harbor until the town fully compensated the East India Company and the customs service for the destroyed tea. The Massachusetts Government Act annulled the

OVERVIEW

ELEVEN BRITISH MEASURES THAT LED TO REVOLUTION

Legislation	Year	
Sugar Act	1764	Placed prohibitive duty on imported sugar; provided for greater regulation of American shipping to suppress smuggling
Stamp Act	1765	Required the purchase of specially embossed paper for newspapers, legal documents, licenses, insurance policies, ships' papers, and playing cards; struck at printers, lawyers, tavern owners, and other influential colonists. Repealed in 1766
Declaratory Act	1766	Asserted the authority of Parliament to make laws binding the colonies "in all cases whatsoever"
Townshend Revenue Acts	1767	Placed import duties, collectible before goods entered colonial markets, on many commodities including lead, glass, paper, and tea. Repealed in 1770
Tea Act	1773	Gave the British East India Company a monopoly on all tea imports to America, hitting at American merchants
Coercive or Intolerable Acts	1774	
Boston Port Bill		Closed Boston harbor
Massachusetts Government Act		Annulled the Massachusetts colonial charter
Administration of Justice Act		Protected British officials from colonial courts by sending them home for trial if arrested
Quartering Act		Legalized the housing of British troops in private homes
Quebec Act		Created a highly centralized government for Canada

colonial charter: delegates to the upper house would no longer be elected by the assembly but henceforth were to be appointed by the king. Civil officers throughout the province were placed under the authority of the royal governor, and the selection of juries was given over to governor-appointed sheriffs. Town meetings, an important institution of the resistance movement, were prohibited from convening more than once a year except with the approval of the governor, who was to control their agendas. With these acts the British terminated the long history of self-rule by communities in the colony of Massachusetts. The Administration of Justice Act protected British officials from colonial courts, thereby encouraging them to vigorously pursue the work of suppression. Those accused of committing capital crimes while putting down riots or collecting revenue, such as the soldiers involved in the Boston Massacre, were now to be sent to England for trial.

Additional measures affected the other colonies and encouraged them to see themselves in league with suffering Massachusetts. The Quartering Act legalized the housing of troops at public expense, not only in taverns and abandoned buildings but also in occupied dwellings and private homes as well.

Finally, in the Quebec Act, the British authorized a permanent government for the territory taken from France during the Seven Years' War. This government was both authoritarian and antirepublican, with a royal government and an appointed council. Furthermore, the act confirmed the feudal system of land tenure along the St. Lawrence. It also granted religious toleration to the Roman Catholic Church and upheld the church's traditional right to collect tithes, thus, in effect, establishing Catholicism as the state religion in Quebec.

To the American colonists, the Quebec Act was a frightening preview of what imperial authorities might have in store for them, and it confirmed the prediction of the Committees of Correspondence that there was a British plot to destroy American liberty.

In May, General Thomas Gage arrived in Boston to replace Hutchinson as governor. The same day, the Boston town meeting called for a revival of nonimportation measures against Britain. In Virginia the Burgesses declared that Boston was enduring a "hostile invasion" and made provision for a "day of fasting, humiliation, and prayer, devoutly to implore the divine interposition for averting the heavy calamity, which threatens destruction to our civil rights and the evils of civil war." For this expression of sympathy, Governor Dunmore suspended the legislature. Nevertheless, throughout the colony on the first of June, funeral bells tolled, flags flew at half mast, and people flocked to the churches.

The First Continental Congress

It was amid this crisis that town meetings and colonial assemblies alike chose representatives for the Continental Congress. The delegates who arrived in Philadelphia in September 1774 included the most important leaders of the American cause. Cousins Samuel and John Adams, the radicals from Massachusetts, were joined by Patrick Henry and George Washington from Virginia and Christopher Gadsden of South Carolina. Many of the delegates were conservatives: John Dickinson and Joseph Galloway of Philadelphia and John Jay and James Duane from New York. With the exception of Gadsden, a hothead who proposed an attack on British forces in Boston, the delegates wished to avoid war and favored a policy of economic coercion.

After one of their first debates, the delegates passed a Declaration and Resolves, in which they asserted that all the colonists sprang from a common tradition and enjoyed rights guaranteed "by the immutable laws of nature, the principles of the English constitution, and the

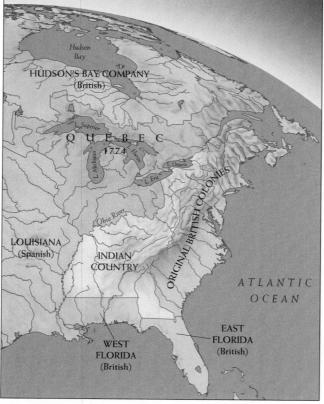

The Quebec Act of 1774 With the Quebec Act, Britain created a centralized colonial government for Canada and extended that colony's administrative control southwest to the Ohio River, invalidating the sea-to-sea boundaries of many colonial charters.

several charters or compacts" of their provinces. Thirteen acts of Parliament, passed since 1763, were declared in violation of these rights. Until these acts were repealed, the delegates pledged, they would impose a set of sanctions against the British. These would include not only the nonimportation and nonconsumption of British goods, but also a prohibition on the export of colonial commodities to Britain or its other colonies.

To enforce these sanctions, the Continental Congress urged that "a committee be chosen in every county, city, and town, by those who are qualified to vote for representatives in the legislature, whose business it shall be attentively to observe the conduct of all persons." This call for democratically elected local committees in each community had important political ramifications. The following year, these groups, known as Committees of Observation and Safety, took over the functions of local government throughout the colonies. They organized militia companies, called extralegal courts, and combined to form colonywide congresses or conventions. By dissolving the colonial legislatures, royal governors unwittingly aided the work of these committees. The committees also scrutinized the activities of fellow citizens, suppressed the expression of Loyalist opinion from pulpit or press, and practiced other forms of coercion. Throughout most of the colonies the committees formed a bridge between the old colonial administrations and the revolutionary governments organized over the next few years. Committees began to link localities together in the cause of a wider American community. It was at this point that people began to refer to the colonies as the American "states."

Lexington and Concord

On September 1, 1774, General Gage sent troops from Boston to seize the stores of cannon and ammunition the Massachusetts militia had stored at armories in Charlestown and Cambridge. In response, the Massachusetts House of Representatives, calling itself the Provincial Congress, created a Committee of Safety empowered to call up the militia. On October 15 the committee authorized the creation of special units, to be known as "minutemen," who stood ready to be called at a moment's notice. The armed militia of the towns and communities surrounding Boston faced the British army, quartered in the city.

In Virginia, at almost the same moment, Patrick Henry predicted that hostilities would soon begin in New England. "Gentlemen may cry peace, peace!—but there is no peace," he thundered in prose later memorized by millions of American schoolchildren. "Is life so dear, or peace so sweet, as to be purchased at the price of chains and slavery? Forbid it, Almighty God! I know not what course others may take, but as for me,

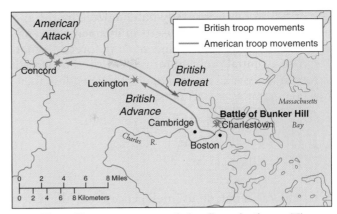

The First Engagements of the Revolution   The first military engagements of the American Revolution took place in the spring of 1775 in the countryside surrounding Boston.

give me liberty or give me death!" Three weeks later, on April 14, General Gage received orders to strike at once against the Massachusetts militia.

On the evening of April 18, 1775, Gage ordered 700 men to capture the store of American ammunition at the town of Concord. Learning of the operation, the Boston committee dispatched two men, Paul Revere and William Dawes, to alert the militia of the countryside. By the time the British forces had reached Lexington, midway to their destination, some seventy armed minutemen had assembled on the green in the center of town, but they were disorganized and confused. "Lay down your arms, you damned rebels, and disperse!" cried one of the British officers. The Americans began to withdraw in the face of overwhelming opposition, but they took their arms with them. "Damn you, why don't you lay down your arms!" someone shouted from the British lines. "Damn them! We will have them!" No order to fire was given, but shots rang out, killing eight Americans and wounding ten others.

The British marched on to Concord, where they burned a small quantity of supplies and cut down a liberty pole. Meanwhile, news of the skirmish at Lexington had spread through the country, and the militia companies of communities from miles around converged on the town. Seeing smoke, they mistakenly concluded that the troops were burning homes. "Will you let them burn the town!" one man cried, and the Americans moved to the Concord bridge. There they attacked a British company, killing three soldiers—the first British casualties of the Revolution. The British immediately turned back for Boston but were attacked by Americans at many points along the way. Reinforcements met them at Lexington, preventing a complete disaster, but by the time they finally marched into Boston, 73 were dead and 202 wounded or missing.

The British troops were vastly outnumbered by the approximately 4,000 Massachusetts militiamen, who suffered 95 casualties. The engagement forecast what would be a central problem for the British: they would be forced to fight an armed population defending their own communities against outsiders.

DECIDING FOR INDEPENDENCE

"We send you momentous intelligence," read the letter received by the Charleston, South Carolina, Committee of Correspondence on May 8, reporting the violence in Massachusetts. Community militia companies mobilized throughout the colonies. At Boston, thousands of militiamen from Massachusetts and the surrounding provinces besieged the city, leaving the British no escape but by sea; their siege would last for nearly a year. Meanwhile, delegates from twelve colonies reconverged on Philadelphia.

The Second Continental Congress

The members of the Second Continental Congress, which opened on May 10, 1775, represented twelve of the British colonies on the mainland of North America. From New Hampshire to South Carolina, Committees of Observation and Safety had elected colonywide conventions, and these extralegal bodies in turn had chosen delegates. Consequently, few conservatives or Loyalists were among them. Georgia, unrepresented at the first session of the Continental Congress, remained absent at the opening of the second. The newest mainland colony, it depended heavily on British subsidies, and its leaders were cautious, fearing both slave and Indian uprisings. But in 1775 the political balance in Georgia shifted in favor of the radicals, and by the end of the summer the colony had delegates in Philadelphia.

Among the delegates at the Continental Congress were many familiar faces and a few new ones, including Thomas Jefferson, a plantation owner and lawyer from Virginia, gifted with one of the most imaginative and analytical minds of his time. All the delegates carried news of the enthusiasm for war that raged in their home provinces. "A frenzy of revenge seems to have seized all ranks of people," said Jefferson. George Washington attended all the sessions in uniform. "Oh that I was a soldier," an envious John Adams wrote to his wife, Abigail. The delegates agreed that defense was the first issue on their agenda.

On May 15, the Second Continental Congress resolved to put the colonies in a state of defense, but the delegates were divided on how best to do it. They lacked the power and the funds to immediately raise and supply an army. After debate and deliberation, John Adams made the practical proposal that the delegates simply designate as a Continental Army the militia forces besieging Boston. On June 14, the Congress resolved to supplement the New England militiamen with six companies of expert riflemen raised in Pennsylvania, Maryland, and Virginia. The delegates agreed that in order to emphasize their national aspirations, they had to select a man from the South to command these New England forces. All eyes turned to George Washington. Although Washington had suffered defeat at the beginning of the Seven Years' War, he had subsequently compiled a distinguished record. On June 15, Jefferson and Adams nominated Washington to be commander-in-chief of all Continental forces, and he was elected by a unanimous vote. He served without salary. The Continental Congress soon appointed a staff of major generals to support him. On June 22, in a highly significant move, the Congress voted to finance the army with an issue of $2 million in bills of credit, backed by the good faith of the Confederated Colonies. Thus began the long and complicated process of financing the Revolution.

Canada, the Spanish Borderlands, and the Revolution

How did the rest of North America react to the coming conflict? The Continental Congress contacted many of the other British colonies. In one of their first acts, delegates called on "the oppressed inhabitants of Canada" to join in the struggle for "common liberty." After the Seven Years' War, the British treated Quebec as a conquered province, and French Canadians felt little sympathy for the empire. On the other hand, the Americans were traditional enemies, much feared because of their aggressive expansionism. Indeed, when the Canadians failed to respond positively and immediately, the Congress reversed itself and voted to authorize a military expedition against Quebec to eliminate any possibility of a British invasion from that quarter, thus killing any chance of the Canadians' joining the anti-British cause. This set a course toward the development of the separate nations of the United States and Canada.

There was some sympathy at first for the American struggle in the British island colonies. The legislative assemblies of Jamaica, Grenada, and Barbados declared themselves in accord with the Continental Congress, but the British navy prevented them from sending representatives. A delegation from Bermuda succeeded in getting to Philadelphia, but the Americans were so preoccupied with more pressing matters they were unable to provide any assistance, and the spark of resistance on the island sputtered out. The island colonies would remain aloof from the imperial crisis, largely because the colonists there were dependent on a British military presence to guard against slave revolts. Things at first seemed more promising in Nova Scotia (not then a part of Canada), where many New Englanders had relocated after the expulsion of the Acadians. There had been Stamp Act demonstrations in Halifax, and when the British attempted to recruit among the Nova Scotians for soldiers to serve in Boston, one community responded that since "almost all of us [were] born in New England, [we are] divided betwixt natural affection to our nearest relations and good faith and friendship to our king and country." The British naval stronghold at Halifax, however, secured the province for the empire. Large contingents of British troops also kept Florida (which Britain had divided into the two colonies of East and West Florida) solidly in the empire.

In Cuba, some 3,000 exiled Spanish Floridians, who had fled rather than live under British rule in 1763, clamored for Spain to retake their homeland. Many of them were active supporters of American independence. (Two centuries later there would be thousands of Cuban exiles in Florida.) Spanish authorities in Cuba, who also administered the newly acquired colony of Louisiana, were somewhat torn in their sympathies. They certainly felt no solidarity with the cause of rebellion, which they understood posed a great danger to monarchy and empire. But with painful memories of the British invasion of Havana in 1763, they passionately looked forward to working revenge on their traditional enemy, as well as to regaining control of the Floridas and eliminating the British threat to their Mexican and Caribbean colonies. In 1775, Spain adopted the recommendation of the Havana authorities and declared a policy of neutrality in the looming independence struggle.

Secretly, however, Spain looked for an opportunity to support the Americans. That presented itself in the late spring of 1776, when a contingent of Americans arrived in Spanish New Orleans via the Mississippi River bearing a proposal from patriot forces in Virginia. British naval supremacy was making it impossible to obtain supplies from overseas. Would the Spanish be willing to quietly sell guns, ammunition, and other provisions to the Americans in New Orleans and allow them to be shipped by way of the Mississippi and Ohio Rivers? If they were cooperative, the Americans might be willing to see the Spanish retake possession of the Floridas and administer them as a "protectorate" for the duration of the independence struggle. Authorities forwarded the proposal to Spain, where a few months later the Spanish king and his ministers approved the plan. Havana and New Orleans became important supply centers for the patriots.

Fighting in the North and South

Both North and South saw fighting in 1775 and early 1776. In June the Continental Congress assembled an expeditionary force against Canada. One thousand Americans moved north up the Hudson River corridor, and in November General Richard Montgomery forced the capitulation of Montreal. Meanwhile, Benedict Arnold set out from Massachusetts with another American army, and after a torturous march through the forests and mountains of Maine, he joined Montgomery outside the walls of Quebec. Unlike the assault of British General Wolfe in 1759, however, the American assault failed to take the city. Montgomery and 100 Americans were killed, and another 300 were taken prisoner. Although Arnold held his position, the American siege was broken the following spring by British reinforcements who had come down the St. Lawrence. By the summer of 1776 the Americans had been forced back from Canada.

Elsewhere there were successes. Washington installed artillery on the heights south of Boston, placing the city and harbor within cannon range. General William Howe, who had replaced Gage, had little choice but to evacuate the city. In March the British sailed out of Boston harbor for the last time, heading north to Halifax with at least 1,000 American Loyalists. In the South, American militia rose against the Loyalist forces of Virginia's Governor Dunmore, who had alienated the planter class by promising freedom to any slave who would fight with the British. After a decisive defeat of his forces, Dunmore retreated to British naval vessels, from which he shelled and destroyed much of the city of Norfolk, Virginia, on January 1, 1776. In North Carolina, the rebel militia crushed a Loyalist force at the Battle of Moore's Creek Bridge near Wilmington in February, ending British plans for an invasion of that province. The British decided to attack Charleston, but at Fort Moultrie in Charleston harbor an American force turned back the assault. It would be more than two years before the British would try to invade the South again.

No Turning Back

Hopes of reconciliation died with the mounting casualties. The Second Continental Congress, which was rapidly assuming the role of a new government for all the provinces, reconvened in September 1775 and received news of the king's proclamation that the colonies were in formal rebellion. Although the delegates disclaimed any intention of denying the sovereignty of the king, they now moved to organize an American navy. They declared British vessels open to capture and authorized privateering. The Congress

The Manner in which the American Colonies Declared themselves INDEPENDENT of the King of ENGLAND, a 1783 English print. Understanding that the coming struggle would require the steady support of ordinary people, in the Declaration of Independence the upper-class men of the Continental Congress asserted the right of popular revolution and the great principle of human equality.

SOURCE: The Granger Collection.

proposed to offer "simple fact, plain argument, and common sense" on the crisis. For years Americans had defended their actions by wrapping themselves in the mantle of British traditions. But Paine argued that the British system rested on "the base remains of two ancient tyrannies," aristocracy and monarchy, neither of which was appropriate for America. Paine placed the blame for the oppression of the colonists on the shoulders of King George. *Common Sense* was the single most important piece of writing during the Revolutionary era, selling more than 100,000 copies within a few months of its publication in January 1776. It reshaped popular thinking and put independence squarely on the agenda.

In April, the North Carolina convention, which operated as the revolutionary replacement for the old colonial assembly, became the first to empower its delegates to vote for a declaration of independence. News that the British were recruiting a force of German mercenaries to use against the Americans provided an additional push toward what now began to seem inevitable. In May the Continental Congress voted to recommend that the individual states move as quickly as possible toward the adoption of state constitutions. When John Adams wrote, in the preamble to this statement, that "the exercise of every kind of authority under the said crown should be totally suppressed," he sent a strong signal that the delegates were on the verge of approving a momentous declaration.

The Declaration of Independence

On June 7, 1776, Richard Henry Lee of Virginia offered a motion to the Continental Congress: "That these united colonies are, and of right ought to be, free and independent states, that they are absolved from all allegiance to the British crown, and that all political connection between them and the state of Great Britain is, and ought to be, totally dissolved." After some debate, a vote was postponed until July, but a committee composed of John Adams, Thomas Jefferson, Benjamin Franklin, Roger Sherman of Connecticut, and Robert Livingston of New York was asked to prepare a draft declaration of American independence. The committee assigned the writing to Jefferson.

The intervening month allowed the delegates to sample the public discussion and debate and receive instructions from their state conventions. By the end of the month, all the states but New York had authorized a vote for independence. When the question came up for debate again on July 1, a large majority in the Continental Congress supported independence. The final vote, taken on July 2, was twelve in favor of independence, none against, with New York abstaining. The delegates then turned to the declaration itself and made a number of changes in Jefferson's draft, striking

took further steps toward de facto independence when it authorized contacts with foreign powers through its agents in Europe. In the spring of 1776, France, hoping that the creation of a new American nation might provide the opportunity of gaining a larger share of the colonial trade while also diminishing British power, joined Spain in approving the shipping of supplies to the rebellious provinces. The Continental Congress then declared colonial ports open to the trade of all nations but Britain.

The emotional ties to Britain proved difficult to break. But in 1776 help arrived in the form of a pamphlet written by Thomas Paine, a radical Englishman recently arrived in Philadelphia. In *Common Sense*, Paine

CHRONOLOGY

1713	France cedes Acadia to Britain	1764	Sugar Act
1745	New Englanders capture Louisburg	1765	Stamp Act and Stamp Act Congress
1749	French send an expeditionary force down the Ohio River	1766	Declaratory Act
1753	French begin building forts from Lake Erie to the Ohio	1767	Townshend Revenue Acts
1754	Albany Congress	1768	Treaties of Hard Labor and Fort Stanwix
1755	British General Edward Braddock defeated by a combined force of French and Indians	1770	Boston Massacre
	Britain expels Acadians from Nova Scotia	1772	First Committee of Correspondence organized in Boston
1756	Seven Years' War begins in Europe	1773	Tea Act
1757	William Pitt becomes prime minister		Boston Tea Party
1758	Louisburg captured by the British for the second time	1774	Intolerable Acts
			First Continental Congress
1759	British capture Quebec		Dunmore's War
1763	Treaty of Paris	1775	Fighting begins at Lexington and Concord
	Pontiac's uprising		Second Continental Congress
	Proclamation of 1763 creates "Indian Country"	1776	Americans invade Canada
			Thomas Paine's *Common Sense*
	Paxton Boys massacre		Declaration of Independence

out, for example, a long passage condemning slavery. In this and a number of other ways the final version was somewhat more cautious than the draft, but it was still a stirring document.

Its central section reiterated the "long train of abuses and usurpations" on the part of King George that had led the Americans to their drastic course; there was no mention of Parliament, the principal opponent since 1764. But it was the first section that expressed the highest ideals of the delegates:

We hold these truths to be self-evident, that all men are created equal, that they are endowed by their creator with certain unalienable rights, that among these are life, liberty, and the pursuit of happiness. That to secure these rights, governments are instituted among men, deriving their just powers from the consent of the governed. That whenever any form of government becomes destructive of these

ends, it is the right of the people to alter or to abolish it, and to institute a new government, laying its foundation on such principles, and organizing its powers in such form, as to them shall seem most likely to effect their safety and happiness.

There was very little debate in the Continental Congress about these principles. The delegates, mostly men of wealth and position, realized that the coming struggle for independence would require the steady support of ordinary people, so they asserted this great principle of equality and the right of revolution. There was little debate about the implications or potential consequences. Surely no statement would reverberate more through American history; the idea of equality inspired the poor as well as the wealthy, women as well as men, blacks as well as whites.

But it was the third and final section that may have contained the most meaning for the delegates: "For the support of this declaration, with a firm reliance on the protection of divine providence, we mutually pledge to each other our lives, our fortunes, and our sacred honor." In voting for independence, the delegates proclaimed their community, but they also committed treason against their king and empire. They could be condemned as traitors, hunted as criminals, and stand on the scaffold to pay for their sentiments. On July 4, 1776, these men approved the text of the Declaration of Independence without dissent.

CONCLUSION

Great Britain emerged from the Seven Years' War as the dominant power in North America. Yet despite its attempts at strict regulation and determination of the course of events in its colonies, it faced consistent resistance and often complete failure. Perhaps British leaders felt as John Adams had when he attended the first session of the Continental Congress in 1774: how could a motley collection of "ambassadors from a dozen belligerent powers" effectively organize as a single, independent, and defiant body? The British underestimated the political consensus that existed among the colonists about the importance of "republican" government. They also underestimated the ability of the colonists to inform one another, to work together, to build a sentiment of nationalism that cut across the boundaries of ethnicity, region, and economic status. Through newspapers, pamphlets, Committees of Correspondence, community organizations, and group protest, the colonists discovered the concerns they shared, and in so doing they fostered a new American identity. Without that identity it would have been difficult for them to consent to the treasonous act of declaring independence, especially when the independence they sought was from an international power that dominated much of the globe.

REVIEW QUESTIONS

1. How did overwhelming British success in the Seven Years' War lead to an imperial crisis in British North America?
2. Outline the changes in British policy toward the colonies from 1750 to 1776.
3. Trace the developing sense of an American national community over this same period.
4. What were the principal events leading to the beginning of armed conflict at Lexington and Concord?
5. How were the ideals of American republicanism expressed in the Declaration of Independence?

RECOMMENDED READING

Benedict Anderson, *Imagined Communities: Reflections on the Origin and Spread of Nationalism*, rev. ed. (1991). An argument that the essential first act of national consciousness is the effort to create a community that encompasses more than just local individuals and groups.

Fred Anderson, *The Crucible of War: The Seven Years' War and the Fate of Empire in British North America, 1754–1766* (2000). A new and powerful history of the war, arguing that it created a "hollow British empire."

Bernard Bailyn, *The Ideological Origins of the American Revolution* (1967). Whereas other accounts stress economic or social causes, this classic argument emphasizes the role of ideas in the advent of the Revolution. Includes an analysis of American views of the imperial crisis.

David A. Copeland, *Debating the Issues in Colonial Newspapers: Primary Documents on Events of the Period* (2000). A rich collection of eighteenth-century newspaper articles, with extensive coverage of the role of the press in the coming of the Revolution.

Eric Foner, *Tom Paine and Revolutionary America* (1976). Combines a biography of Paine with a community study of the Revolution in Philadelphia and Pennsylvania.

William H. Hallahan, *The Day the Revolution Began: 19 April 1775* (2000). How the news of Lexington and Concord spread across the world.

Francis Jennings, *Empire of Fortune: Crowns, Colonies, and Tribes in the Seven Years' War in America* (1988). The French and Indian War examined from the point of view of the Iroquois Confederacy. This is opinionated but exciting history.

Pauline Maier, *American Scripture: Making the Declaration of Independence* (1997). The deep background of this foundation of American democracy.

Richard L. Merritt, *Symbols of American Community, 1735–1775* (1966). A study of colonial newspapers that provides evidence for a rising sense of national community. The French and Indian War emerges as the key period for the growth of nationalist sentiment.

William R. Nester, *"Haughty Conquerors": Amherst and the Great Indian Uprising of 1763* (2000). The underlying causes of Pontiac's rebellion, the fighting itself, and the consequences.

ON THE WEB

http://www.loc.gov/exhibits/british/brit-2.html

A Library of Congress site, this web page contains a variety of Revolutionary War documents, primary sources, and graphics that range from Washington's Commission as Commander of the Continental Army to a French painting of the British surrender at Yorktown. Political cartoons and period maps are also contained within this site.

http://www.historyplace.com/unitedstates/revolution/teaparty.htm

This site contains the statement of a participant in the Boston Tea Party.

http://www.iath.virginia.edu/seminar/unit1/mob.html

This instructional site from the University of Virginia contains two political cartoons, both about the Boston Tea Party, but from the contrasting views of both the American patriot and the British. Also linked on this site is a copy of the Paul Revere engraving of the Boston Massacre.

http://www.constitution.org/bcp/dor_sac.htm

Contained on this page is the Declaration of Rights of the Stamp Act Congress, October 19, 1765.

http://www.law.ou.edu/hist/albplan.html

The University of Oklahoma Law School has posted the Albany Plan of Union of 1754 on this web page.

http://www.prenhall.com/faragherbrief/map6.1

In this exploration, consider the principal military engagements of the Seven Years' War. How did the Indian trade affect the war? Which military defeats dealt the worst blows to the French?

http://www.prenhall.com/faragherbrief/map6.2

Examine the boundaries set by the Quebec Act of 1774. How did they contribute to rising tensions between the colonists and imperial authorities?

The Invention of the Liberty Bell

The First Continental Congress of 1774 met in Carpenters' Hall, the downtown headquarters of one of Philadelphia's guilds. When the Congress reassembled in 1775, it moved to the more commodious State House two blocks away. It was there that the delegates adopted the Declaration of Independence in 1776 and the Articles of Confederation in 1777. Those occasions were commemorated by the tolling of a large bell in the building's steeple. In 1787 the nation's leaders drafted the United States Constitution in the same building, and later that year the State House bell rang upon its ratification by the states.

The State House (today more commonly known as Independence Hall) and the Liberty Bell are two of the most famous symbols of the nation's struggle for independence. Yet in the decades following the Revolution few Americans knew or cared about their existence. Just as Patriot leaders had to imagine and construct the idea of a national community, so these historical memorials had to be deliberately created and invented.

When the state of Pennsylvania moved its capital out of Philadelphia in 1799, it abandoned the State House and the bell. No one gave any thought to preserving them as relics of the nation's founding. The building, dating from the 1740s, was a beautiful Georgian structure, but by the turn of the century it was falling apart. The bell, cast by order of the Pennsylvania Assembly in 1752 to mark the fiftieth anniversary of representative government in the province, was inscribed with a Biblical passage: "PROCLAIM LIBERTY THROUGHOUT ALL THE LAND UNTO ALL THE INHABITANTS THEREOF." But Philadelphians were not particularly sentimental about it. Early in its history the bell developed hairline fractures, resulting in a harsh and shrill tone. By the early nineteenth century the bell was mostly forgotten. Misuse and vandalism caused the fractures in its surface to grow worse, and on one occasion, when rung to celebrate Washington's birthday, it cracked so badly it was rendered completely useless. Authorities made arrangements to scrap it.

But the bell was rescued in the 1830s by the emerging antislavery movement, which adopted it as a symbol of the uncompleted promise of American liberty. In 1837 a poem entitled "The Liberty Bell" appeared in the national abolitionist newspaper, *The Liberator:*

*Our Liberty Bell! let its startling tone
Abroad o'er a slavish land be thrown! . . .*

Antislavery advocates began publication of a series known as The Liberty Bell, annual volumes of stories, poems, and essays devoted to the cause of emancipation. Thus, the bell was named and made famous by a movement directed against the power of slavery. By 1852 so many visitors to the Philadelphia State House were asking to see the bell, it was placed on public display.

Today the Liberty Bell is displayed in a special pavilion on the mall in front of Independence Hall in Philadelphia.

SOURCE: © Richard Cummins/CORBIS.

Thus did the cracked Liberty Bell become a symbol of a divided rather than a united national community. Abolitionists used it to criticize the South. In one antislavery story a slave owner visits Independence Hall and ridicules the inscription he reads on the bell. Those sentiments are wrong, he says, the few should rule the many. "That is the way we do in the South. We have outgrown not only the sentiment inscribed on the bell, but the Declaration of Independence also." The bell cracked, he says, "because the doctrine is false." Suddenly a sad, ghostly voice issues from the bell. "The Lord, seeing that I should speak ever after to a nation of hypocrites," it says, "inflicted upon me this hideous crack, that whenever I did speak, there should issue from me nothing but a miserable clatter. . . . Nor shall I ever speak again in clear and ringing tones, till Liberty has been proclaimed to all the land, to all the inhabitants thereof." During the Civil War the Liberty Bell became one of the most prominent representations of the Union cause, and by war's end it was beloved in the North and loathed in the South.

In the aftermath of the war, the Liberty Bell was reinvented once again as a symbol of the national community. In 1876 the Centennial Exposition in Philadelphia adopted the bell as its most prominent icon. A huge illuminated replica that stood at the entrance became one of the most popular attractions. The bell was promoted as a symbol of the unity of the nation at the moment of its creation, a reminder to Americans of their joint effort in the cause of independence, and a call to Americans from South and North to reunite in the aftermath of the Civil War. The bell was shipped to numerous expositions around the country — in New Orleans, Chicago, Atlanta, Boston, St. Louis, and finally to San Francisco as part of a triumphant railroad tour of much

Visitors to the 1876 Centennial Exhibition in Philadelphia were offered a wide assortment of souvenirs featuring the Liberty Bell. The token is marked "1776" and "1876" and "Liberty Bell," and the silk bookmark features a portrait of George Washington along with the bell. In the aftermath of the Civil War the Liberty Bell was used as a symbol of national unity.

SOURCE: Liberty Bell Museum.

of the country. By World War I, when the Liberty Bell played a prominent role in the campaign to sell war bonds ("Liberty Bonds"), the use of the bell in the campaign against slavery had been suppressed and forgotten. Historical memorials are what we make of them. ∎

CHAPTER

SEVEN

THE CREATION OF THE UNITED STATES

▶ 1 7 7 6 – 1 7 8 6

CHAPTER OUTLINE

AMERICAN COMMUNITIES

A National Community Evolves at Valley Forge

A DRUM ROLL USHERED IN A JANUARY MORNING IN 1778, SUMMONING the Continental Army to roll call. Along a two-mile line of log cabins, doors slowly opened and ragged men stepped out onto the frozen ground of Valley Forge. "There comes a soldier," wrote army surgeon Albigense Waldo. "His bare feet are seen through his worn-out shoes, his legs nearly naked from the tattered remains of an only pair of stockings, his breeches not sufficient to cover his nakedness, his shirt hanging in strings, his hair disheveled, his face meagre." The reek of foul straw and unwashed bodies filled the air. "No bread, no soldier!" The chant began as a barely audible murmur, then was picked up by men all along the line. "No bread, no soldier! No bread, no soldier!" At last the chanting grew so loud it could be heard at General Washington's headquarters, a mile away. The 11,000 men of the American army were surviving on little more than "firecake," a mixture of flour and water baked hard before the fire that, according to Waldo, turned "guts to pasteboard." Two thousand men were without shoes; others were without blankets and had to sit up all night about the fires to keep from freezing. Addressing the Continental Congress, Washington wrote, "Three or four days of bad weather would prove our destruction."

Valley Forge was to become a national symbol of endurance. After marching hundreds of weary miles and suffering a series of terrible defeats at the hands of a British force nearly twice their number, the soldiers of the Continental Army had retreated to this winter headquarters only to find themselves at the mercy of indifferent local suppliers. Contractors demanded exorbitant rates for food and clothing, rates the Congress had refused to pay, and as a result local farmers preferred to deal with the British, who paid in pounds sterling, not depreciated Continental currency.

The 11,000 men of the Continental Army, who had not been paid for nearly six months, were divided into sixteen brigades composed of regiments from nine states. An unsympathetic observer described them as "a vagabond army of ragamuffins," and indeed many of the men were drawn from the ranks of the poor and disadvantaged: indentured servants, landless farmers, and nearly a thousand African Americans, both slave and free. Most of the men came from thinly settled farm districts or small towns where precautions regarding sanitation had been unnecessary. Every thaw revealed ground covered with "much filth and nastiness," and officers ordered sentinels to fire on any man "easing himself elsewhere than at ye vaults." Typhoid fever and other infectious diseases spread quickly. Along with dysentery, malnutrition, and exposure, these diseases claimed as many as 2,500 lives that winter. More than 700 women—wives, lovers, cooks, laundresses, and prostitutes—lived at Valley Forge that winter, and they were kept busy nursing the sick and burying the dead.

"What then is to become of this army?" Washington worried during the depth of the winter. But six months later the force he marched out of Valley Forge was considerably stronger for its experience there. Most important were the strong relationships that formed among the men, twelve of whom bunked together in each cabin, grouped by state regiments and brigade. In these units they fashioned "a band of brotherhood" and "shared with each other their hardships, dangers, and sufferings," wrote common soldier Joseph Plumb Martin. And they "sympathized with each other in trouble and sickness, assisted in bearing each other's burdens, [and] endeavored to conceal each other's faults." During the coming trials of battle, Washington, who referred to his staff as "family," would rely greatly on the bonds of affection his men had developed during that hard winter. As psychologists know today, it is this sense of community that contributes most to success in warfare.

To some American Patriots—as the supporters of the Revolution called themselves— the European-style Continental Army betrayed the ideals of the citizen-soldier and the autonomy of local communities that were central tenets of the Revolution. Washington argued strongly, however, that the Revolution could not be won without a national army insulated from politics and able to withstand the shifting popular mood. Moreover, through the developing sense of community among these men—who came from hundreds of localities and a variety of ethnic backgrounds—the Continental soldiers became living examples of the egalitarian ideals of the Revolution. They were a popular democratic force that counterbalanced the conservatism of the new republic's elite leadership. The national spirit they built at Valley Forge would sustain them through four more years of war and provide momentum for the long process of forging a national political system out of the persistent localism of American politics. "I admire them tremendously!" wrote one European officer serving with Washington. "It is incredible that soldiers composed of men of every age, even children of fifteen, of whites and blacks, almost naked, unpaid, and rather poorly fed, can march so well and withstand fire so steadfastly." Asked to explain why his men served, another officer declared: "Nothing but virtue and that great principle, the love of our country." ■

Valley
Forge

KEY TOPICS

- The major alignments and divisions among Americans during the American Revolution

- Major military campaigns of the Revolution

- The Articles of Confederation and the role of the Confederation Congress during the Revolutionary War

- The states as the setting for significant political change

- The economic crisis in the aftermath of the American Revolution

---

THE WAR FOR INDEPENDENCE

At the beginning of the Revolution, the British had the world's best-equipped and most disciplined army, as well as a navy that was unopposed in American waters. But they greatly underestimated the American capacity to fight. They also misperceived the sources of the conflict. Seeing the rebellion as the work of a small group of disgruntled conspirators, initially they defined their objective as defeating this Patriot opposition. In the wake of a military victory, they believed, they could easily reassert political control. But the geography of eastern North America offered no single vital center whose conquest would end the war. The Patriots had the advantage of fighting on their own ground and among a population thinly spread over a territory stretching along 1,500 miles of coastline and extending 100 miles or more into the interior. When the British succeeded in defeating the Patriots in one area, resistance would spring up in another. The key factor in the outcome of the war for independence, then, was the popular support for the American cause.

The Patriot Forces

Most American men of fighting age had to face the call to arms. From a population of approximately 350,000 eligible men, more than 200,000 saw action, though no more than 25,000 were engaged at any one time. More than 100,000 served in the Continental Army, under Washington's command and the authority of the Continental Congress; the other soldiers served in Patriot militia companies.

These militias—armed bodies of men drawn from local communities—proved important in the defense of their own areas, for they had homes as well as local rep-

utations to protect. Because men preferred to serve with their neighbors in local companies rather than subject themselves to the discipline of the regular service, the states failed to meet their quotas for regiments in the Continental Army. Serving short terms of enlistment, often with officers of their own choosing, militiamen resisted discipline. Indeed, in the face of battle, militia companies demonstrated appalling rates of desertion.

The failings of the militias in the early battles of the war sobered Congress, and it both greatly enlarged state quotas for the army and extended the term of service to three years or the war's duration. To spur enlistment Congress offered bounties, regular wages, and promises of free land after victory.

Discipline was essential in a conflict in which men fired at close range, charged each other with bayonets, and engaged in hand-to-hand combat. According to the best estimates, a total of 25,674 American men died in the Revolution, approximately 6,000 from wounds suffered in battle, 10,000 from the effects of disease, the rest as prisoners of war or missing in action. Regiments of the Continental Army experienced the highest casualty rates, sometimes 30 or 40 percent. Indeed, the casualty rate over all was higher than in any other American conflict except the Civil War. In most areas the war claimed few civilian lives, for it was confined largely to direct engagements between the armies. In the backcountry and in regions of the South, however, where Patriot and Loyalist militias waged vicious campaigns, noncombatant casualties were considerable.

Both the Continentals and the militias played important political roles as well. At a time when Americans identified most strongly with their local communities or their states, the Continental Army, through experiences like the Valley Forge winter, evolved into a powerful force for nationalist sentiment. But shortages of food and pay led to many army mutinies. In the most serious incident, among the

Pennsylvania Line in January 1781, enlisted men killed one officer, wounded two others, and set off from their winter quarters in New Jersey for Philadelphia to ask Congress to uphold its commitments. As they marched they were joined by British agents who encouraged them to go over to the king. Enraged at this attempt at subversion, the mutineers hanged the agents and gave up their resistance. Angry as they were at Congress, they were Americans first and hated the British. Over 100,000 men from every state served in the Continental Army, contributing mightily to the unity of purpose—the formation of a national community—that was essential to the process of nation making.

In most communities Patriots had seized control of local government during the period of committee organizing in 1774 and 1775 (see Chapter 6), and with war imminent they pressed the obligation to serve in a Patriot militia upon most eligible men. Probably the most important role of the Patriot militias was to force even the most apathetic of Americans to think seriously about the Revolution and to choose sides under the scrutiny of their neighbors.

As men marched off to war, many women assumed the management of family farms and businesses. Abigail Adams, for example, ran the Adams family's farm at Quincy for years. The Boston home of Mercy Otis Warren, daughter of James Otis, was a center of Patriot political activity. When the fighting shifted to their locales, women volunteered as seamstresses, cooks, nurses, and even spies.

When the months of fighting lengthened into years, many women left their homes to join husbands and lovers, fathers and brothers, in army encampments. Some were officially employed, but most voluntarily took care of their own men, and many fought with them side by side. Best known among the women who stayed by their husbands' sides even in camp were Martha Washington and Catherine Greene, wives of the two most important American generals of the war. But less socially prominent women were remembered as well. Mary Ludwig Hays (later McCauley) earned the name "Molly Pitcher" for her courage in bringing water to the Patriots during the Battle of Monmouth in June 1778. When her husband was overcome by heat, Mary Hays took his place at the cannon. In another instance, when Margaret Corbin's husband died in battle she stepped into his position. Other women, such as Deborah Sampson of Massachusetts, disguised themselves as men and enlisted.

The Loyalists

Not all Americans were Patriots. Many sat on the fence, confused by the conflict and waiting for a clear turn in the tide of the struggle before declaring their allegiance. About a fifth of the population, perhaps as many as half a million people, remained loyal to the British crown. They called themselves Loyalists, but were known to Patriots as Tories, the popular name for the conservative party in England, which traditionally supported the authority of the king over Parliament. Loyalism was strongest in the Lower South, weakest in New England. Loyalists included members of ethnic minorities who had been persecuted by the dominant majority, such as the Highland Scots of the Carolinas and western New York, and southern tenant farmers who had Patriot landlords. Moreover, many slaves and most Indians, the latter fearing aggressive expansion by independent American states, identified with the Loyalists.

Patriots passed state treason acts that prohibited speaking or writing against the Revolution. They also punished Loyalists by issuing bills of attainder, a legal process (later made illegal by the United States Constitution) by which Loyalists lost their civil rights and their property. In some areas, notably New York, South Carolina, Massachusetts, and Pennsylvania, Loyalists faced mob violence.

The most infamous American supporter of the British cause was Benedict Arnold. Arnold was a hero of the early battles of the Revolution on the American side. But in 1779, angry and resentful about what he perceived to be assignments and rank below his station, he became a paid informer of General Henry Clinton, head of the British army in New York City. In 1780 Patriots uncovered Arnold's plot to betray the strategic post of West Point, which he commanded. After fleeing to the British, who paid him a handsome stipend and pension, he became the most hated man in America. During the last two years of the war he led British raids against his home state as well as against Virginia, and after the Revolution he lived in England until his death in 1801.

The British strategy for suppressing the Revolution depended on mobilizing the Loyalists, but in most areas this proved impossible. As many as 50,000 Loyalists, however, fought for the king during the Revolution. As many as 80,000 Loyalists fled the country during and after the Revolution. Many went to England or the British West Indies, but the largest number settled in Canada; the Canadian provinces of Ontario, Nova Scotia, and New Brunswick honor the Loyalist refugees as founders. Loyalist property was confiscated by the states and sold at public auction. Although the British government compensated many for their losses, most Loyalists were unhappy exiles. Despite their disagreement with the Patriots on essential political questions, they remained Americans, and they mourned the loss of their country.

The Campaign for New York and New Jersey

During the winter of 1775–76 the British developed a strategic plan for the war. From his base at Halifax, Nova Scotia, Sir William Howe was to take his army to New York City, which the British navy would make impregnable. From there Howe was to drive north along the Hudson, while another British army marched south from Canada to Albany. The two armies would converge, cutting New England off from the rest of the colonies, then turn eastward to reduce the rebellious Yankees into submission. Washington, who had arrived at Boston to take command of the militia forces there in the summer of 1775, anticipated this strategy, and in the spring of 1776 he shifted his forces southward toward New York.

In early July, as Congress was taking its final vote on the Declaration of Independence, the British began their operation at New York City, landing 32,000 men, a third of them Hessian mercenaries (from the German state of Hesse), on Staten Island. The Americans, meanwhile, set up fortified positions across the harbor in Brooklyn. Attacking in late August, the British inflicted heavy casualties on the Americans, and the militia forces under Washington's command proved unreliable under fire. The Battle of Long Island ended in disaster for the Patriots, and they were forced to withdraw across the East River to Manhattan.

The British now offered Congress an opportunity to negotiate, and on September 6, Benjamin Franklin, John Adams, and Edward Rutledge sat down with General Howe and his brother, Admiral Richard Howe, on Staten Island. But the meeting broke up when the Howes demanded repeal of the Declaration of Independence. The stage was set for another round of fighting. Six days later the British invaded Manhattan island, and only an American stand at Harlem Heights prevented the destruction of a large portion of the Patriot army. Enjoying naval control of the harbor, the British quickly outflanked the American positions. In a series of battles over the next few months, they forced Washington back at White Plains and overran the American posts of Fort Washington and Fort Lee, on either side of the Hudson River. By November the Americans were fleeing south across New Jersey in a frantic attempt to avoid the British under General Charles Cornwallis.

With morale desperately low, whole militia companies deserted; others, announcing the end of their terms of enlistment, left for home. American resistance seemed to be collapsing all around Washington. But rather than fall back farther, which would surely have meant the dissolution of his entire force, he decided to risk a counterattack. On Christmas night 1776, he led 2,400 troops back across the Delaware, and the next morning defeated the Hessian forces in a surprise attack on their headquarters at Trenton, New Jersey. The Americans inflicted further heavy losses on the British at Princeton, then drove them all the way back to the environs of New York City.

Although these small victories had little strategic importance, they salvaged American morale. As Washington settled into winter headquarters at Morristown, he realized he had to pursue a defensive strategy, avoiding direct confrontations with the British while checking their advances and hurting them wherever possible.

The Northern Campaigns of 1777

The fighting with the American forces had prevented Howe from moving north up the Hudson River, and the British advance southward from Canada had been stalled by American resistance at Lake Champlain. In 1777, however, the British decided to replay their strategy. From Canada they dispatched General John Burgoyne with nearly 8,000 British and German troops. Howe was to move his force from New York, first taking the city of Philadelphia, the seat of the Continental Congress, and then moving north to meet Burgoyne.

Fort Ticonderoga fell to Burgoyne on July 6, but by August the general found himself bogged down and harassed by Patriot militias in the rough country south of Lake George. After several defeats in September at the hands of an American army commanded by General Horatio Gates, Burgoyne retreated to Saratoga. There his army was surrounded by a considerably larger force of Americans, and on October 19, lacking alternatives, he surrendered his nearly 6,000 men. It would be the biggest British defeat until Yorktown, decisive because it forced the nations of Europe to recognize that the Americans had a fighting chance to win their Revolution.

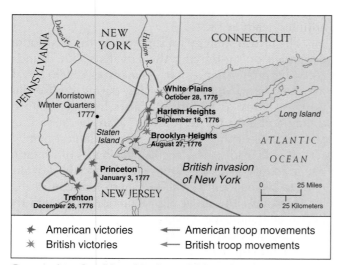

Campaign for New York and New Jersey, 1775–1777

The Americans were less successful against Howe. A force of 15,000 British troops left New York in July, landing a month later, at the northern end of Chesapeake Bay. At Brandywine Creek the British outflanked the Americans, inflicting heavy casualties and forcing a retreat. Ten days later, the British routed the Americans a second time with a frightful bayonet charge at Paoli that left many Patriots dead. When British troops occupied Philadelphia on September 26, Congress had already fled. Washington attempted a valiant counterattack at Germantown on October 4, but initial success was followed by miscoordination that eventually doomed the operation.

After this campaign the Continentals headed for winter quarters at Valley Forge, a few dozen miles from Philadelphia, the bitterness of their defeats muted somewhat by news of the surrender at Saratoga. In taking Philadelphia, the British had gained the most important city in North America, but it proved to have little strategic value. Central government was virtually nonexistent, and so the unified effort suffered little disruption. At the end of two years of fighting, the British strategy for winning the war had to be judged a failure.

The French Alliance and the Spanish Borderlands

During these first two years of fighting, the Americans were sustained by loans from France and Spain, allies against Britain. Both saw an opportunity to win back North American territories lost to Great Britain in the Seven Years' War. The Continental Congress maintained a diplomatic delegation in Paris headed by Benjamin Franklin. Through 1777 Franklin was unable to convince France to commit to an alliance.

In England, meanwhile, the Whig opposition argued strongly against the war. When, in December 1777, British Prime Minister Lord North received the news of Burgoyne's surrender, he dispatched agents to begin peace discussions with Franklin in Paris. Fears of British conciliation with the revolutionaries, as well as the victory at Saratoga, finally persuaded French Foreign Minister Vergennes to tie France to the United States. In mid-December he informed Franklin that the king's council had decided to recognize American independence.

In February 1778, the American delegation submitted to Congress a treaty of commerce and alliance it had negotiated with the French. In the treaty, to take effect upon a declaration of war between France and Britain, the French pledged to "maintain effectually the liberty, sovereignty, and independence" of the United States. France agreed to guarantee to the United States all the "northern parts of America" as well as other "conquests" made in the war, while the United States

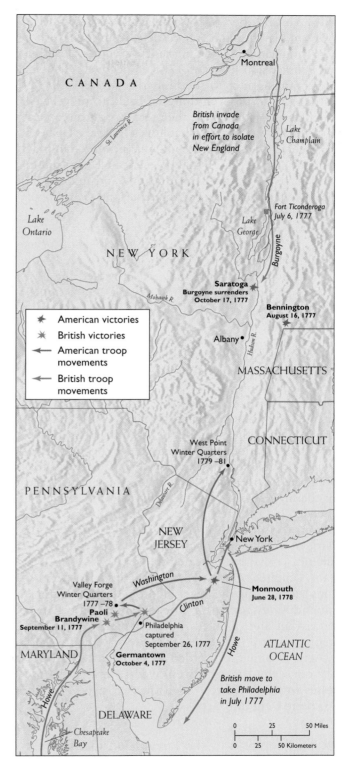

Northern Campaigns, 1777–1778

promised to recognize French acquisitions of British islands in the West Indies. Warfare between France and Britain broke out in June.

A year later Spain also entered the war. But the Spanish pursued an independent strategy against the

British, taking the weakly defended Mississippi River towns of Natchez and Baton Rouge from the British in 1779, and winning the important Gulf ports of Mobile and Pensacola in 1780 and 1781, respectively. The first French ambassador to the United States arrived with instructions to do everything he could to prevent the Americans from enlarging their territory at the expense of the Spanish borderland colonies. Like the Spanish, the French also feared the potential power of an independent United States. Many American leaders did indeed have expansionist aspirations and understood that the wartime alliance with France and tacit support of Spain were expedients.

Worried over the consequences of French involvement, in the spring of 1778 Lord North sent a peace commission to America with promises to repeal the parliamentary legislation that had provoked the crisis in the first place and pledging never again to impose revenue taxes on the colonies. But the Continental Congress declared that any person coming to terms with the peace commission would be labeled a traitor; the only possible topics of negotiation were the withdrawal of British forces and the recognition of American independence.

When France entered the war, the British were forced to rethink their military strategy. With the West Indies at risk, they shipped 5,000 troops from New York to the Caribbean, and suceeded in beating back a French attack. Fearing the arrival of the French fleet along the North American coast, the new British commander in America, General Henry Clinton, evacuated Philadelphia in June 1778. In hot pursuit were Washington's Continentals, fresh out of Valley Forge. At the Battle of Monmouth on June 28, the British blunted the American drive and retreated to New York. The Americans, centered at West Point, took up defensive positions surrounding the lower Hudson. Confidence in an impending victory now spread through the Patriot forces. But after a failed American-French joint campaign against British forces at Newport, Rhode Island, General Washington settled for a defensive strategy. Although the Americans enjoyed several small successes in the Northeast over the next two years, the war there went into a stall.

Indian Peoples and the Revolution in the West

At the beginning of the conflict both sides solicited the support of the Indians. A committee of the Continental Congress reported that "securing and preserving the friendship of Indian nations appears to be a subject of the utmost moment to these colonies." Most concerned about the stance of the Iroquois Confederacy—long one of the most potent political forces in colonial North America—a delegation from Congress told the Iroquois

that the conflict was a "family quarrel" and urged them to keep out of it. British agents, on the other hand, pressed the Iroquois to unite against the Americans. Many Indian people were reluctant to get involved: "We are unwilling to join on either side of such a contest," an Oneida chief responded. "Let us Indians be all of one mind, and live with one another, and you white people settle your own disputes between yourselves."

Ultimately, however, the British were more persuasive. It became clear to Indians that a Patriot victory would mean the extension of American settlements into their homelands. Native peoples fought in the Revolution for some of the same reasons Patriots did—for political independence, cultural integrity, and the protection of their land and property—but Indian fears of American expansion led them to oppose the Patriot rhetoric of natural rights and the equality of all men. Almost all the tribes that engaged in the fighting did so on the side of the British.

British officials marshaled the support of Cherokees, Creeks, Choctaws, and Chickasaws in the South, supplying them with arms from the British arsenal at Pensacola until it was taken by the Spanish in 1781. The consequence was a ferocious Indian war in the southern backcountry. In the summer of 1776, a large number of Cherokees, led by the warrior chief Dragging Canoe (*Tsiyu-Gunsini*), attacked dozens of American settlements. It took hard fighting before Patriot militia companies managed to drive the Cherokees into the mountains, destroying many of their towns. Although the Cherokees eventually made an official peace, sporadic violence between Patriots and Indians continued along the southern frontier.

Among the Iroquois of New York, the Mohawk leader Joseph Brant (*Thayendanegea*) succeeded in bringing most Iroquois warriors into the British camp, although he was opposed by the chiefs of the Oneidas and Tuscaroras, who supported the Patriots. In 1777 and 1778, Iroquois and Loyalist forces raided the northern frontiers of New York and Pennsylvania. In retaliation an American army invaded the Iroquois homelands in 1779. Supported by Oneida and Tuscarora warriors, the Americans destroyed dozens of western villages and thousands of acres of crops. For the first time since the birth of their confederacy in the fifteenth century, the Iroquois were fighting each other.

Across the mountains, the Ohio Indians formed an effective alliance under the British at Detroit, and in 1777 and 1778 they sent warriors south against pioneer communities in western Virginia and Kentucky that had been founded in defiance of the Proclamation of 1763. Boonesborough, Kentucky, was nearly destroyed by repeated attacks, and the Americans barely held out. Virginian George Rogers Clark countered by organizing an expedition of Kentucky militia against the old

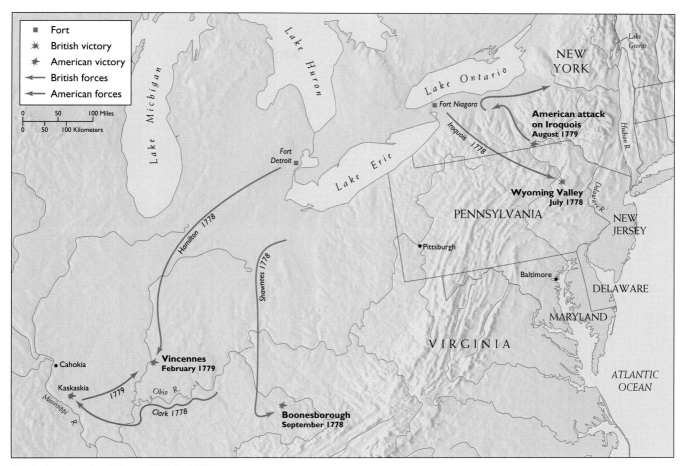

Fighting in the West, 1778–1779

French settlements in the Illinois country, which were controlled by the British. They suceeded in taking the British post at Kaskaskia in the summer of 1778, and in early 1779, in a daring winter raid on Vincennes, they captured Colonel Henry Hamilton, British commander in the West, infamously known as "the Scalp Buyer" because of the bounty he had placed on Patriots' lives.

But Clark lacked the strength to attack the strategic British garrison at Detroit. Coordinating his Iroquois forces with those in Ohio, Brant mounted a new set of offensives that cast a shadow over Clark's successes. Raids back and forth across the Ohio River by Indians and Americans claimed hundreds of lives over the next three years. The war in the West would not end with the conclusion of hostilities in the East. With barely a pause, the fighting in the trans-Appalachian West between Americans and Indians would continue for another two decades.

The War in the South

The most important fighting of the Revolution took place in the South. General Clinton regained the ini-

tiative for Britain in December 1778 by sending a force from New York against Georgia, the weakest of the colonies. The British crushed the Patriot militia at Savannah and began to organize the Loyalists in an effort to reclaim the colony. Several American counterattacks failed, including one in which the French fleet bombarded Savannah. Encouraged by their success in Georgia, the British decided to apply the lessons learned there throughout the South. This involved a fundamental change from a strategy of military conquest to one of pacification. Territory would be retaken step by step, then handed over to Loyalists who would reassert colonial authority loyal to the crown. In October 1779, Clinton evacuated Rhode Island, the last British stronghold in New England, and proceeded with 8,000 troops for a campaign against Charleston. Outflanking the American defenders, Clinton forced the surrender of more than 5,000 troops in May—the most significant American defeat of the war. Horatio Gates, the hero of Saratoga, led a detachment of Continentals southward, but in August they were defeated by General Cornwallis at Camden, South Carolina. Patriot resistance collapsed in the Lower South, and

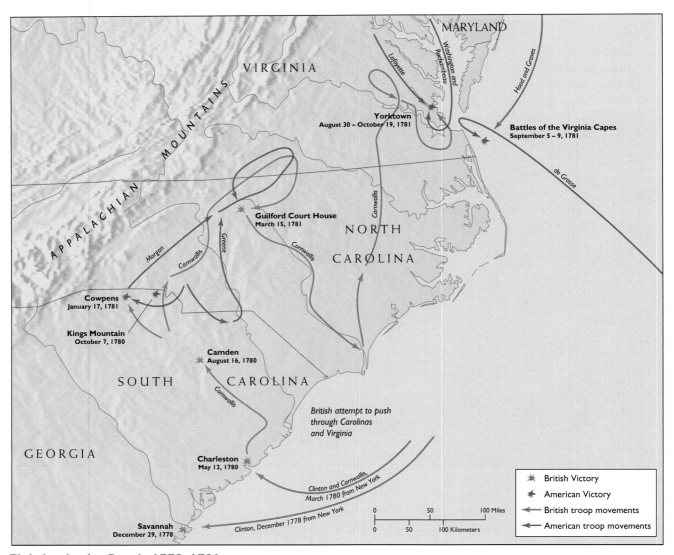

Fighting in the South, 1778–1781

American fortunes were suddenly at their lowest ebb since the beginning of the war.

The southern campaign was marked by vicious violence between partisan militias of Patriots and Loyalists. The violence peaked in September 1780 with Cornwallis's invasion of North Carolina, where the Patriots were stronger and better organized. There the British found their southern strategy untenable: plundering towns and farms in order to feed the army in the interior had the effect of producing angry support for the Patriots.

Into 1781 the Continentals and Patriot militias waged what General Greene called a fugitive war of hit and run against the British. "I am quite tired of marching about the country in quest of adventures," Cornwallis wrote. Finally deciding he would not be able to hold the Carolinas as long as Virginia remained a base

of support and supply for the Americans, he led his army north in the summer of 1781. After marauding through the Virginia countryside he reached the Chesapeake, where he expected reinforcements from New York. The British withdrawal from North Carolina allowed Greene to reestablish Patriot control of the Lower South.

Yorktown

While the British raged through the South, the stalemate continued in the Northeast. In the summer of 1780, taking advantage of the British evacuation of Rhode Island, the French landed 5,000 troops at Newport under the command of General Rochambeau. But it was not until the spring of 1781 that the general risked joining his force to Washington's Continentals north of New York. They planned a campaign against the city, but in August Washington learned that the French Caribbean fleet was headed for the Chesapeake. Washington saw the opportunity for a decisive turn if only he and Rochambeau could move their troops south in coordination with the French naval operation, locking Cornwallis into his camp at Yorktown. Leaving a small force behind as a decoy, Washington and Rochambeau moved quickly down the coast to the Virginia shore.

More than 16,000 American and French troops had converged on the almost 8,000-man British garrison at Yorktown by mid-September. "If you cannot relieve me very soon," Cornwallis wrote to Clinton in New York, "you must expect to hear the worst." French and American heavy artillery hammered the British unmercifully until the middle of October. Cornwallis found it impossible to break the siege, and after the failure of a planned retreat across the York River, he opened negotiations for the surrender of his army. Two days later, on October 19, 1781, Cornwallis, pleading illness, sent his second-in-command, General Charles O'Hara, to surrender. O'Hara first approached General Rochambeau, but the Frenchman waved him toward Washington. It was almost incomprehensible to the British that they would be surrendering to former subordinates. Everyone knew this was an event of incalculable importance, but few guessed it was the end of the war, for the British still controlled New York.

In London, at the end of November, Lord North received the news "as he would have taken a ball in the breast," reported the colonial secretary. "Oh God!" he moaned, "it is all over!" British fortunes were at low ebb in India, the West Indies, Florida, and the Mediterranean; the cost of the war was enormous; and there was little support among the public and members of Parliament for it. King George III wished to press on, but North submitted his resignation, and in March 1782 the king was forced to accept the counsel of Lord Rockingham, who favored granting Americans their independence.

THE UNITED STATES IN CONGRESS ASSEMBLED

The motion for independence, offered to the Continental Congress by Richard Henry Lee on June 7, 1776, called for a confederation of the states. The Articles of Confederation, the first written constitution of the United States, created a national government of sharply limited powers. This arrangement reflected the concerns of people fighting to free themselves from a coercive central government.

The Articles of Confederation

The debate over confederation that took place in the Continental Congress following the Declaration of Independence made it clear that the delegates favoring a loose union of autonomous states outnumbered those who wanted a strong central government. The following year a consensus finally emerged. In November 1777, the Articles of Confederation were formally adopted by the Continental Congress and sent to the states for ratification. The Articles created a national assembly, called the Congress, in which each state had a single vote. Delegates, selected annually in a manner determined by the individual state legislatures, could serve no more than three years out of six. A presiding president elected annually by Congress was eligible no more than one year out of three. Votes would be decided by a simple majority of the states, except for major questions, which would require the agreement of nine states.

Congress was granted national authority in the conduct of foreign affairs, matters of war and peace, and maintenance of the armed forces. It could raise loans, issue bills of credit, establish a coinage, and regulate trade with Indian peoples, and it was to be the final authority in jurisdictional disputes between states. It was charged with establishing a national postal system as well as a common standard of weights and measures. Lacking the power to tax citizens directly, however, the national government was to apportion its financial burdens among the states according to the extent of their surveyed land. The Articles explicitly guaranteed the sovereignty of the individual states, reserving to them all powers not expressly delegated to Congress. Ratification or amendment required the agreement of all thirteen states. This constitution thus created a national government of specific yet sharply circumscribed powers.

The legislatures of twelve states soon voted in favor of the Articles, but final ratification was held up for more than three years by the state of Maryland. Representing the interests of states without claims to lands west of the Appalachians, Maryland demanded that states cede to Congress their western claims, the new nation's most valuable resource, for "the good of the whole." It was 1781 before Virginia, the state with the largest western claims, broke the log-jam by promising to cede its lands. Maryland then agreed to ratification, and in March the Articles of Confederation took effect.

Financing the War

Congress financed the Revolution through grants and loans from friendly foreign powers and by issuing paper currency. The total foreign subsidy by the end of the war approached $9 million, but this was insufficient to back the circulating Continental currency that Congress had authorized, the face value of which had risen to $200 million. Congress called on the states to raise taxes, payable in Continental dollars, so that this currency could be retired. But most of the states were unwilling to do this. In fact, the states resorted to printing currency of their own, which totaled another $200 million by the end of the war. The results of this growth in the money supply were the rapid depreciation of Continental currency and runaway inflation. People who received fixed incomes for services—Continental soldiers, for example, as well as merchants, landlords, and other creditors—were devastated. When Robert Morris, one of the wealthiest merchants in the country, became secretary of finance in May 1781, Continental currency had ceased to circulate; things of no value were said to be "not worth a Continental."

Morris persuaded Congress to charter the Bank of North America in Philadelphia, the first private commercial bank in the United States. There he deposited large quantities of gold and silver coin and bills of exchange obtained through loans from Holland and France. He then issued new paper currency backed by this supply. Once confidence in the bank had developed, Morris was able to begin supplying the Continental Army through private contracts. He was also able to meet the interest payments on the debt, which in 1783 he estimated to be about $30 million.

Negotiating Independence

Peace talks between the United States and Great Britain opened in July 1782, when Benjamin Franklin sat down with the British emissary in Paris. Congress had issued its first set of war aims in 1779. The fundamental demands were recognition of American independence and withdrawal of British forces. The American negotiators were to press for as much territory as possible, including Canada, and guarantees of the American right to fish the North Atlantic. As for its French ally, Congress instructed the commissioners to be guided by friendly advice, but also by "knowledge of our interests, and by your own discretion, in which we repose the fullest confidence." In June 1781, partly as a result of French pressure, Congress issued a new set of instructions: the commissioners were to settle merely for a grant of independence and withdrawal of troops, and to be subject to the guidance and control of the French in the negotiations.

Franklin, John Jay, and John Adams, the peace commissioners in Paris, were aware of French attempts to manipulate the outcome of negotiations and to limit potential American power. In violation of instructions and treaty obligations, and without consulting the French, they signed a preliminary treaty with Britain in November 1782. The British were delighted at the thought of separating the wartime allies. In the treaty, Britain acknowledged the United States as "free, sovereign & independent" and agreed to withdraw its troops from all forts within American territory "with all convenient speed." They guaranteed Americans "the right to take fish" in northern waters. The American commissioners pressed the British for Canada, but settled for western territorial boundaries extending to the Mississippi. Britain received American promises to erect "no lawful impediments" to the recovery of debts, to cease confiscating Loyalist property, and to try to persuade the states to fairly compensate Loyalist exiles. Finally, the two nations agreed to unencumbered navigation of the Mississippi. The American commissioners had accomplished an astounding coup. The peace terms, they wrote to Congress, "appear to leave us little to complain of and not much to desire."

France was thus confronted with an accomplished fact. When the French criticized the commissioners, the Americans responded by hinting that resistance to the treaty provisions could result in a British–American alliance. France thereupon quickly made an agreement of its own with the British.

Though left out of the negotiations, Spain claimed sovereignty over much of the trans-Appalachian territory granted to the United States as a result of its successful campaign against the British on the Mississippi and the Gulf Coast. Spain also arranged a separate peace with Great Britain, in which it won the return of Florida. The final Treaty of Paris—actually a series of separate agreements among the United States, Great Britain, France, and Spain—was signed at Versailles on September 3, 1783.

The Crisis of Demobilization

During the two years between the surrender at Yorktown and the signing of the Treaty of Paris, the British continued to occupy New York City, Charleston, and a series of western posts. The Continental Army remained on wartime alert, with some 10,000 men and an estimated 1,000 women encamped at Newburgh, New York, north of West Point. The soldiers had long been awaiting their pay and were very concerned about the postwar bounties and land warrants promised them. The most serious problem, however, lay not among the enlisted men but in the officer corps.

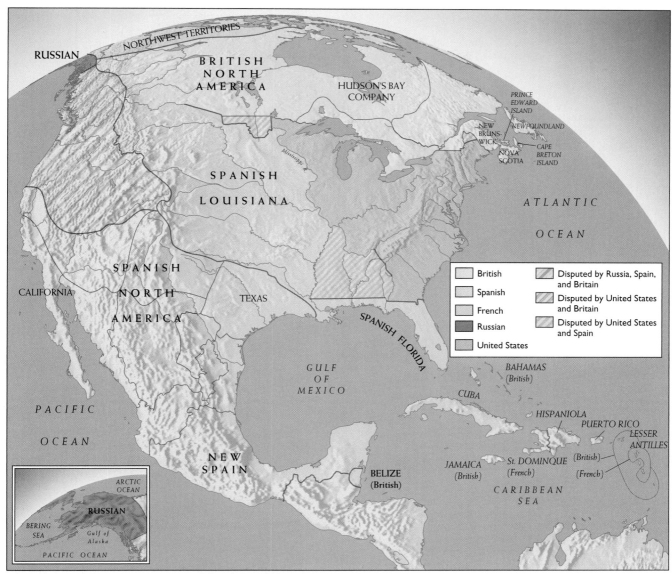

North America after the Treaty of Paris, 1783   The map of European and American claims to North America was radically altered by the results of the American Revolution.

Continental officers had extracted a promise from Congress of life pensions at half pay in exchange for enlistment for the duration of the war. By 1783, however, Congress had still not made specific provisions for veteran's pensions. With peace at hand, officers began to fear that the army would be disbanded before the problem was resolved, and they would lose whatever power they had to pressure Congress. In January 1783, a group of prominent senior officers petitioned Congress, demanding that pensions be converted to a bonus equal to five years of full pay. On Washington's urging, Congress agreed to do this.

As for the common soldiers, they wanted simply to be discharged. In May 1783, Congress voted the soldiers three months' pay as a bonus and instructed

Washington to begin dismissing them. Some troops remained at Newburgh until the British had evacuated New York in November, but by the beginning of 1784 the Continental Army had shrunk to no more than a few hundred men.

The Problem of the West

Even during the Revolution thousands of Americans migrated west, and after the war settlers poured over the mountains and down the Ohio River. Thousands of Americans pressed against the Indian country north of the Ohio River, and destructive violence continued along the frontier. British troops continued to occupy posts in the Northwest and encouraged Indian attacks

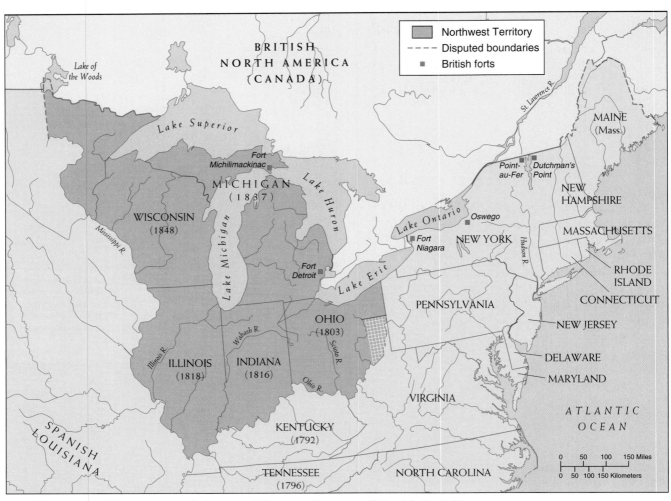

The Northwest Territory and the Land Survey System of the United States

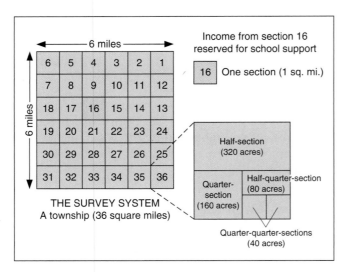

The Land Ordinance of 1785 created an ordered system of survey (revised by the Northwest Ordinance of 1787), dividing the land into townships and sections.

on vulnerable settlements. Spain refused to accept the territorial settlement of the Treaty of Paris, and they closed the port of New Orleans to Americans, effectively blockading the Mississippi River. Westerners who saw that route as their primary access to markets were outraged.

John Jay, appointed secretary for foreign affairs by the Confederation Congress in 1784, attempted to negotiate with the British for withdrawal from the Northwest, but was told that was not possible until all outstanding debts from before the war were settled. Jay also negotiated with the Spanish for guarantees of territorial sovereignty and commercial relations, but they insisted that the Americans relinquish free navigation of the Mississippi. Congress would approve no treaty under those conditions, and under these frustrating circumstances, some Westerners considered leaving the Confederation. There were prominent Kentuckians who advocated rejoing the British, while others, including George Rogers Clark and General James Wilkinson, secretly worked for the Spanish as informants and spies. The people of the West "stand as it were upon a pivot," wrote Washington in 1784 after a trip down the Ohio. "The touch of a feather would turn them any way." In the West, local community interest continued to override the fragile development of national community sentiment.

In 1784, Congress took up the problem of extending national authority over the West. Legislation was drafted, principally by Thomas Jefferson, providing for "Government for the Western Territory." The legislation proposed a remarkably democratic colonial policy. The western public domain would eventually be divided into states, fully the equal of the original thirteen, with guarantees of self-government and republican institutions. Once the population of a territory numbered 20,000, the residents could call a convention and establish a constitution and government of their own choosing. And once the population grew to equal that of the smallest of the original thirteen states, the territory could petition for statehood, provided it agreed to remain forever a member of the Confederation. Congress accepted these proposals but rejected by a vote of seven to six Jefferson's clause forever prohibiting slavery in the West.

Passed the following year, the Land Ordinance of 1785 provided for the survey and sale of western lands. To avoid the chaos of overlapping surveys and land claims that had characterized Kentucky, the authors of the ordinance created an ordered system of survey, dividing the land into townships composed of thirty-six sections of one square mile (640 acres) each. This measure would have an enormous impact on the North American landscape, as can be seen by anyone who has flown over the United States and looked down at the patchwork pattern. Jefferson argued that land ought to be given away to actual settlers. But, eager to establish a revenue base for the government, Congress provided for the auction of public lands for not less than one dollar per acre. In the treaties of Fort Stanwix in 1784 and Fort McIntosh in 1785, congressional commissioners forced the Iroquois and some of the Ohio Indians to cede a portion of their territory in what is now eastern Ohio, and surveyors were immediately sent there to divide up the land. These treaties were not the result of negotiation; the commissioners dictated the terms by seizing hostages and forcing compliance. The first surveyed lands were not available for sale until the fall of 1788. In the meantime, Congress, desperate for revenue, sold a tract of more than 1.5 million acres to a new land company, the Ohio Company, for a million dollars.

Thousands of Westerners chose not to wait for the official opening of the public land north of the Ohio River but settled illegally. In 1785 Congress raised troops and evicted many of them, but once the troops left the squatters returned. The persistence of this problem convinced many congressmen to revise Jefferson's democratic territorial plan. In the Northwest Ordinance of 1787, Congress established a system of government for the territory north of the Ohio. Three to five states were to be carved out of the giant Northwest Territory and admitted "on an equal footing with the original states in all respects whatsoever." Slavery was prohibited. But the initial guarantee of self-government in Jefferson's plan was replaced by the rule of a congressionally appointed court of judges and governor. Once the free white male population of the territory had grown to 5,000, these citizens would be permitted to choose an assembly, but the governor was given the power of absolute veto on all territorial legislation. National interest would be imposed on the localistic western communities.

The creation of the land system of the United States was the major achievement of the Confederation government. But there were other important accomplishments. Under the Articles of Confederation, Congress led the country through the Revolution and its commissioners negotiated the terms of a comprehensive peace treaty. In organizing the departments of war, foreign affairs, the post office, and finance, the Confederation government created the beginnings of a national bureaucracy.

REVOLUTIONARY POLITICS IN THE STATES

Despite these accomplishments, most Americans focused not on the Confederation government in Philadelphia but on the governments of their own states. During the revolutionary era, most Americans identified politically and socially with their local communities and states rather than with the American nation. People spoke of "these United States," emphasizing the plural. The single national community feeling of the Revolution was overwhelmed by persistent localism. The states were the setting for the most important political struggles of the Confederation period and for long afterwards.

The Broadened Base of Politics

The political mobilization that took place in 1774 and 1775 greatly broadened political participation. Mass meetings in which ordinary people expressed their opinions, voted, and gained political experience were common, not only in the cities but in small towns and rural communities as well. During these years, a greater proportion of the population began to participate in elections. Compared with the colonial assemblies, the new state legislatures included more men from rural and western districts—farmers and artisans as well as lawyers, merchants, and large landowners. For example, many delegates to the Massachusetts provincial congress of 1774 were men from small farming communities who lacked formal education and owned little property.

This transformation was accompanied by a dramatic shift in the political debate. During the colonial period, when only the upper crust of society had been truly engaged in the political process, the principal argument took place between the Tory and Whig positions. The Tory position, argued by royal officials, was that colonial governments were simply convenient instruments of the king's prerogative, serving at his pleasure. Colonial elites, seeking to preserve and increase their own power, had argued for stronger assemblies. They used traditional Whig arguments about the need for a balanced government, represented by the governor, the upper house, and the assembly. This debate was ended by the Revolution. The Tory position lost all legitimacy. For the first time in American history, democracy became a term of approval. Patriots who took a Whig position on balanced government found themselves challenged by farmers, artisans, and other ordinary people armed with a new and radical democratic ideology.

One of the first post-Revolution debates focused on the appropriate governmental structure for the new states. The thinking of democrats was indicated by the title of a New England pamphlet of 1776: *The People the Best Governors*. Power, the anonymous author argued, should be vested in a single, popularly elected assembly. The people, the pamphlet said, "best know their wants and necessities, and therefore are best able to govern themselves." The ideal form of government, according to democrats, was the community or town meeting, in which the people set their own tax rates, created a militia, controlled their own schools and churches, and regulated the local economy. State government was necessary only for coordination among communities.

Conservative Americans took up the Whig argument on the need for a balanced government. The "unthinking many," wrote another pamphleteer, should be checked by a strong executive and an upper house. Both of these would be insulated from popular control by property qualifications and long terms in office, the latter designed to draw forth the wisdom and talent of the country's wealthiest and most accomplished men. The greatest danger, according to conservatives, was the possibility of majority tyranny, which might lead to the violation of property rights and to dictatorship.

"We must take mankind as they are," one conservative wrote, "and not as we could wish them to be."

Declarations of Rights

Fourteen states—the original thirteen plus Vermont—adopted constitutions between 1776 and 1780. Each of these documents was shaped by debate between radicals and conservatives, democrats and Whigs, and reflected a political balance of power. The constitutions of Pennsylvania, Maryland, and New York typified the political range of the times. Pennsylvania instituted a radical democracy, Maryland created a conservative set of institutions designed to keep citizens and rulers as far apart as possible, and New York adopted a system somewhere in the middle.

One of the most important innovations of the state constitutions was a guarantee of rights patterned on the Virginia Declaration of Rights of June 1776. Written by George Mason—a wealthy planter, democrat, and brilliant political philosopher—the Virginia declaration set a distinct tone in its very first article: "That all men are by nature equally free and independent, and have certain inherent rights, . . . namely, the enjoyment of life and liberty, with the means of acquiring and possessing property and pursuing and obtaining happiness and safety." The fifteen articles declared, among other things, that sovereignty resided in the people, that government was the servant of the people, and that the people had the "right to reform, alter, or abolish" that government. There were guarantees of due process and trial by jury in criminal prosecutions, and prohibitions of excessive bail and "cruel and unusual punishments." Freedom of the press was guaranteed as "one of the great bulwarks of liberty," and the people were assured of "the free exercise of religion, according to the dictates of conscience."

Eight state constitutions included a general declaration of rights similar to the first article of the Virginia declaration; others incorporated specific guarantees. A number of states proclaimed the right of the people to engage in free speech and free assembly, to instruct their representatives, and to petition for the redress of grievances—rights either inadvertently or deliberately omitted from Virginia's declaration. These declarations were important precedents for the Bill of Rights, the first ten amendments to the federal Constitution. Indeed, George Mason of Virginia was a leader of the democrats who insisted that the Constitution stipulate such rights.

A Spirit of Reform

The political upheaval of the Revolution raised the possibility of other reforms in American society. The

1776 Constitution of New Jersey, by granting the vote to "all free inhabitants" who met the property requirements, enfranchised women as well as men. The number of women voters eventually led to male protests and a new state law explicitly limiting the right to vote to "free white male citizens."

The New Jersey controversy may have been an anomaly, but women's participation in the Revolution wrought subtle but important changes. In 1776 Abigail Adams wrote to her husband John Adams, away at the Continental Congress, "In the new code of laws which I suppose it will be necessary for you to make I desire you would remember the ladies, and be more generous and favourable to them than your ancestors." In the aftermath of the Revolution, there was evidence of increasing sympathy in the courts for women's property rights and fairer treatment of women's petitions for divorce. And the postwar years witnessed an increase in opportunities for women seeking an education. From a strictly legal and political point of view, the Revolution may have done little to change women's role in society, but it did seem to help change expectations.

The most steadfast reformer of the day was Thomas Jefferson, who after completing work on the Declaration of Independence returned to Virginia to take a seat in its House of Delegates. In 1776 he introduced a bill that abolished the law of entails, which had confined inheritance to particular heirs in order that landed property remain undivided. Jefferson believed that "entail" and "primogeniture" (inheritance of all the family property by the firstborn son)—legal customs long in effect in aristocratic England—had no place in a republican society. The legislation had little practical effect because few estates were entailed, but the repeal was symbolically important, for it repudiated an ancient aristocratic custom. By 1790, every state but one had followed Virginia's lead (Rhode Island finally acted in 1798).

Jefferson's other notable success was his Bill for Establishing Religious Freedom. Indeed, he considered this document one of his greatest accomplishments. At the beginning of the Revolution, there were established churches—denominations officially supported and funded by the government—in nine of the thirteen colonies: the Congregationalists in Massachusetts, New Hampshire, and Connecticut and the Anglicans in New York and in the South. (See also Chapter 5 for a discussion of colonial religion.) Established religion was increasingly opposed in the eighteenth century, in part because of Enlightenment criticism of the power it had over free and open inquiry, but, more important, because of the growing sectarian diversity produced by the religious revival of the Great Awakening.

African Americans and the Revolution

For most African Americans there was little to celebrate in the American victory, for it perpetuated the institution of slavery. Few people were surprised when thousands of black fighters and their families departed with the Loyalists and the British at the end of the war, settling in the West Indies, Canada, and Africa. Most of these refugees were fugitive slaves rather than committed Loyalists. Virginia and South Carolina were said to have lost 30,000 and 25,000 slaves as a result of the war.

To many white Americans there was an obvious contradiction in waging a war for liberty while continuing to support the institution of slavery. Slavery was first abolished in the state constitution of Vermont in 1777, and in Massachusetts and New Hampshire in 1780 and 1784, respectively. Pennsylvania, Connecticut, and Rhode Island adopted systems of gradual emancipation during these years, freeing the children of slaves at birth. By 1804 every northern state had provided for abolition or gradual emancipation, although as late as 1810, 30,000 African Americans remained enslaved in the North.

In the Upper South, revolutionary idealism, the Christian egalitarianism of Methodists and Baptists, and a shift from tobacco farming to the cultivation of cereal grains such as wheat and corn combined to weaken the commitment of many planters to the slave system. There was a great increase in "manumissions," grants of freedom to slaves by individual masters. In the Upper South there was a small but important movement to encourage gradual emancipation by convincing masters to free their slaves in their wills. George Washington not only freed several hundred of his slaves upon his death but developed an elaborate plan for apprenticeship and tenancy for the able-bodied, and lodging and pensions for the aged. Planters in the Lower South, however, heavily dependent as they were on slave labor, resisted the growing calls for an end to slavery. Between 1776 and 1786 all the states but South Carolina and Georgia prohibited or heavily taxed the international slave trade, and this issue became an important point of conflict at the Constitutional Convention in 1787 (see Chapter 8).

Perhaps the most important result of these developments was the growth of the free African American population; from a few thousand in 1750, this population grew to more than 200,000 by the end of the century. Largely excluded from the institutions of white Americans, the African American community now had enough strength to establish schools, churches, and other institutions of its own. At first this development was opposed. In Williamsburg, Virginia, for instance, the leader of a black congregation was seized and whipped when he attempted to gain recognition from the Baptist Association. But by the 1790s, the Williamsburg African

This portrait of the African American poet Phillis Wheatley was included in the collection of her work published in London in 1773, when she was only twenty. Kidnapped in Africa when a girl, then purchased off the Boston docks, she was more like a daughter than a slave to the Wheatley family, and later married and lived as a free woman of color before her untimely death in 1784.

SOURCE: © Bettman/CORBIS.

Church had grown to over 500 members, and the Baptist Association reluctantly recognized it. In Philadelphia, Reverend Absalom Jones established St. Thomas's African Episcopal Church. The incorporation of the word "African" in the names of churches, schools, and mutual benefit societies reflected the pride African Americans took in their heritage.

A small group of African American writers rose to prominence in the revolutionary era. Benjamin Banneker published a popular almanac that both white and black Americans consulted. The most famous African American writer, however, was Phyllis Wheatley, who came to public attention when her *Poems on Various Subjects, Religious and Moral* appeared in London in 1773, while she was still a domestic slave in Boston. Kidnapped in Africa as a young girl and converted to Christianity during the Great Awakening, Wheatley wrote poems that combined her piety and a concern for her people.

Economic Problems

During the Revolution, the shortage of goods resulting from the British blockade, the demand for supplies by the army and the militias, and the flood of paper currency issued by the Congress and the states combined to create the worst inflation that Americans have ever experienced. Continental dollars traded against Spanish dollars at the rate of 3 to 1 in 1777, 40 to 1 in 1779, and 146 to 1 in 1781, by which time Congress had issued more than $190 million in Continentals. Most of this paper money ended up in the hands of merchants, who paid only a fraction of its face value. There was a popular outcry at the incredible increase in prices, and communities and states in the North responded with laws regulating wages and prices.

The sponsors of wage and price schedules often blamed high prices on hoarding and profiteering. Although it is doubtful that such practices caused the inflation, many merchants did gouge their customers. Many communities experienced demonstrations and food riots; men and women demanded fair prices, and when they did not receive them, they broke into storehouses and took what they needed. People organized local committees to monitor economic activity and punish wrongdoers.

After the war, inflation was suddenly replaced by depression. Political revolution could not alter economic realities: the independent United States continued to be a supplier of raw materials and an importer of manufactured products, and Great Britain remained its most important trading partner.

With few exports to offset all the imports, the trade deficit with Britain for the period 1784–86 rose to approximately £5 million. The deficit acted like a magnet, drawing hard currency from American accounts. Short of hard currency, the commercial banks in the United States insisted on immediate repayment of old loans and refused to issue new ones. The country was left with very little coin in circulation. It added up to a serious depression, lasting from 1784 to 1788. At their lowest level, in 1786, prices had fallen by 25 percent.

The depression struck while the country was burdened with the huge debt incurred during the Revolution. The total debt owed by the national and state governments amounted to more than $50 million in 1785. Not allowed to raise taxes on its own, the Confederation Congress requisitioned the states for the funds necessary for debt repayment. The states in turn taxed their residents. At a time when there was almost no money in circulation, people rightly feared being crushed by the burden of private debt and public taxes. Thus, the economic problem became a political problem.

State Remedies

Where there were manufacturing interests, as in the Northeast, states erected high tariffs to curb imports and protect infant industries. But shippers could avoid

CHRONOLOGY

1775	Lord Dunmore, royal governor of Virginia, appeals to slaves to support Britain
1776	July: Declaration of Independence
	August: Battle of Long Island initiates retreat of Continental Army
	September: British land on Manhattan Island
	December: George Washington counterattacks at Trenton
1777	Slavery abolished in Vermont
	September: British General William Howe captures Philadelphia
	October: British General John Burgoyne surrenders at Saratoga
	November: Continentals settle into winter quarters at Valley Forge
	December: France recognizes American independence
1778	June: France enters the war
	June: Battle of Monmouth hastens British retreat to New York
	July: George Rogers Clark captures Kaskaskia
	December: British capture Savannah
1779	Spain enters the war
1780	February: British land at Charleston
	July: French land at Newport
	September: British General Charles Cornwallis invades North Carolina
1781	February: Robert Morris appointed superintendent of finance
	March: Articles of Confederation ratified
	October: Cornwallis surrenders at Yorktown
1782	Peace talks begin
1783	March: Washington mediates issue of officer pensions
	September: Treaty of Paris signed
	November: British evacuate New York
1784	Treaty of Fort Stanwix
	Postwar depression begins
1785	Land Ordinance of 1785
	Treaty of Fort McIntosh
1786	Jefferson's Bill for Establishing Religious Freedom
	Rhode Island currency law
	Shays' Rebellion

these duties simply by unloading their cargo in neighboring seaboard states that lacked tariffs; domestic merchants then distributed the products overland. To be effective, commercial regulation had to be national. Local sentiment had to give way to the unity of a national community.

The most controversial economic remedies were those designed to relieve the burden on debtors and ordinary taxpayers. In some areas, farmers called for laws permitting payment of taxes or debts in goods and commodities, a kind of institutionalized barter. More commonly, farmers and debtors pressed their state governments for legal tender laws, which would require creditors to accept at specified rates of exchange a state's paper currency—regardless of its worth—for all debts public and private.

Understandably, creditors opposed such a plan. But farmers were strong enough to enact currency laws in seven states during the depression. For the most part, these were modest programs that worked rather well, caused little depreciation, and did not result in the problems feared by creditors. In most instances, the notes were loaned to farmers, who put up the value of their land as collateral.

Shays' Rebellion

The combination of political uncertainty and economic instability developed into a crisis in a rural uprising of Massachusetts communities that shook the nation in 1786. Farmers in the western part of the state had been hit particularly hard during the depression, when country merchants pressed them to pay their debts in hard currency they didn't have. About a third of all male heads of household were sued for debt during the 1780s, and the county jails were filled with debtors who couldn't pay. Dozens of towns petitioned the state government for relief, but the legislature, dominated by urban and merchant interests, rejected legal tender and paper currency laws. During the spring and summer of 1786, farmers throughout the rural parts of the state mustered their community militia companies and closed the courts—precisely what they had done during the Revolution.

This uprising quickly became known as Shays' Rebellion, after Daniel Shays, one of the leaders of the "committee of the people" who had also been a leader in the Revolution. Although the rebellion was most widespread in Massachusetts, similar disorders occurred in every other New England state except Rhode Island, where the farmers had already taken power. There were incidents outside New England as well.

The crisis ended in Massachusetts when a militia force raised in communities from the eastern part of the state marched west and crushed the Shaysites in January 1787 as they marched on the armory in Springfield. Fifteen of the leaders were subsequently sentenced to death; two were hanged before the remainder were pardoned, and several hundred farmers had to swear an oath of allegiance to the state. In fact, these men had wanted little more than temporary relief from their indebtedness, and rural discontent quickly disappeared once the depression began to lift in 1788.

The most important consequence of Shays' Rebellion was its effect on conservative nationalists unhappy with the distribution of power between the states and national government under the Articles of Confederation. The uprising "wrought prodigious changes in the minds of men respecting the powers of government," wrote the Secretary of War Henry Knox. "Everybody says they must be strengthened and that unless this shall be effected, there is no security for liberty and property." It was time, he declared, "to clip the wings of a mad democracy."

CONCLUSION

The Revolution was a tumultuous era, marked by violent conflict between Patriots and Loyalists, masters and slaves, settlers and Indian peoples. The advocates of independence emerged successful, largely because of their ability to pull together and to begin to define their national community. But fearful of the power of central authority, Americans created a relatively weak national government. By the mid-1780s, however, many nationalists were paraphrasing Washington's question of 1777: "What then is to become of this nation?" Most Americans would seek to answer that question by attempting to reform the national government and build a strong new national community.

REVIEW QUESTIONS

1. Assess the relative strengths of the Patriots and the Loyalists in the American Revolution.
2. What roles did Indian peoples and African Americans play in the Revolution?
3. Describe the structure of the Articles of Confederation. What were its strengths and weaknesses?
4. How did the Revolution affect politics within the states?
5. What were the issues in Shays' Rebellion? How do they help to illustrate the political conflict in the nation during the 1780s?

RECOMMENDED READING

Thomas Fleming, *Liberty! The American Revolution* (1997). This well-written account—derived from a public television series—includes wonderful contemporary images.

Merrill Jensen, *The New Nation: A History of the United States during the Confederation, 1781–1789* (1950). Still the standard work on the 1780s.

Max M. Mintz, *Seeds of Empire: The American Revolutionary Conquest of the Iroquois* (1999). The Revolution as a war for the control of Iroquois lands in upstate New York.

Charles Patrick Neimeyer, *America Goes to War: A Social History of the Continental Army* (1996). A detailed look at the men who fought and won the Revolution.

Mary Beth Norton, *Liberty's Daughters: The Revolutionary Experience of American Women, 1750–1800* (1980). A provocative and comprehensive history of women in the Revolutionary era. Treats not only legal and institutional change but also the more subtle changes in habits and expectations.

John W. Pulis, *Moving On: Black Loyalists in the Afro-Atlantic World* (1999). Essays on their military role, but especially on their communities in Canada, Great Britain, and Africa. In each place they remained second-class citizens.

Ray Raphael, *A People's History of the American Revolution: How Common People Shaped the Fight for Independence* (2001). Demonstrates that the Revolution was much more fractious when viewed at the level of those who did the fighting and dying.

Charles Royster, *A Revolutionary People at War* (1979). A pathbreaking study of the Continental Army and popular attitudes toward it. Emphasizes the important role played by the officer corps and the enlisted men in the formation of the first nationalist constituency.

David P. Szatmary, *Shays' Rebellion: The Making of an Agrarian Insurrection* (1980). An excellent study of the famous farmers' rebellion that stimulated conservatives to write the Constitution. Includes a great deal of general background material on the Confederation period, as well as excellent coverage of the specifics of the revolt.

ON THE WEB

http://lcweb.loc.gov/exhibits/religion/

A Library of Congress exhibit, this site details the role of religion in early American history including the colonial, revolutionary, and early national eras.

The following sites are all from Yale University's Avalon Project and consist of key primary documents from the Revolutionary War era to the early national period of the United States:

http://www.yale.edu/lawweb/avalon/arms.htm

This page contains "A Declaration by the Representatives of the United Colonies of North-America, Now Met in Congress at Philadelphia, Setting Forth the Causes and Necessity of Their Taking Up Arms," July 6, 1775.

http://www.yale.edu/lawweb/avalon/declare.htm

This page contains the Declaration of Independence, July 4, 1776.

http://www.yale.edu/lawweb/avalon/diplomacy/france/frtreaty.htm

This page contains links to the several treaties of alliance between France and the United States, 1778.

http://www.yale.edu/lawweb/avalon/artconf.htm

This page contains the Articles of Confederation proposed by Congress on November 15, 1777, and finally in force after ratification by Maryland, March 1, 1781.

http://www.yale.edu/lawweb/avalon/amerdoc/annapoli.htm

This page contains the report of the Annapolis Convention, September 11, 1786, proposing a convention to amend the Articles of Confederation.

http://www.jmu.edu/madison/madison.htm#JudicialReview

Maintained by James Madison University, this site contains links to primary documents related to the public life of James Madison from the Revolution to the end of his presidency.

http://www.historyplace.com/unitedstates/revolution/

This site is the main index page of the The History Place. Scroll down the page to the American War for Independence, which contains both narrative and links to primary documents and graphics on the American Revolution.

http://www.prenhall.com/faragherbrief/map7.1

Examine the impact of the Treaty of Paris on North America's geopolitical landscape. How did the treaty alter the balance of power in North America?

http://www.prenhall.com/faragherbrief/map7.2

Through a series of animated maps, consider the ways in which the Northwest Ordinance affected the admission of new states into the Union. What were the consequences for western lands?

EIGHT

THE UNITED STATES OF NORTH AMERICA

▶ 1786 – 1800

AMERICAN COMMUNITIES

Mingo Creek Settlers Refuse to Pay the Whiskey Tax

IT WAS A HOT JULY AFTERNOON IN 1794 WHEN THE FEDERAL MARSHAL and the tax collector arrived at the backcountry farm of William Miller in Mingo Creek, a community south of Pittsburgh. Like most of his neighbors, Miller had failed to pay the federal excise tax on his homemade whiskey still, and these authorities had come to serve him with a notice to appear in federal court in Philadelphia. "I felt myself mad with passion," said the farmer, knowing that the fine and the cost of the trip back east would ruin him. As the men argued, thirty or forty of Miller's neighbors suddenly appeared, armed with muskets and pitchforks. Members of the Mingo Creek Democratic Society, they had come to fight off this infringement on their liberty. There was an angry confrontation, and someone fired a gun into the air. No one was hit, and after a heated verbal confrontation, the two officials rode off. But the farmers were fuming and decided to make a "citizen's arrest" of the officials the next day.

At Mingo Creek, poverty was the outstanding fact of life. A third of the farm families owned no land but rented or simply squatted on the acres of others. The tax collector or "exciseman" was one of the great landlords of Mingo Creek, not only controlling most of the local wealth but monopolizing political office as well. Other landlords lived outside the community, the most powerful being President George Washington himself, who owned thousands of acres in the West, much of it in the vicinity of Mingo Creek. The president had evicted so many squatters from his land that local people considered him a grasping speculator. Washington returned the compliment by describing these frontier settlers as "a parcel of barbarians" who lived little better than "dogs or cats."

In the Ohio region farm families lived in miserable mud-floored log huts scattered along the creeks of the Monongahela Valley. But despite appearances, the farmers of Mingo Creek were bound together in networks of family and clan, work and barter, religion and politics. The militiamen had acted together in what they perceived to be the interests of their community.

Like all the western territories, this was a violent place in a violent time. No-holds-barred fights at local taverns were common, and travelers remarked on the presence of one-eyed men, the victims of brutal gougings. Everyone knew of men or women lost in the continuing Indian wars.

In 1782 militia companies from the area had taken their revenge by massacring ninety-six unresisting Christian Indians at Gnadenhutten, north of the Ohio River, hacking their bodies and bringing home their scalps as trophies. The new federal government had committed over 80 percent of its operating budget to defeating the Indians, but the failure of its campaigns had left backcountry families resentful.

It was to help pay the costs of these campaigns that Congress had placed the tax on whiskey in 1791. The tax applied to the owners of stills, whether they produced commercially or simply for family and neighbors. Corn was not worth the cost of shipping it east, but whiskey made from corn was another matter, and many a farm family depended on the income from their stills. Farmers throughout America protested that the excise ran counter to the principles of the Revolution. "Internal taxes upon consumption," declared the citizens of Mingo Creek, are "most dangerous to the civil rights of freemen, and must in the end destroy the liberties of every country in which they are introduced." Hugh Henry Brackenridge, editor of the *Pittsburgh Gazette*, argued for a tax on the "unsettled lands which all around us have been purchased by speculating men, who keep them up in large bodies and obstruct the population of the country." In other words, Congress should tax land speculators, like President Washington, instead of backcountry squatters.

Protest followed the course familiar from the Revolution. At first citizens gathered peacefully and petitioned their representatives, but when the tax collectors appeared, there was vigilante action. Faces blackened or covered with handkerchiefs, farmers tarred and feathered the tax men. Although the immediate issue was taxation, larger matters were at stake. The Mingo Creek Democratic Society was part of Thomas Jefferson's political movement that supported republicanism and the French Revolution, in opposition to the conservative principles of the Washington administration. The tax protesters made this linkage explicit when they raised banners proclaiming the French slogan of "Liberty, Equality, Fraternity" and then adding their own phrase, "and No Excise!" In North Carolina the rebels sang:

Some chaps whom freedom's
spirit warms
Are threatening hard to take up
arms,
And headstrong in rebellion rise

'Fore they'll submit to that excise:
Their liberty they will maintain,
They fought for't, and they'll fight again.

But it was only in western Pennsylvania that the protests turned to riot. When the Mingo Creek militia went to arrest the tax collector, several of their number were killed in the confrontation. The tax collector and his family escaped from their house as it was consumed by a fire set by the farmers. In a community meeting afterward, the protesters resolved to attack and destroy Pittsburgh, where the wealthy and powerful local landlords resided. Terrified residents of the town saved the day by welcoming the rebels with free food and drink. "It cost me four barrels of whiskey that day," declared one man, but "I would rather spare that than a single quart of blood." Destruction was averted, but an angry farmer rode through the street waving a tomahawk and warning, "It is not the excise law only that must go down. A great deal more is to be done. I am but beginning yet."

Declaring the Whiskey Rebellion "the first ripe fruit" of the democratic sentiment sweeping the country, President George Washington organized a federal army of 13,000 men, larger than the one he had commanded during the Revolution, and ordered the occupation of western Pennsylvania. Federal soldiers dragged half-naked men from their beds and forced them into open pens, where they remained for days in the freezing rain. Authorities arrested twenty people, and a judge convicted two of treason. The protest gradually died down. Washington pardoned the felons, sparing their lives.

Federal power had prevailed over the local community. In his Farewell Address to the nation the following year Washington warned of an excessive spirit of localism that "agitates the community with ill-founded jealousies and false alarms; kindles the animosity of one part against another; foments occasionally riot and insurrection." But resistance to the excise remained widespread, and no substantial revenue was ever collected from the tax on whiskey. More important, the whiskey rebels had raised some of the most important issues of the day: the power and authority of the new federal government, the relationship of the West to the rest of the nation, the nature of political dissent, and the meaning of the Revolution. ■

Mingo Creek

KEY TOPICS

- The tensions and conflicts between local and national authorities in the decades after the American Revolution

- The struggle to draft the Constitution and to achieve its ratification

- Establishment of the first national government under the Constitution

- The beginning of American political parties

- The first stirrings of an authentic American national culture

---

FORMING A NEW GOVERNMENT

Eight years before the Whiskey Rebellion a similar rural uprising, Shays' Rebellion (see Chapter 7), had solidified beliefs that the powers of the federal government must be increased lest the budding nation wither.

Nationalist Sentiment

Nationalists had long argued for a strengthened union of the states. In general, the nationalists were drawn from the elite circles of American life. "Although there are no nobles in America, there is a class of men denominated 'gentlemen,'" the French ambassador to America wrote home in 1786. "They are creditors, and therefore interested in strengthening the government, and watching over the execution of the law. The majority of them being merchants, it is for their interest to establish the credit of the United States in Europe on a solid foundation by the exact payment of debts, and to grant to Congress powers extensive enough to compel the people to contribute for this purpose." In addition to merchants, the ambassador identified others who leaned toward national government: former officers in the Continental Army whose experience with the Continental Congress had made them firm believers in a stronger central government, and conservatives who wanted to restrain what they considered the excessive democracy of the states.

The economic crisis that followed the Revolutionary War (see Chapter 7) provided the nationalists with their most important opportunity to organize. In March 1785, a group of men from Virginia and Maryland, including James Madison, George Mason, and George Washington, drafted an agreement to present to legislatures recommending uniform commercial regulations, duties, and currency laws. Early the next year, at Madison's urging, the Virginia legislature invited all the states to send representatives to a commercial conference to be held at Annapolis in the fall. Only five states sent strong nationalist delegates to the Annapolis Convention in September 1786. But this time, most Americans agreed that the Articles needed strengthening, especially in regard to commercial regulation and the generation of revenue. Early in 1787 the Confederation Congress cautiously endorsed the plan for a convention "for the sole and express purpose of revising the Articles of Confederation."

The Constitutional Convention

Fifty-five men from twelve states assembled at the Pennsylvania State House in Philadelphia in late May 1787. Rhode Island, where radical localists held power (see Chapter 7), refused to send a delegation. A number of prominent men were missing. Thomas Jefferson and John Adams were serving as ambassadors in Europe, and crusty localist Patrick Henry declared that he "smelt a rat." But most of America's best-known leaders were present: George Washington, Benjamin Franklin, Alexander Hamilton, James Madison, George Mason, Robert Morris. Twenty-nine of them were college educated, thirty-four were lawyers, twenty-four had served in Congress, and twenty-one were veteran officers of the Revolution. At least nineteen owned slaves, and there were also land speculators and merchants. But there were no ordinary farmers or artisans present, and of course no women, African Americans, or Indians. The Constitution was framed by white men who represented America's social and economic elite.

On their first day of work, the delegates agreed to vote by states, as was the custom of Congress. They chose Washington to chair the meeting. James Madison, a young, conservative Virginian with a profound knowledge of history and political philosophy, took voluminous daily minutes of the entire convention. Madison and his fellow Virginians had arrived early and drafted what became known as the Virginia Plan. Presented by Governor Edmund Randolph of Virginia on May 29, it set the convention's agenda.

The authors of the Virginia Plan proposed scrapping the Articles of Confederation in favor of a "consolidated government" having the power to tax and to enforce its laws directly rather than through the states. "A spirit of locality," Madison declared, was destroying "the aggregate interests of the community," by which he meant the great community of the nation. The Virginia Plan would have reduced the states to little more than administrative districts. Representation in the bicameral national legislature was to be based on population districts, the members of the House of Representatives elected by popular vote, but senators chosen indirectly by state legislators so that they might be insulated from democratic pressure. The Senate would lead, controlling foreign affairs and the appointment of officials. An appointed chief executive and a national judiciary would together form a Council of Revision having the power to veto both national and state legislation.

The main opposition to these proposals came from the delegates from small states, who feared being swallowed up by the large ones. After two weeks of debate, William Paterson of New Jersey introduced an alternative, a set of "purely federal" principles known since as the New Jersey Plan. He proposed increasing the powers of the central government but retaining a single-house Congress in which the states were equally represented. After much debate, and a series of votes that split the convention down the middle, the delegates finally agreed to what has been called the Great Compromise: proportional representation in the House, representation by states in the Senate. The compromise allowed the creation of a strong national government while still providing an important role for the states.

Part of this agreement was a second, fundamental compromise that brought together the delegates from North and South. To boost their power in the new government, the southern delegates wanted to include slaves in the population for the purpose of determining state proportional representation, but to exclude them when it came to apportioning taxes. Ultimately it was agreed that five slaves would be counted as equivalent to three freemen—the "three-fifths rule." Furthermore, the representatives of South Carolina and Georgia demanded protection for the slave trade, and after bitter debate the delegates included a provision preventing any federal restriction on the importation of slaves for twenty years. Another article legitimized the return of fugitive slaves from free states. The word "slave" was nowhere used in the text of the Constitution, but these provisions amounted to national guarantees for southern slavery. Although many delegates were opposed to slavery, and regretted having to give in on this issue, they agreed with Madison, who wrote that "great as the evil is, a dismemberment of the union would be worse."

In the ensuing debate on the role of the branches of government the delegates favored a strong federal judiciary with the implicit power to declare acts of Congress unconstitutional. There was also considerable support for a president with veto power to check the legislature.

In early September, the delegates turned their rough draft of the Constitution over to a Committee of Style, which shaped it into an elegant and concise document providing the general principles and basic framework of government. The delegates voted their approval on September 17, 1787, and transmitted the document to Congress, agreeing that it would become operative after ratification by nine states. Despite some congressmen who were outraged that the convention had exceeded its charge of simply modifying the Articles of Confederation, Congress called for a special ratifying convention in each of the states.

Ratifying the New Constitution

The supporters of the new Constitution immediately adopted the name Federalists to describe themselves. In this, as in much of the subsequent process of ratification, the Federalists (or nationalists) grabbed the initiative, and their opponents had to content themselves with the label Anti-Federalists. The critics of the Constitution were by no means a unified group. Because most of them were localists, they represented a variety of social and regional interests. But most believed the Constitution granted far too much power to the central government, weakening the autonomy of communities and states. As local governments "will always possess a better representation of the feelings and interests of the people at large," one critic wrote, "it is obvious that these powers can be deposited with much greater safety with the state than the general government."

All the great political thinkers of the eighteenth century had argued that a republican form of government could work only for small countries. As French philosopher Montesquieu had observed, "In an extensive republic, the public good is sacrificed to a thousand private views." But in *The Federalist*, a brilliant series of essays in defense of the Constitution written in 1787 and 1788 by James Madison, Alexander Hamilton, and John Jay, Madison stood Montesquieu's assumption on its head. Rhode Island had demonstrated that the rights of property might not be protected in even the smallest of states. Asserting that "the most common and durable source of factions has been the various and unequal distribution of property," Madison concluded that the best way to control such factions was to "extend the sphere" of government. Rather than a disability, Madison argued, great size is an advantage: interests are so diverse that no single faction is able to gain control of the state, threatening the freedoms of others.

It is doubtful whether Madison's sophisticated argument, or the arguments of the Anti-Federalists for that matter, made much of a difference in the popular voting in the states to select delegates for the state ratification conventions. The alignment of forces generally followed the lines laid down during the fights over economic issues in the years since the Revolution. Agrarian-localist and commercial-cosmopolitan alignments characterized most of the states. The most critical convention took place in Massachusetts in early 1788. Five states—Delaware, Pennsylvania, New Jersey, Georgia, and Connecticut—had already voted to ratify, but the states with the strongest Anti-Federalist movements had yet to convene. If the Constitution lost in Massachusetts, its fate would be in great danger. At the convention, Massachusetts opponents of ratification enjoyed a small majority. But several important Anti-Federalist leaders, including Samuel Adams, were swayed by the enthusiastic support for the Constitution among Boston's townspeople, and on February 16 the convention voted narrowly in favor of ratification. To no one's surprise, Rhode Island rejected the Constitution in March, but Maryland and South Carolina approved it in April and May. On June 21 New Hampshire became the ninth state to ratify.

New York, Virginia, and North Carolina were left with the decision of whether to join the new Union. Anti-Federalist support was strong in each of these states. North Carolina voted to reject. (It did not join the Union until the next year, followed by a still reluctant Rhode Island in 1790.) In New York the delegates were moved to vote their support by a threat from New York City to secede from the state and join the Union separately if the state convention failed to ratify. The Virginia convention was almost evenly divided, but promises to amend the Constitution to protect the people from the potential abuses of the federal government persuaded enough delegates to produce a victory for the Constitution. The promise of a Bill of Rights was important in the ratification vote of five of the states.

The Bill of Rights

Although the Bill of Rights—the first ten amendments to the Constitution—was adopted during the first session of the new federal Congress, it was first proposed during the debates over ratification. The various state ratification conventions had proposed a grab bag of over 200 potential amendments. Madison set about transforming these into a series of proposals that he introduced into the new Congress in June 1789. Congress passed twelve and sent them to the states, and ten survived the ratification process to become the Bill of Rights in 1791.

The First Amendment prohibits Congress from establishing an official religion and provides for the freedom of assembly. It also ensures freedom of speech, a free press, and the right of petition. The other amendments guarantee the right to bear arms, limit the government's power to quarter troops in private homes, and restrain the government from unreasonable searches or seizures; they assure the people their legal rights under the common law, including the prohibition of double jeopardy, the right not to be compelled to testify against oneself, and due process of law before life, liberty, or property can be taken away. Finally, the unenumerated rights of the people are protected, and the powers not delegated to the federal government are reserved to the states.

The first ten amendments to the Constitution have been a restraining influence on the growth of government power over American citizens. Their provisions have become an admired aspect of the American political tradition throughout the world. The Bill of Rights is the most important constitutional legacy of the Anti-Federalists.

THE NEW NATION

Ratification of the Constitution was followed by the first federal elections—for the Congress and the presidency—and in the spring of 1789 the new federal government assumed power in the temporary capital of New York City. The inauguration of George Washington as the first president of the United States took place on April 30, 1789, on the balcony of Federal Hall, at the corner of Wall and Broad Streets. The first years under the new federal Constitution were especially important for the future, because they shaped the structure of the American nation-state in ways that would be enormously significant for later generations.

The Washington Presidency

Although he dressed in plain American broadcloth at his inauguration and claimed to be content with a plain republican title, Washington was counted among the nationalists. He was anything but a man of the people. By nature reserved and solemn, he chose to ride about town in a grand carriage drawn by six horses and escorted by uniformed liverymen. In the tradition of British royalty, he delivered his addresses personally to Congress and received from both houses an official reply. These customs were continued by John Adams, Washington's successor, but ended by Thomas Jefferson, who denounced them as "rags of royalty." On the other hand, Washington worked hard to adhere to the letter of the Constitution, refusing, for example, to use the veto power except where he thought the Congress had acted unconstitutionally, and personally seeking the "advice and consent" of the Senate.

Congress quickly moved to establish departments to run the executive affairs of state, and Washington soon appointed Thomas Jefferson his secretary of state, Alexander Hamilton to run the Treasury, Henry Knox the War Department, and Edmund Randolph the Justice Department, as attorney general. The president consulted each of these men regularly, and during his first term met with them as a group to discuss matters of policy. By the end of Washington's presidency the secretaries had coalesced in what came to be known as the cabinet, an institution that has survived to the present despite the absence of constitutional authority or enabling legislation. Washington was a powerful and commanding personality, but he understood the importance of national unity, and in his style of leadership, his consultations, and his appointments he sought to achieve a balance of conflicting political perspectives and sectional interests. These intentions would be sorely tested during the eight years of his administration.

An Active Federal Judiciary

The most important piece of legislation to emerge from the first session of Congress was the Judiciary Act of 1789, which implemented the judicial clause of the Constitution, which impowered Congress to determine the number of justices on the Supreme Court and create a system of federal courts. Congress established a high court of six justices (in 1869 this was increased to nine) and established three circuit and thirteen district courts. Strong nationalists argued for a powerful federal legal system that would provide a uniform code of civil and criminal justice throughout the country. But the localists in Congress fought successfully to retain the various bodies of law that had developed in the states. They wanted to preserve local community autonomy. The act gave federal courts limited original jurisdiction, restricting them mostly to appeals from state courts. But it thereby established the principle of federal judicial review of state legislation, despite the silence of the Constitution on this point.

Under the leadership of Chief Justice John Jay, the Supreme Court heard relatively few cases during its first decade. Still, it managed to raise considerable political controversy. In *Chisholm* v. *Georgia* (1793) it ruled in favor of two South Carolina residents who had sued the state of Georgia for the recovery of confiscated property. Thus did the Court overthrow the common law principle that a sovereignty could not be sued without its consent, and it supported the Constitution's grant of federal jurisdiction over disputes "between a state and citizens of another state." Many localists feared that this nationalist ruling threatened the integrity of the states. In response, they proposed the Eleventh Amendment to the Constitution, ratified in 1798, which declared that no state could be sued by citizens from another state.

Hamilton's Controversial Fiscal Program

Fiscal and economic affairs pressed upon the new government. Lacking revenues, and faced with the massive national debt contracted during the Revolution, the government took power in a condition of virtual bankruptcy. Congress passed the Tariff of 1789, a compromise between advocates of protective tariffs (with duties so high that they made foreign products prohibitively expensive, thus "protecting" American products) and those who wanted moderate tariffs that produced income for the federal government. Duties on imported goods, rather than direct taxes on property or incomes, would constitute the bulk of federal revenues until the twentieth century.

In 1790 Treasury Secretary Hamilton submitted a "Report on the Public Credit" in which he recommended that the federal government assume the obligations accumulated by the states during the previous fifteen years and redeem the national debt—owed to both domestic and foreign leaders—by agreeing to a new issue of interest-bearing bonds.

By this means, Hamilton sought to inspire the confidence of domestic and foreign investors in the public credit of the new nation. Congress endorsed his plan to pay off the $11 million owed to foreign creditors but balked at funding the domestic debt of $27 million and assuming the state debts of $25 million. Necessity had forced many individuals to sell off at deep discounts the notes, warrants, and securities the government had issued them during the Revolution. Yet Hamilton now advocated paying these obligations at face value, providing any speculator who held them with fabulous profits. An even greater debate took place over the assumption of the state debts, for some states, mostly those in the South, had already arranged to liquidate them, whereas others had left theirs unpaid. Congress remained deadlocked on these issues for six months, until congressmen from Pennsylvania and Virginia arranged a compromise.

Final agreement, however, was stalled by a sectional dispute over the location of the new national capital. Southerners supported Washington's desire to plant it on the Potomac River, but Northerners argued for Philadelphia. In return for Madison's pledge to obtain enough southern votes to pass Hamilton's debt assumption plan—which Madison had earlier opposed as a "radically immoral" windfall for speculators—northern congressmen agreed to a location for the new federal district on the boundary of Virginia and Maryland. In July 1790, Congress passed legislation moving the temporary capital from New York to Philadelphia until the expected completion of the federal city in the District of Columbia in 1800. Two weeks later it adopted Hamilton's credit program. This was the first of many sectional compromises.

Hamilton now proposed the second component of his fiscal program, the establishment of a Bank of the United States. The bank, a public corporation funded by private capital, would serve as the depository of government funds and the fiscal agent of the Treasury. Congress narrowly approved it, but Madison's opposition raised doubts in the president's mind about the constitutionality of the measure, and Washington solicited the opinion of his cabinet. Here for the first time were articulated the classic interpretations of constitutional authority. Jefferson took a "strict constructionist" position, arguing that the powers of the federal government must be limited to those specifically enumerated in the Constitution. This position came closest to the basic agreement of the men who had drafted the document. Hamilton, on the other hand, reasoned that the Constitution "implied" the power to use whatever means were "necessary and proper" to carry out its enumerated powers—a loose constructionist position. Persuaded by Hamilton's opinion, Washington signed the bill, and the bank went into operation in 1791.

The final component of Hamilton's fiscal program, outlined in his famous "Report on Manufactures," was an ambitious plan, involving the use of government securities as investment capital for "infant industries," and high protective tariffs to encourage the development of an industrial economy. Many of Hamilton's specific proposals for increased tariff protection became part of a revision of duties that took place in 1792. Moreover, his fiscal program as a whole dramatically restored the financial health of the United States. Foreign investment in government securities increased and, along with domestic capital, provided the Bank of the United States with enormous reserves. Its bank notes became the most important circulating medium of the North American commercial economy, and their wide acceptance greatly stimulated business enterprise. "Our public credit," Washington declared toward the end of his first term, "stands on that ground which three years ago it would have been considered as a species of madness to have foretold."

The Beginnings of Foreign Policy

The Federalist political coalition, forged during the ratification of the Constitution, was sorely strained by these debates over fiscal policy. By the middle of 1792, Jefferson, representing the southern agrarians, and Hamilton, speaking for northern capitalists, were locked in a full-scale feud within the Washington administration. Hamilton conducted himself more like a prime minister than a cabinet secretary, greatly offending Jefferson, who considered himself the president's heir apparent. But the dispute went deeper than a mere conflict of personalities. Hamilton stated the difference clearly when he wrote that "one side appears to believe that there is a serious plot to overturn the State governments, and substitute a monarchy to the present republican system," while "the other side firmly believes that there is a serious plot to overturn the general government and elevate the separate powers of the States upon its ruins." The conflict between Hamilton and Jefferson was to grow even more bitter over the issue of American foreign policy.

The commanding event of the Atlantic world during the 1790s was the French Revolution, which had begun in 1789. Most Americans enthusiastically welcomed the fall of the French monarchy. After the people of Paris stormed the Bastille, Lafayette sent Washington the key to its doors as a symbol of the relationship between the two revolutions. But with the beginning of the Reign of Terror in 1793, which claimed upon the guillotine the lives of hundreds of aristocrats, American conservatives began to voice their opposition. The execution of King Louis XVI, and especially the onset of war between revolutionary France and monarchical Great Britain in 1793, firmly divided American opinion.

Most at issue was whether the Franco-American alliance of 1778 required the United States to support France in its war with Britain. All of Washington's cabinet agreed on the importance of American neutrality. With France and Britain prowling for each other's vessels on the high seas, the vast colonial trade of Europe was delivered up to neutral powers, the United States prominent among them. In other words, neutrality meant windfall profits. Jefferson believed it highly unlikely that the French would call upon the Americans to honor the 1778 treaty; the administration should simply wait and see. But Hamilton argued that so great was the danger of American involvement in the war that Washington should immediately declare the treaty "temporarily and provisionally suspended."

These disagreements revealed two contrasting perspectives on the course the United States should chart in international waters. Hamilton and the nationalists believed in the necessity of an accommodation with Great Britain, the most important trading partner of the United States and the world's greatest naval power. Jefferson, Madison, and the democrats, on the other hand, looked for more international independence, less connection with the British, and thus closer relations with Britain's traditional rival, France. They pinned their hopes on the future of American western expansion.

The debate in the United States grew hotter with the arrival in early 1793 of French ambassador Edmond Genêt. Large crowds of supporters greeted him throughout the nation, and among them he solicited contributions and distributed commissions authorizing American privateering raids against the British. Understandably, a majority of Americans still nursed a hatred of imperial Britain, and these people expressed a great deal of sympathy for republican France. Conservatives such as Hamilton, however, favored a continuation of traditional commercial relations with Britain and feared the antiaristocratic violence of the French. Washington sympathized with Hamilton's position, but most of all he wished to preserve American independence and neutrality. Knowing he must act before "Citizen" Genêt (as the ambassador was popularly known) compromised American sovereignty and involved the United States in a war with Britain, the president issued a proclamation of neutrality on April 22, 1793. In it he assured the world that the United States intended to pursue "a conduct friendly and impartial towards the belligerent powers," while continuing to do business with all sides.

Hamilton's supporters applauded the president, but Jefferson's friends were outraged. Throughout the country those sympathetic to France organized Democratic Societies, political clubs modeled after the Sons of Liberty. Society members corresponded with each other, campaigned on behalf of candidates, and lobbied with congressmen. People interpreted the international question in the light of issues of local importance. Thus, the members of the Mingo Creek Democratic Society used enthusiasm for the French Revolution as a way of organizing political opposition to the Washington administration. In a speech to Congress, President Washington denounced what he called these "self-created societies," declaring them "the most diabolical attempt to destroy the best fabric of human government and happiness."

Citizen Genêt miscalculated, however, alienating even his supporters, when he demanded that Washington call Congress into special session to debate

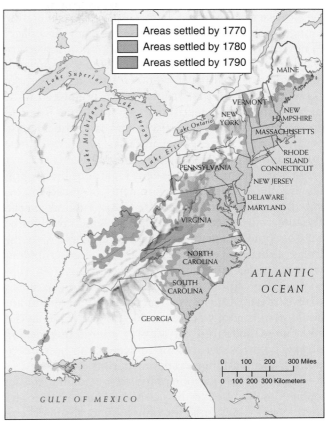

Spread of Settlement: The Backcountry Expands, 1770–1790   From 1770 to 1790 American settlement moved across the Appalachians for the first time. The Ohio Valley became the focus of bitter warfare between Indians and settlers.

neutrality. Jefferson, previously a confidant of the ambassador, now denounced Genêt as "hot-headed" and "indecent towards the President." But these words came too late to save his reputation in the eyes of Washington, and at the end of 1793 Jefferson left the administration. The continuing upheaval in France soon swept Genêt's party from power and he was recalled, but fearing the guillotine, he claimed sanctuary and remained in the United States. During his time in the limelight, however, he furthered the division of the Federalist coalition into a faction identifying with Washington, Hamilton, and conservative principles and a faction supporting Jefferson, Madison, democracy, and the French Revolution.

The United States and the Indian Peoples

Among the many problems of the Washington presidency, one of the most pressing concerned the West. The American attempt to treat the western tribes as conquered peoples after the Revolution had resulted only in further violence and warfare. In the Northwest

Ordinance of 1787 (see Chapter 7), the Confederation Congress abandoned that premise for a new approach. "The utmost good faith shall always be observed towards the Indians," the Ordinance read. "Their lands and property shall never be taken from them without their consent." Yet the Ordinance was premised on the opening of Indian land north of the Ohio River to American settlement, its survey and sale, and the creation of new state governments. The Ordinance pointed in wildly contradictory directions.

The Constitution was silent regarding Indian policy, but the new federal government continued to pursue this inconsistent policy. In 1790 Congress passed the Intercourse Act, the basic law by which the United States would "regulate trade and intercourse with the Indian tribes." To eliminate the abuses of unscrupulous traders, the act created a federal licensing system; subsequent legislation authorized the creation of subsidized trading houses, or "factories," where Indians could obtain goods at reasonable prices. Trade abuses continued unabated for lack of adequate policing power, but these provisions indicated the best intentions of the Washington administration.

To clarify the question of Indian sovereignty, the act declared public treaties between the United States and the Indian nations to be the only legal means of obtaining Indian land. Treaty making, thus, became the procedure for establishing and maintaining relations. In the twentieth century, a number of Indian tribes have successfully appealed for the return of lands obtained by states or individuals in violation of this provision of the Intercourse Act.

On the other hand, one of the federal government's highest priorities was the acquisition of western Indian land to supply a growing population of farmers. The federal government, in fact, was unable to control the flood of settlers coming down the Ohio River. An American expeditionary force was sent to evict the settlers, but inevitably they ended up fighting the Indians. In defense of their homelands, villages of Shawnees, Delawares, and other Indian peoples confederated with the Miamis under their war chief Little Turtle. In the fall of 1790 Little Turtle lured federal forces led by General Josiah Harmar into the confederacy's stronghold in Ohio and badly mauled them. In November 1791 the confederation inflicted an even more disastrous defeat on a large American force under General Arthur St. Clair, governor of the Northwest Territory. More than 900 Americans were killed or wounded, making this the worst defeat of an army by Indians in North American history.

In the aftermath of this defeat the House of Representatives launched the first formal investigation of the executive branch undertaken by the Congress. They found St. Clair's leadership "incompetent," and he soon resigned. Yet few Americans were willint to admit to the contradiction at the heart of American policy. "We acknowledge the Indians as brothers," yet we "seize their lands," Senator Benjamin Hawkins of North Carolina wrote to President Washington. "This doctrine it might be expected would be disliked by the independent Tribes. . . . It is the source of their hostility."

Spanish Florida and British Canada

The position of the United States in the West was made even more precarious by the hostility of Spain and Great Britain, who controlled the adjoining territories. Under the dynamic leadership of King Carlos III and his able ministers, Spain introduced liberal reforms to revitalize the rule-bound economy of its American empire; as a result the economy of New Spain grew rapidly in the 1780s. Moreover, Spain had reasserted itself in North America, acquiring the French claims to Louisiana before the end of the Seven Years' War, expanding into California, seizing the Gulf Coast during the American Revolution, and regaining Florida from Britain in the Treaty of Paris in 1783.

Spain's anti-American policy in the West had several facets. Controlling both sides of the lower Mississippi, they closed the river to American shipping, making it impossible for western American farmers to market their crops through the port of New Orleans. They also sought to create a barrier to American settlement by promoting immigration to Louisiana and Florida. They succeeded in attracting several thousand of the Acadians whom the British had deported during the Seven Years' War. Reassembling their distinctive communities in the bayou country of Louisiana, these tough emigrants became known as the Cajuns. But otherwise the Spanish had little success with immigration and relied mostly on creating a barrier of pro-Spanish Indian nations in the lower Mississippi Valley. To consolidate these gains, in the early 1790s the Spanish constructed two new Mississippi River forts at sites that would later become the cities of Vicksburg and Memphis.

North of the Ohio River the situation was much the same. Thousands of Loyalists had fled the United States in the aftermath of the Revolution and settled in the country north of lakes Ontario and Erie. They were understandably hostile to the new republic. In 1791 the British Parliament passed the Canada Act, creating the province of Upper Canada (later renamed Ontario) and granting the Loyalists limited self-government. To protect this province, British troops remained at a number of posts within American territory at places such as Detroit, where they supplied the Indian nations with arms and ammunition, hoping to create a buffer to American expansion.

Domestic and International Crises

Washington faced the gravest crisis of his presidency in 1794. In the West, the inability of the federal government to subdue the Indians, eliminate the British from the northern fur trade, or arrange with the Spanish for unencumbered use of the Mississippi River stirred frontiersmen to loud protests. There were rumblings of rebellion and secession from western communities. As the opening to this chapter illustrates, this discontent was strengthened by Hamilton's federal excise tax on whiskey, which hit backcountry farmers hardest. In the Old Northwest and Old Southwest, English and Spanish secret agents gave liberal bribes to entice American settlers to quit the Union and join themselves to Canada or Florida. In the Atlantic, Great Britain declared a blockade of France and seized vessels trading with the French West Indies. From 1793 to the beginning of 1794 the British confiscated the cargoes of more than 250 American ships, threatening hundreds of merchants with ruin. The United States was being "kicked, cuffed, and plundered all over the ocean," declared Madison, and in Congress he introduced legislation imposing retaliatory duties on British ships and merchandise.

The Whiskey Rebellion, which broke out in the summer of 1794, thus came at a time when President Washington considered the nation to be under siege. The combination of Indian attack, international intrigue, and domestic insurrection, he believed, created the greatest threat to the nation since the Revolution. In April the president had dispatched Chief Justice John Jay to London to arrange a settlement with the British. At the same time, war seemed increasingly likely, and Washington feared that any sign of federal weakness in the face of western rebellion would invite British or Spanish intervention. With Hamilton's urging he took the decisive course described in the opening of this chapter: he raised a large militia even as he pursued halfhearted negotiations with local authorities and made preparations to occupy the area around Pittsburgh, including Mingo Creek. It is clear now that the president overreacted, for although there was riot and violence in western Pennsylvania, there was no organized insurrection. Nevertheless, his mobilization of federal military power dramatically demonstrated the federal commitment to the preservation of the Union, the protection of the western boundary, and the supremacy of the national over the local community.

This action was reinforced by an impressive American victory against the Indian confederacy. Following the disastrous defeat of St. Clair by Little Turtle, Washington appointed General Anthony Wayne to lead a greatly strengthened American force to subdue the Indian confederacy and secure the Old Northwest. At the battle of Fallen Timbers, fought in the Maumee country of northern Ohio on August 20, 1794, Wayne crushed the Indians. Retreating, the warriors found the gates of Fort Miami closed and barred, the British inside unprepared to engage the powerful American force. The victory set the stage for the Treaty of Greenville in 1795, in which the representatives of twelve Indian nations ceded a huge territory encompassing most of present-day Ohio, much of Indiana, and other enclaves in the Northwest, including the town of Detroit and the tiny village of Chicago.

Jay's and Pinckney's Treaties

The strengthened American position in the West encouraged the British to settle their dispute with the United States so that they might concentrate on defeating republican France. In November 1794, Jay and the British signed an agreement providing for British withdrawal from American soil by 1796, limited American trade with the British East and West Indies, and "most-favored-nation" status for both countries (meaning that each nation would enjoy trade benefits equal to those the other accorded any other nation-state). The treaty represented a solid gain for the young republic. With only a small army and no navy to speak of, the United States was in no position to wage war.

Details of Jay's Treaty leaked out in a piecemeal fashion that inflamed public debate. The treaty represented a victory for Hamilton's conception of American neutrality. The Jeffersonians, on the other hand, were enraged over this accommodation with Great Britain at France's expense. The absence in the treaty of any mention of compensation for the slaves who had fled to the British side during the Revolution alienated Southerners. Throughout the country Democratic Societies and Jeffersonian partisans organized protests and demonstrations. Upon his return to the United States, Jay joked, he could find his way across the country by the light of his burning effigies. Despite these protests, the Senate, dominated by supporters of Hamilton, ratified the agreement in June 1795. In the House, a coalition of Southerners, Westerners, and friends of France attempted to stall the treaty by threatening to withhold the appropriations necessary for its implementation. They demanded that they be allowed to examine the diplomatic correspondence regarding the whole affair, but the president refused, establishing the precedent of "executive privilege" in matters of state.

The deadlock continued until late in the year, when word arrived in Philadelphia that the Spanish had abandoned their claims to the territory south of the Ohio River. Having declared war on revolutionary France, Spain had suffered a humiliating defeat. Fearing the loss of its American empire, the Spanish had suddenly found it expedient to mollify the quarrelsome Americans. In 1795 American envoy Thomas Pinckney negotiated a treaty in which Spain agreed to a boundary with the United States at the 31st parallel and opened the Mississippi to American shipping. This treaty fit the Jeffersonian conception of empire, and congressmen from the West and South were delighted with its terms. But administration supporters demanded their acquiescence in Jay's Treaty before the approval of Pinckney's Treaty.

These two important treaties finally established American sovereignty over the land west of the Appalachians and opened to American commerce a vast market extending from Atlantic ports to the Mississippi Valley. From a political standpoint, however, the events of 1794 and 1795 brought Washington down from his pedestal. Vilified by the opposition press, sick of politics, and longing to return to private life, Washington rejected the offer of a third term.

Washington's Farewell Address

During the last months of his term, Washington published his Farewell Address to the nation. In it argued not for American isolation, but rather for American disinterest in the affairs of Europe. "The great rule of conduct for us in regard to foreign nations is, in extending our commercial relations to have with them as little political connection as possible." Why, he asked "entangle our peace and prosperity in the toils of European ambition, rivalship, interest, humor, or caprice?" Thomas Jefferson, in his Inaugural Address of 1801, paraphrased this first principle of American foreign policy as "peace, commerce, and honest friendship with all nations, entangling alliances with none."

FEDERALISTS AND JEFFERSONIAN REPUBLICANS

The framers of the Constitution envisioned a one-party state in which partisan distinctions would be muted by patriotism and public virtue. "Among the numerous advantages promised by a well constructed Union," Madison had written in *The Federalist*, is "its tendency to break and control the violence of faction." Not only did he fail to anticipate the rise of political parties or factions, but he saw them as potentially harmful to the new nation. Despite the framers' intentions, in the twelve years between the ratification of the Constitution and the federal election of 1800 political parties became a fundamental part of the American system of government.

The Rise of Political Parties

Evident in the debates and votes of Congress from 1789 to 1795 was a series of shifting coalitions. These coalitions first began to polarize into political factions during the debate over Jay's Treaty in 1795, when agrarians, Westerners, Southerners, and supporters of France came together in opposition to the treaty. By the elections of 1796, people had begun to give names to the two factions. The supporters of Hamilton claimed the mantle of Federalism. Forced to find another term, the Jeffersonian opposition became known as the Republicans, meant to imply that the Federalists were really monarchists at heart. Hamilton insisted on labeling his opponents the Anti-Federalists, but historians often call this coalition the Jeffersonian Republicans.

These two political coalitions played a fitful role in the presidential election of 1796, which pitted John Adams, Washington's vice president, against Thomas Jefferson. Partisan organization was strongest in the Middle States, where there was a real contest of political forces, weakest in New England and the South, where sectional loyalty prevailed and organized opposition was weaker. The absence of party discipline was demonstrated when the ballots of the presidential electors, cast in their respective state capitals, were counted in the Senate. Adams was victorious, but the electors chose Jefferson rather than a Federalist for vice president. Thus, the new administration was born divided.

The Adams Presidency

Adams was put in the difficult situation of facing a political opposition led by his own vice president. He nevertheless attempted to conduct his presidency along the lines laid down by Washington, and retained most of the former president's appointees. This arrangement presented Adams with another problem. Although Hamilton had retired the year before, the cabinet remained committed to his advice, actively seeking his opinion and following it. As a result, Adams's authority was further undercut.

On the other hand, Adams benefited from the rising tensions between the United States and France. Angered by Jay's Treaty, the French suspended diplomatic relations at the end of 1796 and inaugurated a tough new policy toward American shipping. During the next two years they seized more than 300 American vessels and confiscated cargoes valued at an estimated $20 million. Hoping to resolve the crisis, Adams sent an American delegation to France. But in dispatches sent back to the United States the American envoys reported that agents of the French foreign ministry had demanded a bribe before any negotiations could be undertaken. Pressed for copies of these dispatches by suspicious Jeffersonian Republicans in

OVERVIEW

THE FIRST AMERICAN PARTY SYSTEM

Federalist Party	Organized by figures in the Washington administration who were in favor of a strong federal government, friendship with the British, and opposition to the French Revolution; its power base was among merchants, property owners, and urban workers tied to the commercial economy. A minority party after 1800, it was regionally strong only in New England.
Democratic Republican Party	Arose as the opposition to the Federalists; its adherents were in favor of limiting federal power; they were sympathetic to the French Revolution and hostile to Great Britain; the party drew strength from southern planters and northern farmers. The majority party after 1800.

Congress, in 1798 Adams released them after substituting the letters X, Y, and Z for the names of the French agents. The documents proved a major liability for the Jeffersonian Republicans, sparking powerful anti-French sentiment throughout the country. To the demand for a bribe, the American delegates had actually answered "Not a sixpence," but in the inflated rhetoric of the day the response became the infinitely more memorable: "Millions for defense, but not one cent for tribute!" The XYZ Affair, as it became known, sent Adams's popularity soaring.

Adams and the Federalists prepared the country for war during the spring of 1798. Congress authorized tripling the size of the army, and Washington came out of retirement to command the force. Fears of a French invasion declined after word arrived of the British naval victory over the French in August 1798 at Aboukir Bay in Egypt, but the "Quasi-War" between France and the United States continued.

The Alien and Sedition Acts

In the summer of 1798 the Federalist majority in Congress, with the acquiescence of President Adams, passed four acts severely limiting both freedom of speech and the freedom of the press and threatening the liberty of foreigners in the United States. Embodying the fear that immigrants, in the words of one Massachusetts Federalist, "contaminate the purity and simplicity of the American character" by introducing dangerous democratic and republican ideas, the Naturalization Act extended the period of residence required for citizenship from five to fourteen years. The Alien Act and the Alien Enemies Act authorized the president to order the imprisonment or deportation of suspected aliens during wartime.

Finally, the Sedition Act provided heavy fines and imprisonment for anyone convicted of writing, publishing, or speaking anything of "a false, scandalous and malicious" nature against the government or any of its officers.

The Federalists intended these repressive laws as weapons to defeat the Jeffersonian Republicans. Led by Albert Gallatin, a Swiss immigrant and congressman from Pennsylvania (replacing Madison, who had retired from politics to devote his time to his plantation), the Jeffersonian Republicans contested all the Federalist war measures and acted as a genuine opposition party, complete with caucuses, floor leaders, and partisan discipline. For the first time, the two parties contested the election of Speaker of the House of Representatives, which became a partisan office. The more effective the Jeffersonian Republicans became, the more treasonous they appeared in the eyes of the Federalists. Disagreement with the administration was misconstrued by the Federalists as opposition to the state itself.

The Federalists thus pursued the prosecution of dissent, indicting leading Jeffersonian Republican newspaper editors and writers, fining and imprisoning at least twenty-five of them. The most vilified was Congressman Lyon, scorned by Federalists as "Ragged Matt the Democrat." Lyon was convicted in July 1798 of publishing libelous statements about President Adams and thrown into a Vermont prison. Later that year, however, he conducted a campaign from his cell and was reelected to Congress.

The Revolution of 1800

The Alien and Sedition Acts were overthrown by the Jeffersonian Republican victory in the national

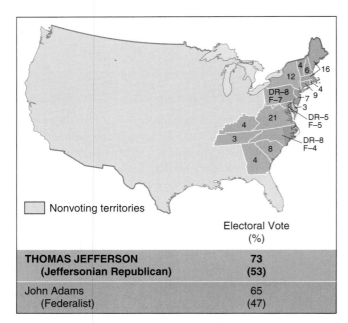

Electoral Vote (%)	
THOMAS JEFFERSON **(Jeffersonian Republican)**	**73** **(53)**
John Adams (Federalist)	65 (47)

The Election of 1800   In the presidential election of 1800, Democratic Republican victories in New York and the divided vote in Pennsylvania threw the election to Jefferson. The combination of the South and these crucial Middle States would keep the Democratic Republicans in control of the federal government for the next generation.

elections of 1800. As the term of President Adams drew to a close, Federalists found themselves seriously divided. In 1799, by releasing seized American ships and requesting negotiations, the French convinced Adams that they were ready to settle their dispute with the United States. The president also sensed the public mood running toward peace. But the Hamiltonian wing of the party, always scornful of public sentiment, continued to beat the drums of war. When Federalists in Congress tried to block the president's attempt to negotiate, Adams threatened to resign and turn the government over to Vice President Jefferson. "The end of war is peace," Adams declared, "and peace was offered me." Adams considered the settlement of this conflict with France to be one of the greatest accomplishments of his career, but it earned him the scorn of conservative Federalists, including Hamilton.

The presidential campaign of 1800 was the first in which Jeffersonian Republicans and Federalists operated as two national political parties. Caucuses of congressmen nominated respective slates: Adams and Charles Cotesworth Pinckney of South Carolina for the Federalists, Jefferson and Aaron Burr of New York for the Jeffersonian Republicans. Both tickets thus represented attempts at sectional balance. The Jeffersonian Republicans presented themselves as the party of traditional agrarian purity, of liberty and states' rights, of "government rigorously frugal and simple," in the words of Jef-

ferson. They were optimistic, convinced that they were riding the wave of the future. Divided and embittered, the Federalists waged a defensive struggle for strong central government and public order, and often resorted to negative campaigning. They denounced Jefferson as an atheist, a Jacobin, and the father of mulatto children. (The first two charges were without foundation, but the last was apparently true, according to the results of recent DNA matching tests. See Chapter 4.)

The balloting for presidential electors took place between October and December 1800. Adams took all the New England states while Jefferson captured the South and West. Jefferson called it "the Revolution of 1800." Party discipline was so effective that one of the provisions of the Constitution was shown to be badly outmoded. By this clause, the candidate receiving a majority of electoral votes became president and the runner-up became vice president. But by casting all their ballots for Jefferson and Burr, Jeffersonian Republican electors unintentionally created a tie and forced the election into the House of Representatives. Because the new Jeffersonian Republican–controlled Congress would not convene until March 1801, the Federalist majority was given a last chance to decide the election. They attempted to make a deal with Burr, who refused but who also would not withdraw his name from consideration. Finally, on the thirty-fifth ballot the Federalists gave up and arranged with their opponents to elect Jefferson without any of them having to cast a single vote in his favor. Congressman Matthew Lyon cast the symbolic final vote in a gesture of sweet revenge. The Twelfth Amendment, creating separate ballots for president and vice president, was ratified in time for the next presidential election.

Democratic Political Culture

Accompanying the rise of partisan politics was a transformation in popular political participation. Consider the custom of celebrating Independence Day. At the beginning of the 1790s, in many communities, the day featured demonstrations of military prowess by veteran officers, followed by banquets for leaders. Relatively few Americans played a direct role. But during the political controversies of the decade a tradition of popular celebration developed. People took to the streets, set off fireworks, erected liberty poles, and listened to readings of the preamble of the Declaration of Independence, which more than any other document encapsulated and symbolized republican ideology. The first of these celebrations took place in Philadelphia, then other large cities, and eventually spread throughout the country. By 1800 the Fourth of July had become the nation's most important holiday.

There was a corresponding increase in the suffrage. In 1789 state regulations limited the franchise to a small percentage of the adult population. Women, African Americans, and Indians could not vote, but neither could a third to a half of all free adult males, who were excluded by tax-paying or property-owning requirements. Moreover, even among the eligible, the turnout was generally low. The traditional manner of voting was *viva voce*, by voice. At the polling place in each community individuals announced their selections aloud to the clerk of elections, who wrote them down. Not surprisingly, this system allowed wealthy men, landlords, and employers of the community to pressure poorer voters.

These practices changed with the increasing competition between Jeffersonian Republicans and Federalists. Popular pressure resulted in the introduction of universal white manhood suffrage in four states by 1800 and the reduction of property requirements in others. Thus was inaugurated a movement that would sweep the nation over the next quarter century. As a consequence voter turnout increased in all the states. The growth of popular interest in politics was a transformation as important as the peaceful transition from Federalists to Jeffersonian Republicans in national government.

"THE RISING GLORY OF AMERICA"

In 1771, Philip Freneau and Hugh Henry Brackenridge addressed their graduating class at Princeton on "The Rising Glory of America." Thus far American contributions to learning and the arts had been slim, they admitted. But they were boundlessly optimistic about the potential of their country. Indeed, judged against the literary and artistic work of individuals in the colonial period, artists and others of the Revolutionary generation accomplished a great deal in their effort to build a national culture.

The Liberty of the Press

At the beginning of the Revolution in 1775 there were thirty-seven weekly or semiweekly newspapers in the thirteen colonies, only seven of which were Loyalist in sentiment. By 1789 the number of papers in the United States had grown to ninety-two, including eight dailies; three papers were being published west of the Appalachians. Relative to population, there were more newspapers in the United States than in any other country in the world—a reflection of the remarkably high literacy rate of the American people

(see Chapter 5). In New England almost 90 percent of the population could read, and even on the frontier, where Brackenridge edited the *Pittsburgh Gazette*, about two-thirds of the males were literate. During the political controversy of the 1790s, the press became the principal medium of Federalist and Jeffersonian Republican opinion, and papers came to be identified by their politics.

The prosecutions under the Sedition Act, however, threatened to curb the further development of the media, and in their opposition to these measures Jeffersonian Republicans played an important role in establishing the principle of a free press. In *An Essay on Liberty of the Press* (1799), the Virginia lawyer George Hay, later appointed to the federal bench by President Jefferson, wrote that "a man may say everything which his passions suggest." Were this not true, he argued, the First Amendment would have been "the grossest absurdity that was ever conceived by the human mind." In his first Inaugural Address, Jefferson echoed this early champion of the freedom of expression. "Error of opinion may be tolerated," he declared, "where reason is left free to combat it."

The Birth of American Literature

The literature of the Revolution understandably reflected the dominating political concerns of the times. The majority of "best-sellers" during the Revolutionary era were political. The most important were Thomas Paine's *Common Sense* (1776) and his series of stirring pamphlets, published under the running title *The American Crisis* (1776–83), the first of which began with the memorable phrase "These are the times that try men's souls."

During the post-Revolutionary years there was an enormous outpouring of American publications. In the cities the number of bookstores grew in response to the demand for reading matter. Perhaps even more significant was the appearance in the countryside of numerous book peddlers who supplied farm households with Bibles, gazettes, almanacs, sermons, and political pamphlets.

Some of the most interesting American books of the postwar years examined the developing American character and proposed that the American, a product of many cultures, was a "new man" with ideas new to the world. John Filson, the author of the *Discovery, Settlement, and Present State of Kentucke* (1784), presented the narrative of one such new man, the Kentucky pioneer Daniel Boone. In doing so, he took an important step toward the creation of that most American of literary genres, the western.

Mason Locke Weems, a man trained as a doctor and ordained an Anglican minister, gave up both these careers in the 1790 for bookselling and writing. Parson

In this 1792 cartoon from the *Lady's Magazine,* the allegorical figure of "Columbia" receives a petition for the "Rights of Woman." In the aftermath of the Revolution, Americans debated the issue of an expanded role for women in the new republic. Many Federalists condemned "women of masculine minds," but there was general agreement among both conservatives and democrats that the time had come for better education for American women.

SOURCE: The Library Company of Philadelphia.

Weems, as he was known, wrote a short biography of the first president. "Washington, you know, is gone!" he wrote to his publisher. "Millions are gaping to read something about him. I am very nearly primed and cocked for 'em." His *Life of Washington* (1800, enlarged edition 1806) became the most popular history of the Revolution and introduced a series of popular and completely fabricated anecdotes, including the story of young George Washington and the cherry tree. The book was a pioneering effort in mass culture, and Weems, as one historian puts it, was "the father of the Father of his Country."

Women on the Intellectual Scene

One of the most interesting literary trends of the 1790s was the growing demand for books that appealed to women readers. Although women's literacy rates continued to be lower than men's, they rose steadily as girls joined boys in common schools. This increase was one of the most important social legacies of the democratic struggles of the Revolutionary era.

Some writers argued that the new republican order ought to provide new roles for women as well as for men. The first avowed feminist in American history was Judith Sargent Murray, who publicly stated her belief that women "should be taught to depend on their own efforts, for the procurement of an establishment in life." She was greatly influenced by the English feminist Mary Wollstonecraft.

There seemed to be general agreement among all parties, however, that the time had come for better-educated and better-informed women. Republican institutions of self-government were widely thought to depend on the wisdom and self-discipline of the American people. Civic virtue, so indispensable for the republic, must be taught at home. Thus were women provided the opportunity to be not simply "helpmates," but people "learned and wise." But they were also expected to be content with a narrow role, not to wish for fuller participation in American democracy.

CONCLUSION

In 1800, the population of Canada numbered about 500,000. Those of European background in New Mexico and the other Spanish North American colonies numbered approximately 25,000. And the Indian people of the continent numbered anywhere from 500,000 to a million. Overwhelming all these groups was the population of the United States, which stood at 5.3 million and was growing at the astounding annual rate of 3 percent.

During the last years of the eighteenth century the United States had adopted a new constitution and established a new national government. It had largely repaid the debt run up during the Revolution and made peace with adversaries abroad and Indian peoples at home. Americans had begun to learn how to channel their disagreements into political struggle. The nation had withstood a first decade of stress, but tensions continued to divide the people. As some of the rebel supporters had promised at the beginning of the Whiskey Rebellion, "their liberty they will maintain, / They fought for't, and they'll fight again." At the beginning of the new century it remained uncertain whether the new nation would find a way to control and channel the energies of an expanding people.

CHRONOLOGY

1786	Annapolis Convention
1787	Constitutional Convention
1787–88	*The Federalist* published
1788	Constitution ratified
	First federal elections
1789	President George Washington inaugurated in New York City
	Judiciary Act
	French Revolution begins
1790	Agreement on site on the Potomac River for the nation's capital
	Indian Intercourse Act
	Judith Sargent Murray publishes "On the Equality of the Sexes"
1791	Bill of Rights ratified
	Bank of the United States chartered
	Alexander Hamilton's "Report on Manufactures"
	Ohio Indians defeat General Arthur St. Clair's army
1793	England and France at war; America reaps trade windfall
	Citizen Genêt affair
	President Washington proclaims American neutrality in Europe
	British confiscate American vessels
	Supreme Court asserts itself as final authority in *Chisholm v. Georgia*
1794	Whiskey Rebellion
	Battle of Fallen Timbers
	Jay's Treaty with the British concluded
1795	Pinckney's Treaty negotiated with the Spanish
	Treaty of Greenville
	Thomas Paine publishes *The Age of Reason*
1796	President Washington's Farewell Address
	John Adams elected president
1797–98	French seize American ships
1798	XYZ Affair
	"Quasi-war" with France
	Alien and Sedition Acts
	Kentucky and Virginia Resolves
1799	Fries's Rebellion
1800	Convention of 1800
	Thomas Jefferson elected president
	Mason Locke Weems publishes *Life of Washington*

REVIEW QUESTIONS

1. Discuss the conflicting ideals of local and national authority in the debate over the Constitution.
2. What were the major crises faced by the Washington and Adams administrations?
3. Describe the roles of Madison and Hamilton in the formation of the first American political parties.
4. What did Jefferson mean when he talked of "the Revolution of 1800"?
5. Discuss the contributions of the Revolutionary generation to the construction of a national culture.

RECOMMENDED READING

Akhil Reed Amar, *The Bill of Rights: Creation and Reconstruction* (1998). A legal analysis arguing that the first ten Amendments were meant to protect the majority from the potential tyranny of the federal government.

William N. Chambers, *Political Parties in a New Nation: The American Experience, 1776–1809* (1963). An introduction to the formation of the American party system. Though several decades old, it remains essential.

Stanley Elkins and Eric McKitrick, *The Age of Federalism* (1993). A massive and informative account of the politics of the 1790s, from the ratification of the Constitution to the election of Jefferson.

Joanne B. Freeman, *Affairs of Honor: National Politics in the New Republic* (2001). A major reassessment of political culture in the new republic, stressing the importance of the culture of honor.

Reginald Horsman, *The Frontier in the Formative Years, 1783–1815* (1970). A sensitive survey of developments in the West, emphasizing that the "western question" was one of the most important facing the young republic.

Jackson Turner Main, *The Antifederalists: Critics of the Constitution, 1781–1788* (1961). A detailed examination of the localist tradition in early American politics. Includes a discussion of the ratification of the Constitution from the point of view of its opponents.

Simon P. Newman, *Parades and the Politics of the Street: Festive Culture in the Early American Republic* (1997). The participation of ordinary Americans in the political culture of the new republic.

Willard Sterne Randall, *George Washington: A Life* (1997). The best one-volume biography of "the Father of his Country."

Thomas P. Slaughter, *The Whiskey Rebellion: Frontier Epilogue to the American Revolution* (1986). A detailed history of the rebellion in western Pennsylvania during the 1790s. Includes a thorough examination of the politics and culture of both the (Jeffersonian) backcountry and the federal government at a moment of crisis.

James M. Smith, *Freedom's Fetters: The Alien and Sedition Laws and American Civil Liberties* (1966). Remains the best overview of the Federalist threat to liberty, as well as the Democratic Republican (Jeffersonian) counterattack.

Bernard A. Weisberger, *American Afire: Jefferson, Adams, and the Revolutionary Election of 1800* (2000). Shows that the election and the transfer of power were victories for popular self-government and that they set a major precedent for all other elections.

Gordon Wood, *The Creation of the American Republic, 1776–1787* (1969). This general survey provides the best overview of the Constitutional Convention.

ON THE WEB

http://www.gwu.edu/~ffcp/exhibit/

A project of George Washington University, the First Federal Congress Project is a rich source of information about the young government from 1789 to 1791. Links lead to good graphics, primary documents, and interesting commentary.

http://lcweb.loc.gov/exhibits/religion/

A Library of Congress exhibit, this site details the role of religion in early American history including the colonial, revolutionary, and early national eras.

http://memory.loc.gov/const/fed/fedpapers.html

The Thomas page maintained by the Library of Congress is a rich source of information about the legislative process in the United States. This site contains the Federalist Papers written by Hamilton, Jay, and Madison in support of the newly proposed federal constitution.

The following sites are all from Yale University's Avalon Project and consist of key primary documents from the early national history of the United States:

http://www.yale.edu/lawweb/avalon/presiden/proclamations/gwproc03.htm

This site contains Washington's proclamation concerning the Whiskey Rebellion as printed in *Claypoole's Daily Advertiser*, August 11, 1794.

http://www.yale.edu/lawweb/avalon/amerdoc/bank-tj.htm

This page contains Jefferson's Opinion on the Constitutionality of a National Bank, 1791.

http://www.yale.edu/lawweb/avalon/amerdoc/bank-ah.htm

This page contains Hamilton's Opinion as to the Constitutionality of the Bank of the United States, 1791.

http://www.yale.edu/lawweb/avalon/const/resolu02.htm

This page contains a Resolution of the First Congress Submitting Twelve Amendments to the Constitution, March 4, 1789.

http://www.prenhall.com/faragherbrief/map8.1

Explore the regional differences that divided the ratification of the Constitution. Why did some regions support the Constitution and others did not?

http://www.prenhall.com/faragherbrief/map8.2

Investigate settlement patterns west of the Appalachians between 1770 and 1790. Why did tension between Indians and settlers increase during this period?

NINE

AN AGRARIAN REPUBLIC

▶ 1790–1824

AMERICAN COMMUNITIES

Expansion Touches Mandan Villages on the Upper Missouri

IN MID-OCTOBER 1804, NEWS ARRIVED AT THE MANDAN VILLAGES, prominently situated on bluffs overlooking the upper Missouri River, that an American expedition led by Meriwether Lewis and William Clark was coming up the river. The principal chiefs, hoping for expanded trade and support against their enemies the Sioux, welcomed these first American visitors. As the expedition's three boats and forty-three men approached the village, Clark wrote, "great numbers on both sides flocked down to the bank to view us." That evening the Mandans welcomed the Americans with an enthusiastic dance and gifts of food.

Since the fourteenth century, when they had migrated from the East, the Mandans had lived along the Missouri, on the edge of the Great Plains in what is now North Dakota. They believed their homeland was "the very center of the world," and indeed it is in the heart of the North American continent. Mandan men hunted buffalo and Mandan women kept storage pits full with abundant crops of corn, beans, squash, sunflowers, and tobacco grown on the fertile soil of the river bottomlands. The Mandan villages were also the central marketplace of the northern Plains; at trading time in late summer they filled with Crows, Assiniboins, Cheyennes, Kiowas, and Arapahoes. Well before any of these people, or those of other tribes, had met a European, they were trading in kettles, knives, and guns acquired from the French and English to the east and leatherwork, glassware, and horses acquired from the Spanish in the Southwest.

The eighteenth century had been a golden age for the Mandan, who with their closely related Hidatsa neighbors numbered about 3,000 in 1804. In each of their five villages, earth lodges surrounded a central plaza. One large ceremonial lodge was used for community gatherings, and each of the other earth lodges was home to a senior woman, her husband, her sisters (perhaps married to the same man as she, for the Mandans practiced polygamy), their daughters and their unmarried sons, along with numerous grandchildren. Matrilineal clans, the principal institution of the community, distributed food to the sick, adopted orphans, cared for the dependent elderly, and punished wrongdoers. A village council of male clan leaders selected chiefs who led by consensus and lost power when people no longer accepted their opinions.

Lewis and Clark had been sent by President Thomas Jefferson to survey the Louisiana Purchase and to find an overland route to the Pacific Ocean. They were also instructed to inform the Indians that they now owed loyalty—and trade—to the American government, thereby challenging British economic control over the lucrative North American fur trade. Meeting with the village chiefs, the Americans offered the Mandans a military and economic alliance. His people would like nothing better, responded Chief Black Cat, for the Mandans had fallen on hard times over the past decade. [Some twenty years earlier], "the smallpox destroyed the greater part of the nation," the chief said. "All the nations before this malady [were] afraid of them, [but] after they were reduced, the Sioux and other Indians waged war, and killed a great many." Black Cat was skeptical that the Americans would deter the Sioux, but Clark reassured him. "We were ready to protect them," Clark reported in his journal, "and kill those who would not listen to our good talk."

The Americans spent the winter with the Mandans, joining in their communal life and establishing firm and friendly relations with them. There were dances and joint hunting parties, frequent visits to the earth lodges, long talks around the fire, and, for many of the men, pleasant nights in the company of Mandan women. Lewis and Clark spent many hours acquiring important geographic information from the Mandans, who drew charts and maps showing the course of the Missouri, the ranges of the Rocky Mountains, and places where one could cross the Continental Divide. The information provided by the Mandans and other Indian peoples to the west was vital to the success of the expedition. Lewis and Clark's "voyage of discovery" depended largely on the willingness of Indian peoples to share their knowledge of the land with the Americans.

Also in need of interpreters who could help them communicate with other Indian communities on their way, the Americans hired several multilingual Frenchmen who lived with the Mandans. They also acquired the services of Sacajawea, the fifteen-year-old Lemhi wife of one of the Frenchmen, who became the only woman to join the westward journey. The presence of Sacajawea and her baby son was a signal, as Clark noted, to "all the

Mandan Villages

Indians as to our friendly intentions"; everyone knew that women and children did not go on war parties.

When the party left the Mandan villages in March, Clark wrote, his men were "generally healthy, except venereal complaints which is very common amongst the natives and the men catch it from them." After an arduous journey across the Rockies, the party reached the Pacific Ocean at the mouth of the Columbia River, where they spent the winter. Overdue and feared lost, they returned in triumph to St. Louis in September 1806. Before long the Americans had established Fort Clark at the Mandan villages, giving American traders a base for challenging British dominance of the western fur trade. The permanent American presence brought increased contact, and with it much more disease. In 1837 a terrible smallpox epidemic carried away the vast majority of the Mandans, reducing the population to fewer than 150. Four Bears, a Mandan chief who had been a child at the time of the Lewis and Clark visit, spoke these last words to the remnants of his people:

> "I have loved the whites," he declared. "I have lived with them ever since I was a boy." But in return for the kindness of the Mandans, the Americans had brought this plague. "I do not fear death, my friends," he said, "but to die with my face rotten, that even the wolves will shrink with horror at seeing me, and say to themselves, that is Four Bears, the friend of the whites." "They have deceived me," he pronounced with his last breath. "Those that I always considered as brothers turned out to be my worst enemies."

In sending Lewis and Clark on their "voyage of discovery" to claim the land and the loyalty of the Mandans and other western Indian communities, President Jefferson was motivated by his vision of an expanding American republic of self-sufficient farmers. During his and succeeding presidencies, expansion became a key element of national policy and pride. Yet, as the experience of the Mandans showed, what Jefferson viewed as enlargement of "the empire for liberty" had a dark side—the destruction, from disease and coerced displacement, of the communities created by America's first peoples. The effects—economic, political, and social—of continental expansion dominate the history of American communities in the first half of the nineteenth century. ■

NORTH AMERICAN COMMUNITIES FROM COAST TO COAST

At first glance, the United States of America in 1800 was little different from the scattered colonies of the pre-Revolution era. Two-thirds of the young nation's people still lived in a long thin line of settlement within fifty miles of the Atlantic coast. From New Hampshire to Georgia, most people lived on farms or in small towns. Because they rarely traveled far from home, people's horizons were limited and local. Nevertheless, the new nation was already transforming itself: between 1790 and 1800, according to the first and second federal censuses, the American population grew from 3.9 million to 5.3 million. Growth by migration was greatest in the trans-Appalachian West, a region that was already home to approximately 100,000 Indians. From 1800 to 1850, in an extraordinary burst of territorial expansion, Americans surged westward all the way to the Pacific. In 1800 few people would have predicted that within fifty years the nation would encompass the entire continent. Then the United States of America was a new and weak nation sharing a continent with many of the world's great powers.

Spanish Colonies

On paper, Spain possessed most of North America, but its control crumbled rapidly in the 1790s, affecting New Spain, the richest colony in Spanish America. Mexico City, with a population of 200,000, was by far the largest and most elegant city on the continent. But there were smoldering problems. Tensions mounted between the Spanish-born *peninsulares*, high officials and bureaucrats, and the native-born *criollos* of Spanish descent, who chafed at their subordination, especially after the success of the American Revolution. In the 1790s there were two abortive criollo

conspiracies on behalf of independence in Mexico City alone. Furthermore, none of New Spain's northern provinces, created to protect the approaches to Mexico's fabulously wealthy silver mines, thrived. In all of the older settlements—San Antonio, Santa Fe, and Tucson—only a handful of persons of Spanish descent lived among a preponderantly native population. This was true even in the northern province, Alta (Upper) California, founded in 1769.

The exception was New Orleans, acquired from France at the end of the Seven Years' War in 1763. New Orleans was becoming a thriving international port. In 1801, it shipped more than $3 million worth of tobacco, sugar, rice, cotton, fruits, and vegetables to Europe. Every year, a greater proportion of products for the New Orleans trade was supplied by Americans living some distance up the Mississippi River. Americans were uncomfortably aware that the city's crucial location at the mouth of the Mississippi meant that whatever foreign nation possessed New Orleans had the power to choke off the flourishing trade in the vast Mississippi Valley river system.

The Caribbean posed other challenges. The rich sugar-producing islands, variously colonies of Spain (Cuba, Puerto Rico, and Santo Domingo), France (Martinique, Guadaloupe, and Saint-Domingue), and Britian (Barbados, Jamaica, and a number of smaller islands), provided 80 to 90 percent of the European supply of sugar. They were all slave societies, with enslaved Africans as the labor force. Thus, they shared with the slaveholding American South a distinctive Afro–North American society that cut across national boundaries. This world was jolted by the 1791 revolt of black slaves in Saint-Domingue, France's richest colony. In 1804, under the leadership of Toussaint L'Ouverture, the former colony, renamed Haiti, became North America's first independent black nation. Its existence struck fear into the hearts of white slaveowners at the same time that it served as a beacon of hope to the enslaved.

This view shows Sitka, the center of Russian activities in Alaska, in 1827. Russian architectural styles and building techniques are apparent in the Church of St. Michael the Archangel in the right background, contrasting with the Asian and Indian origins of most of Sitka's inhabitants.

From an engraving by Freidrich H. von Kittlitz, 1827. Elmer E. Rosmusen Library Rare Books, University of Alaska, Fairbanks.

British and Russian Colonies

British North America had been wrested from the French in the Seven Years' War (see Chapter 6). In 1800, its heart remained the former French colony of Quebec (at that time called the province of Lower Canada), with a predominantly French population of about 160,000. Most of the rest of the settlers elsewhere were American, either Loyalists driven out at the time of the Revolution or simply farmers in search of better land. British authorities discouraged American immigrants from settling among the French, directing them instead either to the Maritime Provinces or to Upper Canada, the first inland colony north of the Great Lakes, established in 1791. Farther west (and closed to settlement) lay Rupert's Land, the great stretch of the Canadian North and West that was administered by the Hudson's Bay Company. To allay popular demands stimulated by the American Revolution, Britain established legislative assemblies in Upper and Lower Canada and in the Maritimes in 1791, but, learning from its American fiasco, Britain kept the legislatures under strong executive control. British North America dominated the continental fur trade and was on friendly terms with many of the native peoples who were part of the trade. This economic grip was a challenge and frustration to many westward-moving Americans.

Finally, Russian settlement of what is now Alaska posed another threat. The Russian American Company, chartered by the tsar in 1799, set up headquarters in Sitka, in what is now the southeastern panhandle of Alaska, in 1802. This was the homeland of the Tlingits, a warrior society, who destroyed the Russians' first fortress in the Tlingit Revolt of 1802. The Russians reestablished Sitka by force in 1804, and over the next generation established Russian settlements along the Pacific coast as far south as Fort Ross, which was just north of San Francisco Bay and well within Spanish territory. The Russian presence in North America was rapidly expanding even as Spain's faltered. In 1800, however, this imperial duel was far from the consciousness of most Americans, who were more concerned about the continuing presence of the British to the north in Canada and the nearby racial powder keg in the Caribbean.

A NATIONAL ECONOMY

In 1800, the United States was a producer of raw materials. The new nation faced the same challenge that developing nations confront today. At the mercy of fluctuating world commodity prices they cannot control, such countries have great difficulty protecting themselves from economic dominance by stronger, more established nations.

The Economy of the Young Republic

In 1800 the United States was predominantly rural and agricultural. In 1800, according to the census, 94 of 100 Americans lived in communities of fewer than 2,500 people, and four of five families farmed the land, either for themselves or for others. Farming families followed centuries-old traditions of working with hand tools and draft animals, producing most of their own food and fiber. Crops were grown for home use rather than for sale. Commodities such as whiskey and hogs (both easy to transport) provided small and irregular cash incomes or items for barter. As late as 1820, only 20 percent of the produce of American farms was consumed outside the local community.

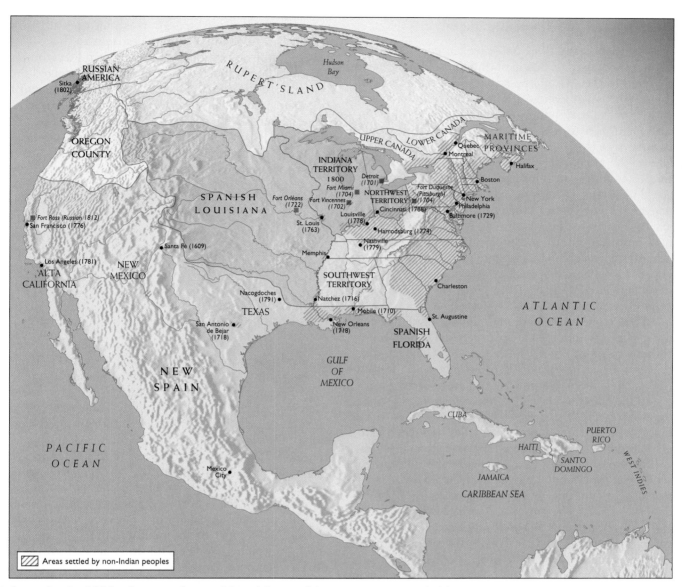

America in 1800   In 1800, the new United States of America was surrounded by territories held by the European powers: British Canada, French Louisiana (secretly ceded that year to France by Spain), Spanish Florida, Spanish Mexico, and Russian Alaska expanding southward along the Pacific coast. Few people could have imagined that by 1850 the United States would span the continent. But the American settlers who had crossed the Appalachians to the Ohio River valley were already convinced that opportunity lay in the West.

In contrast to this pattern, the plantation agriculture of the South was wholly commercial and international. The demand for cotton was growing rapidly in response to the boom in the industrial production of textiles in England and Europe, but extracting the seeds from the fibers of the variety of cotton that grew best in the southern interior required an enormous investment of labor. The cotton gin, which mechanized this process, was invented in 1793, but not until the nineteenth century did cotton assume a commanding place in the foreign trade of the United States.

In 1790, increasing foreign demand for American goods and services hardly seemed likely. Trade with Britain, still the biggest customer for American raw materials, was considerably less than it had been before the Revolution. Britain and France both excluded Americans from their lucrative West Indian trade and taxed American ships with discriminatory duties. It was difficult to be independent in a world dominated by great powers.

Shipping and the Economic Boom

Despite these restrictions on American commerce, the strong shipping trade begun during the colonial era and centered in the Atlantic ports became a major asset in the 1790s, when events in Europe provided America with extraordinary opportunities. The French Revolution, which began in 1789, soon initiated nearly twenty-five years of warfare between Britain and France. All along the Atlantic seaboard, urban centers thrived as American ships carried European goods that could no longer be transported on British ships without danger of French attack (and vice versa). Because America was neutral, its merchants had the legal right to import European goods and promptly reexport them to other European countries. In spite of British and French efforts to prevent the practice (see Chapter 8), reexports amounted to half of the profits in the booming shipping trade.

The vigorous international shipping trade had dramatic effects within the United States. The coastal cities all grew substantially from 1790 to1820. This rapid urbanization was a sign of vigorous economic growth (rather than a sign that poverty was pushing rural workers off the farms, as occurs in some developing countries today), for it reflected expanding opportunities in the cities. In fact, the rapid growth of cities stimulated farmers to produce the food to feed the new urban dwellers.

The long series of European wars also allowed enterprising Americans to seize such lucrative international opportunities as the China trade. In 1784 the *Empress of China* set sail from New York for Canton with forty tons of ginseng. When it returned in 1785 with a cargo of teas, silks, and chinaware, the sponsors of the voyage made a 30 percent profit. Other merchants were quick to follow.

The active American participation in international trade fostered a strong and diversified shipbuilding industry. All the major Atlantic ports boasted expanding shipbuilding enterprises. Demands for speed increased as well, resulting in what many people have regarded as the flower of American shipbuilding, the clipper ship. The narrow-hulled, many-sailed clipper ships of the 1840s and 1850s set records for ships of their size. In 1854, *Flying Cloud*, built in the Boston shipyards of Donald McKay, sailed from New York to San Francisco—a 16,000-mile trip that usually took 150 to 200 days—in a mere 89 days.

THE JEFFERSON PRESIDENCY

At noon on March 4, 1801, Thomas Jefferson walked from his modest boardinghouse through the swampy streets of the new federal city of Washington to the unfinished Capitol. George Washington and John Adams had ridden in elaborate carriages to their inaugurals. Jefferson, although accepting a military honor guard, demonstrated by his actions that he rejected the elaborate, quasi-monarchical style of the two Federalist presidents and their (to his mind) autocratic style of government as well.

For all its lack of pretension, Jefferson's inauguration as the third president of the United States was a momentous occasion in American history, for it marked the peaceful transition from one political party, the Federalists, to their hated rivals, the Jeffersonian Republicans. Beginning in an atmosphere of exceptional political bitterness, Jefferson's presidency was to demonstrate that a strongly led party system could shape national policy without leading either to dictatorship or to revolt. It was a great achievement.

Republican Agrarianism

Jefferson brought to the presidency a clearly defined political philosophy. Behind all the events of his administration (1801–09) and those of his successors in what became known as the Virginia Dynasty (James Madison, 1809–17; James Monroe, 1817–25) was a clear set of beliefs that embodied Jefferson's interpretation of the meaning of republicanism for Americans.

Jefferson's years as ambassador to France in the 1780s were particularly important in shaping his political thinking. Recoiling from the extremes of wealth and poverty he saw there, he came to believe that it was impossible for Europe to achieve a just society that could guarantee to most of its members the "life, liberty and . . . pursuit of happiness" of which he had written in the Declaration of Independence. Only America, he believed, provided fertile earth for the true citizenship necessary to a republican form of government. What America had, and Europe lacked, was room to grow.

Jefferson envisaged a nation of small family farms clustered together in rural communities—an agrarian republic. He believed that only a nation of roughly equal yeoman farmers, each secure in his own possessions and not dependent on someone else for his livelihood, would exhibit the concern for the community good that was essential in a republic. Indeed, Jefferson said that "those who labor in the earth are the chosen people of God," and so he viewed himself, though his "farm" was the large slave-owning plantation of Monticello.

Jefferson's vision of an expanding agrarian republic remains to this day one of our most compelling ideas about America's uniqueness and special destiny. But expansionism contained some negative aspects. The lure of the western lands fostered constant mobility and dissatisfaction rather than the stable, settled communities of yeoman farmers that Jefferson envisaged.

Expansionism caused environmental damage, in particular soil exhaustion—a consequence of abandoning old lands, rather than conserving them, and moving on to new ones. Finally, expansionism bred a ruthlessness toward Indian peoples, who were pushed out of the way for white settlement or who, like the Mandans, were devastated by the diseases that accompanied European trade and contact. Jefferson's agrarianism thus bred some of the best and some of the worst traits of the developing nation.

Jefferson's Government

Thomas Jefferson came to office determined to reverse the Federalist policies of the 1790s and to ensure an agrarian "republic of virtue." Accordingly, he proposed a program of "simplicity and frugality," promising to cut all internal taxes, to reduce the size of the army (from 4,000 to 2,500 men), the navy (from twenty-five ships to seven), and the government staff, and to eliminate the entire national debt inherited from the Federalists. He kept all of these promises, even the last, although the Louisiana Purchase of 1803 cost the Treasury $15 million. This diminishment of government was a key matter of republican principle to Jefferson. If his ideal yeoman farmer was to be a truly self-governing citizen, the federal government must not, Jefferson believed, be either large or powerful.

Perhaps one reason for Jefferson's success was that the federal government he headed was small and unimportant by today's standards. The national government's main service to ordinary people was mail delivery. Everything else—law and order, education, welfare, road maintenance, economic control—rested with state or local governments. Power and political loyalty were still local, not national.

This small national government also explains why for years the nation's capital was so unimpressive. Construction lagged on the President's House and the Capitol. Instead of the imposing dome we know so well today, the early Capitol consisted of two white marble boxes connected by a boardwalk. It is a telling indicator of the true location of national power that a people who had no trouble building new local communities across the continent should have had such difficulty establishing their federal city.

An Independent Judiciary

Although determined to reverse Federalist fiscal policies, Jefferson allowed 132 Federalist office holders to remain at their posts. Jefferson's restraint, however, did not extend to the most notorious Federalist appointees, the so-called midnight judges.

In the last days of the Adams administration, the Federalist-dominated Congress passed several acts that

Tall, ungainly, and diffident in manner, Thomas Jefferson was nonetheless a man of genius, an architect, naturalist, political philosopher, and politician.

SOURCE: Courtesy of the Library of Congress.

created new judgeships and other positions within the federal judiciary. In one of his last acts in office, President Adams appointed Federalists—quickly dubbed the "midnight judges"—to these new positions. William Marbury, whom President Adams had appointed Justice of the Peace for Washington, D.C., and three other appointees sued James Madison, Jefferson's secretary of state, to receive their commissions for their offices. Before the case came to trial, however, Congress, controlled by Jeffersonian Republicans who feared that the losing Federalist Party was trying to use the judiciary to increase the power of the federal government over the states, repealed the acts. This case, *Marbury* v. *Madison*, provoked a landmark decision from the Supreme Court, head of the federal judiciary.

At issue was a fundamental constitutional point: Was the judiciary independent of politics? In his celebrated 1803 decision in *Marbury* v. *Madison*, Chief Justice John Marshall, himself a strong Federalist and an Adams appointee, managed to find a way to please both parties. On the one hand, Marshall proclaimed that the courts had a duty "to say what the law is," thus unequivocally defending the independence of the judiciary and the principle of judicial review. On the other hand, Marshall conceded that the Supreme Court was not empowered by the Constitution to force the executive branch to give Marbury his commission. At first glance, Jefferson's government appeared to have won the battle over Adams's last-minute appointees. But in the long run, Marshall established the principle that only the federal judiciary could decide what was constitutional. This was a vital step in realizing the three-way balance of power among the branches of the federal government—executive (president), legislative (Congress), and judiciary (courts)—envisaged in the Constitution. Equally important, during his long tenure in office (1801–35), Chief Justice Marshall consistently led the Supreme Court in a series of decisions that favored the federal government over state governments. Under Marshall's direction, the Supreme Court became a powerful nationalizing force, often to the dismay of defenders of states' rights.

Opportunity: The Louisiana Purchase

In 1800 the United States was a new and fragile democracy in a world dominated by two contending great powers: Britain and France. If France sought to regain territory that it had once held in North America, this would pose a threat to both American commerce and national security. In 1799, the young general Napoleon Bonaparte seized control of France and began a career of military conquests. As had his predecessors, Napoleon looked at North America as a potential battleground on which to fight the British. In 1800, in a secret treaty, France reacquired the Louisiana Territory, the vast western drainage of the Mississippi and Missouri rivers, from Spain, which had held the region since 1763. From Louisiana, if he chose, Napoleon could launch an attack to regain Canada from the British. As a springboard to a new French North American empire, in 1802 Napoleon sent an army of 30,000 to reconquer Haiti (the former Saint-Domingue) and thereby crush Afro-Caribbean dreams of independence.

Initially, Jefferson offered to buy New Orleans and the surrounding area for $2 million (or up to $10 million, if necessary). As it happened, Napoleon was eager to sell. His army of 30,000 men had just with-

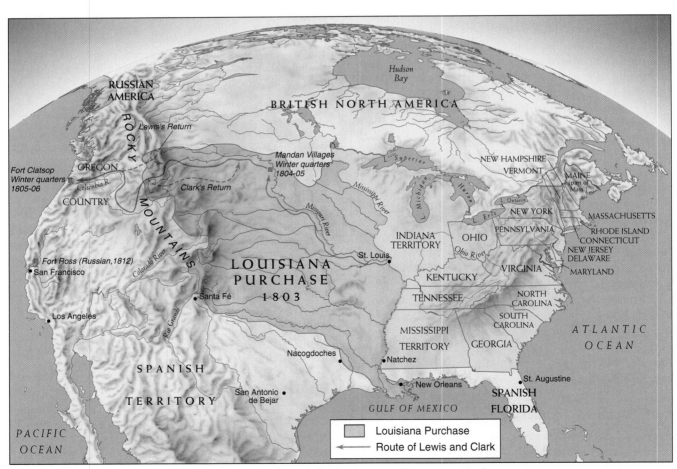

Louisiana Purchase　The Louisiana Purchase of 1803, the largest peaceful acquisition of territory in United States history, more than doubled the size of the nation. The Lewis and Clark expedition (1804–06) was the first to survey and document the natural and human richness of the area. The American sense of expansiveness and continental destiny owes more to the extraordinary opportunity provided by the Louisiana Purchase than to anything else.

drawn from Haiti, defeated by yellow fever as well as by an army of former slaves led by Toussaint L'Ouverture. In the wake of the French defeat, and in need of money for European military campaigns, Napoleon offered the entire Louisiana Territory, including the crucial port of New Orleans, to the Americans for $15 million. Exceeding his instructions, special American envoy James Monroe seized the opportunity and bought the entire Louisiana Territory from Napoleon in Paris in April 1803. Overnight, the size of the United States more than doubled. It was the largest peaceful acquisition of territory in United States history. Jefferson claimed that Louisiana was vital to the nation's republican future. "By enlarging the empire of liberty," Jefferson wrote, "we . . . provide new sources of renovation, should its principles, at any time, degenerate, in those portions of our country which gave them birth." In other words, expansion was essential to liberty.

Incorporating Louisiana

The immediate issue following the Louisiana Purchase was how to treat the French and Spanish inhabitants of the Louisiana Territory. Many people thought that the only way to deal with a population so "foreign" was to wipe out its customs and laws and to impose American ones as quickly as possible. But this did not happen. The incorporation of Louisiana into the American federal system was a remarkable story of adaptation between two different communities—American and French.

In 1803, when the region that is now the state of Louisiana became American property, it had a racially and ethnically diverse population of 43,000 people, of whom only 6,000 were American. French and French-speaking people were numerically and culturally dominant, especially in the city of New Orleans. There the French community effectively challenged the initial American plan of rapidly supplanting French culture and institutions with American ones. The U.S. representative in New Orleans and governor of Lower Louisiana Territory, William Claiborne, came to accept the value of French institutions to the region. As a result, with Claiborne's full support, Louisiana adopted a legal code in 1808 that was based on French civil law rather than English common law. This was not a small concession. French law differed from English law in many fundamental respects, such as in family property (communal versus male ownership), in inheritance (forced heirship versus free disposal), and even in contracts, which were much more strictly regulated in the French system. Remnants of the French legal system remain part of Louisiana state law to this day. In 1812, with the required 60,000 free inhabitants, Louisiana was admitted to the Union. New Orleans remained for

years a distinctively French city, illustrating the flexibility possible under a federal system.

Texas and the Struggle for Mexican Independence

Spain objected, in vain, to Napoleon's 1803 sale of Louisiana to America. For years Spain had attempted to seal off its rich colony of Mexico from commerce with other nations. Now, American Louisiana shared a vague and disputed boundary with Mexico's northern province of Texas (a parcel of land already coveted by some Americans).

Soon Napoleon brought turmoil to all of Mexico. In 1808, having invaded Spain, he installed his brother Joseph Bonaparte as king, forcing Spain's king, Charles IV, to renounce his throne. For the next six years, as warfare convulsed Spain, the country's long-prized New World empire slipped away. Mexico, divided between royalists loyal to Spain and populists seeking social and economic justice for mestizos and Indians, edged bloodily toward independence. Two populist revolts—one in 1810 led by Father Miguel Hidalgo and the other in 1813 led by Father José María Morelos—were suppressed by the royalists, who executed both revolutionary leaders. In 1812 a small force, led by Mexican republican Bernardo Gutiérrez but composed mostly of American adventurers, invaded Texas, captured San Antonio, assassinated the provincial governor Manuel Salcedo, and declared Texas independent. A year later, however, the Mexican republicans were defeated by a royalist army, which then killed suspected collaborators and pillaged the province so thoroughly that the local economy was devastated. The Mexican population declined to fewer than 2,000. Under these circumstances, Mexico's difficult path toward independence seemed, at least to some Americans, to offer yet another opportunity for expansion.

RENEWED IMPERIAL RIVALRY IN NORTH AMERICA

Fresh from the triumph of the Louisiana Purchase, Jefferson scored a major victory over the Federalist Charles Cotesworth Pinckney in the presidential election of 1804, garnering 162 electoral votes to Pinckney's 14. Jefferson's shrewd wooing of moderate Federalists had been so successful that the remaining Federalists dwindled to a highly principled but sectional group, unable to attract voters outside of its home base in New England. Jefferson's Louisiana success was not repeated, however, and few other consequences of the ongoing struggle between Britain and France were so easy to solve.

Problems with Neutral Rights

In his first inaugural address in 1801, Jefferson had announced a foreign policy of "peace, commerce, and honest friendship with all nations, entangling alliances with none." This was a difficult policy to pursue after 1803, when the Napoleonic Wars resumed. By 1805 Napoleon had conquered most of Europe, but Britain, the victor at the great naval battle of Trafalgar, controlled the seas. The United States, trying to profit from trade with both countries, was caught in the middle. The British did not look kindly as their former colonists tried to evade their blockade of the French by claiming neutrality. Beginning in 1805, the British targeted the American reexport trade between the French West Indies and France by seizing American ships that were bringing French West Indian goods to Europe. Angry Americans viewed these seizures as violations of their rights as shippers of a neutral nation.

An even more contentious issue arose from the substantial desertion rate of British sailors. Many deserters promptly signed up on American ships, where they drew better pay and sometimes obtained false naturalization papers as well. The numbers involved were large: as many as a quarter of the 100,000 seamen on American ships were British. Soon the British were stopping American merchant vessels and removing any man they believed to be British, regardless of his papers.

At least 6,000 innocent American citizens suffered forced impressment into the British navy from 1803 to 1812. In 1807 impressment turned bloody when the British ship *Leopard* stopped the American ship *Chesapeake* in American territorial waters and demanded to search for deserters. When the American captain refused, the *Leopard* opened fire, killing three men, wounding eighteen, and removing four deserters (three with American naturalization papers) from the damaged ship. An indignant public protested British interference and the death of innocent sailors.

The Embargo Act

Fully aware that commerce was essential to the new nation, Jefferson was determined to insist on America's right as a neutral nation to ship goods to Europe. He first tried diplomatic protests, then negotiations, and finally threats, all to no avail. In 1806 Congress passed the Non-Importation Act, hoping that a boycott of British goods, which had worked so well during the Revolutionary War, would be effective once again. It was not. Finally, in desperation, Jefferson imposed the Embargo Act in December 1807. This act forbade American ships from sailing to any foreign port, thereby cutting off all exports as well as imports. The intent of

the act was to force both Britian and France to recognize neutral rights by depriving them of American-shipped raw materials.

But the results were a disaster for American trade. The commerce of the new nation, which Jefferson himself had done so much to promote, came to a standstill. Exports fell from $108 million in 1807 to $22 million in 1808, and the nation was driven into a deep depression. There was widespread evasion of the embargo. A remarkable number of ships in the coastal trade found themselves "blown off course" to the West Indies or Canada. Other ships simply left port illegally. Smuggling flourished. Pointing out that the American navy's weakness was due largely to the deep cuts Jefferson had inflicted on it, the Federalists sprang to life with a campaign of outspoken opposition to Jefferson's policy, and they found a ready audience in New England, the area hardest hit by the embargo.

Madison and the Failure of "Peaceable Coercion"

In this troubled atmosphere, Thomas Jefferson despondently ended his second term, acknowledging the failure of what he called "peaceable coercion." He was followed in office by his friend and colleague James Madison of Virginia. Although Madison defeated the Federalist candidate—again Charles Cotesworth Pinkney—by 122 electoral votes to 47, Pinckney's share of the votes was three times what it had been in 1804.

In March 1809, Congress admitted failure and the Embargo Act was repealed. But the struggle to remain neutral in the confrontation between the European giants continued. The next two years saw passage of several acts—among them the Non-Intercourse Act of 1809 and Macon's Bill Number 2 in 1810—that unsuccessfully attempted to prohibit trade with Britain and France unless they ceased their hostile treatment of U.S. shipping. Frustration with the ineffectiveness of government policy mounted.

A Contradictory Indian Policy

The United States also faced other conflicts besides those with Britain and France over neutral shipping rights. In the West, the powerful Indian nations of the Ohio Valley were determined to resist the wave of expansion that had carried thousands of white settlers onto their lands. North of the Ohio River lived the Northwest Confederation of the Shawnees, Delawares, Miamis, Potawatomis, and several smaller tribes. To the south of the Ohio were the so-called

Tecumseh, a Shawnee military leader, and his brother Tenskwatawa, a religious leader called The Prophet, led a pan-Indian revitalization and resistance movement that posed a serious threat to American westward expansion. Tecumseh traveled widely, attempting to build a military alliance on his brother's spiritual message. He achieved considerable success in the Old Northwest, but less in the Old Southwest, where many Indian peoples put their faith in accommodation. Tecumseh's death at the Battle of the Thames (1813) and British abandonment of their Shawnee allies at the end of the War of 1812 brought an end to organized Indian resistance in the Old Northwest.

SOURCE: (A)The Field Museum, #A93851c. (b) Courtesy of the Library of Congress.

"Five Civilized Tribes," the Cherokees, Chickasaws, Choctaws, Creeks, and (in Florida) the Seminoles.

According to the Indian Intercourse Act of 1790, the United States could not simply seize Indian land; it could only acquire it when the Indians ceded it by treaty. But this policy conflicted with the harsh reality of westward expansion. Commonly, settlers pushed ahead of treaty boundaries. When Indian peoples resisted the invasion of their lands, the pioneers fought back and called for military protection. Defeat of an Indian people led to further land cessions. The result for the Indians was a relentless cycle of invasion, resistance, and defeat.

Thomas Jefferson was deeply concerned with the fate of the western Indian peoples. Convinced that Indians had to give up hunting in favor of the yeoman-farmer lifestyle he so favored for all Americans, Jefferson directed the governors of the Northwest Territories to "promote energetically" his vision for civilizing the Indians, which included Christianizing them

and teaching them to read. Many Indian peoples actively resisted these efforts at conversion. An addition, Jefferson's Indian civilization plan was never fully supported by territorial governors and settlers.

After the Louisiana Purchase, Jefferson offered traditionalist Indian groups new lands west of the Mississippi River, where they could live undisturbed by white settlers. But he failed to consider the pace of westward expansion. Less than twenty years later, Missouri, the first trans-Mississippi state, was admitted to the Union. Western Indians like the Mandans, who had seemed so remote, were now threatened by further westward expansion.

Indian Resistance

The Shawnees, a seminomadic hunting and farming tribe (the men hunted, the women farmed) of the Ohio Valley, had resisted white settlement in Kentucky and Ohio since the 1750s. The decisive defeat of the Indian

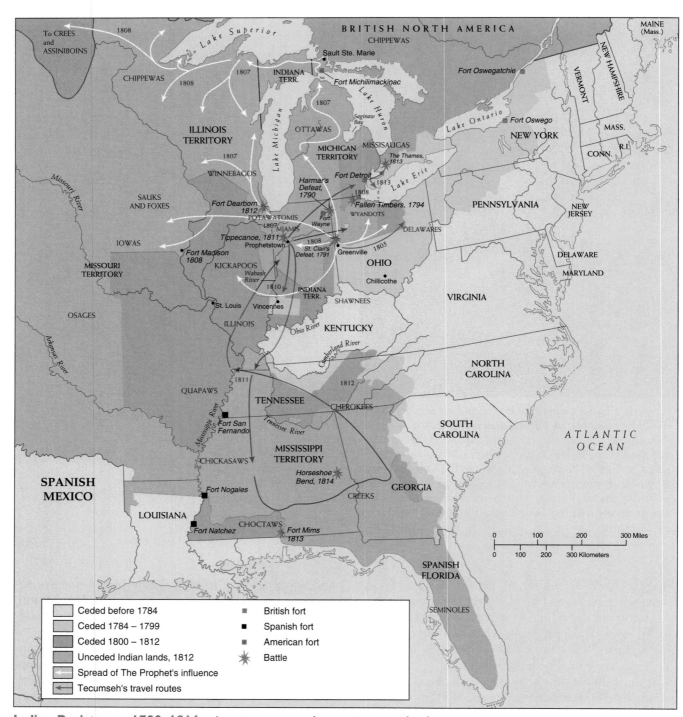

Indian Resistance, 1790–1816   American westward expansion put relentless pressure on the Indian nations in the Trans-Appalachian South and West. The Trans-Appalachian region was marked by constant warfare from the time of the earliest settlements in Kentucky in the 1780s to the War of 1812. Tecumseh's Alliance in the Old Northwest (1809–11) and the Creek Rebellion in the Old Southwest (1813–14) were the culminating struggles in Indian resistance to the American invasion of the Trans-Appalachian region.

Confederacy led by Little Turtle, a Miami Indian, at Fallen Timbers (1794) and the continuing pressure of American settlement, however, had left the Shawnees divided. One group, led by Black Hoof, accepted acculturation. The rest of the tribe tried to maintain traditional ways. Most broke into small bands and tried to eke out a living by hunting, but their numbers were reduced by disease and the survivors were further demoralized by the alcohol offered them illegally by private traders. One group of traditional Shawnees, however, led by the warrior Tecumseh, sought refuge farther west.

But there was no escape from white encroachment. Between 1801 and 1809, William Henry Harrison, governor of Indiana Territory, concluded fifteen treaties with the Delawares, Potawatomis, Miamis, and other tribes. These treaties opened eastern Michigan, southern Indiana, and most of Illinois to white settlement and forced the Indians into ever-smaller reservations. Many of these treaties were obtained by coercion, bribery, and outright trickery, and most Indians did not accept them.

In 1805 Tecumseh's brother, Tenskwatawa, known as The Prophet, began preaching a message of Indian revitalization: a rejection of all contact with the Americans, including the use of American alcohol, clothing, and trade goods, and a return to traditional practices of hunting and farming. He preached an end to quarreling, violence, and sexual promiscuity and to the accumulation of private property. Wealth was valuable only if it was given away, he said. If the Northwest Indians returned to traditional ways, Tenskwatawa promised, "the land will be overturned so that all the white people will be covered and you alone shall inhabit the land."

This was a powerful message, but it was not new. Just six years earlier, Handsome Lake had led the Seneca people of upstate New York in a similar revitalization movement. Tecumseh, however, succeeded in molding his brother's religious following into a powerful pan-Indian military resistance movement. With each new treaty that Harrison concluded, Tecumseh gained new followers among the Northwest Confederation tribes. Significantly, he also had the support of the British, who, after 1807, began sending food and guns to him from Canada.

The pan-Indian strategy was at first primarily defensive, aimed at preventing further westward expansion. But the Treaty of Fort Wayne in 1809, in which the United States gained 3 million acres of Delaware and Potawatomi land in Indiana, led to active resistance. Confronting Harrison directly, Tecumseh argued that the land belonged to the larger community of all the Indian peoples; no one tribe could give away the common property of all. He then warned that any surveyors or settlers who ventured into the 3 million acres would risk their lives.

Tecumseh took his message of common land ownership and military resistance to all the Indian peoples of the Northwest Confederacy. He was not uniformly successful, even among the Shawnees. Black Hoof, for example, refused to join. Tecumseh also recruited, with mixed success, among the tribes south of the Ohio

River. In councils with Choctaws, Chickasaws, Creeks, and Cherokees, he promoted active resistance.

In November 1811, while Tecumseh was still recruiting among the southern tribes, Harrison marched to the pan-Indian village of Tippecanoe with 1,000 soldiers. The 600 to 700 Indian warriors at the town, urged on by Tenskwatawa, attacked Harrison's forces before dawn on November 7, hoping to surprise them. The attack failed, and in the battle that followed the Americans inflicted about 150 Indian casualties, while sustaining about as many themselves. Although Harrison claimed victory, the truth was far different. Dispersed from Tippecanoe, Tecumseh's angry followers fell on American settlements in Indiana and southern Michigan, killing many pioneers and forcing the rest to flee to fortified towns. Tecumseh himself entered into a formal alliance with the British. For western settlers, the Indian threat was greater than ever.

THE WAR OF 1812

Many westerners blamed the British for Tecumseh's attacks on pioneer settlements in the Northwest. British support of western Indians and the long-standing difficulties over neutral shipping rights were the two grievances cited by President Madison when he asked Congress for a declaration of war against Britain on June 1, 1812. Congress obliged him on June 18. But the war had other, more general causes as well.

A rising young generation of political leaders, first elected to Congress in 1810, strongly resented the continuing influence of Britain, the former mother country, on American affairs. These War Hawks, who included such future leaders as Henry Clay of Kentucky and John C. Calhoun of South Carolina, were young Jeffersonian Republicans from the West and South. They found all aspects of British interference, such as impressment of sailors and support for western Indians, intolerable. Eager to assert independence from England once and for all, these young men saw themselves finishing the job begun by the aging revolutionary generation. They also wanted to occupy Florida to prevent runaway slaves from seeking refuge with the Seminole Indians. Westerners wanted to invade Canada, hoping thereby to end threats from British-backed Indians in the Northwest, such as Tecumseh and his followers. As resentments against England and frustrations over border issues merged, the pressure for war—always a strong force for national unity—mounted.

Unaware that the British, seriously hurt by the American trade embargo, were about to adopt a more conciliatory policy, President James Madison yielded to the War Hawks' clamor for action in June 1812,

The War of 1812 On land, the War of 1812 was fought to define the nation's boundaries. In the North, American armies attacked British forts in the Great Lakes region with little success, and the invasion of Canada was a failure. In the South, the Battle of New Orleans made a national hero of Andrew Jackson, but it occurred after the peace treaty had been signed. On the sea, with the exception of Oliver Perry's victory in the Great Lakes, Britain's dominance was so complete and its blockade so effective that British troops were able to invade the Chesapeake and burn the capital of the United States.

and his declaration of war passed the U.S. Senate by the close vote of 19 to 13, the House by 79 to 49. All the Federalists voted against the war. (The division along party lines continued in the 1812 presidential election, in which Madison garnered 128 electoral votes to 89 for his Federalist opponent, DeWitt Clinton.) The vote was sectional, with New England and the Middle States in opposition and the West and South strongly prowar. Thus, the United States entered the War of 1812 more deeply divided along sectional lines than during any other foreign war in American history.

The Americans had a few glorious moments, but on the whole the War of 1812 was an ignominious struggle that gained them little. As a result of Jefferson's economizing, the American army and navy were small and weak. In contrast, the British, fresh from almost ten years of Napoleonic Wars, were in fighting trim. The British navy quickly established a strong blockade, harassing coastal shipping along the Atlantic seaboard and attacking coastal settlements at will. In the most humiliating attack, the British burned Washington in the summer of 1814, forcing the president and Congress to flee. There were a few American military successes. Commodore Oliver Perry's ships defeated a British fleet on Lake Erie in 1813, whereupon Perry sent the famous message "We have met the enemy and they are ours." In early 1815 (after the peace treaty had been signed) Andrew Jackson improbably won a lopsided victory over veteran British troops in the Battle of New Orleans.

The New England states opposed the war. Massachusetts, Rhode Island, and Connecticut refused to provide militia or supplies, and other New England governors turned a blind eye to the flourishing illegal trade across the U.S.–Canadian border. Opposition to the war culminated in the Hartford Convention of 1814, where Federalist representatives from the five New England states met to discuss their grievances. At first the air was full of talk of secession from the Union, but soon cooler heads prevailed.

The convention did insist, however, that a state had the right "to interpose its authority" to protect its citizens against unconstitutional federal laws. This *nullification* threat from Hartford was ignored, for peace with Britain was announced as delegates from the convention made their way to Washington to deliver their message to Congress. There the convention's grievances were treated not as serious business but as an anticlimactic joke.

By 1814 the long Napoleonic Wars in Europe were slowly drawing to a close, and the British decided to end their war with the Americans. The peace treaty, after months of hard negotiation, was signed at Ghent, Belgium, on Christmas Eve in 1814. Like the war itself, the treaty was inconclusive. The major issues of impressment and neutral rights were not mentioned, but the British did agree to evacuate their western posts, and late in the negotiations they abandoned their insistence on a buffer state for neutral Indian peoples in the Northwest.

For all its international inconsequence, the war did have an important effect on national morale. Andrew Jackson's victory at New Orleans allowed Americans to believe that they had defeated the British. It would be more accurate to say that by not losing the war the Americans had ended their own feelings of colonial dependency. Equally important, they convinced the British government to stop thinking of America as its colony.

The War of 1812 was one of America's most divisive wars, arousing more intense opposition than any other American conflict, including Vietnam. Today most historians regard the war as both unnecessary and a dangerous risk to new and fragile ideas of national unity. Fortunately for its future, the United States as a whole came out unscathed, and the Battle of New Orleans had provided last-minute balm for its hurt pride.

The only clear losers of the war were the northwestern Indian nations and their southern allies. With the death of Tecumseh at the Battle of the Thames in 1813 and the defeat of the Southern Creeks in 1814, the last hope of a united Indian resistance to white expansion perished forever. Britain's abandonment of its Indian allies in the Treaty of Ghent sealed their fate. By 1815 American settlers were on their way west again.

DEFINING THE BOUNDARIES

With the War of 1812 behind them, Americans turned, more seriously than ever before, to the tasks of expansion and national development.

Another Westward Surge

The end of the War of 1812 was followed by a westward surge to the Mississippi River that populated the Old Northwest (Ohio, Indiana, Illinois, Michigan, and Wisconsin) and the Old Southwest (western Georgia, Alabama, Mississippi, and Louisiana). The extent of the population redistribution was dramatic: in 1790, about 95 percent of the nation's population had lived in states bordering the Atlantic Ocean; by 1820 fully 25 percent of the population lived west of the Appalachians.

What accounted for the westward surge? There were both push and pull factors. Between 1800 and 1820, the nation's population almost doubled, increasing from 5.3 million to 9.6 million. Overpopulated farmland in all of the seaboard states pushed farmers off the land, while new land pulled them westward. The defeat and removal of Indians in the War of 1812 was another important pull factor.

Geography facilitated lateral westward movement (Northerners tended to migrate to the Old Northwest, Southerners to the Old Southwest). Except in southern Ohio and parts of Kentucky and Tennessee, there was very little contact between regional cultures. New Englanders carried their values and lifestyles directly west and settled largely with their own communities; Southerners did the same.

One section of northern Ohio along Lake Erie, for example, had been Connecticut's western land claim since the days of its colonial charter. Rather than give up the land when the Northwest Territory was established in 1787, Connecticut held onto the Western Reserve (as it was known) and encouraged its citizens to move there. Group settlement was common. General Moses Cleaveland of the Revolutionary War led one of the first groups of Yankees, fifty-two in all. In 1795 they settled the community that bears his name (though not his spelling of it). Many other groups followed, naming towns such as Norwalk after those they had left in Connecticut. These New Englanders brought to the Western Reserve their religion (Congregational), their love of learning (tiny Norwalk soon boasted a three-story academy), and their adamant opposition to slavery.

Western migration in the South was very different. On this frontier, the people clearing the land were doing it not for themselves but to create plantations for slave owners. More than half of the migrants to the Old Southwest after 1812 were involuntary—enslaved African Americans.

After the war, as cotton growing expanded, hopeful slave owners from older parts of the South (Virginia, North and South Carolina, Georgia) flooded into the region. Most of the settlers in the Old Southwest were small farm families living in forest clearings. Most did not own slaves, but they hoped to, for ownership of slaves was the means to wealth. The lifestyle and values of older southern states were quickly replicated on this new frontier.

The western transplantation of distinctive regional cultures explains why, although by 1820 western states accounted for more than a third of all states (eight out of twenty-three), the West did not form a third, unified political region. Although there were common western issues—in particular, the demand for better roads and other transportation routes—communities in the Old

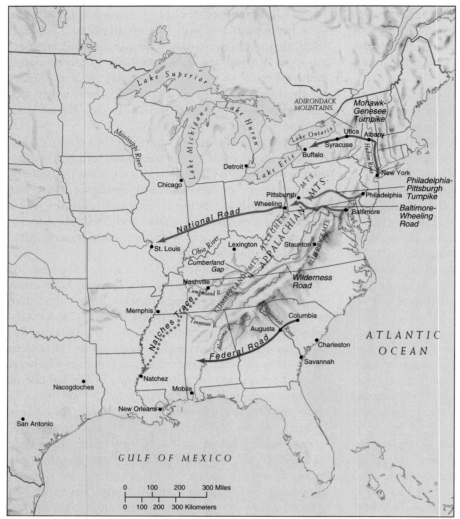

Major Migration Routes, 1800–1820 The barrier of the Appalachian Mountains permitted only a few routes to the west. Settlers from the northern states took the Genesee Turnpike, Middle States migrants favored the Philadelphia-Pittsburgh Turnpike and the National Road, and Southerners used the Wilderness and Federal Roads. Because most westward movement was lateral, regional mixing among western settlers was rare. New Englanders carried their attitudes West, and Southerners did the same.

SOURCE: Donald Meinig, *The Shaping of America*, vol. 2, *Continental America* (New Haven, CT: Yale University Press, 1994).

Northwest, in general, shared New England political attitudes, whereas those in the Old Southwest shared southern attitudes.

The Election of 1816 and the Era of Good Feelings

In 1816 James Monroe, the last of the Virginia Dynasty, was easily elected president over his Federalist opponent Rufus King (183 to 34 electoral votes). This was the last election in which Federalists ran a candidate. Monroe had no opponent in 1820 and was re-elected nearly unanimously (231 to 1). The triumph of the Jeffersonian Republicans over the Federalists seemed complete.

Tall, dignified, dressed in the old-fashioned style of knee breeches and white-topped boots that Washington had worn, Monroe looked like a traditional figure. But his politics reflected changing times. When he visited Boston, as recently as 1815 the heart of a secession-minded Federalist region, he received an enthusiastic welcome, prompting the Federalist *Columbian Centinel* to proclaim an "Era of Good Feelings." The phrase has been applied to Monroe's presidency (1817–25) ever since.

Monroe sought a government of national unity, and he chose men from North and South, Jeffersonian Republicans and Federalists, for his cabinet. He selected John Quincy Adams, a former Federalist, as his secretary of state, virtually assuring that Adams, like his father, would become president. To balance Adams, Monroe picked John C. Calhoun of South Carolina, a prominent War Hawk, as secretary of war. And Monroe supported the American System, a program of national economic development that became identified with Westerner Henry Clay, Speaker of the House of Representatives.

In supporting the American System, Monroe was following President Madison, who had proposed the program in his message to Congress in December 1815. Madison and Monroe broke with Jefferson's agrarianism to embrace much of the Federalist program for economic development, including the chartering of a national bank, a tax on imported goods to protect American manufacturers, and a national system of roads and canals. All three of these had first been proposed by Alexander Hamilton in the 1790s (see Chapter 8). At the time these proposals had met with bitter Jeffersonian Republican opposition. The support that Madison and Monroe gave to Hamilton's ideas following the War of 1812 was a crucial sign of the dynamism of the American knowledged that the federal government had a role to play in fostering the economic and commercial conditions in which both yeoman farmer and merchant could succeed.

In 1816 Congress chartered the Second Bank of the United States for twenty years. Located in Philadelphia, the bank had a capital of $35 million, of which the government contributed $7 million. The bank was to provide the large-scale financing that the smaller state banks could not handle and to create a strong national currency. Because they feared concentrated economic power, Jeffersonian Republicans had allowed the charter of the original Bank of the United States, founded in 1791, to expire in 1811. The Republican about-face in 1816 was a sign that the strength of commercial interests had grown to rival that of farmers, whose distrust for central banks persisted.

The Tariff of 1816 was the first substantial protective tariff in American history. In 1815, British manufacturers, who had been excluded for eight years (from the Embargo Act of 1807 to the end of the War of 1812), flooded the United States market with their products. American manufacturers complained that the British were dumping goods below cost in order to prevent the growth of American industries. Congress responded with a tariff on imported woolens and cottons, on iron, leather, hats, paper, and sugar. The measure had southern as well as northern support, although in later years differences over the passage of higher tariffs would become one of the most persistent sources of sectional conflict.

The third item in the American System, funding for roads and canals—internal improvements, as they came to be known—was more controversial. Monroe and Madison both supported genuinely national (that is, interstate) projects such as the National Road from Cumberland, Maryland, to Vandalia, Illinois. Congressmen, however, aware of the urgent need to improve transportation in general and sensing the political advantages that could accrue to them from directing funds to their districts, proposed spending federal money on local projects. Both Madison and Monroe vetoed such local proposals, believing them to be unconstitutional. Thus it was that some of the most famous projects of the day, such as the Erie Canal, which lay wholly within New York state, and the early railroads, were financed by state or private money.

The support of Madison and Monroe for measures initially identified with their political opposition was an indicator of their realism. The three aspects of the American System—bank, tariff, roads—were all parts of the basic infrastructure that the American economy needed in order to develop. Briefly, during the Era of Good Feelings, politicians agreed about the need for all three. Later, each would be a source of heated partisan argument.

The Diplomacy of John Quincy Adams

The diplomatic achievements of the Era of Good Feelings were due almost entirely to the efforts of one man, John Quincy Adams, Monroe's secretary of state. Adams set himself the task of tidying up the borders of the United States. Two accords with Britain—the Rush-Bagot Treaty of 1817 and the Convention of 1818—fixed the border between the United States and Canada at the 49th parallel and resolved conflicting U.S. and British claims to Oregon with an agreement to occupy it jointly for ten (eventually twenty) years. The American claim to Oregon (present-day British Columbia, Washington, Oregon, northern Idaho, and parts of Montana) was based on China trader Robert Gray's discovery of the Columbia River in 1792 and on the Lewis and Clark expedition of 1804–06.

Adams's major diplomatic accomplishment was the Adams-Onís or Transcontinental Treaty of 1819, in which he skillfully wrested concessions from the faltering Spanish empire. Adams convinced Spain not only to cede Florida but also to drop all previous claims it had to the Louisiana Territory and Oregon. In return, the United States relinquished claims on Texas and assumed responsibility for the $5 million in claims that U.S. citizens had against Spain.

Finally, Adams picked his way through the remarkable changes occurring in Latin America, developing the policy that bears his president's name, the Monroe Doctrine. The United States was the first country outside Latin America to recognize the independence of Spain's former colonies. When the European powers (France, Austria, Russia, and Prussia) began talk of a plan to help Spain recover the lost colonies, what was the United States to do? The British, suspicious of the European powers, proposed a British-American declaration against European intervention in the hemisphere. Others might have been flattered by an approach from the British empire, but Adams would have none of it. Showing the national pride that was so characteristic of the era, Adams insisted on an independent American policy. He, therefore, drafted for the president the hemispheric policy that the United States has followed ever since.

On December 2, 1823, the president presented the Monroe Doctrine to Congress and the world. He called for the end of colonization of the Western Hemisphere by European nations (this was aimed as much at Russia and its Pacific coast settlements as at other European powers). Intervention by European powers in the affairs of the independent New World nations would be considered by the United States a danger to its own peace and safety. Finally, Monroe pledged that the United States would not interfere in the affairs of European countries or in the affairs of their remaining New World colonies.

All of this was a very loud bark from a very small dog. In 1823, the United States lacked the military and economic force to back up its grand statement. In fact, what kept the European powers out of Latin America was British opposition to European intervention, enforced by the Royal Navy. With this string of diplomatic achievements—the treaties with Britain and Spain and the Monroe Doctrine—the position of the United States on the North American continent was transformed. The Spanish presence was diminished, Russian expansion halted, and peace with Britain achieved. As a result, the United States was a much larger and stronger nation.

The Panic of 1819

Across this impressive record of political and economic nation building fell the shadow of the Panic of 1819. A delayed reaction to the end of the War of 1812 and the Napoleonic Wars, the panic forced Americans to come to terms with their economic place in a peaceful world. As British merchant ships resumed trade on routes they had abandoned during the wars, the American shipping boom ended. And as European farm production recovered from the wars, the international demand for American foodstuffs declined and American farmers and shippers suffered.

Domestic economic conditions made matters worse. The western land boom that began in 1815 turned into a speculative frenzy that ended with a sharp contraction of credit by the Second Bank of the United States in 1819. State banks were forced to foreclose on many bad loans. Many small farmers were ruined, and they blamed the faraway Bank of the United States for their troubles. In the 1830s, Andrew Jackson would build a political movement on their resentment.

Urban workers suffered both from the decline in international trade and from manufacturing failures caused by competition from British imports. As they lobbied for local relief, they found themselves deeply involved in urban politics, where they could express their resentment against the merchants and owners who had laid them off. Thus developed another component of Andrew Jackson's new political coalition.

Another confrontation arose over the tariff. Southern planters, hurt by a decline in the price of cotton, began to actively protest the protective tariff, which kept the price of imported goods high even when cotton prices were low. Manufacturers, hurt by British competition, lobbied for even higher rates, which they achieved in 1824 over southern protests. Southerners then began to express doubts about the fairness of a political system in which they were always outvoted.

The Panic of 1819 was a symbol of this transitional time. It showed how far the country had moved since 1800, from Jefferson's republic of yeoman farmers toward a nation dominated by commerce. And the anger and resentment expressed by the groups harmed by the depression—farmers, urban workers, and southern planters—were portents of the politics of the upcoming Jackson era.

The Missouri Compromise

In the Missouri Crisis of 1819–21, the nation confronted the momentous issue that had been buried in the general enthusiasm for expansion: as America moved west, would the largely southern system of slavery expand as well? Until 1819, this question was decided regionally. The Northwest Ordinance of 1787 explicitly banned slavery in the northern section of trans-Appalachia but made no mention of it elsewhere. Because so much of the expansion into the Old Northwest and Southwest was lateral (Northerners stayed in the north, Southerners in the south), there was little conflict over sectional differences. In 1819, however, the sections collided in Missouri, which applied for admission to the Union as a slave state.

The northern states, all of which had abolished slavery by 1819, looked askance at the extension of slavery. Southerners, on the other hand, did not believe Congress had the power to limit the expansion of slavery. They were alarmed that Northerners were considering national legislation on the matter. Slavery, in southern eyes, was a question of property and, therefore, a matter for state rather than federal legislation. Thus, from the very beginning the expansion of slavery raised constitutional issues. Indeed, the aging politician of Monticello, Thomas Jefferson, immediately grasped the seriousness of the question of the expansion of slavery. As he prophetically wrote to a friend, "This momentous question like a fire bell in the night, awakened and filled me with terror. I considered it at once the [death] knell of the Union."

In 1819, Representative James Tallmadge Jr. of New York began more than a year of congressional controversy when he demanded that Missouri agree to the gradual end of slavery as the price of entering the Union. At first, the general public paid little attention, but religious reformers (Quakers prominent among them) organized a number of antislavery rallies in northern cities that made politicians take notice. Former Federalists in the North who had seen their party destroyed by the achievements of Jefferson and his successors in the Virginia Dynasty eagerly seized on the Missouri issue. This was the first time that the growing northern reform impulse had intersected with sectional politics. It was also the first

CHRONOLOGY

1800	Thomas Jefferson elected president
1802	Russian American Company headquarters established at Sitka, Alaska
1803	Louisiana Purchase
	Marbury v. *Madison*
	Ohio admitted to the Union
1804	Lewis and Clark expedition leaves St. Louis
	Thomas Jefferson reelected president
1807	*Chesapeake-Leopard* incident
	Embargo Act
1808	James Madison elected president
1809	Tecumseh forms military alliance among Northwest Confederacy peoples
1811	Battle of Tippecanoe
1812	War of 1812 begins
	James Madison reelected president
	Louisiana admitted to the Union
1814	Treaty of Ghent
1815	Battle of New Orleans
1816	James Monroe elected president
	Congress charters Second Bank of the United States
	Indiana admitted to the Union
1817	Mississippi admitted to the Union
1818	Illinois admitted to the Union
1819	Panic of 1819
	Adams-Onís Treaty
	Alabama admitted to the Union
1819–20	Missouri Crisis and Compromise
1820	James Monroe reelected president
	Maine admitted to the Union
1821	Missouri admitted to the Union as a slave state
1823	Monroe Doctrine

time that southern threats of secession were made openly in Congress.

The Senate debate over the admission of Missouri, held in the early months of 1820, was the nation's first extended debate over slavery. Observers noted the high proportion of free African Americans among the listeners in the Senate gallery. But the full realization that the future of slavery was central to the future of the nation would not become apparent to the general public until the 1850s.

In 1820, Congress achieved compromise over the sectional differences. Henry Clay forged the first of the many agreements that were to earn him the title of "the Great Pacificator" (peacemaker). The Missouri Compromise maintained the balance between free and slave states: Maine (which had been part of Massachusetts) was admitted as a free state in 1820 and Missouri as a slave state in the following year. A policy was also enacted with respect to slavery in the rest of the Louisiana Purchase: slavery was prohibited north of 36° 30′ north latitude—the southern boundary of Missouri—and permitted south of that line. This meant that the vast majority of the Louisiana Territory would be free. In reality, then, the Missouri Compromise could be only a temporary solution, because it left open the question of how the balance between slave and free states would be maintained.

CONCLUSION

In complex ways a developing economy, geographical expansion, and even a minor war helped shape American unity. Local, small, settled, face-to-face communities in both the North and the South began to send their more mobile, expectant members to new occupations in urban centers or west to form new settlements, displacing Indian communities in the process.

The westward movement was the novel element in the American national drama. Europeans believed that large size and a population in motion bred instability and political disintegration. Thomas Jefferson thought otherwise, and the Louisiana Purchase was the gamble that confirmed his guess. The westward population movement dramatically changed the political landscape and Americans' view of themselves.

Expansion would not create the settled communities of yeoman farmers Jefferson had hoped for. Rather, it would breed a nation of restless and acquisitive people and a new kind of national democratic politics that reflected their search for broader definitions of community.

REVIEW QUESTIONS

1. What economic and political problems did the United States face as a new nation in a world dominated by war between Britain and France? How successful were the efforts by the Jefferson, Madison, and Monroe administrations to solve these problems?

2. The anti-European cast of Jefferson's republican agrarianism made it appealing to many Americans who wished to believe in their nation's uniqueness, but how realistic was it?

3. Some Federalists opposed the Louisiana Purchase, warning of the dangers of westward expansion. What are arguments for and against expansion?

4. What contradictions in American Indian policy did the confrontations between Tecumseh's alliance and soldiers and settlers in the Old Northwest reveal? Can you suggest solutions to them?

5. What did the War of 1812 accomplish?

6. What were the issues that made it impossible for the Era of Good Feelings to last?

RECOMMENDED READING

Catharine Allgor, *Parlor Politics: In Which the Ladies of Washington Help Build a City and a Government* (2000). Argues that women played a vital role in the politics of the new capital city.

Stephen E. Ambrose, *Undaunted Courage: Meriweather Lewis, Thomas Jefferson, and the Opening of the American West* (1996). This very popular heroic version of the expedition is told by a master storyteller. It ought, however, to be supplemented by the Ronda version cited below that pays attention to the Indian side of the story.

Frank Bergon, ed., *The Journals of Lewis and Clark* (1989). A handy abridgment of the fascinating history of the expedition. (For more intensive study, Gary Moulton's six-volume unabridged edition of the expedition journals is unsurpassed.)

R. David Edmunds, *Tecumseh and the Quest for Indian Leadership* (1984). A sympathetic portrait.

Joseph J. Ellis, *American Sphinx: The Character of Thomas Jefferson* (1998). An engaging exploration of Jefferson's many contradictions.

John Mack Faragher, *Sugar Creek* (1987). The fullest examination of the lives of pioneers in the Old Northwest.

Donald Hickey, *The War of 1812: A Forgotten Conflict* (1989). Takes a fresh look at the events and historiography of the war.

Drew McCoy, *The Elusive Republic: Political Economy in Jeffersonian America* (1980). The most useful discussion of the ties between expansion and republican agrarianism.

Glover Moore, *The Missouri Controversy, 1819–1821* (1953). The standard account.

Peter S. Onuf, *Jefferson's Empire* (2000). A thoughtful study of Jefferson's ideas about republicanism, empire, and nationalism.

Merrill Peterson, *Thomas Jefferson and the New Nation* (1970). A good one-volume political biography of Jefferson. (The major biography, by Dumas Malone, is a multivolume work.)

James Ronda, *Lewis and Clark among the Indians* (1984). An innovative look at the famous explorers through the eyes of the Indian peoples they encountered.

ON THE WEB

http://supct.law.cornell.edu/supct/cases/historic.htm

The Legal Information Institute of Cornell Law School provides complete transcripts of a few hundred of the most important U.S. Supreme Court decisions. Use this resource to examine the most important decisions of the early Marshall Court, especially *Marbury* v. *Madison* (1803), *Dartmouth College* v. *Woodward* (1819), *McCulloch* v. *Maryland* (1819), *Gibbon* v. *Ogden* (1824), and others.

http://lcweb.loc.gov/exhibits/religion/

A Library of Congress exhibit, this site details the role of religion in early American history including the colonial, revolutionary, and early national eras.

http://etext.virginia.edu/toc/modeng/public/JefVirg.html

This website contains Jefferson's *Notes on the State of Virginia*, written by Jefferson in 1781 and modified in 1782. It is posted by the University of Virginia and describes what Jefferson considered to be an "Agrarian Republic." Other Jefferson documents may be accessed from **http://etext.virginia.edu/jefferson/texts/**.

http://www.prenhall.com/faragherbrief/map9.1

Follow the path of the Lewis and Clark expedition. How did the terrain influence the routes of the journey?

http://www.prenhall.com/faragherbrief/map9.2

Look at the different migration routes favored by Americans between 1800 and 1820. How did westward movement vary by region?

In the Footsteps of Lewis and Clark

As we saw in the chapter opener, in March of 1805 the Lewis and Clark expedition left the hospitable Mandans and headed west, eager to face the unknown challenges that lay between them and the Pacific Ocean. Six months later, however, as the exhausted and starving members of the expedition struggled to find their way through the snow in the Bitterroot Mountains of present-day Montana and Idaho, it appeared that their luck had run out.

Instead, near the present-day town of Weippe, Idaho, the expedition was rescued by a small band of Nez Perce Indians. The Nez Perce fed the weakened party, gave them a chance to regain their strength.and later helped them build canoes and served as guides for the final stage of their journey down the waters of the Columbia River drainage to the Pacific Ocean. When the expedition returned in the spring of 1806, they rested a month with the Nez Perce before recrossing the mountains into present-day Montana. As was their custom with other tribes, Lewis and Clark presented the Nez Perce with a Jefferson medal inscribed on one side with a picture of two clasped hands and the message "Peace and Friendship."

The bicentennial of the Lewis and Clark expedition from St. Louis to the Pacific Ocean occurs in 2003–06. Public interest is high, with millions of tourists expected to visit sites along the route during the bicentennial years. Many of them plan to relive the exploration by literally following in the footsteps of Lewis and Clark. Some of them will find themselves, as the explorers did 200 years ago, in Indian country. Or at least that is the hope of some western Indian tribes who see the bicentennial as a strategic opportunity to tell the Indian side of the expedition's history.

One of the American Indians holding that view is Allen Pinkham of the Nez Perce Tribe, who has been a member of the National Council of the Lewis and Clark Bicentennial since its inception in the mid-1990s. Until recently, most white historians have believed that the hospitality that Indians showed to the expedition along its route was due to the exceptional persuasive power of Lewis and Clark. But Pinkham points out that the Nez Perce were hardly likely to have been persuaded by the group of weakened wanderers they met in the fall of 1805. Every Indian tribe had its own reasons for choosing to help—or not to help—the expedition. The Nez Perce and other Indian groups plan to use the bicentennial to tell their own stories about their encounters with Lewis and Clark.

There are formidable obstacles hindering the Indian effort to be heard. Western history has traditionally been told from the point of view of the white explorers and the settlers who followed them. Most people assume that *real* history didn't begin in the West until white people and written records arrived. The reliance on written material is an important reason for the heroic stature of Lewis and Clark, for historical accounts of the expedition have always relied for evidence on their own journals, supplemented by those of a few of the expedition's soldiers. Although the Nez Perce and other Indians have strong oral traditions about their encounters with Lewis and Clark, most people don't know about them because until recently historians regarded them only as "legend," and, therefore, not as reliable as written evidence. As a result, most Americans have only heard one version of a series of many-sided encounters that occurred as Lewis and Clark found themselves in Indian country.

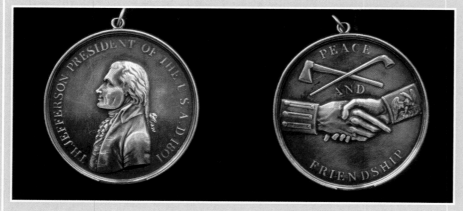

This shows the medal Lewis and Clark presented to the Nez Perce Indians in 1805. One side shows a profile of Thomas Jefferson, with the description "Th. Jefferson, President of the U.S. A.D. 1802," while the clasped hands on the other side promise Peace and Friendship.

SOURCE: National Park Service photo.

This contemporary photograph of Nez Perce tribal member Carla High Eagle leading her children home contains echoes of the past when the Nez Perce were famous for their large herds of spotted Appaloosa horses like the one shown here.

SOURCE: National Park Service Photo.

To ensure that the Indian view is heard, the National Park Service has appointed Otis Halfmoon, a Nez Perce, as tribal liaison for the planning of the NPS traveling exhibit, *Corps of Discovery II: 200 Years to the Future*. In another Park service effort, Gerard Baker, a Mandan-Hidatsa, has been chosen as superintendent of the Lewis and Clark National Historic Trail as well as serving as superintendent of the *Corps of Discovery II* exhibit.

Allen Pinkham and others have worked with the National Council for the Bicentennial to set the proper context for the observation of the bincentnnial. One of the first steps was to refer to the bicentennial as a commemoration, rather than a celebration, thus acknowledging the high price that all Indians paid for discovery. From the Indian point of view, Lewis and Clark brought disaster in their wake: like the Mandans in the chapter opener, every western tribe experienced disease, warfare, and the destruction of their way of life at the hands of white American pioneers. Indian peoples felt betrayed by the same hand that the peace medal promised would clasp forever in friendship.

Yet rather than recrimination, Pinkham sees the bicentennial as a unique opportunity to tell the remarkable story of Indian survival and adaptation. After all, says Pinkham, "After 200 years we're still here. We weren't killed off by disease and warfare." The bicentennial can serve to inform the public about modern Indian life and accomplishments. As the Nez Perce and other western Indians seize the occasion of the bicentennial to tell their own story, they hope to give a new and modern meaning to the two hands clasped together on the Jefferson medal. ■

TEN

THE GROWTH OF DEMOCRACY

▶ 1824 – 1840

AMERICAN COMMUNITIES

Martin Van Buren Forges a New Kind of Political Community

WHEN MARTIN VAN BUREN LEFT ALBANY FOR WASHINGTON IN the fall of 1821 to take up his new position as junior senator from New York, he wrote complacently: "I left the service of the state [of New York] for that of the federal government with my friends in full and almost unquestioned possession of the state government in all its branches, at peace with each other and overflowing with kindly feelings towards myself." Thus did Van Buren sum up more than ten years of intense activity in New York State politics in which he and his allies, nicknamed the Bucktails (for the Indian-inspired insignia, the tail of a buck, that members wore on their hats), created one of the first modern democratic political parties. How could it be, Washington politicians asked, that this short, invariably pleasant but rather nondescript man had triumphed over the renowned DeWitt Clinton?

Tall, handsome, arrogant DeWitt Clinton, governor of New York from 1817 to 1823 (and again from 1825 until his death in 1828), had been swept into office on a tide of enthusiasm for his plan to build a canal the length of the state. Clinton soon gained legislative approval for the project—the Erie Canal—the most ambitious and most successful canal project in an era of canal building. An aristocrat in wealth, connections, and attitude, Clinton represented old-style politics. During his first terms as governor he ran the New York Jeffersonian Republican Party as though it were his personal property, dispensing patronage to relatives and friends (many of whom were Federalists) on the basis of their loyalty to him rather than their political principles.

Martin Van Buren was a new kind of politician. Born in the small, Dutch-dominated town of Kinderhook, New York, Van Buren was the son of a tavern keeper, not a member of the wealthy elite. He grew up with an enduring resentment of the aristocratic landowning families, such as the Van Schaacks and the Van Rensselaers (and, by extension, the Clintons), who disdained him when he was young. Masking his anger with charming manners, Van Buren took advantage of the growing strength of the Jeffersonian Republican Party in New York State to wrest control of the party from Clinton and forge it into a new kind of political organization. Clinton's use of patronage to reward friends at the expense of young party loyalists infuriated Van Buren and other rising politicians. Two years after Clinton became governor, Van Buren wrote bitterly to a friend: "A man to be a sound politician and in any degree useful to his country must be guided by higher and steadier considerations than those of personal sympathy and private regard. . . . In the name of all that is holy, where is the evidence of that towering mind and those superior talents which it has been the business of puffers and toad eaters to attribute to [Clinton]?"

By 1819, Van Buren had gathered together enough other disgruntled Jeffersonian Republicans to form the Bucktail faction and openly challenge Clinton. Two years later, at the state constitutional convention of 1821 (where they made up three-fourths of the delegates), the Bucktails sealed their victory. Meeting in Albany to revise the out-of-date constitution of 1777, the convention voted to streamline the organization of state government and sharply curtail the patronage powers of the governor. To cement these changes, delegates enacted nearly total manhood suffrage: all adult male citizens who paid state or local taxes, served in the militia, or worked on state roads—more than four-fifths of the adult male population—were now eligible to vote directly for state legislators, governor, and members of Congress.

This dramatic democratization of politics reflected the state's changing population. Already the bustling port of New York was the nation's largest city, and the state's commercial opportunities were attracting shrewd Yankee traders from New England, "whose laws, customs and usages," conservative senator Rufus King complained, "differ from those of New York." The old ruling families, failing to recognize the new commercial and social values of the newcomers, were losing their grip on politics. Rising politicians like Van Buren and other Bucktails, in contrast, found opportunity in these changing conditions. Attuned to popular feeling, they responded to the state's growing and increasingly diverse population by creating a new kind of political community. A political party, they maintained, should be

a democratic organization expressing the will of all its members, not an organization dominated by an elite group like Clinton's and bound together only by family ties and political favors. All party members, including leaders, would have to abide by majority rule. Party loyalty, rather than personal opinion or friendship, would be the bond that kept the party together and, rather than aristocratic background, the principal requirement for party leadership. "The first man we see step to the rear," wrote Bucktail Silas Wright Jr., still smarting from the factionalism and favoritism of the Clinton years, "we cut down." In the new party system, there would be no tolerance for politicans who followed their own self-interest rather than the larger good of the party.

By the time he departed for Washington in the fall of 1821, Van Buren had established in Albany a closely knit group of friends and allies who practiced these new political principles. Party decisions, reached by discussion in legislative caucus and publicized by the party newspaper, the *Albany Argus*, were binding on all members and enforced by patronage decisions. The group, dubbed the "Albany Regency," ran New York State politics for twenty years. For all those years Martin Van Buren was in Washington, where he was a major architect of the new democratic politics of mass participation that has been called the Second American Party System. This new movement created, for the first time in American history, national communities of political partisans. Van Buren understood how to create these new communities. Van Buren believed that organization and discipline were essential not for their own sake but because they allowed democracy to flourish. He claimed that what made him different from DeWitt Clinton and earlier politicians was his "faith in the capacity of the masses of the people of our Country to govern themselves, and in their general integrity in the exercise of that function." This unprecedented confidence in popular opinion made American politics and politicians unique in the changing world of the early nineteenth century. ■

KEY TOPICS

- The role of Andrew Jackson's presidency in affirming and solidifying the new democratic politics

- The part played by the transportation revolution in unifying the nation

- Establishment of the basic two-party pattern of American political democracy

- The creation of a distinctive American cultural identity by writers, artists, and their audiences

---

THE NEW DEMOCRATIC POLITICS IN NORTH AMERICA

The early years of the nineteenth century were a time of extraordinary growth and change not only for the United States but also for all the countries of North America. Seen in continental perspective, the American embrace of popular democracy was unusual. Elsewhere crises over popular rights dominated.

Continental Struggles Over Popular Rights

In 1821, after eleven years of revolts (see Chapter 9), Mexico achieved its independence from Spain.

Briefly united under the leadership of Colonel Agustin de Iturbide, Mexico declared itself a constitutional monarchy that promised equality for everyone—peninsulares, criollos, mestizos, and Indians alike. But the initial unity was short-lived. Iturbide reigned as Emperor of Mexico for little more than a year before he was overthrown by a military junta and later executed as a traitor. A series of weak presidents repeatedly invoked emergency powers and relied on the army as they attempted to revive a faltering economy and reconcile the differences between the centralists—the vested interests of clergy, large landowners, and the military—and the federalists, largely criollos and mestizos, who hoped to create a liberal republic modeled on the American one. The strongest of the early presidents was General Antonio Lopez de Santa Anna, elected to the presidency for the first time in 1833. He dominated Mexican politics for the next twenty years, during which he assumed dictatorial, centralized power, surviving the loss of Texas in 1836 and the other northern provinces in 1848 to the United States (see Chapter 15). The unresolved issue of elite versus popular rule continued to undermine the hope for unity, popular

rights, and stable government in an independent Mexico.

The independence of Haiti in 1804 (see Chapter 9) set the pattern for events in many other Caribbean islands in subsequent years. Independence destroyed the sugar industry, for freed slaves refused to perform the killing labor demanded of them on sugar plantations. The British Caribbean islands were racked with revolts. In response, the British Parliament abolished slavery in all British colonies in 1834. As in Haiti, sugar production then plunged. The only island where sugar production increased was Spanish Cuba, where slavery remained legal until 1880. Elsewhere the economic collapse following emancipation destroyed the political authority of local white elites, forcing the British government to impose direct rule. Most of the British possessions in the Caribbean remained Crown Colonies until the 1920s. This sequence of events—revolt, emancipation, economic collapse, loss of local political autonomy—was closely observed by slaveowners in the American South and made them fear for their own futures.

Still a third crisis of popular rights occurred in British North America. In 1837 both Upper and Lower Canada rebelled against the limited representative government that the British government had imposed in the Constitutional Act of 1791. By far the most serious revolt was in predominantly French Lower Canada. Fearing that the true aim of the rebels was independence or, worse, becoming a part of the United States, the British government refused to recognize the French Canadian demand for their own political voice. In 1840, Britain abolished the local government of Lower Canada joined it to Upper Canada in a union that most French Canadians opposed and in which they were a minority. In his report to the British government, Lord Durham announced that the purpose of union was to end the ethnic enmity between British and French by forcing the latter to assimilate and "abandon their vain hopes of nationality." Lord Durham suggested increased colonial self-government, but the British government, fearing further trouble, refused to grant it.

In comparison to these experiences, the rapid spread of suffrage in the United States and the growth of a vibrant but stable democratic political culture seemed extraordinary. But after a brilliant start, in the 1850s the United States, like its neighbors, foundered on sectional differences that not even political democracy could reconcile. (See Chapter 15.)

The Expansion and Limits of Suffrage

Before 1800 most of the original thirteen states had limited the vote to property owners or taxpayers amounting to less than half the white male population.

Westward expansion changed the nature of American politics. The new western states extended the right to vote to all white males over the age of twenty-one. Kentucky entered the Union with universal manhood suffrage in 1792, and Tennessee (1796)

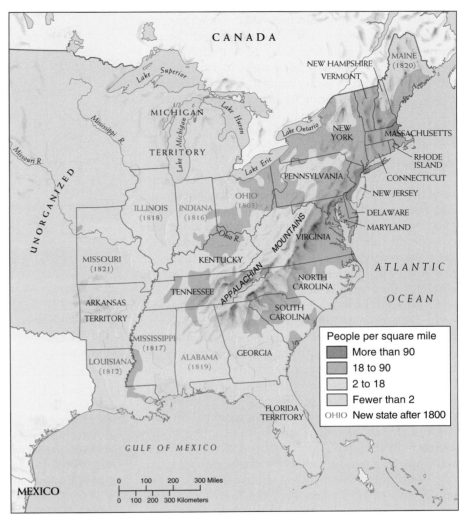

Population Trends: Westward Expansion, 1830   Westward population movement, a trickle in 1800, had become a flood by 1830. Between 1800 and 1830 the U.S. white and African American population more than doubled (from 5.3 million to 12.9 million), but the trans-Appalachian population grew tenfold (from 370,000 to 3.7 million). By 1830 more than a third of the nation's inhabitants lived west of the original thirteen states.

and Ohio (1803) entered with low taxpayer qualifications that approached universal suffrage. Soon older states such as New Jersey (1807) and Maryland (1810) dropped their property qualification for voting. By 1820, most of the older states had followed suit. There were laggards—Rhode Island, Virginia, and Louisiana did not liberalize their voting qualifications until later—but by 1840 more than 90 percent of adult white males in the nation could vote. And they could vote for more officials: governors and (most important) presidential electors were now elected by direct vote rather than chosen by small groups of state legislators.

Universal white manhood suffrage, of course, was far from true universal suffrage: the right to

vote remained barred to most of the nation's free African American males and to women of any race. Only in five New England states (Maine, New Hampshire, Vermont, Massachusetts, and Rhode Island) could free African American men vote before 1865. In most of the other northern states, the right of free African American men to vote was limited, first by custom and later by law. In 1821 in New York, for example, the same Bucktail-dominated legislature that voted to extend the franchise to most white men also restricted it among African American men to those with property valued at $250 or more, a very high amount at the time. As a result, only 68 of the nearly 13,000 African Americans in New York City qualified to vote in 1825.

Free African American men were denied the vote in all southern states and, surprisingly, in the new western states as well. The Ohio constitution of 1802 denied African Americans the right to vote, to hold public office, and to testify against white men in court cases. The constitutions of other western states— Illinois, Indiana, Michigan, Iowa, Wisconsin, and (later) Oregon—attempted to solve the "problem" of free African Americans by simply denying them entry into the state at all.

The denial of suffrage to white women stemmed from the patriarchal belief that men headed households and represented the interests of all household members. Even wealthy single women who lived alone were considered subordinate to male relatives and denied the right to vote. (New Jersey had been an exception to this rule until it amended its constitution in 1807 to withdraw the franchise from propertied women.)

Although the extension of suffrage to all classes of white men seemed to indicate that women had no role in public affairs, in fact women's informal involvement in politics grew along with the increasing pace of political activity. At the same time, however, as "manhood" rather than property became the qualification for voting, men began to ignore women's customary political activity and to regard their participation as inappropriate, an attitude that politically active women increasingly resented.

Thus, in a period famous for democratization and "the rise of the common man," the exclusion of important groups—African American men and women of all races—marked the limits of liberalization. It is also true that nowhere else in the world was the right to vote so widespread as it was in the United States. The extension of suffrage to propertyless farm workers and members of the laboring poor in the nation's cities left European observers wondering: Could "mob rule" possibly succeed? The election of 1824 provided the first outline of the answer.

The Election of 1824

The 1824 election marked a dramatic end to the political truce that James Monroe had established in 1817. Five candidates, all of them members of the Republican Party, ran for president: William H. Crawford of Georgia, John Quincy Adams of Massachusetts, Henry Clay of Kentucky, Andrew Jackson of Tennessee, and John C. Calhoun of South Carolina, who withdrew before the election to run for vice president.

Because no candidate had an electoral majority, the election was thrown into the House of Representatives, as in the election of 1800. After some political dealing, Henry Clay threw his support to Adams and

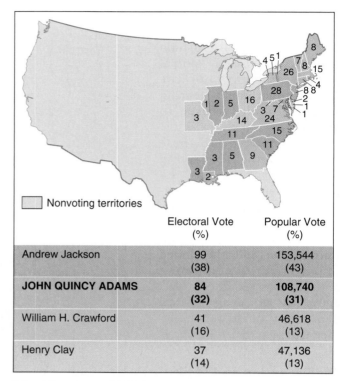

	Electoral Vote (%)	Popular Vote (%)
Andrew Jackson	99 (38)	153,544 (43)
JOHN QUINCY ADAMS	**84 (32)**	**108,740 (31)**
William H. Crawford	41 (16)	46,618 (13)
Henry Clay	37 (14)	47,136 (13)

The Election of 1824   The presidential vote of 1824 was clearly sectional. John Quincy Adams carried his native New England and little else, Henry Clay carried only his own state of Kentucky and two adjoining states, and Crawford's appeal was limited to Virginia and Georgia. Only Andrew Jackson moved beyond the regional support of the Old Southwest to wider appeal and the greatest number of electoral votes. Because no candidate had a majority, however, the election was thrown into the House of Representatives, which chose Adams.

the House elected Adams president. This was customary and proper: the Constitution gave the House the power to decide, and Clay had every right to advise his followers how to vote. But when Adams named Clay his secretary of state, the traditional stepping-stone to the highest office, Jackson's supporters promptly accused them of a "corrupt bargain." Popular opinion, the new element in politics, supported Jackson. John Quincy Adams served four miserable years as president, knowing that Jackson would challenge him, and win, in 1828.

The New Popular Democratic Culture

As the election of 1824 showed, the spread of universal manhood suffrage meant a change in popular attitudes that spelled the end of personal, elitist politics. Politicians in other states shared Van Buren's vision of tightly organized, broad-based political groups. In Virginia a group known as the Richmond Junto had control of state politics by 1816, and in Tennessee the Nashville Junto, masterminded by John Overton, held sway by 1822. In New Hampshire, Isaac Hill's Concord Regency was firmly in control by 1825.

The techniques of mass campaigns—huge political rallies, parades, and candidates with wide name recognition such as military heroes—were quickly adopted by the new political parties. So were less savory techniques such as lavish food and (especially) drink at polling places, which often turned elections into rowdy, brawling occasions.

The spirit that motivated the new mass politics was democratic pride in participation. Political processions were huge affairs, marked by the often spontaneous participation of men carrying badges and party regalia, banners and placards, and portraits of the candidates, accompanied by bands, fireworks, and the shouting and singing of party slogans and songs. The political party provided some of the same satisfactions that popular sports offer today: excitement, entertainment, and a sense of belonging. In effect, political parties functioned as giant national men's clubs. They made politics an immediate and engrossing topic of conversation and argument for men of all walks of life. In this sense, the political party was the political manifestation of a wider social impulse toward community.

The Election of 1828

The election of 1828 was the first to demonstrate the power and effectiveness of the new popular democratic culture and party system. With the help of Martin Van Buren, his campaign manager, Andrew Jackson rode the wave of the new democratic politics to the presidency. Voter turnout in 1828 was more than twice that of 1824. Jackson's party, the Democratic Republicans (they soon dropped "Republicans" and became simply the Democrats), spoke the language of democracy, and they opposed the special privilege personified for them by President John Quincy Adams and his National Republican (as distinguished from the earlier Jeffersonian Republican) Party.

Jackson won 56 percent of the popular vote (well over 80 percent in much of the South and West) and a decisive electoral majority of 178 votes to Adams's 83. The vote was interpreted as a victory for the common man. But the most important thing about Jackson's victory was the coalition that achieved it. The new democratically based political organizations—the Richmond and Nashville juntos, the Albany and Concord regencies, with help from Calhoun's organi-

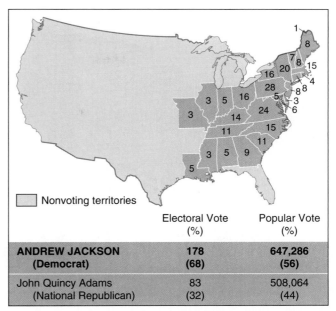

	Electoral Vote (%)	Popular Vote (%)
ANDREW JACKSON (Democrat)	**178 (68)**	**647,286 (56)**
John Quincy Adams (National Republican)	83 (32)	508,064 (44)

The Election of 1828   Andrew Jackson's victory in 1828 was the first success of the new national party system. The coalition of state parties that elected him was national, not regional. Although his support was strongest in the South and West, his ability to carry Pennsylvania and parts of New York demonstrated his national appeal.

zation in South Carolina—worked together to elect him. Popular appeal, which Jackson the military hero certainly possessed, was not enough to ensure victory. To be truly national, a party had to create and maintain a coalition of North, South, and West. The Democrats were the first to do this.

THE JACKSON PRESIDENCY

Andrew Jackson's election ushered in a new era in American politics, an era that historians have called the "Age of the Common Man." Jackson himself, however, was no common man: he was a military hero, a rich slave owner, and an imperious and decidedly undemocratic personality. "Old Hickory," as Jackson was affectionately called, was tough and unbending, just like hickory itself, one of the hardest of woods. Yet he had a mass appeal to ordinary people unmatched—and indeed unsought—by earlier presidents. The secret to Jackson's extraordinary appeal lies in the changing nature of American society. Jackson was the first to respond to the ways in which westward expansion and the extension of the suffrage were changing politics at the national as well as the local and state levels.

Until 1829, presidential inaugurations had been small, polite, and ceremonial occasions. Andrew Jackson's popularity, however, brought a horde of well-wishers to Washington for his inaugural. Conservative critics, dismayed by the disorderly crowd at Jackson's frontier-style open house at the White House, feared "the reign of King Mob" had begun.

SOURCE: Library of Congress.

A Popular President

On March 4, 1829, Andrew Jackson was inaugurated as president of the United States. Jackson himself was still in mourning for his beloved wife Rachel, whose recent death he attributed to the slanders of the campaign. But everyone else was celebrating. The small community of Washington was crowded with strangers, many of them Westerners and common people who had come especially for Jackson's inauguration. Jackson's brief inaugural address was almost drowned out by the cheering of the crowd, and after the ceremony the new president was mobbed by well-wishers. The same unrestrained enthusiasm was evident at a White House reception, where the crowd was large and disorderly. People stood on chairs and sofas to catch glimpses of Jackson and shoved and pushed to reach the food and drink, which were finally carried out to the lawn. In the rush to follow, some people exited through windows rather than the doors. This was the exuberance of democracy in action. It marked something new in American politics. Indeed, Jackson's administration was different from all those before it.

A Strong Executive

Andrew Jackson dominated his administration. Except for Martin Van Buren, whom he appointed secretary of state, he mostly ignored the heads of government departments who made up his official cabinet. Instead he consulted with an informal group, dubbed the "Kitchen Cabinet," made up of Van Buren and old western friends. The Kitchen Cabinet did not include John C. Calhoun, the vice president, or either of the other two great sectional representatives, Henry Clay and Daniel Webster. Jackson never forgave Clay for his role in the "corrupt bargain" of 1825, and he saw Daniel Webster as a representative of his favorite political target, the privileged elite.

Jackson freely used the tools of his office to strengthen the executive branch of government at the expense of the legislature and judiciary. By using the veto more frequently than all previous presidents combined (twelve vetoes compared with nine by the first six presidents), Jackson forced Congress to constantly consider his opinions. Even more important, Jackson's "negative activism" restricted federal activity, thereby allowing more power to remain in state hands.

In one of his most famous and unexpected actions, the veto of the Maysville Road Bill of 1830, Jackson refused to allow federal funding of a southern spur of the National Road in Kentucky, claiming such funding should be left to the state. Like Presidents James Madison and James Monroe before him, Jackson believed that federal funding for extensive and expensive transportation measures was unconstitutional because it infringed on the "reserved powers" the Constitution left to the states. The veto was unexpected because it disappointed Jackson's strongest supporters, Westerners who wanted better transportation. But by addressing his veto message to a popular audience, not just to Congress, and by dramatically portraying federal funding as a threat to the popular political principle of states' rights (and by making it clear that he was not opposed to federal funding of all internal improvements), Jackson actually gained political support. He also had the satisfaction of defeating a measure central to the American System proposed by his western rival, Henry Clay. (See Chapter 9).

INTERNAL IMPROVEMENTS: BUILDING AN INFRASTRUCTURE

Despite the ongoing constitutional debate over who should fund internal improvements, no one argued that they should not be funded at all. On the contrary, ordinary people and politicians of all persuasions agreed that both federal and state governments had an important role in encouraging economic growth and in fostering the development of a national market. And that role included subsidizing the costs of the basic infrastructure—the canals and railroads—that would tie the national market together.

The Transportation Revolution

Between 1800 and 1840 the United States experienced truly revolutionary improvements in transportation. More than any other development, these improvements encouraged Americans to look beyond their local communities to broader ones and to foster the enterprising commercial spirit for which they became so widely known.

The federal government demonstrated its commitment to the improvement of interregional transportation by funding the National Road in 1808, at the time the greatest single federal transportation expense (its eventual cost was $7 million). Built of gravel on a stone foundation, it crossed the Appalachian Mountains at Cumberland, Maryland, thereby opening up the West. Built in stages—to Wheeling, Virginia (now West Virginia), by 1818, to Columbus, Ohio, by 1833, to Vandalia, Illinois, almost at the Mississippi River, by 1850—the National Road tied the East and the West together, providing strong evidence of the nation's commitment to both expansion and cohesion and helping to foster a national community.

Canals and Steamboats

However much they helped the movement of people, the National Road and other roads were unsatisfactory in a commercial sense. Shipments of bulky goods like grain were too slow and expensive by road. Waterborne transportation was much cheaper and still the major commercial link among the Atlantic seaboard states and in the Mississippi-Ohio river system. But before the 1820s most water routes were north-south or coastal (Boston to Charleston, for example); east-west links were urgently needed. Canals turned out to be the answer.

The Erie Canal—the most famous canal of the era—was the brainchild of New York governor DeWitt Clinton, who envisioned a link between New York City and the Great Lakes through the Hudson River and a 364-mile-long canal stretching from Albany to Buffalo. When Clinton proposed the canal in 1817 it was derisively called "Clinton's Ditch"; the longest then existing American canal was only 27 miles long and had taken nine years to build. Nevertheless, Clinton convinced the New York legislature to approve a bond issue for the canal, and investors (New York and

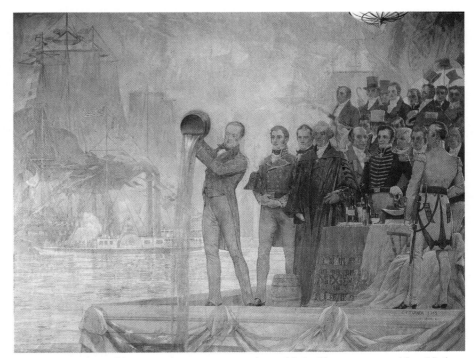

Governor DeWitt Clinton is shown pouring a keg of Lake Erie water into New York Harbor at the *Wedding of the Waters* ceremony on November 4, 1825, marking the official opening of his pet project, the Erie Canal. Initially derided as "Clinton's Ditch," the completion of the 364-mile canal opened America's heartland to settlement and international commerce.

SOURCE: C. Y. Turner, *The Marriage of the Waters.* Mural in DeWitt Clinton High School, New York City. Courtesy of Margaret Yardley Voelker and *American Heritage Magazine.*

British merchants) subscribed to the tune of $7 million, an immense sum for the day.

Building the canal—40 feet wide, 4 feet deep, 364 miles long, with 83 locks and more than 300 bridges along the way—was a vast engineering and construction challenge. In the early stages nearby farmers worked for $8 a month, but when malaria hit the workforce in the summer of 1819, many went home. They were replaced by 3,000 Irish contract laborers, who were much more expensive—50 cents a day plus room and board—but more reliable (if they survived). Local people regarded the Irish workers as different and frightening, but the importation of foreign contract labor for this job was a portent of the future. Much of the heavy construction work on later canals and railroads was performed by immigrant labor.

DeWitt Clinton had promised, to general disbelief, that the Erie Canal would be completed in less than ten years, and he made good on his promise. The canal was the wonder of the age. On October 26, 1825, Clinton declared it open in Buffalo and sent the first boat, the *Seneca Chief*, on its way to New York at the incredible speed of four miles an hour. (Ironically, the Seneca Indians, for whom the boat was named, had been removed from the path of the canal and confined to a small reservation.) The Erie Canal provided easy passage to and from the interior, both for people and for goods. It drew settlers like a magnet from the East and, increasingly, from overseas: by 1830, some 50,000 people a year were moving west on the canal to the rich farmland of Indiana, Illinois, and territory farther west. Earlier settlers now had a national, indeed an international, market for their produce. Moreover, farm families themselves became consumers.

Towns along the canal—Utica, Rochester, Buffalo—became instant cities, each an important commercial center in its own right. Perhaps the greatest beneficiary was New York City, which quickly established a commercial and financial supremacy no other American city could match. The Erie Canal decisively turned New York's merchants away from Europe and toward America's own heartland, building both interstate commerce and a feeling of community.

The phenomenal success of the Erie Canal prompted other states to construct similar waterways to tap the rich interior market. Between 1820 and 1840, $200 million was invested in canal building. No other waterway achieved the success of the Erie, which collected $8.5 million in tolls in its first nine years. Nevertheless, the spurt of canal building ended the geographical isolation of much of the country.

An even more important improvement in water transportation, especially in the American interior, was the steamboat. Robert Fulton first demonstrated

the commercial feasibility of steamboats in 1807, and they were soon operating in the East. Redesigned with more efficient engines and shallower, broader hulls, steamboats transformed commerce on the country's great inland river system: the Ohio, the Mississippi, the Missouri, and their tributaries. Steamboats were extremely dangerous, however; boiler explosions, fires, and sinkings were common, leading to one of the first public demands for regulation of private enterprise in 1838.

Dangerous as they were, steamboats greatly stimulated trade in the nation's interior. There had long been downstream trade on flatboats along the Mississippi River system, but it was limited by the return trip overland on the arduous and dangerous Natchez Trace. For a time, steamboats actually increased the downriver flatboat trade, because boatmen could now make more round trips in the same amount of time, traveling home by steamboat in speed and comfort. The increased river- and canal-borne trade, like the New England shipping boom of a generation earlier, stimulated urban growth and all kinds of commerce.

Railroads

Remarkable as all these transportation changes were, the most remarkable was still to come. Railroads, new in 1830 (when the Baltimore and Ohio Railroad opened with 13 miles of track), grew to an astounding 31,000 miles by 1860. By that date, New England and the Old Northwest had laid a dense network of rails, and several lines had reached west beyond the Mississippi. The South, the least industrialized section of the nation, had fewer railroads. "Railroad mania" surpassed even canal mania as investors—as many as one-quarter of them British—rushed to profit from the new invention.

Early railroads, like the steamboat, had to overcome many technological and supply problems. For some years after the introduction of the railroad, canal boats and coastal steamers carried more freight and at lower cost. It was not until the 1850s that consolidation of local railroads into larger systems began in earnest. But already it was clear that this youngest transportation innovation would have far-reaching social consequences.

Commercial Agriculture in the Old Northwest

Every advance in transportation—better roads, canals, steamboats, railroads—made it easier for farmers to get their produce to market. Improvements in agricultural machinery increased the amount of acreage a farmer could cultivate. These two developments, added to the availability of rich, inexpensive land in the heartland, moved American farmers permanently away from subsistence agriculture and into production for sale.

The impact of the transportation revolution on the Old Northwest was particularly marked. Settlement of the region, ongoing since the 1790s, accelerated. In the 1830s, after the opening of the Erie Canal, migrants from New England streamed into northern Ohio, Illinois, Indiana, southern Wisconsin, and Michigan and began to reach into Iowa.

Government policy strongly encouraged western settlement. The easy terms of federal land sales were an important inducement: terms eased from an initial rate of $2.00 per acre for a minimum of 320 acres in 1800, to $1.25 an acre for 80 acres in 1820. Still, this was too much for most settlers to pay all at once. Some people simply squatted, taking their chances that they could make enough money to buy the land before someone else bought it. Less daring settlers relied on credit, which was extended by banks, storekeepers, speculators, promoters, and, somewhat later, railroads, which received large grants of federal lands.

The very need for cash to purchase land involved western settlers in commercial agriculture from the beginning. Farmers, and the towns and cities that grew up to supply them, needed access to markets for their crops. Canals, steamboats, and railroads ensured that access, immediately tying the individual farm into national and international commercial networks. The long period of subsistence farming that had characterized colonial New England and the early Ohio Valley frontier was superseded by commercial agriculture stimulated by the transportation revolution.

Commercial agriculture in turn encouraged regional specialization. Ohioans shipped corn and hogs first by flatboat and later by steamboat to New Orleans. Cincinnati, the center of the Ohio trade, earned the nickname "Porkopolis" because of the importance of its slaughterhouses. By 1840, the national center of wheat production had moved west of the Appalachians to Ohio. Wheat flowed from the upper Midwest along the Erie Canal to eastern cities and increasingly to Europe.

At the same time, farmers who grew wheat or any other cash crop found themselves at the mercy of far-off markets, which established crop prices; distant canal or railroad companies, which set transportation rates; and the state of the national economy, which determined the availability of local credit. This direct dependence on economic forces outside the control of the local community was something new. So, too, was the dependence on technology, embodied in expensive new machines that farmers often bought on credit.

New tools made western farmers unusually productive. John Deere's steel plow (invented in 1837) cut plowing time in half, making cultivation of larger acreages possible. Seed drills were another important advance. But the most remarkable innovation was Cyrus McCormick's reaper, patented in 1834. Earlier, harvesting had depended on manpower alone. A man could cut two or three acres of wheat a day with a cradle scythe, but with the horse-drawn reaper he could cut twelve acres.

Effects of the Transportation Revolution

Every east-west road, canal, and railroad helped to reorient Americans away from the Atlantic and toward the heartland. This new focus was decisive in the creation of national pride and identity. Transportation improvements such as the Erie Canal and the National Road linked Americans in larger communities of interest beyond the local community in which they lived. Other results were less positive. The technological triumphs of canal building and rail laying fostered a brash spirit of conquest over nature that was to become part of the American myth of the frontier. Furthermore, although every new transportation or communication link broke down local and regional isolation and helped to build a spirit of pride in the nation, it also refocused attention on questions of national politics. The new transportation system caused a subtle political shift, for it strengthened the influence of the North by improving the North's ties with the West more than its ties with the South. In this way, the new modes of communication and transportation served to heat up the politics of the era.

JACKSON AND HIS OPPONENTS: THE RISE OF THE WHIGS

As transportation improvements, increased commercialization, and the new democratic politics drew the people of the United States out of localism into larger networks, fundamental questions about national unity arose. What was the correct balance between local interests—the rights of the states—and the powers of the central government? The men who wrote the federal Constitution in Philadelphia in 1787 had not been able to reach agreement on this question. Because the Constitution deliberately left the federal structure ambiguous, all sectional disagreements automatically became constitutional issues that carried a threat to national unity. The great issues of Jackson's presidency expressed this continuing tension between

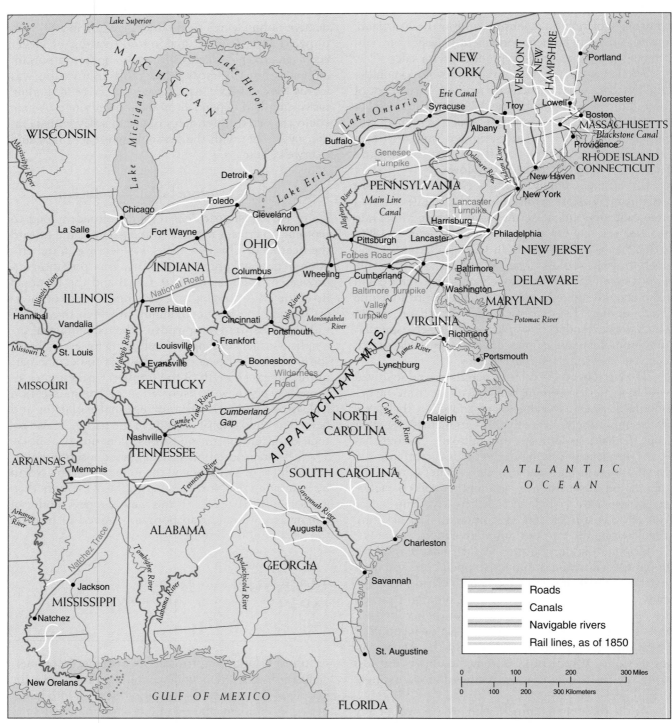

Commercial Links: Rivers, Canals, Roads, 1830, and Rail Lines, 1850 By 1830, the United States was tied together by a network of roads, canals, and rivers. This "transportation revolution" fostered a great burst of commercial activity and economic growth. Transportation improvements accelerated the commercialization of agriculture by getting farmers' products to wider, nonlocal markets. Access to wider markets likewise encouraged new textile and other manufacturers to increase their scale of production. By 1850, another revolutionary mode of transportation, the railroad, had emerged as a vital link to the transportation infrastructure.

nationalism and sectionalism. Jackson's responses to them created such controversy that a permanent opposition—another political party, known as the Whigs—was born.

The Nullification Crisis

The political issue that came to symbolize the divergent sectional interests of North and South, pitting the rights of individual states against the claims of a federal majority, was the protective tariff. As a group, wealthy southern planters were opposed to tariffs, both because duties raised the cost of the luxury goods they imported from Europe and because they believed in the principle of free trade, fearing that American tariffs would cause other countries to retaliate with tariffs against southern cotton. Most southern congressmen, assured that the 1816 tariff was a temporary postwar recovery measure, voted for it. But it was not temporary. As the North industrialized and new industries demanded protection, tariff bills in 1824 and 1828, nicknamed the Tariff of Abominations, raised rates still higher and protected more items. Southerners protested, but they were outvoted in Congress by northern and western representatives.

Southerners in Congress lacked the votes to block the tariff and faced the bleak prospect that their economic interests would always be ignored by the majority. Southern opponents of the tariff insisted that it was not a truly national measure but a sectional one that helped only some groups while harming others. Thus, they claimed, it was unconstitutional because it violated the rights of some of the states.

South Carolina reacted to the Tariff of 1828 with the doctrine of nullification, which upheld the right of a state to declare a federal law null and void and to refuse to enforce it within the state. This was not a new argument. Thomas Jefferson and James Madison had used it in the Kentucky and Virginia Resolves of 1798, which they had written in opposing the Alien and Sedition Acts (see Chapter 8). The Hartford Convention of 1814–15, at which Federalists protested grievances related to the War of 1812, had adopted the same position (see Chapter 9). At issue in each case was the power of the state against that of the federal government.

South Carolina had an important supporter of nullification in the person of John C. Calhoun, who wrote a widely circulated defense of the doctrine, the *Exposition and Protest*, in 1828. Because Calhoun was soon to serve as Andrew Jackson's vice president, he wrote the *Exposition* anonymously. He hoped to use his influence with Jackson to gain support for nullification, but he was disappointed.

Jackson saw nullification a threat to national unity. As he said at a famous exchange of toasts at the annual Jefferson Day dinner in 1830, "Our Federal Union, it must be preserved." In response to Jackson, Calhoun offered his own toast: "The Union—next to our liberty most dear. May we always remember that it can only be preserved by distributing equally the benefits and burdens of the Union." The president and the vice president were, thus, in open disagreement on a matter of crucial national importance. The outcome was inevitable: Calhoun lost all influence with Jackson, and two years later he took the unusual step of resigning the vice presidency. Martin Van Buren was elected to the office for Jackson's second term. Calhoun, his presidential aspirations in ruins, became a senator from South Carolina, and in that capacity participated in the last act of the nullification drama.

In 1832 the nullification controversy became a full-blown crisis. In passing the Tariff of 1832, Congress (in spite of Jackson's disapproval) retained high taxes on woolens, iron, and hemp, although it reduced duties on other items. South Carolina responded with a special convention and an Ordinance of Nullification, in which it rejected the tariff and refused to collect the taxes it required. The state further issued a call for a volunteer militia and threatened to secede from the Union if Jackson used force against it. Jackson responded vehemently, denouncing the nullifiers—"Disunion by armed force is treason"—and obtaining from Congress a Force Bill authorizing the federal government to collect the tariff in South Carolina at gunpoint if necessary. Intimidated, the other southern states refused to follow South Carolina's lead. More quietly, Jackson also asked Congress to revise the tariff. Henry Clay, the Great Pacificator, swung into action and soon, with Calhoun's support, had crafted the Tariff Act of 1833. This measure appeared to meet southern demands by pledging a return to the tariff rate of 1816 (an average of 20 percent) by 1842. The South Carolina legislature, unwilling to act without the support of other southern states, quickly accepted this face-saving compromise and repealed its nullification of the tariff of 1832. In a final burst of bravado, the legislature nullified the Force Bill, but Jackson defused the crisis by ignoring this second nullification.

The nullification crisis was the most serious threat to national unity that the United States had ever experienced. South Carolinians, by threatening to secede, had forced concessions on a matter they believed of vital economic importance. They—and a number of other

Southerners—believed that the resolution of the crisis illustrated the success of their uncompromising tactics. Most of the rest of the nation simply breathed a sigh of relief, echoing Daniel Webster's sentiment, spoken in the heat of the debate over nullification, "Liberty and Union, now and forever, one and inseparable!"

Indian Removal

The official policy of the United States government from the time of Jefferson's administration was to promote the assimilation of Indian peoples by encouraging them to adopt white ways. To Indian groups who resisted "civilization" or who needed more time to adapt, Jefferson offered the alternative of removal from settled areas in the East to the new Indian Territory west of the Mississippi River. Following this logic, at the end of the War of 1812, the federal government signed removal treaties with a number of Indian nations of the Old Northwest, thereby opening up large tracts of land for white settlement (see Chapter 9). In the Southwest, however, the Five Civilized Tribes—the Cherokees, Chickasaws, Choctaws, Creeks, and Seminoles—remained. By the 1830s, under constant pressure from settlers, each of the five

tribes had ceded most of its lands, but sizable self-governing groups lived in Georgia, Alabama, Mississippi, and Florida. All of these (except the Seminoles) had moved far in the direction of coexistence with whites, and they resisted suggestions that they should voluntarily remove themselves.

Despite the evidence of successful adaptation to the dominant white culture, in the 1820s the legislatures of Georgia, Alabama, and Mississippi, responding to pressures from land-hungry whites, voted to invalidate federal treaties granting special self-governing status to Indian lands. Because the federal government, not the states, bore responsibility for Indian policy, these state actions constituted a challenge to federal authority. In this instance, however, unlike the Nullification Crisis, the resisting states had presidential support.

In 1830, at President Jackson's urging, the U.S. Congress passed the hotly debated Indian Removal Act, which appropriated funds for relocation, by force if necessary. When Jackson increased the pressure by sending federal officials to negotiate removal treaties with the southern tribes, most reluctantly signed and prepared to move. The Cherokees, however, fought their removal by using the white man's weapon—the law. At first they seemed to have won: in *Cherokee Nation* v. *Georgia* (1831) and *Worcester* v. *Georgia* (1832) Chief Justice John Marshall ruled that the Cherokees, though not a state or a foreign nation, were a "domestic dependent nation" that could not be forced by the state of Georgia to give up its land against its will. Ignoring the decision, Jackson continued his support for removal.

Faced by the Cherokees' de facto defeat, most of the Choctaws moved west in 1830; the last of the Creeks were forcibly moved by the military in 1836, and the Chickasaws a year later. And in 1838, in the last and most infamous removal, resisting Cherokees were driven west to Oklahoma along what came to be known as the "Trail of Tears." A 7,000-man army escorting them watched thousands (perhaps a quarter of the 16,000 Cherokees) die along the way. Another futile effort to resist removal, the Black Hawk

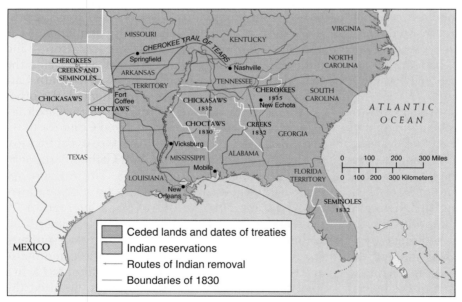

Southern Indian Cessions and Removals, 1830s   Pressure on the five major southern Indian peoples—the Cherokees, Chickasaws, Choctaws, Creeks, and Seminoles—that began during the War of 1812 culminated with their removal in the 1830s. Some groups from every tribe ceded their southern homelands peacefully and moved to the newly established Indian Territory west of Arkansas and Missouri. Some, like the Seminoles, resisted by force. Others, like the Cherokees, resisted in the courts but finally lost when President Andrew Jackson refused to enforce a Supreme Court decision in their favor. The Cherokees, the last to move, were forcibly removed by the U.S. Army along the "Trail of Tears" in 1838.

"war," occurred in the Old Northwest. In 1832, Sac and Fox Indians, led by Black Hawk, attempted to move back to their old tribal grounds in Illinois following removal, but settlers saw the move as an invasion and demanded military protection. Federal troops chased the Black Hawk band to Wisconsin, where more than 300 Indians died in a final battle, and Black Hawk himself was taken prisoner. As in the South, the last of the remaining Indians east of the Mississippi were removed by the end of the 1830s.

The Bank War

In 1816 Congress had granted a twenty-year charter to the Second Bank of the United States. The Bank played a powerful role in the expanding American economy, encouraging the growth of strong and stable financial interests and curbing less stable and irresponsible ones.

The Bank was not a government agency but a private institution, the majority of whose directors were appointed by the government. Its stockholders were some of the nation's richest men (New York's John Jacob Astor and Philadelphia's Stephen Girard among them). The Bank was directed by the erudite and aristocratic Nicholas Biddle of Philadelphia. Biddle, a friend of Thomas Jefferson and an avid amateur scientist, was the editor of the journals of Lewis and Clark.

The Bank, which with thirty branches was the nation's largest, performed a variety of functions: it held the government's money (about $10 million), sold government bonds, and made commercial loans. But its most important function was the control it exercised over state banks. At the time, America lacked a national currency. The money in circulation was a mixture of paper money (U.S. notes and the notes of state banks) and gold and silver coins (specie, or hard currency), many of them of foreign origin. Because state banks tended to issue more paper money than they could back with hard currency, the Bank always demanded repayment of its loans to them in coin. This policy forced state banks to maintain adequate reserves, curbed inflationary pressures (overprinting of their banknotes), and restricted speculative activities such as risky loans. In times of recession, the Bank eased the pressure on state banks, demanding only partial payment in coin. Thus, the Bank acted as a currency stabilizer by helping to control the money supply. It brought a semblance of order to what we today would consider a chaotic money system—coins of various weights and a multitude of state banknotes, many of which were discounted (not accepted at full face value) in other states.

The concept of a strong national bank was supported by the majority of the nation's merchants and businessmen and was a key element in Henry Clay's American System. Nevertheless, the Bank had many opponents. Western land speculators, and many western farmers, chafed at the Bank's tight control over the currency reserves of state banks, claiming it was harmful to western development. Both western farmers and urban workers had bitter memories of the Panic of 1819, which the Bank had caused (at least in part) by sharply cutting back on available credit. Many ordinary people were uneasy not only about the Bank but about banks of all kinds. They believed that a system based on paper currency would be manipulated by bankers in unpredictable and dangerous ways. Among those who held that opinion was Andrew Jackson, who had hated and feared banks ever since the 1790s, when he had lost a great deal of money in a speculative venture.

Nicholas Biddle, urged on by Henry Clay and Daniel Webster, precipitated the conflict by making early application for rechartering the Bank. Congress approved the application in July 1832. Clay and Webster, though well aware of Jackson's antibank feelings, believed the president would not risk a veto in an election year. They were wrong. Jackson immediately decided on a stinging veto, announcing to Van Buren, "The bank . . . is trying to kill me, but I will kill it!"

And kill it he did that same July, with one of the strongest veto messages in American history. Denouncing the Bank as unconstitutional, harmful to states' rights, and "dangerous to the liberties of the people," Jackson presented himself as the spokesman for the majority of ordinary people and the enemy of special privilege. Asserting that the Bank's "exclusive privileges" were benefiting only the rich, Jackson claimed to speak for the "humble members of society—the farmers, mechanics and laborers"—and to oppose injustice and inequality. In short, the veto spoke directly to many of the hopes and fears that Americans felt at this time of exceptionally rapid economic and social change.

Jackson's Reelection in 1832

Jackson's veto message was a great popular success, and it set the terms for the presidential election of 1832. Henry Clay, the nominee of the anti-Jackson forces, lost the battle for popular opinion. Democrats successfully painted Clay as the defender of the Bank and of privilege. His defeat was decisive: he drew only 49 electoral votes, to Jackson's 219.

Although the election was a triumph for Jackson, the Bank War continued. The Bank charter did not expire until 1836, but Jackson, declaring that "the hydra of corruption is only scotched, not dead," decided to kill the Bank by transferring its $10 million in government deposits to favored state banks ("pet banks," critics called them). Cabinet members objected, as did the Senate, but Jackson responded that the election had given him a popular mandate to act against the Bank. The president was the direct representative of the people, he claimed, and could act upon the popular will, regardless of the opinion of Congress or even the cabinet. Short of impeachment, there was nothing Congress could do to prevent Jackson from acting on his expansive—and novel—interpretation of presidential powers.

Whigs, Van Buren, and the Election of 1836

But there was someone outside Congress with power to respond: the Bank's director, Nicholas Biddle. "This worthy President thinks that because he has scalped Indians . . . he is to have his way with the Bank," Biddle commented. "He is mistaken." As the government withdrew its deposits, Biddle abruptly called in the Bank's commercial loans, thereby causing a sharp panic and recession in the winter of 1833–34. Merchants, businessmen, and southern planters were all furious— at Jackson. His opponents, only a loose coalition up to this time, coalesced into a formal opposition party that called itself the Whigs. Evoking the memory of the Patriots who had resisted King George III in the American Revolution, the new party called on everyone to resist tyrannical "King Andrew." Just as Jackson's own calls for popular democracy had appealed to voters in all regions, so his opponents overcame their sectional differences to unite in opposition to his economic policies and arbitrary methods.

Vice President Martin Van Buren, Jackson's designated successor, won the presidential election of 1836 because the Whigs, unable to agree on a common presidential candidate, ran four sectional candidates. The Whig defeat drove home the weakness of the traditional sectional politics, but the closeness of the popular vote showed that the basis for a united national opposition did exist. In 1840, the Whigs would prove that they had learned this lesson.

The Panic of 1837

Meanwhile, the consequences of the Bank War continued. The recession of 1833–34 was followed by a wild speculative boom, caused as much by foreign investors as by the expiration of the Bank. Many new state banks were chartered that were eager to give loans, the price of cotton rose rapidly, and speculation in western lands was feverish (in Alabama and Mississippi, the mid-1830s were known as the "Flush Times"). A government surplus of $37 million distributed to the states in 1836 made the inflationary pressures worse. Jackson became alarmed at the widespread use of paper money (which he blamed for the inflation), and in July 1836 he issued the Specie Circular, announcing that the government would accept payment for public lands only in hard currency. At the same time, foreign investors, especially British banks, affected by a world recession, called in their American loans. The sharp contraction of credit led to the Panic of 1837 and a six-year recession, the worst the American economy had yet known.

In 1837, some 800 banks suspended business, refusing to pay out any of their $150 million in deposits. The collapse of the banking system led to business closures and outright failures. In the winter of 1837–38 in New York City alone, one-third of all manual laborers were unemployed and an estimated 10,000 were living in abject poverty. New York laborers took to the streets. Four or five thousand protesters carrying signs reading "Bread, Meat, Rent, Fuel!" gathered at City Hall on February 10, 1838, then marched to the warehouse of a leading merchant, Eli Hart. Breaking down the door, they took possession of the thousands of barrels of flour Hart had stored there rather than sell at what the mob considered a fair price. Policemen and state militia who tried to prevent the break-in were beaten by the angry mob. Not until 1843 did the economy show signs of recovery.

In neither 1837 nor 1819 did the federal government take any action to aid victims of economic recession. No banks were bailed out, no bank depositors were saved by federal insurance, no laid-off workers got unemployment payments. Nor did the government undertake any public works projects or pump money into the economy. All of these steps, today seen as essential to prevent economic collapse and to alleviate human suffering, were unheard of in 1819 and 1837. Soup kitchens and charities were mobilized in major cities, but only by private, volunteer groups, not by local or state governments. Panics and depressions were believed to be natural stages in the business cycle, and government intervention was considered unwarranted—although it was perfectly acceptable for government to intervene to promote growth. As a result, workers, farmers, and members of the new business middle class suddenly realized that participation in America's booming economy was very dangerous. The rewards could be great, but so could the penalties.

Martin Van Buren (quickly nicknamed "Van Ruin") spent a dismal four years in the White House presiding over bank failures, bankruptcies, and massive unemployment. Van Buren, who lacked Jackson's compelling personality, could find no remedies to the depression.

OVERVIEW

THE SECOND AMERICAN PARTY SYSTEM

Democrats	First organized to elect Andrew Jackson to the presidency in 1828. The Democratic Party spoke for Jeffersonian democracy, expansion, and the freedom of the "common man" from interference from government or from financial monopolies like the Bank of the United States. It found its power base in the rural South and West and among some northern urban workers. The Democratic Party was the majority party from 1828 to 1860.
Whigs	Organized in opposition to Andrew Jackson in the early 1830s. Heir to Federalism, the Whig Party favored a strong role for the national government in the economy (for example, it promoted Henry Clay's American System) and supported active social reform. Its power base lay in the North and Old Northwest among voters who benefited from increased commercialization and among some southern planters and urban merchants. The Whigs won the elections of 1840 and 1848.

His misfortune gave the opposition party, the newly formed Whigs, their opportunity.

THE SECOND AMERICAN PARTY SYSTEM

The political struggles of the Jackson era, coupled with the dramatic social changes caused by expansion and economic growth, created the basic pattern of American politics: two major parties, each with at least some appeal among voters of all social classes and in all sections of the country. That pattern, which we call the "Second American Party System," remains to this day.

Whigs and Democrats

There were genuine differences between the Whigs and the Democrats, but they were not sectional differences. Instead, the two parties reflected just-emerging class and cultural differences. The Democrats, as they themselves were quick to point out, had inherited Thomas Jefferson's belief in the democratic rights of the small, independent yeoman farmer. They had nationwide appeal, especially in the South and West, the most rural regions. Most Democratic voters were opposed to the rapid social and economic changes that accompanied the transportation revolution.

The Whigs were themselves often the initiators and beneficiaries of economic change and were more receptive to it. Heirs of the Federalist belief in the importance of a strong federal role in the national economy (see Chapter 8), they supported the elements of Henry Clay's American System: a strong central government, the Bank of the United States, a protective tariff, and internal improvements. In fact, when it came to improvements, the Whigs wanted to improve people as well as roads. Religion was an important element in political affiliation, and many Whigs were members of evangelical reforming denominations. Reformers believed that everyone, rich and poor, was capable of the self-discipline that would lead to a good life. Thus, Whigs favored government intervention in both economic and social affairs, calling for education and social reforms, such as temperance, that aimed to improve the ordinary citizen. The Whigs' greatest strength was in New England and the northern part of the West (the Old Northwest), the areas most affected by commercial agriculture and factory work.

The Campaign of 1840

In 1840, the Whigs set out to beat the Democrats at their own game. Passing over the ever-hopeful Henry Clay, the Whigs nominated a man as much like Andrew Jackson as possible, the aging Indian fighter William Henry Harrison, former governor of the Indiana Territory from 1801 to 1812. In an effort to duplicate Jackson's winning appeal to the South as well as the West, the Whigs balanced the ticket by nominating a Southerner, John Tyler, for vice president. The campaign slogan was "Tippecanoe and Tyler too" (Tippecanoe was the site of Harrison's famous victory over Tecumseh's Indian confederation in 1811). As if this were not enough, Whigs made Harrison out to be

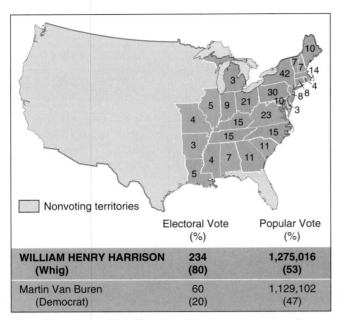

	Electoral Vote (%)	Popular Vote (%)
WILLIAM HENRY HARRISON (Whig)	**234 (80)**	**1,275,016 (53)**
Martin Van Buren (Democrat)	60 (20)	1,129,102 (47)

Nonvoting territories

The Election of 1840 The Whigs triumphed in the election of 1840 by beating the Democrats at their own game. Whigs could expect to do well in the commercializing areas of New England and the Old Northwest, but their adopted strategy of popular campaigning worked well in the largely rural South and West as well, contributing to Harrison's victory. The Whigs' choice of John Tyler as vice presidential candidate, another strategy designed to appeal to southern voters, backfired when Harrison died and Tyler, who did not share Whig principles, became America's first vice president to succeed to the presidency.

a humble man who would be happy to live in a log cabin, although he actually lived in a large and comfortable house. Thus began another long-lived political legend. The Whigs reached out to ordinary people with torchlight parades, barbecues, songs, coonskin caps, bottomless jugs of hard cider, and claims that Martin Van Buren, Harrison's hapless opponent, was a man of privilege and aristocratic tastes. Nothing could be further from the truth: Van Buren was the son of a tavern keeper.

The Whig campaign tactics, added to the popular anger at Van Buren because of the continuing depression, gave Harrison a sweeping electoral victory, 234 votes to 60. Even more remarkable, the campaign achieved the greatest voter turnout up to that time (and rarely equaled since), 80 percent.

The Whig Victory Turns to Loss: The Tyler Presidency

Although the Whig victory of 1840 was a milestone in American politics, the triumph of Whig principles was short-lived. William Henry Harrison, who was

sixty-eight, died of pneumonia a month after his inauguration. For the first time in American history the vice president stepped up to the presidency. Not for the last time, important differences between the dead president and his successor reshaped the direction of American politics.

John Tyler of Virginia was a former Democrat who had left the party because he disagreed with Jackson's autocratic style. The Whigs had sought him primarily for his sectional appeal and had not inquired too closely into his political opinions, which turned out to be anti-Whig as well as anti-Jackson. President Tyler vetoed a series of bills embodying all the elements of Henry Clay's American System: tariffs, internal improvements, a new Bank of the United States. In exasperation, congressional Whigs forced Tyler out of the party, and his entire cabinet of Whigs resigned. To replace them, Tyler appointed former Democrats like himself. Thus, the Whig triumph of 1840, one of the clearest victories in American electoral politics, was negated by the stalemate between Tyler and the Whig majority in Congress. The Whigs were to win only one more election, that of 1848.

AMERICAN ARTS AND LETTERS

Jackson's presidency was a defining moment in the development of an American identity. His combination of western belligerency and combative individualism was the strongest statement of American distinctiveness since Thomas Jefferson's agrarianism. Did Jackson speak for all of America? The Whigs did not think so. And the definitions of American identity that were beginning to emerge in popular culture and in intellectual circles were more complex than the message coming from the White House. Throughout the nation, however, there was a widespread interest in information and literature of all kinds. The Age of the Common Man would prove to be the period when American writers and painters found the national themes that allowed them to produce the first distinctively American literature and art.

Popular Cultures and the Spread of the Written Word

A print revolution had begun in 1826 when a reform organization, the American Tract Society, installed the country's first steam-powered press. Three years later the new presses had turned out 300,000 Bibles and 6 million religious tracts, or pamphlets. The greatest growth, however, was in newspapers that reached a mass audience. The number of newspapers soared from 376 newspapers in 1810 to 1,200 in 1835. Packed with articles that today would be considered libelous and scandalous, newspapers were entertaining and popular reading, and they rapidly became a key part of democratic popular culture.

Newspapers and pamphlets fostered a variety of popular cultures as well. For western readers, the Crockett almanacs offered a mix of humorous stories and tall tales attributed to Davy Crockett (the boisterous Tennessee "roarer" who died defending the Alamo in 1836) along with meteorological and climate information. In New York City the immensely popular "penny papers" (so called from their price), the *New York Morning Post* and the *New York Sun*, began appearing in 1833. These papers, with lurid headlines such as "Double Suicide," and "Secret Tryst," fed the same popular appetite for scandal as did other popular publications such as the *Police Gazette* magazine; pamphlets about murder trials, swindlers, and pirates; and temperance dime novels. Throughout the country, religious literature was still most widely read, but a small middle-class audience existed for literary magazines and, among women especially, for sentimental magazines and novels.

Accompanying all these changes in print communication was an invention that outsped them all: the telegraph, so innovative that its inventor spent years fruitlessly seeking private funds to back its application. Finally, with financing from the federal government, Samuel F. B. Morse sent his first message from Washington to Baltimore in 1844. Soon messages in Morse code would be transmitted instantaneously across the continent. The impact of this revolutionary invention, the first to separate the message from the speed at which a human messenger could travel, was immediate. The timeliness of information available to the individual, from important national news to the next train's arrival time, vastly increased. Distant events gained new and exciting immediacy. Everyone's horizon and sense of community was widened.

Creating a National American Culture

For all the improvements in communication, the United States was a provincial culture, still looking to Britain for values, standards, and literary offerings. In the early years of the nineteenth century, eastern seaboard cities actively built the cultural foundation that would nurture American art and literature. Philadelphia's American Philosophical Society, founded by Benjamin Franklin in 1743, boasted a distinguished roster of scientists, including Thomas Jefferson—concurrently its president and president of the United

States—and Nicholas Biddle, Jackson's opponent in the Bank War. Culturally, Boston ran a close second to Philadelphia, founding the Massachusetts General Hospital (1811) and the Boston Athenaeum (1807), a gentlemen's library and reading room. Southern cities were much less successful in supporting culture. Charleston had a Literary and Philosophical Society (founded in 1814), but the widely dispersed residences of the southern elite made urban cultural institutions difficult to sustain. Thus, unwittingly, the South ceded cultural leadership to the North.

The cultural picture was much spottier in the West. A few cities, such as Lexington, Kentucky, and Cincinnati, Ohio, had civic cultural institutions, and some transplanted New Englanders maintained connections with New England culture. Most pioneers were at best uninterested and at worst actively hostile to traditional literary culture. This was neither from lack of literacy nor from a failure to read. Newspaper and religious journals both had large readerships in the West: The *Methodist Christian Advocate*, for example, reached 25,000 people yearly (compared with the *North American Review*'s 3,000). The frontier emphasis on the practical was hard to distinguish from antiintellectualism.

Thus, in the early part of the nineteenth century, the gap between the intellectual and cultural horizons of a wealthy Bostonian and a frontier farmer in Michigan widened. Part of the unfinished task of building a national society was the creation of a national culture that could fill this gap. For writers and artists, the challenge was to find distinctively American themes.

Of the eastern cities, New York produced the first widely recognized American writers. In 1819, Washington Irving published *The Sketch Book*, thus immortalizing Rip Van Winkle and the Headless Horseman. Within a few years James Fenimore Cooper's Leather-stocking novels (of which *The Last of the Mohicans*, published in 1826, is the best known) achieved wide success in both America and Europe. Cooper's novels established the long American experience of westward expansion, of which the conquest of the Indians was a vital part, as a serious and distinctive American literary theme.

It was New England, however, that claimed to be the forge of American cultural independence from Europe. As Ralph Waldo Emerson proclaimed in "The American Scholar," a lecture he delivered in 1837 to the Harvard faculty, "Our day of dependence, our long apprenticeship to the learning of other lands, draws to a close." He went on to encourage American writers to find inspiration in the ordinary details of daily life. His message of cultural self-sufficiency was one that Americans were eager to hear.

Asher Durand, a member of the Hudson River School of landscape painting, produced this work, *Kindred Spirits*, in 1849 as a tribute to Thomas Cole, the school's leader. Cole is one of the figures depicted standing in a romantic wilderness.
SOURCE: Asher B. Durand, *Kindred Spirits*, 1849. Oil on canvas. The New York Public Library, New York.

Artists and Builders

Artists were as successful as novelists in finding American themes. Thomas Cole, who came to America from England in 1818, applied the British romantic school of landscape painting to American scenes. He founded the Hudson River school of American painting, a style and subject matter frankly nationalistic in tone.

The western painters—realists such as Karl Bodmer and George Catlin as well as the romantics who followed them, like Albert Bierstadt and Thomas Moran—drew on the dramatic western landscape and its peoples. Another unusual western painter, John James Audubon, could at first find no publisher in this country for his striking and sometimes grotesque etchings of American birds. George Caleb Bingham, an accomplished genre painter, produced somewhat tidied-up scenes of real-life American workers, such as flatboatmen on the Missouri River. All these painters found much to record and to celebrate in American life. Ironically, the inspiration for the most prevalent theme, the American wilderness, was profoundly endangered by the rapid western settlement of which the nation was so proud.

The haste and transiency of American life are nowhere so obvious as in the architectural record of this era, which is sparse. The monumental neoclassical style (complete with columns) that Jefferson had recommended for official buildings in Washington continued to be favored for public buildings elsewhere and by private concerns trying to project an imposing image, such as banks. But in general Americans were in too much of a hurry to build for the future, and in balloon-frame construction they found the perfect technique for the present. Balloon-frame structures—which consist of a basic frame of wooden studs fastened with crosspieces top and bottom—could be put up quickly, cheaply, and without the help of a skilled carpenter. Covering the frame with wooden siding was equally simple, and the resultant dwelling was as strong, although not as well insulated, as a house of solid timber or logs. Balloon-frame construction was first used in Chicago in the 1830s, where it created the city almost instantly. The four-room balloon-frame house, affordable to many who could not have paid for a traditionally built dwelling, became standard in that decade. This was indeed housing for the common man and his family.

CHRONOLOGY

1817	Erie Canal construction begins
1818	National Road completed to Wheeling, Virginia (now West Virginia)
1821	Martin Van Buren's Bucktails defeat DeWitt Clinton in New York
	Mexican independence from Spain
1824	John Quincy Adams elected president by the House of Representatives
1825	Erie Canal opens
1826	First American use of the steam-powered printing press
1828	Congress passes "Tariff of Abominations"
	Andrew Jackson elected president
	John C. Calhoun publishes *Exposition and Protest* anonymously
1830	Jackson vetoes Maysville Road Bill
	Congress passes Indian Removal Act
	Baltimore and Ohio Railroad opens
1832	Nullification Crisis begins
	Jackson vetoes renewal of Bank of the United States charter
	Jackson reelected president
1833	National Road completed to Columbus, Ohio
1834	Cyrus McCormick patents the McCormick reaper
	Whig party organized
	British abolish slavery in their Caribbean colonies
1836	Jackson issues Specie Circular
	Martin Van Buren elected president
1837	John Deere invents steel plow
	Ralph Waldo Emerson first presents "The American Scholar"
	Panic of 1837
1838	Cherokee removal along the "Trail of Tears"
1840	Whig William Henry Harrison elected president
	Act of Union merges Upper and Lower Canada
1841	John Tyler assumes presidency at the death of President Harrison
1844	Samuel F. B. Morse operates first telegraph

CONCLUSION

Andrew Jackson's presidency witnessed the building of a strong national party system based on nearly universal white manhood suffrage. At the same time that the nation expanded politically (nine new western states were admitted between 1800 and 1840), construction of new roads, canals, and railroads, and other improvements in transportation and communication, created the infrastructure that united the nation physically. Sectionalism and localism seemed to have been replaced by a more national consciousness that was clearly expressed in the two national political parties, the Whigs and the Democrats. The Second American Party System created new democratic political communities united by common political opinions.

But as the key battles of the Jackson presidency—the Nullification Crisis, Indian removal, the Bank War—showed, the forces of sectionalism resisted the strong nationalizing tendencies of the era. As the next two chapters will show, economic and social forces continued to force the South and the North apart.

REVIEW QUESTIONS

1. What reasons might a person of the 1820s and 1830s give for opposing universal white manhood suffrage? Suffrage for free African American men? For women of all races?
2. Opponents believed that Andrew Jackson was unsuited in both political experience and temperament to be president of the United States, yet his presidency is considered one of the most influential in American history. Explain the changes in political organization and attitude that made his election possible.
3. Both the Nullification Crisis and Indian removal raised the constitutional issue of the rights of a minority in a nation governed by majority rule. What rights, in your opinion, does a minority have, and what kinds of laws are necessary to defend those rights?
4. Why was the issue of government support for internal improvements so controversial? Who benefited from the transportation revolution? Who lost ground?
5. What were the key differences between Whigs and Democrats? What did each party stand for? Who were their supporters? What were the links between each party's programs and party supporters?
6. What distinctive American themes did the writers, artists, and builders of the 1820s and 1830s express in their works? Are they still considered American themes today?

RECOMMENDED READING

Donald B. Cole, *The Presidency of Andrew Jackson* (1993). In this recent work, Jackson is seen as just as influential but less commanding and more ambiguous in his political attitudes than in earlier studies.

Ronald P. Formisano, *The Transformation of Political Culture: Massachusetts Parties, 1790s–1840s* (1983). One of many detailed studies that have contributed to our understanding of the development of the second party system.

William W. Freehling, *Prelude to Civil War* (1966). An examination of the Nullification Crisis that stresses the centrality of slavery to the dispute.

Paul W. Gates, *The Farmer's Age: Agriculture, 1815–1860* (1966). The standard source on the growth of commercial agriculture.

Michael Holt, *The Rise and Fall of the American Whig Party* (1999). A massive study that covers its subject in detail.

Reeve Huston, *Land and Freedom: Rural Society, Popular Protest, and Party Politics in Antebellus New York* (2000). How rural ways of life and the Anti-Rent Wars became a part of Jacksonian politics.

John Lauritz Larson, *Internal Improvement: National Public Works and the Promise of Popular Government in the Early United States* (2001). Links internal improvements with political attitudes toward government and examines how they changed.

Jean V. Matthews, *Toward a New Society: American Thought and Culture, 1800–1830* (1991). A valuable survey of American attitudes toward religion, politics, science, nature, and culture in the early nineteenth century.

Simon Newman, *Parades and the Politics of the Street* (1997). Examines how festive culture became an expression of popular political culture.

Robert Remini, *Andrew Jackson and the Source of American Freedom* (1981). An account of Jackson's White House years by his major biographer.

Carol Sheriff, *The Artificial River: The Erie Canal and the Paradox of Progress, 1817–1862* (1996). Shows how the building of the canal changed personal lives and fostered religious beliefs in human perfectability.

Alan Taylor, *William Cooper's Town: Power and Persuasion on the Frontier of the Early American Republic* (1995). The Pulitzer Prize–winning study of the founding and development of Cooperstown, New York, by the father of novelist James Fenimore Cooper. An engrossing study of the effects of the democratization of politics.

George Rogers Taylor, *The Transportation Revolution, 1815–1860* (1951). The indispensable book on all aspects of the American economy during this period.

Harry L. Watson, *Liberty and Power: The Politics of Jacksonian America* (1990). An excellent recent overview of Jacksonian politics.

ON THE WEB

http://www.history.rochester.edu/canal/index.htm

This site is maintained by the History Department of the University of Rochester and offers a good history of the Erie Canal. The site connects to archives of records concerning the Erie Canal and other sites related to canal history.

http://xroads.virginia.edu/~HYPER/DETOC/toc_indx.html

The University of Virginia has posted on this page an electronic version of Alexis de Tocqueville's *Democracy in America*. It details Tocqueville's travels in the United States in 1831 and his observations of the American people.

http://ngeorgia.com/history/nghisttt.html

A site for tourism in North Georgia, this page also contains a wealth of information about the Trail of Tears and the Indian Removal of the Jackson era. Compare it to this Missouri tourism site on the Trail of Tears: **http://rosecity.net/tears/**.

http://www.whitehouse.gov/history/presidents/aj7.html

This page contains general information about the Jackson presidency and connects to other White House pages on all the presidents.

http://www.prenhall.com/faragherbrief/map10.1

Analyze the changes in white male suffrage between 1800 and 1830. Why were less wealthy white males, women, and African Americans excluded from voting?

http://www.prenhall.com/faragherbrief/map10.2

Through a series of interactive maps, look at the impact of canals, steamboats, and improved roads on travel time between 1800 and 1857. What effect did the transportation revolution have on national identity?

ELEVEN
THE SOUTH AND SLAVERY

▶ 1 7 9 0 s – 1 8 5 0 s

CHAPTER OUTLINE

AMERICAN COMMUNITIES
Natchez-under-the-Hill

THE WHARFMASTER HAD JUST OPENED THE PUBLIC AUCTION OF CONfiscated cargoes in the center of Natchez when a great cry was heard. An angry crowd of flatboatmen, Bowie knives in hand, was storming up the bluffs from the Mississippi shouting, as the local newspaper reported, "threats of violence and death upon all who attempted to sell and buy their property." It was November 1837, and the town council had just enacted a restrictive tax of $10 per flatboat, a measure designed to rid the wharf district known as Natchez-under-the-Hill of the most impoverished and disreputable of the flatboatmen. The council had made its first confiscation of cargo after nine captains refused to pay this tax. As the boatmen approached, merchants and onlookers shrank back in fear. But the local authorities had called out the militia, and a company of farmers and planters now came marching into the square with their rifles primed and lowered. "The cold and sullen bayonets of the Guards were too hard meat for the Arkansas toothpicks," reported the local press, and "there was no fight." The boatmen sullenly turned and went back down the bluffs. It was the first confrontation in the "Flatboat Wars" that erupted as Mississippi ports tried to bring their troublesome riverfronts under regulation.

The first European to take notice of this "land abundant in subsistence" was a member of Hernando de Soto's expedition in the sixteenth century. The area was "thickly peopled" by the Natchez Indians, he wrote. It was not until the French established the port of Fort Rosalie in the 1720s, however, that Europeans settled in the area. The French destroyed the highly organized society of the Natchez Indians in the 1730s and the port became a major Mississippi River trading center. From Fort Rosalie, French traders bought deerskins, for which there was a large export market, from Choctaw, Chickasaw, and Creek hunters. During the same period, some Africans who had been imported by the French to work as slaves on plantations found roles in the French-Indian trade as boatmen, hunters, soldiers, and interpreters.

When the Spanish took control of the territory in 1763 they laid out the new town of Natchez high on the bluffs, safe from Mississippi flooding. Fort Rosalie, rechristened Natchez-under-the-Hill, continued to flourish as the produce grown by American farmers in Kentucky and Tennessee moved downriver on flatboats. Thus, Americans became the newest additions to the ethnic diversity of this well-established trading center. When Americans took possession of Mississippi in 1798, the district surrounding the port became the most important center of settlement in the Old Southwest. Once again this abundant land of rich, black soil became thickly peopled, but this time with cotton planters and their African American slaves.

Under-the-Hill gained renown as the last stop for boatmen before New Orleans. There were often as many as 150 boats drawn up at the wharves. The crowds along the riverfront, noted John James Audubon, who visited in the 1820s, "formed a medley which it is beyond my power to describe." Mingling among American rivermen of all descriptions were trappers and hunters in fur caps, Spanish shopkeepers in bright smocks, French gentlemen from New Orleans in velvet coats, Indians wrapped in their trade blankets, African Americans both free and slave—a pageant of nations and races. Clapboard shacks and flatboats dragged on shore and converted into storefronts served as grog shops, card rooms, dance halls, and hotels. Whorehouses with women of every age and color abounded.

On the bluffs, meanwhile, the town of Natchez had become the winter home to the southwestern planter elite. They built their mansions with commanding views of the river. A visitor attending a ball at one of these homes was dazzled by the display: "Myriads of wax candles burning in wall sconces, sparkling chandeliers, entrancing music, the scent of jasmine, rose and sweet olive, the sparkle of wine mellowed by age, the flow of wit and brilliant repartee, all were there." Sustaining this American aristocracy was the labor of thousands of enslaved men and women, who lived in the squalid quarters behind the great house and worked the endless fields of cotton. It was they who made possible the greatest accumulations of wealth in early nineteenth-century America.

The Natchez planters, their wealth and confidence growing with cotton's growing dominance of the local economy, found Under-the-Hill an increasing irritant. The Under-the-Hill elite, —gamblers, saloon keepers, and pimps—disturbed the social boundary when they began staying at hotels and even building town houses in Natchez town. And in the wake of the slave revolt led by Nat Turner in Virginia in 1831, in which fifty-five white people were killed, the planters began to feel increasingly threatened by the racial mingling of the riverfront.

In the late 1830s the Natchez elite was jolted by rumors that their slaves were conspiring to murder them during Fourth of July celebrations while Under-the-Hill desperadoes looted their mansions. The rumors reinforced the growing conviction among planters that they could no longer tolerate the polyglot community of the riverfront. The measures that ultimately provoked the flatboatmen's threats in November 1837 soon followed.

In response to these threats, the planters issued an extralegal order giving all the gamblers, pimps, and whores of Under-the-Hill twenty-four hours to evacuate the district. As the Mississippi militia sharpened their bayonets, panic swept the wharves, and that night dozens of flatboats loaded with a motley human cargo headed for the more tolerant community of New Orleans. Other river ports issued similar orders of expulsion. "The towns on the river," one resident remembered, "became purified from a moral pestilence which the law could not cure." Three years later a great tornado hit Under-the-Hill, leveling the shacks that had served so long as a rendezvous for the rivermen, and gradually the Mississippi reclaimed the old river bottom.

These two communities—Natchez, home to the rich slave-owning elite, and Natchez-under-the-Hill, the bustling polyglot trading community—epitomize the paradox of the American South in the early nineteenth century. Enslaved African Americans grew the region's most lucrative crop, cotton. On the resulting profits, aristocratic Southerners built a sumptuous and distinctive lifestyle for themselves. The boatmen and traders of Natchez-under-the-Hill who brought the cotton and other products to market were vital to the planters' prosperity. But the polyglot racial and social mixing of Natchez-under-the-Hill threatened the system of control, built on a rigid distinction between free white people and enslaved black people by which the planters maintained slavery. Because the slave owners could not control the boatmen, they expelled them. This defensive reaction—to seal off the world of slavery from the wider commercial world— exposed the vulnerability of the slave system at the very moment of its greatest commercial success. ■

Natchez

KEY TOPICS

- The domination of southern life by the slave system

- The economic implications of cotton cultivation

- The creation of African American communities under slavery

- The social structure of the white South and its increasing defensivenesss

---

COTTON AND SOUTHERN EXPANSION

Slavery had long dominated southern life. African American slaves grew the great export crops of the colonial period—tobacco, rice, and indigo—on which slave owners' fortunes were made, and their presence shaped southern society and culture (see Chapter 4). Briefly, in the early days of American independence, the slave system waned, only to be revived by the immense profitability of cotton in a newly industrializing world. The overwhelming economic success of cotton and of the slave system on which it depended created a distinctive regional culture quite different from that developing in the North.

The Cotton Gin and Expansion into the Old Southwest

Short-staple cotton had long been recognized as a crop ideally suited to southern soils and growing conditions. But it had one major drawback: the seeds were so difficult to remove from the lint that it took an entire day to hand-clean a single pound of cotton. The invention in 1793 that made cotton growing profitable was the result of collaboration between a young Northerner named Eli Whitney, recently graduated from Yale College, and Catherine Greene, a South Carolina plantation owner and widow of Revolutionary War General Nathanael Greene, who had hired Whitney to tutor her children. Whitney built a prototype cotton engine, dubbed "gin" for short, a simple device consisting of a hand-cranked cylinder with teeth that tore the lint away from the seeds. At Greene's suggestion, the teeth were made of wire. With the cotton gin it was possible to clean more than fifty pounds of cotton a day. Soon large and small planters in the inland regions of Georgia and South Carolina had begun to grow cotton. By 1811, this area was producing 60 million pounds of cotton a year, and exporting most of it to England.

Other areas of the South quickly followed South Carolina and Georgia into cotton production. New land was wanted because cotton growing rapidly depleted the soil. The profits to be made from cotton growing drew a rush of southern farmers into the so-called black belt—an area stretching through western Georgia, Alabama, and Mississippi that was blessed with excep-

The South Expands, 1790–1850   This map shows the dramatic effect cotton production had on southern expansion. From the original six states of 1790, westward expansion, fueled by the search for new cotton lands, added another six states by 1821, and three more by 1850.

tionally fertile soil. Following the War of 1812, Southerners were seized by "Alabama Fever." In one of the swiftest migrations in American history, white Southerners and their slaves flooded into western Georgia and the areas that would become Alabama and Mississippi (the Old Southwest). On this frontier, African American pioneers (albeit involuntary ones) cleared the forests, drained the swamps, broke the ground, built houses and barns, and planted the first crops. This migration caused the population of Mississippi to double and that of Alabama to grow sixteenfold between 1810 and 1820.

Like the simultaneous expansion into the Old Northwest, settlement of the Old Southwest took place at the expense of the region's Indian population (see Chapter 9). Beginning with the defeat of the Creeks at Horseshoe Bend in 1814 and ending with the Cherokee forced migration along the "Trail of Tears" in 1838, the Five Civilized Tribes—the Cherokees, Chickasaws, Choctaws, Creeks, and Seminoles—were forced to give up their lands and move to Indian Territory (see Chapter 10).

On the southern frontier, as on the northern frontier, the killing, confinement, and removal of Indian peoples was the result of white expansion and settlement motivated by the hunger for land and profit. In the South, however, there was an additional motivation, rooted in slavery, for Indian removal: there was simply no room in the southern social order for anything other than white and black, master and slave. Literate, slave-owning "redskins" confused this simple picture: they were too "civilized" to be like slaves, but the wrong color to be masters. Thus, southern Indian removal, like southern expansion, was dictated by the needs of the slave system.

Changing Attitudes toward Slavery

In the flush of freedom following the American Revolution, all the northern states abolished slavery or passed laws for gradual emancipation and a number of slave owners in the Upper South freed their slaves (see Chapter 7). Thomas Jefferson, ever the optimist, claimed that "a total emancipation with the consent of the masters" could not be too far in the future. Nevertheless, southern legislatures were unwilling to write steps toward emancipation into law, preferring to depend on the charity of individual slave owners. Between 1776 and 1786 all the states except South Carolina and Georgia either banned or heavily taxed the international slave trade. Following the successful slave revolt in Haiti in 1791 all the southern states banned the importation of foreign slaves, fearing that Caribbean revolutionaries might incite their own slaves to rebellion.

But attitudes rapidly changed in the South following the invention of the cotton gin in 1793 and the realization of the riches to be made from cotton. White Southerners believed that only African slaves could be forced to work day after day, year after year, at the rapid and brutal pace required in the cotton fields of large plantations in the steamy southern summer. As the production of cotton climbed higher every year in response to a seemingly inexhaustible international demand, so too did the demand for slaves and the conviction of Southerners that slavery was an economic necessity.

It was clear, however, that national opinion found the international slave trade abhorrent, and on January 1, 1808, the earliest date permitted by the Constitution, a bill to abolish the importation of slaves became law. Although a small number of slaves continued to be smuggled from Africa, the growth of the slave labor force after 1808 depended primarily on natural increase. And the ban on foreign importations vastly increased the importance of the internal slave trade.

The Internal Slave Trade

The cotton boom caused a huge increase in the domestic slave trade. Plantation owners in the Upper South (Delaware, Kentucky, Maryland, Virginia, and Tennessee) sold their slaves to meet the demand for labor in the new and expanding cotton-growing regions of the Old Southwest.

Cumulatively, between 1820 and 1860 nearly 50 percent of the slave population of the Upper South took part against their will in southern expansion. More slaves—an estimated 1 million—were uprooted by this internal slave trade and enforced migration in the early nineteenth century than were brought to North America during the entire time the international slave trade was legal (see Chapter 4).

Purchased by slave traders from owners in the Upper South, slaves were gathered together in notorious "slave pens" in places like Richmond and Charleston and then moved south by train or boat. In the interior, they were carried as cargo on steamboats on the Mississippi River, hence the dreaded phrase "sold down the river." Often slaves moved on foot, chained together in groups of fifty or more known as "coffles." Arriving at a central market in the Lower South like Natchez, New Orleans, or Mobile, the slaves, after being carefully inspected by potential buyers, were sold at auction to the highest bidder.

Although popular stereotype portrayed slave traders as unscrupulous outsiders who persuaded kind and reluctant masters to sell their slaves, the historical truth is much harsher. Traders, far from being shunned by slave-owning society, were often respected community members. Similarly, the sheer scale of the slave trade makes it impossible to believe that slave owners only reluctantly parted with their slaves at times of economic distress. Instead, it is clear that many owners sold slaves and separated slave families not out of necessity but to increase their profits.

The Economics of Slavery

The insatiable demand for cotton was a result of the technological and social changes that we know today as the Industrial Revolution. Beginning early in the eighteenth century, a series of inventions resulted in the mechanized spinning and weaving of cloth in the world's first factories in the north of England. The ability of these factories to produce unprecedented amounts of cotton cloth revolutionized the world economy. The invention of the cotton gin came at just the right time. British textile manufacturers were eager to buy all the cotton that the South could produce.

Indeed, the export of cotton from the South was the dynamic force in the developing American economy in the period 1790–1840. Just as the international slave trade had been the dynamic force in the Atlantic economy of the eighteenth century (see Chapter 4), southern slavery financed northern industrial development in the nineteenth century.

The connection between southern slavery and northern industry was very direct. Most mercantile services associated with the cotton trade (insurance, for example) were in northern hands and, significantly, so was shipping. This economic structure was not new. In colonial times, New England ships dominated the African slave trade. Some New England families invested some of their profits in the new technology of textile manufacturing in the 1790s. Other merchants made their money from cotton shipping and brokerage.

Cotton Culture

Cotton cultivation created a different kind of society in the South than in the North. At a time when the North was experiencing the greatest spurt of urban growth in the nation's history, southern cities did not keep pace. Charleston, for example, one of America's five largest cities in 1800, had a population of only 41,000 in 1860, compared with Boston's 177,840 and Baltimore's 212,418. The one exception was New Orleans, the great port at the mouth of the extensive Mississippi River transportation system. In 1860 New Orleans was the nation's fifth largest city, with a population of 169,000. The nine other leading cities were all northern or western. Most of the South remained

rural: less than 3 percent of Mississippi's population lived in cities of more than 2,500 residents, and only 10 percent of Virginia's did. There was no question that concentration on plantation agriculture diverted energy and resources from the South's cities. The agrarian ideal, bolstered by the cotton boom, encouraged the antiurban and anticommercial sentiments of many white Southerners.

The failure of the South to industrialize at the northern rate was not a matter of ignorance but of choice. Southern capital was tied up in land and slaves, and Southerners, buoyed by the world's insatiable demand for cotton, saw no reason to invest in economically risky railroads, canals, and factories. Nor were they eager to introduce the disruptive factor of free wage labor into the tightly controlled slave system. Cotton was safer.

Thus, the cotton boom created a distinctive regional culture. Although cotton was far from being the only crop (the South actually devoted more acreage to corn than to cotton in 1860), its vast profitability affected all aspects of society.

TO BE A SLAVE

The slave population, estimated at 700,000 in 1790, grew to more than 4 million in 1860. After 1808 (when official American participation in the international slave trade ceased) the growth occurred because of natural increase—that is, through births within the slave population. A distinctive African American slave community, which had first emerged in the eighteenth century (see Chapter 4), matured in the early years of the nineteenth century.

The Maturing of the American Slave System

The explosive growth of cotton plantations changed the nature of southern slave labor. In 1850, 55 percent of all slaves were engaged in cotton growing. Another 20 percent labored to produce other crops: tobacco (10 percent), rice, sugar, and hemp. About 15 percent of all slaves were domestic servants, and the remaining 10 percent worked in mining, lumbering, industry, and construction.

Cotton growing concentrated slaves on plantations, in contrast to the more dispersed distribution on smaller farms in earlier generations. Although more than half of all slave owners owned five slaves or fewer, 75 percent of all slaves now lived in groups of ten or more. This disproportionate distribution could have a major impact on a slave's life, for it was a very different matter to be the single slave of a small farmer as opposed to being a member of a 100-person black community on a large plantation. The size of cotton plantations fostered the growth of African American slave communities.

On the other hand, the westward expansion of cotton undermined the stability of these communities. As expansion to the Southwest accelerated, so did the demand for slaves in the newly settled regions, thus fueling the internal slave trade. Slaves were increasingly clustered in the Lower South, as Upper South slave owners sold slaves "down the river" or migrated westward with their entire households. An estimated 1 million slaves migrated involuntarily to the Lower South between 1820 and 1860.

Finally, of all the New World slave societies, the one that existed in the American South was the only one that grew by natural increase rather than through the constant importation of captured Africans. This fact alone made the African American community of the South different from the slave societies of Cuba, the Caribbean islands, and Brazil. The first thing to understand, then, are the circumstances of survival and growth.

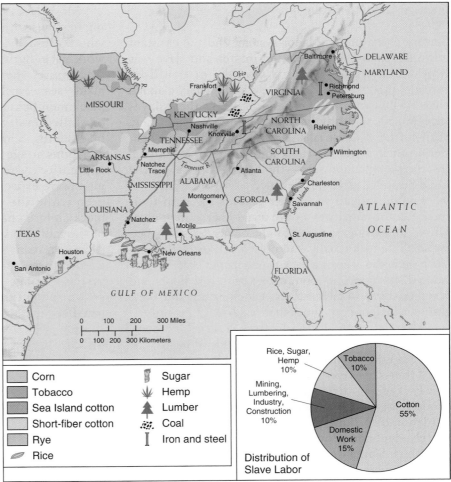

Agriculture, Industry, and Slavery, 1850   The distribution of the slave population in the South was determined by agricultural and industrial patterns. In 1850, 55 percent of all slaves worked in cotton, 10 percent in tobacco, and another 10 percent in rice, sugar, and hemp. Ten percent worked in mining, lumbering, industry, and construction, and 15 percent worked as domestic servants. Slaves were not generally used to grow corn, the staple crop of the yeoman farmer.

The Challenge to Survive

Slave owners thought of the health of their slaves in several ways. First and foremost, they demanded labor from their slaves, and they provided the food, housing, and clothing to keep them healthy enough to work. They also wanted them to be healthy enough to reproduce, for every slave baby increased the wealth of the owner. These sometimes contradictory demands were played out in the lives of slave women.

Mortality rates for slave children under five were twice those for their white counterparts. Historians now say that mortality was high because pregnant black women were inadequately nourished, worked too hard, or were too frequently pregnant, giving birth to six to eight children at year-and-a-half intervals. At the time, owners often accused women of smothering their infants by rolling over them when asleep.

Health remained a lifelong issue for slaves. Malaria and infectious diseases such as yellow fever and cholera were endemic in the South. White people as well as black died, as the life expectancy figures for 1850 show: 40–43 years for white people and 30–33 years for African Americans. Slaves were more at risk because of the circumstances of slave life: poor housing, poor diet, and constant, usually heavy work. Sickness was chronic: 20 percent or more of the slave labor force on most plantations were sick at any one time. Many owners believed sick slaves were only "malingering." Because of the poor medical knowledge of the time, they failed to realize that adequate diet, warm housing, and basic sanitation might have prevented the pneumonia and dysentery that killed or weakened many slaves and that exacted an especially high toll on very young children.

From Cradle to Grave

Slavery was a lifelong labor system, and the constant and inescapable issue between master and slave was how much work the slave would—or could be forced—to do. Southern white slave owners claimed that by housing, feeding, and clothing their slaves from infancy to death they were acting more humanely than northern industrialists who employed people only during their working years. But in spite of occasional instances of manumission—the freeing of a slave—the child born of a slave was destined to remain a slave.

Children lived with their parents (or with their mother if the father was a slave on another farm or plantation) in housing provided by the owner. Slaves owned by small farmers usually had only a bed or mattress to sleep on in the attic or a back room. Larger slave owners housed slaves in one-room cabins with dirt floors and few furnishings (a table, stools, a cooking pot and a few dishes, a bed, or corn-shuck mattresses).

Masters supplied food to their slaves. One common ration for a week was three pounds of meat, four quarts of corn meal, and some molasses for each person. Often slaves were encouraged to supplement their diet by keeping their own gardens, and by hunting—though not, of course, with guns. The opportunity to garden and to hunt, in other words not to be completely dependent on their masters, was one slaves cherished. Slaves were also provided with clothes, usually of rough homespun cloth: two shirts, two pairs of pants, and a pair of shoes a year for men, and enough cloth for women to make an equal number of smocks for themselves and their children yearly. This clothing was barely adequate, and in severe winters slaves suffered badly.

From birth to about age seven, slave children played with one another and with white children, observing and learning how to survive. They saw the penalties: black adults, perhaps their own parents, whipped for disobedience; black women, perhaps their own sisters, violated by white men. And they might see one or both parents sold away as punishment or for financial gain. They would also see signs of white benevolence: special treats for children at holidays, appeals to loyalty from the master or mistress, perhaps friendship with a white child.

The children would learn slave ways of getting along: apparent acquiescence in white demands; pilfering; malingering, sabotage, and other methods of slowing the relentless work pace. Fanny Kemble, a British actress married to a Georgian, was quick to note the pretense in the "outrageous flattery" she received from her husband's slaves. But many white Southerners genuinely believed that their slaves were both less intelligent and more loyal than they really were.

Most slaves spent their lives as field hands, working in gangs with other slaves under a white overseer, who was usually quick to use his whip to keep up the work pace. But there were other occupations. In the "big house" there were jobs for women as cooks, maids, seamstresses, laundresses, weavers, and nurses. Black men became coachmen, valets, and gardeners, or skilled craftsmen—carpenters, mechanics, and blacksmiths. Some children began learning these occupations at age seven or eight, often in an informal apprentice system. Other children, both boys and girls, were expected to take full care of younger children while the parents were working. Of course, black children had no schooling of any kind: in most of the southern states, it was against the law to teach a slave to read, although indulgent owners often rewarded their "pet" slaves by teaching them in spite of the law. At age twelve, slaves were considered full grown and put to work in the fields or in their designated occupation.

House Servants

At first glance, working in the big house might seem to have been preferable to working in the fields. Physically it was much less demanding, and house slaves were often better fed and clothed. They also had much more access to information, for white people, accustomed to servants and generally confident of their loyalty, often forgot their presence and spoke among themselves about matters of interest to the slaves: local gossip, changes in laws or attitudes, policies toward disobedient or rebellious slaves.

For many white people, one of the worst surprises of the Civil War was the eagerness of their house slaves to flee. Considered by their masters the best treated and the most loyal, these slaves were commonly the first to leave or to organize mass desertions. Even the Confederacy's first family, President Jefferson Davis and his wife Varina, were chagrined by the desertion of their house servants in 1864.

From the point of view of the slave, the most unpleasant thing about being a house servant (or the single slave of a small owner) was the constant presence of white people. There was no escape from white supervision. Many slaves who were personal maids and children's nurses were required to live in the big house and rarely saw their own families. Cooks and other house servants were exposed to the tempers and whims of all members of the white family, including the children, who prepared themselves for lives of mastery by practicing giving orders to slaves many times their own age. And house servants, more than any others, were forced to act grateful and ingratiating. The demeaning images of Uncle Tom and the ever-smiling mammy derive from the roles slaves learned as the price of survival. At the same time, genuine intimacy was possible, especially between black nurses and white children. But these were bonds that the white children were ultimately forced to reject as the price of joining the master class.

Artisans and Skilled Workers

A small number of slaves were skilled workers: weavers, seamstresses, carpenters, blacksmiths, mechanics. More slave men than women achieved skilled status (partly because many jobs considered appropriate for women, like cooking, were not thought of as skilled). Solomon Northup, a northern free African American kidnapped into slavery, explained in his 1853 narrative, *Twelve Years a Slave*, that he had been forced to do a variety of work. He had had three owners and had been hired out repeatedly as a carpenter and as a driver of other slaves in a sugar mill; he had also been hired out to clear land for a new Louisiana plantation and to cut sugar cane. Black people worked as lumberjacks (of the 16,000 lumber workers in the South, almost all were slaves), as miners, as deckhands and stokers on Mississippi riverboats, as stevedores loading cotton on the docks of Charleston, Savannah, and New Orleans, and sometimes as workers in the handful of southern factories. Because slaves were their masters' property, the wages of the slave belonged to the owner, not the slave.

The extent to which slaves made up the laboring class was most apparent in cities. A British visitor to Natchez in 1835 noted slave "mechanics, draymen, hostelers, labourers, hucksters and washwomen and the heterogeneous multitude of every other occupation." In the North, all these jobs were performed by white workers. In part, because the South failed to attract as much immigrant labor as the North, southern cities offered both enslaved and free black people opportunities in skilled occupations such as blacksmithing and carpentering that free African Americans in the North were denied.

Field Work and the Gang System of Labor

A full 75 percent of all slaves were field workers, and it was these workers who were most directly affected by the labor system employed on cotton plantations. Cotton was a crop that demanded nearly year-round labor: from planting in April to constant hoeing and cultivation through June to a picking season that began in August and lasted until December. The work was less skilled than on tobacco or sugar plantations, but more constant. Owners divided their slaves into gangs of twenty to twenty-five, a commu-

nal labor pattern reminiscent of parts of Africa, but with a crucial difference—these workers were supervised by overseers with whips. Field hands, both men and women, worked from "can see to can't see" (sunup to sundown) summer and winter, and frequently longer at harvest, when eighteen-hour days were common. Work days were shorter in the winter, perhaps only ten hours.

Work was tedious in the hot and humid southern fields, and the overseer's whip was never far away. Cotton growing was hard work: plowing and planting, chopping weeds with a heavy hoe, and picking the ripe cotton from the stiff and scratchy bolls at the rate of 150 pounds a day. A strong, hardworking slave—a "prime field hand"—was valuable property, worth at least $1,000 to the master. Slaves justifiably took pride in their strength, but aged fast. Poor diet, heavy labor, and the constant threat of the whip undermined health. When they were too old to work, they took on other tasks within the black community, such as caring for young children. Honored by the slave community, the elderly were tolerated by white owners, who continued to feed and clothe them until their deaths. Few actions show the hypocrisy of southern paternalism more clearly than the speed with which white owners evicted their elderly slaves in the 1860s when the end of the slave system was in sight.

Sold "Down the River"

The experience of slaves who were sold or forced by their owners to migrate to the newly opened cotton lands of the Southwest sheds light on the dynamics and tensions underlying the South's cotton-induced prosperity. Although some owners brought existing slave communities with them, the most common experience was that of the individual slave, forcibly separated from family and kin and sent alone with other strangers to a new life far away. For these individual slaves, migration to the Southwest was a long ordeal.

Upper South slaveowners sold slaves to large trading firms, who collected them during the summer in slave pens in Baltimore, Richmond, Nashville, and other northern cities. When the weather cooled, slaves were sent south in chains on foot in coffles, by sailing ship, or by steamboat on the Mississippi to be sold in New Orleans. There, in the streets outside of large slave pens near the French Quarter, thousands of slaves were displayed and sold each year. Dressed in new clothes provided by the traders and exhorted by the traders to walk, run, and otherwise show their stamina, slaves were presented to buyers. For their part, suspicious buyers, unsure that traders and slaves themselves were truthful, poked, prodded, and frequently stripped male and female slaves to be sure they were as healthy as the traders claimed. Aside from obvious signs of illness, buyers often looked for scars on a slave's back: too many scars were a sign of the frequent whippings that a rebellious or "uppity" slave had provoked.

Once sold, slaves could face a variety of conditions. A number, especially in the early years of settlement in the Old Southwest, found themselves in frontier circumstances. Young male slaves were chosen for the backbreaking work of cutting trees and clearing land for cultivation. Some worked side by side with their owners to clear the land for small farms devoted to raising food for immediate consumption. In these circumstances slaves were often highly self-reliant and expected by owners to hunt and fish to supplement the basic diet. This relatively cooperative and permissive attitude was also evident on larger farms engaged in the variety of tasks required in mixed farming. But uniformity and strict discipline were the rule on cotton plantations. Owners eager to clear land rapidly so as to make quick profits often drove the clearing crews at an unmerciful pace. And they attempted to impose strict discipline and a rapid pace on the work gangs that planted, hoed, and harvested cotton. Slaves from other parts of the South, used to more individual and less intense work, hated the cotton regime and most of all hated the overseers who enforced it. They also fought to retain their rights to supplement the owner-supplied diet with their own garden produce and by hunting.

Thus, the new land in the Old Southwest that appeared to offer so much opportunity for owners bred tensions caused by forcible sale and migration, by the organization and pace of cotton cultivation, and by the owners' efforts to abrogate what slaves saw as traditional rights.

THE AFRICAN AMERICAN COMMUNITY

Surely no group in American history has faced a harder job of community building than the black people of the antebellum South. Living in intimate, daily contact with their oppressors, African Americans nevertheless created an enduring culture of their own, a culture that had far-reaching and lasting influence on all of southern life and American society as a whole (see Chapter 4). Within their own communities, African American values and attitudes, and especially their own forms of Christianity, played a vital part in shaping a culture of endurance and resistance.

Few African Americans were unfortunate enough to live their lives alone among white people. Over half of all slaves lived on plantations with twenty or more other slaves, and others, on smaller farms, had links with slaves on nearby properties. Urban slaves were able to make and sustain so many secret contacts with other African Americans in cities or towns that slave owners wondered whether slave discipline could be maintained in urban settings. There can be no question that the bonds among African Americans were what sustained them during the years of slavery.

In law, slaves were property, to be bought, sold, rented, worked, and otherwise used (but not abused or killed) as the owner saw fit. But slaves were also human beings, with feelings, needs, and hopes. Even though most white Southerners believed black people to be members of an inferior, childish race, all but the most brutal masters acknowledged the humanity of their slaves. Furthermore, as a practical matter, white owners had long since learned that unhappy or rebellious slaves were poor workers. White masters learned to live with the two key institutions of African American community life: the family and the African American church.

Slave Families

No southern state recognized slave marriages in law. Most owners, though, not only recognized but encouraged them, sometimes even performing a kind of wedding ceremony for the couple. Masters sometimes tried to arrange marriages, but slaves usually found their own mates, sometimes on their own plantation, sometimes elsewhere. Masters encouraged marriage among their slaves, believing it made the men less rebellious, and for economic reasons they were eager for the slave women to have children.

Whatever marriages meant to the masters, to slaves they were a haven of love and intimacy in a cruel world and the basis of the African American community. Husbands and wives had a chance, in their own cabins, to live their own lives among loved ones. Husband and wife cooperated in loving and sheltering their children and teaching them survival skills. Above all, family meant continuity. Parents made great efforts to teach their children the family history and to surround them with a supportive and protective kinship network.

The strength of these ties is shown by the many husbands, wives, children, and parents who searched for each other after the Civil War when slavery came to an end. As the ads in black newspapers indicate, some family searches went on into the 1870s and 1880s, and many ended in failure.

Given the vast size of the internal slave trade, fear of separation was constant—and real. Separations of slave families were common. One in every five slave marriages was broken, and one in every three children sold away from their families. These figures clearly show that slave owners' support for slave marriages was secondary to their desire for profits.

In the face of constant separation, slave communities attempted to act like larger families. Following practices developed early in slavery, children were taught to respect and learn from all the elders, to call all adults of a certain age "aunt" or "uncle," and to call children of their own age "brother" or "sister" (see Chapter 4). Thus, in the absence of their own family, separated children could quickly find a place and a source of comfort in the slave community to which they had been sold.

The kinship of the entire community, where old people were respected and young ones cared for, represented a conscious rejection of white paternalism. The slaves' ability, in the most difficult of situations, to structure a community that expressed their values, not those of their masters, was extraordinary. Equally remarkable was the way in which African Americans reshaped Christianity to serve their needs.

African American Religion

Slaves brought religions from Africa but were not allowed to practice them, for white people feared religion would create a bond among slaves that might lead to rebellion. African religions managed to survive in the slave community in forms that white people considered as "superstition" or "folk belief," such as the medicinal use of roots by conjurers. Religious ceremonies survived, too, in late-night gatherings deep in the woods where the sound of drumming, singing, and dancing could not reach white ears (see Chapter 4).

Most masters of the eighteenth century made little effort to Christianize their slaves, afraid they might take the promises of universal brotherhood and equality too literally. The Great Awakening, which swept the South after the 1760s, introduced many slaves to Christianity, often in mixed congregations with white people (see Chapter 5). The transformation was completed by the Second Great Awakening, which took root among black and white Southerners in the 1790s. The number of African American converts, preachers, and lay teachers grew rapidly, and a distinctive form of Christianity took shape.

The first African American Baptist and Methodist churches were founded in Philadelphia in 1794 by the Reverend Absalom Jones and the Reverend Richard Allen. In 1816, the Reverend Allen joined with African American ministers from other cities to form the African

Five generations of one family on a South Carolina plantation are gathered together for this 1862 picture, providing living evidence of the importance of kinship in the building of African American communities.

SOURCE: Library of Congress.

Methodist Episcopal (AME) denomination. By the 1830s, free African American ministers like Andrew Marshall of Savannah and many more enslaved black preachers and lay ministers preached, sometimes secretly, to slaves. Their message was one of faith and love, of deliverance, of the coming of the promised land.

African Americans found in Christianity a powerful vehicle to express their longings for freedom and justice. But why did their white masters allow it? Some white people, themselves converted by the revivals, doubtless believed that they should not deny their slaves the same religious experience. But the evangelical religion of the early nineteenth century was also a powerful form of social control. Southern slave owners, seeking to counteract the appeal of African American religion, expected their Christianity to make their slaves obedient and peaceful. Forbidding their slaves to hold their own religious gatherings, owners insisted that their slaves attend white church services. Slaves were quick to realize the owners' purpose. As a former Texas slave recalled: "We went to church on the place and you ought to heard that preachin'. Obey your massa and missy, don't steal chickens and eggs and meat, but nary a word 'bout havin' a soul to save." But at night, away from white eyes, they held their own prayer meetings.

In churches and in spontaneous religious expressions, the black community made Christianity its own. Fusing Christian texts with African elements of group activity, such as the circle dance, the call-and-response pattern, and, above all, group singing, black people created a unique community religion full of emotion, enthusiasm, and protest. Nowhere is this spirit more compelling than in the famous spirituals: "Go Down Moses," with its mournful refrain "Let my people go"; the rousing "Didn't My Lord Deliver Daniel . . . and why not every man"; the haunting "Steal Away."

Nevertheless, this was not a religion of rebellion, for that was unrealistic for most slaves. Black Christianity was an enabling religion: it helped slaves to survive, not as passive victims of white tyranny but as active opponents of an oppressive system that they daily protested in small but meaningful ways.

Freedom and Resistance

Whatever their dreams, most slaves knew they would never escape. Almost all successful escapes in the nineteenth century (approximately 1,000 a year) were from the Upper South (Delaware, Maryland, Virginia, Kentucky, and Missouri). A slave in the Lower South or the Southwest simply had too far to go to reach freedom. In addition, white Southerners were determined to prevent escapes. Slave patrols were a common sight on southern roads. Any black person without a pass from his or her master was captured (usually roughly) and returned home to certain punishment. But despite almost certain recapture,

Harriet Tubman escaped in 1849 from slavery in Maryland and returned nineteen times to free almost 300 other slaves. Here Tubman (at left), the most famous "conductor" on the Underground Railroad, is shown with some of those she led to freedom.

SOURCE: Sophia Smith Collection, Smith College.

slaves continued to flee and to help others do so. Escaped slave Harriet Tubman of Maryland, who made nineteen rescue missions freeing 300 slaves in all, had extraordinary determination and skill.

Slaves who knew they could not reach freedom still frequently demonstrated their desire for liberty or their discontent over mistreatment by taking unauthorized leave from their plantation. Hidden in nearby forests or swamps, provided with food smuggled by other slaves from the plantation, the runaway might return home after a week or so, often to rather mild punishment. Temporary flight by any slave was a warning sign of discontent that a wise master did not ignore.

Slave Revolts

The ultimate resistance, however, was the slave revolt. Southern history was dotted with stories of former slave conspiracies and rumors of current plots (see Chapter 4). Every white Southerner knew about the last-minute failure of Gabriel Prosser's insurrection in Richmond in 1800 and the chance discovery of Denmark Vesey's plot in Charleston in 1822. But when in 1831, Nat Turner actually started a rebellion in which a number of white people were killed, southern fears were greatly magnified.

A literate man, Nat Turner was a lay preacher, but he was also a slave. It was Turner's intelligence and strong religious commitment that made him a leader in the slave community and, interestingly, these very same qualities led his master, Joseph Travis, to treat him with kindness even though Turner had once run away for a month after being mistreated by an overseer. Turner began plotting his revolt after a religious vision in which he saw "white spirits and black spirits engaged in battle"; "the sun was darkened—the thunder rolled in the Heavens, and blood flowed in streams." Turner and five other slaves struck on the night of August 20, 1831, first killing Travis, who, Turner said, "was to me a kind master, and placed the greatest confidence in me; in fact, I had no cause to complain of his treatment of me."

Moving from plantation to plantation and killing a total of fifty-five white people, the rebels numbered sixty by the next morning, when they fled from a group of armed white men. More than forty blacks were executed after the revolt, including Turner, who was captured accidentally after he had hidden for two months in the woods. Thomas R. Gray, a white lawyer to whom Turner dictated a lengthy confession before his death, was impressed by Turner's composure. "I looked on him," Gray said, "and my blood curdled in my veins." If intelligent, well-treated slaves such as Turner could plot revolts, how could white Southerners ever feel safe?

Gabriel's Rebellion, the Denmark Vesey plot, and Nat Turner's Revolt were the most prominent examples of organized slave resistance, but they were far from the only ones. Conspiracies and actual or rumored slave resistance began in colonial times (see Chapter 4) and never ceased. These plots exposed the truth white Southerners preferred to ignore: Only force kept Africans and African Americans enslaved, and because no system of control could ever be total, white Southerners could never be completely safe from the possibility of revolt. Nat Turner brought white Southerners' fears to the surface. After 1831, the possibility of slave insurrection was never far from their minds.

Free African Americans

Another source of white disquiet was the growing number of free African Americans. By 1860, nearly 250,000 free black people lived in the South. For most, freedom dated from before 1800, when antislavery feeling among slave owners in the Upper South was widespread and cotton cultivation had yet to boom.

Most free black people lived in the countryside of the Upper South, where they worked as tenant farmers or farm laborers. Urban African Americans were much more visible. Life was especially difficult for female-headed families because only the most menial work—street peddling and laundry work, for example—was available to free black women. The situation for African American males was somewhat better. Although they were discriminated against in employment and in social life, there were opportunities for skilled black craftsmen in trades such as blacksmithing and carpentry. Cities such as Charleston, Savannah, and Natchez were home to flourishing free African American communities that formed their own churches and fraternal orders.

Throughout the South in the 1830s, state legislatures tightened black codes—laws concerning free black people. Free African Americans could not carry firearms, could not purchase slaves (unless they were members of their own family), and were liable to the criminal penalties meted out to slaves (that is, whippings and summary judgments without a jury trial). They could not testify against whites, hold office, vote, or serve in the militia. In other words, except for the right to own property, free blacks had no civil rights.

THE WHITE MAJORITY

Two-thirds of all Southerners did not own slaves, yet slave owners dominated the social and political life of the region. Who were the two-thirds of white Southerners who did not own slaves, and how did they live? Throughout the South, slave owners occupied the most productive land: tobacco-producing areas in Virginia and Tennessee, coastal areas of South Carolina and Georgia where rice and cotton grew, sugar lands in Louisiana, and large sections of the cotton-producing black belt, which stretched westward from South Carolina to Texas. Small farmers, usually without slaves, occupied the rest of the rural land and a small middle class lived in the cities of the South.

The Middle Class

In the predominantly rural South, cities provided a home for a commercial middle class of merchants, bankers, factors (agents), and lawyers on whom the agricultural economy depended to sell its produce to a world market. Urban growth lagged far behind the North. The cities that grew were major shipping centers for agricultural goods: the river cities of Louisville, St. Louis, Memphis, and New Orleans, and the cotton ports of Mobile and Savannah. Formal educational institutions, libraries, and cultural activities were located in cities, and so were the beginnings of the same kind of entreprenurial and commercial spirit so evident in the North.

The effort of William Gregg of South Carolina to establish the cotton textile industry illustrates some of the problems facing southern entrepreneurs. Gregg became convinced that textile factories were a good way to diversify the southern economy and to provide a living for poor whites. He enthusiastically publicized the findings of his tour of northern textile mills, but found a cool reception. His request to the planter-dominated South Carolina legislature for a charter of incorporation for a textile mill passed by only one vote. In 1846 he built a model mill and a company town in Graniteville, South Carolina, that attracted poor white families as employees. Gregg adapted southern paternalism to industry, providing a school and churches and prohibiting alcohol and dancing, yet paying his workers 20 percent less than northern wages.

John Letcher, a lawyer and politician in Lexington, Virginia, had typical moderate, urban, middle-class attitudes. A Democrat, he served four terms in the U.S. Congress in the 1850s, where he acquired a reputation as a moderate in favor of limited government, earning the nickname "Honest John Letcher, Watchdog of the

Treasury." Elected governor of Virginia in 1860, he led his state out of the Union once the Civil War began and devoted his efforts to unity in pursuit of Confederate war aims. Like some other members of the urban middle class, he owned only enough slaves (a family with children) to do the domestic work for his own family, and at one time, early in his career, he had favored gradual emancipation.

Many southern planters scorned members of the commercial middle class like Letcher and Gregg because they had to please their suppliers and customers, and thus lacked, in their eyes, true independence. No one cherished his independence more than the yeoman farmer.

Yeomen

The word "yeoman," originally a British term for a farmer who works his own land, is often applied to independent farmers of the South, most of whom lived on family-sized farms. Although yeoman farmers sometimes owned a few slaves, in general they and their families worked their land by themselves. Typical of the yeoman-farmer community was northwestern Georgia, once home to the Creeks and Cherokees, but now populated by communities of small farmers who grew enough vegetables to feed their families, including corn, which they either ate themselves or fed to hogs. In addition, these farmers raised enough cotton every year (usually no more than one or two bales) to bring in a little cash.

Where yeomen and large slave owners lived side by side, as in the Georgia black belt where cotton was the major crop, slavery again provided a link between the rich and middle class. Large plantation owners often bought food for their slaves from small local farmers, ground the latter's corn in the plantation mill, ginned their cotton, and transported and marketed it as well. But although planters and much smaller yeomen were part of a larger community network, in the black belt the large slave owners were clearly dominant. Only in their own up-country communities did yeomen feel truly independent.

Poor White People

Not all small farmers were on an equal footing. One-third of the farmers in the Georgia up-country were tenant farmers. Some were farmers' sons, striking out on their own while waiting to inherit their fathers' land. But others were poor whites with little hope of improving their condition. From 30 to 50 percent of all southern white people were landless, a proportion similar to that in the North. But the existence of slavery affected the opportunities for southern poor white people. Slaves made up the permanent, stable workforce in agriculture and in many skilled trades. Many poor white people led highly transient lives in search of work, such as doing farm labor at harvest time, which was only temporary. Others were tenant farmers working under share-tenancy arrangements that kept them in debt to the landowner.

Relationships between poor whites and black slaves were complex. White men and women often worked side by side with black slaves in the fields and were socially and sexually intimate with enslaved and free African Americans. White people engaged in clandestine trade to supply slaves with items like liquor that slave owners prohibited, helped slaves to escape, and even (in an 1835 Mississippi case) were executed for their participation in planning a slave revolt. At the same time, the majority of poor white people insisted, sometimes violently, on their racial superiority over blacks. For their part, many African American slaves, better dressed, better nourished, and healthier, dismissed them as "poor white trash." But the fact was that the difficult lives of poor whites, whom one contemporary described as "a third class of white people," served to blur the crucial racial distinction between independent whites and supposedly inferior, dependent black people on which the system of slavery rested.

Yeoman Values

In 1828 and 1832, southern yeomen and poor white men voted overwhelmingly for Andrew Jackson. They were drawn variously to his outspoken policy of ruthless expansionism, his appeals to the common man, and his rags-to-riches ascent from poor boy to rich slave owner. It was a career many hoped to emulate. The dominance of the large planters was due at least in part to the ambition of many yeomen, especially those with two or three slaves, to expand their holdings and become rich. These farmers, enthusiastic members of the lively democratic politics of the South, supported the leaders they hoped to join.

But for a larger group of yeomen, independence and not wealth was most important. Many southern yeomen lived apart from large slaveholders, in the up-country regions where plantation agriculture was unsuitable. The very high value southern yeomen placed on freedom grew directly from their own experience as self-sufficient property-owning farmers in small, family-based communities and from the absolute, patriarchal control they exercised over their own wives and children. This was a way of life that southern "plain folk" were determined to preserve. It made them resistant to the economic opportunities and challenges that capitalism and industrialization posed for northern farmers, which southern yeomen perceived as encroachments on their freedom.

The irony was that the freedom yeomen so prized rested on slavery. White people could count on slaves to perform the hardest and worst labor, and the degradation of slave life was a daily reminder of the freedom they enjoyed in comparison. Slavery meant that all white people, rich and poor, were equal in the sense that they were all free. This assumption of white skin privilege had formed in the eighteenth century as slavery became the answer to the South's labor problem (see Chapter 4). The democratization of politics in the early nineteenth century and the enactment of nearly universal white manhood suffrage perpetuated the belief in white skin privilege, even though the gap between rich and poor white people was widening.

PLANTERS

Remarkably few slave owners fit the popular stereotype of the rich and leisured plantation owner with hundreds of acres of land and hundreds of slaves. Only 36 percent of southern white people owned slaves in 1830, and only 2.5 percent owned fifty slaves or more. Just as yeomen and poor whites were diverse, so, too, were southern slave owners.

Small Slave Owners

The largest group of slave owners were small yeomen taking the step from subsistence agriculture to commercial production. To do this in the South's agricultural economy, they had to own slaves. But upward mobility was difficult. Owning one or two slaves increased farm production only slightly, and it was hard to accumulate the capital to buy more. One common pattern was for a slave owner to leave one or two slaves to farm while he worked another job (this arrangement usually meant that his wife had assumed responsibility for their supervision). In other cases, small farmers worked side by side with their slaves in the fields. In still other cases, owners hired out their slaves to larger slave owners.

In every case, the owner was economically vulnerable: a poor crop or a downturn in cotton prices could wipe out his gains and force him to sell his slaves. When times improved, he might buy a new slave or two and try again, but getting a secure footing on the bottom rung of the slave-owner ladder was very difficult. The roller-coaster economy of the early nineteenth century did not help matters, and the Panic of 1837 was a serious setback to many small farmers.

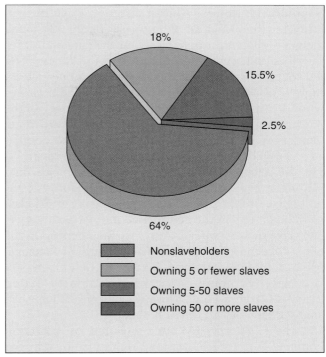

Slaveholding and Class Structure in the South, 1830   The great mass of the southern white population were yeoman farmers. In 1830, slave owners made up only 36 percent of the southern white population; owners of more than fifty slaves constituted a tiny 2.5 percent. Yet they and the others who were middling planters dominated politics, retaining the support of yeomen who prized their freedom as white men above class-based politics.

SOURCE: U.S. Bureau of the Census.

For a smaller group of slave owners, the economic struggle was not so hard. Middle-class professional men—lawyers, doctors, and merchants—frequently managed to become large slave owners because they already had capital (the pay from their professions) to invest in land and slaves. Sometimes they received payment for their services not in money but in slaves. These owners were the most likely to own skilled slaves—carpenters, blacksmiths, and other artisans— and to rent them out for profit. By steady accumulation, the most successful members of this middle class were able to buy their way into the slave-owning elite and to confirm that position by marrying their sons or daughters into the aristocracy.

The Planter Elite

The slave-owning elite, those 2.5 percent who owned fifty slaves or more, enjoyed the prestige, the political leadership, and the lifestyle to which many white

Southerners aspired. Almost all great slave owners inherited their wealth. They were rarely self-made men, although most tried to add to the land and slaves they had inherited. Men of wealth and property had led southern politics since colonial times, but increasingly after 1820 it was men from the middle classes who were most often elected to political office. As the nation moved toward universal manhood suffrage, planters tried to learn how to appeal to the popular vote, but most never acquired "the common touch." It was the smaller slave owners who formed a clear majority in every southern state legislature before 1860.

The eastern seaboard had first given rise to a class of rich planters in the colonial period. As Southerners and slave owning spread westward, membership in the elite broadened to include the new wealth of Alabama, Mississippi, Louisiana, and Texas. The rich planters of the Natchez community were popularly called "nabobs" (from a Hindi word for Europeans who had amassed fabulous wealth in India).

The extraordinary concentration of wealth in Natchez—in 1850 it was the richest county in the nation—fostered a self-consciously elite lifestyle that derived not from long tradition but from suddenly acquired riches.

Plantation Life

The urban life of the Natchez planters was unusual. Many wealthy planters, especially those on new lands in the Old Southwest, lived in isolation on their plantations with their families and slaves. Through family networks, common boarding school experience, political activity, and frequent visiting, the small new planter elite consciously worked to create and maintain a distinctive lifestyle that was modeled on that of the English aristocracy, as Southerners understood it. This entailed a large estate, a spacious, elegant mansion, and lavish hospitality. For men, the gentlemanly lifestyle meant immersion in masculine activities such as hunting, soldiering, or politics, and a touchy concern with "honor" that could lead to duels and other acts of bravado. Women of the slave-owning elite, in contrast, were expected to be gentle, charming, and always welcoming of relatives, friends, and other guests.

But this gracious image was at odds with the economic reality. Large numbers of black slaves had to be forced to work to produce the wealth of the large plantations. A large plantation was an enterprise that required many hands, many skills, and a lot of management. Large plantation owners might have overseers or black drivers to supervise field work, but frequently they themselves had direct financial control of daily operations.

A paternalistic ideology infused the life of large plantations that permitted the planter elite to rationalize their use of slaves and the submissiveness they demanded of wives. According to this ideology, each plantation was a family composed of both black and white. The master, as head of the plantation, was head of the family, and the mistress was his "helpmate." The master was obligated to provide for all of his family, both black and white, and to treat them with humanity. In return, slaves were to work properly and do as they were told, as children would. Most elite slave owners spoke of their position of privilege as a duty and a burden. (Their wives were even more outspoken about the burdensome aspects of supervising slave labor, which they bore more directly than their husbands.) John C. Calhoun spoke for many slave owners when he described the plantation as "a little community" in which the master directed all operations so that the abilities and needs of every member, black and white, were "perfectly harmonized." Convinced of their own benevolence, slave owners expected not only obedience but also gratitude from all members of their great "families."

The Plantation Mistress

Southern paternalism not only laid special burdens on plantation mistresses but put restrictions on their lives and activities not experienced by northern women of the same social rank. The difficulties experienced by these in some ways quite privileged women illustrate the way the slave system affected every aspect of the personal life of slave owners.

Plantation mistresses spent most of their lives tending "family" members—including slaves—in illness and in childbirth, and supervising their slaves' performance of such daily tasks as cooking, housecleaning, weaving, and sewing. In addition, the plantation mistress often had to spend hours, even days, of behind-the-scenes preparation for the crowds of guests she was expected to welcome in her role as elegant and gracious hostess.

Despite the reality of the plantation mistress's daily supervision of an often extensive household, she did not rule it: her husband did. The plantation master was the source of authority to whom wife, children, and slaves were expected to look for both rewards and punishments. A wife who challenged her husband or sought more independence from him threatened the entire paternalistic system of control. After all, if she were not dependent and obedient, why should slaves be? In addition, although many southern women were deeply affected by evangelical religion and exhortations to care for those in need, their response was personal rather than social. Enlisting in reform movements like their northern counterparts would have been far too threatening to the system of slave control to be tolerated in the South, for it might have led slaves to believe that their lives, too, could be improved.

Many southern women also suffered deeply from their isolation from friends and kin. Sometimes the isolation of life on rural plantations could be overcome by long visits, but women with many small children and extensive responsibilities found it difficult to leave. Plantation masters, on the other hand, often traveled widely for political and business reasons.

Plantation women in the Old Southwest, many of whom had moved unwillingly and now were far from their families on the eastern seaboard, were particularly lonely. Mary Kendall wrote, "For about three weeks I did not have the pleasure of seeing one white female face, there being no white family except our own upon the plantation." She was surrounded by women, but the gap between the white mistress and her black slaves was generally unbridgeable.

Although on every plantation black women served as nursemaids to young white children and as lifelong maids to white women, usually accompanying them when they moved as brides into their own homes, there are few historical examples of genuine sympathy and understanding of black women by white women of the slave-owning class. Few of the latter seemed to understand the sadness, frustration, and despair often experienced by their lifelong maids, who were forced to leave their own husbands and children to serve in their mistresses' new homes. A number of southern women did rail against "the curse of slavery," but few meant the inhumanity of the system; most were actually complaining about the extra work entailed by housekeeping with slaves. Years later many former slaves remembered their mistresses as being kinder than their masters, but fully a third of such accounts mention cruel whippings and other punishments by white women.

Coercion and Violence

There were generous and benevolent masters, but most large slave owners believed that constant discipline and coercion were necessary to make slaves work hard. Some slave owners used their slaves with great brutality. Owners who killed slaves were occasionally brought to trial (and usually acquitted), but no legal action was taken in the much more frequent cases of excessive punishment, general abuse, and rape. All southern slave owners, not just those who experienced the special tensions of new and isolated plantations in

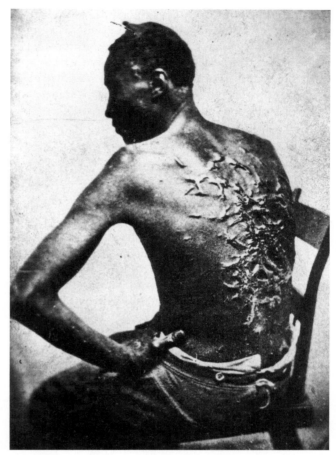

This Louisiana slave named Gordon was photographed in 1863 after he had escaped to Union lines during the Civil War. He bears the permanent scars of the violence that lay at the heart of the slave system. Few slaves were so brutally marked, but all lived with the threat of beatings if they failed to obey.

SOURCE: National Archives and Records Administration.

the Old Southwest, were engaged in a constant battle of wills with their slaves that owners frequently resolved by violence.

One of the most common violations of the paternalistic code of behavior (and of southern law) was the sexual abuse of female slaves by their masters. Usually, masters forcibly raped their women slaves at will, and slave women had little hope of defending themselves from these attacks. Sometimes, however, long-term intimate relationships between masters and slaves developed.

It was rare for slave owners to publicly acknowledge fathering slave children or to free these children, and black women and their families were helpless to protest their treatment. Equally silenced was the master's wife, who for reasons of modesty as well as her subordinate position was not supposed to notice either

her husband's infidelity or his flagrant crossing of the color lines. As Mary Boykin Chesnut, wife of a South Carolina slave owner, vehemently confided to her diary: "God forgive us, but ours is a monstrous system. . . . Like the patriarchs of old, our men live all in one house with their wives and their concubines, and the mulattoes one sees in every family partly resemble the white children."

THE DEFENSE OF SLAVERY

"Slavery informs all our modes of life, all our habits of thought, lies at the basis of our social existence, and of our political faith," announced South Carolina planter William Henry Trescot in 1850, explaining why the South would secede from the Union before giving up slavery. Slavery bound white and black Southerners together in tortuous ways that eventually led, as Trescot had warned, to the Civil War.

The sheer numbers of African Americans reinforced white people's perpetual fears of black retaliation for the violence exercised by the slave master.

Every rumor of slave revolts, real or imagined, kept those fears alive. The basic question was this: What might slaves do if they were not controlled?

Developing Proslavery Arguments

Southerners increasingly sought to justify slavery. They found justifications for slavery in the Bible and in the histories of Greece and Rome, both slave-owning societies. The strongest defense was a legal one: the Constitution allowed slavery. Though never specifically mentioned in the final document, slavery had been a major issue between North and South at the Constitutional Convention in 1787. In the end, the delegates agreed that seats in the House of Representatives would be apportioned by counting all of the white population and three-fifths of the black people (Article I, Section 2, Paragraph 3); they included a clause requiring the return of runaway slaves who had crossed state lines (Article IV, Section 2, Paragraph 3); and they agreed that Congress could not abolish the international slave trade for twenty years (Article I, Section 9, Paragraph 1). There was absolutely no question: the Constitution did recognize slavery.

The Missouri Crisis of 1819–20 alarmed most Southerners, who were shocked by the evidence of widespread antislavery feeling in the North. South Carolinians viewed Denmark Vesey's conspiracy, occurring only two years after the Missouri debate, as an example of the harm that irresponsible northern antislavery talk could cause. After Nat Turner's revolt in 1831, Governor John Floyd of Virginia blamed the uprising on "Yankee peddlers and traders" who supposedly told slaves that "all men were born free and equal." Thus, northern antislavery opinion and the fear of slave uprisings were firmly linked in southern minds.

After Nat Turner

In 1831 the South began to close ranks in defense of slavery. Several factors contributed to this regional solidarity. Nat Turner's revolt was important, linked as it was in the minds of many South-

Population Patterns in the South, 1850 In South Carolina and Mississippi the enslaved African American population outnumbered the white population; in four other Lower South states the percentage was above 40 percent. These ratios frightened many white Southerners. White people also feared the free black population, though only three states in the Upper South and Louisiana had free black populations of over 3 percent. Six states had free black populations that were so small (less than 1 percent) as to be statistically insignificant.

erners with antislavery agitation from the North. Militant abolitionist William Lloyd Garrison began publishing the *Liberator*, the newspaper that was to become the leading antislavery organ, in 1831. The British gave notice that they would soon abolish slavery on the sugar plantations of the West Indies, an action that seemed to many Southerners much too close to home. Emancipation for West Indian slaves came in 1834. Finally, 1831 was the year before the Nullification Crisis (see Chapter 10) was resolved. Although the other southern states did not support the hotheaded South Carolinians who called for secession, they did sympathize with the argument that the federal government had no right to interfere with a state's special interest (namely, slavery).

In 1835, a crowd broke into a Charleston post office, made off with bundles of antislavery literature, and set an enormous bonfire, to fervent state and regional acclaim. By 1835, every southern legislature had tightened its laws concerning control of slaves. For example, they tried to blunt the effect of abolitionist literature by passing laws forbidding slaves to learn how to read. By 1860, it is estimated, only 5 percent of all slaves could read. Slaves were forbidden to gather for dances, religious services, or any kind of organized social activity without a white person present. Other laws made manumission illegal and placed even more restrictions on the lives of free black people.

Attempts were made to stifle all open debate about slavery within the South; dissenters were pressured to remain silent or to leave. A few, such as James G. Birney and Sarah and Angelina Grimké of South Carolina, left for the North to act on their antislavery convictions, but most chose silence. Southern politicians painted melodramatic pictures of a beleaguered white South hemmed in on all sides by "fanatic" antislavery states, while at home Southerners were forced to contemplate what might happen when they had "to let loose among them, freed from the wholesome restraints of patriarchal authority . . . an idle, worthless, profligate set of free negroes" whom they feared would "prowl the . . . streets at night and [haunt] the woods during the day armed with whatever weapons they could lay their hands on."

Finally, southern apologists moved beyond defensiveness to develop proslavery arguments. One of the first to do this was James Henry Hammond, elected a South Carolina congressman in 1834. In 1836 Hammond delivered a major address to Congress in which he denied that slavery was evil. Rather, he claimed, it had produced "the highest toned, the purest, best organization of society that has ever existed on the face of the earth."

In 1854 another southern spokesman, George Fitzhugh, asserted that "the negro slaves of the South are the happiest, and, in some sense, the freest people in the world" because all the responsibility for their care was borne by concerned white masters. Fitzhugh contrasted southern paternalism with the heartless individualism that ruled the lives of northern "wage slaves."

Changes in the South

In spite of these defensive and repressive proslavery measures, which made the South seem monolithic in northern eyes, there were some surprising indicators of dissent. Most came from up-country nonslaveholders. One protest occurred in the Virginia state legislature in 1832, when non-slave-holding delegates, alarmed by the Nat Turner rebellion, forced a two-week debate on the merits of gradual abolition. In the final vote, abolition was defeated 73 to 58. The subject was never raised again.

But slavery was not a static system. From the 1830s on, financial changes increasingly underlined class differences between southern whites. It was harder to become a slaveholder: from 1830 to 1860 slave owners declined from 36 to 25 percent of the population.

An even more alarming trend was evident in southern cities, where the slave system was disintegrating. The number of urban slaves had greatly decreased because plantation owners deeply distrusted the effect of cities on the institution of slavery. Urban slaves led much more informed lives than rural ones and were often in daily contact with free black and urban poor whites. Many slaves were hired out and a number even hired out their own time, making them nearly indistinguishable from northern "free labor." Other urban slaves worked in commercial and industrial enterprises in jobs that were nearly indistinguishable from those of whites. Planters viewed all of these changes with suspicion, yet they also had to acknowledge that southern cities were successful and bustling centers of commerce.

In North Carolina, disputes between slave owners and nonslaveholders erupted in print in 1857, when Hinton Helper published an attack on slavery in a book titled *The Impending Crisis*. His protest was an indicator of the growing tensions between the haves and the have-nots in the South. Equally significant, though, Helper's book was published in New York, where he was forced to move once his views became known.

In spite of these signs of tension and dissent, the main lines of the southern argument were drawn in

CHRONOLOGY

1790s	Second Great Awakening	1832–38	"Flush Times": second wave of westward expansion
	Black Baptist and African Methodist Episcopal churches founded	1832	Virginia legislature debates and defeats a measure for gradual emancipation
1793	Cotton gin invented		
1800	Gabriel Prosser's revolt discovered in Virginia	1834	Britain frees slaves throughout the empire, including in its Caribbean colonies
1806	Virginia tightens law on manumission of slaves	1835	Charleston crowd burns abolitionist literature
1808	Congress prohibits U.S. participation in the international slave trade		Tightening of black codes completed by southern legislatures
1816–20	"Alabama Fever": migration to the Old Southwest	1836	Congress passes "gag rule" to prevent discussion of antislavery petitions
1819–20	Missouri Crisis		James Henry Hammond announces to Congress that slavery is not evil
1822	Denmark Vesey's conspiracy in Charleston	1846	William Gregg opens model textile mill at Graniteville, South Carolina
1831	Nat Turner's revolt in Virginia	1854	George Fitzhugh publishes *Sociology for the South*, a defense of slavery
	William Lloyd Garrison begins publishing antislavery newspaper, the *Liberator*	1857	Hinton Helper publishes *The Impending Crisis*, an attack on slavery
1832	Nullification Crisis		

the 1830s and remained fixed thereafter. The defense of slavery stifled debate within the South, prevented a search for alternative labor systems, and narrowed the possibility of cooperation in national politics. In time, it made compromise impossible.

CONCLUSION

The amazing growth of cotton production after 1793 transformed the South and the nation. Physically, the South expanded explosively westward. Cotton production was based on the labor of African American slaves, who built strong communities under extremely difficult circumstances. The cohesion of African American families and the powerful faith of African American Christianity were the key community elements that bred a spirit of endurance and resistance. White Southerners, two-thirds of whom did not own slaves, denied their real dependence on slave labor by claiming equality in white skin privilege, while slave owners boasted of their own paternalism. In the 1830s, the South defensively closed ranks against real and perceived threats to the slave system. In this sense, the white South was nearly as trapped as the African American slaves they claimed to control. And in defending the slave system, the South was increasingly different from the dynamic capitalist free-labor system that was gaining strength in the North.

REVIEW QUESTIONS

1. How did cotton production after 1793 transform the social and political history of the South? How did the rest of the nation benefit? In what way was it an "international phenomenon"?
2. What were the two key institutions of the African American slave community? How did they function, and what beliefs did they express?
3. The circumstances of three very different groups—poor whites, educated and property-owning American Indians, and free African Americans—put them outside the dominant southern equations of white equals free and black equals slave. Analyze the difficulty each group encountered in the slave-owning South.
4. Who were the yeoman farmers? What was their interest in slavery?
5. Southern slaveholders claimed that their paternalism justified their ownership of slaves, but paternalism implied obligations as well as privileges. How well do you think slaveholders lived up to their paternalistic obligations?
6. How did slave owners justify slavery? How did their defense change over time?

RECOMMENDED READING

Ira Berlin, *Slaves without Masters* (1974). A full portrait of the lives of free black people in the South before the Civil War.

Charles C. Bolton, *Poor Whites of the Antebellum South: Tenants and Laborers in Central North and Northeast Mississippi* (1994). A careful consideration of a hitherto "invisible" population.

Orville Vernon Burton, *In My Father's House Are Many Mansions: Family and Community in Edgefield, South Carolina* (1985). A detailed community study that considers the farms, families, and everyday relations of white and black people in the period 1850–80.

Thomas D. Clark and John D. W. Guice, *Frontiers in Conflict: The Old Southwest, 1795–1830* (1989). Considers the Indian nations and their removal, white settlement, and the economic development of the region.

Catherine Clinton, *The Plantation Mistress: Woman's World in the Old South* (1982). Illustrates how slavery shaped the lives of elite white women. The exclusive focus on white women, however, neglects the black women with whom they lived on a daily basis.

Drew Gilpin Faust, *James Henry Hammond and the Old South* (1982). This outstanding biography uses the complex and interesting story of one man's life and ambitions to tell a larger story about southern attitudes and politics.

Lacy K. Ford Jr., *Origins of Southern Radicalism: The South Carolina Upcountry, 1800–1860* (1988). One of a growing number of studies of up-country non-slaveholders and their commitment to liberty and equality.

Eugene Genovese, *Roll, Jordan, Roll: The World the Slaves Made* (1974). The landmark book that redirected the attention of historians from slaves as victims to the slave community as an active participant in the paternalism of the southern slave system.

Steven Hahn, *The Roots of Southern Populism: Yeoman Farmers and the Transformation of the Georgia Upcountry, 1850–1890* (1983). One of the first studies of the changing world of southern yeomen.

Walter Johnson, *Soul by Soul: Life Inside the Antebellum Slave Market* (1999). A fascinating study of the workings and meanings of the New Orleans slave markets.

Peter Kolchin, *American Slavery 1619–1877* (1993). A well-written, comprehensive survey.

Bruce Levine, *Half Slave and Half Free: The Roots of Civil War* (1992). A useful survey of the different lines of development of the northern and southern economies and the political conflicts between the regions.

Stephanie McCurry, *Masters of Small Worlds: Yeoman Households, Gender Relations, and the Political Culture of the Antebellum South Carolina Low Country* (1995). A study of yeomen that links their prized political and economic independence with their strong patriarchal control over their own families.

Donald P. McNeilly, *The Old South Frontier: Cotton Plantations and the Formation of Arkansas Society, 1819–1861* (2000). Traces slavery and society in Arkansas from frontier to cotton plantations.

James Oakes, *The Ruling Race: A History of American Slaveholders* (1982). Oakes disagrees with Genovese's characterization of paternalism and sees slave owners instead as entrepreneurial capitalists. Especially useful for distinguishing the various classes of slave owners.

Brenda Stevenson, *Life in Black and White: Family and Community in the Slave South* (1996). A careful study of families, black and white, in Louden County, Virginia, that illustrates the difficulties both free and enslaved African American families faced.

Michael Tadman, *Speculators and Slaves: Masters, Traders, and Slaves in the Old South* (1989). Examines the extent, organization, and values of the internal slave trade.

ON THE WEB

http://memory.loc.gov/ammem/aaohtml/exhibit/aopart1.html#01b

The greatest fear that southern slave owners held was of potential slave rebellions. This American Memory exhibit from the Library of Congress chronicles some of the actual slave revolts within the United States and provides other primary documents related to slave rebellions and the abolitionist movement.

http://vi.uh.edu/pages/mintz/primary.htm

This is a site of original narratives and documents relating to the history of slavery in the eighteenth and nineteenth centuries maintained by members of the history department of the University of Houston. Useful in the context of this chapter are the narratives of slaves from the nineteenth century, but notice that many are dated after the Civil War. This reflects their publication dates, but the descriptions are from the pre-Civil-War era.

http://lcweb.loc.gov/rr/print/082_slave.html

This site is the Library of Congress exhibition called "Images of African-American Slavery and Freedom" from the Prints and Photographs Division. It contains two pages of prints and photographs portraying slavery, mainly of the pre-Civil War era, though some Civil War photos are present. It provides a good visual image of the institution of slavery.

http://www.prenhall.com/faragherbrief/map11.1

Consider the relationship between cotton production and westward expansion. What impact did this have on the Indian population of the South?

http://www.prenhall.com/faragherbrief/map11.2

Examine the role of slave labor in the South. Why was slave labor more prevalent in certain types of agriculture and industries, and not in others?

TWELVE

INDUSTRY AND THE NORTH

▶ 1 7 9 0 s – 1 8 4 0 s

AMERICAN COMMUNITIES

Women Factory Workers Form a Community in Lowell, Massachusetts

IN THE 1820s AND 1830s, YOUNG FARM WOMEN FROM ALL OVER NEW England flocked to Lowell to work a twelve-hour day in one of the first cotton textile factories in America. Living six to eight to a room in nearby boardinghouses, the women of Lowell earned an average of $3 a week. Some also attended inexpensive nighttime lectures or classes. Lowell, considered a model factory town, drew worldwide attention. As one admirer of its educated workers said, Lowell was less a factory than a "philanthropic manufacturing college."

The Boston investors who financed Lowell were businessmen, not philanthropists, but they wanted to keep Lowell free of the dirt, poverty, and social disorder that made English factory towns notorious. Built in 1823, Lowell boasted six neat factory buildings grouped around a central clock tower, the area pleasantly landscaped with flowers, shrubs, and trees. Housing was similarly well ordered: a Georgian mansion for the company agent; trim houses for the overseers; row houses for the mechanics and their families; and boardinghouses, each supervised by a responsible matron, for the workforce that made Lowell famous—young New England farm women.

The choice of young women as factory workers seemed shockingly unconventional. In the 1820s and 1830s, young unmarried women simply did not live alone; they lived and worked with their parents until they married. In these years of growth and westward expansion, however, America was chronically short of labor, and the Lowell manufacturers were shrewd enough to realize that young farm women were an untapped labor force. For farmers' sons, the lure of acquiring their own farms in the West was much stronger than factory wages, but for their sisters, escaping from rural isolation and earning a little money was an appealing way to spend a few years before marriage. To attract respectable young women, Lowell offered supervision both on the job and at home, with strict rules of conduct, compulsory religious services, cultural opportunities such as concerts and lectures, and cash wages.

When they first arrived in Lowell, the young women were often bewildered by the large numbers of townspeople and embarrassed by their own rural clothing and ways of speech. The air of the mill was hot, humid, and full of cotton lint, and the noise of the machinery—"The buzzing and hissing and whizzing of pulleys and rollers and spindles and flyers"—was constant. Very quickly, however, other women workers—often their own sisters or neighbors who had preceded them to the mill—helped them adjust. It was company policy for senior women to train the newcomers. The work itself was simple, consisting largely of knotting broken threads on spinning machines and power looms. Most women enjoyed the work. They were not bothered by the long hours; farm people were accustomed to long days. One woman wrote home: "The work is not disagreeable. It tried my patience sadly at first, but in general I like it very much. It is easy to do, and does not require very violent exertion, as much of our farm work does."

The most novel aspect of textile mills was a rigid work schedule. Power-driven machinery operated at a sustained, uniform pace throughout every mill; human workers had to learn to do the same. Each mill published elaborate schedules and imposed fines and penalties on latecomers. It was this kind of precise work schedule that represented the single largest change from preindustrial work habits; it was the hardest for workers to adjust to. Moreover, each mill positioned one or two overseers on every floor to make sure the pace was maintained. Men held these positions, and they earned more than the women who made up most of the workforce; this arrangement was unquestioned.

Why did young women come to Lowell? Some worked out of need and some to add to their family's income, but most regarded Lowell as an opportunity. It was escape from rural isolation and from parental supervision, a chance to buy the latest fashions and learn "city ways," to attend lectures and concerts, to save for a dowry or to pay for an education. As writer Lucy Larcom, one of the most famous workers, said, the young farm women who came to Lowell sought "an opening into freer life." Working side by side and living in com-

pany boardinghouses with six to twelve other women, some of whom might be relatives or friends from home, the Lowell women built a close, supportive community for themselves.

The owners of Lowell made large profits. They also drew praise for their carefully managed community with its intelligent and independent workforce. But their success was short-lived. In the 1830s, because of competition and poor economic conditions, the owners imposed wage cuts and work speedups that their model workforce did not take lightly. Although the Lowell women had been brought together under a system of paternalistic control, the close bonds they forged in the boardinghouses gave them the courage and solidarity to "turn out" in spontaneous protests, which were, however, unsuccessful in reversing the wage cuts. By 1850 the "philanthropic manufacturing college" was no more. The original Lowell workforce of New England farm girls had been replaced by poor Irish immigrants of both sexes, who tended more machines for much less pay than their predecessors. Now Lowell was simply another mill town.

The history of Lowell epitomizes the process by which the North (both the New England and the Middle Atlantic states) began to change from a society composed largely of self-sufficient farm families (Jefferson's "yeoman farmers") to one of urban wageworkers in an industrial economy. Industrialization did not occur overnight. Large factories were not common until the 1880s, but by that decade most workers had already experienced a fundamental change in their working patterns. Once under way, the market revolution changed the very basis of community: how people worked, how they thought, how they lived. In the early years of the nineteenth century, northern communities led this transformation, fostering attitudes far different from those prevalent in the South. ■

Lowell

KEY TOPICS

- Preindustrial ways of working and living

- The nature of the market revolution

- The effects of industrialization on workers in early factories

- Ways the market revolution changed the lives of ordinary people

- The emergence of the middle classs

PREINDUSTRIAL WAYS OF WORKING

The Lowell mill was a dramatic example of the ways factories changed traditional ways of working and living. When Lowell began operation, 97 percent of all Americans still lived on farms, and most work was done in or near the home. There was a community network of barter and mutual obligation. Work was slow, unscheduled, and task oriented. A rural artisan worked when he had orders, responding to demand, not to the clock. "Home" and "work" were not separate locations or activities, but intermixed.

Urban Artisans and Workers

In urban areas, skilled craftsmen had controlled preindustrial production since the early colonial period. Trades were perpetuated through a formal system of apprenticeship in which a boy went to work in the shop of a master, usually at the age of twelve or fourteen. Over the next three to seven years the young apprentice learned all aspects of the craft, gaining increasing responsibility and status as the day approached when he could strike out on his own. During that time, the master not only taught the apprentice his trade but housed, fed, and clothed him. Usually the apprentice lived with the master craftsman and was treated more like a member of the family than an employee. Thus, the family-learning model used on farms was formalized in the urban apprenticeship system. At the end of the contract period, the apprentice became a journeyman craftsman. Journeymen worked for wages in the shop of a master craftsman until they had enough capital to set up shop for themselves.

Although women as well as men did task-oriented skilled work, the formal apprenticeship system was exclusively for men. Because it was assumed that women would marry, most people thought that all girls needed to learn were domestic skills. Women who needed or wanted work, however, found a small niche of respectable occupations as domestic servants, laundresses, or seamstresses, often in the homes of the wealthy, or as cooks in small restaurants or as food vendors on the street. Some owned and managed boardinghouses. Prostitution, another common female occupation (especially in seaport cities), was not respectable.

Patriarchy in Family, Work, and Society

Like the farm family, an entire urban household was commonly organized around one kind of work. Usually the family lived at the shop or store, and all family members worked with the craftsman at his trade. A printer's wife, for example, would be capable of keeping most of the shop's functions going in the printer's absence and of supervising the work of apprentices and her children. Some artisans, like blacksmiths, needed shops separate from their homes but probably relied on their children to fetch and carry and to help with some of the work. Others, like bakers, who generally had to get up in the middle of the night to perform their work, relied on their wives to sell their products during the day.

In both rural and urban settings, working families were organized along strictly patriarchal lines. The man had unquestioned authority to direct the lives and work of family members and apprentices and to decide on occupations for his sons and marriages for his daughters. His wife had many crucial responsibilities—feeding, clothing, child rearing, taking care of apprentices, and all the other domestic affairs of the household—but in all these duties she was subject to the direction of her husband. Men were heads of families and bosses of artisanal shops; although entire families were engaged in the enterprise, the husband and father was the trained craftsman, and assistance by the family was informal and generally unrecognized.

The patriarchal organization of the family was reflected in society as a whole. Legally, men had all the power: neither women nor children had property or legal rights. For example, a married woman's property belonged to her husband, a woman could not testify on her own behalf in court, and in the rare cases of divorce the husband kept the children, for they were considered his property. When a man died, his son or sons inherited his property. The basic principle was that the man, as head of the household, represented the common interests of everyone for whom he was responsible—women, children, servants, apprentices. He thus controlled everything of value, and he alone could vote for political office.

The Social Order

In this preindustrial society everyone, from the smallest yeoman farmer to the largest urban merchant, had a fixed place in the social order. The social status of artisans was below that of wealthy merchants but decidedly above that of common laborers. Yeoman farmers, less grand than large landowners, ranked above tenant farmers and farm laborers. Although men of all social ranks mingled in their daily work, they did not mingle as equals, for great importance was placed on rank and status, which were distinguished by dress and manner. Although by the 1790s many artisans who owned property were voters and vocal participants in urban politics, few directly challenged the traditional authority of the rich and powerful to run civic affairs. The rapid spread of universal white manhood suffrage after 1800 democratized politics (see Chapter 10). At the same time, economic changes undermined the preindustrial social order. New York cabinetmaker Duncan Phyfe and sailmaker Stephen Allen amassed fortunes from their operations. Allen when he retired, was elected mayor of New York, customarily a position reserved for gentlemen. These artisans owed much of their success to the ever-expanding effects of the economic upheaval known as the market revolution.

THE MARKET REVOLUTION

The market revolution, the most fundamental change American communities ever experienced, was the outcome of three interrelated developments: rapid improvements in transportation (see Chapter 10), commercialization, and industrialization. Improved transportation allowed both people and goods to move with new ease and speed. Commercialization involved the replacement of household self-sufficiency and barter with the production of goods for a cash market. And industrialization involved the use of power-driven machinery to produce goods once made by hand.

The Accumulation of Capital

In the northern states, the business community was composed largely of merchants in the seaboard cities: Boston, Providence, New York, Philadelphia, and Baltimore. Many had made substantial profits in the international shipping boom of the period 1790–1807 (as discussed in Chapter 9). Such extraordinary opportunities attracted enterprising people. John Jacob Astor, who had arrived penniless from Germany in 1784, made his first fortune in the Pacific Northwest fur trade with China and eventually dominated the fur trade in the United States through his American Fur Company. Astor made a second fortune in New York real estate, and when he retired in 1834 with $25 million he was reputed to be the wealthiest man in America. Many similar stories of success, though not so fabulous as Astor's, demonstrated that risk-takers might reap rich rewards in international trade.

When the early years of the nineteenth century posed difficulties for international trade, some of the nation's wealthiest men turned to local investments. In Providence, Rhode Island, Moses Brown and his son-in-law William Almy began to invest some of the profits the Brown family had reaped from a worldwide trade in iron, candles, rum, and African slaves in the new manufacture of cotton textiles. Cincinnati merchants banded together to finance the building of the first steamboats to operate on the Ohio River.

Much of the capital for the new investments came from banks, both those in seaport cities that had been established for the international trade. But an astonishing amount of capital was raised through family

WEALTH IN BOSTON, 1687–1848				
Percent of	Percent of Wealth Held			
the Population	1687	1771	1833	1848
Top 1 percent	10%	16%	33%	37%
Top 10 percent	42	65	75	82
Lowest 80 percent	39	29	14	4

This table tracing the distribution of wealth in Boston reflects the gains made by merchants during the international shipping boom of 1790–1807 and the way in which intermarriage between wealthy families consolidated these gains.

connections. In the late eighteenth century, members of the business communities in the seaboard cities had begun to consolidate their position and property by intermarriage. In Boston, such a strong community developed that when Francis Cabot Lowell needed $300,000 in 1813 to build the world's first automated cotton mill in Waltham, Massachusetts (the prototype of the Lowell mills), he had only to turn to his family network.

Southern cotton provided the capital for continuing development. Because Northerners built the nation's ships, controlled the shipping trade, and provided the nation's banking, insurance, and financial services, the astounding growth in southern cotton exports enriched northern merchants almost as much as southern planters. In 1825, for example, of the 204,000 bales of cotton shipped from New Orleans, about one-third (69,000) were transshipped through the northern ports of New York, Philadelphia, and Boston. Although imperfectly understood at the time, the development of northern industry was paid for by enslaved African American labor. The fact is that the surprising wealth that cotton brought to southern planters fostered the market revolution.

The Putting-Out System

Initially, the American business community invested not in machinery and factories but in the "putting-out system" of home manufacture, thereby expanding and transforming it. In this significant departure from preindustrial work, people still produced goods at home but under the direction of a merchant, who "put out" the raw materials to them, paid them a certain sum per finished piece, and sold the completed item to a distant market. A look at the shoe industry in Lynn, Massachusetts, shows how the putting-out system transformed American manufacturing.

Long a major center of the shoe industry, Lynn, in 1800, produced 400,000 pairs of shoes—enough for every fifth person in the country. The town's 200 master artisans and their families, including journeymen and apprentices, worked together in hundreds of small home workshops called "ten-footers" (from their size, about ten feet square). The artisans and journeymen cut the leather, the artisans' wives and daughters did the binding of the upper parts of the shoe, the men stitched the shoe together, and children and apprentices helped where needed. In the early days, the artisan commonly bartered his shoes for needed products. Sometimes an artisan sold his shoes to a larger retailer in Boston or Salem. Although production of shoes in Lynn increased yearly from 1780 to 1810 as markets widened, shoes continued to be manufactured in traditional artisanal ways.

The investment of merchant capital in the shoe business changed everything. In Lynn, a small group of Quaker shopkeepers and merchants, connected by family, religious, and business ties, took the lead in reorganizing the trade. Financed by the bank they founded in 1814, Lynn capitalists like Micajah Pratt built large, two-story central workshops to replace the scattered ten-footers. Pratt employed a few skilled craftsmen to cut leather for shoes, but he put out the rest of the shoemaking to less-skilled workers who were no longer connected by family ties. Individual farm women and children sewed the uppers, which, when completed, were soled by farm men and boys. Putting-out workers were paid on a piecework basis; the men and boys earned more than the women and children but much less than a master craftsman or a journeyman. This arrangement allowed the capitalist to employ much more labor for the same investment than with the traditional artisan workshop. Shoe production increased enormously: the largest central shop in 1832 turned out ten times more shoes than the largest shopkeeper had sold in 1789. Gradually the putting-out system and central workshops replaced artisan's shops. Some artisans became wealthy owners of workshops, but most became wage earners, and the apprenticeship system eventually disappeared.

The putting-out system moved the control of production from the individual artisan households to the merchant capitalists, who could now control labor costs, production goals, and shoe styles to fit certain markets. For example, the Lynn trade quickly monopolized the market for cheap boots for southern slaves and western farmers, leaving workshops in other cities to produce shoes for wealthier customers. This specialization of the national market—indeed, even thinking in terms of a national market—was new. Additionally, and most important from the capitalist's point of view, the owner of the business controlled the workers and could cut back or expand the labor force as economic and marketplace conditions warranted. The unaccustomed severity of economic slumps like the Panics of 1819 and 1837 made this flexibility especially desirable.

While the central workshop system prevailed in Lynn and in urban centers like New York City, the putting-out system also fostered a more dispersed form of home production. By 1810 there were an estimated 2,500 so-called outwork weavers in New England, operating handlooms in their own homes. Other crafts that rapidly became organized according to the putting-out system were flax and wool spinning, straw braiding, glove making, and the knitting of stockings. For example, the palm-leaf hat industry that supplied farm laborers and slaves in the South and West relied completely on women and children, who braided the straw for the hats at home part-time. Absorbed into families' overall domestic routines, the outwork activity seemed small, but the size of the industry itself was surprising: in 1837, 33,000 Massachusetts women braided palm-leaf hats, whereas only 20,000 worked in the state's cotton textile mills. They were producing for a large national market, made possible by the dramatic improvements in transportation that occurred between 1820 and 1840.

The Spread of Commercial Markets

Although the putting-out system meant a loss of independence for artisans such as those in Lynn, Massachusetts, New England farm families liked it. From their point of view, the work could easily be combined with domestic work, and the pay was a new source of income that they could use to purchase mass-produced goods rather than spend the time required to make these things themselves. It was in this way that farm families moved away from the local barter system and into a larger market economy.

Commercialization, or the replacement of barter by a cash economy, did not happen immediately or uniformly throughout the nation. Fixed prices for goods produced by the new principles of specialization and division of labor appeared first along established trade routes. Rural areas in established sections of the country that were remote from trade routes continued in the old ways. Strikingly, however, western farming frontiers were commercial from the very start (see Chapter 10). The existence of a cash market was an important spur to westward expansion.

British Technology and American Industrialization

Important as were the transportation revolution and the commercialization made possible by the putting-out system, the third component of the market revolution, industrialization, brought the greatest changes to personal lives. Begun in Britain in the eighteenth century, industrialization was the result of a series of technological changes in the textile trade. In marked contrast to the putting-out system, in which capitalists had dispersed work into many individual households, industrialization required workers to concentrate in factories and pace themselves to the rhythms of power-driven machinery.

The simplest and quickest way for America to industrialize was to copy the British, but the British, well aware of the value of their machinery, enacted laws forbidding its export and even the emigration of skilled workers. Over the years, however, Americans managed to lure a number of British artisans to the United States.

In 1789 Samuel Slater, who had just finished an apprenticeship in the most up-to-date cotton spinning factory in England, disguised himself as a farm laborer and slipped out of England without even telling his mother good-bye. In Providence, Rhode Island, he met Moses Brown and William Almy, who had been trying without success to duplicate British industrial technology. Having carefully committed the designs to memory before leaving England, Slater promptly built copies of the latest British machinery for Brown and Almy. Slater's mill, as it became known, began operation in 1790. It was the most advanced cotton mill in America.

Following British practice, Slater drew his workforce primarily from among young children (ages seven to twelve) and women, whom he paid much less than the

This early nineteenth-century watercolor shows Slater's mill, the first cotton textile mill in the United States, which depended on the waterpower of Pawtucket Falls for its energy. New England was rich in swiftly flowing streams that could provide power to spinning machines and power looms.

SOURCE: Rhode Island Historical Society.

handful of skilled male workers he hired to keep the machines working. The yarn spun at Slater's mill was then put out to local home weavers, who turned it into cloth on handlooms. As a result, home weaving flourished in areas near the mill, giving families a new opportunity to make money at a task with which they were already familiar.

Soon many other merchants and mechanics followed Slater's lead, and the rivers of New England were soon dotted with mills wherever waterpower could be tapped.

The Lowell Mills

Another way to deal with British competition was to beat the British at their own game. With the intention of designing better machinery, a young Bostonian, Francis Cabot Lowell, made an apparently casual tour of British textile mills in 1810. Lowell, the founder of the Lowell mills described in the opening of this chapter, made a good impression on his English hosts, who were pleased by his interest and his intelligent questions. They did not know that each night, in his hotel room, Lowell made sketches from memory of the machines he had inspected during the day.

Lowell was more than an industrial spy, however. When he returned to the United States, he went to work with a Boston mechanic, Paul Moody, to improve on the British models. Lowell and Moody not only made the machinery for spinning cotton more efficient, but they also invented a power loom. This was a great advance, for now all aspects of textile manufacture, from the initial cleaning and carding (combing) to the production of finished lengths of cloth, could be gathered together in the same factory. Such a mill required a much larger capital investment than a small spinning mill such as Slater's, but Lowell's family network gave him access to the needed funds. In 1814 he opened the world's first integrated cotton mill in Waltham, near Boston. It was a great success: in 1815, the Boston Associates (Lowell's partners) made profits of 25 percent, and their efficiency allowed them to survive the intense British competition following the War of 1812 (see Chapter 9). Many smaller New England mills did not survive. The lesson was clear: size mattered.

The Boston Associates took the lesson to heart, and when they moved their enterprise to a new location in 1823, they thought big. They built an entire town at the junction of the Concord and Merrimack Rivers where the village of East Chelmsford stood, renaming it Lowell in memory of Francis, who had died, still a young man, in 1817. As the opening of this chapter describes, the new industrial community boasted

six mills and company housing for all the workers. In 1826 the town had 2,500 inhabitants; ten years later the population was 17,000.

Family Mills

Lowell was unique. No other textile mill was ever such a showplace. None was as large, integrated so many tasks, or relied on such a homogeneous workforce. Its location in a new town was also unusual. Much more common in the early days of industrialization were small rural spinning mills, on the model of Slater's first mill, built on swiftly running streams near existing farm communities. Because the owners of smaller mills often hired entire families, their operations came to be called family mills. The employment pattern at these mills followed that established by Slater at his first mill in 1790. Children aged eight to twelve, whose customary job was "doffing" (changing) bobbins on the spinning machines, made up 50 percent of the workforce. Women and men each made up about 25 percent of the workforce, but men had the most skilled and best-paid jobs.

Relations between these small rural mill communities and the surrounding farming communities were often difficult, as the history of the towns of Dudley and Oxford, Massachusetts, shows. Samuel Slater, now a millionaire, built three small mill communities near these towns in the early years of the nineteenth century. Each consisted of a small factory, a store, and cottages and a boardinghouse for workers. Slater's mills provided a substantial amount of work for local people, putting out to them both the initial cleaning of the raw cotton and the much more lucrative weaving of the spun yarn. But in spite of this economic link, relations between Slater and his workers on one side and the farmers and shopkeepers of the Dudley and Oxford communities on the other were stormy. They disagreed over the building of mill dams (essential for the mill power supply, these dams sometimes flooded local fields), over taxes, over the upkeep of local roads, and over schools. The debates were so constant, and so heated, that in 1831 Slater petitioned the Massachusetts General Court to create a separate town, Webster, that would encompass his three mill communities. For their part, the residents of Dudley and Oxford became increasingly hostile to Slater's authoritarian control, which they regarded as undemocratic. Their dislike carried over to the workers as well. Disdaining the mill workers for their poverty and transiency, people in the rural communities began referring to them as "operatives," making them somehow different in their work roles from themselves. Industrial work thus led to new social distinctions.

"The American System of Manufactures"

Not all American industrial technology was copied from British inventions, for there were many home-grown inventors. The concept of interchangeable parts, realized first in gun manufacturing, was so unusual that the British soon dubbed it the American system. Standardized production quickly revolutionized the manufacture of items as simple as nails and as complicated as clocks. American businesses mass-produced high-quality goods for ordinary people earlier in America than in Britain or any European country. The availability of these goods was a practical demonstration of American beliefs in democracy and equality.

In 1798 Eli Whitney contracted with the government to make 10,000 rifles in twenty-eight months, an incredibly short period had he been planning to produce each rifle by hand in the traditional way. Whitney's ideas far outran his performance. It took him ten years to fulfill his contract, and even then he had not managed to perfect the production of all the rifle parts. Two other New Englanders, Simeon North and John Hall, created milling machines that could grind parts to the required specifications and brought the concept to fruition, North in 1816 and Hall in 1824. When the system of interchangeable machine-made parts was adopted by the other national armory, at Springfield, Massachusetts, the Springfield rifle got its name.

Other Factories

Although cotton textile mills were the first and best known of the early factories, some factories produced other items, among them metal and iron. Like the textile mills, many of these factories were rural because they depended on natural water sources for power or because they needed to be near their raw materials, such as iron ore. And like the early textile mills, these first heavy industries initially coexisted with the traditional artisanal system.

The rapid development of the steamship industry in Cincinnati illustrates both the role of merchant capital and the coexistence of old and new production methods. Cincinnati's first steamboat, financed by local merchant capital, was commissioned in 1816. It proved so successful that by 1819 one-quarter of all western steamboats were being built in Cincinnati. At the same time, much of the detail work on the steamboat was performed by traditional artisans such as cabinetmakers, upholsterers, tinsmiths, and blacksmiths, who did record-breaking amounts of work in their small, independent shops. In this way, new factory methods and industrial techniques were often coupled with old craft techniques.

FROM ARTISAN TO WORKER

The changes wrought by the market revolution had major and lasting effects on ordinary Americans. The proportion of wage laborers in the nation's labor force rose from 12 percent in 1800 to 40 percent by 1860. Most of these workers were employed in the North, and almost half were women, performing outwork in their homes. The young farm woman who worked at Lowell for a year or two, then returned home; the master craftsman in Lynn who expanded his shop with the aid of merchant capital; the home weaver who prospered on outwork from Slater's mill—all were participating, often unknowingly, in fundamental personal and social changes.

Personal Relationships

The immense increase in productivity made possible by the principles of division of labor and specialization effectively destroyed artisan production and the apprenticeship system. For example, in New York by the mid-1820s, tailors and shoemakers were teaching apprentices only a few simple operations, in effect using them as helpers. Printers undercut the system by hiring partly trained apprentices as journeymen. In almost every trade, apprentices no longer lived with the master's family, and their parents received cash payment for the child's work. Thus, in effect, the apprenticeship system was replaced by child labor.

The breakdown of the patriarchal relationship between the master craftsman and his workers became an issue in the growing political battle between the North and the South over slavery. Southern defenders of slavery compared their cradle-to-grave responsibility to their slaves with northern employers' "heartless" treatment of their "wage slaves." Certainly the new northern employer assumed less responsibility for individual workers than had the traditional artisan. Although the earliest textile manufacturers, like those at Lowell, provided housing for their workers, workers soon became responsible for their own food and housing. Moreover, northern employers felt no obligation to help or care for old or disabled workers. Southerners were right: this was a heartless system. But Northerners were also right: industrialization was certainly freer than the slave system, freer even than the hierarchical craft system, although it sometimes offered only the freedom to starve.

Mechanization and Women's Work

Industrialization posed a major threat to the status and independence of skilled male workers. In trade after trade, mechanization meant that most tasks could be performed by unskilled labor. In fact, work in the textile mills was so simple that children came to form a large part of the workforce.

Mechanization changed the nature of women's work as well. The industrialization of textiles—first in spinning, then in weaving—relieved women of a time-consuming home occupation. To supplement family income, women now had the choice of following textile work into the factory or finding other kinds of home work.

The 1820s saw the birth of the garment industry. In New York City, employers began hiring women to sew ready-made clothing, at first rough, unfitted clothing for sailors and southern slaves, but later overalls and shirts for Westerners and finer items, such as men's shirts. Most women performed this work at low piecework rates in their homes. Although by 1860 Brooks Brothers, the famous men's clothing firm, had 70 "inside" workers in a model central workshop, the firm relied primarily on putting out sewing to 3,000 women who worked at home. The gendered division of labor disadvantaged women outworkers. The low pay and seasonal nature of the industry became notorious. Manufacturers in the garment trade made their profits not from efficient production but by obtaining intensive labor for very low wages. The lower the piece rate, the more each woman, sewing at home, had to produce to earn enough to live. The invention of the sewing machine only made matters worse. Manufacturers dropped their piecework rates still lower, and some women found themselves working fifteen to eighteen hours a day, producing more than they ever had but earning the same pay.

The Cash Economy

Another effect of the market revolution was the transformation of a largely barter system into a cash economy. For example, a farm woman might pay in butter and eggs for a pair of shoes handmade for her by the local shoemaker. A few years later that same woman, now part of the vast New England outwork industry, might buy ready-made footwear with the cash she had earned from braiding straw for hats. Community economic ties were replaced by distant, sometimes national ones.

The pay envelope became the only direct contact between factory worker and (often absentee) owner. For workers, this change was both unsettling and liberating. On the minus side, workers were no longer part of a settled, orderly, and familiar community. On the plus side, they were now free to labor wherever they could, at whatever wages their skills or their bargaining power could command. That workers took their freedom seriously is evidenced by the very high rate of turnover—50 percent a year—in the New England textile mills.

But if moving on was a sign of increased freedom of opportunity for some workers, for others it was an unwanted consequence of the market revolution. In New England, for example, many quite prosperous artisans and farmers faced disruptive competition from factory goods and western commercial agriculture. They could remain where they were only if they were willing to become factory workers or commercial farmers. Often the more conservative choice was to move west and try to reestablish one's traditional lifestyle on the frontier.

Free Labor

At the heart of the industrializing economy was the notion of free labor. Originally, "free" referred to individual economic choice—that is, to the right of workers to move to another job rather than be held to a position by customary obligation or the formal contract of apprenticeship or journeyman labor. But "free labor" soon came to encompass as well the range of attitudes—hard work, self-discipline, and a striving for economic independence—that were necessary for success in a competitive, industrializing economy. These were profoundly individualistic attitudes, and owners cited them in opposing labor unions and the use of strikes to achieve wage goals.

For their part, many workers were inclined to define freedom more collectively, arguing that their just grievances as free American citizens were not being heard. As a group of New Hampshire female workers rhetorically asked, "Why [is] there . . . so much want, dependence and misery among us, if forsooth, we are freemen and freewomen?"

Early Strikes

Rural women workers led some of the first strikes in American labor history. In 1824, in one of the first of these actions, women workers at a Pawtucket, Rhode Island, textile mill led their co-workers, female and male, out on strike to protest wage cuts and longer hours.

More famous were the strikes that the women at the model mill at Lowell led. The first serious trouble came in 1834, when 800 women participated in a spontaneous turnout to protest a wage cut of 25 percent. The owners were shocked and outraged by the strike, considering it both unfeminine and ungrateful. The workers, however, were bound together by a sense of sisterhood and were protesting not just the attack on their economic independence but the blow to their position as "daughters of freemen still." Nevertheless, the wage cuts were enforced, as were more cuts in 1836, again in the face of a turnout. Many women simply packed their clothes in disgust and returned home to the family farm.

A NEW SOCIAL ORDER

The market revolution reached into every aspect of life, down to the most personal family decisions. It also fundamentally changed the social order, creating a new middle class with distinctive habits and beliefs.

Wealth and Class

There had always been social classes in America. Since the early colonial period planters in the South and merchants in the North had comprised a wealthy elite. Somewhere below the elite but above the mass of people were the "middling sort": a small professional group that included lawyers, ministers, schoolteachers, doctors, public officials, some prosperous farmers, prosperous urban shopkeepers and innkeepers, and a few wealthy artisans such as Boston silversmith Paul Revere. "Mechanics and farmers"—artisans and yeoman farmers—made up another large group, and the laboring poor, consisting of ordinary laborers, servants, and marginal farmers were below them. At the very bottom were the paupers—those dependent on public charity—and the enslaved. This was the "natural" social order that fixed most people in the social rank to which they were born.

The market revolution ended this stable and hierarchical social order, creating the dynamic and unstable one we recognize today: upper, middle, and working classes, whose members all share the hope of climbing as far up the social ladder as they can. This social mobility was new.

The major transformation came in the lives of the "middling sort." The market revolution downgraded many independent artisans but elevated others, like Duncan Phyfe and Stephen Allen of New York. Other formerly independent artisans or farmers (or more frequently, their children) joined the rapidly growing ranks of managers and white-collar workers such as accountants, bank tellers, clerks, bookkeepers, and insurance agents. Occupational opportunities shifted dramatically in just one generation. In Utica, New York, for example, 16 percent of the city's young men held white-collar jobs in 1855, compared with only 6 percent of their fathers. At the same time, 15 percent fewer younger men filled artisanal occupations than older men.

These new white-collar workers owed not only their jobs but their lifestyles to the new structure and organization of industry. The new economic order demanded certain habits and attitudes of workers: sobriety, responsibility, steadiness, and hard work. Thus, a new middle class with distinctively new attitudes was formed.

Religion and Personal Life

Religion, which had undergone dramatic changes since the 1790s, played a key role in the emergence of the new attitudes. The Second Great Awakening had supplanted the orderly and intellectual Puritan religion of early New England. The new evangelistic religious spirit, which stressed the achievement of salvation through personal faith, was more democratic and more enthusiastic than the earlier faith. The concept of original sin, the cornerstone of Puritan belief, was replaced by the optimistic belief that a willingness to be saved was enough to ensure salvation. Conversion and repentance were now community experiences, often taking place in huge revival meetings in which an entire congregation focused on the sinners about to be saved. The converted bore a heavy personal responsibility to demonstrate their faith in their own daily lives through morally respectable behavior. In this way the new religious feeling fostered individualism and self-discipline.

In 1825, in Utica, New York, and other towns along the recently opened Erie Canal, evangelist Charles G. Finney began a series of dramatic revival meetings. His spellbinding message reached both rich and poor, converting members of all classes to the new evangelistic religion. In 1830, made famous by these gatherings, Finney was invited by businessmen to preach in Rochester. Prayer meetings were held in schools and businesses, impromptu religious services in people's homes. Middle-class women in particular carried Finney's message by prayer and pleading to the men of their families, who found that evangelism's stress on self-discipline and individual achievement helped them adjust to new business conditions.

The New Middle-Class Family

The market revolution and the new evangelism also affected women's family roles. Women took the lead in making certain their families joined them in converting to the new, more emotional approach to religion. And when production moved into the hands of paid factory workers, the husband's direct connection with the household was broken: he became a manager of workers, and was no longer the undisputed head of a family unit that combined work and personal life.

Wives, on the other hand, remained at home, where they were still responsible for cooking, cleaning, and other domestic tasks, but no longer contributed directly to what had been the family enterprise. Instead, women took on a new responsibility, that of providing a quiet, well-ordered, relaxing refuge from the pressures of the industrial world. Catharine Beecher's *Treatise on Domestic Economy*, first published in 1841, became the standard housekeeping guide for a generation of middle-class American women. In it, Beecher combined innovative ideas for household design (especially in the kitchen, where she introduced principles of organization) with medical information, child-rearing advice, recipes, and numerous discussions of the mother's moral role in the family. The book clearly filled a need: for many pioneer women, it was the only book besides the Bible that they carried west with them.

As the work roles of middle-class men and women diverged, so did social attitudes about appropriate male and female characteristics and behavior. Men were expected to be steady, industrious, responsible, and painstakingly attentive to their business. They had little choice: in the competitive, uncertain, and rapidly changing business conditions of the early nineteenth century, these qualities were essential for men who hoped to hold their existing positions or to get ahead. In contrast, women were expected to be nurturing, gentle, kind, moral, and selflessly devoted to their families. They were expected to operate within the "woman's sphere"—the home.

The maintenance or achievement of a middle-class lifestyle required the joint efforts of husband and wife. More cooperation between them was called for than in the preindustrial, patriarchal family. The nature of the new, companionate marriage that evolved in response to the market revolution was reflected most clearly in decisions concerning children.

The invention of photography made possible family portraits that earlier were too expensive for all but the wealthiest. This portrait of the Edward Miner Gallaudet family, photographed by Mathew Brady in the 1860s, exhibits the gender differences expected in the middle-class family: strong, self-reliant men and softer, more clinging women.

SOURCE: Mathew Brady/Brown Brothers.

Family Limitation

Middle-class couples chose to have fewer children than their predecessors. Children who were being raised to succeed in the middle class placed considerable demands on family resources: They required more care, training, and education than children who could be put to work at traditional tasks at an early age. The dramatic fall in the birthrate during the nineteenth century (from an average of seven children per woman in 1800 to five in 1860) is evidence of conscious decisions about family limitation, first by members of the new middle class and later by working-class families. Few couples used mechanical methods of contraception such as the condom, partly because these were difficult to obtain and partly because most people associated their use with prostitution and the prevention of venereal disease rather

than with family planning. Instead, people used birth control methods that relied on mutual consent: coitus interruptus (withdrawal before climax), the rhythm method (intercourse only during the woman's infertile period), and, most often, abstinence or infrequent intercourse.

When mutual efforts at birth control failed, married women often sought a surgical abortion, a new technique that was much more reliable than the folk remedies women had always shared among themselves. Surgical abortions were widely advertised after 1830, and widely used, especially by middle-class married women seeking to limit family size. Some historians estimate that one out of every four pregnancies was aborted in the years 1840–60 (about the same rate as in 1990). The rising rate of abortion by married women (in other words, its use as birth control) prompted the first legal bans; by 1860, twenty states had outlawed the practice.

Accompanying the interest in family limitation was a redefinition of sexuality. Doctors generally recommended that sexual urges be controlled, but they believed that men would have much more difficulty exercising such control than women, partly because, they also believed, women were uninterested in sex. (Women who were visibly interested ran the risk of being considered immoral or "fallen," and thereupon shunned by the middle class.)

Many women of the late eighteenth century wanted to be free of the medical risks and physical debility that too-frequent childbearing brought, but they had little chance of achieving that goal until men became equally interested in family limitation. The rapid change in attitudes toward family size that occurred in the early nineteenth century has been repeated around the world as other societies undergo the dramatic experience of industrialization. It is a striking example of the ways economic changes affect our most private and personal decisions.

Middle-Class Children

Child rearing had been shared in the preindustrial household, boys learning farming or craft skills from their fathers while girls learned domestic skills from their mothers. The children of the new middle class, however, needed a new kind of upbringing, one that involved a long period of nurturing in the beliefs and personal habits necessary for success. Mothers assumed primary responsibility for this training, in part because fathers were too busy but also because people believed that women's superior qualities of gentleness, morality, and loving watchfulness were essential to the task.

Fathers retained a strong role in major decisions concerning children, but mothers commonly turned to other women for advice on daily matters. Through their churches, women formed maternal associations for help in raising their children to be religious and responsible.

Middle-class families sacrificed to keep their sons in school or in training for their chosen professions, and they often housed and fed their sons until the

In a time before ready-made clothing was available, middle-class women used *Godey's Ladies Book* as a pattern book, taking elaborate fashion illustrations such as this one from 1856 to local seamstresses, or remaking older dresses to fit the current trends.

SOURCE: ©Bettmann/CORBIS.

CHRONOLOGY

1790	Samuel Slater's first mill opens in Rhode Island
1793	Cotton gin invented
1798	Eli Whitney contracts with the federal government for 10,000 rifles, which he undertakes to produce with interchangeable parts
1807	Embargo Act excludes British manufactures
1810	Francis Cabot Lowell tours British textile factories First steamboat on the Ohio River
1812	Micajah Pratt begins his own shoe business in Lynn, Massachusetts
1813	Francis Cabot Lowell raises $300,000 to build his first cotton textile factory at Waltham, Massachusetts
1815	War of 1812 ends; British competition in manufactures resumes
1816	First protective tariff
1820s	Large-scale outwork networks develop in New England
1823	Lowell mills open
1824	John Hall successfully achieves interchangeable parts at Harpers Ferry armory Women lead strike at Pawtucket textile mill
1825	Erie Canal opens
1830	Charles G. Finney's Rochester revivals
1834	First strike at Lowell mills
1841	Catharine Beecher's *Treatise on Domestic Economy* published
1845	New England Female Labor Reform Association formed

young men had "established" themselves financially and could marry. Mothers took the lead in an important informal activity: making sure their children had friends and contacts that would be useful when they were old enough to consider careers and marriage. Matters such as these, rarely considered by earlier generations living in small communities, now became important in the new middle-class communities of America's towns and cities.

Contrary to the growing myth of the self-made man, middle-class success was not a matter of individual achievement. Instead it was usually based on a family strategy in which fathers provided the money and mothers the nurturance. The reorganization of the family described in this section was successful: from its shelter and support emerged generations of ambitious, responsible, and individualistic middle-class men. But

although boys were trained for success, this was not an acceptable goal for their sisters. Women were trained to be the nurturing, silent "support system" that undergirded male success. And women were also expected to ease the tensions of the transition to new middle-class behavior by acting as models and monitors of traditional values.

CONCLUSION

The market revolution involved three transformations: improvements in transportation, commercialization, and industrialization. Each began at different times. The transportation revolution (discussed in Chapter 10), usually dated from 1825 (the year of the opening of the Erie Canal), accelerated with the building of railroads in the 1830s and 1840s. Commercialization began earlier, around 1805, as a consequence of the reorganization of manufacturing through the putting-out system by northern entrepreneurs. After 1805, the cash purchase of items manufactured elsewhere slowly eroded local barter arrangements. American industrialization began with Samuel Slater's small cotton spinning mill in Rhode Island in 1790, but the most famous early example was the mill town of Lowell, Massachusetts, whose factories opened in 1823. These three transformations, taken together, constituted the market revolution that, by changing the ways people worked, changed how they thought.

REVIEW QUESTIONS

1. What changes in preindustrial life and work were caused by the market revolution?
2. This chapter argues that when people begin doing new kinds of work, their beliefs and attitudes change. Give three examples of such changes described in the chapter. Can you think of other examples?
3. Discuss the opinion offered by historian David Potter that mass production has been an important democratizing force in American politics. Do you agree? Why or why not?
4. Consider the portrait of the nineteenth-century middle-class family offered in this chapter and imagine yourself as a member of such a family. What new aspects of family relations would you welcome? Which would be difficult? Why?

RECOMMENDED READING

Christopher Clark, *The Roots of Rural Capitalism: Western Massachusetts, 1780–1860* (1990). The most thorough examination to date of how the commercial spirit changed rural life.

Alan Dawley, *Class and Community: The Industrial Revolution in Lynn* (1976). A pathbreaking study of the shift from artisanal to wage labor.

Thomas Dublin, *Women at Work: The Transformation of Work and Community in Lowell, Massachusetts, 1826–1860* (1979). A careful look at the female workers of Lowell and their changing conditions.

Thomas Dublin, *Transforming Women's Work: New England Lives in the Industrial Revolution* (1994). A thoughtful study of the effects of women's outwork.

Karen Halttunen, *Confidence Men and Painted Women: A Study of Middle-Class Culture in America* (1982). Shows the importance of sentimentalism to the new middle class.

David Houndshell, *From the American System to Mass Production, 1800–1932* (1984). How an entire network of New England "mechanics" contributed to the invention of interchangeable parts.

Shawn Johansen, *Family Men: Middle-Class Fatherhood in Early Industrializing America* (2001). New research on the domestic involvement of fathers.

Paul Johnson, *A Shopkeeper's Millennium: Society and Revivals in Rochester, New York, 1815–1837* (1978). A study of the changing relationship between masters and workers in Rochester.

Bruce Laurie, *Artisans into Workers: Labor in Nineteenth-Century America* (1989). Using many specific examples, this book traces the changes in labor described in this chapter.

Jonathan Prude, *The Coming of Industrial Order: Town and Factory Life in Rural Massachusetts, 1810–1860* (1983). A major source of information on family mills.

Steven J. Ross, *Workers on the Edge: Work, Leisure and Politics in Industrializing Cincinnati, 1788–1890* (1985). Studies the growth of wage labor in a major western city.

Mary Ryan, *The Making of the Middle Class* (1981). A study of Utica, New York, demonstrating the role of women in the family strategies of the new middle class.

Charles Sellers, *The Market Revolution: Jacksonian America, 1815–1846* (1991). A synthesis of the political, religious, and economic change of the period.

Christine Stansell, *City of Women: Sex and Class in New York, 1789–1860* (1983). Explores women's work and the social dynamics of rapidly growing New York City.

ON THE WEB

http://www.loc.gov/exhibits/british/brit-5.html

A Library of Congress site, this web page chronicles the parallel industrial development of the United States and Great Britain, including inventions, tools, and machines that both nations promoted. It contains period drawings and descriptions of locomotives to telegraph instruments from the 1780s to the 1850s. It does proceed on into the twentieth century, but the focus is on the earlier period.

http://www.fordham.edu/halsall/mod/ robinson-lowell.html

This site maintained by Fordham University contains Mary Robinson's account of the Lowell Mill girls.

http://www.state.vt.us/vhs/educate/change/ pages/reform/lowell.html

A collection of letters from a young farm girl who traveled from her home to work in the Lowell, Massachusetts, textile mills is published on this site by the Vermont Historical Society. Links exist to other pages with interesting Vermont state history.

http://www.kentlaw.edu/ilhs/lowell.html

A series of primary documents relating to the Lowell textile mills is posted on this site, which is maintained by the Illinois Labor History Society. The most interesting include the official rules governing both the factory and the boarding-house lives of mill workers and a legislative investigation by the Massachusetts legislature into working conditions at Lowell.

http://www.nps.gov/lowe/loweweb/ Lowell%20History/prologue.htm

This National Park Service site concerns the Lowell National Historical Park. Look at the site map on the left of this page for links to NPS electronic brochures on life in the town of Lowell in PDF format. These brochures contain a wealth of interesting information and photos.

http://www.prenhall.com/faragherbrief/map12.1

Think about the connections between work, home, and the environment in Lowell, Massachussetts, during this period. How did the plan of the town affect the people who lived there?

http://www.prenhall.com/faragherbrief/map12.2

Use these interactive maps to look at the growth of cotton textile manufacturing between 1810 and 1840. How did this growth transform the way people lived and worked?

THIRTEEN

COMING TO TERMS WITH THE NEW AGE

▷ 1820s – 1850s

AMERICAN COMMUNITIES

Seneca Falls: Women Reformers Respond to the Market Revolution

IN THE SUMMER OF 1848, A SMALL ADVERTISEMENT APPEARED IN AN UP-state New York newspaper announcing a "convention to discuss the social, civil, and religious condition and rights of woman," to be held at Seneca Falls on July 19 and 20.

Charlotte Woodward, a nineteen-year-old glove maker who did out-work in her rural home, saw the advertisement and persuaded six friends to join her in the forty-mile journey to the convention. "At first we travelled quite alone," she recalled. "But before we had gone many miles we came on other wagon-loads of women, bound in the same direction. As we reached different crossroads we saw wagons coming from every part of the country, and long before we reached Seneca Falls we were a procession."

To the surprise of the convention organizers, almost 300 people—men as well as women—attended the two-day meeting. The focus of their discussions was the Declaration of Sentiments, a petition for women's rights modeled on the Declaration of Independence. "We hold these truths to be self-evident," it announced: "That all men and women are created equal." Men had deprived women of legal rights, of the right to own their own property, of custody of their children in cases of di-vorce, of the right to higher education (at that time only Oberlin Col-lege and Mount Holyoke Female Seminary admitted women), of full participation in religious worship and activity, and of the right to vote. After discussion, the attendees approved all the resolutions, and all but the last of them, which a minority found too radical, unanimously. "Why Lizzie, thee will make us ridiculous!" Quaker Lucretia Mott had ex-claimed when Elizabeth Cady Stanton proposed the voting rights mea-sure. Indeed the newspapers reporting on the convention thought the demand for the vote was ridiculously unfeminine. But the group that as-sembled in Seneca Falls was undeterred. Buoyed by the success of this first women's rights convention, they promptly planned another one three weeks later in New York's largest upstate city, Rochester, to reach new supporters and to develop strategies to implement their resolutions.

The fight for women's rights was only one of many reform move-ments that emerged in the United States in the wake of the economic and social disruptions of the market revolution. The Seneca Falls region was itself deeply affected by that revolution. A farming frontier in 1800, it had been drawn into national commerce in 1828 when it was reached by an offshoot of the Erie Canal. It was drawn even further into the modern age when the railroad arrived in 1841. A village of 200 in 1824, Seneca Falls had grown to a town of over 4,000 by 1842. It was now a center for flour milling (in 1845, the nine mills in the town produced a total of 2,000 barrels of flour a day) and manufacturing, and a hub of the outwork network of which Charlotte Woodward was a part. Swamped by newcomers (among them a growing number of poor Irish Catholics), the inhabitants of Seneca Falls struggled to maintain a sense of community. They formed volunteer organizations of all kinds—religious, civic, social, educational, recreational. And they became active participants in reform movements seeking to counteract the effects of industrialization, rapid growth, and the influx of newcomers.

Many reformers belonged to liberal religious groups with wide social perspectives. Perhaps a third of those attending the women's rights convention, for example, were members of the Wesleyan Methodist Society of Seneca Falls, which had broken with the national Methodist organization because it would not take a strong stand against slavery. Another quarter were Progressive Quakers of the nearby town of Waterloo, who had broken with their national organization for the same reason. Seneca Falls had been the site of a "Temperance Reformation" in the early 1840s, and many attendees at the Women's Rights convention were also active in the temperance movement, a more limited but extremely popular reform cause dedicated to promoting abstinence from alcohol.

The idea for the Women's Rights convention emerged during a meeting in early July 1848, between Lucretia Mott—a Philadelphia Quaker and the nation's best-known woman reformer—and Elizabeth Cady Stanton of Seneca Falls, wife of a well-known antislavery orator and niece of a leading reform philanthropist. Reflecting her many concerns, Mott had just finished a tour of the new penitentiary at Auburn and a nearby Indian reservation and was visiting her sister in Waterloo. Stanton

called for tea to renew her acquaintance with Mott, and it was in this context of friendship and shared concern for reform that the two began planning the convention that was held two weeks later.

Stanton and her family had moved from Boston, where, she remembered, they had "near neighbors, a new home with all the modern conveniences, and well-trained servants." Living in a house on the outskirts of Seneca Falls, her three children suffering from malaria, she had none of those things.

As she and Mott spoke of the changes that would be necessary to allow women to care for their families but have energy left over to reform "the wrongs of society," the idea of a women's rights convention was born. The women's rights movement that took shape from this convention proved exceptionally long-lasting. Stanton, soon to form a working partnership with former temperance worker Susan B. Anthony, devoted the rest of her life to women's rights.

But what of Charlotte Woodward, a local farm girl, unaware of the national reform community? Why was she there? In this age of hopefulness and change she wanted a better life for herself. She was motivated, she said, by "all the hours that I sat and sewed gloves for a miserable pittance, which, after it was earned, could never be mine." By law and custom her father, as head of the household, was entitled to her wages. "I wanted to work," she explained, "but I wanted to choose my task and I wanted to collect my wages." The reforming women of Seneca Falls, grouped together on behalf of social improvement, had found in the first women's rights convention a way to speak for the needs of working women such as Charlotte Woodward as well as for themselves.

All over the North, in communities like Seneca Falls as well as in cities like New York, Americans gathered together in reform organizations to try to solve the problems that the market revolution posed for work, family life, personal and social values, and urban growth. Through these organizations local women and men became participants in wider communities of concern. ■

KEY TOPICS

- The new social problems that accompanied urbanization and immigration

- The responses of reformers

- The origins and political effects of the abolitionist movement

- The involvement of women in reform efforts

URBAN AMERICA

Although the market revolution affected all aspects of American life, nowhere was its impact so noticeable as in the cities.

The Growth of Cities

The market revolution dramatically increased the size of America's cities, with the great seaports leading the way. The proportion of America's population living in cities increased from only 7 percent in 1820 to almost 20 percent in 1860, a rate of growth greater than at any other time in the country's history. The nation's five largest cities in 1850 were the same as in 1800, with one exception. New York, Philadelphia, Baltimore, and Boston still topped the list, but New Orleans had edged out Charleston (see Chapters 9 and 11). The rate of urban growth was extraordinary. All four Atlantic seaports grew at least 25 percent each decade between 1800 and 1860, and often much more. New York, which grew from 60,000 in 1800 to 202,600 in 1830 and to more than 1 million in 1860, emerged as the nation's most populous city, its largest port, and its financial center.

Philadelphia, which had been the nation's largest city in 1800, was half the size of New York in 1850. Nevertheless, its growth was substantial—from 70,000 in 1800 to 389,000 in 1850 and to 565,529 in 1860. Philadelphia became as much an industrial as a commercial city.

Baltimore, with 212,418 residents in 1860, was about half the size of Philadelphia. The city's merchants, hoping to counter the threat posed by the Erie Canal to their trade links with the trans-Appalachian West, financed the nation's first important railroad, the Baltimore and Ohio, which began operation in 1830. Although Baltimore remained the east coast center of the tobacco trade with Europe, by 1850 its major partner in foreign trade was Brazil, to which it shipped flour and from which it imported coffee.

Boston, in colonial times, had dominated the triangular trade linking Britain and the West Indies. By 1860, with a population of 177,840, the city had emerged as the center of a new triangular trade: the ships of Boston merchants carried New England cotton cloth, shoes, and other manufactured goods to the South, delivered southern cotton to British and European ports, and returned to Boston with European manufactured goods. Boston still dominated the China trade as well.

New Orleans, fed by the expansion of cotton throughout the South and commercial agriculture in the Mississippi Valley, had a population of 168,675 in 1860, and this population, as had been true in 1800, was the most racially diverse of any large city. In the 1850s, New Orleans handled about half the nation's cotton exports and by 1860, its exports—$5 million in 1815—had risen to $107 million.

The market revolution oriented the attention of each of these major seaports away from the oceans and toward trade with the nation's interior. Prosperous merchants in these cities now depended on American exports rather than European imports for their profits.

Another result of the market revolution was the appearance of "instant" cities at critical points on the new transportation network. Utica, New York, once a frontier trading post, was transformed by the opening of the Erie Canal into a commercial and manufacturing center. Chicago, on the shores of Lake Michigan, was transformed by the coming of the railroad into a major junction for water and rail transport. The city, which emerged as a fur trading center around Fort Dearborn, an army post built in 1803, had become, by the 1850s, a hub of trade boasting grain storage facilities, slaughterhouses, and warehouses of all kinds. Farm implement manufacturers such as Cyrus McCormick built manufacturing plants there to serve the needs of Midwest farmers. By 1860 Chicago had a population of

100,000, making it the nation's eighth largest city (after Cincinnati and St. Louis).

Patterns of Immigration

One of the key aspects of urban growth was a surge in immigration to the United States that began in the 1820s and accelerated dramatically after 1830. From an annual figure of about 20,000 in 1831, immigration ballooned to a record 430,000 in 1854 before declining in the years prior to the Civil War. The proportion of immigrants in the population jumped from 1.6 percent in the 1820s to 11.2 percent in 1860. In the nation's cities, the proportion was vastly larger: by 1860, nearly half of New York's population (48 percent) was foreign-born.

Most of the immigrants to the United States during this period came from Ireland and Germany. Political unrest and poor economic conditions in Germany and the catastrophic Potato Famine of 1845–1850 in Ireland were responsible for an enormous surge in immigration from those countries between 1845 and 1854. The starving, desperate "Famine Irish" who crowded into eastern seaports were America's first large refugee group. Between them, the Germans and the Irish represented the largest influx of non-English immigrants the country had known (many Americans found the Irish dialect as strange as a foreign language). They were also the poorest: most of the Irish arrived destitute. In addition, most of the Irish and half of the Germans were Catholics, an unwelcome novelty to many Protestant Americans.

The influx of mostly poor, mostly Catholic foreigners provoked nativist hostility among many Protestant, native-born Americans, including many leaders of the major reform movements (see Chapter 15). It would be a mistake, however, to think that immigration was unwelcome to everyone. Industries needed willing workers, and western states were eager for settlers. In 1852 Wisconsin appointed a commissioner of emigration with responsibility for attracting Europeans to the state.

Immigrant labor fueled the nation's expanding economy and helped turn wilderness into farmland. Many of the changes in industry and transportation that accompanied the market revolution would have been impossible without immigrants. Irish contract workers, for example, were essential to the completion of the Erie Canal in 1825.

Few immigrants found life in the United States pleasant or easy. In addition to the psychological difficulties of leaving a home and familiar ways behind, most immigrants endured harsh living and working conditions. America's cities were unprepared for the social problems posed by large numbers of immigrants. Until the 1880s, the task of receiving immigrants fell completely on cities and states, not the federal government. New York City, by far the largest port of entry, did not even establish an official reception center until 1855, when Castle Garden, at the bottom of Manhattan Island (near present-day Battery Park), was so designated.

Irish Immigration

The first major immigrant wave to test American cities was caused by the catastrophic Irish Potato Famine of 1845–49. Irish emigration to the United States dated from colonial times; young people who knew they could not hope to own land in Ireland had long looked to America for better opportunities. Indeed, from 1818 to 1845, at least 10,000 Irish emigrated yearly. But in the latter year Ireland's green fields of potato plants turned black with blight. The Irish had two choices: starve or leave. One million people died, and another 1.5 million emigrated, the majority to the United States. Starving, diseased (thousands died of typhus during the voyage), and destitute, hundreds of thousands (250,000 in 1851 alone) disembarked in the east coast ports of New York, Philadelphia, Boston, and Baltimore. Lacking the money to go inland and begin farming, they remained in the cities. Crowded together in miserable housing, desperate for work at any wages, foreign in their religion and pastimes (drinking and fighting, their critics said), tenaciously nationalistic and bitterly anti-British, they created ethnic enclaves of a kind new to American cities.

The largest numbers of Irish came to New York, which managed to absorb them. But Boston, a much smaller and more homogeneous city, was overwhelmed by the Irish influx. By 1850, a quarter of Boston's population was Irish, most of them recent immigrants. Boston, the home of Puritanism and the center of American intellectualism, did not welcome illiterate Irish Catholic peasants. All over the city in places of business and in homes normally eager for domestic servants the signs went up: "No Irish Need Apply."

German Immigration

Germans, like the Irish, had a long history of emigration to America. The nineteenth-century immigration of Germans began somewhat later and more slowly than that of the Irish, but by 1854 it had surpassed the Irish influx. Some German peasants, like the Irish, were driven from their homeland by potato blight in the mid-1840s. But the typical German immigrant was a small farmer or artisan dislodged by the same market forces at work in America: the industrialization of production and consolidation and the commercialization of farming. There was also a small group of middle-class liberal intellectuals who left the German states (Germany was not yet a unified nation) after 1848 when attempts at revolution had failed. On the whole, German migrants were not as poor as the Irish, and they could afford to move out of the east coast seaports to other locations.

The first two major ports of embarkation for the Germans were Bremen (in northern Germany) and Le Havre (in northern France), which were also the main ports for the importation of American tobacco and cotton. The tobacco boats bore the Bremen passengers to Baltimore, and the cotton ships took them to New Orleans, a major entry point for European immigrants until the Civil War. From these ports, many Germans made their way up the Mississippi and Ohio valleys, where they settled in Pittsburgh, Cincinnati, and St. Louis and on farms in Ohio, Indiana, Missouri, and Texas.

German agricultural communities took a distinctive form that fostered cultural continuity. Immigrants formed predominantly German towns by clustering, or taking up adjoining land. A small cluster could support German churches, German-language schools, and German customs and thereby attract other Germans, some directly from Europe and some from other parts of the United States. Such communities reinforced the traditional values of German farmers, such as persistence, hard work, and thrift.

Another area attracting immigrants in the early nineteenth century was Gold Rush California, which drew, among others, numbers of Chinese (see Chapter 14). The Chinese who came to California worked in the mines, most as independent prospectors. Other miners disliked their industriousness and their clannishness. By the mid-1860s, Chinese workers made up 90 percent of the laborers building the Central Pacific Railroad, replacing more expensive white laborers and sowing the seeds of the long-lasting hostility of American workers toward Chinese. In the years to come, as hostility against the Chinese broke into violence, Chinatowns in San Francisco and elsewhere served a vital function as safe refuges for the Chinese who remained in the United States.

Class Structure and Living Patterns in the Cities

Although per capita income in America is estimated to have doubled between 1800 and 1850, the gap between rich and poor increased and became glaringly apparent in the nation's cities. The benefits of the market revolution were unequally distributed. In the cities there was a very small group of wealthy people with a net worth of more than $5,000 (about 3 percent of the population), a very large group of poor people with a net worth of $100 or less (nearly 70 percent), and a middle class with incomes in between (25–30 percent).

Differences in income affected every aspect of urban life. Very poor families, including almost all new immigrants, performed unskilled labor in jobs where the future was uncertain at best, lived in cheap rented housing, moved frequently, and depended on more than one income to survive. Artisans and skilled workers with incomes of $500 or more could live adequately, though often in cramped quarters that also served as their shops. A middle-class family with an income of more than $1,000 a year could live comfortably in a house of four to six rooms complete with carpeting, wallpaper, and good furniture. The very rich built mansions and large town houses and staffed them with many servants. In the summer they left the cities for country estates or homes at seaside resorts such as Newport, Rhode Island, which attracted wealthy families from all over the country.

Early nineteenth-century cities lacked municipal water supplies, sewers, and garbage collection. People drank water from wells, used outdoor privies that often contaminated the water supply, and threw garbage and slop out the door to be foraged by roaming herds of pigs. Clearly, this was a recipe for disease, and every American city suffered epidemics of sanitation-related diseases such as yellow fever, cholera, and typhus. Philadelphia's yellow fever epidemic of 1793 caused 4,000 deaths and stopped all business with the outside world for more than a month.

Yet the cities were slow to take action. In part this was due to poor medical understanding of disease but at least equally to expense. In response to the yellow fever epidemic, Philadelphia completed a city water system in 1801, but users had to pay a fee, and only the richest subscribed in the early days. Neither New York nor Boston had a public water system until the 1840s. Garbage collection remained a private service, and cities charged property owners for the costs of sewers, water mains, and street paving. Poorer areas of the cities could not afford the costs.

Provision of municipal services forced residential segregation. Richer people clustered in neighborhoods that had the new amenities. Increasingly, the poor clustered in bad neighborhoods that became known as slums. The worst New York slum in the nineteenth century was Five Points, a stone's throw from city hall. There, immigrants, free black people, and criminals were crammed into rundown buildings known in the slang of the time as "rookeries." Notorious gangs of thieves and pickpockets with names such as the Plug Uglies and the Shirt Tails dominated the district. Starvation and murder were commonplace.

After 1830, when urban growth was augmented by increasing immigration from Europe, middle-class Americans increasingly saw slums as the home of strange and foreign people, who deserved less than American-born citizens. In this way, residential patterns came to embody larger issues of class and citizenship.

Ethnic Neighborhoods

To poverty-stricken Irish immigrants, these same slums represented not only family ties and familiar ways but also community support as they learned how to survive in new surroundings. Isolated partly by their own beliefs (for Catholics fully reciprocated the hatred and fear that Protestants had showed them), Irish immigrants created their own communities in Boston and New York, their major destinations. They raised the money to erect Catholic churches with Irish priests. They established parochial schools with Irish nuns as teachers and sent their children to them in preference to the openly anti-Catholic public schools. They formed mutual aid societies based on kinship or town of origin in Ireland. Men and women formed religious and social clubs, lodges, and brotherhoods and their female auxiliaries. Irishmen manned fire and militia companies as well. This dense network of associations served the same purpose that social welfare organizations do today: providing help in time of need and offering companionship in a hostile environment.

Germans who settled in urban areas also built their own ethnic enclaves—"Little Germanies"—in which they sought to duplicate the rich cultural life of German cities. Like the Irish, the Germans formed church societies, mutual benefit societies, and fire and militia companies to provide mutual support. The Germans also

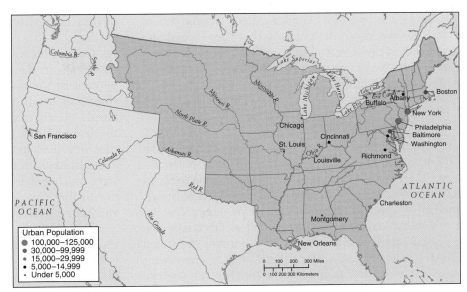

American Cities, 1820

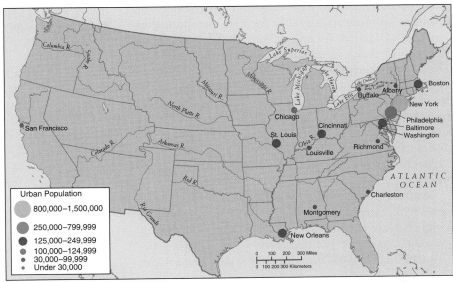

American Cities, 1860   The cities of North America grew more rapidly between 1820 and 1860 than at any other time in the nation's history. Eastern seaport cities remained the largest, but New York grew to twice the size of the second largest city, Philadelphia. New York's growth, due in large part to the increase in trade following the opening of the Erie Canal, illustrates the importance of trade between port cities and the nation's interior. Inland river cities like Cincinnati and St. Louis and the great Mississippi seaport of New Orleans grew rapidly. San Francisco, Louisville, and Buffalo—still villages in 1820—grew also, but Chicago, which rapidly emerged as a hub for both water and rail transport, surpassed them all.

SOURCE: *Statistical Abstract of the United States.*

formed networks of leisure organizations: singing societies, debating and political clubs, concert halls like New York's Beethoven Hall, theaters, turnvereins (gymnastics associations), and beer gardens. They published German-language newspapers as well.

Ethnic clustering, then, allowed new immigrants to hold onto aspects of their culture that they valued and to transplant them to American soil. Many native-born Americans, however, viewed ethnic neighborhoods with deep suspicion.

Urban Popular Culture

The size, diversity, and changing working conditions in American cities bred a new, rougher, urban popular culture. Taverns that served as neighborhood centers of drink and sociability were also frequent centers of brawls and riots. Community groups such as fire engine companies that had once included men of all social classes now attracted rough young laborers who formed their own youth gangs and defended "their" turf against other gangs. Some trades, such as that of butcher, became notorious for starting fights in taverns and grog shops.

Theaters, which had been frequented by men of all social classes, provided another setting for violence. By the 1830s, middle-class and upper-class men withdrew to more respectable theaters to which they could bring their wives and daughters. Workers found new amusements in theaters such as the Lafayette Circus, which featured dancing girls and horseback riders as well as theatrical acts. Another popular urban working-class amusement was the blackface minstrel show. White actors (often Irish) blacked their faces and entertained audiences with songs (including the famous "Dixie," written by an Irishman as a blackface song), dances, theatrical skits, and anti-black political jokes.

Another challenge to middle-class respectability came from the immensely popular "penny papers," which began publication in 1833, and the rapidly growing number of political papers (see Chapter 10). This exuberant urban popular culture was unquestionably a part of the same new democratic political spirit that led to the great upsurge in political participation discussed in Chapter 10. And it was the inspiration for some of America's most innovative writers, foremost among them urban journalist, Democratic Party activist, and poet Walt Whitman, who distilled his passionate love for the variety and commonness of the American people in *Leaves of Grass*, a book of free-verse poems published in 1855. Regarded at the time as scandalous because of its frank language, Whitman's poetry nevertheless captured the driving energy and democratic spirit of the new urban popular culture. In a rather more sinister way, so did the writings of Edgar Allan Poe, who found the inspiration for his gothic horror stories such as "The Murders in the Rue Morgue" (1841) and "The Mystery of Marie Roget" (1842) not in Europe (as his titles might suggest) but in contemporary American crimes.

Urban Life of Free African Americans

By 1860, there were nearly half a million free African Americans in the United States, constituting about 11 percent of the country's total black population. More than half of all free African Americans lived in the North, mostly in cities. Philadelphia and New York had the largest black communities: 22,000 African Americans in Philadelphia and 12,500 in New York (another 4,313 lived just across the East River in Brooklyn). There were much smaller but still significant black communities in the New England cities of Boston, Providence, and New Haven and in Ohio cities like Cincinnati.

Free African Americans in northern cities faced residential segregation (except for the domestic servants who lived in with white families), pervasive job discrimination, segregated public schools, and severe limitations on their civil rights. In addition to these legal restrictions there were matters of custom: African Americans of all economic classes endured daily affronts, such as exclusion from public concerts, lectures, and libraries, and segregation or exclusion from public transportation.

In common with Irish and German immigrants, African Americans created defenses against the larger hostile society by building their own community structures. They formed associations for aiding the poorest members of the community, for self-improvement, and for socializing. Tired of being insulted by the white press, African American communities supported their own newspapers. The major community organization was the black Baptist or African Methodist Episcopal (AME) church, which served, as one historian put it, as "a place of worship, a social and cultural center, a political meetingplace, a hiding place for fugitives, a training ground for potential community leaders, and one of the few places where blacks could express their true feelings."

Employment prospects for black men deteriorated from 1820 to 1850. Those who had held jobs as skilled artisans were forced from their positions, and their sons denied apprenticeships, by white mechanics and craftsmen who were themselves suffering from the effects of the market revolution. Limited to day labor, African Americans found themselves in direct competition with the new immigrants, especially the Irish, for jobs. On the waterfront, black men lost their jobs as carters and longshoremen to the Irish. One of the few occupations to remain open to them was that of seaman. More than 20 percent of all American sailors in 1850 were black, and over the years their ranks included an increasing number of runaway slaves. The pay was poor and the conditions miserable, but many black men found more equality aboard ship than they did ashore. Mothers, wives, and

Free African Americans suffered many forms of discrimination, but as this 1850 daguerreotype of an unknown woman shows, they sought to achieve the same levels of education and economic comfort as other Americans.

SOURCE: Zelsa P. Mackay Collection. Courtesy George Eastman House.

daughters were left ashore to work as domestic servants (in competition with Irishwomen), washerwomen, and seamstresses.

THE LABOR MOVEMENT AND URBAN POLITICS

Universal white manhood suffrage and the development of mass politics (see Chapter 10), coupled with the rapid growth of cities, changed urban politics. The traditional leadership role of the wealthy elite waned. In their place were professional politicians whose job it was to make party politics work. In New York and in other large cities, this change in politics was spurred by working-class activism.

The Tradition of Artisanal Politics

Protests by urban workers had been an integral part of the older social order controlled by the wealthy elite. In the eighteenth century, when only men of property could vote, such demonstrations usually indicated widespread discontent or economic difficulty among workers. They served as a warning signal that the political elite rarely ignored.

By the 1830s the status of artisans and independent craftsmen in the nation's cities had changed. Workers' associations came to include defensive and angry workes who were acutely conscious of their declining status in the economic and social order. Tentatively at first, but then with growing conviction, they became active defenders of working-class interests.

What was new was the open antagonism between workers and employers. The community of interest between masters and workers in preindustrial times broke down. Workers realized they had to depend on other workers, not employers, for support. In turn, employers and members of the middle class began to take urban disorders much more seriously than their grandfathers might have done.

The Union Movement

Urban worker protest against changing conditions quickly took the form of party politics. The Workingmen's Party was founded in Philadelphia in 1827, and chapters quickly formed in New York and Boston as well. Using the language of class warfare—"two distinct classes . . . those that live by their own labor and they that live upon the labor of others"—the "Workies" campaigned for the ten-hour day and the preservation of the small artisanal shop. They also called for the end of government-chartered monopolies—banks were high on the list. And they were in favor of a public school system and cheap land in the West. Although the Workies themselves did not survive as a party, Jacksonian Democrats were quick to pick up on some of their themes. The Democrats attracted many Workingmen's votes in 1832.

Both major parties competed for the votes of urban workers. Nevertheless, neither major political party really spoke to the primary need of workers—for well-paid, stable jobs that assured them independence and respect. Unsatisfied with the response of political parties, workers turned to labor organization to achieve their goals.

Between 1833 and 1837 a wave of strikes in New York City cut the remaining ties between master craftsmen and the journeymen who worked for them. In 1833, journeymen carpenters struck for higher wages. Workers in fifteen other trades came to their support, and within a month the strike was won. The lesson was obvious: if skilled workers banded together across craft lines, they could improve their conditions. The same year, representatives from nine different craft groups formed the General Trades Union (GTU) of

New York. By 1834 similar groups had sprung up in over a dozen cities. In 1834 representatives of several local GTUs met in Baltimore and organized the National Trades Union (NTU). In its founding statement the NTU criticized the "unjustifiable distribution of the wealth of society in the hands of a few individuals," which had created for working people "a humiliating, servile dependency, incompatible with . . . natural equality."

Convinced that unions were dangerous, New York employers took striking journeymen tailors to court in 1836. Judge Ogden Edwards pronounced the strikers guilty of conspiracy and declared unions un-American. The GTU responded with a mass rally at which Judge Edwards was burned in effigy. A year later, stunned by the effects of the Panic of 1837, the GTU collapsed. The founding of these general unions, a visible sign of a class-based community of interest among workers, is generally considered to mark the beginning of the American labor movement. However, these early unions included only white men in skilled trades who made up only a small percentage of all workers. The majority of workers—men in unskilled occupations, all free African Americans, and all women—were excluded.

Big-City Machines

As America's cities experienced unprecedented growth, the electorate mushroomed. In New York, for example, the number of voters grew from 20,000 in 1825 to 88,900 in 1855. Furthermore, by 1855 half of the voters were foreign-born. At the time, America was the only country in the world where propertyless white men had the vote. The job of serving this largely working-class electorate and making the new mass political party work at the urban level fell to a new kind of career politician—the boss—and a new kind of political organization—the machine.

In New York City, the Tammany Society, begun in the 1780s as a fraternal organization of artisans, slowly evolved into the key organization of the new mass politics. Tammany, which was affiliated with the national Democratic Party, reached voters by using many of the techniques of mass appeal made popular earlier by craft organizations—parades, rallies, current songs, and party newspapers.

Along with these new techniques of mass appeal went new methods of organization: a tight system of political control beginning at the neighborhood level with ward committees and topped by a chairman of a citywide general committee. At the citywide level, ward leaders—bosses—bartered the loyalty and votes of their followers for positions on the city payroll for party members and community services for their neighborhood. This was machine politics. Through it workers, although they lacked the political or organizational strength to challenge the harmful effects of the market revolution, could use their numbers to ameliorate some of its effects at the local level. Machine politics served to mediate increasing class divisions and ethnic diversity as well. The machines themselves offered personal ties and loyalties—community feeling—to recent arrivals in the big cities (increasingly, immigrants from Europe) and help in hard times to workers who cast their votes correctly.

SOCIAL REFORM MOVEMENTS

As the opening of this chapter describes, the earliest response to the dislocations caused by the market revolution was community based and voluntary. The reform message was vastly amplified by inventions such as the steam printing press, which made it possible to publish reform literature in great volume. Soon there were national networks of reform groups.

Alexis de Tocqueville commented on the vast extent of American voluntary associations and their many purposes. "In no country in the world," he noted, "has the principle of association been more successfully used, or more unsparingly applied to a multitude of different objects, than in America."

Evangelism, Reform, and Social Control

Evangelical religion was fundamental to social reform. Men and women who had been converted to the enthusiastic new faith assumed personal responsibility for making changes in their own lives. Members of evangelistic religions expected to convert the world and create the perfect moral and religious community on earth. Much of America was swept by the fervor of moralistic reform, and it was the new middle class, who applied new notions of morality to the movement, that set the agenda for reform.

Reform efforts arose from the recognition that the traditional methods of small-scale local relief were no longer adequate. Reformers realized that large cities had to make large-scale provisions for social misfits and that institutional rather than private efforts were needed. This thinking was especially true of the institutional reform movements that began in the 1830s, such as the push for insane asylums. At this time, of course, the federal government provided no such relief.

A second characteristic of the reform movements was a belief in the basic goodness of human nature. All reformers believed that the condition of the unfortunate—the poor, the insane, the criminal—would improve in a wholesome environment. Thus, insane asylums were built in rural areas, away from the noise and stress of the cities, and orphanages had strict rules that were meant to encourage discipline and self-reliance. Prison reform carried this sentiment to the extreme. On the theory that bad social influences were largely responsible for crime, some "model" prisons completely isolated prisoners from one another, making them eat, sleep, work, and do required Bible reading in their own cells. The failure of these prisons to achieve dramatic changes for the better in their inmates (a number of isolated prisoners went mad, and some committed suicide) or to reduce crime was one of the first indications that reform was not a simple task.

A third characteristic of the reform movements was their moralistic dogmatism. Reformers were certain they knew what was right and were determined to see their improvements enacted. It was a short step from developing individual self-discipline to imposing discipline on others. The reforms that were proposed thus took the form of social controls. Lazy, sinful, intemperate, or unfit members of society were to be reformed for their own good, whether they wanted to be or not. This attitude was bound to cause controversy; by no means did all Americans share the reformers' beliefs, nor did those for whom it was intended always take kindly to being the targets of the reformers' concern.

Indeed, some aspects of the social reform movements were harmful. The evangelical Protestantism of the reformers promoted a dangerous hostility to Catholic immigrants from Ireland and Germany that repeatedly led to urban riots. The temperance movement, in particular, targeted immigrants for their free drinking habits. Seeking uniformity of behavior rather than tolerance, the reformers thus helped to promote the virulent nativism that infected American politics between 1840 and 1860 (see Chapter 15).

Regional and national reform organizations quickly grew from local projects to deal with social problems such as drinking, prostitution, mental illness, and crime. In 1828, for example, Congregationalist minister Lyman Beecher joined other ministers in forming a General Union for Promoting the Observance of the Christian Sabbath; the aim was to prevent business on Sundays. The Sabbath reformers engaged in political action but remained aloof from direct electoral politics, stressing their religious mission. In any case, sabbatarianism was controversial. Workingmen (who usually worked six days a week) were angered when the General Union forced the Sunday closure of their favorite taverns and were quick to vote against the Whigs, the party perceived to be most sympathetic to reform thinking.

Education and Women Teachers

Women became deeply involved in reform movements through their churches. Nearly every church had a maternal association, where mothers gathered to discuss ways to raise their children as true Christians. These associations reflected a new and more positive definition of childhood. The Puritans had believed that children were born sinful and that their wills had to be broken before they could become godly. Educational reformers, however, tended to believe that children were born innocent and needed gentle nurturing and encouragement if they were to flourish. At home, mothers began to play the central role in child rearing. Outside the home, women helped spread the new public education pioneered by Horace Mann, secretary of the Massachusetts State Board of Education.

Although literacy had long been valued, especially in New England, schooling since colonial times had been a private enterprise and a personal expense. Town grammar schools, required in Massachusetts since 1647, had been supported primarily by parents' payments, with some help from local property taxes. In 1827, Massachusetts pioneered compulsory education by legislating that public schools be supported by public taxes. Soon schooling for white children between the ages of five and nineteen was common, although, especially in rural schools, the term might be only a month or so long. Uniformity in curriculum and teacher training, and the grading of classes by ability—measures pioneered by Horace Mann in the 1830s—quickly caught on in other states. In the North and West (the South lagged far behind), more and more children went to school, and more and more teachers, usually young single women, were hired to teach them.

The spread of public education created the first real career opportunity for women. The great champion of teacher training for women was Catharine Beecher, daughter of Lyman, who clearly saw her efforts as part of the larger work of establishing "the moral government of God." By 1850 women were dominant in primary school teaching, which had come to be regarded as an acceptable occupation for educated young women during the few years between their own schooling and marriage. For some women, teaching was a great adventure; they enthusiastically volunteered to be "schoolmarms" on the distant western frontiers of Wisconsin and Iowa or to be missionary teachers in distant lands. For others, a few years of teaching was quite enough. Low pay (half of what male schoolteachers earned) and community supervision (women teachers had to board with families in the community) were probably sufficient to make almost any marriage proposal look appealing.

Temperance

The largest reform organization of the period, the American Society for the Promotion of Temperance, founded in 1826, boasted more than 200,000 members by the mid-1830s. Dominated by evangelicals, local chapters used revival methods—lurid temperance tracts detailing the evils of alcohol, large prayer and song meetings, and heavy group pressure—to encourage young men to stand up, confess their bad habits, and "take the pledge" not to drink. Here again, women played an important role.

Traditionally, drinking had been a basic part of men's working lives. It concluded occasions as formal as the signing of a contract and accompanied such informal activities as card games. Drink was a staple offering at political speeches, rallies, and elections. Much of the drinking was well within the bounds of sociability, but the widespread use (more than seven gallons of hard liquor per capita in 1830—more than twice as much as today's rate) must have encouraged drunkenness.

There were many reasons to support temperance. Men drank hard cider and liquor—whiskey, rum—in abundance. Heavy-drinking men hurt their families economically by spending their wages on drink. Excessive drinking also led to violence and crime, both within the family and in the larger society. But there were other reasons for the temperance movement. The new middle class, preoccupied with respectability, morality, and efficiency, found the old easygoing drinking ways unacceptable. As work patterns changed, employers banned alcohol at work and increasingly considered drinking men not only unreliable but immoral. Temperance became a social and political issue. Whigs, who embraced the new morality, favored it; Democrats, who in northern cities consisted increasingly of immigrant workers, were opposed.

The Panic of 1837 affected the temperance movement. Whereas most temperance crusaders in the 1820s had been members of the middle class, the long depression of 1837–43 prompted artisans and skilled workers to give up or at least cut down substantially on drinking. Forming associations known as Washington Temperance Societies, these workers spread the word that temperance was the workingman's best chance to survive economically and to maintain his independence. Their wives, gathered together in Martha Washington Societies, were frequently even more committed to temperance than their husbands.

By the mid-1840s alcohol consumption had been more than halved, to less than two gallons per capita, about the level of today. Concern over drinking would remain constant throughout the nineteenth century and into the twentieth.

Moral Reform, Asylums, and Prisons

Alcohol was not the only "social evil" that reform groups attacked. Another was prostitution, which was common in the nation's port cities. The customary approach of evangelical reformers was to "rescue" prostitutes, offering them the salvation of religion, prayer, and temporary shelter. The success rate was not very high. As an alternative to prostitution, reformers usually offered domestic work, a low-paying and restrictive occupation that many women scorned. Nevertheless, campaigns against prostitution, generally organized by women, continued throughout the nineteenth century. One of the earliest and most effective antiprostitution groups was the Female Moral Reform Society. Founded by evangelical women in New York in 1834 (the first president was Lydia Finney), it boasted 555 affiliates throughout the country by 1840.

Another dramatic example of reform was the asylum movement, spearheaded by the woman evangelist Dorothea Dix. In 1843, Dix horrified the Massachusetts state legislature with the results of her several years of study into the conditions to which insane women were subjected. Dix's efforts led to the establishment of a state asylum for the insane in Massachusetts and to similar institutions in other states. Between 1843 and 1854 Dix traveled more than 30,000 miles to publicize the movement for humane treatment of the insane. By 1860 twenty-eight states had public institutions for the insane.

Other reformers were active in related causes, such as prison reform and the establishment of orphanages, homes of refuge, and hospitals. Model penitentiaries were built in Auburn and Ossining (known as "Sing Sing"), New York, and in Philadelphia and Pittsburgh. Characterized by strict order and discipline, these prisons were supposed to reform rather than simply incarcerate their inmates, but their regimes of silence and isolation caused despair more often than rehabilitation.

Utopianism and Mormonism

Amid all the political activism and reform fervor of the 1830s, a few people chose escape into utopian communities and new religions. The upstate New York area along the Erie Canal was the seedbed for this movement, just as it was for evangelical revivals and reform movements like the Seneca Falls convention. The area was so notable for its reform enthusiasms that it has been termed "the Burned-Over District," a reference to the waves of reform that swept through like forest fires.

Apocalyptic religions tend to spring up in places experiencing rapid social change. The Erie Canal region, which experienced the full impact of the market revolution in the early nineteenth century, was such a place. A second catalyst is hard times, and the prolonged depression that began with the Panic of 1837 led some people to embrace a belief in imminent catastrophe. The Millerites (named for their founder, William Miller) believed that the Second Coming of Christ would occur on October 22, 1843. In anticipation, members of the church sold their belongings and bought white robes for their ascension to heaven. When the Day of Judgment did not take place as expected, most of Miller's followers drifted away. But a small group persisted. Revising their expectations, they formed the core of the Seventh-Day Adventist faith, which is still active today.

The Shakers, founded by "Mother" Ann Lee in 1774, were the oldest utopian group. An offshoot of the Quakers, the Shakers espoused a radical social philosophy that called for the abolishment of the traditional family in favor of a family of brothers and sisters joined in equal fellowship. Despite its insistence on celibacy, the Shaker movement grew between 1820 and 1830, eventually reaching twenty settlements in eight states with a total membership of 6,000. The Shaker's simple and highly structured lifestyle, their isolation from the changing world, and their belief in equality drew new followers, especially among women.

The most successful of the nineteenth-century communitarian movements was also a product of the Burned-Over District. In 1830, a young man named Joseph Smith founded the Church of Jesus Christ of Latter-Day Saints, based on the teachings of the Book of Mormon, which he claimed to have received from an angel in a vision.

Initially, Mormonism, as the new religion became known, seemed little different from the many other new religious groups and utopian communities of the time. But under the benevolent but absolute authority of its patriarch, Joseph Smith, it rapidly gained distinction for its extraordinary communitarianism. Close cooperation and hard work made the Mormon community successful, attracting both new followers and the animosity of neighbors, who resented Mormon exclusiveness and economic success. The Mormons were harassed in New York and driven west to Ohio and then Missouri. Finally they seemed to find an ideal home in Nauvoo, Illinois, where in 1839 they built a model community, achieving almost complete self-government and isolation from non-Mormon neighbors. But in 1844, dissension within the community over Joseph Smith's new doctrine of polygamy (marriage between one man and more than one woman, simultaneously) gave outsiders a chance to intervene. Smith and his brother were arrested peacefully but were killed by a mob from which their jailers failed to protect them.

The beleaguered Mormon community decided to move beyond reach of harm. Led by Brigham Young, the Mormons migrated in 1846 to the Great Salt Lake in present-day Utah. After several lean years (once a grasshopper plague was stopped by the providential arrival of sea gulls, who ate the insects), the Mormon method of communal settlement proved successful. Their hopes of isolation were dashed, however, by the California Gold Rush of 1849.

ANTISLAVERY AND ABOLITIONISM

The antislavery feeling that was to play such an important role in the politics of the 1840s and 1850s also had its roots in the religious reform movements that began in the 1820s and 1830s. Three groups—free African Americans, Quakers, and militant white reformers—worked to bring an end to slavery, but each in different ways.

The American Colonization Society

The first official attempt to "solve" the problem of slavery was a plan for gradual emancipation of slaves (with compensation to their owners) and their resettlement in Africa. This plan was the work of the American Colonization Society, formed in 1817 by northern religious reformers and a number of southern slave owners. The Society was ineffective; by 1830, it had managed to send only 1,400 black people to a colony in Liberia, West Africa.

African Americans' Fight against Slavery

For free African Americans the freedom of other balck people had always been a major goal. Most rejected colonization, insisting instead on a commitment to the immediate end of slavery and the equal treatment of black people in America. By 1830 there were at least fifty black abolitionist societies in the North. These organizations held yearly national conventions, where famous African American abolitionists like Frederick Douglass, Harriet Tubman, and Sojourner Truth spoke. The first African American newspaper, founded in 1827 by John Russwurm and Samuel Cornish, announced its antislavery position in its title, *Freedom's Journal.*

In 1829 David Walker, a free African American in Boston, wrote a widely distributed pamphlet, *Appeal to the Colored Citizens of the World,* that encouraged slave rebellion. White Southerners blamed pamphlets such as these and the militant articles of African American journalists for stirring up trouble among southern slaves, and in particular for Nat Turner's revolt in 1831. The vehemence of white southern reaction testifies to the courage of that handful of determined free African Americans who persisted in speaking for their enslaved brothers and sisters long before most white Northerners even noticed.

This poignant engraving of a chained female slave was made by Patrick Reason, a black artist, in 1835. The accompanying message. "Am I Not a Woman and a Sister?" spoke especially to female abolitionists in the North.

SOURCE: Library of Congress.

Abolitionists

The third and best-known group of antislavery reformers was headed by William Lloyd Garrison. In 1831 Garrison broke with the gradualist persuaders of the American Colonization Society and began publishing his own paper, the *Liberator.* Garrison, the embodiment of moral indignation, was totally incapable of compromise. His approach was to mount a sweeping crusade condemning slavery as sinful and demanding its immediate abolishment. He took the radical step of demanding full social equality for African Americans, referring to them individually as "a man and a brother" and "a woman and a sister." Garrison's determination electrified the antislavery movement, but his inability to compromise limited his effectiveness as a leader.

Moral horror over slavery engaged many Northerners deeply in the abolitionist movement. They flocked to hear firsthand accounts of slavery by Frederick Douglass and Sojourner Truth, and by the white sisters from South Carolina, Angelina and Sarah Grimké. Northerners eagerly read slave narratives and books such as Theodore Weld's 1839 treatise *American Slavery As It Is* (based in part on the recollections of Angelina Grimké, whom Weld had married) that provided graphic details of abuse under slavery. Lyman Beecher's daughter, Harriet Beecher Stowe, was to draw on the Grimké-Weld book for her immensely popular antislavery novel *Uncle Tom's Cabin,* published in 1852.

The style of abolitionist writings and speeches was similar to the oratorical style of the religious revivalists. The abolitionists were confrontational, denunciatory, and personal in their message, much like the evangelical preachers.

They also adopted another tactic of revivalists and temperance workers when, to enhance their powers of persuasion, they began to publish great numbers of antislavery tracts. In 1835 alone they mailed more than a million pieces of antislavery literature to southern states. This tactic drew a backlash: southern legislatures banned abolitionist literature, encouraged the harassment and abuse of anyone distributing it, and looked the other way when proslavery mobs seized and burned it. Most serious, the majority of southern states reacted by toughening laws concerning emancipation, freedom of movement, and all aspects of slave behavior. Ironically, then, the immediate impact of abolitionism in the South was to stifle dissent and make the lives of slaves harder (see Chapter 11).

Even in the North, controversy over abolitionism was common. A tactic that abolitionists borrowed from revivalists—holding large and emotional meetings—opened the door to mob action. Crowds of people often disrupted such meetings, especially those addressed by Theodore Weld, whose oratorical style earned him the title of "the Most Mobbed Man in the United States." William Lloyd Garrison was stoned, dragged through the streets, and on one occasion almost hanged by a Boston mob.

Abolitionism and Politics

Abolitionism began as a social movement but soon intersected with sectional interests and became a national political issue. In the 1830s, massive abolitionist petition drives gathered a total of nearly 700,000 petitions requesting the abolition of slavery and the slave trade in the District of Columbia but were rebuffed by Congress. At southern insistence and with President Andrew Jackson's approval, Congress passed a "gag rule" in 1836 that prohibited discussion of antislavery petitions.

Many Northerners viewed the gag rule and censorship of the mails, which Southerners saw as necessary defenses against abolitionist frenzy, as alarming threats to free speech. First among them was Massachusetts representative John Quincy Adams, the only former president ever to serve in Congress after leaving the executive branch. Adams so publicly and persistently denounced the gag rule as a violation of the constitutional right to petition that it was repealed in 1844.

John Quincy Adams was also a key figure in the abolitionists' one undoubted victory, the fight to free the fifty-three slaves on the Spanish ship *Amistad* and return them to Africa. Although the Africans successfully mutinied against the *Amistad's* crew in 1839, when the ship was found in American waters a legal battle over their "ownership" ensued, during which the Africans themselves were held in jail. Prominent abolitionists, most notably Lewis Tappan, financed the legal fight that went all the way to the Supreme Court, where Adams won the case for the *Amistad* defendants against the American government, which supported the Spanish claim.

Although abolitionist groups raised the nation's emotional temperature, they failed to achieve the moral unity they had hoped for, and they began to splinter. Frederick Douglass and William Lloyd Garrison parted ways when Douglass, refusing to be limited to a simple recital of his life as a slave, began to make specific suggestions for improvements in the lives of free African Americans. When Douglass chose the path of political action, Garrison denounced him as "ungrateful." Douglass and other free African Americans worked under persistent discrimination, even from antislavery whites;

some of the latter refused to hire black people or to meet with them as equals. While many white reformers eagerly pressed for civil equality for African Americans, they did not accept the idea of social equality. On the other hand, black and white "stations" worked closely in the risky enterprise of passing fugitive slaves north over the famous Underground Railroad, as the various routes by which slaves made their way to freedom were called. Contrary to abolitionist legend, however, it was free African Americans, rather than white people, who played the major part in helping the fugitives.

In 1840 the abolitionist movement formally split. The majority moved toward party politics (which Garrison abhorred), founding the Liberty Party and choosing James G. Birney (whom Theodore Weld had converted to abolitionism) as their presidential candidate. Thus, abolitionist movement, which began as an effort at moral reform, took its first major step into politics, and this step in turn led to the formation of the Republican Party in the 1850s and to the Civil War.

THE WOMEN'S RIGHTS MOVEMENT

American women, without the vote or a role in party politics, found a field of activity in social reform movements. There was scarcely a reform movement in which women were not actively involved. Often men were the official leaders of such movements, and some women—especially those in the temperance, moral reform, and abolitionist movements—formed all-female chapters to define and implement their own policies and programs.

The majority of women did not participate in these activities, for they were fully occupied with housekeeping and child rearing (families with five children were the average). A few women—mostly members of the new middle class, who could afford servants—had the time and energy to look beyond their immediate tasks. Led thereby to challenge social restrictions, some, like the Grimké sisters, found that their commitment carried them beyond the limits of what was considered acceptable activity for women.

The Grimké Sisters

Sarah and Angelina Grimké, members of a prominent South Carolina slaveholding family, rejected slavery out of religious conviction and moved north to join a Quaker community near Philadelphia. In the 1830s, these two sisters found themselves drawn into the growing antislavery agitation in the North. Because they knew about slavery firsthand, they were in great demand as speakers. At first they spoke to "parlor meetings" of women only, as was considered proper, but as the meetings got larger and larger, the sisters realized that they had become the first female public speakers in America. In 1837 Angelina Grimké became the first woman to address a meeting of the Massachusetts state legislature.

Whereas male antislavery orators were criticized by the press and by conservative ministers for their abolitionist position, the Grimeké sisters were criticized for speaking out simply because they were women. A letter from a group of ministers cited the Bible in reprimanding the sisters for stepping out of "woman's proper sphere" of silence and subordination. Sarah Grimké answered the ministers in her 1838 *Letters on the Equality of the Sexes and the Condition of Women*, claiming that "men and women were CREATED EQUAL. . . . Whatever is right for a man to do, is right for woman."

Women in the antislavery movement found it a constant struggle to be heard. Some solved the problem of male dominance by forming their own groups, like the Philadelphia Female Anti-Slavery Society. In the antislavery movement and other reform groups as well, men accorded women a secondary role, even when—as was frequently the case—women constituted a majority of the members.

Women's Rights

The Seneca Falls Convention of 1848, the first women's rights convention in American history, was an outgrowth of almost twenty years of female activity in social reform. Every year after 1848 women gathered to hold women's rights conventions and to work for political, legal, and social equality. Over the years, in response to persistent lobbying, states passed property laws more favorable to women and altered divorce laws to allow women to retain custody of children. Teaching positions in higher education opened up to women, as did jobs in some other occupations, and women gained the vote in some states, beginning with Wyoming Territory in 1869. In 1920, seventy-two years after universal woman suffrage was first proposed at Seneca Falls, a woman's right to vote was at last guaranteed in the Nineteenth Amendment to the Constitution.

Women played a vital role in all the social movements of the day. In doing so they implicitly challenged the popular notion of separate spheres for men and women—the public world for him, home and family for her. The separate spheres argument, although it heaped praise on women for their allegedly superior moral qualities, was meant to exclude them from political life. The reforms discussed in this chapter show clearly that women reformers believed they had a right and a duty to propose solutions for the moral and social problems of the day. Empowered by their own religious beliefs and activism, the Seneca Falls reformers spoke for all American women when they demanded an end to the unfair restrictions they suffered as women.

Women's gatherings, like the first women's rights convention in Seneca Falls in 1848 and this meeting of strikers in Lynn in 1860, were indicators of widespread female activism.

SOURCE: Lynn Museum.

CONCLUSION

Beginning in the 1820s, the market revolution changed the size and social order of America's

CHRONOLOGY

1817	American Colonization Society founded
1820s	Shaker colonies grow
1826	American Society for the Promotion of Temperance founded
1827	Workingmen's Party founded in Philadelphia
	Freedom's Journal begins publication
	Public school movement begins in Massachusetts
1829	David Walker's *Appeal to the Colored Citizens of the World* is published
1830	Joseph Smith founds Church of Jesus Christ of Latter-Day Saints (Mormon Church)
	Charles G. Finney's revivals in Rochester
1831	William Lloyd Garrison begins publishing antislavery newspaper, the *Liberator*
1832	Immigration begins to increase
1833	American Anti-Slavery Society founded by William Lloyd Garrison and Theodore Weld
1834	First Female Moral Reform Society founded in New York
	National Trades Union formed

1836	Congress passes "gag rule" to prevent discussion of antislavery petitions
1837	Angelina Grimké addresses Massachusetts legislature
	Sarah Grimké, *Letters on the Equality of the Sexes and the Condition of Women*
	Panic begins seven-year depression
1839	Theodore Weld publishes *American Slavery As It Is*
1840s	New York and Boston complete public water systems
1840	Liberty Party founded
1843	Millerites await the end of the world
	Dorothea Dix spearheads asylum reform movement
1844	Mormon leader Joseph Smith killed by mob
1845	New York creates city police force
	Beginning of Irish Potato Famine and mass Irish immigration into the United States
1846	Mormons begin migration to the Great Salt Lake
1848	Women's Rights Convention at Seneca Falls

preindustrial cities and towns. Immigration, dramatically rapid population growth, and changes in working life and class structure created a host of new urban problems. Older, face-to-face methods of social control no longer worked. To fill the gap, new kinds of associations—the political party, the religious crusade, the reform cause, the union movement—sprang up. These associations were new manifestations of the deep human desire for social connection, for continuity, and—especially in the growing cities—for social order. A striking aspect of these associations was the uncompromising nature of the attitudes and beliefs on which they were based. Most groups were formed of like-minded people who wanted to impose their will on others. Such intolerance boded ill for the future. If political parties, religious bodies, and reform groups were to splinter along sectional lines (as happened in the 1850s), political compromise would be very difficult. In the meantime, however, Americans came to terms with the market revolution by engaging in a passion for improvement. As a perceptive foreign observer, Francis Grund, noted, "Americans love their country not as it is but as it will be."

REVIEW QUESTIONS

1. What impact did the new immigration of the 1840s and 1850s have on American cities?
2. Why did urbanization produce so many problems?
3. What motivated the social reformers of the period? Were they benevolent helpers or dictatorial social controllers? Study several reform causes and discuss similarities and differences among them.
4. Abolitionism differed little from other reforms in its tactics, but the effects of antislavery activism were politically explosive. Why was this so?

RECOMMENDED READING

Tyler Anbinder, *Five Points* (2001). A social history of New York's most notorious slum.

Arthur Bestor, *Backwoods Utopias* (1950). The standard work on utopian communities.

Paul Boyer, *Urban Masses and Moral Order in America, 1820–1920* (1978). Interprets reform as an effort to reestablish the moral order of the preindustrial community.

Amy Bridges, *A City in the Republic: Antebellum New York and the Origins of Machine Politics* (1984). An innovative look at the transition from elite political control to machine politics.

David Grimsted, *American Mobbing, 1828–1865: Toward Civil War* (1998). A national perspective on mob violence, North and South, including political violence.

Oscar Handlin, *Boston's Immigrants: A Study in Acculturation,* rev. ed., (1959). A pathbreaking exploration of conflict and adaptation among Boston's Irish community.

James Oliver Horton and Lois E. Horton, *In Hope of Liberty: Culture, Community and Protest Among Northern Free Blacks, 1700–1860* (1997). A fine portrait that adds the perspective of change over time to earlier studies.

Eric Lott, *Love and Theft: Blackface Minstrelsy and the American Working Class* (1993). Explores the complicated relationships between working-class amusements and racial attitudes.

Steven Mintz, *Moralists and Modernizers: America's Pre-Civil War Reformers* (1995). A brief but inclusive study of reforms and reformers.

David Roediger, *The Wages of Whiteness* (1991). Explores the links between artisanal republicanism, labor organization, and white racism.

David Rothman, *The Discovery of the Asylum: Social Order and Disorder in the New Republic* (1971). Explores institutional reforms.

Mary Ryan, *Civic Wars: Democracy and Public Life in the American City During the Nineteenth Century* (1997). A study of New York, New Orleans, and San Francisco that argues that urban popular culture was "meeting-place democracy" in action.

Kathryn Sklar, *Catharine Beecher: A Study in American Domesticity* (1973). An absorbing "life and times" that explores the possibilities and limits of women's roles in the early nineteenth century.

Sean Wilentz, *Chants Democratic: New York City and the Rise of the American Working Class, 1788–1850* (1983). An important book, rooted in social history, that reveals how workers acted upon their understanding of republicanism in confronting the changes wrought by the market revolution.

ON THE WEB

http://www.loc.gov/exhibits/british/brit-4.html

This Library of Congress site chronicles the parallel development of the British and the American abolitionist movements in the early to middle nineteenth century. It contains drawings, descriptions, and primary documents of the abolitionist cause. It also documents the woman's suffrage movement and carries that theme into the twentieth century.

http://www.osv.org/education/docs/ antislavery/debate.htm

This Old Sturbridge Village site contains primary documents relating to the Grimké sisters and their debates with Catharine E. Beecher who opposed public involvement by women in the abolition movement.

http://www.osv.org/education/docs/ antislavery/hartford.htm

http://www.osv.org/education/docs/ antislavery/bostriot.htm

These Old Sturbridge Village sites contain statements by Northerners in opposition to the abolition movement. Cited as primary documents in these sites are "A Declaration of the Sentiments of the People of Hartford, Regarding the Measures of the Abolitionists," and an antiabolitionist editorial in *The Hampshire Gazette*, October 28, 1835.

http://www.prenhall.com/faragherbrief/map13.1

Explore the many religious revivals and reform movements in the Burned-Over District in the 1830s and 1840s. Why were they strongest in this region of the country?

http://www.prenhall.com/faragherbrief/map13.2

Through a series of interactive maps, follow the progress of the Mormon community westward. Why did the Mormons settle near the Great Salt Lake?

AMERICAN COMMUNITIES

Texans and Tejanos "Remember the Alamo!"

FOR THIRTEEN DAYS IN FEBRUARY AND MARCH 1836, A FORCE OF 187 Texans held the mission fortress known as the Alamo against a siege by 5,000 Mexican troops under General Antonio López de Santa Anna, president of Mexico. Santa Anna had come north to subdue rebellious Texas, the northernmost part of the Mexican province of Coahuila y Tejas, and to place it under central authority. On March 6 he ordered a final assault, and in brutal fighting that claimed over 1,500 Mexican lives, his army took the mission. All the defenders were killed, including Commander William Travis and the well-known frontiersmen Jim Bowie and Davy Crockett. It was a crushing defeat for the Texans, but the cry "Remember the Alamo!" rallied their remaining forces, which, less than two months later, routed the Mexican army and forced Santa Anna to grant Texas independence from Mexico. Today the Alamo, in San Antonio, is one of the most cherished historic shrines in the United States.

But memory is selective: some things tend to be forgotten. Within a generation of the uprising few remembered that many Tejanos, Spanish-speaking people born in Texas, had joined with American settlers fighting for Texas independence. The Americans were concentrated in the central and eastern portions of the huge Texas territory, where during the 1820s the Mexican government had authorized several colonies managed by *empresarios* (land agents) like Stephen F. Austin. These settler communities consisted mostly of farmers from the Mississippi Valley, who introduced slavery and cotton growing to the rich lands of coastal and upland Texas.

The Tejano community, descended from eighteenth-century Spanish and Mexican settlers, included wealthy rancheros who raised cattle on the shortgrass prairies of south Texas, as well as the cowboys known as *vaqueros* and the *peónes*, or poor tenant farmers. Although there was relatively little contact between the Americans and Tejanos, their leaders interacted in San Antonio, the center of regional government. The Tejano elite welcomed the American immigrants and were enthusiastic about their plans for the economic development of Texas. Many Americans married into elite Tejano families, who hoped that by thus assimilating and sharing power with the Americans they could not only maintain but strengthen their community.

The Mexican state, however, was politically and socially unstable during these first years after its successful revolt against Spain in 1821.

Liberals favored a loose federal union, conservatives a strong central state. As a northern frontier province, Texas did not have the benefits of statehood; as a result most Tejanos found themselves taking the liberal side in the struggle, opting for more local control over government activities. When, in 1828, the conservative centralists came to power in Mexico City and decided the Americans had too much influence in Texas, many Tejanos rose up with the Americans in opposition. In 1832, the Tejano elite of San Antonio and many prominent rancheros went on record in favor of provincial autonomy and a strong role for the Americans.

One of the leaders of the San Antonio community was the wealthy ranchero Juan Nepomuceno Seguín. As Santa Anna's army approached from the south, Seguín recruited a company of Tejano volunteers and joined the American force inside the walls of the Alamo. During the siege, Commander Travis sent Seguín and some of his men for reinforcements. Stopped by Mexican troops on his way across the lines, Seguín called out, "*¡Somos paisanos!*" (We are countrymen!), confusing the guards just long enough for Seguín and his men to make their escape despite the hail of gunfire that quickly ensued. Seguín returned from his unsuccessful mission to find the burned bodies of the Alamo defenders, including seven San Antonio Tejanos. *"Texas será libre!"* (Texas shall be free!) Seguín called out as he directed the burial of the Alamo defenders. In April, Seguín led a regiment of Tejanos in the decisive battle of San Jacinto that won independence for Texas.

At first Tejanos were pleased with independence and played an important political role in the new Republic of Texas. The liberal Lorenzo de Zavala was chosen vice president, and Seguín became the mayor of San Antonio. But soon things began to change, illustrating a recurring pattern in the American occupation of new lands—a striking shift in the relations between different cultures in frontier areas. Most commonly, in the initial stage newcomers blended with native peoples, creating a "frontier of inclusion." The first hunters, trappers, and traders on every American frontier—west of the Appalachians, in the Southwest, and in the Far West— married into the local community and tried to learn native ways. Outnumbered Americans adapted to local societies as a matter of simple survival.

A second, unstable stage occurred when the number of Americans increased and they began occupying more and more land or, as in California, "rushing" in great numbers to mine gold, overrunning native communities. The usual result was warfare and the rapid growth of hostility and racial prejudice—all of which was largely absent in earlier days.

A third stage—that of stable settlement—occurred when the native community had been completely "removed" or isolated. In this "frontier of exclusion," racial mixing was rare. Generally, when Europeans pushed American Indians onto reservations they cut themselves off from sources of human history that could have helped them more fully understand the country into which they had moved. And in Texas, American settlers—initially invited in by Mexicans and Tejanos—developed an anti-Mexican passion, regarding all Spanish-speakers as their Mexican enemies rather than their Tejano allies.

Unscrupulous Americans exploited these prejudices to acquire Tejano property. If the rancheros were "sufficiently scared," one wrote, they would "make an advantageous sale of their lands," and if "two or three hundred of our troops should be stationed here, I have no doubt but a man could make some good speculations." Tejanos were attacked and forced from their homes; some of their villages were burned to the ground. "On the pretext that they were Mexicans," Seguín wrote, Americans treated Tejanos "worse than brutes . . . My countrymen ran to me for protection against the assaults or exactions of these adventurers." But even in his capacity as mayor Seguín could do little, and in 1842 he and his family, like hundreds of other Tejano families, fled south to Mexico in fear for their lives.

Thus, the Tejanos became symbols of a romanticized past rather than full participants in the building of western communities. Spanish-speaking communities in Texas, and later in New Mexico and California, like the communities of Indians throughout the West, became conquered peoples. "White folks and Mexicans were never made to live together," a Texas woman told a traveler a few years after the revolution. "The Mexicans had no business here," she said, and the Americans might "just have to get together and drive them all out of the country." The descendants of the first European settlers of the American Southwest had become foreigners in the land their people had lived in for two centuries. ■

San Antonio

KEY TOPICS

■ Continental expansion and the concept of Manifest Destiny

■ The contrasting examples of frontier development in Oregon, Texas, and California

■ How the political effects of expansion heightened sectional tensions

EXPLORING THE WEST

There seemed to be no stopping the expansion of the American people. By 1840 they had occupied all of the land east of the Mississippi River and had organized all of it (except for Florida and Wisconsin) into states. Of the ten states admitted to the Union between 1800 and 1840, all but one were west of the Appalachian Mountains. Less than sixty years after the United States gained its independence, the majority of its population lived west of the original thirteen states. This rapid expansion was caused by the market revolution, and especially the extraordinary expansion of transportation and commerce (see Chapter 12).

Many Americans looked eagerly westward to the vast unsettled reaches of the Louisiana Purchase: to Texas, Santa Fé, and trade with Mexico, and even to the Far West, where New England sea captains had been trading for furs since the 1790s. By 1848 the United States had gained all of these coveted western lands. This chapter examines the way the United States became a continental nation, forming many frontier communities in the process. Exploring the vast continent of North America and gaining an understanding of its geography took several centuries and the efforts of many people.

The Fur Trade

The fur trade, which flourished from the 1670s to the 1840s, was an important spur to exploration on the North American continent. In the 1670s, the British Hudson's Bay Company and its French Canadian rival, Montreal's North West Company, began exploring beyond the Great Lakes in the Canadian West in search of beaver pelts. Traders and trappers for both companies depended on the goodwill and cooperation of the native peoples of the region.

Not until the 1820s were American companies able to challenge British dominance of the trans-Mississippi fur trade. In 1824, William Henry Ashley of the Rocky Mountain Fur Company instituted the "ren-

The artist Alfred Jacob Miller, a careful observer of the western fur trade, shows us a mountain man and his Indian wife in his 1837 *Bourgeois Walker & His Wife*. Both Walker and his wife worked together to trap and prepare beaver pelts for market.

SOURCE: Alfred Jacob Miller, *Bourgeois Walker & His Wife*, 1837. The Walters Art Museum, Baltimore.

dezvous" system. This yearly trade fair, was a boisterous, polyglot, many-day affair at which trappers of many nationalities—Americans and Indian peoples, French Canadians, and métis, as well as Mexicans from Santa Fé and Taos—gathered to trade, drink, and gamble.

Like the British and French before them, most American trappers sought accommodation and friendship with Indian peoples: nearly half of them contracted long-lasting marriages with Indian women, who not only helped in the trapping and curing of furs but also acted as vital diplomatic links between the white and Indian worlds.

For all its adventure, the American fur trade was short-lived. By the 1840s, the population of beaver in western streams was virtually destroyed, and the day of the mountain man was over.

Government-Sponsored Exploration

The federal government played a major role in the exploration and development of the West. The exploratory and scientific aspects of the Lewis and Clark expedition in 1804–6 set a precedent for many government-financed quasi-military expeditions. In 1806 and 1807, Lieutenant Zebulon Pike led an expedition to the Rocky Mountains in Colorado. Major Stephen Long's exploration and mapping of the Great Plains in the years 1819–20 was part of a show of force meant to frighten British fur trappers out of the West. Then, in 1843 and 1844, another military explorer, John C. Frémont, mapped the overland trails to Oregon and California.

Beginning with Long's expedition, the results of these surveys were published by the government, complete with maps, illustrations, and, after the Civil War, photographs. These publications fed a strong popular appetite for pictures of the breathtaking scenery of the Far West and information about its inhabitants. These images of the American West made a powerful contribution to the emerging American self-image. American pride in the land—the biggest of this, the longest of that, the most spectacular of something else—was founded on the images brought home by government surveyors and explorers.

Expansion and Indian Policy

While American artists like Alfred Jacob Miller and George Catlin were painting the way of life of western Indian peoples, eastern Indian tribes were being removed from their homelands to Indian Territory (present-day Oklahoma, Kansas, and Nebraska), a region west of Arkansas, Missouri, and Iowa on the eastern edge of the Great Plains, widely regarded as unfarmable and popularly known as the Great Ameri-

can Desert. The justification for this western removal, as Thomas Jefferson had explained early in the century, was the creation of a space where Indian people could live undisturbed by white people while they slowly adjusted to "civilized" ways. But the government officials who negotiated the removals failed to predict the tremendous speed at which white people would settle the West.

As a result, encroachment on Indian Territory was not long in coming. The territory was crossed by the Santa Fé Trail, established in 1821; in the 1840s the northern part was crossed by the heavily traveled Overland Trails to California, Oregon, and the Mormon community in Utah. In 1854, the government abolished the northern half of Indian Territory, establishing the Kansas and Nebraska Territories in its place and opening them to immediate white settlement. The tribes of the area—the Potawatomis, Wyandots, Kickapoos, Sauks, Foxes, Delawares, Shawnees, Kaskaskias, Peorias, Piankashaws, Weas, Miamis, Omahas, Otos, and Missouris—signed treaties accepting either vastly reduced reservations or allotments. Those who accepted allotments—sections of private land—often sold them, under pressure, to white people. Thus many of the Indian people who had hoped for independence and escape from white pressures in Indian Territory lost both their autonomy and their tribal identity.

The people in the southern part of Indian Territory, in what is now Oklahoma, fared somewhat better. Those members of the southern tribes—the Cherokees, Chickasaws, Choctaws, Creeks, and Seminoles—who had survived the trauma of forcible removal from the Southeast in the 1830s quickly created impressive new communities. The five tribes divided up the territory and established self-governing nations with their own schools and churches. The societies they created were not so different from the American societies from which they had been expelled. The five tribes even carried slavery west with them: an elite economic group established plantations and shipped their cotton to New Orleans like other Southerners. Until after the Civil War, these southern tribes were able to withstand outside pressures and remain the self-governing communities that treaties had assured them they would be.

THE POLITICS OF EXPANSION

America's rapid expansion had many consequences, but perhaps the most significant was that it reinforced Americans' sense of themselves as pioneering people. In the 1890s Frederick Jackson Turner, America's most famous historian, observed that the repeated experience of settling new frontiers across the continent had shaped Americans into a uniquely adventurous, optimistic, and democratic people. Other historians have disagreed with Turner, but there is no question that his view of the frontier long ago won the battle for popular opinion. Ever since the time of Daniel Boone, venturing into the wilderness has held a special place in the American imagination, seen almost as an American right.

Manifest Destiny, an Expansionist Ideology

How did Americans justify their restless expansionism? In 1845 newspaperman John O'Sullivan coined the phrase by which expansionism became famous. It was, he wrote, "our manifest destiny to overspread the continent allotted by Providence for the free development of our yearly multiplying millions." Sullivan argued that Americans had a God-given right to bring the benefits of American democracy to other, more backward peoples—meaning Mexicans and Indians—by force, if necessary. The notion of manifest destiny summed up the powerful combination of pride in what America had achieved and missionary zeal and racist attitudes toward other peoples that lay behind the thinking of many expansionists.

Behind the bravado was some new international thinking about the economic future of the United States. After the devastating Panic of 1837 (see Chapter 10), many politicians became convinced that the nation's prosperity depended on vastly expanded trade with Asia. Senator Thomas Hart Benton of Missouri had been advocating trade with India by way of the Missouri and Columbia rivers since the 1820s (not the easiest of routes, as Lewis and Clark had shown). Soon Benton and others were pointing out how much Pacific trade would increase if the United States held the magnificent harbors of the west coast, among them Puget Sound in the Oregon Country, held jointly with Britain, and the bays of San Francisco and San Diego, both in Mexican-held California.

Expansionism was deeply tied to national politics. O'Sullivan, whose "manifest destiny" became the expansionist watchword, was not a neutral observer: he was the editor of the *Democratic Review*, a party newspaper. Most Democrats were wholehearted supporters of expansion, whereas many Whigs (especially in the North) opposed it. Whigs welcomed most of the changes wrought by industrialization but advocated strong government policies that would guide growth and development within the country's existing boundaries; they feared (correctly) that expansion would raise the contentious issue of the extension of slavery to new territories.

On the other hand, many Democrats feared the industrialization that the Whigs welcomed. Where the Whigs saw economic progress, Democrats saw economic depression (the Panic of 1837 was the worst the nation had experienced), uncontrolled urban growth, and growing social unrest. For many Democrats, the answer to the nation's social ills was to continue to follow Thomas Jefferson's vision of establishing agriculture in the new territories in order to counterbalance industrialization (see Chapter 9). Another factor in the political struggle over expansion in the 1840s was that many Democrats were Southerners, for whom the continual expansion of cotton-growing lands was a matter of social faith as well as economic necessity.

These were politicians' reasons. The average farmer moved west for many other reasons: land hunger, national pride, plain and simple curiosity, and a sense of adventure.

The Overland Trails

The 2,000-mile trip on the Overland Trails from the banks of the Missouri River to Oregon and California usually took seven months, sometimes more. Travel was slow, dangerous, tedious, and exhausting. Forced to lighten their loads as animals died and winter weather threatened, pioneers often arrived at their destination with little food and few belongings. Uprooted from family and familiar surroundings, pioneers faced the prospect of being, in the poignant and much-used biblical phrase, "strangers in a strange land." Yet despite the risks, settlers streamed west: 5,000 to Oregon by 1845 and about 3,000 to California by 1848 (before the discovery of gold).

Pioneers had many motives for making the trip. Glowing reports from Oregon's Willamette Valley, for example, seemed to promise economic opportunity and healthy surroundings, an alluring combination to farmers in the malaria-prone Midwest who had been hard hit by the Panic of 1837. But rational motives do not tell the whole story. Many men were motivated by a sense of adventure, by a desire to experience the unknown, or, as they put it, to "see the elephant." Women were more likely to think of the trip as *A Pioneer's Search for an Ideal Home*, the title that Phoebe Judson chose for her account of her family's 1852 trip to Oregon.

Few pioneers traveled alone, partly because they feared Indian attack (which was rare) but largely because they needed help fording rivers or crossing mountains with heavy wagons. Most Oregon pioneers traveled with their families but usually also joined a larger group, forming a "train." In the earliest years, when the route was still uncertain, trains hired

The Overland Trails, 1840
All the great trails west started at the Missouri River. The Oregon, California, and Mormon Trails followed the Platte River into Wyoming, crossed South Pass, and divided in western Wyoming. The much harsher Santa Fé Trail stretched 900 miles southwest across the Great Plains. All of the trails crossed Indian Territory and, to greater or lesser extent, Mexican possessions as well.

a "pilot," generally a former fur trapper. Often the men of the wagon train drew up semimilitary constitutions, electing a leader. Democratic as this process appeared, not everyone was willing to obey the leader, and many trains experienced dissension and breakups along the trail. But in essence all pioneers— men, women, and children—were part of a new, westward-moving community in which they had to accept both the advantages and disadvantages of community membership.

Wagon trains started westward as soon as the prairies were green (thus ensuring feed for the livestock). The daily routine was soon established. Men took care of the moving equipment and the animals, while the women cooked and kept track of the children. Slowly, at a rate of about fifteen miles a day, the wagon trains moved west along the Platte River, crossing the Continental Divide at South Pass in present-day Wyoming. West of the Rockies the climate was much drier. The long, dusty stretch along the Snake River in present-day southern Idaho finally gave way to Oregon's steep and difficult Blue Mountains and to the dangerous rafting down the Columbia River, in which many drowned and all were drenched by the cold winter rains of the Pacific Northwest. California-

bound migrants faced even worse hazards: the complete lack of water in the Humbolt Sink region of northern Nevada and the looming Sierra Nevadas, which had to be crossed before the winter snows came. (Members of the ill-fated Donner party, snowbound on the Nevada side of that range in 1846–47, resorted to cannibalism before they were rescued.)

In addition to the ever-present tedium and exhaustion, wagon trains were beset by such trail hazards as illness and accident. Danger from Indian attack, which all pioneers feared, was actually very small. It appears that unprovoked white attacks on Indians were more common than the reverse.

In contrast, cholera killed at least a thousand people a year in 1849 and in the early 1850s when it was common along sections of the trail along the Platte River. Spread by contaminated water, cholera caused vomiting and diarrhea, which in turn led to extreme dehydration and death, often in one night. In the afflicted regions, trailside graves were a frequent and grim sight. Drownings were not uncommon, nor were accidental ax wounds or shootings, and children sometimes fell out of wagons and were run over.

By 1860 almost 300,000 people had traveled the Overland Trails to Oregon or California. Ruts from the wagon wheels can be seen in a number of places along the route even today. In 1869, the completion of the transcontinental railroad marked the end of the wagon train era.

Oregon

The American settlement of Oregon provides a capsule example of the stages of frontier development. The first contacts between the region's Indian peoples and Europeans were commercial. Spanish, British, Russian, and American ships traded for sea otter skins from the 1780s to about 1810. Subsequently land-based groups scoured the region for beaver skins as well. In this first "frontier of inclusion" there were frequent, often sexual contacts between Indians and Europeans.

Both Great Britain and the United States claimed the Oregon Country by right of discovery, but in the Convention of 1818 the two nations agreed to occupy it jointly, postponing a final decision on its disposition. In reality, the British clearly dominated the region. In 1824 the Hudson's Bay Company consolidated Britain's position by establishing a major fur trading post at Fort Vancouver, on the banks of the Columbia River. Like all fur-trading ventures, the post exemplified the racial mixing of a "frontier of inclusion." Fort Vancouver housed a polyglot population of eastern Indians (Delawares and Iroquois), local Chinook Indians, French and métis from Canada, British traders, and Hawaiians.

The first permanent European settlers in Oregon were retired fur trappers and their Indian wives and families. They favored a spot in the lush and temperate Willamette Valley that became known as French Prairie, although the inhabitants were a mixed group of Americans, British, French Canadians, Indian peoples, and métis. The next to arrive were Protestant and Catholic missionaries. None of these missionaries was very successful. Epidemics had taken the lives of many of the region's peoples, and those who were left were disinclined to give up their nomadic life and settle down as the missionaries wanted them to do.

Finally, in the 1840s, came the Midwest farmers who would make up the majority of Oregon's permanent settlers, carried on the wave of enthusiasm known as "Oregon fever" and lured by free land and patriotism. By 1845 Oregon boasted 5,000 American settlers, most of them living in the Willamette Valley.

For these early settlers, life was at first very difficult. Most arrived in late autumn, exhausted from the strenuous overland journey. They could not begin to farm until the spring, and so they depended on the earlier settlers for their survival over the winter. In the earliest years American settlers got vital help

from the Hudson's Bay Company, even though its director, John McLoughlin, had been ordered by the British government not to encourage American settlement.

Joint occupancy of Oregon by the Americans and the British continued until 1846. Initially, a peaceful outcome seemed doubtful. President James K. Polk coined the belligerent slogan "Fifty-four Forty or Fight," suggesting that the United States would go to war if it didn't get control of all the territory south of 54°40´ north latitude, the border between Russian Alaska and British Canada. In office, however, Polk was willing to compromise. In June 1846, Britain and the United States concluded a treaty establishing the 49th parallel as the U.S.–Canada border but leaving the island of Vancouver in British hands. In 1849 the Hudson's Bay Company closed Fort Vancouver and moved its operations to Victoria, thus ending the Pacific Northwest's largely successful experience with joint occupancy. Oregon's Donation Land Claim Act of 1850 codified the practice of giving 320 acres to each white male age eighteen or over and 640 acres to each married couple to settle in the territory (African Americans, Hawaiians, and American Indians were excluded).

The white settlers realized that they had to forge strong community bonds if they hoped to survive on their distant frontier. Cooperation and mutual aid were the rule. Until well into the 1850s, residents organized yearly parties that traveled back along the last stretches of the Oregon Trail to help straggling parties making their way to the territory. Kinship networks were strong and vital: many pioneers came to join family who had migrated before them.

Relations with the small and unthreatening disease-thinned local Indian tribes were generally peaceful until 1847, when Cayuse Indians killed the missionaries Marcus and Narcissa Whitman. Their deaths triggered a series of "wars" against the remaining native people. A "frontier of exclusion" had been achieved. Nonetheless, the process by which Oregon became part of the United States (it was admitted as a state in 1859) was relatively peaceful, especially when compared with American expansion into the Spanish provinces of New Mexico and Texas.

The Santa Fé Trade

Commerce with Santa Fé, first settled by colonists from Mexico in 1609 and the center of the Spanish frontier province of New Mexico, had long been desired by American traders. But Spain had forcefully resisted American penetration. For example, Lieutenant Zebulon Pike's Great Plains and Rocky Mountain exploration of 1806–07 ended ignominiously with his capture by Spanish soldiers.

When Mexico gained its independence from Spain in 1821, this exclusionary policy changed. American traders were now welcome in Santa Fé, but the trip over the legendary Santa Fé Trail from Independence, Missouri, was a forbidding 900 miles of arid plains, deserts, and mountains. On the Santa Fé trail, unlike the Oregon Trail, there was serious danger of Indian attack, for neither the Comanches nor the Apaches of the southern high plains tolerated trespassers. In 1825, at the urging of Senator Benton and others, Congress voted federal protection for the Santa Fé Trail, even though much of it lay in Mexican territory. The number of people venturing west in the trading caravans increased yearly because the profits were so great (the first American trader to reach Santa Fé, William Becknell, realized a thousand percent profit). By the 1840s, a few hundred American trappers and traders (called *extranjeros*, or "foreigners") lived permanently in New Mexico. In Santa Fé, some American merchants married daughters of important local families.

Settlements and trading posts soon grew up along the long Santa Fé Trail. One of the most famous was Bent's Fort, on the Arkansas River in what is now eastern Colorado, which did a brisk trade in beaver skins and buffalo robes. Like most trading posts, it had a multiethnic population. In the 1840s the occupants included housekeeper Josefa Tafoya of Taos, whose husband was a carpenter from Pennsylvania; an African American cook; a French tailor from New Orleans; Mexican muleteers; and a number of Indian women, including the two Cheyenne women who were the (successive) wives of William Bent, cofounder of the fort. The three small communities of Pueblo, Hardscrabble, and Greenhorn, spinoffs of Bent's Fort, were populated by men of all nationalities and their Mexican and Indian wives. All three communities lived by trapping, hunting, and a little farming. This racially and economically mixed existence was characteristic of all early trading frontiers except for Texas.

Mexican Texas

In 1821, when Mexico gained its independence from Spain, there were 2,240 Tejano (Spanish-speaking) residents of Texas. Established in 1716 as a buffer against possible French attack on New Spain, the main Texas settlements of Nacogdoches, Goliad, and San Antonio remained small, far-flung frontier outposts (see Chapter 5). As elsewhere in New Spain, society was divided into two classes: the *ricos* (rich), who claimed Spanish descent, and the mixed-blood *pobres* (poor). Tejano town life was traditionally hierarchical, dominated by the ricos, who were connected by blood or marriage

with the great ranching families. The most colorful figures on the ranchos were *mestizo* (mixed-blood) *vaqueros*, renowned for their horsemanship; Americanization of their name made "buckaroos" of the American cowboys to whom they later taught their skills. Most Tejanos were neither ricos nor vaqueros but small farmers or common laborers who led hardscrabble frontier lives. But all Tejanos, rich and poor, faced the constant threat of raids by Comanche Indians.

Legendary warriors, the Comanches raided the small Texas settlements at will and even struck deep into Mexico itself. The nomadic Comanches followed the immense buffalo herds on which they depended for food and clothing. Their relentless raids on the Texas settlements rose from a determination to hold onto this rich buffalo territory, for the buffalo provided all that they wanted. They had no interest in being converted by mission priests or incorporated into mixed-race trading communities.

Americans in Texas

In 1821, seeking to increase the strength of its buffer zone between the heart of Mexico and the marauding Comanches, the Mexican government granted Moses Austin of Missouri an area of 18,000 square miles within the territory of Texas. Moses died shortly thereafter, and the grant was taken up by his son Stephen F. Austin, who became the first American *empresario* (land agent). From the beginning, the American settlement of Texas differed markedly from that of other frontiers. Elsewhere, Americans frequently settled on land to which Indian peoples still held title, or, as in the case of Oregon, they occupied lands to which other countries also made claim. In contrast, the Texas settlement was fully legal: Austin and other empresarios owned their lands as a result of formal contracts with the Mexican government. In exchange, Austin agreed that he and his colonists would become Mexican citizens and would adopt the Catholic religion.

Additionally, in startling contrast with the usual frontier free-for-all, Austin's community was populated with handpicked settlers, Austin insisting that "no frontiersman who has no other occupation than that of hunter will be received—no drunkard, no gambler, no profane swearer, no idler." Austin chose instead prosperous southern slaveowners eager to expand the lands devoted to cotton. Soon Americans (including African American slaves, to whose presence the Mexican government turned a blind eye) outnumbered Tejanos by nearly two to one: in 1830 there were an estimated 7,000 Americans and 4,000 Tejanos living in Texas.

The Austin settlement of 1821 was followed by others, twenty-six in all, concentrating in the fertile

Painted by George Catlin about 1834, this scene, *Comanche Village Life*, shows how the everyday life of the Comanches was tied to buffalo. The women in the foreground are scraping buffalo hide, and buffalo meat can be seen drying on racks. The men and boys may be planning their next buffalo hunt.

SOURCE: Art Resource, N.Y.

river bottoms of east Texas (along the Sabine River) and south central Texas (the Brazos and the Colorado rivers). These large settlements were highly organized farming enterprises whose principal crop was cotton, grown by African American slave labor and sold in the international market. By the early 1830s, Americans in Texas, ignoring the border between Mexican Texas and the United States, were sending an estimated $500,000 worth of goods (mostly cotton) yearly to New Orleans for export.

Austin's colonists and those who settled later were predominantly Southerners who viewed Texas as a natural extension of the cotton frontier in Mississippi and Louisiana (see Chapter 11). These settlers created "enclaves" (self-contained communities) that had little contact with Tejanos or Indian peoples. In fact, although they lived in Mexican territory, most Americans never bothered to learn Spanish. Nor, in spite of Austin's promises, did they become Mexican citizens or adopt the Catholic religion. Yet because of the nature of agreements made by the empresarios, the Americans could not set up local American-style governments like the one created by settlers in Oregon. Like the immigrants who flooded into east coast cities (see Chapter 13) the Americans in Texas were immigrants to another country—but one they did not intend to adapt to.

For a brief period Texas was big enough to hold three communities: Comanche, Tejano, and American. The nomadic Comanches rode the high plains of northern and western Texas, raiding settlements, primarily for horses. The Tejanos maintained their ran-

chos and missions mostly in the South, while American farmers occupied the eastern and south central sections. Each group would fight to hold its land: the Comanches, their rich hunting grounds; the Mexicans, their towns and ranchos; and the newcomers, the Americans, their rich land grants.

The Texas Revolt

The balance between the three communities in Texas was broken in 1828, when centrists gained control of the government in Mexico City and, in a dramatic shift of policy, decided to exercise firm control over the northern province. As the Mexican government restricted American immigration, outlawed slavery, levied customs, duties and taxes, and planned other measures, Americans seethed and talked of rebellion. Bolstering their cause were as many as 20,000 additional Americans, many of them openly expansionist, who flooded into Texas after 1830. These most recent settlers did not intend to become Mexican citizens. Instead, they planned to take over Texas.

Between 1830 and 1836, in spite of the mediation efforts of Austin (who was imprisoned for eighteen months by the Mexican government for his pains), the mood on both the Mexican and the American-Texan sides became more belligerent. In the fall of 1835 war finally broke out. After the disastrous defeat at the Alamo, the Mexican general Antonio López de Santa Anna pursued the remaining army of American and Tejano volunteers commanded by General Sam Houston. On April 21, 1836, at the San Jacinto River in eastern Texas, Santa Anna thought he had Houston trapped at last. Confident of victory against the exhausted Texans, Santa Anna's army rested in the afternoon, failing even to post sentries. Although Houston advised against it, Houston's men voted to attack immediately rather than wait till the next morning. Shouting "Remember the Alamo!" for the first time, the Texans completely surprised their opponents and won an overwhelming victory. On May 14, 1836, Santa Anna signed a treaty fixing the southern boundary of the newly independent Republic of Texas at the Rio Grande. The Mexican Congress, however, repudiated the treaty and refused to recognize Texan independence.

The Republic of Texas

In the eyes of the Mexicans, the American insistence on the Rio Grande boundary was little more than a blatant effort to stake a claim to New Mexico, an older and completely separate Spanish settlement. An effort by the Republic of Texas in 1841 to capture Santa Fé was easily repulsed.

The Republic of Texas was unexpectedly rebuffed in another quarter as well. The U.S. Congress refused to grant it statehood when, in 1837, Texas applied for admission to the Union. Petitions opposing the admission of a fourteenth slave state (there were then thirteen free states) poured into Congress. Congressman (and former president) John Quincy Adams of Massachusetts led the opposition to the admission of Texas.

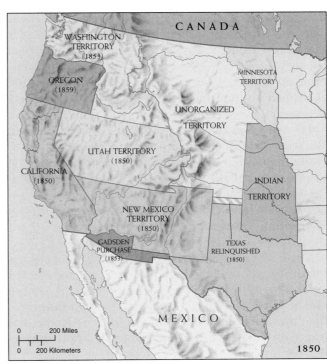

Texas: From Mexican Province to U.S. State

In the space of twenty years, Texas changed shape three times. Initially part of the Mexican province of Coahuila y Tejas, it became the Republic of Texas in 1836, following the Texas Revolt, and was annexed to the United States in that form in 1845. Finally, in the Compromise of 1850 following the Mexican-American War, it took its present shape.

Congress debated and ultimately dropped the Texas application. President Jackson did extend diplomatic recognition to the Republic of Texas, on March 3, 1837, less than twenty-four hours before he left office.

The unresolved conflict with Mexico put heavy stress on American-Tejano relations. Following a temporary recapture of San Antonio by Mexican forces in 1842, positions hardened. Many more of the Tejano elite fled to Mexico, and Americans discussed banishing or imprisoning all Tejanos until the border issue was settled. This was, of course, impossible. Culturally, San Antonio remained a Mexican city long after the Americans had declared independence. The Americans in the Republic of Texas were struggling to reconcile American ideals of democracy with the reality of subordinating those with a prior claim, the Tejanos, to the status of a conquered people.

American control over the other Texas residents, the Indians, was also slow in coming. Although the coastal Indian peoples were soon killed or removed, the Comanches still rode the high plains of northern and western Texas. West of the Rio Grande, equally fierce Apache bands were in control. Both groups soon learned to distrust American promises to stay out of their territory, and they did not hesitate to raid settlements and to kill trespassers. Not until after the Civil War and major campaigns by the U.S. Army were these fierce Indian tribes conquered.

Texas Annexation and the Election of 1844

Texans continued to press for annexation to the United States, while at the same time seeking recognition and support from Great Britain. The idea of an independent and expansionist republic on its southern border that might gain the support of America's traditional enemy alarmed many Americans. Annexation thus became an urgent matter of national politics. This issue also added to the troubles of a governing Whig Party that was already deeply divided by the policies of John Tyler, who had become president by default when William Harrison died in office (see Chapter 10). Tyler raised the issue of annexation in 1844, hoping thereby to ensure his reelection, but the strategy backfired. Presenting the annexation treaty to Congress, Secretary of State John Calhoun awakened sectional fears by connecting Texas with the urgent need of southern slave owners to extend slavery.

In a storm of antislavery protest, Whigs rejected the treaty proposed by their own president and ejected Tyler himself from the party. In his place, they chose Henry Clay, the party's longtime standard-bearer, as their presidential candidate. Clay took a noncommittal stance on Texas, favoring annexation, but only if Mexico approved. Since Mexico's emphatic disapproval was well known, Clay's position was widely interpreted as a politician's effort not to alienate voters on either side of the fence.

In contrast, in the Democratic Party wholehearted and outspoken expansionists seized control. Sweeping aside their own senior politician, Van Buren, who like Clay tried to remain uncommitted, the Democrats nominated their first "dark horse" candidate, James K. Polk of Tennessee. They enthusiastically endorsed Polk's platform, which called for "the re-occupation of Oregon and the re-annexation of Texas at the earliest practicable period."

Polk won the 1844 election by the narrow margin of 40,000 popular votes (although he gained 170 electoral votes to Clay's 105). An ominous portent for the Whigs was the showing of James G. Birney of the Liberty Party, who polled 62,000 votes, largely from northern antislavery Whigs. Birney's third-party campaign was the first political sign of the growing strength of antislavery opinion. Nevertheless, the 1844 election was widely interpreted as a mandate for expansion. Thereupon John Tyler, in one of his last actions as president, pushed through Congress a joint resolution (which did not require the two-thirds approval by the Senate necessary for treaties) for the annexation of Texas.

THE MEXICAN–AMERICAN WAR

James K. Polk lived up to his campaign promises. In 1846 he peacefully added Oregon south of the 49th parallel to the United States; in 1848, following the Mexican-American War, he acquired Mexico's northern provinces of California and New Mexico as well. Thus, with the annexation of Texas, the United States, in the short space of three years, had added 1.5 million square miles of territory, an increase of nearly 70 percent. Polk was indeed the "manifest destiny" president.

Origins of the War

In the spring of 1846, just as the controversy over Oregon was drawing to a peaceful conclusion, tensions with Mexico grew more serious. Because the United States accepted the Texas claim of all land north of the Rio Grande, it found itself embroiled in a border dispute with Mexico. In June 1845, Polk sent General Zachary Taylor to Texas, and by October a force of 3,500 Americans was on the Nueces River with orders to defend Texas in the event of a Mexican invasion.

Polk had something bigger than border protection in mind. He coveted the continent clear to the

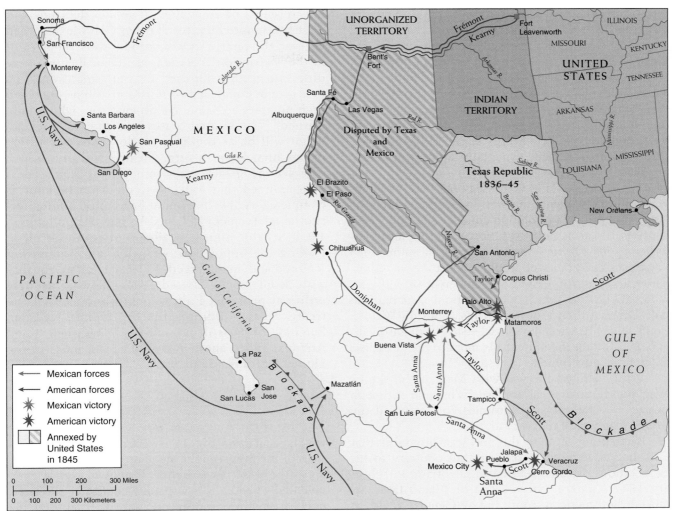

The Mexican-American War, 1846–1848   The Mexican-American War began with an advance by U.S. forces into the disputed area between the Nueces River and the Rio Grande in Texas. The war's major battles were fought by General Zachary Taylor in northern Mexico and General Winfield Scott in Vera Cruz and Mexico City. Meanwhile Colonel Stephen Kearny secured New Mexico and, with the help of the U.S. Navy and John C. Frémont's troops, California.

Pacific Ocean. At the same time that he sent Taylor to Texas, Polk secretly instructed the Pacific naval squadron to seize the California ports if Mexico declared war. He also wrote the American consul in Monterey, Thomas Larkin, that a peaceful takeover of California by its residents—Spanish Mexicans and Americans alike—would not be unwelcome.

In November 1845, Polk sent a secret envoy, John Slidell, to Mexico with an offer of $30 million or more for the Rio Grande border in Texas and Mexico's provinces of New Mexico and California. When the Mexican government refused even to receive Slidell, an angry Polk ordered General Taylor and his forces south to the Rio Grande, into the territory that Mexicans considered their soil. In April 1846 a brief skirmish between American and Mexican soldiers broke out in the disputed zone. Polk seized on the

event, sending a war message to Congress: "Mexico has passed the boundary of the United States, has invaded our territory and shed American blood upon American soil. . . . War exists, and, notwithstanding all our efforts to avoid it, exists by the act of Mexico herself." This last claim of President Polk's was, of course, contrary to fact. On May 13, 1846, Congress declared war on Mexico.

Mr. Polk's War

From the beginning, the Mexican-American War was politically divisive. Whig critics in Congress, among them a gawky young congressman from Illinois named Abraham Lincoln, questioned Polk's account of the border incident. They accused the president of misleading Congress and of maneuvering the country into an unnecessary war. It is with these suspicions that the history of congressional concern over the way presidents have exercised their war powers begins. The issue would again be prominent, for example, more than a hundred years later during the Vietnam War and in the Reagan years. As the Mexican-American War dragged on and casualties and costs mounted—13,000 Americans and 50,000 Mexicans died and the United States spent $97 million—opposition increased, especially among northern antislavery Whigs.

The northern states witnessed both mass and individual protests against the war. In Massachusetts, the legislature passed a resolution condemning Polk's declaration of war as unconstitutional, and philosopher-writer Henry David Thoreau went to jail rather than pay the taxes he believed would support the war effort. Thoreau's dramatic gesture was undercut by his aunt, who paid his fine after he had spent only one night in jail. Thoreau then returned to his cabin on Walden Pond, where he wrote his classic essay "Civil Disobedience," justifying the individual's moral right to oppose an immoral government.

Whigs termed the war with Mexico "Mr. Polk's War," but the charge was not just a Whig jibe. Although he lacked a military background, Polk assumed the overall planning of the war's strategy.

By the end of 1846 the northern provinces that Polk had coveted were secured, but contrary to his expectations, Mexico refused to negotiate. In February 1847, General Santa Anna of Alamo fame attacked the American troops led by General Taylor at Buena Vista but was repulsed by Taylor's small force. A month later, in March 1847, General Winfield Scott launched an amphibious attack on the coastal city of Veracruz and rapidly captured it. After six months of brutal fighting against stubborn Mexican resistance, American troops reacted bitterly to their high casualty rates by retaliating against Mexican citizens with acts of murder, robbery, and rape. Scott finally took Mexico City in September, and Mexican resistance came to an end.

With the American army went a special envoy, Nicholas Trist, who delivered Polk's terms for peace. In the Treaty of Guadalupe Hidalgo, signed February 2, 1848, Mexico ceded its northern provinces of California and New Mexico (which included present-day Arizona, Utah, Nevada, and part of Colorado) and accepted the Rio Grande as the boundary of Texas. The United States agreed to pay Mexico $15 million and assume about $2 million in individual claims against that nation.

When Trist returned to Washington with the treaty, however, Polk was furious. He had actually recalled Trist after Scott's sweeping victory, intend-

ing to send a new envoy with greater demands, but Trist had ignored the recall order. "All Mexico!" had become the phrase widely used by those in favor of further expansion, Polk among them. But two very different groups opposed further expansion. The first group, composed of northern Whigs, included such notables as Ralph Waldo Emerson, who grimly warned, "The United States will conquer Mexico, but it will be as the man swallows arsenic, which brings him down in turn. Mexico will poison us." The second group was composed of Southerners who realized that Mexicans could not be kept as conquered people but would have to be offered territorial government as Louisiana had been offered in 1804. Senator John C. Calhoun of South Carolina, leading the opposition, warned against admitting "colored and mixed-breed" Mexicans "on an equality with people of the United States." Bowing to these political protests, Polk reluctantly accepted the treaty. A later addition, the $10 million Gadsden Purchase of parts of present-day New Mexico and Arizona, added another 30,000 square miles to the United States in 1853.

The Press and Popular War Enthusiasm

The Mexican-American War was the first war in which regular, on-the-scene reporting by representatives of the press caught the mass of ordinary citizens up in the war's daily events. Thanks to the recently invented telegraph, newspapers could get the latest news from their reporters, who were among the world's first war correspondents. The "penny press," with more than a decade's experience of reporting urban crime and scandals, was quick to realize that the public's appetite for sensational war news was apparently insatiable. For the first time in American history, accounts by journalists, and not the opinions of politicians, became the major shapers of popular attitudes toward a war.

The reports from the battlefield united Americans in a new way: they became part of a temporary but highly emotional community linked by newsprint and buttressed by public gatherings. In the spring of 1846, news of Zachary Taylor's victory at Palo Alto prompted the largest meeting ever held in the cotton textile town of Lowell, Massachusetts. In May 1847, New York City celebrated the twin victories at Veracruz and Buena Vista with fireworks, illuminations, and a "grand procession" estimated at 400,000 people. Generals Taylor and Scott became overnight heroes, and in time both became presidential candidates. Exciting, sobering, and terrible, war news had a deep hold on the popular imagination. It was a lesson newspaper publishers never forgot.

CALIFORNIA AND THE GOLD RUSH

In the early 1840s California was inhabited by many seminomadic Indian tribes whose people numbered approximately 50,000. There were also some 7,000 *Californios*, descendants of the Spanish Mexican pioneers who had begun to settle in 1769.

Russian-Californio Trade

The first outsiders to penetrate the isolation of Spanish California were not Americans but Russians. Evading Spanish regulations, Californios traded with the Russian American Company in Sitka, Alaska. A mutually beneficial barter of California food for iron tools and woven cloth from Russia was established in 1806. This arrangement became even brisker after the Russians settled Fort Ross (near present-day Mendocino) in 1812. Agricultural productivity declined after 1832, when the Mexican government ordered the secularization of the California missions, and the Russians regretfully turned to the rich farms of the Hudson's Bay Company in the Pacific Northwest for their food supply. In 1841, they sold Fort Ross, and the Russian-Californio connection came to an end.

Early American Settlement

It was Johann Augustus Sutter, a Swiss who had settled in California in 1839, becoming a Mexican citizen, who served as a focal point for American settlement in the 1840s. Sutter held a magnificent land grant in the Sacramento Valley. At the center of his holdings was Sutter's Fort, a walled compound that was part living quarters and part supply shop for his vast cattle ranch, which was run largely on forced Indian labor. In the 1840s, Sutter offered valuable support to the handful of American overlanders who chose California over Oregon, the destination preferred by most pioneers. Most of these Americans, keenly aware that they were interlopers in Mexican territory, settled near Sutter in California's Central Valley, away from the Californios clustered along the coast.

The 1840s immigrants made no effort to intermarry with the Californios or to conform to Spanish ways. They were bent on taking over the territory. In June 1846 these Americans banded together at Sonoma in the Bear Flag Revolt (so called because their flag bore a bear emblem), declaring independence from Mexico. The American takeover of California was not confirmed until the Treaty of Guadalupe Hidalgo in 1848. In the meantime, California was regarded by most Americans merely as a remote, sparsely populated frontier, albeit one with splendid potential.

Gold!

In January 1848 carpenter James Marshall noticed small flakes of gold in the millrace at Sutter's Mill (present-day Coloma). But not until autumn did the East Coast hear the first rumors about the discovery of gold in California. The reports were confirmed in mid-November when an army courier arrived in Washington carrying a tea caddy full of gold dust and nuggets. The spirit of excitement and adventure so recently aroused by the Mexican-American War was now directed toward California, the new El Dorado. Thousands left farms and jobs and headed west, by land and by sea, to make their fortune. Later known as "forty-niners" for the year the gold rush began in earnest, these people came from all parts of the United States—and, indeed, from all over the world. They transformed what had been a quiet ranching paradise into a teeming and tumultuous community in search of wealth in California's rivers and streams.

Eighty percent of the forty-niners were Americans. They came from every state. The Gold Rush was an eye-opening expansion of their horizons for the many who had known only their hometown folks before. The second largest group of migrants were from nearby Mexico and the west coast of Latin America (13 percent). The remainder came from Europe and Asia.

The presence of Chinese miners surprised many Americans. Several hundred Chinese arrived in California in 1849 and 1850, and in 1852 more than 20,000 landed in San Francisco hoping to share in the wealth of "Gum Sam" (Golden Mountain).

In 1849, as the gold rush began in earnest, San Francisco, the major entry port and supply point, sprang to life. From a settlement of 1,000 in 1848 it grew to a city of 35,000 in 1850. This surge suggested that the real money to be made in California was not in panning for gold but from feeding, clothing, housing, provisioning, and entertaining the miners. Among the first to learn that lesson was the German Jewish immigrant Levi Strauss, who sold so many tough work pants to miners that his name became synonymous with his product. The white population of California jumped from an estimated pre–Gold Rush figure of 11,000 to more than 100,000 by 1852. California was admitted into the Union as a state in 1850.

Mining Camps

As had occurred in San Francisco, most mining camps boomed almost instantly to life, but unlike San Francisco, they were empty again within a few years. They were generally dirty and dreary places. Most miners lived in tents or hovels, unwilling to take time from mining to build themselves decent quarters. They cooked monotonous meals of beans, bread, and bacon,

Chinese first came to California in 1849 attracted by the Gold Rush. Frequently, however, they were forced off their claims by intolerant whites. Rather than enjoy an equal chance in the gold fields, they were often forced to work as servants or in other menial occupations.

SOURCE: Courtesy of the California History Room, California State Library, Sacramento, California.

or, if they had money, bought meals at expensive restaurants and boardinghouses (where the table might be no more than a plank over two flour barrels). They led a cheerless, uncomfortable, and unhealthy existence, especially during the long, rainy winter months, with few distractions apart from the saloon, the gambling hall, and the prostitute's crib.

Most miners were young, unmarried, and unsuccessful. Only a small percentage ever struck it rich in California. Increasingly, those who stayed on in California had to give up the status of independent miners and become wage earners for large mining concerns.

As in San Francisco, a more reliable way to earn money in the camps was to supply the miners. Every mining community had its saloonkeepers, gamblers, prostitutes, merchants, and restauranteurs. Like the miners themselves, these people were transients, always ready to pick up and move at the word of a new gold strike. The majority of women in the early mining camps were prostitutes. Some grew rich or married respectably, but most died young of drugs, venereal disease, or violence. Most of the other women were hardworking wives of miners, and in this predominantly male society they made good money doing domestic work: keeping boardinghouses, cooking, doing laundry.

Partly because few people put any effort into building communities—they were too busy seeking gold—violence was endemic in mining areas, and much of it was racial. Discrimination, especially against Chinese, Mexicans, and African Americans, was common. Frequently miners' claims were "jumped": thieves would rob them of the gold they had accumulated, kill them, or chase them away, and then file their own claim for the victims' strike. Or unscrupulous miners might use the law to their advantage to secure the claims of others without violence—for example, by taking advantage of the prohibitively high mining tax on foreigners.

By the mid-1850s, the immediate effects of the Gold Rush had passed. California had a booming population, a thriving agriculture, and a corporate mining industry. The Gold Rush also left California with a population that was larger, more affluent, and (in urban San Francisco) more culturally sophisticated than that in other newly settled territories. It was also significantly more multicultural than the rest of the nation, for many of the Chinese and Mexicans, as well as immigrants from many European countries, remained in California after the Gold Rush subsided. But the Gold Rush left some permanent scars, and not just on the foothills landscape: the virtual extermination of the California Indian peoples, the dispossession of many Californios who were legally deprived of their land grants, and the growth of racial animosity toward the Chinese in particular.

THE POLITICS OF MANIFEST DESTINY

In three short years, from 1845 to 1848, the territory of the United States grew an incredible 70 percent, and a continental nation took shape. This expansion, pushed by economic desires and feelings of American cultural superiority, led directly to the emergence of the divisive issue of slavery as the dominant issue in national politics.

The Wilmot Proviso

In 1846, almost all the northern members of the Whig Party opposed Democratic president James Polk's belligerent expansionism on antislavery grounds. Northern Whigs correctly feared that expansion would reopen the issue of slavery in the territories. But the outpouring of popular enthusiasm for the Mexican-American War convinced most Whig congressmen that they needed to vote military appropriations for the war in spite of their misgivings.

Ironically it was not the Whigs but a freshman Democratic congressman from Pennsylvania, David Wilmot, who opened the door to sectional controversy over expansion. In August 1846, only a few short months after the beginning of the Mexican-American War, Wilmot proposed, in an amendment to a military appropriations bill, that slavery be banned in all the territories acquired from Mexico. He was ready, Wilmot said, to "sustain the institutions of the South as they exist," but not to extend them. In the debate and voting that followed, something new and ominous occurred: southern Whigs joined southern Democrats to vote against the measure, while Northerners of both parties supported it. Sectional interest had triumphed over party loyalty. Wilmot's Proviso triggered the first breakdown of the national party system and reopened the debate about the place of slavery in the future of the nation.

The Wilmot Proviso was so controversial that it was deleted from the necessary military appropriations bills during the Mexican-American War. But in 1848, following the Treaty of Guadalupe Hidalgo, the question of the expansion of slavery could no longer be avoided or postponed. Antislavery advocates from the North argued with proslavery Southerners in a debate that was much more prolonged and more bitter than in the Missouri Crisis debate of 1819. Civility quickly wore thin: threats were uttered and fistfights broke out on the floor of the House of Representatives. The Wilmot Proviso posed a fundamental challenge to both parties. Neither the Democrats nor the Whigs could take a strong stand on the amendment because neither party could get its northern and southern wings to agree.

The Free-Soil Movement

Why did David Wilmot propose this controversial measure? Wilmot, a northern Democrat, was propelled not by ideology but by the pressure of practical politics. The

---

OVERVIEW

EXPANSION CAUSES THE FIRST SPLITS IN THE SECOND AMERICAN PARTY SYSTEM

1844	Whigs reject President John Tyler's move to annex Texas and expel him from the Whig Party. Southern Democrats choose expansionist James K. Polk as their presidential candidate, passing over Martin Van Buren, who is against expansion.
	Liberty Party runs abolitionist James Birney for president, attracting northern antislavery Whigs.
1846	The Wilmot Proviso, proposing to ban slavery in the territories that might be gained in the Mexican-American War, splits both parties: southern Whigs and Democrats oppose the measure; northern Whigs and Democrats support it.
1848	The new Free-Soil Party runs northern Democrat Martin Van Buren for president, gaining 10 percent of the vote from abolitionists, antislavery Whigs, and some northern Democrats. This strong showing by a third party causes Democrat Lewis Cass to lose the electoral votes of New York and Pennsylvania, allowing the Whig Zachary Taylor to win.

dramatic rise of the Liberty Party, founded in 1840 by abolitionists, threatened to take votes away from both the Whig and the Democratic parties. The Liberty Party won 62,000 votes in the 1844 presidential election, all in the North. This was more than enough to deny victory to the Whig candidate, Henry Clay.

The Liberty Party took an uncompromising stance against slavery. The party proposed to prohibit the admission of slave states to the Union, end slavery in the District of Columbia, and abolish the interstate slave trade that was vital to the expansion of cotton growing into the Old Southwest (see Chapter 11). Liberty Party members also favored denying office to all slaveholders (a proposal that would have robbed all the southern states of their senators). Liberty Party doctrine was too uncompromising for the mass of northern voters, who immediately realized that the southern states would leave the Union before accepting it. Still, as the 1844 vote indicated, many Northerners opposed slavery. From this sentiment the Free-Soil Party was born.

Free-soilers were willing to allow slavery to continue in the existing slave states because they supported the Union, not because they approved of slavery. They were unwilling, however, to allow the extension of slavery to new and unorganized territory. If the South were successful in extending slavery, they argued, northern farmers who moved west would find themselves competing at an economic disadvantage with large planters using slave labor. Free-soilers also insisted that the northern values of freedom and individualism would be destroyed if the slave-based southern labor system were allowed to spread.

In reality many free-soilers meant "antiblack" when they said "antislavery." They proposed to ban all African American people from the new territories (a step that four states—Indiana, Illinois, Iowa, and Oregon—took but did not always enforce), thus "solving" the race issue by ignoring it.

The Election of 1848

A swirl of emotions—pride, expansionism, sectionalism, abolitionism, free-soil sentiment—surrounded the election of 1848. The Treaty of Guadalupe Hidalgo had been signed earlier in the year, and the vast northern Mexican provinces of New Mexico and California and the former Republic of Texas had been incorporated into the United States. But the issues raised by the Wilmot Proviso remained to be resolved, and every candidate had to have an answer to the question of whether slavery should be admitted in the new territories.

Lewis Cass of Michigan, the Democratic nominee for president (Polk, in poor health, declined to run for a second term), proposed to apply the doctrine of popu-

lar sovereignty to the crucial slave–free issue. This democratic-sounding notion of leaving the decision to the citizens of each territory was based on the Jeffersonian faith in the common man's ability to vote both his own self-interest and the common good. In fact, however, popular sovereignty was an admission of the nation's failure to resolve sectional differences. Moreover, the doctrine of popular sovereignty was deliberately vague about when a territory would choose its status. Would it do so during the territorial stage? at the point of applying for statehood? Clearly, this question was crucial, for no slave owner would invest in new land if the territory could later be declared free, and no abolitionist would move to a territory that was destined to become a slave state. Cass hoped his ambiguity on this point would win him votes in both North and South.

For their part, the Whigs passed over perennial candidate Henry Clay and turned once again to a war hero, General Zachary Taylor. Taylor, a Louisiana slaveholder, refused to take a position on the Wilmot Proviso, allowing both northern and southern voters to hope that he agreed with them. Privately, Taylor opposed the expansion of slavery. In public, he evaded the issue by running as a war hero and a national leader who was above sectional politics.

The deliberate vagueness of the two major candidates displeased many northern voters. An uneasy mixture of disaffected Democrats (among them David Wilmot) and Whigs joined former Liberty Party voters to support the candidate of the Free-Soil Party, former president Martin Van Buren. Van Buren, angry at the Democratic Party for passing him over in 1844 and displeased with the growing southern dominance of the Democratic Party, ran as a spoiler. He knew he could not win the election, but he could divide the Democrats. In the end, Van Buren garnered 10 percent of the vote (all in the North). The vote for the Free-Soil Party cost Cass the electoral votes of New York and Pennsylvania, and General Zachary Taylor won the election with only 47 percent of the popular vote. This was the second election after 1840 that the Whigs had won by running a war hero who could duck hard questions by claiming to be above politics. Uncannily, history was to repeat itself: Taylor, like William Henry Harrison, died before his term was completed, and the chance he offered to maintain national unity—if ever it existed—was lost.

CONCLUSION

In the decade of the 1840s, westward expansion took many forms, from relatively peaceful settlement in Oregon, to war with Mexico over Texas, to the overwhelming numbers of gold rushers who changed California forever.

CHRONOLOGY

1609	First Spanish settlement in New Mexico
1670s	British and French Canadians begin fur trade in western Canada
1716	First Spanish settlements in Texas
1769	First Spanish settlement in California
1780s	New England ships begin sea otter trade in Pacific Northwest
1790	First American ship visits Hawaii
1803	Louisiana Purchase
1804–06	Lewis and Clark expedition
1806	Russian-Californio trade begins
1806–07	Zebulon Pike's expedition across the Great Plains to the Rocky Mountains
1819–20	Stephen Long's expedition across the Great Plains
1821	Hudson's Bay Company gains dominance of western fur trade
	Mexico seizes independence from Spain
	Santa Fé Trail opens, soon protected by U.S. military
	Stephen F. Austin becomes first American empresario in Texas
1824	First fur rendezvous sponsored by Rocky Mountain Fur Company
	Hudson's Bay Company establishes Fort Vancouver in Oregon Country

1830	Indian Removal Act moves eastern Indians to Indian Territory
1834	Jason Lee establishes first mission in Oregon Country
1835	Texas revolts against Mexico
1836	Battles of the Alamo and San Jacinto
	Republic of Texas formed
1843–44	John C. Frémont maps trails to Oregon and California
1844	Democrat James K. Polk elected president on an expansionist platform
1845	Texas annexed to the United States as a slave state
	John O'Sullivan coins the phrase "manifest destiny"
1846	Oregon question settled peacefully with Britain
	Mexican-American War begins
	Bear Flag Revolt in California
	Wilmot Proviso
1847	Cayuse Wars begin in Oregon
	Americans win battles of Buena Vista, Veracruz, and Mexico City
1848	Treaty of Guadalupe Hidalgo
	Free-Soil Party captures 10 percent of the popular vote in the North
	General Zachary Taylor, a Whig, elected president
1849	California Gold Rush

The election of 1848, virtually a referendum on manifest destiny, yielded ironic results. James K. Polk, who presided over the unprecedented expansion, did not run for a second term, and thus the Democratic Party gained no electoral victory to match the military one. The electorate that had been so thrilled by the war news voted for a war hero—who led the anti-expansionist Whig Party. The election was decided by Martin Van Buren, the Free-Soil candidate who voiced the sentiments of the abolitionists, a reform group that had been insignificant just a few years before. The amazing expansion achieved by the Mexican-American War—America's manifest destiny—made the United States a continental nation but stirred up the issue that was to tear it apart. Sectional rivalries and fears now dominated every aspect of politics. Expansion, once a force for unity, now divided the nation into Northerners and Southerners, who could not agree on the community they shared—the federal Union.

REVIEW QUESTIONS

1. Define and discuss the concept of manifest destiny.
2. Trace the different ways in which the frontiers in Oregon, Texas, and California moved from frontiers of inclusion to frontiers of exclusion.
3. Take different sides (Whig and Democrat) and debate the issues raised by the Mexican-American War.
4. Referring back to Chapter 13, compare the positions of the Liberty Party and the Free-Soil Party. Examine the factors that made the free-soil doctrine politically acceptable to many and abolitionism so controversial.

RECOMMENDED READING

Arnoldo De Leon, *The Tejano Community, 1836–1900* (1982). Traces the changing status of Tejanos after Texas came under the control of American Texans.

John Mack Faragher, *Women and Men on the Overland Trail* (1979). One of the first books to consider the experience of women on the journey west.

William Goetzman, *Exploration and Empire: The Explorer and the Scientist in the Winning of the American West* (1966). Considers the many government-sponsored explorations of the West.

Julie Roy Jeffrey, *Converting the West: A Biography of Narcissa Whitman* (1991). Makes a clear connection between the missionary Whitman's evangelical upbringing and her failure to understand the culture of Oregon's Cayuse Indians.

Robert W. Johannsen, *To the Halls of the Montezumas: The Mexican War in the American Imagination* (1985). A lively book that explores the impact of the Mexican-American War on public opinion.

Susan Johnson, *Roaring Camp: The Social World of the California Gold Rush* (2000). A beautifully written study of the varieties of mining camp experience.

Paul D. Lack, *The Texas Revolutionary Experience: A Political and Social History, 1835–1836* (1992). A political and social history that stresses the chaotic and discordant nature of the Texas Revolt.

Janet Lecompte, *Pueblo, Hardscrabble, Greenhorn: The Upper Arkansas, 1832–1856* (1978). A social history that portrays the racial and ethnic diversity of the trading frontier.

Michael Morrison, *Slavery and the American West: The Eclipse of Manifest Destiny and the Coming of the Civil War* (1997). In a study of competing ideas over the future of the West, the author stresses the links between expansion and sectional disagreements.

Malcolm Rohrbough, *Days of Gold: The California Gold Rush and the American Nation* (1997). A lively history that emphasizes the effects of this "great American epic" on the national self-image.

David J. Weber, *The Mexican Frontier, 1821–1846: The American Southwest under Mexico* (1982). A fine study of the history of the Southwest before American conquest. The author is a leading borderlands historian.

Richard White, *"It's Your Misfortune and None of My Own": A History of the American West* (1991). A major reinterpretation that focuses on the history of the region itself rather than on the westward expansion of Americans. Pays much more attention to Spanish Mexicans and Indian peoples than earlier texts.

ON THE WEB

http://www.xmission.com/~drudy/
mtman/mmarch.html

This site contains a number of primary documents relating to the history of western exploration in the early nineteenth century, including parts of the journals of Lewis and Clark and others. Navigation back to the home site of the Mountain Men and Fur Trade Home Page leads to other sites relating to western exploration.

http://www.boondocksnet.com/cartoons/mc16.html

Boondocksnet is a collection of political cartoons; this specific site relates to the Mexican War and the issues that followed that event.

http://www.yale.edu/lawweb/avalon/
diplomacy/guadhida.htm

The official text of the Treaty of Guadalupe Hidalgo ending the Mexican War and expanding U.S. territory to include the Mexican Cession.

http://www.calhist.org/frost1/lettersheets/
lettersheets.html

The California Historical Society has posted an interesting collection of "lettersheets" of the Gold Rush era that contains pictures, narrative, and primary documents of the mining experience.

http://www.prenhall.com/faragherbrief/map14.1

Examine the routes taken by major expeditions westward between 1804 and 1830. What role did they play in shaping U. S. Policy in the West?

http://www.prenhall.com/faragherbrief/map14.2

Consider the strategies of each side in the Mexican-American War. Why was the United States more successful than Mexico in achieving its goals?

▶ Remembering the Alamo

The Alamo is the number-one tourist attraction in the state of Texas. Located in a small but tranquil park, remote from the noise and traffic of surrounding downtown San Antonio, the site evokes feelings of hushed reverence and respect for the famous Anglo American heroes—William Barret Travis, Jim Bowie, and Davy Crockett—of the gallant but futile 1836 defense described in the chapter opener.

Today, only the chapel remains from the much larger Mission San Antonio de Valero established in 1718. Only the popular nickname—the Alamo—remains from the first soldiers, a troop of Spanish cavalry who came from the Mexican town of El Alamo in 1801 when the mission became a military fort. There are no signs of the 1836 battle itself aside from a few relics preserved inside the chapel. A brass plaque affixed to the wall of the chapel notes this varied history from mission to fort to finally, in defeat, into the "Cradle of Texas Liberty." What remains of the Alamo today and what is commemorated serves as an example of how long-ago choices about what to preserve continue to shape our present-day understanding of our historic past.

In the aftermath of the 1836 battle the legend of the famous defeat at the Alamo grew and was used by some people, as the chapter opener shows, to consolidate American control by fostering antiMexican sentiment. But until 1883 the Alamo itself was used for a variety of practical purposes by the U.S. Army and commercial interests. By 1883, when the Catholic Church sold the chapel to the State of Texas for $20,000, very little remained of the original grounds. A growing San Antonio encroached on all sides: the convent adjacent to the chapel, a remnant of the original

This modern photograph of the Alamo chapel by the well-known landscape photographer David Muench conveys the romantic and rather nostalgic atmosphere of the site that describes itself as "the Cradle of Texas liberty."

SOURCE: © David Muench/CORBIS.

mission, was used as a store and commercial museum. There was a livery stable and blacksmith shop behind the chapel, a public meat market and several saloons across the way. At this point, local boosters alert to its tourist potential joined with Texas patriots to limit the commercialism and demand that the Alamo be preserved as a memorial to the 1836 battle.

The preservation of the Alamo was entrusted by the Texas State Legislature to the San Antonio Chapter of the Daughters of the Republic of Texas. The custodianship of historic sites by exclusive women's groups such as the Daughters of the American Revolution and the Mount Vernon Ladies Association was common throughout the United States at the time. Usually this meant that control over historic sites was kept firmly in the hands of wealthy Anglo women. But membership in the Daughters of the Republic of Texas was open to *all* women who could trace their ancestry to persons who settled in Texas before 1846. In the 1890s the president of the San Antonio chapter of the DRT was Adina De

This sculpture is part of the Alamo Cenotaph, a memorial to the slain defenders of the Alamo that was erected in Alamo Plaza in 1940. The two prominent figures are the famous defenders William B. Travis (in uniform) and Davy Crockett. Photograph by Lee Snider.

SOURCE: ©Lee Snider/CORBIS.

custodianship, and the Alamo chapel, surrounded by a memorial park and wall, assumed its present-day form.

Today, nearly a century after its preservation as a historic site, the Battle of the Alamo has flared anew. The state-appointed guardians of the Alamo, the Daughters of the Republic of Texas, are under attack for their lack of historical professionalism. Although custodianship of historic sites by elite women's groups was common a century ago, today professionals trained to consider the full historic record are much more likely to administer and preserve such sites. The most sustained protest, however, has come from the Texans of Mexican heritage who feel that the Tejano role in defense of the Alamo (as described in the chapter opener) has not received enough attention, and that the Spanish colonial history of the site has been ignored. In part, these protests reflect the growing political power of Mexican Americans in Texas, which in turn is based on population. In San Antonio itself, more than sixty percent of the city's occupants are Mexican American. As at other historic sites around the country, this ongoing struggle reflects deeper social changes: Mexican Americans see changes in the Alamo as a matter of equity and historical accuracy, while many Anglo-Texans oppose change in the name of tradition. This unresolved controversy reminds us that there is more than one version of the past, thus making the question of who interprets history much more than an academic matter.

Zavala, granddaughter of the Tejano patriot who became the first Vice President of Texas, Lorenzo de Zavala. Adina De Zavala, with the help of her sister DRT member, the wealthy Clara Driscoll, led the effort to raise money to preserve the Alamo site.

No sooner had the DRT obtained control of the Alamo than disagreement arose. In a bitter controversy sometimes called the "Second Battle of the Alamo" De Zavala and Driscoll disagreed about the relative importance of the buildings. De Zavala wanted to retain the full history of the site as a mission and fort while Driscoll, in common with most Anglo-Americans of her time, preferred to emphasize only the chapel as a shrine to the well-known Anglo heroes of the 1836 battle. Driscoll won: the convent was partially demolished, De Zavala and her supporters were legally barred from

FIFTEEN

THE COMING CRISIS

▶ The 1850s

AMERICAN COMMUNITIES

Illinois Communities Debate Slavery

ON SEVEN OCCASIONS THROUGH THE LATE SUMMER AND AUTUMN of 1858, in each of the seven small Illinois towns of Ottawa, Freeport, Jonesboro, Charleston, Galesburg, Quincy, and Alton, thousands of Illinois farmers and townspeople put aside their daily routines and customary chores; climbed into carriages, farm wagons, carts, and conveyances of all sorts; and converged on their local town green. Entertained by brass bands, pageantry, and vast quantities of food and local gossip, they waited impatiently for the main event, the chance to take part in the debate on the most urgent question of the day—slavery. Two Illinois politicians—Democratic Senator Stephen A. Douglas and his Republican challenger, Springfield lawyer Abraham Lincoln, the principal figures in the debates—presented their views in three hours of closely reasoned argument. But they did not speak alone. Cheers, boos, groans, and shouted questions from active, engaged listeners punctuated all seven of the now famous confrontations between the two men. Although commonly referred to as the Lincoln-Douglas debates, these were really community events in which Illinois citizens— who, as did Americans everywhere, held varying political beliefs—took part. Some individuals were proslavery, some antislavery, and many were undecided, but all were agreed that democratic politics gave them the means to air their opinions and resolve their differences.

"The prairies are on fire," announced the *New York Evening Post* correspondent who covered the debates. "It is astonishing how deep an interest in politics this people take." The reason was clear: by 1858, the American nation was in deep political crisis. The decade-long effort to solve the problem of the future of slavery had failed. For most of this time Washington politicians trying to build broad national parties with policies acceptable to voters in both the North and the South had done their best not to talk about slavery. Thus, that the Lincoln-Douglas debates were devoted to one issue alone—slavery and the future of the Union—showed how serious matters had become.

Democrat Stephen Douglas was the leading Democratic contender for the 1860 presidential nomination, but before he could mount a campaign for national office he had first to win reelection to the Illinois seat he had held in the U.S. Senate for twelve years. His vote against allowing slavery in Kansas had alienated him from the strong southern wing of his own party and had put him in direct conflict with its top leader, President James Buchanan. Because the crisis of the Union was so severe and Douglas's role so pivotal, his reelection campaign clearly previewed the 1860 presidential election. For the sake of its future, the Republican Party had to field a strong opponent: it found its candidate in Abraham Lincoln.

Lincoln had represented Illinois in the House of Representatives in the 1840s but had lost political support in 1848 because he had opposed the Mexican-American War. Developing a prosperous Springfield law practice, he had been an influential member of the Illinois Republican Party since its founding in 1856. Although he had entered political life as a Whig, Lincoln was radicalized by the issue of the extension of slavery. Even though his wife's family were Kentucky slave owners, Lincoln's commitment to freedom and his resistance to the spread of slavery had now become absolute: for him, freedom and Union were inseparable.

Much less well known than Douglas, Lincoln was the underdog in the 1858 Senate race, and thus it was he who challenged Douglas to debate. As they squared off in each of the seven Illinois towns, Douglas and Lincoln were an amusing sight. Douglas was short (5 feet, 4 inches) and his build was very square; his nickname was the "Little Giant." Lincoln, on the other hand, was very tall (6 feet, 4 inches) and very thin. Both were eloquent and powerful speakers—and they had to be. The three-hour debates were held without amplification of any kind. Nevertheless, in every town, audiences of 10,000 to 15,000 listened attentively and responded vocally to each speaker's long and thought-packed arguments.

Douglas had many strengths going into the debates. He spoke for the Union, he claimed, pointing out that the Democratic Party was a national party whereas the Republican Party was only sectional. He repeatedly appealed to the racism of much of his audience with declarations such as, "I would not blot out the great inalienable rights of the white men for all the negroes that ever existed!" He repeatedly called his opponent a "Black Republican," implying that Lincoln and his party favored the social equality of whites and blacks, even race mixing.

Lincoln did not believe in the social equality of the races, but he did believe wholeheartedly that slavery was a moral wrong. Pledging the Republican Party to the "ultimate extinction" of slavery, Lincoln continually warned that Douglas's position would lead to the opposite result: the spread of slavery everywhere. Although in this argu-ment Lincoln was addressing the northern fear of an expansionist "slave power," he strove at the same time to present himself as a moderate. He did not favor the breakup of the Union, but he never wavered from his antislavery stance.

The first of the seven debates, held in Ottawa on Saturday, August 21, 1858, showed not only the seriousness but the exuberance of the democratic politics of the time. By early morning the town was jammed with people. The clouds of dust raised by carriages driving to Ottawa, one observer complained, turned the town into "a vast smoke house." By one o'clock the town square was filled to overflowing. At two o'clock, just as the debate was about to begin, the wooden awning over the speakers' platform collapsed under the weight of those sitting on it, delaying the start for half an hour. But then the debate got under way, enthralling an estimated 12,000 people. Ottawa, in northern Illinois, was pro-Republican, and the audience heckled Douglas unmercifully. At the second debate, a week later in Freeport, Douglas's use of the phrase "Black Republicans" drew angry shouts of "White, white" from the crowd. But as the debates moved south in the state, where Democrats predominated, the tables were turned, and Lincoln sometimes had to plead for a chance to be heard.

Although Douglas won the 1858 senatorial election in Illinois, the acclaim that Lincoln gained in the famous debates helped establish the Republicans' claim to be the only party capable of stopping the spread of slavery and made Lincoln himself a strong contender for the Republican presidential nomination in 1860. But the true winners of the Lincoln-Douglas debates were the people of Illinois who gathered peacefully to discuss the most serious issue of their time. The young German immigrant Carl Schurz, who attended the Quincy debate, was deeply impressed by its democratic character. He noted, "There was no end of cheering and shouting and jostling on the streets of Quincy that day. But in spite of the excitement created by the political contest, the crowds remained very good-natured, and the occasional jibes flung from one side to the other were uniformly received with a laugh." The Illinois people who participated in the community debates of 1858 showed the strong faith Americans held in their democratic institutions and the hope—finally shattered in the election of 1860—that a lasting political solution to the problem of slavery could be found. ■

Illinois

AMERICA IN 1850

In 1850, after half a century of rapid growth and change, America was a very different nation from the republic of 1800. Geographic expansion, population increase, economic development, and the changes wrought by the market revolution had transformed the struggling new nation. Economically, culturally, and politically Americans had forged a strong sense of national identity.

Expansion and Growth

America was now a much larger nation than it had been in 1800. Through war and diplomacy, the coun-

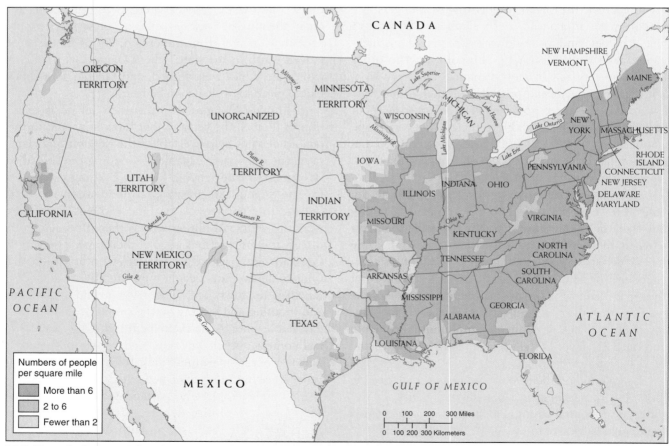

U.S. Population and Settlement, 1850   By 1850, the United States was a continental nation. Its people, whom Thomas Jefferson had once thought would not reach the Mississippi River for forty generations, had not only passed the river but leapfrogged to the west coast. In comparison to the America of 1800 (see the map on p. 157) the growth was astounding.

try had grown to continental dimensions, more than tripling in size from 890,000 to 3 million square miles. Its population had increased enormously: from 5.3 million in 1800 to more than 23 million, 4 million of whom were African American slaves and 2 million new immigrants, largely from Germany and Ireland. Comprising just sixteen states in 1800, America in 1850 had thirty-one, and more than half of the population lived west of the Appalachians.

America was also much richer: it is estimated that real per capita income doubled between 1800 and 1850. Southern cotton, which had contributed so much to American economic growth, continued to be the nation's principal export, but it was no longer the major influence on the domestic economy. The development of manufacturing in the Northeast and the increased economic importance of the Midwest had serious domestic political implications. As the South's share of responsibility for economic growth waned, so did its political importance—at least in the eyes of many Northerners. Thus, the very success of the United States both in geographic expansion and economic development served to undermine the role of the slave South in national politics and to hasten the day of open conflict between it and the free-labor North and Midwest.

Political Parties and Slavery

The Second American Party System forged in the great controversies of Andrew Jackson's presidency (see Chapter 10) was a national party system. In their need to mobilize great masses of recently enfranchised voters to elect a president every four years, politicians created organized party structures that overrode deeply rooted sectional differences. Politicians from all sections of the country cooperated because they knew their party could not succeed without national appeal. At a time when the ordinary person still had very strong sectional loyalties, the mass political party created a national community of like-minded voters. Yet, by the election of 1848, sectional interests were eroding the political "glue" in both parties. Although each party still appeared united, sectional fissures already ran deep.

Political splits were preceded by divisions in other social institutions. Disagreements about slavery had already split the country's great religious organizations into northern and southern groups, the Presbyterians in 1837, the Methodists in 1844, and the Baptists in

1845. (Some of these splits turned out to be permanent. The Southern Baptist Convention, for example, is still a separate body.) The abolitionists had been posing this simple yet uncompromising choice between slavery or freedom since the 1830s. Moreover, they had been insisting on a compelling distinction: as Liberty Party spokesman Salmon P. Chase said, "Freedom is national; slavery only is local and sectional."

States' Rights and Slavery

But was freedom national and slavery sectional, or was it the other way around? Southern politicians took the latter view, as their foremost spokesman, South Carolina's John C. Calhoun, made ringingly clear throughout his long career.

This poster advertises *Uncle Tom's Cabin*, the bestselling novel by Harriet Beecher Stowe. This poignant story of long-suffering African American slaves had an immense impact on Northern popular opinion, swaying it decisively against slavery. In that respect, the poster's boast, "the greatest book of the age" was correct.

SOURCE: ©Bettmann/CORBIS.

In 1850, the three men who had long represented America's three major regions attempted to resolve the political crisis brought on by the applications of California and Utah for statehood. Henry Clay is speaking; John C. Calhoun stands third from right; and Daniel Webster is seated at the left with his head in his hand. Both Clay and Webster were ill, and Calhoun died before the Compromise of 1850 was arranged by a younger group of politicians led by Stephen A. Douglas.

SOURCE: Library of Congress.

Constitution was the only protection for slave owners, whose right to own slaves (a fundamental right in southern eyes) was being attacked. Calhoun's position on the territories quickly became southern dogma: anything less than full access to the territories was unconstitutional. Slavery, Calhoun and other Southerners insisted, had to be national.

As Congressman Robert Toombs of Georgia put the case in 1850, there was very little room for compromise:

> I stand upon the great principle that the South has the right to an equal participation in the territories of the United States. . . . She will divide with you if you wish it, but the right to enter all or divide I shall never surrender. . . . Deprive us of this right and appropriate the common property to yourselves, it is then your government, not mine. Then I am its enemy. . . . Give us our just rights, and we are ready . . . to stand by the Union. . . . Refuse [them], and for one, I will strike for independence.

In 1828 Calhoun had begun the protracted Nullification Crisis by asserting the constitutional right of states to "nullify" national laws that were harmful to their interests (see Chapter 10). Calhoun argued, as others have since, that the states' rights doctrine protected the legitimate rights of a minority in a democratic system governed by majority rule.

In 1847, Calhoun responded to the 1846 Wilmot Proviso with an elaboration of the states' rights argument. In spite of the apparent precedents of the Northwest Ordinance of 1787 and the Missouri Compromise, Calhoun argued that Congress did not have a constitutional right to prohibit slavery in the territories. The territories, he said, were the common property of all the states, north and south, and Congress could not discriminate against slave owners as they moved west. On the contrary, Calhoun argued, slave owners had a constitutional right to the protection of their property wherever they moved. Of course, Calhoun's legally correct description of African American slaves as property enraged abolitionists. But on behalf of the South, Calhoun was expressing the belief—and the fear—that his interpretation of the

Northern Fears of "The Slave Power"

The words of Southerners like Calhoun and Toombs confirmed for many Northerners the warnings of antislavery leaders that they were endangered by a menacing "slave power." Liberty Party leader James Birney, in a speech in 1844, was the first to add this phrase to the nation's political vocabulary. "The slave power," Birney explained, was a group of aristocratic slave owners who not only dominated the political and social life of the South but conspired to control the federal government as well, posing a danger to free speech and free institutions throughout the nation.

Birney's warnings about "the slave power" seemed in 1844 merely the overheated rhetoric of an extremist group of abolitionists. But the defensive southern political strategies of the 1850s were to convince an increasing number of northern voters that "the slave power" did in fact exist. Thus in northern eyes the South became a demonic monolith that threatened the national government.

Two Communities, Two Perspectives

Ironically, it was a common belief in expansion that made the arguments between Northerners and Southerners so irreconcilable. Southerners had been the strongest supporters of the Mexican-American War, and they still hoped to expand into Cuba, believing that the slave system must grow or wither. On the other hand, although many northern Whigs had opposed the Mexican-American War, most did so for antislavery reasons, not because they opposed expansion. The strong showing of the Free-Soil Party (which evolved out of the Liberty Party) in the election of 1848 (getting 10 percent of the popular vote) was proof of that. Basically, both North and South believed in manifest destiny, but each on its own terms.

Similarly, both North and South used the language of basic rights and liberties in the debate over expansion. But free-soilers were speaking of personal liberty, whereas Southerners meant their right to own a particular kind of property (slaves) and to maintain a way of life based on the possession of that property.

By 1850, North and South had created fixed stereotypes of the other. To antislavery Northerners, the South was an economic backwater dominated by a small slave-owning aristocracy that lived off the profits of forced labor and deprived poor whites of their democratic rights and the fruits of honest work. The slave system was not only immoral but a drag on the entire nation, for, in the words of Senator William Seward of New York, it subverted the "intelligence, vigor and energy" that were essential for national growth. In contrast, the dynamic and enterprising commercial North boasted a free labor ideology that offered economic opportunity to the common man and ensured his democratic rights (see Chapter 12).

Things looked very different through southern eyes. Far from being economically backward, the South, through its export of cotton, was, according to Southerners, the great engine of national economic growth from which the North benefited. Slavery was not only a blessing to an inferior race but also the cornerstone of democracy, for it ensured the freedom and independence of all white men without entailing the bitter class divisions that marked the North. Slave owners accused northern manufacturers of hypocrisy for practicing "wage slavery" without the paternal benevolence they claimed to bestow on their slaves.

By the early 1850s, these vastly different visions of the North and the South—the result of many years of political controversy—had become fixed, and the chances of national reconciliation increasingly slim.

THE COMPROMISE OF 1850

By 1850 the issue raised by the Wilmot Proviso—whether slavery should be extended to the new territories—could no longer be ignored. Overnight, the California Gold Rush had turned a remote frontier into a territory with a booming population. In 1849 both California and Utah applied for statehood. Should these territories be admitted as slave or free states? A simmering border war between Texas, a slave state, and New Mexico, which seemed likely to be a free state, had to be settled, as did the issue of the debts Texas had incurred as an independent republic. Closer to home, antislavery forces demanded the end of slavery in the District of Columbia, while slave owners complained that Northerners were refusing to return escaped slaves, as federal law mandated.

Debate and Compromise

The Compromise of 1850 was the final act in the political careers of the three aging men who in the public mind best represented America's sections: Westerner Henry Clay; Southerner John C. Calhoun; and Daniel Webster, spokesman for the North. It was sadly appropriate to the bitter sectional argument of 1850 that the three men contributed great words to the debate but that the compromise itself was enacted by younger men.

On July 9, 1850, in the midst of the debate, President Zachary Taylor died of acute gastroenteritis. When Vice President Millard Fillmore assumed the presidency, however, he helped adjust the Compromise of 1850 to southern liking. Fillmore was a moderate northern Whig and more prosouthern than the southern-born Taylor had been. Moreover, although Clay had assembled all the necessary parts of the bargain, it was not he but members of a younger political generation, and in particular the rising young Democrat from Illinois, Stephen Douglas, who drove the Compromise of 1850 through Congress. The final product consisted of five separate bills (it had been impossible to obtain a majority for a comprehensive measure), embodying three separate compromises.

First, California was admitted as a free state, but the status of the remaining former Mexican possessions was left to be decided by popular sovereignty (a vote of the territory's inhabitants) when they applied for statehood. (Utah's application for statehood was not accepted until 1896 because of controversy over the Mormon practice of polygamy.) The result was, for the time being, fifteen slave states and sixteen free states. Second, Texas (a slave state) was required to cede land to New Mexico Territory (free or slave status undecided). In return, the federal government assumed $10 million of debts Texas had incurred before it became a state. Finally, the slave trade, but not slavery itself, was ended in the District of Columbia, but a stronger fugitive slave law was enacted.

Jubilation and relief greeted the news that compromise had been achieved. In Washington, where the anxiety and concern had been greatest, drunken crowds serenaded Congress, shouting, "The Union is saved!" That was certainly true for the moment, but analysis of the votes on the five bills that made up the compromise revealed no consistent majority. The sectional splits within each party that had existed before the compromise remained. In the country as a whole, the feeling was that the problem of slavery in the territories had been solved. Senator Salmon P. Chase of Ohio soberly noted, "The question of slavery in the territories has been avoided. It has not been settled." And many Southerners felt that their only real gain in the contested compromise was the Fugitive Slave Law, which quickly turned out to be an inflammatory measure.

The Fugitive Slave Act

From the early days of their movement, northern abolitionists had urged slaves to escape, promising assistance and support when they reached the North. Northerners had long been appalled by professional slave catchers, who zealously seized African Americans in the North and took them south into slavery again. Most abhorrent in northern eyes was that captured black people were at the mercy of slave catchers because they had no legal right to defend themselves. In more than one case, a northern free African American was captured in his own community and helplessly shipped into slavery.

The Fugitive Slave Law, enacted in 1850, dramatically increased the power of slave owners to capture escaped slaves. The full authority of the federal government now supported slave owners, and although fugitives were guaranteed a hearing before a federal commissioner, they were not allowed to testify on their own behalf. Furthermore, the new law imposed federal penalties on citizens who protected or assisted fugitives or who did not cooperate in their return. In Boston, the center of the American abolitionist movement, reaction to the Fugitive Slave Law was fierce. When an escaped slave named Shadrach Minkins was seized in February 1851, a group of African American men broke into the courtroom, overwhelmed the federal marshals, seized Minkins, and sent him safely to Canada. Although the action had community support—a Massachusetts jury defiantly refused to convict the perpetrators—many people, including Daniel Webster and President Fillmore, condemned it as "mob rule."

The federal government responded with overwhelming force. In April 1851, 300 armed soldiers

OVERVIEW

THE GREAT SECTIONAL COMPROMISES

Missouri Compromise	1820	Admits Missouri to the Union as a slave state and Maine as a free state; prohibits slavery in the rest of the Louisiana Purchase Territory north of 36°30'.
		Territory Covered: The entire territory of the Louisiana Purchase, exclusive of the state of Louisiana, which had been admitted to the Union in 1812.
Compromise of 1850	1850	Admits California to the Union as a free state, settles the borders of Texas (a slave state); sets no conditions concerning slavery for the rest of the territory acquired from Mexico.
		Territory Covered: The territory that had been part of Mexico before the end of the Mexican-American War and the Treaty of Guadalupe Hidalgo (1848): part of Texas, California, Utah Territory (now Utah, Nevada, and part of Colorado), and New Mexico Territory (now New Mexico and Arizona).

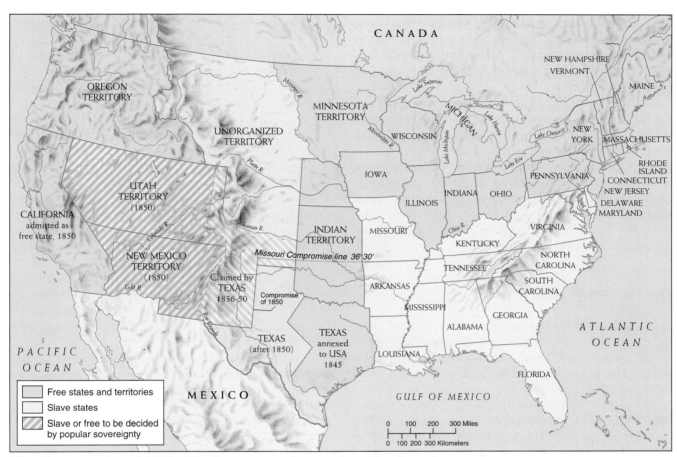

The Compromise of 1850   The Compromise of 1850 reflected heightened sectional tensions by being even messier and more awkward than the Missouri Compromise of 1820. California was admitted as a free state, the borders of Texas were settled, and the status of the rest of the former Mexican territory was left to be decided later by popular sovereignty. No consistent majority voted for the five separate bills that made up the compromise.

were mobilized to prevent the rescue of Thomas Sims, who was being shipped back into slavery. In the most famous case in Boston, a biracial group of armed abolitionists led by Unitarian clergyman Thomas Wentworth Higginson stormed the federal courthouse in 1854 in an attempt to save escaped slave Anthony Burns. The rescue effort failed, and a federal deputy marshal was killed. President Pierce sent marines, cavalry, and artillery to Boston to reinforce the guard over Burns and ordered a federal ship to be ready to deliver the fugitive back into slavery. When the effort by defense lawyers to argue for Burns's freedom failed, Bostonians raised money to buy his freedom. But the U.S. attorney, ordered by the president to enforce the Fugitive Slave Law in all circumstances, blocked the purchase. The case was lost, and Burns was marched to the docks through streets lined with sorrowing abolitionists. Buildings were shrouded in black and draped with American flags hanging upside down, while bells tolled as if for a funeral.

The Burns case radicalized many Northerners. Conservative Whig George Hilliard wrote to a friend, "When it was all over, and I was left alone in my office, I put my face in my hands and wept. I could do nothing less." During the 1850s, 322 black fugitives were sent back into slavery; only 11 were declared free. Northern popular sentiment and the Fugitive Slave Law, rigorously enforced by the federal government, were increasingly at odds.

In this volatile atmosphere, escaped African Americans wrote and lectured bravely on behalf of freedom. Frederick Douglass, the most famous and eloquent of the fugitive slaves, spoke out fearlessly in support of armed resistance. Openly active in the underground network that helped slaves reach safety in Canada, Douglass himself had been constantly in danger of capture until his friends bought his freedom in 1847. Harriet Jacobs, who escaped to the North after seven years in hiding in the South, wrote bitterly in her *Incidents in the Life of a Slave Girl* (1861) that the Fugitive Slave Law made her feel that "I was, in fact, a slave in New York, as subject to slave laws as I had been in a slave state. . . . I had been chased during half my life, and it seemed as if the chase was never to end."

The Fugitive Slave Law made slavery national and forced northern communities to confront what that meant. Although most people were still unwilling to grant social equality to the free African Americans who lived in the northern states, more and more had come to believe that the institution of slavery was wrong. Northern protests against the Fugitive Slave Law bred suspicion in the South and encouraged secessionist thinking. These new currents of public opinion were reflected in the election of 1852.

The Election of 1852

The first sign of the weakening of the national party system in 1852 was the difficulty both parties experienced at their nominating conventions. After fifty-two ballots, the Whigs nominated General Winfield Scott (a military hero like the party's previous two candidates) rather than sitting President Fillmore. Many southern Whigs were angered and alienated by the choice and either abstained during the voting, like Georgia's Alexander Stephens, or, like Robert Toombs, cast a protest vote for the Democratic candidate. Although southern Whigs were still elected to Congress, their loyalty to the national party was strained to the breaking point. The Whigs never again fielded a presidential candidate.

The Democrats had a wider variety of candidates: Lewis Cass of popular sovereignty fame; Stephen Douglas, architect of the Compromise of 1850; and James Buchanan, described as a "Northern man with Southern principles." Cass, Douglas, and Buchanan competed for forty-nine ballots, each strong enough to block the others but not strong enough to win. Finally the party turned to a handsome, affable nonentity, Franklin Pierce of New Hampshire, who was thought to have southern sympathies. Uniting on a platform pledging "faithful execution" of all parts of the Compromise of 1850, including the Fugitive Slave Law, Democrats polled well in the South and in the North. Most Democrats who had voted for the Free-Soil Party in 1848 voted for Pierce. So, in record numbers, did immigrant Irish and German voters, who were eligible for citizenship after three years' residence. The strong immigrant vote for Pierce was a sign of the strength of the Democratic machines in northern cities (see Chapter 13). Pierce easily won the 1852 election, 254 electoral votes to 42.

"Young America": The Politics of Expansion

Pierce entered the White House in 1853 on a wave of good feeling. Massachusetts Whig Amos Lawrence reported, "Never since Washington has an administration commenced with the hearty [good] will of so large a portion of the country." This goodwill was soon strained by Pierce's support for the expansionist adventures of the "Young America" movement.

The "Young America" movement began as a group of writers and politicans in the New York Democratic Party who believed in the democratic and nationalistic promise of "manifest destiny" (a term coined by one of their members, John Sullivan). By the 1850s, however, their lofty goals had shrunk to a desire to conquer Central America and Cuba. When in 1858 the perennial conflict between centrists and liberals in Mexico broke into civil war, the fighting served to convince some southerners that Mexico was ripe for conquest, but ironically, before they could act, America's own Civil War intervened.

During the Pierce administration, several private "filibusters" (from the Spanish *filibustero*, meaning an "adventurer" or "pirate") invaded Caribbean and Central American countries, usually with the declared intention of extending slave territory.

The Pierce administration, not directly involved in the filibustering, *was* deeply involved in an effort to obtain Cuba. In part, the effort was prompted by abortive slave revolts in Cuba in 1843–44, which led some Cuban slave owners to want annexation to the United States so that slavery could continue. In 1854, Pierce authorized his minister to Spain, Pierre Soulé, to try to force the unwilling Spanish to sell Cuba for $130 million. Soulé met in Ostend, Belgium, with the American ministers to France and England, John Mason and James Buchanan, to compose the offer. At first appealing to Spain to recognize the deep affinities between the Cubans and American Southerners that made them "one people with one destiny," the document went on to threaten to "wrest" Cuba from Spain if necessary. This amazing document, which became known as the Ostend Manifesto, was soon leaked to the press. Deeply embarrassed, the Pierce administration was forced to repudiate it.

The complicity between the Pierce administration and proslavery expansionists was foolhardy and lost it the northern goodwill with which it had begun. The sectional crisis that preceded the Compromise of 1850 had made obvious the danger of reopening the territorial issue. Ironically, it was not the Young America expansionists but the prime mover of the Compromise of 1850, Stephen A. Douglas, who reignited the sectional struggle over slavery expansion.

THE CRISIS OF THE NATIONAL PARTY SYSTEM

In 1854, Douglas introduced the Kansas-Nebraska Act and thereby reopened the question of slavery in the territories. Douglas knew he was taking a political risk, but he believed he could satisfy both his expansionist aims and his presidential ambitions. He was wrong. Instead, he pushed the national party system into crisis, first killing the Whigs and then destroying the Democrats.

The Kansas-Nebraska Act

Douglas introduced the Kansas-Nebraska Act opening the territory to white settlement because he was an ardent advocate of a transcontinental railroad that he believed would foster American democracy and commerce. He wanted the rail line to terminate in Chicago (in his own state of Illinois) rather than in St. Louis (a rival city), and to achieve that aim, the land west of Iowa and Missouri had to be organized into territories (the first step toward statehood). To get Congress to agree to the organization of the territories, however, he needed the votes of southern Democrats, who were unwilling to support him unless the new territory was open to slavery.

Douglas thought he was solving his problem by proposing that the status of slavery in the new territories be governed by the principle of popular sovereignty. Douglas thought Southerners would support his bill because of its popular sovereignty provision and Northerners because it favored a northern route for the transcontinental railroad. Douglas chose to downplay the price he had to pay for southern support—by allowing the possibility of slavery in the new territories his bill in effect repealed the Missouri Compromise of 1820, which barred slavery north of latitude 36°30'.

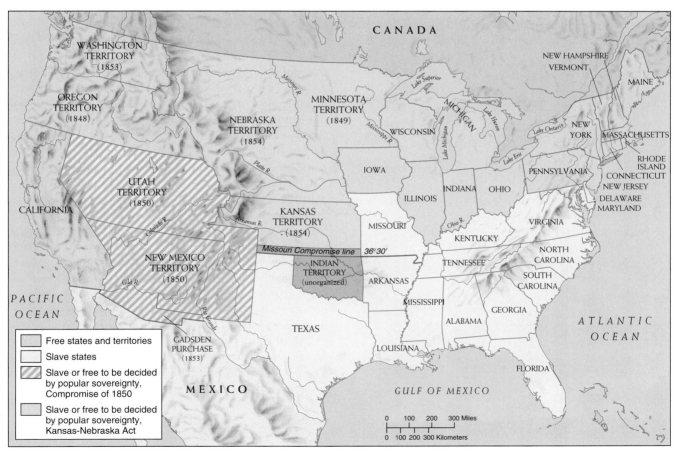

The Kansas-Nebraska Act, 1854   The Kansas-Nebraska Act, proposed by Stephen A. Douglas in 1854, opened the central and northern Great Plains to settlement. The act had two major faults: it robbed Indian peoples of half the territory guaranteed to them by treaty, and, because it repealed the Missouri Compromise Line, it opened up the lands to warring proslavery and antislavery factions.

The Kansas-Nebraska bill passed, but it badly strained the major political parties. Southern Whigs voted with southern Democrats in favor of the measure, northern Whigs rejected it absolutely, creating an irreconcilable split that left Whigs unable to field a presidential candidate in 1856. The damage to the Democratic Party was almost as great. In the congressional elections of 1854, northern Democrats lost two-thirds of their seats (a drop from ninety-one to twenty-five), giving the southern Democrats (who were solidly in favor of slavery extension) the dominant voice both in Congress and within the party.

Douglas had committed one of the greatest miscalculations in American political history. A storm of protest arose throughout the North. More than 300 large anti-Nebraska rallies occurred during congressional consideration of the bill, and the anger did not subside. Douglas, who confidently believed that "the people of the North will sustain the measure when they come to understand it," found himself shouted down more than once at public rallies when he tried to explain the bill.

The Kansas-Nebraska bill shifted a crucial sector of northern opinion: the wealthy merchants, bankers, and manufacturers, called the "Cotton Whigs," who had economic ties with southern slave owners and had always disapproved of abolitionist activity. Convinced that the bill would encourage antislavery feeling in the North, Cotton Whigs urged southern politicians to vote against it, only to be ignored. Passage of the Kansas-Nebraska Act convinced many northern Whigs that compromise with the South was impossible.

In Kansas in 1854, hasty treaties were concluded with the Indian tribes who owned the land. Some, such as the Kickapoos, Shawnees, Sauks, and Foxes, agreed to relocate to small reservations. Others, like the Delawares, Weas, and Iowas, agreed to sell their lands to whites. Still others, such as the Cheyennes and Sioux, kept the western part of Kansas Territory (now Colorado)—until gold was discovered there in 1859. Once the treaties were signed, both proslavery and antislavery white settlers began to pour in, and the battle was on.

Kansas soon became a bloody battleground as the two factions struggled to secure the mandate of "popular sovereignty." Free-soilers in Lawrence received shipments of heavy crates, innocuously marked "BOOKS" but actually containing Sharps repeating rifles, sent by eastern supporters. For their part, proslavery "border ruffians" from Missouri—already heavily armed, with Bowie knives in their boots, revolvers at their waists, rifles slung from their shoulders, and swords at their sides—called for reinforcements. David Atchison exhorted Alabamans: "Let your young men come forth to Missouri and Kansas! Let them come well armed!"

In the summer of 1856, these lethal preparations exploded into open warfare. First, proslavery forces burned and looted the town of Lawrence. The Free State Hotel, among other buildings, was burned to the ground. In retaliation, a grim old man named John Brown led his sons in a raid on the proslavery settlers of Pottawatomie Creek, killing five unarmed people. A wave of violence ensued. Armed bands roamed the countryside, and burnings and killings became commonplace. John Brown and his followers were just one of many bands of marauding murderers who were never arrested, never brought to trial, and never stopped from committing further violence. Peaceful residents of large sections of rural Kansas were repeatedly forced to flee to the safety of military forts when rumors of one or another armed band reached them.

VOTING IN KICKAPOO.

This engraving shows "Border Ruffians" from Missouri lining up to vote for slavery in the Kickapoo, Kansas Territory election of 1855. The widespread practice of illegal voting and of open violence earned Kansas the dreadful nickname of "Bleeding Kansas."

SOURCE: The Granger Collection.

The Politics of Nativism

Meanwhile, sectional pressures continued to reshape national politics. The breakup of the Whig Party left a political vacuum that was filled with one of the strongest bursts of nativism, or anti-immigrant feeling, in American history and by the rapid growth of the new American Party, which formed in 1850 to give political expression to nativism. The new party was in part a reaction to the Democratic Party's success in capturing the support of the rapidly growing population of mostly Catholic foreign-born voters. Irish immigrants in particular voted Democratic, both in reaction to Whig hostility (as in Boston) and because of their own antiblack prejudices. Frquently in competition with free African Americans for low-paying jobs, Irish immigrants were more likely to share the attitudes of Southerners than those of abolitionists.

This 1855 cartoon by Nathaniel Currier illustrates the Know Nothings' fear of an antidemocratic Catholic "invasion" of America. As the shamrock caught by the boathook is meant to indicate, Irish Catholics were a special target of Know Nothing suspicion.

SOURCE: Courtesy of the Library of Congress.

The reformist and individualistic attitudes of many Whigs inclined them toward nativism. Many Whigs disapproved of the new immigrants because they were poor, Catholic, and often disdainful of the temperance movement. The Catholic Church's opposition to the liberal European revolutions of 1848 also fueled anti-Catholic fears. If America's new Catholic immigrants opposed the revolutions in which other Americans took such pride (believing them to be modeled on the American example), how could the future of America's own democracy be ensured? Finally, nativist Whigs held immigration to be solely responsible for the increases in crime and the rising cost of relief for the poor that accompanied the astoundingly rapid urban growth of the 1830s and 1840s (see Chapter 13).

Nativism drew former Whigs, especially young men in white-collar and skilled blue-collar occupations, to the new American Party. At the core of the party were several secret fraternal societies open only to native-born Protestants who pledged never to vote for a Catholic, on the grounds that all Catholics took their orders straight from the pope in Rome. When questioned about their beliefs, party members maintained secrecy by answering, "I know nothing"—hence the popular name for American Party members, the Know-Nothings.

Know-Nothings scored startling victories in northern state elections in 1854, winning control of

the legislature in Massachusetts and polling 40 percent of the vote in Pennsylvania. But in the 1850s, no party could ignore slavery, and in 1855 the American Party split into northern (antislavery) and southern (proslavery) wings. Soon after this split, many people who had voted for the Know-Nothings shifted their support to another new party, one that combined many characteristics of the Whigs with a westward-looking, expansionist, free-soil policy. This was the Republican Party, founded in 1854.

The Republican Party and the Election of 1856

Many constituencies found room in the new Republican Party. Its supporters included many former northern Whigs who opposed slavery absolutely, many Free-Soil Party supporters who opposed the expansion of slavery but were willing to tolerate it in the South, and many northern reformers concerned about temperance and Catholicism. The Republicans also attracted the economic core of the old Whig Party—the merchants and industrialists who wanted a strong national government to promote economic growth by supporting a protective tariff, transportation improvements, and cheap land for western farmers. In quieter times it would have taken this party a

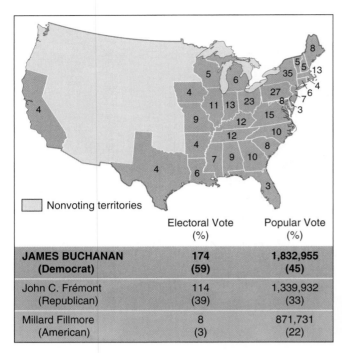

	Electoral Vote (%)	Popular Vote (%)
JAMES BUCHANAN (Democrat)	**174 (59)**	**1,832,955 (45)**
John C. Frémont (Republican)	114 (39)	1,339,932 (33)
Millard Fillmore (American)	8 (3)	871,731 (22)

The Election of 1856 Because three parties contested the 1856 election, Democrat James Buchanan was a minority president. Although Buchanan alone had national support, Republican John Frémont won most of the free states, and Millard Fillmore of the American Party gained 40 percent of the vote in most of the slave states.

while to sort out all its differences and become a true political community. But because of the sectional crisis, the fledgling party nearly won its very first presidential election.

The immediate question facing the nation in 1856 was which new party, the Know-Nothings or the Republicans, would emerge the stronger. But the more important question was whether the Democratic Party could hold together. The two strongest contenders for the Democratic nomination were President Pierce and Stephen A. Douglas. Douglas had proposed the Kansas-Nebraska Act and Pierce had actively supported it. Both men, therefore, had the support of the southern wing of the party. But it was precisely their support of this act that made Northerners oppose both of them. The Kansas-Nebraska Act's divisive effect on the Democratic Party now became clear: no one who had voted on the bill, either for or against, could satisfy both wings of the party. A compromise candidate was found in James Buchanan of Pennsylvania, the "Northern man with Southern principles." Luckily for him, he had been ambassador to Great Britain at the time of the Kansas-Nebraska Act and, thus, had not had to commit himself.

The election of 1856 appeared to be a three-way contest that pitted Buchanan against explorer John C. Frémont of the Republican Party and the American

OVERVIEW

POLITICAL PARTIES SPLIT AND REALIGN

Whig Party	Ran its last presidential candidate in 1852. The candidate, General Winfield Scott, alienated many southern Whigs, and the party was so split it could not field a candidate in 1856.
Democratic Party	Remained a national party through 1856, but Buchanan's actions as president made southern domination of the party so clear that many northern Democrats were alienated. Stephen Douglas, running as a northern Democrat in 1860, won 29 percent of the popular vote; John Breckinridge, running as a southern Democrat, won 18 percent.
Liberty Party	Antislavery party; ran James G. Birney for president in 1844. He won 62,000 votes, largely from northern antislavery Whigs.
Free-Soil Party	Ran Martin Van Buren, former Democratic president, in 1848. Gained 10 percent of the popular vote, largely from Whigs but also from some northern Democrats.
American (Know-Nothing) Party	Nativist party made striking gains in 1854 congressional elections, attracting both northern and southern Whigs. In 1856, its presidential candidate Millard Fillmore won 21 percent of the popular vote.
Republican Party	Founded in 1854. Attracted many northern Whigs and northern Democrats. Presidential candidate John C. Frémont won 33 percent of the popular vote in 1856; in 1860 Abraham Lincoln won 40 percent and was elected in a four-way race.

(Know-Nothing) Party's candidate, former president Millard Fillmore. In fact, the election was two separate contests, one in the North and one in the South. The southern race was between Buchanan and Fillmore, the northern race between Buchanan and Frémont. Buchanan won the election with only 45 percent of the popular vote because he was the only national candidate. But the Republicans, after studying the election returns, claimed "victorious defeat," for they realized that in 1860 the addition of just two more northern states to their total would mean victory. Furthermore, the Republican Party had clearly defeated the American Party in the battle to win designation as a major party. These were grounds for great optimism—and for great concern, for the Republican Party was a sectional rather than a national party; it drew almost all its support from the North. Southerners viewed its very existence as an attack on their vital interests. Thus, the rapid rise of the Republicans posed a growing threat to national unity.

THE POLITICAL QUADRILLE
Music by Dred Scott

This political cartoon shows the devastating impact of the Supreme Court's 1857 *Dred Scott* decision on politics and the election of 1860. Dred Scott, shown with a fiddle in the middle, plays for (clockwise from upper right): Republican Abraham Lincoln and an African American woman; John Bell with an Indian; Northern Democrat Stephen A. Douglas with an Irishman; and Southern Democrat John Breckinridge with President James Buchanan, the "Northern Democrat with Southern sympathies."

SOURCE: Courtesy of the Library of Congress.

THE DIFFERENCES DEEPEN

In one dreadful week in 1856 the people of the United States heard, in quick succession, about the looting and burning of Lawrence, Kansas, about John Brown's retaliatory massacre at Pottawatomie, and about unprecedented violence on the Senate floor. In the last of these incidents, Senator Charles Sumner of Massachusetts suffered permanent injury in a vicious attack by Congressman Preston Brooks of South Carolina. Trapped at his desk, Sumner was helpless as Brooks beat him so hard with his cane that it broke. A few days earlier, Sumner had given an insulting antislavery speech. Using the abusive, accusatory style favored by abolitionists, he had singled out for ridicule Senator Andrew Butler of South Carolina, Preston Brooks's uncle. In Brooks's mind, he was simply avenging an intolerable affront to his

uncle's honor. So far had the behavioral codes of North and South diverged that each man found his own action perfectly justifiable and the action of the other outrageous.

The *Dred Scott* Decision

Although James Buchanan firmly believed that he alone could hold together the nation so riven by hatred and violence, his self-confidence outran his abilities. He was so deeply indebted to the strong southern wing of the Democratic Party that he could not take the impartial actions necessary to heal "Bleeding Kansas." And his support for a momentous prosouthern decision by the Supreme Court further aggravated sectional differences.

In *Dred Scott* v. *Sandford*, decided on March 6, 1857, two days after James Buchanan was sworn in, a southern-dominated Supreme Court attempted—and failed—to solve the political controversy over slavery. Dred Scott had been a slave all his life. His owner, army surgeon John Emerson, had taken Scott on his military assignments during the 1830s to Illinois (a free state) and Wisconsin Territory (a free territory, north of the Missouri Compromise line). During that time Scott married another slave, Harriet, and their daughter Eliza was born in free territory. Emerson and the Scotts then returned to Missouri (a slave state) and there, in 1846, Dred Scott sued for his freedom and that of his wife and his daughter born in Wisconsin Territory (who as women had no legal standing of their own) on the grounds that residence in free lands had made them free.

In his decision, Chief Justice Roger B. Taney of Maryland declared the Missouri Compromise unconstitutional. Taney asserted that the federal government had no right to interfere with the free movement of property throughout the territories. Taney was in effect making John C. Calhoun's states' rights position, always considered an extremist southern position, the law of the land. He then dismissed the *Dred Scott* case on the grounds that only citizens could bring suits before federal courts and that black people—slave or free—were not citizens. With this bold judicial intervention into the most heated issue of the day, Taney intended to settle the controversy over the expansion of slavery once and for all. Instead, he enflamed the conflict.

The five southern members of the Supreme Court concurred in Taney's decision, as did one Northerner, Robert C. Grier. Historians have found that President-elect Buchanan had pressured Grier, a fellow Pennsylvanian, to support the majority. Two of the three other Northerners vigorously dissented, and the last voiced other objections. This was clearly a sectional decision, and the response to it was sectional. Southerners expressed great satisfaction and strong support for the Court. Many northerners disagreed so strongly with the *Dred Scott* decision that for the first time they found themselves seriously questioning the power of the Supreme Court to establish the "law of the land."

For the Republican Party, the *Dred Scott* decision represented a formidable challenge. By invalidating the Missouri Compromise, the decision swept away the free-soil foundation of the party. But to directly challenge a Supreme Court decision was a weighty matter. The most sensational Republican counterattack—made by both Abraham Lincoln and William Seward—was the accusation that President Buchanan had conspired with the southern Supreme Court justices to subvert the American political system by withholding the decision until after the presidential election. Lincoln also raised the frightening possibility that "the next *Dred Scott* decision" would legalize slavery even in free states that abhorred it. President Buchanan's response to events in Kansas, including the

drafting of a proslavery constitution, also stoked political antagonisms.

The Lecompton Constitution

In Kansas the doctrine of popular sovereignty led to continuing civil strife and the political travesty of two territorial governments. The first election of officers to a territorial government in 1855 produced a lopsided proslavery outcome that was clearly the result of illegal voting by Missouri border ruffians. Free-soilers protested by forming their own government, giving Kansas both a proslavery territorial legislature in Lecompton and a free-soil government in Topeka. Because free-soil voters boycotted a June 1857 election for a convention to write a constitution for the territory once it reached statehood, the convention had a proslavery majority that wrote the proslavery Lecompton constitution and then applied to Congress for admission to the Union under its terms. In the meantime, in October free-soil voters had participated in relatively honest elections for the territorial legislature, elections that returned a clear free-soil majority. Nevertheless, Buchanan, in the single most disastrous mistake of his administration, endorsed the proslavery constitution because he feared the loss of the support of southern Democrats. It seemed that Kansas would enter the Union as a sixteenth slave state, making the number of slave and free states equal.

Unexpected congressional opposition came from none other than Stephen Douglas, author of the legislation that had begun the Kansas troubles in 1854. Now, in 1857, in what was surely the bravest step of his political career, Douglas opposed the Lecompton constitution on the grounds that it violated the principle of popular sovereignty. He insisted that the Lecompton constitution must be voted upon by Kansas voters in honest elections (as indeed Buchanan had initially promised). Defying James Buchanan, his own president, Douglas voted with the majority in Congress in April 1858 to refuse admission to Kansas under the Lecompton constitution. In a new referendum, the people of Kansas also rejected the Lecompton constitution, 11,300 to 1,788. Kansas was finally admitted as a free state in January 1861.

The defeat of the Lecompton constitution did not come easily. There was more bloodshed in Kansas, more violence in Congress, and conflict on still another level—the Democratic Party was breaking apart. Douglas had intended to preserve the Democrats as a national party, but instead he lost the support of the southern wing. Summing up these events, Congressman

Alexander Stephens of Georgia wrote glumly to his brother: "All things here are tending my mind to the conclusion that the Union cannot and will not last long."

The Panic of 1857

Adding to the growing political tensions was the short but sharp depression of 1857 and 1858. Technology played a part. In August 1857, the failure of an Ohio investment house—the kind of event that had formerly taken weeks to be widely known—was the subject of a news story flashed immediately over telegraph wires to Wall Street and other financial markets. A wave of panic selling ensued, leading to business failures and slowdowns that threw thousands out of work. The major cause of the panic was a sharp but temporary downturn in agricultural exports to Britain, and recovery was well under way by early 1859.

This painting by Charles G. Rosenberg and James H. Cafferty shows a worried crowd exchanging the latest news on Wall Street during the Panic of 1857. This was the first economic depression in which the telegraph played a part by carrying bad financial news in the West to New York much more rapidly than in the past.

SOURCE: J. Cafferty & C. Rosenberg/Museum of the City of New York.

Because it affected cotton exports less than northern exports, the Panic of 1857 was less harmful to the South than to the North. Southerners took this as proof of the superiority of their economic system to the free-labor system of the North. It seemed that all matters of political discussion were being drawn into the sectional dispute. The next step toward disunion was an act of violence perpetrated by the grim abolitionist from Kansas, John Brown.

John Brown's Raid

In the heated political mood of the late 1850s, some improbable people became heroes. None was more improbable than John Brown, the self-appointed avenger who had slaughtered unarmed proslavery men in Kansas in 1856. In 1859, Brown proposed a wild scheme to raid the South and start a general slave uprising. He believed, as did most northern abolitionists, that discontent among southern slaves was so great that such an uprising needed only a spark to get going. Significantly, free African Americans—among them Frederick Douglass—did not support Brown, thinking his plan to raid the federal arsenal at Harpers Ferry, Virginia, was doomed to failure. They were right. On October 16, 1859, Brown led a group of twenty-two white and African American men against the arsenal. However, he had made no provision for escape. Even more incredible, he had not notified the Virginia slaves whose uprising it was supposed to initiate. In less than a day the raid was over. Eight of Brown's men (including two of his sons) were dead, no slaves had joined the fight, and Brown himself was captured. Moving quickly to prevent a lynching by local mobs, the state of Virginia tried and convicted Brown (while he was still weak from the wounds of battle) of treason, murder, and fomenting insurrection.

Ludicrous in life, possibly insane, Brown was nevertheless a noble martyr. In his closing speech prior to sentencing, Brown was magnificently eloquent: "Now, if it is deemed necessary that I should forfeit my life for the furtherance of the end of justice, and mingle my blood further with the blood of my children and with the blood of millions in this slave country whose rights are disregarded by wicked, cruel, and unjust enactments, I say, let it be done."

Brown's death by hanging on December 2, 1859, was marked throughout northern communities with public rites of mourning not seen since the death of George Washington. Church bells tolled, buildings were draped in black, ministers preached sermons, prayer meetings were held, abolitionists issued eulogies. Ralph Waldo Emerson said that Brown would

JOHN BROWN AT HARPER'S FERRY.

In a contemporary engraving, John Brown and his followers are shown trapped inside the armory at Harpers Ferry in October 1859. Captured, tried, and executed, Brown was regarded as a martyr in the North and a terrorist in the South.

SOURCE: The Granger Collection.

"make the gallows as glorious as the cross," and Henry David Thoreau called him "an angel of light." Not all Northerners supported Brown's action, but many people did support the antislavery cause that he represented.

Brown's raid shocked the South because it aroused the greatest fear—that of slave rebellion. Southerners believed that northern abolitionists were provoking slave revolts, a suspicion apparently confirmed when documents captured at Harpers Ferry revealed that Brown had the financial support of half a dozen members of the northern elite. These "Secret Six"—Gerrit Smith, George Stearns, Franklin Sanborn, Thomas Wentworth Higginson, Theodore Parker, and Samuel Gridley Howe—had been willing to finance armed attacks on the slave system.

Even more shocking to Southerners than the raid itself was the extent of northern mourning for Brown's death. Although the Republican Party disavowed Brown's actions, Southerners simply did not believe the party's statements. Senator Robert Toombs of Georgia warned that the South would "never permit this Federal government to pass into the traitorous hands of the Black Republican party." Talk of secession as the only possible response became common throughout the South.

THE SOUTH SECEDES

By 1860, sectional differences had caused one national party, the Whigs, to collapse. The second national party, the Democrats, stood on the brink of dissolution. Not only the politicians but ordinary people in both the North and the South were coming to believe there was no way to avoid what in 1858 William Seward (once a Whig, now a Republican) had called an "irrepressible conflict."

The Election of 1860

The split of the Democratic Party into northern and southern wings that had occurred during President Buchanan's tenure became official at the Democratic nominating conventions in 1860. The party convened first in Charleston, South Carolina, the center of secessionist agitation. It was the worst possible location in which to attempt to reach unity. Although Stephen Douglas had the support of the plurality of delegates, he did not have the two-thirds majority necessary for nomination. As the price of their support, Southerners insisted that Douglas support a federal slave code—a guarantee that slavery would be protected in the territories. Douglas could not agree without violating his own belief in popular sovereignty and losing his northern support. After ten days, fifty-nine ballots, and two southern walkouts, the convention ended where it had begun: deadlocked.

In June, the Democrats met again in Baltimore. The Douglasites, recognizing the need for a united party, were eager to compromise wherever they could, but most southern Democrats were not. More than a third of the delegates bolted. Later, holding a convention of their own, they nominated Buchanan's vice president John C. Breckinridge of Kentucky. The remaining two-thirds of the Democrats nominated Douglas, but everyone knew that a Republican victory was inevitable. To make matters worse, some southern Whigs joined with some border-state nativists to form the Constitutional Union Party, which nominated John Bell of Tennessee.

Republican strategy was built on the lessons of the 1856 "victorious defeat." The Republicans planned to carry all the states Frémont had won, plus Pennsylvania, Illinois, and Indiana. The two leading Republican contenders were Senator William H. Seward of New York and Abraham Lincoln of Illinois. Seward, the party's best-known figure, had enemies among party moderates, who thought he was too radical, and among nativists with whom he had clashed in the New York Whig Party. Lincoln, on the other hand, appeared new, impressive, more moderate than Seward, and certain to carry Illinois. Lincoln won the nomination on the third ballot.

The election of 1860 presented voters with one of the clearest choices in American history. On the key issue of slavery, Breckinridge supported its extension to the territories; Lincoln stood firmly for its exclusion. Douglas attempted to hold the middle ground with his principle of popular sovereignty; Bell vaguely favored compromise as well. The Republicans offered other platform planks designed to appeal to northern voters: support for a homestead act (free western lands), for a transcontinental railroad, for other internal improvements, and for a higher tariff. Although they spoke clearly against the extension of slavery, Republicans sought to dispel their radical abolitionist image. The Republican platform condemned John Brown's raid as "the gravest of crimes," repeatedly denied that Republicans favored the social equality of black people, and strenuously affirmed that they sought to preserve the Union. In reality, Republicans simply did not believe the South would secede if Lincoln won. In this the Republicans were not alone; few Northerners believed southern threats—Southerners had threatened too many times before.

The only candidate who spoke urgently and openly about the impending threat of secession was Douglas. Breaking with convention, Douglas campaigned personally, in both the North and, bravely, in the hostile South, warning of the danger of dissolution and presenting himself as the only truly national candidate. Realizing his own chances for election were slight, he told his private secretary, "Mr. Lincoln is the next President. We must try to save the Union. I will go South."

In accordance with tradition, Lincoln did not campaign for himself, but many other Republicans spoke for him. The Republicans did not campaign in the South; Breckinridge did not campaign in the North. Each side was, therefore, free to believe the worst about the other. All parties, North and South, campaigned with oratory, parades and rallies, free food and drink. Even in the face of looming crisis, this presidential campaign was the best entertainment of the day.

The mood in the Deep South was close to mass hysteria. Rumors of slave revolts—in Texas, Alabama, and South Carolina—swept the region, and vigilance committees sprang up to counter the supposed threat. In the South Carolina up-country, the question of secession dominated races for the state legislature. Candidates who advocated "patriotic forbearance" if Lincoln won were soundly defeated. The very passion and excitement of the election campaign moved Southerners toward extremism. Even the weather—the worst drought and heat wave the South had known for years—contributed to the tension.

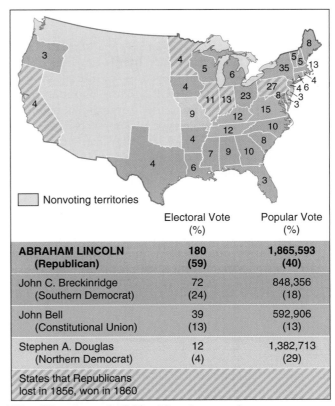

	Electoral Vote (%)	Popular Vote (%)
ABRAHAM LINCOLN (Republican)	**180 (59)**	**1,865,593 (40)**
John C. Breckinridge (Southern Democrat)	72 (24)	848,356 (18)
John Bell (Constitutional Union)	39 (13)	592,906 (13)
Stephen A. Douglas (Northern Democrat)	12 (4)	1,382,713 (29)

Nonvoting territories. States that Republicans lost in 1856, won in 1860

The Election of 1860   The election of 1860 was a sectional election. Lincoln won no votes in the South, Breckinridge none in the North. The contest in the North was between Lincoln and Douglas, and although Lincoln swept the electoral vote, Douglas's popular vote was uncomfortably close. The large number of northern Democratic voters opposed to Lincoln was a source of political trouble for him during the Civil War.

The election of 1860 produced the second highest voter turnout in U.S. history (81.2 percent, topped only by 81.8 percent in 1876). The election turned out to be two regional contests: Breckinridge versus Bell in the South, Lincoln versus Douglas in the North. Breckinridge carried eleven slave states with 18 percent of the popular vote; Bell carried Virginia, Tennessee, and Kentucky with 13 percent of the popular vote. Lincoln won all eighteen of the free states (he split New Jersey with Douglas) and almost 40 percent of the popular vote. Douglas carried only Missouri, but gained nearly 30 percent of the popular vote. Lincoln's electoral vote total was overwhelming: 180 to a combined 123 for the other three candidates. But although Lincoln had won 54 percent of the vote in the northern states, his name had not even appeared on the ballot in ten southern states. The true winner of the 1860 election was sectionalism.

The South Leaves the Union

The results of the election shocked Southerners. They were humiliated and frightened by the prospect of becoming a permanent minority in a political system dominated by a party pledged to the elimination of slavery. In southern eyes the Republican triumph meant they would become unequal partners in the federal enterprise, their way of life (the slave system) existing on borrowed time.

The governors of South Carolina, Alabama, and Mississippi, each of whom had committed his state to secession if Lincoln were elected, immediately issued calls for special state conventions. At the same time, calls went out to southern communities to form vigilance committees and volunteer militia companies. Cooperationists (the term used for those opposed to immediate secession) were either intimi-

dated into silence or simply left behind by the speed of events.

On December 20, 1860, a state convention in South Carolina, accompanied by all the hoopla and excitement of bands, fireworks displays, and huge rallies, voted unanimously to secede from the Union. In the weeks that followed, conventions in six other southern states (Mississippi, Florida, Alabama, Georgia, Louisiana, and Texas) followed suit, with the support, on average, of 80 percent of their delegates. Although there was genuine division of opinion in the South, especially in Georgia and Alabama, along customary up-country–low-country lines, none of the Deep South states held anywhere near the number of Unionists that Republicans had hoped. Throughout the South, secession occurred because Southerners no longer believed they had a choice.

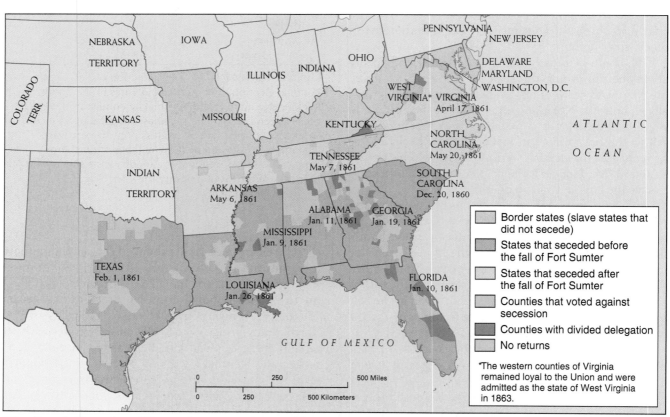

The South Secedes The southern states that would constitute the Confederacy seceded in two stages. The states of the Lower South seceded before Lincoln took office. Arkansas and three states of the Upper South—Virginia, North Carolina, and Tennessee—waited until after the South fired on Fort Sumter. And four border slave states—Delaware, Maryland, Kentucky and Missouri—chose not to secede. Every southern state (except South Carolina) was divided on the issue of secession, generally along up-country–low-country lines. In Virginia, this division was so extreme that West Virginia split off to become a separate nonslave state and was admitted to the Union in 1863.

OVERVIEW

THE IRREPRESSIBLE CONFLICT

Declaration of Independence	1776	Thomas Jefferson's denunciation of slavery deleted from the final version.
Northwest Ordinance	1787	Slavery prohibited in the Northwest Territory (north of the Ohio River).
Constitution	1787	Slavery unmentioned but acknowledged in Article I, Section 2, counting three-fifths of all African Americans, slave and free, in a state's population; and in Article I, Section 9, which barred Congress from prohibiting the international slave trade for twenty years.
Louisiana Purchase	1803	Louisiana admitted as a slave state in 1812; no decision about the rest of Louisiana Purchase.
Missouri Compromise	1820	Missouri admitted as a slave state, but slavery prohibited in Louisiana Purchase north of 36°30'.
Wilmot Proviso	1846	Proposal to prohibit slavery in territory that might be gained in Mexican-American War causes splits in national parties.
Compromise of 1850	1850	California admitted as free state; Texas (already admitted in 1845) is a slave state; the rest of Mexican Cession to be decided by popular sovereignty. Ends the slave trade in the District of Columbia, but a stronger Fugitive Slave Law, leading to a number of violent recaptures, arouses northern antislavery opinion.
Kansas-Nebraska Act	1854	At the urging of Stephen A. Douglas, Congress opens Kansas and Nebraska Territories for settlement under popular sovereignty. Open warfare between proslavery and antislavery factions breaks out in Kansas.
Lecompton Constitution	1857	President James Buchanan's decision to admit Kansas to the Union with a proslavery constitution is defeated in Congress.
***Dred Scott* Decision**	1857	The Supreme Court's denial of Dred Scott's case for freedom is welcomed in the South, condemned in the North.
John Brown's Raid and Execution	1859	Northern support for John Brown shocks the South.
Democratic Party Nominating Conventions	1860	The Democrats are unable to agree on a candidate; two candidates, one northern (Stephen A. Douglas) and one southern (John C. Breckinridge) split the party and the vote, thus allowing Republican Abraham Lincoln to win.

In every state that seceded, the joyous scenes of South Carolina were repeated as the decisiveness of action replaced the long years of anxiety and tension. People danced in the streets, most believing the North had no choice but to accept secession peacefully. They ignored the fact that eight other slave states—Delaware,

Maryland, Kentucky, Missouri, Virginia, North Carolina, Tennessee, and Arkansas—had not acted—though the latter four states would secede after war broke out. Just as Republicans had miscalculated in thinking southern threats a mere bluff, so secessionists now miscalculated in believing they would be able to leave the Union in peace.

The North's Political Options

What should the North do? Buchanan, indecisive as always, did nothing. The decision, thus, rested with Abraham Lincoln, even before he officially became president. One possibility was compromise, and many proposals were suggested, ranging from full adoption of the Breckinridge campaign platform to reinstatement of the Missouri Compromise line. Lincoln cautiously refused them all, making it clear that he would not compromise on the extension of slavery, which was the South's key demand. He hoped, by appearing firm but moderate, to discourage additional southern states from seceding while giving pro-Union Southerners time to organize. He succeeded in his first aim but not in the second. Lincoln and most of the Republican Party had seriously overestimated the strength of pro-Union sentiment in the South.

A second possibility, suggested by Horace Greeley of the *New York Tribune*, was to let the seven seceding states "go in peace." This is what many secessionists expected, but too many Northerners—including Lincoln himself—believed in the Union for this to happen. As Lincoln said, what was at stake was "the necessity of proving that popular government is not an absurdity. We must settle this question now, whether in a free government the minority have the right to break up the government whenever they choose." The third possibility was force, and this was the crux of the dilemma. Although he believed their action was wrong, Lincoln was loath to go to war to force the seceding states back into the Union. On the other hand, he refused to give up federal powers over military forts and customs posts in the South. These were precisely the powers the seceding states had to command if they were to function as an independent nation. A confrontation was bound to come.

Establishment of the Confederacy

In February, delegates from the seven seceding states met in Montgomery, Alabama, and created the Confederate States of America. They wrote a constitution that was identical to the Constitution of the United States, with a few crucial exceptions: it strongly supported states' rights and made the abolition of slavery practically impossible. These two clauses did much to define the Confederate enterprise.

The Montgomery convention passed over the fire-eaters—the men who had been the first to urge secession—and chose Jefferson Davis of Mississippi as president and Alexander Stephens of Georgia as vice president of the new nation. Both men were known as moderates. The choice of moderates was deliberate, for the strategy of the new Confederate state was to argue that secession was a normal, responsible, and expectable course of action, and nothing for the North to get upset about. This was the theme that President Jefferson Davis of the Confederate States of America struck in his Inaugural Address, delivered to a crowd of 10,000 from the steps of the State Capitol at Montgomery, Alabama, on February 18, 1861. "We have changed the constituent parts," Davis said, "but not the system of our Government." Secession was a legal and peaceful step that, Davis said, quoting from the Declaration of Independence, "illustrates the American idea that governments rest on the consent of the governed . . . and that it is the right of the people to alter or abolish them at will whenever they become destructive of the ends for which they were established."

Lincoln's Inauguration

The country as a whole waited to see what Abraham Lincoln would do, which at first appeared to be very little. In Springfield, Lincoln refused to issue public statements before his inaugural (although he sent many private messages to Congress and to key military officers), for fear of making a delicate situation worse. Similarly, during a twelve-day whistle-stopping railroad trip east from Springfield, he was careful to say nothing controversial. Eastern intellectuals, already suspicious of a mere "prairie lawyer," were not impressed. Finally, hard evidence of an assassination plot forced Lincoln to abandon his whistle-stops at Harrisburg and, protected by Pinkerton detectives, he traveled incognito into Washington, "like a thief in the night," as he complained. These signs of moderation and caution did not appeal to an American public with a penchant for electing military heroes. Americans wanted leadership and action.

Lincoln continued, however, to offer nonbelligerent firmness and moderation. And at the end of his Inaugural Address on March 4, 1861, as he stood ringed by federal troops called out in case of a Confederate attack, the new president offered unexpected eloquence:

> I am loath to close. We are not enemies, but friends. We must not be enemies. Though passion may have strained, it must not break our bonds of affection. The mystic chords of memory, stretching from every battlefield, and patriot grave, to every living heart and hearthstone, all over this broad land, will yet swell the chorus of the Union, when again touched, as surely they will be, by the better angels of our nature.

CHRONOLOGY

1820	Missouri Compromise
1828–32	Nullification Crisis
1846	Wilmot Proviso
1848	Treaty of Guadalupe Hidalgo ends Mexican-American War Zachary Taylor elected president Free-Soil Party formed
1849	California and Utah seek admission to the Union as free states
1850	Compromise of 1850 California admitted as a free state American (Know-Nothing) Party formed Zachary Taylor dies, Millard Fillmore becomes president
1851	North reacts to Fugitive Slave Law Harriet Beecher Stowe's *Uncle Tom's Cabin* published
1852	Franklin Pierce elected president
1854	Ostend Manifesto Kansas-Nebraska Act Treaties with Indians in northern part of Indian Territory renegotiated Republican Party formed as Whig Party dissolves
1856	Burning and looting of Lawrence, Kansas John Brown leads Pottawatomie massacre Attack on Senator Charles Sumner James Buchanan elected president
1857	*Dred Scott* decision President Buchanan accepts proslavery Lecompton constitution in Kansas Panic of 1857
1858	Congress rejects Lecompton constitution Lincoln-Douglas debates
1859	John Brown's raid on Harpers Ferry
1860	Four parties run presidential candidates Abraham Lincoln elected president South Carolina secedes from Union
1861	Six other Deep South states secede Confederate States of America formed Lincoln takes office

CONCLUSION

Americans had much to boast about in 1850. Their nation was vastly larger, richer, and more powerful than it had been in 1800. But the issue of slavery was slowly dividing the North and the South, two communities with similar origins and many common bonds. The following decade was marked by frantic efforts at political compromise, but politics had failed: the issue of slavery was irreconcilable. The only remaining recourse was war. But although Americans were divided, they were still one people. That made the war, when it came, all the more terrible.

REVIEW QUESTIONS

1. What aspects of the remarkable economic development of the United States in the first half of the nineteenth century contributed to the sectional crisis of the 1850s?

2. How might the violent efforts by abolitionists to free escaped slaves who had been recaptured and the federal armed enforcement of the Fugitive Slave Act have been viewed differently by Northern merchants (the so-called Cotton Whigs), Irish immigrants, and abolitionists?

3. Consider the course of events in "Bloody Kansas" from Douglas's Kansas-Nebraska Act to the congressional rejection of the Lecompton constitution. Were these events the inevitable result of the political im-

passe in Washington, or could other decisions have been taken that would have changed the outcome?

4. The nativism of the 1850s that surfaced so strongly in the Know-Nothing Party was eclipsed by the crisis over slavery. But nativist sentiment has been a recurring theme in American politics. Discuss why it was strong in the 1850s and why it has emerged periodically since then.

5. Evaluate the character and actions of John Brown. Was he the hero proclaimed by northern supporters or the terrorist condemned by the South?

6. Imagine that you lived in Illinois, home state to both Douglas and Lincoln, in 1860. How would you have voted in the presidential election, and why?

RECOMMENDED READING

William L. Barney, *The Secessionist Impulse: Alabama and Mississippi in 1860* (1974). Covers the election of 1860 and the subsequent conventions that led to secession.

Don E. Fehrenbacher, *The Dred Scott Case: Its Significance in American Law and Politics* (1978). A major study by the leading historian on this controversial decision.

Eric Foner, *Free Soil, Free Labor, Free Men: The Ideology of the Republican Party before the Civil War* (1970). A landmark effort that was among the first studies to focus on the free labor ideology of the North and its importance in the political disputes of the 1850s.

Lacey K. Ford Jr., *Origins of Southern Radicalism: The South Carolina Upcountry, 1800–1860* (1988). One of a number of recent studies of the attitudes of up-country farmers in South Carolina who supported secession wholeheartedly.

Homan Hamilton, *Prologue to Conflict: The Crisis and Compromise of 1850* (1964). The standard source on the Compromise of 1850.

Bruce Levine, *Half Slave and Half Free: The Roots of the Civil War* (1992). Good survey of the contrasting attitudes of North and South.

Alice Nichols, *Bleeding Kansas* (1954). The standard source on the battles over Kansas.

David M. Potter, *The Impending Crisis, 1848–1861* (1976). A comprehensive account of the politics leading up to the Civil War.

Anne C. Rose, *Voices of the Marketplace: American Thought and Culture, 1830–1860* (1995). A new study that considers the effects of the concepts of Christianity, democracy, and capitalism on American cultural life.

Kenneth M. Stampp, *America in 1857: A Nation on the Brink* (1990). A study of the "crucial" year by a leading southern historian.

Albert J. Von Frank, *The Trials of Anthony Burns: Freedom and Slavery in Emerson's Boston* (1998). An eloquent study of the trial and the links between transcendentalist and abolitionist opinion.

Edward L. Widmer, *Young America: The Flowering of Democracy in New York City* (1999). Recovers the idealism of the early years of this literary/political movement and traces its decline.

ON THE WEB

http://jefferson.village.virginia.edu/vshadow2/

The University of Virginia has undertaken a project, called *Valley of the Shadow*, to portray two communities, one northern and the other southern, from the years immediately before until immediately after the Civil War. The Valley of the Shadow Project presents primary documents from private and public sources for Augusta County, Virginia, and Franklin County, Pennsylvania. The resources here are extensive and growing and include newspapers, letters, diaries, photographs, maps, church records, population census, agricultural census, and military records. For this chapter focus on the records for the pre-Civil War era.

http://www.toptags.com/aama/docs/geocodes.htm

This interesting site contains the slave codes of the State of Georgia for the year 1848. Notice the frequency with which capital punishment is the penalty for a transgression by a slave.

http://www.fordham.edu/halsall/mod/1850fugitive.html

This site contains the complete text of the Fugitive Slave Act of September 18, 1850.

http://www.ets.uidaho.edu/eng321/utc_images/

Images taken from one of the many published versions of Harriet Beecher Stowe's *Uncle Tom's Cabin* are posted on this website.

http://www.prenhall.com/faragherbrief/map15.1

Think about the differences in population density in the United States at this time. What were the reasons behind these growth patterns?

http://www.prenhall.com/faragherbrief/map15.2

Explore the reasons behind secession. Why were some states quicker to secede than others?

SIXTEEN

THE CIVIL WAR

▷ 1 8 6 1 – 1 8 6 5

CHAPTER OUTLINE

AMERICAN COMMUNITIES

Mother Bickerdyke Connects Northern Communities to Their Boys at War

IN MAY 1861 THE REVEREND EDWARD BEECHER INTERRUPTED HIS CUStomary Sunday service at Brick Congregational Church in Galesburg, Illinois, to read a disturbing letter to the congregation. Two months earlier, Galesburg had proudly sent 500 of its young men off to join the Union army. They had not yet been in battle. Yet, the letter reported, an alarming number were dying of diseases caused by inadequate food, medical care, and sanitation at the crowded military camp in Cairo, Illinois. Most army doctors were surgeons, trained to operate and amputate on the battlefield. They were not prepared to treat soldiers sick with dysentery, pneumonia, typhoid, measles—all serious, frequently fatal diseases that could often be cured with careful nursing. The letter writer, appalled by the squalor and misery he saw around him, complained of abuses by the army. The Union army, however, was overwhelmed with the task of readying recruits for battle and had made few provisions for their health when they were not in combat.

The shocked and grieving members of Beecher's congregation quickly decided to send not only supplies but one of their number to inspect the conditions at the Cairo camp and to take action. In spite of warnings from a veteran of the War of 1812 that army regulations excluded women from encampments, the congregation voted to send their most qualified member, Mary Ann Bickerdyke, a middle-aged widow who made her living as a "botanic physician." This simple gesture of community concern launched the remarkable Civil War career of "the Cyclone in Calico," who defied medical officers and generals alike in her unceasing efforts on behalf of ill, wounded, and convalescent Union soldiers.

"Mother" Bickerdyke, as she was called, let nothing stand in the way of helping her "boys." When she arrived in Cairo, she immediately set to work cleaning the hospital tents and the soldiers themselves, and finding and cooking nourishing food for them. Ordered to leave by the hospital director, who resented her interference, she blandly continued her work. When he reported her to the commanding officer, General Benjamin Prentiss, she quickly convinced the general to let her stay. "I talked sense to him," she later said.

From a peacetime point of view, what Mother Bickerdyke was doing was not unusual. Every civilian hospital had a matron who made sure patients were supplied with clean bed linen and bandages and were fed the proper convalescent diet. But in the context of the war—the sheer number of soldiers, the constant need to set up new field hospitals and commandeer scarce food for an army on the move—it was unusual indeed and required an unusual person. A plain spoken, hardworking woman, totally unfazed by rank or tender masculine egos, Mother Bickerdyke single-mindedly devoted herself to what she called "the Lord's work." The ordinary soldiers loved her; wise generals supported her. Once, when an indignant officer's wife complained about Bickerdyke's rudeness, General William Tecumseh Sherman joked, "You've picked the one person around here who outranks me. If you want to lodge a complaint against her, you'll have to take it to President Lincoln."

By their actions, Mother Bickerdyke and others like her exposed the War Department's inability to meet the needs of the nation's first mass army. And like the Galesburg congregation, other communities all over the North rallied to make up for the department's shortcomings with supplies and assistance. The efforts of women on the local level—for example, to make clothing for men from their communities who had gone off to the war—quickly took on national dimensions. The Women's Central Association of Relief (WCAR), whose organizers were mostly reformers experienced in the abolitionist, temperance, and education movements, eventually had 7,000 chapters throughout the North. Its volunteers raised funds, made and collected a variety of items—food, clothes, medicine, bandages, and more than 250,000 quilts and comforters—and sent them to army camps and hospitals. Volunteers also provided meals, housing, and transportation to soldiers on furlough. All told, association chapters supplied an estimated $15 million worth of goods to the Union troops.

In June 1861, responding to requests by officials of the WCAR for formal recognition of the organization, President Abraham Lincoln created the United States Sanitary Commission and gave it the power to investigate and advise the Medical Bureau. Henry Bellows, a Unitarian clergyman, became president of the organization, and Frederick Law Olmsted, the author of influential books about the slaveholding South and later the designer of New York's Central Park, was named its executive secre-

tary. The commission's more than 500 "sanitary inspectors" (usually men) instructed soldiers in such matters as water supply, placement of latrines, and safe cooking.

Although at first she worked independently and remained suspicious of all organizations (and even of many other relief workers), in 1862 Mother Bickerdyke was persuaded to become an official agent of "the Sanitary," as it was known. The advantage to her was access to the commission's warehouses and the ability to order from them precisely what she needed. The advantage to the Sanitary was that Mother Bickerdyke was an unequaled fundraiser. In speaking tours throughout Illinois, she touched her female listeners with moving stories of wounded boys whom she had cared for as if they were her own sons. Her words to men were more forceful. It was a man's business to fight, she said. If he was too old or ill to fight with a gun, he should fight with his dollars. With the help of Bickerdyke's blunt appeals, the Sanitary raised $50 million for the Union war effort.

As the Civil War continued, Mother Bickerdyke became a key figure in the medical support for General Ulysses S. Grant's campaigns along the Mississippi River. She was with the army at Shiloh, and as Grant slowly fought his way to Vicksburg, she set up convalescent hospitals in Memphis. Grant authorized her to commandeer any army wagons she needed to transport supplies. Between fifty and seventy "contrabands" (escaped former slaves) worked on her laundry crew. On the civilian side, the Sanitary Commission authorized her to draw on its supply depots in Memphis, Cairo, Chicago, and elsewhere. She was, thus, in a practical sense a vital "middlewoman" between the home front and the battlefield—and in a symbolic and emotional sense too, as a stand-in for all mothers who had sent their sons to war.

The Civil War was a community tragedy, ripping apart the nation's political fabric and producing more casualties than any other war in the nation's history. Yet in another sense, it was a community triumph. Local communities directly supported and sustained their soldiers on a massive scale in unprecedented ways. As national unity failed, the strength of local communities, symbolized by Mother Bickerdyke, endured. ■

Memphis

KEY TOPICS

■ The social and political changes created by the unprecedented nature and scale of the Civil War

■ The major military campaigns of the war

■ The central importance of the end of slavery to the war efforts of North and South

---

COMMUNITIES MOBILIZE FOR WAR

A neutral observer in March 1861 might have seen ominous similarities. Two nations—the United States of America (shorn of seven states in the Deep South) and the Confederate States of America—each blamed the other for the breakup of the Union. Two new presidents—Abraham Lincoln and Jefferson Davis—each faced the challenging task of building and maintaining national unity. Two regions—North and South—scorned each other and boasted of their own superiority. But the most basic similarity was not yet apparent: both sides were unprepared for the ordeal that lay ahead.

Fort Sumter: The War Begins

In their Inaugural Addresses, both Abraham Lincoln and Jefferson Davis prayed for peace but positioned themselves for war. Careful listeners to both addresses realized that the two men were on a collision course.

Fort Sumter, a major federal military installation, sat on a granite island at the entrance to Charleston harbor.

So long as it remained in Union hands, Charleston, the center of secessionist sentiment, would be immobilized. Thus, it was hardly surprising that Fort Sumter would provide President Lincoln with his first crisis.

On April 6, Lincoln notified the governor of South Carolina that he was sending a relief force to the fort carrying only food and no military supplies. On April 10 Davis ordered General P.G.T. Beauregard to demand the surrender of Fort Sumter and to attack it if the garrison did not comply. On April 12, as Lincoln's relief force neared Charleston harbor, Beauregard opened fire. Two days later, the defenders surrendered and the Confederate Stars and Bars rose over Fort Sumter.

The Call to Arms

Even before the attack on Fort Sumter, the Confederate Congress had authorized a volunteer army of 100,000 men to serve for twelve months. There was no difficulty finding volunteers. Men flocked to enlist, and their communities sent them off in ceremonies featuring bands, bonfires, and belligerent oratory. For these early recruits, war was a patriotic adventure.

This Currier and Ives lithograph shows the opening moment of the Civil War. On April 12, 1861, Confederate General P. G. T. Beauregard ordered the shelling of Fort Sumter in Charleston harbor. Two days later, Union Major Robert Anderson surrendered and mobilization began for what turned out to be the most devastating war in American history.

SOURCE: The Granger Collection, New York .

The "thunderclap of Sumter" startled the North into an angry response. The apathy and uncertainty that had prevailed since Lincoln's election disappeared, to be replaced by strong feelings of patriotism. On April 15, Lincoln issued a proclamation calling for 75,000 state militiamen to serve in the federal army for ninety days. Enlistment offices were swamped with so many enthusiastic volunteers that many men were sent home. Free African Americans, among the most eager to serve, were turned away.

The mobilization in Chester, Pennsylvania, was typical of the northern response to the outbreak of war. A patriotic rally was held at which a company of volunteers (the first of many from the region) calling themselves the "Union Blues" were mustered into the Ninth Regiment of Pennsylvania Volunteers amid cheers and band music. As they marched off to Washington (the gathering place for the Union army), companies of home guards were organized by the men who remained behind. Within a month, the women of Chester had organized a county-wide system of war relief that sent a stream of clothing, blankets, bandages, and other supplies to the local troops and provided assistance to their families at home. Such relief organizations, some formally organized, some informal, emerged in every community, North and South, that sent soldiers off to the Civil War. These organizations not only played a vital role in supplying the troops but maintained the human, local link on which so many soldiers depended. In this sense, every American community accompanied its young men to war.

The Border States

The first secession, between December 20, 1860, and February 1, 1861, had taken seven Deep South states out of the Union. Now, in April, the firing on Fort Sumter and Lincoln's call for state militias forced the other southern states to take sides. Courted—and pressured—by both North and South, four states of the Upper South (Virginia, Arkansas, Tennessee, and North Carolina) joined the original seven in April and May 1861. Virginia's secession tipped the other three toward the Confederacy. The capital of the Confederacy was now moved to Richmond. This meant that the two capitals—Richmond and Washington—were less than 100 miles apart.

Still undecided was the loyalty of the northernmost tier of slave-owning states: Missouri, Kentucky, Maryland, and Delaware. Each controlled vital strategic assets. Missouri not only bordered the Mississippi River but controlled the routes to the west. Kentucky controlled the Ohio River. The main railroad link with the West ran through Maryland and the hill region of western Virginia (which split from Virginia to become the free state of West Virginia in 1863). Delaware controlled access to Philadelphia. Finally, were Maryland to secede, the nation's capital would be completely surrounded by Confederate territory.

Delaware was loyal to the Union (less than 2 percent of its population were slaves), but Maryland's loyalty was divided. Lincoln took swift and stern measures to secure Maryland's loyalty. He stationed Union troops along Maryland's crucial railroads, declared martial law in Baltimore, and arrested the suspected ringleaders of the pro-Confederate mob and held them without trial. In July, he ordered the detention of thirty-two secessionist legislators and many sympathizers. Thus was Maryland's loyalty to the Union ensured.

This was the first of a number of violations of basic civil rights during the war, all of which the president justified on the basis of national security.

An even bloodier division occurred in Missouri, where old foes from "Bleeding Kansas" faced off. The proslavery governor and most of the legislature fled to Arkansas, where they declared a Confederate state government in exile. Unionists remained in St. Louis and declared a provisional government that lasted until 1865. Although Missouri had been saved for the Union, the federal military was unable to stop the guerrilla warfare that raged there.

Finally, Lincoln kept Kentucky in the Union by accepting its declaration of neutrality at face value and looking the other way as it became the center of a huge illegal trade with the Confederacy through neighboring Tennessee. By the summer of 1861, Unionists controlled most of the state.

That Delaware, Maryland, Missouri, and Kentucky chose to stay in the Union was a severe blow to the Confederacy. Among them, the four states could have added 45 percent to the white population and military manpower of the Confederacy and 80 percent to its manufacturing capacity. Almost as damaging, the decision of four slave states to stay in the Union punched a huge hole in the Confederate argument that the southern states were forced to secede to protect the right to own slaves.

The Battle of Bull Run

Once sides had been chosen and the initial flush of enthusiasm had passed, the nature of the war, and the mistaken notions about it, soon became clear. The event that shattered the illusions was the First Battle of Bull Run, at Manassas Creek in Virginia in July 1861. Confident of a quick victory, a Union army of 35,000 men marched south, crying "On to Richmond!" So lighthearted and unprepared was the Washington community that the troops were accompanied not only by journalists but by a crowd of politicians and sightseers. At first the Union troops held their ground against the 25,000 Confederate troops commanded by General P. G. T. Beauregard (of Fort Sumter fame). But when 2,300 fresh Confederate troops arrived as reinforcements, the untrained northern troops broke ranks in an uncontrolled retreat that swept up the frightened sightseers as well. Soldiers and civilians alike retreated in disarray to Washington.

Bull Run was sobering—and prophetic. The Civil War was the most lethal military conflict in American history, leaving a legacy of devastation on the battlefield and desolation at home. It claimed the lives of nearly 620,000 soldiers, more than the the First and Second World Wars combined. One out of every four soldiers who fought in the war never returned home.

The Relative Strengths of North and South

Over all, in terms of both population and productive capacity, the Union seemed to have a commanding edge over the Confederacy. The North had two and a half times the South's population (22 million to 9 million, of whom 3.5 million were slaves) and enjoyed an even greater advantage in industrial capacity (nine times that of the South). The North produced almost all of the nation's firearms (97 percent), had 71 percent of its railroad mileage, and produced 94 percent of its cloth and 90 percent of its footwear. The North seemed able to feed, clothe, arm, and transport all the soldiers it chose. These advantages were ultimately to prove decisive. But in the short term the South had important assets to counter the advantage of the North.

The first was the nature of the struggle. The most basic principle of the defense of home and community united almost all white southerners, regardless of their views about slavery. The North would have to invade the South and then control it against guerrilla opposition in order to win.

Second, the military disparity was less extreme than it appeared. Although the North had manpower, its troops were mostly untrained. Moreover, the South, because of its tradition of honor and belligerence (see Chapter 11), appeared to have an advantage in military leaders, the most notable of whom was Robert E. Lee.

Finally, it was widely believed that slavery would work to the South's advantage, for slaves could continue to do the vital plantation work while their masters went off to war. Because of the crucial role of southern cotton in industrialization. Southerners were confident that the British and French need for southern cotton would soon bring those countries to recognize the Confederacy as a separate nation.

GOVERNMENTS ORGANIZE FOR WAR

The Civil War forced the federal government to assume powers unimaginable just a few years before. Abraham Lincoln took as his primary task to lead and unify the nation in his responsibility as commander in chief. He found the challenge almost insurmountable. Jefferson Davis's challenge was even greater. He had to create a Confederate nation out of a loose grouping of eleven states, each believing strongly in states' rights. Yet in the Confederacy, as in the Union, the conduct of the war required central direction.

Lincoln as War President

Lincoln's first task as president was to assert control over his own cabinet. Because he had few national contacts outside the Republican Party, Lincoln chose to staff his cabinet with other Republicans, including two who had been his rivals for the presidential nomination: Treasury Secretary Salmon P. Chase, a staunch abolitionist, and Secretary of State William Seward. That the Republican Party was a not-quite-jelled mix of former Whigs, abolitionists, moderate Free-Soilers, and even some prowar Democrats made Lincoln's task as party leader much more difficult than it might otherwise have been.

After the fall of Fort Sumter, military necessity prompted Lincoln to call up the state militias, order a naval blockade of the South, and vastly expand the military budget.

Although James K. Polk had assumed responsibility for overall American military strategy during the Mexican-American War (see Chapter 14), Lincoln was the first president to act as commander-in-chief in both a practical and a symbolic way. His involvement in military strategy sprang from his realization that a civil war presented problems different from those of a foreign war of conquest. Lincoln wanted above all to persuade the South to rejoin the Union, and his every military move was dictated by the hope of eventual reconciliation—hence, his cautiousness, and his acute sense of the role of public opinion.

Expanding the Power of the Federal Government

The greatest expansion in government power during the war was in the War Department, which by early 1862 was faced with the unprecedented challenge of feeding, clothing, and arming 700,000 Union soldiers. Initially the government relied on the individual states to equip and supply their vastly expanded militias. States often contracted directly with textile mills and shoe factories to clothe their troops. In many northern cities, volunteer groups sprang up to recruit regiments, buy them weapons, and send them to Washington. Other such community groups, like the one in Chester, Pennsylvania, focused on clothing and providing medical care to soldiers. By January 1862 the War Department, under the able direction of Edwin M. Stanton, a former Democrat from Ohio, was able to perform many basic functions of procurement and supply without too much delay or corruption. But the size of the Union army and the complexity of fully supplying it demanded constant efforts at all levels—government, state, and community—throughout the war. Thus, in the matter of procurement and supply, as in mobilization, the battlefront was related to the home front on a scale that Americans had not previously experienced.

The need for money for the vast war effort was pressing. Treasury Secretary Chase worked closely with Congress to develop ways to finance the war. They naturally turned to the nation's economic experts—private bankers, merchants, and managers of large businesses. With the help of Philadelphia financier Jay Cooke, the Treasury used patriotic appeals to sell war bonds to ordinary people in amounts as small as $50. This was the first example in American history of the mass financing of war. Additional sources of revenue were sales taxes and the first federal income tax, (which affected only the affluent).

Most radical of all was Chase's decision—which was authorized only after a bitter congressional fight—to print and distribute Treasury notes (paper money). Until then, the money in circulation had been a mixture of coins and state bank notes issued by 1,500 different state banks. The Legal Tender Act of February 1862 created a national currency. Because of its color, the paper bank notes were popularly known as "greenbacks." In 1863, Congress passed the National Bank Act, which prohibited state banks from issuing their own notes and forced them to apply for federal charters.

The national currency was widely recognized as a major step toward centralization of economic power in the hands of the federal government. Such a measure would have been unthinkable if southern Democrats had still been part of the national government. The absence of southern Democrats also made possible passage of a number of Republican economic measures not directly related to the war.

Although the outbreak of war overshadowed everything else, the Republican Party in Congress was determined to fulfill its campaign pledge of a comprehensive program of economic development. Republicans quickly passed the Morrill Tariff Act (1861); by 1864, this and subsequent measures had raised tariffs to more than double their prewar rate. In 1862 and 1864, Congress created two federally chartered corporations to build a transcontinental railroad—the Union Pacific Railroad Company, to lay track westward from Omaha, and the Central Pacific, to lay track eastward from California. Two other measures, both passed in 1862, had long been sought by Westerners. The Homestead Act gave 160 acres of public land to any citizen who agreed to live on the land for five years, improve it by building a house and cultivating some of the land, and pay a small fee. The Morrill Land Grant Act gave states public land that would allow them to finance land-grant colleges offering education to ordinary citizens in practical skills such as agriculture, engineering, and military science. Coupled with this act, the establishment of a federal Department of Agriculture in 1862 gave American farmers a big push toward modern commercial agriculture.

These were powerful nationalizing forces. They connected ordinary people to the federal government in new ways. Although many of the executive war powers lapsed when the battles ended, the accumulation of strength by the federal government was never reversed.

Diplomatic Objectives

To Secretary of State William Seward fell the job of making sure that Britain and France did not extend diplomatic recognition to the Confederacy. Although southerners had been certain that the need for cotton would gain them European support, they were wrong. British public opinion would not countenance the recognition of a new nation based on slavery. British cotton manufacturers found economic alternatives, first using up their backlog of southern cotton and then turning to Egypt and India for new supplies.

In 1861, a bankrupt Mexico suffered the ignominy of a joint invasion by British, Spanish, and French troops determined to collect the substantial debts owed by Mexico to their nations. This was a serious violation of Mexican independence, just the kind of European intervention that the Monroe Doctrine had been formulated to prevent (see Chapter 9). When it became clear that France was bent on conquest, Britian and Spain withdrew, and Mexican forces repelled the French troops on May 5, 1862. Ever since, Mexico has celebrated *El Cinco de Mayo*. France eventually prevailed and installed the Austrian archduke Maximilian as emperor. In normal times, the French conquest could have led to war with the United States, but fearing that France might recognize the Confederacy or invade Texas, Seward had to content himself with refusing to recognize the new Mexican government.

Jefferson Davis as Confederate President

Although Jefferson Davis had held national cabinet rank (as secretary of war under President Franklin Pierce), had experience as an administrator, and was a former military man (none of which was true of Abraham Lincoln), he was unable to hold the Confederacy together. Perhaps no one could have.

Davis's first cabinet of six men, appointed in February 1861, included a representative from each of the states of the first secession except Mississippi, which was represented by Davis himself. This careful attention to the equality of the states pointed to the fundamental problem that Davis was unable to overcome. Although he saw the need for unity, he was unable to impose it. Soon his autonomous style of leadership—he wanted to decide every detail himself—angered his generals, alienated cabinet members, and gave southern governors reason to resist his orders. After the first flush of patriotism had passed, the Confederacy never lived up to its hope of becoming a unified nation.

Confederate Disappointments in Diplomacy and the Economy

The failure of "cotton diplomacy" was a crushing blow. White Southerners were stunned that Britain and France would not recognize their claim to independence. Well into 1863, the South hoped that a decisive battlefield victory would change the minds of cautious Europeans. In the meantime, plantations continued to grow cotton, but the Confederacy withheld it from market, hoping that lack of raw material for their textile mills would lead the British and French to recognize the Confederacy. The British reacted indignantly, claiming that the withholding of cotton was economic blackmail, and found new sources of cotton. In 1862, when the Confederacy ended the embargo and began to ship its great surplus, the world price of cotton plunged. Then too, the Union naval blockade, weak at first, began to take effect. Cotton turned out to be not so powerful a diplomatic weapon after all.

Perhaps the greatest southern failure was in the area of finances. At first the Confederate government tried to raise money from the states, but governors refused to impose new taxes. By the time uniform taxes were levied in 1863, it was too late. Heavy borrowing and the printing of great sums of paper money produced runaway inflation (a ruinous rate of 9,000 percent per annum by 1865, compared with 80 percent in the North). Inflation, in turn, caused incalculable damage to morale and prospects for unity.

After the initial surge of volunteers, enlistment in the military fell off, as it did in the North also. In April 1862, the Confederate Congress passed the first draft law in American history, and the Union Congress followed suit in March 1863. The southern law declared that all able-bodied men between eighteen and thirty-five were eligible for three years of military service. Purchase of substitutes was allowed, as in the North, but in the South the price was uncontrolled, rising eventually to $10,000 in Confederate money. The most disliked part of the draft law was a provision exempting one white man on each plantation with twenty or more slaves. This provision not only seemed to disprove the earlier claim that slavery freed white men to fight, but it aroused class

resentments. A bitter phrase of the time complained, "It's a rich man's war but a poor man's fight."

Contradictions of Southern Nationalism

In the early days of the war, Jefferson Davis successfully mobilized feelings of regional identity and patriotism. Many Southerners felt part of a beleaguered region that had been forced to resist northern tyranny. But most Southerners felt loyalty to their own state and local communities, not to a Confederate nation. The strong belief in states' rights and aristocratic privilege undermined the Confederate cause. Some Southern governors resisted potentially unifying actions such as moving militias outside their home states. Broader measures, such as general taxation, were widely evaded by rich and poor alike. The inequitable draft was only one of many things that convinced the ordinary people of the South that this was a war for privileged slave owners, not for them. With its leaders and citizens fearing (perhaps correctly) that centralization would destroy what was distinctively southern, the Confederacy was unable to mobilize the resources—financial, human, and otherwise—that might have prevented its destruction by northern armies.

THE FIGHTING THROUGH 1862

Just as political decisions were often driven by military necessity, the basic northern and southern military strategies were affected by political considerations as much as by military ones. The initial policy of limited war, thought to be the best route to ultimate reconciliation, ran into difficulties because of the public's impatience for victories. But victories, as the mounting slaughter made clear, were not easy to achieve.

The War in Northern Virginia

The initial northern strategy, dubbed by critics the Anaconda Plan (after the constrictor snake), envisaged slowly squeezing the South with a blockade at sea and on the Mississippi River. Lincoln accepted the basics of the plan, but public clamor for a fight pushed him to agree to the disastrous Battle of Bull Run and then to a major buildup of Union troops in northern Virginia under General George B. McClellan.

Dashing in appearance, McClellan was extremely cautious in battle. In March 1862, after almost a year spent drilling the raw Union recruits and after repeated exhortations by an impatient Lincoln, McClellan committed 120,000 troops to what became known as the

The contrast between the hope and valor of these young southern volunteer soldiers, photographed shortly before the first battle of Bull Run, and the later advertisements for substitutes is marked. Southern exemptions for slave owners and lavish payment for substitutes increasingly bred resentment among the ordinary people of the South.

SOURCE: (a) Cook Collection. Valentine Museum Library/Richmond History Center; (b) Library of Congress.

SUBSTITUTE NOTICES.

WANTED—A SUBSTITUTE for a conscript, to serve during the war. Any good man over the age of 35 years, not a resident of Virginia, or a foreigner, may hear of a good situation by calling at Mr. GEORGE BAGBY'S office, Shockoe Slip, to-day, between the hours of 9 and 11 A. M.   [jy 9—1t*]   A COUNTRYMAN.

WANTED—Two SUBSTITUTES—one for artillery, the other for infantry or cavalry service. Also, to sell, a trained, thoroughbred cavalry HORSE.   Apply to   DR. BROOCKS, Corner Main and 12th streets, or to
    T. T. BROOCKS,
jy 9—3t*   Petersburg, Va.

WANTED—Immediately, a SUBSTITUTE. A man over 35 years old, or under 18, can get a good price by making immediate application to Room No. 50, Monument Hotel, or by addressing "J. W.," through Richmond P. O.   jy 9—1t*

WANTED—A SUBSTITUTE, to go into the 24th North Carolina State troops, for which a liberal price will be paid. Apply to me at Dispatch office this evening at 4 o'clock P. M.
jy 9—1t*   R. R. MOORE.

WANTED—A SUBSTITUTE, to go in a first-rate Georgia company of infantry, under the heroic Jackson. A gentleman whose health is impaired, will give a fair price for a substitute. Apply immediately at ROOM, No. 13, Post-Office Department, third story, between the hours of 10 and 3 o'clock.   jy 9—6t*

WANTED—Two SUBSTITUTES for the war. A good bonus will be given. None need apply except those exempt from Conscript. Apply to-day at   GEORGE I. HERRING'S,
jy 9—1t*   Grocery store, No. 56 Main st.

Peninsular campaign. The objective was to capture Richmond, the Confederate capital. McClellan had his troops and their supplies ferried in 400 ships from Washington to Fortress Monroe, near the mouth of the James River, an effort that took three weeks. Inching up the James Peninsula, by June McClellan's troops were close enough to Richmond to hear the church bells ringing—but not close enough for victory. In a series of battles known as the Seven Days, Robert E. Lee boldly counterattacked, repeatedly catching McClellan off guard. In August, Lincoln, disappointed by McClellan's inaction, ordered him to abandon the campaign and return to the capital.

Jefferson Davis, like Abraham Lincoln, was an active commander-in-chief. After the Seven Days victories, Davis supported a Confederate attack on Maryland. But in the brutal battle of Antietam on September 17, 1862, which claimed more than 5,000 dead and 19,000 wounded, McClellan's army checked Lee's advance. Lee retreated to Virginia, inflicting terrible losses on northern troops at Fredericksburg when they again made a thrust toward Richmond in December 1862. The war in northern Virginia was stalemated: neither side was strong enough to win, but each was too strong to be defeated.

Shiloh and the War for the Mississippi

Although most public attention was focused on the fighting in Virginia, battles in Tennessee and along the Mississippi River proved to be the key to eventual Union victory. The rising military figure in the West was Ulysses S. Grant, who had once resigned from the service because of a drinking problem. In February 1862, Grant captured Fort Henry and Fort Donelson, on the Tennessee and Cumberland rivers, establishing Union control of much of Tennessee.

Moving south with 28,000 men, Grant met a 40,000-man Confederate force commanded by General Albert Sidney Johnston at Shiloh Church in April 1862. After two days of bitter and bloody fighting in the rain, the Confederates withdrew. The losses on both sides were enormous: the North lost 13,000 men, the South 11,000, including General Johnston, who bled to death. Grant kept moving, capturing Memphis in June and beginning a campaign to eventually capture Vicksburg, Mississippi, in November. Earlier that year, naval forces under Admiral David Farragut had captured New Orleans and then continued up the Mississippi River. By the end of 1862 it was clearly only a matter of time before the entire river would be in Union hands.

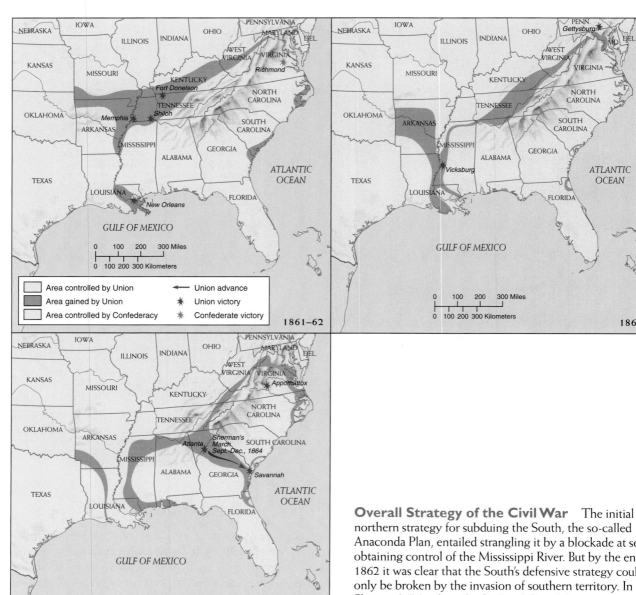

Area controlled by Union — Union advance
Area gained by Union ✳ Union victory
Area controlled by Confederacy ✳ Confederate victory
1861–62

1863

1864–65

Overall Strategy of the Civil War The initial
northern strategy for subduing the South, the so-called
Anaconda Plan, entailed strangling it by a blockade at sea and
obtaining control of the Mississippi River. But by the end of
1862 it was clear that the South's defensive strategy could
only be broken by the invasion of southern territory. In 1864,
Sherman's "March to the Sea" and Grant's hammering tactics
in northern Virginia brought the war home to the South.
Lee's surrender to Grant at Appomattox Courthouse on April
9, 1865, ended the bloodiest war in the nation's history.

The War in the Trans-Mississippi West

Although only one western state, Texas, seceded from
the Union, the Civil War was fought in small ways in
many parts of the West. Southern hopes for the extension of slavery into the Southwest were reignited by
the war, and the just-announced discovery of gold in
Colorado impelled the Confederacy to attempt to capture it. Texans mounted an attack on New Mexico,
which they had long coveted, and kept their eyes on
the larger prizes of Arizona and California. A Confederate force led by General Henry H. Sibley occupied
Santa Fé and Albuquerque early in 1862 without resis-

tance, thus posing a serious Confederate threat to the
entire Southwest. Confederate hopes were dashed,
however, by a ragtag group of 950 miners and adventurers organized into the first Colorado Volunteer Infantry Regiment. After an epic march of 400 miles
from Denver, which was completed in thirteen days
despite snow and high winds, the Colorado militia
stopped the unsuspecting Confederate troops in the
Battle of Glorieta Pass on March 26–28, 1862. This
dashing action, coupled with the efforts of California
militias to safeguard Arizona and Utah from seizure by
Confederate sympathizers, secured the Far West for
the Union.

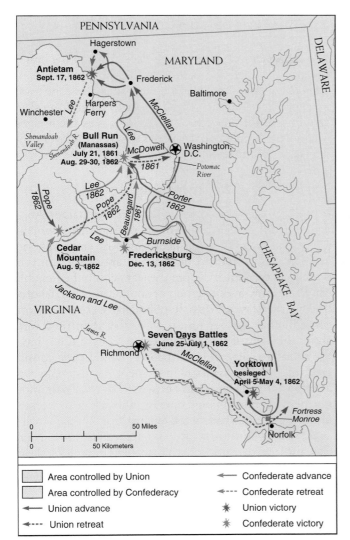

Major Battles in the East, 1861–1862   Northern Virginia was the most crucial and the most constant theater of battle. The prizes were the two opposing capitals, Washington and Richmond, only 70 miles apart. By the summer of 1862, George B. McClellan, famously cautious, had achieved only stalemate in the Peninsular campaign. He did, however, turn back Robert E. Lee at Antietam in September.

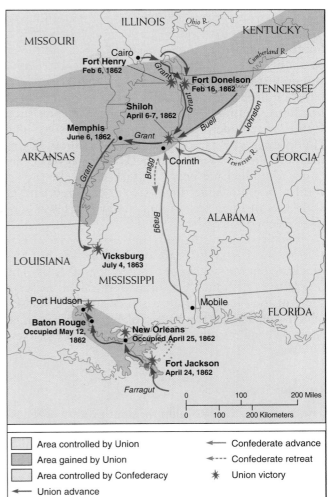

Major Battles in the West, 1862–1863   Ulysses S. Grant waged a mobile war, winning at Fort Henry and Fort Donelson in Tennessee in February 1862 and at Shiloh in April, and capturing Memphis in June. He then laid siege to Vicksburg, as Admiral David Farragut captured New Orleans and began to advance up the Mississippi River.

Other military action in the West was less decisive. The chronic fighting along the Kansas-Missouri border set a record for brutality when Confederate William Quantrill's Raiders made a predawn attack on Lawrence, Kansas, in August 1863, massacring 150 inhabitants and burning the town. Another civil war took place in Indian Territory, south of Kansas. The southern Indian tribes who had been removed there from the Old Southwest in the 1830s included many who were still bitter over the horrors of their removal by federal troops, and they sympathized with the Confederacy. Union victories at Pea Ridge (in northwestern

Arkansas) in 1862 and near Fort Gibson (in Indian Territory) in 1863 secured the area for the Union but did little to stop dissension among the Indian groups themselves. After the Civil War the victorious federal government used the tribes' wartime support for the Confederacy as a justification for demanding further land cessions.

The hostilities in the West showed that no part of the country, and none of its inhabitants, could remain untouched by the Civil War.

The Naval War

The Union's naval blockade of the South, intended to cut off commerce between the Confederacy and the rest of the world, was initially unsuccessful. The U.S.

Navy had only thirty-three ships with which to blockade 189 ports along 3,500 miles of coastline. Southern blockade runners evaded Union ships with ease: only an estimated one-eighth of all Confederate shipping was stopped in 1862. Moreover, the Confederacy licensed British-made privateers to strike at northern shipping. In a two-year period one such Confederate raider, the *Alabama*, destroyed sixty-nine Union ships with cargoes valued at $6 million. Beginning in 1863, however, as the Union navy became larger, the blockade began to take effect. In 1864 a third of the blockade runners were captured, and in 1865 half of them. As a result, fewer and fewer supplies reached the South.

For the Union, the most successful naval operation in the first two years of the war was not the blockade but the seizing of exposed coastal areas. The Sea Islands of South Carolina were taken, as were some of the North Carolina islands and Fort Pulaski, which commanded the harbor of Savannah, Georgia. Most damaging to the South was the capture of New Orleans.

The Black Response

The capture of Port Royal in the South Carolina Sea Islands in 1861 was important for another reason. Whites fled at the Union advance, but 10,000 slaves greeted the troops with jubilation and shouts of gratitude. Union troops had unwittingly freed these slaves in advance of any official Union policy on the status of slaves in captured territory.

Early in the war, an irate Southerner who saw three of his slaves disappear behind Union lines at Fortress Monroe, Virginia, demanded the return of his property, citing the Fugitive Slave Law. The Union commander, Benjamin Butler, replied that the Fugitive Slave Law no longer applied and that the escaped slaves were "contraband of war." News of Butler's decision spread rapidly among the slaves in the region of Fortress Monroe. Two days later, eight runaway slaves appeared; the next day, fifty-nine black men and women arrived at the fort. Union commanders had found an effective way to rob the South of its basic workforce. The "contrabands," as they were known, were put to work building fortifications and doing other useful work in northern camps.

As Union troops drove deeper into the South, the black response grew. When Union General William Tecumseh Sherman marched his army through Georgia in 1864, 18,000 slaves—entire families, people of all ages—flocked to the Union lines. By the war's end, nearly a million black people, fully a quarter of all the slaves in the South, had "voted with their feet" for the Union.

THE DEATH OF SLAVERY

The overwhelming response of black slaves to the Union advance changed the nature of the war. As increasing numbers of slaves flocked to Union lines, the conclusion was unmistakable: the southern war to defend the slave system did not have the support of slaves themselves. Any northern policy that ignored the issue of slavery and the wishes of the slaves was unrealistic.

The Politics of Emancipation

In 1862, as the issue of slavery loomed ever larger, Abraham Lincoln, acutely aware of divided northern opinion, inched his way toward a declaration of emancipation. Lincoln was correct to be worried about the unity of opinion in the North. Before the war, within the Republican Party, only a small group of abolitionists had favored freeing the slaves. Most Republicans were more concerned about the expansion of slavery than they were about the lives of slaves themselves. They did not favor the social equality of black people, whom they considered inferior. The free-soil movement, for example, was as often antiblack as it was antislave. For their part, most northern Democrats were openly antiblack. Irish workers in northern cities had rioted against free African Americans, with whom they often competed for jobs. There was also the question of what would become of slaves who were freed. Even the most fervent abolitionists had refused to face up to this issue. Northern Democrats effectively played on racial fears in the 1862 congressional elections, warning that freed slaves would pour into northern cities and take jobs from white laborers.

Nevertheless, the necessities of war edged Lincoln toward a new position. Following the Union victory at Antietam in September 1862, Lincoln issued a preliminary decree: unless the rebellious states returned to the Union by January 1, 1863, he would declare their slaves "forever free." Although Lincoln did not expect the Confederate states to surrender because of his proclamation, the decree increased the pressure on the South by directly linking the slave system to the war effort. Thus the freedom of black people became part of the struggle. Frederick Douglass, the voice of black America, wrote, "We shout for joy that we live to record this righteous decree."

On January 1, 1863, Lincoln duly issued the final Emancipation Proclamation, which turned out to be just as tortuous as his earlier responses to public opinion. The proclamation freed the slaves in the areas of rebellion—the areas the Union did not control—but specifically exempted slaves in the border states and in former Confederate areas conquered by the Union. Lincoln's purpose was to meet the abolitionist demand for a war against slavery while not losing the support of conservatives, especially in the border states. But the proclamation was so equivocal that Lincoln's own secretary of state, William Seward, remarked sarcastically, "We show our sympathy with slavery by emancipating slaves where we cannot reach them and holding them in bondage where we can set them free."

One group greeted the Emancipation Proclamation with open celebration. On New Year's Day, hundreds of African Americans gathered outside the White House and cheered the president. Realizing the symbolic importance of the proclamation, free African Americans predicted that the news would encourage southern slaves either to flee to Union lines or refuse to work for their masters. Both of these things were already happening as African Americans seized on wartime changes to reshape white-black relations in the South. In one sense, then, the Emancipation Proclamation simply gave a name to a process already in motion.

Abolitionists set about moving Lincoln beyond his careful stance in the Emancipation Proclamation. Reformers such as Elizabeth Cady Stanton and Susan B. Anthony lobbied and petitioned for a constitutional amendment outlawing slavery. Congress, at Lincoln's urging, approved and sent to the states a statement banning slavery throughout the United States. Quickly ratified by the Union states in 1865, the statement became the Thirteenth Amendment to the Constitution.

Black Fighting Men

As part of the Emancipation Proclamation, Lincoln gave his support for the first time to the recruitment of black soldiers. Early in the war, eager black volunteers had been bitterly disappointed at being turned away. Many, like Robert Fitzgerald, a free African American from Pennsylvania, found other ways to serve the Union cause. Fitzgerald first drove a wagon and mule for the Quartermaster Corps, and later, in spite of persistent seasickness, he served in the Union navy. After the Emancipation Proclamation, however, Fitzgerald was able to do what he had wanted to do all along: be a soldier. He enlisted in the Fifth Massachusetts Cavalry, a regiment that, like all the units in which black soldiers served, was 100 percent African American but commanded by white officers.

In Fitzgerald's company of eighty-three men, half came from slave states and had run away to enlist; the other half came mostly from the North but also from Canada, the West Indies, and France. Other regiments had volunteers from Africa. The proportion of volunteers from the loyal border states (where slavery was still legal) was upwards of 25 percent—a lethal blow to the slave system in those states.

After a scant two months of training, Fitzgerald's company was sent on to Washington and thence to battle in northern Virginia. Uncertain of the reception they would receive in northern cities with their history of antiblack riots, Fitzgerald and his comrades were pleasantly surprised. "We are cheered in every town we pass through," he wrote in his diary. "I was surprised to see a great many white people weeping as the train moved South." White people had reason to cheer: black volunteers, eager and willing to fight, made up 10 percent of the Union army. Nearly 200,000 African Americans (one out of every five black males in the nation) served in the Union army or navy. A fifth of them—37,000—died defending their own freedom and the Union.

Military service was something no black man could take lightly. African American soldiers faced prejudice within the army and had to prove themselves in battle.

Furthermore, the Confederates hated and feared African American troops and threatened to treat any captured black soldier as an escaped slave subject to

This painting, *The Storming of Fort Wagner*, shows the attack on the fort near Charleston, South Carolina, by the 54th Massachusetts African American Regiment on July 18, 1863. The attack failed, and more than half the members of this first Union all-black regiment and their white commanding officer, Robert Gould Shaw, were killed.

SOURCE: Courtesy of the Library of Congress.

execution. On at least one occasion, the threats were carried out. In 1864 Confederate soldiers massacred 262 black soldiers at Fort Pillow, Tennessee, after they had surrendered. Although large-scale episodes such as this were rare (especially after President Lincoln threatened retaliation), smaller ones were not. On duty near Petersburg, Virginia, Robert Fitzgerald's company lost a picket to Confederate hatred: wounded in the leg, he was unable to escape from Confederate soldiers, who smashed his skull with their musket butts.

Another extraordinary part of the story of the African American soldiers was their reception by black people in the South, who were overjoyed at the sight of armed black men, many of them former slaves themselves, wearing the uniform of the Union army. As his regiment entered Wilmington, North Carolina, one soldier wrote, "Men and women, old and young, were running throughout the streets, shouting and praising God. We could then truly see what we have been fighting for."

African American soldiers were not treated equally by the Union army. They were segregated in camp, given the worst jobs, and paid less than white soldiers ($10 a month rather than $13). Although they might not be able to do much about the other kinds of discrimination, the men of the Fifty-fourth Massachusetts found an unusual way to protest their unequal pay: they refused to accept it, preferring to serve the army for free until it decided to treat them as free men. The protest was effective; in June 1864 the War Department equalized the wages of black and white soldiers.

THE FRONT LINES AND THE HOME FRONT

Civil War soldiers wrote millions of letters home, more proportionately than in any American war. Their letters are a testament to the patriotism of both Union and Confederate troops, for the story they tell is frequently one of slaughter and horror.

The Toll of War

In spite of early hopes for what one might call a "brotherly" war, one that avoided excessive brutality, Civil War battles were appallingly deadly. One reason was technology: improved weapons, particularly modern rifles, had much greater range and accuracy than the muskets they replaced. Another was that almost all Union and Confederate generals remained committed to the conventional military doctrine of massed infantry offensives—the "Jomini doctrine"—that they had learned in their military classes at West Point. Part

of this strategy had been to "soften up" a defensive line with artillery before an infantry assault, but now the range of the new rifles made artillery itself vulnerable to attack. As a result, generals relied less on "softening up" than on immense numbers of infantrymen, hoping that enough of them would survive the withering rifle fire to overwhelm the enemy line. Enormous casualties were a consequence of this basic strategy.

Medical ignorance was another factor in the casualty rate. Because the use of antiseptic procedures was in its infancy, men often died because minor wounds became infected. Gangrene was a common cause of death. Disease was an even more frequent killer, taking twice as many men as were lost in battle. The overcrowded and unsanitary conditions of many camps were breeding grounds for smallpox, dysentery, typhoid, pneumonia, and, in the summer, malaria.

Yet another factor was that both North and South were completely unprepared to handle the supply and health needs of their large armies. Twenty-four hours after the battle of Shiloh, most of the wounded still lay on the field in the rain. Many died of exposure; some, unable to help themselves, drowned.

Army Nurses

Many medical supplies that the armies were unable to provide were donated by the United States Sanitary Commission in the North, as described in the opening of this chapter, and by women's volunteer groups in the South. But in addition to supplies, there was also an urgent need for skilled nurses. Under the pressure of wartime necessity, and over the objections of most army doctors, women became army nurses. Hospital nursing, previously considered a job only disreputable women would undertake, now became a suitable vocation for middle-class women. Under the leadership of veteran reformer Dorothea Dix of the asylum movement (see Chapter 13), and in cooperation with the Sanitary Commission (and with the vocal support of Mother Bickerdyke), by the war's end more than 3,000 northern women had worked as paid army nurses and many more as volunteers.

One of the volunteers was Ellen Ruggles Strong of New York, who, over her husband's objections, insisted on nursing in the Peninsular campaign of 1862. "The little woman has come out amazingly strong during these two months," George Templeton Strong wrote in his diary with a mixture of pride and condescension. "Have never given her credit for a tithe of the enterprise, pluck, discretion, and force of character that she has shown. God bless her." Other women organized other volunteer efforts outside the Sanitary Commission umbrella. Perhaps the best known was Clara Barton, who had been a government clerk before the war and consequently knew a number of influential members of Congress. Barton organized nursing and the distribution of medical supplies; she also used her congressional contacts to force reforms in army medical practice, of which she was very critical.

Southern women were also active in nursing and otherwise aiding soldiers, though the South never boasted a single large-scale organization like the Sanitary Commission. The women of Richmond volunteered when they found the war on their doorstep in the summer of 1862. During the Seven Days Battles, thousands of wounded poured into Richmond; many died in the streets because there was no room for them in hospitals. Richmond women first established informal "roadside hospitals" to meet the need, and their activities expanded from there. As in the North, middle-class women at first faced strong resistance from army doctors and even their own families, who believed that a field hospital was "no place for a refined lady." Kate Cumming of Mobile, who nursed in Corinth, Mississippi, after the Battle of Shiloh, faced down such reproofs, though she confided to her diary that nursing wounded men was very difficult: "Nothing that I had ever heard or read had given me the faintest idea of the horrors witnessed here." She and her companion nurses persisted and became an important part of the Confederate medical services. For southern women, who had been much less active in the public life of their communities than their northern reforming sisters, this Civil War activity marked an important break with prewar tradition.

Although women had made important advances, most army nurses and medical support staff were men. One volunteer nurse was the poet Walt Whitman, who visited wounded soldiers in the hospital in Washington, D.C. Horrified at the suffering he saw, Whitman also formed a deep admiration for the "incredible dauntlessness" of the common soldier in the face of slaughter and privation. While never denying the senselessness of the slaughter, Whitman nevertheless found hope in the determined spirit of the common man and woman.

The Life of the Common Soldier

The conditions experienced by the eager young volunteers of the Union and Confederate armies included mas-

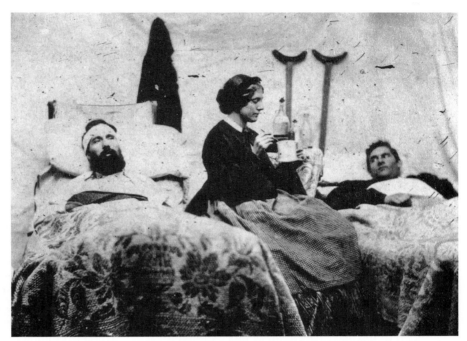

Nurse Ann Bell shown preparing medicine for a wounded soldier. Prompted by the medical crisis of the war, women such as Bell and "Mother" Bickerdyke actively participated in the war effort as nurses.

SOURCE: Center of Military History, U.S. Army.

sive, terrifying, and bloody battles, apparently unending, with no sign of victory in sight. Soldiers suffered from the uncertainty of supply, which left troops, especially in the South, without uniforms, tents, and sometimes even food. They endured long marches over muddy, rutted roads while carrying packs weighing fifty or sixty pounds. Disease was rampant in their dirty, verminous, and unsanitary camps, and hospitals were so dreadful that more men left them dead than alive.

Many soldiers had entered military service with unrealistic, even romantic ideas about warfare. Reality was a rude shock. Desertion was common: an estimated one of every nine Confederate soldiers and one of every seven Union soldiers deserted. Unauthorized absence was another problem. At Antietam, Robert E. Lee estimated that unauthorized absence reduced his strength by a third to a half.

Wartime Politics

In the earliest days of the war, Northerners had joined together in support of the war effort. Democrat Stephen A. Douglas, Lincoln's defeated rival, paid a visit to the White House to offer Lincoln his support. Within a month, Douglas was dead at age forty-eight. The Democrats had lost the leadership of a broad-minded man who might have done much on behalf of northern unity. By 1862 Democrats had split into two factions: the War

Democrats and the Peace Democrats, derogatorily called "Copperheads" (from the poisonous snake).

The Democratic Party remained a powerful force in northern politics. It had received 44 percent of the popular vote in the North in the 1860 election and its united opposition to the emancipation of slaves explains much of Lincoln's equivocal action on this issue. But the Peace Democrats went far beyond opposition to emancipation, denouncing the draft, martial law, and the high-handed actions of "King Abraham."

The leader of the Copperheads, Clement Vallandigham, a former Ohio congressman, advocated an armistice and a negotiated peace that would "look only to the welfare, peace and safety of the white race, without reference to the effect that settlement may have on the African." Western Democrats, he threatened, might form their own union with the South, excluding New England with its radical abolitionists and high-tariff industrialists. Lincoln could not afford to take Vallandigham's threats lightly. Besides, he was convinced that some Peace Democrats were members of secret societies—the Knights of the Golden Circle and the Sons of Liberty—that had been conspiring with the Confederacy. In 1862, Lincoln proclaimed that all people who discouraged enlistments in the army or otherwise engaged in disloyal practices would be subject to martial law. In all, 13,000 people were arrested and imprisoned, including Vallandigham, who was exiled to the Confederacy. Lincoln rejected all protests, claiming that his arbitrary actions were necessary for national security.

Lincoln also faced challenges from the radical faction of his own party. As the war continued, the Radicals gained strength. The most troublesome was Salmon P. Chase, who in December 1862 caused a cabinet crisis when he encouraged Senate Republicans to complain that Secretary of State William Seward was "lukewarm" in his support for emancipation. This Radical challenge was a portent of the party's difficulties after the war, which Lincoln did not live to see—or prevent.

Economic and Social Strains on the North

Wartime needs caused a surge in northern economic growth, but the gains were unequally distributed. Early in the war, some industries suffered: textile manufacturers could not get cotton, and shoe factories that had made cheap shoes for slaves were without a market. But other industries boomed—boot making, shipbuilding, and the manufacture of woolen goods such as blankets and uniforms, to give just three examples. Coal mining expanded, as did ironmaking, especially the manufacture of iron rails for railroads. Agricultural goods were in great demand, promoting further mech-

anization of farming. The McCormick brothers grew rich from sales of their reapers. Women, left to tend the family farm while the men went to war, found that with mechanized equipment they could manage the demanding task of harvesting.

Meeting wartime needs enriched some people honestly, but speculators and profiteers also flourished, as they have in every war. By the end of the war, government contracts had exceeded $1 billion. Not all of this business was free from corruption. New wealth was evident in every northern city.

For most people, the war brought the day-to-day hardship of inflation. During the four years of the war, the North suffered an inflation rate of 80 percent, or nearly 15 percent a year. This annual rate, three times what is generally considered tolerable, did much to inflame social tensions. Wages rose only half as much as prices, and workers responded by joining unions and striking. Manufacturers, bitterly opposed to unions, freely hired strikebreakers (many of whom were African Americans, women, or immigrants) and formed organizations of their own to prevent further unionization and to blacklist union organizers. Thus both capital and labor moved far beyond the small, localized confrontations of the early industrial period. The formation of large-scale organizations, fostered by wartime demand, laid the groundwork for the national battle between workers and manufacturers that would dominate the last part of the nineteenth century.

Another major source of social tension was conscription. The Union introduced a draft in March 1863. Especially unpopular in the 1863 draft law was a provision that allowed the hiring of substitutes or the payment of a commutation fee of $300. Substitution had been accepted in all previous European and American wars, but the Democratic Party made it an inflammatory issue. Pointing out that $300 was almost a year's wages for an unskilled laborer, they denounced the draft law (88 percent of Democratic congressmen had voted against it). They appealed to popular resentment by calling it "aristocratic legislation" and to fear by running headlines such as "Three Hundred Dollars or Your Life."

Conscription was often marred by favoritism and prejudice. Local officials called up many more poor than rich men and selected a higher proportion of immigrants than nonimmigrants. In reality, however, only 7 percent of all men called to serve actually did so. About 25 percent hired a substitute, another 45 percent were exempted for "cause" (usually health reasons), and another 20–25 percent simply failed to report to the community draft office. Nevertheless, by 1863 many northern urban workers believed that the slogan "a rich man's war but a poor man's fight," though coined in the South, applied to them as well.

The New York City Draft Riots

In the spring of 1863 there were protests against the draft throughout the North. Riots and disturbances broke out in many cities, and several federal enrollment officers were killed. The greatest trouble occurred in New York City between July 13 and July 16, 1863, where a wave of working-class looting, fighting, and lynching claimed the lives of 105 people, many of them African American. The rioting, the worst up to that time in American history, was quelled only when five units of the U.S. Army were rushed from the battlefield at Gettysburg, where they had been fighting Confederates the week before.

The riots had several causes. Anger at the draft and racial prejudice were what most contemporaries saw. From a historical perspective, however, the riots had less to do with the war than with the urban growth and tensions described in Chapter 13.

Ironically, African American men, a favorite target of the rioters' anger, were a major force in easing the national crisis over the draft. Though they had been barred from service until 1863, in the later stages of the war African American volunteers filled much of the manpower gap that the controversial draft was meant to address.

The Failure of Southern Nationalism

The war brought even greater changes to the South. As in the North, war needs led to expansion and centralization of government control over the economy. In many cases, Jefferson Davis himself initiated government control (over railroads, shipping, and war production, for example), often in the face of protest or inaction by governors who favored states' rights. The expansion of government brought sudden urbanization, a new experience for the predominantly rural South. The population of Richmond, the Confederate capital, almost tripled, in large part because the Confederate bureaucracy grew to 70,000 people. Because of the need for military manpower, a good part of the Confederate bureaucracy consisted of women, who were referred to as "government girls". All of this—government control,

A black man is lynched during the New York City Draft Riots in July 1863. Free black people and their institutions were major victims of the worst rioting in American history until then. The riots were less a protest against the draft than an outburst of frustration over urban problems that had been festering for decades.

SOURCE: Culver Pictures, Inc.

urban growth, women in the paid workforce—was new to Southerners, and not all of it was welcomed.

Even more than in the North, the voracious need for soldiers fostered class antagonisms. When small yeoman farmers went off to war, their wives and families struggled to farm on their own, without the help of mechanization, which they could not afford, and without the help of slaves, which they had never owned. But wealthy men could be exempted from the draft if they had more than twenty slaves. Furthermore, many upper-class Southerners—at least 50,000—avoided military service by paying liberally ($5,000 and more) for substitutes. In the face of these inequities, desertions from the Confederate army soared.

Worst of all was the starvation. The North's blockade and the breakdown of the South's transportation system restricted the availability of food in the South, and these problems were vastly magnified by runaway inflation. Prices in the South rose by an unbelievable 9,000 percent. Speculation and hoarding by the rich made matters even worse. In the spring of 1863 food riots broke out in four Georgia cities (Atlanta among them) and in North Carolina. In Richmond, more than a thousand people, mostly women, broke into bakeries and snatched loaves of bread, crying "Bread! Bread! Our children are starving while the rich roll in wealth!" When the bread riot threatened to turn into general looting, Jefferson Davis himself appealed to the crowd to disperse—but found he had to threaten the rioters with gunfire before they would leave. A year later, Richmond stores sold eggs for $6 a dozen and butter for $25 a pound. One woman wept, "My God! How can I pay such prices? I have seven children; what shall I do?"

Increasingly, the ordinary people of the South, preoccupied with staying alive, refused to pay taxes, to provide food, or to serve in the army. Soldiers were drawn home by the desperation of their families as well as the discouraging course of the war. By January 1865 the desertion rate had climbed to 8 percent a month.

At the same time, the life of the southern ruling class was irrevocably altered by the changing nature of slavery. By the end of the war, one-quarter of all slaves had fled to the Union lines, and those who remained often stood in a different relationship to their owners. As white masters and overseers left to join the army, white women were left behind on the plantation to cope with shortages, grow crops, and manage the labor of slaves. Lacking the patriarchal authority of their husbands, white women found that white-black relationships shifted, sometimes drastically (as when slaves fled) and sometimes more subtly. Slaves increasingly made their own decisions about when and how they would work, and they refused to accept the punishments that would have accompanied this insubordination in prewar years.

Peace movements in the South were motivated by a confused mixture of realism, war weariness, and the animosity of those who supported states' rights and opposed Jefferson Davis. The anti-Davis faction was led by his own vice president, Alexander Stephens, who early in 1864 suggested a negotiated peace. Peace sentiment was especially strong in North Carolina, where more than a hundred public meetings in support of negotiations were held in the summer of 1863. Davis would have none of it. The peace sentiment, which grew throughout 1864, flourished outside the political system in secret societies such as the Heroes of America and the Red Strings. As hopes of Confederate victory slipped away, conflict expanded beyond the battlefield to include the political struggles that southern civilians were fighting among themselves.

THE TIDE TURNS

As Lincoln's timing of the Emancipation Proclamation showed, by 1863 the nature of the war was changing. The proclamation freeing the slaves struck directly at the southern home front and the civilian workforce. That same year, the nature of the battlefield war changed as well: The Civil War became the first total war.

The Turning Point of 1863

In the summer of 1863 the moment finally arrived when the North could begin to hope for victory. But for the Union army the year opened with stalemate in the East and slow and costly progress in the West. For the South, 1863 represented its highest hopes for military success and for diplomatic recognition by Britain or France.

Attempting to break the stalemate in northern Virginia, General Joseph "Fighting Joe" Hooker and a Union army of 130,000 men attacked a Confederate army half that size at Chancellorsville in May. In response, Robert E. Lee daringly divided his forces, sending General Thomas "Stonewall" Jackson and 30,000 men on a day-long flanking movement that caught the Union troops by surprise. Although Jackson was killed (shot by his own men by mistake), Chancellorsville was a great Confederate victory; there were 17,000 Union losses. However, Confederate losses were also great: 13,000 men, representing more than 20 percent of Lee's army.

Though weakened, Lee moved to the attack. In June, in his second and most dangerous single thrust into Union territory, he moved north into Maryland and Pennsylvania. His purpose was as much political as military: he hoped that a great Confederate victory would lead Britain and France to intervene in the war and demand a negotiated peace. The ensuing Battle of Gettysburg, July 1–3, 1863, was another horrible slaughter. The next day a Union officer reported, "I tried to ride over the field but could not, for dead and wounded lay too thick to guide a horse through them."

Lee retreated from the field, leaving more than one-third of his army behind—28,000 men killed, wounded, or missing. His great gamble had failed; he never again mounted a major offensive.

The next day, July 4, 1863, Ulysses S. Grant took Vicksburg, Mississippi, after a costly siege. The combined news of Gettysburg and Vicksburg dissuaded Britain and France from recognizing the Confederacy and checked the northern peace movement. It also tightened the North's grip on the South, for the Union now controlled the entire Mississippi River. In November, Generals Grant and Sherman broke the Confederate hold on Chattanooga, Tennessee, thereby opening the way to Atlanta.

Grant and Sherman

In March 1864, President Lincoln called Grant east and appointed him general in chief of all the Union forces. Lincoln's critics were appalled. Grant was an uncouth Westerner (like the president) and (unlike the president) was rumored to have a drinking problem. Lincoln replied that if he knew the general's brand of whiskey, he would send a barrel of it to every commander in the Union army.

Grant devised a plan of strangulation and annihilation. While he took on Lee in northern Virginia, he sent General William Tecumseh Sherman to defeat Confederate general Joe Johnston's Army of Tennessee, which was defending the approach to Atlanta. Both Grant and Sherman exemplified the new kind of warfare. They aimed to inflict maximum damage on the fabric of southern life, hoping that the South would choose to surrender rather than face total destruction. This decision to broaden the war so that it directly affected civilians was new in American military history and prefigured the total wars of the twentieth century.

In northern Virginia, Grant pursued a policy of destroying civilian supplies. He said he "regarded it as humane to both sides to protect the persons of those found at their homes, but to consume everything that could be used to support or supply armies." One of those supports was slaves. Grant welcomed fleeing slaves to Union lines and encouraged army efforts to put them to work or enlist them as soldiers.

But the most famous example of the new strategy of total war was General Sherman's 1864 march through Georgia.

On September 2, 1864, Sherman captured Atlanta. The battle had been fierce, and the city lay in ruins, but the rest of Georgia now lay open to him. In November, Sherman set out to march the 285 miles to the coastal city of Savannah, living off the land and destroying everything in his path. His military purpose was to tighten the noose around Robert E. Lee's army in northern Virginia by cutting off Mississippi, Alabama, and Georgia from the rest of the Confederacy. But his second purpose, openly stated, was to "make war so terrible" to the people of the South, to "make them so sick of war that generations would pass away before they would again appeal to it." Accordingly, he told his men to seize, burn, or destroy everything in their path (but, significantly, not to harm civilians).

Terrifying to white southern civilians, Sherman was initially hostile to black Southerners as well. In the interests of speed and efficiency, his army turned away many of the 18,000 slaves who flocked to it in Georgia, causing a number to be recaptured and reenslaved. This callous action caused such a scandal in Washington that Secretary of War Edwin Stanton arranged a special meeting in Georgia with Sherman and twenty African American ministers who spoke for the freed slaves. This meeting in itself was extraordinary: no one had ever before asked slaves what they wanted. Equally extraordinary was Sherman's response in Special Field Order 15, issued in January 1865: he set aside more than 400,000 acres of Confederate land to be given to the freed slaves in forty-acre parcels. This was war of a kind that white Southerners had never imagined.

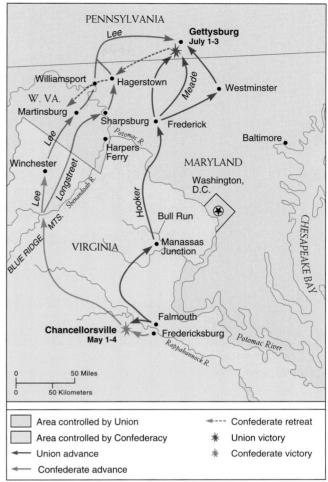

The Turning Point: 1863   In June, Lee boldly struck north into Maryland and Pennsylvania, hoping for a victory that would cause Britain and France to demand a negotiated peace on Confederate terms. Instead, he lost the hard-fought battle of Gettysburg, July 1–3. The very next day, Grant's long siege of Vicksburg succeeded. These two great Fourth of July victories turned the tide in favor of the Union. The Confederates never again mounted a major offensive. Total Union control of the Mississippi now exposed the Lower South to attack.

Far to the North, a much smaller unimaginable event occurred in October, when twenty-six Confederate sympathizers invaded St. Albans Vermont, robbing three banks, setting fires, killing a man—and then escaping over the border into Canada. When a Montreal magistrate released the men on a technicality, American military authorities threatened retaliation if Canadian authorities ever again allowed such an event. Canada was not unprepared for an American attack, but the defenders were British troops: the uncertain diplomatic and naval issues between the Union and Britain had led to the stationing of 14,000 troops to Canada, the largest number of British troops in North America since the War of 1812. The St. Albans incident, minor in itself, caused

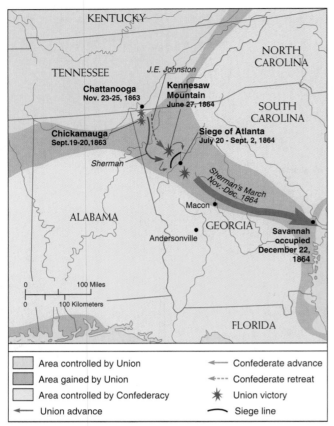

Sherman's Campaign in Georgia, 1864 Ulysses S. Grant and William Tecumseh Sherman, two like-minded generals, commanded the Union's armies in the final push to victory. While Grant hammered away at Lee in northern Virginia, Sherman captured Atlanta in September (a victory that may have been vital to Lincoln's reelection) and began his March to the Sea in November 1864.

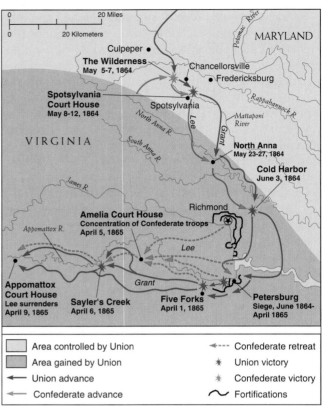

The Final Battles in Virginia, 1864–1865 In the war's final phase early in 1865, Sherman closed one arm of a pincers by marching north from Savannah while Grant attacked Lee's last defensive positions in Petersburg and Richmond. Lee retreated from them on April 2 and surrendered at Appomattox Courthouse on April 9, 1865.

both the British government and Canadian officials to think seriously about how to defend against the possibility of future American invasions. The answer was obvious: the Canadian provinces, which by 1860 stretched from one coast to the other, would need to be united. In 1867, all of the Canadian provinces joined in confederation and henceforth were known as the Dominion of Canada. In this way, a small Confederate pinprick helped to foster the unity of America's large northern neighbor.

The 1864 Election

The war complicated the 1864 presidential election. Lincoln was renominated during a low period. Opposed by the Radicals, who thought he was too conciliatory toward the South, and by Republican conservatives, who disapproved of the Emancipation Proclamation, Lincoln had little support within his own party.

The Democrats had an appealing candidate: General George McClellan, who proclaimed the war a failure and proposed an armistice to end it. Other Democrats played shamelessly on the racist fears of the urban working class, accusing Republicans of being "negro-lovers" and warning that racial mixing lay ahead.

A deeply depressed Lincoln fully expected to lose the election. "I am going to be beaten," he told an army officer in August 1864, "and unless some great change takes place badly beaten." A great change did take place: Sherman captured Atlanta on September 2. Jubilation swept the North: some cities celebrated with 100-gun salutes. Lincoln won the election with 55 percent of the popular vote. Seventy-eight percent of the soldiers voted for him rather than for their former commander. The vote probably saved the Republican Party from extinction. Furthermore, the election was important evidence of northern support for Lincoln's policy of unconditional surrender for the South. There would be no negotiated peace; the war would continue.

Nearing the End

As Sherman devastated the lower South, Grant was locked in struggle with Lee in northern Virginia. Grant did not favor subtle strategies. He bluntly said, "The art of war is simple enough. Find out where your enemy is. Get at him as soon as you can. Strike at him as hard as you can, and keep moving on." Following this plan, Grant eventually hammered Lee into submission, but at enormous cost. Lee inflicted heavy losses on the Union army: almost 18,000 at the battle of the Wilderness, more than 8,000 at Spotsylvania, and 12,000 at Cold Harbor. At Cold Harbor, Union troops wrote their names and addresses on scraps of paper and pinned them to their backs, so certain were they of being killed or wounded in battle. Grim and terrible as Grant's strategy was, it proved effective. Rather than pulling back after his failed assaults, he kept moving South, finally settling in for a prolonged siege of Lee's forces at Petersburg. The North's great advantage in population finally began to tell. There were more Union soldiers to replace those lost in battle, but there were no more white Confederates.

In desperation, the South turned to what had hitherto been unthinkable: arming slaves to serve as soldiers in the Confederate army. As Jefferson Davis said in February 1865, "We are reduced to choosing whether the negroes shall fight for or against us." But—and this was the bitter irony—the African American soldiers and their families would have to be promised freedom or they would desert to the Union at the first chance they had. Even though Davis's proposal had the support of General Robert E. Lee, the Confederate Congress balked at first. As one member said, "If slaves make good soldiers our whole theory of slavery is wrong." Finally, on March 13, the Confederate Congress authorized a draft of black soldiers—without mentioning freedom. Although two regiments of African American soldiers were immediately organized in Richmond, it was too late. The South never had to publicly acknowledge the paradox of having to offer slaves freedom so that they would fight to defend slavery.

By the spring of 1865, public support for the war simply disintegrated in the South. Starvation, inflation,

This striking photograph by Thomas C. Roche shows a dead Confederate soldier, killed at Petersburg on April 3, 1865, only six days before the surrender at Appomattox. The new medium of photography conveyed the horror of the war with a gruesome reality to the American public.

SOURCE: Thomas C. Roche/Library of Congress.

dissension, and the prospect of military defeat were too much. In February, Jefferson Davis sent his vice president, Alexander Stephens, to negotiate terms at a peace conference at Hampton Roads. Lincoln would not countenance anything less than full surrender, so the conference failed and southern resistance faded away.

Appomattox

In the spring of 1865 Lee and his remaining troops, outnumbered two to one, still held Petersburg and Richmond. Starving, short of ammunition, and losing men in battle or to desertion every day, Lee retreated from Petersburg on April 2. The Confederate government fled Richmond, stripping and burning the city. Seven days later, Lee and his 25,000 troops surrendered to Grant at Appomattox Court House. Grant treated Lee with great respect and set a historic precedent by giving the Confederate troops parole. This meant they could not subsequently be prosecuted for treason. Grant then sent the starving army on its way with three days' rations for every man. Jefferson Davis, who had hoped to set up a new government in Texas, was captured in Georgia on May 10. The war was finally over.

Abraham Lincoln toured Richmond, the Confederate capital, just hours after Jefferson Davis had fled. This photograph, taken April 4, 1865, shows Yankee cavalry horses in the foreground and the smoldering city in the background. It gives a sense of the devastation suffered by the South and the immense task of rebuilding and reconciliation that Lincoln would not live to accomplish.

SOURCE: Library of Congress.

Death of a President

Sensing that the war was near its end, Abraham Lincoln visited Grant's troops when Lee withdrew from Petersburg on April 2. Thus it was that Lincoln came to visit Richmond, and to sit briefly in Jefferson Davis's presidential office, soon after Davis had left it. As Lincoln walked the streets of the burned and pillaged city, black people poured out to see him and surround him, shouting "Glory to God! Glory! Glory! Glory!" Lincoln in turn said to Admiral David Porter: "Thank God I have lived to see this. It seems to me that I have been dreaming a horrid dream for four years, and now the nightmare is gone." Lincoln had only the briefest time to savor the victory. On the night of April 14, President and Mrs. Lincoln went to Ford's Theater in Washington. There Lincoln was shot at point-blank range by John Wilkes Booth, a Confederate sympathizer. He died the next day. For the people of the Union, the joy of victory was muted by mourning for their great leader.

CONCLUSION

In 1865, a divided people had been forcibly reunited by battle. Their nation, the United States of America, had been permanently changed by civil war. Devastating losses among the young men of the country would affect not only their families but all of postwar society. Politically, the deepest irony of the Civil War was that only by fighting it had America become completely a nation. For it was the war that broke down local isolation. Ordinary citizens in local communities, North and South, developed a national perspective as they sent their sons and brothers to be soldiers, their daughters to be nurses and teachers. The question now was whether this strengthened but divided national community, forged in battle, could create a just peace.

CHRONOLOGY

1861	March: Morrill Tariff Act
	April: Fort Sumter falls; war begins
	April: Mobilization begins
	April–May: Virginia, Arkansas, Tennessee, and North Carolina secede
	June: United States Sanitary Commission established
	July: First Battle of Bull Run
	December: French troops arrive in Mexico, followed by British and Spanish forces in January.
1862	February: Legal Tender Act
	February: Battles of Fort Henry and Fort Donelson
	March: Battle of Pea Ridge
	March–August: George B. McClellan's Peninsular campaign
	March: Battle of Glorieta Pass
	April: Battle of Shiloh
	April: Confederate Conscription Act
	April: David Farragut captures New Orleans
	May: *Cinqo de Mayo*: Mexican troops repel Franch invaders
	May: Homestead Act
	June–July: Seven Days Battles
	July: Pacific Railway Act
	July: Morrill Land Grant Act
	September: Battle of Antietam
	December: Battle of Fredericksburg
1863	January: Emancipation Proclamation
	February: National Bank Act
	March: Draft introduced in the North
	April: Richmond bread riot
	May: Battle of Chancellorsville
	June: French occupy Mexico City
	July: Battle of Gettysburg
	July: Surrender of Vicksburg
	July: New York City Draft Riots
	November: Battle of Chattanooga
	November: Union troops capture Brownsville, Texas
1864	March: Ulysses S. Grant becomes general in chief of Union forces
	April: Fort Pillow massacre
	May: Battle of the Wilderness
	May: Battle of Spotsylvania
	June: Battle of Cold Harbor
	June: Maximillian becomes Emperor of Mexico
	September: Atlanta falls
	October: St. Albans incident
	November: Abraham Lincoln reelected president
	November–December: William Tecumseh Sherman's March to the Sea
1865	April: Richmond falls
	April: Robert E. Lee surrenders at Appomattox
	April: Lincoln assassinated
	December: Thirteenth Amendment to the Constitution becomes law

REVIEW QUESTIONS

1. At the outset of the Civil War, what were the relative advantages of the North and the South, and how did they affect the final outcome?

2. In the absence of the southern Democrats, in the early 1860s the new Republican Congress was able to pass a number of party measures with little opposition. What do these measures tell you about the historical roots of the Republican Party? More generally, how do you think we should view legislation passed in the absence of the customary opposition, debate, and compromise?

3. The greatest problem facing Jefferson Davis and the Confederacy was the need to develop a true feeling of nationalism. Can the failure of this effort be blamed on Davis's weakness as a leader alone, or are there other causes?

4. In what ways can it be said that the actions of African Americans, both slave and free, came to determine the course of the Civil War?

5. Wars always have unexpected consequences. List some of these consequences both for soldiers and for civilians in the North and in the South.

6. Today Abraham Lincoln is considered one of our greatest presidents, but he did not enjoy such approval at the time. List some of the contemporary criticisms of Lincoln and evaluate them.

RECOMMENDED READING

Jeanie Attie, *Patriotic Toil: Northern Women and the American Civil War* (1998). A fine study of women's activities in the U.S. Sanitary Commission.

Iver Bernstein, *The New York City Draft Riots* (1990). A social history that places the famous riots in the context of the nineteenth century's extraordinary urbanization.

David J. Eocher, *The Longest Night* (2001). The most recent and perhaps the longest (990 pages) and most detailed military history of the Civil War.

Paul Escott, *After Secession: Jefferson Davis and the Failure of Confederate Nationalism* (1978). A thoughtful study of Davis's record as president of the Confederacy.

Drew Gilpin Faust, *Mothers of Invention: Women of the Slaveholding South in the American Civil War* (1996). A major study that considers the importance of gender at the white South's "moment of truth."

Alvin Josephy, *The Civil War in the West* (1992). A long-needed study, by a noted western historian, of the course of the war in the Trans-Mississippi West.

Bryan and Nelson Langford, eds. *Eye of the Storm: A Civil War Odyssey* (2000). The richly illustrated diary of a Union soldier, including his captivity at Andersonville.

James M. McPherson, *The Negro's Civil War: How American Negroes Felt and Acted during the War for the Union* (1965). One of the earliest documentary collections on African American activity in wartime.

———, *Battle Cry of Freedom: The Civil War Era* (1988). An acclaimed, highly readable synthesis of much scholarship on the war.

———, *The Atlas of the Civil War* (1994). Detailed battle diagrams with clear descriptions.

Pauli Murray, *Proud Shoes: The Story of an American Family* (1956). Murray tells the proud story of her African American family and her grandfather, Robert Fitzgerald.

Phillip Shaw Paludan, *"A People's Contest": The Union at War, 1861–1865* (1988). A highly successful social history of the North during the war.

ON THE WEB

http://www.schistory.org/displays/ index.html#plantations

The exhibits page of the South Carolina Historical Society contains some interesting drawings and photos from the Civil War period. The site is expanding with more material planned. Also of interest are the plantation photos, which are post-Civil War, the photos of African American life in South Carolina in the 1920s, and the Revolutionary War sites.

http://www.history.navy.mil/photos/sh-us-cs/ csa-sh/csa-name.htm

This U.S. Navy history site contains a pictorial history of the Confederate navy with drawings, paintings, and photographs of Confederate ships with some short historical commentary. The U.S. Navy has yet to post a comparable site for the Union navy, but Union ships can be found by searching the naval photographic records by ship name at **http://www.history.navy.mil/photos/ sh-usn/usn-name.htm**. Each thumbnail sketch beside the name of listed vessels contains enough information to indicate if it is of Civil War vintage.

http://lcweb.loc.gov/rr/print/081_cwaf.html

This Library of Congress exhibit is entitled "Photographs of African Americans During the Civil War: A List of Images in the Civil War Photograph Collection" and comes from the Prints and Photographs Division. Many of the photographs archived here contain thumbnail copies that can be enlarged. Particularly interesting are the photos of "colored troops" and those of "contrabands," a Union term for runaway slaves who have reached the Union army lines.

http://www.prenhall.com/faragherbrief/map16.1

Consider the military strategies of the North and the South. How did each side's strategies reflect its larger goals?

http://www.prenhall.com/faragherbrief/map16.2

Follow Lee's campaign northward. What was he hoping to achieve and why was his defeat at Gettysburg the war's turning point?

AMERICAN COMMUNITIES

Hale County, Alabama: From Slavery to Freedom in a Black Belt Community

ON A BRIGHT SATURDAY MORNING IN MAY 1867, 4,000 FORMER slaves eagerly streamed into the town of Greensboro, bustling seat of Hale County in west-central Alabama. They came to hear speeches from two delegates to a recent freedmen's convention in Mobile and to find out about the political status of black people under the Reconstruction Act just passed by Congress. Tensions mounted in the days following this unprecedented gathering as military authorities began supervising voter registration for elections to the upcoming constitutional convention that would rewrite the laws of Alabama. On June 13, John Orrick, a local white, confronted Alex Webb, a politically active freedman, on the streets of Greensboro. Webb had recently been appointed a voter registrar for the district. Orrick swore he would never be registered by a black man and shot Webb dead. Hundreds of armed and angry freedmen formed a posse to search for Orrick but failed to find him. Galvanized by Webb's murder, 500 local freedmen formed a chapter of the Union League, the Republican Party's organizational arm in the South. The chapter functioned as both a militia company and a forum to agitate for political rights.

Violent political encounters between black people and white people were common in southern communities in the wake of the Civil War. The war had destroyed slavery and the Confederacy but left the political and economic status of newly emancipated African Americans unresolved. Communities throughout the South struggled over the meaning of freedom in ways that reflected their particular circumstances. The 4 million freed people constituted roughly one-third of the total southern population, but the black–white ratio in individual communities varied enormously. In some places the Union army had been a strong presence during the war, hastening the collapse of the slave system and encouraging experiments in free labor. Other areas had remained relatively untouched by the fighting. In some areas small farms prevailed; in others, including Hale County, large plantations dominated economic and political life.

West-central Alabama had emerged as a fertile center of cotton production just two decades before the Civil War. There, African Americans, as throughout the South's black belt, constituted more than three-quarters of the population. The region was virtually untouched by fighting until the very end of the Civil War. But with the arrival of federal troops in the spring of 1865, African Americans in Hale County, like their counterparts elsewhere, began to challenge the traditional organization of plantation labor.

One owner, Henry Watson, found that his entire workforce had deserted him at the end of 1865. "I am in the midst of a large and fertile cotton growing country," Watson wrote to a partner. "Many plantations are entirely without labor, many plantations have insufficient labor, and upon none are the laborers doing their former accustomed work." Black women refused to work in the fields, preferring to stay home with their children and tend garden plots. Nor would male field hands do any work, such as caring for hogs, that did not directly increase their share of the cotton crop.

Above all, freed people wanted more autonomy. Overseers and owners, thus, grudgingly allowed them to work the land "in families," letting them choose their own supervisors and find their own provisions. The result was a shift from the gang labor characteristic of the antebellum period, in which large groups of slaves worked under the harsh and constant supervision of white overseers, to the sharecropping system, in which African American families worked small plots of land in exchange for a small share of the crop. This shift represented less of a victory for newly freed African Americans than a defeat for plantation owners, who resented even the limited economic independence it forced them to concede to their black workforce.

Only a small fraction—perhaps 15 percent—of African American families were fortunate enough to be able to buy land. The majority settled for some version of sharecropping, while others managed to rent land from owners, becoming tenant farmers. Still, planters throughout Hale County had to change the old routines of plantation labor. Local African Americans also organized politically. In 1866 Congress had passed the Civil Rights Act and sent the Fourteenth Amendment to the Constitution to the states for ratification; both promised full citizenship rights to former slaves. Hale County freedmen joined the Republican Party and local Union League chapters. They used their new political power to press for better labor contracts, demand greater autonomy for the black workforce, and agitate for the more radical goal of land confiscation and redistribution. "The colored people are very anxious to get land of their own to live upon independently; and they want money to buy stock to make crops," reported one black Union League organizer. "The only way to get these necessaries is to give our votes to the [Republican] party . . . making every effort possible to bring these blessings about by reconstructing the State." Two Hale County former slaves, Brister Reese and James K. Green, won election to the Alabama state legislature in 1869.

It was not long before these economic and political gains prompted a white counterattack. In the spring of 1868, the Ku Klux Klan—a secret organization devoted to terrorizing and intimidating African Americans and their white Republican allies—came to Hale County. Disguised in white sheets, armed with guns and whips, and making nighttime raids on horseback, Klansmen flogged, beat, and murdered freed people. They intimidated voters and silenced political activists. Planters used Klan terror to dissuade former slaves from leaving plantations or organizing for higher wages.

With the passage of the Ku Klux Klan Act in 1871, the federal government cracked down on the Klan, breaking its power temporarily in parts of the former Confederacy. But no serious effort was made to stop Klan terror in the west Alabama black belt, and planters there succeeded in reestablishing much of their social and political control.

The events in Hale County illustrate the struggles that beset communities throughout the South during the Reconstruction era after the Civil War. The destruction of slavery and the Confederacy forced African Americans and white people to renegotiate their old economic and political roles. These community battles both shaped and were shaped by the victorious and newly expansive federal government in Washington. In the end, Reconstruction was only partially successful. Not until the "Second Reconstruction" of the twentieth-century civil rights movement would the descendants of Hale County's African Americans begin to enjoy the full fruits of freedom—and even then not without challenge. ■

Greensboro

```
────────────────────── KEY TOPICS ──────────────────────

■ Competing political plans for          ■ The political and social legacy of
  reconstructing the defeated Confederacy   Reconstruction in the southern states

■ Difficult transition from slavery to freedom   ■ Post–Civil War transformations in the
  for African Americans                        economic and political life of the North
```

THE POLITICS OF RECONSTRUCTION

When General Robert E. Lee's men stacked their guns at Appomattox, the bloodiest war in American history ended. Although President Abraham Lincoln insisted early on that the purpose of the war was to preserve the Union, by 1863 it had evolved as well into a struggle for African American liberation. Indeed, the political, economic, and moral issues posed by slavery were the root cause of the Civil War, and the war ultimately destroyed slavery, although not racism, once and for all.

The Civil War also settled the Constitutional crisis provoked by the secession of the Confederacy and its justification in appeals to states' rights. The name "United States" would from now on be understood as a singular rather than a plural noun, signaling an important change in the meaning of American nationality. The old notion of the United States as a voluntary union of sovereign states gave way to the new reality of a single nation in which the federal government took precedence over the individual states.

The Defeated South

The white South paid an extremely high price for secession, war, and defeat. In addition to the battlefield casualties, the Confederate states sustained deep material and psychological wounds. Much of the best agricultural land lay waste. Many towns and cities—including Richmond, Atlanta, and Columbia, South Carolina—were in ruins. By 1865, the South's most

precious commodities, cotton and African American slaves, no longer were measures of wealth and prestige. Retreating Confederates destroyed most of the South's cotton to prevent its capture by federal troops. What remained was confiscated by Union agents as contraband of war. The former slaves, many of whom had fled to Union lines during the latter stages of the war, were determined to chart their own course in the reconstructed South as free men and women.

It would take the South's economy a generation to overcome the severe blows dealt by the war. In 1860 the South held roughly 25 percent of the nation's wealth; a decade later it controlled only 12 percent.

Decorating the Graves of Rebel Soldiers, *Harper's Weekly*, August 17, 1867. After the Civil War, both Southerners and Northerners created public mourning ceremonies honoring fallen soldiers. Women led the memorial movement in the South, which, by establishing cemeteries and erecting monuments, offered the first cultural expression of the Confederate tradition. This engraving depicts citizens of Richmond, Virginia, decorating thousands of Confederate graves with flowers at the Hollywood Memorial Cemetery on the James River. A local women's group raised enough funds to transfer over 16,000 Confederate dead from northern cemeteries for reburial in Richmond.

SOURCE: The Granger Collection.

Many white Southerners resented their conquered status, and white notions of race, class, and "honor" died hard. A white North Carolinian, for example, who had lost almost everything dear to him in the war—his sons, home, and slaves—recalled in 1865 that in spite of all his tragedy he still retained one thing. "They've left me one inestimable privilege—to hate 'em. I git up at half-past four in the morning, and sit up till twelve at night, to hate 'em."

Emancipation proved the most bitter pill for white Southerners to swallow, especially the planter elite. Conquered and degraded, and in their view robbed of their slave property, white people responded by regarding African Americans more than ever as inferior to themselves. Emancipation, however, forced white people to redefine their world. The specter of political power and social equality for African Americans made racial order the consuming passion of most white Southerners during the Reconstruction years. In fact, racism can be seen as one of the major forces driving Reconstruction and, ultimately, undermining it.

Abraham Lincoln's Plan

By late 1863, Union military victories had convinced President Lincoln of the need to fashion a plan for the reconstruction of the South (see Chapter 16). Lincoln based his reconstruction program on bringing the seceded states back into the Union as quickly as possible. His Proclamation of Amnesty and Reconstruction of December 1863 offered "full pardon" and the restoration of property, not including slaves, to white Southerners willing to swear an oath of allegiance to the United States and its laws, including the Emancipation Proclamation. Prominent Confederate military and civil leaders were excluded from Lincoln's offer, though he indicated that he would freely pardon them.

The president also proposed that when the number of any Confederate state's voters who took the oath of allegiance reached 10 percent of the number who had voted in the election of 1860, this group could establish a state government that Lincoln would recognize as legitimate. Fundamental to this Ten Percent Plan was acceptance by the reconstructed governments of the abolition of slavery. Lincoln's plan was designed less as a blueprint for Reconstruction than as a way to shorten the war and gain white people's support for emancipation.

Lincoln's amnesty proclamation angered those Republicans—known as Radical Republicans—who advocated not only equal rights for the freedmen but a tougher stance toward the white South. In July 1864, Senator Benjamin F. Wade of Ohio and Congressman Henry W. Davis of Maryland, both Radicals, proposed a harsher alternative to the Ten Percent Plan. The Wade-Davis bill required 50 percent of a seceding state's white male citizens to take a loyalty oath before elections could be held for a convention to rewrite the state's constitution. The Radical Republicans saw Reconstruction as a chance to effect a fundamental transformation of southern society. They thus wanted to delay the process until war's end and to limit participation to a small number of southern Unionists. Lincoln viewed Reconstruction as part of the larger effort to win the war and abolish slavery. He wanted to weaken the Confederacy by creating new state governments that could win broad support from southern white people. The Wade-Davis bill threatened his efforts to build political consensus within the southern states, and Lincoln, therefore, pocket-vetoed it, by refusing to sign it within ten days of the adjournment of Congress.

As Union armies occupied parts of the South, commanders had improvised a variety of arrangements involving confiscated plantations and the African American labor force. For example, in 1862 General Benjamin F. Butler began a policy of transforming slaves on Louisiana sugar plantations into wage laborers under the close supervision of occupying federal troops. Butler's policy required slaves to remain on the estates of loyal planters, where they would receive wages according to a fixed schedule, as well as food and medical care for the aged and sick. Abandoned plantations would be leased to northern investors.

In January 1865, General William T. Sherman issued Special Field Order 15, setting aside the Sea Islands off the Georgia coast and a portion of the South Carolina low-country rice fields for the exclusive settlement of freed people. Each family would receive forty acres of land and the loan of mules from the army—the origin, perhaps, of the famous call for "forty acres and a mule" that would soon capture the imagination of African Americans throughout the South. Sherman's intent was not to revolutionize southern society but to relieve the demands placed on his army by the thousands of impoverished African Americans who followed his march to the sea. By the summer of 1865 some 40,000 freed people, eager to take advantage of the general's order, had been settled on 400,000 acres of "Sherman land."

Conflicts within the Republican Party prevented the development of a systematic land distribution program. Still, Lincoln and the Republican Congress supported other measures to aid the emancipated slaves. In March 1865 Congress established the Freedmen's Bureau. Along with providing food, clothing, and fuel to destitute former slaves, the bureau was charged with supervising and managing "all the abandoned lands in the South and the control of all subjects relating to refugees and freedmen." The act that established the bureau also stated that forty acres of abandoned or confiscated land could be leased to freed slaves or white Unionists, who would have an option to purchase after three years and "such title thereto as the United States can convey."

On April 14, 1865, white attending the theater in Washington, President Lincoln was shot by John Wilkes Booth. At the time of his assassination, Lincoln's Reconstruction policy remained unsettled and incomplete. In its broad outlines the president's plans had seemed to favor a speedy restoration of the southern states to the Union and a minimum of federal intervention in their affairs. But with his death the specifics of postwar Reconstruction had to be hammered out by a new president, Andrew Johnson of Tennessee, a man whose personality, political background, and racist leanings put him at odds with the Republican-controlled Congress.

Andrew Johnson and Presidential Reconstruction

Andrew Johnson, a Democrat and former slaveholder, was a most unlikely successor to the martyred Lincoln. By trade a tailor, educated by his wife, Johnson overcame his impoverished background and served as state legislator, governor, and U.S. senator. Throughout his career Johnson had championed yeoman farmers and viewed the South's plantation aristocrats with contempt.

In 1864 the Republicans, in an appeal to northern and border state "War Democrats," nominated Johnson for vice president. But despite Johnson's success in Tennessee and in the 1864 campaign, many Radical Republicans distrusted him. In the immediate aftermath of Lincoln's murder, however, Johnson appeared to side with those Radical Republicans who sought to treat the South as a conquered province. But support for Johnson quickly faded as the new president's policies unfolded. Johnson defined Reconstruction as the province of the executive, not the legislative branch, and he planned to restore the Union as quickly as possible. He blamed individual Southerners—the planter elite—rather than entire states for leading the South down the disastrous road to secession.

In the spring of 1865 Johnson granted amnesty and pardon, including restoration of property rights except slaves, to all Confederates who pledged loyalty to the Union and support for emancipation. Fourteen classes of Southerners, mostly major Confederate officials and wealthy landowners, were excluded. But these men could apply individually for presidential pardons. During his tenure Johnson pardoned roughly 90 percent of those who applied. Significantly, he instituted this plan while Congress was not in session. Johnson also appointed provisional governors for seven of the former Confederate states and set highly favorable terms for readmission in the Union. By the fall of 1865 ten of the eleven Confederate states claimed to have met Johnson's requirements to reenter the Union.

Andrew Johnson used the term "restoration" rather than "reconstruction." A lifelong Democrat with ambitions to be elected president on his own in 1868, Johnson hoped to build a new political coalition composed of northern Democrats, conservative Republicans, and southern Unionists. Firmly committed to white supremacy, he opposed political rights for the freedmen. Johnson's open sympathy for his fellow white Southerners, his antiblack bias, and his determination to control the course of Reconstruction placed him on a collision course with the powerful Radical wing of the Republican Party.

The Radical Republican Vision

Most Radicals were men whose careers had been shaped by the slavery controversy. At the core of their thinking lay a deep belief in equal political rights and

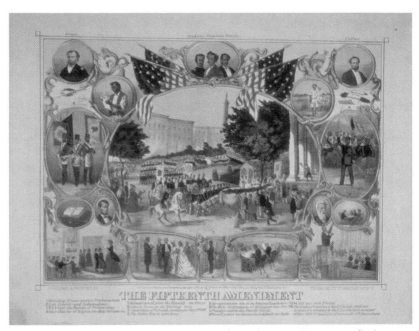

The Fifteenth Amendment, 1870. The Fifteenth Amendment, ratified in 1870, stipulated that the right to vote could not be denied "on account of race, color, or previous condition of servitude." This illustration expressed the optimism and hopes of African Americans generated by this Constitutional landmark aimed at protecting black political rights. Note the various political figures (Abraham Lincoln, John Brown, Frederick Douglass) and movements (abolitionism, black education) invoked here, providing a sense of how the amendment culminated a long historical struggle.

SOURCE: Courtesy of the Library of Congress.

equal economic opportunity, both guaranteed by a powerful national government. They argued that once free labor, universal education, and equal rights were implanted in the South, that region would be able to share in the North's material wealth, progress, and fluid social mobility.

In the Radicals' view, the power of the federal government would be central to the remaking of southern society, especially in guaranteeing civil rights and suffrage for freedmen. In the most far-reaching proposal, Representative Thaddeus Stevens of Pennsylvania called for the confiscation of 400 million acres belonging to the wealthiest 10 percent of Southerners to be redistributed to black and white yeomen and northern land buyers. "The whole fabric of southern society must be changed," Stevens told Pennsylvania Republicans in September 1865, "and never can it be done if this opportunity is lost. How can republican institutions, free schools, free churches, free social intercourse exist in a mingled community of nabobs and serfs? If the South is ever to be made a safe republic let her lands be cultivated by the toil of the owners."

Northern Republicans were especially outraged by the stringent "black codes" passed by South Carolina, Mississippi, Louisiana, and other states. These were designed to restrict the freedom of the black labor force and keep freed people as close to slave status as possible. Laborers who left their jobs before contracts expired would forfeit wages already earned and be subject to arrest by any white citizen. Vagrancy, very broadly defined, was punishable by fines and involuntary plantation labor. Apprenticeship clauses obliged black children to work without pay for employers. Some states attempted to bar African Americans from land ownership. Other laws specifically denied African Americans equality with white people in civil rights, excluding them from juries and prohibiting interracial marriages.

The black codes underscored the unwillingness of white Southerners to accept the full meaning of freedom for African Americans. The Radicals, although not a majority of their party, were joined by moderate Republicans as growing numbers of Northerners grew suspicious of white southern intransigence and the denial of political rights to freedmen. When the Thirty-ninth Congress convened in December 1865, the large Republican majority prevented the seating of the white Southerners elected to Congress under President Johnson's provisional state governments. Republicans also established the Joint Committee on Reconstruction. After hearing extensive testimony from a broad range of witnesses, it concluded that not only were old Confederates back in power in the South but that black codes and racial violence required increased protection for African Americans.

As a result, in the spring of 1866, Congress passed two important bills designed to aid African Americans.

The landmark Civil Rights bill, which bestowed full citizenship on African Americans, overturned the 1857 *Dred Scott* decision and the black codes. It defined all persons born in the United States (except Indian peoples) as national citizens, and it enumerated various rights, including the rights to make and enforce contracts, to sue, to give evidence, and to buy and sell property. Under this bill, African Americans acquired "full and equal benefit of all laws and proceedings for the security of person and property as is enjoyed by white citizens."

Congress also voted to enlarge the scope of the Freedmen's Bureau, empowering it to build schools and pay teachers, and also to establish courts to prosecute those charged with depriving African Americans of their civil rights. The bureau achieved important, if limited, success in aiding African Americans. Bureau-run schools helped lay the foundation for southern public education. The bureau's network of courts allowed freed people to bring suits against white people in disputes involving violence, nonpayment of wages, or unfair division of crops. The very existence of courts hearing public testimony by African Americans provided an important psychological challenge to traditional notions of white racial domination.

An angry President Johnson vetoed both of these bills. But his intemperate attacks on the Radicals—he damned them as traitors unwilling to restore the Union—united moderate and Radical Republicans and they succeeded in overriding the vetoes. Congressional Republicans, led by the Radical faction, were now unified in challenging the president's power to direct Reconstruction and in using national authority to define and protect the rights of citizens.

In June 1866, fearful that the Civil Rights Act might be declared unconstitutional and eager to settle the basis for the seating of southern representatives, Congress passed the Fourteenth Amendment. The amendment defined national citizenship to include former slaves ("all persons born or naturalized in the United States") and prohibited the states from violating the privileges of citizens without due process of law. It also empowered Congress to reduce the representation of any state that denied the suffrage to males over twenty-one. Republicans adopted the Fourteenth Amendment as their platform for the 1866 congressional elections and suggested that southern states would have to ratify it as a condition of readmission. President Johnson, meanwhile, took to the stump in August to support conservative Democratic and Republican candidates. His unrestrained speeches often degenerated into harangues, alienating many voters and aiding the Republican cause.

For their part, the Republicans began an effective campaign tradition known as "waving the bloody shirt"—reminding northern voters of the hundreds of thousands of Yankee soldiers left dead or maimed by the war. In the November 1866 elections, the Republicans increased their majority in both the House and the Senate and gained control of all the northern states. The stage was now set for a battle between the president and Congress. Was it to be Johnson's "restoration" or Congressional Reconstruction?

Congressional Reconstruction and the Impeachment Crisis

United against Johnson, Radical and moderate Republicans took control of Reconstruction early in 1867. In March, Congress passed the First Reconstruction Act over Johnson's veto. This act divided the South into five military districts subject to martial law. To achieve restoration, southern states were first required to call new constitutional conventions, elected by universal manhood suffrage. Once these states had drafted new constitutions, guaranteed African American voting rights, and ratified the Fourteenth Amendment, they were eligible for readmission to the Union.

Congress also passed several laws aimed at limiting Johnson's power. One of these, the Tenure of Office Act, stipulated that any officeholder appointed by the president with the Senate's advice and consent could not be removed until the Senate had approved a successor. In this way, congressional leaders could protect Republicans, such as Secretary of War Edwin M. Stanton, entrusted with implementing Congressional Reconstruction. In August 1867, with Congress adjourned, Johnson suspended Stanton and appointed General Ulysses S. Grant interim secretary of war. This move enabled the president to remove generals in the field that he judged to be too radical and replace them with men who were sympathetic to his own views. It also served as a challenge to the Tenure of Office Act. In January 1868, when the Senate overruled Stanton's suspension, Grant broke openly with Johnson and vacated the office. Stanton resumed his position and barricaded himself in his office when Johnson attempted to remove him once again.

Outraged by Johnson's relentless obstructionism, and seizing upon his violation of the Tenure of Office Act as a pretext, Radical and moderate Republicans in the House of Representatives again joined forces and voted to impeach the president by a vote of 126 to 47 on February 24, 1868, charging him with eleven counts of high crimes and misdemeanors. To ensure the support of moderate Republicans, the articles of impeachment focused on violations of the Tenure of Office Act, leaving unstated the Republicans' real reasons for wanting the president removed: Johnson's political views and his opposition to the Reconstruction Acts.

Reconstruction of the South, 1866–1877 Dates for the readmission of former Confederate states to the Union and the return of Democrats to power varied according to the specific political situations in those states.

An influential group of moderate Senate Republicans feared the damage a conviction might do to the constitutional separation of powers. They also worried about the political and economic policies that might be pursued by Benjamin Wade, the president pro tem of the Senate and a leader of the Radical Republicans, who, because there was no vice president, would succeed to the presidency if Johnson were removed from office. Behind the scenes during his Senate trial, Johnson agreed to abide by the Reconstruction Acts. In May, the Senate voted 35 for conviction, 19 for acquittal—one vote shy of the two-thirds necessary for removal from office. Johnson's narrow acquittal established the precedent that only criminal actions by a president—not political disagreements—warranted removal from office.

The Election of 1868

By the summer of 1868, seven former Confederate states (Alabama, Arkansas, Florida, Louisiana, North Carolina, South Carolina, and Tennessee) had ratified the revised constitutions, elected Republican governments, and ratified the Fourteenth Amendment. They had thereby earned readmission to the Union. Though Georgia, Mississippi, Texas, and Virginia still awaited readmission, the presidential election of 1868 offered some hope that the Civil War's legacy of sectional hate and racial tension might finally ease.

Republicans nominated Ulysses S. Grant, the North's foremost military hero. Grant enjoyed tremendous popularity after the war, especially when he broke with Johnson. Totally lacking in political experience, Grant admitted after receiving the nomination that he had been forced into it in spite of himself.

Significantly, at the very moment that the South was being forced to enfranchise former slaves as a prerequisite for readmission to the Union, the Republicans rejected a campaign plank endorsing black suffrage in the North. Their platform left "the question of suffrage in all the loyal States . . . to the people of those States." State referendums calling for black suffrage failed in eight northern states between 1865 and 1868, succeeding only in Iowa and Minnesota. The Democrats, determined to reverse Congressional Reconstruction, nominated Horatio Seymour, former governor of New York and a longtime foe of emancipation and supporter of states' rights.

The Ku Klux Klan, founded as a Tennessee social club in 1866, threatened, whipped, and murdered black and white Republicans to prevent them from voting. This terrorism enabled the Democrats to carry Georgia and Louisiana, but it ultimately cost the Democrats votes in the North. In the final tally, Grant carried twenty-six of the thirty-four states for an electoral college victory of 214 to 80. But he received a popular majority of less than 53 percent, beating Seymour by only 306,000 votes. Significantly, more than 500,000 African American voters cast their ballots for Grant, demonstrating their overwhelming support for the Republican Party. The Republicans also retained large majorities in both houses of Congress.

In February 1869, Congress passed the Fifteenth Amendment, providing that "the right of citizens of the United States to vote shall not be denied or abridged . . . on account of race, color, or previous condition of servitude." To enhance the chances of ratification, Congress required the three remaining unreconstructed states—Mississippi, Texas, and Virginia—to ratify both the Fourteenth and Fifteenth Amendments before readmission. They did so and rejoined the Union in early 1870. The Fifteenth Amendment was ratified in February 1870. In the narrow sense of simply readmitting the former Confederate states to the Union, Reconstruction was complete.

Woman Suffrage and Reconstruction

Many women's rights advocates had long been active in the abolitionist movement. The Fourteenth and Fifteenth Amendments, which granted citizenship and the vote to freedmen, both inspired and frustrated these activists. For example, Elizabeth Cady Stanton and Susan B. Anthony, two leaders with long involvement in both

---

OVERVIEW

RECONSTRUCTION AMENDMENTS TO THE CONSTITUTION, 1865–1870

Amendment and Date Passed by Congress	Main Provisions	Ratification Process (3/4 of all states including ex-Confederate states required)
13 (January 1865)	Prohibited slavery in the United States	December 1865 (27 states, including 8 southern states)
14 (June 1866)	• Conferred national citizenship on all persons born or naturalized in the United States • Reduced state representation in Congress proportionally for any state disfranchising male citizens • Denied former Confederates the right to hold state or national office • Repudiated Confederate debt	July 1868 (after Congress makes ratification a prerequisite for readmission of ex-Confederate states to the Union)
15 (February 1869)	Prohibited denial of suffrage because of race, color, or previous condition of servitude	March 1870 (ratification required for readmission of Virginia, Texas, Mississippi, and Georgia)

Susan B. Anthony (1820–1906) and Elizabeth Cady Stanton (1815–1902), the two most influential leaders of the woman suffrage movement, ca. 1892. Anthony and Stanton broke with their longtime abolitionist allies after the Civil War when they opposed the Fifteenth Amendment. They argued that the doctrine of universal manhood suffrage it embodied would give constitutional authority to the claim that men were the social and political superiors of women. As founders of the militant National Woman Suffrage Association, Stanton and Anthony established an independent woman suffrage movement with a broader spectrum of goals for women's rights and drew millions of women into public life during the late nineteenth century.

SOURCE: The Susan B. Anthony House, Rochester, NY.

the antislavery and feminist movements, objected to the inclusion of the word "male" in the Fourteenth Amendment. "If that word 'male' be inserted," Stanton predicted in 1866, "it will take us a century at least to get it out."

Insisting that the causes of the African American vote and the women's vote were linked, Stanton, Anthony, and Lucy Stone founded the American Equal Rights Association in 1866. The group launched a series of lobbying and petition campaigns to remove racial and sexual restrictions on voting from state constitutions. Throughout the nation, the old abolitionist organiza-

tions and the Republican Party emphasized passage of the Fourteenth and Fifteenth Amendments and withdrew funds and support from the cause of woman suffrage. Disagreements over these amendments divided suffragists for decades.

The radical wing, led by Stanton and Anthony, opposed the Fifteenth Amendment, arguing that ratification would establish an "aristocracy of sex," enfranchising all men while leaving women without political privileges. They argued for a Sixteenth Amendment that would secure the vote for women. Other women's rights activists, including Lucy Stone and Frederick Douglass, asserted that "this hour belongs to the Negro." They feared a debate over woman suffrage at the national level would jeopardize passage of the two amendments.

By 1869 woman suffragists had split into two competing organizations: the moderate American Woman Suffrage Association (AWSA), which sought the support of men, and the more radical all-female National Woman Suffrage Association (NWSA). For the NWSA, the vote represented only one part of a broad spectrum of goals inherited from the Declaration of Sentiments manifesto adopted at the first women's rights convention held in 1848 at Seneca Falls, New York (see Chapter 13).

Although women did not win the vote in this period, they did establish an independent suffrage movement that eventually drew millions of women into political life. The NWSA in particular demonstrated that self-government and democratic participation in the public sphere were crucial for women's emancipation. The failure of woman suffrage after the Civil War was less a result of factional fighting than of the larger defeat of Radical Reconstruction and the ideal of expanded citizenship.

THE MEANING OF FREEDOM

The deep desire for independence from white control formed the underlying aspiration of newly freed slaves. For their part, most southern white people sought to restrict the boundaries of that independence. As individuals and as members of communities transformed by emancipation, former slaves struggled to establish economic, political, and cultural autonomy. They built on the twin pillars of slave culture—the family and the church—to consolidate and expand African American institutions and thereby laid the foundation for the modern African American community.

Emancipation greatly expanded the choices available to African Americans. It helped build confidence in their ability to effect change without deferring to white people. Freedom also meant greater uncertainty and risk. But the vast majority of African Americans were more than willing to take their chances.

Moving About

The first impulse of many emancipated slaves was to test their freedom. The simplest, most obvious way to do this involved leaving home. By walking off a plantation, coming and going without restraint or fear of punishment, African Americans could savor freedom. Throughout the summer and fall of 1865, observers in the South noted enormous numbers of freed people on the move.

Yet many who left their old neighborhoods returned soon afterward to seek work in the general vicinity, or even on the plantation they had left. Many wanted to separate themselves from former owners but not from familial ties and friendships. Others moved away altogether, seeking jobs in nearby towns and cities. Many former slaves left predominantly white counties, where they felt more vulnerable and isolated, for new lives in the relative comfort of predominantly black communities. Many African Americans, attracted by schools, churches, and fraternal societies as well as the army, preferred the city. Between 1865 and 1870, the African American population of the South's ten largest cities doubled, while the white population increased by only 10 percent.

Disgruntled planters had difficulty accepting African American independence. During slavery, they had expected obedience, submission, and loyalty from African Americans. Now many could not understand why so many former slaves wanted to leave despite urgent pleas to continue working at the old place. Many freed people went out of their way to reject the old subservience. Moving about freely was one way of doing this, as was refusing to tip one's hat to white people, ignoring former masters or mistresses in the streets, and refusing to step aside on sidewalks. After encountering an African American who would not step aside, Eliza Andrews, a Georgia plantation mistress, complained, "It is the first time in my life that I have ever had to give up the sidewalk to a man, much less to negroes!" When freed people staged parades, dances, and picnics to celebrate their new freedom, as they did, for example, when commemorating the Emancipation Proclamation, white people invariably condemned them angrily for "insolence," "outrageous spectacles," or "putting on airs."

The African American Family

Emancipation allowed freed people to strengthen family ties. For many former slaves, freedom meant the opportunity to reunite with long-lost family members. To track down relatives, freed people trekked to faraway places, put ads in newspapers, sought the help of Freedmen's Bureau agents, and questioned anyone who might have information about loved ones. Many thousands of family reunions, each with its own story, took place after the war.

Thousands of African American couples who had lived together under slavery streamed to military and civilian authorities and demanded to be legally married. By 1870, the two-parent household was the norm for a large majority of African Americans.

Emancipation brought changes to gender roles within the African American family as well. Black men could now serve on juries, vote and hold office; black women, like their white counterparts, could not. Freedmen's Bureau agents designated the husband as household head and established lower wage scales for women laborers. African American editors, preachers, and politicians regularly quoted the biblical injunction that wives submit to their husbands.

African American men asserted their male authority, denied under slavery, by insisting their

An overflow congregation crowds into Richmond's First African Baptist Church in 1874. Despite their poverty, freed people struggled to save, buy land, and erect new buildings as they organized hundreds of new black churches during Reconstruction. As the most important African American institution outside the family, the black church, in addition to tending to spiritual needs, played a key role in the educational and political life of the community.

SOURCE: The Granger Collection.

wives work at home instead of in the fields. Yet African American women continued to work outside the home, engaging in seasonal field labor for wages or working a family's rented plot. Most rural black families barely eked out a living and, thus, the labor of every family member was essential to survival. The key difference from slave times was that African American families themselves, not white masters and overseers, decided when and where women and children worked.

African American Churches and Schools

The creation of separate African American churches proved the most lasting and important element of the energetic institution building that went on in postemancipation years. Before the Civil War, southern Protestant churches had relegated slaves and free African Americans to second-class membership. Black worshipers were required to sit in the back during services, they were denied any role in church governance, and they were excluded from Sunday schools. Even in larger cities, where all-black congregations sometimes built their own churches, the law required white pastors. In rural areas, slaves preferred their own preachers to the sermons of local white ministers who quoted Scripture to justify slavery and white supremacy.

In communities around the South, African Americans now pooled their resources to buy land and build their own churches. Before these structures were completed, they might hold services in a railroad boxcar, where Atlanta's First Baptist Church began, or in an outdoor arbor, the original site of the First Baptist Church of Memphis. By late 1866 Charleston's African American community could boast of eleven churches in the city—five Methodist, two Presbyterian, two Episcopalian, one Baptist, and one Congregational. In rural areas, different denominations frequently shared the same church building. Churches became the center not only for religious life but for many other activities that defined the African American community: schools, picnics, festivals, and political meetings. They also helped spawn a host of organizations devoted to benevolence and mutual aid, such as burial societies, Masonic lodges, temperance clubs, and trade associations.

The church became the first social institution fully controlled by African Americans. In nearly every community ministers, respected for their speaking and organizational skills, were among the most influential leaders. By 1877 the great majority of black Southerners had withdrawn from white-dominated churches and belonged to black Baptist or Methodist churches.

African American communities received important educational aid from outside organizations. By 1869 the Freedmen's Bureau was supervising nearly 3,000 schools serving over 150,000 students throughout the South.

Over half the roughly 3,300 teachers in these schools were African Americans, many of whom had been free before the Civil War. Other teachers included dedicated northern white women volunteers. Throughout the South in 1865 and 1866, African Americans raised money to build schoolhouses, buy supplies, and pay teachers. Black artisans donated labor for construction, and black families offered room and board to teachers.

Land and Labor after Slavery

Most newly emancipated African Americans aspired to quit the plantations and to make new lives for themselves. Leaving the plantation was not as simple as walking off. Some freed people did find jobs in railroad building, mining, ranching, or construction work. Others raised subsistence crops and tended vegetable gardens as squatters. The majority hoped to become self-sufficient farmers. Many former slaves believed they were entitled to the land they had worked throughout their lives. General Oliver O. Howard, chief commissioner of the Freedmen's Bureau, observed that many "supposed that the Government [would] divide among them the lands of the conquered owners, and furnish them with all that might be necessary to begin life as an independent farmer." This perception was not merely a wishful fantasy. Frequent reference in the Congress and the press to the question of land distribution made the idea of "forty acres and a mule" not just a pipe dream but a matter of serious public debate.

Above all, African Americans sought economic autonomy, and ownership of land promised the most independence. "Give us our own land and we take care of ourselves," was how one former slave saw it. "But widout land, de ole massas can hire us or starve us, as dey please." At the Colored Convention in Montgomery, Alabama, in May 1867, delegates argued that the property now owned by planters had been "nearly all earned by the sweat of our brows, not theirs. It has been forfeited to the government by the treason of its owners, and is liable to be confiscated whenever the Republican Party demands it." But by 1866 the federal government had already pulled back from the various wartime experiments involving the breaking up of large plantations and the leasing of small plots to individual families. President Johnson directed General Howard of the Freedmen's Bureau to evict tens of thousands of freed people settled on confiscated and abandoned land in southeastern Virginia, southern Louisiana, and the Georgia and South Carolina low country. These evictions created a deep sense of betrayal among African Americans. A former Mississippi slave, Merrimon Howard, bitterly noted that African Americans had been left with "no land, no house, not so much as a place to lay our head. . . . We were friends on the

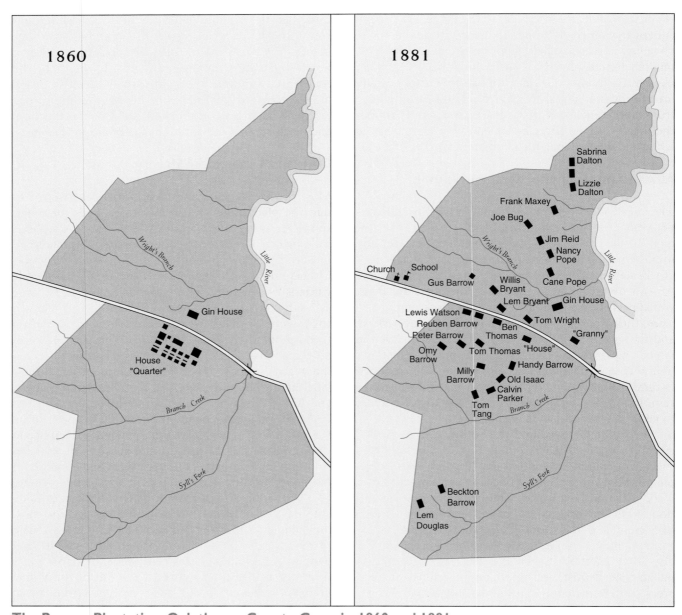

The Barrow Plantation, Oglethorpe County, Georgia, 1860 and 1881 (approx. 2,000 acres) These two maps, based on drawings from *Scribner's Monthly*, April 1881, show some of the changes brought by emancipation. In 1860 the plantation's entire black population lived in the communal slave quarters, right next to the white master's house. In 1881 black sharecropper and tenant families lived on individual plots, spread out across the land. The former slaves had also built their own school and church.

march, brothers on the battlefield, but in the peaceful pursuits of life it seems that we are strangers."

By the late 1860s, sharecropping, had emerged as the dominant form of working the land. Sharecropping represented a compromise between planters and former slaves. Under sharecropping arrangements, individual families contracted with landowners to be responsible for a specific plot. Large plantations were thus broken into family-sized farms. Generally, sharecropper families received one-third of the year's crop if

the owner furnished implements, seed, and draft animals, or one-half if they provided their own supplies. African Americans preferred sharecropping to gang labor, as it allowed families to set their own hours and tasks and offered freedom from white supervision and control. For planters, the system stabilized the workforce by requiring sharecroppers to remain until the harvest and to employ all family members. It also offered a way around the chronic shortage of cash and credit that plagued the postwar South.

By 1880 about 80 percent of the land in the black belt states—Mississippi, Alabama, and Georgia—had been divided into family-sized farms. Nearly three-quarters of black Southerners were sharecroppers. Through much of the black belt, family and community were one. Often several families worked adjoining parcels of land in common, pooling their labor in order to get by. Men usually oversaw crop production. Women went to the fields seasonally during planting or harvesting, but they mainly tended to household chores and child care. In addition, women frequently held jobs that might bring in cash, such as raising chickens or taking in laundry. The cotton harvest engaged all members of the community, from the oldest to the youngest.

The Origins of African American Politics

Inclusion rather than separation was the objective of early African American political activity. In 1865 and 1866, African Americans throughout the South organized scores of mass meetings, parades, and petitions that demanded civil equality and the right to vote. In the cities, the growing web of churches and fraternal societies helped bolster early efforts at political organization.

Hundreds of African American delegates, selected by local meetings or churches, attended statewide political conventions held throughout the South in 1865 and 1866. Previously free African Americans, as well as black ministers, artisans, and veterans of the Union army, tended to dominate these proceedings, setting a pattern that would hold throughout Reconstruction. Convention debates sometimes reflected the tensions within African American communities, such as friction between poorer former slaves and better-off free black people, or between lighter- and darker-skinned African Americans. But most of these state gatherings concentrated on passing resolutions on issues that united all African Americans. The central concerns were suffrage and equality before the law.

The passage of the First Reconstruction Act in 1867 encouraged even more political activity among African Americans. The military started registering the South's electorate, ultimately enrolling approximately 735,000 black and 635,000 white voters in the ten unreconstructed states. Five states—Alabama, Florida, Louisiana, Mississippi, and South Carolina—had black electoral majorities. Fewer than half the registered white voters participated in the elections for state constitutional conventions in 1867 and 1868. In contrast, four-fifths of the registered black voters cast ballots in these elections. Much of this new African American political activism was channeled through local Union League chapters throughout the South.

Begun during the war as a northern, largely white middle-class patriotic club, the Union League now be-

W. L. Sheppard, "Electioneering at the South," *Harper's Weekly*, July 25, 1868. Throughout the Reconstruction-era South, newly freed slaves took a keen interest in both local and national political affairs. The presence of women and children at these campaign gatherings illustrates the importance of contemporary political issues to the entire African American community.

SOURCE: Library of Congress.

came the political voice of the former slaves. Union League chapters brought together local African Americans, soldiers, and Freedmen's Bureau agents to demand the vote and an end to legal discrimination against African Americans. It brought out African American voters, instructed freedmen in the rights and duties of citizenship, and promoted Republican candidates.

In 1867 and 1868, the promise of Radical Reconstruction enlarged the scope of African American political participation and brought new leaders to the fore. Many were teachers, preachers, or others with useful skills, such as literacy. For most ordinary African Americans, politics was inseparable from economic issues, especially the land question. Grass-roots political organizations frequently intervened in local disputes with planters over the terms of labor contracts. African American political groups closely followed the congressional debates over Reconstruction policy and agitated for land confiscation and distribution. Perhaps most important, politics was the only arena where black and white Southerners might engage each other on an equal basis.

SOUTHERN POLITICS AND SOCIETY

By the summer of 1868, when the South had returned to the Union, the majority of Republicans believed the task of Reconstruction to be finished. Ultimately, they put their faith in a political solution to the problems facing the vanquished South. That meant nurturing a viable two-party system in the southern states, where no Republican Party had ever existed. If that could be accomplished, Republicans and Democrats would compete for votes, offices, and influence, just as they did in northern states.

Yet over the next decade the political structure created in the southern states proved too restricted and fragile to sustain itself. Federal troops were needed to protect Republican governments and their supporters from violent opposition. Congressional action to monitor southern elections and protect black voting rights became routine. Despite initial successes, southern Republicanism proved an unstable coalition of often conflicting elements, unable to sustain effective power for very long. By 1877, Democrats had regained political control of all the former Confederate states.

Southern Republicans

Three major groups composed the fledgling Republican coalition in the postwar South. The first group, African American voters, made up a large majority of southern Republicans throughout the Reconstruction era.

The second group consisted of white Northerners, derisively called "carpetbaggers" by native white Southerners. Most carpetbaggers combined a desire for personal gain with a commitment to reform the "unprogressive" South by developing its material resources and introducing Yankee institutions such as free labor and free public schools. Most were veterans of the Union army who stayed in the South after the war. Others included Freedmen's Bureau agents and businessmen who had invested capital in cotton plantations and other enterprises. Although they made up a tiny percentage of the population, carpetbaggers played a disproportionately large role in southern politics. They won a large share of Reconstruction offices, particularly in Florida, South Carolina, and Louisiana and in areas with large African American constituencies.

The third major group of southern Republicans were the native whites pejoratively termed "scalawags." They had even more diverse backgrounds and motives than the northern-born Republicans. Loyalists during the war and traditional enemies of the planter elite (most were small farmers), these white Southerners looked to the Republican Party for help in settling old scores and relief from debt and wartime devastation.

Deep contradictions strained the alliance of these three groups. Southern Republicans touted themselves as the "party of progress and civilization" and promised a new era of material progress for the region. Republican state conventions in 1867 and 1868 voiced support for internal improvements, public schools, debt relief, and railroad building. Yet few white Southerners iden-

tified with the political and economic aspirations of African Americans. Moderate elements more concerned with maintaining white control of the party, and to ecouraging economic investment in the region, outnumbered and defeated "confiscation radicals" who focused on obtaining land for African Americans.

Reconstructing the States: A Mixed Record

With the old Confederate leaders barred from political participation, and with carpetbaggers and newly enfranchised African Americans representing many of the plantation districts, Republicans managed to dominate the ten southern constitutional conventions of 1867–69. Most of these conventions produced constitutions that expanded democracy and the public role of the state. The new documents guaranteed the political and civil rights of African Americans, and they abolished property qualifications for officeholding and jury service, as well as imprisonment for debt. They created the first state-funded systems of education in the South, to be administered by state commissioners. The new constitutions also mandated establishment of orphanages, penitentiaries, and homes for the insane. In 1868, only three years after the end of the war, Republicans came to power in most of the southern states. By 1869, new constitutions had been ratified in all the old Confederate states. "These constitutions and governments," one South Carolina Democratic newspaper vowed bitterly, "will last just as long as the bayonets which ushered them into being, shall keep them in existence, and not one day longer."

Republican governments in the South faced a continual crisis of legitimacy that limited their ability to legislate change. They had to balance reform against the need to gain acceptance, especially by white Southerners. Their achievements were thus mixed. In the realm of race relations there was a clear thrust toward equal rights and against discrimination. Republican legislatures followed up the federal Civil Rights Act of 1866 with various antidiscrimination clauses in new constitutions and laws prescribing harsh penalties for civil rights violations. African Americans could now be employed in police forces and fire departments, serve on juries, school boards, and city councils, and they could hold public office at all levels of government.

Segregation, though, became the norm in public school systems. African American leaders often accepted segregation because they feared that insistence on integrated education would jeopardize funding for the new school systems. African Americans opposed constitutional language requiring racial segregation in schools; most African Americans were less interested in the abstract ideal of integrated education than in ensuring educational opportunities for their children and employment for African American teachers.

Segregation in railroad cars and other public places was more objectionable to African Americans. By the early 1870s, as black influence and assertiveness grew, laws guaranteeing equal access to transportation and public accommodation were passed in many states. By and large, though, such civil rights laws were difficult to enforce in local communities.

In economic matters, Republican governments failed to fulfill African Americans' hopes of obtaining land. Few former slaves possessed the cash to buy land in the open market, and they looked to the state for help. Republicans tried to weaken the plantation system and promote black ownership by raising taxes on land. Yet even when state governments seized land for nonpayment of taxes, the property was never used to help create black homesteads.

Republican leaders envisioned promoting northern-style capitalist development—factories, large towns, and diversified agriculture—through state aid. Much Republican state lawmaking was devoted to encouraging railroad construction. Between 1868 and 1872 the southern railroad system was rebuilt and over 3,000 new miles of track added, an increase of almost 40 percent. But in spite of all the new laws, it proved impossible to attract significant amounts of northern and European investment capital. The obsession with railroads withdrew resources from education and other programs. As in the North, it also opened the doors to widespread corruption and bribery of public officials. Railroad failures eroded public confidence in the Republicans' ability to govern. The "gospel of prosperity" ultimately failed to modernize the economy or solidify the Republican Party in the South.

White Resistance and "Redemption"

The emergence of a Republican Party in the reconstructed South brought two parties but not a two-party system to the region. The opponents of Reconstruction, the Democrats, refused to acknowledge Republicans' right to participate in southern political life. In their view, the Republican Party, supported primarily by the votes of former slaves, was the partisan instrument of the northern Congress. Since Republicans controlled state governments, this denial of legitimacy meant, in effect, a rejection of state authority itself.

From 1870 to 1872 the Ku Klux Klan fought an ongoing terrorist campaign against Reconstruction governments and local leaders. Although not centrally organized, the Klan was a powerful presence in nearly every southern state. It acted as a kind of guerrilla military force in the service of the Democratic Party, the planter class, and all those who sought the restoration of white supremacy. In October 1870, after Republicans carried Laurens County in South Carolina, bands of white people drove 150 African Americans from their homes and murdered 13 black and white Republican activists. In March 1871, three African Americans were arrested in Meridian, Mississippi, for giving "incendiary" speeches. At their court hearing, Klansmen killed two of the defendants and the Republican judge, and thirty more African Americans were murdered in a day of rioting. The single bloodiest episode of Reconstruction era violence took place in Colfax, Louisiana, on Easter Sunday 1873. Nearly 100 African Americans were murdered after they failed to hold a besieged courthouse during a contested election.

Southern Republicans looked to Washington for help. In 1870 and 1871 Congress passed three Enforcement Acts designed to counter racial terrorism. These declared that interference with voting was a federal offense. The acts provided for federal supervision of voting, and authorized the president to send the army and to suspend the writ of habeas corpus in districts declared to be in a state of insurrection. The most sweeping measure was the Ku Klux Klan Act of April 1871, which made the violent infringement of civil and political rights a federal crime punishable by the national government. Attorney General Amos T. Akerman prosecuted hundreds of Klansmen in North Carolina and Mississippi. In October 1871 President Grant sent federal troops to occupy nine South Carolina counties and rounded up thousands of Klan members. By the election of 1872, the federal government's intervention had helped break the Klan and restore a semblance of law and order.

The Civil Rights Act of 1875 outlawed racial discrimination in theaters, hotels, railroads, and other public places. But the law proved more an assertion of principle than a direct federal intervention in southern affairs. Enforcement required African Americans to take their cases to the federal courts, a costly and time-consuming procedure.

As wartime idealism faded, northern Republicans became less inclined toward direct intervention in southern affairs. They had enough trouble retaining political control in the North. In 1874 the Democrats gained a majority in the House of Representatives for the first time since 1856. Key northern states also began to fall to the Democrats. Northern Republicans slowly abandoned the freedmen and their white allies in the South.

Gradually, conservative Democrats "redeemed" one state after another. Virginia and Tennessee led the way in 1869, North Carolina in 1870, Georgia in 1871, Texas in 1873, and Alabama and Arkansas in 1874. In Mississippi, white conservatives employed violence and intimidation to wrest control in 1875 and "redeemed" the state the following year. Republican infighting in Louisiana in 1873 and 1874 led to a series of

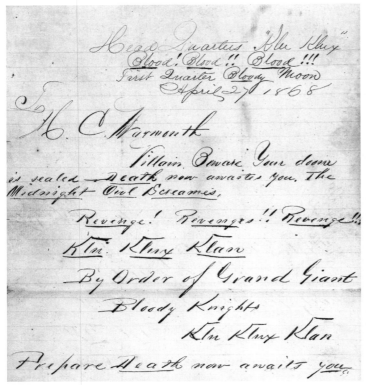

The Ku Klux Klan emerged as a potent political and social force during Reconstruction, terrorizing freed people and their white allies. An 1868 Klan warning threatens Louisiana governor Henry C. Warmoth with death. Warmoth, an Illinois-born "carpetbagger," was the state's first Republican governor. Two Alabama Klansmen, photographed in 1868, wear white hoods to hide their identities.

SOURCE: (a) University of North Carolina Southern Historical Collection; (b) Rutherford B. Hayes Presidential Center.

contested election results, including bloody clashes between black militia and armed whites, and finally to "redemption" by the Democrats in 1877. Once these states returned to Democratic rule, African Americans faced obstacles to voting, more stringent controls on plantation labor, and deep cuts in social services.

Several Supreme Court rulings involving the Fourteenth and Fifteenth Amendments effectively constrained federal protection of African American civil rights. In the so-called Slaughterhouse cases of 1873, the Court issued its first ruling on the Fourteenth Amendment. The cases involved a Louisiana charter that gave a New Orleans meat-packing company a monopoly over the city's butchering business on the grounds of protecting public health. A rival group of butchers had sued, claiming the law violated the Fourteenth Amendment, which prohibited states from depriving any person of life, liberty, or property without due process of law. The Court held that the Fourteenth Amendment protected only the former slaves, not butchers, and that it protected only national citizenship rights, not the regulatory powers of states. The ruling in effect denied the original

intent of the Fourteenth Amendment—to protect against state infringement of national citizenship rights as spelled out in the Bill of Rights.

Three other decisions curtailed federal protection of black civil rights. In *United States* v. *Reese* (1876) and *United States* v. *Cruikshank* (1876), the Court restricted congressional power to enforce the Ku Klux Klan Act. Future prosecution would depend on the states rather than on federal authorities. In these rulings the Court held that the Fourteenth Amendment extended the federal power to protect civil rights only in cases involving discrimination by states; discrimination by individuals or groups was not covered. The Court also ruled that the Fifteenth Amendment did not guarantee a citizen's right to vote; it only barred certain specific grounds for denying suffrage—"race, color, or previous condition of servitude." This interpretation opened the door for southern states to disfranchise African Americans for allegedly nonracial reasons. States back under Democratic control began to limit African American voting by passing laws restricting voter eligibility through poll taxes and property requirements.

Finally, in the 1883 Civil Rights Cases decision, the Court declared the Civil Rights Act of 1875 unconstitutional, holding that the Fourteenth Amendment gave Congress the power to outlaw discrimination by states, but not by private individuals. The majority opinion held that black people must no longer "be the special favorite of the laws." Together, these Supreme Court decisions marked the end of federal attempts to protect African American rights until well into the next century.

White Yeomen, White Merchants, and "King Cotton"

The Republicans' vision of a "New South" remade along the lines of the northern economy failed to materialize. Instead, the South declined into the country's poorest agricultural region. Cotton growing had defined the economic life of large plantations in the coastal regions and black belt communities of the antebellum South. In the post–Civil War years "King Cotton" expanded its realm, as greater numbers of small white farmers found themselves forced to switch from subsistence crops to growing cotton for the market.

The spread of the "crop lien" system as the South's main form of agricultural credit forced more and more farmers into cotton growing.

A chronic shortage of capital and banking institutions made local merchants and planters the sole source of credit. They advanced loans to sharecroppers and tenant farmers only in exchange for a lien, or claim, on the year's cotton crop, and they often charged usurious interest rates on advances, while marking up the prices of the goods they sold in their stores. Thus, at the end of the year, sharecroppers and tenants found themselves deep in debt to stores (many owned by Northerners) for seed, supplies, and clothing.

The near total dominance of "King Cotton" inhibited economic growth across the region. Unlike midwestern and western farm towns burgeoning from trade in wheat, corn, and livestock, southern communities found themselves almost entirely dependent on the price of one commodity as more and more farmers

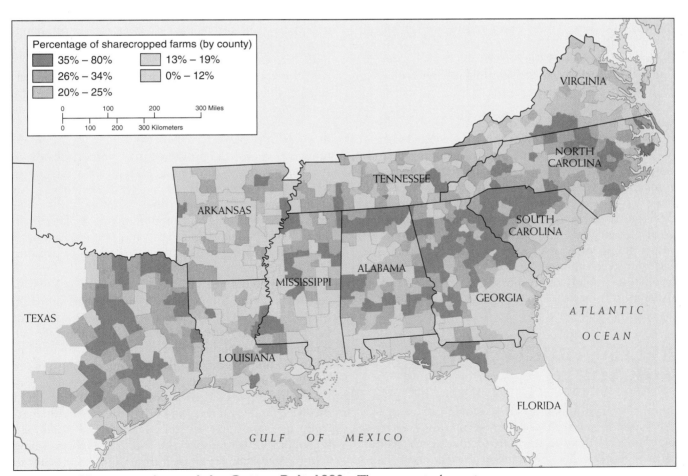

Southern Sharecropping and the Cotton Belt, 1880   The economic depression of the 1870s forced increasing numbers of southern farmers, both white and black, into sharecropping arrangements. Sharecropping was most pervasive in the cotton belt regions of South Carolina, Georgia, Alabama, Mississippi, and east Texas.

turned to cotton growing as the only way to obtain credit. Expanding production depressed prices. Competition from new cotton centers in the world market, such as Egypt and India, accelerated the downward spiral. As cotton prices declined alarmingly, from roughly eleven cents per pound in 1875 to five cents in 1894, per capita wealth in the South fell steadily; by the 1890s it equaled only one-third that of the East, Midwest, or West. Cotton dependency also prevented planters from acquiring the capital to purchase the farm equipment needed to profitably cultivate wheat or corn.

By 1880 about one-third of white farmers and nearly three-quarters of African American farmers in the cotton states were sharecroppers or tenants. Many former slaves and poor white people had tried subsistence farming in the undeveloped backcountry. Yet to obtain precious credit, most found themselves forced to produce cotton for market and, thus, became enmeshed in the debt-ridden crop lien system. In the up-country and newer areas of cultivation, cotton-dominated commercial agriculture, with landless tenants and sharecroppers as the main workforce, had replaced the more diversified subsistence economy of the antebellum era.

With their power based on control of credit and marketing, merchants emerged as a new economic elite unconnected to the antebellum planters whose power had rested on the ownership of land and slaves. But within both the new towns and the old planter elite, white families increasingly defined their social position by celebrating a certain type of ideal household. Women found meaning in their role as upholders of domestic virtue by creating a comfortable home environment and tending to the needs of children and husbands. Men were to be of strong moral fiber and to provide material support for the family. These elite ideals, articulated in magazines, schools, sermons, and other public discourse, rested on a belief that one's ability to reach the standards of womanhood and manhood rested solely upon moral character and individual choice.

RECONSTRUCTING THE NORTH

Abraham Lincoln liked to cite his own rise as proof of the superiority of the northern system of "free labor" over slavery. But the triumph of the North brought with it fundamental changes in the economy, labor relations, and politics that brought Lincoln's ideal vision into question. The spread of the factory system, the growth of large and powerful corporations, and the rapid expansion of capitalist enterprise all hastened the

development of a large unskilled and routinized workforce. Rather than becoming independent producers, more and more workers found themselves consigned permanently to wage labor.

The old Republican ideal of a society bound by a harmony of interests had become overshadowed by a grimmer reality of class conflict. A violent national railroad strike in 1877 was broken only with the direct intervention of federal troops. Northern society, like the society of the South, appeared more hierarchical than equal. That same year the last federal troops withdrew from their southern posts, marking the end of the Reconstruction era. By then, the North had undergone its own "reconstruction" as well.

The Age of Capital

In the decade following Appomattox, the North's economy continued the industrial boom begun during the Civil War. By 1873, America's industrial production had grown 75 percent over the 1865 level. By that time, too, the number of nonagricultural workers in the North had surpassed the number of farmers. Between 1860 and 1880 the number of wage earners in manufacturing and construction more than doubled, from 2 million to over 4 million.

The railroad business both symbolized and advanced the new industrial order. Shortly before the Civil War, enthusiasm mounted for a transcontinental line. Private companies took on the huge and expensive job of construction, but the federal government funded the project, providing the largest subsidy in American history. An 1864 act bestowed a subsidy of $15,000 per mile of track laid over smooth plains country and varying larger amounts up to $48,000 per mile in the foothills and mountains of the Far West. The Union Pacific employed gangs of Irish American and African American workers to lay track heading west from Omaha, while the Central Pacific brought in more than 10,000 men from China to handle the difficult work in the Sierra Nevada mountain region. On May 10, 1869, Leland Stanford, the former governor of California and president of the Central Pacific Railroad, traveled to Promontory Point in Utah Territory to hammer a ceremonial golden spike, marking the finish of the first transcontinental line.

Railroads paved the way for the rapid settlement of the West, and both rural and urban areas grew dramatically over the next several decades. The combined population of Minnesota, the Dakotas, Nebraska, and Kansas, for example, jumped from 300,000 in 1860 to over 2 million in 1880. In the fifty years after 1870, the nation's railroad system expanded to more than a quarter million miles—more than all the rest of the world's railroad track combined.

Railroad corporations became America's first big businesses. Railroads required huge outlays of investment capital, and their growth increased the economic power of banks and investment houses centered in Wall Street. Bankers often gained seats on the boards of directors of these railroad companies, and their access to capital sometimes gave them the real control of railways. A new breed of aggressive entrepreneur sought to ease cutthroat competition by absorbing smaller companies and forming "pools" that set rates and divided the market. A small group of railroad executives, including Cornelius Vanderbilt, Jay Gould, Collis P. Huntington, and James J. Hill, amassed unheard-of fortunes. When he died in 1877, Vanderbilt left his son $100 million. By comparison, a decent annual wage for working a six-day week was around $350.

Railroad promoters, lawyers, and lobbyists became ubiquitous figures in Washington and state capitals, wielding enormous influence among lawmakers. Railroads benefited enormously from government subsidies. Between 1862 and 1872, Congress alone awarded more than 100 million acres of public lands to railroad companies and provided them over $64 million in loans and tax incentives.

Some of the nation's most prominent politicians routinely accepted railroad largesse. The worst scandal of the Grant administration grew out of corruption involving railroad promotion. As a way of diverting funds for the building of the Union Pacific Railroad, an inner circle of Union Pacific stockholders created the dummy Crédit Mobilier construction company. In return for political favors, a group of prominent Republicans received

COMPLETION OF THE PACIFIC RAILROAD—MEETING OF LOCOMOTIVES OF THE UNION AND CENTRAL PACIFIC LINES: THE ENGINEERS SHAKE HANDS.

Completion of the transcontinental railroad, May 10, 1869, as building crews for the Union Pacific and Central Pacific meet at Promontory Point, Utah. The two locomotive engineers salute each other, while the chief engineers for the two railroads shake hands. Construction had begun simultaneously from Omaha and Sacramento in 1863, with the help of generous subsidies from Congress. Work crews, consisting of thousands of ex-soldiers, Irish immigrants, and imported Chinese laborers, laid nearly 1,800 miles of new track, New York.

SOURCE: The Granger Collection, New York.

stock in the company. When the scandal broke in 1872, it politically ruined Vice President Schuyler Colfax and led to the censure of two congressmen.

Other industries also boomed in this period, especially those engaged in extracting minerals and processing natural resources. Railroad growth stimulated expansion in the production of coal, iron, stone, and lumber, and these also received significant government aid. For example, under the National Mineral Act of 1866, mining companies received millions of acres of free public land. Oil refining enjoyed a huge expansion in the 1860s and 1870s. As with railroads, an early period of fierce competition soon gave way to concentration. By the late 1870s, John D. Rockefeller's Standard Oil Company controlled almost 90 percent of the nation's oil-refining capacity.

Liberal Republicans and the Election of 1872

With the rapid growth of large-scale, capital-intensive enterprises, Republicans increasingly identified with the interests of business rather than the rights of freedmen or the antebellum ideology of "free labor." The old Civil War–era Radical Republicans had declined in influence. State Republican parties now organized themselves around the spoils of federal patronage rather than grand causes such as preserving the Union or ending slavery. Despite the Crédit Mobilier affair, Republicans had no monopoly on political scandal. In 1871 New York City newspapers reported the shocking story of how Democratic Party boss William M. Tweed and his friends had systematically stolen tens of millions from the city treasury. The "Tweed Ring" had received enormous bribes and kickbacks from city contractors and businessmen. But to many, the scandal represented only the most extreme case of the routine corruption that now plagued American political life.

By the end of President Grant's first term, a large number of disaffected Republicans sought an alternative. The Liberal Republicans, as they called themselves, emphasized the doctrines of classical economics, stressing the law of supply and demand, free trade, defense of property rights, and individualism. They called for a return to limited government, arguing that bribery, scandal, and high taxes all flowed from excessive state interference in the economy.

Liberal Republicans were also suspicious of expanding democracy. They believed that politics ought to be the province of "the best men"—educated and well-to-do men like themselves, devoted to the "science of government." They proposed civil service reform as the best way to break the hold of party machines on patronage.

Although most Liberal Republicans had enthusiastically supported abolition, the Union cause, and equal rights for freedmen, they now opposed continued federal intervention in the South. The national government had done all it could for the former slaves; they must now take care of themselves. "Root, Hog, or Die" was the harsh advice offered by Horace Greeley, editor of the *New York Tribune.* In the spring of 1872 a diverse collection of Liberal Republicans nominated Greeley to run for president. A longtime foe of the Democratic Party, Greeley nonetheless won that party's presidential nomination as well. He made a new policy for the South the center of his campaign against Grant. All Americans, Greeley urged, must put the Civil War behind them and "clasp hands across the bloody chasm."

Grant easily defeated Greeley, carrying every state in the North and winning 56 percent of the popular vote. Most Republicans were not willing to abandon the regular party organization, and "waving the bloody shirt" was still a potent vote-getter. But the 1872 election accelerated the trend toward federal abandonment of African American citizenship rights. The Liberal Republicans quickly faded as an organized political force. But their ideas helped define a growing conservative consciousness among the northern public. Their agenda included retreat from the ideal of racial justice, hostility toward trade unions, suspicion of working-class and immigrant political power, celebration of competitive individualism, and opposition to government intervention in economic affairs.

The Depression of 1873

In the fall of 1873 the postwar boom came to an abrupt halt as a severe financial panic triggered a deep economic depression. The collapse resulted from commercial overexpansion, especially speculative investing in the nation's railroad system. By 1876 half the nation's railroads had defaulted on their bonds. Over the next two years more than 100 banks folded and 18,000 businesses shut their doors. The depression that began in 1873 lasted sixty-five months—the longest economic contraction in the nation's history until then.

The human toll of the depression was enormous. As factories began to close across the nation, the unemployment rate soared to about 15 percent. In many cities the jobless rate was much higher; roughly one-quarter of New York City workers were unemployed in 1874. Many thousands of men took to the road in search of work, and the "tramp" emerged as a new and menacing figure on the social landscape. The Pennsylvania Bureau of Labor Statistics noted that never before had "so many of the working classes, skilled and unskilled . . . been moving from place to place seeking employment that was not to be had." Farmers were also hard hit by the depression. Agricultural output continued to grow, but prices and land values fell sharply. As prices for their crops fell, farmers had a more difficult time repaying their fixed loan obligations; many sank deeper into debt.

Mass meetings of workers in New York and other cities issued calls to government officials to create jobs through public works. But these appeals were rejected. Indeed, many business leaders and political figures denounced even meager efforts at charity. They saw the depression as a natural, if painful, part of the business cycle, one that would allow only the strongest enterprises (and workers) to survive.

The depression of the 1870s prompted workers and farmers to question the old free-labor ideology that celebrated a harmony of interests in northern society. More people voiced anger at and distrust of large corporations that exercised great economic power from outside their communities.

The Electoral Crisis of 1876

With the economy mired in depression, Democrats looked forward to capturing the White House in 1876. New scandals plaguing the Grant administration also weakened the Republican Party. In 1875, a conspiracy surfaced between distillers and U.S. revenue agents to cheat the government out of millions in tax revenues. The government secured indictments against more than 200 members of this "Whiskey Ring," including Orville E. Babcock, Grant's private secretary. Though acquitted, thanks to Grant's intervention, Babcock resigned in disgrace. In 1876, Secretary of War William W. Belknap was impeached for receiving bribes for the sale of trading posts in Indian Territory, and he resigned to avoid conviction.

Democrats nominated Governor Samuel J. Tilden of New York, who brought impeccable reform credentials to his candidacy. In 1871 he had helped expose and prosecute the "Tweed Ring" in New York City. As governor he had toppled the "Canal Ring," a graft-ridden scheme involving inflated contracts for repairs on the Erie Canal. In their platform, the Democrats linked the issue of corruption to an attack on Reconstruction policies. They blamed the Republicans for instituting "a corrupt centralism."

Republican nominee Rutherford B. Hayes, governor of Ohio, also sought the high ground. As a lawyer in Cincinnati he had defended runaway slaves. Later he had distinguished himself as a general in the Union army. Hayes promised, if elected, to support an efficient civil service system, to vigorously prosecute officials who betrayed the public trust, and to introduce a system of free universal education.

On an election day marred by widespread vote fraud and violent intimidation, Tilden received 250,000 more popular votes than Hayes. But Republicans refused to concede victory, challenging the vote totals in the electoral college. Tilden garnered 184 uncontested electoral votes, one shy of the majority required to win, while Hayes received 165. The problem centered in 20 disputed votes from Florida, Louisiana, South Carolina, and Oregon. In each of the three southern states two sets of electoral votes were returned. In Oregon, which Hayes had unquestionably carried, the Democratic governor nevertheless replaced a disputed Republican elector with a Democrat.

The crisis was unprecedented. In January 1877 Congress moved to settle the deadlock, establishing an Electoral Commission composed of five senators, five representatives, and five Supreme Court justices; eight were Republicans and seven were Democrats. The commission voted along strict partisan lines to award all the contested electoral votes to Hayes. Outraged by this decision, Democratic congressmen threatened a filibuster to block Hayes's inauguration. Violence and stalemate were avoided when Democrats and Republicans struck a compromise in February. In return for Hayes's ascendance to the presidency, the Republicans promised to appropriate more money for southern

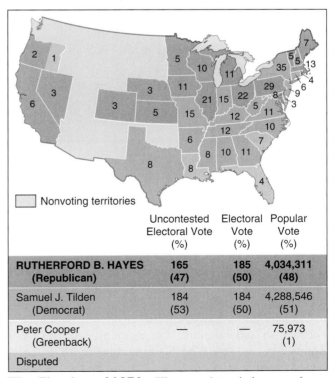

	Nonvoting territories

	Uncontested Electoral Vote (%)	Electoral Vote (%)	Popular Vote (%)
RUTHERFORD B. HAYES (Republican)	**165 (47)**	**185 (50)**	**4,034,311 (48)**
Samuel J. Tilden (Democrat)	184 (53)	184 (50)	4,288,546 (51)
Peter Cooper (Greenback)	—	—	75,973 (1)
Disputed			

The Election of 1876   The presidential election of 1876 left the nation without a clear-cut winner.

CHRONOLOGY

1865	Freedmen's Bureau established
	Abraham Lincoln assassinated
	Andrew Johnson begins Presidential Reconstruction
	Black codes begin to be enacted in southern states
	Thirteenth Amendment ratified
1866	Civil Rights Act passed
	Congress approves Fourteenth Amendment
	Ku Klux Klan founded
1867	Reconstruction Acts, passed over President Johnson's veto, begin Congressional Reconstruction
	Tenure of Office Act
	Southern states call constitutional conventions
1868	President Johnson impeached by the House, but acquitted in Senate trial
	Fourteenth Amendment ratified
	Most southern states readmitted to Union
	Ulysses S. Grant elected president
1869	Congress approves Fifteenth Amendment
	Union Pacific and Central Pacific tracks meet at Promontory Point in Utah Territory

	Suffragists split into National Woman Suffrage Association and American Woman Suffrage Association
1870	Fifteenth Amendment ratified
1871	Ku Klux Klan Act passed
	"Tweed Ring" in New York City exposed
1872	Liberal Republicans break with Grant and Radicals, nominate Horace Greeley for president
	Crédit Mobilier scandal
	Grant reelected president
1873	Financial panic and beginning of economic depression
	Slaughterhouse cases
1874	Democrats gain control of House for first time since 1856
1875	Civil Rights Act
1876	Disputed election between Samuel Tilden and Rutherford B. Hayes
1877	Electoral Commission elects Hayes president
	President Hayes dispatches federal troops to break Great Railroad Strike and withdraws last remaining federal troops from the South

internal improvements, to appoint a Southerner to Hayes's cabinet, and to pursue a policy of noninterference ("home rule") in southern affairs.

Shortly after assuming office, Hayes ordered removal of the remaining federal troops in Louisiana and South Carolina. Without this military presence to sustain them, the Republican governors of those two states quickly lost power to Democrats. "Home rule" meant Republican abandonment of freed people, Radicals, carpetbaggers, and scalawags. It also effectively nullified the Fourteenth and Fifteenth Amendments and the Civil Rights Act of 1866. The "Compromise of 1877" completed repudiation of the idea, born during the Civil War and pursued during Congressional Reconstruction, of a powerful federal government protecting the rights of all American citizens.

CONCLUSION

Reconstruction succeeded in the limited political sense of reuniting a nation torn apart by the Civil War. The Radical Republican vision, emphasizing racial justice, equal civil and political rights guaranteed by the Fourteenth and Fifteenth Amendments, and a new southern economy organized around independent small farmers, never enjoyed the support of the majority of its party or the northern public. The federal government's failure to pursue land reform left former slaves without the economic independence needed for full emancipation. Yet the newly autonomous black family, along with black-controlled churches, schools, and other social institutions, provided the foundations for the modern African American community.

Even as the federal government retreated from the defense of equal rights for black people, it took a more aggressive stance as the protector of business interests. The Hayes administration responded decisively to one of the worst outbreaks of class violence in American history by dispatching federal troops to several northern cities to break the Great Railroad Strike of 1877. In the aftermath of Reconstruction, the struggle between capital and labor had clearly replaced "the southern question" as the number one political issue of the day. "The overwhelming labor question has dwarfed all other questions into nothing," wrote an Ohio Republican. "We have home questions enough to occupy attention now."

REVIEW QUESTIONS

1. How did various visions of a "reconstructed" South differ? How did these visions reflect the old political and social divisions that had led to the Civil War?
2. What key changes did emancipation make in the political and economic status of African Americans? Discuss the expansion of citizenship rights in the post–Civil War years. To what extent did women share in the gains made by African Americans?
3. What role did such institutions as the family, the church, the schools, and the political parties play in the African American transition to freedom?
4. How did white Southerners attempt to limit the freedom of former slaves? How did these efforts succeed, and how did they fail?
5. Evaluate the achievements and failures of Reconstruction governments in the southern states.
6. What were the crucial economic changes occurring in the North and South during the Reconstruction era?

RECOMMENDED READING

Paul A. Cimbala and Randall M. Miller, eds., *The Freedmen's Bureau and Reconstruction* (1999). A wide ranging collection of the latest scholarship, with special attention to recapturing the historical voices of freed people.

Jane Dailey, *Before Jim Crow: The Politics of Race in Post Emancipation Virginia* (2000). A fine study that focuses on the tension between the drive to establish white supremacy and the struggle for biracial coalitions in post–Civil War Virginia politics.

Laura F. Edwards, *Gendered Strife & Confusion: The Political Culture of Reconstruction* (1997). An ambitious analysis of how gender ideologies played a key role in shaping the party politics and social relations of the Reconstruction-era South.

Michael W. Fitzgerald, *The Union League Movement in the Deep South* (1989). Uses the Union League as a lens through which to examine race relations and the close connections between politics and economic change in the post–Civil War South.

Eric Foner, *Reconstruction: America's Unfinished Revolution, 1863–1877* (1988). The most comprehensive and thoroughly researched overview of the Reconstruction era.

William Gillette, *Retreat from Reconstruction: A Political History, 1867–1878* (1979). Covers the national political scene, with special attention to the abandonment of the ideal of racial equality.

Jacqueline Jones, *Labor of Love, Labor of Sorrow* (1985). Includes excellent material on the work and family lives of African American women in slavery and freedom.

Leon Litwack, *Been in the Storm So Long: The Aftermath of Slavery* (1979). A richly detailed analysis of the transition from slavery to freedom; excellent use of African American sources.

Scott Reynolds Nelson, *Iron Confederacies: Southern Railways, Klan Violence, and Reconstruction* (1999). Pathbreaking analysis of how conservative southern and northern business interests rebuilt the South's railroad system and also achieved enormous political power within individual states.

Edward Royce, *The Origins of Southern Sharecropping* (1993). A sophisticated, tightly argued work of historical sociology that explains how sharecropping emerged as the dominant form of agricultural labor in the post-Civil War South.

ON THE WEB

**http://memory.loc.gov/ammem/aaohtml/
exhibit/aopart5.html**

This American Memory project from the Library of Congress provides primary documents, descriptive narrative, photographs, and drawings of the life of the freedman during Reconstruction. Of particular interest would be the history of the "Exodusters," black freedmen who sought a life for themselves and their families on farms in Kansas during Reconstruction.

http://www.uno.edu/~drcom/Griffith/Birth/

http://www.filmsite.org/birt.html

Each of these sites is related to the 1915 film by D. W. Griffith called *Birth of a Nation* based on the racist book, *The Clansman*. The book and movie portray the history of Reconstruction from the southern point of view and make the Ku Klux Klan the heroes of this movie. The first site is a University of New Orleans collection of short clips from the original film. The second site is a review of the Griffith movie by a film buff.

Reconstruction Era Primary Documents:

**http://www.yale.edu/lawweb/avalon/
presiden/inaug/grant1.htm**

First Inaugural Address of Ulysses S. Grant, March 4, 1869.

**http://www.archives.gov/exhibit_hall/
treasures_of_congress/Images/page_13/44a.html**

Wade-Davis Bill.

http://odur.let.rug.nl/~usa/P/al16/writings/wdveto.htm

Lincoln's veto of the Wade-Davis Bill.

**http://www.nv.cc.va.us/home/nvsageh/Hist122/
Part1/ForceActsEx.htm**

The Force Acts of 1870–1871.

**http://www.yale.edu/lawweb/avalon/presiden/
inaug/grant2.htm**

Second Inaugural Address of Ulysses S. Grant, March 4, 1873.

**http://www.yale.edu/lawweb/avalon/presiden/
inaug/hayes.htm**

Inaugural Address of Rutherford B. Hayes, March 5, 1877.

http://www.prenhall.com/faragherbrief/map17.1

In these interactive maps, consider the politics of Reconstruction in the South. What were the competing plans for reconstructing the southern states?

http://www.prenhall.com/faragherbrief/map17.2

Examine the connections between the environment and the economy in shaping sharecropping in the South. How did this new form of labor affect the lives of former slaves?

EIGHTEEN

CONQUEST AND SURVIVAL

▷ The Trans-Mississippi West, 1860–1900

CHAPTER OUTLINE

AMERICAN COMMUNITIES

The Oklahoma Land Rush

DECADES AFTER THE EVENT, COWBOY EVAN G. BARNARD VIVIDLY recalled the preparations made by settlers when Oklahoma territorial officials announced the opening of No Man's Land to the biggest "land rush" in American history. "Thousands of people gathered along the border. . . . As the day for the race drew near, the settlers practiced running their horses and driving carts." Finally the morning of April 22, 1889, arrived. "At ten o'clock people lined up . . . ready for the great race of their lives." Like many others, Barnard displayed his guns prominently on his hips, determined to discourage competitors from claiming the 160 acres of prime land that he intended to grab for himself.

Evan Barnard's story was one strand in the larger tale of the destruction and creation of communities in the trans-Mississippi West. In the 1830s, the federal government designated what was to become the state of Oklahoma as Indian Territory, reserved for the Five Civilized Tribes (Cherokees, Chickasaws, Choctaws, Creeks, and Seminoles) that had been forcibly removed from their eastern lands. All five tribes had reestablished themselves as sovereign republics in Indian Territory. The Cherokees and Chocktaws became prosperous cotton growers. The Creeks managed large herds of hogs and cattle, and the Chickasaws grazed not only cattle but sheep and goats on their open fields. The Five Tribes also ran sawmills, gristmills, and cotton gins. Indian merchants were soon dealing with other tribespeople as well as licensed white traders and even contracting with the federal government.

The Civil War, however, took a heavy toll on their success. Some tribes, slaveholders themselves, sided with the Confederacy; others with the Union. When the war ended, more than 10,000 people—nearly one-fifth of the population of Indian Territory—had died. To make matters worse, new treaties required the Five Civilized Tribes to cede the entire western half of the territory, including the former northern Indian territory of Nebraska and Kansas, for the resettlement of tribes from other regions.

Western Oklahoma thereby became home to thousands of newly displaced peoples, including the Pawnees, Peorias, Ottawas, Wyandots, and Miamis. Many small tribes readily took to farming and rebuilt their communities. But the nomadic, buffalo-hunting Kiowas, Cheyennes, Comanches, and Arapahoes did not settle so peacefully. They continued to traverse the plains until the U.S. Army finally forced them onto reservations. Eventually, more than 80,000 tribespeople were living on twenty-one separate reservations in western Oklahoma, all governed by agents appointed by the federal government.

The opening of the unassigned far western district of Oklahoma known as No Man's Land to non-Indian homesteading, however, signaled the impending end of Indian sovereignty. Many non-Indians saw this almost 2 million acre strip as a Promised Land, perfect for dividing into thousands of small farms. African Americans, many of whom were former slaves of Indian planters, appealed to the federal government for the right to stake claims there. Another group of would-be homesteaders, known as "Boomers," quickly tired of petitioning and invaded the district in 1880, only to be booted out by the Tenth Cavalry. Meanwhile, the railroads, seeing the potential for lucrative commerce, put constant pressure on the federal government to open No Man's Land for settlement. In 1889 the U.S. Congress finally gave in.

Cowboy Barnard was just one of thousands to pour into No Man's Land on April 22, 1889. Many homesteaders simply crossed the border from Kansas. Southerners, dispossessed by warfare and economic ruin in their own region, were also well represented. Market-minded settlers claimed the land nearest the railroads, and by nightfall of April 22 they had set up tent cities along the tracks. In a little over two months, after 6,000 homestead claims had been filed, the first sod houses appeared, sheltering growing communities of non-Indian farmers, ranchers, and other entrepreneurs.

Dramatic as it was, the land rush of 1889 was only one in a series of events that soon dispossessed Oklahoma's Indians of their remaining lands. First,

the federal government broke up the estates held collectively by various tribes in western Oklahoma, assigning to individuals the standard 160-acre allotment and allowing non-Indian homesteaders to claim the rest. Then, in 1898, Congress passed the Curtis Act, formally dissolving Indian Territory and dispossessing the Five Tribes. Members of the former Indian nations were directed to dismantle their governments, abandon their estates, and join the ranks of other homesteaders. They nevertheless retained many of their tribal customs and managed to regain their sovereign status in 1977.

Later generations of Oklahomans often celebrated their historic ties to the Indian nations. At formal ceremonies marking statehood, just before the newly elected governor took the oath of office, a mock wedding ceremony united a tough and virile cowboy with a demure and submissive Indian maiden. By this time, in 1907, tribespeople were outnumbered in Oklahoma by ten to one.

By this time also, nearly one-quarter of the entire population of the United States lived west of the Mississippi River. Hundreds of new communities, supported primarily by cattle ranching, agriculture, mining, or other industries, had not only grown with the emerging national economy but helped to shape it in the process. The newcomers displaced communities that had formed centuries earlier. They also drastically transformed the physical landscape. Through their activities and the support of Easterners, the United States realized an ambition that John L. O'Sullivan had described in 1845 as the nation's "manifest destiny to overspread the continent" and remake it in a new image. ■

Indian Territory (Oklahoma)

KEY TOPICS

- The impact of western expansion on Indian societies

- The West as an "internal empire" and the development of new technologies and new industries

- The creation of new communities and the displacement of old communities

- The West as myth and legend

INDIAN PEOPLES UNDER SIEGE

The tribespeople living west of the Mississippi River keenly felt the pressure of the gradual incorporation of the West into the nation. The Oregon Trail opened the Northwest to large numbers of non-Indian settlers. In 1846 the United States reached an agreement with Great Britain for the division of the Oregon Country. Then came the addition of the vast territories taken from Mexico following the Mexican-American War. California quickly became a state in 1850, Oregon in 1859. Congress consolidated the national domain in the next decades by granting territorial status to Utah, New Mexico, Washington, Dakota, Colorado, Nevada, Arizona, Idaho, Montana, and Wyoming. The purchase of Alaska in 1867 added an area twice the size of Texas and extended the nation beyond its contiguous borders so that it reached almost to Russia and the North Pole. The federal government made itself the custodian of all these thinly settled regions, permitting limited self-rule, with appointed governors supervising the transition from territorial status to statehood.

Competition for the land and its resources was central to this encounter. Unlike the settlers wedded to the principles of private property, the tribespeople mainly believed that the land belongs to those who revere it across many generations. Their prospects to preserve their ways of life amid this contest dimmed considerably following the discovery of gold in California in 1848, the opening of western lands to homesteaders in 1862, and the completion of the transcontinental railroad in 1869. White settlers, hoping to build a new life for themselves, rushed into these new territories and repeatedly invaded Indian lands west of the Mississippi. Violent outbreaks between white emigrants and Indian peoples became increasingly commonplace. Since the Jefferson administration, federal officials had promoted the assimilation of Indian peoples; they now became even more determined to break up their tribal councils and to bring them into the American mainstream.

On the Eve of Conquest

Before the European colonists reached the New World, tribespeople of the Great Plains, Southwest, and Far West had occupied the lands for more than 20,000 years. Hundreds of tribes, totaling perhaps a million members, had adapted to such extreme climates as the desert aridity of present-day Utah and Nevada, the bitter cold of the northern Great Plains, and the seasonally heavy rain of the Pacific Northwest. Many cultivated maize (corn), foraged for wild plants, fished, or hunted game. Several tribes built cities with several thousand inhabitants and traded across thousands of miles of western territory.

Invasion by the English, Spanish, and other Europeans brought disease, religious conversion, and new patterns of commerce. But geographic isolation still gave many tribes a margin of survival unknown in the East. At the close of the Civil War, approximately 360,000 Indian people still lived in the trans-Mississippi West, the majority of them in the Great Plains.

The surviving tribes adapted to changing conditions. The Plains Indians learned to ride the horses and shoot the guns introduced by Spanish and British traders. Even before they were uprooted and moved across the Mississippi River, the Cherokees had learned English, converted to Christianity, established a constitutional republic, and become a nation of farmers.

Legally, the federal government had long regarded Indian tribes as autonomous nations residing within American boundaries and had negotiated numerous treaties with them over land rights and commerce. But pressured by land-hungry whites, several states had violated these federal treaties so often that the U.S. Congress passed the Indian Removal Act of 1830 (see Chapter 10), which provided funds to relocate all eastern tribes by force if necessary. The Cherokees challenged this legislation, and the Supreme Court ruled in their favor in *Cherokee Nation* v.

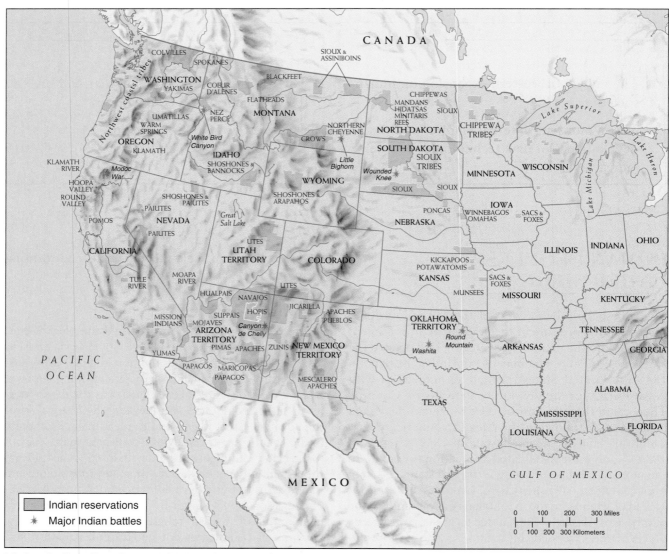

Major Indian Battles and Indian Reservations, 1860–1900 As commercial routes and white populations passed through and occupied Indian lands, warfare inevitably erupted. The displacement of Indians to reservations opened access by farmers, ranchers, and investors to natural resources and to markets.

Georgia (1831). Ignoring the Court's decision, President Andrew Jackson, known as a hardened Indian fighter, forced many tribes to cede their land and remove to Indian Territory. There, it was believed, they might live undisturbed by whites and gradually adjust to "civilized" ways. But soon, the onslaught of white settlers, railroad entrepreneurs, and prospectors rushing for gold pressured tribes to cede millions of their acres to the United States. In 1854, to open the Kansas and Nebraska Territories for white settlement, the federal government simply abolished the northern half of Indian Territory. As demand for resources and land accelerated, the entire plan for a permanent Indian Territory fell apart.

Reservations and the Slaughter of the Buffalo

As early as the 1840s, highly placed officials had outlined a plan to subdue the intensifying rivalry over natural resources and land. Under the terms of their proposal, individual tribes would agree to live within clearly defined zones—reservations—and, in exchange, the Bureau of Indian Affairs would provide guidance while U.S. military forces ensured protection. By the end of the 1850s eight western reservations had been established where Indian peoples were induced to speak English, take up farming, and convert to Christianity.

Several tribes signed treaties, although often under duress. High-handed officials, such as governor

Isaac Stevens of Washington Territory, made no attempt at legitimate negotiations, choosing instead to intimidate or deceive Indian peoples into signing away their lands. State officials moved the Indians onto three reservations after their leaders signed away 45,000 square miles of tribal land. The Suquamish leader Seattle admitted defeat but warned the governor: "Your time of decay may be distant, but it will surely come."

Those tribes that moved to reservations often found federal policies inadequate to their needs. The Medicine Lodge Treaty of 1867 assigned reservations in existing Indian Territory to Comanches, Plains (Kiowa) Apaches, Kiowas, Cheyennes, and Arapahoes, bringing these tribes together with Sioux, Shoshones, and Bannocks. All told, more than 100,000 people found themselves competing intensely for survival. Over the next decade, a group of Quakers appointed by President Ulysses S. Grant attempted to mediate differences among the tribes and to supply the starving peoples with food and seed. At the same time, white prospectors and miners continued to flood the Dakota Territory. Corrupt officials of the Bureau of Indian Affairs routinely diverted funds for their own use and reduced food supplies, a policy promoting malnutrition, demoralization, and desperation.

The nomadic tribes that traditionally hunted and gathered over large territories saw their freedom sharply curtailed. The Lakotas, or Western Sioux, a loose confederation of bands scattered across the northern Great Plains, were one of the largest and most adaptive of all Indian nations. Seizing buffalo-hunting territory from their rivals, the Pawnees and the Crows, the Sioux had learned to follow the herds on horseback. The Sioux were also vision seekers. Young men and women pursued dreams that would provide them guidance for a lifetime; elders themselves followed dreams that might guide the destiny of the entire tribe or nation.

The mass slaughter of the buffalo brought the crisis provoked by the increasing restriction of the nomadic Plains peoples to a peak. In earlier eras, vast herds of buffalo had literally darkened the western horizon. As gunpowder and the railroad came to the range, the number of buffalo fell rapidly. Non-Indian traders avidly sought fur for coats, hide for leather, bones for fertilizer, and heads for trophies. New rifles, like the .50 caliber Sharps, could kill at 600 feet; one sharpshooter bragged of killing 3,000 buffalo. Army commanders encouraged the slaughter, accurately predicting that starvation would break tribal resistance to the reservation system. With their food sources practically destroyed, diseases such as smallpox and cholera (brought by fur traders) sweeping through their villages, and their way of life undermined, many Great Plains tribes, including many Sioux, concluded that they could only fight or die.

The Indian Wars

Under these pressures, a handful of tribes organized themselves and their allies to resist both federal policies and the growing wave of white settlers. The overwhelming majority of tribespeople did not take up arms. But settlers, thousands of them Civil War veterans with weapons close at hand, responded to real or imaginary threats with their own brands of violence.

Large-scale war erupted in 1864. Having decided to terminate all treaties with tribes in eastern Colorado, territorial governor John Evans encouraged a group of white civilians, the Colorado Volunteers, to stage raids through Cheyenne campgrounds. Seeking protection, Chief Black Kettle brought a band of 800 Cheyennes to a U.S. fort and received orders to set up camp at Sand Creek. Feeling secure in this arrangement, Black Kettle sent out most of his men to hunt. Several weeks later, on November 29, 1864, the Colorado Volunteers and soldiers attacked. While Black Kettle held up a U.S. flag and a white truce banner, a disorderly group of 700 men, many of them drunk, slaughtered 105 Cheyenne women and children and 28 men. They mutilated the corpses and took scalps back to Denver to exhibit as trophies. Iron Teeth, a Cheyenne woman who survived, remembered seeing a woman "crawling along on the ground, shot, scalped, crazy, but not yet dead." Months after the Sand Creek Massacre, bands of Cheyennes, Sioux, and Arapahoes were still retaliating, burning civilian outposts and sometimes killing whole families.

The Sioux played the most dramatic roles in the Indian Wars. In 1851, believing the U.S. government would recognize their own rights of conquest over other Indian tribes, the Sioux relinquished large tracts of land as a demonstration of good faith. But within a decade, a mass invasion of miners and the construction of military forts along the Bozeman Trail in Wyoming, the Sioux's principal buffalo range, threw the tribe's future into doubt. During the Great Sioux War of 1865–67, the Oglala Sioux warrior Red Cloud fought the U.S. Army to a stalemate and forced the government to abandon its forts, which the Sioux then burned to the ground. The Treaty of Fort Laramie, signed in 1868, created the Great Sioux Reservation, which included the present state of South Dakota west of the Missouri River, but restored only a temporary peace to the region.

The Treaty of Fort Laramie granted the Sioux the right to occupy the Black Hills, or Paha Sapa, their sacred land, "as long as the grass shall grow," but the discovery of gold soon undermined this guarantee. White prospectors hurriedly invaded the territory. Directed to quash rumors of fabulous deposits of the precious metal, Lieutenant Colonel George Armstrong Custer organized a surveying expedition to the Black Hills during the summer of 1874, but, contrary to plan, the Civil War hero described rich veins of ore that could be cheaply extracted. The U.S. Congress then pushed to acquire the territory for Americans. To protect their land, Sioux, Cheyenne, and Arapaho warriors, ranging between 2,000 and 9,000 in number, moved into war camps during the summer of 1876 and prepared for battle.

After several months of skirmishes and battles between the U.S. Army and Sioux warriors, Lieutenant Colonel Custer decided to rush ahead to a site in Montana that was known to white soldiers as Little Bighorn and to Lakotas as Greasy Grass. This foolhardy move offered the allied Cheyenne and Sioux warriors a perfect opportunity to cut off Custer's logistical and military support. On June 25, 1876, Custer and his troops were wiped out by one of the largest Indian contingents ever assembled, an estimated 2,000 to 4,000 warriors.

"Custer's Last Stand" gave Indian-haters the emotional ammunition to whip up public excitement. After Custer's defeat, spiritual leader Sitting Bull reportedly said, "Now they will never let us rest." By 1877, Sioux leadership in the Indian Wars was ended.

Among the last to hold out against the reservation system were the Apaches in the Southwest. Most Apache bands, unable to tolerate the harsh conditions on the reservation, returned to their old ways of seizing territory and stealing cattle.

Pursued by the U.S. Army, the Apaches earned a reputation as intrepid warriors. Their brilliant strategists and horse-riding braves became legendary for lightning-swift raids followed by quick disappearances. The Kiowas and the Comanches, both powerful tribes, joined the Apaches in one of the bloodiest conflicts, the Red River War of 1874–75. The U.S. Army ultimately prevailed less by military might than by denying Indians access to food. Even after the Red River War, small-scale warfare sputtered on. Not until September 1886, his band reduced to only thirty people, did Geronimo finally surrender, ending the Indian Wars.

The Nez Percé

The Nez Percé (meaning "pierced nose") had been given their name by French Canadian fur trappers, who thought they had seen members of the tribe wearing shells in their septums. For generations the Nez Percé had regarded themselves as good friends to white traders and settlers. Living in the plateau where Idaho, Washington, and Oregon now meet, they had saved the Lewis and Clark expedition from starvation in 1803. The Nez Percé had occasionally assisted American armies against hostile tribes, and many of them were converts to Christianity.

But the discovery of gold on Nez Percé territory in 1860 changed their relations with whites for the worse. Pressed by prospectors and mining companies, government commissioners, in the treaty of 1863, demanded the Nez Percé cede 6 million acres, nine-tenths of their land, at less than ten cents per acre. Some of the Nez Percé leaders agreed to the terms of the treaty, which had been fraudulently signed on behalf of the entire tribe, but others refused. At first, federal officials listened to Nez Percé complaints against the treaty and decided to allow them to remain on their land. But responding to pressure from settlers and politicians, however, they almost immediately reversed their decision, ordering the Nez Percé, including Chief Joseph and his followers, to sell their land and to move onto a reservation.

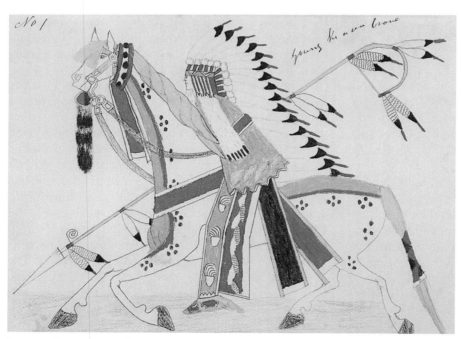

Preparing for a War Expedition, ca. 1887. This sketch on paper was made by an Indian artist, Silverhorn, who had himself taken part in the final revolt of the Kiowas in 1874. He later became a medicine man, and then served as a private in the U.S. Cavalry at Fort Sill, Oklahoma Territory.

SOURCE: Silverhorn, Native American, *Kiowa Preparing for a War Expedition.* From *Sketchbook,* 1887. Graphite ink and crayon. Collection of the McNay Art Museum, Gift of Mrs. Terrell Bartlett.

Intending to comply, Chief Joseph's band set out from the Wallowa Valley with their livestock and all the possessions they could carry. Along the way, some young members of another Indian band traveling with them rode away from camp to avenge the death of one of their own by killing several white settlers. Hoping to explain the situation, a Nez Percé truce team approached U.S. troops. The troops opened fire, and the Indian riders fired back, killing one-third of the soldiers. Brilliantly outmaneuvering vengeful U.S. troops sent to intercept them, the 750 Nez Percé retreated for some 1,400 miles into Montana and Wyoming through mountains and prairies, and across the Bitterroot Range. Over the three and a half months of their journey, Nez Percé braves fought 2,000 regular U.S. troops and eighteen Indian auxiliary detachments in eighteen separate engagements and two major battles. U.S. troops finally trapped the Nez Percé in the Bear Paw Mountains of northern Montana, just 30 miles from the Canadian border. Suffering from hunger and cold, they surrendered.

Promised they would be returned to Oregon, the Nez Percé were sent instead to disease-ridden bottomland near Fort Leavenworth in Kansas, and then to Oklahoma. Arguing for the right of his people to return to their Oregon reservation, Joseph spoke eloquently, through an interpreter, to Congress in 1879. "Treat all men alike. Give them all the same law. Give them all an even chance to live and grow. All men were made by the same Great Spirit Chief," Joseph pleaded. The last remnant of Joseph's band were deported under guard to a non-Nez Percé reservation in Washington, where Chief Joseph died in 1904 "of a broken heart," and where his descendants continue to live in exile to this day.

THE INTERNAL EMPIRE

Since the time of Christopher Columbus, the Americas had inspired in Europeans visions of a land of incredible wealth, free for the taking. In the nineteenth century, the North American continent, stretching across scarcely populated territories toward the Pacific Ocean, revived this fantasy. Determined to make their fortunes, be it from copper in Arizona, wheat in Montana, or oranges in California, numerous adventurers traveled west. As a group they carried out the largest migration and greatest commercial expansion in American history.

But the settlers themselves also became the subjects of a huge "internal empire" whose financial, political, and industrial centers of power remained in the East. Only a small number of settlers actually struck it rich in the great extractive industries—mining, lumbering, ranching, and farming—that ruled the western economy. Meanwhile, older populations—Indian peoples, Hispanic peoples, and more recently settled communities like the Mormons—struggled to create places for themselves in this new order.

Mining Towns

The discovery of gold in California in 1848 roused fortune seekers from across the United States, Europe, and as far away as Chile and China. Within a year, prospecting parties overran the western territories, setting a pattern for intermittent rushes for gold, silver, and copper that extended from the Colorado mountains to the Arizona deserts, from California to Oregon and Washington, and from Alaska to the Black Hills of South Dakota. Mining camps and boomtowns soon dotted what had once been thinly settled regions. The population of California alone jumped from 14,000 in 1848 to 223,856 just four years later. More than any other industry or commercial enterprise, mining fostered western expansion.

The mining industry quickly grew from its treasure-hunt origins into a grand corporate enterprise. The most successful mineowners bought out the smaller claims and built an entire industry around their stakes. They found investors to finance their expansion and used the borrowed capital to purchase the latest in extractive technology, such as new explosives, compressed-air or diamond-headed rotary drills, and wire cable. They gained access to timber to fortify their underground structures and water to feed the hydraulic pumps that washed down mountains. They built smelters to refine the crude ore into ingots and often financed railroads to transport the product to distant markets. By the end of the century, the Anaconda Copper Mining Company, which had mining interests throughout the West, had expanded into hydroelectricity to become one of the most powerful corporations in the nation.

The mining corporations laid the basis for a new economy as well as an interim government and established many of the region's first white settlements. Before the advent of railroads, ore had to be brought out of, and supplies brought into, mining areas by boats, wagons, and mules traveling hundreds of miles over rough territory. The railroad made transportation of supplies and products easier and faster. The shipping trade meanwhile grew into an important industry of its own, employing thousands of merchants, peddlers, and sailors. Gold Hill and nearby Virginia City, Nevada, began as a cluster of small mining camps and by the early 1860s became a thriving urban community of nearly 6,000 people. A decade later, the population had quadrupled, but it subsequently fell sharply as the mines gave out. Men outnumbered women by as much as ten to one, and very few lived with families or stayed very long. They often bunked with male kin and worked alongside friends or acquaintances from their hometown. Some lived unusually well, feasting on oysters trucked in at great expense. The town center was usually the saloon, where, as one observer complained, men "without the restraint of law, indifferent to public opinion, and unburdened by families, drink whenever they feel like it, whenever they have the money to pay for it, and whenever there is nothing else to do."

The western labor movement began in these camps, partly as a response to dangerous working conditions. In the hardrock mines of the 1870s, one of every thirty workers was disabled, one of eighty killed. Miners began to organize in the 1860s, demanding good pay for dangerous and life-shortening work. By the end of the century they had established the strongest unions in the West.

When mineowners' private armies "arrested" strikers or fought their unions with rifle fire, miners burned down the campsites, seized trains loaded with ore, and sabotaged company property. The miners' unions also helped to secure legislation mandating a maximum eight-hour day for certain jobs and workmen's compensation for injuries. Such laws were enacted in Idaho, Arizona, and New Mexico by the 1910s, long before similar laws in most eastern states.

The unions fought hard, but they did so exclusively for the benefit of white workers. The native-born and the Irish and Cornish immigrants (from Cornwall, England) far outnumbered other groups before the turn of the century, when Italians, Slavs, and Greeks began to replace them. Labor unions eventually admitted these new immigrants but refused Chinese, Mexican, and Indian workers.

When prices and ore production fell sharply, not even unions could stop the owners from shutting down the mines and leaving ghost towns in their wake. Often they also left behind an environmental disaster. Hydraulic mining, which used water cannons to blast hillsides and expose gold deposits, drove tons of rock and earth into the rivers and canyons. By the late 1860s southern California's rivers were clogged, producing floods that wiped out towns and farms. In 1893, Congress finally passed the Caminetti Act, giving the state the power to regulate the mines. (The act also created the Sacramento River Commission, which began to replace free-flowing rivers with canals and dams.) Underground mining continued unregulated, using up whole forests for timbers and filling the air with dangerous, sulfurous smoke.

Mormon Settlements

The Mormons (members of the Church of Jesus Christ of Latter-Day Saints) had fled western New York in the 1830s for Illinois and Missouri, only to face greater persecution in the Midwest. When their founder, Joseph Smith, was murdered after proclaiming the doctrine of polygamy (the taking of more than one wife), the community sought refuge in the West. Led by their new prophet, Brigham Young, the Mormons migrated in 1846–47 to the Great Basin in present-day Utah and formed an independent theocratic state called Deseret. However, their dream was cut short in 1850 when Congress set up Utah Territory. In 1857 President James Buchanan declared the Mormons to be in "a state of substantial rebellion" (for being an independent state within U.S. territory) and sent the U.S. Army to occupy the territory.

Although federal troops remained until the outbreak of the Civil War in 1861, the Mormon population continued to grow. By 1870, more than 87,000 Mormons lived in Utah Territory. Contrary to federal law, church officials forbade the selling of land. Mormons instead held property in common. They created sizable settlements complemented by satellite villages joined to communal farmlands and a common pasture. Relying on agricultural techniques learned from local Indian tribes, the Mormons built dams for irrigation and harvested a variety of crops from desert soil. Eventually nearly 500 Mormon communities spread from Oregon to Idaho to northern Mexico.

But as territorial rule tightened, the Mormons saw their unique way of life once again threatened. Preceded by prohibitory federal laws enacted in 1862 and 1874, the Supreme Court finally ruled against polygamy in the 1879 case of *United States* v. *Reynolds*, which granted the freedom of belief but not the freedom of practice. In 1882, Congress passed the Edmunds Act, which effectively disfranchised those who believed in or practiced polygamy and threatened them with fines and imprisonment. Equally devastating was the Edmunds-Tucker Act, passed five years later, which destroyed the temporal power of the Mormon Church by confiscating all assets over $50,000 and establishing a federal commission to oversee all elections in the territory. By the early 1890s, Mormon leaders officially renounced the practice of plural marriage.

Borderland Communities

The Treaty of Guadalupe Hidalgo, which ended the Mexican-American War, allowed the Hispanic people north of the Rio Grande to choose between immigrating to Mexico or staying in what was now the United States. But the new Mexican-American border, one of the longest unguarded boundaries in the world, could not successfully sever communities that had been connected for centuries. What gradually emerged was an economically and socially interdependent zone, the Anglo-Hispanic borderlands linking the United States and Mexico.

Although under the treaty all Hispanics were formally guaranteed citizenship and the "free enjoyment of their liberty and property," local "Anglos" (as the Mexicans called white Americans) often violated these provisions and, through fraud or coercion, took control of the land. The Sante Fe Ring, a group of lawyers, politicians, and land speculators, stole millions of acres from the public domain and grabbed over 80 percent of the Mexicano landholdings in New Mexico alone. More often, Anglos used new federal laws to their own benefit.

For a time, Arizona and New Mexico seemed to hold out hope for a mutually beneficial interaction between Mexicanos and Anglos. A prosperous class of Hispanic landowners, with long-standing ties to Anglos through marriage, had established itself in cities like Albuquerque and Tucson, old Spanish towns that had been founded in the seventeenth and eighteenth centuries. In Las Cruces, New Mexico, an exceptional family such as the wealthy Amadors could shop by mail from Bloomingdales, travel to the World's Fair in Chicago, and send their children to English-language Catholic schools. These Mexican elites, well integrated into the emerging national economy, continued to wield political power as ranchers, landlords, and real estate developers until the end of the century. They secured passage of bills for education in their regions and often served as superintendents of local schools. Several prominent merchants became territorial delegates to Congress.

But the majority of Mexicans who had lived in the mountains and deserts of the Southwest for well over two centuries were less prepared for these changes. Most had worked outside the commercial economy, farming and herding sheep for their own subsistence. Before 1848 they had few contacts with the outside world. With the Anglos came land closures as well as commercial expansion prompted by railroad, mining, and timber industries. Many poor families found themselves crowded onto plots too small for subsistence farming. Many turned to seasonal labor on the new Anglo-owned commercial farms, where they became the first of many generations of poorly paid migratory workers. Other Mexicanos adapted by taking jobs on the railroad or in the mines. By the end of the century Mexicanos had become a predominantly urban population, dependent on wages for survival.

Women were quickly drawn into the expanding network of market and wage relations. They tried to make ends meet by selling produce from their backyard gardens; more often they worked as seamstresses or laundresses. Formerly at the center of a communal society, Mexicanas found themselves with fewer options in the cash economy. What wages they could now earn fell below even the low sums paid to their husbands, and women lost status within both the family and community.

Occasionally, Mexicanos organized to reverse these trends or at least to limit the damage done to their communities. In the border town of Brownsville, Texas, in 1859, Juan Nepomuceno Cortina, known as the Red Robber of the Rio Grande, and sixty of his followers pillaged white-owned stores and killed four Anglos who had gone unpunished for murdering several Mexicans. "Cortina's War" marked the first of several sporadic rebellions. Other Mexicanos organized more peacefully. *El Alianzo Hispano-Americano* (The Hispanic-American Alliance) was formed "to protect and fight for the rights of Spanish Americans" through political action. *Mutualistes* (mutual aid societies) provided sickness and death benefits to Mexican families.

Despite many pressures, Mexicanos preserved much of their cultural heritage. The Roman Catholic Church retained its influence in the community, and most Mexicans continued to turn to the church to baptize infants, to celebrate the feast day of their patron saints, to marry, and to bury the dead. Special saints like the Virgin of Guadalupe and distinctive holy days like the Day of the Dead survived along with fiestas celebrating the change of seasons. Many communities continued to commemorate Mexican national holidays, such as *Cinco de Mayo* (the Fifth of May), marking the Mexican victory over French invaders in the battle of Puebla in 1862. Spanish language and Spanish place names continued to distinguish the Southwest.

Americans had brought in commercial capitalism, their political and legal systems, as well as many of their social and cultural institutions. Ironically, though, even after statehood, white settlers would still be only distant representatives of an empire whose financial, political, and industrial centers remained in the Northeast. Embittered Westerners, along with Southerners, would form the core of a nationwide discontent that would soon threaten to uproot the American political system.

THE CATTLE INDUSTRY

The slaughter of the buffalo made way for the cattle industry, one of the most profitable businesses in the West. Texas longhorns, introduced by the Spanish, numbered over 5 million at the close of the Civil War and represented a potentially plentiful supply of beef for eastern consumers. The Kansas Pacific Railroad provided crucial transportation links to slaughtering and packing houses and commercial distributors in Kansas City, St. Louis, and Chicago.

Drovers pushed herd after herd north from Texas through Oklahoma on the trail marked out by part-Cherokee trader Jesse Chisholm. Great profits were made on Texas steers bought for $7–$9 a head and sold in Kansas for upward of $30. In 1880 nearly 2 million cattle were slaughtered in Chicago alone. For two decades, cattle represented the West's bonanza industry.

Cowboys

The great cattle drives depended on the cowboy, a seasonal or migrant worker. After the Civil War, cowboys—one for every 300–500 head of cattle on the trail—rounded up herds of Texas cattle and drove them as much as 1,500 miles north to grazing ranches or to the stockyards where they were readied for shipping by rail to eastern markets. The boss supplied the horses, the cowboy his own bedroll, saddle, and spurs. The workday lasted from sunup to sundown, with short night shifts for guarding the cattle. Scurvy, a widespread ailment, could be traced to the basic chuckwagon menu of sowbelly, beans, and coffee, a diet bereft of fruits and vegetables. The cowboy worked without protection from rain or hail, and severe dust storms could cause temporary blindness.

In return for his labor, the cowboy received at the best of times about $30 per month. Wages were usually paid in one lump sum at the end of a drive, a policy that encouraged cowboys to spend their money quickly and recklessly. When wages began to fall along with the price of beef, many Texas cowboys struck for higher wages; nearly all Wyoming cowboys struck in 1886. Aided by the legendary camaraderie fostered in the otherwise desolate conditions of the long drive, cowboys, along with miners, were among the first western workers to organize against employers.

Like other parts of the West, the cattle range was ethnically diverse. Between one-fifth and one-third of all workers were Indian, Mexican, or African American. Some African American cowboys were sons of former slaves who had been captured from the African territory of Gambia, where cattle raising was an age-old art. Unlike Mexicans, they earned wages comparable to those paid to Anglos and especially during the early years worked in integrated drover parties. By the 1880s, as the center of the cattle industry shifted to the more settled regions around the northern ranches, African Americans were forced out, and they turned to other kinds of work. The majority of Anglo cowboys also came from the South and remained loyal to the racial hierarchy of the Confederacy.

Cowgirls and Prostitutes

Although few women worked as trail hands, they did find jobs on the ranches, usually in the kitchen or laundry. The majority of women attended to domestic chores, caring for children and maintaining the household. Their daughters, however, enjoyed better prospects. By the end of the century, women, who as girls had accompanied their fathers in outside chores, were riding astride, "clothespin style," roping calves, branding cattle or cutting their ears to mark them, and castrating bulls.

In cattle towns as well as mining camps, many women worked as prostitutes. During the first cattle drive to Abilene in 1867, a few women were so engaged; but by the following spring, Cowman Joseph McCoy's assistant recalled, "they came in swarms, & as the weather was warm 4 or 5 girls could huddle together in a tent very comfortably." Although some women worked in trailside "hoghouses," the best-paid prostitutes congregated in "brothel districts" or "tenderloins." Dodge city had two: one with white prostitutes for white patrons; another with black prostitutes for both white and black men.

Perhaps 50,000 women engaged in prostitution west of the Mississippi during the second half of the nineteenth century. Like most cowboys, most prostitutes were unmarried and in their teens or twenties. Often fed up with underpaid jobs in dressmaking or domestic service, they found few alternatives to prostitution in the cattle towns, where the cost of food and lodging was notoriously high. Still, earnings in prostitution were slim. In the best of times, a fully employed Wichita prostitute might earn $30 per week, nearly two-thirds of which would go for room and board.

Community and Conflict on the Range

The combination of prostitution, gambling, and drinking discouraged the formation of stable communities. Personal violence was notoriously commonplace on the streets and in the barrooms of cattle towns and mining camps populated mainly by young, single men. But contrary to popular belief, gunfights were relatively rare. Local police officers, such as Wyatt Earp and James "Wild Bill" Hickok, worked mainly to keep order among drunken cowboys.

After the Civil War, violent crime, assault, and robbery rose sharply throughout the United States. In the West, the most prevalent crimes were horse theft and cattle rustling, which peaked during the height of the open range period and then fell back by the 1890s. Death by legal hanging or illegal lynching—at "necktie parties" in which the victims were "jerked to Jesus"—was the usual sentence.

The "range wars" of the 1870s produced violent conflicts. By this time, both farmers and sheep herders were encroaching on the fields where cattle had once grazed freely. Sheep chew grass down to its roots, making it practically impossible to raise cattle on land they have grazed. Farmers meanwhile set about building fences to protect their domestic livestock and property. Great cattle barons fought back against farmers by ordering cowboys to cut the new barbed-wire fences.

The cattle barons, eager for greater profits and often backed by foreign capital, overstocked their herds, and eventually the cattle began to deplete the limited supply of grass. Finally, during 1885–87, a combination of summer drought and winter blizzards killed 90 percent of the cattle in the northern Plains. Many big ranchers fell into bankruptcy. Along the way, they often took out their grievances against the former cowboys who had gathered small herds for themselves. They charged these small ranchers with cattle rustling, taking them to court or, in some cases, rounding up lynching parties. As one historian has written, violence was "not a mere sideshow" but "an intrinsic part of western society."

FARMING COMMUNITIES ON THE PLAINS

The vision of a huge fertile garden extending from the Appalachians to the Pacific Ocean had inspired Americans since the early days of the republic. But the first explorers who actually traveled through the Great Plains quashed this dream. "The Great Desert" was the name they gave to the region stretching west from Kansas and Nebraska, north to Montana and the Dakotas, and south again to Oklahoma and Texas. Few trees fended off the blazing sun of summer or promised a supply of lumber for homes and fences. The occasional river or stream flowed with "muddy gruel" rather than pure, sweet water. Economically, the entire region appeared as hopelessly barren as it was vast. It took massive improvements in both transportation and farm technology—as well as unrelenting advertising and promotional campaigns—to open the Great Plains to widescale agriculture.

The Homestead Act

The Homestead Act of 1862 offered the first incentive to prospective white farmers. This act granted a quarter section (160 acres) of the public domain free to any settler who lived on the land for at least five years and improved it; or a settler could buy the land for $1.25 per acre after only six months' residence. Restricting its provisions to unmarried women, the Homestead Act encouraged adventurous and hard-working women to file between 5 and 15 percent of the claims, which allowed approximately 400,000 households to build farms for themselves.

Homesteaders achieved their greatest success in the central and upper Midwest where the soil was rich and weather relatively moderate. But those settlers lured to the Great Plains by descriptions of land "carpeted with soft grass—a sylvan paradise" found themselves locked in a fierce struggle with the harsh climate and arid soil.

Rather than filing a homestead claim with the federal government, most settlers acquired their land outright. State governments and land companies usually held the most valuable land near transportation and markets, and the majority of farmers were willing to pay a hefty price for these benefits. A few women speculators did very well, particularly in the Dakotas, where they acquired acreage under the generous terms of the Homestead Act, not to farm but to sell when prices for land increased. The big-time land speculators gained even more, plucking choice locations at bargain prices. Although the Homestead Act did spark the largest migration in American history, it did not lay the foundation for a nation of prosperous family farms.

Populating the Plains

The rapid settlement of the West could not have taken place without the railroad. Although the Homestead Act offered prospective farmers free land, it was the railroad that promoted settlement, brought people to their new homes, and carried crops and cattle to eastern markets. The railroads, therefore, wielded tremendous economic and political power throughout the West. Their agents—reputed to know every cow in the district—made major decisions regarding territorial welfare. In designing routes and locating depots, railroad companies put whole communities "on the map," or left them behind.

The western railroads directly encouraged settlement. Unlike the railroads built before the Civil War, which followed the path of villages and towns, the western lines preceded settlement. Bringing people west became their top priority, and the railroad companies conducted aggressive promotional and marketing campaigns. Agents enticed Easterners and Europeans alike with long-term loans and free transportation by rail to distant points in the West. The railroads also sponsored land companies to sell parcels of their own huge allotments from the federal government.

More than 2 million Europeans, many recruited by professional promoters, settled the Great Plains between 1870 and 1900. Some districts in Minnesota seemed to be virtual colonies of Sweden; others housed the largest number of Finns in the New World. Nebraska, whose population as early as 1870 was 25 percent foreign-born, concentrated Germans, Swedes, Danes, and Czechs. But Germans outnumbered all other immigrants by far. A smaller portion of European immigrants reached Kansas, still fewer the territories to the south where Indian and Hispanic peoples and African Americans remained the major ethnic populations.

Many immigrants found life on the Great Plains difficult but endurable. The German-speaking Russians who settled the Dakotas discovered soil similar to that of their homeland but weather that was even more severe. Having earlier fled religious persecution in Germany for Russia, they brought with them heavy coats and the technique of using sun-dried bricks to build houses in areas where lumber was scarce. These immigrants often provided examples for other settlers less familiar with such harsh terrain.

Having traveled the huge distance with kin or members of their Old World villages, immigrants tended to form tight-knit communities on the Great Plains. Many married only within their own group. For example, only 3 percent of Norwegian men married women of a different ethnic background. Like many Mexicanos in the Southwest, several immigrant groups retained their languages well into the twentieth century, usually by sponsoring parochial school systems and publishing their own newspapers. A few groups closed their communities to outsiders. The Poles who migrated to central Nebraska in the 1880s, for example, formed an exclusive settlement; and the German Hutterites, who disavowed private property, lived as much as possible in seclusion in the Bon Homme colony of South Dakota, established in 1874.

Among the native-born settlers of the Great Plains, the largest number had migrated from states bordering the Mississippi River. Settling as individual families rather than as whole communities, they faced an exceptionally solitary life on the Great Plains. The prospect of doing better, which brought most homesteaders to the Great Plains in the first place, caused many families to keep seeking greener pastures. Mobility was so high that between one-third and one-half of all households pulled up stakes within a decade.

Communities eventually flourished in prosperous towns, like Grand Island, Nebraska; Coffeyville, Kansas; and Fargo, North Dakota, that served the larger agricultural region. Built alongside the railroad, they grew into commercial centers, home to banking, medical, legal, and retail services. But closeness did not necessarily promote social equality or even friendship. A social hierarchy based on education (for the handful of doctors and lawyers) and, more important, investment property (held mainly by railroad agents and bankers) governed relationships between individuals and families. Reinforced by family ties and religious and ethnic differences, this hierarchy often persisted across several generations.

Work, Dawn to Dusk

By the 1870s the Great Plains, once the home of buffalo and Indian hunters, was becoming a vast farming region populated mainly by immigrants from Europe and white Americans from east of the Mississippi. In place of the first one-room shanties, sod houses, and log cabins stood substantial frame farmhouses, along with a variety of other buildings like barns, smokehouses, and stables. But the built environment took nothing away from the predominating vista—the expansive fields of grain.

Most farm families survived, and prospered if they could, through hard work, often from dawn to dusk. Men's activities in the fields tended to be seasonal, with heavy work during planting and harvest; at other times, their labor centered on construction or repair of buildings and on taking care of livestock. Women's activities were usually far more routine, week in and week out: cooking and canning of seasonal fruit and vegetables, washing, ironing, churning cream for butter, and keeping chickens for their eggs. Women might occasionally take in boarders, usually young men working temporarily in railroad construction, and they tended to the young children. Many women complained about the ceaseless drudgery, especially when they watched their husbands invest in farm equipment rather than in domestic appliances. Others, relished the challenge.

Milking the cows, hauling water, and running errands to neighboring farms could be done by the children, once they had reached the age of nine or so. The "one-room school," where all grades learned together, taught the basics of literacy and arithmetic that a future farmer or commercial employee would require.

The harsh climate and unyielding soil nevertheless forced all but the most reclusive families to seek out friends and neighbors. Neighbors might agree to work together haying, harvesting, and threshing grain. They also traded their labor, calculated by the hour, for use of equipment or for special assistance. A well-to-do farmer might "rent" his threshing machine in exchange for a small cash fee and, for instance, three days' labor. His wife might barter her garden produce for her neighbor's bread and milk or for help during childbirth or disability.

Much of this informal barter, however, resulted from lack of cash rather than a lasting desire to cooperate. When annual harvests were bountiful, even the farm woman's practice of bartering goods with neighbors and local merchants—butter and eggs in return for yard goods or seed—diminished sharply, replaced by cash transactions. Still, wheat production proved unsteady in the last half of the nineteenth century, and few farm families could remain reliant wholly on themselves.

For many farmers, the soil simply would not yield a livelihood, and they often owed more money than they took in. Start-up costs, including the purchase of land and equipment, put many farmers deep in debt to local creditors. Some lost their land altogether. By the turn of the century, more than one-third of all farmers in the United States were tenants on someone else's land.

Again and again foreclosures wiped out the small landowner through dips in commodity prices, bad decisions, natural disasters, or illness. The swift growth of rural population soon ended. Although writers and orators alike continued to celebrate the family farm as the source of virtue and economic well-being, the hard reality of big money and political power told a far different story.

THE WORLD'S BREADBASKET

During the second half of the nineteenth century commercial farms employed the most intensive and extensive methods of agricultural production in the world. Hard-working farmers brought huge numbers of acres under cultivation, while new technologies allowed them to achieve unprecedented levels of efficiency in the planting and harvesting of crops. As a result, western agriculture became increasingly tied to international trade, and modern capitalism soon ruled western agriculture, as it did the mining and cattle industries.

New Production Technologies

Only after the trees had been cleared and grasslands cut free of roots could the soil be prepared for planting. But as farmers on the Great Plains knew so well, the sod west of the Mississippi did not yield readily to cultivation and often broke the cast-iron plows typically used by eastern farmers. Farther west, some farmers resorted to drills to plant seeds for crops such as wheat and oats. Even in the best locations, where loamy, fertile ground had built up over centuries into eight or more

inches of decayed vegetation, the preliminary breaking, or "busting," of the sod required hard labor. But, as a North Dakota settler wrote to his wife back in Michigan, after the first crop the soil became as "soft as can be, any team [of men and animals] can work it."

In 1837 John Deere had designed his famous "singing plow" that easily turned prairie grasses under and turned up even highly compacted soils. Around the same time, Cyrus McCormick's reaper began to be used for cutting grain; by the 1850s his factories were turning out reapers in mass quantities. The harvester, invented in the 1870s, drew the cut stalks upward to a platform where two men could bind them into sheaves; by the 1880s an automatic knotter tied them together. Drastically reducing the number of people traditionally required for this work, the harvester increased the pace many times over. The introduction of mechanized corn planters and mowing or raking machines for hay all but completed the technological arsenal.

In the 1890s, the U.S. commissioner of labor measured the impact of technology on farm productivity. Before the introduction of the wire binder in 1875, he reported, a farmer could not plant more than 8 acres of wheat if he were to harvest it successfully without help; by 1890 the same farmer could rely on his new machine to handle 135 acres with relative ease and without risk of spoilage. The improvements in the last half of the century allowed an average farmer to produce up to ten times more than was possible with the old implements.

Scientific study of soil, grain, and climatic conditions was another factor in the record output. Beginning in the mid-nineteenth century, federal and state governments added inducements to the growing body of expertise, scientific information, and hands-on advice. Through the Morrill Act of 1862, "land-grant" colleges acquired space for campuses in return for promising to institute agricultural programs. The Department of Agriculture, which attained cabinet-level status in 1889, and the Weather Bureau (transferred from the War Department in 1891) also made considerable contributions to farmers' knowledge. The federal Hatch Act of 1887, which created a series of state experimental stations,

HAND V. MACHINE LABOR ON THE FARM, CA. 1880				
	Time Worked		**Labor Cost**	
Crop	Hand	Machine	Hand	Machine
Wheat	61 hours	3 hours	$3.55	$0.66
Corn	39 hours	15 hours	3.62	1.51
Oats	66 hours	7 hours	3.73	1.07
Loose Hay	21 hours	4 hours	1.75	0.42
Baled Hay	35 hours	12 hours	3.06	1.29

provided for basic agricultural research, especially in the areas of soil minerals and plant growth. Many states added their own agricultural stations, usually connected with state colleges and universities.

Nature nevertheless often reigned over technological innovation and seemed in places to take revenge against these early successes. West of the 98th meridian—a north-south line extending through western Oklahoma, central Kansas and Nebraska, and eastern Dakota—perennial dryness due to an annual rainfall of less than 20 inches constantly threatened to turn soil into dust and to break plows on the hardened ground. Summer heat burned out crops and ignited grass fires. Mountains of winter snows turned rivers into spring torrents that flooded fields; heavy fall rains washed crops away. Even good weather invited worms and flying insects to infest the crops. During the 1870s grasshoppers in clouds a mile long ate everything organic, including tree bark and clothes.

Producing for the Market

Farming changed in important ways during the last third of the nineteenth century. Although the family remained the primary source of labor, farmers tended to put more emphasis on production for exchange rather than for home use. They continued to plant vegetable gardens and often kept fowl or livestock for the family's consumption, but farmers raised crops mainly for the market and measured their own success or failure in terms of cash products.

Wheat farmers in particular prospered. With the world population increasing at a rapid rate, the international demand for wheat was enormous, and American farmers made huge profits from the sale of this crop. Wheat production ultimately served as a barometer of the agricultural economy in the West. Farmers in all corners of the region, from Nebraska to California, expanded or contracted their holdings and planned their crops according to the price of wheat.

The new machines and expanding market did not necessarily guarantee success. Land, draft animals, and equipment remained very expensive, and start-up costs could keep a family in debt for decades. A year of good returns often preceded a year of financial disaster. Weather conditions, international markets, and railroad and steamship shipping prices all proved equally unpredictable and heartless.

The new technology and scientific expertise favored the large, well-capitalized farmer over the small one. The majority of farmers with fewer resources expanded at more modest rates. Between 1880 and 1900, average farm size in the seven leading grain-growing states increased from 64.4 acres to more than 100 acres.

California Agribusiness

The trend toward big farms reached an apex in California, where farming as a business surpassed farming as a way of life. Farms of nearly 500 acres dominated the California landscape in 1870; by the turn of the century, two-thirds of the state's arable land was in 1,000-acre farms. As land reformer and social commentator Henry George noted, California was "not a country of farms but a country of plantations and estates."

This scale of production made California the national leader in wheat production by the mid-1880s. But it also succeeded dramatically with fruit and vegetables. Large- and medium-sized growers, shrewdly combined in cooperative marketing associations during the 1870s and 1880s, used the new refrigerator cars to ship their produce in large quantities to the East and even to Europe. By 1890, cherries, apricots, and oranges, packed with mountains of ice, made their way into homes across the United States.

By 1900, California had become the model for American agribusiness, not the home of self-sufficient homesteaders but the showcase of heavily capitalized farm factories. Machines soon displaced animals and even many people. Many Californios tried to hold onto their traditional forms of labor if not their land, only to become the backbone of the state's migrant workforce. Intense battles in the state legislature over land and irrigation rights underscored the message that powerful forces had gathered in California to promote large-scale agricultural production.

The Toll on the Land

The new inhabitants often looked past the existing flora and fauna toward a landscape remade strictly for commercial purposes. The changes they produced in some areas were nearly as cataclysmic as those that occurred during the Ice Age.

Banishing many existing species, farmers "improved" the land by introducing exotic plants and animals—that is, biological colonies indigenous to other regions and continents. Farmers also unintentionally introduced new varieties of weeds, insect pests, and rats. Surviving portions of older grasslands and meadows eventually could be found only alongside railroad tracks, in graveyards, or inside national parks.

Numerous species disappeared altogether or suffered drastic reduction. The grizzly bear, for example, an animal exclusive to the West, could once be found in large numbers from the Great Plains to California and throughout much of Alaska; by the early decades of the twentieth century, one nature writer estimated that only 800 survived, mostly in Yellowstone National Park. At the same time the number of wolves declined from perhaps as many as 2 million to just 200,000. By the mid-1880s, no more than 5,000 buffalo survived in the entire United States, and little remained of the once vast herds but great heaps of bones sold for $7.50 per ton.

The slaughter of the buffalo had a dramatic impact, not only on the fate of the species but also on the grasslands of the Great Plains. Over all, the biological diversity of the region had been drastically reduced. Having killed off the giant herds, ranchers and farmers quickly shifted to cattle and sheep production. Unlike the roaming buffalo, these livestock did not range widely and soon devoured the native grasses down to their roots. With the ground cover destroyed, the soil eroded and became barren. By the end of the century, huge dust storms formed across the windswept plains.

In 1873 the U.S. Congress passed the Timber Culture Act, which allotted homesteaders an additional 160 acres of land in return for planting and cultivating forty acres of trees. Because residence was not required, and because tree planting could not be assessed for at least thirteen years, speculators filed for several claims at once, then turned around and sold the land without having planted a single tree. Although some forests were restored, neither the weather nor the soil improved.

Large-scale commercial agriculture also took a heavy toll on inland waters. Before white settlement, rainfall had drained naturally into lakes and underground aquifers, and watering spots were abundant throughout the Great Plains. Farmers mechanically rerouted and dammed water to irrigate their crops, causing many bodies of water to disappear and the water table to drop significantly. Successful farmers pressed for ever greater supplies of water. In 1887 the state of California formed irrigation districts, securing bond issues for the construction of canals, and other western states followed. But by the 1890s, irrigation had seemed to reach its limit without federal support. The Newlands or National Reclamation Act of 1902 added 1 million acres of irrigated land, and state irrigation districts added more than 10 million acres. Expensive to taxpayers, and ultimately benefiting corporate farmers rather than small landowners, these projects further diverted water and totally transformed the landscape.

Although western state politicians and federal officials debated water rights for decades, they rarely considered the impact of water policies on the environment. The need to maintain the water supply indirectly led to the creation of national forests and the Forest Service. Western farmers supported the General Land Revision Act of 1891, which gave the president the power to establish forest reserves to protect watersheds against the threats posed by lumbering, overgrazing, and forest fires. In the years that followed, President Benjamin Harrison established fifteen forest reserves exceeding 16 million acres, and President Grover Cleveland added more than 21 million acres. But only in 1897 did the secretary of the interior finally gain the authority to regulate the use of these reserves.

The Forest Management Act of 1897 and the National Reclamation Act of 1902 set the federal government on the path of large-scale regulatory activities. The Forest Service was established in 1905, and in 1907 forest reserves were transferred from the Department of the Interior to the Department of Agriculture. The federal government would now play an even larger role in economic development of the West, dealing mainly with corporate farmers and ranchers eager for improvements.

THE WESTERN LANDSCAPE

The public east of the Mississippi craved stories about the West and visual images of its sweeping vistas. Artists and photographers built their reputations in what they saw and imagined. Scholars, from geologists and botanists to historians and anthropologists, toured the trans-Mississippi West in pursuit of new data. The region and its peoples came to represent what was both unique and magnificent about the American landscape.

Nature's Majesty

By the end of the century, scores of writers had described spectacular, breathtaking natural sites like the Grand Tetons and High Sierras, vast meadows of waving grasses and beautiful flowers, expansive canyons and rushing white rivers, and exquisite deserts covered with sagebrush or dotted with flowering cactus and enticing precisely for their stark qualities.

Moved by such evidence, the federal government began to set aside huge tracts of land as nature reserves. In 1864 Congress passed the Yosemite Act, which placed the spectacular cliffs and giant sequoias under the management of the state of California. Meanwhile, explorers returned to the East awestruck by the varied terrain of the Rocky Mountains, the largest mountain chain in North America. In 1872 Congress named Yellowstone the first national park. Yosemite and Sequoia in California, Crater Lake in Oregon, Mount Ranier in Washington, and Glacier in Montana all became national parks between 1890 and 1910.

Landscape painters, particularly the group that became known as the Rocky Mountain School, also piqued the public's interest in western scenery. In the 1860s, German-born Albert Bierstadt, equipped with a camera, traveled the Oregon Trail. Using his photographs as inspiration, Bierstadt painted mountains so wondrous that they seemed nearly surreal, projecting a divine aura behind the majesty of nature. His "earthscapes"—huge canvases with exacting details of animals and plants—thrilled viewers and sold for tens of thousands of dollars.

The Legendary Wild West

By the end of the century, many Americans, rich and poor alike, imagined the West as a land of promise and opportunity and, above all, of excitement and adventure. Future president Theodore Roosevelt helped to promote this view. Soon after his election to the New York State Assembly in 1882, Roosevelt was horrified to see himself lampooned in the newspapers as a dandy and weakling. A year later, after buying a ranch in South Dakota, he began to reconstruct his public image. He wrote three books recounting his adventures in the West, claiming that they had not only instilled in him personal bravery and "hardihood" but self-reliance. The West, as Roosevelt insisted, meant "vigorous manhood."

The first "westerns," the "dime novels" that sold in the 1860s in editions of 50,000 or more, reflected these myths. Competing against stories about pirates, wars, crime, and sea adventures, westerns outsold the others. Edward Zane Carroll Judson's *Buffalo Bill, the King of the Border Men,* first published in 1869, spawned hundreds of other novels, thousands of stories, and an entire magazine devoted to Buffalo Bill. Real-life African American cowboy Nat Love lived on in the imaginations of many generations as Edward L. Wheeler's dime novel hero "Deadwood Dick," who rode the range as a white cowboy in black clothes in over thirty stories. His girlfriend "Calamity Jane"—"the most reckless buchario in ther Hills"—also took on mythic qualities.

Railroad promoters and herd owners actively promoted these romantic and heroic images. Cowman Joseph McCoy staged Wild West shows in St. Louis and Chicago, where Texas cowboys entertained prospective buyers by roping calves and breaking horses. Many cowboys played up this imaginary role, dressing and talking to match the stories told about them. The first professional photographers often made their living touring the West, setting up studios where cowboys and prostitutes posed in elaborate costumes.

The former Pony Express rider, army scout, and famed buffalo hunter William F. Cody hit upon the idea of an extravaganza that would bring the legendary West to those who could never experience it in person. "Buffalo Bill" Cody made sharpshooter Annie Oakley a star performer. Entrancing crowds with her stunning accuracy with pistol or rifle, Oakley shot dimes in midair and cigarettes from her husband's mouth. Cody also hired Sioux Indians and hundreds of cowboys to perform in mock stagecoach robberies and battles. With far less fanfare, many veteran cowboys enlisted themselves on "dude ranches" for tourists or performed as rope twirlers or yodeling singers in theaters across the United States.

The "American Primitive"

New technologies of graphic reproduction encouraged painters and photographers to provide new images of the West, authentic as well as fabricated. A young German American artist, Charles Schreyvogel, saw Buffalo Bill's tent show in Buffalo and decided to make the West his life's work. His canvases depicted Indian warriors and U.S. cavalry fighting furiously but without blood and gore. Charles Russell, a genuine cowboy, painted the life he knew but also indulged in imaginary scenarios, producing paintings of buffalo

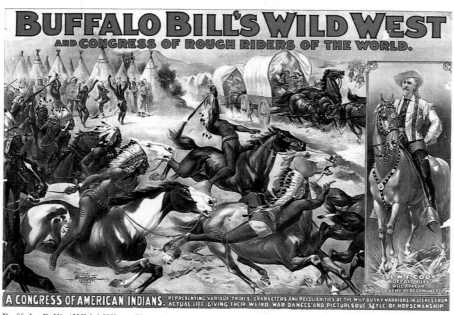

Buffalo Bill's "Wild West Show" poster from 1899. William Cody's theatrical company toured the United States and Europe for decades, reenacting various battles and occasionally switching to football (cowboys versus Indians). Cody's style set the pace for both rodeos and western silent films.

SOURCE: Library of Congress.

hunts and first encounters between Indian peoples and white explorers.

Frederic Remington, the most famous of all the western artists, left Yale Art School to visit Montana in 1881, became a Kansas sheep herder and tavern owner, and then returned to painting. Painstakingly accurate in physical details, especially of horses, his paintings celebrated the "winning of the West" from the Indian peoples.

Painters and photographers led the way for scholarly research on the various Indian societies. The early ethnographer and pioneer of fieldwork in anthropology Lewis Henry Morgan devoted his life to the study of Indian family or kinship patterns, mostly of eastern tribes such as the Iroquois, who adopted him into their Hawk Clan.

One of the most influential interpreters of the cultures of living tribespeople was the pioneering ethnographer Alice Cunningham Fletcher. In 1879, Fletcher met Suzette (Bright Eyes) La Flesche of the Omaha tribe, who was on a speaking tour to gain support for her people, primarily to prevent their removal from tribal lands. Well known as an expert on Omaha music, Fletcher also supported the Omahas' campaign to gain individual title to tribal lands, eventually drafting legislation that was enacted by Congress as the Omaha Act of 1882.

While white settlers and the federal government continued to threaten the survival of tribal life, Indian lore became a major pursuit of scholars and amateurs alike. Adults and children delighted in turning up ar-

rowheads. Fraternal organizations such as the Elks and Eagles borrowed tribal terminology. The Boy Scouts and Girl Scouts, the nation's premier youth organizations, used tribal lore to instill strength of character. And the U.S. Treasury stamped images of tribal chiefs and buffalo on the nation's most frequently used coins.

THE TRANSFORMATION OF INDIAN SOCIETIES

In 1871, the U.S. government formally ended the treaty system, eclipsing without completely abolishing the sovereignty of Indian nations. Still, the tribes persisted. Using a mixture of survival strategies from farming and trade to the leasing of reservation lands, they both adapted to changing conditions and maintained old traditions.

Reform Policy and Politics

For decades, reformers, mainly from the Protestant churches, had lobbied Congress for a program of salvation through assimilation, and they looked to the Board of Indian Commissioners, created in 1869, to carry out this mission. The board often succeeded in mediating conflicts among the various tribes crowded onto reservations but made far less headway in converting them to Christianity or transforming them into prosperous

OVERVIEW

MAJOR INDIAN TREATIES AND LEGISLATION OF THE LATE NINETEENTH CENTURY

1863	Nez Percé Treaty	Signed illegally on behalf of the entire tribe in which the Nez Percé abandoned 6 million acres of land in return for a small reservation in northeastern Oregon. Led to Nez Percé wars, which ended in 1877 with the surrender of Chief Joseph.
1867	Medicine Lodge Treaty	Assigned reservations in existing Indian Territory to Comanches, Plains (Kiowa), Appaches, Kiowas, Cheyennes, and Arapahoes, bringing these tribes together with Sioux, Shoshones, Bannocks, and Navajos.
1868	Treaty of Fort Laramie	Successfully ended Red Cloud's war by evacuating federal troops from Sioux Territory along the Bozeman Trail; additionally granted Sioux ownership of the western half of South Dakota and rights to use Powder River county in Wyoming and Montana.
1871		Congress declares end to treaty system.
1887	Dawes Severalty Act	Divided communal tribal land, granting the right to petition for citizenship to those Indians who accepted the individual land allotment of 160 acres. Successfully undermined sovereignty.

farming communities. The majority of Indian peoples lived in poverty and misery, deprived of their traditional means of survival and more often than not subjected to fraud by corrupt government officials and private suppliers. Reformers who observed these conditions firsthand nevertheless remained unshaken in their belief that tribespeople must be raised out of the darkness of ignorance into the light of civilization.

Some reformers were genuinely outraged by the government's continuous violation of treaty obligations and the military enforcement of the reservation policy. One of the most influential was Helen Hunt Jackson, a noted poet and author of children's stories. Her book-length exposé, *A Century of Dishonor*, published in 1881, detailed the plight of Indian peoples.

The Dawes Severalty Act, passed by Congress in 1887, established federal Indian policy for decades to come. The act allowed the president to distribute land not to tribes but to individuals legally "severed" from their tribes. Those individuals who accepted the land allotment of 160 acres and agreed to allow the government to sell unallotted tribal lands (with some funds set aside for education) could petition to become citizens of the United States. A little over a decade after its enactment, many reformers believed that the Dawes Act had resolved the basis of the "Indian problem." Hollow Horn Bear, a Sioux chief, offered a different opinion, judging the Dawes Act to be "only another trick of the whites."

The Dawes Act successfully undermined tribal sovereignty but offered little compensation. Indian religions and sacred ceremonies were banned, the telling of legends and myths forbidden, and shaman and medicine men imprisoned or exiled for continuing their traditional practices. "Indian schools" forbade Indian languages, clothing styles, and even hair fashions in order to "kill the Indian . . . and save the man," as one schoolmaster put it.

Treated as savages, Indian children fled most white schools. Nor did adults receive much encouragement to become property holders. Government agencies allotted them inferior farmland, inadequate tools, and little training for agricultural self-sufficiency. Seeing scant advantage in assimilating, only a minority of adults dropped their tribal religion for Christianity or their communal ways for the accumulation of private property. Within the next forty years, the Indian peoples lost 60 percent of the reservation land remaining in 1887 and 66 percent of the land allotted to them as homesteaders. The tenets of the Dawes Act were not reversed until 1934. In that year, Congress passed the Indian Reorganization Act, which affirmed the integrity of Indian cultural institutions and returned some land to tribal ownership (see Chapter 24).

The Ghost Dance

After the passage of the Dawes Severalty Act, one more cycle of rebellion remained for the Sioux. In 1888, the Paiute prophet Wovoka, ill with scarlet fever, had a vision during a total eclipse of the sun. In his vision, the Creator told him that if the Indian peoples learned to love each other, they would be granted a special place in the afterlife. The Creator also gave him the Ghost Dance, which the prophet performed for others and soon spread throughout

In 1890, the celebrated artist Frederic Remington (1861–1909) produced this color sketch of Oglala Sioux at the Pine Ridge Indian Reservation in South Dakota. By this time, Remington had established himself as a leading illustrator of western themes, including the Indian Wars. He had traveled extensively in the West, gathering information, making sketches, and taking photographs, which he later used at his studio in New Rochelle, New York. Remington sold his illustrations to major magazines, including *Harper's Weekly*.

The ghost dance of 1890, pictured here, provided artists like Remington with vivid imagery. The dancers wore brightly patterned robes and shirts, some decorated with stars symbolizing the coming of a new age for the Indians.

SOURCE: Frederic Remington, *Oglala Sioux performing the Ghost Dance at the Pine Ridge Indian Agency, South Dakota, 1890*/The Granger Collection, New York.

the tribe. The Sioux came to believe that when the day of judgment came, all Indian peoples who had ever lived would return to their lost world and white peoples would vanish from the earth.

White Americans took the Ghost Dance as a warning of tribal retribution rather than a religious ceremony. As thousands of Sioux danced to exhaustion, local whites intolerantly demanded the practice be stopped. A group of the Sioux led by Big Foot, now fearing mass murder, moved into hiding in the Bad Lands of South Dakota. After a skirmish, the great leader Sitting Bull and his young son lay dead.

The Seventh Calvary pursued the Sioux Ghost Dancers and 300 undernourished Sioux, freezing and without horses, to Wounded Knee Creek on the Pine Ridge Reservation. There, on December 29, 1890, while the peace-seeking Big Foot, who had personally raised a white flag of surrender, lay dying of pneumonia, they were surrounded by soldiers armed with automatic guns. The U.S. troops expected the Sioux to surrender their few remaining weapons, but an accidental gunshot from one deaf brave who misunderstood the command caused panic on both sides.

Within minutes, 200 Sioux had been cut down and dozens of soldiers wounded, mostly by their own cross fire. For two hours soldiers continued to shoot at anything that moved—mostly women and children straggling away.

Black Elk later recalled, "I can see that something else died there in the bloody mud, and was buried in the blizzard. A people's dream died there. It was a beautiful dream. . . . The nation's hoop is broken and scattered. There is no center any longer, and the sacred tree is dead."

Endurance and Rejuvenation

Not even an insular, peaceful agricultural existence on semiarid, treeless terrain necessarily provided protection. Nor did a total willingness to peacefully accept white offers prevent attack. The Pimas of Arizona, for instance, had a well-developed agricultural system adapted to a scarce supply of water, and they rarely warred with other tribes. After the arrival of white settlers, they integrated Christian symbolism into their religion, learned to speak English, and even fought with the U.S. cavalry against the Apaches. Still, the Pimas saw their lands stolen, their precious waterways diverted, and their families impoverished.

A majority of tribes, especially smaller ones, sooner or later reached numbers too low to maintain their collective existence. The Quapaws, for example, formally disbanded in the aftermath of the Dawes Severalty Act. Later generations petitioned the federal government and regained tribal status, established ceremonial grounds and cultural centers (or bingo halls),

and built up one of the most durable powwows in the state. Even so, much of the tribal lore that had underpinned distinct identity had simply vanished.

A small minority of tribes, grown skillful in adapting to dramatically changing circumstances, managed to persist and even grow. The Cheyennes had found themselves caught geographically between aggressive tribes in the Great Lakes region and had migrated into the Missouri area, where they split into small village-sized communities. By the mid-nineteenth century they had become expert horse traders on the Great Plains, well prepared to meet the massive influx of white settlers by shifting their location frequently. They avoided the worst of the pestilence that spread from the diseases white people carried, and likewise survived widespread intermarriage with the Sioux in the 1860s and 1870s. Instructed to settle, many Cheyenne took up elements of the Christian religion and became farmers, also without losing their tribal identity.

The Navajos experienced an extraordinary renewal, largely because they built a life in territory considered worthless by whites. Having migrated to the Southwest from the northwestern part of the continent perhaps 700 years ago, the Diné ("the People") as they called themselves had already survived earlier invasions by the Spanish. In 1863 they had been conquered again through the cooperation of hostile tribes led by the famous Colonel Kit Carson. Their crops burned, their fruit trees destroyed, 8,000 Navajo were forced in the 300-mile "Long Walk" to the desolate Bosque Redondo reservation, where they nearly starved. Four years later, the Indian Bureau allowed the severely reduced tribe to return to a fraction of its former lands.

By 1880 the Navajos' population had returned to nearly what it had been before their conquest by white Americans. Quickly depleting the deer and antelope on their hemmed-in reservation, they had to rely on sheep alone as a food reserve during years of bad crops. With their wool rugs and blankets much in demand in the East, the Navajos increasingly turned to crafts, including eventually silver jewelry as well as weaving, to survive. Although living on the economic margin, they persevered to become the largest Indian nation in the United States.

The nearby Hopis, like the Navajos, survived by stubbornly clinging to lands unwanted by white settlers and by adapting to drastically changing conditions. A famous tribe of "desert people," the Hopis had lived for centuries in their cliff cities. Their highly developed theological beliefs, peaceful social system, sand paintings, and kachina dolls interested many educated and influential whites. The resulting publicity helped them gather the public supporters and financial resources needed to fend off further threats to their reservations.

Fortunate northwestern tribes remained relatively isolated from white settlers until the early twentieth

CHRONOLOGY

1848	Treaty of Guadalupe Hidalgo
1849–60s	California Gold Rush
1853	Gadsden Purchase
1858	Comstock Lode discovered
1859	Cortina's War in South Texas
1862	Homestead Act makes free land available
	Morrill Act authorizes "land-grant" colleges
1865–67	Great Sioux War
1866	Texas cattle drives begin
	Medicine Lodge Treaty established reservation system
	Alaska purchased
1869	Board of Indian Commissioners created
	Buffalo Bill, the King of the Border Men, sets off "Wild West" publishing craze
1870s	Grasshopper attacks on the Great Plains
1872	Yellowstone National Park created
1873	Timber Culture Act
	Red River War
1874–75	Sioux battles in Black Hills of Dakotas
1876	Custer's Last Stand
1877	Defeat of the Nez Percé
1881	Helen Hunt Jackson, *A Century of Dishonor*
1882	Edmunds Act outlaws polygamy
1885–87	Droughts and severe winters cause the collapse of the cattle boom
1887	Dawes Severalty Act
1890	Sioux Ghost Dance movement
	Massacre of Lakota Sioux at Wounded Knee
	Census Bureau announces the end of the frontier line
1887	Forest Management Act gives the federal government authority over forest reserves

century, although they had begun trading with white visitors centuries earlier. Northwestern peoples relied largely on salmon and other resources of the region's rivers and bays. In potlatch ceremonies, leaders redistributed tribal wealth and maintained their personal status and the status of their tribe by giving lavish gifts to invited guests. Northwest peoples also made intricate wood carvings, including commemorative "totem" poles, that recorded their history and identified their regional status. Northwestern peoples maintained their cultural integrity in part through connections with kin in Canada, as did southern tribes with kin in Mexico. In Canada and Mexico, native populations suffered less pressure from new populations and retained more tribal authority than in the United States.

Indian nations approached their nadir as the nineteenth century came to a close. The descendants of the great pre-Columbian civilizations had been conquered by foreigners, their population reduced to fewer than 250,000. Under the pressure of assimilation, the remaining tribespeople became known to non-Indians as "the

vanishing Americans." It would take several generations before Indian sovereignty experienced a resurgence.

CONCLUSION

In 1890 the director of the U.S. Census announced that the nation's "unsettled area has been so broken into by isolated bodies of settlement that there can hardly be said to be a frontier line." The development of the West met the nation's demands for mineral resources for its expanding industries and agricultural products for the people of the growing cities. Envisioning the West as a cornucopia whose boundless treasures would offer themselves to the willing pioneer, most of the new residents failed to calculate the odds against their making a prosperous livelihood as miners, farmers, or petty merchants. Nor could they appreciate the long-term consequences of the violence they brought with them from the battlefields of the Civil War to the far reaches of the West.

REVIEW QUESTIONS

1. Discuss the role of federal legislation in accelerating and shaping the course of westward expansion.
2. How did the incorporation of western territories into the United States affect Indian nations such as the Sioux or the Nez Percé? Discuss the causes and consequences of the Indian Wars. Discuss the significance of reservation policy and the Dawes Severalty Act for tribal life.
3. What were some of the major technological advances in mining and in agriculture that promoted the development of the western economy?
4. Describe the unique features of Mexicano communities in the Southwest before and after the mass immigration of Anglos. How did changes in the economy affect the patterns of labor and the status of women in these communities?
5. What role did the Homestead Act play in western expansion? How did farm families on the Great Plains divide chores among their members? What factors determined the likelihood of economic success or failure?
6. Describe the responses of artists, naturalists, and conservationists to the western landscape. How did their photographs, paintings, and stories shape perceptions of the West in the East?

RECOMMENDED READING

William Cronon, George Miles, and Jay Gitlin, eds., *Under an Open Sky: Rethinking America's Western Past* (1992). A useful collection of essays. Reinterpreting older evidence and adding new data, these essays stress the bitter conflicts over territory, the racial and gender barriers against democratic community models, and the tragic elements of western history.

Jon Gjerde, *The Minds of the West: Ethnocultural Evolution in the Rural Middle West, 1830–1914* (1997). A combination cultural and economic history that weighs the importance of ethnicity in the shaping of American identities in the farming regions of the Middle West. Gjerde pays close attention to the religious institutions and systems of belief of European immigrants as the basis of community formation.

Lisbeth Haas, *Conquests and Historical Identities in California, 1769–1936* (1995). A multiethnic history, centered in San Juan Capistrano, that examines the political intersection of geography and community formation. The author studies the processes of Americanization among the Spanish and Indian populations who settled this land.

Robert V. Hine and John Mack Faragher, *The American West: A New Interpretive History* (2000). A sweeping, amply illustrated survey of western history with reference to recent scholarship. The authors emphasize Native Americans and include rich material on ethnicity, the environment, and the role of women.

John C. Hudson, *Making the Corn Belt: A Geographical History of Middle-Western Agriculture* (1994). An ecologically oriented study of corn growing that traces its development from Indians to Southerners moving westward.

Andrew C. Isenberg, *The Destruction of the Bison: An Environmental History, 1750–1920* (2000). A rich study of the forces behind the near-extinction of the bison with special attention to the interplay among Indians, Euroamericans, and the environment of the Great Plains. Isenberg constructs a narrative that is as much cultural as economic in framing the problem.

Karl Jacoby, *Crimes Against Nature: Squatters, Poachers, Thieves, and the Hidden History of American Conservation* (2001). A complex analysis of the origins of national parks in the Adirondacks, Yellowstone, and the Grand Canyon. Rather than focusing on the individuals and groups that led the conservation of vast public lands, Jacoby switches perspective to focus on those who were dispossessed by the process.

Elizabeth Jameson and Susan Armitage, eds., *Writing the Range* (1997). A collection of essays on women in the West that presents an inclusive historical narrative based on the experiences of women of differing backgrounds, races, and ethnic groups.

Katherine M. B. Osburn, *Southern Ute Women: Autonomy and Assimilation on the Reservation, 1887–1934* (1998). Presents a careful analysis of the impact of the Dawes Act on the role and status of women among the Southern Ute. Osburn acknowledges the changes brought by the Office of Indian Affairs programs on the reservations but emphasizes the resistance of the Ute and the retention of old ways.

Glenda Riley, *Building and Breaking Families in the American West* (1996). Essays covering the variety of cultures in the American West and organized topically to highlight courtship, marriage and intermarriage, and separation and divorce.

Thomas E. Sheridan, *Los Tucsonenses: The Mexican Community in Tucson, 1854–1941* (1986). A highly readable account of Mexican-American communities in the Southwest. Sheridan shows how a midcentury accommodation of Anglos and Mexicanos faded with the absorption of the region into the national economy and with the steady displacement of Mexicano community from its agricultural landholdings.

Liping Zhu, *A Chinaman's Chance: The Chinese on the Rocky Mountain Mining Frontier* (1997). Studies the mining communities of Chinese in the Boise Basin of Idaho. Zhu emphasizes the success the Chinese enjoyed not only as miners but as merchants in the face of discriminatory practices and laws.

ON THE WEB

http://www.lib.utah.edu/spc/photo/cent1.html
http://www.lib.utah.edu/spc/photo/cent2.html
http://www.lib.utah.edu/150/
http://www.lib.utah.edu/spc/photo/photo2.html

These sites connect to the University of Utah, Marriott Library photo archive collections and provide visual images, some very good quality, of early Utah history.

http://www.pbs.org/weta/thewest/resources/archives/index.htm

Prepared by the Public Broadcasting Service (PBS) to accompany its video, *The West*, this very large collection contains both photographs and primary documents on westward expansion during the nineteenth century. Focus attention on the period 1860–1900. This archive is very large.

http://www.vcnevada.com/history.htm

A short narrative history of Virginia City, silver mining, and the Virginia and Truckee Railroad.

http://www.calliope.org/gold/gold3.html

Short narrative history of the Comstock Lode.

http://dmla.clan.lib.nv.us/docs/museums/reno/his-soc.htm

Nevada Historical Society site. Navigate to the online (virtual) exhibits for a fine narrative history of the Indians of Nevada with good photos. Other interesting exhibits are pages also available.

http://w3.arizona.edu/~azhist/health.htm

Narrative history of old healing practices of Arizona residents: Mexican, Indian, and pioneer; posted by the Arizona Historical Society.

http://dizzy.library.arizona.edu/images/

Links through the University of Arizona to interesting historical exhibits on Western history, Mexican history and railroad history.

http://www.smithsonianmag.si.edu/smithsonian/issues97/dec97/bosque.html

This site contains information about the Navajo exile to Bosque Redondo, called the Long Walk.

http://www.prenhall.com/faragherbrief/map18.1

Explore the conflicts between Indians and white settlers from 1860 to 1900. Why were the Indians forcibly removed to reservations?

http://www.prenhall.com/faragherbrief/map18.2

Pan across a map of the West during the period 1860–1900. How did the growth of railroads and mining impact the environment and the lives of native peoples?

NINETEEN

THE INCORPORATION OF AMERICA

▶ 1 8 6 5 – 1 9 0 0

AMERICAN COMMUNITIES

Packingtown, Chicago, Illinois

APPROACHING PACKINGTOWN, THE NEIGHBORHOOD ADJOINING the Union Stockyards, the center of Chicago's great meatpacking industry, one noticed first the pungent odor, a mixture of smoke, fertilizer, and putrid flesh, blood, and hair from the slaughtered animals. A little closer, the stench of the uncovered garbage dump blended in. Finally one crossed "Bubbly Creek," a lifeless offshoot of the Chicago River, aptly named for the effect of the carbolic acid gas that formed from the decaying refuse poured in by the meatpacking plants. Railroads crisscrossed the entire area, bringing in thousands of animals each day and carrying out meat for sale in markets across the country.

Packingtown occupied about one square mile of land bounded by stockyards, packing plants, and freight yards. With a population of 30,000 to 40,000 at the end of the nineteenth century, it was a rapidly growing community of old and new immigrants who depended on the meatpacking industry for their livelihood. An average household included six or seven people—parents, two or three children, and two or three boarders. They lived typically in wooden houses divided into four or more flats. Although Irish, Germans, Bohemians, Poles, Lithuanians, and Slovaks were squeezed together in this solidly working-class neighborhood, strong ethnic identities persisted. Few households included residents of more than one nationality, and interethnic marriages were rare. Nearly everyone professed the Roman Catholic faith, yet each ethnic group maintained its own church and often its own parochial school, where children were taught in their parents' language. Political organizations, fraternal societies, and even gymnastic clubs and drama groups reflected these ethnic divisions.

The one local institution that bridged the different groups was the saloon. Located on virtually every street corner, saloons offered important services to the community, hosting weddings and dances, providing meeting places for trade unions and fraternal societies, and cashing paychecks. During the frequent seasons of unemployment, Packingtown workers spent a lot of time in saloons. Here they often made friends across ethnic divisions, an extension of their common work experience in the nearby stockyard and packinghouses.

Most of the meatpacking industry's first "knife men"—the skilled workers in the "killing gangs" that managed the actual slaughtering and cutting operations—were German and Irish. Many had learned their butcher's craft in the Old Country. Below them were the common laborers, mainly recent immigrants from eastern Europe. Having no previous experience in meatpacking, these workers found themselves in the lowest-paid jobs, such as the by-product manufacturing of glue and oleo. A sizable portion had never before earned wages. They soon discovered, as one Lithuanian laborer put it, that "money was everything and a man without money must die." But the money available—a daily wage of $2 (or less)—was often not enough. The death rate from tuberculosis in Packingtown was thought to be the highest in Chicago and among the highest in the nation.

The Packingtown community, small and insular as it seemed to the residents, was bound into an elaborate economic network that reached distant parts of the United States, transforming the way farmers raised livestock and grains, railroads operated, and consumers ate their meals. These workers helped make Chicago a gateway city, a destination point for raw materials coming in from the West as well as a point of export for products of all kinds.

Chicago meatpackers, led by the "big five" of Armour, Cudahy, Morris, Schwarzschild and Sulzberger, and Swift, expanded more than 900 percent between 1870 and 1890, dominating the national market for meat and establishing a standard for monopoly capitalism in the late nineteenth century. In the process, they also became the city's largest manufacturing employer. They built huge, specialized factories during the 1860s and 1870s that speeded the killing process and—thanks to mountains of ice brought by rail from ponds and lakes—operated year round. The introduction of an efficiently refrigerated railroad car in the 1880s made it possible to ship meat nationwide. Consumers had long believed that only meat butchered locally was safe to eat, but now cheap Chicago-packed beef and pork began to appear on every meateater's table. Local packinghouses throughout the Midwest succumbed to the ruthless competition from Chicago.

Chicago's control of the mass market for meat affected all aspects of the industry. Midwestern farmers practically abandoned raising calves on open pastures. Instead, they bought two-year-old steers from the West and fattened them on homegrown corn in feedlots, making sure that bulk went into edible parts rather than muscle and bone. The feedlot—a kind of rural factory—replaced pasture just as pasture had earlier supplanted prairie grasslands.

Few of the workers in Chicago's stockyards had seen a farm since they left their homelands. But as the working hands of what poet Carl Sandburg would later call the "Hog butcher for the world, . . . City of the big shoulders," they played their part, along with the farmer, the grain dealer, the ironworker, the teamster, and many others in bringing together the neighboring countryside, distant regions, and the city in a common endeavor. ■

Chicago

KEY TOPICS

- The rise of big business and the formation of the national labor movement
- The transformation of southern society
- The growth of cities
- The Gilded Age
- Changes in education
- Commercial amusements and organized sports

THE RISE OF INDUSTRY, THE TRIUMPH OF BUSINESS

At the time of the Civil War, the typical American business firm was a small enterprise, owned and managed by a single family, and producing goods for a local or regional market. By the turn of the century, businesses depending on large-scale investments had organized as corporations and grown to unforeseen size. These mammoth firms could afford to mass-produce goods for national and even international markets. At the helm stood unimaginably wealthy men such as Andrew Carnegie, Philip Danforth Armour, Jay Gould, and John D. Rockefeller, all powerful leaders of a new national business community.

A Revolution in Technology

In the decades after the Civil War, American industry transformed itself into a new wonder of the world. The Centennial Exposition of 1876, held in Philadelphia, celebrated not so much the American Revolution 100 years earlier as the industrial and technological promise of the century to come. Its central theme was power. In the main building—at the time the largest on earth—the visiting emperor of Brazil marked the opening day by throwing a switch on a giant steam engine. Examining the telephone, which he had never before seen in operation, he gasped, "My God, it talks!" Patented that year by Alexander Graham Bell, the telephone signaled the rise of the United States to world leadership in industrial technology.

The year 1876 also marked the opening of Thomas Alva Edison's laboratory in Menlo Park, New Jersey. Three years later, his research team hit upon its most marketable invention, an incandescent lamp that burned for more than thirteen hours. By 1882 the Edison Electric Light Company had launched its service in New York City's financial district.

By this time American inventors, who had filed nearly half a million patents since the close of the Civil War, were previewing the marvels of the next century. Henry Ford, working as an electrical engineer for the Detroit Edison Company, was already experimenting with the gasoline-burning internal combustion engine and designing his own automobile. By 1900 American companies had produced more than 4,000 automobiles. The prospect of commercial aviation emerged in 1903 when Wilbur and Orville Wright staged the first airplane flight near Kitty Hawk, North Carolina.

A major force behind economic growth was the vast transcontinental railroad, completed in 1869. The addition of three more major rail lines (the Southern Pacific; the Northern Pacific; and the Atchison, Topeka, and Santa Fe) in the early 1880s, and the Great Northern a decade later, completed the most extensive transportation network in the world. As the nation's first big business, railroads linked cities in every state and served a nationwide market for goods. Freight trains carried the bountiful natural resources, such as iron, coal, and minerals that supplied the raw materials for industry, as well as food for the growing urban populations.

The monumental advances in transportation and communication facilitated the progressively westward relocation of industry. The geographic center of manufacturing (as computed by the gross value of products) was near the middle of Pennsylvania in 1850, in western Pennsylvania by 1880, and near Mansfield, Ohio, in 1900.

Industry grew at a pace that was not only unprecedented but previously unimaginable. In 1865 the annual production of goods was estimated at $2 billion; by 1900 it stood at $13 billion, transforming the United States from fourth to first in the world in terms of productivity.

Mechanization Takes Command

This second industrial revolution depended on many factors, but none was more important than the application of new technologies to increase the productivity of labor and the volume of goods. Machines, factory managers, and workers together created a system of continuous production by which more could be made, and faster, than anywhere else on earth. Higher productivity depended not only on machinery and technology but also on economies of scale and speed, reorganization of factory labor and business management, and the unparalleled growth of a market for goods of all kinds.

All these changes depended in turn on anthracite coal, a new source of fuel, which was widely used after 1850. Reliable and inexpensive sources of energy made possible dramatic changes in the industrial uses of light, heat, and motion. Equally important, coal fueled the great open-hearth furnaces and mills of the iron and steel industry. By the end of the century, the U.S. steel industry was the world's largest.

New systems of mass production replaced wasteful and often chaotic practices and speeded up the delivery of finished goods. In the 1860s meatpackers set up one of the earliest production lines. This "disassembly line" displaced patterns of hand labor that were centuries old. The production line became standard in most areas of manufacturing.

Sometimes the invention of a single machine could instantly transform production, mechanizing every stage from processing the raw material to packaging the product. The cigarette-making machine, patented in 1881, shaped the tobacco, encased it in an endless paper tube, and snipped off the tube at cigarette-length intervals. This machine could produce more than 7,000 cigarettes per hour, replacing the worker who at best made 3,000 per day. After a few more improvements, fifteen machines could meet the total demand for American cigarettes. Within a generation, continuous production also revolutionized the making of furniture, cloth, grain products, soap, and canned goods; the refining, distilling, and processing of animal and vegetable fats; and eventually the manufacture of automobiles.

The Expanding Market for Goods

To distribute the growing volume of goods, businesses demanded new techniques of marketing and merchandising. For generations, legions of sellers, or "drummers," had worked their routes, pushing goods, especially hardware and patent medicines, to individual buyers and retail stores. The appearance of mail-order houses after the Civil War accompanied the consolidation of the railroad lines and the expansion of the postal system. Rates were lowered for freight and postage alike, and railroad stations opened post offices and sold money orders. By 1896 rural free delivery had reached distant communities.

Growing directly out of these services, the successful Chicago-based mail-order houses drew rural and urban consumers into a common marketplace. Sears, Roebuck and Company and Montgomery Ward offered an enormous variety of goods, from shoes to buggies to gasoline stoves and cream separators. The Sears catalogue offered Armour's summer sausage as well as Aunt Jemima's Pancake Flour and Queen Mary Scotch Oatmeal, both made of grains that came from the agricultural heartland. In turn, the purchases made by farm families through the Sears catalogue sent cash flowing into Chicago.

The chain store achieved similar economies of scale. By 1900, a half-dozen grocery chains had sprung up. The largest was A&P, originally named the Great Atlantic and Pacific Tea Company to celebrate the completion of the transcontinental railroad. Frank and Charles Woolworth offered inexpensive variety goods in five-and-ten-cent stores. Hurt financially by this competition, community-based retailers headed the lobby for antichain legislation.

Opening shortly after the Civil War, department stores began to take up much of the business formerly enjoyed by specialty shops, offering a spectrum of services that included restaurants, rest rooms, ticket agencies, nurseries, reading rooms, and post offices. Elegantly appointed with imported carpets, sweeping marble staircases, and crystal chandeliers, the department store raised retailing to new heights. By the close of the century, the names of Marshall Field of Chicago, Filene's of Boston, The Emporium of San Francisco, Wanamaker's of Philadelphia, and Macy's of New York had come to represent the splendors of those great cities as well as the apex of mass retailing.

Advertising lured customers to the department stores, the chains, and the independent neighborhood shops. The advertising revolution began in 1869, when Francis Wayland Ayer founded the earliest advertising agency, but the firm did not hire its first full-time copy writers until 1891. Ayer's handled the accounts of such companies as Montgomery Ward, Procter & Gamble, and the National Biscuit Company. With the help of this new sales tool, gross revenues of retailers raced upward from $8 million in 1860 to $102 million in 1900.

Integration, Combination, and Merger

The business community aspired to exercise greater control of the economy and to enlarge the commercial empire. From the source of raw materials to the organization of production, from the conditions of labor to the climate of public opinion, business leaders acted shrewdly. Economic cycles alternating between rapid growth and sharp decline also promoted the rise of big business. Major economic setbacks in 1873 and 1893 wiped out weaker competitors, allowing the strongest firms to rebound swiftly and to expand their sales and scale of operation during the recovery period.

Businesses grew in two distinct, if overlapping, ways. Through *vertical integration* a firm gained control of production at every step of the way—from raw materials through processing to transport and merchandising of the finished items. In 1899 the United Fruit Company began to build a network of wholesale houses, and within two years it had opened distribution centers in twenty-one major cities. Eventually it controlled an elaborate system of Central American plantations and temperature-controlled shipping and storage facilities for its highly perishable bananas. The firm became one of the nation's largest corporations.

The second means of growth, *horizontal combination*, entailed gaining control of the market for a single product. The most famous case was the Standard Oil Company, founded by John D. Rockefeller in 1870. Operating out of Cleveland in a highly competitive but lucrative field, Rockefeller first secured preferential rates from railroads eager to ensure a steady supply of oil. He then convinced or coerced other local oil operators to sell their stock to him. The Standard Oil Trust, established in 1882, controlled over 90 percent of the nation's oil-refining industry.

In 1890 Congress passed the Sherman Antitrust Act to restore competition by encouraging small business. Ironically, the courts interpreted the law in ways that inhibited the organization of trade unions (on the ground that they restricted the free flow of labor) and actually helped the consolidation of business. More than 2,600 firms vanished between 1898 and 1902 alone. By 1910 the industrial giants that would dominate the American economy until the last half of the twentieth century— U.S. Rubber, Goodyear, American Smelting and Refining, Anaconda Copper, General Electric, Westinghouse, Nabisco, Swift and Company, Armour, International Harvester, Eastman Kodak, and American Can—had already formed.

The Gospel of Wealth

Ninety percent of the nation's business leaders were Protestant, and the majority attended church services regularly. They attributed their personal achievement to hard work and perseverance and made these the principal tenets of a new faith that imbued the pursuit of wealth with old-time religious zeal.

One version of this "gospel of wealth" justified the ruthless behavior of entrepreneurs who accumulated unprecedented wealth and power through shady deals and conspiracies. Speculator Jay Gould wrung his fortune, it was widely believed, from the labor of others. He rose quickly from his modest origins through a series of unsavory financial maneuvers and such high-handed measures as sending armed employees to seize a factory.

Speculation in railroads proved to be Gould's forte. He took over the Erie Railroad, paying off New York legislators to get the state to finance its expansion, and he acquired the U.S. Express Company by pressuring and tricking its stockholders. When threatened with arrest, Gould sold off his shares for $9 million and moved on to the Union Pacific, where he cut wages, precipitated strikes, and manipulated elections in the western and Plains states. Tired of being caricatured in the press as a great swindler, he bought the leading newspapers.

Andrew Carnegie offered a strikingly different model. A poor immigrant from Scotland, Carnegie spent his boyhood studying bookkeeping at night while working days in a textile mill. In 1852 he became the personal secretary of the superintendent of the Pennsylvania Railroad's western division. He learned quickly and soon stepped into the superintendent's job. While improving passenger train service, he invested brilliantly to build funds for his next venture.

Carnegie built an empire in steel. A genius at vertical integration, he undercut his competitors by using the latest technology and designing his own system of cost analysis. By 1900 Carnegie managed the most efficient steel mills in the world, which accounted for one-third of the nation's output. When he sold out to J. P. Morgan's new United States Steel Corporation in 1901, his personal share of the proceeds came to $225 million.

Carnegie was well known as a civic leader. From one point of view, he was a factory despot who underpaid his employees and ruthlessly managed their working conditions. But to the patrons of the public libraries, art museums, concert halls, colleges, and universities that he funded, Carnegie appeared to be the single greatest philanthropist of the age. By the time he died, he had given away his massive personal fortune.

LABOR IN THE AGE OF BIG BUSINESS

Like the gospel of wealth, the "gospel of work" affirmed the dignity of hard work, the virtue of thrift, and the importance of individual initiative. But unlike business leaders, the philosophers of American working people did not believe in riches as the proof of work well done, or in the lust for power as the driving force of progress. On the contrary, they contended that honesty and competence should become the badge of the morally responsible citizen.

This faith inspired a slender minority, less than 3 percent of the workforce, to form unions in various trades and industries. Despite its small size, the labor movement represented the most significant and lasting response of workers to the rise of big business and the consolidation of corporate power.

The Wage System

The accelerating growth of industry, especially the steady mechanization of production, dramatically changed employer-employee relations and created new categories of workers. Both in turn fostered competition among workers and created conditions often hazardous to health.

For most craft workers, the new system destroyed long-standing practices, chipped away at their customary autonomy. Frederick Winslow Taylor, the pioneer of scientific management, explained that managers must "take all the important decisions . . . out of the hands of workmen." Teams of ironworkers, for example, had previously set the rules of production as well as their wages while the company supplied equipment and raw materials. Once steel replaced iron, most companies gradually introduced a new system. Managers now constantly supervised workers, set the pace of production and rate of payment, and introduced new, faster machinery that made many skills obsolete. In the woodworking trades, highly skilled cabinetmakers, who for generations had brought their own tools to the factory, were largely replaced with "green hands"—immigrants, including many women—who with only minimal training and close supervision could operate new woodworking machines at cheaper rates of pay.

Not all trades conformed to this pattern. The garment industry, for example, retained older systems of labor along with the new. The highly mechanized factories employed hundreds of thousands of young immigrant women, while the outwork system, established well before the Civil War, contracted ever-larger numbers of families to work in their homes on sewing machines or by hand. Paid by the piece, all workers labored faster and longer to forestall a dip in wages.

Industrial expansion also offered new opportunities for women to work outside the home. African American and immigrant women found employment in trades least affected by technological advances, such as domestic service. In contrast, English-speaking white women moved into the better-paying clerical and sales positions in the rapidly expanding business sector. After the typewriter and telephone came into widespread use in the 1890s, the number of women employed in office work rose even faster. At the turn of the century, 8.6 million women worked outside their homes—nearly triple the number in 1870.

By contrast, African American men found themselves excluded from many fields. In Cleveland, for example, the number of black carpenters declined after 1870, just as the volume of construction was rapidly increasing. African American men were also systematically driven from restaurant service and barred from newer trades such as boilermaking, plumbing, electrical work, and paperhanging, which European immigrants secured for themselves.

Discriminatory or exclusionary practices fell hardest on workers recruited earlier from China to work in the mines, in the construction of the railroads, and in market gardening. From the 1860s on, many Chinese established laundries and restaurants in west coast cities where they were viewed as potential competitors by white workers and proprietors of small businesses. A potent and racist anti-Chinese movement organized to protest "cheap Chinese labor" and to demand a halt to Chinese immigration. By the late 1870s white rioters were insistently calling for deportation measures and razing Chinese neighborhoods. In 1882 Congress passed the Chinese Exclusion Act, which suspended Chinese immigration, limited the civil rights of resident Chinese, and forbade their naturalization.

For even the best-placed wage earners, the new workplace could be unhealthy, even dangerous. Meatpacking produced its own hazards—the dampness of the pickling room, the sharp blade of the slaughtering knife, and the noxious odors of the fertilizer department. Factory owners often failed to mark high-voltage wires, locked fire doors, and allowed the emission of toxic fumes. Extractive workers, such as coal and copper miners, labored in mineshafts where the air could suddenly turn poisonous and where cave-ins were possible and deadly.

Except for federal employees, who had been granted the eight-hour day in 1868, most workers still toiled upward of ten or twelve hours daily.

Moreover, steady employment was rare. Between 1866 and 1897, fourteen years of prosperity stood against seventeen of hard times. The major depressions of 1873–79 and 1893–97 were the worst in the nation's history up to that time. Three "minor" recessions (1866–67, 1883–85, and 1890–91) did not seem insignificant to the millions who lost their jobs.

The Knights of Labor

The Noble and Holy Order of the Knights of Labor, founded by a group of Philadelphia garment cutters in 1869, grew to become the largest labor organization in the nineteenth century. Led by Grand Master Workman Terence V. Powderly, the order sought to bring together all wage earners regardless of skill. The Knights endorsed a variety of reform measures—child labor reform, a graduated income tax, more land set aside for homsteading, the abolition of contract labor, and monetary reform—to offset the power of the industrialists. They believed that the "producing classes," once freed from the grip of corporate monopoly and the curses of ignorance and alcohol, would transform the United States into a genuinely democratic society.

The Knights promoted economic cooperation as the alternative to the wage system and advocated a system of producers' cooperatives. In these factories workers collectively made all decisions on prices and wages and shared all the profits. The Knights also ran small cooperative cigar shops and grocery stores, often housed in their own assembly buildings. Successful for a time, most cooperatives could not compete against the heavily capitalized enterprises and ultimately failed.

The Knights reached their peak during the great campaign for a shorter workday. The Eight-Hour League, led by Ira Steward, advocated a "natural" rhythm of eight hours for work, eight hours for sleep, and eight hours for leisure. After staging petition campaigns, marches, and a massive strike in New York City, the movement collapsed during the economic recession of the 1870s. The Knights helped revive it in the next decade, and this time the campaign aroused widespread support from consumers, who boycotted brands of beer, bread, and other products made in longer-hour shops. Finally, during the first weeks of May 1886, more than a third of a million workers walked off their jobs. Approximately 200,000 of them won shorter hours.

The eight-hour campaign swelled the ranks of the Knights of Labor. The organization grew from a few thousand in 1880 to nearly three-quarters of a million six years later. Nearly 3,000 women formed their own "ladies assemblies" or joined mixed locals. Leonora Barry, appointed to organize women, helped to increase their share of membership to 10 percent. African Americans also joined the Knights—20,000 to 30,000 nationally—mainly in separate assemblies within the organization.

In Chicago, the shorter-hours campaign ended in tragedy. On May 4, 1886, following a series of confrontations between strikers and authorities, a protest against police violence at Haymarket Square seemed to be ending quietly until someone threw a bomb that killed one policeman and left seven others fatally wounded. Police responded by firing wildly into the crowd, killing an equal number. After Chicago authorities arrested anarchist leaders, a sensational trial ended in death sentences, although no evidence linked the accused to the bombing. Four of the convicted were hanged, one committed suicide, and three other "Haymarket Martyrs," as they were called, remained jailed until pardoned in 1893 by Illinois governor John Peter Altgeld.

The Knights of Labor had suffered an irreparable setback. Employers' associations successfully pooled funds to rid their factories of troublesome organizers and announced that companies would no longer bargain with unions. The wage system had triumphed.

The American Federation of Labor

The events of 1886 also signaled the rise of a very different kind of organization, the American Federation of Labor (AFL). Unlike the Knights, the AFL accepted the wage system. Following a strategy of "pure and simple unionism," the AFL sought to gain recognition of its union status to bargain with employers for better working conditions, higher wages, and shorter hours. In return, it offered compliant firms the benefit of amenable day-to-day relations with the most highly skilled wage earners. Only if companies refused to bargain in good faith would union members strike.

The new federation, with twelve national unions and 140,000 affiliated members, declared war on the Knights of Labor. In the wake of the Haymarket tragedy and the collapse of the eight-hour movement, the AFL pushed ahead of its rival by organizing craft workers. AFL president Samuel Gompers refused to include unskilled workers, racial minorities, women, and immigrants, believing they were impossible to organize and even unworthy of equal status. Under his leadership, the AFL member became the "aristocrat of labor," the best-paid worker in the world.

Although craft unionism represented only a small minority of working Americans—about 10 percent at the end of the century—local federations of skilled workers often played important roles in their communities. They may not have been able to slow the steady advance of mechanization, which diminished the craft worker's autonomy and eliminated some of the most desirable jobs, but AFL members managed to make their presence felt. Local politicians courted their votes, and Labor Day, first celebrated in the 1880s, became a national holiday in 1894.

THE NEW SOUTH

At the turn of the century southern industries lagged far behind enterprises in other regions of the country. Their progress was held back by dependence on northern finance capital, continued reliance on cotton production, and the legacy of slavery.

An Internal Colony

In the 1870s a vocal and powerful new group of Southerners headed by Henry Woodfin Grady, editor of the *Atlanta Constitution*, insisted that the region enjoyed a great potential in its abundant natural resources of coal, iron, turpentine, tobacco, and lumber. Arguing against those planters who aspired to rejuvenate the agricultural economy based on the cultivation of a few staple crops, this group forcefully promoted industrial development and welcomed northern investors.

Northern investors secured huge concessions from southern state legislatures, including land, forest, and mineral rights and large tax exemptions. Exploiting the incentives, railroad companies laid over 22,000 miles of new track, connecting the region to national markets and creating new cities. By 1890 a score of large railroad companies, centered mainly in New York, held more than half of all the track in the South.

Northerners also employed various means to protect their investments from southern competition. By the late 1870s, southern merchants, with help from foreign investors, had begun to run iron factories around Birmingham, Alabama. Southern iron production was soon encroaching on the northeastern market. To stave off this competition, Andrew Carnegie ordered the railroads to charge higher freight fees to Birmingham's iron producers. New York bankers later succeeded in expatriating Birmingham's profits through stock ownership in southern firms. After the turn of the century, U.S. Steel simply bought out the local merchants and took over much of Birmingham's production.

The production of cotton textiles followed a similar course. Powerful merchants and large landowners, realizing that they could make high profits by controlling the cotton crop from field to factory, promoted the vertical integration of the cotton industry. The number of mills in the South grew from 161 in 1880 to 400 in 1900. Southern investors supplied large amounts of the capital for the industrial expansion and technological improvements. The latest machines ran the new mills, and the South boasted the first factory fully equipped with electricity. Production in the four leading cotton-manufacturing states—North Carolina, South Carolina, Georgia, and Alabama—skyrocketed, far outpacing the New England mills.

Recognizing the potential for great profit in these new factories with their cheap labor, northern manufacturers, including many New England mill owners, shifted their investments to the South. By the 1920s, northern investors held much of the South's wealth, including the major textile mills, but returned through employment or social services only a small share of the profits to the region's people.

The governing role of capital investments from outside the region reinforced long-standing relationships. Even rapid industrialization—in iron, railroads, and textiles—did not carry the same consequences achieved in the North. The rise of the New South reinforced, rather than diminished, the region's status as the nation's internal colony.

Southern Labor

The advance of southern industry did little to improve the working lives of most African Americans. African American men did find work with the railroads; in booming cities like Atlanta they even gained skilled positions in the construction trades and worked as bricklayers, carpenters, and painters. For the most part, however, African Americans were limited to unskilled, low-paying jobs. In the textile mills and cigarette factories, which employed both black and white workers, the workforce was rigidly segregated. African Americans were assigned mainly to janitorial jobs and rarely worked alongside the white workers who tended the machines. Nearly all African American women who earned wages did so as household workers.

Locals of the all-white carpenters' union maintained a segregation policy so absolute that if too few members were available for a job, the union would send for out-of-town white workers rather than employ local members of the black carpenters' union. In an Atlanta mill in 1897, 1,400 white women operatives went on strike when the company proposed to hire two black spinners.

Only at rare moments did southern workers unite across racial lines. In the 1880s, the Knights of Labor briefly organized both black and white workers. But when white politicians and local newspapers began to raise the specter of black domination, the Knights were forced to retreat. Across the region their assemblies collapsed. Other unions remained the exclusive preserve of white skilled workers.

Wages throughout the South were low for both black and white workers. In the 1880s, when investors enjoyed profits ranging from 30 percent to 75 percent, southern mill workers earned as little as 12 cents per hour. Black men earned at or below the poverty line of $300 per year, while black women rarely earned more than $120, and white women about $220, annually. The poorest paid workers were children, the mainstay of southern mill labor.

As industry expanded throughout the nation, so too did the number of children earning wages. This was especially so in the South. In 1896 only one in twenty Massachusetts mill workers was younger than sixteen, but one in four North Carolina cotton mill operatives was that age or younger. Traditions rooted in the agricultural economy reinforced the practice of using the labor of all family members, even the very young. Seasonal labor, such as picking crops or grinding sugarcane, put families on the move, making formal education all but impossible. Not until well into the twentieth century did compulsory school attendance laws effectively restrict child labor in the South.

A system of convict labor also thrived in the South. Bituminous coal mines and public work projects of all kinds, especially in remote areas, employed disciplinary methods and created living and working conditions reminiscent of slavery. African Americans constituted up to 90 percent of the convict workforce. Transported and housed like animals—chained together by day and confined in portable cages at night—these workers suffered high mortality rates. Southern leaders took pride in what they called the "good roads movement"—the chief use of convict labor—as proof of regional progress.

The Transformation of Piedmont Communities

The impact of the New South was nowhere greater than in the Piedmont, the region extending from southern Virginia and the central Carolinas into northern Alabama and Georgia. After 1870, long-established farms and plantations gave way to railroad tracks, textile factories, numerous mill villages, and a few sizable cities. By the turn of the century, five Piedmont towns had populations over 10,000. Even more dramatic was the swelling number of small towns with populations between 1,000 and 5,000—from fourteen in 1870 to fifty-two in 1900. Once the South's backcountry, the Piedmont now surpassed New England in the production of yarn and cloth to stand first in the world.

Rural poverty and the appeal of a new life encouraged many farm families to strike out for a mill town. Those with the least access to land and credit—mainly widows and their children and single women—were the first to go into the mills. Then families sent their children. As the agricultural crisis deepened, more and more people abandoned the countryside entirely for what they called "public work."

A mill community typically comprised rows of single-family houses, a small school, several churches, a company-owned store, and the home of the superintendent who governed everyone's affairs. Millworkers frequently complained that they had no private life at all. A federal report published shortly after the turn of the century concluded that "all the affairs of the village and the conditions of living of all the people are regulated entirely by the mill company. Practically speaking, the company owns everything and controls everything, and to a large extent controls everybody in the mill village."

The processing of raw tobacco employed thousands of African American women, who sorted, stripped, stemmed, and hung tobacco leaves as part of the redrying process. After mechanization was introduced, white women took jobs as cigarette rollers, but black women kept the worst, most monotonous jobs in the tobacco factories. The women shown in this photograph are stemming tobacco in a Virginia factory while their white male supervisor oversees their labor.

SOURCE: Valentine Richmond History Center.

Mill superintendents also relied on schoolteachers and clergy to set the tone of community life. They hired and paid the salaries of Baptist and Methodist ministers to preach a faith encouraging workers to be thrifty, orderly, temperate, and hardworking. The schools, similarly subsidized by the company, reinforced the lesson of moral and social discipline required of industrial life and encouraged students to follow their parents into the mill. But it was mainly young children between six and eight years old who attended school. When more hands were needed in the mill, superintendents plucked out these youngsters and sent them to join their older brothers and sisters who were already at work.

Piedmont mill villages like Greenville, South Carolina, and Burlington, Charlotte, and Franklinville, North Carolina, nevertheless developed a cohesive character typical of isolated rural communities. The new residents maintained many aspects of their agricultural pasts, tilling small gardens and keeping chickens, pigs, and cows in their yards. Factory owners rarely paved roads or sidewalks or provided adequate sanitation. Mud, flies, and diseases such as typhoid fever flourished. Millworkers endured poverty and health hazards by strengthening community ties through intermarriage. Within a few generations, most of the village residents had, according to one study, "some connection to each other, however distant, by marriage," blood, or both. Even the men and women without families boarded in households where privacy was scarce and collective meals created a familylike atmosphere. Historians have called this complex of intimate economic, family, and community ties the customs of incorporation.

THE INDUSTRIAL CITY

Before the Civil War, manufacturing had centered in the countryside, in burgeoning factory towns such as Lowell, Massachusetts, and Troy, New York. By the end of the nineteenth century, 90 percent of all manufacturing took place in cities. The metropolis stood at the center of the growing industrial economy, a magnet drawing raw material, capital, and labor, and a key distribution point for manufactured goods. The industrial city inspired both great hope and great trepidation. Civic leaders often bragged about its size and rate of growth; immigrants wrote to their countryfolk of its pace, both exciting and exhausting.

Populating the City

The population of cities grew at double the rate of the nation's population as a whole. In 1860 only sixteen cities had more than 50,000 residents. By 1890 one-third of all Americans were city dwellers. Eleven cities claimed more than 250,000 people.

The nation's largest cities—New York, Chicago, Philadelphia, St. Louis, Boston, and Baltimore—achieved international fame for the size and diversity of their populations. Many of their new residents had migrated from rural communities within the United States. Between 1870 and 1910, an average of nearly 7,000 African Americans moved north each year, hoping to escape the poverty and oppression prevailing in the South and to find better-paying jobs. By the end of the century, nearly 80 percent of African Americans in the North lived in urban areas.

Immigrants and their children were the major source of urban population growth in the late nineteenth century. Most of those in the first wave of immigration, before the Civil War, had settled in the countryside. In contrast, after the war it was the industrial city that drew the so-called new immigrants, who came primarily from eastern and southern Europe. By the turn of the century Chicago had more Germans than all but a few German cities and more Poles than most Polish cities; New York had more Italians than a handful of the largest Italian cities, and Boston had nearly as many Irish as Dublin. In almost every group except the Irish, men outnumbered women.

Like rural migrants, immigrants came to the American city to take advantage of the expanding opportunities for employment. While many hoped to build a new home in the land of plenty, many others intended to work hard, save money, and return to their families in the Old Country. In the 1880s, for example, nearly half of all Italian, Greek, and Serbian men returned to their native lands. Others could not return to their homelands or did not wish to. Jews, for instance, had emigrated to escape persecution in Russia and Russian-dominated Polish and Romanian lands. A Yiddish writer later called this generation the "Jews without Jewish memories. . . . They shook them off in the boat when they came across the seas. They emptied out their memories."

Of all groups, Jews had the most experience with urban life. Forbidden to own land in most parts of Europe and boxed into *shtetls* (villages), Jews had also formed thriving urban communities in Vilna, Berlin, London, and Vienna. Many had worked in garment manufacturing, in London's East End, for example, and followed a path to American cities like New York, Rochester, Philadelphia, or Chicago where the needle trades flourished.

Bohemians settled largely in Chicago, Pittsburgh, and Cleveland. French Canadians, a relatively small group of a few hundred thousand, emigrated from Quebec and settled almost exclusively in New England and upper New York State. Finding work mainly in textile mills, they transformed smaller industrial cities like Woonsocket, Rhode Island, into French-speaking communities. Cubans, themselves often first- or second-generation immigrants from Spain, moved to Ybor City, a section of Tampa, Florida, to work in cigar factories. Still other groups tended toward cities dominated by fishing, shoemaking, or even glassblowing, a craft carried directly from the Old Country. Italians, the most numerous among the new immigrants, settled mainly in northeastern cities, laying railroad track, excavating subways, and erecting buildings.

Resettlement in an American city did not necessarily mark the end of the immigrants' travels. Newcomers, both native-born and immigrant, moved frequently from one neighborhood to another and from one city to another. American cities experienced a total population turnover three or four times during each decade of the last half of the century.

The Urban Landscape

Faced with a population explosion and an unprecedented building boom, the cities encouraged the creation of many beautiful and useful structures, including commercial offices, sumptuous homes, and efficient public services. At the same time, cities did little to improve the conditions of the majority of the population who worked in dingy factories and lived in crowded tenements. Open space rapidly decreased as American cities grew.

American streets customarily followed a simple gridiron pattern. Builders leveled hills, filled ponds, and pulled down any farms or houses in the way. City officials usually lacked any master plan save the idea of endless expansion. Factories often occupied the best sites, typically near waterways, where goods could be easily transported and chemical wastes dumped.

Built by the thousands after the Civil War, the tenement was designed to maximize the use of space. A typical tenement sat on a lot 25 feet by 100 feet and rose to five stories. There were four families on each floor, each with three rooms. By 1890 New York's Lower East Side packed more than 700 people per acre into back-to-back buildings, producing one of the highest population densities in the world.

At the other end of the urban social scale, New York's Fifth Avenue, St. Paul's Summit Avenue, Chicago's Michigan Avenue, and San Francisco's Nob Hill fairly gleamed with new mansions and town houses. Commonwealth Avenue marked Boston's fashionable Back Bay district, built on a filled-in 450-acre tidal flat. State engineers planned this community, with its magnificent boulevard, uniform five-story brownstones, and back alleys designed for deliveries. Back Bay opened onto the Fenway Park system designed by the nation's premier landscape architect, Frederick Law Olmsted.

The industrial city established a new style of commercial and civic architecture. Using fireproof materials, expanded foundations, and internal metal construction,

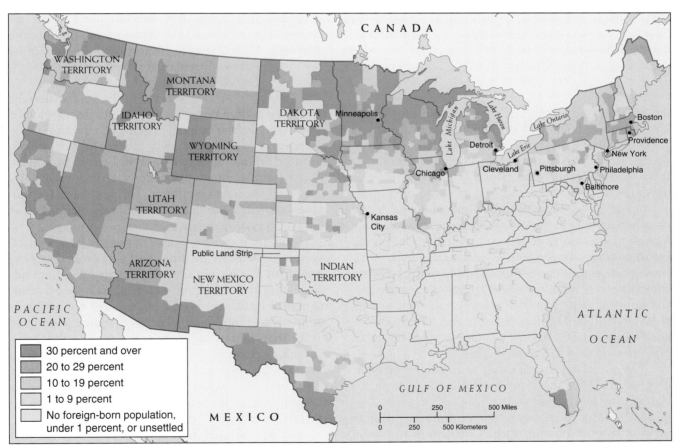

Population of Foreign Birth by Region, 1880   European immigrants after the Civil War settled primarily in the industrial districts of the northern Midwest and parts of the Northeast. French Canadians continued to settle in Maine, Cubans in Florida, and Mexicans in the Southwest, where earlier immigrants had established thriving communities.

SOURCE: From Historical Atlas of the United States 1st edition by Lord/Lord. © 1952. Reprinted with permission of Wadsworth, a division of Thomson Learning: www.thomsonrights.com. Fax 800-730-2215.

In his watercolor *The Bowery at Night*, painted in 1885, W. Louis Sonntag, Jr. shows a New York City scene transformed by electric light. Electricity transformed the city in other ways as well, as seen in the electric streetcars and elevated railroad.

SOURCE: *The Bowery at Night*, 1885. Watercolor. Museum of the City of New York.

than before. By 1895 more than 800 communities operated systems of electrically powered cars or trolleys. In 1902 New York opened its subway system, which would grow to become the largest in the nation.

The City and the Environment

By making it possible for a great number of workers to live in communities distant from their place of employment, mass transportation also allowed the metropolitan region to grow dramatically. By the end of the nineteenth century, suburban trains were bringing nearly 100,000 riders daily into the city of Chicago. Outside Boston, suburbs like Dorchester and Brookline sprang up, offering many professional workers quiet residential retreats from the city's busy downtown.

Electric trolleys eliminated the tons of waste from horsecars that had for decades fouled city streets. But the new rail systems also increased congestion and created new safety hazards for pedestrians. Elevated trains, designed to avoid these problems, placed entire communities under the shadow of noisy and rickety wooden platforms. Despite many technological advances, the quality of life in the nation's cities did not necessarily improve.

Modern water and sewer systems now constituted a hidden city of pipes and wires mirroring the growth of the visible city above ground. These advances did not, however, eradicate serious environmental or health problems. Most cities continued to dump sewage into nearby bodies of water. Moreover, rather than outlawing upriver dumping by factories, municipal governments usually moved to establish separate clean-water systems through the use of reservoirs. But downriver communities began to complain about the unendurable stench from the diverted flow.

The unrestricted burning of coal to fuel the railroads and to heat factories and homes after 1880 greatly intensified urban air pollution. Noise levels continued to rise in the most compacted living and industrial areas. Overcrowded conditions and inadequate sanitary facilities bred tuberculosis, smallpox, and scarlet fever, among other contagious diseases. Children's diseases like whooping cough and measles spread

the era's talented young architects focused on the factory and office building. Concentrating as many offices as possible in the downtown areas, they fashioned hundreds of buildings from steel, sometimes decorating them with elaborate wrought-iron facades. The office building could rise seven, ten, even twenty stories high.

In the 1890s, influenced by American wealth and its enhanced role in the global economy, city planners turned to the monumental or imperial style, laying grand concrete boulevards at enormous public cost. New sports amphitheaters spread pride in the city's accomplishments, and huge new art galleries, museums, and concert halls promoted urban excitement as well as cultural uplift. The imperial style also increased congestion and noise, making the city a more desirable place to visit than to live in.

The city also inspired other architectural marvels. Opened in 1883, the Brooklyn Bridge won wide acclaim as the most original American construction. Designed by John Roebling, who died from an accident early in its construction, and by his son Washington Roebling, who became an invalid during its construction, the bridge was considered an aesthetic and practical wonder.

Like the railroad but on a smaller scale, streetcars and elevated railroads changed business dramatically because they moved traffic of many different kinds— information, people, and goods—faster and farther rapidly through many poor neighborhoods. Only after the turn of the century, amid an intensive campaign against municipal corruption, did laws and administrative practices address the serious problems of public health (see Chapter 21).

Meanwhile the distance between the city and the countryside narrowed. Naturalists had hoped for large open spaces—a buffer zone—to preserve farmland and wild areas, protect future water supplies, and diminish regional air pollution. However, nearby rural lands not destined for private housing or commercial development became sites for water treatment and sewage plants, garbage dumps, and graveyards—services essential to the city's growing population.

CULTURE AND SOCIETY IN THE GILDED AGE

The growth of industry and spread of cities had a profound impact on all regions of the United States. During the final third of the nineteenth century the standard of living climbed, although unevenly and erratically. Real wages (pay in relation to the cost of living) rose, fostering improvements in nutrition, clothing, and housing. More and cheaper products were within the reach of all but the very poor. Food from the farms became more abundant and varied—grains for bread or beer; poultry, pork, and beef; fresh fruits and vegetables from California. Although many Americans continued to acknowledge the moral value of hard work, thrift, and self-sacrifice, the explosion of consumer goods and services promoted sweeping changes in behavior and beliefs.

"Conspicuous Consumption"

Labeled the "Gilded Age" by humorist and social critic Mark Twain, the era following the Civil War favored the growth of a new class united in its pursuit of money and leisure. The well-to-do enjoyed great status throughout the nineteenth century, but only after the war did upper-class Americans form national networks to consolidate their power. Business leaders built diverse stock portfolios and often served simultaneously on the boards of several corporations. Similarly, they intertwined their interests by joining the same religious, charitable, athletic, and professional societies. Their wives and children vacationed together in the sumptuous new seashore and mountain resorts, while they themselves made deals at their leisure in new downtown social clubs and on the golf links of suburban country clubs. Just as Dun and Bradstreet ranked the leading corporations, the Social Register

identified the 500 families that controlled most of the nation's wealth.

According to economist and social critic Thorstein Veblen, the rich had created a new style of "conspicuous consumption." A vice president of the Chicago & Northwestern Railroad, Perry H. Smith, built his marble palace in the style of the Greek Renaissance. Its ebony staircase was trimmed in gold, its butler's pantry equipped with faucets not only for hot and cold water but for iced champagne. The women who oversaw these elaborate households themselves served as measures of their husbands' status, according to Veblen, by adorning themselves in jewels, furs, and dresses of the latest Paris design.

Perhaps no display of wealth matched the ostentation of the "cottages" of Newport, Rhode Island, where the rich created a summer community centering on consumption. Architect H. H. Richardson and his protégés built manor houses more magnificent than the English homes they mimicked. Here wealthy young men and women engaged in new amateur sports such as polo, rowing, and lawn tennis. Young and old alike joined in yachting and golf tournaments.

The wealthy also became the leading patrons of the arts as well as the chief importers of art treasures from Europe and Asia. They provided the bulk of funds for the new symphonies, operas, and ballet companies, which soon rivaled those of Continental Europe. Nearly all major museums and art galleries were founded during the last decades of the nineteenth century.

Gentility and the Middle Class

A new middle class, very different from its predecessor, formed during the last half of the century. The older middle class comprised the owners or superintendents of small businesses, doctors, lawyers, teachers, and ministers and their families. The new middle class included these professionals but also the growing number of salaried employees—the managers, technicians, clerks, and engineers who worked in the complex web of corporations and government. Long hours of labor earned their families a modest status and sufficient income to live securely in style and comfort. For as little as $10 a month, a family could finance the construction of a suburban retreat from the noise, filth, and dangers of the city. Assisted by modern transportation systems, men often traveled one to two hours each day, five or six days a week, to their city offices and back again. Women and children stayed behind.

Middle-class women found themselves devoting a large part of their day to housework. They frequently employed one or two servants but relied increasingly on the many new household appliances to get their work done. Improvements in the kitchen stove, such as the conversion from wood fuel to gas, saved a lot of time. Yet, simultaneously, with the widespread circulation of cookbooks and recipes in newspapers and magazines, as well as the availability of new foods, the preparation of meals became more complex and time-consuming. Similarly, the new carpet sweepers surpassed the broom in efficiency, but the fashionable high-napped carpeting demanded more care. Rather than diminishing with technological innovation, household work expanded to fill the time available.

Almost exclusively white, Anglo-Saxon, and Protestant, the new middle class embraced "culture" not for purposes of conspicuous consumption but as a means of self-improvement and moral uplift. Whole families visited the new museums and art galleries. The middle class also provided the bulk of patrons for the new public libraries.

Middle-class families applied the same standards to their leisure activities. Hiking was a favorite among both men and women. Roller skating and ice skating, which became crazes shortly after the Civil War, took place in specially designed rinks in almost every major town. By the 1890s, the "safety" bicycle had also been marketed. It replaced the large-wheel variety, which was difficult to keep upright. A good-quality "bike" cost $100 and, like the piano, was a symbol of middle-class status.

Leisure became the special province of middle-class childhood. Removed from factories and shops and freed from many domestic chores, children enjoyed creative play and physical activity. The toy market boomed, and lower printing prices helped children's literature flourish. Uplifting classics as *Little Women* and *Black Beauty* were popular.

Life in the Streets

Immigrants often weighed the material abundance they found in the United States against their memories of the Old Country. One could "live better" here, but only by working much harder. In letters home, immigrants described the riches of the new country but warned friends and relatives not to send weaklings, who would surely die of stress and strain amid the alien and intense commercialism of American society. In many immigrant communities, alcoholism and suicide rates soared. Embittered German immigrants called their new land *Malhuerica*, "misfortune"; Jews called it *Ama Reka*, Hebrew for "without soul"; and Slavs referred to it as *Dollerica*.

Many newcomers, having little choice about their place of residence, concentrated in districts marked off by racial or ethnic lines. In San Francisco, city ordinances prevented Chinese from operating laundries in most of the city's neighborhoods, effectively confining

the population to Chinatown. In Los Angeles and San Antonio, Mexicans lived in distinctive barrios. In most cities, African American families were similarly compelled to remain in the dingiest, most crime-ridden, and dangerous sections of town.

The working-class home did not necessarily ensure privacy or offer protection from the dangers of the outside world. In the tenements, families often shared their rooms with other families or paying boarders. During the summer heat, adults, children, and boarders alike competed for a sleeping place on the fire escape or roof, and all year round noise resounded through paper-thin walls. But so complex and varied were income levels and social customs that no single pattern emerged. Packingtown's Slovaks, Lithuanians, and Poles, for example, frequently took in boarders, yet Bohemians rarely did. Neither did the skilled iron rollers who worked at the Carnegie Steel Company in Homestead, Pennsylvania. These well-paid craft workers often owned their own homes, boasting parlors and even imported Belgian carpets. At the other extreme, Italian immigrants, who considered themselves fortunate to get work with a shovel, usually lived in overcrowded rented apartments, just a paycheck away from eviction.

The intersection of Orchard and Hester Streets on New York's Lower East Side, photographed ca. 1905. Unlike the middle classes, who worked and played hidden away in offices and private homes, the Jewish lower-class immigrants who lived and worked in this neighborhood spent the greater parts of their lives on the streets.

SOURCE: The Granger Collection.

Whether it was a small cottage or a tenement flat, the working-class home involved women and children in routines of household labor without the aid of the new mechanical devices. In addition to cooking and cleaning, women used their cramped domestic space for work that provided a small income. They gathered their children—and their husbands after a hard day's labor—to sew garments, wrap cigars, string beads, or paint vases for a contractor who paid them by the piece. And they cooked and cleaned for the boarders whose rent supplemented the family income.

Despite working people's slim resources, their combined buying power created new and important markets for consumer goods. Often they bought shoddy replicas of products sold to the middle class: cheaper canned goods, inferior cuts of meat, and partially spoiled fruit. Several leading clothing manufacturers specialized in inexpensive ready-to-wear items, usually copied from patterns designed for wealthier consumers but constructed hastily from flimsy materials. Patent medicines for ailments caused by working long periods in cramped conditions sold well in working-class communities, where money for doctors was scarce. Their high alcohol content might lift a person's spirits, if only temporarily.

The close quarters of the urban neighborhood allowed immigrants to preserve many Old World customs. In immigrant communities such as Chicago's Packingtown, Pittsburgh's Poletown, New York's Lower East Side, or San Francisco's Chinatown, people usually spoke their native language while visiting their friends and relatives. In good weather they walked and talked, an inexpensive pastime common in European cities. Immigrants also recreated Old World religious institutions such as the temple, church, or synagogue, or secular institutions such as German family-style taverns or Russian Jewish tearooms. They replicated their native cuisine and married, baptized children, and buried their dead according to Old World customs.

In the cosmopolitan cities, immigrants, by being innovative entrepreneurs as well as the best customers, helped to shape the emerging popular culture. Ragtime, for example, quickly found its way north from Storyville, the red-light district of New Orleans. Created by African American and creole bands, ragtime captivated those teenage offspring of immigrants who rushed to the new dance halls.

When developers realized that "wholesome fun" for the masses could pay better than upper-class leisure or lower-class vice, they decided to transform Coney Island into a magnificent seaside park filled with ingenious amusements such as water slides, mechanized horse races, carousels, roller coasters, and fun houses. Here, millions of working-class people enjoyed cheap thrills that offset the hardships of their working lives.

CULTURES IN CONFLICT, CULTURE IN COMMON

The new commercial entertainments gave Americans from various backgrounds more in common than they would otherwise have had. On New York's Lower East Side, for instance, theater blossomed with dramas that Broadway would adopt years later, while children dreamed of going "uptown" where the popular songs they heard on the streets were transcribed onto sheet music and sold in stores throughout the city.

Education

Business and civic leaders realized that the welfare of society now depended on an educated population, one possessing the skills and knowledge required to keep both industry and government running. In the last three decades of the nineteenth century, the idea of universal free schooling, at least for white children, took hold. Kindergartens in particular flourished. St. Louis, Missouri, opened the first public school kindergarten in 1873, and by the turn of the century more than 4,000 similar programs throughout the country enrolled children between the ages of three and seven. The number of public high schools, increased from 160 in 1870 to 6,000 by the end of the century.

Agricultural colleges formed earlier in the century developed into institutes of technology and took their places alongside the prestigious liberal arts colleges. The Morrill Federal Land Grant Act of 1862 funded a system of state colleges and universities for teaching agriculture and mechanics "without excluding other scientific and classic studies." One of the most important developments occurred in the area of research and graduate studies, pioneered in this country in 1876 by Johns Hopkins University. By the end of the century several American universities, including Stanford University and the University of Chicago, offered advanced degrees in the arts and sciences.

This expansion benefited women, who previously had had little access to higher education. After the Civil War, a number of women's colleges were founded, beginning in 1865 with Vassar, which set the academic standard for the remainder of the century. Smith and Wellesley followed in 1875, Bryn Mawr in 1885. By the end of the century, 125 women's colleges offered a first-rate education comparable to that given to men at Harvard, Yale, or Princeton. Meanwhile, coeducation grew at an even faster rate; women constituted 21 percent of undergraduate enrollments in 1870, 32 percent in 1880, and 40 percent in 1910.

An even greater number of women enrolled in vocational courses. The first training school for nurses opened in Boston in 1873, followed in 1879 by a diet kitchen that taught women to become cooks in the city's hospitals. Founded in 1877, the Women's Educational and Industrial Union offered a multitude of classes to Boston's wage-earning women, ranging from elementary French and German, to drawing, watercoloring, and oil and china painting, to dressmaking and millinery, stenography and typing, as well as crafts less familiar to women, such as upholstering, cabinetmaking, and carpentry. In the early 1890s, when the entering class at a large women's college like Vassar still averaged under 100, the Boston Women's Educational and Industrial Union reported that its staff of 83 served an estimated 1,500 clients per day. By that time, one of its most well-funded programs was a training school for domestic servants.

The leaders of the business community had also begun to promote manual training for working-class and immigrant boys. Craft unionists in several cities actively opposed this development, preferring their own methods of apprenticeship to training programs they could not control. But local associations of merchants and manufacturers lobbied hard for "industrial education" and raised funds to supplement the public school budget. By 1895 all elementary and high schools in the city offered courses that trained working-class boys for future jobs in industry and business.

The expansion of education did not benefit all Americans or benefit them all in the same way. Because African Americans were prohibited from enrolling in colleges attended by white students, special colleges were founded in the southern states shortly after the Civil War. All-black Atlanta and Fisk universities both soon offered a rigorous curriculum in the liberal arts. Educator Booker T. Washington encouraged African Americans to resist "the craze for Greek and Latin learning" and to strive for practical instruction. In 1881 he founded the Tuskegee Institute in Alabama to provide industrial education and moral uplift. Black colleges, including Tuskegee, trained so many teachers that by the century's end the majority of black schools were staffed by African Americans.

Leisure and Public Space

Most large cities set aside open land for leisure-time use by residents. New York's Central Park opened for ice skating in 1858, providing a model for urban park systems across the United States. The parks were rolling expanses, cut across by streams and pathways and footbridges and set off by groves of trees, ornamental shrubs, and neat flower gardens. According to the designers' vision, the urban middle class might find here a respite from the stresses of modern life.

The working classes had their own ideas about the use of parks and open land. Trapped in overcrowded tenements or congested neighborhoods, they wanted space for sports, picnics, and lovers' trysts. Young people openly defied ordinances that prohibited play on the grassy knolls, while their elders routinely voted against municipal bonds that did not include funds for more recreational space in their communities. Immigrant ward representatives on the Pittsburgh city council, for instance, argued that band shells for classical music meant little to their constituents, while spaces suitable for sports meant much.

Public drinking of alcoholic beverages, especially on Sunday, provoked similar disputes. Pittsburgh's "blue laws," forbidding businesses to open on Sunday, were rigidly enforced when it came to neighborhood taverns, while large firms like the railroads enjoyed exemptions. Nevertheless, many working people, especially beer-loving German immigrants, continued to treat Sunday as their one day of relaxation and gathered in large numbers for picnics in the city's parks.

National Pastimes

Toward the end of the century, middle-class urban dwellers began to seek out ragtime bands and congregated in nightclubs and even on the rooftops of posh hotels to listen and dance and even to drink.

Vaudeville, the most popular form of commercial entertainment since the 1880s, also bridged middle- and working-class tastes. Drawing on a variety-show tradition of singers, dancers, comedians, jugglers, and acrobats, who had entertained Americans since colonial days, "vaude" became a big business that made ethnic and racial stereotypes and the daily frustrations of city life into major topics of amusement.

Sports, however, outdistanced all other commercial entertainments in appealing to all kinds of fans and managing to create a sense of national identity. No doubt the most popular parks in the United States were the expanses of green surrounded by grandstands and marked by their unique diamond shape—the baseball field. Baseball clubs formed in many cities, and shortly after the Civil War traveling teams with regular schedules made baseball a professional sport. The formation of the National League in 1876 encouraged other spectator sports, but for generations baseball remained the most popular.

Rowdy behavior gave the game a working-class ambience. Team owners, themselves often proprietors of local breweries, counted heavily on beer sales in the parks. To attract more subdued middle-class fans, the National League raised admission prices, banned the sale of alcohol, and observed Sunday blue laws. Catering to a working-class audience, the American Association kept the price of admission low, sold liquor, and played ball on Sunday.

CHRONOLOGY

1862	Morrill Act authorizes "land-grant" colleges
1869	Knights of Labor founded
1870	Standard Oil founded
1871	Chicago Fire
1873	Financial panic brings severe depression
1876	Baseball's National League founded
	Alexander Graham Bell patents the telephone
1879	Thomas Edison invents the incandescent bulb
	Depression ends
1881	Tuskegee Institute founded
1882	Peak of immigration to the United States (1.2 million) in the nineteenth century
	Chinese Exclusion Act passed
	Standard Oil Trust founded
1883	William Graham Sumner published the social Darwinist classic *What Social Classes Owe to Each Other*
1886	Campaigns for eight-hour workday peak
	Haymarket riot and massacre discredit the Knights of Labor
	American Federation of Labor founded
1890	Sherman Antitrust Act passed
1893	Stock market panic precipitates severe depression
1895	Coney Island opens
1896	Rural free delivery begins
1900	Andrew Carnegie's *Gospel of Wealth* recommends honesty and fair dealing
1901	U.S. Steel Corporation formed

Entrepreneur Albert G. Spalding brought order to often chaotic baseball, but at a price. Manager and then president of the Chicago White Stockings, Spalding quickly came to see baseball as a source of multiple profits. He procured the exclusive rights to manufacture the official ball and the rule book, while producing large varieties of other sporting equipment. Meanwhile, he built impressive baseball parks in Chicago with seating for 10,000 and special private boxes above the grandstands for the wealthy.

Spalding also succeeded in tightening the rules of participation in the sport. He prevented players from negotiating a better deal and leaving the team that originally signed them. He encouraged his player-manager "Cap" Anson to forbid the White Stockings from playing against any team with an African American member, effectively setting a segregation standard for professional baseball. African Americans organized their own traveling teams. In the 1920s they formed the Negro Leagues, which produced some of the nation's finest ballplayers.

As attendance continued to grow, the enthusiasm for baseball straddled major social divisions, bringing together Americans of many backgrounds, if only on a limited basis. Although it interested relatively few women, sports news riveted the attention of men from all social classes. Loyalty to the "home team" helped to create an urban identity, while individual players became national heroes.

CONCLUSION

By the end of the nineteenth century, industry and the growing cities had opened a new world for Americans. Fresh from Europe or from the native countryside, ordinary urban dwellers struggled to form communities of fellow newcomers through work and leisure, in the factory, the neighborhood, the ballpark, and the public school. Meanwhile, their "betters," the wealthy and the new middle class, made and executed the decisions of industry and marketing, established the era's grand civic institutions, and set the tone for high fashion and art.

Rich and poor alike shared many aspects of the new order. Yet inequality persisted and increased, as much a part of the new order as the Brooklyn Bridge or advertising. During the mostly prosperous 1880s, optimists believed that unfair treatment based on region, on class, and perhaps even on race and gender might ease in time. By the depressed 1890s, however, these hopes had worn thin, and the lure of overseas empire appeared as one of the few goals that held together a suffering and divided nation.

REVIEW QUESTIONS

1. Discuss the sources of economic growth in the decades after the Civil War. Historians often refer to this period as the era of the "second industrial revolution." Do you agree with this description?
2. Describe the impact of new technologies and new forms of production on the routines of industrial workers. How did these changes affect African American and women workers in particular? What role did trade unions play in this process?
3. Choose one major city, such as Boston, New York, Chicago, Birmingham, or San Francisco, and discuss changes in its economy, population, and urban space in the decades after the Civil War.
4. Discuss the role of northern capital in the development of the New South. How did the rise of indus-

try affect the lives of rural Southerners? Analyze these changes from the point of view of African Americans.
5. How did urban life change during the Gilded Age? How did economic development affect residential patterns? How did the middle class aspire to live during the Gilded Age? How did their lifestyles compare with those of working-class urbanites?
6. How did the American educational system change to prepare children for their adult roles in the new industrial economy?
7. How did the rise of organized sports and commercial amusements reflect and shape social divisions at the end of the century? Which groups were affected most (or least) by new leisure activities?

RECOMMENDED READING

Cindy S. Aron, *Working at Play: A History of Vacations in the United States* (1999). Covers the expansion of vacations from wealthy families to the middle class in the nineteenth century. Aron examines several types of settings, ranging from the grand summer hotels and posh resorts to camping vacations in the new national parks.

James R. Barrett, *Work and Community in the Jungle* (1987). A very close study of the Packingtown district of Chicago, Illinois, at the turn of the century. Barrett describes the transformation of animals to meat in great stockyards and processing plants. He also provides rich documentation of neighborhood life.

Alfred D. Chandler Jr., *The Visible Hand: The Managerial Revolution in American Business* (1977). A highly acclaimed study of corporate management. Chandler shows how the rapid growth in the scale of business, as well as its influence in public life, brought about a new type of executive with skills for national decision making and close links with others of his kind.

William Cronon, *Nature's Metropolis* (1991). Analyzes the changing economic and political relationship between the city of Chicago and the surrounding countryside. Cronon demonstrates through a variety of evidence the tight interdependence of urban and rural regions.

Herbert G. Gutman, *Work, Culture and Society in Industrializing America: Essays in American Working-Class and Social History* (1977). Influential essays on the formation of working-class communities in the nineteenth century. Gutman focuses on the role of

immigrants in transforming the values and belief systems of working-class Americans in the throes of industrialization.

Alice Kessler-Harris, *Out to Work: A History of Wage-Earning Women in the United States* (1982). A comprehensive survey of women's increasing participation in the labor force. Kessler-Harris documents women's role in trade unions and the impact on family patterns and ideas about women's roles in American society.

Kenneth L. Kusmer, *A Ghetto Takes Shape, Black Cleveland, 1870–1930* (1976). A keen analysis of a long-standing African American community. Kusmer shows how blacks suffered downward mobility and increased segregation as their skilled jobs and small-business opportunities were given to European immigrants.

Lawrence H. Larsen, *The Rise of the Urban South* (1985). Studies of the changing South. In Larson's view, the true New South was the city, for relatively few had lived there before the late nineteenth century, but rural values remained vital, especially in religious life and voting patterns.

David F. Noble, *America by Design: Science, Technology and the Rise of Corporate Capitalism* (1977). A view of scientific advancement and its connections with the expanding economy. Noble shows how scientific breakthroughs were often created for, but especially adapted to, corporate purposes.

Dave Roediger and Franklin Rosemont, eds., *Haymarket Scrapbook* (1986). A large, beautifully illustrated book about the events and consequences of the Haymarket tragedy.

Roy Rosenzweig, *Eight Hours for What We Will: Workers and Leisure in an Industrial City, 1870–1920* (1983). Analyzes class and cultural conflicts over recreational space. This valuable book treats the city park as the arena for conflict over whether public community life should be uplifting (devoted to nature walks and concerts) or entertaining (for drinking, courting, and amusement).

Alan Trachtenberg, *The Incorporation of America: Culture and Society in the Gilded Age* (1982). One of the best and most readable overviews of the post–Civil War era. Trachtenberg devotes great care to describing the rise of the corporation to the defining institution of national life, and the reorientation of culture to reflect the new middle classes employed by the corporation.

ON THE WEB

http://trainweb.org/wnyrhs/historyFrame1Source1.htm

An interesting article appears at this site on the history of railroading in western New York State in conjunction with the 1901 Pan-American Exposition and is sponsored by the western New York Railway Historical Society. Written by the Society's resident historian, Greg Jandura, this article also discusses the use of the railroad in the presidential elections of the 1890s. The Society is a hobbyist group, so many links exist to sites relating to the hobby of railroad historical preservation.

http://www.fordham.edu/halsall/mod/1889carnegie.html

Andrew Carnegie's article containing the concepts of the Gospel of Wealth appeared in the *North American Review* in June 1889. It outlined his beliefs regarding the obligations that fall upon any man who realizes great wealth within his lifetime.

http://www.history.rochester.edu/fuels/tarbell/Main.htm

The University of Rochester has posted this electronic version of Ida Tarbell's famous history of John D. Rockefeller's Standard Oil Company as it was printed in 1904 in *McClure's*.

http://www.financialhistory.org/photo-history.htm

A flattering family history of those immediately around John D. Rockefeller, Sr., including his parents, wife, and himself, this site was posted by the Museum of American Financial History located in New York City. The home page of this institution can be located at **http://www.financialhistory.org/**.

http://douglass.speech.nwu.edu/grad_a12.htm

This site contains Henry W. Grady's "The New South" speech given December 22, 1886, before the New England Society of New York.

http://www.prenhall.com/faragherbrief/map19.1

Explore patterns of industry in each region of the United States in 1900. Why did industrial patterns differ from region to region?

http://www.prenhall.com/faragherbrief/map19.2

Consider the percentages of foreign-born residents in the different regions of the United States in 1900. Why did immigrants tend to settle in some regions and not in others?

Representing Chicago's History

Packingtown occupies a unique niche in Chicago's historical memory in that it came to represent the very essence of the city. As the poet Carl Sandburg wrote, Chicago was "the city of big shoulders," "hog butcher to the world." There was a certain grittiness and muscularity about the Midwestern metropolis that for generations delighted residents and intrigued visitors.

This image of Chicago began to circulate widely after the publication of Upton Sinclair's muckraking novel, *The Jungle*. Commissioned by a socialist newspaper to write a novel about immigrant workers in the meat packing houses, Sinclair collected a $500 advance and spent nearly two months researching the working and living conditions of Packingtown. In *The Jungle*, which was published in 1905, he described in vivid detail the blood and guts of the killing floors and the squalid neighborhood that adjoined the stock yards. His story revolved around a family of recent immigrants from Lithuania, and he provided close descriptions of their everyday life, down to the clothes they wore. Sinclair, a socialist himself, hoped to mobilize his read-

Established in 1865, Chicago's Union Stockyards was processing more than 9 million livestock by the turn of the century. "The Yards" covered more than a square mile of land on the city's South Side. The livestock, brought in by trainloads, were held in pens until moved to the "killing floors" for slaughter. It wasn't a "pretty sight," as one Chicagoan remarked, but the meatpacking industry "put Chicago into contention as a world-class city."
SOURCE: © CORBIS.

ers to overthrow the system that created the grave social injustices that put so much strain on the immigrant community, but he succeeded mainly in buttressing a campaign for the regulation of the food industry. "I aimed at the public's heart," he lamented, "and by accident hit it in the stomach." Partly in a response to his best-selling novel, Congress passed the Pure Food and Drug Act and the Meat Inspection Act in 1906. But *The Jungle*, which within a few years sold more than 150,000 copies and was published in 17 languages, also enhanced Packingtown's reputation as symbol of the industrial city at its prime.

Despite Sinclair's intention, *The Jungle* helped to make Packingtown the focal point of Chicago history. By the time of its publication, the Union Stock Yards were already attracting tourists from all over the world. In 1893, more people went to see the killing floors than the famed world's fair, the Columbian Exposition. Ironically, Sinclair's vivid descriptions of the gore further piqued their curiosity about work and life in Packingtown. Well into the 1940s, the big packinghouses like Armour and Swift's maintained a special visitors entrance for tourists who continued to come by the trainload to see the way meat was mass produced.

Chicagoans themselves nurtured this aspect of their history. They took pride in being the center of the meat packing industry, which, after steel, reigned for nearly a century as the city's largest industry. They described the Union Stock Yards as one of the wonders of the world. They even bragged about the notorious stench of the neighborhood. As one longtime member of the community noted, "the first memory" of anybody from Packingtown was "the overpowering smell from the packing houses and the fertilizer plants." Scratch any Chicagoan, a popular saying went, and some stockyard smell would come out. Contrary to Sinclair's intention to expose the degradation of Packingtown's residents, Chicagoans took pride in themselves as survivors of harsh conditions. However, by end of the twentieth century, few Chicagoans could nurture this memory.

Since its origin as a primarily German and Irish neighborhood in the 1860s and transformation into a community of Eastern European immigrants when the stockyards were at their peak, slaughtering 15 million livestock a year and employing 44,000 people, Packingtown underwent a series of dramatic changes. After

World War II, as a consequence of the decentralization of the meat packing industry, the stock yards began a period of sharp decline. By the late 1950s, when some of the biggest firms closed their doors, new populations moved in. Meanwhile, postwar prosperity had encouraged the majority of Poles and Lithuanians to find cleaner jobs in other industries and to flee to the suburbs. Mexicans and African Americans took their place and stayed. At one time there were a dozen Polish-American Catholic parishes; after 1971, when the Union Stock Yards finally shut down, the parishes that remained were Mexican. In the 1980s, the City of Chicago, partnering with the Back of the Yards Council, a community organization founded in the late 1930s, launched a redevelopment plan that laid the foundation for the Stockyards Industrial Park. The new complex of small businesses and retail stores employed about one-third the number of workers as the packing houses and retained a link to the past in name only. All that remained of the scenes made famous by Upton Sinclair and celebrated by Chicagoans themselves was the limestone arch that marks the entryway to the old stockyards complex. By the time Chicago designated the old stone gate as an official landmark in 1972, only the memories of old-timers kept this chapter of Chicago's history alive.

By the end of the twentieth century, a new generation of Chicagoans were poised to celebrate not the city's gritty past but its future in finance, service, and tourist industries. In 1999, the city sponsored "Cows on Parade," a public art project that brought to downtown sidewalks more than 200 "cows" made of a fiberglass-polyester mixture and painted in a rainbow of colors and a variety of styles. One cow perched atop a skateboard, for example, another was on skis. The cows had cute names, such as Rhinestone Cowgirl, Cowbelle de Fruits, and Wow Cow. Local businesses and art patrons vied to purchase a cow of their own for a standard fee of $3,500, and at the end of the summer they could either take home their trophy or donate it to a public auction for charity. "Cows on Parade" enchanted children, tourists, and the thousands of office workers who filled the downtown skyscrapers—including the Sears Tower, which, since 1974, stood as the city's new source of pride as the tallest building in the nation.

A few Chicagoans, however, complained that "Cows on Parade" had supplanted the stockyards as the city's chief symbol and, in the process, obliterated

The Chicago Department of Cultural Affairs promoted the *Cows on Parade* exhibit by presenting the 320 cows on display as "works of art to be treasured" as well as "worthy trophies of Chicago history." Chicago multimedia artist Joyce Martin Perz fashioned the cow shown here, "Jazz Chicago! Merci Henri!" as a tribute to the French modernist artist Henri Matisse. It was one of several cows featured in the "Mooseum Campus," which was located near the downtown. SOURCE: © AFP/CORBIS.

much of its history. "Chicago seems to be erasing its gritty, less-glitzy past," one local critic observed. "The hog (and cattle) butcher to the world," he added, "has become a Technicolor, DisneyQuest, chrome-and-glass kinda town." Another detractor refused to relinquish the time-tested symbol, insisting that the "true monument to Chicago's past" was not the whimsical cows currently on display but "a bull named Sherman." Named after one of the founders of the Union Stock yard, John B. Sherman, this rugged bust of the prize-winning steer still tops the old stone gate.

But what remains of the historical memory of Chicago as the nation's premier industrial city and community of hard-working Eastern European immigrants?

During the summer of 1999, while upscale Chicago basked in the publicity garnered from "Cows on Parade," the new residents of what had once been Packingtown displayed their own cows, a trio of colorfully painted figures contributed not by the big-name artists who crafted the downtown versions but by local schoolchildren and community groups. Few Chicagoans from other parts of the city bothered to visit them. "And there they sit," as one nostalgic observer recorded at the time: "No tourists or cameras. Just three forgotten cows marking Chicago's forgotten past." ■

AMERICAN COMMUNITIES

The Cooperative Commonwealth

EDWARD BELLAMY'S *LOOKING BACKWARD* (1888), THE CENTURY'S best-selling novel after Harriet Beecher Stowe's *Uncle Tom's Cabin*, tells the story of a young man who awakens in the year 2000 after a sleep lasting more than 100 years. He is surprised to learn that Americans had solved their major problems. Poverty, crime, war, taxes, air pollution—even housework—no longer exist. Nor are there politicians, capitalists, bankers, or lawyers. Most amazing, gone is the great social division between the powerful rich and the suffering poor. In the year 2000 everyone lives in material comfort, happily and harmoniously. No wonder Bellamy's hero shudders at the thought of returning to the late nineteenth century, a time of "worldwide bloodshed, greed and tyranny."

Community and cooperation are the key concepts in Bellamy's utopian tale. The nation's businesses, including farms and factories, have been given over to the collective ownership of the people. Elected officials now plan the production and distribution of goods for the common well-being. With great efficiency, they even manage huge department stores and warehouses full of marvelous manufactured goods and oversee majestic apartment complexes with modern facilities for cooking, dining, and laundering. To get the necessary work done, an industrial army enlists all adult men and women, but automated machinery has eliminated most menial tasks. The workday is only four hours; vacations extend to six months of each year. At forty-five everyone retires to pursue hobbies, sports, and culture.

Bellamy envisioned his technological utopia as promoting the "highest possible physical, as well as mental, development for everyone." There was nothing fantastic in this plan, the author insisted. It simply required Americans to share equally the abundant resources of their land. If the nation's citizens actually lived up to their democratic ideals, Bellamy declared, the United States would become a "cooperative commonwealth," that is, a nation governed by the people for their common welfare.

Bellamy, a journalist and writer of historical fiction from Chicopee Falls, Massachusetts, moved thousands of his readers to action. His most ardent fans endorsed his program for a "new nation" and formed the Nationalist movement, which by the early 1890s reached an apex of 165 clubs. Terence V. Powderly of the Knights of Labor declared himself a Nationalist. Many leaders of the woman suffrage movement also threw in their support. They endorsed *Looking Backward*'s depiction of marriage as a union of "perfect equals" and admired Bellamy's sequel, *Equality*

(1897), which showed how women might become "absolutely free agents" by ending their financial dependence on men.

During the 1890s Bellamy's disciples actually attempted to create new communities along the lines set forth in *Looking Backward*. The best known and longest lasting of these settlements was established in Point Loma, California, in 1897. Situated on 330 acres, with avenues winding through gardens and orchards newly planted with groves of eucalyptus trees, Point Loma was known for its physical beauty. Many young married couples chose to live in small bungalows, which were scattered throughout the colony's grounds; others opted for private rooms in a large communal building. Either way, they all met twice daily to share meals and usually spent their leisure hours together. On the ocean's edge the residents constructed an outdoor amphitheater and staged plays and concerts.

The colony's founder, Katherine Tingley, described Point Loma as "a practical illustration of the possibility of developing a higher type of humanity." No one earned wages, but all 500 residents lived comfortably. They dressed simply in clothes manufactured by the community's women. The majority of the men worked in agriculture. They conducted horticultural experiments that yielded new types of avocados and tropical fruits and eventually produced over half of the community's food supply. Children, who slept in a special dormitory from the time they reached school age, enjoyed an outstanding education. They excelled in the fine arts, including music and drama, and often demonstrated their talents to audiences in nearby San Diego.

The Point Loma community never met all its expenses, but with the help of donations from admirers across the country it remained solvent for decades. Baseball entrepreneur Albert Spalding, who lived there during his retirement, helped make up the financial deficit. As late as the 1950s the community still had some seventy-five members living on about 100 acres of land.

Even relatively successful cooperative communities such as Point Loma, however, could not bring about the changes that Bellamy hoped to see, and he knew it. Only a mobilization of citizens nationwide could overturn the existing hierarchies and usher in the egalitarian order depicted in *Looking Backward*. Without such a rigorous challenge, the economic and political leadership that had been emerging since the Civil War would continue to consolidate its power and become even further removed from popular control.

The last quarter of the nineteenth century saw just such a challenge, producing what one historian calls "a moment of democratic promise." Ordinary citizens sought to renew the older values of community through farm and labor organizations as well as philanthropic and charitable societies. They could not clearly see, however, that the fate of the nation depended increasingly on events beyond its territorial boundaries. Business leaders and politicians had proposed their own vision of the future: an American empire extending to far distant lands. ■

Point Loma

KEY TOPICS

- The growth of federal and state governments and the consolidation of the modern two-party system

- The development of mass protest movements

- Economic and political crisis in the 1890s

- The United States as a world power

- The Spanish-American War

TOWARD A NATIONAL GOVERNING CLASS

The basic structure of government changed dramatically in the last quarter of the nineteenth century. Mirroring the fast-growing economy, public administration expanded at all levels—municipal, county, state, and federal—and took on greater responsibility for regulating society, especially market and property relations.

This expansion offered ample opportunities for politicians who were eager to compete against one another for control of the new mechanisms of power. Political campaigns, especially those staged for the presidential elections, became mass spectacles, and votes became precious commodities. The most farsighted politicians attempted to rein in the growing corruption and to promote both efficiency and professionalism in the expanding structures of government.

The Growth of Government

Before the Civil War, local governments attended mainly to the promotion and regulation of trade and relied on private enterprise to supply vital services such as fire protection and water supply. As cities became more responsible for their residents' well-being, they introduced professional police and firefighting forces and began to finance school systems, public libraries, and parks. This expansion demanded huge increases in local taxation.

At the national level, mobilization for the Civil War and Reconstruction had demanded an unprecedented degree of coordination, and the federal government continued to expand under the weight of new tasks and responsibilities. Federal revenues also skyrocketed, from $257 million in 1878 to $567 million in 1900. The administrative bureaucracy also grew dramatically, from 50,000 employees in 1871 to 100,000 only a decade later.

The modern apparatus of departments, bureaus, and cabinets took shape amid this upswing. The Department of Agriculture was established in 1862 to provide information to farmers and to consumers of farm products. The Department of the Interior, which had been created in 1849, grew into the largest and most important federal department after the Post Office. It came to comprise more than twenty agencies, including the Bureau of Indian Affairs, the U.S. Geological Survey, and the Bureau of Territorial and International Affairs. The Department of the Treasury, responsible for collecting federal taxes and customs as well as printing money and stamps, grew from 4,000 employees in 1873 to nearly 25,000 in 1900.

The nation's first independent regulatory agency took charge of the nation's most important industry. The Interstate Commerce Commission (ICC) was created in 1887 to bring order to the growing patchwork of state laws concerning railroads. The five-member commission appointed by the president approved freight and passenger rates set by the railroads. The ICC could take public testimony on possible violations, examine company records, and generally oversee enforcement of the law. This set a precedent for future regulation of trade as well as for positive government—that is, for the intervention of the government into the affairs of private enterprise.

The Machinery of Politics

Only gradually did Republicans and Democrats adapt to the demands of governmental expansion. The Republican Party continued to run on its Civil War record, pointing to its achievements in reuniting the nation and in passing new reform legislation. Democrats, by contrast, sought to reduce the influence of the federal government, slash expenditures, repeal legislation, and protect states' rights. While Republicans held on to their longtime constituencies, Democrats gathered support from southern white voters and immigrants newly naturalized in the North. But neither party commanded a clear majority of votes until the century drew to a close.

Presidents in the last quarter of the century— Rutherford B. Hayes (1877–81), James A. Garfield (1881), Chester A. Arthur (1881–85), Grover Cleveland (1885–89), Benjamin Harrison (1889–93), and Cleveland again (1893–97)—did not espouse a clear philosophy of government. They willingly yielded power to Congress and the state legislatures. Only 1 percent of the popular vote separated the presidential candidates in three of five elections between 1876 and 1892. Congressional races were equally tight, less than 2 percentage points separating total votes for Democratic and Republican candidates in all but one election in the decade before 1888.

Both political parties operated essentially as state or local organizations. Successful politicians responded primarily to the particular concerns of their constituents. To please local voters, Democrats and Republicans repeatedly crosscut each other by taking identical positions on controversial issues.

The rising costs of maintaining local organizations and orchestrating mammoth campaigns drove party leaders to seek ever-larger sources of revenue. Winners often seized and added to the "spoils" of office through an elaborate system of payoffs. Legislators who supported government subsidies for railroad corporations, for instance, commonly received stock in return and sometimes cash bribes. At the time, few politicians or business leaders regarded these practices as unethical.

At the local level, powerful bosses and political machines dominated both parties. Democrats William Marcy Tweed of New York's powerful political organization, Tammany Hall, and Michael "Hinky Dink" Kenna of Chicago specialized in giving municipal jobs to loyal voters and holiday food baskets to their families.

A large number of federal jobs, meanwhile, changed hands each time the presidency passed from one party to another. More than 50 percent of all federal jobs were patronage positions—nearly 56,000 in 1881—jobs that could be awarded to loyal supporters as part of the "spoils" of the winner. Observers estimated that decisions about congressional patronage filled one-third of all legislators' time. No wonder Bellamy's utopian community operated without politicians and political parties.

The Spoils System and Civil Service Reform

As early as 1865, Republican representative Thomas A. Jenckes of Rhode Island proposed a bill for civil service reform. Congress feared that such a measure would hamper candidates in their relentless pursuit of votes. Finally, a group consisting of mainly professors, newspaper editors, lawyers, and ministers organized the Civil Service Reform Association and enlisted Democratic Senator George H. Pendleton to sponsor reform legislation.

In January 1883, a bipartisan congressional majority passed the Pendleton Civil Service Reform Act. This measure allowed the president to create, with Senate approval, a three-person commission to draw up a set of guidelines for executive and legislative appointments. The commission established a system of standards for various federal jobs. The Pendleton Act also barred political candidates from soliciting campaign contributions from government workers. Patronage did not disappear, but public service did improve.

Many departments of the federal government took on a professional character similar to that which doctors, lawyers, and scholars were imposing on their fields through regulatory societies such as the American Medical Association and the American Historical Association. At the same time, the federal judiciary began to act more aggressively to establish the parameters of government. With the Circuit Courts of Appeals Act of 1891, Congress granted the U.S. Supreme Court the right to review all cases at will.

Despite these reforms, many observers still viewed government as a reign of outsiders, people pulling the levers of the party machinery or spending money to influence important decisions. Edward Bellamy agreed. He advised Americans to organize their communities for the specific purpose of wresting control of government from the hands of politicians.

FARMERS AND WORKERS ORGANIZE THEIR COMMUNITIES

In the late 1860s farmers and workers began to organize their respective communities. Though short on financial resources, farmers and workers waged the most significant challenge to the two-party system since the Civil War: the populist movement.

The Grange

In many farming communities, the headquarters of the fraternal society, known as the Grange (a word for "farm"), became the center of social activity, the site of summer dinners and winter dances.

The Grange movement spread rapidly, especially in areas where farmers were experiencing their greatest hardships. Great Plains farmers barely survived the blizzards, grasshopper infestations, and droughts of the early 1870s. Meanwhile, farmers throughout the trans-Mississippi West and the South watched the prices for grains and cotton fall year by year in the face of growing competition from producers in Canada, Australia, Argentina, Russia, and India. In the hope of improving

The symbols chosen by Grange artists represented their faith that all social value could be traced to honest labor and most of all to the work of the entire farm family. The hardworking American required only the enlightenment offered by the Grange to build a better community.

SOURCE: Library of Congress.

their condition through collective action, many farmers joined their local Grange. The Patrons of Husbandry soon swelled to more than 1.5 million members.

Grangers blamed hard times on a band of "thieves in the night"—especially railroads and banks—that charged exorbitant fees for service. They fumed at American farm equipment manufacturers, such as Cyrus McCormick, who sold farm equipment more cheaply in Europe than in the United States. To purchase equipment and raw materials, farmers borrowed money and accrued debts averaging twice that of Americans not engaged in business.

Grangers mounted their greatest assault on the railroad corporations. By bribing state legislators, railroads enjoyed a highly discriminatory rate policy, commonly charging farmers more to ship their crops short distances than over long hauls. In 1874 several midwestern states responded to pressure and passed a series of so-called Granger laws establishing maximum shipping rates. Grangers also complained to their lawmakers about the price-fixing policies of grain wholesalers, warehousers, and operators of grain elevators. In 1873

the Illinois legislature passed a Warehouse Act establishing maximum rates for storing grains.

Determined to buy less and produce more, Grangers established local grain elevators, set up retail stores, and even manufactured some of their own farm machinery.

The deepening depression of the late 1870s wiped out most of these cooperative programs. By 1880 Grange membership had fallen to 100,000. Meanwhile, the Supreme Court overturned most of the key legislation regulating railroads. Despite these setbacks, the Patrons of Husbandry had nonetheless promoted a model of cooperation that would remain at the heart of agrarian protest movements until the end of the century.

The Farmers' Alliance

Agrarian unrest did not end with the downward turn of the Grange but instead moved south. In the 1880s farmers organized in communities where both poverty and the crop-lien system prevailed (see Chapter 17).

In 1889, several regional organizations joined forces to create the National Farmers' Alliance and Industrial Union. Within a year the combined movement claimed 3 million white members. Separately, the Colored Farmers' Alliance and Cooperative Union grew from its beginnings in Texas and Arkansas in 1888 and quickly spread across the South to claim more than a million members of its own.

In the South, the falling price of cotton underscored the need for action, and farmers readily translated their anger into intense loyalty to the one organization pledged to improve their lot. With more than 500 chapters in Texas alone, and cooperative stores complemented by the cooperative merchandising of crops, the Southern Farmers' Alliance became a viable alternative to the capitalist marketplace—if only temporarily.

The Northern Farmers' Alliance took shape in the Great Plains states, drawing upon larger organizations in Minnesota, Nebraska, Iowa, Kansas, and the Dakota Territory. During 1886 and 1887, summer drought followed winter blizzards and ice storms, reducing wheat harvests by one-third on the Plains. Locusts and cinch bugs ate much of the rest. As if this were not enough, prices on the world market fell sharply for what little remained. By 1890 the Kansas Alliance alone claimed 130,000 members.

Grangers had pushed legislation that would limit the salaries of public officials, provide public school students with books at little or no cost, establish a program of teacher certification, and widen the admissions policies of the new state colleges. But only rarely did they put up candidates for office. In comparison, the Farmers' Alliance had few reservations about taking political stands or entering electoral races. By 1890 the alliances had gained control of the Nebraska legislature and held the balance of power in Minnesota and South Dakota.

Workers Search for Power

The depression following the Panic of 1873, which produced 25 percent unemployment in many cities, served as a catalyst for workers to organize their communities.

The railroad, which played a key role in the industrial and urban transformations following the Civil War, became the focus of protests by workers and farmers alike. Nonetheless, the railroad corporations were unprepared for the Great Uprising of 1877, the first nationwide strike. The strike began in Martinsburg, West Virginia, where workers protesting a 10 percent wage cut uncoupled all engines. No trains would run, they promised, until wages were restored. Within a few days, the strike had spread along the railroad routes to New York, Buffalo, Pittsburgh, Chicago, Kansas City, and San Francisco. In all these cities, workers in various industries and masses of the unemployed formed angry crowds, defying armed militia ordered to disperse them by any means. The crowds halted train traffic, sometimes pulling up entire rails and seizing carloads of food for hungry families. Energized by the activity, workers in St. Louis even took over the city's administration.

The rioting persisted for nearly a week. Fearing a "national insurrection," President Hayes set a precedent by calling in the U.S. Army to suppress the strike. In Pittsburgh, federal troops equipped with semiautomatic machine guns fired into a crowd and killed more than twenty people. By the time the strike finally ended, more than 100 people were dead.

Memories of the Uprising of 1877 haunted business and government officials for decades, prompting the creation of the National Guard and the construction of armories in working-class neighborhoods. Workers also drew lessons from the events. Before the end of the century, more than 6 million workers would strike in industries ranging from New England textiles to southern tobacco factories to western mines. While the Farmers' Alliance put up candidates in the South and Plains states, workers launched labor parties in dozens of industrial towns and cities.

In New York City, popular economist and land reformer Henry George, with the ardent support of the city's Central Labor Council and the Knights of Labor, put himself forward in 1886 as candidate for mayor on the United Labor Party ticket. His best-selling book *Progress and Poverty* (1879) advocated a sweeping tax on all property to generate enough revenue to allow all Americans to live in comfort.

Tammany Hall delivered many thousands of the ballots cast for George straight into the Hudson River. Nevertheless, George managed to finish a respectable second with 31 percent of the vote, running ahead of young patrician Theodore Roosevelt. Although his

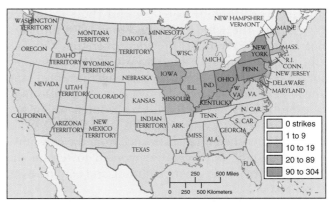

Strikes by State, 1880   Most strikes after the Uprising of 1877 could be traced to organized trades, concentrated in the manufacturing districts of the Northeast and Midwest.

SOURCE: Carville Earle, *Geographical Inquiry and American Historical Problems* (Stanford, CA: Stanford University Press, 1992).

campaign ended in defeat, George had issued a stern warning to the entrenched politicians. Equally important, his impressive showing encouraged labor groups in other cities to form parties.

In the late 1880s labor parties won seats on many city councils and state legislatures. The Milwaukee People's Party elected the mayor, a state senator, six assemblymen, and one member of Congress. In smaller industrial towns where workers outnumbered the middle classes, labor parties did especially well. In Rochester, New Hampshire, with a population of only 7,000, workers, mainly shoemakers, elected a majority slate, from city council to mayor.

Women Build Alliances

Women helped build both the labor and agrarian protest movements while campaigning for their own rights as citizens. With perhaps 65,000 women members at its peak, the Knights of Labor ran day-care centers for the children of wage-earning mothers and occasionally even set up bakery cooperatives to reduce the drudgery of cooking.

The Grangers issued a charter to a local chapter only when women were well represented on its rolls, and in the 1870s delegates to its conventions routinely gave speeches endorsing woman suffrage and even dress reform. In both the Northern and Southern Alliances, women made up perhaps one-quarter of the membership, and several advanced through the ranks to become leading speakers and organizers.

Women in both the Knights of Labor and the Farmers' Alliance found their greatest leader in Frances E. Willard, the most famous woman of the nineteenth century. Willard assumed that women, who guarded their families' physical and spiritual welfare, would, if granted the right to vote, extend their influence throughout the whole society. From 1878 until her death in 1897, Willard presided over the Woman's Christian Temperance Union (WCTU), at the time the largest organization of women in the world, and encouraged her numerous followers to "do everything." She mobilized nearly 1 million women to, in her words, "make the whole world HOMELIKE." WCTU members preached total abstinence from the consumption of alcohol, but they also worked to reform the prison system, eradicate prostitution, and eliminate the wage system.

Under Willard's leadership, the WCTU grew into the major force behind the campaign for woman suffrage, far surpassing the American Woman Suffrage Association and the National Woman Suffrage Association. By 1890, when the two rival suffrage associations merged to form the National American Woman Suffrage Association, the WCTU had already pushed the heart of the suffrage campaign into the Great Plains states and the West. In Iowa, Nebraska, Colorado, and especially Kansas, agitation for the right to vote provided a political bridge among women organized in the WCTU, Farmers' Alliance, Knights of Labor, and various local suffrage societies.

Farmer-Labor Unity

In December 1890 the Farmers' Alliance called a meeting at Ocala, Florida, to press for a national third-party movement. This was a risky proposition because the Southern Alliance hoped to capture control of the Democratic Party, whereas many farmers in the Plains states voted Republican. In some areas, however, the Farmers' Alliance established its own parties, put up full slates of candidates for local elections, won majorities in state legislatures, and even sent a representative to Congress. Reviewing these successes, delegates at Ocala decided to push ahead and form a national party, and they appealed to other farm, labor, and reform organizations to join them. In February 1892, representatives from the Farmers' Alliance, the Knights of Labor, and the National Colored Farmers' Alliance, among others, met in St. Louis. The 1,300 delegates adopted a platform for the new People's Party. It called for government ownership of railroads, banks, and telegraph lines, prohibition of large landholding companies, a graduated income tax, an eight-hour workday, and restriction of immigration. The People's Party convened again in Omaha in July 1892 and nominated James Baird Weaver of Iowa for president and, to please the South, the Confederate veteran James Field from Virginia for vice president.

The Populists, as supporters of the People's Party styled themselves, quickly became a major factor in American politics. Although Democrat Grover Cleveland regained the presidency in 1892 (he had previously served from 1885 to 1889), Populists scored a string of local victories. They elected three governors, ten representatives to Congress, and five senators. Despite poor showings among urban workers east of the Mississippi, Populists looked forward to the next round of state elections in 1894. But the great test would come with the presidential election in 1896.

THE CRISIS OF THE 1890s

A series of events in the 1890s shook the confidence of many citizens in the reigning political system. But nothing was more unsettling than the severe economic depression that consumed the nation and lasted for five years. Many feared—while others hoped—that the entire political system would topple.

Financial Collapse and Depression

The collapse of the Philadelphia and Reading Railroad, followed by the downfall of the National Cordage Company, precipitated a crash in the stock market and sent waves of panic splashing over banks across the country. In a few months, more than 150 banks went into receivership and hundreds more closed; nearly 200 railroads and more than 15,000 businesses also slipped into bankruptcy. Agricultural prices continued to plummet until they reached new lows. The economy slowly began to pick up again in 1897, but the new century arrived before prosperity returned.

In many cities, unemployment rates reached 25 percent; Samuel Gompers, head of the American Federation of Labor (AFL), estimated nationwide unemployment at 3 million. Few people starved, but millions suffered. Inadequate diets prompted a rise in communicable diseases, such as tuberculosis and pellagra. Unable to buy food, clothes, or household items, families learned to survive with the barest minimum.

Tens of thousands "rode the rails" or went "on the tramp" to look for work, hoping that their luck might change in a new city or town. Vagrancy laws (enacted during the 1870s) forced many into prison. In New York City alone, with more than 20,000 homeless people, thousands ended up in jail. Newspapers warned against this "menace" and blamed the growing crime rates on the "dangerous classes."

Another Populist, Jacob Sechler Coxey, decided to gather the masses of unemployed into a huge army and then to march to Washington, D.C., to demand from Congress a public works program. On Easter Sunday, 1894, Coxey left Massillon, Ohio, with several hundred followers. Communities across the country welcomed the marchers, but U.S. attorney general Richard C. Olney, a former lawyer for the railroad companies, conspired with state and local officials to halt them. Only 600 men and women reached the nation's capital, where the police first clubbed and then arrested the leaders for trespassing on the grass. "Coxey's Army" quickly disbanded, but not before voicing the public's growing impatience with government apathy toward the unemployed.

Strikes and Labor Solidarity

Meanwhile, in several locations the conflict between labor and capital had escalated to the brink of civil war. Wage cuts in the silver and lead mines of northern Idaho led to one of the bitterest conflicts of the decade. To put a brake on organized labor, mineowners had formed a "protective association," and in March 1892 they announced a lower wage scale throughout the Coeur d'Alene district. After the miners' union refused to accept the cut, the owners locked out all union members and brought in strikebreakers by the trainload. Unionists tried peaceful methods of protest. But after three months of stalemate, they loaded a railcar with explosives and blew up a mine. Strikebreakers fled while mineowners appealed to the Idaho governor for assistance. More than 300 union members were herded into bullpens, where they were kept under unsanitary conditions for several weeks before their trial. Ore production meanwhile resumed with "scab" labor, and by November, when the troops were withdrawn, the mineowners declared a victory. But the miners' union survived, and most members eventually regained their jobs.

At Homestead, Pennsylvania, members of the Amalgamated Iron, Steel and Tin Workers, the most powerful union of the AFL, had carved out an admirable position for themselves in the Carnegie Steel Company. Well paid, proud of their skills, the unionists customarily directed their unskilled helpers without undue influence of company supervisors. But, determined to gain control over every stage of production, Carnegie and his chairman, Henry C. Frick, decided not only to lower wages but also to break the union.

In 1892, when the Amalgamated's contract expired, Frick announced a drastic wage cut. He also ordered a wooden stockade built around the factory, with grooves for rifles and barbed wire on top. When Homestead's city government refused to assign police to disperse the strikers, Frick dispatched a barge carrying a private army armed to the teeth. Gunfire broke out and continued throughout the day. After the governor sent the Pennsylvania National Guard to restore order, Carnegie's factory reopened, with strikebreakers doing the work.

After four months, the union was forced to concede a crushing defeat, not only for itself but, in effect, for all steelworkers. The Carnegie company reduced its workforce by 25 percent, lengthened the workday, and cut wages 25 percent for those who remained on the job. If the Amalgamated Iron, Steel and Tin Workers, known throughout the industry as the "aristocrats of labor," could be brought down, less-skilled workers could expect little from the corporate giants. Within a decade, every major steel company operated without union interference.

But the spirit of labor solidarity did not die. Just two years after the strikes at Coeur d'Alene and Homestead, the greatest railway strike since 1877 again dramatized the extent of collusion between the government and corporations to crush the labor movement.

Pullman, Illinois, just south of Chicago, had been constructed as a model industrial community. Its creator and proprietor, George M. Pullman, had manufactured luxurious "sleeping cars" for railroads since 1881. He built his company as a self-contained community, with the factory at the center, surrounded by modern cottages, a library, churches, parks, an independent water supply, even its own cemetery, but no saloons. The Pullman Palace Car Company deducted rent, library fees, and grocery bills from each worker's weekly wages. In good times workers enjoyed a decent livelihood, although many resented Pullman's autocratic control of their daily affairs.

When times grew hard, the company cut wages by as much as one-half, in some cases down to less than $1 a day. Charges for food and rent remained unchanged. Furthermore, factory supervisors sought to make up for declining profits by driving workers to produce more. In May 1894, after Pullman fired members of a committee that had drawn up a list of grievances, workers voted to strike.

Pullman workers found their champion in Eugene V. Debs, who had recently formed the American Railway Union (ARU) in order to bring railroad workers across the vast continent into one organization. Debs, the architect of the ARU's victory over the Great Northern rail line just one month earlier, advised caution, but delegates to an ARU convention voted to support a nationwide boycott of all Pullman cars. This action soon turned into a sympathy strike by railroad workers across the country. Support for the strike was especially strong in the western states.

Compared to the Uprising of 1877, the orderly Pullman strike at first produced little violence. ARU officials urged strikers to ignore all police provocations and hold their ground peacefully. But Attorney General Richard C. Olney, claiming that the ARU was disrupting mail shipments (actually Debs had banned such interference), issued a blanket injunction against the strike. On July 4, President Cleveland sent federal troops to Chicago, over Illinois governor John Peter Altgeld's objections. After a bitter confrontation that left thirteen people dead and more than fifty wounded, the army dispersed the strikers. For the next week, railroad workers in twenty-six other states resisted federal troops, and a dozen more people were killed. On July 17, the strike finally ended when federal marshals arrested Debs and other leaders.

Assailing the arrogance of class privilege that encouraged the government to use brute force against its citizens, Debs concluded that the labor movement could not regain its dignity under the present system. An avid fan of Bellamy's *Looking Backward*, he came out of jail committed to the ideals of socialism and in 1898 helped to form a political party dedicated to its principles.

Tens of thousands of people supported Debs. Declining nomination on the Populist ticket in 1896, he ran for president as a socialist in 1900 and in four subsequent elections. The odds against him grew with the scale of the booming economy, but Debs made his point on moral grounds.

The Social Gospel

Like Edward Bellamy, a growing number of Protestant and Catholic clergy and lay theologians noted a discrepancy between the ideals of Christianity and prevailing attitudes toward the poor. Like Bellamy, they could no longer sanction an economic system that allowed so many to toil long hours under unhealthy conditions and for subsistence wages. They demanded that the church lead the way to a new cooperative order.

Ministers called for civil service reform and the end of child labor. Supporting labor's right to organize and, if necessary, to strike, they petitioned government officials to regulate corporations and place a limit on profits. Local Protestant ministers and community leaders sought to restore what they considered the true spirit of Christianity. Although the social gospel spread most rapidly through the northern industrial cities, southern African Americans espoused their own version. They reinterpreted the Gospel as Jesus' promise to emancipate their race from satanic white power brokers. The biblical republic of "Beulahland" became their model of redemption.

Catholics, doctrinally more inclined than Protestants to accept poverty as a natural condition, joined the social gospel movement in smaller numbers. In the early 1880s Polish Americans broke away from the Roman Catholic Church to form the Polish National Church, which was committed to the concerns of working people. Irish Americans, especially prominent in the Knights of Labor, encouraged priests to ally

themselves with the labor movement. Pope Leo XIII's encyclical *Rerum Novarum* (1891) endorsed the right of workers to form trade unions.

Women guided the social gospel movement in their communities. In nearly every city, groups of women affiliated with various evangelical Protestant sects raised money to establish small, inexpensive residential hotels for working women, whose low wages rarely covered the price of safe, comfortable shelter. Many of these groups joined to form the Young Women's Christian Association (YWCA), which by 1900 had more than 600 local chapters. The "Y" sponsored a range of services for needy Christian women, ranging from homes for the elderly and for unmarried mothers to elaborate programs of vocational instruction and physical fitness. Meanwhile Catholic lay women and nuns served the poor women of their faith, operating numerous schools, hospitals, and orphanages.

POLITICS OF REFORM, POLITICS OF ORDER

The severe hardships of the 1890s, following a quarter of a century of popular unrest and economic uncertainty, led to a crisis in the two-party system, making the presidential election of 1896 a turning point in American politics.

The Free Silver Issue

Grover Cleveland owed his victory in 1892 over Republican incumbent Benjamin Harrison to the predictable votes of the Democratic "solid South" and to the unanticipated support of such northern states as Illinois and Wisconsin, whose German-born voters turned against the increasingly nativist Republicans. But when the economy collapsed the following year, Cleveland and the Democrats who controlled Congress faced a public eager for action. Convinced that the economic crisis was "largely the result of financial policy . . . embodied in unwise laws," the president called a special session of Congress to reform the nation's currency.

For generations, reformers had advocated "soft" currency—that is, an increase in the money supply that would loosen credit. During the Civil War the federal government took decisive action, replacing state bank notes with a national paper currency popularly called "greenbacks" (from the color of the bills). Then in 1873 the Coinage Act tightened the money supply by eliminating silver from circulation, prompting farmers who depended on credit to call it "the Crime of '73." This measure actually had little real impact on the economy but opened the door to yet more tinkering.

The Sherman Silver Purchase Act of 1890 directed the Treasury to increase the amount of currency coined from silver mined in the West and also permitted the U.S. government to print paper currency backed by the silver. In turn, Westerners who stood to benefit most from this reform, agreed to support the McKinley Tariff of 1890 that, in establishing the highest import duties yet on foreign goods, pleased the business community.

Following the crash of 1893, as the economy fell into ruins, a desperate President Cleveland demanded the repeal of the Sherman Act, insisting that only the gold standard could pull the nation out of depression. By exerting intense pressure on congressional Democrats, Cleveland succeeded in October 1893, but not without ruining his chances for renomination. The midterm elections in 1894 brought the largest shift in congressional power in American history: the Republicans gained 117 seats, while the Democrats lost 113. The "Silver Democrats" of Cleveland's own party vowed revenge and began to look to the Populists, mainly Westerners and farmers who favored "free silver"—that is, the unlimited coinage of silver. Republicans confidently began to prepare for the presidential election of 1896, known as the "battle of the standards."

Populism's Last Campaigns

Populists had been buoyed by the 1894 election, which delivered to their candidates nearly 1.5 million votes, a gain of 42 percent over their 1892 totals. They made impressive inroads into several southern states. Still, even in the Midwest where Populists doubled their vote, they managed to win less than 7 percent of the total.

As Populists prepared for the 1896 election, they found themselves at a crossroad: What were they to do with the growing popularity of Democrat William Jennings Bryan? A spellbinding orator, Bryan won a congressional seat in 1890. After seizing the Populist slogan "Equal Rights to All, Special Privilege to None," Bryan became a major contender for president of the United States.

Noting the surging interest in free silver, Bryan became its champion. For two years before the 1896 election, Bryan wooed potential voters in a speaking tour that took him to every state in the nation. Pouring new life into his divided party, Bryan pushed Silver Democrats to the forefront.

At the 1896 party convention, the thirty-six-year-old orator thrilled delegates with his evocation of agrarian ideals. "Burn down your cities and leave our farms," Bryan preached, "and your cities will spring up again as if by magic; but destroy our farms and the grass will grow in the streets of every city in the country." What became one of the most famous speeches in American political history closed on a yet more dramatic note. Spreading his arms to suggest the crucified Christ figure, Bryan pledged to answer all demands for a gold standard by saying, "You shall not press down upon the brow of labor this crown of thorns, you shall not crucify mankind upon a cross of gold." The next day, Bryan won the Democratic presidential nomination.

The Populists feared that the growing emphasis on currency would overshadow their more important planks calling for government ownership of the nation's railroads and communications systems. As the date of their own convention approached, delegates divided over strategy: they could endorse Bryan and give up their independent status; or they could run an independent campaign and risk splitting the silver vote.

In the end, the Populists nominated Bryan for president and chose one of their own ranks, the popular Georgian Tom Watson, for the vice presidential candidate. Most of the state Democratic Party organizations, however, refused to put the "fusion" ticket on the ballot, and Bryan and his Democratic running mate Arthur Sewall simply ignored the Populist campaign.

The Republican Triumph

After Cleveland's blunders, Republicans anticipated an easy victory in 1896, but Bryan's nomination, as party stalwart Mark Hanna warned, "changed everything." Luckily, they had their own handsome, knowledgeable, courteous, and ruthless candidate, Civil War veteran William McKinley.

The Republican campaign in terms of sheer expense and skill of coordination outdid all previous campaigns and established a precedent for future presidential elections. Hanna guided a strategy that raised up to $7 million and outspent Bryan more than ten to one. Using innumerable pamphlets, placards, hats, and parades, Republicans advertised their promise to "rebuild out of the ruins of the last four years the stately mansions of national happiness, prosperity and self-respect." McKinley even invited voters to his home, managing to attract as many as 750,000 people to his famous "Front Porch." In the campaign's final two weeks, organizers dispatched 1,400 speakers to spread the word. Fearful that the silver issue could divide their own ranks, Republicans stepped around it while emphasizing the tariff. Delivering a hard-hitting negative camapign, they consistently cast adversary Bryan as a dangerous naysayer.

McKinley triumphed in the most important presidential election since Reconstruction. Bryan managed to win 46 percent of the popular vote but failed

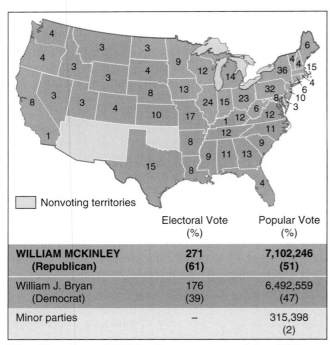

Nonvoting territories

	Electoral Vote (%)	Popular Vote (%)
WILLIAM MCKINLEY (Republican)	**271 (61)**	**7,102,246 (51)**
William J. Bryan (Democrat)	176 (39)	6,492,559 (47)
Minor parties	–	315,398 (2)

The Election of 1896   Democratic candidate William Jennings Bryan carried most of rural America but could not overcome Republican William McKinley's stronghold in the populous industrial states.

to carry the Midwest, West Coast, or Upper South. Moreover, the free silver campaign rebuffed traditionally Democratic urban voters who feared that soft money would bring higher prices. Many Catholics uncomfortable with Bryan's Protestant moral piety also deserted the Democrats. Finally, neither the reform-minded middle classes nor impoverished blue-collar workers were convinced that Bryan's grand reform vision really included them. The Populist following, disappointed and disillusioned, dwindled away.

Once in office, McKinley promoted a mixture of probusiness and expansionist measures. He supported the Dingley Tariff of 1897, which raised import duties to an all-time high. In 1897 McKinley also encouraged Congress to create the United States Industrial Commission, which would plan business regulation; in 1898 he promoted a bankruptcy act that eased the financial situation of small businesses; and he proposed the Erdman Act of the same year, which established a system of arbitration to avoid rail strikes. The Supreme Court ruled in concert with the president, finding eighteen railways in violation of antitrust laws and granting states the right to regulate hours of labor under certain circumstances.

McKinley's triumph ended the popular challenge to the nation's governing system. With prosperity returning by 1898 and nationalism rising swiftly, McKinley encouraged Americans to go for "a full dinner pail," the

winning Republican slogan of the 1900 presidential election.

Nativism and Jim Crow

Campaign rhetoric aside, McKinley and Bryan differed only slightly on the major problems facing the nation in 1896. Neither Bryan the reformer nor McKinley the prophet of prosperity addressed the escalation of racism and nativism (anti-immigrant feeling) throughout the nation.

Toward the end of the century, many political observers noted, the nation's patriotic fervor took on a strongly nationalistic and antiforeign tone. Striking workers and their employers alike tended to blame "foreigners" for the hard times. Semisecret organizations such as the American Protective Association sprang up to defend American institutions. Fourth of July orators continued to celebrate freedom and liberty but more often boasted about the might and power of their nation.

In the South, local and state governments codified racist ideology by passing discriminatory and segregationist legislation, which became known as Jim Crow laws. The phrase, dating from the early decades of the nineteenth century, was made popular by a white minstrel in black face who used the name "Jim Crow" to characterize all African Americans. Before the Civil War, abolitionists described segregated railroad cars as "Jim Crow." By the end of the century, "Jim Crow" referred to the customs of segregation that were becoming codified by law and practice throughout the South. With nine of every ten black Americans living in this region, the significance of this development was sweeping.

"The supremacy of the white race of the South," New South promoter Henry W. Grady declared in 1887, "must be maintained forever . . . because the white race is the superior race." To secure their privileges, Grady and other white Southerners acted directly to impose firm standards of segregation and domination and to forestall any appearance of social equality. State after state in the South enacted new legislation to cover facilities such as restaurants, public transportation, and even drinking fountains. Signs "White Only" and "Colored" appeared over theaters, parks, rooming houses, and toilets. In banks, post offices, and stores, blacks were required to wait until all whites had been served, and special rules prohibited such common practices as trying on shoes or hats before purchasing them.

The United States Supreme Court upheld the new discriminatory legislation. Its decisions in the *Civil Rights Cases* (1883) overturned the Civil Rights Act of 1875, and in *Plessy* v. *Ferguson* (1896) the Court upheld a Louisiana state law formally segregating railroad cars on the basis of the "separate but equal" doctrine. In *Cumming* v. *Richmond County Board of Education* (1899), the Court allowed separate schools for blacks and whites, even where facilities for African American children did not exist.

Southern states enacted new literacy tests and property qualifications for voting, demanding proof of $300 to $500 in property and the ability to read and write. Loopholes permitted poor whites to vote even under these conditions, except where they threatened the Democratic Party's rule. "Grandfather clauses," invented in Louisiana, exempted from all restrictions those who had been entitled to vote on January 1, 1867, together with their sons and grandsons, a measure that effectively enfranchised whites while barring African Americans. In 1898, the Supreme Court ruled that poll taxes and literacy requirements enacted in order to prevent blacks (and some poor whites) from voting were a proper means of restricting the ballot to "qualified" voters. By this time, only 5 percent of the southern black electorate voted, and African Americans were barred from public office and jury service.

Racial violence escalated. Not only race riots but also thousands of lynchings took place. Between 1882 and the turn of the century, the number of lynchings usually exceeded 100 each year; 1892 produced a record 230 deaths (161 black, 69 white). Mobs often burned or dismembered victims in order to drag out their agony and entertain the crowd of onlookers. Announced in local newspapers, lynchings became public spectacles for entire white families, and railroads sometimes offered special excursion rates for travel to these events.

Antilynching became the one-woman crusade of Ida B. Wells, young editor of a black newspaper in Memphis. After three local black businessmen were lynched in 1892, Wells vigorously denounced the outrage, blaming the white business competitors of the victims. Her stand fanned the tempers of local whites, who destroyed her press and forced the outspoken editor to leave the city.

Wells launched an international movement against lynching, lecturing across the country and in Europe, demanding an end to the silence about this barbaric crime. Her work also inspired the growth of a black women's club movement. The National Association of Colored Women was founded in 1896.

"IMPERIALISM OF RIGHTEOUSNESS"

Many Americans attributed the crisis of 1893–97 not simply to the collapse of the railroads and the stock market but also to basic structural problems: an overbuilt economy and an insufficient market for goods.

Profits from total sales of manufactured and agricultural products had grown substantially over the level achieved in the 1880s, but output increased even more rapidly. While the number of millionaires shot up from 500 in 1860 to more than 4,000 in 1892, the majority of working people lacked enough income to buy back a significant portion of what they produced. As Republican Senator Albert J. Beveridge of Indiana put it, "We are raising more than we can consume . . . making more than we can use. Therefore, we must find new markets for our produce, new occupation for our capital, new work for our labor."

The White Man's Burden

In 1893 historian Frederick Jackson Turner read his famous essay, "The Significance of the Frontier in American History," at the meeting of the American Historical Association, which was held in Chicago at the time of the World's Fair, less than two months after the nation's economy had collapsed. A complex of more than 400 buildings, newly constructed in beaux arts design, commemorated the four hundredth anniversary of Columbus's landing.

Agriculture Hall showcased the production of corn, wheat, and other crops and featured a gigantic globe encircled by samples of American-manufactured farm machinery. The symbolism was evident: all eyes were on world-wide markets for American products. Another building housed a model of a canal cut across Nicaragua, suggesting the ease with which American traders might reach Asian markets if transport ships could travel directly from the Caribbean to the Pacific.

The World's Fair also "displayed" representatives of the people who populated foreign lands. The Midway Plaisance, a strip nearly a mile long and more than 600 feet wide, was an enormous sideshow of recreated Turkish bazaars and South Sea island huts. There were Javanese carpenters, Dahomean drummers, Egyptian swordsmen, and Hungarian Gypsies as well as Eskimos, Syrians, Samoans, and Chinese. Very popular was the World Congress of Beauty, parading "40 Ladies from 40 Nations" dressed in native costume.

By celebrating the brilliance of American industry and simultaneously presenting the rest of the world's people as a source of exotic entertainment, the planners of the fair delivered a powerful message. Former abolitionist Frederick Douglass, who attended the fair on "Colored People's Day," objected to the stark contrast setting off Anglo-Saxons from people of color, an opposition between "civilization" and "savagery."

The Chicago World's Fair gave material shape to prevalent ideas about the superiority of American civilization and its racial order. At the same time, by showcasing American industries, it made a strong case for commercial expansion abroad. Social gospeler Josiah Strong, a Congregational minister who had begun his career trying to convert Indians to Christianity, provided a timely synthesis. Linking economic and spiritual expansion, Strong advocated an "imperialism of righteousness" by the white Americans, who were best suited to "Christianizing" and civilizing others with their "genius for colonizing." It was the white American, Strong argued, who had been "divinely commissioned to be, in a peculiar sense, his brother's keeper." Many newspaper reporters and editorialists agreed that it would be morally wrong for Americans to shirk what the British poet Rudyard Kipling called the "White Man's Burden."

Foreign Missions

The push for overseas expansion coincided with a major wave of religious evangelism and foreign missions. Early in the nineteenth century, Protestant missionaries, hoping to fulfill what they believed to be a divine command to carry God's message to all peoples and to win converts for their church, had focused on North America. Many disciples, like Josiah Strong himself, headed west and stationed themselves on Indian reservations. Others worked among the immigrant populations of the nation's growing cities. As early as the 1820s, however, a few missionaries had traveled to the Sandwich Islands (Hawai'i) in an effort to supplant the indigenous religion with Christianity. After the Civil War, following the formation of the Women's Union Missionary Society of Americans for Heathen Lands, the major evangelical Protestant denominations all sponsored missions directed at foreign lands.

By the 1890s, college campuses blazed with missionary excitement, and the intercollegiate Student Volunteers for Foreign Missions spread rapidly. Young Protestant women rushed to join foreign missionary societies. By 1915, more than 3 million women had enrolled in forty denominational missionary societies, surpassing in size all other women's organizations in the United States.

By 1898 Protestants claimed to have made Christians of more than 80,000 Chinese, a tiny portion of the population but a significant stronghold for American interests in their nation. The missionaries did more than spread the gospel. They taught school, provided rudimentary medical care, offered vocational training programs, and sometimes encouraged young men and women to pursue a college education in preparation for careers in their homelands.

Outside the churches proper, the YMCA and YWCA, which had set up nondenominational missions for the working poor in many American cities, also embarked on a worldwide crusade to reach non-Christians.

A close observer ironically suggested that the United States had three great occupying forces: the army, the navy, and the "Y."

Missionaries played an important role both in generating public interest in foreign lands and in preparing the way for American economic expansion. As Josiah Strong aptly put it, "Commerce follows the missionary."

An Overseas Empire

Business and political leaders also had set their sights on distant lands. In the 1860s, Secretary of State William Henry Seward, under Abraham Lincoln and then under Andrew Johnson, correctly predicted that foreign trade would play an increasingly important part in the American economy. Between 1870 and 1900 exports more than tripled, from about $400 million to over $1.5 billion, with textiles and agricultural products leading the way. But as European markets for American goods began to contract, business and political leaders of necessity looked more eagerly to Asia as well as to lands closer by.

Since the American Revolution, many Americans had regarded all nearby nations as falling naturally within their own territorial realm, destined to be acquired when opportunity allowed. Seward advanced these imperialist principles in 1867 by negotiating the purchase of Alaska (known at the time as Seward's Icebox) from Russia for $7.2 million. Meanwhile, with European nations launched on their own imperialist missions in Asia and Africa, the United States increasingly viewed the Caribbean as an "American lake" and all of Latin America as a vast potential market for U.S. goods. The crisis of the 1890s transformed this long-standing desire into a perceived economic necessity. Unlike European imperialists, powerful Americans dreamed of empire without large-scale permanent military occupation and costly colonial administration.

Americans focused their expansionist plans on the Western Hemisphere, determined to dislodge the dominant power, Great Britain. In 1867, when Canada became a self-governing dominion, American diplomats hoped to annex their northern neighbor, believing that Great Britain would gladly accede in order to concentrate its imperial interests in Asia. But Great Britain refused to give up Canada, and the United States backed away. Central and South America proved more accommodating to American designs.

Republican stalwart James G. Blaine, secretary of state under presidents Garfield and Harrison, determined to work out a Good Neighbor policy (a phrase coined by Henry Clay in 1820). Bilateral treaties with Mexico, Colombia, the British West Indies, El Salvador, and the Dominican Republic allowed American business to dominate local economies, importing their raw materials at low prices and flooding their local markets with goods manufactured in the United States. Often American investors simply took over the principal industries of these small nations, undercutting national business classes.

The Good Neighbor policy depended, Blaine knew, on peace and order in the Latin American states. In 1883, wishing to enforce treaties and protect overseas investments, Congress appropriated funds to build up American seapower. Beginning with ninety small ships, over one-third of them wooden, the navy grew quickly to include modern steel fighting ships. The hulls of these ships were painted a gleaming white, and the armada was known as the Great White Fleet.

The annexation of Hawai'i on July 7, 1898, followed nearly a century of economic penetration and diplomatic maneuver. American missionaries, who had arrived in the 1820s to convert Hawai'ians to Christianity, began to buy up huge parcels of land and to subvert the existing feudal system of landholding. They also encouraged American businesses to buy into sugar plantations, and by 1875 U.S. corporations

dominated the sugar trade. In 1887 a new treaty allowed the United States to build a naval base at Pearl Harbor on the island of Oahu.

The next year, American planters took a step further, arranging the overthrow of the weak king Kalakaua and securing a new government allied to their economic interests. In 1891, the new ruler, Queen Liliuokalani, struck back by issuing a constitution granting her more discretionary power. The U.S. minister, prompted by the pineapple magnate Sanford B. Dole, responded by calling for military assistance. On January 16, 1893, U.S. sailors landed on Hawai'i to protect American property. Liliuokalani was deposed, a new provisional government was installed, and Hawai'i was proclaimed an American protectorate (a territory protected and partly controlled by the United States). President Cleveland refused to consider annexation, but five years later McKinley affirmed a joint congressional resolution under which Hawai'i would become an American territory in 1900. The residents of Hawai'i were not consulted about this momentous change in their national identity.

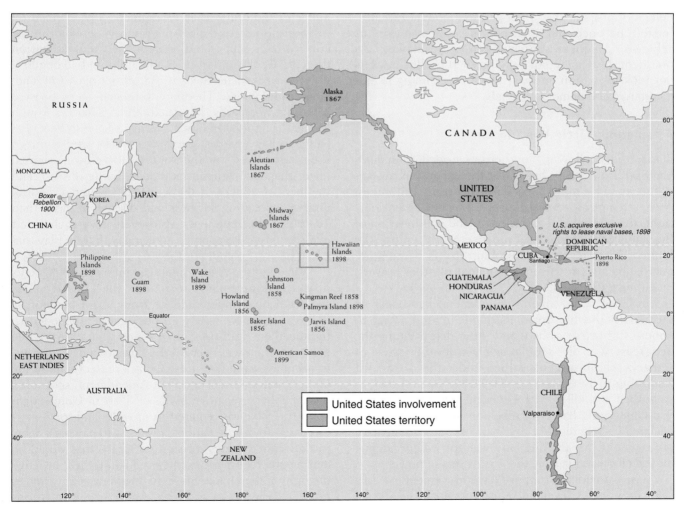

The American Domain, ca. 1900   The United States claimed numerous islands in the South Pacific and intervened repeatedly in Latin America to secure its economic interests.

Hawai'i was often viewed as a steppingstone to the vast Asian markets. To accelerate railroad investment and trade, a consortium of New York bankers created the American China Development Company in 1896. They feared, however, that the tottering Manchu dynasty would fall to European, Russian, and Japanese colonial powers, which would then prohibit trade with the United States. Secretary of State John Hay responded in 1899 by proclaiming the Open Door policy. According to this doctrine, outlined in notes to six major powers, the United States enjoyed the right to advance its commercial interests anywhere in the world, at least on terms equal to those of the other imperialist nations. The Chinese marketplace was too important to lose.

THE SPANISH-AMERICAN WAR

During his 1896 campaign, William McKinley firmly committed himself to the principle of economic expansion. It was for him the proper alternative to Edward Bellamy's program for a cooperative commonwealth. Indeed, he once described his "greatest ambition" as achieving American supremacy in world markets. As president, McKinley not only reached out for markets but took his nation into war while proclaiming its humanitarian and democratic goals.

A "Splendid Little War" in Cuba

Before the Civil War, Southerners hoped to acquire Cuba, still owned by Spain, for the expansion of slavery in its sugar mills, tobacco plantations, and mines. After attempting several times to buy the island outright, the United States settled for the continuation of the status quo. Throughout the nineteenth century, the United States resolved to protect Spain's sovereignty over Cuba against the encroachment of other powers, including Cuba itself.

In Cuba, a movement for independence began in the mid-1860s when Spain, its empire in ruins, began to impose stiff taxes on the island. After defeat during the Ten Years War of 1868–78 and yet another series of setbacks, the insurgents rallied under the nationalist leadership of José Martí. In May 1895 Spanish troops ambushed and killed Martí, turning him into a martyr and fanning the flames of rebellion. By July, the rebels declared Cuba a republic and established a rudimentary government. Meanwhile, the war for independence moved closer to Havana, the island's seat of power.

Many Americans supported the movement for *Cuba Libre*. President Cleveland refused to back the Cuban revolutionaries and instead urged Spain to grant the island a limited autonomy. Even when Congress passed a resolution in 1896 welcoming the future independence of Cuba, Cleveland and his advisers demurred.

After he took over the office, President McKinley also drew back. In his Inaugural Address he declared, "We want no wars of conquest; we must avoid the temptation of territorial aggression." The tide turned, however, when Spain appeared unable to maintain order. In early 1898 public indignation, whipped up by tabloid press headlines and sensational stories, turned into frenzy on February 15, when an explosion ripped through the battleship USS *Maine*, stationed in Havana harbor ostensibly to rescue American citizens.

McKinley, suspecting war was close, had already begun to prepare for intervention. Newspapers ran banner headlines charging a Spanish conspiracy, although there was no proof. The impatient public meanwhile demanded revenge for the death of 266 American sailors.

Finally, on April 11, McKinley asked Congress for a declaration of war against Spain. Yet Congress barely passed the war resolution on April 25, and only with the inclusion of an amendment by Senator Henry Teller of Colorado that disclaimed "any disposition or intention to exercise sovereignty, jurisdiction or control over said island, except for the pacification thereof." By the end of April, the fighting had begun.

Ten weeks later the war was all but over. On land, Lieutenant Colonel Theodore Roosevelt—who boasted of killing Spaniards "like jackrabbits"—led his Rough Riders to victory. On July 3, the main Spanish fleet near Santiago Bay was destroyed; two weeks later Santiago itself surrendered, and the war drew to a close. Although fewer than 400 Americans died in battle, disease and the inept treatment of the wounded created a medical disaster, spreading sickness and disease to more than 20,000 in the regiments. Roosevelt nevertheless felt invigorated by the conflict, agreeing with John Hay that it had been a "splendid little war."

On August 12, at a small ceremony in McKinley's office marking Spain's surrender, the United States secured Cuba's independence from Spain but not its own sovereignty. American businesses proceeded to tighten their hold on Cuban sugar plantations, while U.S. military forces oversaw the formation of a constitutional convention that made Cuba a protectorate of the United States. Under the Platt Amendment, sponsored by Republican senator Orville H. Platt of Connecticut in 1901, Cuba was required to provide land for American bases; to devote national revenues to pay back debts to the United States; to sign no treaty that would be detrimental to American interests; and to acknowledge the right of the United States to intervene at any time to protect its interests in Cuba. After American troops withdrew from Cuba, the terms of the Platt amendment were incorporated into the Cuban-American Treaty of

1903. This treaty, which remained in place until 1934, paved the way for American domination of the island's sugar industry and contributed to anti-American sentiment among Cuban nationalists.

War in the Philippines

The Philippines, another of Spain's colonies, seemed an especially attractive prospect, its 7,000 islands a natural way station to the markets of mainland Asia. In 1897 Assistant Secretary of the Navy Theodore Roosevelt and President McKinley had discussed the merits of taking the Pacific colony in the event of war with Spain. At the first opportunity, McKinley acted to bring these islands into the U.S. strategic orbit. Shortly after Congress declared war on Spain, on May 4, the president dispatched 5,000 troops to occupy the Philippines. George Dewey, a Civil War veteran who commanded the American Asiatic Squadron, was ordered to "start offensive action." During the first week of the conflict, he demolished the Spanish fleet in Manila Bay through seven hours of unimpeded target practice. Once the war ended, McKinley pledged "to educate the Filipinos, and to uplift and civilize and Christianize them." But after centuries of Spanish rule, the majority of islanders—already Christians—were eager to create their own nation.

The Filipino rebels, like the Cubans, at first welcomed American troops and fought with them against Spain. But when the Spanish-American War ended and they perceived that American troops were not preparing to leave, the rebels, led by Emilio Aguinaldo, turned against their former allies and attacked the American base of operations in Manila in February 1899. Predicting a brief skirmish, American commanders seriously underestimated the population's capacity to endure great suffering for the sake of independence.

U.S. troops had provoked this conflict in various ways. Military leaders, the majority veterans of the Indian Wars, commonly described the natives as "gugus," and reported themselves, as one said, as "just itching to get at the niggers." While awaiting action, American soldiers repeatedly insulted or physically abused civilians, raped Filipino women, and otherwise whipped up resentment.

The resulting conflict took the form of modern guerrilla warfare, with brutalities on both sides. By the time the fighting slowed down in 1902, 4,300 American lives had been lost, and one of every five Filipinos had died in battle or from starvation or disease. On some of the Philippine islands, intermittent fighting lasted until 1935.

The conquest of the Philippines, which remained a U.S. territory until 1946, evoked for its defenders the vision of empire. Once again, Josiah Strong pro-

claimed judgment over an era. His famous treatise *Expansion* (1900) roundly defended American overseas involvements by carefully distinguishing between freedom and independence. People could achieve freedom, he argued, only under the rule of law. And because white Americans had proven themselves superior in the realm of government, they could best bring "freedom" to nonwhite peoples by setting aside the ideal of national independence for a period of enforced guidance. Many began to wonder, however, whether the United States could become an empire without sacrificing its democratic spirit, and to ask whether the subjugated people were really so fortunate under the rule of the United States.

Critics of Empire

No mass movement formed to forestall U.S. expansion, but distinguished figures like Mark Twain, Andrew Carnegie, William Jennings Bryan, and Harvard philosopher William James voiced their opposition

"Uncle Sam Teaches the Art of Self-Government," editorial cartoon, 1898. Expressing a popular sentiment of the time, a newspaper cartoonist shows the rebels as raucous children who constantly fight among themselves and need to be brought into line by Uncle Sam. The Filipino leader, Emilio Aguinaldo, appears as a dunce for failing to learn properly from the teacher. The two major islands where no uprising took place, Puerto Rico and Hawai'i, appear as passive but exotically dressed women, ready to learn their lessons.

SOURCE: Library of Congress.

CHRONOLOGY

1867	Grange founded
	Secretary of State Seward negotiates the purchase of Alaska
1874	Tompkins Square Riot
	Granger laws begin to regulate railroad shipping rates
1877	Rutherford B. Hayes elected president
	Great Uprising of 1877
1879	Henry George publishes *Progress and Poverty*
1881	President James A. Garfield assassinated; Chester A. Arthur becomes president
1883	Pendleton Act passed
1884	Grover Cleveland elected president
1887	Interstate Commerce Act creates the Interstate Commerce Commission
1888	Edward Bellamy publishes *Looking Backward*
	National Colored Farmers' Alliance and Cooperative Union formed
	Benjamin Harrison elected president
1889	National Farmers' Alliance and Industrial Union formed
1890	Sherman Silver Purchase Act
	McKinley tariff enacted
	National American Woman Suffrage Association formed
1891	National Women's Alliance formed
	Populist (People's) Party formed
1892	Coeur d'Alene miners' strike
	Homestead strike
	Ida B. Wells begins crusade against lynching
1893	Western Federation of Miners formed
	Financial panic and depression
	World's Columbian Exhibition opens in Chicago
1894	"Coxey's Army" marches on Washington, D.C.
	Pullman strike and boycott
1896	*Plessy* v. *Ferguson* upholds segregation
	William McKinley defeats William Jennings Bryan for president
1897	Dingley tariff again raises import duties to an all-time high
1898	Eugene V. Debs helps found Social Democratic Party
	Hawai'i is annexed
	Spanish-American War begins
	Anti-Imperialist League formed
1899	*Cumming* v. *Richmond County Board of Education* sanctions segregated education
	Secretary of State John Hay announces Open Door policy
	Guerrilla war begins in the Philippines
1900	Gold Standard Act
	Josiah Strong publishes *Expansion*

strongly. Organized protest to military action, especially against the widely reported atrocities in the Philippines, owed much to the Anti-Imperialist League, which was founded by a small group of prominent Bostonians. In historic Faneuil Hall, which had witnessed the birth of both the American Revolution and the antislavery movement, a mass meeting was convened in June 1898 to protest the "insane and wicked ambition which is driving the nation to ruin." Within a few months, the league reported 25,000 members. Most supported American economic expansion but advocated free trade rather than political domination as the means to reach this goal.

A few outspoken anti-imperialists, such as former Illinois governor John Peter Altgeld, openly toasted Filipino rebels as heroes. Morrison Swift, leader of the Coxey's Army contingent from Massachusetts, formed a Filipino Liberation Society and sent antiwar materials to American troops. Others, such as Samuel Gompers, a league vice president, felt no sympathy for conquered peoples but simply wanted to prevent colonized nonwhites from immigrating into the United States and "inundating" American labor.

Military leaders and staunch imperialists did not distinguish between racist and nonracist antiimperialists. They called all dissenters "unhung traitors" and demanded their arrest. Newspaper editors accused universities of harboring antiwar professors, although college students as a group were enthusiastic supporters of the war.

Most Americans put aside their doubts and welcomed the new era of imperialism. Untouched by the private tragedies of dead or wounded American soldiers and the mass destruction of civilian society in the Philippines, the vast majority could approve Theodore Roosevelt's defense of armed conflict: "No triumph of peace is quite so great as the supreme triumphs of war."

CONCLUSION

The conflicts marking the last quarter of the nineteenth century that pitted farmers, workers, and the proprietors of small businesses against powerful outside interests had offered Americans an important moment of democratic promise. By the end of the century, however, the rural and working-class campaigns to retain a large degree of self-government in their communities had been defeated, their organizations destroyed, their autonomy eroded. The rise of a national governing class and its counterpart, the large bureaucratic state, established new rules of behavior, new sources of prestige, and new rewards for the most successful citizens.

But the nation would pay a steep price, in the next era, for the failure of democratic reform. Regional antagonisms, nativist movements against the foreign-born, and above all deepening racial tensions blighted American society. As the new century opened, progressive reformers moved to correct flaws in government while accepting the framework of a corporate society and its overseas empire.

REVIEW QUESTIONS

1. Discuss some of the problems accompanying the expansion of government during the late nineteenth century. What role did political parties play in this process? Explain how a prominent reformer such as James Garfield might become a leading "machine" politician?

2. What were the major causes and consequences of the Populist movement of the 1880s and 1890s? Why did the election of 1896 prove so important to the future of American politics?

3. Discuss the role of women in both the Grange and the People's Party. What were their specific goals?

4. Discuss the causes and consequences of the financial crisis of the 1890s. How did various reformers and politicians respond to the event? What kinds of programs did they offer to restore the economy or reduce poverty?

5. How did the exclusion of African Americans affect the outcome of populism? Explain the rise of Jim Crow legislation in the South, and discuss its impact on the status of African Americans.

6. Describe American foreign policy during the 1890s. Why did the United States intervene in Cuba and the Philippines? What were some of the leading arguments for and against overseas expansion?

RECOMMENDED READING

Ruth Bordin, *Woman and Temperance: The Quest for Power and Liberty, 1873–1900* (1981). Relates the history of the WCTU to other campaigns for women's emancipation in the late nineteenth century and highlights the leadership of Frances E. Willard. Bordin demonstrates the central position temperance occupied in the political struggles of the era.

Matthew Freye Jacobson, *Barbarian Virtues: The United Sates Encounters Foreign Peoples at Home and Abroad, 1876–1917* (2000). Links the histories of immigration and empire-building to examine public discussions about foreign people, especially their "fitness" for self-government. Jacobson casts the search for markets as backdrop for cultural history.

Michael Kazin, *The Populist Persuasion: An American History* (1995, rev. ed., 1998). A fresh interpretation of Populist-style movements through the nineteenth and twentieth centuries that suggests such movements can be either "right" or "left" depending on circumstances.

Walter LaFeber, *The New Empire: An Interpretation of American Expansion, 1860–1898* (1963, 1998). The best overview of U.S. imperial involvement in the late nineteenth century. LaFeber shows how overseas commitments grew out of the economic expansionist assumptions of American leaders and expanded continuously, if often chaotically, with the opportunities presented by the crises experienced by the older imperial powers.

Leon F. Litwack, *Trouble in Mind: Black Southerners in the Age of Jim Crow* (1998). An expansive social history of the first generation of African Americans born in freedom and surviving a period of extraordinary violent and repressive race relations in the South. Litwack examines the retrenchment of their political and civil rights but emphasizes their resourcefulness and resistance.

Nell Irvin Painter, *Standing at Armageddon: The United States, 1877–1919* (1987). Presents a broad overview of racial and industrial conflicts and the political movements that formed in their wake. Painter attempts to show how this period proved decisive to the future history of the United States.

Emily S. Rosenberg, *Spreading the American Dream: American Economic and Cultural Expansion, 1890–1945* (1982). Insightfully examines the significance of expansionist ideology. Rosenberg studies the cultural and social roots of American foreign policy.

Elizabeth Sanders, *Roots of Reform: Farmers, Workers, and the American State, 1877–1917* (1999). A painstaking reconstruction of the legislative history of congressional bills with emphasis on the lobbying of dirt farmers as well as their search for allies. Sanders, a political scientist, shines new light on familiar conflicts between debtors and creditors and the political processes of the Gilded Age.

David O. Stowell, *Streets, Railroads, and the Great Strike of 1877* (1999). Examines in close detail the uprising of 1877 in Buffalo, Albany, and Syracuse, New York, casting the strike simultaneously as a struggle between workers and the railroad corporations and an attempt by the community to protest against usurpation of streets by the trains. Stowell emphasizes the importance of the urban setting of this strike and provides ample data on the physical injuries inflicted by trains on local residents.

William Appleman Williams, *Empire as a Way of Life: An Essay on the Causes and Character of America's Present Predicament* (1982). A lucid general exploration of American views of empire. Williams shows that Americans allowed the idea of empire and, more generally, economic expansion, to dominate their concept of democracy, especially in the last half of the nineteenth century.

ON THE WEB

http://www.history.navy.mil/photos/events/spanam/eve-pge.htm

This is a U.S. Navy historical site containing photographs with informative captions from the Spanish-American War era. It proves a blessing to the naval history buff but also contains interesting photos for the general historian such as the Hawaiian annexation ceremony at the Old Government Building (Iolani Palace), August 12, 1898, and photographs of the wreck of the USS *Maine* and the Havana funeral ceremonies for her crew. This site is rich and growing in graphic primary materials.

http://oyez.nwu.edu/

The Oyez Project of Northwestern University provides information on Supreme Court decisions, especially the written Court opinions. For this chapter search for *Plessy* v. *Ferguson* (1896) and, in particular, examine the dissenting opinion of Justice John M. Harlan before looking at the interesting facts in his bibliography attached to the *Plessy* records.

http://memory.loc.gov/ammem/aaohtml/exhibit/aopart6.html

This American Memory exhibition from the Library of Congress describes the America of African Americans from the 1870s to World War I as Booker T. Washington gained prominence as a black leader.

http://www.boondocksnet.com/gallery/us_intro.html
http://www.boondocksnet.com/gallery/ads_index.html

Boondocksnet presents political cartoons and commercial advertisements of America's age of imperialism and the Spanish-American War on this site. The cartoons and ads are clear and easily studied but may not be copied.

http://www.prenhall.com/faragherbrief/map20.1

Consider the global reach of America in 1900. What fueled this expansion overseas?

http://www.prenhall.com/faragherbrief/map20.2

Look at both theaters of action in the Spanish-American War. What did the United States gain from victories in each of these conflicts?

TWENTY-ONE

URBAN AMERICA AND THE PROGRESSIVE ERA

▶ 1900–1917

AMERICAN COMMUNITIES

The Henry Street Settlement House: Women Settlement House Workers Create a Community of Reform

A SHY AND FRIGHTENED YOUNG GIRL APPEARED IN THE DOORWAY OF A weekly home-nursing class for women on Manhattan's Lower East Side. The teacher beckoned her to come forward. Tugging on the teacher's skirt, the girl pleaded in broken English for the teacher to come home with her. "Mother," "baby," "blood," she kept repeating. The teacher gathered up the sheets that were part of the interrupted lesson in bed making. The two hurried through narrow, garbage-strewn, foul-smelling streets, then groped their way up a pitch-dark, rickety staircase. They reached a cramped, two-room apartment, home to an immigrant family of seven and several boarders. There, in a vermin-infested bed, encrusted with dried blood, lay a mother and her newborn baby. The mother had been abandoned by a doctor because she could not afford his fee.

The teacher, Lillian Wald, was a twenty-five-year-old nurse at New York Hospital. Years later she recalled this scene as her baptism by fire and the turning point in her life. Born in 1867, Wald had enjoyed a comfortable upbringing in a middle-class German Jewish family in Rochester. Despite her parents' objections, she had moved to New York City to become a professional nurse. Resentful of the disdainful treatment nurses received from doctors and horrified by the inhumane conditions at a juvenile asylum she worked in, Wald determined to find a way of caring for the sick in their neighborhoods and homes. With nursing school classmate Mary Brewster, Wald rented a fifth-floor walk-up apartment on the Lower East Side and established a visiting nurse service. The two provided professional care in the home to hundreds of families for a nominal fee of 10 to 25 cents. They also offered each family they visited information on basic health care, sanitation, and disease prevention. In 1895, philanthropist Jacob Schiff generously donated a red brick Georgian house on Henry Street as a new base of operation.

The Henry Street Settlement stood in the center of perhaps the most overcrowded neighborhood in the world, New York's Lower East Side. Roughly 500,000 people were packed into an area only as large as a midsized Kansas farm. Population density was about 500 per acre, roughly four times the figure for the rest of New York City and far more concentrated than even the worst slums of London or Calcutta. A single city block might have as many as 3,000 residents. Home for most Lower

East Siders was a small tenement apartment that might include paying boarders squeezed in alongside the immediate family. Residents were mostly recent immigrants from southern and eastern Europe: Jews, Italians, Germans, Greeks, Hungarians, Slavs. Men, women, and children toiled in the garment shops, small factories, retail stores, breweries, and warehouses to be found on nearly every street. An Irish-dominated machine controlled local political affairs.

The Henry Street Settlement became a model for a new kind of reform community composed essentially of college-educated women who encouraged and supported one another in a wide variety of humanitarian, civic, political, and cultural activities. Settlement house living arrangements closely resembled those in the dormitories of such new women's colleges as Smith, Wellesley, and Vassar. Like these colleges, the settlement house was an "experiment," but one designed, in settlement house pioneer Jane Addams's words, "to aid in the solution of the social and industrial problems which are engendered by the modern conditions of urban life." Unlike earlier moral reformers who tried to impose their ideas from outside, settlement house residents lived in poor communities and worked for immediate improvements in the health and welfare of those communities. Yet, as Addams and others repeatedly stressed, the college-educated women were beneficiaries as well. The settlement house allowed them to preserve a collegial spirit, satisfy the desire for service, and apply their academic training.

With its combined moral and social appeal, the settlement house movement attracted many educated young women and grew rapidly. There were six settlement houses in the United States in 1891, some 74 in 1897, more than 200 by 1900, and more than 400 by 1910. Few women made settlement work a career. The average stay was less than five years. Roughly half of those who worked in the movement eventually married.

Those who did make a career of settlement house work, however, typically chose not to marry, and most lived together with female companions. As the movement flourished, settlement house residents called attention to the plight of the poor and fostered respect for different cultural heritages in countless articles and lectures. Leaders of the movement, including Jane Addams, Lillian Wald, and Florence Kelley, emerged as influential political figures during the progressive era.

Wald attracted a dedicated group of nurses, educators, and reformers to live at the Henry Street Settlement. By 1909 Henry Street had more than forty residents, supported by the donations of well-to-do New Yorkers. Wald and her allies convinced the New York Board of Health to assign a nurse to every public school in the city. They lobbied the Board of Education to create the first school lunch programs. They persuaded the city to set up municipal milk stations to ensure the purity of milk. Henry Street also pioneered tuberculosis treatment and prevention. Its leaders became powerful advocates for playground construction, improved street cleaning, and tougher housing inspection. The settlement's Neighborhood Playhouse became an internationally acclaimed center for innovative theater, music, and dance.

As settlement house workers expanded their influence from local neighborhoods to larger political and social circles, they became, in the phrase of one historian, "spearheads for reform." Lillian Wald became a national figure—an outspoken advocate of child labor legislation and woman suffrage and a vigorous opponent of American involvement in World War I. She offered Henry Street as a meeting place to the National Negro Conference in 1909, out of which emerged the National Association for the Advancement of Colored People. It was no cliché for Wald to say, as she did on many occasions, "The whole world is my neighborhood." ■

New York City

KEY TOPICS

- The political, social, and intellectual roots of progressive reform

- Tensions between social justice and social control

- The urban scene and the impact of new immigration

- Political activism by the working class, women, and African Americans

- Progressivism in national politics

THE CURRENTS OF PROGRESSIVISM

Between the 1890s and World War I, a large and diverse number of Americans claimed the political label "progressive." Progressivism is best understood as a varied collection of reform communities, often fleeting, uniting citizens in a host of political, professional, and religious organizations, some of which were national in scope.

As a political movement, progressivism flowered in the soil of several key issues: ending political corruption, bringing more businesslike methods to governing, and offering a more compassionate legislative response to the excesses of industrialism. As a national movement, progressivism reached its peak in 1912, when the four major presidential candidates all ran on some version of a progressive platform.

Three basic attitudes underlay the various crusades and movements that emerged in response to the fears gnawing at large segments of the population. The first was anger over the excesses of industrial capitalism and urban growth. At the same time, progressives shared an essential optimism about the ability of citizens to improve social and economic conditions. They were reformers, not revolutionaries. Second, progressives emphasized social cohesion and common bonds as a way of understanding how modern society and economics actually worked. They largely rejected the ideal of individualism that had informed nineteenth-century economic and political theory. For progressives, poverty and success hinged on more than simply individual character; the economy was more than merely a sum of individual calculations. Progressives thus opposed social Darwinism, with its claim that any effort to improve social conditions would prove fruitless because society is like a jungle in which only the "fittest" survive. Third, progressives believed in the need for citizens to intervene actively, both politically and morally, to improve social conditions. They pushed for a stronger government role in regulating the economy and solving the nation's social problems.

Progressive rhetoric and methods drew on two distinct sources of inspiration. One was evangelical Protestantism, which emphasized both the capacity and the duty of Christians to purge the world of poverty, inequality, and economic greed. A second strain of progressive thought looked to natural and social scientists to develop rational measures for improving the human condition, believing that experts trained in statistical analysis and engineering could make government and industry more efficient. Progressivism, thus, offered an uneasy combination of social justice and social control, a tension that would characterize American reform for the rest of the twentieth century.

Women Spearhead Reform

In the 1890s the settlement house movement had begun to provide an alternative to traditional concepts of private charity and humanitarian reform. Settlement workers found they could not transform their neighborhoods without confronting a host of broad social questions: chronic poverty, overcrowded tenement houses, child labor, industrial accidents, and public health.

Jane Addams founded one of the first settlement houses, Hull House, in Chicago in 1889 after years of struggling to find work and a social identity equal to her talents. Hull House was located in a run-down slum area of Chicago. It had a day nursery, a dispensary for medicines and medical advice, a boardinghouse, an art gallery, and a music school. Addams often spoke of the "subjective necessity" of settlement houses. By this she meant that they gave young, educated women a way to satisfy their powerful desire to connect with the real world.

OVERVIEW

CURRENTS OF PROGRESSIVISM

	Key Figures	Issues	Institutions/Achievements
Local Communities	Jane Addams, Lillian Wald, Florence Kelley, Frederic C. Howe, Samuel Jones	■ Improving health, education, welfare in urban immigrant neighborhoods ■ Child labor, eight-hour day ■ Celebrating immigrant cultures ■ Reforming urban politics ■ Municipal ownership/ regulation of utilities	■ Hull House Settlement ■ Henry Street Settlement ■ National Consumers League ■ New York Child Labor Committee ■ Bureau of Municipal Research
State	Robert M. LaFollette, Hiram Johnson, Al Smith	■ Limiting power of railroads, other corporations ■ Improving civil service ■ Direct democracy ■ Applying academic scholarship to human needs	■ "Wisconsin Idea" ■ State Workmen's Compensation ■ Unemployment Insurance ■ Public utility regulation
	James K. Vardaman, Hoke Smith	■ Disfranchisement of African Americans	■ Legalized segregation
National	Theodore Roosevelt	■ Trustbusting ■ Conservation and Western development ■ National regulation of corporate and financial excesses	■ Reclamation Bureau (1902) ■ U.S. Forest Service (1905) ■ Food and Drug Administration (1906) ■ Meat Inspection Act (1906) ■ Hepburn Act–ICC (1906)
	Woodrow Wilson	■ National regulation of corporate and financial excesses ■ Reform of national banking	■ Graduated Income Tax (1913) ■ Federal Reserve Act (1913) ■ Clayton Antitrust Act (1914) ■ Federal Trade Commission (1914)
Intellectual/ Cultural	Jacob Riis	■ Muckraking	■ *How the Other Half Lives* (1890)
	Lincoln Steffens, Ida Tarbell, Upton Sinclair, S. S. McClure		■ *Shame of the Cities* (1902) ■ *History of Standard Oil* (1904) ■ *The Jungle* (1906) ■ *McClure's Magazine*
	John Dewey	■ Education reform	■ *Democracy and Education* (1916)
	Louis Brandeis	■ Sociological jurisprudence	■ *Muller v. Oregon* (1908)
	Edwin A. Ross	■ Empowering "ethical elite"	■ *Social Control* (1901)

Social reformer Florence Kelley helped direct the support of the settlement house movement behind groundbreaking state and federal labor legislation. In 1893, she wrote a report detailing the dismal condi- tions in sweatshops and the effects of long hours on the women and children who worked in them. This re- port became the basis for landmark legislation in Illi- nois that limited women to an eight-hour workday,

Photographer Lewis Hine, one of the pioneers of social documentary photography, made this evocative 1908 portrait of "Mamie," a typical young spinner working at a cotton mill in Lancaster, South Carolina. The National Child Labor Committee hired Hine to help document, publicize, and curb the widespread employment of children in industrial occupations. "These pictures," Hine wrote, "speak for themselves and prove that the law is being violated."

SOURCE: Lewis Hine (American, 1874–1940), *A Carolina Spinner,* 1908. Gelatin silver print, 4 3/4 × 7 in. Milwaukee Art Museum, Gift of the Sheldon M. Barnett Family. (M1973.83).

barred children under fourteen from working, and abolished tenement labor. Moving to Henry Street Settlement in 1898, Kelley served as general secretary of the new National Consumers' League. With Lillian Wald she established the New York Child Labor Committee and pushed for the creation of the U.S. Children's Bureau, established in 1912.

Kelley, Addams, Wald, and their circle consciously used their power as women to reshape politics in the progressive era. Electoral politics and the state were historically male preserves, but female social progressives turned their gender into an advantage. They built upon the tradition of female moral reform, where women had long operated outside male-dominated political institutions to agitate and organize.

The Urban Machine

By the turn of the century Democratic Party machines, usually dominated by first- and second-generation Irish, controlled the political life of most large American cities. The keys to machine strength were disciplined organization and the delivery of essential services to both immigrant communities and business elites. Recent immigrants in particular faced frequent

unemployment, sickness, and discrimination. In exchange for votes, machine politicians offered their constituents a variety of services. These included municipal jobs in the police and fire departments, work at city construction sites, intervention with legal problems, and food and coal during hard times.

For those who did business with the city— construction companies, road builders, realtors—staying on the machine's good side was simply another business expense. In exchange for valuable franchises and city contracts, businessmen routinely bribed machine politicians and contributed liberally to their campaign funds. George Washington Plunkitt, a stalwart of New York's Tammany Hall machine, good-naturedly defended what he called "honest graft": making money from inside information on public improvements. "It's just like lookin' ahead in Wall Street or in the coffee or cotton market."

Organized prostitution and gambling, patronized largely by visitors to the city, could flourish only when "protected" by politicians who shared in the profits. Many machine figures began as saloonkeepers, and liquor dealers and beer brewers provided important financial support for "the organization." Vaudeville and burlesque theater, boxing, horse racing, and professional baseball were other urban enterprises with economic and political links to machines.

On New York City's Lower East Side, where the Henry Street Settlement was located, Timothy D. "Big Tim" Sullivan embodied the popular machine style. Critics charged that Sullivan controlled the city's gambling and made money from prostitution. But Big Tim, who had risen from desperate poverty, remained enormously popular with his constituents until his death in 1913. Sullivan, whose district included the largest number of immigrants and transients in the city, provided shoe giveaways and free Christmas dinners to thousands every winter. To help pay for these and other charitable activities, he informally taxed the saloons, theaters, and restaurants in the district. Sullivan also made a fortune through his investments in Vaudeville and the early movie business.

State legislatures, controlled by Republican rural and small-town elements, proved a formidable check on what city-based machines could accomplish. Reform campaigns that publicized excessive graft and corruption sometimes led voters to throw machine-backed mayors and aldermen out of office. And there were never enough patronage jobs for all the people clamoring for appointments. In the early twentieth century, to expand their base of support, political machines in the Northeast began concentrating more on passing welfare legislation beneficial to working-class and immigrant constituencies. In New York, for example, Tammany Hall figures such as Robert Wagner, Al Smith, and Big Tim Sullivan worked with middle-class progressive groups to pass child labor laws, factory safety regulations, worker compensation plans, and other efforts to make government more responsive to social needs. Urban machines also began to champion cultural pluralism, opposing prohibition and immigration restrictions and defending the contributions made by new ethnic groups in the cities.

Political Progressives and Urban Reform

Political progressivism originated in the cities. It was both a challenge to the power of machine politics and a response to deteriorating urban conditions. City governments, especially in the Northeast and industrial Midwest, seemed hardly capable of providing the basic services needed to sustain large populations. For example, an impure water supply left Pittsburgh with one of the world's highest rates of death from typhoid, dysentery, and cholera. Most New York City neighborhoods rarely enjoyed street cleaning, and playgrounds were nonexistent.

Reformers placed much of the blame for urban ills on the machines and looked for ways to restructure city government. Reformers revised city charters in favor of stronger mayoral power and expanded use of appointed administrators and career civil servants.

Business and professional elites became the biggest boosters of structural reforms in urban government. In the summer of 1900 a hurricane in the Gulf of Mexico unleashed a tidal wave on Galveston, Texas. To cope with this disaster, leading businessmen convinced the state legislature to replace the mayor-council government with a small board of commissioners. Each commissioner was elected at large, and each was responsible for a different city department. Under this plan voters could more easily identify and hold accountable those responsible for city services. The city commission, enjoying both policy-making and administrative powers, proved very effective in rebuilding Galveston. By 1917 nearly 500 cities, including Houston, Oakland, Kansas City, Denver, and Buffalo, had adopted the commission form of government. Another approach, the city manager plan, gained popularity in small and midsized cities. In this system, a city council appointed a professional, nonpartisan city manager to handle the day-to-day operations of the community.

Progressive politicians who focused on the human problems of the industrial city championed a different kind of reform, one based on changing policies rather than the political structure. In Cleveland, wealthy businessman Thomas L. Johnson served as mayor from 1901 to 1909. He emphasized both efficiency and social welfare. His popular program included lower streetcar fares, public baths, milk and meat inspection, and an expanded park and playground system.

Progressivism in the Statehouse: West and South

Their motives and achievements were mixed, but progressive politicians became a powerful force in many state capitals. In Wisconsin, Republican dissident Robert M. La Follette forged a coalition of angry farmers, small businessmen, and workers with his fiery attacks on railroads and other large corporations. Leader of the progressive faction of the state Republicans, "Fighting Bob" won three terms as governor (1900–06), then served as a U.S. senator until his death in 1925. As governor he pushed through tougher corporate tax rates, a direct primary, an improved civil service code, and a railroad commission designed to regulate freight charges. La Follette used faculty experts at the University of Wisconsin to help research and write his bills. Other states began copying the "Wisconsin Idea"—the application of academic scholarship and theory to the needs of the people.

In practice, La Follette's railroad commission accomplished far less than progressive rhetoric claimed. Ordinary consumers did not see lower passenger fares or reduced food prices. And as commissioners began to realize, the national reach of the railroads limited the effectiveness of state regulation. Although La Follette championed a more open political system, he also enrolled state employees in a tight political machine of his own. The La Follette family would dominate Wisconsin politics for forty years.

Western progressives displayed the greatest enthusiasm for institutional political reform. In the early 1900s, Oregon voters approved a series of constitutional amendments designed to strengthen direct democracy. The two most important were the *initiative*, which allowed a direct vote on specific measures put on the state ballot by petition, and the *referendum*, which allowed voters to decide on bills referred to them by the legislature. Other reforms included the direct *primary*, which allowed voters to cross party lines, and the *recall*, which gave voters the right to remove elected officials by popular vote. Widely copied throughout the West, all these measures intentionally weakened political parties.

Southern progressives supported the push toward a fully segregated public sphere. Between 1900 and 1910 southern states strengthened "Jim Crow" laws requiring separation of races in restaurants, streetcars, beaches, and theaters. Schools were separate but hardly equal. A 1916 Bureau of Education study found that per capita expenditures for education in southern states averaged $10.32 a year for white children and $2.89 for black children. And African American teachers received far lower salaries than their white counterparts. Black taxpayers, in effect, subsidized improved schools for whites, even as they saw their own children's educational opportunities deteriorate. The legacy of southern progressivism was, thus, closely linked to the strengthening of the legal and institutional guarantees of white supremacy.

New Journalism: Muckraking

Changes in journalism helped fuel a new reform consciousness by drawing the attention of millions to urban poverty, political corruption, the plight of industrial workers, and immoral business practices. As early as 1890, journalist Jacob Riis had shocked the nation with his landmark book *How the Other Half Lives,* a portrait of New York City's poor. A Danish immigrant who arrived in New York City in 1871, Riis became a newspaper reporter, covering the police beat and learning about the city's desperate underside. Riis's book included a remarkable series of photographs he had taken in tenements, lodging houses, sweatshops, and saloons, which had a powerful impact on a whole generation of urban reformers.

Within a few years, magazine journalists had turned to uncovering the seamier side of American life. The key innovator was S. S. McClure, a young Midwestern editor who in 1893 started America's first large-circulation magazine, *McClure's.* Charging only a dime for his monthly, McClure effectively combined popular fiction with articles on science, technology, travel, and recent history. He attracted a new readership among the urban middle class.

In 1902 McClure began hiring talented reporters to write detailed accounts of the nation's social problems. Lincoln Steffens's series *The Shame of the Cities* (1902) revealed the widespread graft at the center of American urban politics. He showed how big-city bosses routinely worked hand in glove with businessmen seeking lucrative municipal contracts for gas, water, electricity, and mass transit. Ida Tarbell, in her *History of the Standard Oil Company* (1904), thoroughly documented how John D. Rockefeller ruthlessly squeezed out competitors with unfair business practices.

McClure's and other magazines discovered that "exposure journalism" paid off handsomely in terms of increased circulation. A series such as Steffens's fueled reform campaigns that swept individual communities. Between 1902 and 1908, magazines were full of articles exposing insurance scandals, patent medicine frauds, and stock market swindles. Upton Sinclair's 1906 novel *The Jungle,* a socialist tract set among Chicago packinghouse workers, exposed the filthy sanitation and abysmal working conditions in the stockyards and the meatpacking industry. In an effort to boost sales, Sinclair's publisher devoted an entire issue of a monthly magazine it owned, *World's Work,* to articles and photographs that substantiated Sinclair's devastating portrait.

SOCIAL CONTROL AND ITS LIMITS

Many middle- and upper-class Protestant progressives feared that immigrants and large cities threatened the stability of American democracy. They worried that alien cultural practices were disrupting what they viewed as traditional American morality. Viewing themselves as part of what sociologist Edward Ross called the "ethical elite," progressives often believed they had a mission to frame laws and regulations for the social control of immigrants, industrial workers, and African Americans. This was the moralistic and frequently xenophobic side of progressivism, and it provided a powerful source of support for the regulation of drinking, prostitution, leisure activities, and schooling. Organizations devoted to social control constituted other versions of reform communities. These attempts at moral reform met with mixed success.

The Prohibition Movement

During the last two decades of the nineteenth century, the Woman's Christian Temperance Union had grown into a powerful mass organization. The WCTU appealed especially to women angered by men who used alcohol and then abused their wives and children. But local WCTU chapters put their energy into nontemperance activities as well, including homeless shelters, Sunday schools, prison reform, child nurseries, and woman suffrage. By 1911 the WCTU, with a quarter million members, was the largest women's organization in American history.

Other temperance groups had a narrower focus. The Anti-Saloon League, founded in 1893, began by organizing local-option campaigns in which rural counties and small towns banned liquor within their geographical limits. It drew much of its financial support from local businessmen, who saw a link between closing a community's saloons and increasing the productivity of workers. The league was a one-issue pressure group that played effectively on antiurban and anti-immigrant prejudice.

The battle to ban alcohol revealed deep ethnic and cultural divides within America's urban communities. Opponents of alcohol were generally "pietists," who viewed the world from a position of moral absolutism. These included native-born, middle-class Protestants associated with evangelical churches along with some old-stock Protestant immigrant denominations. Opponents of prohibition were generally "ritualists" with less arbitrary notions of personal morality. These were largely new-stock, working-class Catholic and Jewish immigrants, along with some Protestants, such as German Lutherans.

The Social Evil

Many of the same reformers who battled the saloon and drinking also engaged in efforts to eradicate prostitution. Crusades against "the social evil" had appeared at intervals throughout the nineteenth century. But they reached a new level of intensity between 1895 and 1920.

Between 1908 and 1914 exposés of the "white slave traffic" became a national sensation. Dozens of books, articles, and motion pictures alleged an international conspiracy to seduce and sell girls into prostitution. Most of these materials exaggerated the practices they attacked. They also made foreigners, especially Jews and southern Europeans, scapegoats for the sexual anxieties of native-born whites. In 1910 Congress passed legislation that permitted the deportation of foreign-born prostitutes or any foreigner convicted of procuring or employing them. That same year, the Mann Act made it a federal offense to transport women across state lines for "immoral purposes."

The progressive bent for defining social problems through statistics was nowhere more evident than in these reports. Vice commission investigators combed red-light districts, tenement houses, hotels, and dance halls, drawing up detailed lists of places where prostitution took place. They interviewed prostitutes, pimps, and customers. These reports agreed that commercialized sex was a business run by and for the profit and pleasure of men. They also documented the dangers of venereal disease to the larger community. The highly publicized vice reports were effective in forcing police crackdowns in urban red-light districts.

For wage-earning women, prostitution was a rational choice in a world of limited opportunities. Maimie Pinzer, a prostitute, summed up her feelings in a letter to a wealthy female reformer: "I don't propose to get up at 6:30 to be at work at 8 and work in a close, stuffy room with people I despise, until dark, for $6 or $7 a week! When I could, just by phoning, spend an afternoon with some congenial person and in the end have more than a week's work could pay me." The antivice crusades succeeded in closing down many urban red-light districts and larger brothels, but these were replaced by the streetwalker and call girl, who were more vulnerable to harassment and control by policemen and pimps.

The Redemption of Leisure

For large numbers of working-class adults and children, leisure meant time and money spent at vaudeville and burlesque theaters, amusement parks, dance halls, and motion picture houses. For many cultural traditionalists, the flood of new urban commercial amusements posed a grave threat: "Commercialized leisure" must be controlled by the community, if it is to become an agency of civilization rather than the reverse," warned Cleveland progressive Frederic C. Howe in 1914.

By 1908 movies had become the most popular form of cheap entertainment in America. One survey estimated that 11,500 movie theaters attracted 5 million patrons each day. For 5 or 10 cents "nickelodeon" theaters offered programs that might include a slapstick comedy, a western, a travelogue, and a melodrama. Early movies were most popular in the tenement and immigrant districts of big cities, and with children. As the films themselves became more sophisticated and as "movie palaces" began to replace cheap storefront theaters, the new medium attracted a large middle-class clientele as well.

Progressive reformers seized on the new medium as an alternative to the older entertainment traditions, such as concert saloons and burlesque theater, that had been closely allied with machine politics and the vice economy. In 1909, New York City movie producers and exhibitors joined with the reform-minded People's Institute to establish the voluntary National Board of Censorship (NBC). Movie entrepreneurs, most of whom were themselves immigrants, sought to shed the stigma of the slums, attract more middle-class patronage, and increase profits. A revolving group of civic activists reviewed new movies, passing them, suggesting changes, or condemning them. Local censoring committees all over the nation subscribed to the board's weekly bulletin. They aimed at achieving what John Collier of the NBC called "the redemption of leisure." By 1914 the NBC was reviewing 95 percent of the nation's film output.

WORKING-CLASS COMMUNITIES AND PROTEST

The Industrial Revolution, which had begun transforming American life and labor in the nineteenth century, reached maturity in the early twentieth. In 1900, out of a total labor force of 28.5 million, 16 million people worked at industrial occupations and 11 million on farms. By 1920, in a labor force of nearly 42 million, almost 29 million were in industry, but farm labor had declined to 10.4 million. The world of the industrial worker included large manufacturing towns in New England; barren mining settlements in the West; primitive lumber and turpentine camps in the South; steelmaking and coal-mining cities in Pennsylvania and Ohio; and densely packed immigrant ghettos from New York to San Francisco, where workers toiled in garment trade sweatshops.

All these industrial workers shared the need to sell their labor for wages in order to survive. At the same time, differences in skill, ethnicity, and race proved powerful barriers to efforts at organizing trade unions that could bargain for improved wages and working conditions. So, too, did the economic and political power of the large corporations that dominated much of American industry. These years saw many labor struggles that created effective trade unions or laid the groundwork for others. Industrial workers also became a force in local and national politics, adding a chorus of insistent voices to the calls for social justice.

New Immigrants from Two Hemispheres

On the eve of World War I, close to 60 percent of the industrial labor force was foreign-born. In the nineteenth century, much of the overseas migration had come from the industrial districts of northern and western Europe. English, Welsh, and German artisans had brought with them skills critical for emerging industries such as steelmaking and coal mining. Unlike their predecessors, nearly all the new Italian, Polish, Hungarian, Jewish, and Greek immigrants lacked industrial skills. They, thus, entered the bottom ranks of factories, mines, mills, and sweatshops.

These new immigrants had been driven from their European farms and towns by several forces, including the undermining of subsistence farming by commercial agriculture; a falling death rate that brought a shortage of land; and religious and political persecution. American corporations also sent agents to recruit cheap labor. Except for Jewish immigrants, a majority of whom fled virulent anti-Semitism in Russia and Russian Poland, most newcomers planned on earning a stake and then returning home.

The decision to migrate usually occurred through social networks—people linked by kinship, personal acquaintance, and work experience. These "chains," extending from places of origin to specific destinations in the United States, helped migrants cope with the considerable risks entailed by the long and difficult journey. A study conducted by the U.S. Immigration Commission in 1909 found that about 60 percent of the new immigrants had their passage arranged by immigrants already in America.

The low-paid, backbreaking work in basic industry became nearly the exclusive preserve of the new immigrants. In 1907, of the 14,359 common laborers employed at Pittsburgh's U.S. Steel mills, 11,694 were eastern Europeans. For twelve-hour days and seven-day weeks, two-thirds of these workers made less than $12.50 a week, one-third less than $10.00. This was far less than the $15.00 that the Pittsburgh Associated Charities had estimated as the minimum for providing necessities for a family of five. Small

IMMIGRATION TO THE UNITED STATES (1901–1920)		
Total: 14,532,000		% of Total
Italy	3,157,000	22%
Austria-Hungary	3,047,000	21
Russia and Poland	2,524,000	17
Canada	922,000	6
Great Britain	867,000	6
Scandinavia	709,000	5
Ireland	487,000	3
Germany	486,000	3
France and Low Countries (Belgium, Netherlands, Switz.)	361,000	2
Mexico	268,000	2
West Indies	231,000	2
Japan	213,000	2
China	41,000	*
Australia and New Zealand	23,000	*

*Less than 1% of total

SOURCE: U.S. Bureau of the Census, *Historical Statistics of the United States from Colonial Times to 1970*, Washington, DC, 1975.

wonder that the new immigration was disproportionately male. One-third of the immigrant steelworkers were single. Workers with families generally supplemented their incomes by taking in single men as boarders.

Between 1898 and 1907 more than 80,000 Japanese entered the United States. The vast majority were young men working as contract laborers in the West. American law prevented Japanese immigrants (the *Issei*) from obtaining American citizenship, because they were not white. Most Japanese settled near Los Angeles, where they established small communities centered around fishing, truck farming, and the flower and nursery business. In 1920 Japanese farmers produced 10 percent of the dollar volume of California agriculture on 1 percent of the farm acreage.

Mexican immigration also grew in these years, providing a critical source of labor for the West's farms, railroads, and mines. Economic and political crises spurred tens of thousands of Mexico's rural and urban poor to emigrate north. Large numbers of seasonal agricultural workers regularly came up from Mexico to work in the expanding sugar beet industry, and then returned. But between 1900 and 1914, the number of people of Mexican descent living and working in the United States tripled, from roughly 100,000 to 300,000.

Urban Ghettos

By 1920, immigrants and their children constituted almost 60 percent of the population of cities over 100,000. The sheer size and dynamism of these cities made the immigrant experience more complex than in smaller cities and more isolated communities. Workers in the urban garment trades toiled for low wages and suffered layoffs, unemployment, and poor health. But conditions in the small, labor-intensive shops of the clothing industry differed significantly from those in the large-scale, capital-intensive industries like steel.

New York City had become the center of both Jewish immigration and America's huge ready-to-wear clothing industry. The city's Jewish population was 1.4 million in 1915, almost 30 percent of its inhabitants. In small factories, lofts, and tenement apartments some 200,000 people, most of them Jews, some of them Italians, worked in the clothing trades. Most of the industry operated on the grueling piece-rate, or task, system, in which manufacturers and subcontractors paid individuals or teams of workers to complete a certain quota of labor within a specific time.

The garment industry was highly seasonal. A typical workweek was sixty hours, with seventy common during busy season. But there were long stretches of unemployment in slack times. Even skilled cutters, all men, earned an average of only $16 per week. Unskilled workers, nearly all of them young single women, made only $6 or $7 a week.

In November 1909 two New York garment manufacturers responded to strikes by unskilled women workers by hiring thugs and prostitutes to beat up pickets. The strikers won the support of the Women's Trade Union League, a group of sympathetic female reformers that included Lillian Wald, Mary Dreier, and prominent society figures. At a dramatic mass meeting in Cooper Union Hall, Clara Lemlich, a teenage working girl speaking in Yiddish, made an emotional plea for a general strike. She called for everyone in the crowd to take an old Jewish oath: "If I turn traitor to the cause I now pledge, may this hand wither from the arm I now raise." The Uprising of the 20,000, as it became known, swept through the city's garment district.

The strikers demanded union recognition, better wages, and safer and more sanitary conditions. Hundreds of them were arrested, and many were beaten by police. After three cold months on the picket line, the strikers returned to work without union recognition. But the International Ladies Garment Workers Union (ILGWU), founded in 1900, did gain strength and negotiated contracts with some of the city's shirtwaist makers. The strike was an important breakthrough in the drive to organize unskilled workers into industrial unions.

On March 25, 1911, the issues raised by the strike took on new urgency when a fire raced through three floors of the Triangle Shirtwaist Company. As the flames spread, workers found themselves trapped by exit doors that had been locked from the outside. Fire escapes were nonexistent. Within half an hour, 146 people, mostly young Jewish women, had been killed by smoke or had leaped to their death. In the bitter aftermath, women progressives led by Florence Kelley and Frances Perkins of the National Consumers' League joined with Tammany Hall leaders Al Smith, Robert Wagner, and Big Tim Sullivan to create a New York State Factory Investigation Commission. Under Perkins's vigorous leadership, the commission conducted an unprecedented round of public hearings and on-site inspections, leading to a series of state laws that dramatically improved safety conditions and limited the hours for working women and children.

The AFL: "Unions, Pure and Simple"

Following the depression of the 1890s, the American Federation of Labor (AFL) emerged as the strongest and most stable organization of workers. Samuel Gompers's strategy of recruiting skilled labor into unions organized by craft had paid off. Union membership climbed from under 500,000 in 1897 to 1.7 million by 1904. The national unions—the United Mine Workers of America, the Brotherhood of Carpenters and Joiners, the International Association of Machinists—represented workers of specific occupations in collective bargaining. Trade autonomy and exclusive jurisdiction were the ruling principles within the AFL.

But the strength of craft organization also gave rise to weakness. In 1905 Gompers told a union gathering in Minneapolis that "caucasians" would not "let their standard of living be destroyed by negroes, Chinamen, Japs, or any others." Each trade looked mainly to the welfare of its own. Many explicitly barred women and African Americans from membership. There were some important exceptions. The United Mine Workers of America (UMWA) followed a more inclusive policy, recruiting both skilled underground pitmen and the unskilled aboveground workers. The UMWA even tried to recruit strikebreakers brought in by coal operators. With 260,000 members in 1904, the UMWA became the largest AFL affiliate.

AFL unions had a difficult time holding on to their gains. Economic slumps, technological changes, and aggressive counterattacks by employer organizations could be devastating. Trade associations using management-controlled efficiency drives fought union efforts to regulate output and shop practices. The National Association of Manufacturers (NAM), a group of smaller industrialists founded in 1903, launched an "open shop" campaign to eradicate unions altogether. "Open shop" was simply a new name for a workplace where unions were not allowed.

Unfriendly judicial decisions also hurt organizing efforts. In 1906 a federal judge issued a permanent injunction against an iron molders strike at the Allis Chalmers Company of Milwaukee. In the so-called Danbury Hatters' Case (*Loewe v. Lawler*, 1908), a federal court ruled that secondary boycotts, aimed by strikers at other companies doing business with their employer were illegal. Not until the 1930s would unions be able to count on legal support for collective bargaining and the right to strike.

The IWW: "One Big Union"

Some workers developed more radical visions of labor organizing. In company towns, where a single large corporation was dominant, miners suffered from low wages, poor food, and primitive sanitation, as well as injuries and death from frequent cave-ins and explosions. In response to the brutal realities of labor organizing in the West, in 1905, leaders of the Western Federation of Miners, the Socialist Party, and various radical groups gathered in Chicago to found the Industrial Workers of the World (IWW). The IWW charter proclaimed bluntly, "The working class and the employing class have nothing in common. . . . Between these two classes a struggle must go on until the workers of the world unite as a class, take possession of the earth and the machinery of production, and abolish the wage system."

William D. "Big Bill" Haywood, an imposing, one-eyed, hard-rock miner, emerged as the most influential and flamboyant spokesman for the IWW, or Wobblies, as they were called. Haywood, a charismatic speaker and effective organizer, regularly denounced the AFL for its conservative emphasis on organizing skilled workers by trade. The Wobblies concentrated their efforts on miners, lumberjacks, sailors, "harvest stiffs," and other casual laborers. Openly contemptuous of bourgeois respectability, the IWW stressed the power of collective direct action on the job—strikes and, occasionally, sabotage.

The IWW briefly became a force among eastern industrial workers, tapping the rage and growing militance of the immigrants and unskilled. In 1909, an IWW–led steel strike at McKees Rocks, Pennsylvania, challenged the power of U.S. Steel. In the 1912 "Bread and Roses" strike in Lawrence, Massachusetts, IWW organizers turned a spontaneous walkout of textile workers into a successful struggle for union recognition.

These battles gained the IWW a great deal of sympathy from radical intellectuals, along with public scorn from the AFL and employers' groups. The IWW failed to establish permanent organizations in the eastern cities, but it remained a force in the lumber camps, mines, and wheat fields of the West. In spite of its militant rhetoric, the IWW concerned itself with practical gains. "The final aim is revolution," said one Wobbly organizer, "but for the present let's see if we can get a bed to sleep in, water enough to take a bath in and decent food to eat." But when the United States entered World War I, the Justice Department used the IWW's anticapitalist rhetoric and antiwar stance to crush it.

WOMEN'S MOVEMENTS AND BLACK AWAKENING

The New Woman

The settlement house movement discussed in the opening of this chapter was just one of the new avenues of opportunity that opened to progressive era women. A steady proliferation of women's organizations attracted growing numbers of educated, middle-class women in the early twentieth century. With more men working in offices, more children attending school, and family size declining, the middle-class home was emptier. At the same time, more middle-class women were graduating from high school and college.

The women's club movement combined an earlier focus on self-improvement and intellectual pursuits with newer benevolent efforts on behalf of working women and children. The Buffalo Union, for example, sponsored art lectures for housewives and classes in typing, stenography, and bookkeeping for young working women. It also maintained a library, set up a "noon rest" downtown where women could eat lunch, and ran a school for training domestics. In Chicago the Women's Club became a powerful ally for reformers. For many middle-class women the club movement provided a new kind of female-centered community.

Other women's associations made even more explicit efforts to bridge class lines between middle-class homemakers and working-class women. The National Consumers' League (NCL), started in 1898 by Maud Nathan and Josephine Lowell, sponsored a "white label" campaign in which manufacturers who met safety and sanitary standards could put NCL labels on their food and clothing. Under the dynamic leadership of Florence Kelley, the NCL took an even more aggressive stance by publicizing labor abuses in department stores and lobbying for maximum-hour and minimum-wage laws in state legislatures. In its efforts to protect home and housewife, worker and consumer, the NCL embodied the ideal of "social housekeeping."

Birth Control

The phrase "birth control," coined by Margaret Sanger around 1913, described her campaign to provide contraceptive information and devices for women. Sanger had seen her own mother die at age forty-nine after bearing eleven children. In 1910, Sanger was a thirty-year-old nurse and housewife living with her husband and three children in a New York City suburb. Excited by a socialist lecture she had attended, she convinced her husband to move to the city, where she threw herself into the bohemian milieu. She became an organizer for the IWW, and in 1912 she wrote a series of articles on female sexuality for a socialist newspaper.

When postal officials confiscated the paper for violating obscenity laws, Sanger left for Europe to learn more about contraception. She returned to New York determined to challenge the obscenity statutes with her own magazine, the *Woman Rebel*. Sanger's journal celebrated female autonomy, including the right to sexual expression and control over one's body. When she distributed her pamphlet *Family Limitation*, postal inspectors confiscated copies and she found herself facing forty-five years in prison. In October 1914 she fled to Europe again.

An older generation of feminists had advocated "voluntary motherhood," or the right to say no to a husband's sexual demands. The new birth control advocates embraced contraception as a way of advancing sexual freedom for middle-class women as well as responding to the misery of those working-class women who bore numerous children while living in poverty. Sanger returned to the United States in October 1915. After the government dropped the obscenity charges, she embarked on a national speaking tour. In 1916 she again defied the law by opening a birth control clinic in a working-class neighborhood in Brooklyn and offering birth control information without a physician present. Arrested and jailed, she gained more publicity for her crusade. Within a few years, birth control leagues and clinics could be found in every major city and most large towns in the country.

Racism and Accommodation

African Americans endured a deeply racist popular culture that made hateful stereotypes of black people a normal feature of political debate and everyday life. White southern politicians and writers claimed that African Americans had undergone a natural "reversion to savagery" upon the end of slavery. In northern cities "coon songs," based on gross caricatures of black life, were extremely popular in theaters and as sheet music. Like the antebellum minstrel shows, these songs reduced African Americans to creatures of pure appetite for food, sex, alcohol, and violence.

In this political and cultural climate, Booker T. Washington won recognition as the most influential black leader of the day. Born a slave in 1856, Washington was educated at Hampton Institute in Virginia, one of the first freedmen's schools devoted to industrial education. In 1881 he founded Tuskegee Institute, a black school in Alabama devoted to industrial and moral education. He became the leading spokesman for racial accommodation, urging blacks to focus on economic improvement and self-reliance, as opposed to political and civil rights. His widely read autobiography, *Up from Slavery* (1901), stands as a classic narrative of an American self-made man. Written with a shrewd eye toward cementing his support among white Americans, it stressed the importance of learning values such as frugality, cleanliness, and personal morality. But Washington also gained a large following among African Americans, especially those who aspired to business success. Publicly he insisted that "agitation of questions of social equality is the extremest folly." But privately Washington also spent money and worked behind the scenes trying to halt disfranchisement and segregation.

Racial Justice, the NAACP, Black Women's Activism

Washington's focus on economic self-help remained deeply influential in African American communities long after his death in 1915. But alternative black voices challenged his racial philosophy while he lived. In the early 1900s, scholar and activist W. E. B. Du Bois created a significant alternative to Washington's leadership. A product of the black middle class, Du Bois had been educated at Fisk University and Harvard, where in 1895 he became the first African American to receive a Ph.D. Through essays on black history, culture, education, and politics, Du Bois explored the concept of "double consciousness." Black people, he argued, would always feel the tension between an African heritage and their desire to assimilate as Americans.

Du Bois criticized Booker T. Washington's philosophy for its acceptance of "the alleged inferiority of the Negro." The black community, he argued, must fight for the right to vote, for civic equality, and for higher education for the "talented tenth" of their youth. In 1905 Du Bois and editor William Monroe Trotter brought together a group of educated black men to oppose Washington's conciliatory views. Discrimination they encountered in Buffalo, New York, prompted the men to move their meeting to Niagara Falls, Ontario. The Niagara movement protested legal segregation, the exclusion of blacks from labor unions, and the curtailment of voting and other civil rights.

The Niagara movement failed to generate much change. But in 1909 many of its members, led by Du Bois, attended a National Negro Conference held

In July 1905, a group of African American leaders met in Niagara Falls, Ontario, to protest legal segregation and the denial of civil rights to the nation's black population. This portrait was taken against a studio backdrop of the falls. In 1909, the leader of the Niagara movement, W. E. B. Du Bois (second from right, middle row) founded and edited *The Crisis*, the influential monthly journal of the National Association for the Advancement of Colored People.

SOURCE: Photographs and Print Division, Schomburg Center for Research in Black Culture, The New York Public Library, Astor, Lenox and Tilden Foundations.

at the Henry Street Settlement in New York. A new, interracial organization emerged from this conference, the National Association for the Advancement of Colored People. Du Bois was the only black officer of the original NAACP.

The disfranchisement of black voters in the South severely curtailed African American political influence. In response, African American women created new strategies to challenge white supremacy and improve life in their communities. As Sallie Mial, a North Carolina Baptist home missionary, told her male brethren, "We have a peculiar work to do. We can go where you cannot afford to go." Founded in 1900, the Women's Convention of the National Baptist Convention, the largest black denomination in the United States, offered African American women a new public space to pursue reform work and "racial uplift." They organized settlement houses and built playgrounds; they created day-care facilities and kindergartens; they campaigned for women's suffrage, temperance, and advances in public health.

NATIONAL PROGRESSIVISM

Theodore Roosevelt and Presidential Activism

The assassination of William McKinley in 1901 made forty-two-year-old Theodore Roosevelt the youngest man to ever hold the office of president. Born to a wealthy New York family in 1858, Roosevelt overcame a sickly childhood through strenuous physical exercise and rugged outdoor living. After graduating from Harvard he immediately threw himself into a career in the rough and tumble of New York politics. He won election to the state assembly, ran an unsuccessful campaign for mayor of New York, served as president of the New York City Board of Police Commissioners, and went to Washington as assistant secretary of the navy. During the Spanish-American War, he won national fame as leader of the Rough Rider regiment in Cuba. Upon his return, he was elected governor of New York and then in 1900 vice president. Roosevelt viewed the presidency as a "bully pulpit"—a platform from which he could exhort Americans to reform their society—and he aimed to make the most of it.

Roosevelt was a uniquely colorful figure, a shrewd publicist, and a creative politician. He preached the virtues of "the strenuous life," and he believed that educated and wealthy Americans had a special responsibility to serve, guide, and inspire those less fortunate. In style, Roosevelt made key contributions to national progressivism. He knew how to inspire and guide public opinion. He stimulated discussion and aroused curiosity like no one before him. In 1902 Roosevelt demonstrated his unique style of activism when he personally intervened in a bitter strike by anthracite coal miners. Using public calls for conciliation, a series of White House bargaining sessions, and private pressure on the mine owners, Roosevelt secured a settlement that won better pay and working conditions for the miners, but without recognition of their union. Roosevelt also pushed for efficient government as the solution to social problems. Unlike most nineteenth-century Republicans, who had largely ignored economic and social inequalities, Roosevelt frankly acknowledged them. Administrative agencies run by experts, he believed, could find rational solutions that could satisfy everyone.

Trustbusting and Regulation

One of the first issues Roosevelt faced was growing public concern with the rapid business consolidations taking place in the American economy. In 1902 he directed the Justice Department to begin a series of prosecutions under the Sherman Antitrust Act. The first target was the Northern Securities Company, a huge merger of transcontinental railroads brought about by financier J. P. Morgan. The deal would have created a giant holding company controlling nearly all the long-distance rail lines from Chicago to California. The Justice Department fought the case all the way through a hearing before the Supreme Court. In *Northern Securities* v. *United States* (1904), the Court held that the stock transactions constituted an illegal combination in restraint of interstate commerce.

This case established Roosevelt's reputation as a "trustbuster." During his two terms, the Justice Department filed forty-three cases under the Sherman Antitrust Act to restrain or dissolve business monopolies. Roosevelt viewed these suits as necessary to publicize the issue and assert the federal government's ultimate authority over big business. But he did not really believe in the need to break up large corporations. Unlike many progressives, who were nostalgic for smaller companies and freer competition, Roosevelt accepted centralization as a fact of modern economic life and considered government regulation the best way to deal with big business.

After easily defeating Democrat Alton B. Parker in the 1904 election, Roosevelt felt more secure in pushing for regulatory legislation. In 1906 Roosevelt responded to public pressure for greater government intervention and, overcoming objections from a conservative Congress, signed three important measures into law. The Hepburn Act strengthened the Interstate Commerce Commission (ICC), established in 1887 as the first independent regulatory agency, by authorizing it to set maximum railroad rates and inspect financial records. The Pure Food and Drug Act established the Food and Drug Administration (FDA), which tested and approved drugs before they went on the market. The Meat Inspection Act (passed with help from the shocking publicity surrounding Upton Sinclair's muckraking novel *The Jungle*) empowered the Department of Agriculture to inspect and label meat products.

But regulatory legislation found advocates among American big business as well. Large meatpackers such as Swift and Armour strongly supported stricter federal regulation as a way to drive out smaller companies that could not meet tougher standards. The new laws also helped American packers compete more profitably in the European export market by giving their meat the official seal of federal inspectors.

As a naturalist and outdoorsman, Theodore Roosevelt also believed in the need for government regulation of the natural environment. He worried about the destruction of forests, prairies, streams, and the wilderness. In 1905 he created the U.S. Forest Service and named conservationist Gifford Pinchot to head it. Pinchot recruited a force of forest rangers to manage the reserves. By 1909 total timber and forest reserves had

increased from 45 to 195 million acres, and more than 80 million acres of mineral lands had been withdrawn from public sale.

Republican Split

By the end of his second term, Roosevelt had moved beyond the idea of regulation to push for the most far-reaching federal economic and social programs ever proposed. He saw the central problem as "how to exercise . . . responsible control over the business use of vast wealth."

In 1908, Roosevelt kept his promise to retire after a second term. He chose Secretary of War William Howard Taft as his successor. Taft easily defeated Democrat William Jennings Bryan in the 1908 election. During Taft's presidency, the gulf between "insurgent" progressives and the "stand pat" wing split the Republican Party wide open. To some degree, the battles were as much over style as substance. Compared with Roosevelt, the reflective and judicious Taft brought a much more restrained concept of the presidency to the White House. He supported some progressive measures, including the constitutional amendment legalizing a graduated income tax (ratified in 1913), safety codes for mines and railroads, and the creation of a federal Children's Bureau (1912). But in a series of bitter political fights involving tariff, antitrust, and conservation policies, Taft alienated Roosevelt and many other progressives.

After returning from an African safari and a triumphant European tour in 1910, Roosevelt threw himself back into national politics. He directly challenged Taft for the Republican Party leadership. In a dozen bitter state presidential primaries (the first ever held), Taft and Roosevelt fought for the nomination. Although Roosevelt won most of these contests, the old guard still controlled the national convention and renominated Taft in June 1912. Roosevelt's supporters stormed out, and in August the new Progressive Party nominated Roosevelt and Hiram Johnson of California as its presidential ticket. The platform called for woman suffrage, the eight-hour day, prohibition of child labor, minimum-wage standards for working women, and stricter regulation of large corporations.

The Election of 1912: A Four-Way Race

With the Republicans so badly divided, the Democrats sensed a chance for their first presidential victory in twenty years. They chose Governor Woodrow Wilson of New Jersey as their candidate. Although not nearly as well known nationally as Taft and Roosevelt, Wilson had built a strong reputation as a reformer. The son of a Virginia Presbyterian minister, Wilson spent most of his early career in academia. He studied law at the University of Virginia and then earned a Ph.D. in political science from Johns Hopkins. After teaching history and political science at several schools, he became president of Princeton University in 1902. In 1910, he won election as New Jersey's governor, running against the state Democratic machine. He won the Democratic nomination for president with the support of many of the party's progressives, including William Jennings Bryan.

Wilson declared himself and the Democratic Party to be the true progressives. Crafted largely by progressive lawyer Louis Brandeis, Wilson's platform was far more ambiguous than Roosevelt's. The New Freedom emphasized restoring conditions of free competition and equality of economic opportunity. Wilson did favor a variety of progressive reforms for workers, farmers, and consumers. But in sounding older, nineteenth-century Democratic themes of states' rights and small government, Wilson argued against allowing the federal government to become as large and paternalistic as Roosevelt advocated.

Socialist party nominee Eugene V. Debs offered the fourth and most radical choice to voters. The Socialists had more than doubled their membership since 1908, to more than 100,000. On election days Socialist strength was far greater than that, as the party's candidates attracted increasing numbers of voters. By 1912 more than a thousand Socialists held elective office in thirty-three states and 160 cities. Geographically, Socialist strength had shifted to the trans-Mississippi South and West.

Debs and the Socialists also took credit for pushing both Roosevelt and Wilson farther toward the left. Both the Democratic and Progressive Party platforms contained proposals that had been considered extremely radical only ten years earlier.

In the end, the divisions in the Republican Party gave the election to Wilson. He won easily, polling 6.3 million votes to Roosevelt's 4.1 million. Taft came in third with 3.5 million. Eugene Debs won 900,000 votes, 6 percent of the total, for the strongest Socialist showing in American history. Even though he won with only 42 percent of the popular vote, Wilson swept the electoral college with 435 votes to Roosevelt's 88 and Taft's 8, giving him the largest electoral majority up to that time. In several respects, the election of 1912 was the first "modern" presidential race. It featured the first direct primaries, challenges to traditional party loyalties, an issue-oriented campaign, and a high degree of interest group activity.

Woodrow Wilson's First Term

As president, Wilson followed Roosevelt's lead in expanding the activist dimensions of the office. He became more responsive to pressure for a greater federal role in regulating business and the economy. This increase in direct lobbying—from hundreds of local and national re-

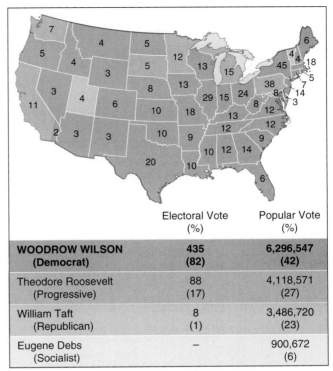

	Electoral Vote (%)	Popular Vote (%)
WOODROW WILSON (Democrat)	**435 (82)**	**6,296,547 (42)**
Theodore Roosevelt (Progressive)	88 (17)	4,118,571 (27)
William Taft (Republican)	8 (1)	3,486,720 (23)
Eugene Debs (Socialist)	–	900,672 (6)

The Election of 1912   The split within the Republican Party allowed Woodrow Wilson to become only the second Democrat since the Civil War to be elected president. Eugene Debs's vote was the highest ever polled by a Socialist candidate.

form groups, Washington-based organizations, and the new Progressive Party—was itself a new and defining feature of the era's political life. With the help of a Democratic-controlled Congress, Wilson pushed through a significant battery of reform proposals.

The Underwood-Simmons Act of 1913 substantially reduced tariff duties on a variety of raw materials and manufactured goods, including wool, sugar, agricultural machinery, shoes, iron, and steel. Taking advantage of the newly ratified Sixteenth Amendment, which gave Congress the power to levy taxes on income, it also imposed the first graduated tax (up to 6 percent) on personal incomes. The Federal Reserve Act that same year restructured the nation's banking and currency system. It created twelve Federal Reserve Banks, regulated by a central board in Washington. Member banks were required to keep a portion of their cash reserves in the Federal Reserve Bank of their district. By giving central direction to banking and monetary policy, the Federal Reserve Board diminished the power of large private banks.

Wilson also supported the Clayton Antitrust Act of 1914, which replaced the old Sherman Act of 1890 as the nation's basic antitrust law. The Clayton Act reflected the growing political clout of the American Federation of Labor. It exempted unions from being

CHRONOLOGY

1889	Jane Addams founds Hull House in Chicago
1890	Jacob Riis publishes *How the Other Half Lives*
1895	Booker T. Washington addresses Cotton States Exposition in Atlanta, emphasizing an accommodationist philosophy
	Lillian Wald establishes Henry Street Settlement in New York
1898	Florence Kelley becomes general secretary of the new National Consumers' League
1900	Robert M. La Follette elected governor of Wisconsin
1901	Theodore Roosevelt succeeds the assassinated William McKinley as president
1904	Lincoln Steffens publishes *The Shame of the Cities*
1905	President Roosevelt creates U.S. Forest Service and names Gifford Pinchot head
	Industrial Workers of the World is founded in Chicago
1906	Upton Sinclair's *The Jungle* exposes conditions in the meatpacking industry
	Congress passes Pure Food and Drug Act and Meat Inspection Act and establishes Food and Drug Administration
1908	In *Muller v. Oregon* the Supreme Court upholds a state law limiting maximum hours for working women

1909	Uprising of 20,000 garment workers in New York City's garment industries helps organize unskilled workers into unions
	National Association for the Advancement of Colored People (NAACP) is founded
1911	Triangle Shirtwaist Company fire kills 146 garment workers in New York City
	Socialist critic Max Eastman begins publishing *The Masses*
1912	Democrat Woodrow Wilson wins presidency, defeating Republican William H. Taft, Progressive Theodore Roosevelt, and Socialist Eugene V. Debs
	Bread and Roses strike involves 25,000 textile workers in Lawrence, Massachusetts
	Margaret Sanger begins writing and speaking in support of birth control for women
1913	Sixteenth Amendment, legalizing a graduated income tax, is ratified
1914	Clayton Antitrust Act exempts unions from being construed as illegal combinations in restraint of trade
	Federal Trade Commission is established
	Ludlow Massacre occurs
1916	National Park Service is established

construed as illegal combinations in restraint of trade, and it forbade federal courts from issuing injunctions against strikers. But Wilson adopted the view that permanent federal regulation was necessary for checking the abuses of big business. The Federal Trade Commission (FTC), established in 1914, sought to give the federal government the same sort of regulatory control over corporations that the ICC had over railroads.

On social issues, Wilson proved more cautious in his first two years. His initial failure to support federal child labor legislation and rural credits to farmers angered many progressives. A Southerner, Wilson also sanctioned the spread of racial segregation in federal offices. As the reelection campaign of 1916 approached, Wilson worried about defections from the labor and social justice wings of his party. He proceeded to support a rural credits act providing government capital to federal farm banks, as well as federal aid to agricultural extension programs in schools. He also came out in favor of child labor reform and a worker compensation bill for federal employees. But by 1916 the dark cloud of war in Europe had already begun to cast its long shadow over progressive reform.

CONCLUSION

The American political and social landscape was significantly altered by progressivism, but these shifts reflected the tensions and ambiguities of progressivism itself. Nearly every new election law had the effect of excluding some people from voting while including others. For African Americans, progressivism largely meant disfranchisement from voting altogether. Direct primary laws eliminated some of the most blatant abuses of big-city machines, but in cities and states dominated by one party, the majority party's primary effectively decided the general election. Stricter election laws made it more difficult for third parties to get on the ballot. Voting itself steadily declined in these years.

Over all, party voting became a less important form of political participation. Interest group activity, congressional and statehouse lobbying, and direct appeals to public opinion gained currency as ways of influencing government. Business groups such as the National Association of Manufacturers and individual trade associations were among the most active groups pressing their demands on government. Political action often shifted from legislatures to the new administrative agencies and commissions created to deal with social and economic problems. Popular magazines and journals grew significantly in both number and circulation, becoming more influential in shaping and appealing to national public opinion.

Social progressives and their allies could point to significant improvements in the everyday lives of ordinary Americans. On the state level, real advances had been made through a range of social legislation covering working conditions, child labor, minimum wages, and worker compensation. Social progressives, too, had discovered the power of organizing into extra-party lobbying groups such as the National Consumers' League and the National American Woman Suffrage Association. Yet the tensions between fighting for social justice and the urge toward social control remained unresolved. The emphasis on efficiency, uplift, and rational administration often collided with humane impulses to aid the poor, the immigrant, the slum dweller. The large majority of African Americans, blue-collar workers, and urban poor remained untouched by federal assistance programs.

Progressives had tried to confront the new realities of urban and industrial society. What had begun as a discrete collection of local and state struggles had by 1912 come to reshape state and national politics. Politics itself had been transformed by the calls for social justice. Federal and state power would now play a more decisive role than ever in shaping work, play, and social life in local communities.

REVIEW QUESTIONS

1. Discuss the tensions within progressivism between the ideals of social justice and the urge for social control. What concrete achievements are associated with each wing of the movement? What were the driving forces behind them?
2. Describe the different manifestations of progressivism at the local, state, and national levels. To what extent did progressives redefine the role of the state in American politics?
3. What gains were made by working-class communities in the progressive era? What barriers did they face?
4. How did the era's new immigration reshape America's cities and workplaces? What connections can you draw between the new immigrant experience and progressive era politics?
5. Analyze the progressive era from the perspective of African Americans. What political and social developments were most crucial, and what legacies did they leave?
6. Evaluate the lasting impact of progressive reform. How do the goals, methods, and language of progressives still find voice in contemporary America?

RECOMMENDED READING

Robert M. Crunden, *Ministers of Reform: The Progressives' Achievement in American Civilization, 1889–1920* (1982). Emphasizes the moral and religious traditions of middle-class Protestants as the core of the progressive ethos.

Alan Dawley, *Struggles for Justice: Social Responsibility and the Liberal State* (1991). Offers an important interpretation of progressivism that focuses on how the working class and women pushed the state toward a more activist role in confronting social problems.

Susan A. Glenn, *Daughters of the Shtetl: Life and Labor in the Immigrant Generation* (1990). A sensitive analysis of the experiences of immigrant Jewish women in the garment trades.

Dewey Grantham, *Southern Progressivism: The Reconciliation of Progress and Tradition* (1982). Examines the contradictions within the southern progressive tradition.

Morton Keller, *Regulating a New Society: Public Policy and Social Change in America, 1900–1930* (1994). A comprehensive study of public policymaking on local and national levels in early twentieth-century America.

Arthur Link and Richard L. McCormick, *Progressivism* (1983). The best overview of progressivism and electoral politics.

Daniel T. Rodgers, *Atlantic Crossings: Social Politics in A Progressive Age* (1998). A magisterial work of comparative history focusing on the transnational conversations that deeply influenced American progressive thinkers and reformers.

Elizabeth Sanders, *Roots of Reform: Farmers, Workers, and the American State, 1877–1917* (1999). Arguing for the centrality of agrarian movements in shaping progressive era reform, Sanders explores the irony of how these efforts led to an increasingly bureaucratic state.

Kathryn Kish Sklar, *Florence Kelley and the Nation's Work* (1995). The first installment in a two-volume biography, this book brilliantly brings Florence Kelley alive within the rich context of late nineteenth-century women's political culture.

Christine Stansell, *American Moderns: Bohemian New York and the Creation of a New Century* (2000). Vividly written account that places radical politics and "New Women" at the center of the shaping of modernism.

ON THE WEB

http://www.archives.gov/exhibit_hall/ picturing_the_century/portfolios/port_hine.html

This small collection of child labor and industrial photos was the work of Lewis Hine and the National Child Labor Committee. Be sure to click on the hot button for more information on Hine whose career stretched from the progressive era into the New Deal. More Hine photos are available on the following Library of Congress site **http://lcweb.loc.gov/rr/ print/coll/207-b.html.**

http://oyez.nwu.edu/cases/cases.cgi

The Oyez Project of Northwestern University provides information on Supreme Court decisions, especially the written Court opinions. Use the search program of this site to find *Muller v. Oregon*, 208 U.S. 412 (1908) to examine the details of the landmark progressive case supporting Oregon's laws that protected women workers.

http://www.yale.edu/amstud/inforev/riis/title.html

Yale University maintains this hypertext version of Jacob Riis's *How the Other Half Lives*, a classic 1890 study of tenement live in New York City. This hypertext version contains many of the original images of the Riis book.

http://lcweb.loc.gov/rr/print/070_immi.html

This Library of Congress exhibit is entitled: "Selected Images of Ellis Island and Immigration, ca. 1880–1920" from the Prints and Photographs Division and shows a dozen photographs of immigrants arriving at Ellis Island.

http://www.ilr.cornell.edu/trianglefire/

Cornell University has posted a comprehensive online history of the Triangle Waistshirt Company Fire (1911), which includes an unusually large collection of contemporary photographs, editorial cartoons, and documents.

Battle for the Lower East Side

Uniformed young women, part of the Visiting Nurse Service founded by Lillian Wald, leave the Henry Street Settlement for their rounds among tenement families of New York's Lower East Side. By the early 1900s the service was sending scores of trained nurses on tens of thousands of visits every year to provide health care for the poor.

SOURCE: ©Bettman/CORBIS.

When Lillian Wald opened the doors of the Henry Street Settlement House in 1893, the surrounding Lower East Side of New York was the poorest and most polyglot neighborhood in the city, as well as the most overcrowded quarter in the world. Settlement house workers dedicated themselves to helping recent immigrants and the working poor cope with lives scarred by poverty, disease, poor food, and dank tenements. Henry Street Settlement offered a variety of programs, including a free visiting nurse service, advice on cooking and child rearing, art classes, a theater, and a music school. Wald and other settlement house leaders soon saw that, in order to improve the miserable conditions they observed in their communities, they needed to get involved in larger political struggles to improve sanitation, health care, housing, and education. Henry Street Settlement often made common cause in these battles with some of the other political activists who flourished in the Lower East Side community, including socialists, anarchists, trade unionists, woman suffragists, socially conscious artists, and public health reformers.

Over most of the twentieth century the character of the Lower East Side remained fairly stable, though its dominant ethnic groups changed. By the 1950s the Italian, German, and Eastern European Jewish immigrants had largely moved away, while Puerto Ricans, Ukranians, and Asians poured in. But regardless of ethnicity, the neighborhood was still one of the city's poorest, and decent affordable housing remained difficult to get. Tens of thousands of poor working class people still lived in old, dilapidated nineteenth century tenements. The neighborhood's historic reputation as a center for political and cultural radicalism also attracted newcomers. Many Beat poets and jazz musicians settled there in the 1950s, and during the 1960s and 70s the area became a magnet for hippies, rock bands, and young runaways. Local concert halls like the Fillmore East and C.B.G.B.'s, cheap ethnic restaurants, funky clothing shops, and a flourishing drug culture also made the area something of a tourist attraction for young people from around the country and the world. Tompkins Square, a ten-acre park that provided the only swatch of green in the neighborhood, became a popular rallying point for anti-Vietnam War protest, the Black Panther Party, and other political causes.

But by the late 1980s two new groups appeared on the scene and their presence sparked tense debate over the historical legacy of the Lower East Side. Hundreds of homeless people began living in Tompkins Square Park, and hundreds of "squatters" occupied abandoned buildings in the surrounding blocks. The area's homeless represent only a small fraction of New York's total, estimated to be in the tens of thousands. At the same time, a wave of young urban professionals arrived, attracted by the downtown Manhattan location and old apartments newly renovated by real estate developers. Young couples expecting to enjoy the grassy park were afraid to walk near the grungy shantytown that had sprung up. "We've had an ongoing battle," said the Rev. George Kuhn of nearby St. Brigid's Church, "between the people who believe they are going to be displaced here and the people who are moving into the area." A loose coalition of neighborhood squatters, young radicals, artists, and punk rockers took up the cause of the homeless, defending their right to live in the park and attacking the influx of "yuppies." These protesters invoked the Lower East Side's historic traditions of tolerance and sympathy for the down and out. In the summer of 1988 the city announced it would enforce a 1 a.m. curfew in Tompkins Square Park, setting the stage for a violent confrontation. On August 7 over 400 riot equipped police swept through the park, forcibly removing the homeless colony, and clashing with hundreds of demonstrators. Throughout the night, angry protesters hurled bottles, fireworks, and insults as squads of policemen on horseback charged into crowds on nearby streets.

In the bitter aftermath of the riot, deep disagreements over the meaning of the neighborhood's history emerged. "We've always had a fairly diverse, progressive tradition," said Barbara Ingram who ran Children's Liberation daycare center and expressed support for the homeless. "It's something that everyone has tried to protect, because this community *is* different. In this neighborhood, people try to show concern for one another." Tom Calley, a 24 year-old artist and self-described anarchist, thought "this trouble in the park has been great. It's been a rallying point for people who once fought, like blacks and whites." "We can't ignore this problem any longer," argued another young political organizer. "The homeless shouldn't have been carted off, and a lot of activists are going to be demonstrating here this summer." But

Maryann Williams, who with her husband and young daughter had just moved to the neighborhood, spoke for many newcomers: "I sympathize with the homeless. I consider myself pro-homeless. But people don't have a right to live in the park. Isn't it supposed to be for everyone? Or am I crazy?" Some, like the neighborhood's City Councilman Antonio Pagan, denounced the protesters for "living out their revolutionary fantasies. They are white, middle class young people from the suburbs hiding behind the banner of helping the homeless." He noted that "poor and working people have not had access to that park," and he asked, "why should a poor, working class neighborhood serve as the burning torch of homelessness for the city of New York?" Edgy conflict continued for years. The city closed the park for renovations in 1991, once again removing hundreds of homeless. Mass evictions of squatters also continued, as did raucous, sometimes violent protests against these police actions.

Henry Street Settlement celebrated its centennial anniversary in 1993 with a giant street festival and parade. Its current community service programs include a battered women's shelter, a day-care facility, art education, and feeding the homeless. Like Lillian Wald and other settlement house pioneers, today's advocates for the poor insist on connecting their plight to policies made far away from the neighborhood. "The community is overwhelmed by the terrible problems of homelessness and drug abuse," declared the Lower East Side Planning Council, a coalition of churches and synagogues. "The lack of affordable housing is the major reason for this situation." Gentrification has meant skyrocketing rents for apartment dwellers and small businesses. A recent survey showed more than half the area's families pay over 30 percent of their income for housing, and two-thirds reported their apartments had some vital malfunction—no heat, hot water, or electricity. Grinding poverty remains a grim fact of life for much of the Lower East Side, where the median family income is only one-third the city average. The 1997 Broadway musical "Rent" became a smash hit by glamorizing the Lower East Side's roiling world of poverty, struggling artists, yuppie ambition, and escalating housing costs. But as one late 90s protester and longtime resident ironically noted, "Now, for the first time in the Lower East Side's history, the poor can't afford to live here." ▪

New York City police try to control an angry crowd of 400 protesters in Tompkins Square Park in August 1988. These demonstrators opposed the forcible removal of homeless people from the park, as well as the continuing "gentrification" of the surrounding Lower East Side neighborhood.

SOURCE: AP/Wide World Photos.

TWENTY-TWO

WORLD WAR I

▶ 1 9 1 4 – 1 9 2 0

CHAPTER OUTLINE

AMERICAN COMMUNITIES

Vigilante Justice in Bisbee, Arizona

EARLY IN THE MORNING OF JULY 12, 1917, 2,000 ARMED VIGILANTES swept through Bisbee, Arizona, acting on behalf of the Phelps-Dodge mining company and Bisbee's leading businessmen to break a bitter strike that had crippled Bisbee's booming copper industry. The vigilantes seized miners in their homes, on the street, and in restaurants and stores. Any miner who wasn't working or willing to work was herded into Bisbee's downtown plaza, where two machine guns commanded the scene. From the Plaza more than 2,000 were marched to the local baseball park. There mine managers gave them a last chance to return to work. Hundreds accepted and were released. The remaining 1,400 were forced at gunpoint onto a freight train, which took them 173 miles east to Columbus, New Mexico, where they were dumped in the desert.

The Bisbee deportation occurred against a complex backdrop. America had just entered World War I, corporations were seeking higher profits, and labor militancy was on the rise. Bisbee was only one of many American communities to suffer vigilantism during the war. Any number of offenses—not displaying a flag, failing to buy war bonds, criticizing the draft, alleged spying, any apparently "disloyal" behavior—could trigger vigilante action. In western communities like Bisbee, vigilantes used the superpatriotic mood to settle scores with labor organizers and radicals.

Arizona was the leading producer of copper in the United States. With a population of 8,000, Bisbee lay in the heart of the state's richest mining district. The giant Phelps-Dodge Company dominated Bisbee's political and social life. It owned the town's hospital, department store, newspaper, library, and largest hotel. With the introduction of new technology and open pit mining after 1900, unskilled laborers—most of them Slavic, Italian, Czech, and Mexican immigrants—had increasingly replaced skilled American and English-born miners in Bisbee's workforce.

America's entry into the war pushed the price of copper to an all-time high, prompting Phelps-Dodge to increase production. Miners viewed the increased demand for labor as an opportunity to flex their own muscle and improve wages and working conditions. Two rival union locals, one affiliated with the American Federation of Labor (AFL), the other with the more radical Industrial Workers of the World (IWW), or "Wobblies," sought to organize Bisbee's workers. On June 26, 1917, Bisbee's Wobblies went on strike. They demanded better mine safety, an end to discrimination against union workers, and a substantial pay increase. The IWW, making special efforts to attract lower-paid, foreign-born workers to their cause, even hired two Mexican organizers. Although the IWW had only 300 or 400 members in Bisbee, more than half the town's 4,700 miners supported the strike.

The walkout was peaceful, but Walter Douglas, district manager for Phelps-Dodge, was unmoved. "There will be no compromise," he declared, "because you cannot compromise with a rattlesnake." Douglas, Cochise County Sheriff Harry Wheeler, and Bisbee's leading businessmen met secretly to plan the July 12 deportation. The approximately 2,000 men they deputized to carry it out were members of Bisbee's Citizens' Protective League and the Workers Loyalty League. These vigilantes included company officials, small businessmen, professionals, and antiunion workers. Local telephone and telegraph offices agreed to isolate Bisbee by censoring outgoing messages. The El Paso and Southwestern Railroad, a subsidiary of Phelps-Dodge, provided the waiting boxcars.

The participants in this illegal conspiracy defended themselves by exaggerating the threat of organized labor. They also appealed to patriotism and played on racial fears. The IWW opposed American involvement in the war, making it vulnerable to charges of disloyalty. A proclamation, posted in Bisbee the day of the deportation, claimed, "There is no labor trouble—we are sure of that—but a direct attempt to embarrass and injure the government of the United States." Sheriff Wheeler told a visiting journalist he worried that Mexicans "would take advantage of the disturbed conditions of the strike and start an uprising, destroying the mines and murdering American women and children."

An army census of the deportees, who had found temporary refuge at an army camp in Columbus, New Mexico, offered quite a different picture. Of the 1,400 men, 520 owned property in Bisbee. Nearly 500 had already registered for the draft, and more than 200 had purchased Liberty Bonds. More than 400 were married with children; only 400 were members of the IWW. Eighty percent were immigrants, including nearly 400 Mexicans. A presidential mediation committee concluded that "conditions in Bisbee were in fact peaceful and free from manifestations of disorder or violence." The deported miners nonetheless found it difficult to shake the accusations that their strike was anti-American and foreign inspired.

At their camp, the miners organized their own police force and elected an executive committee to seek relief. In a letter to President Wilson, they claimed "Common American citizens here are now convinced that they have no constitutional rights." They promised to return to digging copper if the federal government operated the nation's mines and smelters. IWW leader William D. "Big Bill" Haywood threatened a general strike of metal miners and harvest workers if the government did not return the deportees to their homes. The presidential mediation committee criticized the mine companies and declared the deportation illegal. But it also denied that the federal government had any jurisdiction in the matter. Arizona's attorney general refused to offer protection for a return to Bisbee.

In September, the men began gradually to drift away from Columbus. Only a few ever returned to Bisbee. The events convinced President Wilson that the IWW was a subversive organization and a threat to national security. The Justice Department began planning an all-out legal assault that would soon cripple the Wobblies. But Wilson could not ignore protests against the Bisbee outrage from such prominent and patriotic Americans as Samuel Gompers, head of the American Federation of Labor. To demonstrate his administration's commitment to harmonious industrial relations, the president appointed a special commission to investigate and mediate wartime labor conflicts. But Arizona's mines would remain union free until the New Deal era of the 1930s.

America's entry into the war created a national sense of purpose and an unprecedented mobilization of resources. Unifying the country and winning the war now took precedence over progressive reforms. The war also aroused powerful political emotions and provided an excuse for some citizens to try to cleanse their communities of anyone who did not conform. In a 1918 speech, Arizona State Senator Fred Sutter hailed the benefits of vigilante justice. "And what are the results in Bisbee since the deportation?" he asked. "They are, sir, a practically 100 percent American camp; a foreigner to get a job there today had to give a pretty good account of himself. The mines are today producing more copper than ever before and we are a quiet, peaceful, law-abiding community and will continue so, so long as the IWWs or other enemies of the government let us alone." ■

Bisbee

KEY TOPICS

- America's expanding international role

- From neutrality to participation in the Great War

- Mobilizing the society and the economy for war

- Dissent and its repression

- Woodrow Wilson's failure to win the peace

BECOMING A WORLD POWER

Roosevelt: The Big Stick

Like many of his class and background, Theodore Roosevelt took for granted the superiority of Protestant Anglo-American culture and the goal of spreading its values and influence. He believed that to maintain and increase its economic and political stature, America must be militarily strong. In 1900 Roosevelt summarized his activist views, declaring, "I have always been fond of the West African proverb, 'Speak softly and carry a big stick, you will go far.'"

Roosevelt brought the "big stick" approach to several disputes in the Caribbean region. Since the 1880s, several British, French, and American companies had pursued various plans for building a canal across the Isthmus of Panama, thereby connecting the Atlantic and Pacific Oceans. Roosevelt tried to negotiate a leasing agreement with Colombia, of which Panama was a province. But when the Colombian Senate rejected a final American offer in the fall of 1903, Roosevelt invented a new strategy. A combination of native forces and foreign promoters associated with the canal project plotted a revolt against Colombia. Roosevelt kept in touch with at least one leader of the revolt, Philippe Bunau-Varilla, an engineer and agent for the New Panama Canal Company, and the president let him know that U.S. warships were steaming toward Panama.

On November 3, 1903, just as the USS *Nashville* arrived in Colón harbor, the province of Panama declared itself independent of Colombia. The United States immediately recognized the new Republic of Panama. Less than two weeks later, Bunau-Varilla, serving as a minister from Panama, signed a treaty granting the United States full sovereignty in perpetuity over a ten-mile-wide canal zone. America guaranteed Panama's independence and agreed to pay it $10 million initially and an additional $250,000 a year for the canal zone. Years after the canal was completed, the

U.S. Senate voted another $25 million to Colombia as compensation.

The Panama Canal was a triumph of modern engineering and gave the United States a tremendous strategic and commercial advantage in the Western Hemisphere. It took eight years to build and cost hundreds of poorly paid manual workers their lives. Several earlier attempts to build a canal in the region had failed. But with better equipment and a vigorous campaign against disease, the United States succeeded. In 1914, after $720 million in construction costs, the first merchant ships sailed through the canal.

"The inevitable effect of our building the Canal," wrote Secretary of State Elihu Root in 1905, "must be to require us to police the surrounding premises." Roosevelt agreed. He was especially concerned that European powers might step in if America did not. In 1903 Great Britain, Germany, and Italy had imposed a blockade on Venezuela in a dispute over debt payments owed to private investors. To prevent armed intervention by the Europeans, Roosevelt in 1904 proclaimed what became known as the Roosevelt Corollary to the Monroe Doctrine. "Chronic wrongdoing, or an impotence which results in a general loosening of the ties of civilized society," the statement read, justified "the exercise of an international police power" anywhere in the hemisphere. Roosevelt invoked the corollary to justify U.S. intervention in the region, beginning with the Dominican Republic in 1905. He and later presidents cited the corollary to justify armed intervention in the internal affairs of Cuba, Haiti, Nicaragua, and Mexico.

With the outbreak of the Russo–Japanese War in 1904, Roosevelt worried about the future of the Open Door policy in Asia. In 1899, in a series of diplomatic notes, Secretary of State John Hay had won approval for the so-called Open Door approach, giving all nations equal access to trading and development rights in China. A total victory by Russia or Japan could upset the balance of power in East Asia and threaten American business enterprises there. He became especially concerned after the Japanese scored a series of military victories over Russia and began to loom as a dominant power in East Asia.

Roosevelt mediated a settlement of the Russo-Japanese War at Portsmouth, New Hampshire, in 1905 (for which he was awarded the 1906 Nobel Peace Prize). In this settlement, Japan won recognition of its dominant position in Korea and consolidated its economic control over Manchuria. Yet repeated incidents of anti-Japanese racism in California kept American-Japanese relations strained.

Roosevelt built up American naval strength in the Pacific, and in 1908 he sent battleships to visit Japan in a muscle-flexing display of sea power. In that same year, the two burgeoning Pacific powers reached a reconciliation. The Root-Takahira Agreement affirmed the "existing status quo" in Asia, mutual respect for territorial possessions in the Pacific, and the Open Door trade policy in China.

Wilson: Moralism and Realism in Mexico

Right after he took office in 1913, President Wilson had to face international crises of a scope and complexity unprecedented in U.S. history. Wilson had no experience in diplomacy, but he brought to foreign affairs a set of fundamental principles that combined a moralist's faith in American democracy with a realist's understanding of the power of international commerce. He believed that American economic expansion, accompanied by democratic principles and Christianity, was a civilizing force in the world.

Wilson, like most corporate and political leaders of the day, emphasized foreign investments and industrial exports as the keys to the nation's prosperity. He believed that the United States, with its superior industrial efficiency, could achieve supremacy in world commerce if artificial barriers to free trade were removed. He championed and extended the Open Door principles of John Hay, advocating strong diplomatic and military measures "for making ourselves supreme in the world from an economic point of view." Wilson often couched his vision of a dynamic, expansive American capitalism in terms of a moral crusade. Yet he quickly found that the complex realities of power politics could interfere with moral vision.

Wilson's policies toward Mexico, which foreshadowed the problems he would encounter in World War I, best illustrate his difficulties. The 1911 Mexican Revolution had overthrown the brutally corrupt dictatorship of Porfirio Díaz, and popular leader Francisco Madero had won wide support by promising democracy and economic reform for millions of landless peasants. U.S. businessmen, however, were nervous about the future of their investments, which totaled over $1 billion, an amount greater than Mexico's own investment and more than all other foreign investment in that country combined. Wilson at first gave his blessing to the revolutionary movement, but right before he took office, he was stunned by the ousting and murder of Madero by his chief lieutenant, General Victoriano Huerta. Other nations, including Great Britain and Japan, recognized the Huerta regime, but Wilson refused. He announced that the United States would support only governments that rested on the rule of law. An armed faction opposed to Huerta, known as the Constitutionalists and led by Venustiano Carranza, emerged in northern Mexico. Both sides rejected an effort by Wilson to broker a compromise between

Mexican revolutionary leaders and sometime allies Francisco "Pancho" Villa (center) and Emiliano Zapata (right) are shown at the National Palace in Mexico City, ca. 1916. Zapata's army operated out of a base in the southern agricultural state of Morelos, while Villa's army controlled large portions of Mexico's north. In 1914 Villa captured the imagination of American reformers, journalists, and moviemakers with his military exploits against the oppressive Huerta regime. But in 1916, after several border clashes between his forces and U.S. military units, President Wilson dispatched a punitive expedition in pursuit of Villa.

SOURCE: Culver Pictures, Inc.

them. Carranza, an ardent nationalist, pressed for the right to buy U.S. arms, which he won in 1914. Wilson also isolated Huerta diplomatically by persuading the British to withdraw their support in exchange for American guarantees of English property interests in Mexico.

But Huerta stubbornly remained in power. In April 1914 Wilson used a minor insult to U.S. sailors in Tampico as an excuse to invade. American naval forces bombarded and then occupied Veracruz, the main port through which Huerta received arms shipments. Wilson accepted the offer of the ABC Powers—Argentina, Brazil, and Chile—to mediate the dispute. Huerta rejected a plan for him to step aside in favor of a provisional government. But then in August, Carranza managed to overthrow Huerta. Playing to nationalist sentiment, Carranza too denounced Wilson for his intervention.

As war loomed in Europe, Mexico's revolutionary politics continued to frustrate Wilson. For a brief period Wilson threw his support behind Francisco "Pancho" Villa, Carranza's former ally who now led a rebel army of his own in northen Mexico. But Carranza's forces dealt Villa a major setback in April 1915. In October, its attention focused on the war in Europe, the Wilson administration recognized Carranza as Mexico's de facto president. Meanwhile Pancho Villa, feeling betrayed, turned on the United States and tried to provoke a crisis that might draw Washington into war with Mexico. In 1916, Villa led several raids in Mexico and across the border into the United States that killed a few dozen Americans. The man once viewed by Wilson as a fighter for democracy was now dismissed as a dangerous bandit.

In March 1916, enraged by Villa's defiance, Wilson dispatched General John J. Pershing and an army that eventually numbered 15,000 to capture him. For a year, Pershing's troops chased Villa in vain, penetrating 300 miles into Mexico. The invasion made Villa a symbol of national resistance in Mexico. Skirmishes between American forces and Carranza's army brought the two nations to the brink of war again in June 1916. Wilson prepared a message to Congress asking permission for American troops to occupy all of northern Mexico. But he never delivered it. There was fierce opposition to war with Mexico throughout the country. Perhaps more important, mounting tensions with Germany caused Wilson to hesitate. He told an aide that "Germany is anxious to have us at war with Mexico, so that our minds and our energies will be taken off the great war across the sea." Wilson, thus, accepted negotiations by a face-saving international commission.

Wilson's attempt to guide the course of Mexico's revolution and protect U.S. interests left a bitter legacy of suspicion and distrust in Mexico. It also suggested the limits of a foreign policy tied to a moral vision rooted in the idea of American exceptionalism. Militarism and imperialism, Wilson had believed, were hallmarks of the old European way. American liberal values—rooted in capitalist development, democracy, and free trade—were the wave of the future. Wilson declared that he had no desire to interfere with Mexican sovereignty. But in both cases that is exactly what he did. The United States, he argued, must actively use its enormous moral and material power to create the new order. That principle would soon engage America in Europe's bloodiest war and its most momentous revolution.

THE GREAT WAR

The Guns of August

Only a complex and fragile system of alliances had kept the European powers at peace with each other since 1871. Two great competing camps had evolved by 1907: the Triple Alliance (also known as the Central Powers), which included Germany, Austria-Hungary, and Italy; and the Triple Entente (also known as the Allies), which included Great Britain, France, and Russia. At the heart of this division was the competition between Great Britain, long the world's dominant colonial and commercial power, and Germany, which had powerful aspirations for an empire of its own.

The alliance system managed to keep small conflicts from escalating into larger ones for most of the late nineteenth and early twentieth centuries. But its inclusiveness was also its weakness: the alliance system threatened to entangle many nations in any war that did erupt. On June 28, 1914, Archduke Franz Ferdinand, heir to the throne of the unstable Austro-Hungarian Empire, was assassinated in Sarajevo, Bosnia. The archduke's killer was a Serbian nationalist who believed the Austro-Hungarian province of Bosnia ought to be annexed to neighboring Serbia. Germany pushed Austria-Hungary to retaliate against Serbia, and the Serbians in turn asked Russia for help.

By early August both sides had exchanged declarations of war and begun mobilizing their forces. Germany invaded Belgium and prepared to move across the French border. But after the German armies were stopped at the River Marne in September, the war settled into a long, bloody stalemate. New and grimly efficient weapons, such as the machine gun and the tank, and the horrors of trench warfare meant unprecedented casualties for all involved. Centered in northern France, the fighting killed 5 million people over the next two and a half years.

American Neutrality

The outbreak of war in Europe shocked Americans. President Wilson issued a formal proclamation of neutrality and urged citizens to be "impartial in thought as well as in action."

Both sides bombarded the United States with vigorous propaganda campaigns. The British effectively exploited their bonds of language and heritage with Americans. Reports of looting, raping, and the killing of innocent civilians by German troops circulated widely in the press. Many of these atrocity stories were exaggerated. German propagandists blamed the war on Russian expansionism and France's desire to avenge its defeat by Germany in 1870–71. It is difficult to measure the impact of war propaganda on American public opinion. As a whole, though, it highlighted the terrible human costs of the war and, thus, strengthened the conviction that America should stay out of it.

Economic ties between the United States and the Allies were perhaps the greatest barrier to true neutrality. Early in the war Britain imposed a blockade on all shipping to Germany. The United States, as a neutral country, might have insisted on the right of nonbelligerents to trade with both sides, as required by international law. But in practice, although Wilson protested the blockade, he wanted to avoid antagonizing Britain and disrupting trade between the United States and the Allies. Trade with Germany all but ended while trade with the Allies increased dramatically. As war orders poured in from Britain and France, the value of American trade with the Allies shot up from $824 million in 1914 to $3.2 billion in 1916. Increased trade with the Allies helped produce a great economic boom at home, and the United States became neutral in name only.

Preparedness and Peace

In February 1915, Germany declared the waters around the British Isles to be a war zone, a policy that it would enforce with unrestricted submarine warfare. All enemy shipping, despite the requirements of international law to the contrary, would be subject to surprise submarine attack. Neutral powers were warned that the problems of identification at sea put their ships at risk.

On May 7, 1915, a German U-boat sank the British liner *Lusitania* off the coast of Ireland. Among the 1,198 people who died were 128 American citizens. The *Lusitania* was in fact secretly carrying war materials, and passengers had been warned about a possible attack. Wilson nevertheless denounced the sinking as illegal and inhuman, and the American press loudly condemned the act as barbaric. An angry exchange of diplomatic notes led Secretary of State William Jennings Bryan to resign in protest against a policy he thought too warlike.

Tensions heated up again in March 1916 when a German U-boat torpedoed the *Sussex*, an unarmed French passenger ship, injuring four Americans. President Wilson threatened to break off diplomatic relations with Germany unless it abandoned its methods of submarine warfare. Germany promised that all vessels would be visited prior to attack, but this crisis prompted Wilson to begin preparing for war. The National Security League, active in large eastern cities and bankrolled by conservative banking and commercial interests, helped push for a bigger army and navy and, most important, a system of universal military training. In June 1916, Congress passed the National Defense Act, which more than doubled the size of the regular army. In August, Congress passed a bill that dramatically increased spending for new battleships, cruisers, and destroyers.

Not all Americans supported these preparations for battle, and opposition to military buildup found expression in scores of American communities. As early as August 29, 1914, 1,500 women clad in black had marched down New York's Fifth Avenue in the Woman's Peace Parade. Out of this gathering evolved the American Union against Militarism, which lobbied against the preparedness campaign and against intervention in Mexico. Antiwar feeling was especially strong in the South and Midwest. A group of thirty to fifty House Democrats, led by majority leader Claude Kitchin of North Carolina, stubbornly opposed Wilson's military buildup.

A large reservoir of popular antiwar sentiment flowed through the culture in various ways. Movie director Thomas Ince won a huge audience for his 1916 film *Civilization*, which depicted Christ returning to reveal the horrors of war to world leaders. Two of the most popular songs of 1915 were "Don't Take My Darling Boy Away" and "I Didn't Raise My Boy to Be a Soldier."

Wilson acknowledged the active opposition to involvement in the war by adopting the winning slogan "He Kept Us Out of War" in the 1916 presidential campaign. He made a point of appealing to progressives of all kinds, stressing his support for the eight-hour day and his administration's efforts on behalf of farmers. The war-induced prosperity no doubt helped him to defeat conservative Republican Charles Evans Hughes in a very close election. But Wilson knew that the peace was as fragile as his victory.

Safe for Democracy

By the end of January 1917, Germany's leaders had decided against a negotiated peace settlement, placing their hopes instead in a final decisive offensive against the Allies. On February 1, 1917, with the aim of breaking the British blockade, Germany declared unlimited submarine warfare, with no warnings, knowing that it might bring America into the conflict. In effect, German leaders were gambling that they could destroy the ability of the Allies to fight before the United States would be able to effectively mobilize manpower and resources.

Wilson was indignant and disappointed. Germany had made it impossible for him to preserve his twin goals of U.S. neutrality and freedom of the seas. He broke off diplomatic relations with Germany and called on Congress to approve the arming of U.S. merchant ships. On March 1, the White House shocked the country when it made public a recently intercepted coded message, sent by German foreign secretary Arthur Zimmermann to the German ambassador in Mexico. The Zimmermann note proposed that an alliance be made between Germany and Mexico if the United States entered the war. Zimmermann suggested that Mexico take up arms against the United States and receive in return the "lost territory in New Mexico, Texas, and Arizona." The specter of a German-Mexican alliance helped turn the tide of public opinion in the Southwest, where opposition to U.S. involvement in the war had been strong.

Revelation of the Zimmermann note stiffened Wilson's resolve. He issued an executive order in mid-March authorizing the arming of all merchant ships and allowing them to shoot at submarines. In that month, German U-boats sank seven U.S. merchant ships, leaving a heavy death toll. Anti-German feeling increased, and thousands took part in prowar demonstrations in New York, Boston, Philadelphia, and other cities. Wilson finally called a special session of Congress to ask for a declaration of war.

On April 2, on a rainy night before a packed and very quiet assembly, Wilson made his case. He reviewed the escalation of submarine warfare and said that neutrality was no longer feasible or desirable. But the conflict was not merely about U.S. shipping rights, Wilson argued. He employed highly idealistic language to make the case for war, reflecting his deeply held belief that America had a special mission as mankind's most enlightened and advanced nation: "The world must be made safe for democracy. Its peace must be planted upon the tested foundations of political liberty."

Wilson's eloquent speech won over the Congress, most of the press, and even his bitterest political critics, such as Theodore Roosevelt. On April 6, President Wilson signed the declaration of war. All that remained was to win over the American public.

AMERICAN MOBILIZATION

Selling the War

Just a week after signing the war declaration, Wilson created the Committee on Public Information (CPI) to organize public opinion. It was dominated by its civilian chairman, the journalist and reformer George Creel. Creel quickly transformed the CPI from its original function as coordinator of government news into a sophisticated and aggressive agency for promoting the war. To sell the war, Creel raised the art of public relations to new heights. He enlisted more than 150,000 people to work on a score of CPI committees. They produced more than 100 million pieces of literature—pamphlets, articles, books—that explained the causes and meaning of the war. The CPI also created posters, slides, newspaper advertising, and films to promote the war. It called upon movie stars such as Charlie Chaplin, Mary Pickford, and Douglas Fairbanks to help sell war bonds at huge rallies. Famous journalists like the muckraker Ida Tarbell and well-known artists like Charles Dana Gibson were recruited. Across the nation, a volunteer army of 75,000 "Four Minute Men" gave brief patriotic speeches before stage and movie shows.

The CPI led an aggressively negative campaign against all things German. Posters and advertisements depicted the Germans as Huns, bestial monsters outside the civilized world. German music and literature, indeed the German language itself, were suspect, and were banished from the concert halls, schools, and libraries of many communities. The CPI also urged ethnic Americans to abandon their Old World ties, to become "unhyphenated Americans."

"You're in the Army Now"

Traditionally, the United States had relied on volunteer forces organized at the state level. But volunteer rates after April 6 were less than they had been for the Civil War or the Spanish-American War, reflecting the softness of prowar sentiment. The administration, thus, introduced the Selective Service Act, which provided for the registration and classification for military service of all men between ages twenty-one and thirty-five. To prevent the widespread opposition to the draft that had occurred during the Civil War, the new draft had no unpopular provision allowing draftees to buy their way out of service by paying for a substitute.

On June 5, 1917, nearly 10 million men registered for the draft. There was scattered organized resistance, but overall, registration records offered evidence of national support. A supplemental registration in August 1918 extended the age limits to eighteen and forty-five. Of the 2.8 million men eventually called up for service, about 340,000, or 12 percent, failed to show up. Another 2 million Americans volunteered for the various armed services.

The vast polyglot army posed unprecedented challenges of organization and control. But progressive elements within the administration also saw opportunities for pressing reform measures involving education, alcohol, and sex. Army psychologists gave the new Stanford-Binet intelligence test to all recruits and were shocked to find illiteracy rates as high as 25 percent. The low test scores among recent immigrants and rural African Americans undoubtedly reflected the cultural biases embedded in the tests.

African Americans were organized into totally segregated units, barred entirely from the marines and the Coast Guard, and largely relegated to working as cooks, laundrymen, stevedores, and the like in the army and navy. Thousands of black soldiers endured humiliating, sometimes violent treatment, particularly from southern white officers. African American servicemen faced hostility from white civilians as well, North and South, often being denied service in restaurants and admission to theaters near training camps.

More than 200,000 African Americans eventually served in France, but only about one in five saw combat, as opposed to two out of three white soldiers. Black combat units served with distinction in various divisions of the French army. The all-black 369th U.S. Infantry, for example, saw the first and longest service of any American regiment deployed in a foreign army, serving in the trenches for 191 days. The French government awarded the Croix de Guerre to the entire regiment, and 171 officers and enlisted men were cited individually for exceptional bravery in action. African American soldiers by and large enjoyed a friendly reception from French civilians as well. The contrast with their treatment at home would remain a sore point with these troops upon their return to the United States.

Americans in Battle

Shipping tonnage lost each month to submarine warfare had been reduced to 200,000; the flow of weapons, supplies, and troops continued. No American soldiers were lost on the way to Europe.

President Wilson appointed General John J. Pershing, recently returned from pursuing Pancho Villa in Mexico, as commander of the American Expeditionary Force (AEF). Pershing insisted that the AEF maintain its own identity, distinct from that of the French and British armies. He was also reluctant to send American troops into battle before they had received at least six months' training. The AEF's combat role would be brief but intense: not until early 1918 did AEF units reach the front in large numbers; eight months later the war was over.

In the early spring of 1918 the Germans launched a major offensive that brought them within fifty miles of Paris. In early June about 70,000 AEF soldiers helped the French stop the Germans in the battles of Château-Thierry and Belleau Wood. In July, Allied forces led by Marshal Ferdinand Foch of France, began a counteroffensive designed to defeat Germany once and for all. American reinforcements began flooding the ports of Liverpool in England and Brest and Saint-Nazaire in France. The "doughboys" (a nickname for soldiers dating back to Civil War–era recruits who joined the army for the money) streamed in at a rate of over 250,000 a month. By September, General Pershing had more than a million Americans in his army.

In late September 1918, the AEF took over the southern part of a 200-mile front in the Meuse-Argonne offensive. In seven weeks of fighting, most through terrible mud and rain, U.S. soldiers used more ammunition than the entire Union army had in the four years of the Civil War. The Germans, exhausted and badly outnumbered, began to fall back and look for a ceasefire. On November 11, 1918, the war ended with the signing of an armistice.

The massive influx of American troops and supplies no doubt hastened the end of the war. About two-thirds

African American troops advance toward the sound of gunfire in northern France, 1918. Nearly 400,000 black men served in World War I, but due to the racist beliefs held by most military and political leaders, only 42,000 went into combat. "Many of the white field officers," wrote black Lieutenant Howard H. Long, "seemed far more concerned with reminding their Negro subordinates that they were Negroes than they were in having an effective unit that would perform well in combat."

SOURCE: Brown Brothers.

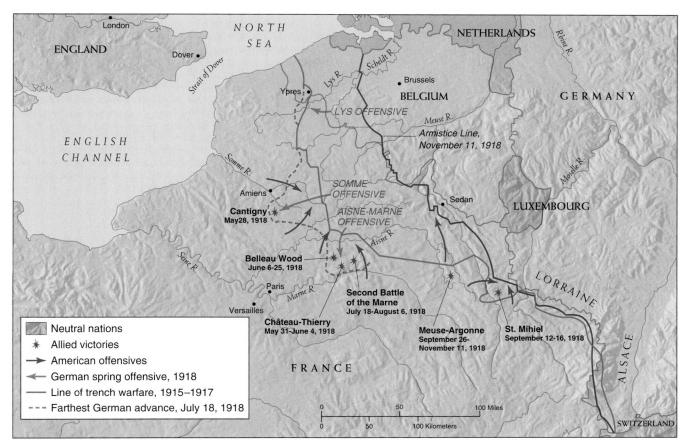

The Western Front, 1918   American units saw their first substantial action in late May, helping to stop the German offensive at the Battle of Cantigny. By September, more than 1 million American troops were fighting in a counteroffensive campaign at St. Mihiel, the largest single American engagement of the war.

of the U.S. soldiers saw at least some fighting, but even they managed to avoid the horrors of the sustained trench warfare that had marked the earlier years of the war. For most Americans at the front, the war experience was a mixture of fear, exhaustion, and fatigue. Their time in France would remain a decisive moment in their lives. In all, more than 52,000 Americans died in battle. Another 60,000 died from influenza and pneumonia, half of these while still in training camp. More than 200,000 Americans were wounded in the war. These figures, awful as they were, paled against the estimated casualties (killed and wounded) suffered by the European nations: 9 million for Russia, more than 6 million for Germany, nearly 5 million for France, and over 2 million each for Great Britain and Italy.

OVER HERE

Organizing the Economy

In the summer of 1917 President Wilson established the War Industries Board (WIB) as a clearinghouse for industrial mobilization to support the war effort. Led by the successful Wall Street speculator Bernard M.

Baruch, the WIB proved a major innovation in expanding the regulatory power of the federal government. The WIB had to balance price controls against war profits. Only by ensuring a fair rate of return on investment could it encourage stepped-up production.

The WIB eventually handled 3,000 contracts worth $14.5 billion with various businesses. Standardization of goods brought large savings and streamlined production. Baruch continually negotiated with business leaders, describing the system as "voluntary cooperation with the big stick in the cupboard." At first Elbert Gary of U.S. Steel refused to accept the government's price for steel and Henry Ford balked at limiting private car production. But when Baruch warned that he would instruct the military to take over their plants, both industrialists backed down.

In August 1917, Congress passed the Food and Fuel Act, authorizing the president to regulate the production and distribution of the food and fuel necessary for the war effort. To lead the Food Administration (FA), Wilson appointed Herbert Hoover, a millionaire engineer who had already won fame for directing a program of war relief for Belgium. He became one of the best-known figures of the war administration.

Hoover imposed price controls on certain agricultural commodities, such as sugar, pork, and wheat. These were purchased by the government and then sold to the public through licensed dealers. The FA also raised the purchase price of grain so that farmers would increase production. But Hoover stopped short of imposing mandatory food rationing, preferring to rely on persuasion, high prices, and voluntary controls.

Hoover's success, like George Creel's at the CPI, depended on motivating hundreds of thousands of volunteers in thousands of American communities. The FA coordinated the work of local committees that distributed posters and leaflets urging people to save food, recycle scraps, and substitute for scarce produce. Hoover exhorted Americans to "go back to simple food, simple clothes, simple pleasures." He urged them to grow their own vegetables. These efforts resulted in a sharp cutback in the consumption of sugar and wheat as well as a boost in the supply of livestock. The resultant increase in food exports helped sustain the Allied war effort.

The enormous cost of fighting the war, about $33 billion, required unprecedentedly large expenditures for the federal government. The tax structure shifted dramatically as a result. Taxes on incomes and profits replaced excise and customs levies as the major source of revenue. The minimum income subject to the graduated federal income tax, in effect only since 1913, was lowered to $1,000 from $3,000, increasing the number of Americans who paid income tax from 437,000 in 1916 to 4,425,000 in 1918. Tax rates were as steep as 70 percent in the highest brackets.

The bulk of war financing came from government borrowing, especially in the form of the popular Liberty Bonds sold to the American public. Bond drives became highly organized patriotic campaigns that ultimately raised a total of $23 billion for the war effort. The administration also used the new Federal Reserve Banks to expand the money supply, making borrowing easier. The federal debt jumped from $1 billion in 1915 to $20 billion in 1920.

The Business of War

Over all, the war meant expansion and high profits for American business. Between 1916 and 1918, Ford Motor Company increased its workforce from 32,000 to 48,000, General Motors from 10,000 to 50,000. Total capital expenditure in U.S. manufacturing jumped from $600 million in 1915 to $2.5 billion in 1918. Corporate profits as a whole nearly tripled between 1914 and 1919, and many large businesses did much better than that. Expanded farm acreage and increased investment in farm machinery led to a jump of 20–30 percent in overall farm production.

The most important and long-lasting economic legacy of the war was the organizational shift toward corporatism in American business. Never before had business and the federal government cooperated so closely. Under war administrators like Baruch and Hoover, entire industries (such as radio manufacturing) and economic sectors (such as agriculture and energy) were organized, regulated, and subsidized. War agencies used both public and private power—legal authority and voluntarism—to hammer out and enforce agreements. Here was the genesis of the modern bureaucratic state.

Labor and the War

The expansion of the wartime economy often meant severe disruptions and discomfort for America's workers. Overcrowding, rapid workforce turnover, and high inflation rates were typical in war-boom communities. In Bridgeport, Connecticut, a center for small-arms manufacturing, the population grew by 50,000 in less than a year. In 1917 the number of families grew by 12,000, but available housing stock increased by only 6,000 units. Chronic congestion became common in many cities.

That same economic expansion, combined with army mobilization and a decline in immigration from Europe, caused a growing wartime labor shortage, so that working people generally enjoyed higher wages and a better standard of living. Trade unions, especially those affiliated with the American Federation of Labor (AFL), enjoyed a sharp rise in membership.

Organized labor's power and prestige, though by no means equal to business's or government's, clearly grew during the war. Samuel Gompers, president of the AFL, pledged the AFL's patriotic support for the war effort, and in April 1918 President Wilson appointed him to the National War Labor Board (NWLB). During 1917 the nation had seen thousands of strikes involving more than a million workers. Wages were usually at issue, reflecting workers' concerns with spiraling inflation and higher prices. The NWLB, co-chaired by labor attorney Frank Walsh and former president William H. Taft, acted as a kind of supreme court for labor, arbitrating disputes and working to prevent disruptions in production. The great majority of these interventions resulted in improved wages and reduced hours of work.

Most important, the NWLB supported the right of workers to organize unions and furthered the acceptance of the eight-hour day for war workers—central aims of the labor movement. It also backed time-and-a-half pay for overtime, as well as the principle of equal pay for women workers. AFL unions gained more than a million new members during the war, and overall union membership rose from 2.7 million in 1914 to more than 5 million by 1920.

If the war boosted the fortunes of the AFL, it also spelled the end for more radical elements of the U.S. labor movement. The Industrial Workers of the World (IWW), unlike the AFL, had concentrated on organizing unskilled workers into all-inclusive industrial unions. The Wobblies denounced capitalism as an unreformable system based on exploitation, and they opposed U.S. entry into the war. IWW leaders advised their members to refuse induction for "the capitalists' war." In September 1917, the Wilson administration responded to appeals from western business leaders for a crackdown on the Wobblies. Justice Department agents, acting under the broad authority of the recently passed Espionage Act, swooped down on IWW offices in more than sixty towns and cities, arresting more than 300 people and confiscating files. The mass trials and convictions that followed broke the back of America's radical labor movement and marked the beginning of a powerful wave of political repression.

Women at Work

For many of the 8 million women already in the labor force, the war meant a chance to switch from low-paying jobs, such as domestic service, to higher-paying industrial employment. About a million women workers joined the labor force for the first time. Of the estimated 9.4 million workers directly engaged in war work, some 2.25 million were women. Of these, 1.25 million worked in manufacturing. Female munitions plant workers, train engineers, drill press operators, streetcar conductors, and mail carriers became a common sight around the country.

In response to the widened range of female employment, the Labor Department created the Women in Industry Service (WIS). Directed by Mary Van Kleeck, the service advised employers on using female labor and formulated general standards for the treatment of women workers. The WIS represented the first attempt by the federal government to take a practical stand on improving working conditions for women. Its standards included the eight-hour day, equal pay for equal work, a minimum wage, the prohibition of night work, and the provision of rest periods, meal breaks, and restroom facilities. These standards had no legal force, however, and WIS inspectors found that employers often flouted them. Women also suffered discrimination over pay. Government surveys found that women's average earnings were roughly half of men's in the same industries.

At war's end, women lost nearly all their defense-related jobs. By 1920, more women who worked outside the home did so in white-collar occupations—as telephone operators, secretaries, and clerks, for example—than in manufacturing or domestic service. The new

awareness of women's work led Congress to create the Women's Bureau in the Labor Department, which continued the WIS wartime program of education and investigation through the postwar years.

Woman Suffrage

The presence of so many new women wageworkers, combined with the highly visible volunteer work of millions of middle-class women, helped finally to secure the vote for women. These women played a key role in the success of the Food Administration, and the Women's Committee of the Council of National Defense included a variety of women's organizations.

Until World War I, the fight for woman suffrage had been waged largely within individual states. Western states and territories had led the way. Ethnocultural divisions between Catholics and Protestants hindered suffrage efforts in the East. The close identification in the East between the suffrage and prohibition movements led many Catholic immigrants and German Lutherans to oppose the vote for women because they feared it would lead to prohibition.

The U.S. entry into the war provided a unique opportunity for suffrage groups to shift their strategy to a national campaign for a constitutional amendment

Members of the National Woman's Party picketed President Wilson at the White House in 1917. Their militant action in the midst of the war crisis aroused both anger and sympathy. The NWP campaign helped push the president and the Congress to accept woman suffrage as a "war measure."

SOURCE: Library of Congress.

granting the vote to women. Under the leadership of Carrie Chapman Catt, the National American Woman Suffrage Association.(NAWSA) threw its support behind the war effort and doubled its membership to 2 million. Catt gambled that a strong show of patriotism would help clinch the century-old fight to win the vote for women. The NAWSA pursued a moderate policy of lobbying Congress for a constitutional amendment and calling for state referendums on woman suffrage.

A young Quaker activist, Alice Paul, injected new energy and more radical tactics into the movement. Dissatisfied with the NAWSA's conservative strategy of quiet lobbying and orderly demonstrations, Paul joined forces with western women voters to form the National Woman's Party. Borrowing from English suffragists, this party pursued a more aggressive and dramatic strategy of agitation. Paul and her supporters picketed the White House, publicly burned President Wilson's speeches, and condemned the president and the Democrats for failing to produce an amendment. Although some in the NAWSA objected to these tactics, Paul's radical approach helped make the NAWSA position—passage of the woman suffrage amendment as a "war measure"—more acceptable to Wilson. In 1917 the president urged Congress to pass a woman suffrage amendment as "vital to the winning of the war." The House did so in January 1918 and a more reluctant Senate approved it in June 1919. Another year of hard work was spent convincing the state legislatures. In August 1920, Tennessee gave the final vote needed to ratify the Nineteenth Amendment to the Constitution, finally making woman suffrage legal nationwide.

Prohibition

Another reform effort closely associated with women's groups triumphed at the same time. The movement to eliminate alcohol from American life had attracted many Americans, especially women, since before the Civil War. Temperance advocates saw drinking as the source of many of the worst problems faced by the working class, including family violence, unemployment, and poverty. By the early twentieth century the Woman's Christian Temperance Union, with a quarter-million members, had become the single largest women's organization in American history.

The moral fervor that accompanied America's entry into the war provided a crucial boost to the cause. With so many breweries bearing German names, the movement benefited as well from the strong anti-German feeling of the war years. Outlawing beer and whiskey would also help to conserve precious grain, prohibitionists argued.

In 1917, a coalition of progressives and rural fundamentalists in Congress pushed through a constitutional amendment providing for a national ban on alcoholic drinks. The Eighteenth Amendment was ratified by the states in January 1919 and became the law of the land one year later. Although Prohibition would create a host of problems in the postwar years, especially as a stimulus for the growth of organized crime, many Americans, particularly native Protestants, considered it a worthy moral reform.

REPRESSION AND REACTION

Muzzling Dissent: The Espionage and Sedition Acts

The Espionage Act of June 1917 became the government's key tool for the suppression of antiwar sentiment. It set severe penalties (up to twenty years' imprisonment and a $10,000 fine) for anyone found guilty of aiding the enemy, obstructing recruitment, or causing insubordination in the armed forces. The act also empowered the postmaster general to exclude from the mails any newspapers or magazines he thought treasonous. Within a year the mailing rights of forty-five newpapers had been revoked.

To enforce the Espionage Act, the government had to increase its overall police and surveillance machinery. Civilian intelligence was coordinated by the newly created Bureau of Investigation in the Justice Department. This agency was reorganized after the war as the Federal Bureau of Investigation (FBI). In May 1918 the Sedition Act, an amendment to the Espionage Act, outlawed "any disloyal, profane, scurrilous, or abusive language intended to cause contempt, scorn, contumely, or disrepute" to the government, Constitution, or flag.

These acts became a convenient vehicle for striking out at socialists, pacifists, radical labor activists, and others who resisted the patriotic tide. The most celebrated prosecution came in June 1918 when federal agents arrested Eugene V. Debs in Canton, Ohio, after he gave a speech defending antiwar protesters. Debs served thirty-two months in federal prison before being pardoned by President Warren G. Harding on Christmas Day 1921.

The Supreme Court upheld the constitutionality of the acts in several 1919 decisions. In *Debs* v. *United States*, the Court affirmed the guilt of Eugene V. Debs for his antiwar speech in Canton, even though he had not explicitly urged violation of the draft laws. In *Abrams* v. *United States*, the Court upheld Sedition Act convictions of four Russian immigrants who had printed pamphlets denouncing American military intervention in the Russian Revolution.

The Great Migration and Racial Tensions

Economic opportunity brought on by war prosperity triggered a massive migration of rural black Southerners to northern cities. From 1914 to 1920, somewhere between 300,000 and 500,000 African Americans left the rural South for the North. Chicago's black population increased by 65,000, or 150 percent; Detroit's by 35,000, or 600 percent. Acute labor shortages led northern factory managers to recruit black migrants to the expanding industrial centers. The Pennsylvania Railroad alone drew 10,000 black workers from Florida and south Georgia. Black workers eagerly left low-paying jobs as field hands and domestic servants for the chance at relatively high-paying work in meatpacking plants, shipyards, and steel mills.

Kinship and community networks were crucial in shaping what came to be called the Great Migration. They spread news about job openings, urban residential districts, and boardinghouses in northern cities. Black clubs, churches, and fraternal lodges in southern communities frequently sponsored the migration of their members, as well as return trips to the South. Single African American women often made the trip first because they could more easily obtain steady work as maids, cooks, and laundresses. Relatively few African American men actually secured high-paying skilled jobs in industry or manufacturing. Most had to settle for work as construction laborers, teamsters, janitors, porters, or other low-paying jobs.

The persistence of lynching and other racial violence in the South no doubt contributed to the Great Migration. But racial violence was not limited to the South. On July 2, 1917, in East St. Louis, Illinois, a ferocious mob of whites attacked African Americans, killing at least 200. Before this riot, some of the city's manufacturers had been steadily recruiting black labor as a way to keep local union demands down. In Chicago, on July 27, 1919, antiblack rioting broke out on a Lake Michigan beach. For two weeks white gangs hunted African Americans in the streets and burned hundreds out of their homes. Twenty-three African Americans and fifteen whites died, and more than 500 were injured.

In both East St. Louis and Chicago, local authorities held African Americans responsible for the violence. President Wilson refused requests for federal intervention or investigation.

Black disillusionment about the war grew quickly. So did a newly militant spirit. A heightened sense of race consciousness and activism was evident among black veterans and the growing black communities of northern cities. Taking the lead in the fight against bigotry and injustice, the NAACP held a national conference in 1919 on lynching. It pledged to defend persecuted African Americans, publicize the horrors of lynch law, and seek federal legislation against "Judge Lynch." By 1919 membership in the NAACP had reached 60,000 and the circulation of its journal exceeded half a million.

Labor Strife

The relative labor peace of 1917 and 1918 dissolved after the armistice. More than 4 million American workers were involved in some 3,600 strikes in 1919 alone. This unprecedented strike wave had several causes. Most of the modest wartime wage gains were wiped out by spiraling inflation and high prices for food, fuel, and housing. With the end of government controls on industry, many employers withdrew their recognition of unions. Difficult working conditions, such as the twelve-hour day in steel mills, were still routine in some industries.

Several of the postwar strikes received widespread national attention. They seemed to be more than simple economic conflicts, and they provoked deep fears about the larger social order. In February 1919, a strike

THE GREAT MIGRATION: BLACK POPULATION GROWTH IN SELECTED NORTHERN CITIES, 1910–1920					
	1910		1920		
City	No.	Percent	No.	Percent	Percent Increase
New York	91,709	1.9%	152,467	2.7%	66.3%
Chicago	44,103	2.0	109,458	4.1	148.2
Philadelphia	84,459	5.5	134,229	7.4	58.9
Detroit	5,741	1.2	40,838	4.1	611.3
St. Louis	43,960	6.4	69,854	9.0	58.9
Cleveland	8,448	1.5	34,451	4.3	307.8
Pittsburgh	25,623	4.8	37,725	6.4	47.2
Cincinnati	19,739	5.4	30,079	7.5	53.2

SOURCE: U.S. Department of Commerce.

in the shipyards of Seattle, Washington, over wages escalated into a general citywide strike involving 60,000 workers. The local press and Mayor Ole Hanson denounced the strikers as revolutionaries. Hanson effectively ended the strike by requesting federal troops to occupy the city.

In September, Boston policemen went out on strike when the police commissioner rejected a citizens' commission study that recommended a pay raise. Massachusetts governor Calvin Coolidge called in the National Guard to restore order and won a national reputation by crushing the strike. The entire police force was fired.

The biggest strike took place in the steel industry, involving some 350,000 steelworkers. Centered in several midwestern cities, this epic struggle lasted from September 1919 to January 1920. The major demands were union recognition, the eight-hour day, and wage increases. The steel companies used black strikebreakers and armed guards to keep the mills running. Elbert Gary, president of U.S. Steel, directed a sophisticated propaganda campaign that branded the strikers as revolutionaries. Public opinion turned against the strike and condoned the use of state and federal troops to break it. The failed steel strike proved to be the era's most bitter and devastating defeat for organized labor.

AN UNEASY PEACE

The Fourteen Points

President Wilson arrived in Paris with the United States delegation in January 1919. He brought with him a plan for peace that he had outlined a year earlier in a speech to Congress on U.S. war aims. The Fourteen Points, as they were called, had originally served wartime purposes: to appeal to antiwar factions in Austria-Hungary and Germany, to convince Russia to stay in the war, and to help sustain Allied morale. As a blueprint for peace, they contained three main elements. First, Wilson offered a series of specific proposals for setting postwar boundaries in Europe and creating new countries out of the collapsed Austro-Hungarian and Ottoman empires. Second, Wilson listed general principles for governing international conduct, including freedom of the seas, free trade, open covenants instead of secret treaties, reduced armaments, and mediation for competing colonial claims. Third, and most important, Wilson called for a League of Nations to help implement these principles and resolve future disputes.

The most controversial element, both at home and abroad, would prove to be the League of Nations, whose covenant called for collective security as the ultimate method of keeping the peace. In the United States, Wilson's critics focused on this provision as an unacceptable surrender of the nation's sovereignty and independence in foreign affairs.

Wilson in Paris

Despite Wilson's devotion to "open covenants," much of the negotiating at Versailles was in fact done in secret among the Big Four: Great Britain, France, the United States and Italy. The ideal of self-determination found limited expression. The independent states of Austria, Hungary, Poland, Yugoslavia, and Czechoslovakia were carved out of the homelands of the beaten Central Powers. But the Allies resisted Wilson's call for independence for the colonies of the defeated nations. A compromise mandate system of protectorates gave the French and British control of parts of the old German and Turkish empires in Africa and West Asia. Japan won control of former German colonies in China. Among those trying, but failing, to influence the treaty negotiations were the sixty-odd delegates to the first Pan African Congress, held in Paris at the same time as the peace talks. The group included Americans W. E. B. Du Bois and William Monroe

Woodrow Wilson, Georges Clemenceau, and David Lloyd George are among the central figures depicted in John Christen Johansen's *Signing of the Treaty of Versailles*. But all the gathered statesmen appear dwarfed by their surroundings.

SOURCE: John Christen Johansen, *Signing of the Treaty of Versailles*, 1919. National Portrait Gallery, Smithsonian Institution, Washington, D.C./Art Resource, New York.

Trotter as well as representatives from Africa and the West Indies. All were disappointed with the failure of the peace conference to grant self-determination to thousands of Africans living in former German colonies.

Another disappointment for Wilson came with the issue of war guilt. He had strongly opposed the extraction of harsh economic reparations from the Central Powers. But the French and British, with their awful war losses fresh in mind, insisted on making Germany pay. The final treaty contained a clause attributing the war to "the aggression of Germany," and a commission later set German war reparations at $33 billion. Bitter resentment in Germany over the punitive treaty helped sow the seeds for the Nazi rise to power in the 1930s.

Hovering over the proceedings was the specter of the Russian Revolution. The repressive and corrupt regime of Czar Nicholas II had been overthrown in March 1917 by a coalition of forces demanding change. The new provisional government, headed by Alexander Kerensky, vowed to keep Russia in the fight against Germany. But the war had taken a terrible toll on Russian soldiers and civilians, and had become very unpopular. The radical Bolsheviks, led by V. I. Lenin, gained a large following by promising "peace, land, and bread," and they began plotting to seize power. The Bolsheviks followed the teachings of German revolutionary Karl Marx, emphasizing the inevitability of class struggle and the replacement of capitalism by communism. In November 1917 the Bolsheviks took control of the Russian government.

The final treaty was signed on June 28, 1919, in the Hall of Mirrors at the Versailles palace. The Germans had no choice but to accept its harsh terms. President Wilson had been disappointed by the secret deals and the endless compromising of his ideals, no doubt underestimating the stubborn reality of power politics in the wake of Europe's most devastating war. He had nonetheless won a commitment to the League of Nations, the centerpiece of his plan, and he was confident that the American people would accept the treaty. The tougher fight would be with the Senate, where a two-thirds vote was needed for ratification.

The Treaty Fight

Preoccupied with peace conference politics in Paris, Wilson had neglected politics at home. His troubles had actually started earlier. Republicans had captured both the House and the Senate in the 1918 elections. Wilson had then made a tactical error by including no prominent Republicans in the U.S. peace delegation. He, therefore, faced a variety of tough opponents to the treaty he brought home.

Wilson's most extreme enemies in the Senate were a group of about sixteen "irreconcilables," opposed to a treaty in any form. Some were isolationist progressives, who opposed the League of Nations as steadfastly as they opposed American entry into the war. Others were racist xenophobes.

The less dogmatic but more influential opponents were led by Republican Henry Cabot Lodge of Massachusetts, powerful majority leader of the Senate. They had strong reservations about the League of Nations, especially the provisions for collective security in the event of a member nation's being attacked. Lodge argued that this provision impinged on congressional authority to declare war and placed unacceptable restraints on the nation's ability to pursue an independent foreign policy. Lodge proposed a series of amendments that would have weakened the League. But Wilson refused to compromise, motivated in part by the long-standing hatred he and Lodge felt toward each other.

In September, Wilson set out on a speaking tour across the country to drum up support for the League and the treaty. The crowds were large and responsive, but they did not change any votes in the Senate. The strain took its toll. On September 25, after speaking in Pueblo, Colorado, the sixty-three-year-old Wilson collapsed from exhaustion. His doctor canceled the rest of the trip. A week later, back in Washington, the president suffered a stroke that left him partially paralyzed. In November, Lodge brought the treaty out of committee for a vote, having appended to it fourteen reservations—that is, recommended changes. A bedridden Wilson stubbornly refused to compromise and instructed Democrats to vote against the Lodge version of the treaty. On November 19, Democrats joined with the "irreconcilables" to defeat the amended treaty, 39 to 55.

Wilson refused to budge. In January, he urged Democrats to either stand by the original treaty or vote it down. The 1920 election, he warned, would be "a great and solemn referendum" on the whole issue. In the final vote, on March 19, 1920, twenty-one Democrats broke with the president and voted for the Lodge version, giving it a majority of 49 to 35. But this was seven votes short of the two-thirds needed for ratification. As a result, the United States never signed the Versailles Treaty, nor did it join the League of Nations. The absence of the United States weakened the League and made it more difficult for the organization to realize Wilson's dream of a peaceful community of nations.

The Red Scare

The revolutionary changes taking place in Russia became an important backdrop for domestic politics. In the United States it became common to blame socialism, the IWW, and trade unionism in general on foreign radicals and alien ideologies. The accusation of Bolshevism became a powerful weapon for turning public opinion against strikers and political dissenters of all kinds.

In fact, by 1919 the American radicals were already weakened and badly split. The Socialist Party had around 40,000 members. Two small Communist Parties, made up largely of immigrants, had a total of perhaps 70,000. In June 1919 simultaneous bombings in eight cities killed two people and damaged the residence of Attorney General A. Mitchell Palmer. With public alarm growing, state and federal officials began a coordinated campaign to root out subversives and their alleged Russian connections.

Palmer used the broad authority of the 1918 Alien Act, which enabled the government to deport any immigrant found to be a member of a revolutionary organization prior to or after coming to the United States. In a series of raids in late 1919, Justice Department agents in eleven cities arrested and roughed up several hundred members of the IWW and the Union of Russian Workers. Little evidence of revolutionary intent was found, but 249 people were deported, including prominent anarchists Emma Goldman and Alexander Berkman. In early 1920, some 6,000 people in thirty-three cities, including many U.S. citizens and noncommunists, were arrested and herded into prisons and bullpens. Again, no evidence of a grand plot was found, but another 600 aliens were deported. The Palmer raids had a ripple effect around the nation, encouraging other repressive measures against radicals.

A report prepared by a group of distinguished lawyers questioned the legality of the attorney general's tactics. Palmer's popularity had waned by the spring of 1920, when it became clear that his predictions of revolutionary uprisings were wildly exaggerated. But the Red Scare left an ugly legacy: wholesale violations of constitutional rights, deportations of hundreds of innocent people, fuel for the fires of nativism and intolerance. Business groups, such as the National Association of Manufacturers, found "Red-baiting" to be an effective tool in postwar efforts to keep unions out of their factories. Indeed, the government-sanctioned Red Scare reemerged later in the century as a powerful political force.

The Election of 1920

Woodrow Wilson had wanted the 1920 election to be a "solemn referendum" on the League of Nations and his conduct of the war. Ill and exhausted, Wilson did not run for reelection. A badly divided Democratic Party compromised on Governor James M. Cox of Ohio as its candidate. A proven vote-getter, Cox distanced himself from Wilson's policies, which had come under withering attack from many quarters.

The Republicans nominated Senator Warren G. Harding of Ohio. A political hack, the handsome and genial Harding had virtually no qualifications to be president, except that he looked like one. Harding's campaign was vague and ambiguous about the Versailles Treaty and almost everything else. "America's present need," he said, "is not heroics but healing; not nostrums but normalcy; not revolution but restoration."

The notion of a "return to normalcy" proved very attractive to voters exhausted by the war, inflation, big government, and social dislocation. Harding won the greatest landslide in history to that date, carrying every state outside the South and taking the popular vote by 16 million to 9 million. Republicans retained their majorities in the House and Senate as well. Socialist Eugene V. Debs, still a powerful symbol of the dream of radical social change, managed to poll 900,000 votes from jail. But the overall vote repudiated Wilson and the progressive movement. Americans seemed eager to pull back from moralism in public and international controversies. Yet many of the economic, social, and cultural changes wrought by the war would accelerate during the 1920s. In truth, there could never be a "return to normalcy."

CONCLUSION

Compared to the casualties and social upheavals endured by the European powers, the Great War's impact on American life might appear slight. Yet the war created economic, social, and political dislocations that helped reshape American life long after Armistice Day. Republican administrations invoked the wartime partnership between government and industry to justify an aggressive peacetime policy fostering cooperation between the state and business. Wartime production needs contributed to what economists later called "the second industrial revolution." Patriotic fervor and the exaggerated specter of Bolshevism were used to repress radicalism, organized labor, feminism, and the entire legacy of progressive reform. The wartime measure of national prohibition evolved into perhaps the most contentious social issue of peacetime. Sophisticated use of sales techniques, psychology, and propaganda during the war helped define the newly powerful advertising and public relations industries of the 1920s. The growing visibility of immigrants and African Americans, especially in the nation's cities, provoked a xenophobic and racist backlash in the politics of the 1920s. More than anything else, the desire for "normalcy" reflected the deep anxieties evoked by America's wartime experience.

CHRONOLOGY

1903	United States obtains Panama canal rights
1905	President Theodore Roosevelt mediates peace treaty between Japan and Russia at Portsmouth Conference
1908	Root-Takahira Agreement with Japan affirms status quo in Asia and Open Door policy in China
1911	Mexican Revolution begins
1914	U.S. forces invade Mexico
	Panama Canal opens
	World War I begins in Europe
	President Woodrow Wilson issues proclamation of neutrality
1915	Germany declares war zone around Great Britain
	German U-boat sinks *Lusitania*
1916	Pancho Villa raids New Mexico, is pursued by General Pershing
	Wilson is reelected
	National Defense Act establishes preparedness program
1917	February: Germany resumes unrestricted submarine warfare
	March: Zimmermann Note, suggesting a German-Mexican alliance, shocks Americans

	April: United States declares war on the Central Powers
	May: Selective Service Act is passed
	June: Espionage Act is passed
	November: Bolshevik Revolution begins in Russia
1918	January: Wilson unveils Fourteen Points
	May: Sedition Act is passed
	June: U.S. troops begin to see action in France
	November: Armistice ends war
1919	January: Eighteenth Amendment (Prohibition) is ratified
	Wilson serves as Chief U.S. negotiator at Paris Peace Conference
	June: Versailles Treaty is signed in Paris
	July: Race riot breaks out in Chicago
	Steel strike begins in several midwestern cities
	November: Palmer raids begin
1920	March: Senate finally votes down Versailles Treaty and League of Nations
	August: Nineteenth Amendment (woman suffrage) is ratified
	November: Warren G. Harding is elected president

REVIEW QUESTIONS

1. What central issues drew the United States deeper into international politics in the early years of the century? How did American presidents justify a more expansive role? What diplomatic and military policies did they exploit for these ends?

2. Compare the arguments for and against American participation in the Great War. Which Americans were most likely to support entry? Which were more likely to oppose it?

3. How did mobilizing for war change the economy and its relationship to government? Which of these changes, if any, spilled over to the postwar years?

4. How did the war affect political life in the United States? What techniques were used to stifle dissent? What was the war's political legacy?

5. To what extent was the war an extension of progressivism?

6. Analyze the impact of the war on American workers. How did the conflict affect the lives of African Americans and women?

7. What principles guided Woodrow Wilson's Fourteen Points? How would you explain the United States' failure to ratify the Treaty of Versailles?

RECOMMENDED READING

Marc Allen Eisner, *From Warfare State to Welfare State: World War I, Compensatory State Building, and the Limits of the Modern Order* (2000). Demonstrates how, to compensate for the limited capacities of the state to wage total war, policymakers incorporated business organizations and structures into the network of committees coordinating the war effort.

Kathleen Kennedy, *Disloyal Mothers and Scurrilous Citizens: Women and Subversion During World War I* (1999). Analyzes the federal government's campaign against antiwar women activists and their refusal to adhere to accepted notions of "patriotic motherhood."

Thomas J. Knock, *To End All Wars: Woodrow Wilson and the Quest for a New World Order* (1992). A persuasive analysis of Wilson's internationalism, its links to his domestic policies, and his design for the League of Nations.

Walter LaFeber, *The American Age* (1989). A fine survey of the history of U.S. foreign policy that includes an analysis of the pre–World War I era.

Paul L. Murphy, *World War I and the Origin of Civil Liberties* (1979). A good overview of the various civil liberties issues raised by the war and government efforts to suppress dissent.

Ronald Schaffer, *America in the Great War: The Rise of the War Welfare State* (1991). Excellent material on how the war transformed the relationship between business and government and spurred improved conditions for industrial workers.

Joe William Trotter Jr., ed., *The Great Migration in Historical Perspective* (1991). An excellent collection of essays examining the Great Migration, with special attention to issues of class and gender within the African American community.

Neil A. Wynn, *From Progressivism to Prosperity: World War I and American Society* (1986). An illuminating account of the social impact of the war on American life. Effectively connects the war experience with both progressive era trends and postwar developments in the 1920s.

Robert H. Zieger, *America's Great War: World War I and the American Experience* (2000). The best new one-volume synthesis on how the war transformed the United States and its role in the world.

Susan Zeiger, *In Uncle Sam's Service: Women Workers with the American Expeditionary Force, 1917–1919* (1999). The first in-depth study of American women's experiences with the armed forces overseas.

ON THE WEB

http://www.history.navy.mil/photos/prs-tpic/ females/yeoman-f.htm

This is a U.S. Navy historical site that records the contributions of women in the Navy during World War I. It contains textual, photographic, and cartoon primary documents.

http://lcweb.loc.gov/rr/print/076_vfw.html

This Library of Congress site presents a selected collection of photographs and some prints from the suffrage movement beginning in the late 1890s, focusing on the war years, and ending with the 1920s. Twenty-one photos and prints are presented on this site relating to suffrage events while seventeen photos of prominent suffrage leaders are portrayed.

http://raven.cc.ukans.edu/~kansite/ww_one/photos/ greatwar.htm

This University of Kansas site contains an extensive collection of World War I photographs, some of very high quality.

http://gulib.lausun.georgetown.edu/dept/speccoll/ amposter.htm

This Georgetown University site contains twenty-five World War I posters.

http://www.prenhall.com/faragherbrief/map22.1

Examine "dollar diplomacy" in the Caribbean. Why was the United States so heavily involved in this region?

http://www.prenhall.com/faragherbrief/map22.2

Chart the progress of the women's suffrage movement. What were the reasons behind the regional differences in support of women's suffrage?

TWENTY-THREE

THE TWENTIES

CHAPTER OUTLINE

AMERICAN COMMUNITIES

The Movie Audience and Hollywood: Mass Culture Creates a New National Community

INSIDE MIDTOWN MANHATTAN'S MAGNIFICENT NEW ROXY THEATER, A sellout crowd eagerly settled in for opening night. Outside, thousands of fans cheered wildly at the arrival of movie stars such as Charlie Chaplin, Gloria Swanson, and Harold Lloyd. A squadron of smartly uniformed ushers guided patrons under a five-story-tall rotunda to some 6,200 velvet-covered seats. The audience marveled at the huge gold and rose-colored murals, classical statuary, plush carpeting, and Gothic-style windows. It was easy to believe newspaper reports that the theater had cost $10 million to build. Suddenly, light flooded the orchestra pit and 110 musicians began playing "The Star Spangled Banner." A troupe of 100 performers took the stage, dancing ballet numbers and singing old southern melodies such as "My Old Kentucky Home" and "Swanee River." Congratulatory telegrams from President Calvin Coolidge and other dignitaries flashed on the screen. Finally, the evening's feature presentation, *The Love of Sunya*, starring Gloria Swanson, began. Samuel L. "Roxy" Rothapfel, the theater's designer, had realized his grand dream—to build "the cathedral of the motion picture."

When Roxy's opened in March 1927, nearly 60 million Americans "worshiped" each week at movie theaters across the nation. The "movie palaces" of the 1920s were designed to transport patrons to exotic places and different times. As film pioneer Marcus Loew put it, "We sell tickets to theaters, not movies." Every large community boasted at least one opulent movie theater. Houston's Majestic was built to represent an ancient Italian garden; it had a ceiling made to look like an open sky, complete with stars and cloud formations. The Tivoli in Chicago featured opulent French Renaissance decor; Grauman's Egyptian in Los Angeles recreated the look of a pharaoh's tomb; and Albuquerque's Kimo drew inspiration from Navajo art and religion.

The remarkable popularity of motion pictures, and later radio, forged a new kind of community. A huge national audience regularly went to the movies, and the same entertainment could be enjoyed virtually anywhere in the country by just about everyone. Movies emerged as the most popular form in the new mass culture, with an appeal that extended far beyond the films themselves, or even the theaters. Americans embraced the cult of celebrity, voraciously consuming fan magazines, gossip columns, and news of the stars. By the 1920s, the production center for this dream world was Hollywood, California, a suburb of Los Angeles that had barely existed in 1890.

Motion picture companies found Hollywood an alluring alternative to the east coast cities where they had been born. Its reliably sunny and dry climate was ideal for year-round filming. Its unique surroundings offered a perfect variety of scenic locations—mountains, desert, ocean—and downtown Los Angeles was only an hour away. Land was cheap and plentiful. And because Los Angeles was the leading nonunion, open-shop city in the country, so was labor. By the early 1920s Hollywood produced more than 80 percent of the nation's motion pictures and was assuming mythical status. The isolation of the town, its great distance from the eastern cities, its lack of traditional sources of culture and learning—all contributed to movie folk looking at life in a self-consciously "Hollywood" way.

With its feel of a modern frontier boomtown, Hollywood was a new kind of American community. It lured the young and cosmopolitan with the promise of upward mobility and a new way of life. Most of the top studio executives were Jewish immigrants from eastern and central Europe. In contrast to most Americans, who hailed from rural areas or small towns, more than half of Hollywood's writers, directors, editors, and actors were born in cities of over 100,000. Two-thirds of its performers were under thirty-five, and three-fourths of its actresses were under twenty-five. More than 90 percent of its writers (women made up one-third to one-half of this key group) had attended college or worked in journalism. The movies this untypical community created evoked the pleasures of leisure, consumption, and personal freedom, redefining the nation's cultural values in the 1920s.

Movie stars dominated Hollywood. Charlie Chaplin, Mary Pickford, Rudolph Valentino, Gloria Swanson, and Douglas Fairbanks became popular idols as much for their highly publicized private lives as for their roles on screen. Many accumulated great wealth, becoming the nation's experts on how to live well. Movie folk built luxurious mansions in a variety of architectural styles and outfitted them with swimming pools, tennis courts, golf courses, and lavish gardens.

Visitors often noted that Hollywood had no museums, art galleries, live theater, or other traditional institutions of high culture. How would the town's wealthy movie elite spend their time and money? By 1916 Charlie Chaplin, a working-class immigrant from the London slums, was earning $10,000 a week for the comedies that made his the most famous face in the world. He recalled trying to figure out what to do with his new wealth. "The money I earned was legendary, a symbol in figures, for I had never actually seen it. I therefore had to do something to prove I had it. So I procured a secretary, a valet, a car, a chauffeur."

Ordinary Americans found it easy to identify with movie stars despite their wealth and status. Unlike industrialists or politicians, stars had no social authority over large groups of employees or voters. They, too, had to answer to a boss, and most had risen from humble beginnings. But above all, Hollywood, like the movies it churned out, represented for millions of Americans new possibilities: freedom, material success, upward mobility, and the chance to remake one's very identity. By the end of the decade the Hollywood "dream factory" had helped forge a national community whose collective aspirations and desires were increasingly defined by those possibilities, even if relatively few Americans realized them during the 1920s. ■

Hollywood

— KEY TOPICS —

- A second industrial revolution that transforms the economy

- The promise and limits of prosperity in the 1920s

- New mass media and the culture of consumption

- Republican Party dominance

- Political and cultural opposition to modern trends

POSTWAR PROSPERITY AND ITS PRICE

The Second Industrial Revolution

The prosperity of the 1920s rested on what historians have called the "second industrial revolution" in American manufacturing, in which technological innovations made it possible to increase industrial output without expanding the labor force. Electricity replaced steam as the main power source for industry in these years, making possible the replacement of older machinery with more efficient and flexible electric machinery.

Much of the newer, automatic machinery could be operated by unskilled and semiskilled workers, and it boosted the overall efficiency of American industry. Thus, in 1929 the average worker in manufacturing produced roughly three-quarters more per hour than he or she had in 1919. The machine industry itself employed more workers than any other manufacturing sector—some 1.1 million in 1929—supplying not only a growing home market but 35 percent of the world market as well.

During the late nineteenth century, heavy industries such as machine tools, railroads, iron, and steel had pioneered mass-production techniques. These industries manufactured what economists call producer-durable goods. In the 1920s, modern mass-production techniques were increasingly applied as well to newer consumer-durable goods such as automobiles, radios, washing machines, and telephones. With more efficient management, greater mechanization, intensive product research, and ingenious sales and advertising methods, the consumer-based industries helped to nearly double industrial production in the 1920s.

The Modern Corporation

In the late nineteenth century, individual entrepreneurs such as John D. Rockefeller in oil and Andrew Carnegie in steel had provided a model for success. They maintained both corporate control (ownership) and business leadership (management) in their enterprises. In the 1920s, a managerial revolution increasingly divorced ownership of corporate stock from the everyday control of businesses. The new corporate ideal was to be found in men such as Alfred P. Sloan of General Motors and Owen D. Young of the Radio Corporation of America.

During the 1920s, the most successful corporations were those that led in three key areas: the integration of production and distribution, product diversification, and the expansion of industrial research. Until the end of World War I, for example, the chemical manufacturer Du Pont had specialized in explosives such as gunpowder. After the war, Du Pont moved aggressively into the consumer market with a diverse array of products. Similarly, the great electrical manufacturers—General Electric and Westinghouse—which had previously concentrated on lighting and power equipment, now diversified into household appliances like radios, washing machines, and refrigerators. The chemical and electrical industries also led the way in industrial research, hiring personnel to develop new products and test their commercial viability.

By 1929 the 200 largest corporations owned nearly half the nation's corporate wealth—that is, physical plant, stock, and property. Half the total industrial income—revenue from sales of goods—was concentrated in 100 corporations. Oligopoly—the control of a market by a few large producers—became the norm. Four companies packed almost three-quarters of all American meat. Another four rolled nine out of every ten cigarettes. National chain grocery stores, clothing shops, and pharmacies began squeezing out local

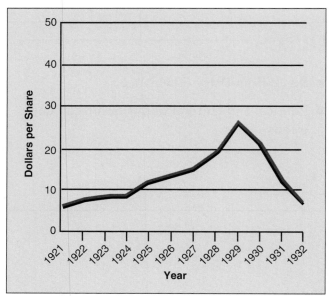

Stock Market Prices, 1921–1932 Common stock prices rose steeply during the 1920s. Although only about 4 million Americans owned stocks during the period, "stock watching" became something of a national sport.

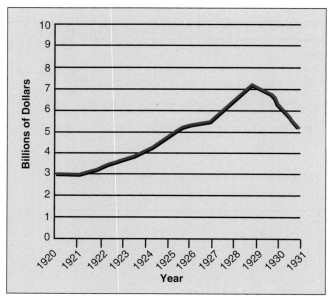

Consumer Debt, 1920–1931 The expansion of consumer borrowing was a key component of the era's prosperity. These figures do not include mortgages or money borrowed to purchase stocks. They reveal the great increase in "installment buying" for such consumer durable goods as automobiles and household appliances.

neighborhood businesses. One grocery chain alone, the Great Atlantic and Pacific Tea Company (A&P), accounted for 10 percent of all retail food sales in America.

A growing class of salaried executives, plant managers, and engineers formed a new elite who made corporate policy without themselves having a controlling interest in the companies they worked for. They stressed scientific management and the latest theories of behavioral psychology in their effort to make their workplaces more productive, stable, and profitable.

Welfare Capitalism

The wartime gains made by organized labor and the active sympathy shown to trade unions by government agencies such as the National War Labor Board troubled most corporate leaders. To challenge the power and appeal of trade unions and collective bargaining, large employers aggressively promoted a variety of new programs designed to improve worker well-being and morale. These schemes, collectively known as welfare capitalism, became a key part of corporate strategy in the 1920s.

One approach was to encourage workers to acquire property through stock-purchase plans or, less frequently, home ownership plans. Other programs offered workers insurance policies covering accidents, illness, old age, and death. Many plant managers and personnel

departments consciously worked to improve safety conditions, provide medical services, and establish sports and recreation programs for workers. But welfare capitalism could not solve the most chronic problems faced by industrial workers: seasonal unemployment, low wages, long hours, and unhealthy factory conditions.

Large corporations also mounted an effective antiunion campaign in the early 1920s called "the American plan," a name meant to associate unionism with foreign and un-American ideas. Backed by powerful business lobbies such as the National Association of Manufacturers and the Chamber of Commerce, campaign leaders called for the open shop, in which no employee would be compelled to join a union. If a union existed, nonmembers would still get whatever wages and rights the union had won—a policy that put organizers at a disadvantage in signing up new members.

The open shop undercut the gains won in a union shop, where new employees had to join an existing union, or a closed shop, where employers agreed to hire only union members. As alternatives, large employers such as U.S. Steel and International Harvester began setting up company unions. Their intent was to substitute largely symbolic employee representation in management conferences for the more confrontational process of collective bargaining.

These management strategies contributed to a sharp decline in the ranks of organized labor. Total union membership dropped from about 5 million in 1920 to

3.5 million in 1926. A large proportion of the remaining union members were concentrated in the skilled crafts of the building and printing trades. A conservative and timid union leadership was also responsible for the trend. The federal government, which had provided limited wartime support for unions, now reverted to a more probusiness posture. The Supreme Court in particular was unsympathetic toward unions, consistently upholding the use of injunctions to prevent strikes, picketing, and other union activities.

The Auto Age

In their classic community study *Middletown* (1929), sociologists Robert and Helen Lynd noted the dramatic impact of the car on the social life of Muncie, Indiana. "Why on earth do you need to study what's changing this country?" asked one lifelong Muncie resident in 1924. "I can tell you what's happening in just four letters: A-U-T-O!" This remark hardly seems much of an exaggeration today. No other single development could match the impact of the postwar automobile explosion on the way Americans worked, lived, and played. The auto industry offered the clearest example of the rise to prominence of consumer durables. During the 1920s, America made approximately 85 percent of all the world's passenger cars. By 1929 the motor vehicle industry was the most productive in the United States in terms of value, producing some 4.8 million cars that year.

This extraordinary new industry had mushroomed in less than a generation. Its great pioneer, Henry Ford, had shown how the use of a continuous assembly line could drastically reduce the number of worker hours required to produce a single vehicle. In 1914, at his sprawling new Highland Park assembly plant just outside Detroit, Ford's system finished one car every ninety minutes. By 1925, cars were rolling off his assembly line at the rate of one every ten seconds.

In 1914 Ford startled American industry by inaugurating a new wage scale: $5 for an eight-hour day. This was roughly double the going pay rate for industrial labor, along with a shorter workday as well. But in defying the conventional economic wisdom of the day, Ford acted less out of benevolence than out of shrewdness. He understood that workers were consumers as well as producers, and the new wage scale helped boost sales of Ford cars. It also reduced the high turnover rate in his labor force and increased worker efficiency. Ford's mass-production system and economies of scale permitted him to progressively reduce the price of his cars, bringing them within the reach of millions of Americans. The famous Model T, thoroughly standardized and available only in black, cost just under $300 in 1924—about three months' wages for the best-paid factory workers.

The auto industry provided a large market for makers of steel, rubber, glass, and petroleum products. It stimulated public spending for good roads and extended the housing boom to new suburbs. Showrooms, repair shops, and gas stations appeared in thousands of communities. New small enterprises, from motels to billboard advertising to roadside diners, sprang up as motorists took to the highway. The rapid development of Florida and California, in particular, was partly a response to the growing influence of the automobile.

For some the car merely reinforced old social patterns, making it easier for them to get to church on Sunday, for example, or visit neighbors. Others used their cars to go to new places, shop in nearby cities, or take vacations. The automobile made leisure, in the sense of getting away from the routines of work and school, a more regular part of everyday life. It undoubtedly also changed the courtship practices of America's youth. Young people took advantage of the car to gain privacy and distance from their parents.

Until 1924 Henry Ford had disdained national advertising for his cars. But as General Motors gained a competitive edge by making yearly changes in style and technology, Ford was forced to pay more attention to advertising. This ad was directed at "Mrs. Consumer," combining appeals to both female independence and motherly duties.

SOURCE: Ford Motor Company.

"What on earth do you want me to do?" complained one "Middletown" high school girl to her anxious father. "Just sit around home all evening?" Many had their first sexual experiences in a car.

Cars also promoted urban and suburban growth. The federal census for 1920 was the first in American history in which the proportion of the population that lived in urban places (those with 2,500 or more people) exceeded the proportion of the population living in rural areas. More revealing of urban growth was the steady increase in the number of big cities. In 1910 there were sixty cities with more than 100,000 inhabitants; in 1920 there were sixty-eight; and by 1930 there were ninety-two. During the 1920s New York grew by 20 percent to nearly 7 million, whereas Detroit, home of the auto industry, doubled its population, to nearly 2 million.

Exceptions: Agriculture, Ailing Industries

Amid prosperity and progress, there were large pockets of the country that lagged behind. Advances in real income and improvements in the standard of living for workers and farmers were uneven at best. During the 1920s, one-quarter of all American workers were employed in agriculture, yet the farm sector failed to share in the general prosperity. The years 1914–19 had been a kind of golden age for the nation's farmers. But with the war's end, American farmers began to suffer from a chronic worldwide surplus of such farm staples as cotton, hogs, and corn.

Prices began to drop sharply in 1920. Cotton, which sold at 37 cents a pound in mid-1920, fell to 14 cents by year's end. By 1921 net farm income was down more than half from the year before. Land values also dropped, wiping out billions in capital investment. Behind these aggregate statistics were hundreds of thousands of individual human tragedies on the nation's 6 million farms.

In the South, farmers' dependency on "King Cotton" deepened, as the region lagged farther behind the rest of the nation in both agricultural diversity and standard of living. Cotton acreage expanded as large and heavily mechanized farms opened up new land in Oklahoma, west Texas, and the Mississippi-Yazoo delta. But in most of the South, from North Carolina to east Texas, small one- and two-mule cotton farms, most under 50 acres, still dominated the countryside. While editors, state officials, and reformers preached the need for greater variety of crops, southern farmers actually raised less corn and livestock by the end of the decade. With few large urban centers and inadequate transportation, even those southern farmers who had access to capital found it extremely difficult to find reliable markets for vegetables, fruit, poultry, or dairy products. The average southern farm had land and buildings worth $3,525; for

northern farms, the figure was $11,029. The number of white tenant farmers increased by 200,000 during the 1920s, while black tenantry declined slightly as a result of the Great Migration. Some 700,000 southern farmers, roughly half white and half black, still labored as sharecroppers. Modern conveniences such as electricity, indoor plumbing, automobiles, and phonographs remained far beyond the reach of the great majority of southern farmers. Widespread rural poverty, poor diet, little access to capital—the world of southern agriculture had changed very little since the days of Populist revolt in the 1890s.

Large sectors of American industry also failed to share in the decade's general prosperity. As oil and natural gas gained in importance, America's coal mines became a less important source of energy. Economic hardship was widespread in many mining communities dependent on coal, particularly in Appalachia and the southern Midwest. And those miners who did work earned lower hourly wages.

The number of miles of railroad track actually decreased after 1920 as automobiles and trucks began to displace trains. In textiles, the women's fashions of the 1920s generally required less material than had earlier fashions, and competition from synthetic fibers such as rayon depressed demand for cotton textiles. To improve profit margins, textile manufacturers in New England and other parts of the Northeast began a long-range shift of operations to the South, where nonunion shops and substandard wages became the rule. Older New England manufacturing centers such as Lawrence, Lowell, Nashua, Manchester, and Fall River were hard hit by this shift. Southern mills increased their work force from 220,000 to 257,000 between 1923 and 1933. By 1933 they employed nearly 70 percent of the workers in the industry. Southern mills generally operated night and day, used the newest labor-saving machinery, and cut back on the wage gains of the World War I years.

THE NEW MASS CULTURE

Advertising Modernity

A thriving advertising industry both reflected and encouraged the growing importance of consumer goods in American life. Previously, advertising had been confined mostly to staid newspapers and magazines and offered little more than basic product information. The successful efforts of the government's Committee on Public Information, set up to "sell" World War I to Americans, suggested that new techniques using modern communication media could convince people to buy a wide range of goods and services. As a profession, advertising reached a higher level of respectability, sophistication, and economic power in American life during the 1920s.

Advertisers began focusing on the needs, desires, and anxieties of the consumer rather than on the qualities of the product. Ad agencies and their clients invested extraordinary amounts of time, energy, and money trying to discover and, to some extent, shape people's beliefs. One of the more spectacular examples of advertising effectiveness involved an old product, Listerine, which had been marketed as a general antiseptic for years by Lambert Pharmaceutical Company. A new ad campaign touting Listerine as a cure for halitosis—a scientific-sounding term for bad breath—boosted Lambert's profits from $100,000 in 1922 to more than $4 million in 1927.

Above all, advertising celebrated consumption itself as a positive good. In this sense the new advertising ethic was a therapeutic one, promising that products would contribute to the buyer's physical, psychic, or emotional well-being. Well-financed ad campaigns were especially crucial for marketing newer consumer goods such as cars, electrical appliances, and personal hygiene products. Total advertising volume in all media—newspapers, magazines, radio, billboards—jumped from $1.4 billion in 1919 to $3 billion in 1929.

Radio Broadcasting

In the fall of 1920, Westinghouse executive Harry P. Davis noticed that amateur broadcasts from the garage of an employee had attracted attention in the local Pittsburgh press. A department store advertised radio sets capable of picking up these "wireless concerts." Davis converted this amateur station to a stronger one at the Westinghouse main plant. Beginning with the presidential election returns that November, station KDKA offered regular nightly broadcasts that were probably heard by only a few hundred people. Radio broadcasting, begun as a service for selling cheap radio sets left over from World War I, would soon sweep the nation.

Before KDKA, wireless technology had been of interest only to the military, the telephone industry, and a few thousand "ham" (amateur) operators who enjoyed communicating with each other. The "radio mania" of the early 1920s was a response to the new possibilities offered by broadcasting. By 1923 nearly 600 stations had been licensed by the Department of Commerce, and about 600,000 Americans had bought radios. Early programs included live popular music, the playing of phonograph records, talks by college professors, church services, and news and weather reports. For millions of Americans, especially in rural areas and small towns, radio provided a new and exciting link to the larger national community of consumption.

Who would pay for radio programs? By the end of the decade commercial (or "toll") broadcasting emerged as the answer. The dominant corporations in the industry—General Electric, Westinghouse, Radio Corporation of America (RCA), and American Telephone and Telegraph (AT&T)—settled on the idea that advertisers would foot the bill for radio. Sponsors advertised directly or indirectly to the mass audience through such shows as the *Eveready Hour*, the *Ipana Troubadors*, and the *Taystee Loafers*.

Radio broadcasting created a national community of listeners, just as motion pictures created one of viewers. NBC and CBS led the way in creating popular radio programs that relied heavily on older cultural forms. The variety show, hosted by vaudeville comedians, became network radio's first important format. Radio's first truly national hit, The *Amos 'n' Andy Show* (1928), was a direct descendant of nineteenth-century "blackface" minstrel entertainment. Radio did more than any previous medium to publicize and commercialize previously isolated forms of American music such as country-and-western, blues, and jazz. Broadcasts of baseball and college football games proved especially popular. By 1930, some 600 stations were broadcasting to more than 12 million homes with radios, or roughly 40 percent of American families. By that time all the elements that characterize the present American system of broadcasting—regular daily programming paid for and produced by commercial advertisers, national networks carrying shows across the nation, and mass ownership of receiver sets in American homes—were in place.

Movie-Made America

The early movie industry, centered in New York and a few other big cities, had made moviegoing a regular habit for millions of Americans, especially immigrants and the working class. They flocked to cheap, storefront theaters, called nickelodeons, to watch short westerns, slapstick comedies, melodramas, and travelogues. With the shift of the industry westward to Hollywood, movies entered a new phase of business expansion.

Large studios such as Paramount, Fox, Metro-Goldwyn-Mayer (M-G-M), Universal, and Warner Brothers dominated the business with longer and more expensively produced movies—feature films. These companies were founded and controlled by immigrants from Europe, all of whom had a talent for discovering and exploiting changes in popular tastes. Adolph Zukor, the Hungarian-born head of Paramount, had been a furrier in New York City. Warsaw-born Samuel Goldwyn, a founder of M-G-M, had been a glove salesman. William Fox, of Fox Pictures, began as a garment cutter in Brooklyn. Most of the immigrant moguls had started in the business by buying or managing small movie theaters before beginning to produce films.

Each studio combined the three functions of production, distribution, and exhibition, and each controlled hundreds of movie theaters around the country. The era of silent films ended when Warner Brothers scored a huge hit in 1927 with *The Jazz Singer,* starring Al Jolson, which successfully introduced sound. New genres—musicals, gangster films, and screwball comedies—soon became popular. The higher costs associated with "talkies" also increased the studios' reliance on Wall Street investors and banks for working capital.

At the heart of Hollywood's success was the star system and the accompanying cult of celebrity. Stars became vital to the fantasy lives of millions of fans. For many in the audience, there was only a vague line separating the on-screen and off-screen adventures of the stars. Studio publicity, fan magazines, and gossip columns reinforced this ambiguity. Young Americans in particular looked to movies to learn how to dress, wear their hair, talk, or kiss.

A New Morality?

Movie stars, radio personalities, sports heroes, and popular musicians became the elite figures in a new culture of celebrity defined by the mass media. They were the model for achievement in the new age. Great events and abstract issues were made real through movie close-ups, radio interviews, and tabloid photos.

One of the most enduring images of the "Roaring Twenties" is the flapper. She was usually portrayed on screen, in novels, and in the press as a young, sexually aggressive woman with bobbed hair, rouged cheeks, and short skirt. She loved to dance to jazz music, enjoyed smoking cigarettes, and drank bootleg liquor in cabarets and dance halls. She could also be competitive, assertive, and a good pal.

Was the flapper a genuine representative of the 1920s? Did she embody the "new morality" that was so widely discussed and chronicled in the media of the day? The flapper certainly did exist, but she was neither as new nor as widespread a phenomenon as the image would suggest. The delight in sensuality, personal pleasure, and rhythmically complex dance and music had long been key elements of subcultures on the fringes of middle-class society: bohemian enclaves, communities of political radicals, African American ghettos, working-class dance halls. In the 1920s, these activities became normative for a growing number of white middle-class Americans, including women. Jazz, sexual experimentation, heavy makeup, and cigarette smoking spread to college campuses.

Several sources, most of them rooted in earlier years, can be found for the increased sexual openness of the 1920s. New psychological and social theories like those of Havelock Ellis, Ellen Key, and Sigmund Freud stressed the central role of sexuality in human experience, maintaining that sex is a positive, healthy impulse that, if repressed, could damage mental and emotional health. The pioneering efforts of Margaret Sanger in educating women about birth control had begun before World War I (see Chapter 21).

Advertisers routinely used sex appeal to sell products. Tabloid newspapers exploited sex with "cheesecake" photos, but they also provided features giving advice on sex hygiene and venereal disease. And movies, of course, featured powerful sex symbols such as Rudolph Valentino, Gloria Swanson, John Gilbert, and Clara Bow. Movies also taught young people an etiquette of sex. One typical eighteen-year-old college student wrote in the motion picture diary she kept for a sociological study: "These passionate pictures stir such longings, desires, and urges as I never expected any person to possess. Just the way the passionate lover held his sweetheart suggests so many beautiful and intimate relations, which even my reenacting a scene does not satisfy any more."

Sociological surveys also suggested that genuine changes in sexual behavior began in the prewar years among both married and single women. Katherine Bement Davis's pioneering study of 2,200 middle-class women, carried out in 1918 and published in 1929, revealed that most used contraceptives and described sexual relations in positive terms. Women born after the turn of the century were twice as likely to have had premarital sex as those born before 1900. The critical change took place in the generation that came of age in the late teens and early twenties. By the 1920s, male and female "morals" were becoming more alike.

THE STATE, THE ECONOMY, AND BUSINESS

Harding and Coolidge

Handsome, genial, and well-spoken, Warren Harding may have looked the part of a president—but acting like one was another matter. Harding was a product of small-town Marion, Ohio, and the machine politics in his native state. Republican Party officials had made a point of keeping Senator Harding, a compromise choice, as removed from the public eye as possible in the 1920 election. They correctly saw that active campaigning could only hurt their candidate by exposing his shallowness and intellectual weakness. Harding understood his own limitations. He sadly told one visitor to the White House shortly after taking office, "I knew that this job would be too much for me."

Harding surrounded himself with a close circle of friends, the "Ohio gang," delegating to them a great deal of administrative power. The president often conducted business as if he were in the relaxed, convivial, and masculine confines of a small-town saloon.

Soon after Harding's death in 1923, a series of congressional investigations revealed a deep pattern of corruption. Attorney General Harry M. Daugherty had received bribes from violators of the Prohibition statutes. He had also failed to investigate graft in the Veterans Bureau, where Charles R. Forbes had pocketed a large chunk of the $250 million spent on hospitals and supplies. The worst affair was the Teapot Dome scandal involving Interior Secretary Albert Fall. Fall received hundreds of thousands of dollars in payoffs when he secretly leased navy oil reserves in Teapot Dome, Wyoming, and Elk Hills, California, to two private oil developers. He eventually became the first cabinet officer ever to go to jail.

But the Harding administration's legacy was not all scandal. Andrew Mellon, an influential Pittsburgh banker, served as secretary of the treasury under all three Republican presidents of the 1920s. One of the richest men in America, and a leading investor in the Aluminum Corporation of America and Gulf Oil, Mellon believed government ought to be run on the same conservative principles as a corporation. His tax program sharply cut taxes for both higher-income brackets and for businesses. By 1926, a person with an income of a million a year paid less than a third of the income tax he or she had paid in 1921. Over all, Mellon's policies succeeded in rolling back much of the progressive taxation associated with Woodrow Wilson.

When Calvin Coolidge succeeded to the presidency, he seemed to most people the temperamental opposite of Harding. Born and raised in rural Vermont, elected governor of Massachusetts, and coming to national prominence only through the 1919 Boston police strike (see Chapter 22), "Silent Cal" was the quintessential New England Yankee. Taciturn, genteel, and completely honest, Coolidge believed in the least amount of government possible. He spent only four hours a day at the office. He was in awe of wealthy men such as Andrew Mellon, and he thought them best suited to make society's key decisions.

Coolidge easily won election on his own in 1924. He benefited from the general prosperity and the contrast he provided with the disgraced Harding. Coolidge defeated little-known Democrat John W. Davis.

In his full term, Coolidge showed most interest in reducing federal spending, lowering taxes, and blocking congressional initiatives. He saw his primary function as clearing the way for American businessmen. They, after all, were the agents of the era's unprecedented prosperity.

Herbert Hoover and the "Associative State"

The most influential figure of the Republican new era was Herbert Hoover, who as secretary of commerce dominated the cabinets of Harding and Coolidge before becoming president himself in 1929. A successful engineer, administrator, and politician, Hoover effectively embodied the belief that enlightened business, encouraged and informed by the government, would act in the public interest. In the modern industrial age, Hoover believed, the government needed only to advise private citizens' groups about what national or international polices to pursue.

Unlike an earlier generation of Republicans, Hoover wanted not just to create a favorable climate for business but to actively assist the business community. He spoke of creating an "associative state," in which the government would encourage voluntary cooperation among corporations, consumers, workers, farmers, and small businessmen. This became the central occupation of the Department of Commerce under Hoover's leadership. Under Hoover, the Bureau of Standards became one of the nation's leading research centers, setting engineering standards for key American industries such as machine tools and automobiles. The bureau also helped standardize the styles, sizes, and designs of many consumer products such as canned goods and refrigerators.

Hoover actively encouraged the creation and expansion of national trade associations. By 1929 there were about 2,000 of them. To some this practice violated the spirit of antitrust laws, but in the 1920s the Justice Department's Antitrust Division took a very lax view of its responsibility. In addition, the Supreme Court consistently upheld the legality of trade associations. Hoover also had a strong influence on presidential appointments to regulatory commissions; most of these went to men who had worked for the very firms the commissions had been designed to supervise. Regulatory commissions thus benefited from the technical expertise brought by industry leaders, but they in turn tended to remain uncritical of the industries they oversaw.

The government, thus, provided an ideal climate for the concentration of corporate wealth and power. The trend toward large corporate trusts and holding companies had been well under way since the late nineteenth century, but it accelerated in the 1920s. By 1929, the 200 largest American corporations owned almost half the total corporate wealth and about a fifth of the total national wealth.

Commerce and Foreign Policy

Throughout the 1920s, Republican leaders pursued policies designed to expand American economic activity abroad. The focus was on friendly nations and investments that would help foreign citizens to buy American goods. Toward this end, Republican leaders urged close cooperation between bankers and the government as a strategy for expanding American investment and economic influence abroad. For Hoover and other policymakers, American business abroad was simply rugged individualism at work around the globe.

American oil, autos, farm machinery, and electrical equipment supplied a growing world market. Much of this expansion took place through the establishment of branch plants overseas by American companies. America's overall direct investment abroad increased from $3.8 billion in 1919 to $7.5 billion in 1929.

The strategy of maximum freedom for private enterprise, backed by limited government advice and assistance, significantly boosted the power and profits of American overseas investors. But in Central and Latin America, in particular, aggressive U.S. investment also fostered chronically underdeveloped economies, dependent on a few staple crops (sugar, coffee, cocoa, bananas) grown for export. U.S. economic dominance in the hemisphere also hampered the growth of democratic politics by favoring autocratic, military regimes that could be counted on to protect U.S. investments.

RESISTANCE TO MODERNITY

Prohibition

The Eighteenth Amendment, banning the manufacture, sale, and transportation of alcoholic beverages, took effect in January 1920. Prohibition was the culmination of a long campaign that associated drinking with the degradation of working-class family life and the worst evils of urban politics. Supporters, a coalition of women's temperance groups, middle-class progressives, and rural Protestants, hailed the new law as "a noble experiment." But it became clear rather quickly that enforcing the new law would be extremely difficult. The Volstead Act of 1919 established a federal Prohibition Bureau to enforce the Eighteenth Amendment. Yet the bureau was severely understaffed, with only about 1,500 agents to police the entire country.

The public demand for alcohol, especially in the big cities, led to widespread lawbreaking. Illegal stills and breweries, as well as liquor smuggled in from Canada, supplied the needs of those Americans who continued to drink. Nearly every town and city had at least one "speakeasy," where people could drink and enjoy music and other entertainment. Local law en-

forcement personnel, especially in the cities, were easily bribed to overlook these illegal establishments. By the early 1920s many eastern states no longer made even a token effort at enforcing the law.

Prohibition gave an enormous boost to violent organized crime. The pattern of organized crime in the 1920s closely resembled the larger trends in American business: smaller operations gave way to larger and more complex combinations. Successful organized crime figures, like Chicago's Al "Scarface" Capone, became celebrities in their own right and received heavy coverage in the mass media.

Organized crime, based on its huge profits from liquor, also made significant inroads into legitimate businesses, labor unions, and city government. By the time Congress and the states ratified the Twenty-first Amendment in 1933, repealing Prohibition, organized crime was a permanent feature of American life.

Immigration Restriction

Sentiment for restricting immigration, growing since the late nineteenth century, reached its peak immediately after World War I. Anti-immigrant feeling reflected major shifts in both the size and makeup of the immigrant stream. The "new immigrants" were mostly Catholic and Jewish, and they were darker-skinned than the "old immigrants." To many Americans they seemed more exotic, more foreign, and less willing and able to assimilate the nation's political and cultural values. They were also relatively poorer, more physically isolated in the nation's cities, and less politically strong than earlier immigrants. In the 1890s, the anti-Catholic American Protective Association called for a curb on immigration, and by exploiting the economic depression of that decade it reached a membership of 2.5 million. In 1894 a group of prominent Harvard graduates, including Henry Cabot Lodge and John Fiske, founded the Immigration Restriction League, providing an influential forum for the fears of the nation's elite. The league used newer scientific arguments, based on a flawed application of Darwinian evolutionary theory and genetics, to support its call for immigration restriction.

Theories of scientific racism, which had become more popular in the early 1900s, reinforced anti-immigrant bias. Eugenicists, who enjoyed considerable vogue in these years, held that heredity determined almost all of a person's capacities and that genetic inferiority predisposed people to crime and poverty. Such pseudoscientific thinking sought to explain historical and social development solely as a function of "racial" differences.

Against this background, the war and its aftermath provided the final push for immigration restriction. The postwar depression coincided with the resumption of massive immigration, bringing much hostile comment on the relationship between rising unemployment and the new influx of foreigners. Sensational press coverage of organized crime figures, many of them Italian or Jewish, also played a part.

In 1921 Congress passed the Immigration Act, setting a maximum of 357,000 new immigrants each year. Quotas limited annual immigration from any European country to 3 percent of the number of its natives counted in the 1910 U.S. census. But restrictionists complained that the new law still allowed too many southern and eastern Europeans in. The Johnson-Reed Immigration Act of 1924 revised the quotas to 2 percent of the number of foreign-born counted for each nationality in the census for 1890, when far fewer southern or eastern Europeans were present in the United States. The maximum total allowed each year was also cut, to 164,000. The quota laws did not apply to Canada, Mexico, or any other nation in the western hemisphere. The immigration restriction laws reversed earlier practices and became a permanent feature of national policy.

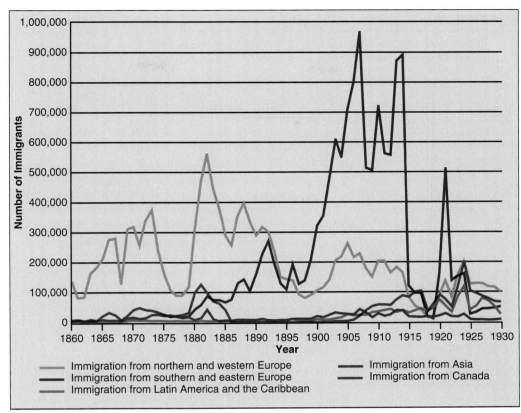

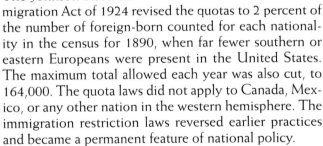

Annual Immigration to the United States, 1860–1930

The Ku Klux Klan

If immigration restriction was resurgent nativism's most significant legislative expression, a revived Ku Klux Klan was its most effective mass movement. The original Klan had been formed in the 1870s. The new Klan, born in Stone Mountain, Georgia, in 1915, was inspired by D. W. Griffith's racist spectacle *The Birth of a Nation,* a film released in that year depicting the original KKK as a heroic organization. The new Klan patterned itself on the secret rituals and antiblack hostility of its predecessor.

When Hiram W. Evans, a dentist from Dallas, became imperial wizard of the Klan in 1922, he hired professional fundraisers and publicists and directed an effective recruiting scheme that paid a commission to sponsors of new members. The Klan advocated "100

percent Americanism" and "the faithful maintenance of White Supremacy." It staunchly supported Prohibition, and it attacked birth control and Darwinism.

By 1924 the new Klan counted more than 3 million members across the country. Its slogan, "Native, White, Protestant Supremacy," proved especially attractive in the Midwest and South, including many cities. Klansmen boycotted businesses, threatened families, and sometimes resorted to violence—public whippings, arson, and lynching—against their chosen enemies. The Klan's targets sometimes included white Protestants accused of sexual promiscuity, blasphemy, or drunkenness, but most victims were African Americans, Catholics, and Jews. Support for Prohibition enforcement probably united Klansmen more than any single issue.

The Klan had a strong presence among delegates to the 1924 Democratic National Convention. The Klan began to fade in 1925 when its Indiana leader, Grand Dragon David C. Stephenson, became involved in a sordid personal affair. Stephenson had picked up a young secretary at a party, got her drunk on bootleg liquor, and then assaulted her on a train. After the woman took poison and died, Stephenson was convicted of manslaughter. With one of its most famous leaders disgraced and in jail, the new Klan began to lose members and influence.

PROMISES POSTPONED

Feminism in Transition

The achievement of the suffrage removed the central issue that had given cohesion to the disparate forces of female reform activism. In addition, female activists of all persuasions found themselves swimming against a national tide of hostility to political idealism. During the 1920s, the women's movement split into two main wings over a fundamental disagreement about female identity. Should activists stress women's differences from men— their vulnerability and the double burden of work and family—and continue to press for protective legislation, such as laws that limited the length of the workweek for women? Or should they emphasize the ways that women were like men—sharing similar aspirations— and push for full legal and civil equality?

In 1920, the National American Woman Suffrage Association reorganized itself as the League of Women Voters. The league represented the historical mainstream of the suffrage movement, those who believed that the vote for women would bring a nurturing sensibility and a reform vision to American politics. Most league members continued working in a variety of reform organizations, and the league itself concentrated on educating the new female electorate, encouraging women to run for office, and supporting laws for the protection of women and children.

A newer, smaller, and more militant group was the National Woman's Party (NWP), founded in 1916 by militant suffragist Alice Paul. The NWP argued that women were still subordinate to men. It opposed protective legislation for women, claiming that such laws reinforced sex stereotyping and prevented women from competing with men in many fields. Largely representing the interests of professional and business women, the NWP focused on passage of a brief Equal Rights Amendment (ERA) to the Constitution, introduced in Congress in 1923: "Men and women shall have equal rights throughout the United States and every place subject to its jurisdiction."

Many of the older generation of women reformers opposed the ERA as elitist, arguing that far more women benefited from protective laws than were injured by them. ERA supporters countered that maximum hours laws or laws prohibiting women from night work prevented women from getting many lucrative jobs. But most women's groups opposed the ERA. These included the League of Women Voters the National Consumers' League, and the Women's Trade Union League. ERA supporters generally stressed individualism, competition, and the abstract language of "equality" and "rights." They dreamed of a labor market that might be one in which women might have the widest opportunity. Anti-ERA forces looked at the labor market as it was, insisting it was more important to protect women from existing exploitation. The NWP campaign failed to get the ERA passed by Congress, but the debates it sparked would be echoed during the feminist movement of the 1970s.

A small number of professional women made real gains in the fields of real estate, banking, and journalism. The press regularly announced new "firsts" for women, such as Amelia Earhart's 1928 airplane flight across the Atlantic. As business expanded, a greater percentage of working women were employed in white-collar positions, as opposed to manufacturing and domestic service. But men still dominated in the higher-paid and managerial white-collar occupations.

The most significant, if limited, victory for feminist reformers was the 1921 Sheppard-Towner Act, which established the first federally funded health care program, providing matching funds for states to set up prenatal and child health care centers. These centers also provided public health nurses for house calls. Although hailed as a genuine reform breakthrough, especially for women in rural and isolated communities, the act aroused much opposition. The NWP disliked it for its assumption that all women were mothers. Birth control advocates such as Margaret Sanger complained that contraception was not part of the program. The American Medical Association (AMA) objected to government-sponsored health care and to nurses who functioned outside the supervision of physicians. By 1929, largely as a result of intense AMA lobbying, Congress cut off funds for the program.

Mexican Immigration

The 1920s brought a dramatic influx of Mexicans to the United States. Mexican immigration, which was not included in the immigration laws of 1921 and 1924, had picked up substantially after the outbreak of the Mexican Revolution in 1911, when political instability and economic hardships provided incentives to cross the border to *El Norte*. According to the U.S. Immigration Service, an estimated 459,000 Mexicans entered the United States between 1921 and 1930, more than double the number for the previous decade. The official count no doubt underrepresented the true numbers of immigrants from Mexico. Many Mexicans shunned the main border crossings at El Paso, Texas; Nogales, Arizona; and Calexico, California, and, thus, avoided paying the $8 head tax and $10 visa fee.

The primary pull was the tremendous agricultural expansion occurring in the American Southwest. Irrigation and large-scale agribusiness had begun transforming California's Imperial and San Joaquin Valleys from arid desert into lucrative fruit and vegetable fields. Cotton pickers were needed in the vast plantations of Lower Rio Grande Valley in Texas and the Salt River Valley in Arizona. The sugar beet fields of Michigan, Minnesota, and Colorado also attracted many Mexican farm workers. American industry had also begun recruiting Mexican workers, first to fill wartime needs and later to fill the gap left by the decline in European immigration.

The new Mexican immigration appeared more permanent than previous waves—that is, more and more newcomers stayed. By 1930, San Antonio's Mexican community accounted for roughly 80,000 people out of a total population of a quarter million. Around 100,000 Mexicans lived in Los Angeles. Substantial Mexican communities also flourished in midwestern cities. Many of the immigrants alternated between agricultural and factory jobs, depending on the seasonal availability of work. Mexican women often worked in the fields alongside their husbands. They also had jobs as domestics and seamstresses or took in laundry and boarders.

Racism and local patterns of residential segregation confined most Mexicans to barrios. Housing conditions were generally poor, particularly for recent arrivals, who were forced to live in rude shacks without running water or electricity. Disease and infant mortality rates were much higher than average, and most Mexicans worked at low-paying, unskilled jobs and received inadequate health care. Legal restrictions passed by states and cities made it difficult for Mexicans to enter teaching, legal, and other professions. Mexicans were routinely banned from local public works projects as well. Many felt a deep ambivalence about applying for American citizenship. Loyalty to the Old Country was strong, and many cherished dreams of returning to live out their days in Mexico.

Ugly racist campaigns against Mexicans were common in the 1920s, especially when "cheap Mexican labor" was blamed for local unemployment or hard times. Stereotypes of Mexicans as "greasers" or "wetbacks" were prevalent in newspapers and movies of the day. Nativist efforts to limit Mexican immigration were thwarted by the lobbying of powerful agribusiness interests.

Mutual aid societies—*mutualistas*—became key social and political institutions in the Mexican communities of the Southwest and Midwest. They provided death benefits and widows' pensions for members and also served as centers of resistance to civil rights violations and discrimination. In 1928, the Federation of Mexican Workers Unions formed in response to a large farm labor strike in the Imperial Valley of California. A group of middle-class Mexican professionals in Texas organized the League of United Latin American Citizens (LULAC) in 1929. The founding of these organizations marked only the beginnings of a long

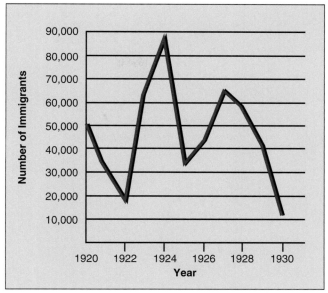

Mexican Immigration to the United States in the 1920s Many Mexican migrants avoided official border crossing stations so they would not have to pay visa fees. Thus, these official figures probably underestimated the true size of the decade's Mexican migration. As the economy contracted with the onset of the Great Depression, immigration from Mexico dropped off sharply.

struggle to bring economic, social, and racial equality to Mexican Americans.

The "New Negro"

The Great Migration spurred by World War I showed no signs of letting up during the 1920s, and African American communities in northern cities grew rapidly. New York City's Harlem began attracting middle-class African Americans in the prewar years. After the war, heavy black migration from the South and the Caribbean encouraged real estate speculators and landlords to remake Harlem as an exclusively black neighborhood.

Harlem emerged as the demographic and cultural capital of black America, but its appeal transcended national borders as mass migration from the Caribbean helped reshape the community. Between 1900 and 1930 some 300,000 West Indians emigrated to the United States, roughly half of whom settled in New York City. By the late 1920s about one-quarter of Harlem's population had been born in Jamaica, Barbados, Trinidad, the Bahamas, and other parts of the Caribbean. Some of the leading cultural, business, and political figures of the era—poet Claude McKay, newspaper publisher P. M. H. Savory, labor organizer Hubert Harrison, black nationalist Marcus Garvey—had roots in the West Indies. Most black Caribbean migrants came from societies where class differences mattered more than racial ones, and many refused to

Black Population, 1920 Although the Great Migration had drawn hundreds of thousands of African Americans to the urban North, the southern states of the former Confederacy still remained the center of the African American population in 1920.

accept racial bigotry without protest. A large number also carried with them entrepreneurial experience that contributed to their success in running small businesses. Intraracial tensions and resentment between American-born blacks and an increasingly visible West Indian population was one reflection of Harlem's transformation into a hemispheric center for black people.

The demand for housing in this restricted geographical area led to skyrocketing rents, but most Harlemites held low-wage jobs. This combination produced extremely overcrowded apartments, unsanitary conditions, and the rapid deterioration of housing stock. Disease and death rates were abnormally high. Yet Harlem also boasted a large middle-class population and supported a wide array of churches, theaters, newspapers and journals, and black-owned businesses. It became a magnet for African American intellectuals, artists, musicians, and writers from all over the world.

Harlem became the political and intellectual center for what writer Alain Locke called the "New Negro." Locke was referring to a new spirit in the work of black writers and intellectuals, an optimistic faith that encouraged African Americans to develop and celebrate their distinctive culture, firmly rooted in the history,

folk culture, and experiences of African American people. This faith was the common denominator uniting the disparate figures associated with the Harlem Renaissance. The assertion of cultural independence resonated in the poetry of Langston Hughes and Claude McKay, the novels of Zora Neale Hurston and Jessie Fauset, the essays of Countee Cullen and James Weldon Johnson, the acting of Paul Robeson, and the blues singing of Bessie Smith.

The newly militant spirit that black veterans had brought home from World War I matured and found a variety of expressions in the Harlem of the 1920s. New leaders and movements began to appear alongside established organizations like the National Association for the Advancement of Colored People. A. Philip Randolph began a long career as a labor leader, socialist, and civil rights activist in these years. Harlem was also headquarters to Marcus Garvey's Universal Negro Improvement Association. Garvey created a mass movement that stressed black economic self-determination and unity among the black communities of the United States, the Caribbean, and Africa. His newspaper, *Negro World*, spoke to black communities around the world, urging black businesses to trade among themselves.

Garvey's best-publicized project was the Black Star Line, a black-owned and -operated fleet of ships that would link people of African descent around the world. But insufficient capital and serious financial mismanagement resulted in the spectacular failure of the enterprise. In 1923, Garvey was found guilty of mail fraud in his fundraising efforts; he later went to jail and was subsequently deported to England. Despite the disgrace, Harlem's largest newspaper, the *Amsterdam News*, explained Garvey's continuing appeal to African Americans: "In a world where black is despised, he taught them that black is beautiful. He taught them to admire and praise black things and black people."

Harlem in the 1920s also became a popular tourist attraction for "slumming" whites. Nightclubs like the Cotton Club were often controlled by white organized crime figures. They featured bootleg liquor, floor shows, and the best jazz bands of the day, led by Duke Ellington, Fletcher Henderson, Cab Calloway, and Louis Armstrong. Yet these clubs were rigidly segregated. Black dancers, singers, and musicians provided the entertainment, but no African Americans were allowed in the audience. Chronicled in novels and newspapers, Harlem became a potent symbol to white America of the ultimate good time. For the vast majority of Harlem residents, the day-to-day reality was depressingly different.

The Election of 1928

The 1928 campaign featured two politicians who represented profoundly different sides of American life. Al Smith, the Democratic nominee for president, was a pure product of New York City's Lower East Side. Smith came from a background that included Irish, German, and Italian ancestry, and he was raised as a Roman Catholic. He rose through the political ranks of New York's Tammany Hall machine. A personable man with a deep sympathy for poor and working-class people, Smith served four terms as governor of New York, pushing through an array of laws reforming factory conditions, housing, and welfare programs.

Herbert Hoover easily won the Republican nomination after Calvin Coolidge announced he would not run for reelection. Hoover epitomized the successful and forward-looking American. An engineer and self-made millionaire, he offered a unique combination of experience in humanitarian war relief, administrative efficiency, and probusiness policies. Hoover was one of the best-known men in America and promised to continue the Republican control of national politics.

Smith himself quickly became the central issue of the campaign. His sharp New York accent, jarring to many Americans who heard it over the radio, marked him clearly as a man of the city. So did his brown derby and fashionable suits, as well as his promise to work for the

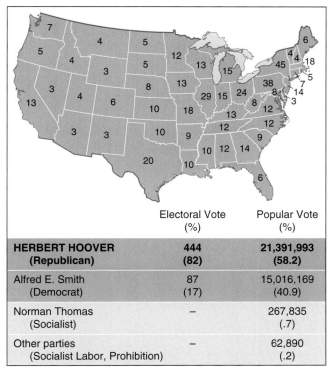

	Electoral Vote (%)	Popular Vote (%)
HERBERT HOOVER (Republican)	**444** **(82)**	**21,391,993** **(58.2)**
Alfred E. Smith (Democrat)	87 (17)	15,016,169 (40.9)
Norman Thomas (Socialist)	–	267,835 (.7)
Other parties (Socialist Labor, Prohibition)	–	62,890 (.2)

The Election of 1928 Although Al Smith managed to carry the nation's twelve largest cities, Herbert Hoover's victory in 1928 was one of the largest popular and electoral landslides in the nation's history.

repeal of Prohibition. As the first Roman Catholic nominee of a major party, Smith also drew a torrent of anti-Catholic bigotry, especially in the South and Midwest.

Hoover polled 21 million votes to Smith's 15 million, and swept the electoral college 444 to 87, including New York State. Even the Solid South, reliably Democratic since the Civil War, gave five states to Hoover—a clear reflection of the ethnocultural split in the party. Yet the election offered important clues to the future of the Democrats. Smith ran better in the big cities of the North and East than any Democrat in modern times. He outpolled Hoover in the aggregate vote of the nation's twelve largest cities and carried six of them, thus pointing the way to the Democrats' future dominance with urban, Northeastern, and ethnic voters.

CONCLUSION

America's big cities, if not dominant politically, now defined the nation's cultural and economic life as never before. The mass media brought cosmopolitan entertainments and values to the remotest small communities. New consumer durable goods associated with mass-production techniques—automobiles, radios, telephones, household appliances—were manufactured largely in cities. The advertising and public relations companies that sang their praises were also distinctly

CHRONOLOGY

1920	Prohibition takes effect
	Warren G. Harding is elected president
	Station KDKA in Pittsburgh goes on the air
	Census reports that urban population is greater than rural population for the first time
1921	First immigration quotas are established by Congress
	Sheppard-Towner Act establishes first federally funded health care program
1922	Washington conference produces Five-Power Treaty, scaling down navies
1923	Equal Rights Amendment is first introduced in Congress
	Harding dies in office; Calvin Coolidge becomes president
1924	Ku Klux Klan is at height of its influence
	Dawes Plan for war reparations stabilizes European economies
	Johnson-Reed Immigration Act tightens quotas established in 1921
1925	Scopes trial pits religious fundamentalism against modernity
	F. Scott Fitzgerald publishes *The Great Gatsby*
1926	National Broadcasting Company establishes first national radio network
1927	McNary-Haugen Farm Relief bill finally passed by Congress but is vetoed by President Coolidge as unwarranted federal interference in the economy
	Warner Brothers produces *The Jazz Singer,* the first feature-length motion picture with sound
	Charles Lindbergh makes first solo flight across the Atlantic Ocean
1928	Kellogg-Briand Pact renounces war
	Herbert Hoover defeats Al Smith for the presidency
1929	Robert and Helen Lynd publish their classic community study *Middletown*

urban enterprises. Even with the curtailing of European immigration, big cities attracted a kaleidoscopic variety of migrants: white people from small towns and farms, African Americans from the rural South, Mexicans from across the border, intellectuals and professionals looking to make their mark.

Many Americans, of course, remained deeply suspicious of postwar cultural and economic trends. Yet the partisans of Prohibition, members of the Ku Klux Klan, and religious fundamentalists usually found themselves on the defensive against what they viewed as alien cultural and economic forces centered in the metropolis. Large sectors of the population did not share in the era's prosperity. But the large numbers who did—or at least had a taste of good times—ensured Republican political dominance throughout the decade. Thus, America in the 1920s balanced dizzying change in the cultural and economic realms with conservative politics.

REVIEW QUESTIONS

1. Describe the impact of the "second industrial revolution" on American business, workers, and consumers. Which technological and economic changes had the biggest impact on American society?
2. Analyze the uneven distribution of the 1920s' economic prosperity. Which Americans gained the most, and which were largely left out?
3. How did an expanding mass culture change the contours of everyday life in the decade following World War I? What role did new technologies of mass communication play in shaping these changes?

What connections can you draw between the "culture of consumption," then and today?
4. What were the key policies and goals articulated by Republican political leaders of the 1920s? How did they apply these to both domestic and foreign affairs?
5. How did some Americans resist the rapid changes taking place in the post–World War I world? What cultural and political strategies did they employ?
6. Discuss the 1928 election as a mirror of the divisions in American society.

RECOMMENDED READING

Nancy F. Cott, *The Grounding of American Feminism* (1987). Includes a sophisticated analysis of the debates among feminists during the 1920s.

Lynn Dumenil, *The Modern Temper: America in the 1920s* (1995). An excellent synthesis of recent scholarship, which emphasizes the ambivalence that many Americans felt toward the emergence of modern society.

James J. Flink, *The Car Culture* (1975). The best single volume on the history of the automobile and how it changed American life.

David J. Goldberg, *Discontented America: The United States in the 1920s* (1999). Focuses on Americans' continuing discomfort with racial, ethnic, religious, and class difference during the decade.

Ellis W. Hawley, *The Great War and the Search for Modern Order* (1979). An influential study of the relations between the state and business and the growth of mass consumer society.

Desmond King, *Making Americans: Immigration, Race, and the Origins of Diverse Democracy* (2000). Fine analysis of the shift of U.S. immigration policies in the 1920s, with special attention to the influence of eugenics, and the long-term consequences of the new restrictive legislation.

Nancy Maclean, *Behind the Mask of Chivalry: The Making of the Second Ku Klux Klan* (1994). An excellent case study of the KKK in Athens, Georgia, with important insights on the Klan's relationship to issues involving gender and class difference.

Roland Marchand, *Advertising the American Dream: Making Way for Modernity, 1920–1940* (1985). A superb, beautifully illustrated account of the rise of the modern advertising industry.

Emily S. Rosenberg, *Spreading the American Dream* (1982). A fine study of American economic and cultural expansion around the world from 1890 to 1945.

Susan Smulyan, *Selling Radio: The Commercialization of American Broadcasting, 1920–1934* (1994). The best analysis of the rise of commercial radio broadcasting in the 1920s.

ON THE WEB

http://jurist.law.pitt.edu/trials17.htm

This University of Missouri–Kansas City Law School site contains a legal analysis of the Sacco-Vanzetti trial.

The Inaugural Addresses of the three Republican presidents of the 1920s:

http://www.bartleby.com/124/pres46.html

Warren G. Harding.

http://www.bartleby.com/124/pres47.html

Calvin Coolidge.

http://www.bartleby.com/124/pres48.html

Herbert Hoover.

http://www.archives.gov/digital_classroom/lessons/volstead_act/volstead_act.html

Several original photographs, primary documents, and the laws relating to Prohibition are posted on this National Archives site.

http://www.law.umkc.edu/faculty/projects/ftrials/scopes/scopes.htm

This University of Missouri–Kansas City Law School site has a very thorough site on the Scopes Monkey Trial (1925).

http://www.top-education.com/Speeches/RTHoover.htm

Herbert Hoover delivered this speech on October 22, 1928, as his acceptance speech for the Republican nomination for president. Here Hoover announced the "near abolition of poverty" and proclaimed the philosophy of rugged individualism.

http://www.prenhall.com/faragherbrief/map23.1

Examine the Great Migration in more detail. Why were African Americans drawn to northern cities?

TWENTY-FOUR

THE GREAT DEPRESSION AND THE NEW DEAL

▶ 1929–1940

CHAPTER OUTLINE

AMERICAN COMMUNITIES

Sit-Down Strike at Flint: Automobile Workers Organize a New Union

IN THE GLOOMY EVENING OF FEBRUARY 11, 1937, 400 TIRED, UNSHAVEN, but very happy strikers marched out of the sprawling automobile factory known as Fisher Body Number 1. Most carried American flags and small bundles of clothing. A makeshift banner on top of the plant announced "Victory Is Ours." A wildly cheering parade line of a thousand supporters greeted the strikers at the gates. Shouting with joy, honking horns, and singing songs, the celebrants marched to two other factories to greet other emerging strikers. After forty-four days, the great Flint sit-down strike was over.

Flint, Michigan, was the heart of production for General Motors, the largest corporation in the world. In 1936 GM's net profits had reached $285 million, and its total assets were $1.5 billion. Originally a center for lumbering and then carriage making, Flint had boomed with the auto industry during the 1920s. Thousands of migrants streamed into the city, attracted by assembly-line jobs averaging about $30 a week. By 1930 Flint's population had grown to about 150,000 people, 80 percent of whom depended on work at General Motors. A severe housing shortage made living conditions difficult. Tar-paper shacks, tents, even railroad cars were the only shelter available for many. Parts of the city resembled a mining camp.

The Great Depression hit Flint very hard. Employment at GM fell from a 1929 high of 56,000 to fewer than 17,000 in 1932. As late as 1938 close to half the city's families were receiving some kind of emergency relief. By that time, as in thousands of other American communities, Flint's private and county relief agencies had been overwhelmed by the needs of the unemployed and their families. Two new national agencies based in Washington, D.C., the Federal Emergency Relief Administration and the Works Progress Administration, had replaced local sources of aid during the economic crisis.

The United Automobile Workers (UAW) came to Flint in 1936 seeking to organize GM workers into one industrial union. The previous year, Congress had passed the National Labor Relations Act (also known as the Wagner Act), which made union organizing easier by guaranteeing the right of workers to join unions and to bargain collectively. The act established the National Labor Relations Board to oversee union elections and prohibit illegal antiunion activities by employers. But the obstacles to labor organizing were still enormous. Unemployment was high, and GM had maintained a vigorous antiunion policy for years. By the fall of 1936, the UAW had signed up only a thousand members. The key moment came with the seizure of two Flint GM plants by a few hundred auto workers on December 30, 1936. The idea was to stay in the factories until strikers could achieve a collective bargaining agreement with General Motors. "We don't aim to keep the plants or try to run them," explained one sit-downer to a reporter, "but we want to see that nobody takes our jobs. We don't think we're breaking the law, or at least we don't think we're doing anything really bad."

The sit-down strike was a new and daring tactic that gained popularity among American industrial workers during the 1930s. In 1936 there were forty-eight sit-downs involving nearly 90,000 workers, and in 1937 some 400,000 workers participated in 477 sit-down strikes. Sit-downs expressed the militant exuberance of the rank and file. As one union song of the day put it:

> When they tie the can to a union man,
> Sit down! Sit down!
> When they give him the sack they'll take him back,
> Sit down! Sit down!
> When the speed up comes, just twiddle your thumbs,
> Sit down! Sit down!
> When the boss won't talk don't take a walk,
> Sit down! Sit down!

The Flint strikers carefully organized themselves into what one historian called "the sit-down community." Each plant elected a strike committee and appointed its own police chief and sanitary engineer. Strikers were divided into "families" of fifteen, each with a captain. No alcohol was allowed, and strikers were careful not to destroy company property. Committees were organized for every conceivable purpose: food, recreation, sanitation, education, and contact with the outside. Sit-downers formed glee clubs and small orchestras to entertain themselves. Using loudspeakers, they broadcast concerts and speeches to their supporters outside the gates. A Women's Emergency Brigade—the strikers' wives, mothers, and daughters—

provided crucial support preparing food and maintaining militant picket lines.

As the sit-down strike continued through January 1937, support in Flint and around the nation grew. Over-all production in the GM empire dropped from 53,000 vehicles per week to 1,500. Reporters and union supporters flocked to the plants. On January 11, in the so-called Battle of Running Bulls, strikers and their supporters clashed violently with Flint police and private GM guards. Michigan governor Frank Murphy, sympathetic to the strikers, brought in the National Guard to protect them. He refused to enforce an injunction obtained by GM to evict the strikers.

In the face of determined unity by the sit-downers, GM gave in and recognized the UAW as the exclusive bargaining agent in all sixty of its factories. The strike was perhaps the most important in American labor history, sparking a huge growth in union membership in the automobile and other mass-production industries. Rose Pesotta, a textile union organizer, described the wild victory celebration in Flint's overflowing Pengelly Building: "People sang and joked and laughed and cried, deliriously joyful. Victory meant a freedom they had never known before. No longer would they be afraid to join unions."

Out of the tight-knit, temporary community of the sit-down strike emerged a looser yet more permanent kind of community: a powerful, nationwide trade union of automobile workers. The UAW struggled successfully to win recognition and collective bargaining rights from other carmakers, such as Chrysler and Ford. The national UAW, like other new unions in the mass-production industries, was composed of locals around the country. The permanent community of unionized auto workers won significant improvements in wages, working conditions, and benefits. Locals also became influential in the political and social lives of their larger communities—industrial cities such as Flint, Detroit, and Toledo. Nationally, organized labor became a crucial component of the New Deal political coalition and a key power broker in the Democratic Party. The new reality of a national community of organized labor would alter the national political and economic landscape for decades to come. ■

Flint

KEY TOPICS

- Causes and consequences of the Great Depression

- The politics of hard times

- Franklin D. Roosevelt and the two New Deals

- The expanding federal sphere in the West

- American cultural life during the 1930s

- Legacies and limits of New Deal reform

HARD TIMES

The Crash

Only about 4 million Americans out of a total population of 120 million owned any stocks when the tumbling of prices on the New York Stock Exchange ended the speculative mania of the 1920s. Many of these stock buyers had been lured into the market through easy-credit, margin accounts. These allowed investors to purchase stocks by making a small down payment (as low as 10 percent), borrowing the rest from a broker, and using the shares as collateral, or security, on the loan.

Although often portrayed as a one- or two-day catastrophe, the Wall Street crash of 1929 was in reality a steep downward slide. The bull market peaked in early September, and prices drifted downward. On October 23 the Dow Jones industrials lost 21 points in one hour, and many large investors concluded the boom was over. The boom itself rested on expectations of continually rising prices; once those expectations began to melt, the market had to decline. On Monday, October 28, the Dow lost 38 points, or 13 percent of its value. On October 29, "Black Tuesday," the bottom seemed to fall out. Over 16 million shares, more than double the previous record, were traded as panic selling took hold. For many stocks no buyers were available at any price.

The situation worsened. The market's fragile foundation of credit, based on the margin debt, quickly crumbled. Many investors with margin accounts had no choice but to sell when stock values fell. Since the shares themselves represented the security for their loans, more money had to be put up to cover the loans when prices declined. By mid-November about $30 billion in the market price of stocks had been wiped out. Half the value of the stocks listed in the *New York Times* index was lost in ten weeks.

The nation's political and economic leaders downplayed the impact of Wall Street's woes. "The fundamental business of the country," President Herbert Hoover told Americans in late October, "is on a sound and prosperous basis." Secretary of the Treasury Andrew Mellon spoke for many in the financial world when he described the benefits of the slump: "It will purge the rottenness out of the system." At the end of 1929 hardly anyone was predicting that a depression would follow the stock market crash.

Underlying Weaknesses

It would be oversimple to say that the stock market crash "caused" the Great Depression. But like a person who catches a chill, the economy after the crash became less resistant to existing sources of infection. The resulting sickness revealed underlying economic weaknesses left over from the previous decade. First, workers and consumers by and large received too small a share of the enormous increases in labor productivity.

Better machinery and more efficient industrial organization had increased labor productivity enormously. But wages and salaries had not risen nearly as much. In effect, the automobile of American capitalism had one foot pressed to the accelerator of production and another on the brake of consumption. Between 1923 and 1929 manufacturing output per worker-hour increased by 32 percent. Wages during the same period rose only 8 percent, or one-quarter the rise in productivity. Moreover, the rise in productivity itself had encouraged overproduction in many industries. The farm sector had never been able to regain its prosperity of the World War I years. Farmers suffered under a triple burden of declining prices for their crops, a drop in exports, and large debts incurred by wartime expansion (see Chapter 23).

The most important weakness in the economy was the extremely unequal distribution of income and wealth. In 1929, the top 0.1 percent of American families (24,000 families) had an aggregate income equal to that of the bottom 42 percent (11.5 million families). The top 5 percent of American families received 30 percent of the nation's income; the bottom 60 percent got only 26 percent. Nearly 80 percent of the nation's families (21.5 million households) had no savings; the top 0.1 percent held 34 percent of all savings.

The stock market crash undermined the confidence, investment, and spending of businesses and the well-to-do. Manufacturers decreased their production and began laying off workers, and layoffs brought further declines in consumer spending and another round of production cutbacks. A spurt of consumer spending might have checked this downward spiral, but consumers had less to spend as industries laid off workers and reduced work hours. With a shrinking market for products, businesses were hesitant to expand. A large proportion of the nation's banking funds were tied to the speculative bubble of Wall Street stock buying. Many banks began to fail as anxious depositors withdrew their funds, which were uninsured. Thousands of families lost their savings to these failures. An 86 percent plunge in agricultural prices between 1929 and 1933, compared to a decline in agricultural production of only 6 percent, brought suffering to America's farmers.

Mass Unemployment

At a time when unemployment insurance did not exist and public relief was completely inadequate, the loss of a job could mean economic catastrophe for workers and their families. Massive unemployment across America became the most powerful sign of a deepening depression. By 1933, 12.6 million workers—over one-quarter of the labor force—were without jobs. Other sources put the figure that year above 16 million, or nearly one out of every three workers. None of these statistics tells us how long people were unemployed or how many Americans found only part-time work.

What did it mean to be unemployed and without hope in the early 1930s? Figures give us only an outline of the grim reality. Many Americans, raised believing that they were responsible for their own fate, blamed themselves for their failure to find work. Contemporary journalists and social workers noted the common feelings of shame and guilt expressed by the unemployed. Even those who did not blame themselves struggled with feelings of inadequacy, uselessness, and despair. One unemployed Houston woman told a relief caseworker, "I'm just no good, I guess. I've given up ever amounting to anything. It's no use."

Joblessness proved especially difficult for men between the ages of thirty-five and fifty-five, the period

in their lives when family responsibilities were heaviest. Nathan Ackerman, a psychiatrist who went to Pennsylvania to observe the impact of prolonged unemployment on coal miners, found an enormous sense of "internal distress":

> They gave each other solace. They were loath to go home because they were indicted, as if it were their fault for being unemployed. . . . The women punished the men for not bringing home the bacon, by withholding themselves sexually . . . These men suffered from depression.

Women found it easier to hold onto jobs, since their labor was cheaper. Female clerks, secretaries, maids, and waitresses earned much less than male factory workers, but their jobs were more likely to survive hard times. Unemployment upset the psychological balance in many families by undermining the traditional authority of the male breadwinner. Men responded in a variety of ways: Some withdrew emotionally; others became angry or took to drinking. A few committed suicide. One Chicago social worker, writing about unemployment in 1934, summed up the strains she found in families: "Fathers feel they have lost their prestige in the home; there is much nagging, mothers nag at the fathers, parents nag at the children. Children of working age who earn meager salaries find it hard to turn over all their earnings and deny themselves even the greatest necessities and as a result leave home."

Pressures on those lucky enough to have a job increased as well. Anna Novak, a Chicago meat packer, recalled the degrading harassment at the hands of foremen: "You could get along swell if you let the boss slap you on the behind and feel you up." Fear of unemployment and a deep desire for security marked the Depression generation. "I mean there's a conditioning here by the Depression," a sanitation worker told an interviewer many years later. "I'm what I call a security cat. I don't dare switch [jobs]. 'Cause I got too much whiskers on it, seniority."

Hoover's Failure

The enormity of the Great Depression overwhelmed traditional—and meager—sources of relief. In most communities across America these sources were a patchwork of private agencies and local government units, such as towns, cities, or counties. They simply lacked the money, resources, and staff to deal with the worsening situation. One West Virginia coal-mining county with 1,500 unemployed miners had only $9,000 to meet relief needs for that year. Unemployed transients, attracted by warm weather, posed a special problem for communities in California and Florida.

By the end of 1931, Los Angeles had 70,000 nonresident jobless and homeless men; new arrivals numbered about 1,200 a day.

There was great irony, even tragedy, in President Hoover's failure to respond to human suffering. He had administered large-scale humanitarian efforts during World War I with great efficiency. Yet he failed to face the facts of the Depression. He resisted the growing calls from Congress and local communities for a greater federal role in relief efforts or public works projects. He worried, as he told Congress after vetoing one measure, about injuring "the initiative and enterprise of the American people." The President's Emergency Committee for Unemployment, established in 1930, and its successor, the President's Organization for Unemployment Relief (POUR), created in 1931, did little more than encourage local groups to raise money to help the unemployed.

Hoover's plan for recovery centered on restoring business confidence. His administration's most important institutional response to the depression was the Reconstruction Finance Corporation (RFC), established in early 1932. The RFC was designed to make government credit available to ailing banks, railroads, insurance companies, and other businesses, thereby stimulating economic activity. The key assumption here was that the credit problem was one of supply (for businesses) rather than demand (from consumers). The RFC managed to save numerous banks and other businesses from going under, but its approach did not hasten recovery.

Protest and the Election of 1932

By 1932, the desperate mood of many Americans was finding expression in direct, sometimes violent protests that were widely covered in the press. On March 7, Communist organizers led a march of several thousand Detroit auto workers and unemployed to the Ford River Rouge factory in nearby Dearborn. When the demonstrators refused orders to turn back, Ford-controlled police fired tear gas and bullets, killing four and seriously wounding fifty others. Some 40,000 people attended a tense funeral service a few days later. Desperate farmers in Iowa organized the Farmers' Holiday Association, aimed at raising prices by refusing to sell produce. In August, some 1,500 farmers turned back cargo trucks outside Sioux City, Iowa, and made a point by dumping milk and other perishables into ditches.

That spring the "Bonus Army" begin descending on Washington, D.C. to demand the cash bonuses that Congress had promised in 1924 to every veteran of World War I. By summer around 20,000 veterans and their families were camped out all over the capital city.

Their lobbying convinced the House to pass a bill for immediate payment, but the Senate rejected the bill and most of the veterans left. At the end of July, U.S. Army troops led by Chief of Staff General Douglas MacArthur forcibly evicted the remaining 2,000 veterans from their encampment. The spectacle of these unarmed and unemployed men, the heroes of 1918, being driven off by bayonets and bullets provided the most disturbing evidence yet of the failure of Hoover's administration.

In 1932, Democrats nominated Franklin D. Roosevelt, governor of New York, as their candidate. Roosevelt's acceptance speech stressed the need for reconstructing the nation's economy. "I pledge you, I pledge myself," he said, "to a new deal for the American people." But his plans for recovery were vague at best. Hoover bitterly condemned Roosevelt's ideas as a "radical departure" from the American way of life. But with the Depression growing worse every day, probably any Democrat would have defeated Hoover. Roosevelt carried forty-two states, taking the electoral college 472 to 59 and the popular vote by about 23 million to 16 million.

FDR AND THE FIRST NEW DEAL

FDR the Man

No president of this century had a greater impact on American life and politics than Franklin Delano Roosevelt. He was born in 1882 in Dutchess County, New York, where he grew up an only child, secure and confident, on his family's vast estate. Franklin's father, James, had made a fortune through railroad investments, but he was already in his fifties when Franklin was born, and it was his mother, Sara Delano, who was the dominant figure in his childhood. Roosevelt's education at Groton, Harvard, and Columbia Law School reinforced the aristocratic values of his family.

In 1905, Franklin married his distant cousin, Anna Eleanor Roosevelt, niece of President Theodore Roosevelt. Eleanor would later emerge as an influential adviser and political force on her own. Franklin turned to politics as a career early on. He was elected as a Democrat to the New York State Senate in 1910, served as assistant navy secretary from 1913 to 1920, and was nominated for vice president by the Democrats in the losing 1920 campaign.

In the summer of 1921 Roosevelt was stricken with polio at his summer home. He was never to walk again without support. The disease strengthened his relationship with Eleanor, who encouraged him not only to fight his handicap but to continue his political career. His patience and determination in fighting the illness transformed him. The wealthy aristocrat, for whom everything had come relatively easy, now personally understood the meaning of struggle and hardship. "Once I spent two years lying in bed trying to move my big toe," he recalled. "After that anything else seems easy."

Elected governor of New York in 1928, Roosevelt served two terms and won a national reputation for reform. As governor, his achievements included instituting unemployment insurance, strengthening child labor laws, providing tax relief for farmers, and providing pensions for the old. As the Depression hit the state, he slowly increased public works and set up a Temporary Emergency Relief Administration. With his eye on the White House, he began assembling a group of key advisers, the "brains trust," who would follow him to Washington. The "brain trusters" shared a faith in the power of experts to set the economy right and a basic belief in government–business cooperation. They rejected the old progressive dream of recreating an ideal society of small producers. Structural economic reform, they argued, must accept the modern reality of large corporate enterprise based on mass production and distribution.

Restoring Confidence

In the first days of his administration Roosevelt conveyed a sense of optimism and activism that helped restore the badly shaken confidence of the nation. "First of all," he told Americans in his Inaugural Address on March 4, 1933, "let me assert my firm belief that the only thing we have to fear is fear itself." The very next day he issued an executive order calling for a four-day "bank holiday" to shore up the country's ailing financial system. Contemporary investigations had revealed a disquieting pattern of stock manipulation, illegal loans to bank officials, and tax evasion that helped erode public confidence in the banking system. Between election day and the inauguration, the banking system had come alarmingly close to shutting down altogether due to widespread bank failures and the hoarding of currency.

Roosevelt, therefore, called for a special session of Congress to deal with the banking crisis as well as with unemployment aid and farm relief. On March 12 he broadcast his first "fireside chat" to explain the steps he had taken to meet the financial emergency. These radio broadcasts became a standard part of Roosevelt's political technique, and they proved enormously successful. They communicated a genuine sense of compassion from the White House.

Congress immediately passed the Emergency Banking Act, which gave the president broad discretionary powers over all banking transactions and foreign

This *New Yorker* magazine cover depicted an ebullient Franklin D. Roosevelt riding to his 1933 inauguration in the company of a glum Herbert Hoover. This drawing typified many mass media images of the day contrasting the different moods and temperaments of the new President and the defeated incumbent.

SOURCE: Franklin D. Roosevelt Library.

exchange. It authorized healthy banks to reopen only under licenses from the Treasury Department and provided for greater federal authority in managing the affairs of failed banks. By the middle of March about half the country's banks, holding about 90 percent of the nation's deposits, were open for business again. Banks began to attract new deposits from people who had been holding back their money. The bank crisis had passed.

The Hundred Days

From March to June of 1933—the "Hundred Days"—FDR pushed through Congress an extraordinary number of acts designed to combat various aspects of the Depression. What came to be called the New Deal was no unified program to end the Depression but rather an improvised series of reform and relief measures, some of which seemed to contradict each other. Roosevelt

OVERVIEW

KEY LEGISLATION OF THE FIRST NEW DEAL ("HUNDRED DAYS," MARCH 9–JUNE 16, 1933)

Legislation	Purpose
Emergency Banking Relief Act	Enlarged federal authority over private banks Government loans to private banks
Civilian Conservation Corps	Unemployment relief Conservation of natural resources
Federal Emergency Relief Administration	Direct federal money for relief, funneled through state and local governments
Agricultural Adjustment Administration	Federal farm-aid based on parity pricing and subsidy
Tennessee Valley Authority	Economic development and cheap electricity for Tennessee Valley
National Industrial Recovery Act	Self-regulating industrial codes to revive economic activity
Public Works Administration	Federal public works projects to increase employment and consumer spending

responded to pressures from Congress, from business, and from organized labor, but he also used his own considerable influence over public opinion to get his way.

Five measures were particularly important and innovative. The Civilian Conservation Corps (CCC), established in March 1933 as an unemployment relief effort, provided work for jobless young men in protecting and conserving the nation's natural resources. Road construction, reforestation, flood control, and national park improvements were some of the major projects performed in work camps across the country. CCC workers received room and board and $30 each month, up to $25 of which had to be sent home to dependents. By the time the program was phased out in 1942, more than 2.5 million youths had worked in some 1,500 CCC camps.

In May, Congress authorized $500 million for the Federal Emergency Relief Administration (FERA). Half the money went as direct relief to the states; the rest was distributed on the basis of a dollar of federal aid for every three dollars of state and local funds spent for relief. This system of outright federal grants differed significantly from Hoover's approach, which provided only for loans. Establishment of work relief projects, however, was left to state and local governments. To direct the FERA Roosevelt turned to Harry Hopkins, an experienced reformer from the world of New York social work. A brilliant administrator with a special commitment to ending discrimination in relief work, Hopkins became the New Deal's most influential figure in relief policies and one of Roosevelt's most trusted advisers.

The Agricultural Adjustment Administration (AAA) was set up to provide immediate relief to the nation's farmers. The AAA established parity prices for basic farm commodities based on the purchasing power that farmers had enjoyed during the prosperous years of 1909 to 1914. That period now became the benchmark for setting the prices of farm commodities. The AAA also incorporated the principle of subsidy, whereby farmers received benefit payments in return for reducing acreage or otherwise cutting production where surpluses existed. The funds for these payments were to be raised from new taxes on food processing.

The AAA raised total farm income and was especially successful in pushing up the prices of wheat, cotton, and corn. But it had some troubling side effects as well. Landlords often failed to share their AAA payments with tenant farmers, and they frequently used benefits to buy tractors and other equipment that displaced sharecroppers. Many Americans were disturbed, too, by the sight of surplus crops, livestock, and milk being destroyed while millions went hungry.

The Southern Tenant Farmers Union (STFU), founded in 1934, emerged as an important voice of protest against AAA policies. The STFU (over half of whose members were black) succeeded in drawing national attention to the plight of sharecroppers and tenant farmers, but it failed to influence national farm policy.

The Tennessee Valley Authority (TVA) proved to be one of the most unique and controversial projects of the New Deal era. The TVA, an independent public corporation, built dams and power plants, produced cheap fertilizer for farmers, and, most significantly, brought cheap electricity for the first time to thousands of people in six southern states. Denounced by some as a dangerous step toward socialism, the TVA stood for decades as a model of how careful government planning could dramatically improve the social and economic welfare of an underdeveloped region.

On the very last of the Hundred Days, Congress passed the National Industrial Recovery Act, the closest attempt yet at a systematic plan for economic recovery. In theory, each industry would be self-governed by a code hammered out by representatives of business, labor, and the consuming public. Once approved by the NRA in Washington, the codes would have the force of law. In practice, almost all the NRA codes were written by the largest firms in any given industry; labor and consumers got short shrift. The sheer administrative complexities involved with code writing and compliance made a great many people unhappy with the NRA's operation.

The Public Works Administration (PWA), led by Secretary of the Interior Harold Ickes, authorized $3.3 billion for the construction of roads, public buildings, and other projects. The idea was to provide jobs and, thus, stimulate the economy through increased consumer spending. Eventually the PWA spent over $4.2 billion building roads, schools, post offices, bridges, courthouses, and other public buildings around the country. In thousands of communities today, these structures remain the most tangible reminders of the New Deal era.

LEFT TURN AND THE SECOND NEW DEAL

Roosevelt's Critics

Criticism of the New Deal came from the right and the left. On the right, pro-Republican newspapers and the American Liberty League, a group of conservative businessmen organized in 1934, denounced Roosevelt and his advisers. Dominated by wealthy executives of Du Pont and General Motors, the league attracted support from a group of conservative Democrats, including Al Smith, the former presidential candidate, who declared the New Deal's laws "socialistic." The league supported anti–New Dealers for Congress, but in the 1934 election Democrats built up their majorities from 310 to 319 in the House and from 60 to 69 in the Senate—an unusually strong showing for the incumbent party in a midterm election.

Some of Roosevelt's staunchest early supporters turned critical. Father Charles E. Coughlin, a Catholic priest in suburban Detroit, attracted a huge national radio audience of 40 million listeners with passionate sermons attacking Wall Street, international bankers, and "plutocratic capitalism." Coughlin at first supported Roosevelt and the New Deal, and he tried to build a

close personal relationship with the president. But by 1934 the ambitious Coughlin, frustrated by his limited influence on the administration, began attacking FDR. Roosevelt was a tool of special interests, he charged, who wanted dictatorial powers.

More troublesome for Roosevelt and his allies were the vocal and popular movements on the left. In California, well-known novelist and socialist Upton Sinclair entered the 1934 Democratic primary for governor. He proposed a $50 a month pension for all poor people over age sixty. Sinclair shocked local and national Democrats by winning the primary easily. He lost a close general election only because the Republican candidate received heavy financial and tactical support from wealthy Hollywood studio executives and frightened regular Democrats.

Huey Long, Louisiana's flamboyant backcountry orator, posed the greatest potential threat to Roosevelt's leadership. Long had captured Louisiana's governorship in 1928 by attacking the state's entrenched oil industry and calling for a radical redistribution of wealth. In office, he significantly improved public education, roads, medical care, and other public services, winning the loyalty of the state's poor farmers and industrial workers. Elected to the U.S. Senate in 1930, Long came to Washington with national ambitions. He at first supported Roosevelt, but in 1934 he began denouncing the New Deal as a failure and organized the Share Our Wealth Society. Long promised that limiting the size of large fortunes would mean a homestead worth $5,000 and a $2,500 annual income for everyone. Although Long's economics were fuzzy at best, he undoubtedly touched a deep nerve with his "Every Man a King" slogan. The Democratic National Committee was shocked when a secret poll in the summer of 1935 revealed that Long might attract 3 or 4 million votes. Only his assassination that September by a disgruntled political enemy prevented Long's third-party candidacy, which might have proved disastrous for FDR.

A newly militant labor movement also loomed as a force to be reckoned with. Section 7a of the National Industrial Recovery Act required that workers be allowed to bargain collectively with employers, through representatives of their own choosing. Though this provision of the NIRA was not enforced, it did help raise expectations and spark union organizing. Almost 1.5 million workers took part in some 1,800 strikes in 1934. But employers resisted unionization nearly everywhere, often with violence and the help of local and state police.

The Second Hundred Days

The popularity of leaders like Sinclair, Townsend, and Long suggested Roosevelt might be losing electoral support among workers, farmers, the aged, and the

OVERVIEW

KEY LEGISLATION OF THE SECOND NEW DEAL (1935–1938)

Legislation	Purpose
Emergency Relief Appropriations Act (1935) (includes Works Progress Administration)	Large-scale public works program for the jobless
Social Security Act (1935)	Federal old-age pensions and unemployment insurance
National Labor Relations Act (1935)	Federal guarantee of right to organize trade unions and collective bargaining
Resettlement Administration (1935)	Relocation of poor rural families Reforestation and soil erosion projects
National Housing Act (1937)	Federal funding for public housing and slum clearance
Fair Labor Standards Act (1938)	Federal minimum wage and maximum hours

unemployed. In early 1935, Roosevelt and his closest advisers responded by turning left and concentrating on a new program of social reform. What came to be called the "Second Hundred Days" marked the high point of progressive lawmaking in the New Deal.

In April the administration pushed through the Emergency Relief Appropriation Act, which allocated $5 billion for large-scale public works programs for the jobless. The major responsible agency here was the Works Progress Administration (WPA), led by Harry Hopkins. Over the next seven years Hopkins oversaw the employment of more than 8 million Americans on a vast array of construction projects: roads, bridges, dams, airports, and sewers. Among the most innovative WPA programs were community service projects that employed thousands of jobless artists, musicians, actors, and writers.

The landmark Social Security Act of 1935 provided for old-age pensions and unemployment insurance. A payroll tax on workers and their employers created a fund from which retirees received monthly pensions after age sixty-five. The unemployment compensation plan established a minimum weekly payment and a minimum number of weeks during which those who lost jobs could collect. The original law failed to cover domestics and farm workers, many of whom were Latinos and African Americans. It also made no provisions for casual laborers or public employees. And to collect unemployment, one had to have first lost a job. But the law, which has since been amended many times, established the crucial principle of federal responsibility for America's most vulnerable citizens.

Another 1935 law, the National Labor Relations Act (often called the Wagner Act for its chief sponsor,

Democratic senator Robert F. Wagner of New York), guaranteed the right of American workers to join or form independent labor unions and bargain collectively for improved wages, benefits, and working conditions. The National Labor Relations Board would conduct secret-ballot elections in shops and factories to determine which union, if any, workers desired as their sole bargaining agent. The law also defined and prohibited unfair labor practices by employers, including firing workers for union activity.

Finally, the Resettlement Administration (RA) produced one of the most utopian New Deal programs, one designed to create new kinds of model communities. The RA helped destitute farm families relocate to more productive areas. It granted loans for purchasing land and equipment, and it directed reforestation and soil erosion projects, particularly in the hard-hit Southwest. Due to lack of funds and poor administration, however, only about 1 percent of the projected 500,000 families were actually moved.

Labor's Upsurge: Rise of the CIO

In 1932 the American labor movement was nearly dead. Yet by 1942, unions claimed more than 10.5 million members, nearly a third of the total nonagricultural workforce. This remarkable turnaround was one of the key events of the Depression era. The growth in the size and power of the labor movement permanently changed the work lives and economic status of millions, as well as the national and local political landscapes.

At the core of this growth was a series of dramatic successes in the organization of workers in large-scale, mass-production industries, such as those producing automobiles, steel, rubber, electrical goods, and textiles.

Workers in these fields had largely been ignored by the conservative, craft-conscious unions that dominated the American Federation of Labor. At the 1935 AFL convention, a group of more militant union officials led by John L. Lewis (of the United Mine Workers) and Sidney Hillman (of the Amalgamated Clothing Workers) formed the Committee for Industrial Organization (CIO). They emphasized the need for opening the new unions to all, regardless of a worker's level of skill. And they differed from nearly all old-line AFL unions by calling for the inclusion of black and women workers. In 1938 CIO unions withdrew from the AFL and reorganized themselves as the Congress of Industrial Organizations.

The gruff son of a Welsh miner, Lewis was articulate, ruthless, and very ambitious. He saw the new legal protection given by the Wagner Act as a historic opportunity. But despite the act—whose constitutionality was unclear until 1937—Lewis knew that establishing permanent unions in the mass-production industries would be a bruising battle. He committed the substantial resources of the United Mine Workers to a series of organizing drives, focusing first on the steel and auto industries. Many CIO organizers were Communists or radicals of other persuasions, and their dedication, commitment, and willingness to work within disciplined organizations proved invaluable in the often dangerous task of creating industrial unions.

Militant rank-and-file unionists were often ahead of Lewis and other CIO leaders. After the dramatic breakthrough in the Flint sit-down strike at General Motors, membership in CIO unions grew rapidly. In eight months, membership in the United Automobile Workers alone soared from 88,000 to 400,000. CIO victories in the steel, rubber, and electrical industries followed, but often at a very high cost. One bloody example of the perils of union organizing was the 1937 Memorial Day Massacre in Chicago. In a field near the struck Republic Steel Mill in South Chicago, police fired into a crowd of union supporters, killing ten workers and wounding scores more.

Over all, the success of the CIO's organizing drives was remarkable. For the first time ever, the labor movement had gained a permanent place in the nation's mass-production industries. Organized labor took its place as a key power broker in Roosevelt's New Deal and the national Democratic Party. Frances Perkins, FDR's secretary of labor and the nation's first woman cabinet member, captured the close relationship between the new unionism and the New Deal: "Programs long thought of as merely labor welfare, such as shorter hours, higher wages, and a voice in the terms of conditions of work, are really essential economic factors for recovery."

The New Deal Coalition at High Tide

Did the American public support Roosevelt and his New Deal policies? Both major political parties looked forward to the 1936 elections as a national referendum, and the campaign itself was an exciting and hard-fought contest. Very few political observers predicted its lopsided result.

Republicans nominated Governor Alfred M. Landon of Kansas, an easygoing, colorless man with little personal magnetism, emphasized a nostalgic appeal to traditional American values. His campaign served as a lightning rod for all those, including many conservative Democrats, who were dissatisfied with Roosevelt and the direction he had taken.

Roosevelt attacked the "economic royalists" who denied that government "could do anything to protect the citizen in his right to work and his right to live." At the same time, FDR was careful to distance himself from radicalism. "It was this administration," he declared, "which saved the system of private profit and free enterprise after it had been dragged to the brink of ruin." As Roosevelt's campaign crossed the country, his advisers were heartened by huge and enthusiastic crowds, especially in large cities like Chicago and Pittsburgh. Still, the vast majority of the nation's newspapers endorsed Landon. And a widely touted "scientific" poll by the Literary Digest forecast a Republican victory in November.

On Election day Roosevelt carried every state but Maine and Vermont, polling 61 percent of the popular vote. The Literary Digest, it turned out, had drawn the sample for its poll from people whose addresses were listed in telephone directories and car registration records, thus omitting the poorer Americans who had no telephones or cars—and who supported Roosevelt. In 1936 the Democrats drew millions of new voters into the political process and at the same time forged a new coalition of voters that would dominate national politics for two generations.

This "New Deal coalition," as it came to be known, included traditional-minded white southern Democrats, big-city political machines, industrial workers of all races, trade unionists, and many Depression-hit farmers. Roosevelt was especially popular among first- and second-generation Catholics and Jews, and the New Deal drew enthusiastic support from millions in the ethnic working class who had never bothered with politics. As one Slovak worker in Chicago's stock yards put it, "Our people did not know anything about the government until the Depression years. In my neighborhood, I don't remember anyone voting." The severity of the Great Depression had overwhelmed the ethnically based support networks—mutual benefit societies, immigrant banks, and religious charities—

that had traditionally helped so many to survive hard times. Working-class voters in large cities like New York, Chicago, Detroit, and Philadelphia increasingly took credit for putting and keeping Democrats in power locally and nationally—and their attitudes toward politics changed. The federal government no longer seemed so remote or irrelevant to their lives. Popular federal programs like Social Security, the WPA, and Home Owners Loan Corporation mortgages changed the consciousness of a generation of the ethnic working class. In exchange for their votes, they now looked to the state—especially the federal government—for relief, protection, and help in achieving the American dream.

THE NEW DEAL AND THE WEST

The Dust Bowl

The southern Great Plains had suffered several drought years in the early 1930s. Such dry spells occurred regularly in roughly twenty-year cycles. But this time the

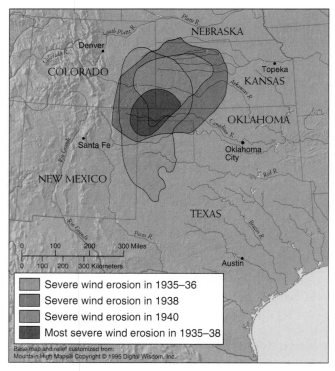

The Dust Bowl, 1935–1940   This map shows the extent of the Dust Bowl in the southern Great Plains. Federal programs designed to improve soil conservation, water management, and farming practices could not prevent a mass exodus of hundreds of thousands out of the Great Plains.

parched earth became swept up in violent dust storms. Black blizzards of dust a mile and a half high rolled across the landscape, darkening the sky and whipping the earth into great drifts of dust that settled over hundreds of miles. Dust storms made it difficult for humans and livestock to breathe and destroyed crops and trees over vast areas.   The hardest-hit regions were western Kansas, eastern Colorado, western Oklahoma, the Texas Panhandle, and eastern New Mexico. It was the calamity in this southern part of the Great Plains that prompted a Denver journalist to coin the phrase "Dust Bowl." Dust storms turned day into night, terrifying those caught in them. "Dust pneumonia" and other respiratory infections afflicted thousands, and many travelers found themselves stranded in automobiles and trains unable to move. The dust storms were largely the consequence of years of stripping the landscape of its natural vegetation. During World War I, wheat fetched record-high prices on the world market, and for the next twenty years Great Plains farmers had turned the region into a vast wheat factory. With native grasses destroyed for the sake of wheat growing, there was nothing left to prevent soil erosion. Dust storms blew away tens of millions of acres of rich topsoil, and thousands of farm families left the region. Those who stayed suffered deep economic and psychological losses from the calamity.

The Department of Agriculture, under Secretary Henry A. Wallace, sought to change farming practices to relieve the distress. The Soil Conservation Service (SCS) conducted research into controlling wind and water erosion, set up demonstration projects, and offered technical assistance, supplies, and equipment to farmers engaged in conservation work on farms and ranches. The SCS pumped additional federal funds into the Great Plains and created a new rural organization, the soil conservation district, which administered conservation regulations locally.

By 1940 the acreage subject to blowing in the Dust Bowl area of the southern Plains had been reduced from roughly 50 million acres to less than 4 million acres. In the face of the Dust Bowl disaster, New Deal farm policies had restricted market forces in agriculture.

While large landowners and ranchers reaped sizable benefits from AAA subsidies and other New Deal programs, tenant farmers and sharecroppers received very little. In the cotton lands of Texas, Oklahoma, Missouri, and Arkansas, thousands of tenant and sharecropper families were forced off the land. They became part of a stream of roughly 300,000 people, disparagingly called "Okies," who migrated to California in the 1930s. Most Okies could find work only as poorly paid agricultural laborers in the fertile San Joaquin and Imperial Valley districts. There they faced discrimination and scorn as "poor white trash" while they struggled to create communities amid the squalor of migrant labor camps. Only with the outbreak of World War II and the pressing demand for labor were migrants able to significantly improve their situation.

Mexican farm laborers faced stiff competition from Dust Bowl refugees. Southwestern communities, responding to racial hostility from unemployed whites and looking for ways to reduce their welfare burden, campaigned to deport Mexicans and Mexican Americans.

Water Policy

The New Deal ushered in an era of large-scale water projects designed to provide irrigation and cheap power and to prevent floods. The long-range impact of these undertakings on western life was enormous. The key government agency in this realm was the Bureau of Reclamation of the Department of the Interior, established under the National Reclamation Act of 1902. Until the late 1920s the bureau's efforts had been of little consequence, providing irrigation for only a very small portion of land. But its fortunes changed when its focus shifted to building huge multipurpose dams designed to control entire river systems.

The first of these projects was the Boulder Dam (later renamed the Hoover Dam). The dam, actually begun during the Hoover administration, was designed to harness the Colorado River, wildest and most isolated of the major western rivers. Its planned benefits included flood prevention, the irrigation of California's Imperial Valley, the supplying of domestic water for southern California, and the generation of cheap electricity for Los Angeles and southern Arizona. Hoover, however, had opposed the public power aspect of the project, arguing that the government ought not to compete with private utility companies. Roosevelt's support forgovernment-sponsored power projects was a significant factor in his winning the political backing of the West in 1932 and subsequent election years.

The success of Boulder Dam transformed the Bureau of Reclamation into a major federal agency with huge resources at its disposal. In 1938 it completed the All-American Canal—an 80-mile channel connecting the Colorado River to the Imperial Valley, with a 130-mile branch to the Coachella Valley. More than a million acres of desert land were opened up to the cultivation of citrus fruits, melons, vegetables, and cotton. Irrigation districts receiving water promised to repay, without interest, the cost of the canal over a forty-year period. This interest-free loan was in effect a huge government subsidy to the private growers who benefited from the canal.

The largest power and irrigation project of all was the Grand Coulee Dam, northwest of Spokane, Washington. Completed in 1941, it was designed to convert the power of the Columbia River into cheap electricity and to irrigate previously uncultivated land, thereby stimulating the economic development of the Pacific Northwest. The construction of Grand Coulee employed tens of thousands of workers and pumped millions of dollars into the region's badly depressed economy. Grand Coulee provided the cheapest electricity in the United States and helped attract new manufacturing to a region previously dependent on the export of raw materials, such as lumber and metals.

The Grand Coulee and smaller dams nearby reduced the Columbia River, long a potent symbol of the western wilderness, to a string of lakes. Spawning salmon could no longer run the river above the dam. In California, the federal guarantee of river water made a relative handful of large farmers fabulously wealthy. But tens of thousands of farm workers, mostly of Mexican descent, labored in the newly fertile fields for very low wages, and their health suffered from contact with pesticides. The Colorado River, no longer emptying into the Pacific, began to build up salt deposits, making its water increasingly unfit for drinking or irrigation. Water pollution in the form of high salinity continues to plague the 2,000-mile river to this day.

DEPRESSION-ERA CULTURE

A New Deal for the Arts

The Depression hit America's writers, artists, and teachers just as hard as blue-collar workers. In 1935, the WPA allocated $300 million for the unemployed in these fields. Over the next four years, Federal Project No. 1, an umbrella agency covering writing, theater, music, and the visual arts, proved to be one of the most innovative and successful New Deal programs. "Federal One," as it was called, offered work to desperate artists and intellectuals, enriched the cultural lives of millions, and left a substantial legacy of artistic and cultural production.

The Federal Writers Project (FWP) employed 5,000 writers on a variety of programs. Most notably, it produced a popular series of state and city guidebooks, each combining history, folklore, and tourism. The 150-volume "Life in America" series included valuable oral histories of former slaves, studies of ethnic and Indian cultures, and pioneering collections of American songs and folk tales. Work on the Writers Project helped many American writers to survive, hone their craft, and go on to great achievement and prominence.

These included Ralph Ellison, Richard Wright, Margaret Walker, John Cheever, Saul Bellow, and Zora Neale Hurston. Novelist Anzia Yezierska recalled a strong spirit of camaraderie among the writers: "Each morning I walked to the Project as lighthearted as if I were going to a party."

The Federal Theater Project, reached as many as 30 million Americans with its productions. Tickets were cheap, and a variety of dramatic forms were made available. Among its most successful productions were the "Living Newspaper" plays based on contemporary controversies and current events.

The Federal Music Project, under Nikolai Sokoloff of the Cleveland Symphony Orchestra, employed 15,000 musicians and financed hundreds of thousands of low-priced public concerts by touring orchestras. The Composers' Forum Laboratory supported new works by American composers such as Aaron Copland and William Schuman.

Among the painters who received government assistance through the FAP were Willem de Kooning, Jackson Pollock, and Louise Nevelson. The FAP employed painters and sculptors to teach studio skills and art history in schools, churches, and settlement houses. It also commissioned artists to paint hundreds of murals on the walls of post offices, meeting halls, courthouses, and other government buildings.

The Documentary Impulse

During the 1930s an enormous number of artists, novelists, journalists, photographers, and filmmakers tried to document the devastation wrought by the Depression in American communities. They also depicted people's struggles to cope with and reverse hard times.

The "documentary impulse" became a prominent style in 1930s cultural expression. The most direct and influential expression of the documentary style was the photograph. In 1935 Roy Stryker, chief of the Historical Section of the Resettlement Administration (later part of the Farm Security Administration), gathered a remarkable group of photographers to help document the work of the agency. These photographers, including Dorothea Lange, Walker Evans, Arthur Rothstein, Russell Lee, Ben Shahn, and Marion Post Wolcott, left us the single most significant visual record of the Great Depression.

That double vision, combining a frank portrayal of pain and suffering with a faith in the possibility of overcoming disaster, could be found in many other cultural works of the period. John Steinbeck's *Grapes of Wrath* (1939) sympathetically portrayed the hardships of Oklahoma Dust Bowl migrants on their way to California. "We ain't gonna die out," Ma Joad asserts near the end of the book. "People is goin' on—changing' a little, maybe, but goin' right on." A similar, if more per-

sonal, ending could be found in Margaret Mitchell's 1936 bestseller *Gone with the Wind*. Although this romantic novel was set in the Civil War–era South, many Americans identified with Scarlett O'Hara's determination to overcome the disaster of war.

Waiting for Lefty

For some, the capitalist system itself, with its enormous disparities of private wealth amid desperate poverty, was the culprit responsible for the Great Depression. Relatively few Americans became Communists or socialists in the 1930s (at its height, the Communist Party of the United States had perhaps 100,000 members), and many of these remained active for only a brief time. Yet Marxist analysis, with its emphasis on class conflict and the failures of capitalism, had a wide influence on the era's thought and writing.

Some writers joined the Communist Party believing it to be the best hope for political revolution. They saw in the Soviet Union an alternative to an American system that appeared mired in exploitation, racial inequality, and human misery. Communist writers, like the novelist Michael Gold and the poet Meridel LeSueur, sought to radicalize art and literature, and they celebrated collective struggle over individual achievement.

A more common pattern for intellectuals, especially when they were young, was brief flirtation with communism. Many African American writers, attracted by the Communist Party's militant opposition to lynching, job discrimination, and segregation, briefly joined the party or found their first supportive audiences there. These included Richard Wright, Ralph Ellison, and Langston Hughes. Many playwrights and actors associated with New York's influential Group Theater were part of the Communist Party orbit in those years. One production of the group, Clifford Odets's *Waiting for Lefty* (1935), depicted a union organizing drive among taxi drivers. At the play's climax, the audience was invited to join the actors in shouting "Strike!" A commercial and political success, it offered perhaps the most celebrated example of radical, politically engaged art.

Left-wing influence reached its height after 1935 during the "Popular Front" period. Alarmed by the rise of fascism in Europe, communists around the world followed the Soviet line of uniting with liberals and all other antifascists. Communists became strong supporters of Roosevelt's New Deal, and their influence was especially strong within the various WPA arts projects. Some 3,200 Americans volunteered for the Communist Party–organized Abraham Lincoln Brigade, which fought in the Spanish civil war on the republican side against the fascists led by Francisco Franco.

Film and Radio in the 1930s

Several film genres proved enormously popular during the 1930s. Gangster films did very well in the early Depression years. They depicted violent criminals brought to justice by society—but along the way they gave audiences a vicarious exposure to the pleasures of wealth, power, and lawbreaking. Social disorder was treated comically in Marx Brothers films. Mae West's popular comedies made people laugh by subverting expectations about sex roles. West was an independent woman, not afraid of pleasure. When Cary Grant asked her, "Haven't you ever met a man who could make you happy?" she replied, "Sure, lots of times."

Movie musicals offered audiences extravagant song-and-dance spectacles, as in Busby Berkeley's *Gold Diggers of 1933* and *42nd Street* (1933). "Screwball comedies" featured sophisticated, fast-paced humor and usually paired popular male and female stars: Clark Gable and Claudette Colbert in *It Happened One Night* (1934), Katharine Hepburn and Cary Grant in *Bringing Up Baby* (1938). A few movies, notably from the Warner Brothers studio, tried to offer a more "socially conscious" view of Depression-era life. By and large, however, Hollywood avoided confronting controversial social or political issues.

The Depression helped radio expand as an influx of talent arrived from the weakened worlds of vaudeville, ethnic theater, and the recording industry. The well-financed networks offered an attractive outlet to advertisers seeking a national audience. Radio programming achieved a regularity and professionalism absent in the 1920s, making it much easier for a listener to identify a show with its sponsor.

Much of network radio was based on older cultural forms. The variety show, hosted by comedians and singers and based on the old vaudeville format, was the first important style. It featured stars like Eddie Cantor, Ed Wynn, Kate Smith, and Al Jolson, who constantly plugged the sponsor's product. The use of a studio audience re-created the human interaction so necessary in vaudeville. The popular comedy show *Amos 'n' Andy* adapted the minstrel "blackface" tradition to the new medium. White comedians Freeman Gosden and Charles Correll used only their two voices to invent a world of stereotyped African Americans for their millions of listeners.

The spectacular growth of the daytime serial, or soap opera, dominated radio drama. Aimed mainly at women working in the home, "soaps" revolved around strong, warm female characters who provided advice and strength to weak, indecisive friends and relatives. Thrillers such as *Inner Sanctum* and *The Shadow* emphasized crime and suspense. These shows made great use of music and sound effects to sharpen their impact.

THE LIMITS OF REFORM

Court Packing

In May 1935, in *Schecter* v. *United States*, the Supreme Court found the National Recovery Administration unconstitutional in its entirety. Its ruling in *Butler* v. *United States*, in early 1936, invalidated the Agricultural Adjustment Administration. The Court was composed mostly of Republican appointees, six of whom were over seventy. Roosevelt looked for a way to get more friendly judges on the high court.

In February 1937, FDR asked Congress for legislation that would expand the Supreme Court from nine to a maximum of fifteen justices. The president would be empowered to make a new appointment whenever an incumbent judge failed to retire upon reaching age seventy. Roosevelt argued that age prevented justices from keeping up with their workload, but few people believed this logic. Newspapers almost unanimously denounced FDR's "court-packing bill."

Even more damaging was the determined opposition from a coalition of conservatives and outraged New Dealers in the Congress, such as Democratic senator Burton K. Wheeler of Montana. As the battle dragged on through the spring and summer, FDR's claims weakened. Conservative justice Willis Van Devanter announced plans to retire, giving Roosevelt the chance to make his first Court appointment.

More important, the Court upheld the constitutionality of some key laws from the second New Deal, including the Social Security Act and the National Labor Relations Act. At the end of August, FDR backed off from his plan and accepted a compromise bill that reformed lower court procedures but left the Supreme Court untouched. FDR lost the battle for his judiciary proposal, but he may have won the war for a more responsive Court. Still, the political price was very high. The Court fight badly weakened Roosevelt's relations with Congress. Many more conservative Democrats now felt free to oppose further New Deal measures.

The Women's Network

The Great Depression and the New Deal brought some significant changes for women in American economics and politics. Most women continued to perform unpaid domestic labor within their homes, work that was not covered by the Social Security Act. A growing minority, however, also worked for wages and salaries outside the home. By 1940, 25.1 percent of the workforce was female. But sexual stereotyping still routinely forced women into low-paying and low-status jobs.

The New Deal brought a measurable, if temporary, increase in women's political influence. For those women

Eleanor Roosevelt on a campaign tour with her husband in Nebraska, 1935. Long active in women's organizations and Democratic Party circles, she used political activity both to maintain her independence and make herself a valuable ally to FDR. "The attitude of women toward change in society," she argued, "is going to determine to a great extent our future in this country."

SOURCE: UPI/CORBIS.

the Federal Emergency Relief Administration, find jobs for 100,000 women, ranging from nursery school teaching to sewing. Roosevelt worked vigorously for anti-lynching legislation, compulsory health insurance, and child labor reform, and she fought racial discrimination in New Deal relief programs. She saw herself as the guardian of "human values" within the administration, a buffer between Depression victims and government bureaucracy. She frequently testified before legislative committees, lobbied her husband privately and the Congress publicly, and wrote a widely syndicated newspaper column.

New Deal agencies opened up spaces for scores of women in the federal bureaucracy. In addition, the social work profession, which remained roughly two-thirds female in the 1930s, grew enormously in response to the massive relief and welfare programs. Yet despite the best efforts of the "women's network," women never constituted more than 19 percent of those employed by work relief programs, even though they made up 37 percent of the unemployed. In sum, although the 1930s saw no radical challenges to existing male and female roles, working-class women and professional women held their own and managed to make some gains.

associated with social reform, the New Deal opened up possibilities to effect change. A "women's network," linked by personal friendships and professional connections, made its presence felt in national politics and government. Most of the women in this network had long been active in movements promoting suffrage, labor law reform, and welfare programs.

Eleanor Roosevelt became a powerful political figure in her own right, actively using her prominence as First Lady to fight for the liberal causes she believed in. She revolutionized the role of the political wife by taking a position involving no institutional duties and turning it into a base for independent action. Privately, she enjoyed great influence with her husband. She was a strong supporter of protective labor legislation for women, and her overall outlook owed much to the social reform tradition of the women's movement.

One of her first public acts as First Lady was to convene a White House Conference on the Emergency Needs of Women in November 1933. She helped Ellen Woodward, head of women's projects in

A New Deal for Minorities?

"The Negro was born in Depression," recalled Clifford Burke. "It only became official when it hit the white man." The old saying among black workers that they were "last hired, first fired" was never more true than during times of high unemployment. With jobs made scarce by the Depression, even traditional "Negro occupations"—domestic service, cooking, janitorial work, elevator operating—were coveted. One white clerk in Florida expressed a widely held view among white Southerners when he defended a lynch mob attack on a store with black employees: "A nigger hasn't got no right to have a job when there are white men who can do the work and are out of work."

The Roosevelt administration made little overt effort to combat racism and segregation. FDR was especially worried about offending the powerful southern Democratic congressmen who were a key element in his political coalition. And local administration of many federal programs meant that most early New Deal programs routinely accepted discrimination. The CCC established separate camps for African Americans. The NRA labor codes tolerated lower wages for black workers doing the same jobs as white workers. African Americans could not get jobs with the TVA. Finally, the Social Security Act excluded domestics and casual laborers—workers whose ranks were disproportionately African Americans—from old-age insurance.

Yet some limited gains were made. President Roosevelt issued an executive order in 1935 banning discrimination in WPA projects. In the cities, the WPA, paying minimum wages of $12 a week, enabled thousands of African Americans to survive. Between 15 and 20 percent of all WPA employees were black people, although African Americans made up less than 10 percent of the nation's population. The Public Works Administration, under Harold Ickes, constructed a number of integrated housing complexes and employed more than its fair share of black workers in construction.

Hard times were especially trying for Mexican Americans as well. As the Great Depression drastically reduced the demand for their labor, they faced massive layoffs, deepening poverty, and deportation. During the 1930s over 400,000 Mexican nationals and their children returned to Mexico, often coerced by local officials unwilling to provide them with relief but happy to offer train fare to border towns. Many native-born Americans argued that deporting Mexicans could reduce unemployment for U.S. citizens. But these claims reflected deep racial prejudice inflamed by the economic crisis.

The New Deal record for minorities was mixed at best. African Americans, especially in the cities, benefited from New Deal relief and work programs, though this assistance was not colorblind. Black industrial workers made inroads into labor unions affiliated with the CIO. The New Deal made no explicit attempt to attack the deeply rooted patterns of racism and discrimination in American life. The deteriorating economic and political conditions faced by Mexicans and Mexican Americans resulted in a mass reverse exodus. Yet by 1936, for the first time ever, a majority of black voters had switched their political allegiance to the Democrats—concrete evidence that they supported the directions taken by FDR's New Deal.

The Roosevelt Recession

The nation's economy had improved significantly by 1937. Unemployment had declined to "only" 14 percent (9 million people), farm prices had improved to 1930 levels, and industrial production was slightly higher than the 1929 mark. Roosevelt, uneasy about the federal deficit, which had grown to more than $4 billion, called for large reductions in federal spending, particularly in WPA and farm programs. Federal Reserve System officials, worried about inflation, tightened credit policies.

The retrenchment brought about a steep recession. The stock market collapsed in August 1937, and industrial output and farm prices plummeted. By March 1938, the jobless rate hovered around 20 percent. As conditions worsened, Roosevelt began to blame the "new depression" on a "strike of capital," claiming businessmen had refused to invest because they wanted to hurt his prestige. In truth, the administration's own severe spending cutbacks were more responsible for the decline.

The blunt reality was that even after five years the New Deal had not brought about economic recovery. Throughout 1937 and 1938 the administration drifted. Roosevelt received conflicting advice on the economy. Some advisers, suspicious of the reluctance of business to make new investments, urged a massive antitrust campaign against monopolies. Others urged a return to the strategy of "priming the economic pump" with more federal spending. Emergency spending bills in the spring of 1938 pumped new life into the WPA and the PWA. But Republican gains in the 1938 congressional elections made it harder than ever to get new reform measures through.

There were a couple of important exceptions. The 1938 Fair Labor Standards Act established the first federal minimum wage (25 cents an hour) and set a maximum work week of forty-four hours for all employees engaged in interstate commerce. The National Housing Act of 1937, also known as the Wagner-Steagall Act, funded public housing construction and slum clearance and provided rent subsidies for low-income families. But by and large, by 1938 the reform whirlwind of the New Deal was over.

CONCLUSION

Far from being the radical program its conservative critics charged, the New Deal did little to alter fundamental property relations or the distribution of wealth. But the New Deal profoundly changed many areas of American life. Over all, it radically increased the role of the federal government in American lives and communities. Western and southern communities in particular were transformed. Relief programs and the Social Security system established at least the framework for a welfare state. The federal government guaranteed the

CHRONOLOGY

1929	Stock market crash
1930	Democrats regain control of the House of Representatives
1932	Reconstruction Finance Corporation established to make government credit available
	Bonus Army marches on Washington
	Franklin D. Roosevelt elected president
1933	Roughly 13 million workers unemployed
	The "hundred days" legislation of the First New Deal
	Twenty-first Amendment repeals Prohibition (Eighteenth Amendment)
1934	Indian Reorganization Act repeals Dawes Severalty Act and reasserts the status of Indian tribes as semisovereign nations
	Growing popularity of Father Charles E. Coughlin and Huey Long, critics of Roosevelt
1935	Second New Deal

	Committee for Industrial Organization (CIO) established
	Dust storms turn the southern Great Plains into the Dust Bowl
	Boulder Dam completed
1936	Roosevelt defeats Alfred M. Landon in reelection landslide
	Sit-down strike begins at General Motors plants in Flint, Michigan
1937	General Motors recognizes United Automobile Workers
	Roosevelt's "Court-packing" plan causes controversy
	Memorial Day Massacre in Chicago demonstrates the perils of union organizing
	"Roosevelt recession" begins
1938	CIO unions withdraw from the American Federation of Labor to form the Congress of Industrial Organizations
	Fair Labor Standards Act establishes the first federal minimum wage

right of workers to join trade unions, and it set standards for minimum wages and maximum hours. In politics, the New Deal established the Democrats as the majority party. Some version of the Roosevelt New Deal coalition would dominate the nation's political life for another three decades.

The New Deal's efforts to end racial and gender discrimination were modest at best. Some of the more ambitious programs, such as subsidizing the arts or building model communities, enjoyed only brief success. Other reform proposals, such as national health insurance, never got off the ground. Conservative counterpressures, especially after 1937, limited what could be changed.

Still, the New Deal did more than strengthen the presence of the national government in people's lives. It also fed expectations that the federal presence would intensify. With the coming of World War II, the direct role of national government in shaping American communities would expand beyond the dreams of even the most ardent New Dealer.

REVIEW QUESTIONS

1. What were the underlying causes of the Great Depression? What consequences did it have for ordinary Americans, and how did the Hoover administration attempt to deal with the crisis?

2. Analyze the key elements of Franklin D. Roosevelt's first New Deal program. To what degree did these succeed in getting the economy back on track and in providing relief to suffering Americans?

3. How did the so-called Second New Deal differ from the first? What political pressures did Roosevelt face that contributed to the new policies?

4. How did the New Deal reshape western communities and politics? What specific programs had the greatest impact in the region? How are these changes still visible today?

5. Evaluate the impact of the labor movement and radicalism on the 1930s. How did they influence American political and cultural life?

6. To what extent were the grim realities of Depression reflected in popular culture? To what degree were they absent?

7. Discuss the long- and short-range effects of the New Deal on American political and economic life. What were its key successes and failures? What legacies of New Deal–era policies and political struggles can you find in contemporary America?

RECOMMENDED READING

Anthony J. Badger, *The New Deal: The Depression Years, 1933–1940* (1989). Very useful overview that emphasizes the limited nature of New Deal reforms.

Alan Brinkley, *The End of Reform: New Deal Liberalism in Recession and War* (1995). A sophisticated analysis of the political and economic limits faced by New Deal reformers from 1937 through World War II.

Lizabeth Cohen, *Making a New Deal: Industrial Workers in Chicago, 1919–1939* (1990). A brilliant study that demonstrates the transformation of immigrant and African American workers into key actors in the creation of the CIO and in New Deal politics and illuminates the complex relationship between ethnic cultures and mass culture.

Michael Denning, *The Cultural Front: The Laboring of American Culture in the Twentieth Century* (1997). A provocative reinterpretation of 1930s culture, emphasizing the impact of the Popular Front and its lasting influence on American modernism and mass culture.

Ronald Edsforth, *The New Deal: America's Response to the Great Depression* (2000). A concise political history of the 1930s, offering an excellent synthesis of the massive secondary literature.

David M. Kennedy, *Freedom From Fear: The American People in Depression and War* (1999). An absorbing, magisterial narrative account of the U.S. experience in depression and war.

Richard Lowitt, *The New Deal and the West* (1984). A comprehensive study of the New Deal's impact in the West, with special attention to water policy and agriculture.

Robert S. McElvaine, *The Great Depression: America, 1929–1941* (1984). The best one-volume overview of the Great Depression. It is especially strong on the origins and early years of the worst economic calamity in American history.

Lois Scharf, *To Work and to Wed* (1980). Examines female employment and feminism during the Great Depression.

Harvard Sitkoff, *A New Deal for Blacks* (1978). Focuses on the narrow gains made by African Americans from New Deal measures, as well as the racism that pervaded most government programs.

ON THE WEB

http://newdeal.feri.org/library/index.htm#4

The New Deal Network is sponsored by the Franklin and Eleanor Roosevelt Institute and based at Columbia University. This web page contains from that site an almost unlimited collection of photographs and graphics from the New Deal agencies established to deal with the problems of the Great Depression. The photos and graphics frequently contain interesting details concerning life during the 1930s.

http://lcweb.loc.gov/rr/print/085_disc.html

This site is a Library of Congress exhibit entitled: "Photographs of Signs Enforcing Racial Discrimination: Documentation by Farm Security Administration–Office of War Information Photographers" from the Prints and Photographs Division. It offers thirty-one photographs from the late 1930s to the early 1940s of racial segregation and the public signs enforcing Jim Crow laws in the South. It is an interesting visual commentary on social and racial history for this period.

http://lcweb.loc.gov/rr/print/128_migm.html

Dorothea Lange's "Migrant Mother" photograph became one of the classic photos illustrating the deprivation and hunger of the Great Depression. This Library of Congress site provides background information on that photo as well as others taken about the same time by Lange. After examining this site, search the Internet for additional sites that document Lange's career as a photographer and illustrate her work during the Great Depression and World War II.

http://www.mhric.org/fdr/fdr.html

This site provides electronic texts of Roosevelt's thirty "Fireside Chats" with the American people during the Great Depression and World War II. The first president to use the radio to directly appeal to the people, these Roosevelt speeches were very effective. Pay close attention to those of the Depression era, especially the first on the banking crisis that had paralyzed the nation in 1933.

http://www.prenhall.com/faragherbrief/map24.1

Through a series of rollover maps, consider the extent of the Dust Bowl from 1935–1940. What were the reasons for this ecological disaster?

http://www.prenhall.com/faragherbrief/map24.2

Consider the many water projects sponsored by federal agencies during the New Deal. Why were many of these projects located in the West?

CHAPTER OUTLINE

AMERICAN COMMUNITIES

Los Alamos, New Mexico

On Monday, July 16, 1945, at 5:29:45 a.m., Mountain War Time, the first atomic bomb exploded in a brilliant flash visible in three states. Within just seven minutes, a huge, multicolored, bell-shaped cloud soared 38,000 feet into the atmosphere and threw back a blanket of smoke and soot to the earth below. The heat generated by the blast was four times the temperature at the center of the sun, and the light produced rivaled that of nearly twenty suns. Even ten miles away people felt a strong surge of heat. The giant fireball ripped a crater a half-mile wide in the ground, fusing the desert sand into glass. The shock wave blew out windows in houses more than 200 miles away. The blast killed every living creature—squirrels, rabbits, snakes, plants, and insects—within a mile and the smells of death lingered for nearly a month.

Very early that morning, Ruby Wilkening had driven to a nearby mountain ridge, where she joined several other women waiting for the blast. Wilkening worried about her husband, a physicist, who was already at the test site. No one knew exactly what to expect, not even the scientists who developed the bomb.

The Wilkenings were part of a unique community of scientists who had been marshaled for war. President Franklin D. Roosevelt, convinced by Albert Einstein and other physicists that the Nazis might successfully develop an atomic bomb, had inaugurated a small nuclear research program in 1939. Soon after the United States entered World War II, the president released resources to create the Manhattan Project and placed it under the direction of the Army Corps of Engineers. By December 1942 a team headed by Italian-born Nobel Prize–winner Enrico Fermi had produced the first chain reaction in uranium under the University of Chicago's football stadium. Now the mission was to build a new, formidable weapon of war, the atomic bomb.

The government moved the key researchers and their families to Los Alamos, New Mexico, a remote and sparsely populated region of soaring peaks, ancient Indian ruins, modern Pueblos, and villages occupied by the descendents of the earliest Spanish settlers. The scientists and their families arrived in March 1943. They occupied a former boys' preparatory school until new houses could be built. Some families doubled up in rugged log cabins or nearby ranches. Telephone service to the outside world was poor, and the mountain roads were so rough that changing flat tires became a tiresome but familiar routine. Construction of new quarters proceeded slowly, causing nasty disputes between the "long-hairs" (scientists) and the "plumbers" (army engineers) in charge of the grounds. Despite the chaos, outstanding American and European scientists eagerly signed up. Most were young, with an average age of twenty-seven, and quite a few were recently married. Many couples began their families at Los Alamos, producing a total of nearly a thousand babies between 1943 and 1949.

The scientists and their families formed an exceptionally close-knit community, united by the need for secrecy and their shared antagonism toward their army guardians. The military atmosphere was oppressive. Homes and laboratories were cordoned off by barbed wire and guarded by military police. Everything, from linens to food packages, was stamped "Government Issue." The scientists were followed by security personnel whenever they left Los Alamos. Several scientists were reprimanded for discussing their work at home, although many of their wives worked forty-eight hours a week in the Technical Area. All outgoing mail was censored. Well-known scientists commonly worked under aliases—Fermi became "Eugene Farmer"—and code names were used for such terms as *atom*, *bomb*, and *uranium fission*. The birth certificates of babies born at Los Alamos listed their place of birth simply as rural Sandoval County, and children registered without surnames at nearby public schools. Even automobile accidents went unreported, and newspapers carried no wedding announcements or obituaries. Only a group thoroughly committed to the war effort could accept such restrictions on personal liberty.

A profound urgency motivated the research team, which included refugees from Nazi Germany and Fascist Italy and a large proportion of Jews. The director of the project, California physicist J. Robert Oppenheimer, promoted a scientific élan that offset the military style of commanding general Leslie Groves. Just thirty-eight, slightly built, and deeply emotional,

"Oppie" personified the idealism that helped the community of scientists overcome whatever moral reservations they held about placing such a potentially ominous weapon in the hands of the government.

In the Technical Area of Los Alamos, Oppenheimer directed research from an office with a desk, long tables, and blackboard along the walls in a typical two-story army building. At seven o'clock each workday morning, the siren dubbed "Oppie's Whistle" called the other scientists to their laboratories to wrestle with the theoretical and practical problems of building an atomic device. Once a week Oppenheimer called together the heads of the various technical divisions to discuss their work in round-table conferences. From May to November 1944, after the bomb had been designed, the key issue was testing it. Many scientists feared a test might fail, scattering the precious plutonium at the bomb's core and discrediting the entire project. Finally, with plutonium production increasing, the Los Alamos team agreed to test "the gadget" at a site 160 miles away.

The unprecedented scientific mobilization at Los Alamos mirrored changes occurring throughout American society as the nation rallied behind the war effort. Sixteen million men and women left home for military service and nearly as many moved to take advantage of wartime jobs. Several states in the South and Southwest experienced huge surges in population. California alone grew by 2 million people, a large proportion from Mexico. Many broad social changes with roots in earlier times—the economic expansion of the West, the erosion of farm tenancy among black people in the South and white people in Appalachia, and the increasing employment of married women—accelerated during the war. The United States, initially reluctant to enter the war, emerged from it the world's leading superpower and free from the weight of the Great Depression. The events of the war eroded old communities, created new ones like Los Alamos, and transformed nearly all aspects of American society. ■

Los Alamos

KEY TOPICS

- The events leading to Pearl Harbor and the declaration of war

- The marshaling of national resources for war

- American society during wartime

- The mobilization of Americans into the armed forces

- The war in Europe and Asia

- Diplomacy and the atomic bomb

THE COMING OF WORLD WAR II

The worldwide Great Depression further undermined a political order that had been shaky since World War I. Production declined by nearly 40 percent, international trade dropped by as much as two-thirds, unemployment rose, and political unrest spread across Europe and Asia. Demagogues played upon nationalist hatreds, fueled by old resentments and current despair, and offered solutions in the form of territorial expansion by military conquest.

Preoccupied with restoring the domestic economy, President Franklin D. Roosevelt had no specific plan to deal with growing conflict elsewhere in the world. Moreover, the majority of Americans strongly opposed foreign entanglements. But as debate over diplomatic policy heated up, terrifying events overseas pulled the nation steadily toward war.

The Shadows of War

War spread first across Asia. Militarist-imperialist leaders in Japan, which suffered economically from loss of trade during the 1930s, determined to make their nation the richest in the world. The Japanese army seized control of Manchuria in 1931 and in 1932 installed a puppet government there. When reprimanded by the League of Nations, Japan simply withdrew from the organization. In 1937 Japan provoked full-scale war with an invasion of northern China. When it seized control of the capital city of Nanking, Japan's army murdered as many as 300,000 Chinese men, women, and children and destroyed much of the city. Within the year Japan controlled all but China's western interior and threatened all Asia and the Pacific.

Meanwhile, the rise of authoritarian nationalism in Italy and Germany cast a dark shadow over Europe. The economic hardships brought on by the Great Depression—and, in Germany, resentment over the harsh terms of the Treaty of Versailles, which ended

World War I—fueled the rise of demagogic mass movements. Glorifying war as a test of national virility, the Italian Fascist dictator Benito Mussolini, who had seized power in 1922, declared, "We have buried the putrid corpse of liberty." In Germany, the National Socialists (Nazis), led by Adolf Hitler, combined militaristic rhetoric with a racist doctrine of Aryan (Nordic) supremacy that claimed biological superiority for the blond-haired and blue-eyed peoples of northern Europe and classified nonwhites, including Jews, as "degenerate races."

Hitler, who became chancellor of Germany in January 1933 with the backing of major industrialists and about a third of the electorate, prepared for war. With his brown-shirted storm troopers ruling the streets, he quickly destroyed opposition parties and effectively made himself dictator of the strongest nation in central Europe. Renouncing the disarmament provisions of the Versailles treaty, he began to rebuild Germany's armed forces.

The prospect of war grew as both Mussolini and Hitler began to act on their imperial visions. In 1935 Italy invaded Ethiopia and formally claimed the impoverished African kingdom as a colony. In 1936 Hitler sent 35,000 troops to occupy the Rhineland, a region demilitarized by the Versailles treaty. When the Spanish Civil War broke out later that year, Italy and Germany both supported the fascist insurrection of General Francisco Franco and then, in November, drew up a formal alliance to become the Rome-Berlin Axis. Hitler was now nearly ready to put into operation his plan to secure *Lebensraum*—living space for Germany's growing population—through further territorial expansion.

After annexing his native Austria, Hitler turned his attention to Czechoslovakia, a country that both Britain and France were pledged by treaty to assist. War seemed imminent. But Britain and France surprised Hitler by agreeing, at a conference in Munich the last week of September 1938, to allow Germany to annex the Sudetenland, a part of Czechoslovakia bordering

Germany. In return, Hitler pledged to stop his territorial advance. Less than six months later, in March 1939, Hitler seized the rest of Czechoslovakia.

By this time, much of the world was aware of the horror of Hitler's regime, especially its virulent racist doctrines. After 1935, when Hitler published the notorious Nuremberg Laws denying civil rights to Jews, the campaign against them became steadily more vicious. On the night of November 9, 1938, Nazi storm troopers rounded up Jews, beating them mercilessly and murdering an untold number. They smashed windows in Jewish shops, hospitals, and orphanages and burned synagogues to the ground. This attack came to be known as *Kristallnacht*, "the Night of Broken Glass." The Nazi government soon expropriated Jewish property and excluded Jews from all but the most menial forms of employment. Pressured by Hitler, Hungary and Italy also enacted laws against Jews.

Roosevelt Readies for War

While Americans looked on anxiously, the twists and turns of world events prompted President Franklin D. Roosevelt to ready the nation for war. In October 1937 he had called for international cooperation to "quarantine the aggressors." But a poll of Congress revealed that a two-thirds majority opposed economic sanctions, calling any such plan a "back door to war." Forced to draw back, Roosevelt nevertheless won from Congress $1 billion in appropriations to enlarge the navy.

Everything changed on September 1, 1939, when Hitler invaded Poland. Committed by treaty to defend Poland against unprovoked attack, Great Britain and France issued a joint declaration of war against Germany two days later. After the fall of Warsaw at the end of the month, the fighting slowed to a near halt. Even along their border, French and German troops did not exchange fire. From the east, however, the invasion continued. Just two weeks before Hitler overran Poland, the Soviet Union had stunned the world by signing a nonaggression pact with its former enemy. The Red Army now entered Poland, and the two great powers proceeded to split the hapless nation between them. Soviet forces then headed north, invading Finland on November 30. The European war had begun.

Calculating that the United States would stay out of the war, Hitler began a crushing offensive against western Europe in April 1940. Using the technique of *Blitzkrieg* (lightning war)—massed, fast-moving columns of tanks supported by air power—that had overwhelmed Poland, Nazi troops moved first against Germany's northern neighbors. After taking Denmark and Norway, the Nazi armored divisions swept over Holland, Belgium, and Luxembourg and sent more

than 338,000 British troops into retreat across the English Channel from Dunkerque. Hitler's army, joined by the Italians, easily conquered France in June 1940. Hitler now turned toward England. In the Battle of Britain, Nazi bombers pounded population and industrial centers while U-boats cut off incoming supplies.

Even with Great Britain under attack, opinion polls indicated Americans' determination to stay out of the war. But most Americans, like Roosevelt himself, believed that the security of the United States depended on both a strong defense and the defeat of Germany. Invoking the Neutrality Act of 1939, which permitted the sale of arms to Britain, France, and China, the president clarified his position: "all aid to the Allies short of war." In May 1940 he began to transfer surplus U.S. planes and equipment to the Allies. In September the president secured the first peacetime military draft in American history, the Selective Service Act of 1940, which sent 1.4 million men to army training camps by July 1941.

President Roosevelt could not yet admit the inevitability of U.S. involvement—especially during an election year. His popularity had dropped with the "Roosevelt recession" that began in 1937, raising doubts that he could win what would be an unprecedented third term. In his campaign he promised voters not to "send your boys to any foreign wars." Roosevelt and his vice presidential candidate Henry Wallace won by a margin of 5 million popular votes over the Republican dark-horse candidate, Wendell L. Willkie of Indiana.

Roosevelt now moved more aggressively to aid the Allies in their struggle with the Axis powers. He proposed a bill that would allow the president to sell, exchange, or lease arms to any country whose defense appeared vital to U.S. security. Passed by Congress in March 1941, the Lend-Lease Act made Great Britain the first beneficiary of massive aid. After Congress authorized the merchant marine to sail fully armed while conveying lend-lease supplies directly to Britain, a formal declaration of war was only a matter of time.

In August 1941 Roosevelt met secretly at sea off Newfoundland with British prime minister Winston Churchill to map military strategy and declare common goals for the postwar world. Known as the Atlantic Charter, their proclamation specified the right of all peoples to live in freedom from fear, want, and tyranny.

Pearl Harbor

Throughout 1940 and much of 1941 the United States focused on events in Europe, but the war in Asia went on. Roosevelt, anticipating danger to American interests in the Pacific, had directed the transfer of the

On the day after the attack on Pearl Harbor, President Franklin D. Roosevelt addressed a joint session of Congress and asked for an immediate declaration of war against Japan. The resolution passed with one dissenting vote, and the United States entered World War II.

SOURCE: National Archives and Records Administration.

can planes and badly damaged the fleet; more than 2,400 Americans were killed and nearly 1,200 wounded. On the same day, Japan struck U.S. bases on the Philippines, Guam, and Wake Island.

On December 8, declaring the attack on Pearl Harbor a day that "will live in infamy," Roosevelt asked Congress for a declaration of war against Japan. With only one dissenting vote— by pacifist Jeannette Rankin of Montana, who had voted against U.S. entry into World War I in 1917—Congress acceded. The United States had not yet declared war on Japan's European allies, but Hitler made that unnecessary when he asked the *Reichstag* on December 11 to support war against the "half Judaized, and the other half Negrified" American nation. Mussolini joined him in the declaration, and the

Pacific Fleet from bases in California to Pearl Harbor, on the island of Oahu, Hawai'i, in May 1940. On September 27 Japan formally joined Germany and Italy as the Asian partner of the Axis alliance.

The United States and Japan each played for time. Roosevelt wanted to save his resources to fight against Germany, while Japan's leaders gambled that America's preoccupation with Europe might allow them to conquer all of Southeast Asia, including the French colonies in Indochina (Vietnam, Cambodia, and Laos) and the British possessions of Burma and India. When Japan occupied Indochina in July 1941, however, Roosevelt responded by freezing Japanese assets in the United States and cutting off its oil supplies.

Confrontation with Japan now looked likely. U.S. intelligence had broken the Japanese diplomatic code, and the president knew that Japan was preparing for war against the Western powers. Roosevelt's advisers expected an attack somewhere in the Pacific and by the end of November placed all American forces there on high alert.

Early Sunday morning, December 7, 1941, Japanese carriers launched an attack on Pearl Harbor that caught American forces completely off guard. Within two hours, Japanese pilots had destroyed nearly 200 Ameri-

United States on the same day recognized that a state of war existed with Germany and Italy. World War II now began for Americans.

ARSENAL OF DEMOCRACY

Late in 1940 President Roosevelt called upon all Americans to make the nation a "great arsenal of democracy." During the next three years, the economic machinery that had failed during the 1930s was swiftly retooled for military purposes, with dramatic results. The Great Depression suddenly ended.

Mobilizing for War

A few days after the United States declared war on Germany, Congress passed the War Powers Act, which established a precedent for executive authority that would endure long after the war's end. The president gained the power to reorganize the federal government and create new agencies; to establish programs censoring all news and information and abridging civil liberties; to seize property owned by foreigners; and even to award government contracts without competitive bidding.

Roosevelt promptly created special wartime agencies. At the top of his agenda was a massive reorientation and management of the economy, and an alphabet soup of new agencies arose to fill any gaps in production.

In June 1942 the president created the Office of War Information (OWI) to coordinate information from the multiplying federal agencies and to engage the press, radio, and film industry in an informational campaign—in short, to sell the war to the American people.

The federal government also sponsored various measures to prevent subversion of the war effort. The Federal Bureau of Investigation (FBI) was kept busy, its appropriation rising from $6 million to $16 million in just two years. The attorney general authorized wiretapping in cases of espionage or sabotage, but the FBI used it extensively—and illegally—in domestic surveillance. The Joint Chiefs of Staff created the Office of Strategic Services (OSS) to assess the enemy's military strength, to gather intelligence information, and to oversee espionage activities. Its head, Colonel William Donovan, envisioned the OSS as an "adjunct to military strategy" and engaged leading social scientists to plot psychological warfare against the enemy.

It cost about $250 million a day to fight the war, and the federal government spent twice as much during the war as during its entire prior history. The federal budget grew to ten times what it had been during the New Deal. The exception to this pattern of expansion was the New Deal itself. As President Roosevelt announced in 1942, "Dr. New Deal" had been replaced by "Dr. Win the War." One by one, New Deal agencies vanished.

Economic Conversion

The decisive factor for victory, even more than military prowess and superior strategy, would be, many observers agreed, the ability of the United States to outproduce its enemies. The country enjoyed many advantages to meet this challenge: a large industrial base, abundant natural resources (largely free from interference by the war), and a civilian population large enough to permit it to increase both its labor force and its armed forces. The war would lift the United States out of the Great Depression and create the biggest economic boom in the history of any nation. But first the entire civilian economy had to be both expanded and transformed for the production of arms and other military supplies.

By the summer of 1941 the federal government was pouring vast amounts into defense production. Six months after the attack on Pearl Harbor its allocations topped $100 billion for equipment and supplies, which exceeded what American firms had produced in any previous war. Facing war orders too large to fill, American industries were now primed for all-out production.

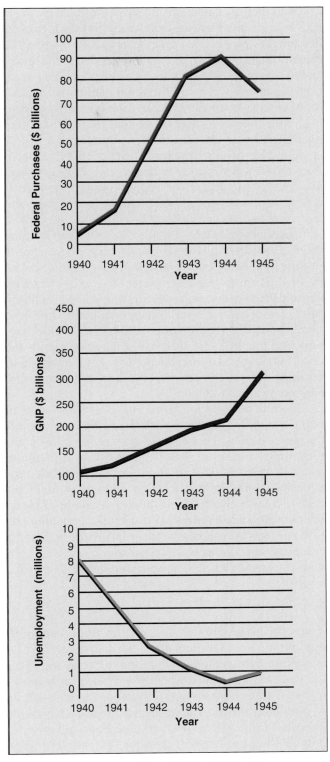

Effects of War Spending, 1940–1945 Wartime spending had a multiplier effect on the U.S. economy. Government contracts with industry rapidly increased the gross national product, and the sharp upswing in production utilized all available workers and sharply reduced unemployment.

SOURCE: Robert L. Heilbroner, *The Economic Transformation of America* (New York: Harcourt, Brace, 1977), p. 205.

With better equipment and more motivation, American workers proved twice as productive as the Germans, five times as productive as the Japanese. No wonder the actual volume of industrial output expanded at the fastest rate in American history. Military production alone grew from 2 percent of the 1939 total gross national product to 40 percent of the 1943 total. "Something is happening," announced *Time* magazine, "that Adolf Hitler does not understand . . . it is the miracle of production."

Defense production transformed entire regions. The impact was strongest in the West—the major staging area for the war in the Pacific—where the federal government spent nearly $40 billion for military and industrial expansion. California secured 10 percent of all federal funds, and by 1944 Los Angeles had become the nation's second largest manufacturing center, only slightly behind Detroit. The South also benefited from 60 of the army's 100 new camps. Its textile factories hummed: the army alone required nearly 520 million pairs of socks and 230 million pairs of pants. The economic boom lifted entire populations out of sharecropping and tenancy into well-paid industrial jobs in the cities and pumped unprecedented profits into southern business. Across the country the rural population decreased by almost 20 percent.

Despite a "Food for Freedom" program, American farmers could not keep up with the rising international demand or even the domestic market for milk, potatoes, fruits, and sugar. The Department of Agriculture reached its goals only in areas such as livestock production, thanks to skyrocketing wholesale prices for meat. The war also speeded the development of large-scale, mechanized production of crops, including the first widespread use of chemical fertilizers and pesticides. By 1945 farm income had doubled, but thousands of small farms had disappeared, never to return.

New Workers

The wartime economy brought an unprecedented number of new workers into the labor force. The *bracero* program, negotiated by United States and Mexico in 1942, opened to Mexicans short-term employment in trades previously closed to them, such as shipbuilding on the Pacific coast. Sioux and Navajos were hired in large numbers to help build military depots and military training centers. African Americans found new opportunities in industry; the number of black workers rose from 2,900,000 to 3,800,000.

The war most dramatically altered the wage-earning patterns of women. The female labor force grew by over 50 percent, reaching 19.5 million in 1945. The rate of growth proved especially high for white women over the age of thirty-five, and for the first time married women became the majority of female wage earners. The employment rate changed comparatively little for African American women; fully 90 percent had been in the labor force in 1940. However, many black women left domestic service for higher-paying jobs in manufacturing.

Neither government nor industry expected women to stay in their jobs when the war ended. Recruitment campaigns targeted "Mrs. Stay-at-Home" yet underscored the temporary aspect of her wartime service. "Rosie the Riveter" appeared in posters and advertisements as the model female citizen, but only "for the duration." In Washington, D.C., women bus drivers were given badges to wear on their uniforms that read: "I am taking the place of a man who went to war."

Compared to the Great Depression, when married women were barred from many jobs, World War II opened up new fields. The number of women automobile workers, for example, jumped from 29,000 to 200,000, that of women electrical workers from 100,000 to 374,000. Polled near the end of the war, the overwhelming majority—75 percent—of women workers expressed a desire to keep working, preferably at the same jobs.

The major advances proved short-lived. As early as 1943 some industries began planning to lay off women as war production wound down. With jobs reserved for returning veterans, women in industry saw their numbers diminish rapidly; as many as 4 million lost their jobs between 1944 and 1946.

Wartime Strikes

Although 17 million new jobs were created during the war, the economic gains were not evenly distributed. Wages increased by as much as 50 percent but never as fast as profits or prices. This widely reported disparity produced one of the most turbulent periods in American labor history.

Labor strife began even before U.S. involvement in World War II. Only two weeks after the 1940 election, workers struck at the Vultee aircraft plant in Los Angeles. After the attorney general denounced the strikers as unpatriotic and the FBI began to harass participants, workers throughout the city walked off their jobs in sympathy with the aircraft workers.

More workers went on strike in 1941, before the United States entered the war, than in any previous year except 1919. Rising production orders and tightening labor markets made strikes feasible: jobs were plentiful, and business leaders, anticipating hefty profits, had reason to settle quickly. This climate prompted a militant union drive at Ford Motor Company's enormous River Rouge plant, and the United Auto Workers (UAW) emerged as one of the most powerful labor organizations in the world.

Once the United States entered the war, the major unions dutifully agreed to no-strike pledges for its duration. The National War Labor Board, with representatives from business and labor, encouraged employers to allow unions in their plants, and unions secured contracts that included automatic dues checkoff, high wages, and new fringe benefits such as pension plans. Total union membership increased from 10.5 million to 14.7 million, with the women's share alone rising from 11 to 23 percent.

Unions also enrolled 1,250,000 African Americans, twice the prewar number. But many white workers resisted this change. "Hate strikes" broke out in plants across the country when African Americans were hired or promoted to jobs customarily held by white workers. For example, at a U.S. Rubber Company factory in Detroit, more than half the workers walked out in 1943 when African American women began to operate the machinery. Such strikes usually ended quickly because black workers refused to back down.

Rank-and-file union members staged other illegal "wildcat" strikes. The most dramatic, a walkout of more than a half-million coal miners in 1943 led by the rambunctious John L. Lewis, withstood the attacks of the government and the press. Roosevelt repeatedly ordered the mines seized, only to find, as Lewis retorted, that coal could not be mined with bayonets. The Democratic majority in Congress passed the first federal antistrike bill, giving the president power to penalize strikers, even to draft them. And yet the strikes grew in size and number, reaching a level greater than in any other four-year period in American history.

THE HOME FRONT

Most Americans thoroughly appreciated the burst of prosperity brought on by wartime production, but they also experienced food rationing, long workdays, and separation from loved ones. Alongside national unity ran deep conflicts on the home front. Racial and ethnic hostilities flared repeatedly and on several occasions erupted in violence.

Families in Wartime

Despite the uncertainties of wartime, or perhaps because of them, men and women rushed into marriage. The surge in personal income caused by the wartime economic boom meant that many young couples could afford to set up their own households—something their counterparts in the 1930s had not been able to do. As one social scientist remarked at the time, "Economic conditions were ripe for a rush to the altar." For other couples, the prospect of separation provided the

incentive. The U.S. Census Bureau estimated that between 1940 and 1943 at least a million more people married than would have been expected had there been no war. The marriage rate skyrocketed, peaking in 1946, but by 1946 the number of divorces also set records.

Housing shortages were acute, and rents were high. So scarce were apartments that taxi drivers became, for an extra fee, up-to-the-minute guides to vacancies. Able to set their own terms, landlords frequently discriminated against families with children and even more so against racial minorities.

Supplying a household was scarcely less difficult. Although retailers extended their store hours into the evenings and weekends, shopping had to be squeezed in between long hours on the job. Extra planning was necessary for purchasing government-rationed staples such as meat, cheese, sugar, milk, coffee, gasoline, and even shoes. Many women found it nearly impossible to manage both a demanding job and a household. This dual responsibility contributed to high turnover and absentee rates in factories.

The care of small children became a major problem. Wartime employment or military service often separated husbands and wives, leaving children in the hands of only one parent. But even when families stayed together, both adults often worked long hours, sometimes on different shifts. Although the War Manpower Commission estimated that as many as 2 million children needed some form of child care, federally funded day-care centers served less than 10 percent of defense workers' children.

Juvenile delinquency rose during the war. With employers often relaxing minimum age requirements for employment, many teenagers quit school for the high wages of factory jobs. In 1944 the U.S. Office of Education and the Children's Bureau inaugurated a back-to-school campaign. Local school boards appealed to employers to hire only older workers, and toward the end of the war the student dropout rate began to decline.

Public health improved greatly during the war. Forced to cut back on expenditures for medical care during the Great Depression, many Americans now spent large portions of their wartime paychecks on doctors, dentists, and prescription drugs. But even more important were the benefits provided to the more than 16 million men inducted into the armed forces and their dependents. Nationally, incidences of such communicable diseases as typhoid fever, tuberculosis, and diphtheria dropped considerably, the infant death rate fell by more than a third, and life expectancy increased by three years. The death rate in 1942, excluding battle deaths, was the lowest in the nation's history.

The Internment of Japanese Americans

After the attack on Pearl Harbor, many Americans feared an invasion of the mainland and suspected Japanese Americans of secret loyalty to an enemy government. On December 8, 1941, the federal government froze the financial assets of those born in Japan, known as Issei, who had been barred from U.S. citizenship. Although a State Department intelligence report certified their loyalty, Japanese Americans— two-thirds of whom were American-born citizens—became the only ethnic group singled out for legal sanctions.

Charges of sedition masked long-standing racial prejudices. The press began to use the word "Jap" in headlines, while political cartoonists employed blatant racial stereotypes. Popular songs appeared with titles like "You're a Sap, Mister Jap, to Make a Yankee Cranky." "The very fact that no sabotage has taken place to date," an army report suggested, with twisted logic, "is a disturbing and confirming indication that action will be taken."

On February 19, 1942, President Roosevelt signed Executive Order 9066, suspending the civil rights of Japanese Americans and authorizing the exclusion of more than 112,000 men, women, and children from designated military areas, mainly in California, but also in Oregon, Washington, and southern Arizona.

During the spring of 1942, Japanese American families received one week's notice to close up their businesses and homes before being transported to one of the ten internment camps managed by the War Relocation Authority. The guarded camps were located as far away as Arkansas, although the majority had been set up in isolated and arid districts of Utah, Colorado, Idaho, Arizona, Wyoming, and California. Karl G. Yoneda described his quarters at Manzanar in northern California:

> There were no lights, stoves, or window panes. My two cousins and I, together with seven others, were crowded into a 25 × 30 foot room. We slept on army cots with our clothes on. The next morning we discovered that there were no toilets or washrooms. . . . We saw GIs manning machine guns in the watchtowers. The barbed wire fence which surrounded the camp was visible against the background of the snow-covered Sierra mountain range. "So this is the American-style concentration camp," someone remarked.

By August, virtually every West Coast resident who had at least one Japanese grandparent had been interned.

The Japanese American Citizens League charged that "racial animosity" rather than military necessity had dictated the internment policy. Despite the protest of the American Civil Liberties Union and several church groups against the abridgment of the civil rights of Japanese Americans, the Supreme Court in *Korematsu v. United States* (1944) upheld the constitutionality of relocation on grounds of national security. By this time a program of gradual release was in place, although the last center, at Tule Lake, California, did not close until March 1946. In protest, nearly 6,000 Japanese Americans renounced their U.S. citizenship. Japanese Americans had lost homes and businesses valued at $500 million in what many historians judge as being the worst violation of American civil liberties during the war. Not until 1988 did the U.S. Congress vote reparations of $20,000 and a public apology to each of the 60,000 surviving victims.

Byron Takashi Tsuzuki, *Forced Removal, Act II*, 1944. This Japanese American artist illustrates the forced relocation of Japanese Americans from their homes to one of ten inland camps in 1942. About 110,000 Japanese Americans were interned during World War II, some for up to four years. Beginning in January 1945, they were allowed to return to the Pacific coast.

SOURCE: Masako Nakagawa.

Civil Rights and Race Riots

Throughout the war, African American activists conducted a "Double V" campaign, mobilizing not only for Allied victory but for their own rights as citizens. "The army is about to take me to fight for democracy," one Detroit resident said, "but I would as leave fight for democracy right here." Black militants demanded, at a minimum, fair housing and equal employment opportunities. President Roosevelt responded in a lukewarm fashion, supporting advances in civil rights that would not, in his opinion, disrupt the war effort.

Before the United States entered the war, A. Philip Randolph, president of both the Brotherhood of Sleeping Car Porters and the National Negro Congress, had organized the March on Washington Movement. Eager to stop the movement, President Roosevelt met with Randolph, who proposed an executive order "making it mandatory that Negroes be permitted to work." Randolph reviewed several drafts before approving the text that became, on June 25, 1941, Executive Order 8802, banning discrimination in defense industries and government. Randolph called off the march but did not disband his all-black March on Washington organization. He remained determined to "shake up white America."

Other civil rights organizations formed during wartime to fight both discrimination and Jim Crow practices, including segregation in the U.S. armed forces. The interracial Congress of Racial Equality (CORE), formed by pacifists in 1942, staged sit-ins at Chicago, Detroit, and Denver restaurants that refused to serve African Americans. Meanwhile, membership in the National Association for the Advancement of Colored People (NAACP), which took a strong stand against discrimination in the military, grew from 50,000 in 1940 to 450,000 in 1946.

The struggle for equality took shape within local communities. In February 1942, when twenty black families attempted to move into new federally funded apartments adjacent to a Polish American community in Detroit, a mob of 700 white protesters halted the moving vans and burned a cross on the project's grounds. The police overlooked the white rioters but arrested black youths. Finally, two months later, 1,000 state troopers supervised the move of these families into the Sojourner Truth Homes, named after the famous abolitionist and former slave.

Racial violence reached its wartime peak during the summer of 1943, when 274 conflicts broke out in nearly fifty cities. In Detroit, where the black population had grown by more than a third since the beginning of the war, twenty-five blacks and nine whites were killed and more than 700 were injured. The poet Langston Hughes, who supported U.S. involvement in the war, wrote:

*Looky here, America
What you done done—
Let things drift
Until the riots come*

*Yet you say we're fighting
For democracy.
Then why don't democracy
Include me?*

*I ask you this question
Cause I want to know
How long I got to fight
BOTH HITLER—AND JIM CROW.*

Zoot-suit Riots

On the night of June 4, 1943, sailors poured into nearly 200 cars and taxis to drive through the streets of East Los Angeles in search of Mexican Americans dressed in zoot suits. The sailors assaulted their victims at random, even chasing one youth into a movie theater and stripping him of his clothes while the audience cheered. Riots broke out and continued for five days.

Two communities had collided, with tragic results. The sailors had only recently been uprooted from their hometowns and regrouped under the strict discipline of boot camp. Now stationed in southern California while awaiting departure overseas, they came face-to-face with Mexican American teenagers wearing long-draped coats, pegged pants, pocket watches with oversized chains, and big floppy hats. To the sailors, the zoot suit was not just a flamboyant fashion. Unlike the uniform the young sailors wore, the zoot suit signaled a lack of patriotism.

The zoot-suiters, however, represented less than 10 percent of their community's youth. More than 300,000 Mexican Americans were serving in the armed forces (a number representing a greater proportion of their draft-age population than other Americans), and they served in the most hazardous branches, the paratrooper and marine corps. Many others were employed in war industries in Los Angeles, which had become home to the largest community of Mexican Americans in the nation. For the first time Mexican Americans were finding well-paying jobs, and, like African Americans, they expected their government to protect them from discrimination.

In Los Angeles, military and civilian authorities eventually contained the zoot-suit riots by ruling several sections of the city off limits to military personnel. The Los Angeles City Council passed legislation making the wearing of a zoot suit in public a criminal offense. Many Mexican Americans expressed concern about their personal safety; some feared that, after the government rounded up the Japanese, they would be the next group sent to internment camps.

Popular Culture and "The Good War"

Global events shaped the lives of American civilians but appeared to touch them only indirectly in their everyday activities. Food shortages, long hours in the factories, and even fears for loved ones abroad did not take away all the pleasures of full employment and prosperity. With money in their pockets, Americans spent freely at vacation resorts, country clubs, racetracks, nightclubs, dance halls, and movie theaters. Sales of books skyrocketed, and spectator sports attracted huge audiences.

Hollywood artists meanwhile threw themselves into a perpetual round of fund-raising and morale-boosting public events. Movie stars called on fans to buy war bonds and to support the troops. Combat films such as *Action in the North Atlantic* made heroes of ordinary Americans under fire, depicting GIs of different races and ethnicities discovering their common humanity. Movies with antifascist themes, such as *Tender Comrade*, promoted friendship among Russians and Americans, while films like *Since You Went Away* portrayed the loyalty and resilience of families with servicemen stationed overseas.

Never to see a single battle, safeguarded by two oceans, many Americans nevertheless experienced the war years as the most intense of their entire lives. Popular music, Hollywood movies, radio programs, and advertisements—all screened by the Office of War Information—encouraged a sense of personal involvement in a collective effort to preserve democracy at home and to save the world from fascism. No one was excluded, no action considered insignificant. Even casual conversation came under the purview of the government, which warned that "Loose Lips Sink Ships."

MEN AND WOMEN IN UNIFORM

During World War I, American soldiers served for a relatively brief period and in small numbers. A quarter-century later, World War II mobilized 16.4 million Americans into the armed forces. Although only 34 percent of men who served in the army saw combat—the majority during the final year of the war—the experience had a powerful impact on nearly everyone.

Creating the Armed Forces

Before the European war broke out in 1939, the majority of the 200,000 men in the U.S. armed forces were employed as military police, engaging in such tasks as patrolling the Mexican border or occupying colonial possessions, such as the Philippines. Neither the army

nor the navy was prepared for the scale of combat World War II entailed. Only the U.S. Marine Corps, which had been planning since the 1920s to wrest control of the western Pacific from Japan, was poised to fight.

On October 16, 1940, National Registration Day, all men between the ages of twenty-one and thirty-six were legally obligated to register for military service. After the United States entered the war, the draft age was lowered to eighteen, and local boards were instructed to choose first from the youngest.

One-third of the men examined by the Selective Service were rejected. Surprising numbers were refused induction because they were physically unfit for military service. For the first time, men were screened for "neuropsychiatric disorders or emotional problems." At a time when only one American in four graduated from high school, induction centers turned away many conscripts because they were functionally illiterate. But those who passed the screening tests joined the best-educated army in history: nearly half of white draftees had graduated from high school and 10 percent had attended college.

The officer corps, whose top-ranking members were from the Command and General Staff School at Fort Leavenworth, tended to be highly professional, politically conservative, and personally autocratic. General Douglas MacArthur, supreme commander in the Pacific theater, was said to admire the discipline of the German army and to disparage political democracy. General Dwight D. Eisenhower, however, supreme commander of the Allied forces in Europe, projected a new and contrasting spirit. Distrusted by MacArthur and many of the older brass, Eisenhower appeared to his troops a model of leadership.

The democratic rhetoric of the war contributed to this transformation. A shortage of officers during World War I had prompted a huge expansion of the Reserve Officer Training Corps, but its drilling and discipline alone could not create good officers, and it was still insufficient to meet the demand for trained officers. Racing to make up for the deficiency, Army Chief of Staff George Marshall opened schools for officer candidates. In 1942, in seventeen-week training periods, these schools produced more than 54,000 platoon leaders. Closer in sensibility to the civilian population, these new officers were the kind of leaders Eisenhower sought.

Most GIs (short for "government issue"), who were the vast majority of draftees, had limited contact with officers at the higher levels and instead forged bonds with their company commanders and men within their own combat units. "Everyone wants someone to look up to when he's scared," one GI explained. Most of all, soldiers depended on the solidarity of the group and the loyalty of their buddies to pull through the war.

Women Enter the Military

With the approach of World War II, Massachusetts Republican congresswoman Edith Nourse Rogers proposed legislation for the formation of a women's corps. The army instead drafted its own bill, which both Rogers and Eleanor Roosevelt supported, creating in May 1942 the Women's Army Auxiliary Corps (WAAC), later changed to Women's Army Corps (WAC). In 1942–43 other bills established a women's division of the navy (WAVES), the Women's Airforce Service Pilots, and the Marine Corps Women's Reserve.

Although barred from combat, women were not necessarily protected from danger. Nurses accompanied the troops into combat in Africa, Italy, and France, treated men under fire, and dug and lived in their own foxholes. More than 1,000 women flew planes, although not in combat missions.

The WACS and WAVES were both subject to hostile commentary and bad publicity. The overwhelming majority of soliders believed that most WACS were prostitutes, and the War Department itself, fearing "immorality" among women in the armed forces, closely monitored their conduct and established much stricter rules for women than for men. The U.S. Marine Corps even used intelligence officers to ferret out suspected lesbians or women who showed "homosexual tendencies" (as opposed to homosexual acts), both causes for dishonorable discharge.

Old Practices and New Horizons

The Selective Service Act, in response to the demands of African American leaders, specified that "there shall be no discrimination against any person on account of race or color." The draft brought hundreds of thousands of young black men into the army, and African Americans enlisted at a rate 60 percent above their proportion of the general population. By 1944 black soliders represented 10 percent of the army's troops, and overall approximately 1 million African Americans served in the armed forces during World War II. The army, however, channeled black recruits into segregated, poorly equipped units, which were commanded by white officers. Secretary of War Henry Stimson refused to challenge this policy, saying that the army could not operate effectively as "a sociological laboratory." The majority served in the Signal, Engineer, and Quartermaster Corps, mainly in construction or stevedore work. Only toward the end of the war, when the shortage of infantry neared a crisis, were African Americans permitted to rise to combat status. The all-black 761st Tank Battalion, the first African American unit in combat, won a Medal of Honor after 183 days in action. And despite the very small number of African Americans admitted to the Air Force, the 99th Pursuit Squadron earned high marks in action against the feared German air force, the Luftwaffe. Even the Marine Corps and the Coast Guard agreed to end their historic exclusion of African Americans, although they recruited and promoted only a small number.

The ordinary black soldier, sailor, or marine experienced few benefits from the late-in-the-war gains of a few. They encountered discrimination everywhere, from the army canteen to the religious chapels. Even the blood banks kept blood segregated by race (although a black physician, Dr. Charles Drew, had invented the process for storing plasma).

The army also grouped Japanese Americans into segregated units, sending most to fight far from the Pacific theater. Better educated than the average soldier, many Nisei soldiers who knew Japanese served state-side as interpreters and translators. When the army decided to create a Nisei regiment, more than 10,000 volunteers stepped forward, only one in five of whom was accepted. The Nisei 442nd fought heroically in Italy and France and became the most decorated regiment in the war.

Despite segregation, the armed forces ultimately pulled Americans of all varieties out of their communities. Many Jews and other second-generation European immigrants, for example, described their stint in the military as an "Americanizing" experience. Many Indian peoples left reservations for the first time, approximately 25,000 serving in the armed forces. Many Navajo "code talkers," for example, who used a special code based on their native language to transmit information among military units, learned English in special classes established by the marines. For many African Americans, military service provided a bridge to postwar civil rights agitation.

Many homosexuals also discovered a wider world. Despite a policy barring them from military service, most slipped through mass screening at induction centers. Moreover, the emotional pressures of wartime, especially the fear of death, encouraged close friendships, and homosexuals in the military often found more room than in civilian life to express their sexual orientation openly. In army canteens, for example, men often danced with one another, whereas in civilian settings they would have been subject to ridicule or even arrest for such activity.

Most soldiers looked back at the war, with all its dangers and discomforts, as the greatest experience they would ever know. As the *New Republic* predicted in 1943, they met fellow Americans from every part of the country and recognized for the first time in their lives "the bigness and wholeness of the United States."

The Medical Corps

The chance of being killed in combat was surprisingly small, estimated at less than 1 in 50, but the risk of injury was much higher. By the time the war ended, the army reported 949,000 casualties, including 175,000 who had been killed in action. Although the European Theater produced the greatest number of casualties, the Pacific held grave dangers in addition to artillery fire. For the soliders fighting in hot, humid jungles, malaria, typhus, diarrhea, or dengue fever posed the most common threat to their lives.

The prolonged stress of combat also took a toll in the form of "battle fatigue." Despite the rigorous screening of recruits, more than 1 million soldiers suffered at one time or another from debilitating psychiatric symptoms, and the number of men discharged for neuropsychiatric reasons was 2.5 times greater than in previous wars. The cause, psychiatrists concluded, was not individual weakness but long stints in the front lines. In France, for example, where soldiers spent up to 200 days in the field without a break from fighting, thousands cracked, occasionally inflicting wounds on themselves in order to be sent home. In 1944 the army concluded that eight months in combat was the maximum and instituted, when replacements were available, a rotation system to relieve exhausted soldiers.

To care for sick and wounded soldiers, the army depended on a variety of medical personnel. Soldiers received first aid training as part of basic training, and they went into battle equipped with bandages to treat minor wounds. For the most part, however, they relied on the talents of trained physicians and medics. The Army Medical Corps sent doctors to the front lines. Working in make-shift tent hospitals, these physicians advanced surgical techniques and, with the use of new "wonder" drugs such as penicillin, saved the lives of many wounded soldiers. Of the soldiers who underwent emergency surgery on the field, more than 85 percent survived. Over all, less than 4 percent of all soldiers who received medical care died as a result of their injuries. Much of the success in treatment came from the use of blood plasma, which reduced the often lethal effect of shock from severe bleeding. By 1945, the American Red Cross Blood Bank, which was formed four years earlier, had collected more than 13 million units of blood from volunteers, converted most of it into dried plasma, and made it readily available throughout the European Theater.

Grateful for the care of skilled surgeons, many soldiers nevertheless named medics the true heroes of the battlefront. Between thirty to forty medics were attached to each infantry battalion, and they were responsible for emergency first-aid and for transporting the wounded to the aid station and if necessary on to the field hospital. Many medics were recruited from the approximately 35,000 conscientious objectors, who were defined by the Selective Service as a person "who, by reason of religious training and belief, is conscientiously opposed to participation in war in any form."

In the military hospitals, American nurses supplied the bulk of care to recovering soldiers. Before World War II, the Army Nurse Corps, created in 1901, was scarcely a military organization, with recruits earning neither military pay nor rank. To overcome the short supply of nurses, Congress extended military rank to nurses in 1944, although only for the duration and for six months after the war ended. In 1945 Congress came close to passing a bill to draft nurses. Like medics, army nurses went first to training centers in the United States, learning how to dig foxholes and dodge bullets before being sent overseas. By 1945, approximately 56,000 women, including 500 African American women, were on active duty in the Army Nurse Corps, staffing medical facilities in every theater of the war.

THE WORLD AT WAR

During the first year of declared war, the Allies remained on the defensive. Hitler's forces held the European Continent and pounded England with aerial bombardments while driving deep into Russia and across northern Africa to take the Suez Canal. The situation in the Pacific was scarcely better. Just two hours after the attack on Pearl Harbor, Japanese planes struck the main U.S. base in the Philippines and demolished half the air force commanded by General Douglas MacArthur. Within a short time, MacArthur was forced to withdraw his troops to the Bataan Peninsula, admitting that Japan had practically seized the Pacific.

But the Allies enjoyed several important advantages: vast natural resources and a skilled workforce with sufficient reserves to accelerate the production of weapons and ammunitions; the determination of millions of antifascists throughout Europe and Asia; and the capacity of the Soviet Union to endure immense losses. Slowly at first, but then with quickening speed, these advantages made themselves felt.

Soviets Halt Nazi Drive

The weapons and tactics of World War II were radically different from those of World War I. Unlike World War I, which was fought by immobile armies kept in trenches by bursts of machine-gun fire, World War II was a war of offensive maneuvers punctuated by surprise attacks. Its chief weapons were tanks and airplanes, combining mobility and concentrated firepower. Also of major importance were artillery and explosives, which according to some estimates accounted for over 30 percent of the casualties. Major improvements in communication systems, mainly two-way radio transmission and radiotelephony that permitted commanders to stay in contact with division leaders, also played a decisive role from the beginning of the war.

Early on, Hitler had used these methods to seize the advantage, purposefully creating terror among the stricken populations of western Europe. In the summer of 1941, he turned his attention to the east, hoping to invade and conquer the Soviet Union before the United States entered the war. But he had to delay the invasion in order to support Mussolini, whose weak army had been pushed back in North Africa and Greece. The attack on Russia did not come until June 22, six weeks later than planned and too late to achieve its goals before the brutal Russian winter began.

The burden of the war now fell on the Soviet Union. From June to September, Hitler's forces overran the Red Army, killing or capturing nearly 3 million soldiers and leaving thousands to die from exposure or starvation. But Nazi commanders did not count on civilian resistance. The Soviets rallied, cutting German supply lines and sending every available resource to Soviet troops concentrated just outside Moscow. After furious fighting and the onset of severe winter weather, the Red Army launched a massive counterattack, catching the freezing German troops off guard. For the first time, the Nazi war machine suffered a major setback.

Turning strategically away from Moscow, during the summer of 1942 German troops headed toward Crimea and the rich oil fields of the Caucasus. Still set on conquering the Soviet Union and turning its vast resources to his own use, Hitler decided to attack Stalingrad, a major industrial city on the Volga River. The Soviets suffered more casualties during the following battles than Americans did during the entire war. But intense house-to-house and street fighting and a massive Soviet counteroffensive took an even greater toll on the Nazi fighting machine. By February 1943, the German Sixth Army had met defeat, overpowered by Soviet troops and weapons. More than 100,000 German soldiers surrendered.

Already in retreat but plotting one last desperate attempt to halt the Red Army, the Germans threw most of their remaining armored vehicles into action at Kursk, in the Ukraine, in July 1943. The clash quickly developed into the greatest land battle in history. More than 2 million troops and 6,000 tanks went into action. After another stunning defeat, the Germans had decisively lost the initiative. Their only option was to delay the advance of the Red Army against their homeland.

Meanwhile, the Soviet Union had begun to recover from its early losses, even as tens of millions of its own people remained homeless and near starvation. Assisted

by the U.S. Lend-Lease program, by 1942 the Soviets were outproducing Germany in many types of weapons and other supplies. Nazi officers and German civilians alike began to doubt that Hitler could win the war. The Soviet victories had turned the tide of the war.

The Allied Offensive

In the spring of 1942, Germany, Italy, and Japan commanded a territory extending from France to the Pacific Ocean. They controlled central Europe and a large section of the Soviet Union as well as considerable parts of China and the southwestern Pacific. But their momentum was flagging. American shipbuilding outpaced the punishment Nazi submarines inflicted on Allied shipping, and sub-sinking destroyers greatly reduced the submarines' threat. The United States far outstripped Germany in the production of landing craft and amphibious vehicles, two of the most important innovations of the war. Also outnumbered by the Allies, the German air force was limited to defensive action. On land, the United States and Great Britain had the trucks and jeeps to field fully mobile armies, while German troops marched in and out of Russia with packhorses.

Still, German forces represented a mighty opponent on the European Continent. Fighting the Nazis almost alone, the Soviets repeatedly appealed for the creation of a Second Front, an Allied offensive against Germany from the west. The Allies focused instead on securing North Africa and then on an invasion of Italy, hoping to move from there into central Europe.

On the night of October 23–24, 1942, near El Alamein in the desert of western Egypt, the British Eighth Army halted a major offensive by the German Afrika Korps, headed by General Erwin Rommel, the famed "Desert Fox." Although suffering heavy losses—approximately 13,000 men and more than 500 tanks—British forces destroyed the Italian North African Army and much of Germany's Afrika Korps. Americans entered the war in Europe as part of Operation Torch, the landing of British and American troops on the coast of Morocco and Algeria in November 1942, the largest amphibious military landing to that date. The Allies then fought their way along the coast, entering Tunis in triumph six months later. With the surrender of a quarter-million Germans and Italians in Tunisia in May 1943, the Allies controlled North Africa and had a secure position in the Mediterranean.

During the North African campaign, the Allies announced that they would accept nothing less than the unconditional surrender of their enemies. In January 1943, Roosevelt and Churchill had met in Casablanca in Morocco and ruled out any possibility of negotiation with the Axis powers. Roosevelt's supporters

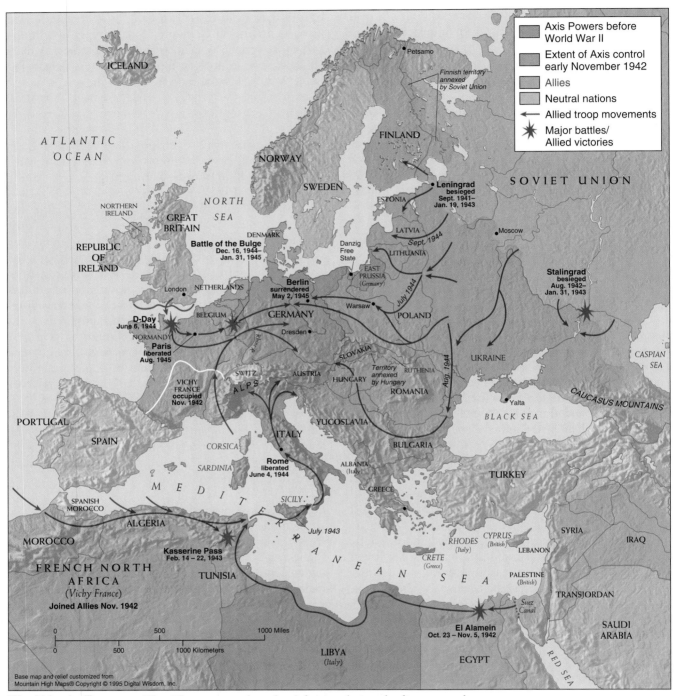

The War in Europe   The Allies remained on the defensive during the first years of
the war, but by 1943 the British and Americans, with an almost endless supply of resources,
had turned the tide.

hailed the policy as a clear statement of goals, a
promise to the world that the scourge of fascism would
be completely banished. Stalin, who did not attend the
meeting, criticized the policy, fearing that it would
only increase the enemy's determination to fight to the
end. Other critics similarly charged that the demand
for total capitulation would serve to prolong the war
and lengthen the casualty list.

Allied aerial bombing further increased pressure on
Germany. Many U.S. leaders believed that in the B-17
Flying Fortress, the air force possessed the ultimate
weapon, "the mightiest bomber ever built." The U.S.
Army Air Corps described this bomber as a "humane"
weapon, capable of hitting specific military targets and
sparing the lives of civilians. But when weather or darkness required pilots to depend on radar for sightings,

they couldn't distinguish clearly between factories and schools or between military barracks and private homes, and bombs might fall within a range of nearly two miles from the intended target. American pilots preferred to bomb during daylight hours, while the British bombed during the night. Bombing missions over the Rhineland and the Ruhr successfully took out many German factories. But the Germans responded by relocating their plants, often dispersing light industry to the countryside.

Determined to break German resistance, the Royal Air Force redirected its main attack away from military sites to cities, including fuel dumps and public transportation. Hamburg was practically leveled. Between 60,000 and 100,000 people were killed, and 300,000 buildings were destroyed. Sixty other cities were hit hard, leaving 20 percent of Germany's total residential area in ruins. The very worst air raid of the war—650,000 incendiary bombs dropped on the city of Dresden, destroying 8 square miles and killing 135,000 civilians—had no military value.

The Allied Invasion of Europe

During the summer of 1943, the Allies began to advance on southern Italy. On July 10, British and American troops stormed Sicily from two directions and conquered the island in mid-August. King Vittorio Emmanuel dismissed Mussolini, calling him "the most despised man in Italy," and Italians, by now disgusted with the Fascist government, celebrated in the streets. Italy surrendered to the Allies on September 8, and Allied troops landed on the southern Italian peninsula. But Hitler sent new divisions into Italy, occupied the northern peninsula, and effectively stalled the Allied campaign. When the European war ended, the German and Allied armies were still battling on Italy's rugged terrain.

Elsewhere in occupied Europe, armed uprisings against the Nazis spread. The brutalized inhabitants of Warsaw's Jewish ghetto repeatedly rose up against their tormentors during the winter and spring of 1943. Realizing that they could not hope to defeat superior forces, they finally sealed off their quarter, executed collaborators, and fought invaders, street by street and house by house. Scattered revolts followed in the Nazi labor camps, where military prisoners of war and civilians were being worked to death on starvation rations.

Partisans were active in many sections of Europe, from Norway to Greece and from Poland to France. Untrained and unarmed by any military standard, organized groups of men, women, and children risked their lives to distribute antifascist propaganda, taking action against rich and powerful Nazi collaborators.

Meanwhile, Stalin continued to push for a second front. Stalled in Italy, the Allies prepared in early 1944

for Operation Overlord, a campaign to retake the Continent with a decisive counterattack through France. American and British forces began by filling the southern half of England with military camps. All leaves were canceled.

The Allied invasion finally began on "D-Day," June 6, 1944. Under steady German fire the Allied fleet brought to the shores of Normandy more than 175,000 troops and more than 20,000 vehicles—an accomplishment unimaginable in any previous war. Although the Germans had responded slowly, anticipating an Allied strike at Calais instead of Normandy, at Omaha Beach they had prepared their defense almost perfectly. Wave after wave of Allied landings met machine-gun and mortar fire, and the tides filled with corpses and those pretending to be dead. Some 2,500 troops died, many before they could fire a shot. Nevertheless, in the next six weeks, nearly 1 million more Allied soldiers came ashore, broke out of Normandy, and prepared to march inland.

As the fighting continued, all eyes turned to Paris, the premier city of Europe. Allied bombers pounded factories producing German munitions on the outskirts of the French capital. As dispirited German soldiers retreated, many now hoping only to survive, the French Resistance unfurled the French flag at impromptu demonstrations on Bastille Day, July 14. On August 10, railway workers staged one of the first successful strikes against Nazi occupiers, and three days later the Paris police defected to the Resistance, which proclaimed in leaflets that "the hour of liberation has come." General Charles de Gaulle, accompanied by Allied troops, arrived in Paris on August 25 to become president of the reestablished French Republic.

One occupied European nation after another now swiftly fell to the Allied armies. But the Allied troops had only reached a resting place between bloody battles.

The High Cost of European Victory

In September 1944 Allied commanders searched for a strategy to end the war quickly. Missing a spectacular chance to move through largely undefended territory and on to Berlin, they turned north instead, intending to open the Netherlands for Allied armies on their way to Germany's industrial heartland. Faulty intelligence reports overlooked a well-armed German division at Arnhem, Holland, waiting to cut Allied paratroopers to pieces. By the end of the battle, the Germans had captured 6,000 Americans.

In a final, desperate effort to reverse the Allied momentum, Hitler directed his last reserves, a quarter-million men, at Allied lines in the Belgian forest of the Ardennes. In what is known as the Battle of the Bulge, the Germans took the Allies by surprise, driving them back 50 miles before they were stopped. This last effort exhausted the German capacity for counterattack. After Christmas day 1944, the Germans fell back, retreating into their own territory.

The end was now in sight. In March 1945 the Allies rolled across the Rhine and took the Ruhr Valley with its precious industrial resources. The defense of Germany, now hopeless, had fallen into the hands of young teenagers and elderly men. By the time of the German surrender, May 8, Hitler had committed suicide in a Berlin bunker and high Nazi officials were planning their escape routes. The casualties of the Allied European campaign had been enormous, if still small compared to those of the Eastern Front: more than 200,000 killed and almost 800,000 wounded, missing, or dead in nonbattle accidents and unrelated illness.

The War in Asia and the Pacific

The war that had begun with Pearl Harbor rapidly escalated into scattered fighting across a region of the world far larger than all of Europe, stretching from Southeast Asia to the Aleutian Islands. Japan followed up its early advantage by cutting the supply routes between Burma and China, crushing the British navy, and seizing the Philippines, Hong Kong, Wake Island, British Malaya, and Thailand. Although China offically joined the Allies on December 9, 1941, and General Stillwell arrived in March as commander of the China-Burma-India theater, the military mission there remained on the defensive. Meanwhile, after tenacious fighting on the Bataan Peninsula and on the island of Corregidor, the U.S. troops not captured or killed retreated to Australia.

At first, nationalist and anticolonial sentiment played into Japanese hands. Japan succeeded with only 200,000 men because so few inhabitants of the imperial colonies of Britain and France would fight to defend them. Japan installed puppet "independent" governments in Burma and the Philippines. But the new Japanese empire proved terrifyingly cruel. Nationalists from Indochina to the Philippines turned against the Japanese, establishing guerrilla armies that cut Japanese supply lines and prepared the way for Allied victory.

Six months after the disaster at Pearl Harbor, the United States began to regain naval superiority in the central Pacific and halt Japanese expansion. In an aircraft carrier duel with spectacular aerial battles during the Battle of the Coral Sea on May 7 and 8, the United States blocked a Japanese threat to Australia. A month later, the Japanese fleet converged on Midway Island, which was strategically vital to American communications and the defense of Hawai'i. American strategists, however, thanks to specialists who had broken Japanese codes, knew when and where the Japanese planned to attack. The two carrier fleets, separated by hundreds of miles,

clashed at the Battle of Midway on June 4. American planes sank four of Japan's vital aircraft carriers and destroyed hundreds of planes, ending Japan's offensive threat to Hawai'i and the west coast of the United States.

But the war for the Pacific was far from over. By pulling back their offensive perimeter, the Japanese concentrated their remaining forces. Their commanders calculated that bitter fighting, with high casualties on both sides, would wear down the American troops. The U.S. command, divided between General Douglas MacArthur in the southwest Pacific and Admiral Chester Nimitz in the central Pacific, needed to develop a counterstrategy to strangle the Japanese import-based economy and to retake strategic islands closer to the homeland.

The Allies launched their counteroffensive campaign on the Solomon Islands and Papua, near New Guinea. American and Australian ground forces fought together through the jungles of Papua, while the marines prepared to attack the Japanese stronghold of Guadalcanal.

For the next two years, the U.S. Navy and Marine Corps, in a strategy known as "island hopping," pushed to capture a series of important atolls from their well-armed Japanese defenders and open a path to Japan. The first of these assaults, which cost more than 1,000 marines their lives, was on Tarawa, in November 1943, in the Gilbert Islands. In subsequent battles in 1944, American forces occupied Guam, Saipan, and Tinian in the Marianas Islands, within air range of the Japanese home islands. In another decisive naval engagement, the Battle of the Philippine Sea, fought in June 1944, the Japanese fleet suffered a crippling loss.

In October 1944, General MacArthur led a force of 250,000 to retake the Philippines. In a bid to defend the islands, practically all that remained of the Japanese navy threw itself at the American invaders in the Battle of Leyte Gulf, the largest naval battle in history. The Japanese lost eighteen ships, leaving the United States in control of the Pacific. The ground fighting in the Philippines, meanwhile, cost 100,000 Filipino civilians their lives and left Manila devastated.

The struggle for the island of Okinawa, 350 miles southwest of the home islands of Japan, proved even more bloody. The invasion of the island, which began on Easter Sunday, April 1, 1945, was the largest amphibious operation mounted by Americans in the Pacific war. It was met by waves of Japanese *kamikaze* ("divine wind") pilots flying suicide missions in planes with a 500-pound bomb and only enough fuel for a one-way flight. On the ground, U.S. troops used flamethrowers, each with three hundred gallons of napalm, against the dug-in Japanese. More Americans died or were wounded here than at Normandy. By the end of June, the fighting had killed more than 200,000 people.

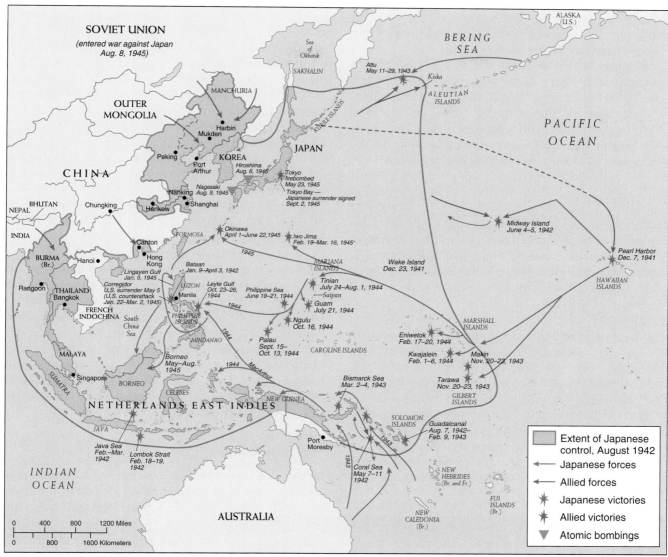

War in the Pacific   Across an ocean battlefield utterly unlike the European theater, Allies battled Japanese troops near their homeland.

Attacks on mainland Japan began to take their toll. U.S. submarines drastically reduced the ability of ships to reach Japan with supplies. Since the taking of Guam, American bombers had been able to reach Tokyo and other Japanese cities, with devastating results. Massive fire bombings burned thousands of civilians alive in their mostly wood or bamboo homes and apartments and left hundreds of thousands homeless.

Japan could not hold out forever. Without a navy or air force, the government could not transport the oil, tin, rubber, and grain needed to maintain its soldiers. Great Britain and particularly the United States, however, pressed for quick unconditional surrender. They had special reasons to hurry. Earlier they had sought a commitment from the Soviet Union to invade Japan, but now they looked beyond the war, determined to

prevent the Red Army from taking any territories held by the Japanese. These calculations and the anticipation that an invasion would be extremely bloody set the stage for the use of a secret weapon that American scientists had been preparing: the atomic bomb.

THE LAST STAGES OF WAR

From the attack on Pearl Harbor until mid-1943, President Roosevelt and his advisers had focused on military strategy rather than on plans for peace. But once the defeat of Nazi Germany appeared in sight, high government officials began to reconsider their diplomatic objectives. Roosevelt wanted both to crush the Axis powers and to establish a system of collective security to prevent another world war. He knew he could not succeed without the cooperation of the other key leaders, Stalin and Churchill.

During 1944 and 1945, the "Big Three" met to hammer out the shape of the postwar world. Although none of these nations expected to reach a final agreement, neither did they anticipate how quickly they would be confronted with momentous global events. It soon became clear that the only thing holding the Allies together was the mission of destroying the Axis.

The Holocaust

Not until the last stages of the war did Americans learn the extent of Hitler's atrocities. As part of his "final solution to the Jewish question," Hitler had ordered the systematic extermination of not only Jews, but Gypsies, other "inferior races," homosexuals, and anyone deemed an enemy of the Reich. Beginning in 1933, and accelerating after 1941, the Nazis murdered millions of people from Germany and the European nations they conquered.

During the war the U.S. government released little information on what came to be known as the Holocaust. Although liberal magazines such as the *Nation* and small committees of intellectuals tried to call attention to what was happening in German concentration camps, major news media like the *New York Times* and *Time* magazine treated reports of the camps and killings as minor news items. As late as 1943, only 43 percent of Americans polled believed that Hitler was systematically murdering European Jews.

Roosevelt and his advisers maintained that the liberation of European Jews depended primarily on a speedy and total Allied victory. When American Jews pleaded for a military strike against the rail lines leading to the notorious extermination camp in Auschwitz, Poland, the War Department replied that Allied armed forces would not be employed "for the purpose of rescuing victims of enemy oppression unless such rescues are the direct result of military operations conducted with the objective of defeating the armed forces of the enemy." In short, the government viewed civilian rescue as a diversion of precious resources.

Allied troops discovered the death camps when they invaded Germany and liberated Poland. When Eisenhower and General George S. Patton visited the Ohrdruf concentration camp in April 1945, they found barracks crowded with corpses and crematories still reeking of burned flesh. "I want every American unit not actually in the front lines to see this place," Eisenhower declared. "We are told that the American soldier does not know what he is fighting for. Now, at least, he will know what he is fighting against." At Buchenwald in the first three months of 1944, more than 14,000 prisoners were murdered. In all, the Holocaust claimed the lives of as many as 6 million Jews, 250,000 Gypsies, and 60,000 homosexuals, among others.

The Yalta Conference

In early February 1945, Roosevelt held his last meeting with Churchill and Stalin at Yalta, a Crimean resort on the Black Sea. Although diplomats avoided the touchy phrase "spheres of influence," it was clear that this principle guided all negotiations. Neither the United States nor Great Britain did more than object to the Soviet Union's plan to retain the Baltic states and part of Poland as a buffer zone to protect it against any future German aggression. In return, Britain planned to reclaim its empire in Asia, and the United States hoped to hold several Pacific islands in order to monitor any military resurgence in Japan. The delegates also negotiated the terms of membership in the United Nations, which had been outlined at a meeting several months earlier.

The biggest and most controversial item on the agenda at Yalta was the Soviet entry into the Pacific war, which Roosevelt believed necessary for a timely Allied victory.

Belsen Camp: The Compound for Women, painted by American artist Leslie Cole, depicts Belsen as the Allied troops found it when they invaded Germany in 1945.

SOURCE: Leslie Cole, *Belsen Camp. The Compound for Women*. Imperial War Museum, London.

After driving a hard bargain involving rights to territory in China, Stalin agreed to declare war against Japan within two or three months of Germany's surrender.

The death of Franklin Roosevelt of a stroke on April 12, 1945, cast a dark shadow over all hopes for long-term, peaceful solutions to global problems. Stung by a Republican congressional comeback in 1942, Roosevelt had rebounded in 1944 to win an unprecedented fourth term as president. In an overwhelming electoral college victory (432 to 99), he had defeated Republican New York governor Thomas E. Dewey. Loyal Democrats continued to link their hopes for peace to Roosevelt's leadership, but the president did not live to witness the surrender of Germany on May 8, 1945. And now, as new and still greater challenges were appearing, the nation's great pragmatic idealist was gone.

The Atomic Bomb

Roosevelt's death made cooperation among the Allied nations much more difficult. His successor, Harry Truman, who had been a Kansas City machine politician, a Missouri judge, and a U.S. senator, lacked diplomatic experience as well as Roosevelt's personal finesse. As a result, negotiations at the Potsdam Conference, held just outside Berlin from July 17 to August 2, 1945, lacked the spirited cooperation characteristic of the wartime meetings of Allied leaders that Roosevelt had attended. The American, British, and Soviet delegations had a huge agenda, including reparations, the future of Germany, and the status of other Axis powers such as Italy. Although they divided sharply over most issues, they held fast to the demand of Japan's unconditional surrender.

It was during the Potsdam meetings that Truman first learned about the successful testing of an atomic bomb in New Mexico. Until this time, the United States had been pushing the Soviet Union to enter the Pacific war as a means to avoid a costly U.S. land invasion. But after Secretary of War Stimson received a cable reading "Babies satisfactorily born," U.S. diplomats concluded that Soviet assistance was no longer needed to bring the war to an end.

On August 3, 1945, Japan wired its refusal to surrender. Three days later, the Army Air Force B-29 bomber *Enola Gay* dropped the bomb that destroyed the Japanese city of Hiroshima. As estimated 40,000 people died instantly; in the following weeks 100,000 more died from radiation poisoning or burns; by 1950 the death toll reached 200,000.

An editorialist wrote in the Japanese *Nippon Times*, "This is not war, this is not even murder; this is pure nihilism . . . a crime against God which strikes at the very basis of moral existence." In the United States, several leading religious publications echoed this view.

The *Christian Century* interpreted the use of the bomb as a "moral earthquake" that made the long-denounced use of poison gas by Germany in World War I utterly insignificant by comparison.

Most Americans learned about the atomic bomb for the first time on August 7, when the news media reported the destruction and death it had wrought in Hiroshima. But concerns about the implications of this new weapon were soon overwhelmed by an outpouring of relief when Japan surrendered on August 14 after a second bomb destroyed Nagasaki, killing another 70,000 people.

The Allied insistence on unconditional surrender and the decision to use the atomic bomb against Japan remain two of the most controversial aspects of the war. Although Truman stated in his memoirs, written much later, that he gave the order with the expectation of saving "a half a million American lives" in ground combat, no such official estimate exists. An intelligence document of April 30, 1946, states, "The dropping of the bomb was the pretext seized upon by all leaders as the reason for ending the war, but . . . [even if the bomb had not been used] the Japanese would have capitulated upon the entry of Russia into the war." There is no question, however, that the use of nuclear force did strengthen the U.S. diplomatic mission. It certainly intimidated the Soviet Union, which would soon regain its status as a major enemy of the United States. Truman and his advisers in the State Department knew that their atomic monopoly could not last, but they hoped that in the meantime the United States could play the leading role in building the postwar world.

CONCLUSION

The new tactics and weapons of the Second World War made warfare incomparably more deadly than before to both military and civilian populations. Between 40 and 50 million people died in World War II—four times the number in World War I—and half the casualties were women and children. More than 405,000 Americans died, and more than 670,000 were wounded. Although slight compared to the casualties suffered by other Allied nations—more than 20 million Soviets died during the war—the human cost of World War II for Americans was second only to that of the Civil War.

Coming at the end of two decades of resolutions to avoid military entanglements, the war pushed the nation's leaders to the center of global politics and into risky military and political alliances that would not outlive the war. The United States emerged the strongest nation in the world, but in a world where the prospects for lasting peace appeared increasingly remote.

If World War II raised the nation's international commitments to a new height, its impact on ordinary

CHRONOLOGY

1931	September: Japan occupies Manchuria
1933	March: Adolf Hitler seizes power
	May: Japan quits League of Nations
1935	October: Italy invades Ethiopia
1935–1937	Neutrality Acts authorize the president to block the sale of munitions to belligerent nations
1937	August: Japan invades China
	October: Franklin D. Roosevelt calls for international cooperation against aggression
1938	March: Germany annexes Austria
	September: Munich Agreement lets Germany annex Sudetenland of Czechoslovakia
	November: *Kristallnacht,* Nazis attack Jews and destroy Jewish property
1939	March: Germany annexes remainder of Czechoslovakia
	August: Germany and the Soviet Union sign nonaggression pact
	September: Germany invades Poland; World War II begins
	November: Soviet Union invades Finland
1940	April–June: Germany's *Bliztkrieg* sweeps over Western Europe
	September: Germany, Italy, and Japan—the Axis powers—conclude a military alliance
	First peacetime military draft in American history
	November: Roosevelt is elected to an unprecedented third term
1941	March: Lend-Lease Act extends aid to Great Britain
	May: German troops secure the Balkans
	A. Philip Randolph plans March on Washington movement for July
	June: Germany invades Soviet Union

	Fair Employment Practices Committee formed
	August: The United States and Great Britain agree to the Atlantic Charter
	December: Japanese attack Pearl Harbor; United States enters the war
1942	January: War mobilization begins
	February: Executive order mandates internment of Japanese Americans
	May–June: Battles of Coral Sea and Midway give the United States naval superiority in the Pacific
	August: Manhattan Project begins
	November: United States stages amphibious landing in North Africa; Operation Torch begins
1943	January: Casablanca Conference announces unconditional surrender policy
	February: Soviet victory over Germans at Stalingrad
	April–May: Coal miners strike
	May: German Afrika Korps troops surrender in Tunis
	July: Allied invasion of Italy
	Summer: Race riots break out in nearly fifty cities
1944	June–August: Operation Overlord and liberation of Paris
	November: Roosevelt elected to fourth term
1945	February: Yalta Conference renews American-Soviet alliance
	February–June: United States captures Iwo Jima and Okinawa in Pacific
	April: Roosevelt dies in office; Harry Truman becomes president
	May: Germany surrenders
	July–August: Potsdam Conference
	August: United States drops atomic bombs on Hiroshima and Nagasaki; Japan surrenders

Americans was not so easy to gauge. Many new communities formed as Americans migrated in mass numbers to new regions that were booming as a result of the wartime economy. Enjoying a rare moment of full employment, many workers new to well-paying industrial jobs anticipated further advances against discrimination. Exuberant at the Allies' victory over fascism and the return of the troops, the majority were optimistic as they looked ahead.

REVIEW QUESTIONS

1. Describe the response of Americans to the rise of nationalism in Japan, Italy, and Germany during the 1930s. How did President Franklin D. Roosevelt ready the nation for war?
2. What role did the federal government play in gearing up the economy for wartime production?
3. How did the war affect the lives of American women?
4. Discuss the causes and consequences of the Japanese American internment program.
5. Describe the role of popular culture in promoting the war effort at home.
6. How did military service affect the lives of those who served in World War II?
7. What were the main points of Allied military strategy in both Europe and Asia?
8. How successful were diplomatic efforts in ending the war and in establishing the terms of peace?

RECOMMENDED READING

Stephen E. Ambrose, *D-Day, June 6, 1944: The Climactic Battle of World War II* (1994). A vivid and extremely readable, moment-by-moment reconstruction of the preparation and battle, relying heavily upon the oral histories of American veterans.

Philip D. Beidler, *The Good War's Greatest Hits: World War II and American Remembering* (1998). Examines the popular culture produced about World War II, such as movies, photographs, cartoons, and books, to show how these sources created a lasting image of World War II as the "good war."

Amy Bentley, *Eating for Victory: Food Rationing and the Politics of Domesticity* (1998). Brings together several areas of scholarship, including the social history of food and women's history, and provides a fascinating overview of rationing programs and Victory Gardens during World War II.

Allan Berube, *Coming Out under Fire: The History of Gay Men and Women in World War Two* (1991). A study of government policy toward homosexuals during the war and the formation of a gay community. Berube offers many insights into the new opportunities offered homosexuals through travel and varied companionship and of the effects of sanctions against them.

Paul Boyer, *By the Bomb's Early Light: American Thought and Culture at the Dawn of the Atomic Age* (1985). An analysis of the intellectual and cultural assumptions in relation to atomic weaponry. Boyer examines the development of a political logic, on the part of President Harry Truman and others, that made use of atomic weapons against the Japanese inevitable.

Wayne S. Cole, *Roosevelt and the Isolationists, 1932–45* (1983). Shows the president and his critics sparring over foreign policy issues. Cole analyzes the complexities of liberal-conservative divisions over war and offers insights into the logic of conservatives who feared the growth of a permanent bureaucratic, militarized state.

Richard M. Dalfiume, *Desegregation of the U.S. Armed Forces: Fighting on Two Fronts, 1939–1953* (1969). Analyzes wartime race relations in the military. By examining the official mechanisms to end discrimination and the remaining patterns of racism in the armed forces, Dalfiume reveals how changing attitudes from the top ran up against old assumptions among enlisted men and women.

Roger Daniels, *Concentration Camps USA: Japanese Americans and World War II* (1981). Perhaps the best account of Japanese American internment. Daniels details the government programs, the experiences of detention and camp life, and the many long-term consequences of lost liberty.

Sherna Berger Gluck, *Rosie the Riveter Revisited: Women, the War, and Social Change* (1987). An oral history–based study of women workers during World War II. Gluck's interviewees reveal the diversity of experiences and attitudes of women workers as well as their common feelings of accomplishment.

Laura Hein and Mark Selden, eds., *Living With the Bomb: American and Japanese Cultural Conflict in the Nuclear Age* (1997). Essays dealing with the ambiguous legacy of the atomic bomb in both the United States and Japan. Reviews the "official story" of the bomb as the symbol of U.S. triumph in the "Good War" in light of the growing number of dissenting voices and the impact of both views on memorials and museum exhibits.

John W. Jeffries, *Wartime America: The World War II Home-front* (1996). Provides a useful synthesis of scholarship and assesses the major differences in the interpretations of leading historians.

Gerald F. Linderman, *The World within War: America's Combat Experience in World War II* (1997). Emphasizes the less glamorous aspects of war, mainly the strains placed on the combat soldiers on the front lines. Linderman examines in especially close detail the grim experiences of army infantrymen and the marine riflemen who fought in the Pacific campaign and provides a nuanced analysis of their complex responses to the horror of war.

Katrina R. Mason, *Children of Los Alamos: An Oral History of the Town Where the Atomic Age Began* (1995). Recollections of those who spent their childhood in Los Alamos. They describe their affection for the geographical setting as well as sense of safety growing up in a community so well protected. They also comment on the ethnic diversity of those who populated the town and on the pride they took in their parents' contribution to building the bomb and ending the war.

Neil R. McMillan, ed., *Remaking Dixie: The Impact of World War II on the American South* (1997). A collection of essays on the impact of World War II on the South that pay special attention to the experiences of African Americans and women. Several authors question the degree to which southern society was transformed by wartime mobilization.

Robert J. Moskin, *Mr. Truman's War: The Final Victories of World War II and the Birth of the Postwar World* (1996). A lively history of the final stages of World War II, including the surrender of Germany and the emergence of postwar foreign policy. Moskin provides an assessment of the impact of the war on social and economic conditions in the United States.

William M. Tuttle, Jr., *"Daddy's Gone to War": The Second World War in the Lives of America's Children* (1993). Draws from 2,500 letters that the author solicited from men and women in their fifties and sixties about their wartime childhood memories.

David S. Wyman, *The Abandonment of the Jews: America and the Holocaust, 1941–1945* (1984). A detailed examination of U.S. immigration policy and response to Hitler's program of genocide. Wyman shows both the indifference of the Roosevelt administration to appeals for Allied protection of Jews and the inclinations of leading American Jewish organizations to stress the formation of a future Jewish state instead of the protection of European Jewry.

ON THE WEB

http://www.loc.gov/exhibits/british/brit-3.html

With political posters, graphic drawings, and cartoons, this Library of Congress site documents the evolution of British-American foreign policy relations from the War of 1812 to the end of World War II. The World War I and World War II sections are particularly important here and include sheet music covers of war songs, photographs of Roosevelt and Churchill, and other primary source materials.

http://www.archives.gov/exhibit_hall/powers_of_persuasion/powers_of_persuasion_home.html

This National Archives site documents posters of World War II. These primary documents will give you a good feel for wartime propaganda on the home front.

http://www.fdrlibrary.marist.edu/wwphotos.html

Available through the Franklin D. Roosevelt Presidential Library are literally hundreds of photographs of the American home front and battlefield action in every theater of the war. Particularly interesting war the women war workers, Mother of the Assembly Line is a photo of two grandmotherly-looking women assembling rifle clips as handily as they might bake an apple pie (see **http://www.fdrlibrary.marist.edu/images/photodb/23-0095a.gif**). Of course, the photo was staged, but that was just good home front wartime propaganda.

http://www.history.navy.mil/photos/sh-fornv/japan/japsh-s/shokaku.htm

http://www.history.navy.mil/photos/sh-fornv/germany/ger-name.htm

These two sites, official U.S. Navy historical records, provide photographs of the major vessels of the Japanese and German fleets during World War II. Of particular interest are the midget submarines used at Pearl Harbor and elsewhere, the aircraft carriers, and Germany's battleships and submarines.

http://lcweb.loc.gov/rr/print/coll/109_anse.html
http://lcweb.loc.gov/rr/print/coll/109-b.html

These two sites connect to the Ansel Adams's photos of the Manzanar Japanese Internment camp of World War II. The collection is small, but instructions are provided about how to search the National Archives for a larger collection.

http://lcweb.loc.gov/rr/print/126_rosi.html

Extensive collection of Library of Congress photos, wartime posters, and cartoons concerning women war industry workers during World War II. Most citations have expandable thumbnail pictures attached.

http://www.prenhall.com/faragherbrief/map25.1

Examine the strategies of the Axis and the Allies. What were the key turning points of the war in Europe?

http://www.prenhall.com/faragherbrief/map25.2

Consider the war in the Pacific in more detail. How did strategies in this theater differ from those in Europe?

COMMUNITY & MEMORY

▶ Exhibiting the *Enola Gay*

When news of the successful detonation of the atomic bomb over Hiroshima reached Los Alamos, New Mexico, horns and sirens blared in exultation. The community took pride in its achievement and, like other Americans, welcomed the prospect of Japan's surrender and the end of the devastating conflict. Chief scientist J. Robert Oppenheimer nevertheless expressed a sentiment equally common at the time, reporting that he was a "little scared of what I have made." Nearly a half-century later, Americans are no more certain about the meaning of this event.

In 1994, a major controversy erupted as the curatorial staff of the Smithsonian Institution's National Air and Space Museum (NASM) circulated their plans for an exhibition on the *Enola Gay*, the B-29 aircraft that carried "Little Boy," the weapon used on the Hiroshima mission. After reading drafts of a script that was to accompany the display, critics charged that the museum staff had crafted a message that was lop-sided at best, anti-American at worst. A writer in *Time* magazine accused the NASM curators of portraying the Japanese as "more or less innocent victims of American beastliness and lust for revenge." A columnist in the *Washington Post* expressed his opinion more bluntly, calling them a bunch of "politically correct pinheads." These judgments came as a surprise to those at the museum who had prepared the script. They had already received a positive report from a group of scholars who had reviewed the draft and judged it, in the words of a distinguished military historian, "comprehensive and dramatic" and needing only a "bit of 'tweaking.'" However, many Air Force veterans strongly disagreed, and they launched a campaign to block the proposed exhibit.

At the center of the controversy were two nagging questions. Both had been addressed by political and military leaders in August 1945 but never answered—and perhaps can never be answered—satisfactorily: Was the atomic bomb necessary to end the war quickly and to save the lives of hundreds of thousands of Americans? Was the decision to deploy the bomb morally unambiguous, given the death toll of Japanese civilians?

The NASM curators had wrestled with these hard questions in preparing the original script. They decided, for example, not to use the conventional estimate of a half-million American lives saved as too high. This figure, they noted, had been projected only after the war had ended and often to rebut critics of the Hiroshima

On his official website, Brigadier General Paul W. Tibbets (USAF Retired) offered for sale replicas of the *Enola Gay*, with signed certificates of authenticity, as well as commemorative coins and stamps, books, and videos about the dropping of the first atomic bomb.

SOURCE: © Reuters NewMedia Inc./CORBIS.

bombing. Instead, the curators relied on the actual wartime estimates by military leaders that projected perhaps tens of thousands of American casualties if a land invasion of Japan were to ensue. They also cited the U.S. Strategic Bombing Survey, which was completed soon after Japan's surrender, that concluded that even without the bomb the war would "certainly" have ended by November or December of 1945.

Many veterans who had served in the Pacific Theater objected strongly even to raising such questions. They continued to have no doubt that Truman had made the decision to drop the atomic bomb to save American lives and to shorten the war. They accused the museum staff of intentionally distorting history. Their collective memory of the battles of Guadacanal, Iwo Jima, and Okinawa, the risks posed by the ground invasion of Japan, and the torture inflicted on prisoners of war in the Japanese death camps ran directly counter to the script that read, "It is possible that there was a last opportunity to end the war without either atomic bombings or an invasion of Japan." The nation's largest veteran organization, the American Legion, issued a public letter to President Clinton calling for the cancellation of the exhibit as planned.

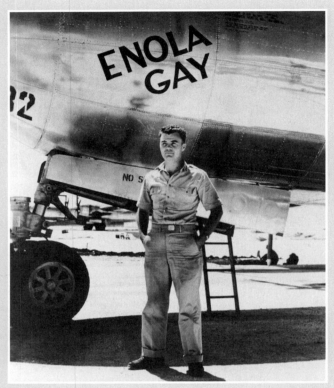

In 1937, Paul W. Tibbets, Jr., enlisted as a flying cadet in the Army Aircorps, and during World war II he became a test pilot for the B-29, the airplane that he helped to redesign to deliver the atomic bomb.

SOURCE: © Bettmann/CORBIS.

The controversy eventually pulled in General Paul W. Tibbets, the pilot of the *Enola Gay* (he had painted his mother's maiden name on the nose of the plane). He, too, objected to the museum staff's "second-guessing the decision to use the atomic weapons." He wanted a simple, straightforward label for the fifty-six feet of fuselage inside the museum hall: "'This airplane was the first one to drop an atomic bomb.'"

Eventually, the U.S. Congress stepped into the fray. The Senate passed a nonbinding resolution reminding the NASM staff of its "obligation to portray history in the proper context of the time." The museum, at the time averaging about 8.2 million visitors a year, more than any other museum in the world, depended mainly on government funding and therefore relied on those who controlled the federal budget, the Congress.

The NASM staff did have support for their plans, particularly among other professional historians. The Organization of American Historians condemned the intervention by members of Congress. An independent group of "historians and scholars" protested this "transparent attempt at historical cleansing."

On June 28, 1995, the exhibit finally opened, although in greatly reduced form. The original plans for photographs of "ground zero" in Hiroshima, for example, were scrapped, and what remained were several restored components of the B-29 aircraft, such as its fuselage, propellers, and cockpit. As to the *Enola Gay's* mission, one photograph featured the crew before take-off, another of the mushroom cloud as seen from the tail gunner's position. The wall text read simply:

> Tibbets piloted the aircraft on its mission to drop an atomic bomb on Hiroshima on Aug. 6, 1945. That bomb and the one dropped on Nagasaki three days later destroyed much of the two cities and caused tens of thousands of deaths. However, the use of the bombs led to the immediate surrender of Japan and made unnecessary the planned invasion of the Japanese home islands. Such an invasion, especially if undertaken for both main islands, would have led to very heavy casualties among American and Allied troops and Japanese civilians and military. It was thought highly unlikely that Japan, while in a very weakened military condition, would have surrendered unconditionally without such an invasion."

"The aircraft speaks for itself in this exhibit," Smithsonian director I. Michael Heyman said, "and, 50 years after its mission, it continues to evoke strong emotions, in those who look at it."

The legacy of the atomic bomb, including the scientific research done at Los Alamos during the 1940s, remains so uncertain and contentious that an attempted explanation of the mission of the *Enola Gay* was abandoned for a celebration of the aircraft's design as an engineering marvel. Historians and military veterans seemed to speak different languages. Meanwhile, a Gallup Poll conducted at the time of the controversy surrounding the *Enola Gay* exhibit indicated that a quarter of Americans did not even know that World War II ended with the explosion of an atomic bomb over Japan. ■

TWENTY-SIX
THE COLD WAR

▶ 1945 – 1952

CHAPTER OUTLINE

AMERICAN COMMUNITIES

University of Washington, Seattle: Students and Faculty Face the Cold War

IN MAY 1948, A PHILOSOPHY PROFESSOR AT THE UNIVERSITY OF WASHington in Seattle answered a knock on his office door. Two state legislators, members of the state's Committee on Un-American Activities, entered. "Our information," they charged, "puts you in the center of a Communist conspiracy."

The accused professor, Melvin Rader, had never been a Communist. A self-described liberal, Rader drew fire because he had joined several organizations supported by Communists. During the 1930s, in response to the rise of Nazism and fascism, Rader had become a prominent political activist in his community. At one point he served as president of the University of Washington Teacher's Union, which had formed during the upsurge of labor organizing during the New Deal. When invited to join the Communist Party, Rader bluntly refused. "The experience of teaching social philosophy had clarified my concepts of freedom and democracy," he later explained. "I was an American in search of a way— but it was not the Communist way."

Despite this disavowal, Rader was caught up in a Red Scare that curtailed free speech and political activity on campuses throughout the United States. At some universities, such as Yale, the Federal Bureau of Investigation (FBI) set up camp with the consent of the college administration, spying on students and faculty, screening the credentials of job or scholarship applicants, and seeking to entice students to report on their friends or roommates. The University of Washington administration turned down the recommendation of the Physics Department to hire J. Robert Oppenheimer because the famed atomic scientist had become a vocal opponent of the arms race and the proliferation of nuclear weapons.

Although one state legislator claimed that "not less than 150 members" of the University of Washington faculty were subversives, the state's Committee on Un-American Activities turned up just six members of the Communist Party. These six were brought up before the university's Faculty Committee on Tenure and Academic Freedom, charged with violations ranging from neglect of duty to failing to inform the university administration of their party membership. Three were ultimately dismissed, while the other three were placed on probation.

What had provoked this paranoia? Instead of peace in the wake of World War II, a pattern of cold war—icy relations—prevailed between the United States and the Soviet Union. Uneasy allies during World War II, the two superpowers now viewed each other as arch-enemies, and nearly all other nations lined up with one or the other of them. Within the United States, the cold war demanded pledges of absolute loyalty from citizens in every institution, from the university to trade unions and from the mass media to government itself.

If not for the outbreak of the cold war, this era would have marked one of the most fruitful in the history of higher education. The Servicemen's Readjustment Act, popularly known as the G.I. Bill of Rights, passed by Congress in 1944, offered stipends covering tuition and living expenses to veterans attending vocational schools or college. By the 1947–48 academic year, the federal government was subsidizing nearly half of all male college students. Between 1945 and 1950, 2.3 million students benefited from the G.I. Bill, at a cost of more than $10 billion.

At the University of Washington the student population in 1946 had grown by 50 percent over its prewar peak of 10,000, and veterans represented fully two-thirds of the student body. A quickly expanded faculty taught into the evening to use classroom space efficiently. Meanwhile, the state legislature pumped in funds for the construction of new buildings, including dormitories and prefabricated units for married students.

According to many observers, a feeling of community flourished among these war-weary undergraduates. Often the first in their families to attend college, they joined fellow students in campaigns to improve the campus. Married, often fathers of young children, they expected university administrators to treat them as adults. They wanted less supervision of undergraduate social life, more affordable housing, and

better cultural opportunities than had previously been the case. On some campuses, film societies and student-run cooperatives vied with fraternities and sororities as centers of undergraduate social activity.

The cold war put a damper on these community-building efforts. FBI director J. Edgar Hoover testified that the college campuses were centers of "red propaganda," full of teachers "tearing down respect for agencies of government, belittling tradition and moral custom and . . . creating doubts in the validity of the American way of life." Due to Communistic teachers and "Communist-line textbooks," a senator lamented, thousands of parents sent "their sons and daughters to college as good Americans," only to see them return home "four years later as wild-eyed radicals."

Although these extravagant charges were never substantiated, several states, including Washington, enacted or revived loyalty-security programs, obligating all state employees to swear in writing their loyalty to the United States and to disclaim membership in any subversive organization. Nationwide, approximately 200 faculty members were dismissed outright and many others were denied tenure. Thousands of students simply left school, dropped out of organizations, or changed friends after "visits" from FBI agents or interviews with administrators. The main effect on campus was the restraint of free speech generally and fear of criticizing U.S. racial, military, or diplomatic policies in particular.

This gloomy mood reversed the wave of optimism that had swept through America only a few years earlier. V-J Day, marking victory over Japan, had erupted into a two-day national holiday of wild celebrations, complete with ticker-tape parades, spontaneous dancing, and kisses for returned G.I. Americans, living in the richest and most powerful nation in the world, finally seemed to have gained the peace they had fought and sacrificed to win. But peace proved fragile and elusive. ■

Seattle

KEY TOPICS

■ Prospects for world peace at end of World War II

■ Diplomatic policy during the cold war

■ The Truman presidency

■ Anticommunism and McCarthyism

■ Cold war culture and society

■ The Korean War

GLOBAL INSECURITIES AT WAR'S END

The war that had engulfed the world from 1939 to 1945 created an international interdependence that no country could ignore. The legendary African American folk singer Leadbelly (Huddie Ledbetter) added a fresh lyric to an old spiritual melody: "We're in the same boat, brother. . . . And if you shake one end you're going to rock the other." Never before, not even at the end of World War I, had hopes been so strong for a genuine "community of nations."

Financing the Future

In 1941 Henry Luce, publisher of *Time, Life,* and *Fortune* magazines, had forecast the dawn of "the American Century." Americans must, he wrote, "accept whole-heartedly our duty and our opportunity as the most powerful and vital nation in the world and in consequence to assert upon the world the full impact of our influence, for such means as we see fit." Indeed, immediately after the bombing of Hiroshima, President Truman pronounced the United States "the most powerful nation in the world—the most powerful nation, perhaps, in all history."

Americans had good reason to be confident about their prospects for setting the terms of reconstruction. Unlike Great Britain and France, the United States had not only escaped the ravages of the war but had actually prospered. By June 1945, the capital assets of manufacturing had increased 65 percent over prewar levels and were equal in value to approximately half the entire world's goods and services.

Yet many Americans recognized that it was the massive government spending associated with wartime industry, rather than New Deal programs, that had ended the nightmare of the 1930s. A great question loomed: What would happen when wartime production slowed and millions of troops returned home?

"We need markets—big markets—in which to buy and sell," answered Assistant Secretary of State for Economic Affairs Will Clayton. Just to maintain the current level of growth, the United States needed an estimated $14 billion in exports—an unprecedented amount. Many business leaders even looked to the Soviet Union as a potential trading partner. With this prospect vanishing, Eastern European markets threatened, and large chunks of former colonial territories closed off, U.S. business and government leaders became determined to integrate Western Europe and Asia into a liberal international economy open to American trade and investment.

During the final stages of the war, President Roosevelt's advisers laid plans to establish U.S. primacy in the postwar global economy. In July 1944 representatives from forty-four Allied nations met at Bretton Woods, New Hampshire, and established the International Bank for Reconstruction and Development (World Bank) and the International Monetary Fund (IMF) to help rebuild war-torn Europe and to assist the nations of Asia, Latin America, and Africa. By stabilizing exchange rates to permit the expansion of international trade, the IMF would deter currency conflicts and trade wars—two maladies of the 1930s that were largely responsible for the political instability and national rivalries leading to World War II. As the principal supplier of funds for the IMF and the World Bank—more than $7 billion to each—the United States, in essence, could unilaterally shape the world economy by determining the allocation of loans.

The Soviet Union participated in the Bretton Woods conference but refused to ratify the agreements that, in essence, allowed the United States to rebuild the world economy along capitalist lines. By spurning both the World Bank and the IMF, the Soviet Union cut off the possibility of aid to its own people as well as to its Eastern European client states and, equally important, isolated itself economically.

The Division of Europe

The Atlantic Charter of 1941 committed the Allies to recognize the right of all nations to self-determination and to renounce all claims to new territories as the spoils of war. The Allied leaders themselves, however, violated the charter's main points before the war had ended by dividing occupied Europe into spheres of influence (see Chapter 25).

So long as Franklin Roosevelt remained alive, this strategy had seemed reconcilable with world peace. The president had balanced his own international idealism with his belief that the United States was entitled to extraordinary influence in Latin America and the Philippines and that other great powers might have similar privileges or responsibilities elsewhere. Roosevelt also recognized the diplomatic consequences of the brutal ground war that had been fought largely on Soviet territory: the Soviet Union's unnegotiable demand for territorial security along its European border.

From the early days of the war, the USSR was intent on reestablishing its 1941 borders, and by the time of the Potsdam Conference in July 1945 the Soviets had not only regained but extended their territory. Much of eastern Europe, including a large portion of Poland and the little Baltic nations, was now under its control as client states.

When the Allies turned to plan the future of Germany, they agreed to dismember Germany and eventually decided to divide the conquered nation into four occupation zones, each governed by one of the Allied nations. But the Allies could not agree on long-term plans. Having borne the brunt of German aggression, France and the USSR both opposed reunification. The latter, in addition, demanded heavy reparations along with a limit on postwar reindustrialization. Roosevelt appeared to agree with the Soviets. But American business leaders, envisioning a new center for U.S. commerce, shared Winston Churchill's hope of rebuilding Germany into a powerful counterforce against the Soviet Union and a strong market for U.S. and British goods.

After the war, continuing disagreements about the future Germany darkened hopes for cooperation between the Soviet Union and the United States. By July 1946, Americans had begun to withhold reparations from their zone and to institute a program of amnesty for former Nazis. Then, in December, the American and British merged their zones and extended an invitation to France and the USSR to join. Although France accepted the offer, the Soviets, fearing a resurgence of united Germany, held out.

The United States and the Soviet Union were now at loggerheads. Twice in the twentieth century, Germany had invaded Russia, and the USSR now interpreted these U.S. moves toward consolidation of Germany an act of supreme hostility. For its part, the United States envisioned a united Germany as a bulwark against Soviet expansion.

The United Nations and Hopes for Collective Security

The dream of postwar international cooperation had been seeded earlier by President Roosevelt. In late summer and fall 1944 at the Dumbarton Oaks Conference in Washington, D.C., and again in April 1945 in San Francisco, the Allies worked to shape the United Nations as an international agency that would arbitrate disputes among members as well as impede aggressors, by military force if necessary.

The terms of membership, however, limited the UN's ability to mediate disputes. Although all member nations enjoyed representation in the General Assembly, only five members (the United States, Great Britain, the Soviet Union, France, and Nationalist China) served permanently on the Security Council, which had the "primary responsibility for the maintenance of international peace and security," and each enjoyed absolute veto power over the decisions of the other members.

The UN achieved its greatest success with its humanitarian programs. Its relief agency provided the war-torn countries of Europe and Asia with billions of dollars for medical supplies, food, and clothing. The UN also dedicated itself to protecting human rights, and its high standards of human dignity owed much to the lobbying of Eleanor Roosevelt, one of the first delegates from the United States.

On other issues, however, the UN operated strictly along lines dictated by the cold war. The Western nations allied with the United States held the balance of power and maintained their position by controlling the admission of new member nations. They successfully excluded Communist China, for example. Moreover, the polarization between East and West made negotiated settlements virtually impossible.

THE POLICY OF CONTAINMENT

In March 1946, in a speech delivered in Fulton, Missouri, Winston Churchill spoke to the new reality. With President Harry Truman at his side, the former British prime minister declared that "an iron curtain has descended across the [European] continent." He called directly upon the United States, standing "at this time at the pinnacle of world power," to recognize its "awe-inspiring accountability to the future" and to act assertively to turn back Soviet expansion.

Although Truman responded cautiously to Churchill's pronouncement, he and his administration ultimately decided to meet the challenge. Within a short time, they were wholeheartedly committed to securing U.S. leadership in the world and, equally important, preventing communism from spreading further. As a doctrine uniting military, economic, and diplomatic strategies, the "containment" of communism also fostered an ideological opposition, an "us"-versus-"them" theme that divided the world into "freedom" and "slavery," "democracy" and "autocracy," and "tolerance" and "coercive force." The Truman Doctrine laid down the first plank in a global campaign against communism.

The Truman Doctrine

Many Americans believed that Franklin D. Roosevelt, had he lived, would have been able to stem the tide of tensions between the Soviet Union and the United States. His successor sorely lacked FDR's talent for diplomacy. More comfortable with machine politicians than with polished New Dealers, the new president liked to talk tough and act defiantly. Just ten days after he took office, Truman complained that U.S.–Soviet negotiations had been a "one-way street." He vowed to "baby" them no longer.

A perceived crisis in the Mediterranean prompted President Truman to show his colors. On February 21, 1947, amid a civil war in Greece, Great Britain informed the U.S. State Department that it could no longer afford to prop up the anti-Communist government there and announced its intention to withdraw all aid. Without U.S. intervention, Truman concluded, Greece, Turkey, and perhaps the entire oil-rich Middle East would fall under Soviet control.

On March 12, 1947, the president made his argument before Congress. Never mentioning the Soviet Union by name, he appealed for all-out resistance to a "certain ideology" wherever it appeared in the world. The preservation of peace and the freedom of all Americans depended, the president insisted, on containing communism.

Congress approved a $400 million appropriation in aid for Greece and Turkey, which helped the monarchy and right-wing military crush the rebel movement. Truman's victory buoyed his popularity for the upcoming 1948 election. It also helped to generate popular support for a campaign against communism, both at home and abroad.

The significance of what became known as the Truman Doctrine far outlasted the events in the Mediterranean: the United States had declared its right to intervene to save other nations from communism. As early as February 1946, foreign-policy adviser George F. Kennan had sent an 8,000-word "long telegram" to the State Department insisting that Soviet fanaticism made cooperation impossible. The USSR intended to extend its realm not by military means alone, he explained, but by "subversion" within "free" nations. It was now the responsibility of the United States, Truman insisted, to safeguard the "Free World" by diplomatic, economic, and, if necessary, military means. He had, in sum, fused anticommunism and internationalism into an aggressive foreign policy.

The Marshall Plan

The Truman Doctrine complemented the European Recovery Program, commonly known as the Marshall Plan. Introduced in a commencement speech at Harvard University on June 5, 1947, by secretary of state and former army chief of staff George C. Marshall, the plan sought to reduce "hunger, poverty, desperation, and chaos" and to restore "the confidence of the European people in the economic future of their own countries and of Europe as a whole." Indirectly, the Marshall plan aimed to turn back both socialist and Communist electoral bids for power in northern and western Europe.

Considered by many historians the most successful postwar U.S. diplomatic venture, the Marshall Plan, in effect brought recipients of aid into a bilateral agreement with the United States. In addition, the western European nations, seventeen in all, ratified the General Agreement on Tariffs and Trade (GATT), which reduced commercial barriers among member nations and opened all to U.S. trade and investment. The plan was costly to Americans, in its initial year taking 12 percent of the federal budget, but effective. Industrial production in the European nations covered by the plan rose by 200 percent between 1947 and 1952. Although deflationary programs cut wages and increased unemployment, profits soared and the standard of living improved.

The Marshall Plan drove a deeper wedge between the United States and the Soviet Union. Although invited to participate, Stalin denounced the plan for what it was, an American scheme to rebuild Germany and to incorporate it into an anti-Soviet bloc. The president readily acknowledged that the Marshall Plan and the Truman Doctrine were "two halves of the same walnut."

The Berlin Crisis and the Formation of NATO

As Stalin recognized, the Marshall Plan also sought to rebuild and integrate the western zones of Germany into unified region compatible with U.S. political and economic interests. Within a year of its introduction, the United States and Britain moved closer to this goal by introducing a common currency in the western

OVERVIEW

MAJOR COLD WAR POLICIES

Policy	Date	Provisions
Truman Doctrine	1947	Pledged the United States to the containment of communism in Europe and elsewhere. The doctrine was the foundation of Truman's foreign policy. It impelled the United States to support any nation whose stability was threatened by communism or the Soviet Union.
Federal Employees Loyalty program and Security Program	1947	Established by Executive Order 9835, this barred Communists and fascists from federal employment and outlined procedures for investigating current and prospective federal employees.
Marshall Plan	1947	U.S. program to aid war-torn Europe, also known as the European Recovery Program. The Marshall Plan was a cornerstone in the U.S. use of economic policy to contain communism.
National Security Act	1947	Established Department of Defense (to coordinate the three armed services), the National Security Council (to advise the president on security issues), and the Central Intelligence Agency (to gather and evaluate intelligence data).
Smith-Mundt Act	1948	Launches an overseas campaign of anti-Communist propaganda.
North Atlantic Treaty Organization (NATO)	1948	A military alliance of twelve nations formed to deter possible aggression of the Soviet Union against Western Europe.
NSC-68	1950	National Security Council Paper calling for an expanded and aggressive U.S. defense policy, including greater military spending and higher taxes.
Internal Security Act (also known as the McCarran Act and the Subversive Activities Control Act)	1950	Legislation providing for the registration of all Communist and totalitarian groups and authorizing the arrest of suspect persons during a national emergency.
Psychological Strategy Board created	1951	Created to coordinate anti-Communist propaganda campaigns.
Immigration and Nationality Act (also known as McCarran-Walter Immigration Act)	1952	Reaffirmed the national origins quota system but tightened immigration controls, barring homosexuals and people considered subversive from entering the United States.

zones. Stalin reacted to this challenge on June 24, 1948, by halting all traffic to West Berlin, formally controlled by the Western allies but situated deep within the Soviet-occupied zone.

The Berlin blockade created both a crisis and an opportunity for the Truman administration to test its mettle. With help from the Royal Air Force, the United States began an around-the-clock airlift of historic proportions—Operation Vittles—that delivered nearly 2 million tons of supplies to West Berliners.

The Soviet Union finally lifted the blockade in May 1949, clearing the way for the Western powers to merge their occupation zones into a single nation, the Federal Republic of West Germany. The USSR countered by establishing the German Democratic Republic in their sector.

The Berlin Crisis made a U.S.-led military alliance against the USSR attractive to western European nations. In April 1949 ten European nations, Canada, and the United States formed the North Atlantic Treaty

Organization (NATO), a mutual defense pact in which "an armed attack against one or more of them . . . shall be considered an attack against them all." NATO complemented the Marshall Plan, strengthening economic ties among the member nations by, according to one analyst, keeping "the Russians out, the Americans in, and the Germans down." It also deepened divisions between eastern and western Europe, making a permanent military mobilization on both sides almost inevitable.

Congress approved $1.3 billion in military aid, which involved the creation of U.S. Army bases and the deployment of American troops abroad. Critics, such as isolationist senator Robert A. Taft, warned that

the United States could not afford to police all Europe without sidetracking domestic policies and undercutting the UN. But opinion polls revealed strong support for Truman's tough line against the Soviets.

Between 1947 and 1949, the Truman administration had defined the policies that would shape the cold war for decades to come. The Truman Doctrine explained the ideological basis of containment; the Marshall Plan put into place its economic underpinnings in western Europe; and NATO created the mechanisms for military enforcement. When NATO extended membership to a rearmed West Germany in May 1955, the Soviet Union responded by creating a counterpart, the Warsaw Pact, including East Germany.

Divided Europe   During the cold war, Europe was divided into opposing military alliances, the North American Treaty Organization (NATO) and the Warsaw Pact (Communist bloc).

Atomic Diplomacy

The policy of containment depended on the ability of the United States to back up its commitments through military means, and Truman invested his faith in the U.S. monopoly of atomic weapons. The United States began to build atomic stockpiles and to conduct tests on the Bikini Islands in the Pacific. By 1950, as a scientific adviser subsequently observed, the United States "had a stockpile capable of somewhat more than reproducing World War II in a single day."

Despite warnings to the contrary by leading scientists, U.S. military analysts estimated it would take the Soviet Union three to ten years to produce an atomic bomb. In August 1949, the Soviet Union proved them wrong by testing its own atomic bomb. "There is only one thing worse than one nation having the atomic bomb," Nobel prize-winning scientist Harold C. Urey said, "that's two nations having it."

Within a few years, both the United States and the Soviet Union had tested hydrogen bombs a thousand times more powerful than the weapons dropped on Hiroshima and Nagasaki in 1945. Both proceeded to stockpile bombs attached to missiles, inaugurating the fateful nuclear arms race that scientists had feared since 1945.

The United States and the Soviet Union were now firmly locked into the cold war. The nuclear arms race imperiled their futures, diverted their economies, and fostered fears of impending doom. Prospects for global peace had dissipated, and despite the Allied victory in World War II, the world had again divided into hostile camps.

COLD WAR LIBERALISM

Truman's aggressive, gutsy personality suited the confrontational mood of the cold war. He linked the Soviet threat in Europe to the need for a strong presidency. Pressed to establish his own political identity, "Give 'em Hell" Harry successfully portrayed himself as a fierce fighter against all challengers, yet loyal to Roosevelt's legacy.

"To Err Is Truman"

Within a year of assuming office, Harry Truman rated lower in public approval than any twentieth-century president except Roosevelt's own predecessor, Herbert Hoover, who had been blamed for the Great Depression. The responsibilities of reestablishing peacetime conditions seemed to overwhelm the new president's administration. "To err is Truman," critics jeered.

In handling the enormous task of reconverting the economy to peacetime production, Truman appeared both inept and mean-spirited. The president faced millions of restless would-be consumers tired of rationing and eager to spend their wartime savings on shiny cars, new furniture, choice cuts of meat, and colorful clothing. The demand for consumer items rapidly outran supply, fueling inflation and creating a huge black market. When Congress proposed to extend wartime price controls, Truman vetoed the bill and prices skyrocketed.

In 1945 and 1946, the country appeared ready to explode. While homemakers protested rising prices by boycotting neighborhood stores, industrial workers struck in unprecedented numbers. Employers, fearing a rapid decline to Depression-level profits, determined to slash wages or at least hold them steady; workers wanted a bigger cut of the huge war profits they had heard about. The spectacle of nearly 4.6 million workers on picket lines alarmed the new president. In May 1946, Truman proposed to draft strikers into the army who refused to return to work under a presidential order. The usually conservative Senate killed this plan.

Congress defeated most of Truman's proposals to revive the New Deal. One week after Japan's surrender, the president introduced a twenty-one-point program that included greater unemployment compensation, higher minimum wages, and housing assistance. Later he added proposals for national health insurance and atomic energy legislation. Congress turned back the bulk of these bills, passing the Employment Act of 1946 only after substantial modification. The act created a new executive body, the Council of Economic Advisers, which would confer with the president and formulate policies for maintaining employment, production, and purchasing power. But the measure did not include funding mechanisms to guarantee full employment, thus falling far short of the bill's intent.

Republicans, sensing victory in the upcoming off-year elections, asked the voters, "Had enough?" Apparently the voters had. They gave Republicans majorities in both houses of Congress and in the state capitols. And in a symbolic repudiation of Roosevelt, they passed an amendment to the Constitution establishing a two-term limit for the presidency.

The Republicans, dominant in Congress for the first time since 1931, prepared a counteroffensive against the New Deal, beginning with an attack on organized labor. Unions had by this time reached a peak in size and prestige, with membership topping 15 million and encompassing nearly 40 percent of all wage earners. Concluding that labor had gone too far, the Republican-dominated Eightieth Congress aimed to outlaw many practices approved by the Wagner Act of 1935 (see Chapter 24).

The Labor-Management Relations Act of 1947, better known as Taft-Hartley Act, brought to an end the closed shop, the secondary boycott, and the use of union dues for political activities. It also mandated an eighty-day cooling-off period in the case of strikes affecting national safety or health. Taft-Hartley furthermore required all union officials to swear under oath that they were not Communists—a cold war mandate that abridged freedoms ordinarily guaranteed by the First Amendment. Unions that refused to cooperate were denied the services of the National Labor Relations Board, which arbitrated strikes and issued credentials to unions.

Truman regained some support from organized labor when he vetoed the Taft-Hartley Act, saying it would "conflict with important principles of our democratic society." Congress, however, overrode his veto, and Truman himself went on to invoke the act against strikers.

The 1948 Election

Harry Truman had considered some of Roosevelt's advisers to be "crackpots and the lunatic fringe." By 1946 Truman had forced out the remaining social planners who had staffed the Washington bureaus for over a decade, including one of the best-loved New Dealers, Secretary of Interior Harold Ickes. Truman also fired the secretary of commerce, Henry Wallace, for advocating a more conciliatory policy toward the Soviet Union.

However, Wallace would not retreat and made plans to run against Truman for president. He pledged to expand New Deal programs by moving boldly to establish full employment, racial equality, and stronger labor unions. He also promised peace with the Soviet Union. As the 1948 election neared, Wallace appeared a viable candidate on the new Progressive party ticket until Truman accused him of being a tool of communists.

Meanwhile, Truman repositioned himself to discredit congressional Republicans. He proposed programs calling for federal funds for education and new housing and a national program of medical insurance that he knew the Republicans would oppose, and he called Congress back for a fruitless special session in 1948. He then hammered away at the Republican controlled "do-nothing Congress" to good effect in his reelection campaign.

To cut Wallace's lead on civil rights, Truman issued executive orders in July 1948 desegregating the armed forces and banning discrimination in the federal civil service. In response, some 300 southern delegates bolted from the Democratic National Convention and formed a States' Rights ("Dixiecrat") ticket, headed by Governor J. Strom Thurmond of South Carolina, known for his segregationist views. With the South as good as lost, and popular New York governor Thomas E. Dewey heading the Republican ticket, Truman appeared hopelessly far from victory.

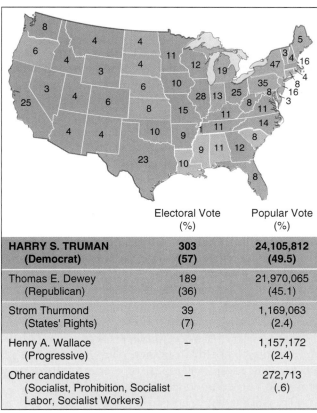

	Electoral Vote (%)	Popular Vote (%)
HARRY S. TRUMAN (Democrat)	**303** **(57)**	**24,105,812** **(49.5)**
Thomas E. Dewey (Republican)	189 (36)	21,970,065 (45.1)
Strom Thurmond (States' Rights)	39 (7)	1,169,063 (2.4)
Henry A. Wallace (Progressive)	–	1,157,172 (2.4)
Other candidates (Socialist, Prohibition, Socialist Labor, Socialist Workers)	–	272,713 (.6)

The Election of 1948 Harry Truman holds up a copy of the *Chicago Tribune* with headlines confidently and mistakenly predicting the victory of his opponent, Thomas E. Dewey. An initially unpopular candidate, Truman made a whistle-stop tour of the country by train to win 49.5 percent of the popular vote to Dewey's 45.1 percent.

SOURCE: UPI/CORBIS.

Yet as the election neared, Truman campaigned vigorously and managed to revive the New Deal coalition. Fear of the Republicans won back the bulk of organized labor, while the recognition of the new

State of Israel in May 1948 helped prevent the defection of many liberal Jewish voters from Democratic ranks. The success of the Berlin airlift also buoyed the president's popularity. By election time, Truman had deprived Henry Wallace of nearly all his liberal support. Meanwhile, Dewey, who had run a hard-hitting campaign against Roosevelt in 1944, expected to coast to victory.

Truman won the popular vote by a margin of 5 percent and trounced Dewey 303 to 189 in the electoral college. Moreover, Democrats again had majorities in both houses of Congress. But, as it turned out, Truman had hit the highest point of his popularity and was about to begin a steady slide downhill.

The Fair Deal

"Every segment of our population and every individual has a right," Truman announced in January 1949, "to expect from our Government a fair deal." The return of Democratic congressional majorities, he hoped, would enable him to translate campaign promises into concrete legislative achievements and expand the New Deal. But a powerful bloc of conservative southern Democrats and midwestern Republicans turned back his domestic agenda.

Truman broke no new ground. Congress passed a National Housing Act in 1949, promoting federally funded construction of low-income housing. It also raised the minimum wage from 40 to 75 cents per hour and expanded the Social Security program to cover an additional 10 million people. Otherwise, Truman made little headway. He and congressional liberals introduced a variety of bills to weaken southern segregationism: a federal antilynching law; outlawing the poll tax; prohibiting discrimination in interstate transportation. These measures were all defeated by southern-led filibusters. Proposals to create a national health insurance plan, provide federal aid for education, and repeal or modify Taft-Hartley remained bottled up in committees.

Truman managed best to lay out the basic principles of cold war liberalism. Toning down the rhetoric of economic equality espoused by the visionary wing of the Roosevelt coalition, his Fair Deal exalted economic growth—not the reapportionment of wealth or political power—as the proper mechanism for ensuring social harmony and national welfare. His administration insisted, therefore, on an ambitious program of expanded foreign trade, while relying on the federal government to encourage high levels of productivity at home. Equally important, Truman further tempered

liberalism by making anticommunism a key element in both foreign policy and the domestic agenda.

THE COLD WAR AT HOME

"Communists . . . are everywhere—in factories, offices, butcher shops, on street corners, in private businesses," Attorney General J. Howard McGrath warned in 1949: "At this very moment [they are] busy at work—undermining your government, plotting to destroy the liberties of every citizen, and feverishly trying in whatever way they can, to aid the Soviet Union." Republican senator Joseph R. McCarthy even claimed to have in his personal possession a list of communists serving secretly in government agencies. By this time, the Communist Party, U.S.A., which had formed in 1919, was steadily losing ground.

Nevertheless, during the earliest days of the cold war, anticommunism already occupied center stage in domestic politics. Thus, FBI director J. Egar Hoover characteristically warned Americans not to be complacent in the face of low numbers of Communists because "for every party member there are ten others ready, willing, and able to do the Party's work" in infiltrating and corrupting "various spheres of American life."

The federal government, with the help of the media, would lead the campaign, finding in the threat of communism a rationale for the massive reordering of its operation and the quieting of the voices of dissent. In this far-reaching quest for security, Americans moved toward a greater concentration of power in government, and, while promising to lead the "free world," allowed many of their own rights to be circumscribed.

The National Security Act of 1947

The imperative of national security destroyed old-fashioned isolation, forcing the United States into international alliances such as NATO and into the role of world leader. "If we falter in our leadership," Truman warned, "we may endanger the peace of the world—and we shall surely endanger the welfare of this nation." Such a responsibiity required a massive amount of resources. Truman went on, therefore, to argue successfully that national security demanded a substantial increase in the size of the federal government, including both military forces and surveillance agencies. Security measures were required to keep the nation in a steady state of preparedness, readily justified during wartime, now extended into the very uneasy peacetime.

The National Security Act of 1947, passed by Congress in July, established the Department of Defense and the National Security Council (NSC) to administer and coordinate defense policies and to advise the president. The Department of Defense replaced the War Department and united the armed forces—the army, navy, and air force—under the jurisdiction of a single secretary with cabinet-level status. The act also created the National Security Resources Board (NSRB) to coordinate plans throughout the government "in the event of war" and, for the first time in American history, to maintain a program of military preparedness in peacetime.

The Department of Defense, together with the NSRB, became the principal sponsor of scientific research during the first ten years of the cold war. It was commonly recognized at the time that World War II had been "a physicists' war," leading to the creation of the ultimate weapon, the atom bomb, but also to major advances in military technology in areas of systems of navigation and detection, strategic targeting, and communication. Many scientists anticipated that, at the end of the war, the special relationship between science and government would continue under the auspices of a new federal agency that would channel funds mainly to universities for basic research under civilian control.

The National Security Act added to this system of defense in 1947 by establishing the Central Intelligence Agency (CIA). With roots in the wartime Office of Strategic Services, the CIA now became a permanent operation devoted to collecting political, military, and economic information for security purposes throughout the world. Although information about the CIA was classified—that is, secret from both Congress and the public—historians have estimated that the agency soon dwarfed the State Department in number of employees and size of budget.

The national security state required a huge workforce. Before World War II, approximately 900,000 civilians worked for the federal government, with about 10 percent engaged in security work; by the beginning of the cold war, nearly 4 million people were on the government's payroll, with 75 percent working in national security agencies.

National security took up increasingly large portions of the nation's resources and required an enormous increase in the size of the defense budget. By the end of Truman's second term, defense allocations accounted for 10 percent of the gross national product, directly or indirectly employed hundreds of thousands of well-paid workers, and subsidized some of the nation's most profitable corporations. This vast financial outlay created the rationale for permanent, large-scale military spending as a basic stimulus to economic growth.

The Loyalty-Security Program

National security also required increased surveillance at home. Within two weeks of proclaiming the Truman Doctrine, the president signed Executive Order 9835 on March 21, 1947, and thereby established a loyalty program for all federal employees. The new Federal Employees Loyalty and Security Program, directed at members of the Communist Party—as well as fascists and anyone guilty of "sympathetic association" with either—in effect established a political test for federal employment. Later amendments added "homosexuals" as potential security risks on the grounds that they might succumb to blackmail by enemy agents.

Many state and municipal governments enacted loyalty programs and required public employees, including teachers at all levels, to sign loyalty oaths. In all, some 6.6 million people underwent loyalty and security checks. An estimated 500 government workers were fired and perhaps as many as 6,000 more chose to resign.

Attorney General Clark aided this effort by publishing a list of hundreds of potentially subversive organizations selected by criteria so vague that any views "hostile or inimical to the American form of government" could make an organization liable for investigation and prosecution. There was, moreover, no right of appeal. The attorney general's list effectively outlawed many political and social organizations, indirectly stigmatizing hundreds of thousands of individuals who had done nothing illegal. Fraternal and social institutions, especially popular among aging European immigrants of various nationalities, were among the largest organizations destroyed. The state of New York, for example, legally dismantled the International Workers' Order, which had provided insurance to nearly 200,000 immigrants and their families. Only a handful of organizations had the funds to challenge the listing legally; most simply closed their doors.

In 1950 Congress overrode the president's veto to pass a bill that Truman called "the greatest danger to freedom of press, speech, and assembly since the Sedition Act of 1798." The Internal Security (McCarran) Act required Communist organizations to register with the Subversive Activities Control Board and authorized the arrest of suspect persons during a national emergency. The Immigration and Nationality Act, also sponsored by Republican senator Pat McCarran of Nevada and adopted in 1952, again over Truman's veto, barred people deemed "subversive" or "homosexual" from becoming citizens or even from visiting the United States. It also empowered the attorney general to deport immigrants who were members of Communist organizations, even if they had become citizens. Challenged repeatedly on constitutional grounds, the Subversive Activities Control Board remained in place until 1973, when it was terminated.

The Red Scare in Hollywood

Anti-Communist Democratic representative Martin Dies of Texas, who had chaired a congressional committee on "un-American activities" since 1938, told reporters at a press conference in Hollywood in 1944:

> Hollywood is the greatest source of revenue in this nation for the Communists and other subversive groups. . . . Two elements stand out in . . . the making of pictures which extoll foreign ideology—propaganda for a cause which seeks to spread its ideas to our people[,] and the "leftist" or radical screenwriters.

A few years later, Dies's successor, J. Parnell Thomas of New Jersey, directed the committee to investigate supposed Communist infiltration of the movie industry.

Renamed and made a permanent standing committee in 1945, the House Un-American Activities Committee (HUAC) had the power to subpoena witnesses and to compel them to answer all questions or face contempt of Congress charges. In well-publicized hearings held in Hollywood in October 1947, the mother of actress Ginger Rogers defended her daughter by saying that she had been duped into appearing in the pro-Soviet wartime film *Tender Comrade* (1943) and "had been forced" to read the subversive line "Share and share alike, that's democracy." HUAC encouraged testimony by "friendly witnesses," including Ronald Reagan and Gary Cooper. The committee intimated many others who feared the loss of their careers into naming former friends and co-workers in order to be cleared for future work in Hollywood.

A small but prominent minority refused to cooperate with HUAC. By claiming the freedoms of speech and association guaranteed by the First and Sixth Amendments to the Constitution, they became known as "unfriendly witnesses." A handful served prison sentences for contempt of Congress.

Hollywood studios refused to employ any writer, director, or actor who refused to cooperate with HUAC. The resulting blacklist remained in effect until the 1960s and limited the production of films dealing directly with social or political issues. Meanwhile, the privately published *Red Channels: The Report of Communist Influence in Radio and Television* (1950) persuaded advertisers to cancel their accounts with many programs considered friendly to the Soviet Union, the United Nations, or liberal causes.

Spy Cases

In August 1948, Whittaker Chambers, a *Time* magazine editor, appeared before HUAC to name Alger Hiss as a fellow Communist in the Washington underground during the 1930s. Hiss, then president of the prestigious Carnegie Endowment for International Peace and former member of FDR's State Department, denied the charges and sued his accuser for slander. A federal grand jury in January 1950 convicted Hiss of perjury (for denying he knew Chambers), and he received a five-year prison term. Hiss was released two years later, still proclaiming his innocence.

Many Democrats, including Truman himself, at first dismissed the allegations against Hiss—conveniently publicized at the start of the 1948 election campaign—as a red herring, a Republican maneuver to gain votes. Nevertheless, the highly publicized allegations against Hiss proved detrimental to Democrats, suggesting that both FDR and Truman had allowed Communists to infiltrate the federal government.

The most dramatic spy case of the era involved Julius Rosenberg, former government engineer, and his wife, Ethel, who were accused of stealing and plotting to convey atomic secrets to Soviet agents during World War II. The government's case against the Rosenbergs rested on the testimony of their supposed accomplices, some of them secretly coached by the FBI. Although the Rosenbergs maintained their innocence to the end, in March 1951 a jury found them guilty of conspiring to commit espionage. The American press showed them no sympathy, but around the world the Rosenbergs were defended by citizens' committees and their convictions protested in large-scale demonstrations. Scientist Albert Einstein, the pope, and the president of France, among many prominent figures, all pleaded for clemency. Julius and Ethel Rosenberg died in the electric chair on June 19, 1953.

McCarthyism

In a sensational Lincoln Day speech to the Republican Women's Club of Wheeling, West Virginia, on February 9, 1950, Republican senator Joseph R. McCarthy of Wisconsin announced that the United States had been sold out by the "traitorous actions of those who have been treated so well by the nation." These "bright young men who have been born with silver spoons in their mouths"—such as Secretary of State Dean Acheson, whom McCarthy called a "pompous diplomat in striped pants, with a phony English accent"—were part of a conspiracy, he charged, of more than 200 Communists working in the State Department.

McCarthy refused to reveal names, however, and a few days later, after a drinking bout, he told persistent reporters: "I'm not going to tell you anything. I just want you to know I've got a pailful [of dirt] . . . and I'm going to use it where it does the most good." Although investigations uncovered not a single Communist in the State Department, McCarthy launched

The tables turned on Senator Joseph McCarthy (1908–57) after he instigated an investigation of the U.S. Army for harboring Communists. A congressional committee then investigated McCarthy for attempting to make the army grant special privileges to his staff aide, Private David Schine. During the televised hearings, Senator McCarthy—shown here with his staff assistant Roy Cohn—discredited himself. In December 1954, the Senate voted to censure him.

SOURCE: Hank Walker/TimePix.

a flamboyant offensive against New Deal Democrats and the Truman administration for failing to defend the nation's security. His name provided the label for the entire campaign to silence critics of the cold war: McCarthyism.

Behind the blitz of publicity, the previously obscure junior senator from Wisconsin had struck a chord. Communism seemed to many Americans to be much more than a military threat—indeed, nothing less than a demonic force capable of undermining basic values. It compelled patriots to proclaim themselves ready for atomic warfare: "Better Dead Than Red." McCarthy also had help from organizations such as the American Legion and the Chamber of Commerce, and prominent religious leaders and union leaders.

Civil rights organizations faced the severest persecution since the 1920s. The Civil Rights Congress and the Negro Youth Council, for instance, were destroyed after frequent charges of Communist influence. W. E. B. Du Bois, the renowned African American historian, and famed concert singer (and former All-American

football hero) Paul Robeson had public appearances canceled and their right to travel abroad abridged.

In attacks on women's organizations and homosexual groups, meanwhile, anti-Communist rhetoric cloaked deep fears about changing sexual mores. Aided by FBI reports, the federal government fired up to sixty homosexuals per month in the early 1950s. Dishonorable discharges from the U.S. armed forces for homosexuality, an administrative procedure without appeal, also increased dramatically. Noted historian Arthur Schlesinger, Jr. suggested that critics of cold war policies were not "real" men or, perhaps, "real" women either.

Joseph McCarthy and his fellow Red-hunters eventually burned themselves out. During televised congressional hearings in 1954, not only did McCarthy fail to prove wild charges of Communist infiltration of the army, but in the glare of the television cameras he appeared deranged. Cowed for years, the Senate finally condemned him for "conduct unbecoming a member."

COLD WAR CULTURE

As the Truman Doctrine clearly specified, the cold war did not necessarily depend on military confrontation; nor was it defined exclusively by a quest for economic supremacy. The cold war embodied the struggle of one "way of life" against another. It was, in short, a contest of values. The president therefore pledged the United States to "contain" communism from spreading beyond the parameters of the Soviet Union and its client states and simultaneously called for fortifications at home. If Americans were to rebuild the world based on their own values, they must rededicate themselves to the defense of their birthright: freedom and democracy.

An Anxious Mood

"We have about 50 percent of the world's wealth," George Kennan noted in 1948, "but only 3.6 percent of its population." Very large pockets of poverty remained, and not all Americans benefited from the postwar abundance. Nonetheless, millions of Americans achieved middle-class status, often through new programs subsidized by the federal government.

Prosperity did not dispel an anxious mood, fueled in part by the reality and the rhetoric of the cold war. Many Americans also feared an economic backslide. If war production had ended the hardships of the Great Depression, how would the economy fare in peacetime? No one could say. Above all, peace itself seemed precarious.

Anxieties intensified by the cold war surfaced as major themes in popular culture. One of the most acclaimed Hollywood films of the era, the winner of nine Academy Awards, *The Best Years of Our Lives* (1946), followed the stories of three returning veterans as they tried to readjust to civilian life. The former soldiers found that the dreams of reunion with family and loved ones that had sustained them through years of fighting now seemed hollow. In some cases, their wives and children had become so self-reliant that the men had no clear function to perform in the household; in other cases, the prospect for employment appeared dim.

The genre of *film noir* (French for "black") deepened this mood into an aesthetic. Movies like *Out of the Past, Detour,* and *They Live by Night* featured stories of ruthless fate and betrayal. Their protagonists were usually strangers or loners falsely accused of crimes or trapped into committing them. The high-contrast lighting of these black and white films accentuated the difficulty of distinguishing friend from foe.

Plays and novels also described alienation and anxiety in vivid terms. Playwright Arthur Miller in *Death of a Salesman* (1949) sketched an exacting portrait of self-destructive individualism. Willy Loman, the play's hero, is obsessively devoted to his career in sales but is nevertheless a miserable failure. Worse, he has trained his sons to excel in personal presentation and style—the very methods prescribed by standard American success manuals—making them both shallow and materialistic. J. D. Salinger's widely praised novel *Catcher in the Rye* (1951) explored the mental anguish of a teenage boy estranged from the crass materialism of his parents.

Hollywood studios played directly into the mounting fears, releasing by 1954 more than forty films with titles such as *I Married a Communist* (1950) and *The Red Menace* (1949) that sensationalized the Communist threat. The television industry sponsored the dramatic series *The Hunter*, featuring the adventures of an American businessman fighting Communist agents throughout the Free World. Few of these films or programs were popular, however.

The Family as Bulwark

Postwar prosperity helped to strengthen the ideal of domesticity, although many Americans interpreted their rush toward marriage and parenthood, as one writer put it, as a "defense—an impregnable bulwark" against the anxieties of the era.

Young couples were marrying younger and producing more children than at any time in the past century. The U.S. Census Bureau predicted that the "baby boom" would be temporary. To everyone's surprise, the birthrate continued to grow at a record pace, peaking at over 118 per 1,000 women in 1957.

The new families who enjoyed postwar prosperity inaugurated a spending spree of trailblazing proportions. "The year 1946," *Life* magazine proclaimed, "finds the U.S. on the threshold of marvels, ranging from runless stockings and shineless serge suits to jet-propelled airplanes that will flash across the country in just a little less than the speed of sound." By the time Harry Truman left office two-thirds of all American households claimed at least one television set.

These two trends—the baby boom and high rates of consumer spending—encouraged a major change in the middle-class family. Having worked during World War II, often in occupations traditionally closed to them, many women wished to continue in full-time employment. Reconversion to peacetime production forced the majority from their factory positions, but most women quickly returned, taking jobs at a faster rate than men and providing half the total growth of the labor force. By 1952, 2 million more wives worked than during the war. Gone, however, were the high-paying unionized jobs in manufacturing. Instead, most women found minimum-wage jobs in the expanding service sector: clerical work, health care and education, and restaurant, hotel, and retail services. Older women whose children were grown might work because they had come to value a job for its own sake. Younger women often worked for reasons of "economic necessity"—that is, to maintain a middle-class standard of living that now required more than one income. Indeed, mothers of young children were the most likely to be employed.

Even though most women sought employment primarily to support their families, they ran up against popular opinion and expert advice urging them to return to their homes. Public opinion registered resounding disapproval—by 86 percent of those surveyed—of a married woman's working if jobs were scarce and her husband could support her. Commentators appealed for a return to an imaginary "traditional" family, where men alone were breadwinners and women stayed happily at home.

This campaign began on a shrill note. Ferdinand Lundberg and Marynia Farnham, in their best-selling *Modern Woman: The Lost Sex* (1947), attributed the "super-jittery age in which we live" to women's abandonment of the home to pursue careers. To counter this trend, they proposed federally funded psychotherapy to readjust women to their housewifely roles and cash subsidies to encourage them to bear more children.

Articles in popular magazines, television shows, and high-profile experts chimed in with similar messages. Talcott Parsons, the distinguished Harvard sociologist, delineated the parameters of the "democratic" family: husbands served as breadwinners while wives— "the emotional hub of the family"—stayed home to care for their families. In the first edition of *Baby and Child Care* (1946), the child-rearing advice manual that soon outsold the Bible, Benjamin Spock similarly advised women to devote themselves full time, if financially possible, to their maternal responsibilities.

Patterns of women's higher education reflected this conservative trend. Having made slight gains during World War II when college-age men were serving in the armed forces or working in war industries, women lost ground after the G.I. Bill created a huge upsurge in male enrollment. Women represented 40 percent of all college graduates in 1940 but only 25 percent a decade later.

With a growing number of middle-class women working to help support their families, these cold war policies and prescriptions worked at cross-purposes. As early as 1947, *Life* magazine registered concern in a thirteen-page feature, "American Woman's Dilemma." How could women comfortably take part in a world beyond the home and at the same time heed the advice of FBI director J. Edgar Hoover, who exhorted the nation's women to fight "the twin enemies of freedom—crime and communism" by fulfilling their singular role as "homemakers and mothers"?

Military-Industrial Communities in the West

All regions of the United States felt the impact of the cold war but perhaps none so directly as the Trans-Mississippi West. Defense spending during World War II had stimulated the western economy and encouraged a mass migration of people eager to find employment in wartime industry. Following the war, many cities successfully converted to peacetime production; Los Angeles, for example, attracted one-eighth of all new business in the nation during the late 1940s. However, the cold war, by reviving defense funding, provided the most important boost to the western economy. The Department of Defense and private corporations and subcontractors generated billions of dollars for research and development of military equipment of various kinds.

The federal government poured so much defense money—nearly 10 percent of the entire military budget—into California that the state's rate of economic growth between 1949 and 1952 outpaced that of the nation as a whole, with nearly 40 percent coming from the manufacture of aircraft alone. Ten years later, it was estimated that one-third of all workers in Los Angeles were employed by defense industries, particularly aerospace, and that their absolute number was far greater than during the peak of production in World War II. The concentration of defense workers was even greater in the suburbs of Los Angeles. Orange Country, for example, grew quickly during the

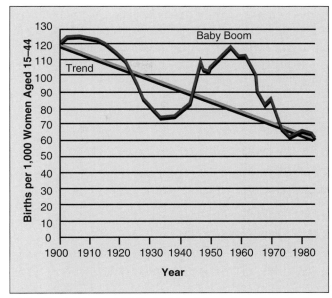

U.S. Birth Rate, 1930–1980   The bulge of the "baby boom," a leading demographic factor in the postwar economy, stands out for this fifty-year period.

cold war to become a major producer of communication equipment. The San Francisco Bay Area also benefited economically from defense spending, and cities such as Sunnyvale, Mountain View, and San Jose began their ascendance as home to the nation's budding high-technology industry.

The cold war also pumped new life into communities that had grown up during World War II. Hanford, Washington, and Los Alamos, New Mexico, both centers of the Manhattan Project, employed a greater number of people in the construction of the cold war nuclear arsenal than in the development of the atom bomb that brought an end to World War II. Los Alamos grew from its rural origins at such a fast pace that thirty years later its population density was one of the highest in the state, second only to the metropolitan region of Albuquerque. The community lost little of its secretive quality, with entry restricted to mainly well-paid workers and residents who could neither own land or homes within its boundary. Meanwhile, the federal government continued to place its distinctive stamp on the architecture, with institutional and purely functional aesthetics governing the design of concrete structures with hospital-green interiors.

New communities accompanied the growth of the U.S. military bases and training camps in the western states. Many of these installations, as well as hospitals and supply depots, not only survived but expanded during the transition from the actual warfare of World War II to the virtual warfare of the cold war. Between 1950 and 1953 approximately twenty western bases were reopened. California became at least a temporary home to more military personnel than any other state, but Texas was not far behind. The availability of public lands with areas of sparse population made western states especially attractive to military planners commissioned to design dangerous and secretive installations such as the White Sands Missile Range in the New Mexican desert.

Zeal for Democracy

World War II revitalized patriotism by rallying Americans to define themselves and their institutions against Nazi and fascist forces abroad. Pledging allegiance to the flag, for example, gained new symbolic meaning as school children were directed to avoid saluting, a gesture now perceived as disturbingly similar to the militaristic Nazi hand-raising, and were instead told to hold their right hand steadily over their heart.

Following the massive V-J Day celebrations that marked the end of World War II, Americans began to retreat from public displays of patriotism but were soon chastized for their "national apathy" by organizations like the Freedoms Foundation of Valley Forge, which aimed to mobilize a "vast articulate, creative army of ministers, teachers, professional people, students, men and women from the farm and factory" to defend "the American Way." Soon, other new groups, such as the American Heritage Foundation, founded in 1947, joined such stalwarts as the American Legion, the Chamber of Commerce, and local business and veterans groups in this endeavor.

In 1948, Attorney General Tom Clark, with the support of President Truman, funding from private donors, and planning by the American Heritage Foundation, put on track the "Freedom Train." Carrying documents illustrating basic American rights and liberties, such as the Bill of Rights and the Constitution, the Freedom Train traveled to various cities across the United States where local citizens got aboard to view various patriotic displays at the average rate of 8,500 people per day. The popular songwriter Irving Berlin memorialized the Freedom Train, lyrically assuring the expectant viewers who endured long lines that inside "you'll find a precious freight."

Patriotic messages also permeated public education. According to guidelines set down by the Truman administration, teachers were to "strengthen national security through education," specifically designing their lesson plans to illustrate the superiority of the American democratic system over Soviet communism. In 1947 the federal Office of Education launched the "Zeal for Democracy" program for implementation by school boards nationwide. The program veered toward propaganda, announcing its intention to "promote and strengthen democratic thinking and practice, just as

the schools of totalitarian states have so effectively promoted the ideals of their respective cultures." Meanwhile, as part of a separate program in civil defense, schoolchildren were taught to "duck" under their desks and "cover" their heads to protect themselves in the event of a surprise nuclear attack by the Soviets.

There were voices of protest to these cold war programs. The black poet Langston Hughes, for example, expressed his skepticism in verse, writing that he hoped the Freedom Train would carry no Jim Crow car. A fearless minority of scholars protested infringements on their academic freedom by refusing to sign loyalty oaths and by writing books pointing out the potential dangers of aggressively nationalistic foreign and domestic policies. But the chilling atmosphere made many individuals reluctant to express contrary opinions or ideas.

END OF THE DEMOCRATIC ERA

Cold war tensions festered in Europe and pushed the United States and Soviet Union to the brink of armed conflict. With so much happening in Europe, neither superpower would have predicted that events in Asia would soon transform their political and ideological competition into a war threatening to destroy the world. Yet, in 1949, Communists in China seized power in the most heavily populated nation in the world. Then, a few months later, in June 1950, Communists threatened to take over all of Korea. The precarious balance of power was seemingly shifting.

The "Loss" of China

At the close of World War II, the United States acted deliberately to secure Japan firmly in its realm. General Douglas MacArthur directed an interim government in a modest reconstruction program that included land reform, the creation of independent trade unions, the abolition of contract marriages, the granting of woman suffrage, sweeping demilitarization, and, eventually, a constitutional democracy that barred Communists from all posts. American leaders worked to rebuild the nation's economy along capitalist lines and integrate Japan, like West Germany, into an anti-Soviet bloc. Japan also housed huge U.S. military bases, thus placing U.S. troops and weapons strategically close to the Soviet Union's Asian rim.

The situation in China could not be handled so easily. After years of civil war, the pro–Western Nationalist government of Jiang Jeishi (Chiang Kai-shek) collapsed. Since World War II, the United States had been sending aid to the unpopular government while warning Jiang that without major reforms the Nationalists were heading for defeat. Moreover, they tried to convince him to accept a coalition government. After refusing to intervene on their behalf, the United States watched as Jiang's troops were finally forced to surrender to the Communists, led by Mao Zedong, who enjoyed the support of the Chinese countryside, where 85 percent of the population lived. Surrendering to Mao the entire China mainland, the defeated Nationalist government withdrew to the island of Formosa (Taiwan). On October 1, 1949, the People's Republic of China (PRC) was formally established.

The news of China's "fall" to communism created an uproar in the United States. The Asia First wing of the Republican Party, which envisioned the Far East rather than Europe as the prime site of U.S. trade and investment, blamed the Truman administration for the "loss" of China.

The Korean War

At the end of World War II, the Allies had divided the small peninsula of Korea, ceded by Japan, at the 38th parallel. Although all parties hoped to reunite the nation under its own government, the line between North and South instead hardened. The United States backed the unpopular government of Syngman Rhee (the Republic of Korea), and the Soviet Union sponsored a rival government in North Korea under Kim Il Sung.

On June 25, 1950, the U.S. State Department received a cablegram reporting a military attack on South Korea by the Communist-controlled North. "If we are tough enough now," President Truman pledged, "if we stand up to them like we did in Greece three years ago, they won't take any next steps." The Soviet Union, on the other hand, regarded the invasion as Kim Il Sung's affair. Despite Soviet disclaimers, Truman sought approval from the UN Security Council to send in troops to South Korea. Because of the absence of the Soviet delegate, who could have vetoed the decision, the Security Council agreed. Two-thirds of Americans polled approved the president's decision to send troops under the command of General Douglas MacArthur.

Military events seemed at first to justify the president's decision. Seoul, the capital of South Korea, had fallen to North Korean troops within weeks of the invasion, and Communist forces continued to push south until they had taken most of the peninsula. The situation appeared grim until Truman authorized MacArthur to carry out an amphibious landing at Inchon, which he did on September 15, 1950. With tactical brilliance and good fortune, the general orchestrated a military campaign that halted the Communist drive. By October, UN troops had retaken South Korea.

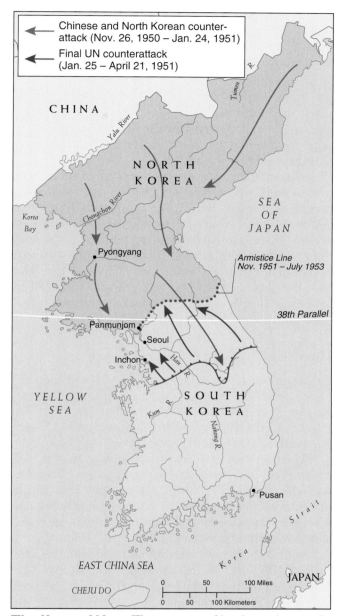

The Korean War The intensity of battles underscored the strategic importance of Korea in the cold war.

Basking in victory, the Truman administration could not resist the temptation to expand its war aims. Hoping to prove that Democrats were not "soft" on communism, the president and his advisers decided to roll back the Communists beyond the 38th parallel. Until this point, China had not been actively involved in the war. But it now warned that any attempt to cross the dividing line would be interpreted as a threat to its own national security. Truman flew to Wake Island in the Pacific on October 15 for a conference with MacArthur, who assured the president of a speedy victory.

MacArthur had sorely miscalculated. Chinese troops massed just above the UN offensive line, at the Yalu River. Suddenly, and without any air support, the Chinese attacked in human waves. MacArthur's force was all but crushed. The Chinese drove the UN troops back into South Korea, where they regrouped along the 38th parallel. By summer 1951 a stalemate had been reached very near the old border. Negotiations for a settlement went on for the next eighteen months amid heavy fighting.

MacArthur tried without success to convince Truman to prepare for a new invasion of Communist territory. Encouraged by strong support at home, he continued to provoke the president by speaking out against official policy, calling for bombing of supply lines in China and a naval blockade of the Chinese coast—actions certain to lead to a Chinese-American war. Finally, on April 10, 1951, Truman dismissed MacArthur for insubordination and other unauthorized activities.

The Price of National Security

By instituting a peacetime draft in 1948 and then ordering American troops into Korea, Truman had bypassed congressional authority. Truman carefully referred to the military deployment not as a U.S. war but as a UN-sanctioned "police action."

The president derived his authority from NSC-68, a paper released to him by the National Security Council in April 1950. NSC-68 pledged the United States not only to drive back Communist influence wherever it appeared but also to "foster the seeds of destruction within the Soviet Union."

Initially reluctant, Truman fulfilled the prescriptions of NSC-68 after the outbreak of the Korean War and agreed to its mandate for a rapid and permanent military buildup. By the time the conflict subsided, the defense budget had quadrupled, and the U.S. Army had grown to 3.6 million, or six times its size at the beginning of the conflict. At the same time, the federal government accelerated the development of both conventional and nonconventional weapons. In the first instance, it began to stockpile nuclear bombs and weapons, including the first hydrogen, or H-bomb, which was tested in November 1952.

The Korean War also provided the rationale for the expansion of anti-Communist propaganda. At the end of World War II President Truman had taken steps to transform the Office of War Information into a peacetime program that operated on a much smaller budget. But by 1948 Congress was ready to pass with bipartisan support the Smith-Mundt Act, designed "to promote the better understanding of the United States among the peoples of the world and to strengthen cooperative international relations." Within a year,

Congress doubled the budget for such programming, granting $3 million to revive the Voice of America, the short-wave international radio program that had been established in 1942. The new legislation also funded the development of film, print media, cultural exchange programs, and exhibitions, and it created a foundation to promote anti-Communist propaganda throughout the world.

The outcome of the Korean War did nothing to improve the case for rolling back communism. Negotiations and fighting proceeded in tandem until the summer of 1953, when a settlement was reached in which both North Korea and South Korea occupied almost the same territory as when the war began. Approximately 54,000 Americans died in Korea; the North Koreans and Chinese lost well over 2 million people. The UN troops had employed both "carpet bombing" (an intense, destructive attack on a given area) and napalm (jellied gasoline bombs), destroying most of the housing and food supplies in both Koreas. True to the pattern of modern warfare, which emerged during World War II, the majority of civilians killed were women and children. Nearly 1 million Koreans were left homeless.

For the United States, the Korean War enlarged the geographical range of the cold war to include East Asia. The war also lined up the People's Republic of China and the United States as unwavering enemies for the next twenty years and heightened the U.S. commitment to Southeast Asia. Moreover, the Korean War, did much to establish an ominous tradition of "unwinnable" conflicts that left many Americans skeptical of official policy.

In retrospect many Americans recognized that Truman, in fighting communism in Korea, had pledged the United States to defend a corrupt government and a brutal dictator. Decades later the Korean War inspired the dark comedy M*A*S*H, adapted for television from the film written by Hollywood screenwriter Ring Lardner, Jr., an "unfriendly witness" before HUAC, who was jailed during the Korean War for contempt of Congress. As late as 1990, members of Congress were still debating the terms of a Korean War memorial. "It ended on a sad note for Americans," one historian has concluded, "and the war and its memories drifted off into a void."

The Election of 1952

There was only one burning issue during the election campaign of 1952: the Korean War. Truman's popularity had wavered continually since he took office in 1945, but it sank to an all-time low in the early 1950s shortly after he dismissed MacArthur as commander of the UN troops in Korea. Congress received thousands of letters and telegrams calling for Truman's impeachment.

CHRONOLOGY

1941	Henry Luce forecasts the dawn of "the American Century"
1944	G.I. Bill of Rights benefits World War II veterans
	International Monetary Fund and World Bank founded
1945	Franklin D. Roosevelt dies in office; Harry S. Truman becomes president
	United Nations charter signed
	World War II ends
	Strike wave begins
	Truman proposes program of economic reforms
1946	Employment Act creates Council of Economic Advisers
	Churchill's Iron Curtain speech
	Atomic Energy Act establishes Atomic Energy Commission
	Republicans win control of Congress
	Benjamin Spock publishes *Baby and Child Care*
1947	Americans for Democratic Action founded
	Truman Doctrine announced; Congress appropriates $400 million in aid for Greece and Turkey
	Federal Employees Loyalty and Security Program established and attorney general's list of subversive organizations authorized
	Marshall Plan announced
	Taft-Hartley Act restricts union activities
	National Security Act establishes Department of Defense, the National Security Council, and the Central Intelligence Agency
	House Un-American Activities Committee hearings in Hollywood
1948	Smith-Mundt Act passed by Congress
	Ferdinand Lundberg and Marynia Farnham publish *Modern Woman: The Lost Sex*
	State of Israel founded
	Berlin blockade begins

	Henry Wallace nominated for president on Progressive Party ticket
	Truman announces peacetime draft and desegregates U.S. armed forces and civil service
	Truman wins election; Democrats sweep both houses of Congress
1949	Truman announces Fair Deal
	North Atlantic Treaty Organization (NATO) created
	Communists, led by Mao Zedong, take power in China
	Berlin blockade ends
	Soviet Union explodes atomic bomb
1950	Alger Hiss convicted of perjury
	Senator Joseph McCarthy begins anti-Communist crusade
	Soviet Union and the People's Republic of China sign an alliance
	Adoption of NSC-68 consolidates presidential war powers
	Korean War begins
	Internal Security (McCarran) Act requires registration of Communist organizations and arrest of Communists during national emergencies
1951	Truman dismisses General Douglas MacArthur
	Psychological Strategy Board created
	Armistice talks begin in Korea
1952	Immigration and Nationality Act retains quota system, lifts ban on immigration of Asian and Pacific peoples, but bans "subversives" and homosexuals
	United States explodes first hydrogen bomb
	Dwight D. Eisenhower wins presidency; Richard Nixon becomes vice president
1953	Julius and Ethel Rosenberg executed for atomic espionage
	Armistice ends fighting in Korea
1954	Army-McCarthy hearings end
1955	Warsaw Pact created

"Oust President Truman" bumper stickers could be seen. MacArthur, meanwhile, returned home a hero, welcomed by more than 7 million fans in New York City alone.

Popular dissatisfaction with Truman increased. Newspapers reported that several agencies had been dealing in 5 percent kickbacks for government contracts. Business and organized labor complained about the price and wage freezes imposed during the Korean War. A late 1951 Gallup poll showed the president's approval rating at 23 percent. In March 1952, Truman announced he would not run for reelection, a decision rare for a president eligible for another term.

In accepting political defeat and disgrace, Truman turned to the popular but uncharismatic governor of Illinois, Adlai E. Stevenson, Jr. Admired for his honesty and intelligence, Stevenson offered no solutions to the conflict in Korea, the accelerating arms race, or the cold war generally. Accepting the Democratic nomination, he candidly admitted that "the ordeal of the twentieth century is far from over," a prospect displeasing to voters aching for peace.

The Republicans made the most of the Democrats' dilemma. Without proposing any sweeping answers of their own, they pointed to all the obvious shortcomings of their opponents. Their campaign strategy, known as "K_1C_2"—Korea, Communism, and Corruption—took steady aim at the Truman administration, and when opinion polls showed that Dwight Eisenhower possessed an "unprecedented" 64 percent approval rating, they found in "Ike" the perfect candidate to head the ticket.

Eisenhower styled himself the representative of "modern Republicanism." He wisely avoided the negative impressions made by the unsuccessful 1948 Republican candidate, Thomas Dewey, who had seemed as aggressive as Truman on foreign policy and simultaneously eager to overturn the New Deal domestic legislation. Eisenhower knew better: voters wanted peace and a limited welfare state. He referred to New Deal reforms as "a solid floor that keeps all of us from falling into the pit of disaster." And athough he did not go into specifics, he promised to end the Korean War with "an early and honorable" peace. Whenever he was tempted to address questions of finance or the economy, his advisers warned him: "The chief reason that people want to vote for you is because they think you have more ability to keep us out of another war."

Meanwhile, Eisenhower's vice presidential candidate, Richard Nixon, waged a relentless and defamatory attack on Stevenson, calling him "Adlai the Appeaser." Senator Joseph McCarthy chimed in, proclaiming that with club in hand he might be able to make "a good American" of Stevenson. A month before the election, McCarthy went on network television with his requisite "exhibits" and "documents," this time purportedly showing that the Democratic presidential candidate had promoted communism at home and abroad. These outrageous charges kept the Stevenson campaign off balance.

The Republican campaign was itself not entirely free of scandal: Nixon had been caught accepting personal gifts from wealthy benefactors. Pleading his case on national television, he described his wife Pat's "good Republican cloth coat" and their modest style of living. He then contritely admitted that he had indeed accepted one gift, a puppy named Checkers that his daughters loved and that he refused to give back. "The Poor Richard Show," as critics called the event, defused the scandal without answering the most important charges.

Unaffected by the scandal, Eisenhower continued to enchant the voters as a peace candidate. Ten days before the election he dramatically announced, "I shall go to Korea" to settle the war. Eisenhower received 55 percent of the vote and carried thirty-nine states, in part because he brought out an unusually large number of voters in normally Democratic areas. He won the popular vote in much of the South and in the northern cities of New York, Chicago, Boston, and Cleveland. Riding his coattails, the Republicans regained narrow control of Congress. The New Deal coalition of ethnic and black voters, labor, northern liberals, and southern conservatives no longer commanded a majority.

CONCLUSION

The election of Dwight Eisenhower helped to diminish the intensity of this dour mood without actually bringing a halt to the conflict. "The Eisenhower Movement," wrote journalist Walter Lippmann, was a "mission in American politics" to restore a sense of community among the American people. In a larger sense, many of the issues of the immediate post–World War II years seemed to have been settled, or put off for a distant future. The international boundaries of communism were frozen with the Chinese Revolution, the Berlin Crisis, and now the Korean War. Meanwhile, at home cold war defense spending had become a permanent part of the national budget, an undeniable drain on tax revenues but an important element in the government contribution to economic prosperity. If the nuclear arms race remained a cause for anxiety, joined by more personal worries about the changing patterns of family life, a sense of relative security nevertheless spread. Prospects for world peace had dimmed, but the worst nightmares of the 1940s had eased as well.

REVIEW QUESTIONS

1. Discuss the origins of the cold war and the sources of growing tensions between the United States and the Soviet Union at the close of World War II.
2. Describe the basic elements of President Harry Truman's policy of containment. How did the threat of atomic warfare affect this policy?
3. Compare the presidencies of Franklin D. Roosevelt and Harry S. Truman, both Democrats.
4. Describe the impact of McCarthyism on American political life. How did the anti-Communist campaigns affect the media? What were the sources of Senator Joseph McCarthy's popularity? What brought about his downfall?
5. How did the cold war affect American culture?
6. Discuss the role of the United States in Korea in the decade after World War II. How did the Korean War affect the 1952 presidential election?
7. Why did Dwight D. Eisenhower win the 1952 presidential election?

RECOMMENDED READING

Mark S. Byrnes, *The Truman Years, 1945–1953* (2000). A concise history of the Truman administration and its role at the moment when the United States became the dominant economic power in the world. Byrnes covers this transformation with particular attention to the way the president helped to shape a view of the world that presented the United States and the Soviet Union as permanent enemies in a struggle for domination. Includes a set of twenty-one key documents and a detailed chronology of events.

Warren I. Cohen, *America in the Age of Soviet Power, 1945–1991* (1993). A highly readable volume in the "Cambridge History of American Foreign Relations" series, this study examines the origins of the cold war in policies ending World War II, including the breakup of the colonial empires, and concludes with the collapse of communism in the Soviet Union in 1991.

Kevin J. Fernlund, ed., *The Cold War American West, 1945–1989* (1998). Ten essays illustrating the impact of the cold war on the region of the United States that housed the bulk of military bases, airfields, nucelar testing grounds, and toxic waste dumps. Presenting a variety of interpretations, the contributors ask a common question: Was the West transformed or deformed by the policies of the growing national security state?

John Fousek, *To Lead the Free World: American Nationalism and the Cultural Roots of the Cold War* (2000). Examines the "public culture" of the cold war through an innovative study of various responses to the official doctrines and declarations of the Truman administration. Fousek pays special attention to the publications of major civil rights organizations and the two largest labor unions of the period and argues that "a broad public consensus" supported Truman's nationalistic foreign policy.

Richard M. Fried, *The Russians Are Coming! The Russians Are Coming!: Pageantry and Patriotism in Cold-War America* (1998). Examines, through vivid example, the creation of the fear of communism and its translation into patriotic zeal. Fried takes as his thesis that rallying the public to "fight" the cold war required as much organization and energy as mobilizing Americans to defend the home front during World War II.

Margot A. Henriksen, *Dr. Strangelove's America: Society and Culture in the Atomic Age* (1997). Argues in a lively fashion that the atomic bomb played the "central, defining role" in American culture and society from 1945 into the early 1980s. Henriksen culls evidence from a wide range of sources, including novels, movies, TV programs, and rock 'n' roll songs.

George Lipsitz, *A Rainbow at Midnight: Labor and Culture in the 1940s* (1994). A vivid account of economic and cultural hopes, uneasiness, and disappointments after World War II. Lipsitz shows how struggles for economic democracy were defeated and how popular culture—for example, country-and-western music and rock 'n' roll, as well as stock car racing and roller derby—arose in blue-collar communities.

Elaine Tyler May, *Homeward Bound: American Families in the Cold War Era* (1988). A lively account of the effects on family life and women's roles of the national mood of "containment." May argues that government policy became part of a popular culture that solidified the cold war era's "feminine mystique."

David G. McCullough, *Truman* (1992). A heroic rendition of Truman's personal life and political career. Through personal correspondence and other documents, McCullough details Truman's view of himself and the generally favorable view of him held by supporters of cold war liberalism.

Patrick McGilligan and Paul Buhle, *Tender Comrades: A Backstory of the Hollywood Blacklist* (1997). A collection of interviews with thirty-five victims of the Hollywood Blacklist, including some of the most important writers, directors, and film stars. The collection is especially valuable for its detailing of film production during the years of World War II and afterward, including the creation of *film noir.*

Joanne Meyerowitz, ed., *Not June Cleaver: Women and Gender in Postwar America, 1945–1960* (1994). A collection of essays that refute the common stereotype of women as homebound during the postwar era.

Stanley Weintraub, *MacArthur's War: Korea and the Undoing of an American Hero* (2000). Tells the story of the downfall of the commander of U.S. forces in the Far East, who was "senior to everyone but God" in the military services. The author additionally offers a detailed description of the horror and ruin accompanying the brutal ground war in Korea.

ON THE WEB

http://www.archives.gov/exhibit_hall/ picturing_the_century/galleries/postwar.html

This site is from the American Memory by the National Archives and includes a small but interesting collection of photos, one of the most interesting being a snapshot of American troops on November 1, 1951, at Yucca Flats, Nevada, being used for experimentation at a test of an atomic bomb. Another interesting photo shows a private family fallout shelter built by Louis Severance in the late 1950s at his home near Akron, Michigan.

http://www.history.navy.mil/photos/events/ wwii-dpl/hd-state/potsdam.htm

Official U.S. Navy photos of President Truman traveling to the Potsdam Conference aboard the USS *Augusta*, some photos at the conference site, and photos of the president on the return voyage. Most photos have a fair amount of information attached in their text.

http://www.historyplace.com/speeches/ ironcurtain.htm

Winston Churchill's "Iron Curtain Speech" delivered March 5, 1946, at Westminster College, in Fulton, Missouri. Here Churchill announces the opening of the Cold War.

http://www.trumanlibrary.org/whistlestop/

This is a rich site on the Truman years and includes speeches, documents, photos, and narrative.

http://korea50.army.mil/

Interesting Korean War 50th Commemoration site. The Interviews and Images sites are particularly useful.

http://www.trumanlibrary.org/whistlestop/ study_collections/korea/large/

Truman Presidential Library site on the Korean War with links to many other sites and to Korean War photographs.

http://www.prenhall.com/faragherbrief/map26.1

Examine Europe during the Cold War. Which countries were aligned with the United States and which with the Soviet Union?

http://www.prenhall.com/faragherbrief/map26.2

Examine the U.S. military campaign in Korea. How did this reflect Truman's doctrine of containment?

CHAPTER OUTLINE

AMERICAN COMMUNITIES

Popular Music in Memphis

THE NINETEEN-YEAR-OLD SINGER WAS PEERING NERVOUSLY OUT OVER the large crowd. He knew that people had come to Overton Park's outdoor amphitheater that hot, sticky July day in 1954 to hear the headliner, country music star Slim Whitman. Sun Records, a local Memphis label, had just released the teenager's first record, and it had begun to receive some airplay on local radio. But the singer and his two bandmates had never played in a setting even remotely as large as this one. And their music defied categories: it wasn't black and it wasn't white; it wasn't pop and it wasn't country. But when the singer launched into his version of a black blues song called "That's All Right," the crowd went wild. "I came offstage," the singer later recalled, "and my manager told me that they was hollering because I was wiggling my legs. I went back out for an encore, and I did a little more, and the more I did, the wilder they went." Elvis Presley had arrived.

Elvis combined a hard-driving, rhythmic approach to blues and country music with a riveting performance style, inventing the new music known as rock 'n' roll. An unprecedented cultural phenomenon, rock 'n' roll was a music made largely for and by teenagers. In communities all over America, rock 'n' roll brought teens together around jukeboxes, at sock hops, in cars, and at private parties. It demonstrated the enormous consumer power of American teens. Rock 'n' roll also embodied a postwar trend accelerating the integration of white and black music. This cultural integration prefigured the social and political integration won by the civil rights movement.

Located halfway between St. Louis and New Orleans on the Mississippi River, Memphis had become a thriving commercial city by the 1850s, with an economy centered on the lucrative cotton trade of the surrounding delta region. It grew rapidly in the post–Civil War years, attracting a polyglot population of white businessmen and planters, poor rural whites and blacks, and German and Irish immigrants. By the early twentieth century Memphis also boasted a remarkable diversity of popular theater and music, including a large opera house, numerous brass bands, vaudeville and burlesque, minstrel shows, jug bands, and blues clubs.

Like most American cities, Memphis enjoyed healthy growth during World War II, with lumber mills, furniture factories, and chemical manufacturing supplementing the cotton market as sources of jobs and prosperity. And like the rest of the South, Memphis was a legally segregated city; whites and blacks lived, went to school, and worked apart. Class differences among whites were important as well. Like thousands of other poor rural whites in these years, Elvis Presley had moved from Mississippi to Memphis in 1949, where his father found work in a munitions plant. The Presleys were poor enough to qualify for an apartment in Lauderdale Courts, a Memphis public housing project. To James Conaway, who grew up in an all-white, middle-class East Memphis neighborhood, people like the Presleys were "white trash." Negroes, he recalled, were "not necessarily below the rank of a country boy like Elvis, but of another universe, and yet there was more affection for them than for some whites."

Gloria Wade-Gayles, who lived in the all-black Foote Homes housing project, vividly remembered that her family and neighbors "had no illusion about their lack of power, but they believed in their strength." For them, strength grew from total immersion in a black community that included ministers, teachers, insurance men, morticians, barbers, and entertainers. "Surviving meant being black, and being black meant believing in our humanity, and retaining it, in a world that denied we had it in the first place."

Yet in the cultural realm, class and racial barriers could be challenged. Elvis Presley grew up a dreamy, shy boy, who turned to music for emotional release and spiritual expression. He soaked up the wide range of music styles available in Memphis. The Assembly of God Church his family attended featured a renowned hundred-voice choir. Elvis and his friends went to marathon all-night "gospel singings" at Ellis Auditorium, where they enjoyed the tight harmonies and emotional style of white gospel quartets.

Elvis also drew from the sounds he heard on Beale Street, the main black thoroughfare of Memphis and one of the nation's most influential centers of African American music. In the postwar years, local black rhythm and blues artists like B. B. King, Junior Parker, and Muddy Waters attracted legions of black and white fans with their emotional power and exciting showmanship. At the Handy Theater on Beale Street, the teenaged Elvis Presley, like thousands of other white young people, heard black performers at the "Midnight Rambles"—late shows for white people only. Elvis himself performed along with black contestants in amateur shows at Beale Street's Palace Theater. Nat D. Williams, a prominent black Memphis disc jockey and music promoter, recalled how black

audiences responded to Elvis's unique style. "He had a way of singing the blues that was distinctive. He could sing 'em not necessarily like a Negro, but he didn't sing 'em altogether like a typical white musician. . . . Always he had that certain humanness about him that Negroes like to put in their songs."

The expansion of the broadcasting and recording industries in the postwar years also contributed to the weakening of racial barriers in the musical realm. Two Memphis radio stations featured the hard-driving rhythm and blues music that was beginning to attract a strong following among young white listeners. These Memphis stations also featured spirituals by African American artists such as Mahalia Jackson and Clara Ward.

Elvis himself understood his debt to black music and black performers. "The colored folks," he told an interviewer in 1956, "been singing and playing it just like I'm doing now, man, for more years than I know. They played it like that in the shanties and in their juke joints and nobody paid it no mind until I goosed it up. I got it from them."

Dissatisfied with the cloying pop music of the day, white teenagers across the nation were increasingly turning to the rhythmic drive and emotional intensity of black rhythm and blues. They quickly adopted rock 'n' roll (the term had long been an African American slang expression for dancing and sexual intercourse) as their music. But it was more than just music: it was also an attitude, a celebration of being young, and a sense of having something that adult authority could not understand or control.

When Sun Records sold Presley's contract to RCA Records in 1956, Elvis became an international star. Records like "Heartbreak Hotel," "Don't Be Cruel," and "Jailhouse Rock" shot to the top of the charts and blurred the old boundaries between pop, country, and rhythm and blues. By helping to accustom white teenagers to the style and sound of black artists, Elvis helped establish rock 'n' roll as an interracial phenomenon. Institutional racism would continue to plague the music business—many black artists were routinely cheated out of royalties and severely underpaid—but the music of postwar Memphis at least pointed the way toward the exciting cultural possibilities that could emerge from breaking down the barriers of race. It also gave postwar American teenagers a newfound sense of community. ■

Memphis

AMERICAN SOCIETY AT MIDCENTURY

The Eisenhower Presidency

Dwight D. Eisenhower's landslide election victory in 1952 set the stage for the first full two-term Republican presidency since that of Ulysses S. Grant. During his eight-year administration, intellectuals and liberals found it easy to satirize and attack Eisenhower for his blandness, his frequent verbal gaffes, his vagueness, and his often contradictory pronouncements. But for Eisenhower, politics demanded conciliation and compromise more than devotion to principle and truth. "The public loves Ike," observed one journalist in 1959. "The less he does the more they love him. That, probably, is the secret. Here is a man who doesn't rock the boat."

In practice, this meant that Eisenhower wanted to run government in a businesslike manner while letting the states and corporate interests guide domestic policy and the economy. Eisenhower appointed nine businessmen to his first Cabinet. Former GM chief Charles Wilson served as secretary of defense and epitomized the administration's economic views with his famous aphorism "What's good for General Motors' business is good for America." In his appointments to the Federal Trade Commission, the Federal Communications Commission, and the Federal Power Commission, Eisenhower favored men congenial to the corporate interests they were charged with regulating. Eisenhower also secured passage in 1953 of the Submerged Lands Act, which transferred $40 billion worth of disputed offshore oil lands from the federal government to the Gulf states. This ensured a greater role for the states and private companies in the oil business and accelerated a trend toward the destruction of the natural environment.

At the same time, Eisenhower accepted the New Deal legacy of greater federal responsibility for social welfare. He rejected calls from conservative Republicans to dismantle the Social Security system. His administration agreed to a modest expansion of Social Security and unemployment insurance and small increases in the minimum wage. Ike also created the Department of Health, Education, and Welfare, appointing Oveta Culp Hobby as the second woman to hold a cabinet post. In agriculture Eisenhower continued the policy of parity payments designed to sustain farm prices. Between 1952 and 1960 federal spending on agriculture jumped from about $1 billion to $7 billion.

After the Korean War ended in 1953, and again in 1958, when the unemployment rate reached 7.5 percent, the economy went into a recession. The administration refused to cut taxes or increase spending to stimulate growth. Eisenhower feared starting an inflationary spiral more than he worried about unemployment or poverty. By the time he left office, Eisenhower could proudly point out that real wages for an average family had risen 20 percent during his term. Combined with low inflation and steady, if modest, growth, the Eisenhower years meant greater prosperity for most Americans.

Subsidizing Prosperity

During the Eisenhower years the federal government played a crucial role in subsidizing programs that helped millions of Americans achieve middle-class status. The Federal Housing Administration (FHA), established in 1934, put the full faith and credit of the federal government behind residential mortgages and attracted new private capital into home building. A typical FHA mortgage required less than 10 percent for a down payment and spread low-interest monthly payments over thirty years.

Yet FHA policies also had long-range drawbacks. FHA insurance went overwhelmingly to new residential developments, usually on the fringes of urban areas, hastening the decline of older, inner-city neighborhoods. It was FHA policy to favor the construction of single-family projects while discouraging multiunit housing, to refuse loans for the repair of older structures and rental units, and to require for any loan guarantee an "unbiased professional estimate" rating the property, the prospective borrower, and the neighborhood. In practice, these estimates resulted in blatant discrimination against communities that were racially mixed. The FHA's Underwriting Manual bluntly warned: "If a neighborhood is to retain stability, it is necessary that properties shall continue to be occupied by the same social and racial classes." FHA policies in effect inscribed the racial and income segregation of suburbia in public policy.

The revolution in American life wrought by the 1944 Servicemen's Readjustment Act, known as the GI Bill of Rights, extended beyond its impact on higher education (see Chapter 26). In addition to educational grants, the act provided returning veterans with low-interest mortgages and business loans, thus subsidizing the growth of the suburbs as well as the postwar expansion of higher education. Through 1956, nearly 10 million veterans received tuition and training benefits under the act. Veteran's Administration–insured loans totaled more than $50 billion by 1962, providing assistance to millions of former GIs who started businesses.

The Federal Highway Act of 1956 gave another key boost to postwar growth, especially in the suburbs. By 1972 the program had become the single largest public works program in American history; 41,000 miles of highway were built at a cost of $76 billion. Federal subsidy of the interstate highway system stimulated both the automobile industry and suburb building. But it also accelerated the decline of American mass transit and older cities. By 1970, the nation possessed the world's best roads and one of its worst public transportation systems.

The shadow of the cold war prompted the federal government to take new initiatives in aid for education. After the Soviet Union launched its first Sputnik satellite in the fall of 1957, American officials worried that the country might be lagging behind the Soviets in training scientists and engineers. The National Defense Education Act (NDEA) of 1958 allocated $280 million in grants for state universities to upgrade their science facilities. The NDEA also created $300 million in low-interest loans for college students, who had to repay only half the amount if they went on to teach in elementary or secondary school after graduation. In addition, the NDEA provided fellowship support for graduate students planning to go into college and university teaching. The NDEA represented a new consensus on the importance of high-quality education to the national interest.

Suburban Life

The suburban boom strengthened the domestic ideal of the nuclear family as the model for American life. Suburban domesticity was usually presented as women's only path to happiness and fulfillment. This cultural image often masked a stifling existence defined by housework, child care, and boredom. In the late 1950s, Betty Friedan, a wife, mother, and journalist, began a systematic survey of her Smith College classmates. She found "a strange discrepancy between the reality of our lives as women and the image to which we were trying to conform." Friedan expanded her research and in 1963 published *The Feminine Mystique*, a landmark book that articulated the frustrations of suburban women and helped to launch a revived feminist movement.

Contemporary journalists, novelists, and social scientists contributed to the popular image of suburban life as essentially dull, conformist, and peopled exclusively by the educated middle class,

This photo, which appeared in a 1950 issue of *Life* magazine, posed a family of pioneer suburbanites in front of their Levittown, New York, home. The prefabricated house was built in 1948.

SOURCE: Bernard Hoffman/Life Magazine/© 1950 TimePix.

yet many new suburbs had a distinctively blue-collar cast. Milpitas, California, for example, grew up around a Ford auto plant about fifty miles outside San Jose. Its residents were blue-collar assembly-line workers and their families, rather than salaried, college-educated, white-collar employees. Self-segregation and zoning ordinances gave some new suburbs distinctively Italian, Jewish, or Irish ethnic identities, similar to older urban neighborhoods. For millions of new suburbanites, architectural and psychological conformity was an acceptable price to pay for the comforts of home ownership, a small plot of land, and a sense of security and status.

Organized Labor and the AFL-CIO

By the mid-1950s American trade unions reached an historic high point in their penetration of the labor market, reflecting the enormous gains made during the organizing drives in core mass-production industries during the New Deal and World War II. Whereas only one in eight nonagricultural workers were union members on the eve of the Great Depression, twenty-five years later the figure stood at one in three. Union influence in political life, especially within the Democratic Party, had also increased. Yet the Republican sweep to power in 1952 meant that for the first time in a generation organized labor was without an ally in the White House. New leaders in the nation's two major labor organizations, the American Federation of Labor (dominated by old line construction and craft unions) and the Congress of Industrial Organizations (centered around unions in mass-production industry), now pushed for a merger of the two rival groups as way to protect and build on the movement's recent gains.

George Meany, the gruff, cigar-chomping head of the AFL, seemed the epitome of the modern labor boss. Originally a plumber, he had worked his way through the AFL bureaucracy and had played a leading role on National War Labor Board during World War II. An outspoken anti-Communist, Meany had pushed the AFL closer to the Democratic Party, and he took pride in never having been on a strike or a picket line. Unions, he believed, must focus on improving the economic well-being of their members. Meany's counterpart in the CIO was Walter Reuther, originally a tool-and-die maker in the auto shops of Detroit. Reuther had come to prominence as a leader of the United Automobile Workers during the tumultuous organizing drives of the 1930s and 1940s. Although he had moved away from his early socialist leanings, Reuther believed strongly that American unions ought to stand for something beyond the bread and butter needs of their members. His support of a broader social vision, including racial equality, aggressive union organizing, and expansion of the welfare state, reflected the

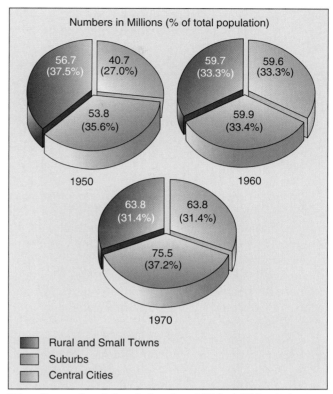

The Growth of the Suburbs, 1950–1970 Suburban growth, at the expense of older inner cities, was one of the key social trends in the twenty-five years following World War II. By 1970, more Americans lived in suburbs than in either inner cities or rural areas.

SOURCE: Adapted from U.S. Bureau of the Census, *Current Censuses, 1930–1970* (Washington, D.C.: U.S. Government Printing Office, 1975).

more militant tradition of CIO unions. Despite their differences, both Meany and Reuther believed a merger of their two organizations offered the best strategy for the labor movement. In 1955 the newly combined AFL-CIO brought some 12.5 million union members under one banner, with Meany as president and Reuther as director of the Industrial Union Department.

The merger marked the apex of trade union membership, and after 1955 its share of the labor market began a slow and steady decline. To be sure, union membership helped bring the trappings of middle-class prosperity to millions of workers and their families: home ownership, higher education for children, travel, and comfortable retirement. But the AFL-CIO showed little commitment to bringing unorganized workers into the fold. Scandals involving union corruption and racketeering hurt the labor movement's public image. In 1957 the AFL-CIO expelled its largest single affiliate, the International Brotherhood of Teamsters, because of its close ties to organized crime. In 1959, after highly publicized hearings into union corruption, Congress passed the Landrum-Griffin Act, which widened government control over union affairs and further restricted union use of picketing and secondary boycotts during strikes.

The Expansion of Higher Education

American higher education experienced rapid growth after the war. The number of students enrolled in colleges and universities climbed from 2.6 million in 1950 to 3.2 million in 1960. It then more than doubled—to 7.5 million—by 1970, as the baby boom generation came of age.

Several factors contributed to this explosion. A variety of new federal programs, including the GI Bill and the National Defense Education Act, helped subsidize college education for millions of new students. Government spending on research and development in universities, especially for defense-related projects, promoted a postwar shift to graduate education and faculty research and away from traditional undergraduate teaching.

Colleges and universities by and large accepted the values of postwar corporate culture. By the mid-1950s, 20 percent of all college graduates majored in business or other commercial fields. The college degree became a requirement for a whole range of expanding white-collar occupations in banking, insurance, real estate, advertising and marketing, and other corporate enterprises. Universities themselves were increasingly run like businesses, with administrators adopting the language of input-output, cost effectiveness, and quality control.

YOUTH CULTURE

The Youth Market

The term "teenager," describing someone between thirteen and nineteen, entered standard usage only at the end of World War II. Birthrates had accelerated gradually during the late 1930s and more rapidly during the war years. The children born in those years had by the late 1950s come of age in a society that, compared with that of their parents and the rest of the world, was uniquely affluent. Together, the demographic growth of teens and the postwar economic expansion created a burgeoning youth market. In 1959, *Life* summarized the new power of the youth market. "Counting only what is spent to satisfy their special teenage demands," the magazine reported, "the youngsters and their parents will shell out about $10 billion this year, a billion more than the total sales of GM."

The increasing uniformity of public school education also contributed to the public recognition of the special status of teenagers. In 1900, about one of every

eight teenagers was in school; by the 1950s, the figure was six out of eight. Psychologists wrote guidebooks for parents, two prominent examples being Dorothy Baruch's *How to Live with Your Teenager* (1953) and Paul Landis's *Understanding Teenagers* (1955). Traditional sources of adult authority and socialization—the marketplace, schools, child-rearing manuals, the mass media—all reinforced the notion of teenagers as a special community, united by age, rank, and status.

"Hail! Hail! Rock 'n' Roll!"

In the recording industry, small independent record labels led the way in aggressively recording African American rhythm and blues artists. Atlantic Records, in New York, developed the most influential galaxy of artists, including Ray Charles, Ruth Brown, the Drifters, Joe Turner, LaVerne Baker, and the Clovers. Chess, in Chicago, had the blues-based, singer-songwriter-guitarists Chuck Berry and Bo Diddley, and the "doo-wop" group the Moonglows. In New Orleans, Imperial had the veteran pianist-singer Fats Domino, while Specialty unleashed the outrageous Little Richard on the world. On radio, over jukeboxes, and in record stores, all of these African American artists "crossed over," adding millions of white teenagers to their solid base of black fans.

The older, more established record companies, such as RCA, Decca, M-G-M, and Capitol, had largely ignored black music. Their response to the new trend was to offer slick, toned-down "cover" versions by white pop singers of rhythm and blues originals. While African American artists began to enjoy newfound mass acceptance, there were limits to how closely white kids could identify with black performers. Also, because of the superior promotional power of the major companies and the institutional racism in the music business, white cover versions almost always outsold the black originals.

The stage was thus set for the arrival of white rock 'n' roll artists who could exploit the new sounds and styles. Elvis Presley burst upon the national scene and created as big a cultural convulsion as anyone in this century. With his carefully pomaded hair, flashy outfits, and sexy sneer, Elvis was a big hit with young female fans and a nightmare for their parents. Elvis reinvented American popular music. As a symbol of rebellious youth and the embodiment of youthful sexuality, Elvis revitalized American popular culture.

Almost Grown

Teenage consumers remade the landscape of popular music into their own turf. The dollar value of annual record sales nearly tripled between 1954 and 1959,

This photo of Elvis Presley singing at a 1956 state fair in Memphis captured his dramatic stage presence. Performing with only a trio, his sound was spare but hard driving. Both the music and Presley's stage moves owed a great deal to African American rhythm and blues artists.

SOURCE: Getty Images, Inc./Hulton Archive Photos.

racist fears that white females might be attracted to black music and black performers. The undercurrent beneath all this opposition was a deep anxiety over the more open expression of sexual feelings by both performers and audiences.

Paralleling the rise of rock 'n' roll was a growing concern with an alleged increase in juvenile delinquency. Gang fights, drug and alcohol abuse, car theft, and sexual offenses received the most attention. The U.S. Senate established a special subcommittee on juvenile delinquency. Highly publicized hearings in 1955 and 1956 convinced much of the public that youthful criminals were terrorizing the country. Although crime statistics do suggest an increase in juvenile crime during the 1950s, particularly in the suburbs, the public perception of the severity of the problem was surely exaggerated.

from $213 million to $603 million. New magazines aimed exclusively at teens flourished. Paradoxically, behavior patterns among white middle-class teenagers in the 1950s and early 1960s exhibited a new kind of youth orientation and at the same time a more pronounced identification with adults.

Postwar affluence multiplied the number of two-car families, making it easier for sixteen-year-olds to win driving privileges formerly reserved for eighteen- year-olds. Girls began dating, wearing brassieres and nylon stockings, and using cosmetics at an earlier age than before—twelve or thirteen rather than fifteen or sixteen. Several factors contributed to this trend, including a continuing decline in the age of menarche (first menstruation), the sharp drop in the age of marriage after World War II, and the precocious social climate of junior high schools (institutions that became widespread only after 1945). By the late 1950s, eighteen had become the most common age at which American females married.

Many observers of the emerging youth culture were disturbed by an apparent decline in parental control over teens. A psychiatrist writing in the *New York Times* described rock 'n' roll as "a cannibalistic and tribalistic kind of a music" and "a communicable disease." Many clergymen and church leaders declared it "the devil's music." Much of the opposition to rock 'n' roll, particularly in the South, played on long-standing

MASS CULTURE AND ITS DISCONTENTS

Television: Tube of Plenty

No mass medium ever achieved such power and popularity as rapidly as television. The three main television networks—NBC, CBS, ABC—grew directly from radio organizations. Nearly all TV stations were affiliated with one or more of the networks; only a handful of independent stations could be found around the country.

The television business, like radio, was based on the selling of time to advertisers who wanted to reach the mass audiences tuning into shows. Radio had offered entire shows produced by and for single sponsors, usually advertisers who wanted a close identification between their product and a star. Sponsors now bought scattered time slots for spot advertisements rather than bankrolling an entire show.

Ad agencies switched their creative energy to producing slick thirty-second commercials rather than entertainment programs. A shift from broadcasting live shows to filming them opened up lucrative opportunities for reruns and foreign export. The total net revenue of the TV networks and their affiliated stations in 1947 was about $2 million; by 1957 it was nearly $1 billion.

Set largely among urban ethnic families, early shows like *I Remember Mama, The Goldbergs, The Life of Riley, Life with Luigi,* and *The Honeymooners* often featured working-class families struggling with the dilemmas posed by consumer society. By the late 1950s all the urban ethnic comedy shows were off the air. A new breed of situation comedies presented nonethnic white, affluent, and insular suburban middle-class families. Shows like *Father Knows Best, Leave It to Beaver, The Adventures of Ozzie and Harriet,* and *The Donna Reed Show* epitomized the ideal suburban American family of the day. Their plots focused on genial crises, usually brought on by children's mischief and resolved by kindly fathers. In retrospect, what is most striking about these shows is what is absent—politics, social issues, cities, white ethnic groups, African Americans, and Latinos were virtually unrepresented.

Television and Politics

As in Hollywood, the cold war chill severely restricted the range of political discussion on television. An important exception was Edward R. Murrow's *See It Now* on CBS—but that show was off the air by 1955. Television news did not come into its own until 1963, with the beginning of half-hour nightly network newscasts. Only then did television's extraordinary power to rivet the nation's attention during a crisis become clear.

Still, some of the ways that TV would alter the nation's political life emerged in the 1950s. Television made Democratic senator Estes Kefauver of Tennessee a national political figure through live coverage of his 1951 Senate investigation into organized crime. It also contributed to the political downfall of Senator Joseph McCarthy in 1954 by showing his cruel bullying tactics during Senate hearings into alleged subversive Communist influence in the army. The 1952 election also brought the first use of TV political advertising for presidential candidates. Ever since then, television image-making has been the single most important element in American electoral politics.

Culture Critics

The urge to denounce the mass media for degrading the quality of American life tended to unite radical and conservative critics. Thus, Marxist writer Dwight Macdonald sounded an old conservative warning when he described "a tepid, flaccid Middlebrow Culture that threatens to engulf everything in its spreading ooze."

Critics of mass culture argued that the audiences for the mass media were atomized, anonymous, and detached. These critics undoubtedly overestimated the power of the media. They ignored the preponderance of research suggesting that most people watched and responded to mass media in family, peer group, and other social settings. The critics also missed the genuine vitality and creative brilliance to be found within mass culture: African American music; the films of Nicholas Ray, Elia Kazan, and Howard Hawks; the experimental television of Ernie Kovacs; the satire of *Mad* magazine.

Some of the sharpest dissents from the cultural conformity of the day came from a group of writers known collectively as the Beats. Led by the novelist Jack Kerouac and the poet Allen Ginsberg, the Beats shared a distrust of the American virtues of progress, power, and material gain. The Beat sensibility celebrated spontaneity, friendship, jazz, open sexuality,

Jack Kerouac, founding voice of the Beat literary movement, in front of a neon-lit bar, ca. 1950. Kerouac's public readings, often to the accompaniment of live jazz music, created a performance atmosphere underlining the connections between his writing style and the rhythms and sensibility of contemporary jazz musicians.

SOURCE: Globe Photos, Inc.

drug use, and the outcasts of American society. Kerouac, born and raised in a working-class French Canadian family in Lowell, Massachusetts, coined the term "beat" in 1948. It meant for him a "weariness with all the forms of the modern industrial state"—conformity, militarism, blind faith in technological progress. Kerouac's 1957 novel *On the Road*, chronicling the tumultuous adventures of Kerouac's circle of friends as they traveled by car back and forth across America, became the Beat manifesto.

Beat writers received a largely antagonistic, even virulent reception from the literary establishment. But millions of young Americans read their work and became intrigued by their alternative visions, which foreshadowed the mass youth rebellion and counterculture to come in the 1960s.

THE COLD WAR CONTINUED

The "New Look" in Foreign Affairs

Secretary of State John Foster Dulles gave shape to the "new look" in American foreign policy in the 1950s. Dulles had been involved in diplomatic affairs since World War I. He brought a strong sense of righteousness to his job, an almost missionary belief in America's responsibility to preserve the "free world" from godless, immoral communism.

Dulles articulated a more assertive policy toward the Communist threat by calling not simply for containment but for a "rollback." The key would be greater reliance on America's nuclear superiority.

The limits of a policy based on nuclear strategy became painfully clear when American leaders faced tense situations that offered no clear way to intervene without provoking full-scale war. In the fall of 1956 Hungarians revolted against their Soviet-dominated Communist rulers, staging a general strike and taking over the streets and factories in Budapest and other cities. The United States opened its gates to thousands of Hungarian refugees, but despite urgent requests, it refused to intervene when Soviet tanks and troops crushed the revolt.

The death of Josef Stalin in 1953 and the worldwide condemnation of his crimes, revealed by his successor, Nikita Khrushchev, in 1956, gave Eisenhower fresh hope for a new spirit of peaceful coexistence between the two superpowers. Khrushchev made a twelve-day trip to America in 1959, a psychological thaw in the cold war.

In early 1960 Khrushchev called for another summit in Paris, to discuss German reunification and nuclear disarmament. Eisenhower, meanwhile, planned his own friendship tour of the Soviet Union. But in May 1960 the Soviets shot down an American U-2 spy plane gathering intelligence on Soviet military installations. The summit collapsed when Eisenhower refused Khrushchev's demands for an apology and an end to the spy flights. The U-2 incident demonstrated the limits of personal diplomacy in resolving the deep structural rivalry between the superpowers.

Eisenhower often provided a moderate voice on issues of defense spending and missile development. The Soviet Union's dramatic launch of Sputnik, the first space-orbiting satellite, in October 1957 upset many Americans' precarious sense of security. In particular, this demonstration of Soviet technological prowess raised fears about Russian ability to deploy intercontinental ballistic missiles (ICBMs) against American cities. Critics attacked the Eisenhower administration for failure to keep up with the enemy. Senator Stuart Symington (D-MO) bluntly warned that, "Unless our defense policies are promptly changed, the Soviets will move from superiority to supremacy." In addition to huge increases in defense spending, some urged a massive program to build "fallout shelters" for the entire population in case of nuclear attack.

Eisenhower rejected these more radical responses. He knew from evidence provided by U-2 spy planes that the Soviet Union in fact trailed far behind the United States in ICBM development, but he kept this knowledge secret. Instead of panicking before Sputnik, he held to a doctrine of "sufficiency": maintaining enough military strength to survive any foreign attack and enough nuclear capability to deliver a massive counterattack. Yet, in Congress a bipartisan majority voted to increase the military budget by another $8 billion in 1958, thereby accelerating the arms race and expanding the defense sector of the economy.

Covert Action

While the United States moderated its stance toward the Soviet Union and its Eastern European satellites, it hardened its policies in the third world. The need for anti-Communist tactics short of all-out military conflict pushed the Eisenhower administration to develop new means of fighting the cold war. The premise rested on encouraging confusion or rivalry within the Communist sphere and on destabilizing or destroying anticapitalist movements around the world.

The Central Intelligence Agency, created in 1947, was perfectly designed for this task. For CIA director, Eisenhower named Allen Dulles, brother of the secretary of state and a former leader in the CIA's World War II precursor, the Office of Strategic Services.

The CIA's mandate was to collect and analyze information, but it did much more under Dulles's command. Thousands of covert agents stationed all over the world carried out a wide range of political activities. Some agents arranged large, secret financial payments to friendly political parties or to foreign trade unions opposed to socialist policies.

Intervening around the World

The Central Intelligence Agency produced a swift, major victory in Iran in 1953. The country's popular prime minister, Mohammed Mossadegh, had nationalized Britain's Anglo-Iranian Oil Company, and the State Department worried that this might set a prece-

dent throughout the oil-rich Middle East. Kermit Roosevelt, CIA chief in Iran, organized and financed an opposition to Mossadegh within the Iranian army and on the streets of Teheran. This CIA-led movement forced Mossadegh out of office and replaced him with Riza Shah Pahlavi. The shah proved his loyalty to his American sponsors by renegotiating oil contracts so as to assure American companies 40 percent of Iran's oil concessions.

The most publicized CIA intervention of the Eisenhower years took place in Guatemala, where a fragile democracy had taken root in 1944. President Jácobo Arbenz Guzmán, elected in 1950, aggressively pursued land reform and encouraged the formation of trade unions. Arbenz also challenged the

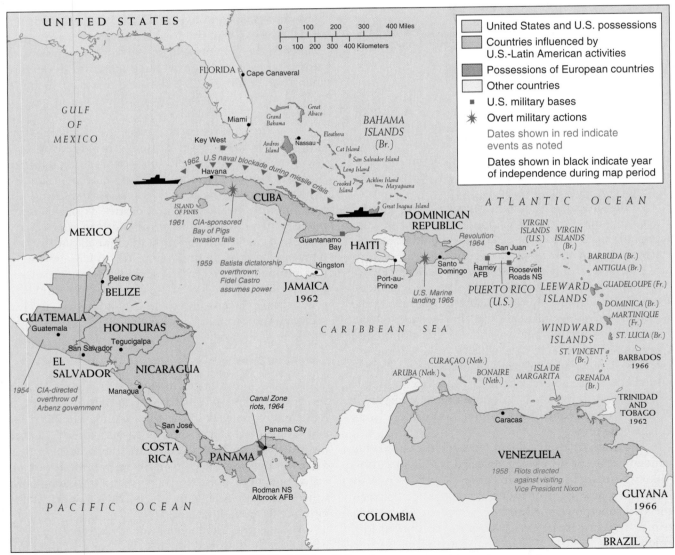

The United States in the Caribbean, 1948–1966   U.S. military intervention and economic presence grew steadily in the Caribbean following World War II. After 1960, opposition to the Cuban Revolution dominated U.S. Caribbean policies.

long-standing dominance of the American-based United Fruit Company by threatening to expropriate hundreds of thousands of acres that United Fruit was not cultivating. The company began intensive lobbying for U.S. intervention. United Fruit linked the land-reform program to the evils of international communism, and the CIA spent $7 million training antigovernment dissidents based in Honduras.

On June 14, 1954, a U.S.-sponsored military invasion began. Guatemalans appealed in vain to the United Nations for help. Meanwhile, President Eisenhower publicly denied any knowledge of CIA activities. The newly appointed military leader, Carlos Castillo Armas, was assassinated in 1957, and a decades-long civil war ensued between military factions and peasant guerrillas.

In Indochina, the United States provided France with massive military aid and CIA cooperation in its desperate struggle to maintain its colonial empire, fighting against the nationalist Vietminh movement, led by Communist Ho Chi Minh. When Vietminh forces surrounded 25,000 French troops at Dien Bien Phu in March 1954, France pleaded with the United States to intervene directly. But Eisenhower, recalling the difficulties of the Korean conflict, rejected this call.

At the same time, Eisenhower feared that the loss of one country to communism would inevitably lead to the loss of others. As he put it, "You have a row of dominoes set up, and you knock over the first one and what will happen to the last one is the certainty that it will go over quickly." According to this so-called domino theory, the "loss" of Vietnam would threaten other Southeast Asian nations, such as Laos, Thailand, the Philippines, and perhaps even India and Australia. After the French surrender at Dien Ben Phu, a conference in Geneva established a cease-fire and a temporary division of Vietnam along the 17th parallel into northern and southern sectors. The Geneva accord called for reunification and national elections in 1956. But the United States, although it had attended the conference along with the Soviet Union and China, refused to sign the accord.

South Vietnamese leader Ngo Dinh Diem, a former Japanese collaborator and a Catholic in a country that was 90 percent Buddhist, quickly alienated many peasants with his corruption and repressive policies. Both Diem and Eisenhower refused to permit the 1956 elections stipulated in Geneva because they knew popular hero Ho Chi Minh would easily win. By 1959 Diem's harsh and unpopular government in Saigon faced a civil war; thousands of peasants had joined guerrilla forces determined to drive him out. Eisenhower's commitment of military advisers and economic aid to South Vietnam, based on cold war assumptions, laid the foundation for the Vietnam War of the 1960s.

Ike's Warning: The Military-Industrial Complex

Throughout the 1950s small numbers of peace advocates in the United States had protested that the increasing reliance on nuclear weapons did not strengthen national security but rather threatened the entire planet with extinction. As he neared retirement, President Eisenhower came to share some of the protesters' anxiety and doubts about the arms race. He chose to devote his Farewell Address, delivered in January 1961, to warning the nation about the dangers of what he termed the "military-industrial complex." Its total influence, he cautioned, "economic, political, even spiritual— is felt in every city, every statehouse, every office of the federal government." The conjunction of a large military establishment and a large arms industry, Eisenhower noted, was new in American history. "The potential for the disastrous rise of misplaced power exists and will persist. We must never let the weight of this combination endanger our liberties or democratic processes."

The old soldier understood perhaps better than most the dangers of raw military force. Eisenhower's public posture of restraint and caution in foreign affairs accompanied an enormous expansion of American economic, diplomatic, and military strength. Yet the Eisenhower years also demonstrated the limits of power and intervention in a world that did not always conform to the simple dualistic assumptions of cold war ideology.

JOHN F. KENNEDY AND THE NEW FRONTIER

The Election of 1960

No one could have resembled Dwight Eisenhower less in personality, temperament, and public image than John Fitzgerald Kennedy. The handsome son of a prominent, wealthy Irish American diplomat, husband of a fashionable, trend-setting heiress, forty-two-year-old JFK embodied youth, excitement, and sophistication.

John F. Kennedy's political career began in Massachusetts, which elected him to the House in 1946 and then the Senate in 1952. Kennedy won the Democratic nomination after a bruising series of primaries in which he defeated party stalwarts Hubert Humphrey of Minnesota and Lyndon B. Johnson of Texas. Vice President Richard M. Nixon, the Republican nominee, was far better known than his younger opponent. The Kennedy campaign stressed its candidate's youth and his image as a war hero. During his World War II tour of duty in the Pacific, Kennedy had bravely rescued one of his crew after their PT boat had been sunk. Kennedy's supporters also pointed to his intellectual

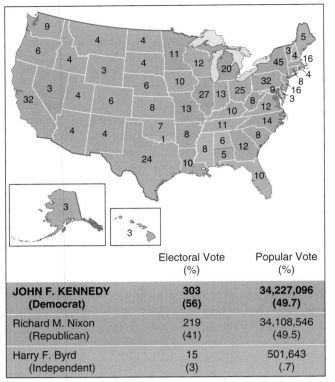

	Electoral Vote (%)	Popular Vote (%)
JOHN F. KENNEDY (Democrat)	**303 (56)**	**34,227,096 (49.7)**
Richard M. Nixon (Republican)	219 (41)	34,108,546 (49.5)
Harry F. Byrd (Independent)	15 (3)	501,643 (.7)

The Election of 1960 Kennedy's popular vote margin over Nixon was only a little over 100,000, making this one of the closest elections in American history.

ability. JFK had won the Pulitzer Prize in 1957 for his book *Profiles in Courage*, which in fact had been written largely by his aides.

The election featured the first televised presidential debates. Nixon appeared nervous and the camera made him look unshaven. Kennedy, in contrast, benefited from a confident manner and telegenic good looks. Both candidates emphasized foreign policy. Nixon defended the Republican record and stressed his own maturity and experience. Kennedy hammered away at the alleged "missile gap" with the Soviet Union and promised more vigorous executive leadership.

Kennedy squeaked to victory in the closest election since 1884. He won by a little more than 100,000 votes out of nearly 69 million cast. Surrounding himself with prestigious Ivy League academics, Hollywood movie stars, and talented artists and writers, he imbued the presidency with an aura of celebrity. The new president's ringing inaugural address ("Ask not what your country can do for you—ask what you can do for your country") had special resonance for a whole generation of young Americans.

New Frontier Liberalism

Kennedy promised to revive the long-stalled liberal domestic agenda. His New Frontier advocated such liberal programs as a higher minimum wage, greater federal aid for education, increased Social Security benefits, medical care for the elderly, support for public housing, and various antipoverty measures. Yet the thin margin of his victory and the stubborn opposition of conservative southern Democrats in Congress made it difficult to achieve these goals. Congress refused, for example, to enact the administration's attempt to extend Social Security and unemployment benefits to millions of uncovered workers.

Congress did approve a modest increase in the minimum wage (to $1.25 per hour), agreed to a less ambitious improvement in Social Security, and appropriated $5 billion for public housing. It also passed the Manpower Retraining Act, appropriating $435 million to train the unemployed. The Area Redevelopment Act provided federal funds for rural, depressed Appalachia. The Higher Education Act of 1963 offered aid to colleges for constructing buildings and upgrading libraries. One of the best-publicized New Frontier programs was the Peace Corps, in which thousands of mostly young men and women traveled overseas for two-year stints in underdeveloped countries. As a force for change, the Peace Corps produced modest results, but it epitomized Kennedy's promise to provide opportunities for service for a new generation of idealistic young people.

Kennedy helped revive the issue of women's rights with his Presidential Commission on the Status of Women, led by Eleanor Roosevelt. One concrete legislative result, the Equal Pay Act of 1963, made it illegal for employers to pay men and women different wages for the same job. The work of the commission contributed to a new generation of women's rights activism.

Kennedy took a more aggressive stance on stimulating economic growth and creating new jobs than had Eisenhower. His administration pushed lower business taxes through Congress, even at the cost of a higher federal deficit. The Revenue Act of 1962 encouraged new investment and plant renovation by easing tax depreciation schedules for business. Kennedy also gained approval for lower U.S. tariffs as a way to increase foreign trade. To help keep inflation down, he intervened in the steel industry in 1961 and 1962, pressuring labor to keep its wage demands low and management to curb price increases.

Kennedy also increased the federal commitment to a wholly new realm of government spending: the space program. The National Aeronautics and Space Administration (NASA) had been established under Eisenhower in response to the Soviet success with Sputnik. In 1961, driven by the cold war motivation of beating the Soviets to the moon and avoiding "another Sputnik," Kennedy won approval for a greatly expanded space program with the goal of landing an American on the moon by the end of the decade. In space, if not on earth, the New Frontier might actually be reached.

Kennedy and the Cold War

During Kennedy's three years in office his approach to foreign policy shifted from aggressive containment to efforts at easing U.S.–Soviet tensions. Certainly when he first entered office, Kennedy and his chief aides considered it their main task to confront the Communist threat. To head the State Department Kennedy chose Dean Rusk, a conservative former assistant to Truman's secretary of state, Dean Acheson. Secretary of Defense Robert McNamara, a Republican and Ford Motor Company executive, was determined to streamline military procedures and weapons buying. Allen Dulles, Eisenhower's CIA director, remained at his post. These and other officials believed with Kennedy that Eisenhower had timidly accepted stalemate when the cold war could have been won.

Between 1960 and 1962 defense appropriations increased by nearly a third, from $43 billion to $56 billion. JFK expanded Eisenhower's policy of covert operations, deploying the army's elite Special Forces as a supplement to CIA covert operations in counterinsurgency battles against third world guerrillas. The Special Forces reflected the president's desire as president to acquire greater flexibility, secrecy, and independence in the conduct of foreign policy.

The limits on the Special Forces and covert action became apparent in Southeast Asia. In Laos, where the United States had ignored the 1954 Geneva agreement and installed a friendly military regime, the CIA-backed government could not defeat Soviet-backed Pathet Lao guerrillas. The president had to arrange with the Soviets to neutralize Laos. In neighboring Vietnam, the situation proved more difficult. When Communist Vietcong guerrillas launched a civil war in South Vietnam against the U.S.–supported government in Saigon, Kennedy began sending hundreds of military advisers to support the rule of Ngo Dinh Diem. In May 1961, in response to North Vietnamese aid to the Vietcong, Kennedy ordered a covert action against Ho Chi Minh's government that included sabotage and intelligence gathering.

Kennedy's approach to Vietnam reflected an analysis of the situation in that country by two aides, General Maxwell Taylor and Walt Rostow, who saw it through purely cold war eyes, ignoring the inefficiency, corruption, and unpopularity of the Diem government. By 1963, with Diem's army unable to contain the Vietcong rebellion, Kennedy had sent nearly 16,000 support and combat troops to South Vietnam. By then, a wide spectrum of South Vietnamese society had joined the revolt against the hated Diem, including highly respected Buddhist monks and their students. Americans watched in horror as television news reports showed footage of Buddhists burning themselves to death on the streets of Saigon—the ultimate protest against Diem's repressive rule. The South Vietnamese army, bloated by U.S. aid and weakened by corruption, continued to disintegrate. In the fall of 1963, American military officers and CIA operatives stood aside with approval as a group of Vietnamese generals removed President Diem, killing him and his top advisers. It was the first of many coups that racked the South Vietnamese government over the next few years.

In Latin America, Kennedy looked for ways to forestall various revolutionary movements that were gaining ground. The erosion of peasant landholdings had accelerated rapidly after 1950. Millions of impoverished peasants were forced to relocate to already overcrowded cities. In 1961 Kennedy unveiled the Alliance for Progress, a ten-year, $100 billion plan to spur economic development in Latin America. Kennedy intended the program as a kind of Marshall Plan that would benefit the poor and middle classes of the continent. The alliance did help raise growth rates in Latin American economies. But the expansion in export crops and in consumption by the tiny upper class did little to aid the poor or encourage democracy. The United States hesitated to challenge the power of dictators and extreme conservatives who were staunch anti-Communist allies. Thus, the alliance soon degenerated into just another foreign aid program, incapable of generating genuine social change.

The Cuban Revolution and the Bay of Pigs

The direct impetus for the Alliance for Progress was the Cuban Revolution of 1959, which loomed over Latin America. The U.S. economic domination of Cuba that began with the Spanish American War (see Chapter 20) had continued through the 1950s. American-owned businesses controlled all of Cuba's oil production, 90 percent of its mines, and roughly half of its railroads and sugar and cattle industries. Havana, the island's capital, was an attractive tourist center for Americans, and U.S. crime syndicates shared control of the island's lucrative gambling, prostitution, and drug trade with dictator Fulgencio Batista. In the early 1950s, a peasant-based revolutionary movement, led by Fidel Castro, began gaining strength in the rural districts and mountains outside Havana.

On New Year's Day 1959, after years of guerrilla war, the rebels entered Havana and seized power amid great public rejoicing. Castro's land-reform program, involving the seizure of acreage from the tiny minority that controlled much of the fertile land, threatened to set an example for other Latin American countries.

Although Castro had not joined the Cuban Communist Party, he turned to the Soviet Union after the United States withdrew economic aid. He began to sell sugar to the Soviets and soon nationalized American-owned oil companies and other enterprises. Eisenhower established an economic boycott of Cuba in 1960, then severed diplomatic relations.

Kennedy inherited from Eisenhower plans for a U.S. invasion of Cuba, including the secret arming and training of Cuban exiles. The CIA drafted the invasion plan, which was based on the assumption that a U.S.-led invasion would trigger a popular uprising of the Cuban people and bring down Castro. Kennedy went along with the plan, but at the last moment decided not to supply an Air Force cover for the operation. On April 17, 1961, a ragtag army of 1,400 counterrevolutionaries led by CIA operatives landed at the Bay of Pigs, on Cuba's south coast. Castro's efficient and loyal army easily subdued them.

The debacle revealed that the CIA, blinded by cold war assumptions, had failed to understand the Cuban Revolution. There was no popular uprising against Castro. Instead, the invasion strengthened Castro's standing among the urban poor and peasants, already attracted by his programs of universal literacy and medical care. An embarrassed Kennedy reluctantly took the blame for the abortive invasion, and his administration was censured time and again by third world delegates to the United Nations. American liberals criticized Kennedy for plotting Castro's overthrow, while conservatives blamed him for not supporting the invasion. Despite the failure, Kennedy remained committed to getting rid of Castro and keeping up the economic boycott. The CIA continued to support anti-Castro operations and launched at least eight attempts to assassinate the Cuban leader.

The Missile Crisis

The aftermath of the Bay of Pigs led to the most serious confrontation of the cold war: the Cuban missile crisis of October 1962. Frightened by U.S. belligerency, Castro asked Soviet premier Khrushchev for military help. Khrushchev responded in the summer of 1962 by shipping to Cuba a large amount of sophisticated weaponry, including intermediate-range nuclear missiles. In early October, U.S. reconnaissance planes found camouflaged missile silos dotting the island. Several Kennedy aides demanded an immediate bombing of Cuban bases, arguing that the missiles had decisively eroded the strategic global advantage the United States had previously enjoyed. Instead Kennedy went on national television on October 22. He announced

the discovery of the missile sites, demanded the removal of all missiles, and ordered a strict naval blockade of all offensive military equipment shipped to Cuba. He also requested an emergency meeting of the UN Security Council and promised that any missiles launched from Cuba would bring "a full retaliatory response upon the Soviet Union." For a tense week, the American public wondered if nuclear Armageddon was imminent. Eyeball to eyeball, the two superpowers waited for each other to blink. On October 26 and 27 Khrushchev yielded, ordering twenty-five Soviet ships off their course to Cuba, thus avoiding a challenge to the American blockade. Khrushchev offered to remove all the missiles in return for a pledge from the United States not to invade Cuba. Khrushchev later added a demand for removal of American weapons from Turkey, as close to the Soviet Union as Cuba is to the United States. On November 20, after weeks of delicate negotiations, Kennedy publicly announced the withdrawal of Soviet missiles and bombers from Cuba. He also pledged to respect Cuban sovereignty, and promised that U.S. forces would not invade the island.

The crisis had passed. The Soviets, determined not to be intimidated again, began the largest weapons buildup in their history. For his part Kennedy, perhaps chastened by this flirtation with nuclear disaster, made important gestures toward peaceful coexistence with the Soviets. In a June 1963 address at American University, Kennedy called for a rethinking of cold war diplomacy. Shortly after, Washington and Moscow set up a "hot line"—a direct phone connection to permit instant communication during times of crisis. More substantial was the Limited Nuclear Test-Ban Treaty, signed in August 1963 by the United States, the Soviet Union, and Great Britain. The treaty prohibited above-ground, outer space, and underwater nuclear weapons tests. It eased international anxieties over radioactive fallout. But underground testing continued to accelerate for years. The limited test ban was perhaps more symbolic than substantive, a psychological breakthrough in East–West relations after a particularly tense three years.

The Assassination of President Kennedy

The assassination of John F. Kennedy in Dallas on November 22, 1963, sent the entire nation into shock and mourning. Tens of millions watched the televised spectacle of Kennedy's funeral, trying to make sense of the brutal murder. Although a special commission found the killing to be the work of a lone assassin, Lee Harvey Oswald, many Americans doubted this conclusion. Kennedy's death gave rise to a host of conspiracy theories, none of which seems provable. We will never

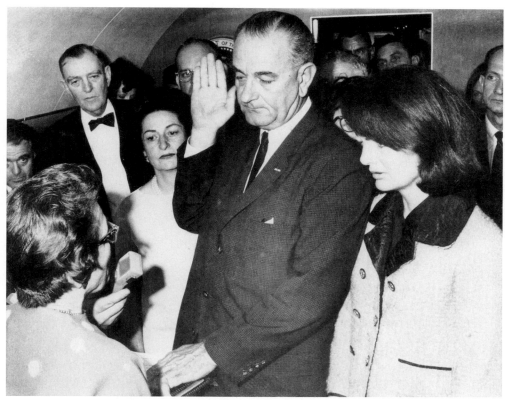

Vice President Lyndon B. Johnson took the oath of office as president aboard *Air Force One* after the assassination of John F. Kennedy, November 22, 1963. Onlookers included the grief-stricken Jacqueline Kennedy (right) and Lady Bird Johnson (left). This haunting photo captured both the shock of Kennedy's assassination and the orderly succession of power that followed.

SOURCE: AP/Wide World Photos.

know, of course, what Kennedy might have achieved in a second term. But in his 1,000 days as president, he demonstrated a capacity to change and grow in office. Having gone to the brink during the missile crisis, he managed to launch new initiatives toward peaceful co-existence. At the time of his death, relations between the United States and the Soviet Union were more amicable than at any time since the end of World War II. Much of the domestic liberal agenda of the New Frontier would be finally implemented by Kennedy's successor, Lyndon B. Johnson, who dreamed of creating a Great Society.

CONCLUSION

America in 1963 still enjoyed the full flush of its postwar economic boom. To be sure, millions of Americans, particularly African Americans and Latinos, did not share in the good times. But millions of others had managed to achieve middle-class status since the early 1950s. An expanding economy, cheap energy, govern-

ment subsidies, and a dominant position in the world marketplace had made the hallmarks of "the good life" available to more Americans than ever. The postwar "American dream" promised home ownership, college education, secure employment at decent wages, affordable appliances, and the ability to travel—for one's children if not for one's self. The nation's public culture—its schools, mass media, politics, advertising—presented a powerful consensus based on the idea that the American dream was available to all who would work for it.

The presidential transition from the grandfatherly Dwight Eisenhower to the charismatic John F. Kennedy symbolized for many a generational shift as well. By 1963 young people had more influence than ever before in shaping the nation's political life, its media images, and its burgeoning consumer culture. Kennedy himself inspired millions of young Americans to pursue public service and to express their political idealism. But even by the time of Kennedy's death, the postwar consensus and the conditions that nurtured it were beginning to unravel.

CHRONOLOGY

1950	David Riesman publishes *The Lonely Crowd*
1952	Dwight D. Eisenhower is elected president
1953	CIA installs Riza Shah Pahlavi as leader of Iran
1954	Vietminh force French surrender at Dien Bien Phu
	CIA overthrows government of Jácobo Arbenz Guzmán in Guatemala
	United States explodes first hydrogen bomb
1955	Jonas Salk pioneers vaccine for polio
	James Dean stars in the movie *Rebel without a Cause*
1956	Federal Highway Act authorizes Interstate Highway System
	Elvis Presley signs with RCA
	Eisenhower is reelected
	Allen Ginsberg publishes *Howl*
1957	Soviet Union launches Sputnik, first space-orbiting satellite
	Jack Kerouac publishes *On the Road*

1958	National Defense Education Act authorizes grants and loans to college students
1959	Nikita Khrushchev visits the United States
1960	Soviets shoot down U-2 spy plane
	John F. Kennedy is elected president
	Almost 90 percent of American homes have television
1961	President Kennedy creates "Green Berets"
	Bay of Pigs invasion of Cuba fails
1962	Cuban missile crisis brings the world to the brink of a superpower confrontation
1963	Report by the Presidential Commission on the Status of Women documents ongoing discrimination
	Betty Friedan publishes *The Feminine Mystique*
	Limited Nuclear Test-Ban Treaty is signed
	President Kennedy is assassinated

REVIEW QUESTIONS

1. How did postwar economic prosperity change the lives of ordinary Americans? Which groups benefited most and which were largely excluded from "the affluent society"?
2. What role did federal programs play in expanding economic opportunities?
3. Analyze the origins of postwar youth culture. How was teenage life different in these years from previous eras? How did popular culture both reflect and distort the lives of American youth?
4. How did mass culture become even more central to American everyday life in the two decades following World War II? What problems did various cultural critics identify with this trend?
5. How did cold war politics and assumptions shape American foreign policy in these years? What were the key interventions the United States made in Europe and the third world?
6. Evaluate the domestic and international policies associated with John F. Kennedy and the New Frontier. What continuities with Eisenhower-era politics do you find in the Kennedy administration? How did JFK break with past practices?

RECOMMENDED READING

Roslayn Fraad Baxandall and Elizabeth Ewen, *Picture Windows: How the Suburbs Happened* (2000). The best new account of postwar suburbs, emphasizing the demand for affordable housing and making fine use of the voices of suburbanites.

Lawrence Freedman, *Kennedy's Wars: Berlin, Cuba, Laos, and Vietnam* (2000). A comprehensive new analysis of JFK's foreign policy, emphasizing the context of cold war liberalism.

James B. Gilbert, *A Cycle of Outrage* (1986). An insightful examination of juvenile delinquency and its treatment by social scientists and the mass media during the 1950s.

Kenneth T. Jackson, *Crabgrass Frontier* (1985). The most comprehensive overview of the history of American suburbs. Jackson provides a broad historical context for understanding postwar suburbanization and offers an excellent analysis of the impact of government agencies such as the Federal Housing Administration.

David E. Kaiser, *American Tragedy: Kennedy, Johnson, and the Origins of the Vietnam War* (2000). The most detailed account yet of how the contradictions of cold war thinking pushed policymakers in three administrations toward an unnecessary and unwinnable war.

Zachary Karabell, *Architects of Intervention: The United States, the Third World, and the Cold War, 1946–1962* (1999). A wide-ranging analysis of U.S. involvement in various third world countries, with special emphasis on the active role played by indigineous, non-American participants.

George Lipsitz, *Time Passages* (1990). An illuminating set of essays charting developments in American popular culture, especially strong analysis of music and early television.

Elaine Tyler May, *Homeward Bound: American Families in the Cold War* (1988). A thoughtful social history linking family life of the 1950s with the political shadow of the cold war.

Grace Palladino, *Teenagers: An American History* (1996). A lively and witty narrative account of the emergence of teenagers as a new social class.

James T. Patterson, *Grand Expectations: Postwar America, 1945–1974* (1996). A comprehensive overview of postwar life that centers on the "grand expectations" evoked by unprecedented prosperity.

Mark J. White, ed., *Kennedy: The New Frontier Revisited* (1998). Wide ranging collection of recent essays that together offer a balanced view of Kennedy's presidency.

ON THE WEB

http://www.lihistory.com/8/chap8cov.htm
This site provides a good overview of Levittown, among the first of the postwar suburbs.

http://www.tvhistory.tv/
Rich site with a detailed history of television and its impact on mass culture.

http://www.english.upenn.edu/~afilreis/50s/home.html
Maintained by the University of Pennsylvania, this is one of the premier sites on the culture of the fifties.

Eisenhower/Kennedy administration primary documents:
http://www.bartleby.com/124/pres54.html
First Inaugural Address of Dwight D. Eisenhower, January 20, 1953.

http://www.bartleby.com/124/pres55.html
Second Inaugural Address of Dwight D. Eisenhower, January 21, 1957.

http://www.ukans.edu/carrie/docs/texts/ddefarew.html
Eisenhower's "Farewell Address," January 17, 1961 (excerpts).

http://www.bartleby.com/124/pres56.html
Inaugural Address of John F. Kennedy, January 20, 1961.

http://www.fordham.edu/halsall/mod/1962kennedy-cuba.html
Kennedy's Address on the Cuban Crisis, October 22, 1962.

http://www.prenhall.com/faragherbrief/map27.1
Compare American intervention in the Caribbean from 1948—1966 with intervention in this region earlier in the twentieth century (Chapter 22). What are the similarities? What are the differences?

AMERICAN COMMUNITIES

The Montgomery Bus Boycott: An African American Community Challenges Segregation

A STEADY STREAM OF CARS AND PEDESTRIANS JAMMED THE STREETS around the Holt Street Baptist Church in Montgomery, Alabama. By early evening a patient, orderly, and determined crowd of more than 5,000 African Americans had packed the church and spilled over onto the sidewalks. Loudspeakers had to be set up for the thousands who could not squeeze inside. After a brief prayer and a reading from Scripture, all attention focused on the twenty-six-year-old minister who was to address the gathering. "We are here this evening," he began slowly, "for serious business. We are here in a general sense because first and foremost we are American citizens, and we are determined to apply our citizenship to the fullness of its means."

Sensing the expectant mood of the crowd, the minister got down to specifics. Rosa Parks, a seamstress and well-known activist in Montgomery's African American community, had been taken from a bus, arrested, and put in jail for refusing to give up her seat to a white passenger on December 1, 1955. Composing roughly half the city's 100,000 people, Montgomery's black community had long endured the humiliation of a strictly segregated bus system. Drivers could order a whole row of black passengers to vacate their seats for one white person. And black people had to pay their fares at the front of the bus and then step back outside and reenter through the rear door. The day of the mass meeting, more than 30,000 African Americans had answered a hastily organized call to boycott the city's buses in protest of Mrs. Parks's arrest. As the minister quickened his cadence and drew shouts of encouragement, he seemed to gather strength and confidence from the crowd. "You know, my friends, there comes a time when people get tired of being trampled over by the iron feet of oppression. There comes a time, my friends, when people get tired of being flung across the abyss of humiliation, when they experience the bleakness of nagging despair."

Even before he concluded his speech, it was clear to all present that the bus boycott would continue for more than just a day. The minister laid out the key principles that would guide the boycott—nonviolence, Christian love, unity. In his brief but stirring address the minister created a powerful sense of communion. "If we are wrong, justice is a lie," he told the clapping and shouting throng. "And we are determined here in Montgomery to work and fight until justice runs down like water and righteousness like a mighty stream." Historians would look back at Montgomery, he noted, and have to say: "'There lived a race of people, black people, fleecy locks and black complexion, of people who had the moral courage to stand up for their rights.' And thereby they injected a new meaning into the veins of history and of civilization."

The Reverend Dr. Martin Luther King, Jr. made his way out of the church amid waves of applause and rows of hands reaching out to touch him. His prophetic speech catapulted him into leadership of the Montgomery bus boycott—but he had not started the movement. When Rosa Parks was arrested, local activists with deep roots in the black protest tradition galvanized the community with the idea of a boycott. Mrs. Parks herself had served for twelve years as secretary of the local NAACP chapter. She was a committed opponent of segregation and was thoroughly respected in the city's African American community. E. D. Nixon, president of the Alabama NAACP and head of the local Brotherhood of Sleeping Car Porters union, saw Mrs. Parks's arrest as the right case on which to make a stand. It was Nixon who brought Montgomery's black ministers together on December 5 to coordinate an extended boycott of city buses. They formed the Montgomery Improvement Association (MIA) and chose Dr. King as their leader. Significantly, Mrs. Parks's lawyer was Clifford Durr, a white liberal with a history of representing black clients. His politically active wife Virginia, for whom Mrs. Parks worked as a seamstress, had been a longtime crusader against the poll tax that prevented many blacks from voting. And two white ministers, Rev. Robert Graetz and Rev. Glenn Smiley, would offer important support to the MIA.

While Nixon organized black ministers, Jo Ann Robinson, an English teacher at Alabama State College, spread the word to the larger black community. Robinson led the Women's Political Council (WPC), an organization of black professional women founded in 1949. With her WPC allies, Robinson wrote, mimeographed, and distributed 50,000 copies of a leaflet telling the story of Mrs. Parks's arrest and urging all African Americans to stay off city buses on December 5. They did. Now the MIA faced the more difficult task of keeping the boycott going. Success depended on providing alternate transportation for the 30,000 to 40,000 maids, cooks, janitors, and other black working people who needed to get to work.

The MIA coordinated an elaborate system of car pools, using hundreds of private cars and volunteer drivers to provide as many as 20,000 rides each day. Many people walked. Local authorities, although shocked by the discipline and sense of purpose shown by Montgomery's African American community, refused to engage in serious negotiations. With the aid of the NAACP, the MIA brought suit in federal court against bus segregation in Montgomery. Police harassed boycotters with traffic tickets and arrests. White racists exploded bombs in the homes of Dr. King and E. D. Nixon. The days turned into weeks, then months, but still the boycott continued. All along, mass meetings in Montgomery's African American churches helped boost morale with singing, praying, and stories of individual sacrifice. One elderly woman, refusing all suggestions that she drop out of the boycott on account of her age, made a spontaneous remark that became a classic refrain of the movement: "My feets is tired, but my soul is rested."

The boycott reduced the bus company's revenues by two-thirds. In February 1956, city officials obtained indictments against King, Nixon, and 113 other boycotters under an old law forbidding hindrance to business without "just cause or legal excuse." A month later King went on trial. A growing contingent of newspaper reporters and TV crews from around the country watched as the judge found King guilty, fined him $1,000, and released him on bond pending appeal. But on June 4, a panel of three federal judges struck down Montgomery's bus segregation ordinances as unconstitutional. On November 13 the Supreme Court affirmed the district court ruling. After eleven hard months and against all odds, the boycotters had won.

The struggle to end legal segregation took root in scores of southern cities and towns. African American communities led these fights, developing a variety of tactics, leaders, and ideologies. With white allies, they engaged in direct-action protests such as boycotts, sit-ins, and mass civil disobedience as well as strategic legal battles in state and federal courts. The movement was not without its inner conflicts. Tensions between local movements and national civil rights organizations flared up regularly. Within African American communities, long-simmering distrust between the working classes and rural folk on the one hand and middle-class ministers, teachers, and business people on the other sometimes threatened to destroy political unity. There were generational conflicts between African American student activists and their elders. But overall, the civil rights movement created new social identities for African Americans and profoundly changed American society. ■

Montgomery

KEY TOPICS

- Legal and political origins of the African American civil rights struggle

- Martin Luther King's rise to leadership

- Student protesters and direct action in the South

- Civil rights and national politics

- Civil Rights Act of 1964 and Voting Rights Act of 1965

- America's other minorities

ORIGINS OF THE MOVEMENT

Civil Rights after World War II

The boom in wartime production spurred a mass migration of nearly a million black Southerners to northern cities. Although racial discrimination in housing and employment was by no means absent in northern cities, greater economic opportunities and political freedom continued to attract rural African Americans after the war. Black people gained significant influence in local political machines in such cities as New York, Chicago, and Detroit. Within industrial unions such as the United Automobile Workers and the United Steel Workers, white and black workers learned the power of biracial unity in fighting for better wages and working conditions.

After the war, civil rights issues returned to the national political stage for the first time since Reconstruction. Black voters had already begun to switch their allegiance from the Republicans to the Democrats during the New Deal. A series of symbolic and substantial acts by the Truman administration solidified that shift. In 1946 Truman created a President's Committee on Civil Rights. Its report, *To Secure These Rights* (1947), set out an ambitious program to end racial inequality. Recommendations included a permanent civil rights division in the Justice Department, voting rights protection, antilynching legislation, and a legal attack on segregated housing. Yet, although he publicly endorsed nearly all the proposals of the new committee, Truman introduced no legislation to make them law.

Truman and his advisers walked a political tightrope on civil rights. They understood that black voters in several key northern states would be pivotal in the 1948 election. At the same time, they worried about the loyalty of white southern Democrats adamantly opposed to changing the racial status quo. In July 1948, the president made his boldest move on behalf of civil rights, issuing an executive order barring segregation in the armed forces. When liberals forced the Democratic National Convention to adopt a strong civil rights plank that summer, a group of outraged Southerners walked out and nominated Governor Strom Thurmond of South Carolina for president on a States' Rights ticket. Thurmond carried four southern states in the election. But with the help of over 70 percent of the northern black vote, Truman barely managed to defeat Republican Thomas E. Dewey in November. The deep split over race issues would continue to rack the national Democratic Party for a generation.

During the war, membership in the National Association for the Advancement of Colored People had mushroomed from 50,000 to 500,000. Working- and middle-class urban black people provided the backbone of this new membership. The NAACP conducted voter registration drives and lobbied against discrimination in housing and employment. Its Legal Defense and Education Fund, vigorously led by special counsel Thurgood Marshall, mounted several significant legal challenges to segregation laws. In *Morgan* v. *Virginia* (1946), the Supreme Court declared that segregation on interstate buses was an undue burden on interstate commerce. Other Supreme Court decisions struck down all-white election primaries, racially restrictive housing covenants, and the exclusion of blacks from law and graduate schools.

The NAACP's legal work demonstrated the potential for using federal courts in attacking segregation. Courts were one place where black people, using the constitutional language of rights, could make forceful arguments that could not be voiced in Congress or at political conventions. But federal enforcement of court decisions was often lacking. In 1947 a group of black and white activists tested compliance with the *Morgan* decision by traveling on a bus through the Upper South. This "Freedom Ride" was cosponsored by the Christian pacifist Fellowship of Reconciliation (FOR) and its recent offshoot, the Congress of Racial Equality (CORE), which was devoted to interracial, nonviolent direct action. In North Carolina, several riders were arrested and sentenced to thirty days on a chain gang for refusing to leave the bus.

Two symbolic "firsts" raised black expectations and inspired pride. In 1947 Jackie Robinson broke the color barrier in major league baseball, winning rookie-of-the-year honors with the Brooklyn Dodgers. Robinson's courage in the face of racial epithets from fans and players paved the way for the black ballplayers who soon followed him to the big leagues. In 1950 United Nations diplomat Ralph Bunche won the Nobel Peace Prize for arranging the 1948 Arab-Israeli truce. Bunche, however, later declined an appointment as undersecretary of state because he did not want to subject his family to the humiliating segregation laws of Washington, D.C.

Cultural change could have political implications as well. Although black musicians had pioneered the development of swing and, earlier, jazz, white band-leaders and musicians had reaped most of the recognition and money from the public. Artists such as Charlie Parker, Dizzy Gillespie, Thelonius Monk, Bud Powell, and Miles Davis revolted against the standard big-band format of swing, preferring small groups and competitive jam sessions to express their musical visions. The new music, dubbed "bebop" by critics and fans, demanded a much more sophisticated knowledge of harmony and melody and featured more complex rhythms and extended improvisation than previous jazz styles. Serious about both their music and the way it was presented, these black artists refused to cater to white expectations of grinning, easygoing black performers.

The Segregated South

The 1896 Supreme Court ruling in *Plessy* v. *Ferguson* had sanctioned the principle of "separate but equal" facilities in southern life. In practice, segregation meant separate but unequal. A tight web of state and local ordinances enforced strict separation of the races in schools, restaurants, hotels, movie theaters, libraries, restrooms, hospitals, even cemeteries, and the facilities for black people were consistently inferior to those for whites. There were no black policemen in the Deep South and only a handful of black lawyers. "A white man," one scholar observed, "can steal from or maltreat a Negro in almost any way without fear of reprisal, because the Negro cannot claim the protection of the police or courts."

In the late 1940s only about 10 percent of eligible southern black people voted, most of these in urban areas. A combination of legal and extralegal measures

Signs designating "White" and "Colored" restrooms, waiting rooms, entrances, benches, and even water fountains were a common sight in the segregated South.

SOURCE: CORBIS.

kept all but the most determined black people disfranchised. Poll taxes, all-white primaries, and discriminatory registration procedures reinforced the belief that voting was "the white man's business." African Americans who insisted on exercising their right to vote, especially in remote rural areas, faced physical violence—beatings, shootings, lynchings.

Outsiders often noted that despite Jim Crow laws (see Chapter 20) contact between blacks and whites was ironically close. The mass of black Southerners worked on white-owned plantations and in white households. One black preacher neatly summarized the nation's regional differences this way: "In the South, they don't care how close you get as long as you don't get too big; in the North, they don't care how big you get as long as you don't get too close." The South's racial code forced African Americans to accept, at least outwardly, social conventions that reinforced their low standing with whites. A black person did not shake hands with a white person, or enter a white home through the front door, or address a white person except formally.

Brown v. Board of Education

Since the late 1930s, the NAACP had chipped away at the legal foundations of segregation. Rather than making a frontal assault on the *Plessy* separate-but-equal rule, civil rights attorneys launched a series of suits seeking complete equality in segregated facilities. The aim of this strategy was to make segregation so prohibitively expensive that the South would be forced to dismantle it. In the 1939 case *Missouri v. ex.rel. Gaines*, the Supreme Court ruled that the University of Missouri law school must either admit African Americans or build another, fully equal law school for them. NAACP lawyers pushed their arguments further, asserting that equality could not be measured simply by money or physical plant. In *McLaurin v. Oklahoma State Regents* (1950), the Court agreed with Thurgood Marshall's argument that regulations forcing a black law student to sit, eat, and study in areas apart from white students inevitably created a "badge of inferiority."

By 1951, Marshall had begun coordinating the NAACP's legal resources for a direct attack on the separate-but-equal doctrine. The goal was to overturn *Plessy* and the constitutionality of segregation itself. For a test case, Marshall combined five lawsuits challenging segregation in public schools. The Supreme Court heard initial arguments on the cases, grouped together as *Brown v. Board of Education*, in December 1952.

In his argument before the Court, Thurgood Marshall tried to establish that separate facilities, by definition, denied black people their full rights as American citizens. He used evidence from psychologists and sociologists demonstrating that black children educated in segregated schools developed a negative self-image and low self-esteem. Chief Justice Earl Warren, eager for a unanimous decision, patiently worked at convincing two holdouts.

On May 17, 1954, Warren read the Court's unanimous decision aloud. "Does segregation of children in public schools solely on the basis of race . . . deprive the children of the minority group of equal educational opportunities?" The chief justice paused. "We believe that it does." Warren made a point of citing several of the psychological studies of segregation's effects. He ended by directly addressing the constitutional issue. Segregation deprived the plaintiffs of the equal protection of the laws guaranteed by the Fourteenth Amendment. "We conclude that in the field of public education the doctrine of 'separate but equal' has no place. Separate educational facilities are inherently unequal." "Any language in *Plessy* v. *Ferguson* contrary to this finding is rejected."

African Americans and their liberal allies around the country hailed the decision and the legal genius of Thurgood Marshall. But the issue of enforcement soon dampened this enthusiasm. To gain a unanimous decision, Warren had had to agree to let the Court delay for one year its ruling on how to implement desegregation. This second *Brown* ruling, handed down in May 1955, assigned responsibility for desegregation plans to local school boards. The Court left it to federal district judges to monitor compliance, requiring only that desegregation proceed "with all deliberate speed." Thus, although the Court had made a momentous and clear constitutional ruling, the need for compromise dictated gradual enforcement by unspecified means.

Crisis in Little Rock

Resistance to *Brown* took many forms. Most affected states passed laws transferring authority for pupil assignment to local school boards. This prevented the NAACP from bringing statewide suits against segregated school systems. Counties and towns created layers of administrative delays designed to stop implementation of *Brown*. Some school boards transferred public school property to new, all-white private "academies." State legislatures in Virginia, Alabama, Mississippi, and Georgia, resurrecting pre–Civil War doctrines, passed resolutions declaring their right to "interpose" themselves between the people and the federal government and to "nullify" federal laws. In 1956, 101 congressmen from the former Confederate states signed the Southern Manifesto, urging their states to refuse compliance with desegregation. President Dwight Eisenhower declined to publicly endorse *Brown*, contributing to the spirit of southern resistance. Privately, the president opposed the *Brown* decision.

In Little Rock, Arkansas, the tense controversy over school integration became a test case of state versus federal power. A federal court ordered public schools to begin desegregation in September 1957, and the local school board made plans to comply. But Governor Orval Faubus, facing a tough reelection fight, decided to make a campaign issue out of defying the court order. He dispatched Arkansas National Guard troops to Central High School to prevent nine black students from entering. For three weeks, armed troops stood guard at the school. Screaming crowds, encouraged by Faubus, menaced the black students, beat up two black reporters, and chanted "Two, four, six, eight, we ain't going to integrate." Moderate whites, such as *Arkansas Gazette* editor Harry Ashmore, opposed Faubus, fearing that his controversial tactics would make it harder to attract new businesses and investment capital to the city.

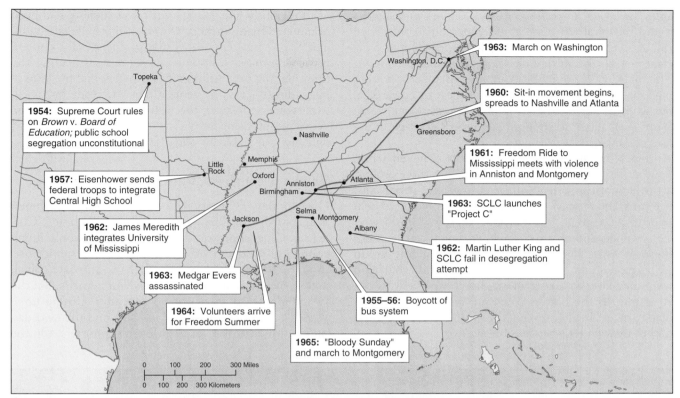

1963: March on Washington

1960: Sit-in movement begins, spreads to Nashville and Atlanta

1954: Supreme Court rules on *Brown* v. *Board of Education;* public school segregation unconstitutional

1961: Freedom Ride to Mississippi meets with violence in Anniston and Montgomery

1957: Eisenhower sends federal troops to integrate Central High School

1963: SCLC launches "Project C"

1962: James Meredith integrates University of Mississippi

1962: Martin Luther King and SCLC fail in desegregation attempt

1963: Medgar Evers assassinated

1955–56: Boycott of bus system

1964: Volunteers arrive for Freedom Summer

1965: "Bloody Sunday" and march to Montgomery

Map of the Civil Rights Movement   Key battlegrounds in the struggle for racial justice in communities across the South.

At first, President Eisenhower tried to intervene quietly, gaining Faubus's assurance that he would protect the nine black children. But when Faubus suddenly withdrew his troops, leaving the black students at the mercy of the white mob, Eisenhower had to move. On September 24 he placed the Arkansas National Guard under federal control and ordered a thousand paratroopers of the 101st Airborne Division to Little Rock. The nine black students arrived in a U.S. Army car. With fixed bayonets, the soldiers protected the students as they finally integrated Central High School in Little Rock. Eisenhower, the veteran military commander, justified his actions on the basis of upholding federal authority and enforcing the law. He also defended his intervention as crucial to national prestige abroad, noting the propaganda victory Faubus had handed to the Soviet bloc. "Our enemies," the President argued, "are gloating over this incident and using it everywhere to misrepresent our whole nation." But he made no endorsement of desegregation. Unfazed, Governor Faubus kept Little Rock high schools closed during the 1958–59 academic year to prevent what he called "violence and disorder."

NO EASY ROAD TO FREEDOM, 1957–62

Martin Luther King and the SCLC

The 381-day Montgomery bus boycott made Martin Luther King a prominent national figure. King himself was an extraordinary and complex man. Born in 1929 in Atlanta, he enjoyed a middle-class upbringing as the son of a prominent Baptist minister. As a graduate student, he was drawn to the social Christianity of American theologian Walter Rauschenbusch, who insisted on connecting religious faith with struggles for social justice. Above all, King admired Mohandas Gandhi, a lawyer turned ascetic who had led a successful nonviolent resistance movement against British colonial rule in India.

A unique blend of traditional African American folk preacher and erudite intellectual, King used his passion and intelligence to help transform a community's pain into a powerful moral force for change. He recognized the need to exploit the momentum of the Montgomery movement. In early 1957, with the help of Bayard Rustin of the War Resister's League and other aides, he brought together nearly 100 black ministers to found the Southern Christian Leadership Conference (SCLC). The clergymen elected King president and his close friend, the Reverend Ralph Abernathy, treasurer. The SCLC called upon black people "to understand that nonviolence is not a symbol of weakness or cowardice, but as Jesus demonstrated, nonviolent resistance transforms weakness into strength and breeds courage in the face of danger."

But King and other black leaders believed white Southerners could be divided roughly into three groups: a tiny minority—often with legal training, social connections, and money—that might be counted on to help overthrow segregation; extreme segregationists who were willing and able to use violence and terror in defense of white supremacy; and a broad middle group who favored and benefited from segregation, but who were unwilling to take personal risks to prevent its destruction. In the battles to come, civil rights leaders made this nuanced view of the white South a central part of their larger political strategy.

Previously, the struggle for racial equality had been dominated by a northern elite focusing on legal action. The SCLC now envisioned the southern black church, preaching massive nonviolent protest, as leading the fight. But the organization failed to generate the kind of mass, direct-action movement that had made history in Montgomery. Instead, the next great spark to light the fire of protest came from what seemed at the time a most unlikely source: black college students.

Sit-Ins: Greensboro, Nashville, Atlanta

On Monday, February 1, 1960, four black freshmen from North Carolina Agricultural and Technical College in Greensboro sat down at the whites-only lunch counter in Woolworth's. They were refused service. Although they could buy pencils or toothpaste, black people were not allowed to eat in Woolworth's. But the four students stayed at the counter until closing time. Word of their actions spread quickly, and the next day they returned with over two dozen supporters. On the

The second day of the sit-in at the Greensboro, North Carolina, Woolworth lunch counter, February 2, 1960. From left: Joseph McNeil, Franklin McCain, Billy Smith, and Clarence Henderson. The Greensboro protest sparked a wave of sit-ins across the South, mostly by college students, demanding an end to segregation in restaurants and other public places.

SOURCE: John G. Moebes/*News & Record Library.*

third day, students occupied sixty-three of the sixty-six lunch counter seats. By Thursday they had been joined by three white students from the Women's College of the University of North Carolina in Greensboro. Scores of sympathizers overflowed Woolworth's and started a sit-in down the street in S. H. Kress. On Friday hundreds of black students and a few whites jammed the lunch counters.

City officials, looking to end the protest, offered to negotiate in exchange for an end to demonstrations. But white business leaders and politicians proved unwilling to change the racial status quo, and the sit-ins resumed on April 1. In response to the April 21 arrest of forty-five students for trespassing, an outraged African American community organized an economic boycott of targeted stores. With the boycott cutting deeply into merchants' profits, Greensboro's leaders reluctantly gave in. On July 25, 1960, the first African American ate a meal at Woolworth's.

During the next eighteen months 70,000 people—most of them black students, a few of them white allies—participated in sit-ins against segregation in dozens of communities. More than 3,000 were arrested. African Americans had discovered a new form of direct-action protest, dignified and powerful, which white people could not ignore. The sit-in movement also transformed participants' self-image, empowering them psychologically and emotionally.

In Nashville, Reverend James Lawson, a northern-born black minister, had led workshops in nonviolent resistance since 1958. Lawson gathered around him a group of deeply committed black students from Nashville colleges who wanted to end segregation through Christian idealism and Gandhian principles. In the spring of 1960 more than 150 Nashville students were arrested in disciplined sit-ins aimed at desegregating downtown lunch counters, and Lawson found himself expelled from the divinity school at Vanderbilt. The Nashville group developed rules of conduct that became a model for protesters elsewhere: "Don't strike back or curse if abused. . . . Show yourself courteous and friendly at all times. . . . Report all serious incidents to your leader in a polite manner. Remember love and nonviolence."

The most ambitious sit-in campaign developed in Atlanta, the South's largest and richest city, home to the region's most powerful and prestigious black community. Led by Julian Bond and Lonnie King, the students formed the Committee on an Appeal for Human Rights. Over the summer they planned a fall campaign of large-scale sit-ins at major Atlanta department stores and a boycott of downtown merchants. Their slogan became "Close out your charge account with segregation, open up your account with freedom." In October 1960 Martin Luther King and thirty-six students were arrested when they sat down in the all-white Magnolia Room restaurant in Rich's Department Store. The campaign stretched on for months, and hundreds of protesters went to jail. The city's business leaders finally relented in September 1961, and desegregation came to Atlanta.

SNCC and the "Beloved Community"

The sit-in movement pumped new energy into the civil rights cause, creating a new generation of activists and leaders. Mass arrests, beatings, and vilification in the southern white press only strengthened the resolve of those in the movement. Students also had to deal with the fears of their families, many of whom had made great sacrifices to send them off to college.

The new student militancy also caused discord within black communities. The authority of local African American elites had traditionally depended on their influence and cooperation with the white establishment. Student calls for freedom disturbed many community leaders worried about upsetting traditional patronage networks. The president of Southern University in Baton Rouge, the largest black college in the nation, suspended eighteen sit-in leaders in 1960 and forced the entire student body of 5,000 to reapply to the college so that agitators could be screened out.

An April 1960 conference of 120 black student activists in Raleigh, North Carolina, underlined the generational and radical aspects of the new movement. The meeting had been called by Ella Baker, executive director of the SCLC. For years Baker had played an important behind-the-scenes role in the civil rights cause, serving as a community organizer and field secretary for the NAACP before heading the staff of the SCLC. She understood the psychological importance of the students' remaining independent of adult control and encouraged the trend toward group-centered leadership among the students. With Baker's encouragement, the conference voted to establish a new group, the Student Nonviolent Coordinating Committee (SNCC).

SNCC's emphasis was on fighting segregation through direct confrontation, mass action, and civil disobedience. SNCC fieldworkers initiated and supported local, community-based activity. Three-quarters of the first fieldworkers were less than twenty-two years old. Leadership was vested in a nonhierarchical Coordinating Committee, but local groups were free to determine their own direction. SNCC people distrusted bureaucracy and structure; they stressed spontaneity and improvisation. Over the next few years SNCC was at the forefront of nearly every major civil rights battle.

The Election of 1960 and Civil Rights

The issue of race relations was kept from center stage during the very close presidential campaign of 1960. As vice president, Richard Nixon had been a leading Republican voice for stronger civil rights legislation. In contrast, Democratic nominee Senator John F. Kennedy had played virtually no role in the congressional battles over civil rights during the 1950s. But during the campaign, their roles reversed. Kennedy praised the sit-in movement as part of a revival of national reform spirit. He declared, "It is in the American tradition to stand up for one's rights—even if the new way is to sit down." While the Republican platform contained a strong civil rights plank, Nixon, eager to court white southern voters, minimized his own identification with the movement. In October, when Martin Luther King, Jr. was jailed after leading a demonstration in Atlanta, Kennedy telephoned King's wife, Coretta Scott King, to reassure her and express his personal support. Kennedy's brother Robert telephoned the judge in the case and angrily warned him that he had violated King's civil rights and endangered the national Democratic ticket. The judge released King soon afterward.

News of this intervention did not gain wide attention in the white South, much to the relief of the Kennedys. The race was tight, and they knew they could not afford to alienate traditional white southern Democrats. But the campaign effectively played up the story among black voters all over the country. Kennedy won 70 percent of the black vote, which helped put him over the top in such critical states as Illinois, Texas, Michigan, and Pennsylvania and secure his narrow victory over Nixon. Many civil rights activists optimistically looked forward to a new president who would have to acknowledge his political debt to the black vote.

But the very closeness of his victory constrained Kennedy on the race question. Democrats had lost ground in the House and Senate, and Kennedy had to worry about alienating conservative southern Democrats who chaired key congressional committees. Passage of major civil rights legislation would be virtually impossible. The new president told leaders such as Roy Wilkins of the NAACP that a strategy of "minimum legislation, maximum executive action" offered the best road to change. The president did appoint some forty African Americans to high federal positions, including Thurgood Marshall to the federal appellate court. He established a Committee on Equal Employment Opportunity, chaired by Vice President Lyndon B. Johnson, to fight discrimination in the federal civil service and in corporations that received government contracts.

Most significantly, the Kennedy administration sought to invigorate the Civil Rights Division of the Justice Department. Robert Kennedy, the new attorney general, began assembling a staff of brilliant and committed attorneys, headed by Washington lawyer Burke Marshall. Kennedy encouraged them to get out of Washington and get into the field wherever racial troubles arose. In early 1961, when Louisiana school officials balked at a school desegregation order, Robert Kennedy warned them that he would ask the federal court to hold them in contempt. When Burke Marshall started court proceedings, the state officials gave in. But the new, more aggressive mood at Justice could not solve the central political dilemma: how to move forward on civil rights without alienating southern Democrats. Pressure from the newly energized southern civil rights movement soon revealed the true difficulty of that problem.

A Freedom Riders' bus burns after being firebombed in Anniston, Alabama, May 14, 1961. After setting the bus afire, whites attacked the passengers fleeing the smoke and flames. Violent scenes like this one received extensive publicity in the mass media and helped compel the Justice Department to enforce court rulings banning segregation on interstate bus lines.

SOURCE: UPI/CORBIS.

Freedom Rides

In the spring of 1961 James Farmer, national director of CORE, announced plans for an interracial Freedom Ride through the South. The goal was to test compliance with court orders banning segregation in interstate travel and terminal accommodations. CORE had just recently made Farmer its leader in an effort to revitalize the organization. He designed the Freedom Ride to induce a crisis, in the spirit of the sit-ins. "Our intention," Farmer declared, "was to provoke the southern authorities into arresting us and thereby prod the Justice Department into enforcing the law of the land." CORE informed the Justice Department and the Federal Bureau of Investigation of its plans, but received no reply.

On May 4 seven blacks and six whites split into two interracial groups and left Washington on public buses bound for Alabama and Mississippi. At first the two buses encountered only isolated harassment and violence as they headed south. But when one bus entered Anniston, Alabama, on May 14, an angry mob surrounded it, smashing windows and slashing tires. Six miles out of town, the tires went flat. A firebomb tossed through a window forced the passengers out. The mob then beat the Freedom Riders with blackjacks, iron bars, and clubs, and the bus burst into flames. A caravan of cars organized by the Birmingham office of the SCLC rescued the wounded. Another mob attacked the second bus in Anniston, leaving one Freedom Rider close to death and permanently brain-damaged.

In Birmingham, a mob of forty whites waited on the loading platform and attacked the bus that managed to get out of Anniston. Although police had been warned to expect trouble, they did nothing to stop the mob from beating the Freedom Riders with pipes and fists, nor did they make any arrests. FBI agents observed and took notes but did nothing. The remaining Freedom Riders decided to travel as a single group on the next lap, from Birmingham to Montgomery, but no bus would take them. Stranded and frightened, they reluctantly boarded a special flight to New Orleans arranged by the Justice Department. On May 17 the CORE-sponsored Freedom Ride disbanded.

But that was not the end of the Freedom Rides. SNCC leaders in Atlanta and Nashville assembled a fresh group of volunteers to continue the trip. On May 20, twenty-one Freedom Riders left Birmingham for Montgomery. The bus station in the Alabama capital was eerily quiet and deserted as they pulled in. But when the passengers left the bus a mob of several hundred whites rushed them, yelling "Get those niggers!" and clubbing people to the ground. As John Lewis, veteran of the Nashville sit-in movement, lay in a pool of blood, a policeman handed him a state court injunction forbidding interracial travel in Alabama. The mob indiscriminately beat journalists and clubbed John Siegenthaler, a Justice Department attorney sent to observe the scene.

The mob violence and the indifference of Alabama officials made the Freedom Ride page-one news around the country and throughout the world. The Kennedy administration, preparing for the president's first summit meeting with Soviet premier Nikita Khrushchev, saw the situation as a threat to its international prestige. The attorney general called for a cooling-off period, but Martin Luther King, Jr., James Farmer, and the SNCC leaders announced that the Freedom Ride would continue. When Robert Kennedy warned that the racial turmoil would embarrass the president in his meeting with Khrushchev, Ralph Abernathy of the SCLC replied, "Doesn't the attorney general know that we've been embarrassed all our lives?"

A bandaged but spirited group of twenty-seven Freedom Riders prepared to leave Montgomery for Jackson, Mississippi, on May 24. To avoid further violence Robert Kennedy arranged a compromise through Mississippi senator James Eastland. In exchange for a guarantee of safe passage through Mississippi, the federal government promised not to interfere with the arrest of the Freedom Riders in Jackson. This Freedom Ride and several that followed thus escaped violence. But more than 300 people were arrested that summer. Sticking to a policy of "jail, no bail," Freedom Riders clogged the prison, where they endured beatings and intimidation by prison guards that went largely unreported in the press. Their jail experiences turned most of them into committed core leaders of the student movement.

The Justice Department eventually petitioned the Interstate Commerce Commission to issue clear rules prohibiting segregation on interstate carriers. By creating a crisis, the Freedom Rides had forced the Kennedy administration to act. The Freedom Rides exposed the ugly face of southern racism to the world. At the same time, they reinforced white resistance to desegregation. The jailings and brutality experienced by Freedom Riders made clear to the civil rights community the limits of moral suasion alone for effecting change.

The Albany Movement: The Limits of Protest

Where the federal government chose not to enforce the constitutional rights of black people, segregationist forces tenaciously held their ground, especially in the more remote areas of the Deep South. In Albany, a small city in southwest Georgia, activists from SNCC, the NAACP, and other local groups formed a coalition known as the Albany movement. Starting in October

1961 and continuing for more than a year, thousands of Albany's black citizens marched, sat in, and boycotted as part of a citywide campaign to integrate public facilities and win voting rights. More than a thousand people spent time in jail. In December, the arrival of Martin Luther King, Jr. and the SCLC transformed Albany into a national symbol of the struggle.

But the gains at Albany proved minimal. Albany police chief Laurie Pritchett shrewdly deprived the movement of the kind of national sympathy won by the Freedom Riders. Pritchett filled the jails with black demonstrators, kept their mistreatment to a minimum, and prevented white mobs from running wild. "We met 'nonviolence' with 'nonviolence,'" he boasted.

By late 1962 the Albany movement had collapsed, and Pritchett proudly declared the city "as segregated as ever." One activist summed up the losing campaign: "We ran out of people before he ran out of jails." Albany showed that mass protest without violent white reaction and direct federal intervention could not end Jim Crow.

In the fall of 1962 James Meredith, an air force veteran, tried to register as the first black student at the University of Mississippi. Governor Ross Barnett defied a federal court order and personally blocked Meredith's path at the admissions office. When Barnett refused to assure Robert Kennedy that Meredith would be protected, the attorney general dispatched 500 federal marshals to the campus. Over the radio, Barnett encouraged resistance to the "oppressive power of the United States," and an angry mob of several thousand whites, many of them armed, laid siege to the campus on September 30. A night of violence left 2 people dead and 160 marshals wounded, 28 from gunfire. President Kennedy ordered 5,000 army troops onto the campus to stop the riot. A federal guard remained to protect Meredith, who graduated the following summer.

THE MOVEMENT AT HIGH TIDE, 1963–65

Birmingham

At the end of 1962, Martin Luther King, Jr. and his SCLC allies decided to launch a new campaign against segregation in Birmingham, Alabama. After the failure in Albany, King and his aides looked for a way to shore up his leadership and inject new momentum into the freedom struggle.

Working closely with local civil rights groups led by the longtime Birmingham activist Reverend Fred Shuttlesworth, the SCLC carefully planned its campaign. The strategy was to fill the city jails with protest-ers, boycott downtown department stores, and enrage Public Safety Commissioner Eugene "Bull" Connor. In April, King arrived with a manifesto demanding an end to racist hiring practices and segregated public accommodations and the creation of a biracial committee to oversee desegregation. Connor's police began jailing hundreds of demonstrators, including King himself, who defied a state court injunction against further protests.

Held in solitary confinement for several days, King managed to write a response to a group of Birmingham clergy who had deplored the protests. King's *Letter from Birmingham Jail* was soon widely reprinted and circulated as a pamphlet. It set out the key moral issues at stake, and scoffed at those who claimed the campaign was illegal and ill timed. King wrote:

> We know through painful experience that freedom is never voluntarily given by the oppressor; it must be demanded by the oppressed. . . . For years now I have heard the word "Wait!" It rings in the ear of every Negro with a piercing familiarity. This "Wait" has almost always meant "Never."

After King's release on bail, the campaign intensified. In early May, Bull Connor's forces began using high-powered water cannons, billy clubs, and snarling police dogs to break up demonstrations. Millions of Americans reacted with horror to the violent scenes from Birmingham shown on national television. Many younger black people, especially from the city's poor and working-class districts, began to fight back, hurling bottles and bricks at police. On May 10, mediators from the Justice Department negotiated an uneasy truce. The SCLC agreed to an immediate end to the protests. In exchange, businesses would desegregate and begin hiring African Americans over the next three months, and a biracial city committee would oversee desegregation of public facilities.

King claimed the events in Birmingham represented "the most magnificent victory for justice we've ever seen in the Deep South." But whites such as Bull Connor and Governor George Wallace denounced the agreement. When bombs rocked SCLC headquarters and the home of King's brother, a Birmingham minister, enraged blacks took to the streets and pelted police and firefighters with stones and bottles. President Kennedy ordered 3,000 army troops into the city and prepared to nationalize the Alabama National Guard. The violence receded, and white business people and politicians began to carry out the agreed-upon pact. But in September a bomb killed four black girls in a Birmingham Baptist church, reminding the city and the world that racial harmony was still a long way off.

The civil rights community now drew support from millions of Americans, black and white, who were inspired by the protesters and repelled by the face of southern bigotry. At the same time, Birmingham changed the nature of black protest. The black unemployed and working poor who joined in the struggle brought a different perspective from that of the students, professionals, and members of the religious middle class who had dominated the movement before Birmingham. They cared less about the philosophy of nonviolence and more about immediate gains in employment and housing and an end to police brutality. "Freedom now!" they cried.

JFK and the March on Washington

The growth of black activism and white support convinced President Kennedy the moment had come to press for sweeping civil rights legislation. In June 1963, Alabama governor George Wallace threatened to personally block the admission of two black students to the state university. Only the deployment of National Guard troops, placed under federal control by the president, ensured the students' safety and their peaceful admission into the University of Alabama.

It was a defining moment for Kennedy. On June 11 the president went on national television and offered his personal endorsement of the civil rights activism. "Today we are committed to a worldwide struggle to promote and protect the rights of all who wish to be free. And when Americans are sent to Vietnam or West Berlin, we do not ask for whites only . . . Are we to say to the rest of the world, and much more importantly, to each other, that this is a land of the free except for Negroes?" Reviewing the racial situation, Kennedy told his audience that "We face . . . a moral crisis as a country and a people. . . . It is a time to act in the Congress, in your state and local legislative body, and, above all, in all our daily lives." The next week Kennedy asked Congress for a broad law that would ensure voting rights, outlaw segregation in public facilities, and bolster federal authority to deny funds for discriminatory programs.

Movement leaders lauded the president's initiative. Yet they understood that racial hatred still haunted the nation. Only a few hours after Kennedy's television speech, a gunman murdered Medgar Evers, leader of the Mississippi NAACP, outside his home in Jackson, Mississippi. To pressure Congress and demonstrate the urgency of their cause, a broad coalition of civil rights groups planned a massive, nonviolent March on Washington.

The Kennedy administration originally opposed the march, fearing it would jeopardize support for the president's civil rights bill in Congress. But as plans for the

rally solidified, Kennedy reluctantly gave his approval. Leaders from the SCLC, the NAACP, SNCC, the Urban League, and CORE—the leading organizations in the civil rights community—put aside their tactical differences to forge a broad consensus for the event. John Lewis, the young head of SNCC, who had endured numerous brutal assaults, planned a speech that denounced the Kennedys as hypocrites. Randolph, the acknowledged elder statesman of the movement, convinced Lewis at the last moment to tone down his remarks. "We've come this far," he implored. "For the sake of unity, change it."

On August 28, 1963, more than a quarter of a million people, including 50,000 whites, gathered at the Lincoln Memorial to rally for "jobs and freedom." Americans from all walks of life joined the largest political assembly in the nation's history until then. At the end of a long, exhilarating day of speeches and freedom

Reverend Dr. Martin Luther King, Jr., acknowledging the huge throng at the historic March on Washington for "jobs and freedom," August 28, 1963. The size of the crowd, the stirring oratory and song, and the live network television coverage produced one of the most memorable political events in the nation's history.

SOURCE: AP/Wide World Photos.

songs, Martin Luther King, Jr. stirred the crowd with his dream for America:

> I have a dream today that one day this nation will rise up and live out the true meaning of its creed: "We hold these truths to be self-evident—that all men are created equal." . . . When we allow freedom to ring, when we let it ring from every village and every hamlet, from every state and every city, we will be able to speed up that day when all of God's children—black men and white men, Jews and Gentiles, Protestants and Catholics—will be able to join hands and sing in the words of the old Negro spiritual, "Free at last! Free at last! Thank God Almighty, we are free at last!"

LBJ and the Civil Rights Act of 1964

An extraordinary demonstration of interracial unity, the March on Washington stood as the high-water mark in the struggle for civil rights. But the assassination of John F. Kennedy on November 22, 1963, in Dallas threw an ominous cloud over the whole nation and the civil rights movement in particular. In the Deep South, many ardent segregationists welcomed the president's death because of his support for civil rights.

Lyndon Baines Johnson, Kennedy's successor, had never been much of a friend to civil rights. Johnson had built a career as one of the shrewdest and most powerful Democrats in Congress. Throughout the 1950s he had worked to obstruct the passage and enforcement of civil rights laws—though as vice president he had ably chaired Kennedy's working group on equal employment. Civil rights activists looked upon Johnson warily as he took over the Oval Office.

As president, Johnson realized that he faced a new political reality, one created by the civil rights movement. Eager to unite the Democratic Party and prove himself as a national leader, he seized on civil rights as a golden political opportunity. Throughout the early months of 1964, the new president let it be known publicly and privately that he would brook no compromise on civil rights.

Johnson exploited all his skills as a political insider. He cajoled, flattered, and threatened key members of the House and Senate. Working with the president, the fifteen-year-old Leadership Conference on Civil Rights coordinated a sophisticated lobbying effort in Congress. The House passed the bill in February by a 290–130 vote. The more difficult fight would be in the Senate, where a southern filibuster promised to block the bill or weaken it. But by June, Johnson's persistence had paid off and the southern filibuster had collapsed.

On July 2, 1964, Johnson signed the Civil Rights Act of 1964. Every major provision had survived intact.

This landmark law represented the most significant civil rights legislation since Reconstruction. It prohibited discrimination in most places of public accommodation; outlawed discrimination in employment on the basis of race, color, religion, sex, or national origin; outlawed bias in federally assisted programs; authorized the Justice Department to institute suits to desegregate public schools and other facilities; created the Equal Employment Opportunity Commission; and provided technical and financial aid to communities desegregating their schools.

Mississippi Freedom Summer

While President Johnson and his liberal allies won the congressional battle for the new civil rights bill, activists in Mississippi mounted a far more radical and dangerous campaign than any yet attempted in the South. In the spring of 1964, a coalition of workers led by SNCC launched the Freedom Summer project, an ambitious effort to register black voters and directly challenge the iron rule of segregation. Mississippi stood as the toughest test for the civil rights movement, racially and economically. It was the poorest, most backward state in the nation, and had remained largely untouched by the freedom struggle. African Americans constituted 42 percent of the state's population, but fewer than 5 percent could register to vote. Median black family income was under $1,500 a year, roughly one-third that of white families. A small white planter elite controlled most of the state's wealth, and a long tradition of terror against black people had maintained the racial caste system.

Bob Moses of SNCC and Dave Dennis of CORE planned Freedom Summer as a way of opening up this closed society to the glare of national publicity. The project recruited over 900 volunteers, mostly white college students, to aid in voter registration, teach in "freedom schools," and help build a "freedom party" as an alternative to Mississippi's all-white Democratic Party. Organizers expected violence, which was precisely why they wanted white volunteers. Dave Dennis later explained their reasoning: "The death of a white college student would bring on more attention to what was going on than for a black college student getting it."

The predictions of violence proved accurate. On June 21, while most project volunteers were still undergoing training in Ohio, three activists disappeared in Neshoba County, Mississippi, when they went to investigate the burning of a black church that was supposed to serve as a freedom school. Six weeks later, after a massive search belatedly ordered by President Johnson, FBI agents discovered the bodies of the three—white activists Michael Schwerner and Andrew Goodman, and a local black activist, James Chaney—buried in an earthen dam. Goodman and Schwerner

OVERVIEW

LANDMARK CIVIL RIGHTS LEGISLATION, SUPREME COURT DECISIONS, AND EXECUTIVE ORDERS

Year	Decision, law, or executive order	Significance
1939	*Missouri v. ex.rel.Gaines*	Required University of Missouri Law School either to admit African Americans or build another fully equal law school
1941	Executive Order 8802 (by President Roosevelt)	Banned racial discrimination in defense industry and government offices; established Fair Employment Practices Committee to investigate violations
1946	*Morgan v. Virginia*	Ruled that segregation on interstate buses violated federal law and created an "undue burden" on interstate commerce
1948	Executive Order 9981 (by President Truman)	Desegregated the U.S. armed forces
1950	*McLaurin v. Oklahoma State Regents*	Ruled that forcing an African American student to sit, eat, and study in segregated facilities was unconstitutional because it inevitably created a "badge of inferiority"
1950	*Sweatt v. Painter*	Ruled that an inferior law school created by the University of Texas to serve African Americans violated their right to equal protection and ordered Herman Sweatt to be admitted to University of Texas Law School
1954	*Brown v. Board of Education of Topeka I*	Declared "separate educational facilities are inherently unequal," thus overturning *Plessy v. Ferguson* (1896) and the "separate but equal" doctrine as it applied to public schools
1955	*Brown v. Board of Education of Topeka II*	Ordered school desegregation to begin with "all deliberate speed," but offered no timetable
1957	Civil Rights Act	Created Civil Rights Division within the Justice Department
1964	Civil Rights Act	Prohibited discrimination in employment and most places of public accommodation on basis of race, color, religion, sex, or national origin; outlawed bias in federally assisted programs; created Equal Employment Opportunity Commission
1965	Voting Rights Act	Authorized federal supervision of voter registration in states and counties where fewer than half of voting age residents were registered; outlawed literacy and other discriminatory tests in voter registration

had been shot once; Chaney had been severely beaten before being shot three times. Over the summer, at least three other civil rights workers died violently. Project workers suffered 1,000 arrests, 80 beatings, 35 shooting incidents, and 30 bombings in homes, churches, and schools.

Within the project, there were simmering problems. Black veterans of SNCC resented the affluent white volunteers, many of whom had not come to terms with their own racial prejudices. Sexual tensions between black male and white female volunteers also strained relations. A number of black and white

women, began to raise the issue of women's equality as a companion goal to racial equality. The day-to-day reality of violent reprisals, police harassment, and constant fear took a hard toll on everyone.

The project did manage to rivet national attention on Mississippi racism, and it got 60,000 black voters signed up to join the Mississippi Freedom Democratic Party (MFDP). In August 1964 the MFDP sent a slate of delegates to the Democratic National Convention looking to challenge the credentials of the all-white regular state delegation. Lyndon Johnson opposed the seating of the MFDP because he wanted to avoid a divisive floor fight. He was already concerned that Republicans might carry a number of southern states in November. But MFDP leaders and sympathizers gave dramatic testimony before the convention, detailing the racism and brutality in Mississippi politics. "Is this America," asked Fannie Lou Hamer, "the land of the free and the home of the brave, where we are threatened daily because we want to live as decent human beings?" Led by vice presidential nominee Senator Hubert Humphrey, Johnson's forces offered a compromise that would have given the MFDP a token two seats on the floor. Bitter over what they saw as a betrayal, the MFDP delegates turned the offer down. Within SNCC, the defeat of the MFDP intensified African American disillusionment with the Democratic Party and the liberal establishment.

Malcolm X and Black Consciousness

Frustrated with the limits of nonviolent protest and electoral politics, younger activists within SNCC found themselves increasingly drawn to the militant rhetoric and vision of Malcolm X, who since 1950 had been the preeminent spokesman for the black nationalist religious sect, the Nation of Islam (NOI). Founded in Depression-era Detroit by Elijah Muhammad, the NOI, like the followers of black nationalist leader Marcus Garvey in the 1920s (see Chapter 23) aspired to create a self-reliant, highly disciplined, and proud community—a separate "nation" for black people. During the 1950s the NOI (also called Black Muslims) successfully organized in northern black communities. It operated restaurants, retail stores, and schools as models for black economic self-sufficiency.

The man known as Malcolm X had been born Malcolm Little in 1925 and raised in Lansing, Michigan. His father, a preacher and a follower of Marcus Garvey, was killed in a racist attack by local whites. In his youth, Malcolm led a life of petty crime, eventually serving a seven-year prison term for burglary. While in jail he educated himself and converted to the Nation of Islam. He took the surname "X" to symbolize his original African family name, lost through slavery. Emerging from jail in 1952, he became a dynamic organizer, editor, and speaker for the Nation of Islam. He encouraged his audiences to take pride in their African heritage and to consider armed self-defense rather than relying solely on nonviolence.

Malcolm ridiculed the integrationist goals of the civil rights movement. Black Muslims, he told audiences, do not want "to integrate into this corrupt society, but to separate from it, to a land of our own, where we can reform ourselves, lift up our moral standards, and try to be godly." In his best-selling *Autobiography of Malcolm X* (1965), he admitted that his position was extremist. "The black race here in North America is in extremely bad condition. You show me a black man who isn't an extremist," he argued, "and I'll show you one who needs psychiatric attention."

In 1964, troubled by Elijah Muhammad's personal scandals (he faced paternity suits brought by two young female employees) and eager to find a more politically effective approach to improving conditions for blacks, Malcolm X broke with the Nation of Islam. He made a pilgrimage to Mecca, the Muslim holy city, where he met Islamic peoples of all colors and underwent a "radical alteration in my whole outlook about 'white' men." He returned to the United States as El-Hajj Malik El-Shabazz, abandoned his black separatist views, and founded the Organization of Afro-American Unity.

On February 21, 1965, Malcolm X was assassinated during a speech at Harlem's Audubon Ballroom. His assailants were members of a New Jersey branch of the NOI, possibly infiltrated by the FBI. "More than any other person," remarked black author Julius Lester, "Malcolm X was responsible for the new militancy that entered The Movement in 1965." SNCC leader John Lewis thought Malcolm had been the most effective voice "to articulate the aspirations, bitterness, and frustrations of the Negro people," forming "a living link between Africa and the civil rights movement in this country." As much as anyone, Malcolm X pointed the way to a new black consciousness that celebrated black history, black culture, the African heritage, and black self-sufficiency.

Selma and the Voting Rights Act of 1965

Lyndon Johnson won reelection in 1964 by a landslide, capturing 61 percent of the popular vote. Of the 6 million black people who voted in the election, 2 million more than in 1960, an overwhelming 94 percent cast their ballots for Johnson. With Democrats in firm control of both the Senate and the House, Johnson and his staff began drafting a tough voting rights bill in late 1964, partly with an eye toward countering Republican gains in the Deep South with newly registered black and Democratic voters. Martin Luther King and the SCLC shared this goal of passing a strong voting rights law that would provide southern black people with direct federal protection of their right to vote.

Once again, movement leaders plotted to create a crisis that would arouse national indignation, pressure Congress, and force federal action. Selma, Alabama, because of its notorious record of preventing black voting, was selected as the target. Sensing that county sheriff Jim Clark might be another Bull Connor, King arrived in Selma in January 1965, just after accepting the Nobel Peace Prize in Oslo. King, the SCLC staff, and SNCC workers led daily marches on the Dallas County Courthouse, where hundreds of black citizens tried to get their names added to voter lists. By early February, Clark had imprisoned more than 3,000 protesters.

Despite the brutal beating of Reverend James Bevel, a key SCLC strategist, and the killing of Jimmy Lee Jackson, a young black demonstrator in nearby Marion, the SCLC failed to arouse the level of national indignation it sought. Consequently, in early March SCLC staffers called on black activists to march from Selma to Montgomery, where they planned to deliver a list of grievances to Governor Wallace. On Sunday, March 7, while King preached to his church in Atlanta, a group of 600 marchers crossed the Pettus Bridge on the Alabama River, on their way to Montgomery. A group of mounted, heavily armed county and state lawmen blocked their path and ordered them to turn back. When the marchers did not move, the lawmen attacked with billy clubs and tear gas, driving the protesters back over the bridge in a bloody rout. More than fifty marchers had to be treated in local hospitals.

The dramatic "Bloody Sunday" attack received extensive coverage on network television, prompting a national uproar. Demands for federal intervention poured into the White House from all over the country. King issued a public call for civil rights supporters to come to Selma for a second march on Montgomery. But a federal court temporarily enjoined the SCLC from proceeding with the march. King found himself trapped. He reluctantly accepted a face-saving compromise: in return for a promise from Alabama authorities not to harm marchers, King would lead his followers across the Pettus Bridge, stop, pray briefly, and then turn back. This plan outraged the more militant SNCC activists and sharpened their distrust of King and the SCLC.

But just when it seemed the Selma movement might die, white racist violence revived it. A gang of white toughs attacked four white Unitarian ministers who had come to Selma to participate in the march. One of them, Reverend James J. Reeb of Boston, died of multiple skull fractures. His death brought new calls for federal action. On March 15, President Johnson delivered a televised address to a joint session of Congress to request passage of a voting rights bill. In a stirring speech, the president fused the political power of his office with the moral power of the movement. "Their cause must be our cause, too. Because it is not just Negroes, but really all of us who must overcome the crippling legacy of bigotry and injustice. And," he concluded firmly, invoking the movement's slogan, "we shall overcome." Johnson also prevailed upon federal judge Frank Johnson to issue a ruling allowing the march to proceed, and he warned Governor Wallace not to interfere.

On March 21 Martin Luther King led a group of more than 3,000 black and white marchers out of Selma

Voting rights demonstrators rallied in front of the state capitol in Montgomery, Alabama, March 25, 1965, after a four day, fifty-four-mile trek from Selma. The original 3,000 marchers were joined by over 30,000 supporters by the end of their journey.
SOURCE: 2001 © Matt Herron c/o Mira.com.

on the road to Montgomery. Four days later they arrived at the Alabama statehouse. Their ranks had been swelled by more than 30,000 supporters, including hundreds of prominent politicians, entertainers, and black leaders.

In August 1965 President Johnson signed the Voting Rights Act into law. It authorized federal supervision of registration in states and counties where fewer than half of voting-age residents were registered. It also outlawed literacy and other discriminatory tests that had been used to prevent blacks from registering to vote. Between 1964 and 1968, black registrants in Mississippi leaped from 7 percent to 59 percent of the statewide black population; in Alabama, from 24 percent to 57 percent. In those years the number of southern black voters grew from 1 million to 3.1 million. For the first time in their lives, black Southerners in hundreds of small towns and rural

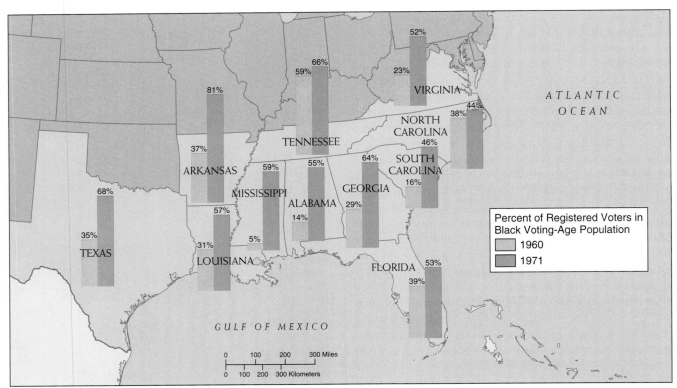

Impact of the Voting Rights Act of 1965 Voter registration among African Americans in the South increased significantly between 1960 and 1971.

communities could enjoy full participation in American politics. Ten years after the Montgomery bus boycott, the civil rights movement had reached a peak of national influence and interracial unity.

FORGOTTEN MINORITIES, 1945–65

The historic injustices of slavery, racism, and segregation gave a moral and political urgency to the black struggle for full citizenship rights. Yet other minorities as well had long been denied their civil rights. After World War II, Latinos, Indian peoples, and Asian Americans began making their own halting efforts to improve their political, legal, and economic status. By the late 1960s, the success of the black civil rights movement had inspired these minority groups to adopt more militant strategies of their own.

Mexican Americans

The Mexican American community in the West and Southwest included both longtime U.S. citizens—who found white authorities nonetheless unwilling to recognize their rights—and noncitizen immigrants

from Mexico. After World War II, several Mexican American political organizations sought to secure equal rights and equal opportunity for their community by stressing its American identity. The most important of these groups were the League of United Latin American Citizens (LULAC), founded in Texas in 1928, and the G.I. Forum, founded in Texas in 1948 by Mexican American veterans of World War II. Both emphasized the learning of English, assimilation into American society, improved education, and the promotion of political power through voting. LULAC successfully pursued two important legal cases that anticipated *Brown* v. *Board of Education*. In *Mendez* v. *Westminster*, a 1947 California case, and in the 1948 *Delgado* case in Texas, the Supreme Court upheld lower-court rulings that declared segregation of Mexican Americans unconstitutional. LULAC won another significant legal battle in the 1954 *Hernandez* decision, in which the Supreme Court ended the exclusion of Mexican Americans from Texas jury lists.

Mexican migration to the United States increased dramatically during and after World War II. The *bracero* program, a cooperative effort between the U.S. and Mexican governments, brought some 300,000 Mexicans to the United States during the war as temporary agricultural and railroad workers. American agribusiness came to depend on Mexicans as a key source of cheap farm labor, and the program continued after the war. Most braceros endured harsh work, poor food, and substandard housing in the camps in which they lived. Some migrated into the newly emerging barrio neighborhoods in cities such as San Antonio, Los Angeles, El Paso, and Denver. Many braceros and their children became American citizens, but most returned to Mexico. Another group of postwar Mexican immigrants were the *mojados*, or "wetbacks," so called because many swam across the Rio Grande River to enter the United States illegally.

In 1954, in an effort to curb the flow of undocumented immigrants from Mexico, the Eisenhower administration launched the massive "Operation Wetback." Over the next three years Immigration Service agents rounded up some 3.7 million allegedly illegal migrants and sent them back over the border. Immigration agents made little effort to distinguish the so-called illegals from braceros and Mexican American citizens. Many families were broken up, and thousands who had lived in the United States for a decade or more found themselves deported. Many deportees were denied basic civil liberties, such as due process, and suffered physical abuse and intimidation. Among Mexican Americans, Operation Wetback left a bitter legacy of deep mistrust and estrangement from Anglo culture and politics.

Puerto Ricans

The United States took possession of the island of Puerto Rico in 1898, during the final stages of the Spanish-American War. The Jones Act of 1917 made the island an unincorporated territory of the United States and granted U.S. citizenship to all Puerto Ricans. Over the next several decades, Puerto Rico's economic base shifted from a diversified, subsistence-oriented agriculture to a single export crop—sugar. U.S. absentee owners dominated the sugar industry. Puerto Rico's sugar industry grew enormously profitable, but few island residents benefited from this expansion. By the 1930s, unemployment and poverty were widespread and the island was forced to import its foodstuffs.

Small communities of Puerto Rican migrants had begun to form in New York City during the 1920s. The largest was on the Upper East Side of Manhattan—*el barrio* in East Harlem. During the World War II, labor shortages led the federal government to sponsor the recruitment of Puerto Rican workers for industrial jobs in New Jersey, Philadelphia, and Chicago. But the "great migration" took place from 1945 to 1964.

The advent of direct air service between Puerto Rico and New York in 1945 made the city easily accessible. By 1970 there were about 800,000 Puerto Ricans in New York—more than 10 percent of the city's population. New Puerto Rican communities also took root in Connecticut, Massachusetts, New Jersey, and the Midwest.

George Gillette (left foreground), chairman of the Fort Berthold Indian Council, wept as Secretary of Interior J. A. Krug signed a contract buying 155,000 acres of the tribe's best land in North Dakota for a reservoir project, May 20, 1948. "The members of the tribal council sign this contract with heavy hearts," Gillette said.

SOURCE: CORBIS.

The experience of Puerto Rican migrants both resembled and differed from that of other immigrant groups in significant ways. Like Mexican immigrants, Puerto Ricans were foreign in language, culture, and experience, yet unlike them they entered the United States as citizens. In New York, Puerto Ricans found themselves barred from most craft unions, excluded from certain neighborhoods, and forced to take jobs largely in the low-paying garment industry and service trades. Puerto Rican children were not well served by a public school system insensitive to language differences and too willing to track Spanish-speaking students into obsolete vocational programs.

By the early 1970s, Puerto Rican families were substantially poorer on average than the total population of the country, and they had the lowest median income of any Latino groups. The steep decline in manufacturing jobs and in the garment industry in New York during the 1960s and 1970s hit the Puerto Rican community especially hard. So did the city's fiscal crisis, which brought sharp cuts in funding for schools, health care, libraries, government jobs, and other public services traditionally available to immigrant groups. The structural shift in the U.S. economy away from manufacturing and toward service and high-technology jobs reinforced the Puerto Rican community's goal of improving educational opportunities for its members. The struggle to establish and improve bilingual education in schools became an important part of this effort.

Indian Peoples

The postwar years also brought significant changes in the status and lives of Indian peoples. Congress reversed the policies pursued under the New Deal, which had stressed Indian sovereignty and cultural independence. Responding to a variety of pressure groups, including mining and other economic interests wishing to exploit the resources on Indian reservations, Congress adopted a policy known as "termination," designed to cancel Indian treaties and terminate sovereignty rights. In 1953, Congress passed House Concurrent Resolution 108, which allowed Congress to terminate a tribe as a political entity by passing legislation specific to that tribe. Supporters of termination had varied motives, but the policy added up to the return of enforced assimilation for solving the "Indian problem."

Between 1954 and 1962, Congress passed twelve termination bills covering more than sixty tribes, nearly all in the West. Even when tribes consented to their own termination, they discovered that dissolution brought unforeseen problems. For example, members of the Klamaths of Oregon and the Paiutes of Utah received large cash payments from the division of tribal assets. But after these one-time payments were spent, members had to take poorly paid, unskilled jobs to survive. Many Indian peoples became dependent on state social services and slipped into poverty and alcoholism.

Along with termination, the federal government gave greater emphasis to a relocation program aimed at speeding up assimilation. The Bureau of Indian Affairs encouraged reservation Indians to relocate to cities, where they were provided housing and jobs. For some, relocation meant assimilation, intermarriage with whites, and the loss of tribal identity. Others, homesick and unable to adjust to an alien culture and place, either returned to reservations or wound up on the margins of city life.

By the early 1960s, a new movement was emerging to defend Indian sovereignty. The National Congress of American Indians (NCAI) condemned termination, calling for a review of federal policies and a return to self-determination. The NCAI led a political and educational campaign that challenged the goal of assimilation and created a new awareness among white people that Indians had the right to remain Indians. When the termination policy ended in the early 1960s, it had affected only about 3 percent of federally recognized Indian peoples.

Taking their cue from the civil rights movement, Indian activists used the court system to reassert sovereign rights. Indian and white liberal lawyers, many with experience in civil rights cases, worked through the Native American Rights Fund, which became a powerful force in western politics. A series of Supreme Court decisions, culminating in *United States* v. *Wheeler* (1978), reasserted the principle of "unique and limited" sovereignty. The Court recognized tribal independence except where limited by treaty or Congress.

The Indian population had been growing since the early years of the century, but most reservations had trouble making room for a new generation. Indians suffered increased rates of poverty, chronic unemployment, alcoholism, and poor health. The average Indian family in the early 1960s earned only one-third of the average family income in the United States. Those who remained in the cities usually became "ethnic Indians," identifying themselves more as Indians than as members of specific tribes. By the late 1960s, ethnic Indians had begun emphasizing civil rights over tribal rights, making common cause with African Americans and other minorities. The National Indian Youth Council (NIYC), founded in 1960, tried to unite the two causes of equality for individual Indians and special status for tribes. But the organization faced difficult contradictions between a common Indian identity, emphasizing Indians as a single ethnic group, and tribal identity, stressing the citizenship of Indians in separate nations.

Asian Americans

The harsh relocation program of World War II devastated the Japanese American community on the west coast (see Chapter 25). But the war against Nazism also helped weaken older notions of white superiority and racism. During the war the state of California had aggressively enforced an alien land law by confiscating property declared illegally held by Japanese. In November 1946 a proposition supporting the law appeared on the state ballot. But, thanks in part to a campaign by the Japanese American Citizens League (JACL) reminding voters of the wartime contributions of Nisei (second-generation Japanese Americans) soldiers, voters overwhelmingly rejected the referendum. Two years later the Supreme Court declared the law unconstitutional, calling it "nothing more than outright racial discrimination."

The 1952 Immigration and Nationality Act (see Chapter 26) removed the old ban against Japanese immigration, and also made Issei (first-generation Japanese Americans) eligible for naturalized citizenship. Japanese Americans, who lobbied hard for the new law, greeted it with elation. "It gave the Japanese equality with all other immigrants," said JACL leader Harry Takagi, "and that was the principle we had been struggling for from the very beginning." By 1965 some 46,000 immigrant Japanese, most of them elderly Issei, had taken their citizenship oaths.

CHRONOLOGY

1941	Executive Order 8802 forbids racial discrimination in defense industries and government
1946	In *Morgan* v. *Virginia*, U.S. Supreme Court rules that segregation on interstate buses is unconstitutional
	President Harry Truman creates the Committee on Civil Rights
1947	Jackie Robinson becomes the first African American on a major league baseball team
1948	President Truman issues executive order desegregating the armed forces
1954	In *Brown* v. *Board of Education*, Supreme Court rules segregated schools inherently unequal
1955	Supreme Court rules that school desegregation must proceed "with all deliberate speed"
	Montgomery bus boycott begins
1956	Montgomery bus boycott ends in victory as the Supreme Court affirms a district court ruling that segregation on buses is unconstitutional
1957	Southern Christian Leadership Conference (SCLC) is founded
	President Dwight Eisenhower sends in federal troops to protect African American students integrating Little Rock, Arkansas, high school
1960	Sit-in movement begins as four college students sit at a lunch counter in Greensboro, North Carolina, and ask to be served
	Student Nonviolent Coordinating Committee (SNCC) founded

1960	Board of Indian Commissioners is created
	Buffalo Bill, the King of the Border Men, sets off "Wild West" publishing craze
1961	Freedom Rides begin
1962	James Meredith integrates the University of Mississippi
	The Albany movement fails to end segregation in Albany, Georgia
1963	SCLC initiates campaign to desegregate Birmingham, Alabama
	Medgar Evers, leader of the Mississippi NAACP, is assassinated
	March on Washington; Martin Luther King, Jr. delivers his historic "I Have a Dream" speech
1964	Mississippi Freedom Summer project brings students to Mississippi to teach and register voters
	President Johnson signs the Civil Rights Act of 1964
	Civil rights workers Michael Schwerner, James Chaney, and Andrew Goodman are found buried in Philadelphia, Mississippi
	Mississippi Freedom Democratic Party (MFDP) is denied seats at the 1964 Democratic Presidential Convention
1965	SCLC and SNCC begin voter registration campaign in Selma, Alabama
	Malcolm X is assassinated
	Civil rights marchers walk from Selma to Montgomery
	Voting Rights Act of 1965 is signed into law

In 1965 Congress passed a new Immigration and Nationality Act, abolishing the national-origins quotas and providing for the admission each year of 170,000 immigrants from the Eastern Hemisphere and 120,000 from the Western Hemisphere. The new law set a limit of 20,000 per country from the Eastern Hemisphere—these immigrants to be admitted on a first-come, first-served basis—and established preference categories for professional and highly skilled immigrants.

The 1965 act would have a profound effect on Asian American communities, opening the way for a new wave of immigration. In the twenty years following the act, the number of Asian Americans soared from 1 million to 5 million. Four times as many Asians settled in the

United States in this period as in the entire previous history of the nation. This new wave also brought a strikingly different group of Asian immigrants to America. In 1960 the Asian American population was 52 percent Japanese, 27 percent Chinese, and 20 percent Filipino. In 1985, the composition was 21 percent Chinese, 21 percent Filipino, 15 percent Japanese, 12 percent Vietnamese, 11 percent Korean, 10 percent Asian Indian, 4 percent Laotian, and 3 percent Cambodian. These newcomers included significant numbers of highly educated professionals and city dwellers, a sharp contrast with the farmers and rural peoples of the past.

CONCLUSION

The mass movement for civil rights was arguably the most important domestic event of the twentieth century. The struggle that began in Montgomery, Alabama, in December 1955 ultimately transformed race relations in thousands of American communities. By the early 1960s this community-based movement had placed civil rights at the very center of national political life. It achieved its greatest successes by invoking the law of the land to destroy legal segregation and win individual freedom for African Americans. The Civil Rights Act of 1964 and the Voting Rights Act of 1965 testified to the power of an African American and white liberal coalition. Yet the persistence of racism, poverty, and ghetto slums challenged a central assumption of liberalism: that equal protection of constitutional rights would give all Americans equal opportunities in life. By the mid-1960s, many black people had begun to question the core values of liberalism, the benefits of alliance with whites, and the philosophy of nonviolence. At the same time, a conservative white backlash against the gains made by African Americans further weakened the liberal political consensus.

In challenging the persistence of widespread poverty and institutional racism, the civil rights movement called for deep structural changes in American life. By 1967, Martin Luther King, Jr. was articulating a broad and radical vision linking the struggle against racial injustice to other defects in American society. "The black revolution," he argued, "is much more than a struggle for the rights of Negroes. It is forcing America to face all its interrelated flaws—racism, poverty, militarism, and materialism. It is exposing evils that are deeply rooted in the whole structure of our society." Curing these ills would prove far more difficult than ending legal segregation.

REVIEW QUESTIONS

1. What were the key legal and political antecedents to the civil rights struggle in the 1940s and early 1950s? What organizations played the most central role? Which tactics continued to be used, and which were abandoned?

2. How did African American communities challenge legal segregation in the South? Compare the strategies of key organizations, such as the NAACP, SNCC, SCLC, and CORE.

3. Discuss the varieties of white resistance to the civil rights movement. Which were most effective in slowing the drive for equality?

4. Analyze the civil rights movement's complex relationship with the national Democratic Party between 1948 and 1964. How was the party transformed by its association with the movement? What political gains and losses did that association entail?

5. What legal and institutional impact did the movement have on American life? How did it change American culture and politics? Where did it fail?

6. What relationship did the African Americans who struggled for civil rights have with other American minorities? How—if at all—did these minorities benefit? Did they build their own versions of the movement?

RECOMMENDED READING

Taylor Branch, *Parting the Waters: America in the King Years, 1954–1963* (1988); *Pillar of Fire: America in the King Years, 1963–1965* (1998). A deeply researched and monumental narrative history of the southern civil rights movement organized around the life and influence of Reverend Martin Luther King, Jr.

Clayborne Carson, *In Struggle: SNCC and the Black Awakening of the 1960s* (1981). The most comprehensive history of the Student Nonviolent Coordinating Committee, arguably the most important civil rights organization. Carson stresses the evolution of SNCC's radicalism during the course of the decade.

William Chafe, *Civilities and Civil Rights: Greensboro, North Carolina, and the Black Struggle for Equality* (1980). Examines the community of Greensboro from 1945 to 1975. Chafe focuses on the "etiquette of civility" and its complex relationship with the promise of racial justice, along with black protest movements and relations between the city's blacks and whites.

David Chappell, *Inside Agitators: White Southerners in the Civil Rights Movement* (1994). A thoughtful and sophisticated analysis of the varying roles played by whites in the movement.

Mary L. Dudziak, *Cold War Civil Rights: Race and the Image of American Democracy* (2000). Excellent analysis of the connections between the struggle for racial equality in America and the nation's contest with communism abroad.

Sara Evans, *Personal Politics: The Roots of Women's Liberation in the Civil Rights Movement and the New Left* (1979). A pathbreaking study showing the important connections between the struggle for black rights and the rebirth of feminism.

Aldon D. Morris, *The Origins of the Civil Rights Movement: Black Communities Organizing for Change* (1984). An important study combining history and social theory. Morris emphasizes the key role of ordinary black people, acting through their churches and other community organizations before 1960.

Howell Raines, *My Soul Is Rested: Movement Days in the Deep South Remembered* (1977). The best oral history of the civil rights movement, drawing from a wide range of participants and points of view. It is brilliantly edited by Raines, who covered the events as a journalist.

Jo Ann Gibson Robinson, *The Montgomery Bus Boycott and the Women Who Started It.* ed. David J. Garrow (1987). An important memoir by one of the key behind-the-scenes players in the Montgomery bus-boycott. Robinson stresses the role of middle- and working-class black women in the struggle.

Robert Weisbrot, *Freedom Bound: A History of America's Civil Rights Movement* (1990). One of the best single-volume syntheses of the movement. Weisbrot is especially strong on the often turbulent relations between black activists and white liberals and the relationship between civil rights and broader currents of American reform.

ON THE WEB

http://supct.law.cornell.edu/supct/cases/historic.htm

The Legal Information Institute of Cornell Law School provides complete transcripts of a few hundred of the most important U.S. Supreme Court decisions. Use this resource to examine the most important decisions of the Warren Court, especially *Brown* v. *Board of Education of Topeka, Kansas* (1954), *Brown II* (1955), *Gideon* v. *Wainright* (1963), *Escobedo* v. *Illinois* (1964), *Baker* v. *Carr* (1962), *Miranda* v. *Arizona* (1966), and others.

http://www.angelfire.com/pa/marchonwashington/

An interesting, detailed description of the 1963 March on Washington.

http://www.mecca.org/~crights/wash.html

A short description of the 1963 March on Washington that acknowledges the debt owed to A. Philip Randolph. Navigate to **http://www.civilrightsmuseum.org/** and visit the home site of the National Civil Rights Museum that sponsors this page.

http://www.usbr.gov/laws/civil.html

Links to the full legal text of the Civil Rights Acts of 1957, 1960, 1964, and 1968.

http://hcl.chass.ncsu.edu/garson/dye/docs/votrit65.htm

Full legal text of the Voting Rights Act of 1965.

http://www.prenhall.com/faragherbrief/map28.1

Examine the chronology of the Civil Rights Movement. How did the *Brown* decision pave the way for subsequent events?

http://www.prenhall.com/faragherbrief/map28.2

Consider the impact of the Voting Rights Act on the number of registered African American voters in the South. In which states was the increase in voters particularly dramatic?

▶ Flying the "Stars and Bars"

In 1956 African American citizens in Montgomery, Alabama, successfully boycotted the city's segregated bus lines, thus sparking a nonviolent mass movement to end legalized segregation in the South. Nearly a century earlier, on the eve of the Civil War, Montgomery had hosted a convention that created the Confederate States of America. As both the "cradle of the Confederacy" and the birthplace of the modern civil rights movement, it's not surprising that Montgomery, Alabama, has been the site of bitter conflict over the meaning and use of the Confederate flag. Indeed, during the 1990s, widespread controversy in the South over displays of the Confederate flag reflected both the fierce pride many white Southerners maintained for the "Lost Cause" and the enormous changes wrought by the civil rights movement of the 1950s and 1960s. The fight over the flag and what it represents provides a perfect example of how communities struggle over the meaning of their history. For as William Faulkner, the South's most distinguished novelist, once put it: "The past is not dead, it isn't even past."

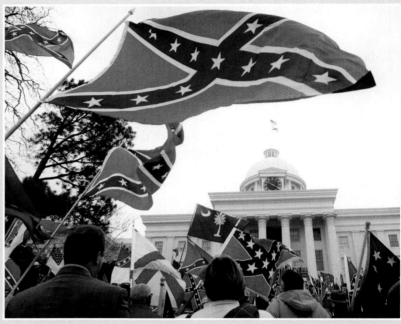

In March 2000 thousands of demonstrators rallied outside the Capitol in Montgomery, calling on state officials to once again fly the Confederate flag over the building. This rally was organized by the League of the South, an organization dedicated to celebrating white Southern history and culture.

SOURCE: AP/Wide World Photos.

Throughout the South, the revived use of the Confederate flag began as part of the white backlash against the campaign to end legal segregation. In 1963 Alabama Gov. George C. Wallace ordered the Confederate battle flag to fly on top of the state capitol to protest a visit by Attorney General Robert F. Kennedy, who had come to Montgomery to discuss desegregation of the state's schools. The flag, which had white stars on a blue X-shape against a red background, was the same design as the battle flag carried in the field by Confederate troops during the Civil War. The battle flag flew over the dome, along with the national and state flags, until the spring of 1992, when they were taken down during renovation work. By then, the Confederate flag had become a cultural icon of regional pride and enduring belief in white supremacy in many parts of the South. And around the nation, others adopted it as an all-purpose symbol of rebellion and resistance to authority,

displayed on posters, clothing, bumper stickers, and featured in music videos.

But for most African Americans the Confederate flag meant something quite different. In the summer of 1988 fourteen black state legislators were arrested for trespassing on state property when they attempted to scale a chain-link fence and remove the flag. Rep. Alvin Holmes, one of those arrested, said, "When I walk up the Capitol steps, instead of seeing the American flag, the flag that I served under when I was in the United States Army, I see a flag that represents treason, sedition, slavery, and oppression toward my people."

In December 1992 Montgomery prepared to re-dedicate the 141-year-old state Capitol after a $28 million restoration. When Gov. Guy Hunt insisted that the "Stars and Bars" continue to fly over the building, 24 African American legislators boycotted the ceremony in protest. Rep. Holmes filed a lawsuit asking for

In the early 1960s three flags flew over the Alabama State Capitol in Montgomery, representing the United States, Alabama, and the Confederacy. Governor George Wallace had insisted on flying the Confederate "Stars and Bars" as a protest against the civil rights movement. It was removed in 1992 after demonstrations and a court challenge led by African American state legislators.

SOURCE: © Reuters NewMedia Inc./CORBIS.

an injunction, claiming an 1896 state law prohibited any flags other than the Alabama and U.S. flags from flying above the Capitol. Alabama citizens expressed a wide range of opinions on the subject. Most whites insisted the old symbol was about regional identity and pride, not race. John Napier, a retired Air Force colonel and leader of the Sons of Confederate veterans argued, "We celebrate our civil rights history. There are those of us who feel the earlier struggle should be commemorated historically, too. While we're running around naming streets for Rosa Parks, which I have no problem with, you're getting into removing all the symbols of the Confederacy." African Americans, for whom the flag symbolized slavery, racism, and segregation, tried to distinguish between private and public displays. "I see nothing wrong with someone flying the Confederate flag even on their front lawn or putting it on their bumper stickers," said Earl Shinhoster, an official of the NAACP. "I do, however, see something wrong when the state promotes something that many people find offensive."

As with the Montgomery bus boycott of 1956, the economic implications of the controversy were not lost on the city's the business community and political leaders. Anna Bishop, spokeswoman for the Montgomery Chamber of Commerce, noted that, "Business people are realizing that the flag contributes to a negative image for Alabama."

The Alabama State Business Council told Gov. Hunt in a letter that "the Confederate flag is detrimental to our image and is dividing our citzenry." Neal Wade of the Economic Development Partnership of Alabama asserted, "Anything that causes division within a state makes it less attractive to a potential employer, particularly from overseas."

In January 1993, just a few weeks after the dedication of the renovated Capitol, Judge William Gordon of Alabama Circuit Court in Montgomery ruled that the 1896 state law did indeed prohibit the state from flying the "Stars and Bars" over the state Capitol. The new governor, Jim Folsom, announced that he would not challenge the decision, and that the Confederate battle flag would fly instead across the street at the First White House of the Confederacy. "This has been a divisive issue in our state," he said, "and I believe it is time we put it behind us and move our state forward." Still, in many parts of the country private and public displays of the Confederate flag have persisted—and so have the continued and deeply felt debates over the historical meanings embedded within it. ■

TWENTY-NINE

WAR ABROAD, WAR AT HOME

▶ 1 9 6 5 – 1 9 7 4

AMERICAN COMMUNITIES

Uptown, Chicago, Illinois

DURING FREEDOM SUMMER OF 1964, WHILE TEAMS OF NORTHERN college students traveled south to join voter registration campaigns among African Americans, a small group moved to Chicago to help the city's poor people take control of their communities and to demand better city services. They targeted a neighborhood known as Uptown, a one-mile-square section five miles north of the Loop, the city center. The residents, many only recently transplanted from the poverty of the Appalachian South, lived in crowded tenements or in once elegant mansions now subdivided into tiny, run-down apartments. Four thousand people lived on just one street running four blocks, 20 percent of them on welfare. Chicago civic authorities had also selected this neighborhood for improvement. Designating it a Conservation Area under the terms of the Urban Renewal Act, they applied for federal funds in order to upgrade the housing for middle-income families and, in effect, to clear out the current residents. In contrast, the student organizers intended to mobilize the community "so as to demand an end to poverty and the construction of a decent social order."

With the assistance of the Packinghouse Workers union, the students formed Jobs or Income Now (JOIN), opened a storefront office, and invited local residents to work with them to halt the city's plans. They spent hours and hours listening to people, drawing out their ideas and helping them develop scores of additional programs. Confronting the bureaucracy of the welfare and unemployment compensation offices stood high on their list. They also campaigned against Mayor Richard Daley's policy of "police omnipresence" that had a fleet of squad cars and paddy wagons continually patrolling the neighborhood. To curb police harassment, they demanded the creation of civilian review boards. They also helped establish new social clubs, a food-buying cooperative, a community theater, and a health clinic. Within a few years, Uptown street kids had formed the Young Patriots organization, put out a community newspaper, *Rising Up Angry*, and staffed free breakfast programs.

Chicago JOIN was one of ten similar projects sponsored by Students for a Democratic Society (SDS). Impatient with the nation's chronic poverty and cold war politics, twenty-nine students from nine universities had met in June 1960 to form a new kind of campus-based political organization. SDS soon caught the attention of liberal students, encouraging them, as part of the nation's largest college population to date, to make their voices heard. By its peak in 1968, SDS had 350 chapters and between 60,000 and 100,000 members. Its principle of participatory democracy—with its promise to give people control over the decisions affecting their lives—appealed to a wider following of more than a million students.

In June 1962, in Port Huron, Michigan, the founding members of SDS issued a declaration of principles, drafted mainly by graduate student Tom Hayden. "We are people . . . bred in at least modest comfort, housed now in universities," *The Port Huron Statement* opened, "looking uncomfortably to the world we inherit." The dire effects of poverty and social injustice, it continued, were not the only dismaying things about American society. A deeper ailment plagued American politics. Everyone, including middle-class students with few material wants, suffered from a sense of "loneliness, estrangement, and alienation." *The Port Huron Statement* defined SDS as a new kind of political movement that would bring people "out of isolation and into community." Through participatory democracy, not just the poor but all Americans could overcome their feelings of "powerlessness [and hence] resignation before the enormity of events." As one organizer explained, programs like JOIN were attempts to create a poor people's movement as well as a means for students themselves to live an "authentic life" outside the constraints of middle-class society.

SDS began with a campaign to reform the university, especially to disentangle the financial ties between campus-based research programs and the military-industrial complex. Later it expanded to the nation's cities, sending small groups of students to live and organize in the poor communities of Boston, Louisville, Cleveland, and Newark as well as Chicago. Ultimately, few of these projects succeeded in mobilizing the poor to political action. Protests against local government did little to combat unemployment, and campaigns for better garbage collection or more playgrounds rarely evolved into lasting movements. Nevertheless, organizers did succeed in

bringing many neighborhood residents "out of isolation and into community." By late 1967, SDS prepared to leave JOIN in the hands of the people it had organized, which was its goal from the beginning.

Initially, even Lyndon Baines Johnson promoted the ideal of civic participation. The Great Society, as the president called his domestic program, promised more than the abolition of poverty and racial inequality. In May 1964, at the University of Michigan, the president described his goal as a society "where every child can find knowledge to enrich his mind and to enlarge his talents," where "the city of man serves not only the needs of the body and the demands of commerce but the desire for beauty and the hunger for community."

By 1967 the Vietnam War had upset the domestic agendas of both SDS and the Johnson administration. If SDSers had once believed they could work with liberal Democrats to reduce poverty in the United States, they now interpreted social injustice at home as the inevitable consequence of dangerous and destructive foreign policies pursued by liberals and conservatives alike. SDS threw its energies into the movement against the war in Vietnam. President Johnson, meanwhile, pursued a foreign policy that would swallow up the funding for his own plans for a war on poverty and would precipitate a very different war at home, Americans against Americans. As hawks and doves lined up on opposite sides, the Vietnam War created a huge and enduring rift. SDS member Richard Flacks had warned that the nation had to "choose between devoting its resources and energies to maintaining military superiority and international hegemony or rechanneling those resources and energies to meeting the desperate needs of its people." Ultimately, even President Johnson himself understood that the "bitch of a war" in Asia ruined "the woman I really loved—the Great Society." The dream of community did not vanish, but consensus appeared increasingly remote as the United States fought—and eventually lost— the longest war in its history. ■

Chicago

KEY TOPICS

- Widening U.S. involvement in the war in Vietnam

- The "sixties generation" and the antiwar movement

- Poverty and urban crisis

- The election of 1968

- The rise of "liberation" movements

- The Nixon presidency and the Watergate conspiracy

VIETNAM: AMERICA'S LONGEST WAR

The Vietnam War had its roots in the Truman Doctrine and its goal of containing communism (see Chapter 26). After the defeat of the French by the Communist forces of Ho Chi Minh in 1954, Vietnam emerged as a major zone of cold war contention. President John Kennedy called it "the cornerstone of the Free World in Southeast Asia, the keystone in the arch, the finger in the dike," a barrier to the spread of communism throughout the region and perhaps the world. President Lyndon Johnson sounded the same note at the beginning of his presidency. With American security at stake, he concluded, Americans had little choice but to fight.

Vietnam was not Valley Forge, however, and the United States ultimately paid a huge price for its determination to turn back communism in Indochina. More than 50,000 Americans died in an unwinnable overseas war that only deepened divisions at home.

Johnson's War

Although President Kennedy had greatly increased the number of military advisors in South Vietnam (see Chapter 27), it was his successor, Lyndon B. Johnson, who made the decision to engage the United States in a major war there. At first, Johnson simply hoped to stay the course in Vietnam. Facing a presidential election in November 1964, he knew that a major military setback would cripple his election campaign. But he was equally determined to avoid the fate of President Truman, who had bogged down politically after "losing" China to communism and producing a stalemate in Korea.

Throughout the winter and spring of 1964, as conditions grew steadily worse in South Vietnam,

Johnson and his advisors quietly laid the groundwork for a sustained bombing campaign against North Vietnam. In early August, they found a pretext to set this plan in motion. After two U.S. destroyers in the Gulf of Tonkin, off the coast of North Vietnam, reported attacks by North Vietnamese patrol boats, Johnson retaliated by ordering air strikes against bases in North Vietnam.

Johnson now appealed to Congress to pass a resolution giving him the authority "to take all necessary measures" and "all necessary steps" to defend U.S. armed forces and to protect Southeast Asia "against aggression or subversion." This Tonkin Gulf resolution, secretly drafted six weeks before the incident for which it was named, passed the Senate on August 7 with only two dissenting votes and moved unanimously through the House. It served, in Undersecretary of State Nicholas Katzenbach's words, as the "functional equivalent" of a declaration of war.

Ironically, Johnson had campaigned for the presidency with a call for restraint in Vietnam. This strategy helped him win a landslide victory over conservative Republican Barry Goldwater of Arizona. With the election behind him, Johnson faced a hard decision. The limited bombing raids against North Vietnam had failed to slow the movement of the Communist Vietcong forces across the border into the South. Meanwhile, the government in Saigon, the capital city of South Vietnam, appeared near collapse. Faced with the prospect of a Communist victory, the president chose to escalate U.S. involvement in Vietnam massively.

Deeper into the Quagmire

In early February 1965, Johnson found a rationale to justify massive bombing of the North. The Vietcong had fired at the barracks of the U.S. Marine base at

Refugees, Binh Dinh Province, 1967. The massive bombing and ground combat broke apart the farming communities of South Vietnam, creating huge numbers of civilian casualties and driving millions into quickly constructed refugee camps or already overcrowded cities. Approximately 25 percent of the South Vietnamese population fled their villages, many never to return.

SOURCE: Photo by Philip Jones Griffiths. Magnum Photos, Inc.

the airfields where bombing runs began. But six week later, 50,000 U.S. troops were in Vietnam. By November 1965 the total topped 165,000, and more troops were on the way. But even after Johnson authorized a buildup to 431,000 troops in mid-1966, victory was still nowhere in sight.

The strategy pursued by the Johnson administration and implemented by General William Westmoreland—a war of attrition—was based on the premise that continued bombing would eventually exhaust North Vietnam's resources. Meanwhile, U.S. ground forces would defeat the Vietcong in South Vietnam, forcing its soldiers to defect and supporters to scatter, thereby restoring political stability to South Vietnam's pro-Western government. As Johnson once boasted, the strongest military power in the world surely could crush a Communist rebellion in a "pissant" country of peasants.

In practice, the United States wreaked havoc in South Vietnam, tearing apart its society and bringing ecological devastation to its land. Intending to locate and eradicate the support network of the Vietcong, U.S. ground troops conducted search-and-destroy missions throughout the countryside. They attacked villagers and their homes. Seeking to ferret out Vietcong sympathizers, U.S. troops turned at any one time as many as 4 million people—approximately one-quarter of the population of South Vietnam—into refugees. By late 1968, the United States had dropped more than 3 million tons of bombs on Vietnam, and eventually delivered more than three times the tonnage dropped by the Allies on all fronts during World War II. Using herbicides to defoliate forest, the United States also conducted the most destructive chemical warfare in history.

Several advisers urged the president to inform the American people about his decisions on Vietnam, even to declare a state of national emergency. But Johnson feared he would lose momentum on domestic reform, including his antipoverty programs, if he drew attention to foreign policy. Seeking to avoid "undue excitement in the Congress and in domestic public opinion," he held to a course of intentional deceit.

Pleiku in the central highlands of Vietnam, killing eight and wounding more than 100 Americans. Waving the list of casualties, the president rushed into an emergency meeting of the National Security Council to announce that the time had passed for keeping "our guns over the mantel and our shells in the cupboard." He ordered immediate reprisal bombing of North Vietnam and one week later, on February 13, authorized Operation Rolling Thunder, a campaign of gradually intensifying air attacks.

Once Rolling Thunder had begun, President Johnson found it increasingly difficult to speak frankly with the American public about his policies. Initially, he announced that only two battalions of marines were being assigned to Danang to defend

The Credibility Gap

Johnson's popularity had surged at the time of the Tonkin Gulf resolution, skyrocketing in one day from 42 to 72 percent, according to a Louis Harris poll. But afterward it waned rapidly. The war dragged on. Every night network television news reported the soaring American body count, from 26 per week in 1965 to 180 in 1967. No president had worked so hard to control the news media, but by 1967 Johnson found himself badgered at press conferences by reporters who accused the president of creating a credibility gap.

Scenes of human suffering and devastation recorded by television cameras increasingly undermined the administration's moral justification of the war with claims that it was a necessary defense of freedom and democracy in South Vietnam. During the early 1960s, network news had either ignored Vietnam or had been patriotically supportive of U.S. policy. Beginning with a report on a ground operation against the South Vietnamese village of Cam Ne by Morley Safer for CBS News in August 1965, however, the tenor of news reporting changed. Although government officials described the operation as a strategic destruction of "fortified Vietcong bunkers," the *CBS Evening News* showed pictures of Marines setting fire to the thatched homes of civilians. After CBS aired Safer's report, President Johnson complained bitterly to the news director. But more critical commentary soon followed. By 1967, according to a noted media observer, "every subject tended to become Vietnam." Televised news reports now told of new varieties of American cluster bombs, which released up to 180,000 fiberglass shards, and showed the nightmarish effects of the defoliants used on forests in South Vietnam to uncover enemy strongholds.

Coverage of the war in the print media also became more skeptical of Johnson's policies. By 1967 independent news teams were probing the government's official claims. Harrison Salisbury, Pulitzer Prize–winning *New York Times* reporter, questioned the administration's claims that its bombing of the North precisely targeted military objectives, charging that U.S. planes had bombed the population center of Hanoi, capital of North Vietnam, and intentionally ravaged villages in the South. As American military deaths climbed at the rate of more than 800 per month during the first half of 1967, newspaper coverage of the war focused yet more intently on such disturbing events.

The most vocal congressional critic of Johnson's war policy was Democratic senator J. William Fulbright of Arkansas, who chaired the Senate Foreign Relations Committee and who had personally speeded the passage of the Tonkin Gulf resolution. A strong supporter of the cold war, Fulbright had decided that the war in Vietnam was unwinnable and destructive to domestic reform. In *Arrogance of Power*, a book published in 1966 that became a national bestseller, he proposed a negotiated withdrawal from a neutralized Southeast Asia. Fulbright persuaded prominent Democrats in Congress, such as Frank Church, Mike Mansfield, and George McGovern, to put aside their personal loyalty to Johnson and oppose his conduct of the war. In 1967 the Congress passed a nonbinding resolution appealing to the United Nations to help negotiate an end to hostilities. Meanwhile, some of the nation's most trusted European allies called for restraint in Vietnam.

The impact of the war, which cost Americans $21 billion per year, was also felt at home. Johnson convinced Congress to levy a 10 percent surcharge on individual and corporate taxes. Later adjustments in the national budget tapped the Social Security fund, heretofore safe from interference. Inflation raced upward, fed by spending on the war. Johnson replaced advisers who questioned his policy, but as casualties multiplied, more and more Americans began to question his handling of the war.

A GENERATION IN CONFLICT

As the war in Vietnam escalated, Americans from all walks of life demanded an end to U.S. involvement. But between 1965 and 1971, its years of peak activity, it had a distinctly generational character. At the forefront were the baby boomers who were just coming of age.

This so-called sixties generation, the largest generation in American history, was also the best educated. By the late 1960s, nearly half of all young adults between the ages of 18 and 21 were enrolled in college. In 1965 there were 5 million college students; in 1973 the number had doubled to 10 million. Public universities made the largest gains; by 1970 eight had more than 30,000 students apiece. Although a small minority, groups of students began to combine protest against the war in Vietnam with a broader, penetrating critique of American society. Through music, dress, and even hairstyle, they expressed a deep estrangement from the values and aspirations of their parents' generation. As early as 1967, when opposition to the war had begun to swell, "flower children" were putting daisies in the rifle barrels of troops stationed to quash campus protests, providing a seemingly innocent counterpoint to the grim news of slaughter abroad.

These young people promoted a "culture of life" against the "culture of death" symbolized by the war. Campus organizations such as SDS, which had begun in the early 1960s in an attempt to build community, now turned against the government.

"The Times They Are A-Changin'"

The first sign of a new kind of protest was the free speech movement at the University of California at Berkeley in 1964. That fall, civil rights activists returned to the 27,000-student campus from Freedom Summer in Mississippi. They soon began to picket Bay Area stores that practiced discrimination in hiring and to recruit other students to join them. When the university administration moved to prevent them from setting up information booths on campus, eighteen groups protested, including the arch-conservative Students for Goldwater, claiming that their right to free speech had been abridged. The administration responded by sending police to break up the protest rally and arrest participants. University president Clark Kerr met with students, agreed not to press charges, and seemed set to grant them a small space on campus for political activity. Then, under pressure from conservative regents, Kerr reversed himself and announced in November that the university planned to press new charges against the free speech movement's leaders. On December 2 a crowd of 7,000 gathered to protest this decision. Joining folk singer Joan Baez in singing "We Shall Overcome," a group of 1,000 people marched toward the university's administration building, where they planned to stage a sit-in until Kerr rescinded his order. The police arrested nearly 800 protestors in the largest mass arrest in California history.

Mario Savio, a Freedom Summer volunteer and philosophy student, explained that the free speech movement wanted more than just the right to conduct political activity on campus. He spoke for many students when he complained that the university had become a faceless bureaucratic machine rather than a community of learning.

Across the country college students began to demand a say in the structuring of their education. Brown University students, for example, demanded a revamp of the curriculum that would eliminate all required courses and make grades optional. Students also protested campus rules that treated students as children instead of as adults. After a string of campus protests, most large universities, including the University of California, relinquished *in loco parentis* (in the place of parents) policies and allowed students to live off-campus and to set their own hours.

Across the bay in San Francisco, other young adults staked out a new form of community—a counterculture. In 1967, the "Summer of Love," the population of the Haight-Ashbury district swelled by 75,000 as youthful adventurers gathered for the most celebrated "be-in" of the era. They congregated in "the Haight" to listen to music, take drugs, and "be" with each other. "If you're going to San Francisco," a popular rock group sang, "be sure to wear some flowers in your hair . . . you're going to meet some gentle people there." In the fall, the majority returned to their own communities, often bringing with them a new lifestyle.

The generational rebellion took many forms, including a revolution in sexual behavior that triggered countless quarrels between parents and their maturing sons and daughters. During the 1960s more teenagers experienced premarital sex—by the decade's end three-quarters of all college seniors had engaged in sexual intercourse—and far more talked about it openly than in previous eras. "We've discarded the idea that the loss of virginity is related to degeneracy," one college student explained. Many heterosexual couples chose to live together outside marriage, a practice few parents condoned. A much smaller but significant number formed communes—approximately 4,000 by 1970—where members could share housekeeping and child care as well as sexual partners.

Mood-altering drugs played a large part in this counterculture. Harvard professor Timothy Leary urged young people to "turn on, tune in, drop out" and also advocated the mass production and distribution of LSD (lysergic acid diethylamide), which was not criminalized until 1968. Marijuana, illegal yet readily available, was often paired with rock music in a collective ritual of love and laughter. Singer Bob Dylan taunted adults with the lyrics of his hit single, "Everybody must get stoned."

Music played a large part in defining the counterculture. With the emergence of rock 'n' roll in the 1950s, popular music had begun to express a deliberate generational identity (see Chapter 27), a trend that gained momentum with the emergence of the British rock group The Beatles in 1964. Folk music, which had gained popularity on campuses in the early 1960s with the successful recordings of Peter, Paul, and Mary, Phil Ochs, and Judy Collins, as well as Joan Baez, continued to serve the voice of protest. Shortly after Freedom Summer, folk singer Bob Dylan issued a warning to parents:

> *Your sons and your daughters*
> *are beyond your command*
> *Your old road is*
> *rapidly agin'.*
> *Please get out of the new one*
> *If you can't lend your hand*
> *For the times they are a-changin'.*

At a farm near Woodstock, New York, more than 400,000 people gathered in August 1969 for a three-day rock concert and to give witness to the ideals of the counterculture. Thousands took drugs while security officials and local police stood by.

The Woodstock Nation, as the counterculture was mythologized, did not actually represent the senti-ments of most young Americans. But its attitudes and styles, especially its efforts to create a new community, did speak for the large minority seeking a peaceful alternative to the intensifying climate of war. "We used to think of ourselves as little clumps of weirdos," rock star Janis Joplin explained. "But now we're a whole new minority group." The slogan "Make Love, Not War" linked generational rebellion and opposition to the U.S. invasion of Vietnam.

From Campus Protest to Mass Mobilization

Three weeks after the announcement of Operation Rolling Thunder in 1965, peace activists called for a day-long boycott of classes so that students and faculty might meet to discuss the war. At the University of Michigan in Ann Arbor, more than 3,000 students turned out for sessions held through the night because

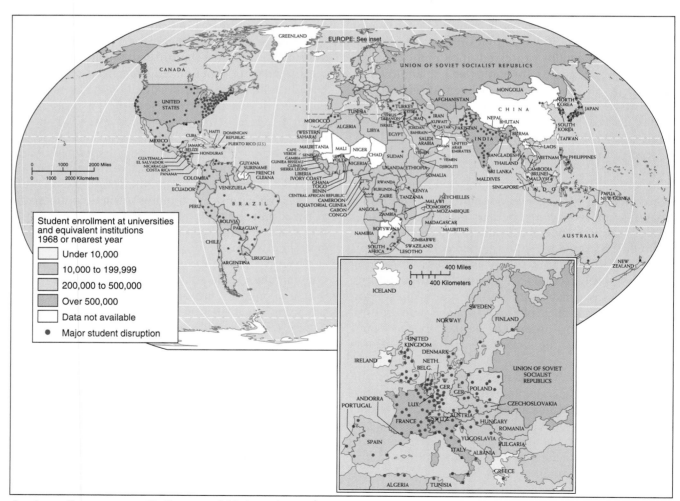

Antiwar Protests on College and University Campuses, 1967–1969
Campus-based protests against the war in Vietnam, at first centered on the East Coast and in California, spread to nearly every region of the country and around the world by the decade's end.

university administrators had bowed to the pressure of state legislators and had refused to cancel classes. During the following weeks, "teach-ins" spread across the United States and to Europe and Japan as well.

Students also began to protest against war-related research on their campuses. The expansion of higher education in the 1960s had depended largely on federally funded programs, including military research on counterinsurgency tactics and new chemical weapons. Student protesters demanded an end to these programs and, receiving no response from university administrators, turned to civil disobedience. In October 1967, the Dow Chemical Company, manufacturers of napalm, a form of jellied gasoline often used against civilians in Vietnam, sent job recruiters to the University of Wisconsin at Madison despite warnings that a group of students would try to prevent them from conducting interviews. A few hundred students staged a sit-in at the building where the recruitment interviews were scheduled, and 2,000 onlookers gathered outside. Ordered by university administrators to disperse the crowd, the city's police broke glass doors, dragged students through the debris, and clubbed those who refused to move. Suddenly the campus erupted. Students chanted *Sieg Heil* at the police, who attempted to disperse them with tear gas and Mace. Undergraduate students and their teaching assistants boycotted classes for a week. During the next three years, the momentum grew, and demonstrations took place on campuses in every region of country.

Many student strikes and demonstrations merged opposition to the war with other campus and community issues. At Columbia University, students struck in 1968 against the administration's plans to build a new gymnasium in a city park used by residents of neighboring Harlem. In the Southwest, Mexican American students demonstrated against the use of funds for military projects that might otherwise be allocated to antipoverty and educational programs.

In April 1967, a day-long antiwar rally at the Sheep Meadow in Manhattan's Central Park drew more than 300,000 people Meanwhile, 60,000 protesters turned out in San Francisco. By summer, Vietnam Veterans Against the War had begun to organize returning soldiers and sailors, encouraging them to cast off the medals and ribbons they had won in battle.

The steadily increasing size of antiwar demonstrations provoked conservatives and prowar Democrats to take a stronger stand in support of the war. Several newspaper and magazine editorialists called for the arrest of antiwar leaders on charges of treason. Secretary of State Dean Rusk, appearing on NBC's *Meet the Press*, expressed his concern that "authorities in Hanoi"

might conclude, incorrectly, that the majority of Americans did not back their president and that "the net effect of these demonstrations will be to prolong the war, not to shorten it."

Many demonstrators themselves concluded that mass mobilizations alone had little impact on U.S. policy. Some sought to serve as moral witnesses. Despite a congressional act of 1965 providing for a five-year jail term and a $10,000 fine for destroying a draft card, nearly 200 young men destroyed their draft cards at the April Sheep Meadow demonstration and encouraged approximately a half-million more to resist the draft or refuse induction. Two Jesuit priests, Daniel and Philip Berrigan, raided the offices of the draft board in Catonsville, Maryland, in May 1968 and poured homemade napalm over records. Other activists determined to "bring the war home." An estimated 40,000 bombing incidents or bomb threats took place from January 1969 to April 1970; more than $21 million of property was damaged, and forty-three people were killed. Most of the perpetrators were never identified. Parallel wars were now being fought, one between two systems of government in Vietnam, another between the American government and masses of its citizens. Those Americans sent to Vietnam were caught in between.

Teenage Soldiers

Whereas the average age of the World War II soldier was twenty-six, the age of those who fought in Vietnam hovered around nineteen. Until late 1969 the Selective Service System—the draft—gave deferments to college students and to workers in selected occupations while recruiting hard in poor communities, advertising the armed forces as a provider of vocational training and social mobility. Working-class young men, disproportionately African American and Latino, signed up in large numbers under these inducements. They also bore the brunt of combat. Whereas college graduates constituted only 12 percent of all soldiers and 9 percent of those who were killed in combat, high school dropouts were the most likely to serve in Vietnam and by far the most likely to die there. These disparities created a rupture that would last well past the end of the war.

Yet the soldiers were not entirely isolated from the changes affecting their generation. G.I.s in significant numbers smoked marijuana, listed to rock music, and participated in the sexual revolution. But most condemned antiwar protest as the expressions of their privileged peers who did not have to fight. As the war dragged on, however, some soldiers began to show their frustration. By 1971 many G.I.s were putting peace symbols on their combat helmets, joining anti-war demonstrations, and staging their own events such as "Armed Farces Day." Sometimes entire companies refused to carry out duty assignments or even to enter battle. A smaller number took revenge by "fragging" reckless commanding officers with grenades meant for the enemy. Some African American soldiers complained about being asked to fight "a white man's war" and emblazoned their helmets with slogans like "No Gook Ever Called Me Nigger."

The nature of the war fed feelings of disaffection in the armed forces. U.S. troops entering South Vietnam expected a warm welcome from the people whose homeland they had been sent to defend. Instead, they encountered anti-American demonstrations and placards with slogans like "End Foreign Dominance of Our Country." Hostile Vietnamese civilians viewed the Americans as invaders. The enemy avoided open engagements in which the Americans could benefit from their superior arms and air power. Soldiers found themselves instead stumbling into booby traps as they chased an elusive guerrilla foe through deep, leech-infested swamps and dense jungles swarming with fire ants. They could never be sure who was friend and who was foe. Patently false U.S. government press releases that heralded glorious victories and extolled the gratitude of Vietnamese civilians deepened bitterness on the front lines.

Vietnam veterans returned to civilian life quietly and without fanfare, denied the glory earned by the combat veterans of previous wars. They reentered a society divided over the cause for which they had risked their lives. Tens of thousands suffered debilitating physical injuries. As many as 40 percent of them came back with drug dependencies or symptoms of post-traumatic stress disorder, haunted and depressed by troubling memories of atrocities. Moreover, finding and keeping a job proved to be particularly hard in the shrinking economy of the 1970s.

WARS ON POVERTY

During the early 1960s, the civil rights movement spurred a new awareness of and concern with poverty. What good was winning the right to sit at a lunch counter if one could not afford to buy a hamburger?

One of the most influential books of the times, Michael Harrington's *The Other America* (1962), added fuel to this fire. Harrington argued that one-fifth of the nation—as many as 40 to 50 million people—suffered from bad housing, malnutrition, poor medical care, and other deprivations of poverty. He documented the miseries of what he called the "invisible

land of the other Americans," the rejects of society who simply did not exist for affluent suburbanites or the mass media.

These arguments motivated President Johnson to expand the antipoverty program that he had inherited from the Kennedy administration. "That's my kind of program," he told his advisers. "It will help people. I want you to move full speed ahead on it." Ironically, it was another kind of war that ultimately undercut his aspiration to wage "an unconditional war on poverty."

The Great Society

In his State of the Union message in 1964, Johnson announced his plans to build a Great Society. Over the next two years, he used the political momentum of the civil rights movement and the overwhelming Democratic majorities in the House and Senate to push through the most ambitious reform program since the New Deal. In August 1964 the Economic Opportunity Act launched the War on Poverty. It established an Office of Economic Opportunity (OEO), which coordinated a network of federal programs designed to increase opportunities in employment and education.

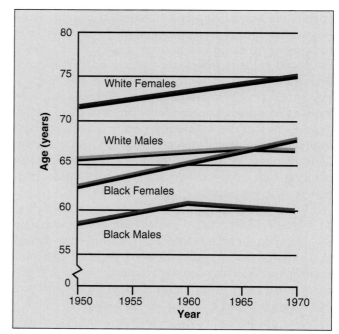

Comparative Figures on Life Expectancy at Birth by Race and Sex, 1950–1970 Shifting mortality statistics suggested that the increased longevity of females increasingly cut across race lines but did not diminish the difference between white people and black people as a whole.

The programs had mixed results. The Job Corps provided vocational training mostly for urban black youth considered unemployable. Housed in dreary barrackslike camps far from home, trainees often found themselves learning factory skills that were already obsolete. The Neighborhood Youth Corps managed to provide work for about 2 million young people aged sixteen to twenty-one. But nearly all of these were low-paying, make-work jobs. Educational programs proved more successful. VISTA (Volunteers in Service to America) was a kind of domestic Peace Corps that brought several thousand idealistic volunteers into poor communities for social service work.

The most innovative and controversial element of the OEO was the Community Action Program (CAP). The program invited local communities to establish community action agencies (CAAs), to be funded through the OEO. The Economic Opportunity Act included language requiring these agencies to be "developed, conducted, and administered with the maximum feasible participation of residents of the areas and members of the groups served." In theory, as the SDS organizers had also believed, community action would empower the poor by giving them a direct say in mobilizing resources to attack poverty.

By 1966 the OEO was funding more than 1,000 CAAs, mostly in the black neighborhoods of big cities. The traditional powers in cities—mayors, business elites, and political machines—generally resisted institutional change. They looked at CAAs as merely another way to dispense services and patronage, with the federal government picking up the tab. A continual tug-of-war over who should control funding and decision making plagued the CAP in most cities, sparking intense power struggles that helped to cripple the antipoverty effort. Such was the case in Chicago, where Mayor Richard Daley demanded absolute control over the allocation of federal funds.

The most successful and popular offshoots of the CAAs were the so-called national-emphasis programs, designed in Washington and administered according to federal guidelines. The Legal Services Program, staffed by attorneys, helped millions of poor people in legal battles with housing authorities, welfare departments, police, and slumlords. Head Start and Follow Through reached more than 2 million poor children and significantly improved the long-range educational achievement of participants.

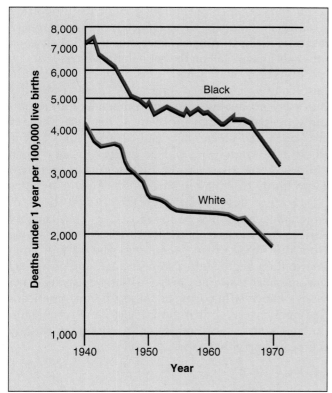

Comparative Figures on Infant Mortality by Race, 1940–1970 The causes of infant mortality such as inadequate maternal diets, prenatal care, and medical services were all rooted in poverty, both rural and urban. Despite generally falling rates of infant mortality, nonwhite people continued to suffer the effects more than white people.

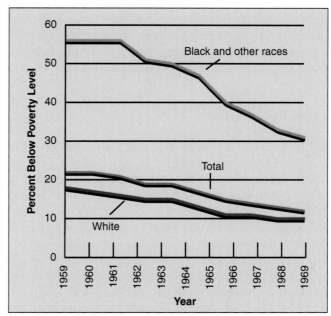

Percent of Population Below Poverty Level, by Race, 1959–1969
Note: The poverty threshold for a nonfarm family of four was $3,743 in 1969 and $2,973 in 1959.

SOURCE: *Congressional Quarterly, Civil Rights: A Progress Report,* 1971, p. 46.

Comprehensive Community Health Centers—one-stop clinics—provided basic medical services to poor patients who could not afford to see doctors. Upward Bound helped low-income teenagers develop the skills and confidence needed for college. Birth control programs dispensed contraceptive supplies and information to hundreds of thousands of poor women.

But the root cause of poverty lay in unequal income distribution. The Johnson administration never committed itself to the redistribution of income or wealth. Spending on social welfare jumped from 7.7 percent of the gross national product in 1960 to 16 percent in 1974. But roughly three-quarters of social welfare payments went to the nonpoor. The largest sums went to Medicare, established by Congress in 1965 to provide basic health care for the aged, and to expanded Social Security payments and unemployment compensation.

The War on Poverty, like the Great Society itself, became a forgotten dream. "More than five years after the passage of the Economic Opportunity Act," a 1970 study concluded, "the war on poverty has barely scratched the surface. Most poor people have had no contact with it, except perhaps to hear the promises of a better life to come." Having made the largest commitment to federal spending on social welfare since the New Deal, Johnson could take pride in the gains scored in the War on Poverty. At the same time, he had raised expectations higher than could be reached without a more drastic redistribution of economic and political power. Even in the short run, the president could not sustain the welfare programs and simultaneously fight a lengthy and expensive war abroad.

Crisis in the Cities

With funds for new construction limited during the Great Depression and World War II, and the postwar boom taking place in the suburbs, the housing stock in the cities diminished and deteriorated. The Federal Housing Administration had encouraged this trend by insuring loans to support the building of new homes in suburban areas (see Chapter 27). The federal government also encouraged "redlining," which left people in poor neighborhoods without access to building loans. In these areas, the supply of adequate housing declined sharply. Slumlords took advantage of this situation, collecting high rents while allowing their properties to deteriorate. City officials meanwhile appealed for federal funds under Title I of the 1949 Housing Act to upgrade housing. Designed as a program of civic revitalization, these urban renewal projects more often than not sliced apart poor neighborhoods with new highways, demolished them in favor of new office complexes, or, as in Chicago's Uptown, favored new developments for the middle class rather than the poor. In 1968 a federal survey showed that 80 percent of those residents who had been displaced under this program were nonwhite.

Urban employment opportunities declined along with the urban housing stock. The industries and corporations that had lured working men and women to the cities a century earlier either automated their plants, thus scaling back their workforces, or relocated to the suburbs or other regions, such as the South and Southwest, that promised lower corporate taxes and nonunion labor. Nationwide, military spending prompted by the escalation of the Vietnam War brought the unemployment rate down from 6 percent, where it was in 1960, to 4 percent in 1966, where it remained until the end of the decade. Black unemployment, however, was nearly twice that of white unemployment. In northern cities, the proportion of the workforce employed in the higher-paying manufacturing jobs declined precipitously while the proportion working in minimum-wage service industries rose at a fast rate. In short, African Americans were losing good jobs and steadily falling farther behind whites.

Pollution, which had long plagued traffic-congested cities like Los Angeles and industrial cities like steel-producing Pittsburgh, became an increasingly pervasive urban problem. Cities like Phoenix that once had clean air began to issue smog alerts. Pointing to high levels of lead in the blood of urban children, scientists warned of the long-term threat of pollution to public health.

Despite deteriorating conditions, millions of Americans continued to move to the cities, mainly African Americans from the Deep South, white people from the Appalachian Mountains, and Latinos from Puerto Rico. By the mid-1960s, African Americans had become near majorities in the nation's decaying inner cities. The vast majority of these African Americans fled rural poverty only to find themselves earning minimum wages at best and living in miserable, racially segregated neighborhoods.

Urban Uprisings

These deteriorating conditions brought urban pressures to the boiling point in the mid-1960s. In the "long, hot summers" of 1964 to 1968 the nation was rocked by more than 100 urban uprisings.

The first major uprising erupted in August 1965 in the Watts section of Los Angeles. Here, the male unemployment rate hovered around 30 percent. Watts lacked health-care facilities—the nearest hospital was twelve miles away—and in a city with little public transportation, fewer than one-fifth of its residents owned cars. It took only a minor arrest to set off the uprising, which quickly spread outward for fifty miles. Throwing rocks and bottles through store windows, participants reportedly shouted, "This is for Selma! This is for Birmingham!" and "Burn, baby, burn!" Nearly 50,000 people turned out, and 20,000 National Guard troops were sent in. After six days, 34 people lay dead, 900 were injured, and 4,000 more had been arrested. Los Angeles chief of police William H. Parker blamed civil rights workers, the mayor accused Communists, and both feigned ignorance when the media reported that white police assigned to "charcoal alley," their name for the Watts district, had for years referred to their nightsticks as "nigger knockers."

The following summer, large-scale uprisings occurred in San Francisco, Milwaukee, Dayton, and Cleveland. On July 12, 1967, in Newark, New Jersey, a city with severe housing shortages and the nation's highest black unemployment rate, the beating and arrest of a black taxi driver by a white police officer provoked a widespread protest. Five days of looting and burning of white-owned buildings ended with twenty-five people dead. One week later the Detroit "Great Rebellion" began. This time a vice squad of the Detroit police had raided a bar and arrested the after-hours patrons. Army tanks and paratroopers were brought in to quell the massive disturbance, which lasted a week and left 34 people dead and 7,000 under arrest.

The uprisings seemed at first to prompt badly needed reforms. After Watts, President Johnson set up a task force headed by Deputy Attorney General Ramsey Clark and allocated funds for a range of antipoverty programs. Several years later the Kerner Commission, headed by Governor Otto Kerner of

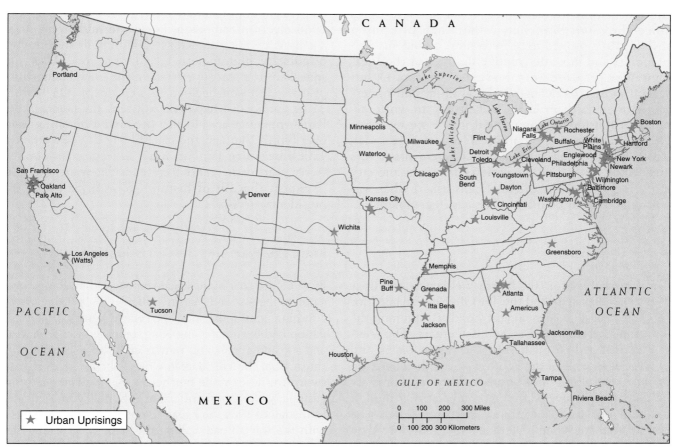

Urban Uprisings, 1965–1968   After World War II urban uprisings precipitated by racial conflict increased in African American communities. In Watts in 1965 and in Detroit and Newark in 1967, rioters struck out at symbols of white control of their communities, such as white-owned businesses and residential properties.

Illinois, studied the riots and found that the participants in the uprisings were not the poorest or least-educated members of their communities. They suffered instead from heightened expectations sparked by the civil rights movement and Johnson's promise of a Great Society, expectations that were not to be realized.

But Congress ignored the commission's warning that "our nation is moving toward two societies, one black, one white—separate and unequal." Moreover, the costs of the Vietnam War left little federal money for antipoverty programs. Senator William Fulbright noted, "Each war feeds on the other, and, although the President assures us that we have the resources to win both wars, in fact we are not winning either of them."

1968

The urban uprisings of the summer of 1967 marked the most drawn-out violence in the United States since the Civil War. But, rather than offering a respite, 1968 proved to be even more turbulent. The bloodiest and most destructive fighting of the Vietnam War resulted in a hopeless stalemate that soured most Americans on the conflict and undermined their faith in U.S. invincibility in world affairs. Disillusionment deepened in the spring when two of the most revered political leaders were struck down by assassins' bullets. Once again protesters and police clashed on the nation's campuses and city streets, and millions of Americans asked what was wrong with their country. Why was it so violent?

The Tet Offensive

On January 30, 1968, the North Vietnamese and their Vietcong allies launched the Tet Offensive (named for the Vietnamese lunar new year holiday), stunning the U.S. military command in South Vietnam. The Vietcong managed to push into the major cities and provincial capitals of the South, as far as the courtyard of the U.S. embassy in Saigon. U.S. troops ultimately halted the offensive, suffering comparatively modest casualties of 1,600 dead and 8,000 wounded. The North Vietnamese and Vietcong suffered more than 40,000 deaths, about one-fifth of their total forces. Civilian casualties ran to the hundreds of thousands. As many as 1 million South Vietnamese became refugees, their villages totally ruined.

The Tet Offensive, despite the U.S. success in stopping it, shattered the credibility of American officials who had repeatedly claimed the enemy to be virtually beaten. Television and press coverage—including scenes of U.S. personnel shooting from the embassy windows in Saigon—dismayed the public. Americans saw the beautiful, ancient city of Hue devastated almost beyond recognition. Television newscasters began to warn parents: "The following scenes might not be suitable viewing for children."

The United States had chalked up a major military victory during the Tet Offensive but lost the war at home. For the first time, polls showed strong opposition to the war, 49 percent concluding that the entire operation in Vietnam was a mistake. Meanwhile, in Rome, Berlin, Paris, and London, students and others turned out in huge demonstrations to protest U.S. involvement in Vietnam. At home, sectors of the antiwar movement began to shift from resistance to open rebellion.

The Tet Offensive also opened a year of political drama at home. Congress resoundingly turned down a request for a general increase in troops issued by General Westmoreland. President Johnson, facing the 1968 election campaign, knew the odds were now against him. He watched as opinion polls showed his popularity plummet to an all-time low. After he squeaked to a narrow victory in the New Hampshire primary, Johnson decided to step down. On March 31 he announced he would not seek the Democratic Party's nomination. He also declared a bombing halt over North Vietnam and called Hanoi to peace talks, which began in Paris in May. Like Truman almost thirty years earlier, and despite his determination not to repeat that bit of history, Johnson had lost his presidency in Asia.

King, the War, and the Assassination

By 1968 the civil rights leadership stood firmly in opposition to the war, and Martin Luther King, Jr. had reached a turning point in his life. The Federal Bureau of Investigation had been harassing King, tapping his telephones and spreading malicious rumors about him. Despite the threat from the FBI (Bureau Chief J. Edgar Hoover had sworn to "destroy the burrhead"), King abandoned his customary caution in criticizing U.S. policy in Vietnam. In the fall of 1965, he began to connect domestic unrest with the war abroad, calling the U.S. government the "greatest purveyor of violence in the world today." As he became more militant in opposing the war, King lost the support of liberal Democrats who remained loyal to Johnson. King refused to compromise.

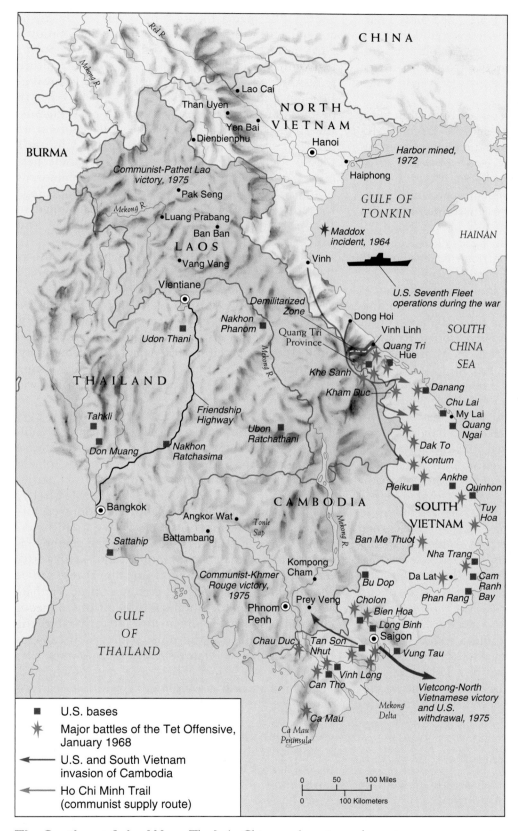

The Southeast Asian War The Indo-Chinese subcontinent, home to long-standing regional conflict, became the center of a prolonged war with the United States.

In the spring of 1968 King chose Memphis, Tennessee, home of striking sanitation workers, as the place to inaugurate a Poor People's Campaign for peace and justice. April 4, 1968, as he stepped out on the balcony of his motel, King was shot and killed by a lone assassin, James Earl Ray.

Throughout the world crowds turned out to mourn King's death. Student Nonviolent Coordinating Committee leader Stokely Carmichael stormed, "When white America killed Dr. King, she declared war on us." Riots broke out in more than 100 cities. Chicago Mayor Richard Daley ordered his police to shoot to kill. In Washington, D.C., U.S. Army units set up machine guns outside the Capitol and the White House. By week's end, nearly 27,000 African Americans had been jailed.

The Democratic Campaign

The dramatic events of the first part of the year had a direct impact on the presidential campaign. For those liberals dissatisfied with Johnson's conduct of the war, and especially for African Americans suffering the loss of their greatest national leader, New York senator Robert F. Kennedy emerged as the candidate of choice. Kennedy enjoyed a strong record on civil rights, and, like King, he had begun to interpret the war as a mirror of injustice at home. Kennedy insisted during the Tet Offensive that "our nation must be told the truth about this war, in all its terrible reality." On this promise he began to build a campaign for the Democratic nomination.

Ironically, Kennedy faced an opponent who agreed with him, Minnesota senator Eugene McCarthy. The race for the Democratic nomination positioned McCarthy, the witty philosopher, against Kennedy, the charismatic campaigner. McCarthy garnered support from liberal Democrats and white suburbanites. On college campuses his popularity with idealistic students was so great that his campaign became known as the "children's crusade." Kennedy reached out successfully to African Americans and Latinos and won all but the Oregon primary.

Kennedy appeared to be the Democratic Party's strongest candidate as June 4, the day of the California primary, dawned. But as the final tabulation of his victory came in just past midnight, Robert Kennedy was struck down by the bullet of an assassin, a Jordanian national named Sirhan Sirhan.

Vice President Hubert H. Humphrey, a longtime presidential hopeful, was now the sole Democrat with the credentials to succeed Johnson. But his reputation as a cold war Democrat had become a liability. In the 1950s Humphrey had delivered stirring addresses for civil rights and antipoverty legislation; yet he also sponsored repressive cold war measures and supported huge defense appropriations that diverted needed funds from domestic programs. He fully supported the Vietnam War and had publicly scorned peace activists as cowardly and un-American. Incongruously calling his campaign the "Politics of Joy," Humphrey simultaneously courted Democrats who grimly supported the war and the King-Kennedy wing, which was sickened by it.

Humphrey skillfully cultivated the Democratic power brokers. Without entering a single state primary, he lined up delegates loyal to city bosses, labor leaders, and conservative southern Democrats. As the candidate least likely to rock the boat, he had secured his party's nomination well before delegates met in convention.

"The Whole World Is Watching!"

The events surrounding the Democratic convention in Chicago, August 21–26, demonstrated how deep the divisions within the United States had become. Antiwar activists had called for a massive demonstration at the delegates' hotel and at the convention center. The media focused, however, on the plans announced by the "Yippies," or Youth International Party, a largely imaginary organization of politicized hippies led by jokester and counterculture guru Abbie Hoffman. Yippies called for a Festival of Life, including a "nude-in" on Lake Michigan beaches and the release of a greased pig—Pigasus, the Yippie candidate for president. Still reeling from the riots following King's assassination, Chicago's Mayor Richard Daley refused to issue parade permits. According to later accounts, he sent hundreds of undercover police into the crowds to encourage rock throwing and generally to incite violence so that retaliation would appear necessary and reasonable.

Daley's strategy boomeranged when his officers staged what a presidential commission later termed a "police riot," randomly assaulting demonstrators, casual passersby, and television crews filming the events. For one of the few times in American history, the media appeared to join a protest against civil authorities. Angered by the embarrassing publicity, Daley sent his agents to raid McCarthy's campaign headquarters, where Democrats opposed to the war had gathered.

Inside the convention hall, a raging debate over a peace resolution underscored the depth of the division within the party over the war. Representative Wayne Hays of Ohio lashed out at those who substituted "beards for brains . . . [and] pot [for] patriotism." When the resolution failed, McCarthy delegates put on black armbands and followed folk singer Theodore Bikel in singing "We Shall Overcome." Later, as tear gas used against the demonstrators outside turned the amphitheater air acrid, delegates heard the beaming Humphrey praise Mayor Daley and Johnson's conduct of the Vietnam War. When Senator Abraham Ribicoff of Connecticut addressed the convention and protested the "Gestapo tactics" of the police, television cameras focused on Mayor Daley saying, "You Jew son of a bitch . . . , go home!" The crowd outside chanted, "The whole world is watching! The whole world is watching!" Indeed, through satellite transmission, it was.

Protest and social strain spread worldwide. Across the United States the antiwar movement picked up steam. In Paris, students took over campuses and workers occupied factories. Young people scrawled on the walls such humorous and half-serious slogans as "Be Realistic, Demand the Impossible!" Similar protests against authority occurred in eastern Europe. In Prague, Czechoslovakia, students wearing blue jeans and singing Beatles songs threw rocks at Soviet tanks. Meanwhile, demonstrations in Japan, Italy, Ireland, Germany, and England all brought young people into the streets to demand democratic reforms in their own countries and an end to the war in Vietnam.

THE POLITICS OF IDENTITY

The tragic events of 1968 brought whole sectors of the counterculture into political activism. With great media fanfare, gay liberation and women's liberation movements emerged in the late 1960s. By the early 1970s, young Latinos, Asian Americans, and Indian peoples had pressed their own claims. In different ways, these groups drew their own lessons from the nationalist movement that formed in the wake of Malcolm X's death—Black Power. Soon, "Brown Power," "Yellow Power," and "Red Power" became the slogans of movements constituted distinctly as new communities of protest.

Black Power

Derived from a century-long tradition of black nationalism, the key tenets of Black Power were self-determination and self-sufficiency. National conferences of activists, held annually beginning in 1966, adopted separatist resolutions, including a plan to partition the United States into black and white nations. Black Power also promoted self-esteem by affirming the unique history and heritage of African peoples.

The movement's boldest expression was the Black Panther Party for Self-Defense, founded in Oakland, California, in 1966 by Huey P. Newton and Bobby Seale. Armed self-defense was the Panthers' strategy, and they adopted a paramilitary style—black leather jackets, shoes, black berets, and firearms—that infuriated local authorities. Monitoring local police, a practice Panthers termed "patrolling the pigs," was their major activity. In several communities, Panthers also ran free breakfast programs for schoolchildren, established medical clinics, and conducted educational classes.

For a time the Panthers became folk heroes. Persecuted by local police and the FBI—there were more than thirty raids on Panther offices in eleven states during 1968 and 1969—the Panthers were arrested, prosecuted, and sentenced to long terms in jail that effectively destroyed the organization.

Black Power nevertheless continued to grow during the late 1960s and became a multifaceted movement. The Reverend Jesse Jackson, for example, rallied African Americans in Chicago to boycott the A&P supermarket chain until the firm hired 700 black workers. A dynamic speaker and skillful organizer, Jackson encouraged African Americans to support

The war in Vietnam contributed to the growing racial militancy in the United States. African Americans served on the front lines in Vietnam in disproportionate numbers, and many came to view the conflict as a "white man's war."

SOURCE: James Meredith march through Mississippi. Photo by Matt Herron. Media Image Resource Alliance (0001A089).

their own businesses and services. His program, Operation Breadbasket, strengthened community control. By 1970 it had spread beyond Chicago to fifteen other cities.

Cultural nationalism became the most enduring component of Black Power. In their popular book *Black Power* (1967), Stokely Carmichael and Charles V. Hamilton urged African Americans "to assert their own definitions, to reclaim their history, their culture; to create their own sense of community and togetherness." Thousands of college students responded by calling for more scholarships and for more classes on African American history and culture.

Meanwhile, trend setters put aside Western dress for African-style dashikis and hairdos, and black parents gave their children African names. Many well-known African Americans such as Imamu Amiri Baraka (formerly LeRoi Jones), Muhammad Ali (formerly Cassius Clay), and Kwame Touré (formerly Stokely Carmichael) rejected their "slave names." The African American holiday Kwanzaa began to replace Christmas as a seasonal family celebration. This deepening sense of racial pride and solidarity was summed up in the popular slogan "Black Is Beautiful."

Sisterhood Is Powerful

Like Black Power, the women's liberation movement especially attracted women who had been active in civil rights, SDS, and campus antiwar movements. These women resented the sexist attitudes and behaviors of their fellow male activists. Impatient with the legislative reforms promoted by NOW, and angered by the sexism of SNCC and SDS, these women proclaimed "Sisterhood Is Powerful." "Women are an oppressed class. Our oppression is total, affecting every facet of our lives," read the Redstocking Manifesto of 1969. "We are exploited as sex objects, breeders, domestic servants, and cheap labor."

The women's liberation movement developed a scathing critique of patriarchy—that is, the power of men to dominate all institutions, from the family to business to the military to the protest movements themselves. Patriarchy, they argued, was the prime cause of exploitation, racism, and war. Outraged and sometimes outrageous, radical feminists, as they called themselves, conducted "street theater" at the 1968 Miss America Beauty Pageant in Atlantic City, crowning a live sheep as queen and "throwing imple-

ments of female torture" (bras, girdles, curlers, and copies of the *Ladies' Home Journal*) into a "freedom trash can."

The media focused on the audacious acts and brazen pronouncements of radical feminists, but the majority involved in the women's liberation movement were less flamboyant women who were simply trying to rise above the limitations imposed on them because of their sex. Most of their activism took place outside the limelight in consciousness-raising (CR) groups. CR groups, which multiplied by the thousands in the late 1960s and early 1970s, brought women together to discuss the relationship between public events and private lives, particularly between politics and sexuality. Here women shared their most intimate feelings toward men or other women and established the constituency for the movement's most important belief, expressed in the aphorism "The personal is political." Believing that no aspect of life lacked a political dimension, women in these groups explored the power dynamics of the institutions of family and marriage as well as the workforce and government.

Participants in the women's liberation movement engaged in a wide range of activities. Some staged sit-ins at *Newsweek* to protest demeaning media depictions of women. Others established health clinics, day-care centers, rape crisis centers, and shelters for women fleeing abusive husbands or lovers. The women's liberation movement also had a significant educational impact. Feminist bookstores and publishing companies, such as the Feminist Press, reached out to eager readers. Scholarly books such as Kate Millett's *Sexual Politics* (1970) found a wide popular audience. By the early 1970s, campus activists were demanding women's studies programs and women's centers. Like black studies, women's studies programs included traditional academic goals, such as the generation of new scholarship, but also encouraged personal change and self-esteem. Between 1970 and 1975, as many as 150 women's studies programs had been established. The movement continued to grow; by 1980 nearly 30,000 women's studies courses were offered at colleges and universities throughout the United States.

The women's liberation movement remained, however, a bastion of white middle-class women. The appeal to sisterhood did not unite women across race or class or even sexual orientation. Lesbians, who charged the early leaders of NOW with homophobia, found large pockets of "heterosexism" in the women's liberation movement and broke off to form their own organizations. Although some

OVERVIEW

PROTEST MOVEMENTS OF THE 1960S

Year	Organization/ Movement	Description
1962	Students for a Democratic Society (SDS)	Organization of college students that became the largest national organization of left-wing white students. Calling for "participatory democracy," SDS involved students in community-based campaigns against poverty and for citizens' control of neighborhoods. SDS played a prominent role in the campaign to end the war in Vietnam.
1964	Free Speech Movement	Formed at the University of California at Berkeley to protest the banning of on-campus political fund-raising. Decried the bureaucratic character of the "multiuniversity" and advocated an expansion of student rights.
1965	Anti-Vietnam War Movement	Advocated grass-roots opposition to U.S. involvement in Southeast Asia. By 1970 a national mobilization committee organized a demonstration of a half-million protesters in Washington, D.C.
1965	*La raza*	A movement of Chicano youth to advance the cultural and political self-determination of Mexican Americans. *La raza* included the Brown Berets, which addressed community issues, and regional civil rights groups such as the Crusade for Social Justice, formed in 1965.
1966	Black Power	Militant movement that emerged from the civil rights campaigns to advocate independent institutions for African Americans and pride in black culture and African heritage. The idea of Black Power, a term coined by Stokely Carmichael, inspired the formation of the paramilitary Black Panthers.
1968	American Indian Movement (AIM)	Organization formed to advance the self-determination of Indian peoples and challenge the authority of the Bureau of Indian Affairs. Its most effective tactic was occupation. In February, 1973, AIM insurgents protesting land and treaty violations occupied Wounded Knee, South Dakota, the location of an 1890 massacre, until the FBI and BIA agents drove them out.
1968	Women's Liberation	Movement of mainly young women that took shape following a protest at the Miss America Beauty Pageant. Impatient with the legislative reforms promoted by the National Organization for Women, founded in 1966, activists developed their own agenda shaped by the slogan "The Personal Is Political." Activities included the formation of "consciousness-raising" groups and the establishment of women's studies programs.
1968	Asian American Political Alliance (AAPA)	Formed at the University of California at Berkeley, the AAPA was one of the first pan-Asian political organizations to struggle against racial oppression. The AAPA encouraged Asian Americans to claim their own cultural identity and to protest the war against Asian peoples in Vietnam.
1969	Gay Liberation	Movement to protest discrimination against homosexuals and lesbians that emerged after the Stonewall Riots in New York City. Unlike earlier organizations such as the Mattachine Society, which focused on civil rights, Gay Liberationists sought to radically change American society and government, which they believed were corrupt.

African American women were outraged at the posturing of Black Power leaders like Stokely Carmichael, who joked that "the only position for women in SNCC is prone," the majority remained wary of white women's appeals to sisterhood. African American women formed their own "womanist" movement to address their distinct cultural and political concerns. Similarly, by 1970 a Latina feminist movement had begun to address issues uniquely relevant to women of color in an Anglo-dominated society.

Gay Liberation

The gay community had been generations in the making but only gained visibility during World War II (see Chapter 25). By the mid-1950s, two pioneering homophile organizations, the Mattachine Society and the Daughters of Bilitis, were campaigning to reduce discrimination against homosexuals in employment, the armed forces, and all areas of social and cultural life. Other groups, such as the Society for Individual Rights, rooted themselves in New York's Greenwich Village, San Francisco's North Beach, and other centers of gay night life. But it was during the tumultuous 1960s that gay and lesbian movements encouraged many men and women to proclaim publicly their sexual identity: "Say It Loud, Gay Is Proud."

The major event prompting gays to organize grew out of repeated police raids of gay bars and the harassment of their patrons. On Friday, June 27, 1969, New York police raided the Stonewall Inn, a well-known gay bar in Greenwich Village, and provoked an uprising of angry homosexuals that lasted the entire night. The next day, "Gay Power" graffiti appeared on buildings and sidewalks throughout the neighborhood. The Stonewall Riot, as it was called, sparked a new sense of collective identity among many gays and lesbians and touched off a new movement for both civil rights and liberation. Gay men and women in New York City formed the Gay Liberation Front (GLF), announcing themselves as "a revolutionary homosexual group of men and women formed with the realization that complete sexual liberation for all people cannot come about unless existing social institutions are abolished. We reject society's attempt to impose sexual roles and definitions of our nature. We are stepping outside these roles and simplistic myths. We are going to be who we are." The GLF also took a stand against the war in Vietnam and supported the Black Panthers. It

quickly adopted the forms of public protest, such as street demonstrations and sit-ins, developed by the civil rights movement and given new direction by antiwar protesters.

Changes in public opinion and policies followed. As early as 1967 a group of Episcopal priests had urged church leaders to avoid taking a moral position against same-sex relationships. The San Francisco–based Council on Religion and Homosexuality established a network for clergy sympathetic to gay and lesbian parishioners. In 1973 the American Psychiatric Association, which since World War II had viewed homosexuality as a treatable mental illness, reclassified it as a normal sexual orientation. Meanwhile, there began a slow process of decriminalization of homosexual acts between consenting adults. In 1975 the U.S. Civil Service Commission ended its ban on the employment of homosexuals.

The Chicano Rebellion

By the mid-1960s young Mexican Americans adopted the slang term *Chicano*, in preference to Mexican American, to express a militant ethnic nationalism. Chicano militants demanded not only equality with white people but cultural and political self-determination. Tracing their roots to the heroic Aztecs, they identified *la raza* (the race or people) as the source of a common language, religion, and heritage.

Students played a large role in shaping the Chicano movement. In East Los Angeles, high school students staged "blowouts" or strikes to demand educational reform and a curricular emphasis on the history, literature, art, and language of Mexican Americans. Fifteen thousand students from five Los Angeles schools struck against poor educational facilities. The police conducted a mass arrest of protesters, and within a short time students in San Antonio and Denver were conducting their own blowouts, holding placards reading "Teachers, Sí, Bigots, No!" By 1969, on September 16, Mexican Independence Day, high school students throughout the Southwest skipped classes in the First National Chicano Boycott. Meanwhile, students organized to demand Mexican American studies on their campuses. In 1969, a group staged a sit-in at the administrative offices of the University of California at Berkeley, which one commentator called "the first important public appearance of something called Brown Power."

Chicano nationalism inspired a variety of regional political movements in the late 1960s. One of these, Rodolfo "Corky" Gonzales's Crusade for Justice, formed in 1965 to protest the failure of the Great Society's antipoverty programs. A former boxer and popular poet, Gonzales was especially well liked by barrio youth and college students. He led important campaigns for greater job opportunities and land reform throughout the Southwest well into the 1970s. In Colorado and New Mexico, the *Alianza Federal de Mercedes*, formed in 1963 by Reies López Tijerina, fought to reclaim land fraudulently appropriated by white settlers. The Texas-based *La Raza Unida Party* (LRUP), meanwhile, increased Mexican American representation in local government and established social and cultural programs.

Mexican American activists, even those who won local office, soon discovered that economic power remained out of community hands. Stifled by poverty, ordinary Mexican Americans had less confidence in the political process, and many fell back into apathy after early hopes of great, sudden change. Despite these setbacks, a sense of collective identity had been forged among many Mexican Americans.

The Chicano movement found vivid expression in the performing and visual arts and in literature. *Teatro*, comprising film and drama, drew creatively on Mexican and Anglo cultural forms to explore the political dimensions of Mexican American society. *La Carpa de los Rasquachis (The Tent of the Underdogs)*, appeared in 1974 as the first full-length Chicano play and was subsequently staged in many communities. One of the most popular and visible media was the mural, often based on the works of Mexican masters such as Diego Rivera. Chicano muralists painted an estimated 1,500 murals on public buildings throughout their communities, from the exteriors of retail shops to freeway overpasses, even to large drainage pipes. Artistic expression found its way into music and dance. The rock group *Los Lobos*, for example, dedicated their first recorded album to the United Farm Workers. One of the most important writers to capture the excitement of the Chicano movement was Oscar Zeta Acosta, whose *Revolt of the Cockroach*, published in 1973, renders into fiction some of the major events of the era.

Labor activist Cesar Chavez spearheaded the organization of Chicano agricultural workers into the United Farm Workers (UFW), the first successful union of migrant workers. In 1965, a strike of grape pickers in the fields around Delano, California, and a nationwide boycott of table grapes brought Chevez and the UFW into the media spotlight. Like Martin Luther King, Jr., he advocated nonviolent methods for achieving justice and equality.

SOURCE: EPA Documercia (1927–1933) National Archives and Records Administration.

Red Power

The phrase "Red Power," attributed to Vine Deloria, Jr., commonly expressed a growing sense of supratribal Indian identity. At the forefront of this movement was the American Indian Movement (AIM), which was founded in 1968. Its members represented mainly urban Indian communities, and its leaders were young and militant. Like the Black Panthers and Brown Berets, AIM was initially organized to monitor law enforcement practices such as police harassment and brutality. It soon played a major role in building a network of urban Indian centers, churches, and philanthropic organizations and in establishing the "powwow circuit" that publicized news of protest activities across the country. Skillful in attracting attention from the news media, AIM quickly inspired a plethora of new publications and local chapters. Many young Indians turned to their elders to learn tribal ways, including traditional dress and spiritual practices.

The major catalyst of Red Power was the occupation of the deserted federal prison on Alcatraz Island in San Francisco Bay on November 20, 1969. A group of eighty-nine Indians, identifying themselves as "Indians of All Tribes," claimed the island according to the terms of an 1868 Sioux treaty that gave Indians rights to unused federal property on Indian land. The group demanded federal funds for a multifaceted cultural and educational center. For the next year and a half, an occupation force averaging around 100 and a stream of visitors from a large number of tribes celebrated the occupation. Although the protestors ultimately failed to achieve their specific goals, they had an enormous impact on the Indian community. With the occupation at Alcatraz, a participant testified, "we got back our worth, our pride, our dignity, our humanity." At the same time, the occupation fostered a new identity, a multitribal ethnicity —the American Indian.

The most dramatic series of events of the Red Power movement began in 1972, when Indian activists left the cities to return to their rural roots. In November, AIM staged an event known as the "Trail of Broken Treaties" that culminated in a week-long occupation of the Bureau of Indian Affairs in Washington, D.C. Emphasizing treaty violation rather than civil rights, AIM insurgents then moved to the Pine Ridge Reservation, the site of the 1890 massacre at Wounded Knee, South Dakota, where in the spring of 1973 they began a siege that lasted ten weeks. AIM activists demanded the removal of the leader of the Oglala Lakota, whom they believed to be a corrupt puppet of the Bureau of Indian Affairs, and the restoration of treaty rights. Dozens of FBI agents then invaded under shoot-to-kill orders, leaving two Indians dead and an unknown number of casualties on both sides.

Several tribes won in court, by legislation or by administrative fiat, small parts of what had earlier been taken from them. Despite these victories, tribal lands continued to suffer from industrial and government waste dumping and other commercial uses. On reservations and in urban areas with heavy Indian concentrations, alcohol abuse and ill health remained serious problems.

The 1960s also marked the beginning of an "Indian Renaissance" in literature. New books like Vine Deloria, Jr.'s *Custer Died for Your Sins* (1969) and the classic *Black Elk Speaks* (1961), reprinted from the 1930s, reached millions of readers inside and outside Indian communities. A wide variety of Indian novelists, historians, and essayists, such as Pulitzer Prize–winning N. Scott Momaday and Leslie Silko, followed up these successes, and fiction and nonfiction works about Indian life and lore continued to attract a large audience.

The Asian American Movement

In 1968 students at the University of California at Berkeley founded the Asian American Political Alliance (AAPA), one of the first pan-Asian political organizations bringing together Chinese, Japanese, and Filipino American activists. Similar organizations soon appeared on campuses throughout California and spread quickly to the East Coast and Midwest.

These groups took a strong stand against the war in Vietnam, condemning it as a violation of the national sovereignty of the small Asian country. They also protested the racism directed against the peoples of Southeast Asia, particularly the practice common among American soldiers of referring to the enemy as "Gooks." This racist epithet, first used to denigrate Filipinos during the Spanish-American War, implied that Asians were something less than human and, therefore, proper targets for slaughter. In response, Asian American activists rallied behind the people of Vietnam and proclaimed racial solidarity with their "Asian brothers and sisters."

Between 1968 and 1973, major universities across the country introduced courses on Asian American studies, and a few, such as the City College of New York, set up interdisciplinary departments. Meanwhile, artists, writers, documentary filmmakers, oral historians, and anthropologists worked to recover the Asian American past. Maxine Hong Kingston's *Woman Warrior: A Memoir of a Girlhood among Ghosts* (1976) became a major bestseller.

Looking to the example of the Black Panthers, young Asian Americans also took their struggle into the community. In 1968, activists presented the San Francisco municipal government with a list of grievances about conditions in Chinatown, particularly the poor housing and medical facilities, and organized a protest march down the neighborhood's main street. They led a communitywide struggle to save San Francisco's International Hotel, a low-income residential facility mainly for Filipino and Chinese men, which was ultimately leveled for a new parking lot.

Community activists ranging from college students to neighborhood artists worked in a variety of campaigns to heighten public awareness. The Redress and Reparations Movement, initiated by Sansei (third-generation Japanese Americans), for example, encouraged students to ask their parents about their wartime experiences and prompted older civil rights organizations, such as the Japanese American Citizens League, to bring forward the issue of internment. At the same time, trade union organizers renewed labor organizing among new Asian workers, mainly in service industries, such as hotel and restaurant work, and in clothing manufacturing. Other campaigns reflected the growing diversity of the Asian population. Filipinos, the fastest-growing group, organized to protest the destructive role of U.S.-backed Philippine dictator Ferdinand Marcos. Students from South Korea similarly denounced the repressive government in their homeland. Samoans sought to publicize the damage caused by nuclear testing in the Pacific Islands. Ultimately, however, in blurring intergroup differences, the Asian American movement failed to reach the growing populations of new immigrants, especially the numerous Southeast Asians fleeing their devastated homeland.

THE NIXON PRESIDENCY

The sharp divisions among Americans in 1968, mainly due to President Johnson's policies in Vietnam, paved the way for the election of Richard Milhous Nixon. The new Republican president inherited not only an increasingly unpopular war but a nation riven by internal discord. Without specifying his plans, he promised a "just and honorable peace" in Southeast Asia and the restoration of law and order at home. Yet, once in office, Nixon puzzled both friends and foes. He ordered unprecedented illegal government action against private citizens while agreeing with Congress to enhance several welfare programs and improve environmental protection. He widened and intensified the war in Vietnam, yet made stunning moves toward détente with the People's Republic of China. An architect of the cold war in the 1950s, Nixon became the first president to foresee its end. Nixon worked hard in the White House, centralizing authority and reigning defiantly as an "Imperial President"—until he brought himself down.

The Southern Strategy

In 1968, Republican presidential contender Richard Nixon deftly built on voter hostility toward youthful protesters and the counterculture. He represented, he said, the "silent majority"—those Americans who worked, paid taxes, and did not demonstrate, picket, or protest loudly, "people who are not haters, people who love their country." Recovering from defeats in elections for the presidency in 1960 and the governorship of California in 1962, Nixon declared himself the one candidate who could restore law and order to the nation.

After signing the landmark Civil Rights Act of 1964, President Johnson said privately, "I think we just delivered the South to the Republicans for a long time to come." Republican strategists moved quickly to make this prediction come true. They also recognized the growing electoral importance of the Sunbelt, where populations grew with the rise of high-tech industries and retirement communities. A powerful conservatism dominated this region, home to many military bases, defense plants, and an increasingly influential Protestant evangelism. Nixon appealed directly to these voters by promising to appoint to federal courts judges who would undercut liberal interpretations of civil rights and be tough on crime.

Nixon selected as his running mate Maryland governor Spiro T. Agnew, known for his vitriolic oratory. Agnew treated dissent as near treason. The 1968 campaign underscored the antiliberal sentiment of the

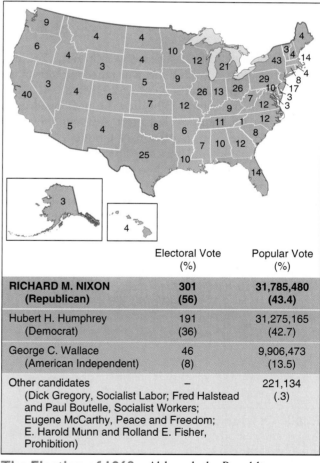

	Electoral Vote (%)	Popular Vote (%)
RICHARD M. NIXON (Republican)	**301 (56)**	**31,785,480 (43.4)**
Hubert H. Humphrey (Democrat)	191 (36)	31,275,165 (42.7)
George C. Wallace (American Independent)	46 (8)	9,906,473 (13.5)
Other candidates (Dick Gregory, Socialist Labor; Fred Halstead and Paul Boutelle, Socialist Workers; Eugene McCarthy, Peace and Freedom; E. Harold Munn and Rolland E. Fisher, Prohibition)	–	221,134 (.3)

The Election of 1968 Although the Republican Nixon-Agnew team won the popular vote by only a small margin, the Democrats lost in most of the northern states that had voted Democratic since the days of FDR. Segregationist Governor George Wallace of Alabama polled more than 9 million votes.

voting public. The most dramatic example was the relative success of Alabama governor George Wallace's third-party bid for the presidency. Wallace took state office in 1963 promising white Alabamans "Segregation now! Segregation tomorrow! Segregation forever!" In 1968 he waged a national campaign around a conservative hate list that included school busing, antiwar demonstrations, and urban uprisings. Winning only five southern states, Wallace nevertheless captured 13.5 percent of the popular vote.

The Nixon-Agnew team squeaked to victory, capturing the popular vote by the slim margin of 43.4 percent to Humphrey and Maine senator Edmund Muskie's 42.7 percent but taking nearly all the West's electoral votes. Bitterly divided by the campaign, the Democrats would remain out of presidential contention for over two decades, except when the Republicans suffered scandal and disgrace. The Republicans in 1968 had paved the way for the conservative ascendancy.

Nixon's War

Nixon promised to bring "peace with honor." Yet, despite this pledge, the Vietnam War raged for four more years before a peace settlement was reached.

Much of the responsibility for the prolonged conflict rested with Henry A. Kissinger. A dominating personality on the National Security Council, Kissinger insisted that the United States could not retain its global leadership by appearing weak to either allies or enemies. Brilliant and ruthless, Kissinger helped Nixon centralize foreign policymaking in the White House. Together, they overpowered those members of the State Department who had concluded that the majority of Americans no longer supported the war.

In public Nixon followed a policy of "Vietnamization." On May 14, 1969, he announced that the time was approaching "when the South Vietnamese . . . will be able to take over some of the fighting." During the next several months, he ordered the withdrawal of 60,000 U.S. troops. Hoping to placate public opinion, Nixon also intended to "demonstrate to Hanoi that we were serious in seeking a diplomatic settlement." In private, with Kissinger's guidance, Nixon mulled over the option of a "knockout blow" to the North Vietnamese.

On April 30, 1970, Nixon made one of the most controversial decisions of his presidency. Without seeking congressional approval, Nixon ordered U.S. troops to invade the tiny nation of Cambodia. Nixon had hoped in this way to end North Vietnamese infiltration into the South, but he had also decided to live up to what he privately called his "wild man" or "mad bomber" reputation. The enemy would be unable to anticipate the location or severity of the next U.S. strike, Nixon reasoned, and would thus feel compelled to negotiate.

Nixon could not have predicted the outpouring of protest that followed the invasion of Cambodia. The largest series of demonstrations and police-student confrontations in the nation's history took place on campuses and in city streets. At Kent State University in Ohio, twenty-eight National Guardsmen apparently panicked, shooting into an unarmed crowd of about 200 students, killing four and wounding nine. Ten days later, on May 14, at Jackson State University, a black school in Mississippi, state troopers entered a campus dormitory and began shooting wildly, killing two students and wounding twelve others. Demonstrations broke out on fifty campuses.

The nation was shocked. Thirty-seven college and university presidents signed a letter calling on the president to end the war. A few weeks later the Senate adopted a bipartisan resolution outlawing the use of funds for U.S. military operations in Cambodia, starting July 1, 1970. Although the House rejected the resolution, Nixon saw the writing on the wall. He had planned to negotiate a simultaneous withdrawal of North Vietnamese and U.S. troops, but he could no longer afford to hold out for this condition.

The president, still goaded by Kissinger, did not accept defeat easily. In February 1971 Nixon directed the South Vietnamese army to invade Laos and cut supply lines, but the demoralized invading force suffered a quick and humiliating defeat. Faced with

> **In view of the developments since we entered the fighting in Vietnam, do you think the United States made a mistake sending troops to fight in Vietnam?**
>
> | | |
> |---|---|
> | Yes | 52% |
> | No | 39 |
> | No opinion | 9 |
>
> Interviewing Date 1/22–28/1969, Survey #774-K, Question #6/Index #45

Public Opinion on the War in Vietnam By 1969 Americans were sharply divided in their assessments of the progress of the war and peace negotiations. The American Institute of Public Opinion, founded in 1935 by George Gallup, charted a growing dissatisfaction with the war in Vietnam.

SOURCE: From *The Gallup Poll*, 1935-1971 by George Gallup, copyright © 1972 by American Institute of Public Opinion. Used by permission of Random House, Inc.

enemy occupation of more and more territory during a major offensive in April 1972, Nixon ordered the mining of North Vietnamese harbors and directed B-52s to conduct massively destructive bombing missions in Cambodia and North Vietnam.

Nixon also sent Kissinger to Paris for secret negotiations with delegates from North Vietnam. They agreed to a cease-fire specifying the withdrawal of all U.S. troops and the return of all U.S. prisoners of war. Knowing these terms ensured defeat, South Vietnam's president refused to sign the agreement. On Christmas Day 1972, hoping for a better negotiating position, Nixon ordered one final wave of bomb attacks on North Vietnam's cities. To secure a halt to the bombing, the North Vietnamese offered to resume negotiations. But the terms of the Paris Peace Agreement, signed by North Vietnam and the United States in January 1973, differed little from the settlement Nixon could have procured in 1969, costing hundreds of thousands of deaths that might have been prevented. Beginning in March 1973, the withdrawal of U.S. troops left the outcome of the war a foregone conclusion. By December of that year only fifty American military personnel remained, and the government of South Vietnam had no future.

In April 1975 North Vietnamese troops took over Saigon, and the Communist-led Democratic Republic of Vietnam soon united the small nation. The war was finally over. It had cost the United States 58,000 lives and $150 billion. The country had not only failed to achieve its stated war goal but had lost an important post in Southeast Asia. Equally important, the policy of containment introduced by President Truman had proved impossible to sustain.

While Nixon was maneuvering to bring about "peace with honor," the chilling crimes of war had already begun to haunt Americans. In 1971 the army court-martialed a young lieutenant, William L. Calley, Jr., for the murder of "at least" twenty-two Vietnamese civilians during a 1968 search-and-destroy mission subsequently known as the My Lai Massacre. Calley's platoon had destroyed a village and slaughtered more than 350 unarmed South Vietnamese, raping and beating many of the women before killing them. "My Lai was not an isolated incident," one veteran attested, but "only a minor step beyond the standard official United States policy in Indochina." Commander of the platoon at My Lai, Calley was first sentenced to life imprisonment before being given a reduced term of ten years. The secretary of the army paroled Calley after he served three years under house arrest in his apartment.

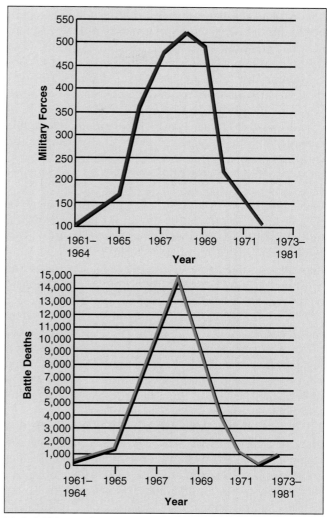

U.S. Military Forces in Vietnam and Casualties, 1961–1981   The United States government estimated battle deaths between 1969 and 1973 for South Vietnamese troops at 107,504 and North Vietnamese and Vietcong at more than a half-million. Although the United States suffered fewer deaths, the cost was enormous.

SOURCE: U.S. Department of Defense, *Selected Manpower Statistics*, annual, and unpublished data; beginning 1981, National Archives and Records Service, "Combat Area Casualty File" (3-330-80-3).

"The China Card"

Apart from Vietnam, Nixon's foreign policy defied the expectations of liberals and conservatives alike. Actually, he followed traditions of previous Republican moderates such as Herbert Hoover and Dwight Eisenhower, who had so effectively "proved" their anticommunism that they could conciliate international foes without undermining their popularity at home. Nixon added a new page, however—a policy of détente that replaced U.S.–Soviet bipolarity with multilateral relations.

Nixon could cultivate relations with the People's Republic of China, a rising world power more rigidly Communist than the Soviet Union, to form an alliance against the Soviet Union. And he could easily persuade the Soviet Union to cooperate on trade agreements, thus limiting the two nations' ruthless competition to control governments in Asia, the Middle East, and Africa. Opponents of the Vietnam War accused Nixon of double dealing, while conservatives howled at any compromise with Communist governments. But Nixon persisted in his plans, anticipating an end to the cold war on American terms.

Playing the "China card" was the most dramatic of the president's moves. Early in his political career Nixon had avidly supported the arch-conservative China lobby. But as president he considered the People's Republic of China too important to be isolated by the West and too obviously hostile to the Soviet Union to be discounted as a potential ally.

"Ping-pong diplomacy" began in April 1971, when the Chinese hosted a table tennis team from the United States. Henry Kissinger embarked on a secret mission a few months later. Finally, in February 1972, Richard and Pat Nixon flew to Beijing, where they were greeted by foreign minister Zhou Enlai and a band playing "The Star-Spangled Banner."

It was a momentous and surprising event, one that marked a new era in East-West diplomacy. Nixon claimed that he had succeeded in bridging "16,000 miles and twenty-two years of hostility." The president's move successfully increased diplomatic pressure on the Soviet Union but simultaneously weakened the Nationalist Chinese government in Taiwan, which now slipped into virtual diplomatic obscurity.

Next the president went to Moscow to negotiate with Soviet leader Leonid Brezhnev, who was anxious about U.S. involvement with China and eager for economic assistance. Declaring, "There must be room in this world for two great nations with different systems to live together and work together," Nixon offered to sell $1 billion of grain to the Soviets. Winning the favor of American wheat farmers, this deal simultaneously relieved U.S. trade deficits and crop surpluses. Afterward, the Soviet leader became visibly more cautious about supporting revolutions in the third world. Nixon also completed negotiations of the Strategic Arms Limitation Treaty (SALT, known later as SALT I). A limited measure, SALT I represented the first success at strategic arms control since the opening of the cold war and a major public relations victory for the leaders of the two superpowers.

Nixon's last major diplomatic foray proved far less effective. The president sent Kissinger on a two-year mission of "shuttle diplomacy" to mediate Israeli-Arab disputes, to ensure the continued flow of oil, and to increase lucrative U.S. arms sales to Arab countries. The Egyptians and Israelis agreed to a cease-fire in their October 1973 Yom Kippur War, but little progress toward peace in the area was achieved.

Domestic Policy

Nixon deeply desired to restore order in American society. "We live in a deeply troubled and profoundly unsettled time," he noted. "Drugs, crime, campus revolts, racial discord, draft resistance—on every hand we find old standards violated, old values discarded." Despite his hostility to liberalism, however, Nixon had some surprises for conservatives. Determined to win reelection in 1972, he supported new Social Security benefits and subsidized housing for the poor and oversaw the creation of the Environmental Protection Agency and the Occupational Safety and Health Administration. Most notable was his support, under the guidance of Democratic adviser Daniel P. Moynihan, for the Family Assistance Plan, which proposed a minimal income for the poor in place of welfare benefits. Conservatives judged the plan too generous while liberals found it inadequate. Moreover, the plan was expensive. Bipartisan opposition ultimately killed the bill.

Nixon also embraced a policy of fiscal liberalism. Early in 1971 he accepted the idea of deficit spending. Later that year he ordered a first: he took the nation off the gold standard. Subsequently, the dollar's value would float on the world market rather than being tied to the value of gold. His ninety-day freeze on wages, rents, and prices, designed to halt the inflation caused by the massive spending on the Vietnam War, also closely resembled Democratic policies. Finally, Nixon's support of "black capitalism"—adjustments or quotas favoring minority contractors in construction projects—created an explosive precedent for "set-aside" programs later blamed on liberals.

Nixon lined up with conservatives, however, on most civil rights issues and thus enlarged southern Republican constituencies. He accepted the principle of school integration but rejected the busing programs required to implement racial balance. His nominees to the Supreme Court were far more conservative than those appointed by Eisenhower. Warren E. Burger, who replaced Chief Justice Earl Warren, steered the Court away from the liberal direction it had taken since the 1950s.

One of the most newsworthy events of Nixon's administration was a distant result of President Kennedy's determination to outshine the Soviets in outer space (see Chapter 27). On July 21, 1969, the lunar module of Apollo 11 descended to the moon's Sea of Tranquility. As millions watched on television, astronauts Neil Armstrong and Buzz Aldrin stepped out to plant an American flag and to bear the message, "We came in peace for all mankind."

WATERGATE

At times Richard Nixon expressed his yearning for approval in strange ways. A few days after the bombing of Cambodia in May 1970, he wandered out of the White House alone at 5:00 in the morning to talk to antiwar demonstrators. He tried to engage them in small talk about football and pleaded, "I know that probably most of you think I'm an SOB, but I want you to know I understand just how you feel." According to H. R. Haldeman, one of Nixon's closest advisers, the student killings at Kent State deeply troubled the president.

Yet only a few months later Nixon ordered illegal wiretaps of news professionals. He also reaffirmed his support of Central Intelligence Agency (CIA) surveillance of U.S. citizens and organizations—a policy specifically forbidden by the CIA charter—and encouraged members of his administration to spy on Democrats planning for the 1972 election campaign. When news of these illegal activities surfaced, one of the most canny politicians in American history found himself the first president since Andrew Johnson to face the likelihood of impeachment proceedings.

Foreign Policy as Conspiracy

Nixon's conduct of foreign policy offered early clues into his political character. Although he had welcomed the publicity surrounding his historic moves toward détente with the Soviet Union and normalized relations with China, Nixon generally handled the nation's foreign affairs in surreptitious fashion. But as opposition to the Vietnam War mounted in Congress, he began to face hard questions about this practice. As early as 1970, Republicans as well as Democrats had condemned covert operations in foreign countries. In response, the president, the Department of State, and the CIA developed plans to tighten security even further. Nixon issued a tough mandate against all leaks of information by government personnel, news specialists, or politicians.

At the time, apart from the highly publicized tour to China, Nixon revealed little about his policy for other parts of the globe. Unknown to most Americans, he accelerated the delivery of arms supplies to foreign dictators, including the shah of Iran, Ferdinand Marcos of the Philippines, and the regime of Pieter William Botha in South Africa. His CIA assistants trained and aided SAVAK, the Iranian secret police force notorious for torturing political dissidents. They also stood behind the South African government in its effort to curtail the activities of the antiapartheid African National Congress. In Latin America, Nixon provided financial assistance and military aid to repressive regimes such as that of Anastasio Somoza of Nicaragua, notorious for its blatant corruption and repeated violations of human rights.

Still more controversial was Nixon's plan to overthrow the legally elected socialist government of Salvador Allende in Chile. With the assistance of nongovernment agencies, such as the AFL-CIO's American Institute for Free Labor Development, the CIA destabilized the regime by funding right-wing parties, launching demonstrations, and preparing the Chilean army for a coup. In September 1973, a military junta killed President Allende and captured, tortured, or murdered thousands of his supporters. Nixon and Kissinger warmly welcomed the new ruler, Augusto Pinochet, granting him financial assistance to restabilize the country.

Toward the end of Nixon's term, members of Congress who had been briefed on these policies began to break silence, and reports of clandestine operations flooded the media. Several former CIA agents issued anguished confessions of their activities in other countries. More troubling to Nixon, in spite of all his efforts the United States continued to lose ground as a superpower.

The Age of Dirty Tricks

As Nixon approached the 1972 reelection campaign, he tightened his inner circle of White House staff who assisted him in withholding information from the public, discrediting critics, and engaging in assorted "dirty tricks." Circle members solicited illegal contributions for the campaign and laundered the money through Mexican bank accounts. They also formed a secret squad, "the plumbers," to halt the troublesome leaks of information. This team, headed by former CIA agent E. Howard Hunt and former FBI agent G. Gordon Liddy, assisted in conspiracy at the highest levels of government.

The first person on the squad's "hit list" was Daniel Ellsberg, a former researcher with the Department of Defense, who in 1971 had turned over to the press secret documents outlining the military history of American involvement in Vietnam. The so-called Pentagon Papers exposed the role of presidents and military leaders in deceiving the public and Congress about the conduct of the United States in Southeast Asia. Nixon sought to bar publication by the *New York Times*, but the Supreme Court ruled in favor of the newspaper on the basis of the First Amendment. Within weeks, a complete version of the Pentagon Papers became a best-selling book, and in 1972 the *New York Times* won a Pulitzer Prize for the series of articles. Frustrated in his attempt to suppress the report, Nixon directed the Department of Justice to prosecute Ellsberg on charges of conspiracy, espionage, and theft. Meanwhile, Hunt and Liddy, seeking to discredit Ellsberg, broke into the office of his former psychiatrist. They found nothing that would make their target less heroic in the eyes of an increasingly skeptical public, and by 1973 the charges against Ellsberg were dropped after the Nixon administration itself stood guilty of misconduct.

At the same time, Nixon ran a skillful negative campaign charging George McGovern, the liberal Democrat who had won his party's nomination on the first ballot, with supporting "abortion, acid [LSD], and amnesty" for those who had resisted the draft or deserted the armed forces. The Republicans also informed the news media that McGovern's running mate, Senator Thomas Eagleton, had once undergone electric shock therapy for depression, thus forcing his resignation from the Democratic team. Voter turnout fell to an all-time low, and McGovern lost every state but Massachusetts. (Later, when Nixon faced disgrace, bumper stickers appeared reading, "Don't Blame Me, I'm from Massachusetts.")

The Committee to Re-Elect the President (CREEP) enjoyed a huge war chest and spent a good portion on dirty tricks designed to divide the Democrats and discredit them in the eyes of the voting public. The most ambitious plan—wiretapping the Democratic National Committee headquarters—backfired.

On June 17, 1972, a security team had tripped up a group of intruders hired by CREEP to install listening devices in the Washington, D.C., Watergate apartment and office complex where the Democrats were headquartered. The police arrested five men, who were later found guilty of conspiracy and burglary. Although Nixon disclaimed any knowledge of the plan, two *Washington Post* reporters, Bob Woodward and Carl Bernstein, followed a trail of evidence back to the nation's highest office.

Televised Senate hearings opened to public view more than a pattern of presidential wrongdoing: they showed an attempt to impede investigations of the Watergate case. Testifying before the committee, a former Nixon aide revealed the existence of secret tape recordings of conversations held in the Oval Office. After special prosecutor Archibald Cox refused to allow Nixon to claim executive privilege and withhold the tapes, the president ordered Cox fired. This "Saturday Night Massacre," as it came to be called, further tarnished Nixon's reputation and swelled curiosity about the tapes. On June 24, 1974, the Supreme Court voted unanimously that Nixon had to release the tapes to a new special prosecutor, Leon Jaworski.

The Fall of the Executive

Although incomplete, the Watergate tapes proved damning. They documented Nixon's ravings against his enemies, including anti-Semitic slurs, and his conniving efforts to harass private citizens through federal agencies. The tapes also proved that Nixon had not only known about plans to cover up the Watergate break-in but had ordered it. The news media enjoyed a field day with the revelations. In July 1974, the House Judiciary Committee adopted three articles of impeachment, charging Nixon with obstructing justice.

Charges of executive criminality had clouded the Nixon administration since his vice president had resigned in disgrace. In 1972 Spiro Agnew had admitted accepting large kickbacks while serving as governor of Maryland. Pleading no contest to this and to charges of federal income tax evasion, Agnew had resigned from office in October 1973. Gerald Ford, a moderate Republican representative from Michigan, had replaced him and now stood in the wings while the president's drama unfolded.

Facing certain impeachment by the House of Representatives, Richard Nixon became, on August 9, 1974, the first U.S. president to resign from office.

CONCLUSION

The resignations of Richard Nixon and Spiro Agnew brought little to relieve the feeling of national exhaustion that attended the Vietnam War. U.S. troops had pulled out of Vietnam in 1973 and the war officially ended in 1975, but bitterness lingered over the unprecedented—and, for many, humiliating—defeat. Morover, confidence in the government's

CHRONOLOGY

1964 President Lyndon Johnson calls for "an unconditional war on poverty" in his state of the union address

Tonkin Gulf resolution

The Economic Opportunity Act establishes the Office of Economic Opportunity

Free speech movement gets under way at University of California at Berkeley

Johnson defeats conservative Barry Goldwater for president

1965 President Johnson authorizes Operation Rolling Thunder, the bombing of North Vietnam

Teach-ins begin on college campuses

First major march on Washington for peace is organized

Watts uprising begins a wave of rebellions in black communities

1966 J. William Fulbright publishes *The Arrogance of Power*

Black Panther Party is formed

National Organization for Women (NOW) is formed

1967 Antiwar rally in New York City draws 300,000

Vietnam Veterans against the War is formed

Uprisings in Newark, Detroit, and other cities

Hippie "Summer of Love"

1968 U.S. ground troops levels in Vietnam number 500,000

Tet Offensive in Vietnam, followed by international protests against U.S. policies

Martin Luther King, Jr. is assassinated; riots break out in more than 100 cities

Vietnam peace talks begin in Paris

Robert Kennedy is assassinated

Democratic National Convention, held in Chicago, nominates Hubert Humphrey; "police riot" against protesters

Richard Nixon elected president

American Indian Movement (AIM) founded

1969 Woodstock music festival marks the high tide of the counterculture

Stonewall Riot in Greenwich Village sparks the gay liberation movement

Apollo 11 lands on the moon

1970 U.S. incursion into Cambodia sparks campus demonstrations; students killed at Kent State and Jackson State universities

Women's Strike for Equality marks the fiftieth anniversary of the woman suffrage amendment

1971 Lieutenant William Calley, Jr. court-martialed for My Lai Massacre

New York Times starts publishing the Pentagon Papers

1972 Nixon visits China and Soviet Union

SALT I limits offensive intercontinental ballistic missiles

Intruders attempting to "bug" Democratic headquarters in the Watergate complex are arrested

Nixon is reelected in a landslide

Nixon orders Christmas Day bombing of North Vietnam

1973 Paris Peace Agreement ends war in Vietnam

FBI seizes Indian occupants of Wounded Knee, South Dakota

Watergate burglars tried; congressional hearings on Watergate

CIA destabilizes elected Chilean government, which is overthrown

Vice President Spiro T. Agnew resigns

1974 House Judiciary Committee adopts articles of impeachment against Nixon

Nixon resigns the presidency

highest office was severely shaken. The passage of the War Powers Act in 1973, written to compel any future president to seek congressional approval for armed intervention abroad, dramatized both the widespread suspicion of presidential intentions and a yearning for peace. But the positive dream of community that had inspired Johnson, King, and a generaton of student activists could not be revived. No other vision took its place.

In 1968 seven prominent antiwar protesters had been brought to trial for allegedly conspiring to disrupt the Democratic National Convention in Chicago. Just a few years later, the majority of Americans had concluded that presidents Johnson and Nixon had conspired to do far worse. They had intentionally deceived the public about the nature and fortunes of the war. This moral failure signaled a collapse at the center of the American political system. Since Dwight Eisenhower left office warning of the potential danger embedded in the "military-industrial complex," no president had survived the presidency with his honor intact.

REVIEW QUESTIONS

1. Discuss the events that led up to and contributed to U.S. involvement in Vietnam. How did U.S. involvement in the war affect domestic programs?

2. Discuss the reasons the protest movement against the Vietnam War started on college campuses. Describe how these movements were organized and how the opponents of the war differed from the supporters.

3. Discuss the programs sponsored by Johnson's plan for a Great Society. What was their impact on urban poverty in the late 1960s?

4. What was the impact of the assassinations of Martin Luther King, Jr. and Robert Kennedy on the election of 1968? How were various communities affected?

5. How were the "politics of identity" movements different from earlier civil rights organizations? In what ways did the various movements resemble one another?

6. Why did Richard Nixon enjoy such a huge electoral victory in 1972? Discuss his foreign and domestic policies. What led to his sudden downfall?

RECOMMENDED READING

John A. Andrew III, *Lyndon Johnson and the Great Society* (1998). An assessment of the Great Society, with special emphasis on the two major issues of civil rights and poverty. Andrew discusses Johnson's aspirations and the obstacles that kept them out of reach.

Keith Beattie, *The Scar That Binds: American Culture and the Vietnam War* (1998). Examines memoirs, war novels and films, and the Vietnam Veterans Memorial in Washington, D.C., to discuss the cultural legacy of the war.

Alexander Bloom, ed., *Long Time Gone: Sixties America Then and Now* (2001). Ten essays covering various aspects of the social and political movements of the 1960s. The authors draw out the meaning of the "sixties" for today and dispel commonplace myths by providing accurate information and a sound context for interpretation.

Jane F. Gerhard, *Desiring Revolution: Second-Wave Feminism and the Rewriting of American Sexual Thought, 1920–1982* (2001). Discusses the background of the feminist side of the sexual revolution with special attention to popular versions of Freud's theories. Gerhard discusses disagreements among feminists on the meaning and experience of sexual liberation.

Michael H. Hunt, *Lyndon Johnson's War: America's Cold War Crusade in Vietnam, 1945–1968* (1996). Tracks Johnson's decisions to wage all-out war in Vietnam. Hunt interprets Johnson's actions as consistent with the cold war foreign policy that had prevailed since the Truman administration and its pledge to "contain" communism.

Rebecca E. Klatch, *A Generation Divided: The New Left, the New Right, and the 1960s* (1999). Compares and contrasts the respective roles of Students for a Democratic Society and the conservative Young Americans for Freedom on college campuses. Klatch, a sociologist, presents lengthy oral interviews with former student activists in both camps.

Joan Morrison and Robert K. Morrison, eds., *From Camelot to Kent State: the Sixties Experience in the Words of Those Who Lived It* (2001). A collection of 59 oral histories with a range of people who lived through the 1960s. The volume includes stories of better-known activists, such as Eldridge Cleaver and Abbie Hoffman, as well as those who were soldiers in Vietnam or student activists. This edition also contains many photographs.

Joseph Tilden Rhea, *Race Pride and the American Identity* (1997). Examines American Indians, Asian Americans, Latinos, and African Americans in their search for recognition. Rhea emphasizes the importance of political struggles and their impact on historical consciousness, including the establishment of historical sites and museums.

Ruth Rosen, *The World Split Open: How the Modern Women's Movement Changed America* (2000). Discusses the impact of women's liberation on American politics, business, and family life. Through extensive archival research and interviews, Rosen provides compelling evidence for the magnitude of change accompanying second-wave feminism.

Anthony Summers, *The Arrogance of Power: The Secret World of Richard Nixon* (2000). A popular biography of Nixon's life from his early political career in California through his presidency. Summers drew on more than a thousand interviews, including those with Nixon's psychotherapist, to portray the former president's erratic behavior and mental instability during as well as before the disastrous Watergate affair.

Marilyn B. Young, *The Vietnam Wars, 1945–1990* (1991). An excellent overview of the involvement of the French and the American military and diplomatic forces in Vietnam from the 1910s to 1975, and of the various movements against them. Young presents a thematic continuity that highlights the nationalism of the Vietnamese as ultimately more powerful than the troops and weaponry of their opponents.

ON THE WEB

http://www.yale.edu/lawweb/avalon/tonkin-g.htm

Text of President Johnson's address to Congress on the Gulf of Tonkin incident and the Joint Resolution of Congress H.J. RES 1145, August 7, 1964.

http://archives.seattletimes.nwsource.com/ cgi-bin/texis.cgi/web/vortex/ display?slug=tett&date=19980130

A *Seattle Times* assessment of the impact of the Tet Offensive of 1968.

http://www.gwu.edu/~nsarchiv/NSAEBB/ NSAEBB48/supreme.html

Interesting discussion and links on the Pentagon Papers and the court battle to publish that document.

http://www.washingtonpost.com/ wp-srv/style/longterm/books/chap1/daythepr.htm

Washington Post commentary on the Pentagon Papers.

http://www.pbs.org/wgbh/amex/vietnam/ trenches/mylai.html

Short but detailed PBS description of the My Lai incident.

http://www.lib.berkeley.edu/MRC/watergate.html

RealAudio recordings of the Nixon White House tapes. Visit the National Archives link listed here for interesting information concerning the preservation of those tapes.

http://www.washingtonpost.com/wp-srv/national/ longterm/watergate/chronology.htm

Washington Post timeline of the Watergate events leading to Nixon's resignation with links to *Washington Post* news stories of the day.

http://www.prenhall.com/faragherbrief/map29.1

Consider the geographical distribution of urban uprising from 1965—1968. What were the main factors behind urban unrest?

http://www.prenhall.com/faragherbrief/map29.2

Examine those states which sizable Indian reservations. How did the Civil Rights Act affect Indian identity?

AMERICAN COMMUNITIES

Grass-Roots Conservatism in Orange County, California

I N 1962 BEE GATHRIGHT, A BROWNIE LEADER AND MOTHER OF THREE young girls, listened to a neighbor's casual request. Would she allow the patio of her suburban Garden Grove home to be used for a meeting bringing together neighbors to hear a talk about liberalism and conservatism by a man from the nearby Knott's Berry Farm Freedom Center? Gathright agreed and found the meeting to be a revelation: "This is when I discovered that I was a conservative," she recalled three decades later. She soon arranged for the speaker to address a larger audience at the local public school. Gathright began to read widely in books and newspapers "because I began to hear that the Communists were going to bury us, were going to take over the world . . . I was afraid." She convinced her skeptical husband Neil, an aerospace engineer, to share her new-found activism. They attended study groups and soon joined the California Republican Assembly, a volunteer organization dedicated to electing conservatives to office. In 1964 the Gathrights' home served as a local headquarters for the presidential campaign of conservative Arizona Senator Barry Goldwater. After winning the Republican nomination Goldwater lost the election to President Lyndon Johnson in one of the biggest landslides in American electoral history. Most political commentators and analysts believed Goldwater's crushing defeat proved that "far Right" conservatism had little future in American politics.

Orange County in the 1960s and 1970 had thousands of "kitchen table" activists like the Gathrights, and they began a transformation of American conservatism and American politics that would culminate in the election of Ronald Reagan as president in 1980. Most of them were middle-class men and women, including large numbers of professionals and people with small businesses. Many were recent migrants to California, attracted by job opportunities in aerospace. Bee Gathright herself had arrived after World War II from Iowa, taking a job as an executive secretary at Douglas Aircraft in Santa Monica. Orange County's 800 square miles lie at the geographic center of the Southern California basin, and large lemon and orange groves dominated the economy until the 1940s. The Second World War and Cold War defense-related spending accelerated Orange County's growth as companies like Hughes Aircraft, Autonetics, and Beckman Instruments created over 30,000 new manufacturing jobs in defense and electronics between 1950 and the early 1960s. The strong demand for housing spurred a highly profitable construction boom and a roaring real estate market. By 1960, over

700,000 people lived in Orange County, an increase of nearly 400 percent since 1940, and the population doubled again to almost 1.5 million by 1970.

While Barry Goldwater's 1964 campaign had ignited great enthusiasm in Orange County, his national defeat forced conservatives to consider how they might shed the "extremism" label and put more emphasis on winning office. In 1966 they succeeeded in electing Ronald Reagan as governor. A former Hollywood actor and New Deal liberal, Reagan had evolved in the 1950s into an effective conservative spokesman and a prominent Republican Party activist. His gubernatorial campaign stressed limiting state support for welfare and other social services, while expanding state power to enforce law and order.

Reagan's electoral success in California, as well as Richard Nixon's election as president in 1968, signaled an important new turn for American conservatives in the 1970s. They still championed anticommunism, but no longer engaged in the kind of loose talk about using nuclear weapons that had hurt Goldwater. They attacked the growth of "big government," but no longer spoke openly about repealing popular New Deal programs like Social Security. Instead, they responded to the concerns over "social issues" that increasingly troubled and mobilized Orange County's grass-roots activists. These issues were largely defined by a "backlash" against the antiwar movement, counterculture, feminist activism, and urban riots, and an emphasis on so-called family issues, in which opposition to sex education, obscenity, abortion rights, and gay liberation were all linked together. On the economic side, conservatives began to tap a deep well of resentment over rising property taxes and high inflation.

Two of the central themes of this new conservatism found powerful expression in Orange County, and resonated with millions of Americans well beyond it. One was the so-called tax revolt led by Howard Jarvis, a flamboyant campaigner long active in Southern California conservative circles. Saying he had been energized and inspired by local taxpayer-protest meetings, Jarvis told his supporters, "Lower taxes and less government became my holy grail. . . . The only way to cut government spending is not to give them the money in the first place." Jarvis relied on local networks to gather 1.3 million signatures to get his Proposition 13 on the ballot— a constitutional amendment that slashed the property tax rate

from 3 percent to 1 percent of a home's market value, and strictly limited future tax increases. After its passage in 1978, the "tax revolt" soon spread to other states and attracted millions to the conservative message of limiting government and lowering taxes.

Orange County was a center of the second new force reshaping conservatism, the spectacular growth of "born again" evangelical Christianity. Fundamentalist sects had long been associated with the rural poor of the South. But Orange County's religious revival demonstrated how educated professionals and middle class suburbanites were also turning to "born again" Christianity in their search for spirituality and meaning, as a rejection of "permissiveness," and as a way to assert order amidst rapid cultural and social change. One of the most successful fundamentalist ministers was the Reverend Chuck Smith, who pioneered the use of Christian folk music, adopted countercultural symbols and motifs, and conducted mass ocean baptisms in Corona del Mar. By 1978 his mother church in Costa Mesa, Calvary Chapel, had 25,000 members. They found community not only in Sunday services but in a wide range of tightly organized activities: Bible study groups, summer retreats, "singles' fellowships," prayer breakfasts, and "Christian" consumer culture, which allowed people to simultaneously embrace faith, modern business techniques, and worldly goods.

The political implications of the new evangelicalism became clear by the late 1970s. Most fundamentalist preachers tied their sermons and prophesies to conservative political themes, especially fears about the decline of morality and of American power in the world. Reverend Chuck Smith warned that "the decline of the economy and government of the United States will open the doors to the rise of the anti-Christ to world power."

Newly politicized Christian voters worked diligently to elect Ronald Reagan President in 1980. In Orange County they helped Reagan get 68 percent of the vote, the most lopsided victory of any large county in the nation. For Bee Gathright, the former Goldwater supporter who by then had shifted her energies to Christian missionary work, Reagan's victory provided a national vindication of her years of grass-roots activism. For her, as for so many others in Orange County, the "Christian movement" and the conservative movement had become one and the same. ■

Three Mile Island

KEY TOPICS

- Structural shifts in the economy

- The Ford and Carter presidencies

- Crisis in the cities and environment

- Community politics and the rise of the New Right

- Iran hostage crisis

- The Reagan Republican presidential victory

- Reagan's domestic and foreign policies

- The growth of inequality

THE OVEREXTENDED SOCIETY

In the 1970s Americans faced an unfamiliar combination of skyrocketing prices, rising unemployment, and low economic growth. Economists termed this novel condition "stagflation." By 1975, the unemployment rate had reached nearly 9 percent, its highest level since the Great Depression, and it remained close to 7 percent for most of the rest of the decade. Inflation, meanwhile, reached double digits.

The United States had come to a turning point in its economic history. Emerging from World War II as the most prosperous nation in the world and retaining this status through the 1960s, the country suddenly found itself falling behind western Europe and Japan. Polls conducted at the end of the 1970s revealed that a majority of Americans believed that conditions would worsen.

A Troubled Economy

In October 1973 gasoline prices nearly doubled, jumping from 40 to nearly 70 cents per gallon. Several states responded to the shortage by introducing rationing programs.

The oil crisis began suddenly, although it had been decades in the making. The United States, which used about 70 percent of all oil produced in the world, had found the domestic supply sufficient until the late 1950s. But rising demand had outstripped national reserves, and by 1973 the nation was importing one-third of its crude oil, mainly from the Middle East. In that year, following the Arab-Israeli War, oil prices skyrocketed. On Octo-

ber 17, the Organization of Petroleum Exporting Countries (OPEC), a cartel of mainly Arab oil producers, announced an embargo on oil shipments to Israel's allies, including the United States.

President Nixon responded to the embargo by creating an "energy czar" and paving the way for the creation of the Department of Energy in 1977. He ordered a 10 percent reduction in air travel and appealed to Congress to lower speed limits on interstate highways to 55 miles per hour and to extend daylight-saving time into the winter months.

With the cost of gasoline, oil, and electricity up, many other prices also rose, from apartment rents and telephone bills to restaurant checks. As oil prices continued to rise through the 1970s, many Americans also began to look suspiciously at the pricing practices of U.S. oil companies. Whatever the causes, the oil crisis played a major role in the economic downturn.

The economic downturn, according to many experts, had deeper roots in the failure of the United States to keep up with the rising industrial efficiency of Western Europe and Japan. Manufacturers from Asia, Latin America, and Europe now offered consumers cheaper and better products, including automobiles, long considered the monopoly of Detroit. U.S. automakers, determined to reduce costs, turned to "outsourcing"—that is, making cars and trucks from parts cheaply produced abroad and imported into the United States as semifinished materials (which were subject to a lower tariff than finished goods.) In high-tech electronics, the United States scarcely competed against Japanese-produced televisions, radios, tape players, cameras, and computers. An AFL-CIO leader complained that the United States was becoming "a nation of hamburger

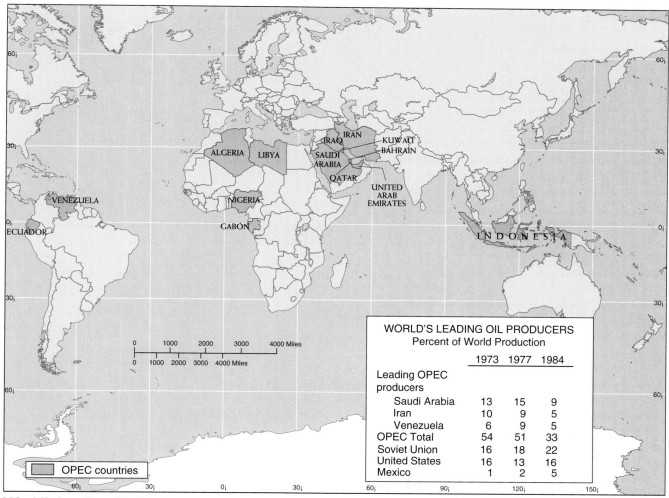

WORLD'S LEADING OIL PRODUCERS Percent of World Production			
	1973	1977	1984
Leading OPEC producers			
Saudi Arabia	13	15	9
Iran	10	9	5
Venezuela	6	9	5
OPEC Total	54	51	33
Soviet Union	16	18	22
United States	16	13	16
Mexico	1	2	5

World's Leading Oil Producers

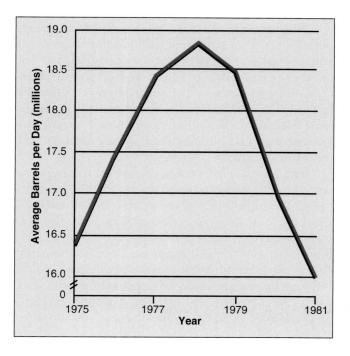

Decline of U.S. Oil Consumption, 1975–1981

SOURCE: Department of Energy, *Monthly Energy Review,* June 1982.

stands . . . a country stripped of industrial capacity and meaningful work."

The situation in agriculture was still more grim. The huge increase in oil prices translated into higher gasoline and fertilizer costs, forcing farmers to borrow heavily from banks. Soon the high interest rates on borrowed money threw many family farmers into a state of permanent indebtedness. When overseas sales declined at the end of the 1970s, tens of thousands defaulted on loans and lost their farms to banks and credit companies, ending a way of life generations old.

Blue-Collar Blues

In past decades labor unions had typically responded to inflation by negotiating new contracts or, if necessary, striking for higher pay. But while factories closed, the National Labor Relations Board increasingly ruled in favor of management, making the organization of new union locals far more difficult. Between 1970 and 1982 the AFL-CIO lost nearly 30 percent of its membership. Union-backed meaures now routinely failed in Congress, despite the Democratic majority.

Typical of hard times, women in increasing numbers sought jobs to support their families. By 1980 more than half of all married women and nearly 60 percent of mothers with children between the ages of six and seventeen were in the labor force. Yet despite these statistical changes, women had lost ground relative to men. In 1955 women earned 64 percent of the average wages paid to men; in 1980 they earned only 59 percent. The reason for this dip was that women were clustered in the clerical and service trades where the lowest wages prevailed.

African American women made some gains. Through Title VII of the Civil Rights Act, which outlawed work place discrimination by sex or race, and the establishment of the Equal Employment Opportunity Commission to enforce it, they managed to climb the lower levels of the job ladder. By 1980, northern black women's median earnings were about 95 percent of white women's earnings.

In contrast, Hispanic women, whose labor force participation leaped by 80 percent during the decade, were restricted to a very few poorly paid occupations. Puerto Ricans found jobs in the garment industry of the Northeast; Mexican Americans more typically worked as domestics or agricultural laborers in the Southwest. Neither group earned much more than the minimum wage.

Sunbelt/Snowbelt Communities

By the 1970s the Sunbelt offered a rare showplace of American prosperity. It boasted a gross product greater than many nations and more cars, television sets, houses, and even miles of paved roads than the

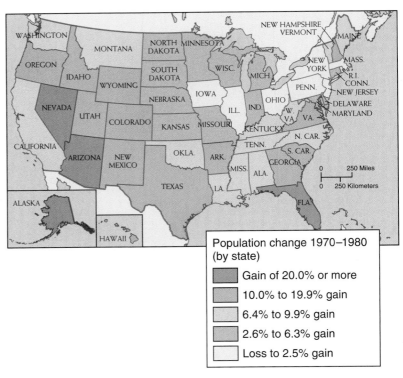

Population Shifts, 1970–1980 Industrial decline in the Northeast coincided with an economic boom in the Sunbelt, encouraging millions of Americans to head for warmer climates and better jobs.

rest of the United States. Large influxes of immigrants from Latin America, the Caribbean, and Asia combined with the shift of Americans from the depressed Northeast to boost the region's population.

This increase had been made possible by a huge outlay of federal funds, including defense spending and the allocation of Social Security funds. The number of residents over the age of sixty-five increased by 30 percent during the 1970s, reaching 26 million by 1980. Armed with retirement packages won decades earlier, huge "golden age" migrations created new communities in Florida, Arizona, and southern California.

The South witnessed a dramatic turnaround in demographic and economic trends. While manufacturing and highly subsidized agribusiness flourished, southern cities reversed the century-long trend of out-migration among African Americans. The Southwest and West changed yet more dramatically. Aided by air conditioning, water diversions, public improvements, and large-scale development, California became the nation's most populous state; Texas moved to third, behind New York. Former farms and deserts were turned almost overnight into huge metropolitan areas by the automobile and suburbs. Phoenix grew from 664,000 in 1960 to 1,509,000 in 1980, Las Vegas from 127,000 to 463,000.

Much of the Sunbelt wealth tended to be temporary or sharply cyclical, producing a boom-and-bust economy of sudden expansion and disordered sprawl. Corporate office buildings in cities such as Houston emptied almost as fast as they filled. Income was also distributed very unevenly. Older Hispanic populations made only modest gains, while recent Mexican immigrants and Indian peoples suffered from a combination of low wages and poor public services. The Sunbelt states concentrated their tax and federal dollars on strengthening police forces, building roads or sanitation systems for the expanding suburbs, and creating budget surpluses, in contrast to eastern and midwestern states that continued to spend significantly on public housing, education, and mass transit.

The "Snowbelt" (or "Rustbelt") states meanwhile suffered severe population losses accompanying the sharp decline of industry. Of the nineteen metropolitan areas that lost population during the 1970s, all were old manufacturing centers, topped by New York, Cleveland, Pittsburgh, Boston, Philadelphia, and Buffalo.

A feeling of defeat intensified in the aging industrial cities of the Monogahela River valley in western Pennsylavnia. Since the late ninteeenth century, "Mon Valley" had proudly stood as the steelmaking center of the nation and much of the world. With the decline of steel production, however, major firms such as U.S. Steel increased investments in overseas mining and mineral processing companies, some of which worked closely with foreign steelmakers. This policy of "disinvestment" had a devastating impact on the people and communities who for generations had helped build the nation's basic industries. During the 1980s the Mon Valley lost 30,000 people, or 10 percent of its population.

New York City offered a more spectacular example. A fiscal crisis in 1975 forced liberal mayor Abraham Beame to choose between wage freezes for public employees and devastating cuts and layoffs. Eventually, with the municipal government teetering on the brink of bankruptcy, he chose both. In response to cutbacks in mass transit and the deterioration of municipal services, a large sector of the middle class fled. At the same time, the proportion of poor people rose from 15 percent in 1969 to nearly 25 percent fourteen years later.

"Lean Years" Presidents: Ford and Carter

Gerald R. Ford and Jimmy Carter presided over not only a depressed economy but a nation of disillusioned citizens. Replacing Nixon in August 1974, Gerald Ford reassured the public that "our long national nightmare is over"—then quickly pardoned Nixon for all the federal crimes he may have committed. The pardon reinforced public cynicism toward government and Ford in particular.

Ford, who issued more vetoes of major bills than any other president in the twentieth century but saw Congress override most of them, struck most Americans as a pleasant person of modest ability. First Lady Betty Ford was the shining star of the White House. She broke ranks with other Republicans to champion the Equal Rights Amendment. She also won praise for her courage in discussing her mastectomy for breast cancer and her voluntary entry into a substance abuse clinic for a drinking problem.

Ford banked on his incumbency for the 1976 election and welcomed Senator Robert Dole of Kansas as his running mate. Democrats chose Jimmy Carter, a former one-term governor of Georgia, who depicted himself as an antipolitician, an outsider, and someone who was independent of the Washington establishment. When Carter told his mother he was running for president, she reportedly asked, "President of what?"

A "born again" Christian, Carter had been born in Plains, Georgia, in 1924. A successful Southern politician, Carter promoted regional development. In seeking the nomination, he declined to call himself a liberal, offering instead personal integrity as his chief qualification for the nation's highest office.

Carter campaigned as a moderate on domestic policy issues. Counting on support from both conservative and southern voters who would ordinarily vote Republican, he defended existing entitlement programs while opposing Senator Edward Kennedy's call for comprehensive health coverage. He capitalized on Ford's unpopular Nixon pardon and, with his running mate Senator Walter Mondale of Minnesota, won with just over 50 percent of the popular vote and a 297-to-240 margin in the Electoral College.

In office, Carter seemed to many observers enigmatic, even uninterested in the presidency. His most successful innovation, deregulation of the airlines, brought lower fares for millions of passengers. But by freeing banks from congressional control, he inadvertently encouraged bad investments, outright fraud, and a round of disastrous bank failures. Inflation proved to be his worst enemy. As older Americans could recognize, half of all the inflation since 1940 had occurred in just ten years. Carter could not deliver on his promise to turn the economy around. By the time he left office in 1980, a majority of those polled agreed that "the people running the country don't really care what happens to you."

COMMUNITIES AND POLITICS

The mass demonstrations of the 1960s gave way in the 1970s to a style of political mobilization centered squarely in communities. Unlike national elections, which after 1968 registered increasing voter apathy, local campaigns brought a great many people to the voting booth and into newly organized voluntary associations.

The New Urban Politics

In many cities, new groups came into political power. In several college towns, such as Berkeley, California, and Eugene, Oregon, both of which had been centers of political activism during the 1960s, student coalitions were formed to secure seats for their candidates on city councils. In 1973 labor unions, college students, and community groups in Madison, Wisconsin, elected a former student activist to the first of three terms as mayor.

African American candidates scored impressive victories during the 1970s. The newly elected African American mayor of Atlanta, Maynard Jackson, concluded that "politics is the civil rights movement of the 1970s." By 1978, 2,733 African Americans held elected offices in the South, ten times the number a decade earlier. Voters had elected African American mayors in New Orleans and Atlanta. In other parts of the country, black mayors, such as Coleman Young in Detroit, Richard Hatcher in Gary, and Tom Bradley in Los Angeles, held power along with many minor black officials.

Other racial or ethnic groups advanced more slowly, rarely in proportion to their actual numbers in the population. Mexican Americans had already won offices in Crystal City, Texas, and in 1978 took control of a major city council, in San Antonio, for the first time. They also scored electoral victories in other parts of Texas and in New Mexico and developed strong neighborhood or ward organizations in southern California. Puerto Ricans

elected a handful of local officials in New York, mostly in the Bronx. Asian Americans advanced in similar fashion in parts of Hawai'i.

The fiscal crises of the 1970s nevertheless undercut these efforts to reform municipal government. Most new officials found themselves unable to make the sweeping changes they had promised during their campaigns. Community-based job programs could not counteract the effects of factory shutdowns and the disappearance of industrial jobs. Affirmative action programs aroused cries of "reverse discrimination" from angered whites who felt that minorities' progress had been registered at their expense. Conservatives put forward their own candidates, charging that government at all levels favored minorities, the jobless, and criminals over the law-abiding, hardworking, tax-paying majority.

The City and the Neighborhood

The Community Development Act of 1974, signed by President Ford, combined federal grant programs for cities into a single program and put mayors and city managers directly in charge of spending. With grants totaling $8.4 billion over three years, city governments could allocate funds as they saw fit and encourage citizens to take part in local planning. Groups of preservationists organized to save historic buildings and public spaces, to form land trusts for acquiring and refurbishing old houses, and to turn vacant lots into neighborhood parks.

Local and national foundations joined federal agencies in funding Community Development Corporations (CDCs) through a series of antipoverty agencies. These community groups promoted "development banks" that would facilitate "sweat equity"—that is, the granting of low-interest mortgage loans to buyers willing to rebuild or refurbish dilapidated housing. They also acted to prevent local banks from closing when a neighborhood became mainly black.

In 1979 President Carter's National Commission on Neighborhoods recommended the strenthening of local institutions "to reorganize our society . . . to a new democratic system of grass-roots involvement." But advocacy groups often learned to their dismay that foundations and federal agencies with money to spend resisted local decision making. While the economy worsened, mortgages moved out of reach for most buyers, and rents in many locations doubled. Local preservationists' dreams sometimes became nightmarish. "Gentrification" often accompanied restoration, with poor residents displaced by the more prosperous Americans who craved the increasingly fashionable old homes.

The Endangered Environment

On March 28, 1979, a series of mechanical problems and judgment errors at the nuclear generating facility at Three Mile Island (TMI), near Harrisburg, Pennsylvania, led to the formation of a dangerously explosive hydrogen bubble and posed the danger of a catastrophic core meltdown. After the news broke, nearly 150,000 residents fled their homes. Ten days later, the Nuclear Regulatory Commission announced that any danger of explosion had passed, but what had seemed an isolated event in one community had already grown into a regional phenomenon with national repercussions. Massive demonstrations against nuclear power followed the accident, concluding in a rally of more than 200,000 people in New York City. Groups organized in many communites to defeat referendums to fund new nuclear power facilities or rallied around candidates who promised to shut down existing ones. Of the ninety-six under construction and the thirty more planned at the time of the TMI crisis, only a handful were completed.

Earlier in the 1970s, the discovery of high rates of cancer and birth defects in Love Canal, near Buffalo, New York, had offered compelling evidence of a growing danger to many American communities. Here toxic wastes dumped by the Hooker Chemical Laboratory had oozed into basements and backyards, and homemaker Lois Gibbs organized a vigorous publicity campaign to draw attention to the grim situation. Meanwhile, outraged Florida residents realized that the damming of the Everglades for sugar production and housing developments, undertaken by the Army Corps of Engineers decades earlier, had degraded thousands of acres of wilderness, eliminating natural filtration systems and killing millions of birds and other species.

Even before the energy crisis, many Americans had begun to make changes in their own ways of living. Many families began to save glass bottles and newspapers for reuse. Some began to reduce or eliminate their consumption of beef, since beef is far more costly and uses more resources to produce than grain. Backyard vegetable gardens became popular, as did grocers who stocked organic foods.

The environmentalist movement grew stronger in long-standing organizations, such as the Audubon Society and the Wilderness Society. The Sierra Club, formed in 1892 as a small society of western mountain hikers, grew to 100,000 members in 1970 and to 500,000 over the next decade. New groups sprang up in response to the energy crisis, often devoted to developing renewable energy sources such as solar power.

Cutting across nearly all population groups and regions, environmentalists reached such traditionally conservative areas as the Deep South with warnings of the dangers of toxic wastes, the destruction of wetlands, and the ruin of fishing industries. Sometimes campaigns succeeded in blocking massive construction projects, such as nuclear energy plants; more often they halted small-scale destruction of a natural habitat or historic urban district. These campaigns made the public more aware of the consequences of private and government decisions about the environment.

Responding to organized pressure groups, Congress passed scores of bills designed to protect endangered species, reduce pollution caused by automobile emissions, limit and ban the use of some pesticides, and control strip-mining practices. The Environmental Protection Agency (EPA), established in 1970, grew to become the federal government's largest regulatory agency, employing more than 10,000 people by the end of the decade.

Environmentalists enjoyed only limited success in bringing about large-scale changes in policy. Cities often avoided congressional mandates for reduction in air pollution by requesting lengthy extensions of deadlines for compliance. Despite the introduction of lead-free gasoline, the air in major metropolitan areas grew no better in the long run because automobile traffic increased at a fast pace. Environmentalists lost an important campaign with the approval of the Alaskan Pipeline, 800 miles of pipe connecting oil fields with refining facilities.

Small-Town America

A host of unresolved problems, ranging from air pollution to rising crime rates to higher taxes, encouraged a massive exodus from the nation's cities. Between 1970 and 1975, for every 100 people relocating to metropolitan areas, 138 moved out. Newer residential communities in small towns and in formerly rural areas grew at a fast pace, attracting retirees and others seeking solace or security.

Government programs such as mortgage guarantees and low-interest financing on individual homes promoted these large "low-density" developments of single-family houses. In many regions, the countryside gradually disappeared into "exurbia," a trend that population experts Peter A. Morison and Judith P. Wheeler attributed to the American "wish to love one's neighbor but keep him at arm's length." Opinion poles suggested that many Americans wanted to live in a small town that was not a suburb but was still no more than thirty miles from a major city.

Soon even small towns developed their own suburbs, usually moderate-income tracts of ranch houses squeezed between older wood-frame colonial or Victorian farmhouses. Federal subsidies for the construction of sewerage and water lines, originally intended to aid rural communities, now became springboards for further development. Ironically, shopping malls on former farmland drained commercial activity from the small-town centers, channeling the benefits of development to chain stores rather than to local merchants.

Some communities organized to oppose these trends. Following the publication of E. F. Schumacher's *Small Is Beautiful* (1973), groups of people began to question the advantages of "bigness" and its toll on humanity. They principally sought to rebuild communities on a smaller scale and therefore campaigned to preserve the environment by opposing further development and the construction of new highways, nuclear energy generating plants, and toxic dumps. In Vermont, liberal "hippies" and "back-to-the-landers" joined traditionally conservative landowners to defeat a 1974 gubernatorial plan to attract developers. In other locales, such as the Berkshire Mountains of Massachusetts, community land trusts were organized to encourage common ownership of the land. "From coast to coast," the *New York Times* reported, "environmental, economic and social pressures have impelled hundreds of cities and towns to adopt limitations on the size and character of their populations." To encourage public discussion of land-use issues, President Carter created the Small Community and Rural Development Policy group. Many small towns, especially those in the Plains states, meanwhile collapsed from failing family farms and small businesses, leaving rundown schools, inadequate medical care, and abandoned movie theaters and grocery stores. Only nursing homes and funeral parlors continued to thrive.

THE NEW CONSERVATISM

Sizable numbers of taxpayers resented the tax hikes required to fund government programs that benefited minorities, provided expanded social services for the poor, or protected the environment at the expense of economic development. In 1978 California voters staged a "taxpayers' revolt," approving Proposition 13, which cut property taxes and government revenues for social programs and education. In other economically hard-pressed urban areas, white voters who resented the gains made by African Americans and Latinos formed a powerful backlash movement. By the end of the decade, the only substantial increase in voter participation was among conservatives.

The New Right

The largest New Right constituency united behind major conservative religious and political leaders to promote what they viewed as traditional values. Evangelical Christians became the backbone of key organizations such as the National Conservative Political Action Committee and, most especially, Moral Majority.

Conservative political organizations were among the first to employ direct-mail campaigns. Greater success came from the work of televangelists. By the late 1960s, televangelists such as Pat Robertson and Jim Bakker frequently mixed conservative political messages with appeals to prayer. Falwell's *Old-Time Gospel Hour* was broadcast over 200 television stations and 300 radio stations each week. Christian broadcasters generally endorsed Falwell's faith that "the free-enterprise system is clearly outlined in the Book of Proverbs of the Bible." By the end of the 1970s more than 1,400 radio stations and thirty TV stations specialized in religious broadcasts that reached an audience of perhaps 20 million weekly.

The Reverend Jerry Falwell formed Moral Majority as a political lobbying group to advocate tough laws against homosexuality and pornography, to promote a reduction of government services (especially welfare payments to poor families), and to increase spending for a stronger national defense.

Jesse Helms was the first major politician to appeal directly to the New Right and to build his own impressive fund-raising empire with its help. A North Carolina journalist who had fought the integration of public schools and defended the Ku Klux Klan, he had often attacked Martin Luther King, Jr. as a Communist-influenced demagogue. Helms entered national politics as a Goldwater supporter in 1964 and ran for the Senate in 1972. Carried to victory with Nixon's success in North Carolina, Helms immediately promoted a host of conservative bills as well as federal support for regional tobacco interests.

He introduced legislation to allow automobile owners or dealers to disconnect mandatory antipollution devices. He also defended the Watergate break-ins as necessary to offset the "traitorous conduct" of antiwar activists. By 1978 he had raised $8.1 million, the largest amount ever, for his successful reelection campaign. Helms built a powerful, loyal, and wealthy following.

The political surge rightward gained intellectual respectability from neoconservatives, former liberals who blamed the social movements of the 1960s for the demoralization of the nation. The American Enterprise Institute and the Heritage Foundation, heavily supported by major corporations, established major research centers for conservative scholars. These and other foundations also funded campus publications attacking welfare programs, affirmative action, and environmentalism.

Anti-ERA, Antiabortion

The New Right rallied support for a balanced budget amendment to the Constitution, sought unsuccessfully to return prayer to the public schools, and endorsed the Supreme Court's approval of the death penalty in 1977. Practically all the New Right's campaigns emphasized restoration of the "traditional family values" undermined, they alleged, by the women's liberation movement.

The defeat of the Equal Rights Amendment (ERA) stood at the top of the New Right agenda. Approved by Congress in March 1972, nearly fifty years after its introduction (see Chapter 22), the ERA stated: "Equality of rights under the law shall not be denied or abridged by the United States or by any State on account of sex." Endorsed by both the Democratic and Republican Parties, the amendment appeared likely to be ratified by the individual states. Nearly all mainstream women's organizations, including the Girl Scouts of America, endorsed the ERA. Even the AFL-CIO retracted its long-standing opposition and endorsed the amendment.

Cued by this groundswell of support in favor of the ERA, the New Right swung into action. Phyllis Schlafly, a self-described suburban housewife and popular conservative lecturer, headed the STOP ERA campaign, describing the amendment's supporters as "a bunch of bitter women seeking a constitutional cure for their personal problems." The New Right mounted large, expensive campaigns in each swing state and overwhelmed pro-ERA resources. Although thirty-five states had ratified the ERA by 1979, the amendment

remained three votes short of passage. Despite a three-year extension, the ERA died in 1982.

The New Right also waged a steady campaign against abortion, which the women's liberation movement had defined as a woman's right rather than a mere medical issue. In 1973 the Supreme Court had ruled in *Roe* v. *Wade* that state laws decreeing abortion a crime during the first two trimesters of pregnancy constituted a violation of a woman's right to privacy. Opponents of *Roe* rallied for a constitutional amendment defining conception as the beginning of life and arguing that the "rights of the unborn" supersede a woman's right to control her own body. The Roman Catholic Church organized the first antiabortion demonstrations after the Supreme Court's decision and sponsored the formation of the National Right to Life Committee, which claimed 11 million members by 1980.

Antiabortion groups also picketed Planned Parenthood counseling centers, intimidating potential clients. They rallied against government-subsidized day-care centers and against sex education programs in public schools. A small minority turned to more extreme actions and bombed dozens of abortion clinics.

"The Me Decade"

The shift in the political winds of the 1970s registered not only the rise of the New Right but also the disengagement of a sizable number of Americans from politics altogether. In 1976 novelist Tom Wolfe coined the phrase the "Me Decade" to describe an era obsessed with personal well-being and emotional security. Health foods and diet crazes, a mania for physical fitness, and a quest for happiness through therapy involved millions of middle-class Americans. Historian Christopher Lasch provided his own label for this enterprise in the title of his best-selling book *The Culture of Narcissism: American Life in an Age of Diminishing Expectations* (1978).

The rise of the "human potential movement" provided a vivid example of this trend. The most successful was Erhard Seminars Training (EST), a self-help program blending insights from psychology and mysticism. Founded by Werner Erhard (a former door-to-door seller of encyclopedias), the institute taught individuals to form images of themselves as successful and satisfied. Through sixty hours of intensive training involving playacting and humiliation, participants learned one major lesson: "You are the one and only source of your experience. You created it." Priced at $400 for a series of two weekend sessions, EST peaked at 6,000 participants per month, grossing $25 million in revenue in 1980.

Transcendental meditation (TM) promised a short-cut to mental tranquility and found numerous advocates among Wall Street brokers, Pentagon officials, and star athletes. Techniques of TM were taught in more than 200 special teaching centers and practiced by a reputed 350,000 devotees.

Religious cults also formed in large numbers during the 1970s. The Unification Church, founded by the Korean Reverend Sun Myung Moon, extracted intense personal loyalty from its youthful disciples, dubbed by the media as "Moonies." Moon's financial empire, which included hundreds of retail businesses and the conservative *Washington Star*, proved highly lucrative and kept his church solvent despite numerous lawsuits. By contrast, Jim Jones's People's Temple, an interracial movement organized in the California Bay Area, ended in a mass murder and suicide when Jones induced more than 900 of his followers to drink cyanide-laced Kool-Aid in a remote retreat in Guyana in 1978.

Popular music expressed and reinforced many of these trends. The songs of community and hope common in the late 1960s gave way to songs of nostalgia, despair, or nihilism. Bruce Springsteen, whose lyrics lamented the disappearance of the white working class, became the decade's most popular new rock artist. At the same time, heavy metal bands such as Kiss, as well as punk and new wave artists underscored themes of decadence and futility. Meanwhile country and western music hit its peak with crossover hits and numerous new all-C&W radio stations. Charismatic stars like Willie Nelson sang melodic refrains reeking of loneliness and nostalgia and appealing to older, white, working-class Americans.

ADJUSTING TO A NEW WORLD

In April 1975 the North Vietnamese struck Saigon and easily captured the city as the South Vietnamese army, now without U.S. assistance, fell apart. All fighting stopped within a few weeks, and Saigon was renamed Ho Chi Minh City. Vietnam was reunited under a government dominated by Communists. For many Americans, this outcome underscored the futility of U.S. involvement in the Vietnam War.

By the mid-1970s a new realism seemed to prevail in U.S. diplomacy. Presidents Ford and Carter, as well as their chief advisers, acknowledged that the cost of fighting the Vietnam War had been too high, speeding the decline of the United States as the world's reigning superpower. The realists shared with dissatisfied nationalists a single goal: "No More Vietnams."

A Thaw in the Cold War

The military defeat in Vietnam forced the makers of U.S. foreign policy to reassess priorities. The United States must continue to defend its "vital interests," declared Ford's secretary of state Henry Kissinger, but must also recognize that "Soviet-American relations are not designed for tests of manhood." Both nations had experienced a decline of power in world affairs. And both were suffering from the already enormous and relentlessly escalating costs of sustaining a prolonged cold war.

At the close of World War II, the United States could afford to allocate huge portions of its ample economic resources to maintaining and enlarging its global interests. Soon, however, military and defense expenses began to grow at a much faster rate than the economy itself. Whereas the Korean War had cost around $69.5 billion, the Vietnam War cost $172.2 billion. Clandestine operations, alliance building, and weapons production accounted for many billions of dollars more.

Military spending at this level eventually took its toll on the American economy, especially as the federal government increasingly relied on deficit spending in an attempt to cover the bill. The federal debt, which stood at $257 billion in 1950, had jumped to $908 billion by 1980, and an increasingly large part of the federal budget went to paying just the interest on this debt. At the same time, military spending diverted funds from programs that could have strengthened the economy. The results were disastrous. While the United States endured falling productivity levels and rates of personal savings, and a disappearing skilled workforce, other nations rushed ahead.

The Soviet Union, whose economy suffered even greater setbacks from defense spending, joined the United States in moving toward détente. The signing of SALT I, the first Strategic Arms Limitation Treaty, during Nixon's administration, followed by the U.S. withdrawal from Vietnam, encouraged new efforts to negotiate on strategic arms control. In November 1974, Ford and Soviet leader Leonid Brezhnev met in Vladivostok to set the terms of SALT II, and President Carter secured the final agreement in 1979. However, the treaty failed to

President Carter signs the Middle East Peace Treaty with Egyptian President Anwar Sadat and Israeli Prime Minister Menachem Begin, in Washington, D.C., March 1979. President Carter had invited both leaders to Camp David, the presidential retreat in Maryland, where for two weeks he mediated between them on territorial rights to the West Bank and Gaza Strip. Considered Carter's greatest achievement in foreign policy, the negotiations, known as the Camp David Peace Accords, resulted in not only the historic peace treaty but also the Nobel Peace Prize for Begin and Sadat.

SOURCE: CORBIS.

win confirmation from the Senate when the Soviet Union invaded Afghanistan in December 1979.

Although repeated conflicts in the third world continued to slow the pace toward détente, leaders in both the United States and the Soviet Union usually recognized that their economic well-being depended on a reduction in defense spending.

Foreign Policy and "Moral Principles"

When he took office, President Carter presented his lack of experience in foreign affairs as an asset. "We've seen a loss of morality," he noted, "and we're ashamed."

The "soul" of his policy would be an "absolute" commitment to human rights.

Carter condemned policies that allowed the United States to support "right-wing monarchs and military dictators" in the name of anticommunism. In 1976 a powerful human rights lobby pressured Congress to pass a bill that required the secretary of state to report annually on the status of human rights in all countries receiving aid from the United States and to cut off assistance to any country with a record of "gross violations." Carter's secretary of state, Cyrus R. Vance, and the assistant secretary for human rights and humanitarian affairs, Pat Derrian, worked to punish or at least to censure repressive military regimes in

Brazil, Argentina, and Chile. For the first time, leading U.S. diplomats spoke out against the South African apartheid regime.

In line with this policy, Carter attempted to institute reforms at the Central Intelligence Agency (CIA), particularly to halt the blatant intervention in the affairs of foreign governments. He appointed Admiral Stansfield Turner, a Rhodes scholar, as director and ordered a purge of the "rogue elephants" who had pursued covert operations in Southeast Asia during the Vietnam War. "The CIA must operate within the law," Carter insisted. Under Turner, however, these reforms remained incomplete; they later proved temporary.

Carter nearly triumphed in the Middle East. Early in his administration, Carter met privately with Israeli prime minister Menachem Begin to encourage conciliation with Egypt. When negotiations between the two countries stalled in 1978, Carter brought Begin together with Egyptian president Anwar el-Sadat for a thirteen-day retreat at Camp David, Maryland.

The Camp David Accords, signed in September 1978, set the formal terms for peace in the region. Egypt became the first Arab country to recognize Israel's right to exist, as the two nations established mutual diplomatic relations for the first time since the founding of Israel in 1948. In return, Egypt regained control of the Sinai Peninsula, including important oil fields and airfields. In 1979 Begin and Sadat shared the Nobel Prize for Peace.

But disappointment lay ahead. Carter staked his hopes for regional peace on the final achievement of statehood, or at least political autonomy, for Palestinians in a portion of their former lands now occupied by the Israelis. The accords specified that Israel would eventually return to its approximate borders of 1967. However, although Begin agreed to dismantle some Israeli settlements in the Sinai, the Israeli government continued to sponsor more and more Jewish settlements, expropriating Palestinian holdings. The final status of the Palestinians remained in limbo, as did that of Jerusalem, which many Christians and Muslims felt should be an autonomous holy city. Meanwhile Sadat grew increasingly isolated within the Arab world. In 1981 he was asassinated by Islamic fundamentalists.

Carter scored his biggest moral victory in foreign affairs by paving the way for Panama to assume the ownership, operation, and defense of the Panama Canal Zone. Negotiations with Panama had begun during Johnson's administration, following riots by Panamanians against U.S. territorial rule in their country. Carter pressured the Senate to ratify new treaties in 1978 (by a vote of 68 to 32) that would turn the Panama Canal over to Panama by the year 2000.

(Mis)Handling the Unexpected

Mired in problems inherited from his predecessors, Carter often found himself disoriented by contradictory advice. Carter's Secretary of state Cyrus Vance recommended well-planned negotiations to soothe Soviet–U.S. relations and resolve disagreements with third world nations. But national security adviser Zbigniew Brzezinski, a bitterly anti-Communist Polish exile, adhered to cold war policies and interpreted events in even remote sections of Africa or South America as plays in a zero-sum game: wherever the United States lost influence, the Soviet Union gained, and vice versa. Despite Carter's commitment to human rights, he allowed U.S. policy to resume cold war postures.

In 1979 the overthrow of the brutal Nicaraguan dictatorship of Anastasio Somoza, long-time ally of the United States, left Carter without a succcessor to support. When the new Sandinista revolutionary government pleaded for help, Congress turned down Carter's request for $75 million in aid to Nicaragua. Meanwhile, in El Salvador, the Carter administration continued to back a repressive government even after the assassination of Oscar Romero, a Catholic archbishop and opposition leader. Following the rape and murder of four U.S. Catholic church women, apparently by the ultraright Salvadoran armed forces trained in the United States, peace activists and other Americans pleaded with Carter to withhold further military aid. Conservatives meanwhile demanded yet more funds to bolster the repressive anti-Communist regime.

African nations vacillated between allying with the United States and courting the Soviet Union. In this tricky political territory, UN ambassador (and former civil rights leader) Andrew Young, the first major African American diplomat assigned to Africa, could not persuade Carter to recognize the antiapartheid government of Angola, which had invited 20,000 Cuban troops to help in its fight against South African–backed rebels. Nor did Carter's and Young's verbal criticisms of the South African regime, unaccompanied by economic sanctions, satisfy black Africans. After Carter fired Young for having met secretly with officials of the Palestine Liberation Organization (PLO), the president proved even less effective in negotiating with antiapartheid leaders.

The Soviet invasion of Afghanistan produced a major stalemate. In December 1979, 30,000 Soviet troops invaded their neighbor to put down a revolt by Islamic fundamentalists against the weakening Soviet-backed government. The invasion succeeded mainly in heating up the civil war, which the American press quickly labeled the "Russian Vietnam." As the war bogged down, Americans heard familiar stories, this time of Soviet soldiers using drugs and expressing disillusionment with their government.

President Carter responded to these events with his own corollary to the Monroe Doctrine. The so-called Carter Doctrine asserted the determination of the United States to protect its interests in yet another area of the world, the Persian Gulf. Carter acted on the advice of Brzezinski, who believed that the Soviet Union would soon try to secure for itself a warm-water port on the gulf, an area rich in oil and now vital to U.S. interests. The president backed up his increasingly hard-line policies by halting exports of grain and high technology to the Soviet Union, supporting Afghani resistance against the Russians, and by cancelling American participation in the 1980 Moscow Olympics.

By the end of Carter's term, conservatives had swamped liberals within the Democratic Party. With the economy still hurting from the effects of cold war spending, Carter called for ever-larger increases in the military budget. He also signed Presidential Directive 59, guaranteeing the production of weapons alleged necessary to win a prolonged nuclear war. The prospect of peace and détente dried up.

The Iran Hostage Crisis

On November 4, 1979, Iranian fundamentalists seized the U.S. embassy in Tehran and held fifty-two American employees hostage for 444 days. This event made President Carter's previous problems seem small by comparison.

For decades, U.S. foreign policy in the Middle East had depended on a friendly government in Iran. After the CIA had helped to overthrow the reformist, constitutional government and installed the Pahlavi royal family and the shah of Iran in 1953, millions of U.S. dollars had poured into the Iranian economy and the shah's armed forces. President Carter had toasted the shah for his "great leadership" and overlooked the rampant corruption in government and a well-organized opposition. But, by early 1979, a revolution led by Islamic fundamentalist Ayatollah Ruholla Khomeini had overthrown the shah.

After Carter had allowed Mohammad Reza Pahlavi, the deposed shah, to enter the United States to be treated for cancer in November, a group of Khomeini's followers retaliated, storming the U.S. embassy and taking the American staff as hostages.

Cyrus Vance assured Carter that only negotiations could free the Americans. Caught up in a reelection campaign and lobbied by Brzezinski for decisive action, Carter ordered U.S. military forces to stage a nighttime helicopter rescue mission. But a sandstorm caused some of the aircraft to crash and burn, leaving eight Americans dead, their burned corpses displayed by the enraged Iranians. Short of an all-out attack, which surely would have resulted in the hostages' death, Carter had used up his options.

The political and economic fallout was heavy. Cyrus Vance resigned, the first secretary of state in sixty-five years to leave office over a political difference with the president. The price of oil rose by 60 percent. Carter had failed in the one area he had proclaimed central to the future of the United States: energy. He had also violated his own human rights policy, which was intended to be his distinctive mark on American foreign affairs.

The 1980 Election

Carter's prospects for reelection appeared to rest on his conduct of international affairs. If he only could put his human rights policy on a firm ground, move toward lasting peace in the Middle East, or strike a bargain with the Soviets on arms limitation, he might restore voter confidence. If not, his presidency would end after a single term.

Ultimately, Carter's bid for renomination depended more on his incumbency than on his popularity. Delegates at the Democratic National Convention unenthusiastically endorsed Carter along with running mate Walter Mondale. On the Republican side, former California governor Ronald Reagan had been building his campaign since his near nomination in 1976. Former CIA director and Texas oil executive George H. W. Bush, more moderate than Reagan, became the Republican candidate for vice president. Moral Majority placed itself squarely in Reagan's camp, and Senator Jesse Helms's Congressional Club contributed $4.6 million to the campaign.

Reagan repeatedly asked voters, "Are you better off now than you were four years ago?" Although critics questioned Reagan's competence, the attractive, soft-spoken actor shrugged off criticisms while spotlighting the many problems besetting the country.

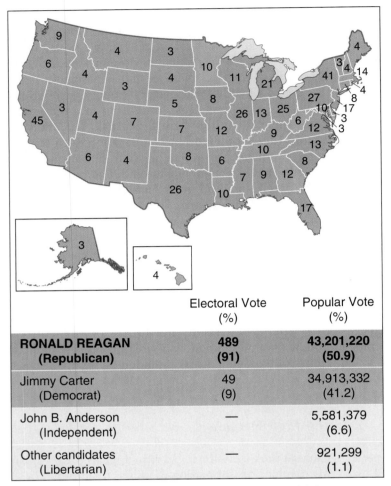

	Electoral Vote (%)	Popular Vote (%)
RONALD REAGAN (Republican)	**489** **(91)**	**43,201,220** **(50.9)**
Jimmy Carter (Democrat)	49 (9)	34,913,332 (41.2)
John B. Anderson (Independent)	—	5,581,379 (6.6)
Other candidates (Libertarian)	—	921,299 (1.1)

The Election of 1980 Ronald Reagan won a landslide victory over incumbent Jimmy Carter, who managed to carry only six states and the District of Columbia. Reagan attracted millions of traditionally Democratic voters to the Republican camp.

The Republican ticket cruised to victory. Carter won only 41.2 percent of the popular vote to Reagan's 50.9 percent, 49 votes in the Electoral College to Reagan's 489. The Republicans won control of the Senate for the first time since 1952 and with the largest majority since 1928. Still, barely half of the eligible voters turned out in the 1980 election, bringing Ronald Reagan into office with a mandate of a thin 25 percent.

THE REAGAN REVOLUTION

The Great Communicator

Ronald Reagan was born in 1911 and raised in the small town of Dixon, Illinois. His father was a sales-man and an alcoholic who had a tough time holding a job. His strong-willed mother was a fundamentalist Christian who kept the family together despite frequent moves. A job with the Works Progress Administration for Reagan's father had helped the family survive the hard times of the Great Depression. Encouraged by his mother, Reagan began acting in church plays and in productions at Eureka College, from which he graduated in 1932.

In 1937 Reagan began a Hollywood acting career that lasted for a quarter-century. Although he was never a big star, on screen he appeared tall, handsome, and affable. In later years, he credited his political success to his acting experience. He told one interviewer: "An actor knows two important things—to be honest in what he's doing and to be in touch with the audience. That's not bad advice for a politician either."

While serving as president of the Screen Actors Guild from 1947 to 1952, Reagan began to distance himself from New Deal liberalism by becoming a leader of the anti-Communist forces in Holly-wood. In 1954 he became the host of a new national television program, General Electric Theater, and began a long stint as a national promoter for GE. In this role he made numerous speeches celebrating the achievements of corporate America and emphasizing the dangers of big government, excessive liberalism, and radical trade unions."

Reagan switched his party affiliation to the Republicans and became a popular fund-raiser and speaker for the California GOP. He took a leading role in conservative Republican Barry Goldwater's 1964 presidential campaign. A televised address on Goldwater's behalf thrust Reagan himself to national prominence. At the core of Reagan's conservative message was an attack on big government. He lashed out at a growing bureaucracy and celebrated the achievements of entrepreneurs unfettered by government regulation or aid.

With the financial backing of a group of wealthy, conservative Californians, Reagan defeated Democratic governor Edmund G. Brown in 1966 and won reelection in 1970. As governor, he cut the state welfare rolls, placed limits on the number of state employees, and funneled a large share of state tax revenues back to local governments. He vigorously attacked student protesters and black militants, thereby tapping into the conservative backlash against the activism of the 1960s.

Reaganomics

During the Reagan presidency, supply-side economic theory, dubbed "Reaganomics," dominated the administration's thinking and helped redirect American economic policy. Supply-side theorists urged a sharp break with the Keynesian policies that had been dominant since the New Deal era (see Chapter 24). Keynesians traditionally favored moderate tax cuts and increases in government spending to stimulate the economy and reduce unemployment during recessions. By putting more money in people's pockets, they argued, greater consumer demand would lead to economic expansion.

By contrast, supply-siders called for simultaneous tax cuts and reductions in public spending. This combination, they claimed, would give private entrepreneurs and investors greater incentives to start businesses, take risks, invest capital, and thereby create new wealth and jobs. Whatever revenues were lost in lower tax rates would be offset by revenue from new economic growth. At the same time, spending cuts would keep the federal deficit under control and thereby keep interest rates down.

Reagan quickly won bipartisan approval for two key pieces of legislation based on these ideas. The Economic Recovery Tax Act of 1981 cut income and corporate taxes by $747 billion over five years. For individuals, the act cut taxes across the board. It also reduced the maximum tax on all income from 70 percent to 50 percent, lowered the maximum capital gains tax—the tax paid on profitable investments—from 28 percent to 20 percent, and eliminated the distinction between earned and unearned income. This last measure proved a boon to the small, richest fraction of the population that derives most of its income from rent, dividends, and interest instead of from wages.

Ronald and Nancy Reagan at the Inaugural Ball, January 20, 1981. The Reagans, supported by a circle of wealthy conservative friends from the business world and Hollywood, brought a lavish style to the White House that helped define the culture of the 1980s.

SOURCE: Photo by Dennis Brack. Black Star (1-81-8930).

With the help of conservative southern and western Democrats in the House, the administration also pushed through a comprehensive program of spending cuts, awkwardly known as the Omnibus Reconciliation Act of 1981. This bill mandated cuts of $136 billion in federal spending for the period 1982–1984, affecting more than 200 social and cultural programs. The hardest-hit areas included federal appropriations for education, the environment, health, housing, urban aid, food stamps, research on synthetic fuels, and the arts. The conservative coalition in the House allowed only one vote on the entire package of spending cuts, a strategy that allowed conservatives to slash appropriations for a wide variety of domestic programs in one fell swoop.

While reducing spending on domestic programs, the Reagan administration greatly increased the defense budget. During the 1980 election campaign, Reagan's calls to "restore America's defenses" helped reinforce the public perception that President Carter had dealt ineffectively with the Iran hostage crisis. Once in office he greatly accelerated a trend already under way during the last two years of the Carter presidency: a sharp increase in defense spending. Over all, the Reagan budgets for military spending totaled $1.6 trillion over five years and indicated a significant shift in federal budget priorities under his administration.

Meanwhile, the Reagan administration created a chilly atmosphere for organized labor. In the summer of 1981, some 13,000 federal employees, all members of the Professional Air Traffic Controllers Organization (PATCO), went on strike. The president retaliated against the strikers by firing them, and the Federal Aviation Administration started a crash program to replace them. Conservative appointees to the National Labor Relations Board and the federal courts toughened its antiunion position.

Reagan appointed conservatives to head the Environmental Protection Agency, the Occupational Safety and Health Administration, and the Consumer Product Safety Commission. These individuals abolished or weakened hundreds of rules governing environmental protection, work-place safety, and consumer protection, all in the interest of increasing the efficiency and productivity of business. The deregulatory fever dominated cabinet departments as well. Secretary of the Interior James Watt opened up formerly protected wilderness areas and wetlands to private developers. Secretary of Transportation Andrew L. "Drew" Lewis, Jr. eliminated regulations passed in the 1970s aimed at reducing air pollution and improving fuel efficiency in cars and trucks.

Following the tenets of supply-side economics, the Reagan administration weakened the Antitrust Division of the Justice Department, the Securities and Exchange Commission, and the Federal Home Loan Bank Board. Large corporations, Wall Street stock brokerages, investment banking houses, and the savings and loan industry were all allowed to operate with a much freer hand than ever before. By the

late 1980s, the unfortunate consequences of this freedom would become apparent in a series of unprecedented scandals in the nation's financial and banking industries.

The Election of 1984

As the 1984 election approached, many Americans expressed doubts about the Reagan administration's defense initiatives. Polls showed that more than 70 percent of Americans favored a nuclear freeze with the Soviet Union. Many observers noted that Reagan also appeared politically vulnerable for his economic policies and cutbacks in social programs.

Hoping to win back disgruntled voters, Democrats chose Carter's vice president, Walter Mondale, as their nominee. As a former senator from Minnesota, Mondale had close ties with the party's liberal establishment and also the support of its more military-minded wing. At the Democratic National Convention, Mondale named Representative Geraldine Ferraro of New York as his running mate, a first for women in American politics. Charismatic speakers such as the Reverend Jesse Jackson, a dynamic disciple of Martin Luther King, Jr., and Governor Mario Cuomo of New York stirred the delegates and many television viewers with their appeals to compassion, fairness, and brotherhood.

Opinion polls showed Mondale running even with Reagan. But the president's enormous personal popularity, along with the booming economy, overwhelmed the Democratic ticket. While Mondale emphasized the growing deficit and called attention to Americans who were left out of prosperity, Reagan cruised above it all. It was "morning again in America," his campaign ads claimed. In one of the biggest landslides in American history, Reagan won 59 percent of the popular vote and carried every state but Minnesota and the District of Columbia.

Recession, Recovery, Fiscal Crisis

Over the course of his two terms in office, Reagan's economic policies had mixed results. In 1982 a severe recession, the worst since the 1930s, gripped the nation. The official unemployment rate reached nearly 11 percent, or more than 11.5 million people. Another 3 million had been out of work so long they no longer actively looked for jobs and therefore were not counted in official statistics. But by the middle of 1983 the economy had begun to recover, and unemployment dropped to about 8 percent while inflation fell below 5 percent. The stock market boomed, pushing the Dow Jones industrial average from 776 in August 1982 to an all-time high of 2,722 in August 1987. The administration took credit for the turnaround, hailing the supply-side fiscal policies that had drastically cut taxes and domestic spending. But critics pointed to other factors: the Federal Reserve Board's tight-money policies, an energy resource glut and a consequent sharp drop in energy prices, and the billions of dollars pumped into the economy for defense spending.

Few doubted, however, that the supply-side formula intensified an ominous fiscal crisis. Although President Reagan had promised to balance the federal budget, his policies had the opposite effect. The national debt grew from $907 billion in 1980 to over $2 trillion in 1986, more than the federal government had accumulated in its entire previous history. Expenditures for paying just the interest on the national debt reached 14 percent of the annual budget in 1988, double the percentage set aside for that purpose in 1974.

In the Reagan years the fiscal crisis became a structural problem with newly disturbing and perhaps permanent implications for the American economy. Big deficits kept interest rates high, as the government drove up the cost of borrowing the money it needed to pay its own bills. Foreign investors, attracted by high interest rates on government securities, pushed up the value of the dollar in relation to foreign currencies. The overvalued dollar made it difficult for foreigners to buy American products, while making overseas good cheaper to American consumers. Basic American industries— steel, autos, textiles—thus found it difficult to compete abroad and at home. In 1980, the United States still enjoyed a trade surplus of $166 billion. By 1987 the nation had an indebtedness to foreigners of $340 billion. Since World War I, the United States had been the world's leading creditor; in the mid-1980s it became its biggest debtor.

In late 1986, the Securities and Exchange Commission (SEC) uncovered the biggest stock scandal in history, in the process revealing the inner workings of high finance in the 1980s. Ivan Boesky, one of the nation's leading stock speculators, admitted to using confidential information about upcoming corporate takeovers to trade stocks illegally. Just two years earlier the dapper Boesky had made more than $100 million on just two deals. Now he agreed to cooperate with SEC investigators.

The biggest fish caught in their net was Michael Milken, a Boesky ally. An investment banker for Drexel Burnham Lambert, Milken perfected the art of corporate raiding through creative manipulation of debt. He showed how enormous profits could be earned from weak firms that were tempting targets for takeovers and mergers. Their debt could be used as tax write-offs; less efficient units could be sold off piecemeal; and more profitable units could be retained, merged, or sold again to form new entities. Instead of borrowing from banks, Milken financed his deals by underwriting high-yield, risky "junk bonds" for companies rated below investment grade. Investors in turn reaped huge profits by selling these junk bonds to hostile-takeover dealers.

Milken and other corporate raiders reshaped the financial world, setting off the greatest wave of buying and selling in American business history. Milken himself made a staggering $550 million in one year alone. Just before filing for bankruptcy in 1990, Drexel Burnham Lambert paid its executives $350 million in bonuses—almost as much as it owed its creditors. Milken was eventually convicted of insider trading and stock fraud and sent to prison.

On Wall Street, the bull market of the 1980s ended abruptly in the fall of 1987. After reaching its new high of 2,722 at the end of August, the Dow Jones average of thirty leading industrial stocks began to slide downward and then crashed. On October 19, the Dow lost almost 23 percent of its value. The panic on the trading floors recalled the pandemonium set off by the stock market crash of 1929.

BEST OF TIMES, WORST OF TIMES

The celebration of wealth, moneymaking, and entrepreneurship dominated much of popular culture, politics, and intellectual life in the 1980s. But grimmer realities lay under the surface. A variety of measures strongly suggested that the nation had moved toward greater inequality, that the middle class was shrinking, and that poverty was on the rise. Two of the most cherished basic assumptions about America—that life would improve for most people and their children, and that membership in the comfortable middle class was available to all who worked for it—looked shaky by the end of the decade.

SHARE OF TOTAL NET WORTH OF AMERICAN FAMILIES		
	1983	1989
Richest 1 percent of families	31%	37%
Next richest 9 percent	35	31
Remaining 90 percent	33	32

SOURCE: *New York Times*, April 21, 1992, from Federal Reserve Survey of Consumer Finances.

NUMBER OF POOR, RATE OF POVERTY, AND POVERTY LINE, 1979–1992		
	1979	1992
Millions of poor	26.1	36.9
Rate of poverty	11.7%	14.5%
Poverty line (family of four)	$7,412	$14,335

SOURCE: U.S. Bureau of the Census, *Current Population Reports: Consumer Income*, Series P-60, Nos. 161 and 185, 1988, 1993. U.S. federal data compiled by Ed Royce, Rollins College.

The Celebration of Wealth

The very wealthy did extremely well during the 1980s. In 1989, the richest 1 percent of American households accounted for 37 percent of the nation's private wealth—up from 31 percent in 1983, a jump of almost 20 percent. This top 1 percent owned more than the bottom 90 percent of Americans.

Other affluent Americans also made huge gains. In 1980 the top 5 percent of families earned 15.3 percent of the nation's total income. By 1992 their share had grown to 17.6 percent, an increase of 15 percent; their average income was $156,000 a year. In 1980 the top 20 percent of families earned 41.6 percent of the nation's total. By 1992 their share had grown to 44.6 percent, an increase of about 7 percent, with an average income of $99,000 a year. In contrast, the bottom 40 percent of families had 16.7 percent of aggregate income in 1980. By 1992 their share had declined to 14.9 percent, a drop of nearly 2 percent, with an average income of about $16,500 a year.

A Two-Tiered Society

During the 1960s, despite the diversion of federal funds to military spending during the Vietnam War, President Johnson's Great Society had brought a higher standard of living to many Americans. By the time Carter took office in 1977, the sinking economy was undercutting these gains. Reagan's supply-side policies enlivened the economy but at the same time widened the gap between rich and poor.

The number and percentage of Americans in poverty grew at an alarming rate. Since the mid-1970s, most of the new jobs clustered in low-paying service and manufacturing sectors and less than half of them paid more than the $11,611 poverty-level income for a family of four. In 1979 the government classified about 26.1 million people as poor, 11.7 percent of the total population; by 1992 the number of poor had reached 36.9 million, or 14.5 percent of the population, and nearly 22 percent of all American children under eighteen lived in poverty.

The widening gap between rich and poor was sharply defined by race. By 1992, 33 percent of all African Americans lived in poverty, as did 29 percent of Hispanics (the rate was especially high among Puerto Ricans, yet low among Cuban Americans). The majority of African Americans, six out of ten, lived in central cities with high unemployment rates, and the bleak prospects took a toll especially on the young. A black child was twice as likely as a white child to die before reaching the first birthday and four times more likely to be killed between the ages of one and four. Among black teenagers, the unemployment rate topped 40 percent; the few jobs available to them were among the lowest-paid in the economy. Meanwhile, the high school dropout rate skyrocketed, and the number of serious crimes, such as burglary, car theft, and murder, perpetrated by children between the ages of ten and seventeen increased at an alarming rate.

Moreover, opportunities for advancement into the middle class were dwindling. By 1980 fewer black students attended integrated schools than in 1954, except in the South, where about half the black students did. The turnabout resulted in part from increasing opposition by white parents to court-ordered school busing, which had served since *Brown* v. *Board of Education* as the principal means of achieving racial balance in urban school systems. During the 1980s the busing controversy nearly disappeared because federal judges hesitated to mandate such programs. But more important was the change in the racial composition of American cities. As a consequence of "white flight" to the suburbs, big-city school systems were serving mainly African American and Latino children, making the issue of integration moot.

New legal rulings closed off important routes to employment in the professions. A 1978 U.S. Supreme

Court decision dealt a sharp blow to affirmative action. To ensure acceptance of a minimum number of minority students, the University of California at Davis Medical School had established a quota system under affirmative action guidelines. In 1973 and 1974 the school denied admission to Allan Bakke, a white student. Bakke sued the university for "reverse discrimination," claiming his academic record was better than that of the sixteen minority students who were admitted. The U.S. Supreme Court handed down a five-to-four decision on June 18, 1978, stating that the use of an "explicit racial classification" in situations where no earlier discrimination had been demonstrated violated the equal protection clause of the Fourteenth Amendment. The Court ordered the University of California to admit Bakke to its medical school. During the 1980s, therefore, affirmative action programs could operate only when "a legacy of unequal treatment" could be proved.

The Feminization of Poverty

Despite a growing rate of labor force participation, the majority of women gainfully employed earned less than a living wage. Even if employed, women usually lost ground following a divorce, especially as new no-fault divorce laws lowered or eradicated alimony. Moreover, the majority of men defaulted on child-support payments within one year after separation. Whereas divorced men enjoyed a sizable increase in their standard of living, divorced women suffered a formidable decline. During the 1970s alone, the number of poor families headed by women increased nearly 70 percent.

A sharp rise in teenage pregnancy reinforced this pattern. Many of these mothers were too young to have gained either the education or skills to secure jobs that would pay enough to support themselves and their children. Even with Aid to Families with Dependent Children (AFDC) payments and food stamps, it was impossible for these single mothers to keep their families above the poverty line. By 1992, female-headed households, comprising 13.7 million people, accounted for 37 percent of the poor. African American and Latino women and their children had by far the highest poverty rates.

Epidemics: Drugs, AIDS, Homelessness

Drug addiction and drug trafficking took on frightening new dimensions in the early 1980s. The arrival of "crack," a cheap, smokable, and highly addictive form of cocaine, made that drug affordable to the urban poor. As crack addiction spread, the drug trade assumed alarming new proportions both domestically and internationally. Crack ruined hundreds of thousands of lives and led to a dramatic increase in crime rates. Studies showed that over half the men arrested in the nation's largest cities tested positive for cocaine. The crack trade spawned a new generation of young drug dealers who were willing to risk jail and death for enormous profits. In city after city, drug wars over turf took the lives of dealers and innocents, both caught in the escalating violence.

The Reagan administration declared a highly publicized "war on drugs," a multibillion-dollar campaign to bring the traffic under control. Critics charged that the war on drugs focused on supply from abroad when it needed to look at demand here at home. They urged more federal money for drug education, treatment, and rehabilitation. Drug addiction and drug use, they argued, were primarily health problems, not law enforcement issues.

In 1981 doctors in Los Angeles, San Francisco, and New York began encountering a puzzling new medical phenomenon. Young homosexual men were dying suddenly from rare types of pneumonia and cancer. The underlying cause was found to be a mysterious new viral disease that destroyed the body's natural defenses against illness, making its victims susceptible to a host of opportunistic infections. Researchers at the Centers for Disease Control (CDC) in Atlanta called the new disease acquired immune deficiency syndrome (AIDS). The virus that causes AIDS is transmitted primarily in semen and blood. Full-blown AIDS might not appear for years after initial exposure to the virus. Thus, one could infect others without knowing one had the disease. Although tests emerged to determine whether one carried HIV, there was no cure. The majority of early AIDS victims were homosexual men who had been infected through sexual contact. Many Americans, thus, perceived AIDS as a disease of homosexuals. But other victims became infected through intravenous drug use, blood transfusions, heterosexual transmission, or birth to AIDS-carrying mothers.

AIDS provoked fear, anguish, and anger. It also brought an upsurge of organization and political involvement. In city after city, the gay community responded to the AIDS crisis with energy and determination. Most gay men changed their sexual habits, practicing "safe sex" to lessen the chances of infection. The Reagan administration, playing to antihomosexual prejudices, largely ignored the epidemic.

In May 1987, members of the Lesbian and Gay Community Services in Downtown Manhattan organized ACT-UP. Protesting what they perceived to be the Reagan administration's mismanagement of the AIDs crisis, they used nonviolent direct action, which often took the form of dramatic acts of civil disobedience. ACT-UP grew to more than 70 chapters in the United States and the world.

SOURCE: AP/Wide World Photos.

One important exception was Surgeon General C. Everett Koop, who urged a comprehensive sex education program in the nation's schools.

Homelessness emerged as a chronic social problem during the 1980s. Often disoriented, shoeless, and forlorn, growing numbers of street people slept over heating grates, on subways, and in parks. Homeless people wandered city sidewalks panhandling and struggling to find scraps of food. Winters proved especially difficult. In the early 1980s, the Department of Housing and Urban Development placed the number of the nation's homeless at between 250,000 and 350,000. But advocates for the homeless estimated that the number was as high as 3 million.

Who were the homeless? Analysts agreed that at least a third were mental patients who had been discharged from psychiatric hospitals amid the deinstitutionalization trend of the the 1970s. Many more were alcoholics and drug addicts unable to hold jobs. But the ranks of the homeless also included female-headed families, battered women, Vietnam veterans, AIDS victims, and elderly people with no place to go. Some critics pointed to the decline in decent housing for poor people and the deterioration of the nation's health-care system as a cause of homelessness.

REAGAN'S FOREIGN POLICY

The Evil Empire

In the early 1980s, the Reagan administration made vigorous anti-Communist rhetoric the centerpiece of its foreign policy. In a sharp turn from President Carter's focus on human rights and President Nixon's pursuit of détente, Reagan described the Soviet Union as "an evil empire . . . the focus of evil in the modern world." The president denounced the growing movement for a nuclear freeze, arguing that "we must find peace through strength."

Administration officials argued that the nation's military strength had fallen dangerously behind that of the Soviet Union during the 1970s. Critics disputed this assertion, pointing out that the Soviet advantage in intercontinental ballistic missiles (ICBMs) was offset by American superiority in submarine-based forces and strategic aircraft. Nonetheless, the administration proceeded with plans to enlarge America's nuclear strike force.

In 1983 President Reagan introduced an unsettling new element into superpower relations when he presented his Strategic Defense Initiative (SDI), the plan for a space-based ballistic-missile defense system that journalists dubbed "Star Wars," after the popular Hollywood film series. This proposal for a five-year $26 billion program promised to give the United States the capacity to shoot down incoming missiles with laser beams and homing rockets. To critics, the plan seemed unworkable, impossibly expensive, and likely to destabilize existing arms treaties. The Reagan administration pressed ahead, spending $17 billion in research before the president left office—without achieving any convincing results.

The Reagan Doctrine and Central America

Declaring the "Vietnam syndrome" over, the president confidently reasserted America's right to intervene anywhere in the world to fight Communist insurgency. The Reagan Doctrine, as this declaration was later called, assumed that all political instability in the third world resulted not from indigenous factors such as poverty or corruption but from the pernicious influence of the Soviet Union. It found its most important expression in Central America, where the United States hoped to reestablish its historical control over the Caribbean basin.

On the economic front, the Caribbean Basin Initiative (CBI) promised to stimulate the Caribbean economy by encouraging the growth of business corporations and a freer flow of capital through $350 million in U.S. aid. Yet Congress refused to play by the rules of free trade, placing stiff tariffs and quotas on imports of shoes, leather goods, and sugar competing with U.S. products. Many Latin American business leaders opposed key parts of the CBI, such as generous tax breaks for foreign investors. They feared that once large multinational corporations entered their markets, the CBI would strengthen the kind of chronic economic dependency that had shaped so much of the region's past.

In El Salvador, the Reagan administration continued to support the repressive regime. Military aid

jumped from $6 million in 1980 to $82 million in 1982, and El Salvador received more U.S. economic assistance than any other Latin American country. By 1983 right-wing death squads, encouraged by military elements within the regime, had tortured and assassinated thousands of opposition leaders. The election in 1984 of centrist president José Napoleón Duarte failed to end the bloody civil war. Some 53,000 Salvadorans, more than one out of every hundred, lost their lives in the conflict.

In Nicaragua, the Reagan administration claimed that the revolutionary Sandinista government posed "an unusual and extraordinary threat to the national security." U.S. officials accused the Sandinistas of shipping arms to antigovernment rebels in El Salvador. In December 1981, Reagan approved a $19 million CIA plan arming and organizing Nicaraguan exiles, known as Contras, to fight against the Sandinista government. As Reagan escalated this undeclared war, the aim became not merely the cutting of Nicaraguan aid to Salvadoran rebels but the overthrow of the Sandinista regime itself.

In 1984 the CIA secretly mined Nicaraguan harbors. When Nicaragua won a judgment against the United States in the World Court over this violation of its sovereignty, the Reagan administration refused to recognize the court's jurisdiction in the case and ignored the verdict. Predictably, the U.S. covert war pushed the Sandinistas closer to Cuba and the Soviet bloc. Meanwhile, U.S. grass-roots opposition to Contra aid grew more vocal and widespread. A number of U.S. communities set up sister city projects offering humanitarian and technical assistance to Nicaraguan communities. Scores of U.S. churches offered sanctuary to political refugees from Central America.

In 1984 Congress reined in the covert war by passing the Boland Amendment, introduced by Democratic Representative Edward Boland of Massachusetts. If forbid government agencies from supporting "directly or indirectly military or paramilitary operations" in Nicaragua. Denied funding by Congress, President Reagan turned to the National Security Council to find a way to keep the Contra war going. Between 1984 and 1986, the NSC staff secretly ran the Contra assistance effort, raising $37 million in aid from foreign countries and private contributors, creating the largest mercenary army in hemispheric history. In 1987 the revelation of this unconstitutional scheme exploded before the public as part of the Iran-Contra affair, the most damaging political scandal of the Reagan years.

Glasnost and Arms Control

Meanwhile, momentous political changes within the Soviet Union led to a reduction in East-West tensions and ultimately the end of the cold war itself. Soviet premier Leonid Brezhnev, in power since 1964, died toward the end of 1982. His successors, Yuri Andropov and Konstantin Chernenko, both died after brief terms in office. But in 1985 a new, reform-minded leader, Mikhail Gorbachev, won election as general secretary of the Soviet Communist Party. Although a lifelong Communist, Gorbachev represented a new generation of disenchanted party members. He initiated a radical new program of economic and political reform under the rubrics of *glasnost* (openness) and *perestroika* (restructuring).

Gorbachev and his advisers opened up political discussion and encouraged criticism of the Soviet economy and political culture. The government released longtime dissidents like Andrei Sakharov from prison and took the first halting steps toward profit-based, private initiatives in the economy. This "new thinking" inspired an unprecedented wave of diverse, often critical perspectives in Soviet art, literature, journalism, and scholarship.

In Gorbachev's view, improving the economic performance of the Soviet system depended first on halting the arms race. Over 10 percent of the Soviet GNP (gross national product) went to defense spending, while the majority of its citizens still struggled to find even the most basic consumer items in shops. Gorbachev thus took the lead in negotiating a halt to the arms race with the United States.

The historical ironies were stunning. Reagan had made militant anticommunism the centerpiece of his administration, but between 1985 and 1988 he had four separate summit meetings with the new Soviet leader. In October 1986, and Gorbachev met in Reykjavík, Iceland, but this summit bogged down over the issue of SDI. Reagan refused to abandon his plan for a space-based defensive umbrella. Gorbachev insisted that the plan violated the 1972 Strategic Arms Limitation Treaty (SALT I) and that SDI might eventually allow the United States to make an all-out attack on the Soviet Union.

After another year of tough negotiating, the two sides agreed to a modest treaty that called for comprehensive, mutual, on-site inspections. It provided an important psychological breakthrough. At one of the summits a Soviet leader humorously announced, "We are going to do something terrible to you Americans—we are going to deprive you of an enemy."

The Iran-Contra Scandal

In 1987 the revelations of the Iran-Contra affair laid bare the continuing contradictions and difficulties attending America's role in world affairs. The affair also demonstrated how overzealous and secretive government officials subverted the Constitution and compromised presidential authority under the guise of patriotism.

The Middle East presented the Reagan administration with its most frustrating foreign policy dilemmas. In October 1983 a terrorist bombing in marine barracks in Lebanon killed 241 American servicemen, and the administration pulled the marines out of Lebanon, shying away from a long-term commitment of U.S. forces in the Middle East.

Terrorist acts, including the seizing of Western hostages and the bombing of commercial airplanes and cruise ships, redefined the politics of the region. These were desperate attempts by small sects, many of them splinter groups associated with the Palestinian cause or Islamic fundamentalism, to inhibit U.S. support of Israel. The Reagan administration insisted that behind international terrorism lay the sinister influence and money of the Soviet bloc, the Ayatollah Khomeini of Iran, and Libyan leader Muammar el-Qaddafi. In the spring of 1986 the president, eager to demonstrate his antiterrorist resolve, ordered the bombing of Tripoli in a failed effort to kill Qaddafi.

As a fierce war between Iran and Iraq escalated, the administration tilted publicly toward Iraq to please the Arab states around the Persian Gulf. But in 1986 Reagan's advisors began secret negotiations with the revolutionary Iranian government. They eventually offered to supply Iran with sophisticated weapons for use against Iraq in exchange for help in securing the release of Americans held hostage by radical Islamic groups in Lebanon.

Subsequent disclosures elevated the arms-for-hostages deal into a major scandal. Some of the money from the arms deal had been secretly diverted into covert aid for the Nicaraguan Contras. The American public soon learned the sordid details from investigative journalists and through televised congressional hearings held during the summer of 1987. In order to escape congressional oversight of the CIA, Reagan and CIA director William Casey had essentially turned the National Security Council, previously a policy-coordinating body, into an operational agency. Under the direction of National Security Advisers Robert McFarlane and later Admiral John Poindexter, the NSC had sold TOW and Hawk missiles to the Iranians, using Israel as a go-between. Millions of dollars from these sales were then given to the Contras in blatant and illegal disregard of the Boland Amendment.

In the televised congressional hearings, NSC staffer and marine lieutenant colonel Oliver North emerged as the figure running what he euphemistically referred to as "the Enterprise." North defiantly defended his actions in the name of patriotism. Some Americans saw the handsome and dashing North as a hero; most were appalled by his and Poindexter's blithe admissions that they had lied to Congress, shredded evidence, and refused to inform the president of details in order to guarantee his "plausible deniability." A blue-ribbon commission led by former senator John Tower of Texas concluded that Reagan himself "did not seem to be aware" of the policy or its consequences. But the Tower Report offered a stunning portrait of a president who was at best confused and far removed from critical policy-making responsibilities.

Ultimately, the Iran-Contra investigation raised more questions than it answered. The full role of CIA director Casey, who died in 1987, particularly his

CHRONOLOGY

1973	*Roe* v. *Wade* legalizes abortion
	Arab embargo sparks oil crisis in the United States
1974	Richard Nixon resigns presidency; Gerald Ford takes office
	President Ford pardons Nixon and introduces anti-inflation program
1975	Unemployment rate reaches nearly 9 percent
	South Vietnamese government falls to communists
	Antibusing protests break out in Boston
1976	Percentage of African Americans attending college peaks at 9.3 percent and begins a decline
	Jimmy Carter is elected president
1977	President Carter announces human rights as major tenet in foreign policy
1978	*Bakke* v. *University of California* decision places new limits on affirmative action programs
	Camp David meeting sets terms for Middle East peace
	California passes Proposition 13, cutting taxes and government social programs
1979	Three Mile Island nuclear accident threatens a meltdown
	Nicaraguan Revolution overthrows Anastasio Somoza
	Iranian fundamentalists seize the U.S. embassy in Tehran and hold U.S. citizens hostage for 444 days
	Soviets invade Afghanistan
1980	Inflation reaches 13.5 percent
	Ronald Reagan is elected president
1981	Reagan adminisration initiates major cuts in taxes and domestic spending
	Military buildup accelerates
	AIDS is recognized and named
1982	Economic recession grips the nation
1983	Reagan announces the Strategic Defense Initiative, labeled "Star Wars" by critics.
	241 marines killed in Beirut terrorist bombing
1985	Mikhail Gorbachev initates reforms— *glasnost* and *perestroika*—in the Soviet Union
1986	Iran-Contra hearings before Congress reveal arms-for-hostages deal and funds secretly and illegally diverted to Nicaraguan rebels

relationships with North and the president, remained murky. The role of Vice President George H. W. Bush remained mysterious as well, and it would return as an issue in the 1992 presidential election. Both North and Poindexter were convicted of felonies, but their convictions were overturned by higher courts on technical grounds. Reagan held fast to his plea of ignorance. When pressed on what had happened, he repeatedly claimed, "I'm still trying to find out."

In December 1992, following his reelection defeat and six years after the scandal broke, President George H. W. Bush granted pardons to six key players in the Iran-Contra affair. The Bush pardons made it unlikely that the full truth about the arms-for-hostages affair would ever be known.

CONCLUSION

The success of conservatives to halt and in some cases actually reverse key trends in American politics, from Franklin Roosevelt's New Deal to Lyndon Johnson's Great Society, was made possible by the legacy of the cold war and the trauma of defeat in Vietnam. But it also owed a great deal to a deepening anxiety of the public about cultural changes and a growing pessimism about the ability of politicians to offer solutions, especially at the national level.

Those community activists struggling to extend the protest movements of the 1960s into an updated, comprehensive reformism encompassing such issues as feminism, ecology, and affirmative action readily recognized that the liberal era had ended.

President Ronald Reagan, a charismatic figure who sometimes invented his own past and seemed to believe in it, offered remedies for a weary and nostalgic nation. By insisting that the rebellious 1960s had been a terrible mistake, lowering national self-confidence along with public morals and faith in the power of economic individualism, he successfully wedded the conservatism of Christian fundamentalists, many suburbanites, and Sunbelt voters with the more traditional conservatism of corporate leaders. In many respects, the Reagan administration actually continued and added ideological fervor to the downscaling of government services and upscaling of military spending already evident under President Jimmy Carter, while offering supporters the hope of a sweeping conservative revolution.

In the end, critics suggested, supporters of Ronald Reagan and Reaganism could not go back to the 1950s—just as the erstwhile rebels of the 1960s could not go back to their favorite era. Economically, conservatives achieved many of their goals, including widespread acceptance of sharper economic divisions within society and fewer restraints on corporations and investments. But socially and culturally, their grasp was much less secure.

REVIEW QUESTIONS

1. Evaluate the significance of the major population shifts in the United States from the 1940s through the 1970s. What was their impact on local and national politics?

2. Discuss the connections between the energy crisis and the rise of the environmental movement.

3. Why was the 1970s dubbed the "Me Decade"? Interpret the decline of liberalism and the rise of conservative political groups. How did these changes affect the outcome of presidential elections?

4. Was the Iran hostage crisis a turning point in American politics or only a thorn in Carter's reelection campaign? How did Iran-Contra affect the Republicans?

5. Describe the central philosophical assumptions behind Reaganomics. What were the key policies by which it was implemented? To what extent were these policies a break with previous economic approaches?

6. Evaluate Reagan's foreign policy. How did it differ from Carter's approach to foreign affairs?

7. Analyze the key structure factors underlying recent changes in American economic and cultural life. Do you see any political solutions for the growth of poverty and inequality?

RECOMMENDED READING

Lee Edwards, *The Conservative Revolution: The Movement That Remade America* (2000). Traces the rise of modern political conservatism from its origins in cold war anticommunism. A longtime conservative activist and writer, Edwards credits much of Reagan's success in office to the presence of a stong, vital, and grass-roots conservative movement.

Frances FitzGerald, *Way Out There in the Blue: Reagan, Star Wars, and the End of the Cold War* (2000). A well-documented study of the conservative mood that made Star Wars both credible and popular among conservatives. FitzGerald provides a sweeping historical context for Star Wars with special attention given to the impact of the cold war on traditional isolationism.

Angela Howard and Sasha Ranae Addams Tarrant, eds., *Reaction to the Modern Women's Movement, 1963 to Present* (1997). A collection of essays covering a wide variety of topics concerning the rise of antifeminism. The editors include excerpts from the writings of leading conservatives and analysis by historians.

John Karaagac, *Between Promise and Policy: Ronald Reagan and Conservative Reformism* (2000). Assesses Reagan's major polities, such as increased funding for federal government and regulatory reform, in light of his professed conservative ideals. Karaagac argues that Reagan wielded ideology as a political weapon to gain support for his programs while acting pragmatically and with a good deal of flexibility on particular issues.

Michael B. Katz, *Improving Poor People: The Welfare State, the "Underclass," and Urban Schools as History* (1995). Provides a broad overview of the history of urban poverty, welfare policy, and public education. Katz examines the "underclass" debates of the 1970s as a function of the interaction between politics and economics within the postindustrial inner city.

William M. LeoGrande, *Our Own Backyard: The United States in Central America, 1977–1992* (1998). Assesses the efforts of the Reagan adminstration to gain congressional approval for funding counterrevolutionary operations in El Salvador and Nicaragua. LeoGrande, a former congressional advisor, based his well-documented and detailed study on declassified State Department records, interviews, as well as conventional published sources.

Melani McAlister, *Epic Encounters: Culture, Media, and U.S. Interests in the Middle East, 1945–2000* (2001). A close reading of American popular culture, including films, television news broadcasts, museum exhibits, and fiction, representing relationship between the Middle East and the United States. McAlister considers the importance of the abundance of oil and the Islamic religion of the Middle East as factors shaping U.S. foreign policy.

Lisa McGirr, *Suburban Warriors: The Origins of the New American Right* (2001). Traces the resurgence of American conservatism by analyzing issues that galvanized grass-roots middle-class activism in 1960s and 1970s Southern California.

Bruce J. Schulman, *The Seventies: The Great Shift in American Culture, Society, and Politics* (2001). Examines the move away from the public-spirited universalism that characterized the New Deal and civil rights movement toward the sovereignty of the free market and celebration of private life. With a geopolitical twist that emphasizes the increasing importance of the Sunbelt, Schulman argues that the conservative 1980s actually began a decade earlier.

Judith Stein, *Running Steel, Running America: Race, Economic Policy, and the Decline of Liberalism* (1998). Discusses the impact of the decline of the U.S. steel industry on its large African American labor force. Stein analyzes trade policy, especially under Carter, that benefited foreign steel producers and led to the closing of American plants.

Robert A. Strong, *Working in the World: Jimmy Carter and the Making of American Foreign Policy* (2000). A collection of nine case studies of international affairs covering Carter's presidency. Strong's goal is not to provide new insight into the central crises of the era but to open a window to the range of presidential responsibilities in the diplomatic arena.

Andrew Szasz, *EcoPopulism: Toxic Waste and the Movement for Environmental Justice* (1994). A careful analysis of a turning point in federal regulation of toxic waste. Szasz shows how the prevention of pollution, previously considered a local issue, through strengthened state and federal regulations became a national issue and a springboard for the environmental movement.

Winifred D. Wandersee, *On the Move: American Women in the 1970s* (1988). A highly readable overview of the changes that brought American women into political life but also kept them at the margins of power. This study includes a close description of the National Organization for Women as well as media personalities, such as Jane Fonda, who gave feminism a public face.

ON THE WEB

http://www.bartleby.com/124/pres60.html

Jimmy Carter's Inaugural Address, January 20, 1977.

http://www.jimmycarterlibrary.org/documents/ hostages.phtml

Description of the Iran hostage crisis as described by the Jimmy Carter presidential library.

http://www.yale.edu/lawweb/avalon/mideast/ campdav.htm

The Camp David Accords brokered by Jimmy Carter in 1978 between Egypt and Israel.

http://www.jimmycarterlibrary.org/documents/ campdavid/letters.phtml

Documents from the Jimmy Carter Presidential Library related to the Camp David Accords.

http://www.bartleby.com/124/pres61.html

Ronald Reagan's First Inaugural Address, January 20, 1981.

http://www.bartleby.com/124/pres62.html

Ronald Reagan's Second Inaugural Address, January 21, 1985.

http://www.bartleby.com/124/pres63.html

George Bush's Inaugural Address, January 20, 1989.

http://www.prenhall.com/faragherbrief/map30.1

Consider the changes in population between 1970 and 1980. How were these changes reflected in the American economy?

THIRTY-ONE

TOWARD A TRANSNATIONAL AMERICA

▶ s i n c e 1 9 8 8

AMERICAN COMMUNITIES

The World Trade Center, New York, as a Transnational Community

TELMO ALVEAR HAD QUIT HIS JOB AS A BUSBOY IN AUGUST 2001 to become a waiter at Windows on the World, a restaurant on the 106th and 107th floors of the North Tower of the World Trade Center (WTC) that was once described by *New York* magazine as "the most spectacular restaurant in the world." The posh restaurant was huge and elegant. Designed originally as part of a private club for the WTC's business clients, Windows on the World could accommodate as many as 1,000 people. In the decade after it opened in 1976, Windows was one of the most successful restaurants in the world, earning revenues that topped $20 million a year. Much of its success came from its fabulous menu, originally planned with the consultation of James Beard, one of the world's most renowned chefs. In the early 1990s, the reputation of Windows began to slip, and following a terrorist attack on the WTC in February 1993, the restaurant closed. But by the time Alvear found a job there, Windows on the World was once again thriving. Celebrity chef Michael Lomonaco was in charge, earning for the restaurant the Visitors Choice Award of "Grand Prize for Best Restaurant Overall." With views on a clear day extending for forty-five miles, and with a wine cellar and liquor stock that was modestly named "The Greatest Bar on Earth," Windows had become a prime tourist attraction and a popular dining spot for some of the most powerful international traders and merchants in the world. "It's more than a restaurant," one reviewer enthused. "It's a New York experience."

And so it was. Not just Windows on the World but the entire World Trade Center had come to represent both the best and worst of New York City, the commercial capital of the world. The twin skyscrapers, which were designed to be the tallest in the world, were audacious. Completed in 1973 at a cost of $400 million, they rose 110 stories above ground and occupied a thirteen-square-block site in Lower Manhattan, conveniently close to Wall Street and the New York Stock Exchange. When the WTC was first built, many New Yorkers, including distinguished architects, complained that the mammoth, boxy structures destroyed the city's unrivaled skyline. They stood too self-assuredly, critics charged, as tasteless monuments to commerce, wealth, and ambition. But over the years, the WTC became a preeminent symbol of the glory of New York and, by extension, the United States. The image of the twin towers was emblazoned on t-shirts and captured on postcards and sold to tourists from all over the world. The WTC provided office space to hundreds of businesses and government agencies and served as a workplace for more than 50,000 people.

The people who worked in the twin towers constituted a remarkable transnational community. Although many were native New Yorkers, a large number were relative newcomers. Alvear himself was one in a huge wave of Hispanic immigration that had been transforming New York City since 1990. Immigrating from Ecuador as a teenager, he represented what census takers term "other Hispanics"—immigrants from South and Central America and the Caribbean who had replaced the Puerto Ricans and Cubans as the city's Hispanic majority. Alvear lived with his wife Blanca and their one-year-old son in Queens and spent his hours away from work at soccer games and dance clubs.

At his job, Alvear worked with and served people from a wide array of national backgrounds. Those who worked at Windows on the World proudly described themselves as a "little United Nations" because they represented just about every nation of the world and spoke nearly as many languages. Representing a wide range of cultures, they were well prepared to deal with the restaurant's equally diverse patrons, tourists from around the world and international traders and executives with offices in the WTC.

The Port Authority of New York and New Jersey, which owned the WTC, rented space primarily to tenants engaged in international commerce. Importers, exporters, freight handlers, steamship lines, oil traders, and insurance organizations were among the long-term renters. Many were multinational businesses, the majority with home offices in the United States, but a sizable number represented financial or commercial operations from Latin America, Asia, Africa, and

Europe. American-based firms such as Verizon Communications, Morgan Stanley, and the Oppenheimer Funds occupied several floors. But Fuji Bank of Japan, Thai Farmers Bank, Zim-American Israeli Shipping Company, and the Bank of Taiwan also had offices there. To promote transnational exchanges, the World Trade Institute, on the 55th floor of the North Tower, sponsored training courses in world trade, seminars for international businesspeople, and even language classes. Many of these firms chose to rent space in the WTC not because their businesses benefited directly from physical proximity to other international traders, but because an address at the WTC offered visibility to firms seeking a high profile in the world of commerce. The WTC offered firms the prestige of working in New York's most imposing landmark, a symbol of American wealth and power.

On September 11, 2001, two commercial jetliners hijacked by terrorists crashed into both towers of the World Trade Center and within an hour both towers had collapsed. Telmo Alvear, who usually worked the night shift, had been covering for a friend that morning. At age twenty-five he perished, along with nearly eighty members of the Hotel and Restaurant Workers Union who, like Alvear, were serving a special breakfast meeting. Nearly 3,000 people—citizens of the United States and eighty other nations—died that day. Uncounted were an unknown number of homeless New Yorkers who had sought what they believed to be a safe haven in the cavernous underground spaces of the WTC.

The WTC symbolized, if any building could, the confidence of American leadership in an era when national borders seemed to melt away. It also symbolized the transnationalism that many believed laid the foundation for a new world order based on the democratic liberalism that Americans treasured. Its vulnerability to surprise attack suggested the fragile nature of the swiftly changing society. ■

New York City

KEY TOPICS

- American foreign policy after the cold war

- The impact of the New Economy and the boom of the 1990s

- Revelations of the 2000 Census

- The Clinton presidency and resurgent conservatism

- Globalization

- International terrorism

A NEW WORLD ORDER

Between 1989 and 1991, Americans watched with amazement as the Soviet empire disintegrated, and the cold war came to an end. But contrary to expectations, this dramatic event did not bring world peace. The end of the cold war let loose a multitude of furies in the form of renewed nationalism, ethnic and religious conflict, and widening divisions between the world's rich and poor. Just as dramatically, as the old geopolitical order disappeared, ideological rivalry shifted to the Middle East and other areas in the world where Islamic militants had forcefully turned against the West.

The Collapse of Communism

The reforms initiated by Mikhail Gorbachev in the mid-1980s, known as *perestroika*, and, more immediately, the failed Soviet war in Afghanistan led to the dissolution of the Soviet Union and to the end of Communist rule throughout Eastern Europe. Beginning in June 1989, when Poland held its first free elections since the close of

Constructed by the Port Authority of New York and New Jersey in the early 1970s, the World Trade Center provided office space to businesses from around the world. The 110-story twin towers dominated the skyline of Lower Manhattan.

SOURCE: © Joseph Sohm; Visions of America/CORBIS (JS1262341).

World War II in 1945, prodemocracy demonstrations forced out long-time Communist leaders in Hungary, Czechoslovakia, Bulgaria, and Romania. Most dramatic of all were the events in East Germany. The Berlin Wall, which for thirty years had loomed as the ultimate symbol of cold war division, came down on November 9, 1989. Hundreds of thousands of East Germans immediately rushed into West Berlin. Popular protest intensified, paving the way for German reunification the following year.

Political changes in the Soviet Union came more slowly, accompanied by such drastically reduced living standards that successful transition to a liberal market economy and democratic political system was uncertain. In March 1989 the Soviet Union held its first open elections since 1917, and a new Congress of People's Deputies replaced the old Communist Party–dominated Supreme Soviet. In the next elections the following year, hundreds of party officials went down in defeat in key Russian cities. In August 1991 party hard-liners made a final attempt to hold on to the old order and staged a coup, placing President Gorbachev under house arrest. Although the coup quickly failed, most of the fifteen republics had meanwhile announced their withdrawal from the Soviet Union. Gorbachev found he could no longer control the government. On Christmas Day 1991 the weary and bitter president of the USSR resigned and recognized the new Commonwealth of Independent States.

The Soviet Union had dissolved, marking the end of the great superpower rivalry that had shaped American foreign policy and domestic politics for nearly a half-century. President Bush described the end of the cold war as an event of "biblical proportions." Many scholars have agreed that the changes rivaled the collapse of European empires during World War I and the rise of the cold war after World War II.

War in the Middle East

On August 2, 1990, 120,000 Iraqi troops backed by 850 tanks swept into neighboring Kuwait and quickly seized control of that tiny monarchy with its rich oil fields. The motives of Saddam Hussein, Iraq's military dictator, were mixed. Like most Iraqis, Hussein believed that oil-rich Kuwait was actually an ancient province of Iraq that had been illegally carved away by British imperial agents in the 1920s as part of the dismemberment of the Ottoman Empire. Control of Kuwait would give Saddam Hussein

control of its huge oil reserves, as well as Persian Gulf ports for his landlocked country. Just emerging from an exhausting and inconclusive eight-year war with Iran, Iraqis also bitterly resented Kuwait's production of oil beyond OPEC quotas, which had helped send the world price of oil plummeting from the highs of the 1970s and early 1980s.

The United States responded swiftly to news of the invasion. Its first concern was that Saddam Hussein also might attack Saudi Arabia, which the United States had defined as vital to its interests as far back as 1943. On August 15, President George H. W. Bush ordered U.S. forces to Saudi Arabia and the Persian Gulf, calling the action Operation Desert Shield. By the middle of October, some 230,000 American troops had been sent to the Persian Gulf.

In early November, President Bush announced a change in policy to what he called "an offensive military option," and the U.S. troop deployment quickly doubled and reached 580,000 by January 1991. Administration officials now demonized Saddam Hussein as another Adolf Hitler. The UN sanctions failed to budge Hussein from Kuwait, and the drift to war now looked inevitable. In January 1991, Congress narrowly passed a joint resolution authorizing the president to use military force.

After a last-minute UN peace mission failed to break the deadlock, President Bush announced, on January 16, 1991, the start of Operation Desert Storm. U.S-led air strikes began forty-two days of massive bombing of Iraqi positions in Kuwait, as well as Baghdad and other Iraqi cities. The ground war, which began on February 24, took only 100 hours to force Saddam Hussein's troops out of Kuwait. Hussein's vaunted military machine—the fourth largest army in the world—turned out to be surprisingly weak. U.S. forces lost only 184 dead, compared to nearly 100,000 Iraqi deaths, mostly from the bombing.

Almost every community in the United States sent men and women to the Gulf, and the vast majority supported Operation Desert Storm. Unlike the media coverage of the Vietnam War, television new reports showed virtually no blood or death. The Pentagon required "military escorts" to accompany all reporters and carefully regulated the release of silent film footage documenting precision bombing runs. Air strikes looked more like video games than bombing attacks, and military officials insisted that the bombing had been limited to Iraqi military targets. But subsequent investigations revealed massive numbers of targeting errors and the devastation of Iraq's infrastructure, from its communications network to its water system.

Victory in the Gulf War rekindled national pride in many people of the United States. But for the 18 million people of Iraq, it produced the worst possible outcome. The ecological damage in the Gulf region was extensive and long-lasting. Oil fires burned out of control. Human rights groups reported an appalling toll among civilians.

The limits of military power to solve complex political and economic disputes became clear in the aftermath of victory. The Persian Gulf war failed to dislodge Saddam Hussein, who remained in power despite CIA attempts to overthrow him and repeated bombings of Iraqi military positions. Trade sanctions did little to weaken his rule, although the economic boycott, which brought increasing hardship to the civilian population, eventually divided the Western powers, leaving the United States and Great Britain isolated in their sanctions against Iraq.

Moreover, regional tensions worsened in the aftermath of the war. In order to gain support from Egypt, Syria, Jordan, and Saudi Arabia to conduct military operations against Iraq, U.S. diplomats had promised to forge a just peace between the Palestinians and Israelis. President Clinton undertook secret negotiations culminating in a Declaration of Principles in Oslo, Norway, in 1993, which for the first time promised security for the Israelis and self-rule for the Palestinians. For their role in this process, Israeli prime minister Itzakh Rabin and Palestinian leader Yassar Arafat were jointly awarded a Nobel Peace Prize. But the assassination of Rabin by an Israeli religious fundamentalist, the continuing buildup of Israeli "settlements" in the occupied West Bank of the Jordan River, and the resulting violence on both sides deprived Clinton of a major diplomatic triumph.

The repercussions of the Gulf War were long-lasting. The leading U.S. ally in the region, the oil-rich kingdom of Saudi Arabia, had served as the launching-pad for the invasion of Iraq, and following the war the Saudis had allowed the continuing presence of U.S. troops and weapons. This occupation of Saudi territory, which included Islamic holy sites, intensified the hatred of Americans among many Muslims and prompted appeals for revenge.

Among those actively opposed to the U.S. role in the region was Saudi millionaire Osama bin Laden, just a few years earlier a close ally of the United States during the Russian invasion of Afghanistan. He now turned squarely against his former arms suppliers and CIA contacts. Using his own funds and a tribal network, bin Laden built his shadowy Al-Qaeda organization, training small groups in terror tactics to be used against Western interests, particularly to force American troops out of the Middle East.

Peacekeeping in the Balkans

The immediate victory in the Persian Gulf and a six-month surge of popularity did little to help President Bush when faced with a formidable candidate, William Jefferson Clinton. Unlike Bush, the last of the World War II veterans to enter the White House, Arkansas governor Clinton belonged to the Vietnam War generation and had opposed U.S. military intervention in Southeast Asia. The electorate awarded him 43 percent of the votes, compared to Bush's 38 percent, and gave the moderate Democrat a solidly Democratic House and Senate.

Despite this strong mandate, Clinton did not enjoy an easy transition. Heightened ethnic nationalism and religious fundamentalism continued to fill the vacuum left by the collapse of communism. Across the globe, from Africa to the Middle East, the Indian subcontinent, and beyond, civil wars created massive civilian casualties and new waves of refugees.

With the collapse of communism, Yugoslavia had quickly fallen to pieces when four of its six states declared independence. Ethnic and religious rivalry among Serbs, Croats, and Muslims living in Bosnia erupted into a violent civil war. Bush and his foreign policy advisers, seeing no threat to American interests, opposed U.S. military intervention. But as reports of "ethnic cleansing"—forced removal and murder of Croats and Muslims by Bosnian Serbs—increased, and as the numbers of refugees grew, Clinton, with congressional support, prepared to act. By late summer 1995, U.S. and NATO fighter pilots were bombing Serbian strong-holds in Bosnia. After negotiating with Yugoslavian president Slobodan Milosevic, on November 27 Clinton announced the Dayton Accords, an agreement drawn up in Dayton, Ohio, and signed in Paris that called for a federated, multiethnic state of Bosnia. An International Protection Force, one-third of whom were U.S. troops, was then installed as peacekeepers.

The worst foreign crisis of Clinton's presidency erupted in Kosovo, a Serbian province about 160 miles east of Italy, across the Adriatic Sea. Milosevic, a Serb nationalist, had terminated the autonomy of the province shortly after he took office in 1989, and in response the ethnic Albanians living there organized their own government and declared their independence the following year. While preoccupied by the civil war in Bosnia, Milosevic paid comparatively little attention to Kosovo. However, in 1997, the virtual collapse of the government of neighboring Albania changed the situation dramatically. Armed Albanians poured into Kosovo and joined the rebel forces. Clashes between Serbs and Albanians intensified, and the fighting soon spread to neighboring Macedonia and to Albania itself.

President Clinton once again attempted to negotiate, but he failed to resolve the problems through diplomacy. After NATO authorized air strikes, he addressed Americans on March 24, 1999, stating that U.S. armed forces had that day joined their allies to attack Serbian forces in Kosovo. On June 10, after a little more than two months of intensive bombing, he reported that the Serbian army was withdrawing from Kosovo and "for the first time in seventy-nine days, the skies over Yugoslavia are silent."

His country in ruins, and voted out of office, Slobodan Milosevic became the first head of state to be brought to trial for war crimes and crimes against humanity by the International War Crimes Tribunal in 2001. Meanwhile, in the Balkans, nationalist and ethnic conflicts continued to flare up, and U.S. peacekeepers remained.

CHANGING AMERICAN COMMUNITIES

The dark side of the post–cold war era seemed to be offset during the 1990s by the unprecedented surge of the U.S. economy and the inclusion of millions of new immigrants, who easily found places for themselves within the rapidly expanding service sector. The patterns of growth indicated a dynamic shift toward a postindustrial economy based upon high technology, wherein today's worker with a high degree of skill and entrepreneurial initiative might be tomorrow's millionaire. After a recession, which had plagued Bush's presidency, bottomed out in 1994, Americans settled in to enjoy record profits, low unemployment rates, and unsurpassed prosperity.

The Boom Years

The economy rather than foreign affairs had fueled the 1992 presidential election campaign. Republi-

cans took credit for forcing the fall of communism and reviving America's military strength. But they had also promised to cut government spending and balance the budget. In 1985, the Republican Congress had enacted, amid great fanfare, the Balanced Budget and Emergency Deficit Reduction Act, more popularly known as Gramm-Rudman after its principal authors, senators Phil Gramm and Warren Rudman. The act mandated automatic spending cuts if the government failed to meet fixed deficit reduction goals leading to a balanced budget by 1991. But just as Bush was about to take office in 1989, many of the nation's savings and loan institutions, which had been deregulated by Reagan, collapsed. Then, on Friday, October 13, 1989, the stock market took its worst nosedive since 1987, signaling the beginning of a major recession. With the national debt reaching an astronomical $4 trillion, the paradoxes of the Reagan-Bush years had become readily apparent.

In the Democrats' campaign headquarters a sign humorously reminded the staff: "It's the economy, stupid." Candidate Bill Clinton promised economic leadership, including deficit reduction and a tax cut for the middle class. He also effectively adopted many of the conservative themes that proved so advantageous to Republicans over the past twelve years. He called for "responsibility" on the part of recipients of social programs, spoke of the importance of stable families, promised to be tough on crime and to reduce the bureaucracy, and stressed the need for encouraging private investment to create new jobs. Economic issues also fueled the independent campaign of Texas billionaire H. Ross Perot, who with his folksy East Texas twang argued that a successful businessman such as himself was better qualified to solve the nation's economic woes than Washington insiders.

The Clinton administration succeeded in breaking the political gridlock caused by the traditional Democratic resistance to the "economic discipline" urged by Republicans. He pursued a strategy his advisors called "triangulation," positioning himself above and between the interests of warring Democrats and Republicans. For example, despite his attacks on the Republicans as radicals, Clinton opposed his own party's efforts to block a Republican plan to dismantle the federal welfare system in place since the New Deal. The new legislation—the Welfare Reform Act—abolished the sixty-year-old Aid to Families with Dependent Children program (AFDC). Poor mothers with dependent children would now have access to aid for only a limited period and only if they were preparing for or seeking work. When Congress passed the act in August of 1996, Clinton held a public signing ceremony and declared "an end to welfare as we know it."

President Clinton pushed two major trade agreements through Congress that built on efforts by the Reagan and Bush administrations to expand markets and encourage "free trade." Approved in November 1993, the North American Free Trade Agreement (NAFTA) eased the international flow of goods, services, and investments among the United States, Mexico, and Canada by eliminating tariffs and other trade barriers. Supplemental agreements called for cooperation on environmental and labor concerns. The stated goal of NAFTA was to improve productivity and living standards through a freer flow of commerce in North America. It created the largest free-trade zone in the world, comprising 360 million people and an annual gross national product of $6 trillion.

In 1994 Congress also approved the General Agreement on Tariffs and Trade (GATT), which slashed tariffs on thousands of goods throughout the world and phased out import quotas imposed by the United States and other industrialized nations. It also established the World Trade Organization (WTO) to mediate commercial disputes among 117 nations.

Critics and supporters of NAFTA and GATT argued over whether the agreements would encourage global competition, thereby boosting American export industries and creating new high-wage jobs for American workers, or simply erode the American industrial base and accelerate environmental degradation. Cities on the U.S.–Mexican border, such as Tijuana and San Diego were clear beneficiaries, but the downside was considerable. New *maquiladora* (factories and assembly plants) lacked pollution controls and spewed tons of toxic wastes into the air and groundwater. Despite the boost from NAFTA, the Mexican peso collapsed, and only a $20 billion bailout of the Mexican economy directed by executive order from the White House on January 31, 1995, prevented a serious depression there.

Perhaps the greatest stimulus to Clinton's economic policy was the soaring stock market of the 1990s, with "tech stocks" leading the way. The record highs of the Bush years, when the Dow Jones index of thirty industrials approached 4,000, paled by comparison to the leap in 1999 when the Dow hit 10,000 in March and then peaked above 11,000 in May. The market remained volatile during the decade, but profits were extraordinarily high. Annual returns on investments, generally under 6 percent during the 1970s, had risen to more than 18 percent.

The down side of the economic boom was nearly invisible. Productivity had risen sharply since the 1970s while labor costs had actually declined, hoisting profits to new levels. But critics observed that while a corporate official had earned around twenty or thirty times the pay of a blue-collar worker at the same company a few decades earlier, corporate executive income was more than two hundred times greater than that of a blue-collar employee. Moreover, "downsizing" became a common strategy for increasing profits levels or defeating negative trends. In the blue-collar sector, industrial jobs continued to disappear as factories closed or companies moved production of textiles, auto parts, and even electronics across borders or overseas. By the second half of 1999, the "dot-com" Internet-related stocks began to tumble, and economic analysts began to wonder if the business cycle had indeed been rendered obsolete.

Silicon Valley

Much of the growth of the 1990s was attributed to the consolidation of the "new economy," a phrased coined by economists in the 1970s to characterize the increasing importance of the service sector, corporate restructuring, and globalization. During the peak years of the new economy, a thirty-by-ten-mile strip of Santa Clara County, California, emerged as both the real and symbolic capital of the most important sector of the new economy—microelectronics. As late as 1960 this region was the major processor of fruits and vegetables in the world; forty years later one-third of the valley's workforce were employed by high-tech companies.

Dubbed "Silicon Valley" in 1971 after the semiconductor chip, which is made of silicon, and which became the basic building block of modern microelectronics, the region flourished thanks to its unique combination of research facilities, investment capital, attractive environment, and a large pool of highly educated people. At first, military contracts predominated, but the consumer electronics revolution of the 1970s fueled an explosive new wave of growth. Silicon Valley firms gave birth to pocket calculators, video games, home computers, cordless telephones, digital watches, and almost every other new development in electronics. It became home to more than 1,700 high-tech firms that specialized in gathering, processing, or distributing information or in manufacturing information technology. Companies like Atari, Apple, and Intel achieved enormous success and became household names. Silicon Valley boasted the greatest concentration of new wealth in the United States.

By the end of the century, Silicon Valley had become a continuous sprawl of two dozen cities between San Francisco and San Jose and the home and work place of a diverse population. The managers and engineers, nearly all of whom were white males, had settled in affluent communities such as Palo Alto, Mountain View, and Sunnyvale. Manual workers on assembly lines and in low-paying service jobs clustered in San Jose and Gilroy. Most of these were Latino, African American, Vietnamese, Cambodian, and Filipino men and women who constituted a cheap, nonunionized labor pool with an extremely high turnover rate.

The prime example of the new economy, Silicon Valley was also part of a global enterprise. Its firms were closely linked to the microelectronic industry of the greater Pacific Rim. The end of the cold war and the accompanying decline in military spending in the United States forced high-tech firms in California into greater competition on the world market and especially against similar companies in Japan, Korea, China, and Malaysia. But many American companies protected themselves against such competition by owning and managing a large share of the plants in these countries.

By the end of the century, the rate of growth showed signs of slowing, as did the infusion of new venture capital into high-tech industries. Young entrepreneurs throughout the Pacific Rim found it more difficult to start successful new companies and to make the leap from a small, start-up company to a large corporation. By this time, scarcity in housing, traffic jams, and an inflated cost of living were already leading many companies and individuals to move out of Silicon Valley.

An Electronic Culture

The technological developments produced in Silicon Valley helped reconfigure cultural life in the United States and the world. Revolutions in computers and telecommunications merged telephones, televisions, computers, cable, and satellites into a global system of information exchange. The new technologies changed the way people worked and played, made the nation's cultural life more homogeneous and played a greater role than ever in shaping politics.

The twin arrivals of cable and the videocassette recorder (VCR) expanded and redefined the power of television. By the end of the 1980s pay cable services and VCRs had penetrated roughly two-thirds of American homes. The VCR revolutionized the way people used their television sets, allowing them to organize program watching around their own schedules. Hollywood studios began releasing movies on videotape, and the rental and sale of movies for home viewing quickly outstripped ticket sales at theaters as the main profit source for filmmakers.

In 1981, a new cable channel called MTV (for Music Television) began airing videos of popular music stars performing their work. The intent was to boost sales of the stars' audio recordings, but the music video soon became a new art form in itself. Artists who best exploited music video, such as Madonna and Michael Jackson, achieved international superstar status. MTV also helped transform smaller, cult musical forms, such as rap and heavy metal, into giant mass-market phenomena. MTV pioneered an imaginative visual style, featuring rapid cutting, animation, and the sophisticated fusion of sound and image.

More than ever, television drove the key strategies and tactics defining American political life. Politicians and their advisers focused intently on a candidate's television image. Issues, positions, and debate all paled alongside the key question: How did it look on television? Fewer citizens voted or took an active role in campaigns, and most relied on television coverage to make their choices. Thus creating an effective television "character" emerged as perhaps the most crucial form of political discourse.

Perhaps no aspect of the electronics culture was more revolutionary than the creation of cyberspace, the conceptual region occupied by people linked through computers and communications networks. It began with ARPANET, the first computer network, which was created by the Department of Defense in the early 1970s. Computer enthusiasts known as "hackers" created unexpected grass-roots spinoffs from ARPANET, including electronic mail, computer conferencing, and computer bulletin board systems. In the mid-1980s the boom in cheap personal computers capable of linking to the worldwide telecommunications network began a population explosion in cyberspace. By then, tens of thousands of researchers and scholars at universities and in private industry were linked to the Internet—the U.S. government-sponsored successor to ARPANET—through their institutions' computer centers. The establishment of the World Wide Web and easy-to-use browser software such as Netscape, introduced in 1994, made the "information highway" accessible to millions of Americans with few computer skills and created a popular communications medium with global dimensions.

By the beginning of the new century, the Census Bureau estimated that more than half of all households had at least one computer and more than 40 percent were connected to the Internet. Nearly 85 percent of classrooms in public schools were online. At work, Americans spent an average of 21 hours per week online. At home, they spent an average of 9.5 hours per week online, gaining access to the Web from independent service providers such as America Online and Earthlink. For a flat monthly fee users could play games, send electronic mail, discuss issues in public forums, and purchase a huge array of goods and services, ranging from books and airline tickets to automobiles and psychotherapy sessions.

These new information technologies gave birth to a media community that transcended national boundaries. During the 1980s, exports from Hollywood to the rest of the world doubled in value. The number of hours of television watched throughout the world nearly tripled. MTV was broadcast to an estimated 250 million households throughout the world. By the mid-1990s there were more television sets in China than in the United States. The growth of cable was phenomenal; in the Netherlands, for example, 98 percent of households received programming by cable.

The New Immigrants and Their Communities

The 2000 census showed that the nation's population during the 1990s grew by 32.7 million, a number greater than that of any other decade in U.S. history. Even the 1950s, which witnessed the post–World War II baby boom, could not compete against a decade marked by a huge number of immigrants and a birthrate that surpassed the death rate. At the beginning of the new millennium, Americans numbered 281.4 million.

The 2000 census confirmed what many Americans had observed over the previous decade in their communities and workplaces. The face of the nation was perceptibly changing and changing on a scale that compared to the first decades of the twentieth century, when immigration from Europe peaked. At the turn of the twenty-first century, more than a third of the nation's population growth came from the influx of new immigrants. Although three-quarters of the newcomers joined many other Americans in flocking to the Sunbelt states, headed by California, Texas, and Florida, they not only helped to reverse population loss in such major urban centers as New York and Chicago and slow the decline in Rustbelt cities like Cleveland, Detroit, and Milwaukee, but also for the first time in any census, they played a major role in the population increase in all fifty states.

The Immigration Act of 1965, passed almost unnoticed in the context of the egalitarian political climate created by the civil rights movement, had revolutionary consequences, some of them unintended. The act abolished the discriminatory national origins quotas that had been in place since the 1920s. It also limited immigration from the Western Hemisphere for the first time, while giving preferences to people from the nations of the Eastern Hemisphere who had specialized job skills and training. This provision created the conditions for Asian immigrants to become the fasting growing ethnic group in the United States. But in setting limits on Western Hemisphere immigration, the 1965 act tempted many thousands of people from Latin American to enter the United States illegally. By the mid-1980s, growing concern over "illegal aliens" had

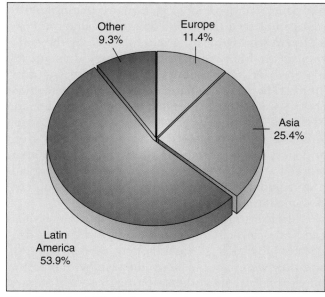

Continent of Birth for Immigrants, 1990–2000
By 2000, the number of foreign-born residents and their children—56 million according to the Census Bureau—had reached the highest level in U.S. history.

become a hotly debated political issue, particularly in the Southwest. The Immigration Reform and Control Act of 1986 marked a break with the past attempts to address this problem. Instead of mass deportation programs, the law offered an amnesty to all undocumented workers who had entered the country since 1982. Four years later, additional revisions of this act enlarged the quota of immigrants, once again giving priority to skilled and professional workers. Hispanics and Asians benefited from these changes in immigration law. Within the twenty fastest-growing cities, the number of Hispanics and Asians increased by approximately 70 percent.

Demographers predicted that Hispanics, who had grown from 22.4 million in 1990 to 35.3 million in 2000, according to census data, would replace African Americans as the largest minority group in the nation by the middle of the twenty-first century. By 1990 Hispanics had already formed over a third of the population of New Mexico, a quarter of the population of Texas, and over 10 percent of the populations of California, Arizona, and Colorado. Nearly a million Mexican Americans lived in Los Angeles alone.

The 2000 census showed that Mexicans were the largest Hispanic group in the United States, at 20.6 million and representing nearly 60 percent of the total Hispanic population. The boom of the U.S. economy in the 1990s, with service, agricultural, and even factory jobs readily available, had provided a significant "pull" for these newcomers. But other factors encouraged many immigrants to make an often difficult and dangerous sojourn. First, a drop in worldwide oil prices followed by the deflation of the Mexican national currency dramatically lowered living standards in Mexico in the mid-1990s. The North American Free Trade Agreement (NAFTA) and the greater integration of the U.S. and Mexican economies brought new jobs but often with increasingly expensive living conditions. Tens and perhaps hundreds of thousands of Mexicans worked in the United States temporarily while planning a permanent move north, with or without legal documentation.

After settling across the border, most new Mexican Americans struggled in low-wage and often dangerous jobs such as meatpacking or construction, and they were more likely to die from workplace injuries than other workers. Through education and success in business, a significant number achieved middle-class status and wealth. But almost 20 percent of Mexican Americans lived below the poverty line. They tended to live in segregated neighborhoods and were less likely than non-Hispanic whites to have health insurance or to own their own homes.

Puerto Rican–born population jumped from 100,000 to roughly 1 million. However, during the 1990s, this trend had begun to reverse, their numbers falling by 12 percent. The smaller but highly influential Cuban population declined even more, by 27 percent. Meanwhile, other Latin populations grew at an extraordinary rate of 50 percent. The Mexican-born population more than doubled, and Filipinos, who often speak Spanish as a first language, increased by 27 percent. Immigrants from the Dominican Republic, now second in population size only to Puerto Ricans, dominated sizable sections of Washington Heights and Brooklyn, while immigrants from various countries in Central and South America created new communities throughout the greater metropolitan region.

The cultural implications for all Americans, not just new New Yorkers, were far-reaching. Children born to the new immigrants of the 1980s and 1990s, despite increasing neighborhood segregation by race, played on the streets together, attended the same schools and often married outside their racial group. In the 2000 census, 6.8 million Americans nationwide listed themselves as multiracial. Identities blurred as popular entertainment created new mixes of traditions and styles. "World beat" music (heavily influenced by "Afro-Pop"), *Alternalationo* (alternative Latin music—a mixture of salsa and merenge), Tejano, Reggae, and other music in fusion mixtures became as common to Manhattan or Los Angeles as to Mexico City or Rio. By the 1990s, the West Indian carnival held annually in Brooklyn at the end of summer had become the most popular ethnic festival in Greater New York City.

Although smaller in number than Hispanics, Asians were the fasting-growing racial group in the United States. The number of Asian Americans soared from 7.3 million in 1990 to approximately 10.2 million in 2000. With a steady flow of professionals and workers skilled in technology into their communities, Chinese Americans maintained their status as the largest Asian ethnicity in the United States. However, other groups grew at faster rates, particularly Indo Americans (from the subcontinent of India), whose numbers doubled during the 1990s to 1.68 million to become the third-largest Asian group. Meanwhile Japanese Americans, once the largest and most influential members of the pan-Asian community, declined. Immigration from Japan had virtually ceased during the decade, while many with pooling family capital and labor to support small businesses. Newcomers selected communities with job opportunities or where family members and friends had settled previously. This "chain migration" is illustrated by the large numbers of Hmongs, a tribal group from Laos, living in Minneapolis and St. Paul. The stream of Hmongs began with church-sponsored refugee programs, then gained momentum as more and more family members followed. As one of the nation's leading states in the resettlement of refugees, Minnesota saw its total Asian population triple, increasing during the 1980s from 26,000 to 78,000, and then nearly doubling in the next decade.

A NEW AGE OF ANXIETY

Despite the prosperity of the 1990s, many Americans experienced an uneasiness that resembled the anxiety of mid-twentieth century, when the world seemed on the brink of nuclear destruction. The threat of communism had expired along with the cold war, but doubts and fears about the fate of their own society had multiplied. So many changes had occurred in just the last three decades of the century that a sense of permanence had disappeared. The new economy had transformed the way Americans worked and played. The new wave of immigration had dramatically altered the demographic landscape. Even the way the nation's leaders conducted themselves appeared not only new but potentially hazardous to the moral order. In addition, many Americans had begun to fear for their personal safety, even within their own communities.

Hmong-origin immigrants were among the fastest-growing Asian groups in the United States in the 1990s. In Minnesota, they were the leading Asian group coming to the state. The Hmong brought traditional clothing as well as entertainments food, and sports and established more than 400 businesses in the Minneapolis-St. Paul region.

SOURCE: Photograph by *The Merced Sun-Star*. AP/Wide World Photos (6090567).

young Japanese Americans married someone of a different race.

Like earlier immigrant groups, new Americans from Korea, Vietnam, and the Philippines tended to cluster in their own communities and maintain a durable group identity. As a whole, Asian Americans made mobility through education a priority, along

The Racial Divide

In the spring of 1992 an upheaval in Los Angeles offered the starkest evidence that racial tensions had not eased. The spark that ignited the worst riot of the century was outrage over police brutality. A year earlier, Rodney King, a black motorist, had been pulled from his vehicle and severely beaten by four white police officers. An amateur videotape of the incident was widely aired on television newshows. When, despite this graphic evidence, a jury acquitted the officers of all but one of eleven counts of assault, several minority communities erupted in anger. Rioters swept through South Central Los Angeles and nearby Koreatown, looting and burning businesses. Fifty-one people were killed, more than $850 million in damage was reported, and about 500 buildings were destroyed before L.A. police and National Guard troops restored order.

More than a quarter-century after the uprising in Watts, the situation in Los Angeles seemed more desperate than ever to most African Americans. The poverty rate in South Los Angeles was 30.3 percent, more than twice the national average. The unemployment rate for adult black males hovered around 40 percent, and a quarter of the population was on welfare. Drug dealing and gang warfare had escalated, reflecting the sense of despair among young people.

The events in Los Angeles exposed the deep animosity among various groups—so much so that the observers referred to the event as a "multicultural riot." Almost 2,000 Korean businesses were destroyed, and Koreans angrily accused the police of making no effort to defend their stores. The division was sharpest, though, between whites and the minority populations. "We are all quite isolated in our own communities," a resident of Westwood, a mostly white middle-class neighborhood, explained. "We don't know and don't care about the problems in the inner cities. Driving to work every day most of us don't even know where South Central is—except many of us saw the fires from that direction when we were stuck in traffic."

The situation in Los Angeles was not unique. The 2000 census showed that segregation was on the rise, and not only in cities but in their surrounding suburbs. For example, in the Atlanta region, which claimed the largest share of black suburbanites in the nation (26 percent), the percent living separately from whites had increased from 52 percent in 1990 to nearly 60 percent by 2000. Similarly, in the nation's schools, the gains from the civil rights era were diminishing and, in some communities, disappearing altogether. A report released in 2001 showed that, despite the increasing racial and ethnic diversity of nation's youth, segregation was becoming more pronounced in grades K–12.

The publicity generated by the arrest of Rodney King fed several major controversies concerning the U.S. criminal justice system. Racial disparities were pronounced, with ethnic and racial minorities accounting for approximately two-thirds of state prison inmates. Based on these figures, the Bureau of Justice estimated that 28 percent of African American men would enter a state or federal prison during their lifetimes.

Various civil liberties groups reviewed these statistics and concluded that African Americans were not necessarily more prone to criminal activity but were far more likely to be stopped, searched, arrested, convicted, and given harsher penalties than white Americans. Critics singled out the practice of "racial profiling" whereby police disportionately stopped African Americans and Latinos as the most likely offenders. By the end of the decade, in a review of various data nationwide, the National Institute of Drug Abuse estimated that although 12 percent of illegal drug users were black, they now made up 50 percent of all drug possession arrestees. By this time, "driving while black" had become a news item in all the major media, leading to the introduction of a bill into the U.S. Senate in 1999 to collect statistics on traffic stops.

The Forces of Fear

During the 1990s and first years of the new century, anxiety about terrorism and random violence escalated. Within their own borders, Americans were actually far safer from terrorist attacks than the citizens of many other countries. Nevertheless, two events—the attack on the World Trade Center 1993 and the destruction of the federal building in Oklahoma City in 1995—alerted Americans to danger at home.

On February 26, 1993, a small group associated with Osama bin Laden bombed the World Trade Center in New York City. The terrorists used a rented van to deliver explosives that demolished an underground parking lot, killed six people, and injured more than a thousand others. Taken in retaliation for U.S. policies in the Middle East, the attack was the most destructive act of terrorism committed within the United States to that time. Despite increased surveillance of terrorist groups, bin Laden's organization struck another lethal blow. On August 7, 1998, car bombings of U.S. embassies in Nairobi, Kenya, and Dar es Salaam, Tanzania, injured more than 5,500 people and killed 225.

The bombing of the Alfred P. Murrah Federal Building in Oklahoma City raised an entirely different specter: terrorism by self-described patriotic

Americans. The perpetrators represented the extremist wing of the New Right, the superpatriot movement, which included groups of people who set up "survivalist" encampments in rural areas and organized themselves into armed militias. Inspired by author William Pierce's *Turner Diaries* (1978), which predicted a revolt of "Aryans" against people of color and the federal government, the patriots found their martyrs in the Branch Davidians and their revenge in Oklahoma.

Two years earlier, on February 28, 1993, agents of the FBI and the Federal Bureau of Alcohol, Tobacco, and Firearms (ATF) had conducted a "search and arrest" operation against the Branch Davidians that turned deadly. Their object was David Koresh, the leader of the ob-

Rescue workers carried an injured man from the ruble of the U.S. Embassy in Nairobi, Kenya. A terrorist bomb killed more than 100 people and injured more than 1,600 on August 8, 1998.

SOURCE: © AFP/CORBIS (FT0047338).

scure religious sect who was suspected of stockpiling illegal firearms and ammunition. After a round of shots, which took the lives of four ATF agents and six Branch Davidians, Koresh's heavily armed followers barricaded themselves in their compound in Waco, Texas. Fifty-one days later, on April 19, government agents brought their siege to a fiery end. Nine Davidians managed to escape the flames engulfing their buildings, while seventy-six others, including twenty-one children, perished.

On April 19, 1995, Timothy McVeigh and his accomplices took revenge for the tragedy in Waco. Shortly after 9:00 A.M., a bomb went off in the federal office building in Oklahoma City, killing 168 people, including 19 children, and injuring more than 500 others. They had chosen April 19, the anniversary of the federal raid at Waco, as their "Date of Doom." Arrested within hours of the bombing on a misdemeanor traffic violation, McVeigh was charged in connection with the crime just three days later. After a trial in federal court and demonstrations both for and against the death penalty, he was executed in June 2001.

Terrorism continued, with many of the attacks politically or ideologically motivated. For example, medical clinics that provided abortion services to

women became a prime target. Often the motivation for acts of domestic terror eluded even experts on the subject. Workers suspended from their jobs, fathers separated from their children, as well as individuals with grudges against the government turned to violence. One of the most highly publicized cases occurred in Littleton, Colorado, a mostly white, middle-class suburb of Denver. On April 20, 1999, two students at Columbine High School, armed with semiautomatic handguns, shotguns, and explosives, opened fire, killing one teacher and twelve of their classmates before killing themselves.

The Culture Wars

In the 1980s and 1990s, moral and social issues, many observers noted, were replacing long-standing political markers such as religion, ethnicity, and socioeconomic class. Whereas the "New Democrats" of Clinton's administration and conservative Republicans differed little on their perception of the appropriate size and power of the federal government, they were at loggerheads over what constituted American values. Thus, what one scholar described as "the struggle to define America" became hotly contested in the 1990s, with politics increasingly centered in discussions about reproductive rights and reproductive technology, homosexuality and gay rights, the curriculum in public schools, codes of speech and standards in the arts, gun control, and scientific developments such as cloning, genetic alteration, and fetal tissue research, and even the validity of Darwin's theory of evolution.

The increasing racial and ethnic diversity of American society, as well as the expansion of rights for groups such as women and gays, had become the impetus for a broad and controversial movement known as "multiculturalism." Unlike earlier conceptions of America as a "melting pot," new metaphors such as "salad bowl" or "mosaic" became popular expressions that emphasized the unique attributes and achievements of formerly marginal groups and recent immigrants. This celebration of diversity played a big part in the campaign strategy of Bill Clinton, and he won a large share of votes by tailoring his appeals to specific groups. Like other Democrats, he received upward of 80 percent of black votes, but he won more votes from Latinos and Asian Americans than any other candidate in American history. On college campuses, multiculturalism marked the high point of the curricular reform that had been ongoing since the late 1960s and early 1970s, when specialized programs in women's studies and African American studies were launched (see Chapter 29).

For many conservatives, multiculturalism had replaced communism as the nation's most dangerous enemy, and they rallied to reinstate what they called universal truths and traditional moral values. University of Chicago professor Allan Bloom's best-selling *The Closing of the American Mind* (1987), for example, argued that the new lesson plans failed to prepare Americans for the responsibility of preserving their democratic legacy.

The culture wars were not restricted to the academic world. Americans divided sharply over many issues, including immigration policy. In 1994, a referendum on California's ballot, Proposition 187, called for making all undocumented aliens ineligible for any welfare services, schooling, and nonemergency medical care, and it required teachers and clinic doctors to report illegal immigrants to the police. Proposition 187 passed by a three to two margin, but it was immediately challenged in the streets and in the courts. In 1998, after several years of legal wrangling, a Los Angeles federal district court judge ruled that Proposition 187 unconstitutionally usurped federal authority over immigration policy. In June 2001, the U.S. Supreme Court ruled that im-

migrants are entitled to same protection by the Constitution as that afforded to citizens.

But the national debate over immigration policy, in which economic issues and racial fears were deeply entangled, continued unabated in California and elsewhere. As one Stanford law professor who had worked to overturn Proposition 187 put it: "Some people genuinely worry about the problem of too many immigrants in a stagnant economy. But for most, economics is a diversion. Underneath it is race."

A similar backlash gathered steam against gays. A major controversy erupted around a push for the legal recognition of marriage for same-sex couples. Although the first lawsuits dated to the early 1970s, in May 1993 the Supreme Court of Hawai'i ruled that the laws barring same-sex couples from getting a marriage license were discriminatory and, therefore, in violation of the state constitution. This highly controversial decision prompted conservative state legislators to propose an amendment to the state constitution barring same-sex marriages, which the Hawai'ian voters overwhelmingly approved in 1998. Meanwhile, several Republicans in the U.S. Congress, fearing that if any state recognized same-sex marriages all other states would be forced to recognize these marriages as legal, sponsored legislation to deny recognition to these unions. In 1996, President Clinton signed the Defense of Marriage Act, which specified that gay couples would be ineligible for spousal benefits provided by federal law. By the end of the century, more than thirty states had enacted similar legislation. Vermont, however, stood alone, becoming the first state to recognize civil unions, allowing same-sex couples to receive many, although not all, of the legal benefits of marriage.

At the end of the century, the antiabortion movement took a new turn by opposing government financing of an area of scientific research that had been growing in importance since the birth of the first test-tube baby in 1981—embryonic stem cell research. Because these microscopic clusters of cells have the potential to grow into any tissue in the body, embryonic stems cells hold promise, scientists believe, for refurbishing or replacing damaged tissues or organs and therefore might prove useful in treating or perhaps even curing diseases such as diabetes, Parkinson's, and Alzheimer's. Conservatives opposed this research because it involves the destruction of human embryos, usually derived from the excess products of *in vitro* fertilization processes and scheduled for disposal by fertility clinics. In 1995, in response to pressure from conservatives groups such as the National

Right to Life Committee, Congress enacted legislation banning the use of federal funds for research that involves the destruction of human embryos. However, in his last year in office, Clinton loosened the ban and thereby generated another round of controversy. Most conservative groups remained firm in their opposition, agreeing with the United States Conference of Catholic Bishops, which insisted "that the government must not treat any living human being as research material, as a mere means for benefit to others."

High Crimes and Misdemeanors

During the 1994 election campaign, the Republicans targeted the key item in Clinton's liberal agenda, reform of the nation's health-care system. President Clinton had appointed Hillary Rodham Clinton to head a task force charged with preparing a sweeping legislative overhaul of health care. The task force sought a political middle ground between conservative approaches, which stressed fine tuning the system by making private insurance available to all, and more liberal approaches, which would have the federal government guarantee health care as a right. Powerful forces such as the Chamber of Commerce, the National Association of Manufacturers, and most Republicans immediately attacked the proposal. The Health Insurance Association of America spent millions of dollars on negative advertisements. In August, as the 1994 election campaign moved into its final phase, the president conceded that his proposal had died in Congress.

Voter turnout was light in most areas, but the majority who voted turned firmly against Clinton. Republicans gained control of both the House and Senate for the first time in forty years—a disaster of historic proportions for Clinton and the Democratic Party. Congress was now dominated by a new breed of younger, ideologically more conservative Republicans led by the new House Speaker, Newt Gingrich of Georgia.

Gingrich, first elected to Congress in 1978, had quickly won a reputation as a formidable polemicist for the Republican Party's far right. With his scathing denunciations of big government and celebration of entrepreneurship, Gingrich challenged Clinton as the key figure setting the nation's political agenda. His priorities were expressed in a set of proposals labeled the "Contract with America." Invoking the "hundred days" of Franklin D. Roosevelt's New Deal in 1933 (see Chapter 24), Gingrich promised to bring all these proposals to a vote in the House within a hundred days. The House did indeed pass much of the "Contract," including a large tax cut, an increase in military spending, cutbacks in federal regulatory power in the environment and at the work place, a tough anticrime bill, and a sharp reduction in federal welfare programs.

Differences with the Senate, however, and the threat of presidential veto ultimately thwarted Gingrich's plans and created conditions that allowed President Clinton to make a political comeback. In December 1995 the Republican-controlled Congress forced a shutdown of the federal government rather than accede to President Clinton's demand for changes in their proposed budget. The result was a public relations disaster for the Republicans. Gingrich's reputation plummeted, and after little more than a year as Speaker he had become one of the most unpopular figures in American politics.

Meanwhile, Clinton undercut the Republicans by adapting many of their positions to his own. He endorsed the goal of a balanced federal budget and declared, in his January 1996 State of the Union message, that "the era of big government is over." With such deft maneuvers, the president set the theme for his 1996 reelection campaign, portraying himself as a reasonable conservative and the Republicans in Congress as conservative radicals.

While the Republican contender, Robert Dole of Kansas, majority leader of the Senate, waged an inept campaign for president, Clinton and his staff crafted a brilliant and well-funded one. Confounding the predictions of the political pundits who had pronounced his political death, the president won a resounding reelection victory in November 1996. He won 49 percent of the popular vote compared to Dole's 41 percent and carried thirty-three states.

During his second term as president, Clinton had to answer many questions about his moral conduct. Real estate deals involving both him and Hillary Rodham Clinton blew up into a major scandal known as Whitewater. More predictive of troubles ahead, a former Arkansas state employee, Paula Jones, charged Clinton with sexual assault during his gubernatorial term. Attorney General Janet Reno, under extreme pressure from conservatives, appointed an independent counsel, former judge Kenneth Starr, to investigate allegations. But in the summer of 1998, Starr delivered to the House Judiciary Committee a report focusing on an extramarital affair that the president conducted with a young White House intern, Monica Lewinsky. Starr's report outlined several potential impeachable offenses, including false testimony under oath, witness tampering, and obstruction of justice, all allegedly committed by the president to keep his relationship with Lewinsky secret.

After agreeing to testify before a grand jury empaneled by Starr—a first for an American president—Clinton made an extraordinary television address to the nation. He defended his legal position and attacked the Starr inquiry as politically motivated. The Congress and the American people at large fiercely debated the nature of the charges against the president: Were they truly impeachable—"high crimes and misdemeanors" as the Constitution put it—or merely part of a partisan political effort to overturn the election of 1996? For only the third time in history, in October 1998, the House of Representatives voted to open an inquiry into possible grounds for the impeachment.

Republicans hoping to reap a wholesale victory from the scandal in the fall elections were bitterly disappointed. Contrary to predictions and traditions in off-term elections, the president's party added seats, trimming the Republican majority in the 105th Congress. Higher than expected turnout from such core constituencies as union members and African Americans (especially in the South) also contributed to the unexpectedly strong Democratic showing. The election also brought a shakeup in the Republican leadership. Newt Gingrich, under pressure from Republican colleagues angry about a campaign strategy that had narrowly focused on Clinton's impeachment problem, announced his resignation as Speaker of the House and from his seat in Congress.

In the aftermath of the 1998 election, most politicians and analysts, and indeed most Americans, believed the impeachment inquiry to be at a dead end. But the House Judiciary Committee, after raucous televised debate, voted to bring four articles of impeachment—charging President Clinton with perjury, obstruction of justice, witness tampering, and abuse of power—to the full House. Neither the 1998 election results, nor polls showing a large majority of Americans opposed to removing the president, curbed the Republican determination to push impeachment through the House and then on to the Senate for trial. On February 12, 1999, the Senate trial concluded with the president's acquittal.

THE NEW MILLENNIUM

At the beginning of the twenty-first century, citizens, politicians, and business and religious leaders had to rethink their basic assumptions about the American way of life. American society had become more stratified along lines of race and income. New immigrant groups, especially from Asia and Latin America, had changed the face of the nation's communities, schools, and work places. New media technologies had made cultural life more homogenized and caused the manipulation of image to become more crucial than ever to both politics and entertainment. The New Economy, service oriented and high tech, had fundamentally altered the way many Americans did business and earned a livelihood, and it depended not only on American consumers heavily burdened with debt but also on an expanding global market.

The end of the cold war had reconfigured global politics, ending the bilateralism that had dominated international affairs since the end of World War II. The United States alone held fast to its superpower status, but this achievement did not necessarily make Americans more secure or safe. The old enemy, Soviet communism, was succeeded by more fanatic, less predictable foes. It was clear that international terrorism was emerging as a persistent threat, as witnessed by yet another terrorist attack, the October 12, 2000, bombing of the USS *Cole* in Aden, Yemen, which cost the lives of seventeen American sailors.

The Election of 2000

After a relatively dull campaign season, the 2000 election played out as high drama. Voters went to the polls as usual on election day, watched as late-night television newscasters projected a victory for the Democratic candidate, Clinton's vice president Al Gore, and then woke up the next morning to learn that perhaps the winner was not the vice president but his Republican opponent, Governor George W. Bush of Texas, son of former president George H. W. Bush. It was clear that Gore and his running mate, Connecticut Senator Joseph Lieberman, had won the popular vote, although by the closest margin since John F. Kennedy defeated Richard Nixon in 1961. In doubt was the number of votes in the Electoral College. At 2:15 A.M., the pollsters who had projected Gore as the winner changed their minds. The cliffhanger in Florida had finally ended with the state's decisive twenty-five electoral votes earmarked for the Republicans. By morning Gore had called Bush to concede. The *New York Times*, however, ran a guarded headline "Bush Appears to Defeat Gore." Only a few hundred votes in Florida gave Bush the edge, and in cases where the margin is so narrow Florida law mandates a machine recount in all sixty-seven counties. Gore soon retracted his concession, putting voters into suspense until the middle of December, when the vice president finally ended his campaign.

Such a spectacular ending to the 2000 campaign could not have been foreseen from the primaries. As the son of a former president, George W. Bush had run a low-key campaign, calling himself a "compassionate conservative" who cared about the underdog and the nation's educational system. He nevertheless did not swerve from the Republican agenda that President Reagan had shaped: tax cuts, strong military defense, and the overhaul of Social Security and Medicare. He also promised relief from environmental regulations, new judicial appointments that would eventually limit reproductive rights, and the restoration of morality to public life. Albert Gore, Jr., also the son of a prominent politician, carried the burden of association with Bill Clinton and waged an uphill battle. More notable was his running mate, Lieberman, the first Jewish candidate for vice president. Dick Cheney, who had served prominently in the senior Bush's administration, balanced the younger Bush's relative lack of experience in federal government. The emergence of consumer advocate Ralph Nader as Green Party candidate added spice to an often dull campaign.

The 2000 campaign played out as the first disputed presidential election since 1876, when Democrat Samuel J. Tilden, who won the popular vote, charged his Republican opponent, Rutherford B. Hayes, with fraudulent vote counting. A similar question of legitimacy hung over the 2000 election. After Florida completed its machine recount of votes, the Democrats requested a hand tally in selected counties where the ballots were in dispute. The Republicans responded by suing in the Miami district court to prohibit the manual recounting. Meanwhile Florida election officials, mainly Republicans, set November 14 as the date to certify the election results, thereby disallowing the returns on overseas ballots which might favor Al Gore. In turn, Democrats sued to extend the deadline. Eventually, appeals by both parties reached the Florida Supreme Court and finally the U.S. Supreme Court, which voted five to four along partisan lines to halt the counting. Time had run out, and on December 12 Gore conceded defeat. With less fanfare than usual, George W. Bush took the oath of office in January 2001.

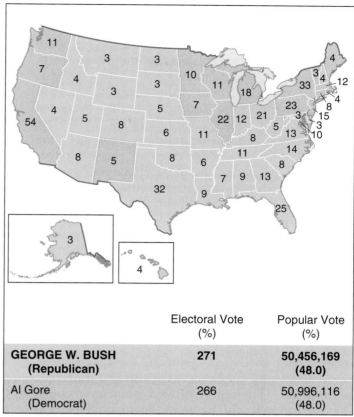

	Electoral Vote (%)	Popular Vote (%)
GEORGE W. BUSH (Republican)	271	**50,456,169** (48.0)
Al Gore (Democrat)	266	50,996,116 (48.0)

The Election of 2000   The 2000 presidential election was the closest one in U.S. history and the first one to be decided by a decision of the Supreme Court.

A Global Community?

Beginning in the 1970s, social scientists began to study and debate the degree to which to which people throughout the world were affected by events happening far from their homelands. The big questions concerning globalization centered on political economy. Now that communism has collapsed, they asked, would a steady expansion of free trade among nations create the basis for a global community?

There were many answers to this question. Some observers argued that the interpenetration of markets and cultural patterns—the enormous sales of Hollywood movies in China, for example—set the stage for other exchanges. Others argued that the global economy depended less on "interpenetration" than "domination" of the marketplace by the industrialized nations. Whereas physical occupation of territory defined the form of colonialism that prevailed before World War II, a new "colonialism" had come into existence since the 1960s that relied on a few multinational corporations controlling distant economies throughout the world. To back up this argument, they referred to a UN report that estimated that about 90 percent of the multinational corporations that did business worldwide were headquartered in the industrialized nations of North America, Europe, and Japan. Known collectively as the Triad, the consortium of these nations, home to only 15 percent of the world's population, produced nearly 75 percent of the world's goods by the late 1990s. Some traditional economists discounted the significance of these developments, insisting that trading activities date to the earliest civilizations and that well-organized transnational economies were the hallmark of the Industrial Age.

What made the current trend toward "globalization" distinctive was, therefore, not the rate of growth but the absolute volume and character of the exchange. Revenues from multinational corporations grew phenomenally at the end of the twentieth century. Because the member nations of the Triad were homes to the world's largest multinational corporations, they also reaped the largest share of the wealth. A UN annual human development report stated that "global inequalities in income and living standards have reached grotesque proportions." The report offered statistics showing that the gap in wealth between the upper 20 percent and the world's poorest people was at the end of the nineteenth century 30 to 1; by 1990 it reached 60 to 1; and by the end of the century it had widened to 74 to 1.

While many political observers and scholars predicted that globalization would bring both free markets and democracy to more and more of the world's people, others became increasingly skeptical. At the turn of the twenty-first century, an international protest movement emerged that targeted the most powerful organization in the global economy, the World Trade Organization (WTO) and the International Monetary Fund (IMF), or World Bank. In November 1999, thousands of protestors converged in Seattle, Washington, site of the annual meeting of the WTO, only to be pushed back by local police. In response, the WTO formulated new procedures for its meetings, secreting delegates behind walls and banning demonstrations from the area near future sites. Nevertheless, confrontations continued, the most dramatic occurring at a meeting of delegates from the eight leading industrial nations in Genoa, Italy, in 2001, which resulted in the death of one protestor.

Experts on globalization could not agree if the trend toward a single international market challenged traditional notions of national sovereignty and laid the foundation for global democracy or if the post–cold war world order was increasingly challenged by civil wars, ethnic and religious clashes, and the breakup of nation-states.

Terrorist Attack on America

On September 11, 2001, hijackers, armed only with knives and box cutters, crashed two jetliners into each of New York's World Trade Center towers, while a third jetliner slammed into the Pentagon in Virginia. A fourth plane, diverted from its terrorist mission by courageous passengers, hurtled to the ground near Pittsburgh. In all, 246 people perished in the four planes. At the sites of the attack, the damage was devastating. At the Pentagon, which had been built to withstand terrorist attacks, a huge explosion followed by fierce fires destroyed a large section of the defense complex. The death toll soon reached 184, including 59 people who had been on board the hijacked airliner. In New York, the number of lives lost was, as Mayor Rudolph W. Giulani said, "horrendous." The collapse of the twin towers, most likely caused by the intense fires propelled by the planes' jet fuel, brought death to thousands, including hundreds of police and rescue workers who had dashed into the buildings to help. At the end of the day, the New York City Fire Department had lost 350 firefighters, nearly thirty times the number ever lost by the department in a single incident. The nation watched in horror as the events vividly unfolded in live newscoverage on TV. The stark images of the second plane hitting the WTC, the dramatic collapse of the buildings, and the fear on the faces of thousands fleeing the sites were replayed over and over again on televisions throughout the world.

While the media recalled Pearl Harbor, President Bush declared the deadly attacks an act of war and vowed to hunt down those responsible for the "evil, despicable acts of terror." Congress, with only one dissenting vote, granted him power to take whatever steps necessary. The Department of Justice began what it described as the largest and most intensive investigation ever conducted, and the president issued a blanket warning to all nations who harbor terrorists. Secretary of State Colin Powell stated clearly, "You're either with us or against us." For the first time ever, NATO invoked the mutual defense clause in its founding treaty, which in effect supported any U.S. military response.

Observers described Bush's response as the defining moment of his presidency, as it was for the lives of many Americans. A patriotic surge found flags displayed on homes and cars—even painted on the faces of children. Millions of Americans rushed to donate blood, and thousands traveled to New York to assist rescue efforts. Prayer vigils were held in churches, synagogues, and mosques, as well as in public buildings and parks. Millions of dollars were soon raised for the relief effort and to assist the families of those who perished.

Many businesses, especially those in the travel, entertainment, or hazardous materials industries, were closed in the days following the attack. Perhaps most dramatic was the unprecedented shutdown of all airports in the United States, stranding thousands around the world. Service returned several days later at greatly reduced levels and with enhanced security. President Bush created a new Cabinet-level agency, Homeland Security, charged with coordinating the efforts of more than forty other agencies to protect Americans against terrorists and to respond to any such attacks. He also allocated millions of dollars to boost the budgets of the Department of Defense, the CIA, and the FBI.

The day following the highly coordinated terrorist attack, President Bush identified the Saudi Arabian Osama bin Laden as the prime suspect. Administration officials linked the airline hijackers, all presumed to be Islamic fundamentalists, to his Al-Qaeda network, which apparently had dispatched them to train at American flight schools. In 1998, bin Laden had issued a decree that granted religious legitimacy to all efforts to expel the United States from the lands of Islam in the Middle East. His network of terrorist cells, which reportedly operated in sixty countries, had directed rage at what they believe to be the global arrogance of the United States—its accumulation of unprecedented wealth when poverty and hopelessness extended across the Middle East.

With bin Laden presumed to be hiding in Afghanistan and supported by the ruling Taliban government, President Bush insisted that the Taliban regime hand over the terrorists "or they will share in their fate." He dispatched U.S. aircraft carriers to join the U.S. forces already assembled in the Persian

The United States conducted air strikes on the village of Rahesh, near the capital city of Kabul, in November 2001 in a military campaign to drive the Taliban from power in Afghanistan.

SOURCE: © AP/Wide World Photos (6051224).

Gulf region, and mobilized reservists for a possible invasion. On October 7, he ordered the first air strikes in Afghanistan, with the stated goal of destroying Al-Qaeda's terrorist training camps and bringing down the Taliban government that was shielding bin Laden.

CONCLUSION

Although the attack on the WTC and the Pentagon stunned and infuriated most Americans, it represented only the most destructive in the series of terrorist attacks that had been levied against the United States since the 1980s. In 1999, the U.S. Commission on National Security/Twenty-first Century, which has been established by Congress to evaluate the nation's defense systems, had concluded that "America will become increasingly vulnerable to hostile attack

CHRONOLOGY

1981	MTV and CNN start broadcasting as cable channels
1986	Immigration Reform and Control Act addresses concerns about illegal aliens
1987	Allan Bloom publishes *The Closing of the American Mind*
1988	Indian Gaming Regulatory Act allows Indian tribes to operate gambling establishments
	George Bush is elected president
	Terrorist attack on Pam Am plane over Lockerbie, Scotland
1989	Tiananmen Square demonstration in China
	Communist authority collapses in Eastern Europe
1990	August: Iraqi invasion of Kuwait leads to massive U.S. military presence in the Persian Gulf
1991	January–February: Operation Desert Storm forces Iraq out of Kuwait
	Operation Rescue launched in Wichita, Kansas
	Soviet Union dissolves into Commonwealth of Independent States
1992	Rodney King verdict sparks rioting in Los Angeles
	UN holds first Earth Summit
	Bill Clinton is elected president
1993	Terrorist bombing of World Trade Center kills six people
	Federal agents conduct seige of Branch Davidian compound in Waco, Texas
	Clinton administration introduces comprehensive health-care reform, but it fails to win passage in Congress
	Congress approves the North American Free Trade Agreement

1994	Republicans win control of Senate and House for first time in forty years
	Congress approves the General Agreement on Tariffs and Trade
	Congress passes the Comprehensive AIDS Revenue Emergency Act
	Congress passes "Defense of Marriage" Act
	California voters approve Proposition 187
1995	Bombing of Alfred P. Murrah Federal Building in Oklahoma City kills 168 people
	Clinton announces Dayton Accords to mediate civil war in Bosnia
1996	Congress passes Welfare Reform Act
	Congress enacts the Antiterrorism and Effective Death Penalty Act
	President Bill Clinton is reelected
1997	Kyoto Protocol endorsed by European Union but not United States
1998	U.S. embassies in Kenya and Tanzania bombed by terrorists
	House of Representatives votes to impeach President Clinton but vote fails in Senate
1999	United States joins NATO forces in Kosovo
	Protesters disrupt meetings of the World Trade Organization in Seattle
2000	USS *Cole* bombed by terrorists
2001	George W. Bush becomes president after contested election
	Terrorists attack World Trade Center and Pentagon
	United States begins military campaign in Afghanistan

on our homeland" and that "Americans will likely die on American soil, possibly in large numbers." The security promised by the end of the cold war seemed more elusive than ever. By early 2002, the Taliban government had collapsed much sooner than antici-

pated by U.S. military advisors. However, the war continued. President Bush, who had asked Americans to be patient "in understanding that it will take time to achieve our goals," broadened the scope and declared a worldwide war on terrorism.

REVIEW QUESTIONS

1. Is the United States entering a "new era" in the twenty-first century? What effects have the globalized economy and the fall of the Soviet Union had on American political life?

2. How is the "new economy" different from the old economy? How has it reshaped American business and financial practices? Explain the relationship between the new economy and electronic media, such as the Internet and cable television.

3. Evaluate the presidency of Bill Clinton. Compare his domestic and foreign policies to those of the Republican presidents who preceded and followed him in office. What was the impact of the scandals that plagued his presidency?

4. Describe the major demographic trends revealed by the 2000 census. Identify the racial and ethnic groups with the greatest gains in population. How have various legislation acts since 1965 af-

fected immigration to the United States? How have communities changed as a result of the influx of new immigrants?

5. The concept of globalization is highly controversial. Are borders between nations "melting away" as some scholars contend? How does this concept square with the description of the United States as the single superpower in the world? Does this concept apply primarily to economics, or is it useful for discussing issues related to culture, media, the environment, and population trends?

6. Earlier scholars predicted that the end of the cold war would bring peace and promote democracy throughout the world. Events, beginning with the Persian Gulf War, have instead suggested a new basis for international affairs. Describe the importance of regional and ethnic conflicts in the Middle East and Central Europe.

RECOMMENDED READING

Angus Kress Gillespie, *Twin Towers: The Life of New York City's World Trade Center* (1999). A detailed history of the buildings, including the political background and the process of design and construction. Gillespie traces the emergence of the World Trade Center as a popular symbol of New York City and center of international commerce.

Mark S. Hamm, *Apocalypse in Oklahoma: Waco and Ruby Ridge Revenge* (1997). Provides a succinct overview of the events leading to the bombing of the federal building in Oklahoma City in 1995, seeing it as an act of murderous revenge.

David Held, ed., *A Globalizing World? Culture, Economics, Politics* (2000). Four essays addressing various aspects of globalization. This slim volume offers a concise summary of the major theories of globalization and compares the contemporary situation with previous eras.

Neil Howe, *Millennials Rising: The Next Generation* (2000). An optimistic assessment of the generation of Americans who were born on or after 1982 and projections for their future. Howe surveys statistics as well as cultural trends and concludes that the rising generation shows a return to conservative family values and a respect for rules.

William G. Hyland, *Clinton's World: Remaking American Foreign Policy* (1999). Evaluates the first post–cold war president's decisions with regard to the major international events of the 1990s. Examines the developing policies toward Russia and Asia. Hyland offers a fairly negative assessment.

Robert K. Kaplan, *The Coming Anarchy: Shattering the Dreams of the Post–Cold War* (2000). Nine essays on international affairs that provide an often disturbing assessment of the prospects for peace. Kaplan discusses the rise of ethnic conflict in regions such as Sierra Leone, Russia, and India and weighs the signficance of increasing tribalistic warfare, the breakdown of central government authority in several nations, and the rise in crime in post-Communist countries.

Judith Millwer, Stephen Engelberg, and William Broad, *Germs: Biological Weapons and America's Secret War* (2001). Beginning with the use of salmonella to poison food in Oregon in 1984, this book narrates the history of biological warfare in the last half of the twentieth century. The authors, veteran reporters for the *New York Times*, argue that the United States is ill equipped to protect its citizens against a serious biological attack.

Jill Nelson, ed., *Police Brutality: An Anthology* (2000). Twelve essays written by scholars, activists, and writers that discuss, from a variety of perspectives, police presence in American communities. Several essays focus on the broad historical dimensions of this issue, tracing the roots back to the time of slavery.

New York Times staffwriters, *The Downsizing of America* (1996). A well-researched account detailing the devastating impact of corporate "downsizing" on American communities and families.

Howard Rheingold, *The Virtual Community* (1994). Very thoughtful examination of the promises and problems posed by the new computer-based technologies associated with "virtual communities."

Micah L. Sifry and Christopher Cerf, eds., *The Gulf War Reader* (1991). An excellent collection of historical essays, government documents, and political addresses that provides a comprehensive overview of the Persian Gulf War.

Janet Thomas, *The Battle in Seattle: The Story Behind and Beyond the WTO* (2000). An impassioned, eyewitness account by a participant in the 1999 demonstrations against the World Trade Organization, which the author describes as a "global tailspin at the end of the century."

ON THE WEB

http://oyez.nwu.edu/

The Oyez Project of Northwestern University provides information on Supreme Court decisions, especially the written Court opinions. The cases of *Bush* v. *Palm Beach County Canvassing Board* (2000) and *Bush* v. *Gore* (2000) were two key U.S. Supreme Court decisions in the presidential election crisis of 2000. Search this site for the written opinions of the justices on these two historical decisions of the Court.

http://www.nytimes.com/learning/general/specials/impeachment/

A *New York Times* site that explains the impeachment process not just in relationship to Clinton, but over the entire history of the United States with all presidents who were either threatened with impeachment, impeached, or censured.

http://www.bartleby.com/124/pres64.html

Bill Clinton's First Inaugural Address, January 21, 1993.

http://www.bartleby.com/124/pres65.html

Bill Clinton's Second Inaugural Address, January 20, 1997.

http://www.bartleby.com/124/pres66.html

George W. Bush's Inaugural Address, January 20, 2001.

http://www.september11.archive.org

An extensive site that serves as a gateway to the many websites devoted to the events of September 11, 2001.

The World Trade Center and Ways of Remembering

The first plane hit the north tower of the World Trade Center at 8:48 A.M. The second plane struck the south tower at 9:03 A.M. The two massive, 110-story "twin towers" soon collapsed into a nightmarish rubble, as millions of disbelieving viewers watched the scene on television. By then many Americans had already begun to speak of the event as the defining moment of their own lifetimes, declaring that they would forever remember where they were and what they were doing when reports of the tragedy reached them. While the events were still unfolding, Americans began to search for ways to place the terrorist attack on America in historical perspective. How would their memories make sense of the experience in the long run? How did the larger context of U.S. history frame the horrible events of September 11, 2001?

Newscasters, commentators, political figures, and ordinary citizens all struggled to find appropriate historical analogies for attacks on the World Trade Center and the Pentagon. They repeatedly invoked two twentieth-century events that seemed to offer at least some parallels. One was the surprise Japanese attack on the American naval fleet anchored in Pearl Harbor, Hawai'i, on December 7, 1941. Both enemy attacks came from the air and lasted just over an hour. The death toll was high in both cases, with 2,403 Americans dead in Pearl Harbor. In his address the next day, President Franklin D. Roosevelt memorialized the date as one "which will live in infamy." "Always will our whole nation remember the character of the onslaught against us," he predicted while asking Congress for a declaration of war against Japan. On September 11, 2001, newscasters almost instantaneously revived President Roosevelt's descriptive phrase. This new "day of infamy," they suggested, carried as much historical weight as the event that brought the United States into World War II.

The second frequently cited historical parallel was the assassination of President John F. Kennedy on November 22, 1963. Kennedy's death and funeral underscored the new power of television to transform a nation into a community witnessing momentous and shocking events as they unfolded. Indeed, millions of Americans had watched in disbelief as Kennedy's accused assassin, Lee Harvey Oswald, was gunned down in a Dallas police station the day after the president had been killed. And

People ran for safety following the collapse of the World Trade Center after the terrorist attack on the New York landmark on September 11, 2001.

SOURCE: Associated Press, AP.

just as Americans would never forget where they were and what they were doing when they heard the news about JFK, so it seemed that the WTC attack would also prove a lifelong marker of memory.

These two historical analogies are far from perfect. Pearl Harbor was a military target, thousands of miles from the mainland; the attack had clearly come from a nation state that had a deep economic and diplomatic rivalry with the United States. In contrast, the September 11 assault came against a symbol of American economic power with no military significance, and it marked the first time that American civilians had ever suffered mass casualties at the hands of a foreign enemy. And that enemy appeared to be not a nation state but rather a shadowy international organization of radical Islamic terrorists. The JFK assassination had surely demonstrated the growing power of television to focus an entire nation's attention. But Americans would never really agree on the cause and meaning of Kennedy's tragic death. For decades, American citizens, abetted by a cottage industry of conspiracy theorists, filmmakers, historians, novelists, and journalists, continued to argue about who was responsible, what motives were in play, and how history might have been different had Kennedy lived.

By the evening of September 11, groups of people across the nation gathered in candlelight vigils to honor the victims of the terrorist attacks. President Bush declared September 14 a National Day of Prayer and Remembrance.

SOURCE: © Reuters New Media Inc./CORBIS.

What role did the media play in shaping our understanding of the events of September 11, 2001? Unlike the bombing of U.S. naval ships in Pearl Harbor, the terrorist attack on the World Trade Center occurred, virtually, before the eyes of millions of Americans. Video cameras caught the image of the second plane hitting the south tower, the panic on the faces of those fleeing the scene, the smoke billowing from the towers, and their sudden collapse. Reporters were soon on the scene to interview eyewitnesses and to pull comments from traumatized survivors. The networks immediately preempted regular programming and allowed millions of Americans to watch in horror as the televised images played and replayed the attack. The newscasters narrated the events, drawing out the analogy with Pearl Harbor, and giving the unfolding story a title, such as "Attack on America" or "Day of Infamy." Within a few days, programmers had edited the videotapes to enhance the drama. They added scenes, such as images of cell phones to remind viewers of the final calls many of the victims made to their loved ones. They overlaid the images of towers collapsing with an unfurling American flag and added patriotic music. To enhance further the emotional impact, they borrowed cinematic techniques, slowing down the pace to draw out the action. They also used jump cuts, juxtaposing in fast time an image of the burning or collapsing towers with a closeup shot of an anguished face of an observer, putting the viewer emotionally into the picture.

But the shaping of historical memory took place on other levels as well. At hundreds of funerals and memorial services held in communities throughout the Greater New York area, many thousands of strangers joined families of the victims in paying respects and trying to make sense of it all. Makeshift memorials sprouted up in lower Manhattan with people leaving flowers, personal notes, and artwork. At the Massachusetts Institute of Technology in Cambridge, Massachusetts, faculty and students built a Reflecting Wall, consisting of a recreated fragment of the familiar World Trade Center façade.

For more long-term efforts at documenting collective memory, historians and museums looked to the Internet. Some 70 history-oriented institutions came together to create a new Internet site, 911history.net, devoted to collecting oral histories and artifacts from the event. And the Library of Congress spearheaded another site, September11.archive.org, which by mid-October had already put online more than 500,000 pages related to the terrorist attacks, ranging from daily news reports to personal memorials. As Diane Kresh of the Library of Congress put it, "The Internet has become for many the public commons, a place where they can come together and talk." A more permanent memorial will no doubt be a part of the reconstruction of Lower Manhattan. Through all these projects, Americans will continue demonstrating how creating historical memory is an active and dynamic process. ■

APPENDIX

THE DECLARATION OF INDEPENDENCE

When in the course of human events it becomes necessary for one people to dissolve the political bands which have connected them with another and to assume, among the powers of the earth, the separate and equal station to which the laws of nature and of nature's God entitle them, a decent respect to the opinions of mankind requires that they should declare the causes which impel them to the separation.

We hold these truths to be self-evident, that all men are created equal; that they are endowed by their Creator with certain unalienable rights; that among these are life, liberty, and the pursuit of happiness. That, to secure these rights, governments are instituted among men, deriving their just powers from the consent of the governed; that, whenever any form of government becomes destructive of these ends, it is the right of the people to alter or to abolish it, and to institute a new government, laying its foundation on such principles, and organizing its powers in such form, as to them shall seem most likely to effect their safety and happiness. Prudence, indeed, will dictate that governments long established should not be changed for light and transient causes; and, accordingly, all experience hath shown that mankind are more disposed to suffer, while evils are sufferable, than to right themselves by abolishing the forms to which they are accustomed. But when a long train of abuses and usurpations, pursuing invariably the same object, evinces a design to reduce them under absolute despotism, it is their right, it is their duty, to throw off such government and to provide new guards for their future security. Such has been the patient sufferance of these colonies, and such is now the necessity which constrains them to alter their former systems of government. The history of the present King of Great Britain is a history of repeated injuries and usurpations, all having, in direct object, the establishment of an absolute tyranny over these States. To prove this, let facts be submitted to a candid world:

He has refused his assent to laws the most wholesome and necessary for the public good.

He has forbidden his governors to pass laws of immediate and pressing importance, unless suspended in their operation till his assent should be obtained; and, when so suspended, he has utterly neglected to attend to them.

He has refused to pass other laws for the accommodation of large districts of people, unless those people would relinquish the right of representation in the legislature, a right inestimable to them and formidable to tyrants only.

He has called together legislative bodies at places unusual, uncomfortable, and distant from the depository of their public records, for the sole purpose of fatiguing them into compliance with his measures.

He has dissolved representative houses, repeatedly for opposing, with manly firmness, his invasions on the rights of the people.

He has refused, for a long time after such dissolutions, to cause others to be elected; whereby the legislative powers, incapable of annihilation, have returned to the people at large for their exercise; the state remaining, in the meantime, exposed to all the danger of invasion from without and convulsions within.

He has endeavored to prevent the population of these States; for that purpose, obstructing the laws for naturalization of foreigners, refusing to pass others to encourage their migration hither, and raising the conditions of new appropriations of lands.

He has obstructed the administration of justice by refusing his assent to laws for establishing judiciary powers.

He has made judges dependent on his will alone for the tenure of their offices and the amount and payment of their salaries.

He has erected a multitude of new offices and sent hither swarms of officers to harass our people and eat out their substance.

He has kept among us, in time of peace, standing armies, without the consent of our legislatures.

He has affected to render the military independent of, and superior to, the civil power.

He has combined with others to subject us to a jurisdiction foreign to our Constitution and unacknowledged by our laws, giving his assent to their acts of pretended legislation—

For quartering large bodies of armed troops among us;

For protecting them, by mock trial, from punishment for any murders which they should commit on the inhabitants of these States;

For cutting off our trade with all parts of the world;

For imposing taxes on us without our consent;

For depriving us, in many cases, of the benefit of trial by jury;

For transporting us beyond seas to be tried for pretended offences;

For abolishing the free system of English laws in a neighboring province, establishing therein an arbitrary government, and enlarging its boundaries, so as to render it at once an example and fit instrument for introducing the same absolute rule into these colonies;

For taking away our charters, abolishing our most valuable laws, and altering, fundamentally, the powers of our governments.

For suspending our own legislatures and declaring themselves invested with power to legislate for us in all cases whatsoever.

He has abdicated government here by declaring us out of his protection and waging war against us.

He has plundered our seas, ravaged our coasts, burnt our towns, and destroyed the lives of our people.

He is, at this time, transporting large armies of foreign mercenaries to complete the works of death, desolation, and tyranny already begun with circumstances of cruelty and perfidy scarcely paralleled in the most barbarous ages, and totally unworthy the head of a civilized nation.

He has constrained our fellow citizens, taken captive on the high seas, to bear arms against their country, to become the executioners of their friends and brethren, or to fall themselves by their hands.

He has excited domestic insurrections amongst us and has endeavored to bring on the inhabitants of our frontiers, the merciless Indian savages, whose known rule of warfare is an undistinguished destruction of all ages, sexes, and conditions.

In every stage of these oppressions, we have petitioned for redress in the most humble terms; our repeated petitions have been answered only by repeated injury. A prince whose character is thus marked by every act which may define a tyrant is unfit to be the ruler of a free people.

Nor have we been wanting in attention to our British brethren. We have warned them, from time to time, of attempts made by their legislature to extend an unwarrantable jurisdiction over us. We have reminded them of the circumstances of our emigration and settlement here. We have appealed to their native justice and magnanimity, and we have conjured them, by the ties of our common kindred, to disavow these usurpations, which would inevitably interrupt our connections and correspondence. They, too, have been deaf to the voice of justice and consanguinity. We must, therefore, acquiesce in the necessity which denounces our separation, and hold them, as we hold the rest of mankind, enemies in war, in peace, friends.

We, therefore, the representatives of the United States of America, in general Congress assembled, appealing to the Supreme Judge of the world for the rectitude of our intentions, do, in the name and by the authority of the good people of these colonies, solemnly publish and declare, that these united colonies are, and of right ought to be, free and independent states: that they are absolved from all allegiance to the British Crown, and that all political connection between them and the state of Great Britain is, and ought to be, totally dissolved; and that, as free and independent states, they have full power to levy war, conclude peace, contract alliances, establish commerce, and to do all other acts and things which independent states may of right do. And, for the support of this declaration, with a firm reliance on the protection of Divine Providence, we mutually pledge to each other our lives, our fortunes, and our sacred honor.

THE CONSTITUTION OF THE UNITED STATES OF AMERICA

We the people of the United States, in order to form a more perfect union, establish justice, insure domestic tranquillity, provide for the common defense, promote the general welfare, and secure the blessings of liberty to ourselves and our posterity, do ordain and establish this Constitution for the United States of America.

Article I

Section 1. All legislative powers herein granted shall be vested in a Congress of the United States, which shall consist of a Senate and House of Representatives.

Section 2. 1. The House of Representatives shall be composed of members chosen every second year by the people of the several States, and the electors in each State shall have the qualifications requisite for electors of the most numerous branch of the State legislature.

2. No person shall be a representative who shall not have attained to the age of twenty-five years, and been seven years a citizen of the United States, and who shall not, when elected, be an inhabitant of that State in which he shall be chosen.

3. Representatives and direct taxes[1] shall be apportioned among the several States which may be included within this Union, according to their respective numbers, which shall be determined by adding to the whole number of free persons, including those bound to service for a term of years, and excluding Indians not taxed, three fifths of all other persons.[2] The actual enumeration shall be made within three years after the first meeting of the Congress of the United States, and within every subsequent term of ten years, in such manner as they shall by law direct. The number of representatives shall not exceed one for every thirty thousand, but each State shall have at least one representative; and until such enumeration shall be made, the State of New Hampshire shall be entitled to choose three, Massachusetts eight, Rhode Island and Providence Plantations one, Connecticut five, New York six, New Jersey four, Pennsylvania eight, Delaware one, Maryland six, Virginia ten, North Carolina five, South Carolina five, and Georgia three.

4. When vacancies happen in the representation from any State, the executive authority thereof shall issue writs of election to fill such vacancies.

5. The House of Representatives shall choose their speaker and other officers; and shall have the sole power of impeachment.

Section 3. 1. The Senate of the United States shall be composed of two senators from each State, chosen by the legislature thereof,[3] for six years; and each senator shall have one vote.

2. Immediately after they shall be assembled in consequence of the first election, they shall be divided as equally as may be into three classes. The seats of the senators of the first class shall be vacated at the expiration of the second year, of the second class at the expiration of the fourth year, and of the third class at the expiration of the sixth year, so that one third may be chosen every second year; and if vacancies happen by resignation, or otherwise, during the recess of the legislature of any State, the executive thereof may make temporary appointments until the next meeting of the legislature, which shall then fill such vacancies.[4]

3. No person shall be a senator who shall not have attained to the age of thirty years, and been nine years a citizen of the United States, and who shall not, when elected, be an inhabitant of that State for which he shall be chosen.

4. The Vice President of the United States shall be President of the Senate, but shall have no vote, unless they be equally divided.

5. The Senate shall choose their other officers, and also a president pro tempore, in the absence of the Vice President, or when he shall exercise the office of the President of the United States.

6. The Senate shall have the sole power to try all impeachments. When sitting for that purpose, they shall be on oath or affirmation. When the President of the United States is tried, the Chief Justice shall preside: and no person shall be convicted without the concurrence of two thirds of the members present.

7. Judgment in cases of impeachment shall not extend further than to removal from office, and disqualification to hold and enjoy any office of honor, trust or profit under the United States: but the party convicted shall nevertheless be liable and subject to indictment, trial, judgment and punishment, according to law.

Section 4. 1. The times, places, and manner of holding elections for senators and representatives, shall be prescribed in each State by the legislature thereof; but the Congress may at any time by law make or alter such regulations, except as to the places of choosing senators.

2. The Congress shall assemble at least once in every year, and such meeting shall be on the first Monday in December, unless they shall by law appoint a different day.

Section 5. 1. Each House shall be the judge of the elections, returns and qualifications of its own members, and a majority of each shall constitute a quorum to do business; but a smaller number may adjourn from day to day, and may be authorized to compel the attendance of absent members, in such manner, and under such penalties as each House may provide.

2. Each House may determine the rules of its proceedings, punish its members for disorderly behavior, and, with the concurrence of two thirds, expel a member.

3. Each House shall keep a journal of its proceedings, and from time to time publish the same, excepting such parts as may in their judgment require secrecy; and the yeas and nays of the members of either House on any question

---

[1]See the Sixteenth Amendment.
[2]See the Fourteenth Amendment.
[3]See the Seventeenth Amendment.

---

[4]See the Seventeenth Amendment.

shall, at the desire of one fifth of those present, be entered on the journal.

4. Neither House, during the session of Congress, shall, without the consent of the other, adjourn for more than three days, nor to any other place than that in which the two Houses shall be sitting.

Section 6. 1. The senators and representatives shall receive a compensation for their services, to be ascertained by law, and paid out of the Treasury of the United States. They shall in all cases, except treason, felony, and breach of the peace, be privileged from arrest during their attendance at the session of their respective Houses, and in going to and returning from the same; and for any speech or debate in either House, they shall not be questioned in any other place.

2. No senator or representative shall, during the time for which he was elected, be appointed to any civil office under the authority of the United States, which shall have been created, or the emoluments whereof shall have been increased, during such time; and no person holding any office under the United States shall be a member of either House during his continuance in office.

Section 7. 1. All bills for raising revenue shall originate in the House of Representatives; but the Senate may propose or concur with amendments as on other bills.

2. Every bill which shall have passed the House of Representatives and the Senate, shall, before it become a law, be presented to the President of the United States; If he approves he shall sign it, but if not he shall return it, with his objections, to that House in which it shall have originated, who shall enter the objections at large on their journal, and proceed to reconsider it. If after such reconsideration two thirds of that House shall agree to pass the bill, it shall be sent, together with the objections, to the other House, by which it shall likewise be reconsidered, and if approved by two thirds of that House, it shall become a law. But in all such cases the votes of both Houses shall be determined by yeas and nays, and the names of the persons voting for and against the bill shall be entered on the journal of each House respectively. If any bill shall not be returned by the President within ten days (Sundays excepted) after it shall have been presented to him, the same shall be a law, in like manner as if he had signed it, unless the Congress by their adjournment prevent its return, in which case it shall not be a law.

3. Every order, resolution, or vote to which the concurrence of the Senate and the House of Representatives may be necessary (except on a question of adjournment) shall be presented to the President of the United States; and before the same shall take effect, shall be approved by him, or being disapproved by him, shall be repassed by two thirds of the Senate and House of Representatives, according to the rules and limitations prescribed in the case of a bill.

Section 8. The Congress shall have the power

1. To lay and collect taxes, duties, imposts, and excises, to pay the debts and provide for the common defense and general welfare of the United States; but all duties, imposts, and excises shall be uniform throughout the United States.

2. To borrow money on the credit of the United States;

3. To regulate commerce with foreign nations, and among the several States, and with the Indian tribes;

4. To establish a uniform rule of naturalization, and uniform laws on the subject of bankruptcies throughout the United States;

5. To coin money, regulate the value thereof, and of foreign coin, and fix the standard of weights and measures;

6. To provide for the punishment of counterfeiting the securities and current coin of the United States;

7. To establish post offices and post roads;

8. To promote the progress of science and useful arts, by securing for limited times to authors and inventors the exclusive right to their respective writings and discoveries;

9. To constitute tribunals inferior to the Supreme Court;

10. To define and punish piracies and felonies committed on the high seas, and offenses against the law of nations;

11. To declare war, grant letters of marque and reprisal, and make rules concerning captures on land and water;

12. To raise and support armies, but no appropriation of money to that use shall be for a longer term than two years;

13. To provide and maintain a navy;

14. To make rules for the government and regulation of the land and naval forces;

15. To provide for calling forth the militia to execute the laws of the Union, suppress insurrections and repel invasions;

16. To provide for organizing, arming, and disciplining the militia, and for governing such part of them as may be employed in the service of the United States, reserving to the States respectively, the appointment of the officers, and the authority of training the militia according to the discipline prescribed by Congress;

17. To exercise exclusive legislation in all cases whatsoever, over such district (not exceeding ten miles square) as may, by cession of particular States, and the acceptance of Congress, become the seat of the government of the United States, and to exercise like authority over all places purchased by the consent of the legislature of the State in which the same shall be, for the erection of forts, magazines, arsenals, dockyards, and other needful buildings; and

18. To make all laws which shall be necessary and proper for carrying into execution the foregoing powers, and all other powers vested by this Constitution in the government of the United States, or any department or officer thereof.

Section 9. 1. The migration or importation of such persons as any of the States now existing shall think proper to admit, shall not be prohibited by the Congress prior to the year one thousand eight hundred and eight, but a tax or duty may be imposed on such importation, not exceeding ten dollars for each person.

2. The privilege of the writ of habeas corpus shall not be suspended, unless when in cases of rebellion or invasion the public safety may require it.

3. No bill of attainder or ex post facto law shall be passed.

4. No capitation, or other direct, tax shall be laid, unless in proportion to the census or enumeration hereinbefore directed to be taken.[5]

5. No tax or duty shall be laid on articles exported from any State.

6. No preference shall be given by any regulation of commerce or revenue to the ports of one State over those of another: nor shall vessels bound to, or from, one State be obliged to enter, clear, or pay duties in another.

7. No money shall be drawn from the treasury, but in consequence of appropriations made by law; and a regular statement and account of the receipts and expenditures of all public money shall be published from time to time.

8. No title of nobility shall be granted by the United States: and no person holding any office of profit or trust under them, shall, without the consent of the Congress, accept of any present, emolument, office, or title, of any kind whatever, from any king, prince, or foreign State.

Section 10. 1. No State shall enter into any treaty, alliance, or confederation; grant letters of marque and reprisal; coin money; emit bills of credit; make any thing but gold and silver coin a tender in payment of debts; pass any bill of attainder, ex post facto law, or law impairing the obligation of contracts, or grant, any title of nobility.

2. No State shall, without the consent of the Congress, lay any imposts or duties on imports or exports, except what may be absolutely necessary for executing its inspection laws: and the net produce of all duties and imposts laid by any State on imports or exports, shall be for the use of the treasury of the United States; and all such laws shall be subject to the revision and control of Congress.

3. No State shall, without the consent of the Congress, lay any duty of tonnage, keep troops, or ships of war in time of peace, enter into any agreement or compact with another State, or with a foreign power, or engage in war, unless actually invaded, or in such imminent danger as will not admit of delay.

Article II

Section 1. 1. The executive power shall be vested in a President of the United States of America. He shall hold his office during the term of four years, and, together with the Vice President, chosen for the same term, be elected, as follows:

2. Each State shall appoint, in such manner as the legislature thereof may direct, a number of electors, equal to the whole number of senators and representatives to which the State may be entitled in the Congress: but no senator or representative, or person holding any office of trust or profit under the United States, shall be appointed an elector.

The electors shall meet in their respective States, and vote by ballot for two persons, of whom one at least shall not be an inhabitant of the same State with themselves. And they shall make a list of all the persons voted for, and of the number of votes for each; which list they shall sign and certify, and transmit sealed to the seat of the government of the United States, directed to the president of the Senate. The president of the Senate shall, in the presence of the Senate and House of Representatives, open all the certificates, and the votes shall then be counted. The person having the greatest number of votes shall be the President, if such number be a majority of the whole number of electors appointed; and if there be more than one who have such majority, and have an equal number of votes, then the House of Representatives shall immediately choose by ballot one of them for President; and if no person have a majority, then from the five highest on the list the said House shall in like manner choose the President. But in choosing the President, the votes shall be taken by States, the representation from each State having one vote; a quorum for this purpose shall consist of a member or members from two thirds of the States, and a majority of all the States shall be necessary to a choice. In every case after the choice of the President, the person having the greatest number of votes of the electors shall be the Vice President. But if there should remain two or more who have equal votes, the Senate shall choose from them by ballot the Vice President.[6]

3. The Congress may determine the time of choosing the electors, and the day on which they shall give their votes; which day shall be the same throughout the United States.

4. No person except a natural born citizen, or a citizen of the United States, at the time of the adoption of this Constitution, shall be eligible to the office of President; neither shall any person be eligible to the office who shall not have attained to the age of thirty-five years, and been fourteen years a resident within the United States.

5. In case of the removal of the President from office, or of his death, resignation, or inability to discharge the powers and duties of the said office, the same shall devolve on the Vice President, and the Congress may by law provide for the case of removal, death, resignation or inability, both of the President and Vice President, declaring what officer shall then act as President, and such officer shall act accordingly until the disability be removed, or a President shall be elected.

6. The President shall, at stated times, receive for his services a compensation which shall neither be increased nor diminished during the period for which he shall have been elected, and he shall not receive within that period any other emolument from the United States, or any of them.

7. Before he enter on the execution of his office, he shall take the following oath or affirmation:—"I do

---

[5]See the Sixteenth Amendment.

[6]Superseded by the Twelfth Amendment.

solemnly swear (or affirm) that I will faithfully execute the office of President of the United States, and will to the best of my ability, preserve, protect and defend the Constitution of the United States."

Section 2. 1. The President shall be commander in chief of the army and navy of the United States, and of the militia of the several States, when called into the actual service of the United States; he may require the opinion in writing, of the principal officer in each of the executive departments, upon any subject relating to the duties of their respective offices, and he shall have power to grant reprieves and pardons for offenses against the United States, except in cases of impeachment.

2. He shall have power, by and with the advice and consent of the Senate, to make treaties, provided two thirds of the senators present concur; and he shall nominate, and by and with the advice and consent of the Senate, shall appoint ambassadors, other public ministers and consuls, judges of the Supreme Court, and all other officers of the United States, whose appointments are not herein otherwise provided for, and which shall be established by law; but the Congress may by law vest the appointment of such inferior officers, as they think proper, in the President alone, in the courts of laws, or in the heads of departments.

3. The President shall have power to fill up all vacancies that may happen during the recess of the Senate, by granting commissions which shall expire at the end of their next session.

Section 3. He shall from time to time give to the Congress information of the state of the Union, and recommend to their consideration such measures as he shall judge necessary and expedient; he may, on extraordinary occasions, convene both Houses, or either of them, and in case of disagreement between them with respect to the time of adjournment, he may adjourn them to such time as he shall think proper; he shall receive ambassadors and other public ministers; he shall take care that the laws be faithfully executed, and shall commission all the officers of the United States.

Section 4. The President, Vice President, and all civil officers of the United States, shall be removed from office on impeachment for, and conviction of, treason, bribery, or other high crimes and misdemeanors.

Article III

Section 1. The judicial power of the United States shall be vested in one Supreme Court, and in such inferior courts as the Congress may from time to time ordain and establish. The judges, both of the Supreme and inferior courts, shall hold their offices during good behavior, and shall, at stated times, receive for their services, a compensation, which shall not be diminished during their continuance in office.

Section 2. 1. The judicial power shall extend to all cases, in law and equity, arising under this Constitution, the laws of the United States, and treaties made, or which shall be made, under their authority;—to all cases of admiralty and maritime jurisdiction;—to controversies to which the United States shall be a party;[7]—to controversies between two or more States;—between a State and citizens of another State;—between citizens of different States;—between citizens of the same State claiming lands under grants of different States, and between a State, or the citizens thereof, and foreign States, citizens or subjects.

2. In all cases affecting ambassadors, other public ministers and consuls, and those in which a State shall be party, the Supreme Court shall have original jurisdiction. In all the other cases before mentioned, the Supreme Court shall have appellate jurisdiction, both as to law and fact, with such exceptions, and under such regulations as the Congress shall make.

3. The trial of all crimes, except in cases of impeachment, shall be by jury; and such trial shall be held in the State where the said crimes shall have been committed; but when not committed within any State, the trial shall be such place or places as the Congress may by law have directed.

Section 3. 1. Treason against the United States shall consist only in levying war against them, or in adhering to their enemies, giving them aid and comfort. No person shall be convicted of treason unless on the testimony of two witnesses to the same overt act, or on confession in open court.

2. The Congress shall have power to declare the punishment of treason, but no attainder of treason shall work corruption of blood, or forfeiture except during the life of the person attained.

Article IV

Section 1. Full faith and credit shall be given in each State to the public acts, records, and judicial proceedings of every other State. And the Congress may by general laws prescribe the manner in which such acts, records and proceedings shall be proved, and the effect thereof.

Section 2. 1. The citizens of each State shall be entitled to all privileges and immunities of citizens in the several States.[8]

2. A person charged in any State with treason, felony, or other crime, who shall flee from justice, and be found in another State, shall on demand of the executive authority of the State from which he fled, be delivered up to be removed to the State having jurisdiction of the crime.

3. No person held to service or labor in one State under the laws thereof, escaping into another, shall, in consequence of any law or regulation therein, be discharged from such service or labor, but shall be delivered up on claim of the party to whom such service or labor may be due.[9]

Section 3. 1. New States may be admitted by the Congress into this Union; but no new State shall be formed or erected within the jurisdiction of any other State, nor any State be formed by the junction of two or more States, or parts of States, without the consent of the legislatures of the States concerned as well as of the Congress.

---

[7]See the Eleventh Amendment.
[8]See the Fourteenth Amendment, Sec. 1.
[9]See the Thirteenth Amendment.

2. The Congress shall have power to dispose of and make all needful rules and regulations respecting the territory or other property belonging to the United States; and nothing in this Constitution shall be so construed as to prejudice any claims of the United States, or of any particular State.

Section 4. The United States shall guarantee to every State in this Union a republican form of government, and shall protect each of them against invasion; and on application of the legislature, or of the executive (when the legislature cannot be convened) against domestic violence.

Article V

The Congress, whenever two thirds of both Houses shall deem it necessary, shall propose amendments to this Constitution, or, on the application of the legislatures of two thirds of the several States, shall call a convention for proposing amendments, which in either case shall be valid to all intents and purposes, as part of this Constitution, when ratified by the legislatures of three fourths of the several States, or by conventions in three fourths thereof, as the one or the other mode of ratification may be proposed by the Congress; Provided that no amendment which may be made prior to the year one thousand eight hundred and eight shall in any manner affect the first and fourth clauses in the ninth section of the first article; and that no State, without its consent, shall be deprived of its equal suffrage in the Senate.

Article VI

1. All debts contracted and engagements entered into, before the adoption of this Constitution, shall be as valid against the United States under this Constitution, as under the Confederation.[10]

2. This Constitution, and the laws of the United States which shall be made in pursuance thereof; and all treaties made, or which shall be made, under the authority of the United States, shall be the supreme law of the land; and the judges in every State shall be bound thereby, any thing in the Constitution or laws of any State to the contrary notwithstanding.

3. The senators and representatives before mentioned, and the members of the several State legislatures, and all executive and judicial officers, both of the United States and of the several States, shall be bound by oath or affirmation to support this Constitution; but no religious test shall ever be required as a qualification to any office or public trust under the United States.

Article VII

The ratification of the conventions of nine States shall be sufficient for the establishment of this Constitution between the States so ratifying the same.

Done in Convention by the unanimous consent of the States present the seventeenth day of September in the year of our Lord one thousand seven hundred and eighty-

seven, and of the independence of the United States of America the twelfth. In witness whereof we have hereunto subscribed our names.

[Names omitted]

* * *

Articles in addition to, and amendment of, the Constitution of the United States of America, proposed by Congress, and ratified by the legislatures of the several States, pursuant to the fifth article of the original Constitution.

Amendment I [First ten amendments ratified December 15, 1791]

Congress shall make no law respecting an establishment of religion, or prohibiting the free exercise thereof; or abridging the freedom of speech, or of the press; or the right of the people peaceably to assemble, and to petition the government for a redress of grievances.

Amendment II

A well regulated militia, being necessary to the security of a free State, the right of the people to keep and bear arms, shall not be infringed.

Amendment III

No soldier shall, in time of peace be quartered in any house, without the consent of the owner, nor in time of war, but in a manner to be prescribed by law.

Amendment IV

The right of the people to be secure in their persons, houses, papers, and effects, against unreasonable searches and seizures, shall not be violated, and no warrants shall issue, but upon probable cause, supported by oath or affirmation, and particularly describing the place to be searched, and the persons or things to be seized.

Amendment V

No person shall be held to answer for a capital or otherwise infamous crime, unless on a presentment or indictment of a grand jury, except in cases arising in the land or naval forces, or in the militia, when in actual service in time of war or public danger; nor shall any person be subject for the same offense to be twice put in jeopardy of life or limb; nor shall be compelled in any criminal case to be a witness against himself, nor be deprived of life, liberty, or property, without due process of law; nor shall private property be taken for public use, without just compensation.

Amendment VI

In all criminal prosecutions, the accused shall enjoy the right to a speedy and public trial, by an impartial jury of the State and district wherein the crime shall have been committed, which district shall have been previously ascertained by law, and to be informed of the nature and cause of the accusation; to be confronted with the witnesses against him; to have compulsory process for obtaining witnesses in his favor, and to have the assistance of counsel for his defense.

[10]See the Fourteenth Amendment, Sec. 4.

Amendment VII

In suits at common law, where the value in controversy shall exceed twenty dollars, the right of trial by jury shall be preserved, and no fact tried by a jury shall be otherwise reexamined in any court of the United States, than according to the rules of the common law.

Amendment VIII

Excessive bail shall not be required, nor excessive fines imposed, nor cruel and unusual punishments inflicted.

Amendment IX

The enumeration in the Constitution of certain rights shall not be construed to deny or disparage others retained by the people.

Amendment X

The powers not delegated to the United States by the Constitution, nor prohibited by it to the States, are reserved to the States respectively, or to the people.

Amendment XI [January 8, 1798]

The judicial power of the United States shall not be construed to extend to any suit in law or equity, commended or prosecuted against one of the United States by citizens of another State, or by citizens or subjects of any foreign State.

Amendment XII [September 25, 1804]

The electors shall meet in their respective States, and vote by ballot for President and Vice President, one of whom, at least, shall not be an inhabitant of the same State with themselves; they shall name in their ballots the person voted for as President, and in distinct ballots the person voted for as Vice President, and they shall make distinct lists of all persons voted for as President and of all persons voted for as Vice President, and of the number of votes for each, which lists they shall sign and certify, and transmit sealed to the seat of the government of the United States, directed to the President of the Senate;—The President of the Senate shall, in the presence of the Senate and House of Representatives, open all the certificates and the votes shall then be counted;—The person having the greatest number of votes for President, shall be the President, if such number be a majority of the whole number of electors appointed; and if no person have such majority, then from the persons having the highest numbers not exceeding three on the list of those voted for as President, the House of Representatives shall choose immediately, by ballot, the President. But in choosing the President, the votes shall be taken by States, the representation from each State having one vote; a quorum for this purpose shall consist of a member or members from two thirds of the States, and a majority of all the States shall be necessary to a choice. And if the House of Representatives shall not choose a President whenever the right of choice shall devolve upon them, before the fourth day of March next following, then the Vice President shall act as President, as in the case of the death or other constitutional disability of the President. The person having the greatest

number of votes as Vice President shall be the Vice President, if such number be a majority of the whole number of electors appointed, and if no person have a majority, then from the two highest numbers on the list, the Senate shall choose the Vice President; a quorum for the purpose shall consist of two thirds of the whole number of Senators, and a majority of the whole number shall be necessary to a choice. But no person constitutionally ineligible to the office of President shall be eligible to that of Vice President of the United States.

Amendment XIII [December 18, 1865]

    Section 1. Neither slavery nor involuntary servitude, except as punishment for crime whereof the party shall have been duly convicted, shall exist within the United States, or any place subject to their jurisdiction.

    Section 2. Congress shall have power to enforce this article by appropriate legislation.

Amendment XIV [July 28, 1868]

    Section 1. All persons born or naturalized in the United States, and subject to the jurisdiction thereof, are citizens of the United States and of the State wherein they reside. No State shall make or enforce any law which shall abridge the privileges or immunities of citizens of the United States; nor shall any State deprive any person of life, liberty, or property, without due process of law; nor deny to any person within its jurisdiction the equal protection of the laws.

    Section 2. Representatives shall be apportioned among the several States according to their respective numbers, counting the whole number of persons in each State, excluding Indians not taxed. But when the right to vote at any election for the choice of electors for President and Vice President of the United States, representatives in Congress, the executive and judicial officers of a State, or the members of the legislature thereof, is denied to any of the male inhabitants of such State, being twenty-one years of age, and citizens of the United States, or in any way abridged, except for participating in rebellion, or other crime, the basis of representation there shall be reduced in the proportion which the number of such male citizens shall bear to the whole number of male citizens twenty-one years of age in such State.

    Section 3. No person shall be a senator or representative in Congress, or elector of President and Vice President, or hold any office, civil or military, under the United States, or under any State, who having previously taken an oath, as a member of Congress, or as an officer of the United States, or as a member of any State legislature, or as an executive or judicial officer of any State, to support the Constitution of the United States, shall have engaged in insurrection or rebellion against the same, or given aid or comfort to the enemies thereof. But Congress may by a vote of two thirds of each House, remove such disability.

    Section 4. The validity of the public debt of the United States, authorized by law, including debts incurred for payment of pensions and bounties for services in suppressing insurrection or rebellion; shall not be questioned.

But neither the United States nor any State shall assume or pay any debt or obligation incurred in aid of insurrection or rebellion against the United States, or any claim for the loss or emancipation of any slave; but all such debts, obligations, and claims shall be held illegal and void.

Section 5. The Congress shall have the power to enforce, by appropriate legislation, the provisions of this article.

Amendment XV [March 30, 1870]

Section 1. The right of citizens of the United States to vote shall not be denied or abridged by the United States or by any State on account of race, color, or previous condition of servitude.

Section 2. The Congress shall have power to enforce this article by appropriate legislation.

Amendment XVI [February 25, 1913]

The Congress shall have power to lay and collect taxes on incomes, from whatever source derived, without apportionment among the several States, and without regard to any census or enumeration.

Amendment XVII [May 31, 1913]

The Senate of the United States shall be composed of two senators from each State, elected by the people thereof, for six years; and each senator shall have one vote. The electors in each State shall have the qualifications requisite for electors of the most numerous branch of the State legislature.

When vacancies happen in the representation of any State in the Senate, the executive authority of such State shall issue writs of election to fill such vacancies: *Provided,* That the legislature of any State may empower the executive thereof to make temporary appointments until the people fill the vacancies by election as the legislature may direct.

This amendment shall not be so construed as to affect the election or term of any senator chosen before it becomes valid as part of the Constitution.

Amendment XVIII[11] [January 29, 1919]

After one year from the ratification of this article, the manufacture, sale, or transportation of intoxicating liquors within, the importation thereof into, or the exportation thereof from the United States and all territory subject to the jurisdiction thereof for beverage purposes is thereby prohibited.

The Congress and the several States shall have concurrent power to enforce this article by appropriate legislation.

This article shall be inoperative unless it shall have been ratified as an amendment to the Constitution by the legislatures of the several States, as provided in the Constitution, within seven years from the date of the submission hereof to the States by Congress.

[11]Repealed by the Twenty-first Amendment.

Amendment XIX [August 26, 1920]

The right of citizens of the United States to vote shall not be denied or abridged by the United States or by any State on account of sex.

Congress shall have the power to enforce this article by appropriate legislation.

Amendment XX [January 23, 1933]

Section 1. The terms of the President and Vice President shall end at noon on the 20th day of January and the terms of Senators and Representatives at noon on the 3d day of January, of the years in which such terms would have ended if this article had not been ratified; and the terms of their successors shall then begin.

Section 2. The Congress shall assemble at least once in every year, and such meeting shall begin at noon on the 3d day of January, unless they shall by law appoint a different day.

Section 3. If, at the time fixed for the beginning of the term of President, the President-elect shall have died, the Vice President-elect shall become President. If a President shall not have been chosen before the time fixed for the beginning of his term, or if the President-elect shall have failed to qualify, then the Vice President-elect shall act as President until a President shall have qualified; and the Congress may by law provide for the case wherein neither a President-elect nor a Vice President-elect shall have qualified, declaring who shall then act as President, or the manner in which one who is to act shall be selected, and such person shall act accordingly until a President or Vice President shall have qualified.

Section 4. The Congress may by law provide for the case of the death of any of the persons from whom, the House of Representatives may choose a President whenever the right of choice shall have devolved upon them, and for the case of the death of any of the persons from whom the Senate may choose a Vice President whenever the right of choice shall have devolved upon them.

Section 5. Sections 1 and 2 shall take effect on the 15th day of October following the ratification of this article.

Section 6. This article shall be inoperative unless it shall have been ratified as an amendment to the Constitution by the legislatures of three-fourths of the several States within seven years from the date of its submission.

Amendment XXI [December 5, 1933]

Section 1. The Eighteenth Article of amendment to the Constitution of the United States is hereby repealed.

Section 2. The transportation or importation into any State, Territory, or possession of the United States for delivery or use therein of intoxicating liquors in violation of the laws thereof, is hereby prohibited.

Section 3. This article shall be inoperative unless it shall have been ratified as an amendment to the Constitution by conventions in the several States, as provided in the Constitution, within seven years from the date of the submission thereof to the States by the Congress.

Amendment XXII [March 1, 1951]

No person shall be elected to the office of the President more than twice, and no person who has held the office of President, or acted as President, for more than two years of a term to which some other person was elected President shall be elected to the office of the President more than once.

But this article shall not apply to any person holding the office of President when this article was proposed by the Congress, and shall not prevent any person who may be holding the office of President, or acting as President, during the term within which this article becomes operative from holding the office of President or acting as President during the remainder of such term.

This article shall be inoperative unless it shall have been ratified as an amendment to the Constitution by the legislatures of three-fourths of the several States within seven years from the date of its submission to the States by the Congress.

Amendment XXIII [March 29, 1961]

Section 1. The District constituting the seat of Government of the United States shall appoint in such manner as the Congress may direct.

A number of electors of President and Vice President equal to the whole number of Senators and Representatives in Congress to which the District would be entitled if it were a State, but in no event more than the least populous State; they shall be in addition to those appointed by the States, but they shall be considered, for the purposes of the election of President and Vice President, to be electors appointed by a State; and they shall meet in the District and perform such duties as provided by the twelfth article of amendment.

Section 2. The Congress shall have power to enforce this article by appropriate legislation.

Amendment XXIV [January 23, 1964]

Section 1. The right of citizens of the United States to vote in any primary or other election for President or Vice President, for electors for President or Vice President, or for Senator or Representative in Congress, shall not be denied or abridged by the United States or any State by reason of failure to pay any poll tax or other tax.

Section 2. The Congress shall have power to enforce this article by appropriate legislation.

Amendment XXV [February 10, 1967]

Section 1. In case of the removal of the President from office or of his death or resignation, the Vice President shall become President.

Section 2. Whenever there is a vacancy in the office of the Vice President, the President shall nominate a Vice President who shall take office upon confirmation by a majority of both Houses of Congress.

Section 3. Whenever the President transmits to the President pro tempore of the Senate and the Speaker of the House of Representatives his written declaration that he is unable to discharge the powers and duties of his office, and until he transmits to them a written declaration to the contrary, such powers and duties shall be discharged by the Vice President as Acting President.

Section 4. Whenever the Vice President and a majority of either the principal officers of the executive departments or of such other body as Congress may by law provide, transmit to the President pro tempore of the Senate and the Speaker of the House of Representatives their written declaration that the President is unable to discharge the powers and duties of his office, the Vice President shall immediately assume the powers and duties of the office as Acting President.

Thereafter, when the President transmits to the President pro tempore of the Senate and the Speaker of the House of Representatives his written declaration that no inability exists, he shall resume the powers and duties of his office unless the Vice President and a majority of either the principal officers of the executive departments or of such other body as Congress may by law provide, transmit within four days to the President pro tempore of the Senate and the Speaker of the House of Representatives their written declaration that the President is unable to discharge the powers and duties of his office. Thereupon Congress shall decide the issue, assembling within forty-eight hours for that purpose if not in session. If the Congress, within twenty-one days after receipt of the latter written declaration, or, if Congress is not in session, within twenty-one days after Congress is required to assemble, determines by two-thirds vote of both Houses that the President is unable to discharge the powers and duties of his office, the Vice President shall continue to discharge the same as Acting President; otherwise, the President shall resume the powers and duties of his office.

Amendment XXVI [June 30, 1971]

Section 1. The right of citizens of the United States who are eighteen years of age or older to vote shall not be denied or abridged by the United States or by any State on account of age.

Section 2. The Congress shall have power to enforce this article by appropriate legislation.

Amendment XXVII [May 8, 1992]

No law, varying the compensation for the services of the Senators and Representatives, shall take effect until an election of Representatives shall have intervened.

PRESIDENTS AND VICE PRESIDENTS

1. George Washington (1789)
   John Adams (1789)

2. John Adams (1797)
   Thomas Jefferson (1797)

3. Thomas Jefferson (1801)
   Aaron Burr (1801)
   George Clinton (1805)

4. James Madison (1809)
   George Clinton (1809)
   Elbridge Gerry (1813)

5. James Monroe (1817)
   Daniel D. Thompkins (1817)

6. John Quincy Adams (1825)
   John C. Calhoun (1825)

7. Andrew Jackson (1829)
   John C. Calhoun (1829)
   Martin Van Buren (1833)

8. Martin Van Buren (1837)
   Richard M. Johnson (1837)

9. William H. Harrison (1841)
   John Tyler (1841)

10. John Tyler (1841)

11. James K. Polk (1845)
    George M. Dallas (1845)

12. Zachary Taylor (1849)
    Millard Fillmore (1849)

13. Millard Fillmore (1850)

14. Franklin Pierce (1853)
    William R. King (1853)

15. James Buchanan (1857)
    John C. Breckinridge (1857)

16. Abraham Lincoln (1861)
    Hannibal Hamlin (1861)
    Andrew Johnson (1865)

17. Andrew Johnson (1865)

18. Ulysses S. Grant (1869)
    Schuyler Colfax (1869)
    Henry Wilson (1873)

19. Rutherford B. Hayes (1877)
    William A. Wheeler (1877)

20. James A. Garfield (1881)
    Chester A. Arthur (1881)

21. Chester A. Arthur (1881)

22. Grover Cleveland (1885)
    T. A. Hendricks (1885)

23. Benjamin Harrison (1889)
    Levi P. Morton (1889)

24. Grover Cleveland (1893)
    Adlai E. Stevenson (1893)

25. William McKinley (1897)
    Garret A. Hobart (1897)
    Theodore Roosevelt (1901)

26. Theodore Roosevelt (1901)
    Charles Fairbanks (1905)

27. William H. Taft (1909)
    James S. Sherman (1909)

28. Woodrow Wilson (1913)
    Thomas R. Marshall (1913)

29. Warren G. Harding (1921)
    Calvin Coolidge (1921)

30. Calvin Coolidge (1923)
    Charles G. Dawes (1925)

31. Herbert C. Hoover (1929)
    Charles Curtis (1929)

32. Franklin D. Roosevelt (1933)
    John Nance Garner (1933)
    Henry A. Wallace (1941)
    Harry S Truman (1945)

33. Harry S Truman (1945)
    Alben W. Barkley (1949)

34. Dwight D. Eisenhower (1953)
    Richard M. Nixon (1953)

35. John F. Kennedy (1961)
    Lyndon B. Johnson (1961)

36. Lyndon B. Johnson (1963)
    Hubert H. Humphrey (1965)

37. Richard M. Nixon (1969)
    Spiro T. Agnew (1969)
    Gerald R. Ford (1973)

38. Gerald R. Ford (1974)
    Nelson A. Rockefeller (1974)

39. James E. Carter Jr. (1977)
    Walter F. Mondale (1977)

40. Ronald W. Reagan (1981)
    George H. W. Bush (1981)

41. George H. W. Bush (1989)
    James D. Quayle III (1989)

42. William J. B. Clinton (1993)
    Albert Gore (1993)

43. George W. Bush (2001)
    Richard Cheney (2001)

PRESIDENTIAL ELECTIONS

Year	Number of States	Candidates	Party	Popular Vote*	Electoral Vote[†]	Percentage of Popular Vote
1789	11	GEORGE WASHINGTON	No party designations		69	
		John Adams			34	
		Other Candidates			35	
1792	15	GEORGE WASHINGTON	No party designations		132	
		John Adams			77	
		George Clinton			50	
		Other Candidates			5	
1796	16	JOHN ADAMS	Federalist		71	
		Thomas Jefferson	Democratic Republican		68	
		Thomas Pinckney	Federalist		59	
		Aaron Burr	Democratic Republican		30	
		Other Candidates			48	
1800	16	THOMAS JEFFERSON	Democratic Republican		73	
		Aaron Burr	Democratic Republican		73	
		John Adams	Federalist		65	
		Charles C. Pinckney	Federalist		64	
		John Jay	Federalist		1	
1804	17	THOMAS JEFFERSON	Democratic Republican		162	
		Charles C. Pinckney	Federalist		14	
1808	17	JAMES MADISON	Democratic Republican		122	
		Charles C. Pinckney	Federalist		47	
		George Clinton	Democratic Republican		6	
1812	18	JAMES MADISON	Democratic Republican		128	
		DeWitt Clinton	Federalist		89	
1816	19	JAMES MONROE	Democratic Republican		183	
		Rufus King	Federalist		34	
1820	24	JAMES MONROE	Democratic Republican		231	
		John Quincy Adams	Independent Republican		1	
1824	24	JOHN QUINCY ADAMS		108,740	84	30.5
		Andrew Jackson		153,544	99	43.1
		William H. Crawford		46,618	41	13.1
		Henry Clay		47,136	37	13.2
1828	24	ANDREW JACKSON	Democrat	647,286	178	56.0
		John Quincy Adams	National Republican	508,064	83	44.0
1832	24	ANDREW JACKSON	Democrat	687,502	219	55.0
		Henry Clay	National Republican	530,189	49	42.4
		William Wirt	Anti-Masonic	33,108	7	2.6
		John Floyd	National Republican		11	

*Percentage of popular vote given for any election year may not total 100 percent because candidates receiving less than 1 percent of the popular vote have been omitted.

[†]Prior to the passage of the Twelfth Amendment in 1804, the electoral college voted for two presidential candidates; the runner-up became Vice-President. Data from *Historical Statistics of the United States, Colonial Times to 1957* (1961), pp. 682–683, and *The World Almanac*.

PRESIDENTIAL ELECTIONS
(continued)

Year	Number of States	Candidates	Party	Popular Vote	Electoral Vote	Percentage of Popular Vote
1836	26	MARTIN VAN BUREN	Democrat	765,483	170	50.9
		William H. Harrison	Whig		73	
		Hugh L. White	Whig		26	
		Daniel Webster	Whig	739,795	14	49.1
		W. P. Mangum	Whig		11	
1840	26	WILLIAM H. HARRISON	Whig	1,274,624	234	53.1
		Martin Van Buren	Democrat	1,127,781	60	46.9
1844	26	JAMES K. POLK	Democrat	1,338,464	170	49.6
		Henry Clay	Whig	1,300,097	105	48.1
		James G. Birney	Liberty	62,300		2.3
1848	30	ZACHARY TAYLOR	Whig	1,360,967	163	47.4
		Lewis Cass	Democrat	1,222,342	127	42.5
		Martin Van Buren	Free Soil	291,263		10.1
1852	31	FRANKLIN PIERCE	Democrat	1,601,117	254	50.9
		Winfield Scott	Whig	1,385,453	42	44.1
		John P. Hale	Free Soil	155,825		5.0
1856	31	JAMES BUCHANAN	Democrat	1,832,955	174	45.3
		John C. Frémont	Republican	1,339,932	114	33.1
		Millard Fillmore	American ("Know Nothing")	871,731	8	21.6
1860	33	ABRAHAM LINCOLN	Republican	1,865,593	180	39.8
		Stephen A. Douglas	Democrat	1,382,713	12	29.5
		John C. Breckinridge	Democrat	848,356	72	18.1
		John Bell	Constitutional Union	592,906	39	12.6
1864	36	ABRAHAM LINCOLN	Republican	2,206,938	212	55.0
		George B. McClellan	Democrat	1,803,787	21	45.0
1868	37	ULYSSES S. GRANT	Republican	3,013,421	214	52.7
		Horatio Seymour	Democrat	2,706,829	80	47.3
1872	37	ULYSSES S. GRANT	Republican	3,596,745	286	55.6
		Horace Greeley	Democrat	2,843,446	*	43.9
1876	38	RUTHERFORD B. HAYES	Republican	4,036,572	185	48.0
		Samuel J. Tilden	Democrat	4,284,020	184	51.0
1880	38	JAMES A. GARFIELD	Republican	4,453,295	214	48.5
		Winfield S. Hancock	Democrat	4,414,082	155	48.1
		James B. Weaver	Greenback-Labor	308,578		3.4
1884	38	GROVER CLEVELAND	Democrat	4,879,507	219	48.5
		James G. Blaine	Republican	4,850,293	182	48.2
		Benjamin F. Butler	Greenback-Labor	175,370		1.8
		John P. St. John	Prohibition	150,369		1.5
1888	38	BENJAMIN HARRISON	Republican	5,447,129	233	47.9
		Grover Cleveland	Democrat	5,537,857	168	48.6
		Clinton B. Fisk	Prohibition	249,506		2.2
		Alson J. Streeter	Union Labor	146,935		1.3

*Because of the death of Greeley, Democratic electors scattered their votes.

PRESIDENTIAL ELECTIONS
(continued)

Year	Number of States	Candidates	Party	Popular Vote	Electoral Vote	Percentage of Popular Vote
1892	44	GROVER CLEVELAND	Democrat	5,555,426	277	46.1
		Benjamin Harrison	Republican	5,182,690	145	43.0
		James B. Weaver	People's	1,029,846	22	8.5
		John Bidwell	Prohibition	264,133		2.2
1896	45	WILLIAM MCKINLEY	Republican	7,102,246	271	51.1
		William J. Bryan	Democrat	6,492,559	176	47.7
1900	45	WILLIAM MCKINLEY	Republican	7,218,491	292	51.7
		William J. Bryan	Democrat; Populist	6,356,734	155	45.5
		John C. Woolley	Prohibition	208,914		1.5
1904	45	THEODORE ROOSEVELT	Republican	7,628,461	336	57.4
		Alton B. Parker	Democrat	5,084,223	140	37.6
		Eugene V. Debs	Socialist	402,283		3.0
		Silas C. Swallow	Prohibition	258,536		1.9
1908	46	WILLIAM H. TAFT	Republican	7,675,320	321	51.6
		William J. Bryan	Democrat	6,412,294	162	43.1
		Eugene V. Debs	Socialist	420,793		2.8
		Eugene W. Chafin	Prohibition	253,840		1.7
1912	48	WOODROW WILSON	Democrat	6,296,547	435	41.9
		Theodore Roosevelt	Progressive	4,118,571	88	27.4
		William H. Taft	Republican	3,486,720	8	23.2
		Eugene V. Debs	Socialist	900,672		6.0
		Eugene W. Chafin	Prohibition	206,275		1.4
1916	48	WOODROW WILSON	Democrat	9,127,695	277	49.4
		Charles E. Hughes	Republican	8,533,507	254	46.2
		A. L. Benson	Socialist	585,113		3.2
		J. Frank Hanly	Prohibition	220,506		1.2
1920	48	WARREN G. HARDING	Republican	16,143,407	404	60.4
		James M. Cox	Democrat	9,130,328	127	34.2
		Eugene V. Debs	Socialist	919,799		3.4
		P. P. Christensen	Farmer-Labor	265,411		1.0
1924	48	CALVIN COOLIDGE	Republican	15,718,211	382	54.0
		John W. Davis	Democrat	8,385,283	136	28.8
		Robert M. La Follette	Progressive	4,831,289	13	16.6
1928	48	HERBERT C. HOOVER	Republican	21,391,993	444	58.2
		Alfred E. Smith	Democrat	15,016,169	87	40.9
1932	48	FRANKLIN D. ROOSEVELT	Democrat	22,809,638	472	57.4
		Herbert C. Hoover	Republican	15,758,901	59	39.7
		Norman Thomas	Socialist	881,951		2.2
1936	48	FRANKLIN D. ROOSEVELT	Democrat	27,752,869	523	60.8
		Alfred M. Landon	Republican	16,674,665	8	36.5
		William Lemke	Union	882,479		1.9
1940	48	FRANKLIN D. ROOSEVELT	Democrat	27,307,819	449	54.8
		Wendell L. Willkie	Republican	22,321,018	82	44.8
1944	48	FRANKLIN D. ROOSEVELT	Democrat	25,606,585	432	53.5
		Thomas E. Dewey	Republican	22,014,745	99	46.0

PRESIDENTIAL ELECTIONS
(continued)

Year	Number of States	Candidates	Party	Popular Vote	Electoral Vote	Percentage of Popular Vote
1948	48	HARRY S TRUMAN	Democrat	24,105,812	303	49.5
		Thomas E. Dewey	Republican	21,970,065	189	45.1
		J. Strom Thurmond	States' Rights	1,169,063	39	2.4
		Henry A. Wallace	Progressive	1,157,172		2.4
1952	48	DWIGHT D. EISENHOWER	Republican	33,936,234	442	55.1
		Adlai E. Stevenson	Democrat	27,314,992	89	44.4
1956	48	DWIGHT D. EISENHOWER	Republican	35,590,472	457[*]	57.6
		Adlai E. Stevenson	Democrat	26,022,752	73	42.1
1960	50	JOHN F. KENNEDY	Democrat	34,227,096	303[†]	49.9
		Richard M. Nixon	Republican	34,108,546	219	49.6
1964	50	LYNDON B. JOHNSON	Democrat	42,676,220	486	61.3
		Barry M. Goldwater	Republican	26,860,314	52	38.5
1968	50	RICHARD M. NIXON	Republican	31,785,480	301	43.4
		Hubert H. Humphrey	Democrat	31,275,165	191	42.7
		George C. Wallace	American Independent	9,906,473	46	13.5
1972	50	RICHARD M. NIXON[‡]	Republican	47,165,234	520	60.6
		George S. McGovern	Democrat	29,168,110	17	37.5
1976	50	JIMMY CARTER	Democrat	40,828,929	297	50.1
		Gerald R. Ford	Republican	39,148,940	240	47.9
		Eugene McCarthy	Independent	739,256		0.9
1980	50	RONALD REAGAN	Republican	43,201,220	489	50.9
		Jimmy Carter	Democrat	34,913,332	49	41.2
		John B. Anderson	Independent	5,581,379		6.6
1984	50	RONALD REAGAN	Republican	53,428,357	525	59.0
		Walter F. Mondale	Democrat	36,930,923	13	41.0
1988	50	GEORGE H. W. BUSH	Republican	48,901,046	426	53.4
		Michael Dukakis	Democrat	41,809,030	111	45.6
1992	50	BILL CLINTON	Democrat	43,728,275	370	43.2
		George Bush	Republican	38,167,416	168	37.7
		H. Ross Perot	United We Stand, America	19,237,247		19.0
1996	50	BILL CLINTON	Democrat	45,590,703	379	49.0
		Bob Dole	Republican	37,816,307	159	41.0
		H. Ross Perot	Reform	7,866,284		8.0
2000	50	GEORGE W. BUSH	Republican	50,456,169	271	48.0
		Al Gore	Democrat	50,996,116	266	48.0
		Ralph Nader	Green	2,767,176	0	3.0

[*]Walter B. Jones received 1 electoral vote.

[†]Harry F. Byrd received 15 electoral votes.

[‡]Resigned August 9, 1974: Vice President Gerald R. Ford became President.

ADMISSION OF STATES INTO THE UNION

State	Date of Admission	State	Date of Admission
1. Delaware	December 7, 1787	26. Michigan	January 26, 1837
2. Pennsylvania	December 12, 1787	27. Florida	March 3, 1845
3. New Jersey	December 18, 1787	28. Texas	December 29, 1845
4. Georgia	January 2, 1788	29. Iowa	December 28, 1846
5. Connecticut	January 9, 1788	30. Wisconsin	May 29, 1848
6. Massachusetts	February 6, 1788	31. California	September 9, 1850
7. Maryland	April 28, 1788	32. Minnesota	May 11, 1858
8. South Carolina	May 23, 1788	33. Oregon	February 14, 1859
9. New Hampshire	June 21, 1788	34. Kansas	January 29, 1861
10. Virginia	June 25, 1788	35. West Virginia	June 20, 1863
11. New York	July 26, 1788	36. Nevada	October 31, 1864
12. North Carolina	November 21, 1789	37. Nebraska	March 1, 1867
13. Rhode Island	May 29, 1790	38. Colorado	August 1, 1876
14. Vermont	March 4, 1791	39. North Dakota	November 2, 1889
15. Kentucky	June 1, 1792	40. South Dakota	November 2, 1889
16. Tennessee	June 1, 1796	41. Montana	November 8, 1889
17. Ohio	March 1, 1803	42. Washington	November 11, 1889
18. Louisiana	April 30, 1812	43. Idaho	July 3, 1890
19. Indiana	December 11, 1816	44. Wyoming	July 10, 1890
20. Mississippi	December 10, 1817	45. Utah	January 4, 1896
21. Illinois	December 3, 1818	46. Oklahoma	November 16, 1907
22. Alabama	December 14, 1819	47. New Mexico	January 6, 1912
23. Maine	March 15, 1820	48. Arizona	February 14, 1912
24. Missouri	August 10, 1821	49. Alaska	January 3, 1959
25. Arkansas	June 15, 1836	50. Hawaii	August 21, 1959

DEMOGRAPHICS OF THE UNITED STATES

POPULATION GROWTH

Year	Population	Percent Increase
1630	4,600	–
1640	26,600	478.3
1650	50,400	90.8
1660	75,100	49.0
1670	111,900	49.0
1680	151,500	35.4
1690	210,400	38.9
1700	250,900	19.2
1710	331,700	32.2
1720	466,200	40.5
1730	629,400	35.0
1740	905,600	43.9
1750	1,170,800	29.3
1760	1,593,600	36.1
1770	2,148,100	34.8
1780	2,780,400	29.4
1790	3,929,214	41.3
1800	5,308,483	35.1
1810	7,239,881	36.4
1820	9,638,453	33.1
1830	12,866,020	33.5
1840	17,069,453	32.7
1850	23,191,876	35.9
1860	31,443,321	35.6
1870	39,818,449	26.6
1880	50,155,783	26.0
1890	62,947,714	25.5
1900	75,994,575	20.7
1910	91,972,266	21.0
1920	105,710,620	14.9
1930	122,775,046	16.1
1940	131,669,275	7.2
1950	150,697,361	14.5
1960	179,323,175	19.0
1970	203,235,298	13.3
1980	226,545,805	11.5
1990	248,709,873	9.8
2000	281,421,906	9.0

Source: *Historical Statistics of the United States* (1975); *Statistical Abstract of the United States* (1991 and 2001).
Note: Figures for 1630–1780 include British colonies within limits of present United States only; Native-American population included only in 1930 and thereafter.

WORKFORCE

Year	Total Number Workers (1000s)	Farmers as % of Total	Women as % of Total	% Workers in Unions
1810	2,330	84	(NA)	(NA)
1840	5,660	75	(NA)	(NA)
1860	11,110	53	(NA)	(NA)
1870	12,506	53	15	(NA)
1880	17,392	52	15	(NA)
1890	23,318	43	17	(NA)
1900	29,073	40	18	3
1910	38,167	31	21	6
1920	41,614	26	21	12
1930	48,830	22	22	7
1940	53,011	17	24	27
1950	59,643	12	28	25
1960	69,877	8	32	26
1970	82,049	4	37	25
1980	108,544	3	42	23
1990	117,914	3	45	16
2000	140,863	3	47	13.5

Source: *Historical Statistics of the United States* (1975); *Statistical Abstract of the United States* (1991, 1996, and 2001).

VITAL STATISTICS
(rates per 1000 population)

Year	Births	Deaths	Marriages	Divorces
1800	55	(NA)	(NA)	(NA)
1810	54.3	(NA)	(NA)	(NA)
1820	55.2	(NA)	(NA)	(NA)
1830	51.4	(NA)	(NA)	(NA)
1840	51.8	(NA)	(NA)	(NA)
1850	43.3	(NA)	(NA)	(NA)
1860	44.3	(NA)	(NA)	(NA)
1870	38.3	(NA)	9.6 (1867)	0.3 (1867)
1880	39.8	(NA)	9.1 (1875)	0.3 (1875)
1890	31.5	(NA)	9.0	0.5
1900	32.3	17.2	9.3	0.7
1910	30.1	14.7	10.3	0.9
1920	27.7	13.0	12.0	1.6
1930	21.3	11.3	9.2	1.6
1940	19.4	10.8	12.1	2.0
1950	24.1	9.6	11.1	2.6
1960	23.7	9.5	8.5	2.2
1970	18.4	9.5	10.6	3.5
1980	15.9	8.8	10.6	5.2
1990	16.7	8.6	9.8	4.7
1998	14.5	8.6	8.3	4.2

Source: *Historical Statistics of the United States* (1975); *Statistical Abstract of the United States* (1999 and 2001).

RACIAL COMPOSITION OF THE POPULATION
(in thousands)

Year	White	Black	Indian	Hispanic	Asian
1790	3,172	757	(NA)	(NA)	(NA)
1800	4,306	1,002	(NA)	(NA)	(NA)
1820	7,867	1,772	(NA)	(NA)	(NA)
1840	14,196	2,874	(NA)	(NA)	(NA)
1860	26,923	4,442	(NA)	(NA)	(NA)
1880	43,403	6,581	(NA)	(NA)	(NA)
1900	66,809	8,834	(NA)	(NA)	(NA)
1910	81,732	9,828	(NA)	(NA)	(NA)
1920	94,821	10,463	(NA)	(NA)	(NA)
1930	110,287	11,891	(NA)	(NA)	(NA)
1940	118,215	12,866	(NA)	(NA)	(NA)
1950	134,942	15,042	(NA)	(NA)	(NA)
1960	158,832	18,872	(NA)	(NA)	(NA)
1970	178,098	22,581	(NA)	(NA)	(NA)
1980	194,713	26,683	1,420	14,609	3,729
1990	208,741	30,517	2,067	22,479	7,467
2000	226,232	35,307	2,434	32,440	11,159

Source: U.S. Bureau of the Census, *U.S. Census of Population: 1940*, vol. II, part 1, and vol. IV, part 1; *1950*, vol. II, part 1; *1960*, vol. I, part 1; *1970*, vol. I, part B; and *Current Population Reports*, P25-1095 and P25-1104; and unpublished data; *Statistical Abstract of the United States*, 2001.

IMMIGRATION, BY ORIGIN
(in thousands)

Period	Europe	Americas	Asia
1820–30	106	12	—
1831–40	496	33	—
1841–50	1,597	62	—
1851–60	2,453	75	42
1861–70	2,065	167	65
1871–80	2,272	404	70
1881–90	4,735	427	70
1891–1900	3,555	39	75
1901–10	8,065	362	324
1911–20	4,322	1,144	247
1921–30	2,463	1,517	112
1931–40	348	160	16
1941–50	621	355	32
1951–60	1,326	997	150
1961–70	1,123	1,716	590
1971–80	800	1,983	1,588
1981–90	706	3,581	2,817
1991–1998	1,086	3,744	2,427

Source: *Historical Statistics of the United States* (1975); *Statistical Abstract of the United States* (1991 and 2001).

TEXT CREDITS

INDEX

SINGLE PC LICENSE AGREEMENT AND LIMITED WARRANTY

READ THIS LICENSE CAREFULLY BEFORE OPENING THIS PACKAGE. BY OPENING THIS PACKAGE, YOU ARE AGREEING TO THE TERMS AND CONDITIONS OF THIS LICENSE. IF YOU DO NOT AGREE, DO NOT OPEN THE PACKAGE. PROMPTLY RETURN THE UNOPENED PACKAGE AND ALL ACCOMPANYING ITEMS TO THE PLACE YOU OBTAINED THEM [[FOR A FULL REFUND OF ANY SUMS YOU HAVE PAID FOR THE SOFTWARE]]. *THESE TERMS APPLY TO ALL LICENSED SOFTWARE ON THE DISK EXCEPT THAT THE TERMS FOR USE OF ANY SHARE-WARE OR FREEWARE ON THE DISKETTES ARE AS SET FORTH IN THE ELECTRONIC LICENSE LOCATED ON THE DISK:*

1. GRANT OF LICENSE and OWNERSHIP: The enclosed computer programs ("Software") are licensed, not sold, to you by Pearson Education, Inc. publishing as Prentice Hall ("We" or the "Company") and in consideration [[of your payment of the license fee, which is part of the price you paid]] [[of your purchase or adoption of the accompanying Company textbooks and/or other materials,]] and your agreement to these terms. We reserve any rights not granted to you. You own only the disk(s) but we and/or our licensors own the Software itself. This license allows you to use and display your copy of the Software on a single computer (i.e., with a single CPU) at a single location for *academic* use only, so long as you comply with the terms of this Agreement. You may make one copy for backup, or transfer your copy to another CPU, provided that the Software is usable on only one computer.

2. RESTRICTIONS: You may *not* transfer or distribute the Software or documentation to anyone else. Except for backup, you may *not* copy the documentation or the Software. You may *not* network the Software or otherwise use it on more than one computer or computer terminal at the same time. You may *not* reverse engineer, disassemble, decompile, modify, adapt, translate, or create derivative works based on the Software or the Documentation. You may be held legally responsible for any copying or copyright infringement that is caused by your failure to abide by the terms of these restrictions.

3. TERMINATION: This license is effective until terminated. This license will terminate automatically without notice from the Company if you fail to comply with any provisions or limitations of this license. Upon termination, you shall destroy the Documentation and all copies of the Software. All provisions of this Agreement as to limitation and disclaimer of warranties, limitation of liability, remedies or damages, and our ownership rights shall survive termination.

4. LIMITED WARRANTY AND DISCLAIMER OF WARRANTY: Company warrants that for a period of 60 days from the date you purchase this SOFTWARE (or purchase or adopt the accompanying textbook), the Software, when properly installed and used in accordance with the Documentation, will operate in substantial conformity with the description of the Software set forth in the Documentation, and that for a period of 30 days the disk(s) on which the Software is delivered shall be free from defects in materials and workmanship under normal use. The Company does *not* warrant that the Software will meet your requirements or that the operation of the Software will be uninterrupted or error-free. Your only remedy and the Company's only obligation under these limited warranties is, at the Company's option, return of the disk for a refund of any amounts paid for it by you or replacement of the disk. THIS LIMITED WARRANTY IS THE ONLY WARRANTY PROVIDED BY THE COMPANY AND ITS LICENSORS, AND THE COMPANY AND ITS LICENSORS DISCLAIM ALL OTHER WARRANTIES, EXPRESS OR IMPLIED, INCLUDING WITHOUT LIMITATION, THE IMPLIED WARRANTIES OF MERCHANTABILITY AND FITNESS FOR A PARTICULAR PURPOSE. THE COMPANY DOES NOT WARRANT, GUARANTEE OR MAKE ANY REPRESENTATION REGARDING THE ACCURACY, RELIABILITY, CURRENTNESS, USE, OR RESULTS OF USE, OF THE SOFTWARE.

5. LIMITATION OF REMEDIES AND DAMAGES: IN NO EVENT, SHALL THE COMPANY OR ITS EMPLOYEES, AGENTS, LICENSORS, OR CONTRACTORS BE LIABLE FOR ANY INCIDENTAL, INDIRECT, SPECIAL, OR CONSE-QUENTIAL DAMAGES ARISING OUT OF OR IN CONNECTION WITH THIS LICENSE OR THE SOFTWARE, INCLUD-ING FOR LOSS OF USE, LOSS OF DATA, LOSS OF INCOME OR PROFIT, OR OTHER LOSSES, SUSTAINED AS A RESULT OF INJURY TO ANY PERSON, OR LOSS OF OR DAMAGE TO PROPERTY, OR CLAIMS OF THIRD PARTIES, EVEN IF THE COMPANY OR AN AUTHORIZED REPRESENTATIVE OF THE COMPANY HAS BEEN ADVISED OF THE POSSIBILITY OF SUCH DAMAGES. IN NO EVENT SHALL THE LIABILITY OF THE COMPANY FOR DAMAGES WITH RESPECT TO THE SOFTWARE EXCEED THE AMOUNTS ACTUALLY PAID BY YOU, IF ANY, FOR THE SOFTWARE OR THE ACCOMPANYING TEXTBOOK. BECAUSE SOME JURISDICTIONS DO NOT ALLOW THE LIMITATION OF LIABILITY IN CERTAIN CIRCUMSTANCES, THE ABOVE LIMITATIONS MAY NOT ALWAYS APPLY TO YOU.

6. GENERAL: THIS AGREEMENT SHALL BE CONSTRUED IN ACCORDANCE WITH THE LAWS OF THE UNITED STATES OF AMERICA AND THE STATE OF NEW YORK, APPLICABLE TO CONTRACTS MADE IN NEW YORK, AND SHALL BENEFIT THE COMPANY, ITS AFFILIATES AND ASSIGNEES. HIS AGREEMENT IS THE COMPLETE AND EXCLUSIVE STATEMENT OF THE AGREEMENT BETWEEN YOU AND THE COMPANY AND SUPERSEDES ALL PRO-POSALS OR PRIOR AGREEMENTS, ORAL, OR WRITTEN, AND ANY OTHER COMMUNICATIONS BETWEEN YOU AND THE COMPANY OR ANY REPRESENTATIVE OF THE COMPANY RELATING TO THE SUBJECT MATTER OF THIS AGREEMENT. If you are a U.S. Government user, this Software is licensed with "restricted rights" as set forth in sub-paragraphs (a)-(d) of the Commercial Computer-Restricted Rights clause at FAR 52.227-19 or in subparagraphs (c)(1)(ii) of the Rights in Technical Data and Computer Software clause at DFARS 252.227-7013, and similar clauses, as applicable.

Should you have any questions concerning this agreement or if you wish to contact the Company for any reason, please contact in writing: Deborah O"Connell, Media Editor for Humanities, Prentice Hall, One Lake Street, Upper Saddle River, NJ 07458.